TCHAIKOVSKY
A Biographical and Critical Study

THE YEARS OF FAME
(1878–1893)

David Brown

TCHAIKOVSKY
A Biographical and Critical Study

THE YEARS OF FAME
(1878–1893)

LONDON
VICTOR GOLLANCZ LTD
1992

First published in Great Britain
in two volumes, 1986 and 1991,
by Victor Gollancz Ltd
14 Henrietta Street, London WC2E 8QJ

First published in Gollancz Paperbacks 1992

A catalogue record for this book is available
from the British Library

ISBN 0 575 05427 1

Printed in Finland by Werner Söderström Oy

To Elizabeth

NOTE ON THE
PAPERBACK EDITION

This paperback edition reproduces exactly the text of the four hardback volumes, though the opportunity has been taken to correct minor errors, to add some minor pieces of information, and to bring the Work List up to date.

David Brown
Braishfield, Hampshire
September 1992

Volume III

THE YEARS OF WANDERING

(1878–1885)

CONTENTS

Preface to Volume III   11

Main Literary Sources for Volume III   13

1 *First Suite and* The Maid of Orléans   15
   A note on the First Suite, and on certain persons and
   places

2 *A New Home: Second Piano Concerto*   64

3 *Ukrainian Summer: Total Isolation*   98

4 *Resurgent Individuality: Piano Trio*   129

5 *Further Uncertainties:* Mazepa   162

6 *A Time of Children: Second Suite*   206
   A note on the Second Suite, and on certain persons

7 *Intimate Insights and Marks of Rehabilitation: Third Suite*   243

8 *A Home of His Own*   274

9 *Balakirev Resurgent: Manfred Symphony*   296

Cumulative Indexes of Works and Persons
appear at the end of Volume IV

ILLUSTRATIONS

Mily Balakirev (1880)
Vladimir Stasov (c.1870)
Alexandra [Sasha] Davïdova and Nataliya [Nata] Pleskaya
Nikolay and Anna [née Davïdova] von Meck
Tchaikovsky in 1884
Tatyana [Tanya] Davïdova
Max Erdmannsdörfer
Eduard Nápravník
Praskovya [Parasha] Tchaikovskaya

PREFACE

THIS VOLUME COVERS the seven years of Tchaikovsky's life following his resignation from the Moscow Conservatoire in 1878. His existence during this period was almost rootless; insofar as he had a home, it was with his sister Sasha and her family at Kamenka in the Ukraine. Otherwise he spent his time in the seclusion of country estates, or wandering restlessly in Western Europe until, in 1885, he took a house at Maidanovo, and settled into the first of a series of homes outside Moscow upon which he was to centre the rest of his life.

It was almost inevitable that a hypersensitive man, as emotionally ravaged as Tchaikovsky had been by the devastating experience of his marriage, should have retreated into an existence as solitary as he could make it. On a personal level he sought only the love of his intimate family and the companionship of his closest friends, and in such an existence the course of his life became correspondingly constricted. For the biographer this poses something of a dilemma: in how much detail should he record a day-to-day existence comprising so many events of a minor nature? It is a problem exacerbated by the ever-increasing abundance of information which survives as the composer's list of works lengthens and his reputation grows. Yet there is, in fact, a very positive value in chronicling this phase, for it is precisely in the slight events of a man's life, and in his routine intercourse with those close to him, that his most fundamental characteristics will emerge. In this present volume, perhaps more than in any of the remaining three, Tchaikovsky is at his most exposed; in his responses to ordinary occurrences and situations we may observe most clearly his idiosyncrasies and rapidly changing moods, his likes and dislikes, loves and hates, his common sense which could rise to wisdom, his kindness and compassion, his improvidence, pettiness, prejudices, his perceptiveness and blindness in assessing personality and behaviour, his openhanded generosity and calculating deviousness, his gentle but constant envy of those whose sexual nature permitted them the experiences and joys of normal family life.

And in the music, too, there is more than one might expect of works conceived within a period when their creator was so emotionally withdrawn, even impaired. Even in these difficult years his lively inventiveness did not desert him, and though few pieces from this phase belong within the first rank of his compositions, even those which are second rank must command our grateful attention when their composer has remained as tuneful and resourceful as Tchaikovsky. Indeed, on occasions he showed himself still capable of matching the quality of his best earlier works and of those yet to come: in portions of the Piano Trio, for instance, or of the opera *Mazepa* – while in the Manfred Symphony, which closes this volume, he triumphantly regained a richness of inspiration and an emotional fullness which proclaimed unequivocally that he was completely and confidently himself again.

The editorial principles and practices of the preceding two volumes are maintained in this one. So, too, I owe a continuing debt to several people who helped in practical ways in those volumes: to Dr Anthea Baird and Mr A. Helliwell (now retired) of London University, and to my undaunted typist, Mrs Miriam Phillips, whose oft-challenged powers of comprehension still so readily solve the calligraphic riddles confronting her on my typescript. As before, my wife receives the dedication, which can be no more than a partial recompense for the help she has given in checking and proof-reading. And, again, the earlier pages of this volume contain material from the Soviet-suppressed volume, *Pisma k rodnïm* (Moscow, 1940), a photo-copy of which has been so generously made available to me by Mrs Alexandra Orlova. To all these, and the others who have contributed in various ways to this volume, my most grateful thanks.

UNIVERSITY OF SOUTHAMPTON   DAVID BROWN
MAY 1985

MAIN LITERARY SOURCES FOR VOLUME III

WITH ABBREVIATIONS

TLP 1–17 TCHAIKOVSKY (P.), *Polnoye sobraniye sochineny: literaturnïye proizvedeniya i perepiska* [Complete edition: literary works and correspondence], 17 vols. (Moscow, 1953–81)

TD TCHAIKOVSKY (P.), *Dnevniki* [Diaries] (Moscow/Petrograd, 1923)

TPB TCHAIKOVSKY (P.), *Pisma k blizkim* [Letters to his family] (Moscow, 1955)

TPJ 1–2 TCHAIKOVSKY (P.), *Perepiska s P. I. Jurgensonom* [Correspondence with Jurgenson], 2 vols. (Moscow, 1938–52)

TPM 1–3 TCHAIKOVSKY (P.), *Perepiska s N. F. von Meck* [Correspondence with Nadezhda von Meck], 3 vols. (Moscow/Leningrad, 1934–6)

TPR TCHAIKOVSKY (P.), *Pisma k rodnïm* [Letters to his relatives] (Moscow, 1940)

TTP *P. I. Chaykovsky: S. I. Taneyev. Pisma* [Tchaikovsky/Taneyev. Letters] (Moscow, 1951)

BVP BALAKIREV (M.), *Perepiska s P. I. Chaykovskim* [Correspondence with Tchaikovsky], reprinted in FRID (E.) [ed.], *M. A. Balakirev: vospominaniya i pisma* [Balakirev: Recollections and letters] (Leningrad, 1962)

DTC DOMBAYEV (G.), *Tvorchestvo P. I. Chaykovskovo* [Tchaikovsky's works] (Moscow, 1958)

TZC 1–3 TCHAIKOVSKY (M.), *Zhizn P. I. Chaykovskovo* [Tchaikovsky's life], 3 vols. (Moscow, 1900–2)

YDGC YAKOVLEV (V.) [ed.], *Dni i godï P. I. Chaykovskovo* [The days and years of Tchaikovsky] (Moscow/Leningrad, 1940)

One musical source is also abbreviated in references:

T50RF TCHAIKOVSKY (P.), *50 Russian Folksongs*, arranged for piano duet by Tchaikovsky (Moscow, 1869)

I

FIRST SUITE AND

THE MAID OF ORLEANS

WHEN TCHAIKOVSKY ARRIVED in St Petersburg on 20 October 1878 he had hoped to resume work on his First Suite and to decide the subject of his next opera, but on the very day of his arrival Alexey Apukhtin's brother died, and Tchaikovsky, himself much upset by this, spent the first days trying to console and distract his old friend. Otherwise he confined his visiting to the numerous members of his family, but this he found a great strain, for by now he had grown far away from most of them. They welcomed him warmly and he tried to be an agreeable guest, but he found very wearing the perpetual requests that he should play the piano and talk about music with people who had little or no understanding of it. Few of these relatives seemed able to grasp why he had left the Conservatoire. As for the many acquaintances he met on the streets, they, so he said, always wanted to probe into his private affairs with questions which made his longing to get away from Russia the stronger. He saw the revival of *Vakula*, was angry with himself for what he saw as its faults, and his discontent increased. Only with his father and twin brothers did he feel really at ease, and but for the fear of hurting them, he would have fled St Petersburg forthwith.

His declared intention was to leave for Clarens in mid-November as soon as a passport could be arranged for his valet, Alexey, but an invitation from his sister Sasha to visit Kamenka before going abroad proved irresistible. He would stay there a month, he decided, perhaps even two, and would then go straight to Italy. Yet again his plans were to be revised. Nadezhda von Meck, his benefactress, was in Florence, and was pressing him to come so that he might spend some time within the same city as she. Since she offered to make all the necessary arrangements for his visit Tchaikovsky could not decline and he entrusted everything to her. He had only one requirement: the accommodation she selected for him must be out of range of those extraneous musical sounds which had so irritated him in Florence on his previous visit, for he was determined to work. His stay with Sasha would be curtailed to one week, but he would appease his sister by promising to return to Kamenka in the spring. On 13 November he was again in Moscow to tie up his affairs and complete the disposal of his apartment and furniture. Having dined some of his closest friends and dropped incognito into a rehearsal of the First Piano Concerto which Nikolay Rubinstein was about to perform yet again at an RMS concert, he collected Alexey and left the next day for the Ukraine.

Tchaikovsky had found himself quite unable to work during his three weeks in St Petersburg, and he hoped that at Kamenka he might resume composition. He was the more irritated, therefore, to discover that the sketches which he had already made for the first three movements of his First Suite had not been packed into his luggage when he left the Russian capital. Being unable to work upon these, he pressed ahead with the projected movements, and when he left his sister's home on 27 November, two more had been outlined, thus completing the suite as he had first envisaged it. During his eleven days at his sister's he joined heartily in her wedding anniversary celebrations and in hunting expeditions. Before his departure he asked Anatoly to forward the missing sketches to Florence, and he had already begun to look ahead to a new project. Browsing through Lev's library he came across Zhukovsky's translation of Schiller's *Die Jungfrau von Orleans*, skimmed through it, and the seed of a new work was sown. In Florence he would first score the suite, 'and then I shall begin to think about an opera, and I think I've finally settled upon Joan of Arc,' he confided to Modest.[1] Having asked Jurgenson to discover whether the libretto of Auguste Mermet's *Jeanne d'Arc*, produced at the Paris Opéra in 1876, was published, he set off for Vienna. Here he forwent an opportunity of hearing Verdi's *Les Vêpres siciliennes* because that opera did not interest him, but the next evening he revelled in a performance of Meyerbeer's *Robert le Diable*. Before leaving the Austrian capital he purchased a copy of another Verdi opera, *Giovanna d'Arco*, for though he considered it a poor work, he thought it might be worth examining the libretto even though this had been drawn only loosely from Schiller. His spirits had plummeted on leaving Kamenka, but when he arrived in Florence on 2 December and saw the splendid accommodation Mrs von Meck had placed at his disposal, with its new grand piano, writing material – even a supply of his favourite cigarettes – he found his morale completely restored.

The tenor of Tchaikovsky's life in Florence was relaxed yet purposeful. As usual he went for walks and read a great deal. Two things marred the idyll. The first was the lack of any music worth hearing in

---

[1] *TLP*7, p. 457; *TPR*, p. 458; *TPB*, p. 180; *DTC*, p. 99.

Florence; almost the only musical pleasure he found came from the vocal score he had purchased there of Massenet's recent opera, *Le Roi de Lahore*. The second was the condition of his twin brothers in St Petersburg. Anatoly would not write, and Tchaikovsky assumed there must be something seriously wrong, while Modest had been plunged into a further bout of self-doubting by Tchaikovsky's friend, Laroche, to whom he had read his unfinished novel, and who had criticized it tactlessly. But the peace and calm of his Florentine abode afforded Tchaikovsky unqualified satisfaction. Out of a sense of duty he wrote his patroness at least one letter a day until she left Florence. She replied with equal zeal, sharing his delight in the great success which 'their symphony' enjoyed when it was performed for the first time in St Petersburg on 7 December, but differing strongly over the merits of Lalo's Violin Concerto which Tchaikovsky felt to be weak ('you are *too much* a musician for him to be able to please you. . . . I like Lalo more than Bizet,' she declared obstinately – and a little aggressively, since she knew perfectly well Tchaikovsky's passionate admiration for the composer of *Carmen*).[2] Kotek's successor as her resident violinist, Wladislaw Pachulski, had ambitions to turn composer, and Tchaikovsky, again out of a sense of duty, coached him twice a week.

So that there should be no danger of their encountering one another accidentally on their separate excursions, Nadezhda von Meck had quietly provided Tchaikovsky with a timetable of her regular routes and outings. At her request he went to see where she was staying, approaching her house close enough to hear the chatter of children's voices from the garden. When she and her family entourage passed his apartment the next day he glimpsed her from a distance. Next she invited him to visit her villa: Pachulski would show him round and he would have to meet no one. No doubt she looked forward to receiving from him an account of his tour so that she could imagine him in her present house, just as she had been able to envisage him in her Moscow home. But he declined the invitation, saying that he would feel embarrassed to think that everybody was hiding because of him. He began, in fact, to feel a growing apprehension at the dangers within these close approaches. 'What if we should meet? How should I behave?' he wrote anxiously to Anatoly on 5 December. 'She apparently isn't in the least afraid of this, for she's even sent me a ticket for the theatre on Saturday, and she'll be there also. . . . Sometimes I even wonder whether now she indeed wants a personal acquaintance, although there's no hint of this in her daily letters. All this makes me

[2] *TPM*1, p. 509.

less than free and, to tell the truth, in the depth of my heart I very much wish she would leave sooner.'[3] Six days later he was expressing even greater alarm. 'N[adezhda] F[ilaretovna] was also in the theatre, and this embarrassed me, just as her proximity in general also constantly embarrasses me. . . . For instance, every morning I see how, when she passes my villa, she stops and tries to see me! [She was, mercifully, very short-sighted.] How ought I to behave? Go to the window and bow? But in such circumstances should I not call out from the window: "Hullo!"?'[4] Yet he had at all costs to keep his uneasiness to himself, and in his letters to her he continued to profess his passionate unqualified joy at her nearness.

Thus encouraged, Mrs von Meck made a further proposal: that Tchaikovsky should postpone the trip he was preparing to make imminently to Paris until February, when she herself intended to visit the French capital. Tchaikovsky was quick to see how, by agreeing to such a close concurrence of itineraries, he was likely to become chained to her. 'There have already been hints in several of her letters that she would like it *always* to be as it is now, that she would *always* take upon herself all concern for my welfare,' he wrote to Modest on 18 December. '. . . Today, she writes to me that she has decided, after Vienna, to go to Paris early in February, and asks me not to go there now, and that if I do not want to go to Vienna (she suggested to me that I should), then that I should now proceed to Clarens, and visit Paris by 13 February. In other words, she wishes me not to live independently in Paris but in a flat which she has rented and provided with all that's necessary. I replied that I have to obtain in Paris materials for an opera (this is true) and that therefore I shall now still go to Paris for several days, but that afterwards I'm prepared to go to Clarens and be in Paris on 13 February. And now, having written this, I'm in a bad temper. You'll say I'm being fussy. That's true, but it's also true that, however tactfully and delicately she may go about it, N[adezhda] F[ilaretovna] still somewhat inhibits my freedom, and that I'd with pleasure turn down her apartment if it were possible, for the money which she gives me is fully adequate for me to flourish.'[5]

Tchaikovsky held to his resolve. On 27 December Nadezhda von Meck and her suite left Florence for Vienna. By this time he had become accustomed to her close presence and to seeing her, and being seen, across a theatre. Even so, he was surprised at his own reaction to

---

[3] *TLP*7, p. 479; *TPM*1, pp. 598–9; *TPR*, p. 463; *TPB*, p. 182; *YDGC*, p. 193 (last sentence only).
[4] *TLP*7, p. 492; *TPM*1, p. 601; *TPR*, p. 467; *TPB*, p. 184.
[5] *TLP*7, p. 519; *TPM*1, p. 605; *TPR*, pp. 473–4.

her going. 'I feel a great longing for her and a great void beyond my expectations. I pass her uninhabited villa with tears in my eyes. . . . What had at first embarrassed and confused me now forms a subject for the most sincere regret,' he admitted to Modest later that day.[6] With her she carried away Tchaikovsky's profuse thanks for all the joy she had made possible for him in Florence, and also a full preliminary assessment of Pachulski's abilities. For the latter he provided a letter of introduction to Anton Door, his old colleague at the Moscow Conservatoire; for Modest he penned a poem on the lily of the valley in remembrance of an expedition they had made together in Florence during the spring to pick Tchaikovsky's favourite flower. 'For the first time in my life I've succeeded in writing some really tolerable verses which are, moreover, *deeply felt*,' he added proudly in his covering letter.[7] On 28 December he set out for Paris.

From the day of his arrival in Florence nearly four weeks earlier Tchaikovsky had determined to establish a creative momentum, and he had wasted no time in scoring the two movements he had with him of his First Suite upon which he had started in the Ukraine during the summer. He had begun the scherzo on 27 August, and by 2 September he could inform Modest that he had set about a second movement. 'I'm writing an *Introduzione e Fuga*. Both these pieces [the Scherzo, and the Introduction and Fugue] will become part of a suite which I want to compose so that I may have a good rest from symphonic music.'[8] Four days more, and he was confessing the extent of his labours to Nadezhda von Meck, and defining clearly the shape which this '*suite* in the style of Lachner' would take.

When I arrived in Verbovka I felt I simply could not resist my inner compulsion, and I therefore hastened to set down on paper sketches of this suite. I worked with such enjoyment, such enthusiasm, that I literally did not notice how the hours flew by. At this moment three movements of this future orchestral piece are ready, a fourth is roughly sketched, while the fifth is in my head. . . . The suite will consist of five movements: (1) Introduction and Fugue, (2) Scherzo, (3) Andante [these were the three movements which were fully sketched], (4) Intermezzo (*Echo du bal*), (5) Rondo. Because I was constantly thinking of you while I was composing this piece, at every stage was asking myself whether this or that bit would please you,

[6] *TLP*7, p. 541; *TPM*1, p. 607; *TPR*, p. 483.

[7] *TLP*7, p. 541; *TPM*1, p. 608; *TPR*, p. 483; *TZC*2, p. 241; *TPB*, p. 191; *YDGC*, p. 198.

[8] *TLP*7, p. 374; *TPB*, p. 173; *DTC*, p. 385.

whether this or that melody would touch you, I cannot dedicate it to anyone other than *my best friend*.[9]

Though the suite's ultimate shape had seemed clear to Tchaikovsky at this early stage, it was to be much modified. Within a week of beginning scoring it in Florence, the two movements he had by him were finished. Unfortunately the rest was still in Russia, and there followed a long period of anxiety and frustration which he filled by setting to work on his new opera, *The Maid of Orléans*. It was the middle of January before at last a much-frayed Tchaikovsky received the missing package, and by then he was so engrossed in the opera that there was no question of redirecting his attention to the orchestral piece. On 6 March, having the day before finished sketching the opera, he at last began some preliminary work on putting the sketches in order, but his labours were only sporadic, and it was 26 April before he could announce that the scoring was completed. At this stage the work still consisted of only five movements, and their sequence was quite different from that in which they were later to appear. In addition, the last two movements (Nos. 4 and 6 in the final order) had titles. Tchaikovsky had listed the work's intended content to Modest while at Kamenka in November:

(1) Introduction and Fugue
(2) Scherzo
(3) Andante melanconico
(4) *March of the Lilliputians*
(5) *Dance of the Giants*

Then in August 1879, when Jurgenson was actually engraving the suite, Tchaikovsky perceived a fundamental defect and wrote urgently to his publisher:

If you haven't yet got to No. 4 I shall be happy in the extreme. Only now has it suddenly occurred to me that all five movements of the suite are in duple time. *This is impossible!* And because No. 4 is of doubtful merit, I have hastened to compose another piece in waltz time to replace this; this is incomparably better. As soon as I've finished the opera, and this will be done in a week, I'll score this new number and will bring it to you by September, together with all the

9 *TPM*1, p. 421; *TLP*7, pp. 375–6; *TZC*2, p. 200; *DTC*, p. 385 (partial).

rest. Is this possible? Shall I be in time? . . . If it's already too late, I ask you all the same to append the new number, for it's impossible to leave the whole suite in one metre. . . . But it would be best of all to cross out No. 4 (the very doubtful one) and insert the new one instead.[10]

The March, however, was to be reprieved, though only after outside intervention. 'You write that the *Marche miniature* ought to be left,' Tchaikovsky observed to Jurgenson on 5 September 1879 from Simaki. '. . . Speaking frankly, I would wish to throw out this rubbish altogether. Moreover, I find *six* movements too many. . . . But the point is that I'm a poor judge of my own pieces until they have been performed. I think *Taneyev* is familiar with the suite. I rely *entirely* upon his judgement. Please send him a note asking him to state his opinion *frankly*.'[11] If Taneyev decided the March was to be retained, the Andante was to be dropped and the order would be Introduction and Fugue, Divertimento (the new movement), Scherzo, March, Gavotte. It was now the Andante's turn to be saved, and when the suite was first performed on 20 December 1879 at an RMS concert in Moscow conducted by Nikolay Rubinstein, the order of the six movements was the one finally established.

Tchaikovsky did not attend the première, for he was in Rome, and Jurgenson must have taken some sly pleasure in reporting to the composer on the reception accorded the new work. 'The first movement went off without fervent expressions of delight. The second evidently pleased. The Andante pleased very much, but the March drew applause which wouldn't stop until it was repeated. The Scherzo was very well received. The Gavotte found the audience by now fatigued and bursting to get away.'[12] Rubinstein claimed that the orchestra found the work difficult, but Tchaikovsky, who was very upset by this report, refused to accept that the objections were valid. '[This complaint] exasperates me, drives me to despair. The more I try to be simple and easy, the less successful are my efforts,' he lamented to Taneyev on 31 December.[13] The suite was heard – and very enthusiastically received – in St Petersburg on 6 April 1880, when again it was the March which scored the greatest success. In fact this movement was to be played frequently as a separate item because of its popularity.

None of Tchaikovsky's three original orchestral suites can count

[10] *TLP8*, pp. 315–16; *TZC2*, p. 301; *TPJ1*, p. 109; *DTC*, p. 387.
[11] *TLP8*, p. 335; *TZC2*, p. 305; *TPJ1*, p. 111.
[12] *DTC*, p. 388.
[13] *TLP8*, p. 473; *DTC*, p. 388; *TTP*, p. 41.

among his most important works. By the time he came to compose the third, and by far the best of them, he believed that he could fully understand what had most strongly drawn him to the form. '[The suite] has for some time been particularly attractive to me because of the freedom it affords the composer not to be inhibited by any traditions, by conventional methods and established rules,' he told Nadezhda von Meck on 28 April 1884.[14] This was a very retrospective view, accurate to a certain point, but one in which Tchaikovsky had forgotten that what had impelled him to essay his first suite some six years before was that it absolved him not only from certain compositional responsibilities but from expressive ones as well. By the summer of 1878 he was quite incapable of finding within himself those reserves of titanic emotional force from which he had forged the first movement of the Fourth Symphony only a year earlier. Deciding that he needed 'a good rest from symphonic music', as he told Modest, he yet did not wish, in shedding the heavier expressive responsibilities, to negate himself to the degree he had done in the Rococo Variations. Instead that same polish and poise he heard as a property of eighteenth-century music was to be achieved within his own idiom; it was to be his equivalent of what he had identified in *Carmen* as *le joli*. But whereas Bizet's music had drawn in full measure upon the passion and violence of a tumultuous tale, Tchaikovsky's First Suite is rooted primarily in the decorative world of the ballet divertissement. However, lest this should all seem too light, even frivolous, a measure of self-conscious highmindedness is afforded by the opening fugue with its earnest introduction (to give the whole suite a frame this opening fugal material returns to close the piece). Tchaikovsky had several times before used extensive fugato sections, notably in the finales of the Second String Quartet and Third Symphony, but only once before, among the Piano Pieces, Op. 21, had he included a full-blown example of the form. The fugue of the First Suite is a thoroughly pedantic specimen in its earlier stretches, impressive as a demonstration of resourcefulness in devising new contrapuntal webs to accompany successive entries of the subject, but ineffably dull as music, despite the Tchaikovskyan rhetoric which begins to tear through the mesh of the contrapuntal net in the latter half of the piece. The mild spicing of the coda merely serves to emphasize how stodgy has been the preceding fare.

What follows in the other five movements is far more palatable, yet rather second-rate, despite some undeniable charm. By now Tchaikovsky knew his own technique and style so well that he could,

[14] *TPM*3, p. 272; *TLP*12, p. 352; *DTC*, p. 403.

when genuine creativity remained unstirred, 'invent himself'. Admittedly there are some nice things in this suite – for example, the first main division of the Divertimento with its halting clarinet opening, and the section which begins with the wistful, slightly folky E flat minor theme in the middle of the Scherzo (otherwise a very pedestrian movement) – but the overall impression is of inconsequence, for here the lightness is not a necessary phase of relaxation to set off or complement more portentous matters, but instead projects a lack of real commitment, a point emphasized when, near the end of the Intermezzo, the watery flow finally thickens into a new più mosso melody of some real emotional allegiance. Otherwise this Intermezzo is little more than blandly melancholy, despite all Tchaikovsky's undeniable skill at melody spinning. It is the only movement susceptible to any kind of sonata interpretation (here exposition and recapitulation without development, but with a markedly extensive coda). As for the other movements, they rely for their effect heavily (the Gavotte) or entirely (the March) upon the exploitation of a particular, arresting kind of scoring. If the Gavotte puts us a little in mind of the debt Prokofiev was to owe Tchaikovsky, the March foretells even more affirmatively the world of Tchaikovsky's own last ballet, *The Nutcracker*, in which he was to exploit so scintillatingly yet excessively his flair for orchestral confectionery. Scored only for treble instruments (violins, bells, triangle and upper woodwind), this trifle lives entirely through its perky, sugar-coated timbres. Glinka had envisaged a similarly delicate, ear-tickling world in the women's chorus that precedes Chernomor's March (and in the trio of the march itself) in Act 4 of *Ruslan*. But whereas that silvery music had been alluringly persuasive, this is merely cute. A foreshadowing of the mirlitons of *The Nutcracker* is detectable also in the passage for three flutes in the Divertimento. Since the suites were not concerned with major expressive issues, there was no problem in listening to them, and they swiftly enjoyed an audience success which did more to spread their composer's fame than many of his more serious, far finer pieces.

As we have seen, within a week of his arrival in Florence Tchaikovsky had exhausted the work he could do upon the First Suite. After a further week of inactivity he could bear it no longer, and he focused his attention upon his other creative project, the opera on Joan of Arc. His determination to compose this had consolidated since leaving Kamenka, and after three days in Florence he was making plans to begin. He would even make a special trip to Paris to collect relevant literary materials, above all Mermet's libretto. So much did his enthusiasm grow that finally, despite the lack of a scenario, let alone a libretto, he could restrain himself no longer and started to devise his own text from Zhukovsky's translation of Schiller. 'Fearfully, excitedly, and not without some diffidence, I have set about the opera,' he announced to his benefactress on 17 December, having that very morning begun composition.[15] She responded by promptly sending him a copy of Henri Wallon's *Jeanne d'Arc* to aid his work. Within four days he had composed the entire scene of Joan's recognition towards the end of Act 2. In fact, so gripped was he by this new subject, so overwhelmed with ideas, and so moved by reading Wallon's account of Joan's terrible end (the only bit in this book which at all impressed him) that it induced a nervous attack which persuaded him he must break off composition. It also gave him an added reason for going to Paris; as he explained to Jurgenson, the excitements and pressures in composing an opera were such 'that I am simply afraid of living in a quiet corner where I have always to be alone with myself. I must have a ready opportunity, by means of the theatre, music, walking along noisy streets, and so on, to divert and distract myself from the exclusive concentration of all my powers upon one subject.'[16] Thus he did no more work on *The Maid of Orléans* until after his visit to Paris.

When he arrived in the French capital he found the noise and bustle of everyone preparing for the New Year in the sharpest contrast to the tranquillity of Florence. Equally contrasted was the cultural fare on offer, and he sampled to the full what Paris could provide during his ten-day stay. Mostly with Alexey or Kotek, who had travelled especially from Berlin and whose expenses Tchaikovsky defrayed, he visited a variety of entertainments, including several performances at the Comédie-Française, where he was vastly impressed by Sarah Bernhardt in Racine's *Andromaque*. At the opposite end of the enjoyment scale was a performance of Gounod's recent *Polyeucte* at the Opéra.

But by far the most distasteful experience of his Paris stay was to receive, via both Jurgenson and Anatoly, intelligence of Antonina's activities. His brother had been approached by an unknown man, claiming to be a relative of Tchaikovsky's wife, who now, the stranger said, wanted a divorce; what were Tchaikovsky's terms? Mindful of Antonina's past vacillations, a deeply distrustful Tchaikovsky stipulated that he was prepared to be divorced on the grounds of '*adultery*, *impotence*, or whatever you like',[17] but that he would do nothing until he returned to Russia, and that would be in his own good time. But for a

[15] *TPM*1, p. 530; *TLP*7, p. 512; *TCZ*2, pp. 236 and 314; *YDGC*, p. 195; *DTC*, p. 99.
[16] *TLP*7, p. 527; *TPJ*1, p. 60.
[17] *TPR*, p. 489.

while he was badly upset. In Florence, he said, he had sometimes thought of Antonina, but there his whole marriage episode had seemed so remote that it might have been no more than a bad dream. Now reality confronted him again, and a nightmare rose up before him. 'What did I not imagine to myself! Amongst other things I had already decided in my own mind that she was instituting criminal proceedings against me, and wished to charge me. Vividly I saw myself in the dock, and though I routed the public prosecutor with my concluding speech, I still perished under the weight of the shameful indictment. In my letters to you I tried not to appear afraid, but in fact I considered myself already quite ruined,' he confessed to Anatoly on 7 January 1879,[18] by which time he had recovered his composure a little. Nevertheless his stay in Paris was poisoned. He became annoyed by Kotek's foibles – and felt ashamed of himself. To Anatoly he admitted that Kotek's 'fondness for women'[19] was irritating him.

While the theatres afforded Tchaikovsky much pleasure, he found the musical life in Paris altogether deplorable on this visit. The one event which might have given him pleasure was the festival concert at the massive Hippodrome at which various celebrated French composers, including Saint-Saëns, Massenet, Gounod and Delibes, were to conduct their own works. But Tchaikovsky mistook the date by one week, and when he arrived he discovered his ticket admitted him to a horse show instead! As for his own operatic enterprises, he obtained a copy of the Mermet libretto, but found it of less use than he had hoped. 'In the end I have come to the conclusion that Schiller's tragedy, although it is not consistent with historical accuracy, still outstrips all other artistic presentations of *Joan* in its depth of psychological truth,' he concluded to Nadezhda von Meck.[20] Having equipped himself with all the literary materials he felt he needed for his opera, including Jules Michelet's *Jeanne d'Arc* and at least one of Jules Barbier's two treatments of the Joan story, and having resigned himself to accepting that the sketches of his suite's first three movements might now be irretrievably lost in the post, he bade farewell to Kotek and left Paris on 9 January. After an enforced delay in Dijon through appalling weather, he and Alexey were in Clarens at their much-loved Pension Richelieu on 11 January. The next day he set about *The Maid of Orléans* in earnest.

The early compositional process of Tchaikovsky's fifth surviving

---

[18] *TPM*1, p. 608; *TPR*, p. 496. This extract is excised in *TLP*7, p. 567.

[19] *TPR*, p. 494. In fact Kotek had contracted syphilis from his earlier escapades; it was probably this which caused Nadezhda von Meck to replace him as her resident violinist.

[20] *TPM*1, p. 560; *TLP*7, p. 566.

opera is far more precisely charted than is the case with its predecessors. 'Today . . . I composed the first chorus of Act 1,' he informed
Mrs von Meck on 12 January. 'The composition of this opera will be
very laborious for me because I have no ready libretto, and have not yet
even worked out fully the plan of the scenario. Meanwhile I have put
together a detailed scheme for the first act, and I am writing the text a
bit at a time, borrowing it mostly, of course, from Zhukovsky, but also
using other sources, and especially Barbier, whose tragedy on the
subject of Joan has many good points.'[21] His method, as he told Anatoly
the next day, was to round off one day's work by preparing the text for
the morrow's music. As usual when deep in composition, he had a
precise daily routine. 'I drink morning coffee with a light breakfast. A
walk while my room is being cleaned. Composing the opera until lunch
[at 1 p.m.]. After lunch a long walk. On returning, reading and writing
the libretto. . . . At 8 p.m. supper with tea. Then letter-writing and
reading. At 11 I go to bed.'[22] His rate of progress fortified his confident
prediction that when he returned to Russia a significant portion of
the opera would be complete. Within two days he had reached the
Peasants' Chorus (No. 4) with which he was very well pleased. The
next day he sat down to Joan's arioso (No. 5); 'at first for some reason it
went slowly – subsequently, by contrast, it really got going . . . and I
didn't notice the passing of time until lunch,' he told Anatoly.[23] Equal
success attended the next day's labours, and the Hymn (No. 6) was
sketched.

The libretto was a very different matter. Although he believed that
the text he was producing was satisfactory, even good, he often had to
wrestle with it. 'This labour will certainly take several days at least off
my life,' he lamented to his patroness. 'It is difficult to convey to you
how tired I get. How many pens do I gnaw to bits before extracting
from myself a few lines! How often do I get up in utter despair because
the rhymes or a certain number of feet will not come out, or because I
am uncertain whether this or that person should be speaking at a
particular moment!'[24] But composition still proceeded swiftly, and on
21 January Act 1 was done. It had taken ten days. Tchaikovsky wasted
no time in launching into Act 2. During the next two days the duet for
Dunois and the King was ready; Tchaikovsky was particularly pleased
with the passage in F major beginning at bar 86. Since the scene of
Joan's recognition had, of course, already been composed in Florence,

[21] *TPM1*, p. 564; *TLP7*, p. 578; *TZC2*, p. 250.
[22] *TLP8*, pp. 15–16; *TZC2*, p. 251; *TPR*, p. 502; *TPB*, p. 199.
[23] *TLP8*, p. 25; *TPR*, p. 504; *TPB*, p. 201; *YDGC*, p. 200 (partial).
[24] *TPM2*, p. 19; *TLP8*, p. 32; *TZC2*, p. 252; *DTC*, p. 101.

Tchaikovsky only required three more days to complete the whole second act. By 26 January half the opera was sketched. That evening he sat down to play through all he had written. He was well satisfied with the total impression. 'If this opera won't be a masterpiece by universal standards, it will certainly be *mine*,' he judged it proudly to Modest. 'It has undoubted simplicity of style. The structures are lucid. In a word, it will be at the very opposite extreme to *Vakula*.'[25]

During all this intensive work Tchaikovsky had several times felt an urgent need for some diversion. He had been reading *Little Dorrit* with enormous enjoyment. 'Dickens and Thackeray are about the only people I forgive for being English. One must add Shakespeare, but he lived at a time when that vile nation was less ignoble,' he told Anatoly,[26] still remembering with bitter rancour Britain's role in the Russo-Turkish war. Reading, however, used mental energy; what he needed was some real respite. Accordingly for two days he did no more to the opera than devise the text for the first scene of Act 3. Then on 29 January he set off to Geneva for twenty-four hours, where he purchased a piano reduction of some quartets by Mozart and Beethoven, the daily playing of one of which was to afford him much delight in the days just ahead. But nothing could distract him from the opera for long. Back in Clarens, he set about Act 3 on 31 January, and completed the first scene on 4 February. Since he wanted to deal with the 'two fundamental and most difficult love scenes'[27] in immediate succession, he plunged the next day into the love duet in Act 4. It did not come easily. 'In general I'm pleased with myself,' he reported to Modest, 'but I'm a bit tired.'[28] It was a full week before he could return to Act 2.

It is clear that Tchaikovsky's rate of composition was slowing. Before going to Geneva he had confessed to fatigue, and now his creative energies were faltering. This is hardly surprising; after all, in little more than three weeks he had sketched music which would occupy some three hundred pages of vocal score. He had been occupied with other things, too. Letter-writing had consumed much time, and he wrote an especially carefully worded letter to Stasov asking him to intercede with Suvorin, the editor/proprietor of *New Time*, to ensure that the violent press attacks which were currently being mounted by this newspaper against Nikolay Rubinstein and his administration of the Conservatoire should be moderated. Tchaikovsky himself would have come out

[25] *TLP*8, p. 48; *TPM*2, p. 597; *TPR*, p. 512; *TPB*, p. 208; *DTC*, p. 103; *YDGC*, p. 202 (partial).
[26] *TLP*8, p. 31; *TPM*2, p. 596; *TPR*, p. 507; *TPB*, pp. 203–4; *YDGC*, p. 201.
[27] *TPM*2, p. 31; *TLP*8, p. 52; *TZC*2, p. 256.
[28] *TLP*8, p. 68; *TZC*2, p. 259; *TPR*, p. 521; *TPB*, p. 213.

publicly against Rubinstein's tormentors, but he feared that they might fall upon him in return with insinuations about his marriage. He felt much mortified when Stasov excused himself from action on Rubinstein's behalf on the grounds that he felt the charges to be justified. Tchaikovsky's lengthy rejoinder, an imposing mixture of uncompromising frankness with dignified tact, is a reminder of that continuing balance and lucidity with which he could observe the personal affairs and problems of others, if not always of himself. To set against such strains and the sheer labour of composition there was the absolute quiet of the Pension Richelieu, the impeccably solicitous hospitality of the family Mayor who ran the hotel, and the enchantment of Lake Geneva with its winter scenery. If it had not been for these blessings his work would not have advanced so far.

His agreement with Nadezhda von Meck was that he should be in Paris on 13 February, but lack of money made a punctual departure impossible, and he had to send an urgent message to his provider for funds. Even before this he had reported that the overture of the opera was now drafted, as well as the whole of Acts 1 and 2, and the first scenes of Acts 3 and 4 respectively; now he used his enforced delay in Clarens to compile the libretto for the second scene of Act 3, and to compose the coronation march which opens it. On 15 February the necessary financial instalment arrived. Two days later the Mayor family, with very visible marks of regret, said goodbye to their sole guest, himself tearful at leaving them. Next day, as he settled himself into the accommodation Mrs von Meck had arranged for him in Paris, he summarized for her his feelings about leaving the place in which he had just passed some five weeks. 'It is very nice to know that there is a corner of Western Europe where I shall always be received with joy, care and friendliness, where my habits and requirements are well known, where they always know how to arrange it so that, while I am there, I feel as though I were at home.'[29]

The stages by which the last quarter of *The Maid of Orléans* came to completion are not clear. Overcoming his initial disinclination to work in the French capital, and having transferred himself to a less luxurious apartment out of earshot of the traffic, Tchaikovsky had, by 22 February, immersed himself in the finale of Act 3. His response to Paris was ambivalent. During his first week there he hungrily dipped into the cultural riches of the city, rejoicing this time not only in the

---

[29] *TPM*2, p. 45; *TLP*8, p. 91. What Tchaikovsky did not know was that his servant Alexey had made the servant, Marie Savion, pregnant. When later in the year Tchaikovsky heard of this, he promptly sent Marie 100 roubles, and subsequently offered to take her under his protection, an offer which was declined.

Comédie-Française but in musical delights, for two of his favourite works were on immediate offer: Weber's *Der Freischütz* at the Opéra, and Berlioz's *La Damnation de Faust* which Colonne was to conduct at the Théâtre du Châtelet, and which in parts moved Tchaikovsky to tears. But at the same time he was yearning for the peace and quiet he had savoured at Clarens, and after a week he felt little inclination to go out, preferring to remain in his room to read. Dostoyevsky's *The Brothers Karamazov* had just begun to appear in the *Russian Herald*, and Tchaikovsky, deeply moved by the first instalment, enthused about it to Mrs von Meck. 'Why, my friend, are you reading Dostoyevsky – this is not for one with your nerves!' was her alarmed rejoinder.[30] He came across another book, Rousseau's *Confessions*, which he, in his turn, felt would be unsuitable reading for her – 'since,' as he explained mysteriously, 'along with continual flashes of genius, it contains an abundance of very cynical declarations which render this book almost unapproachable for women'[31] (as he later revealed, it was Rousseau's descriptions of his amorous escapades which made his *Confessions* 'almost unapproachable' for genteel femininity). He was deeply impressed by Rousseau's understanding of certain of those very traits he found in his own personality. Above all, the Frenchman offered an explanation of why he, an intelligent man, always appeared so gauche when in company. 'Apropos of this,' Tchaikovsky continued to his confidante, 'he enlarges upon the unsociability of his own nature, and on *the intolerable difficulty of maintaining a conversation as a matter of duty* when, for the sake of keeping the conversation going, you have to speak empty words which you do not really mean and which express no true train of thought or feeling.'[32]

This was an experience familiar to Tchaikovsky, as he pointed out most emphatically to Mrs von Meck when she asked him whether he would call upon Turgenev, who was now resident in Paris. He remembered only too well the problems he had had in talking to another author – Tolstoy. There was something, too, in his patroness's attitude towards Tchaikovsky himself which puzzled him. Though her letters were as ardent as ever, she pleaded headaches and eye-strain as reasons for writing to him only once a week instead of every day, as in Florence; moreover, the wish she had constantly displayed in that city to glimpse him daily if possible seemed to have gone. Only occasionally did they observe each other in a theatre or concert hall. Having to write to her

---

[30] *TPM*2, p. 61.
[31] *TPM*2, p. 73; *TLP*8, p. 142; *TZC*2, p. 276.
[32] *TPM*2, p. 73; *TLP*8, p. 143; *TZC*2, p. 276.

less frequently was, however, some relief. For Pachulski he resumed his twice-weekly lessons begun in Florence. All in all, his mood was unsettled, and this did nothing to facilitate composition. Nevertheless, he persisted with his dogged labour and on 1 March he signed the end of Act 4. What exactly remained to be done is uncertain, but even an optimistic Tchaikovsky reckoned there was a full week's work left. In fact, through unusually intensive application, it took only four days. After this he spent a further two days in ordering the sketches of both the opera and the First Suite, and on 8 March he could report *The Maid of Orléans* drafted to the last detail.

Tchaikovsky remained four more days in Paris. The joy he felt at labour brought to a happy conclusion was fortified by seeing that *The Tempest*, already heard under Rubinstein's direction at the Paris Exhibition in the summer, was to be conducted by Colonne in a morning concert at the Théâtre du Châtelet. Yet even here he felt some gloom. 'I know already both that it'll be badly played and that the audience will hiss as has always happened up to now when my works have been given abroad – and therefore it would have been better if they'd played it after I'd left,' he concluded to Modest.[33] During his time in Paris he had remained obdurately incognito, and no one knew of the composer's presence in the audience when *The Tempest* was performed. The discomforts he endured, despite not having to come forward publicly, were vividly recounted to the same brother the day after the concert.

The evening before I had begun to have nausea and diarrhoea. Right up to the very first chords my agony all morning went *crescendo*, and when they were playing I thought I would that very moment expire, my heart ached so much. And my agitation did not arise at all because I was anticipating a failure but because for some time every fresh hearing of any of my works has been attended by the strongest disenchantment with myself. . . . *The Tempest* was given a very tolerable if not first-rate performance. The tempi were absolutely right. It seemed to me that the players were performing diligently, but without love and enthusiasm. . . . When the last chords finished, rather feeble applause was heard; then, as it were, there was a new burst, and then three or four very loud whistles were heard – but then there resounded through the hall cries of Oh! Oh! signifying protest against the whistling, and then everything fell silent.[34]

[33] *TLP*8, p. 129; *TZC*2, p. 270; *TPR*, p. 543; *TPB*, p. 225; *DTC*, p. 358.
[34] *TLP*8, p. 138; *TPM*2, p. 604; *TZC*2, pp. 271–2; *TPR*, pp. 547–8; *TPB*, pp. 227–8; *DTC*, p. 358.

When he had become calmer Tchaikovsky wrote to Colonne an open letter of thanks which was published in *Revue et Gazette Musicale* a week later. *The Tempest* received at least one favourable press notice and, on reflection, Tchaikovsky decided it had not been a disaster.

Except for this very mixed experience Tchaikovsky's days in Paris after completing *The Maid of Orléans* were the pleasantest of his three-week stay, and he completely recaptured his youthful delight in the city, describing for Anatoly's benefit the modish outfit he was now sporting in this most fashion-conscious of metropolises. 'I walk along the streets in a new grey coat (demi-saison) with a most elegant top hat, showing off a silk shirt front with coral studs, and lilac-coloured gloves. Passing the mirrored piers in the Rue de la Paix or on the boulevards, I invariably stop and admire myself. In shop windows I also observe the reflection of my elegant person.'[35] That liking for fine clothes which he had displayed many years before on entering government service had now resurged, but such expenditure drained his exchequer, and when he left Paris on 12 March his funds would take him only as far as Berlin. Here he would have to wait until Jurgenson came to the rescue. He relieved his boredom a little by twice going to hear Bilse's orchestra; on the first occasion the Andante cantabile from Tchaikovsky's own First String Quartet was in the programme, splendidly played by the entire string band. Otherwise the days he had to endure waiting in hope of help from his publisher gave him much cause to regret his earlier extravagance, and the situation became so desperate that Kotek, with whom he was staying, had to pawn his watch. Finally, in desperation at Jurgenson's apparent silence, Tchaikovsky telegraphed his bene-factress in Paris for an advance against his next instalment from her. She responded by return, and on 19 March he could at last escape from Berlin.

Tchaikovsky stayed only six days in St Petersburg before, on 27 March, setting out for Moscow and the first public performance two days later of *Eugene Onegin* by students of the Conservatoire. As we have seen, he returned to St Petersburg early the following morning. Coming straight from the relative freedom – and sometimes positive joys – of Western Europe, he found his antipathy to St Petersburg at its most extreme. Yet again his arrival coincided with a bereavement: the five-year-old son of Vera Butakova – who, as Vera Davïdova, had some twelve years earlier occasioned him so much distress through her passion for him – died, and the grief of the mother deeply affected the former unwilling lover, Tchaikovsky. That persistent social problem,

[35] *TLP8*, p. 133; *TPM2*, p. 605; *TPR*, p. 546.

the nature of which Rousseau had so clearly revealed to him, was one he had to contend with much on his return to the Russian capital, but he had to endure as patiently as he could these meetings with relatives, for his father, now growing daily more enfeebled, begged him to stay until Easter, and Tchaikovsky could hardly refuse what he realized would perhaps be the last request his parent would ever make of him. 'When I look at his wan appearance and thin face my heart contracts at the thought that his end is near,' he confided sadly to Nadezhda von Meck.[36]

But worse torture was to come. Antonina suddenly surfaced and forced a meeting upon him. It was the first time he had seen her since he had fled from her and Moscow eighteen months before, and she ensured that the reunion was as distressing as possible for him. First she watched the house where Tchaikovsky was lodging with Anatoly; the next day, 5 April, she knocked and demanded to see her husband. After she had left, Tchaikovsky recounted all that had happened to Mrs von Meck. Antonina had been asked to wait in Anatoly's study.

Hardly had I appeared than she threw herself on my neck and started to repeat endlessly that she loved only me in the whole world, that she could not live without me, that she agreed to any conditions I wanted so long as I would live with her, and so on. Probably she wanted to work upon me and, through an outpouring of tenderness, to obtain what she had been unable to get through her refusal of a divorce. I cannot tell you in detail the whole succession of scenes with which she tormented me for at least two hours. My brother Anatoly, who heard our conversation from another room, says that I behaved with tact. I tried with as much composure as I could to explain to her that, however blameworthy I might be in respect of her and however much I might wish her every happiness – yet under no circumstances would I ever agree to live with her. I confess it cost me an incredible effort of self-control not to tell her of the feelings of loathing she instils in me. Of course during this she, as always, suddenly digressed and began now to enlarge upon the craftiness of my relatives who had such a pernicious influence upon me in this matter, now to speak of my music to *Onegin* which she finds superb. Then again tears, protestations of love, and so on. I simply did not know how to break off this intolerable scene, and finally seeing that, despite my firm declaration of emphatic unwillingness to live with her, she was still trying to move me with her displays of affection, I asked her to cut

[36] *TPM2*, p. 83; *TLP8*, p. 155; *TZC2*, p. 277.

short her declaration and to think over for several days all I had said to her, after which she would receive from me either a letter or else a personal interview in Moscow. Meanwhile I handed her the extraordinary sum of one hundred roubles for the return journey to Moscow. At this she suddenly became as happy as a child, recounted to me several instances of men who had been in love with her during the winter, and expressed a wish to see my [twin] brothers, who appeared, and whom she showered with expressions of affection and protestations of love despite the fact that for half an hour before she had been calling them her enemies. During all this she behaved as though we were all glad to see her. Finally she left, and as she said goodbye, she asked me where we would see each other today and tomorrow as though she supposed that I was longing for meetings with her. I had to tell her that I could not see her here, and I asked her to go off to Moscow today, which she has promised to do.[37]

Much upset by this meeting, Tchaikovsky reflected that there could be no prospect of negotiating a divorce with a woman so disturbed and irrational (Antonina had declared that the stranger who had sought out Anatoly to open negotiations for divorce was a vile intriguer who was in love with her and was acting against her wishes). But Antonina's campaign was only beginning, and a week later Tchaikovsky was recounting the next skirmish to his confidante.

A certain person, having received from me the wherewithal for her return journey to Moscow, nevertheless thought fit to remain in St Petersburg, and one fine morning I met her walking near our house. It appears that she is living in the very same house as we are. I repeated to her my wish that she should go off to Moscow. . . . She replied that she could not now live far away from me, and that she would go off to Moscow at the same time as I. Then I received from her a long letter with a declaration of her passionate love for me. I did not reply. I shall simply have to flee from this unforeseen persecution of hers, and with this aim I have decided to leave here sooner than I had proposed – namely, on Easter Sunday. I shall remain in Moscow three days; on the Thursday Modest and his Kolya will arrive, along with my niece, Anna, after which we shall continue our journey to Kamenka together.[38]

[37] *TPM*2, pp. 86–7; *TLP*8, pp. 159–60.
[38] *TPM*2, p. 88; *TLP*8, p. 163.

Tchaikovsky would have held to this schedule, had not an indisposition of Kolya necessitated an extra day in Moscow, in consequence of which he had another painful encounter with his wife. Besieging him with her sister, she announced that she wished to commute Tchaikovsky's allowance to her into a lump sum of 15,000 roubles since, she said, she could not work in Russia because of the way people looked upon her, and so had decided to go abroad and devote herself to music. Tchaikovsky, of course, refused; he did not possess the necessary funds, and he knew only too well that Antonina would later return for more. Promising to write her a final reply, he left Moscow on 18 April. These meetings with his wife had made him ill, and it was in a tense, nervous condition that he arrived in Kamenka. There he wrote to Antonina the promised letter, declining her request and adding that he would return to her unopened any communication she sent him. This done, he tried to turn his attention to the pleasures and peace of Kamenka, and to scoring his First Suite.

Tchaikovsky spent the spring and summer of 1879 on estates in the Russian countryside, just as he had done in 1878. Brailov or nearby Simaki, Nizy – above all, Kamenka – all claimed a part of his time. His musical occupations included no composition except for the movement he added to the First Suite in August. Instead he devoted himself entirely to orchestrating and making a piano duet transcription of the suite, and to the far larger labour of scoring *The Maid of Orléans*. All work on the suite was quickly finished, and two days later, on 8 May, he set about the opera. It was an occupation in which he found the greatest pleasure. 'It is difficult to convey the delight you experience when an abstract musical idea takes on a real form as the result of its assignment to this or that instrument or group of instruments. If not the most pleasant, it is one of the pleasantest moments in the compositional process,' he divulged to Nadezhda von Meck while engrossed in *The Maid*.[39] The very appearance of one of his scores gave him pleasure, and corrections and alterations were offensive disfigurations of the page, he told her. Orchestration was tending to become a more extended process with him. Just as his views on what constituted good operatic writing had changed much since *Vakula* in 1874, so his conception of the special requirements of operatic scoring had clarified. At an early stage in his summer's work on *The Maid* he read through Wagner's *Lohengrin* not, as he hastened to make clear, in order to filch certain orchestral combinations, but to see what he might learn of Wagner's methods in general from the opera which he considered the peak of that composer's output.

[39] *TPM*2, p. 139; *TLP*8, p. 254; *TZC*2, p. 293; *YDGC*, p. 214; *DTC*, p. 105.

'The older I get, the more convinced I become that these two branches, i.e. *symphony* and *opera*, are in all respects the extreme opposites,' he told Nadezhda von Meck.[40] The scoring was finally completed on 2 September. Compared to the three or so weeks he had taken to score *Vakula*, the nearly four months of actual labour spent on *The Maid* was surprising, even allowing for the fact that there had been none of the urgent conditions in which the earlier work had been created. It is a measure of the careful thought he gave to matters of balance, colour and contrast that he took so long. 'If it should prove that *The Maid* still does not conform to the requirements of operatic style, then it will be clear to me that those who assert that I am by nature exclusively a symphonist, that I ought to leave the stage alone, are right,' he declared to his patroness as he returned to survey the finished score the following December.[41]

The Maid of Orléans was first produced on 25 February 1881 at the Maryinsky Theatre in St Petersburg. Despite the reputation Tchaikovsky was now beginning to enjoy in Russia, the production left much to be desired. The cast was good and the singers were generally delighted with their music. Nápravník, who was the opera's dedicatee as well as its first conductor, had required some cuts and some revisions in the part of Joan because Mariya Kamenskaya, the singer who was to create the part, was a mezzo-soprano; where Tchaikovsky had to transpose he had to do some rescoring. Some of these revisions pained him, but as he had realized when the same Nápravník had introduced *The Oprichnik* seven years before, this conductor knew his job thoroughly, and he prepared the new opera to the composer's entire satisfaction. The problems lay with the theatre management and with the provision for production. The Imperial Theatres' head of repertoire, Nikolay Lukashevich, attempted to be an autocrat in musical decisions, even on one occasion informing Tchaikovsky that he could not revise his own music without permission. Worst of all, because a vast sum had recently been spent on a new ballet, funds were very low and there was a ruling in force that no new scenery was to be made for new operas, nor was any singer permitted two costumes in one opera. Thus Lionel turned up for the coronation in the garb he had worn on the battlefield, while the set for the square outside the Gothic cathedral of Reims had already served to represent two other locations in earlier operas, having started life as a square in Warsaw. Nearly everything on stage was second-hand, and some of the costumes were threadbare.

[40] *TPM2*, p. 111; *TLP8*, p. 198; *TZC2*, p. 287; *YDGC*, p. 213.
[41] *TPM2*, p. 269; *TLP8*, pp. 445–6; *TZC2*, p. 341; *DTC*, p. 106.

The success of the opera with the first-night audience therefore stemmed entirely from the quality of the performance, which Tchaikovsky agreed was in general very good. 'Kamenskaya sang the whole scene with the angels magnificently and I took eight bows after Act 1,' he reported to Mrs von Meck three days after the première.

> Act 2 also pleased very much. Scene 1 of the third act drew a storm of applause. The second scene [outside Reims Cathedral] was far less successful; the march and the whole scene in general was mounted so wretchedly, grubbily and pitifully that nothing else could be expected. On the other hand Act 4 again pleased very much. Altogether I took twenty-four bows. *Kamenskaya* was superb; she even acted extremely well, which she had never done before. Of the rest the best of all was *Pryanishnikov* who sang Lionel.[42]

Modest remembered that his brother had also singled out for praise Fyodor Stravinsky as Dunois.

The critics were far more doubtful than the first-night audience about the work's merits, and from Cui it drew blistering condemnation (though Tchaikovsky must have been a little consoled to find that his scoring was unreservedly praised by this universal savager). Tchaikovsky must have foreseen this; what probably disturbed him more was the blunt pronouncement of one critic who reaffirmed what Tchaikovsky had heard before, but which he hoped his latest opera would convincingly refute. 'In *The Maid of Orléans* Tchaikovsky has again shown that he is by nature a symphonist and in no way an opera composer,' wrote Pavel Makarov in the *Exchange Gazette*.[43]

The opera did not maintain its apparent initial success. Early next season it had to be dropped because of a persistent throat ailment suffered by Kamenskaya. For the revival in the 1882–3 season Tchaikovsky made some further transpositions in Joan's part to accommodate Kamenskaya and made new cuts, but the opera was soon dropped and was never heard again in Russia in Tchaikovsky's lifetime. Nevertheless it was the first of his operas ever to be given abroad (in Prague in July 1882).

Except for the early, ill-fated *Undine*, which Tchaikovsky had destroyed after it had failed to secure production, *The Maid of Orléans* was Tchaikovsky's first opera from a non-Russian literary source. The basic text was Schiller's play, *Die Jungfrau von Orleans*, translated (as had been

---

[42] *TPM*2, p. 478; *TLP*10, pp. 32–3; *TZC*2, pp. 453–4; *DTC*, p. 110.
[43] *DTC*, p. 110; *YDGC*, p. 252.

de la Motte Fouqué's *Undine*) by Zhukovsky. In the following summary of the plot the major excisions made by Tchaikovsky after completing the music are enclosed in square brackets:

ACT I. *A country setting, on one side a chapel with an ikon of the Virgin, on the other a tall leafy oak on the bank of a stream.*
Some girls are singing as they decorate the oak with garlands (No. 1). Thibaut, Raimond and Joan enter (No. 2). Thibaut reproves the girls for singing in such circumstances; Paris has fallen to the English, the King is a fugitive, and their own future has an imminent uncertainty. He counsels his daughter, Joan, in such circumstances to seek a protector; he wishes her to marry Raimond. When Joan remains silent, Raimond, despite his love for her, urges her father not to press her into marriage. 'Let her young life blossom freely as before,' he declares (bar 51). 'If it is not the Lord's will, my longed-for hour will not come!' There develops a terzetto, Raimond professing further his readiness to forgo his joy, while Thibaut continues reproachfully to remonstrate with his daughter, the chorus now supporting his plea. But Joan herself struggles with her inner feelings, and in the following scene (No. 3), she discloses timidly that she has been given a different destiny. Thibaut is furious, and alleges that Joan's pact is not with heaven but with the devil, and he asks her angrily why she repairs at night to the crossroads to listen to the mountain wind, and why she is constantly beneath this oak tree which has long been a haunt of evil. As Thibaut warns Joan of the punishment God will mete out to her, Raimond remains incredulous.

Suddenly the glow of a fire is seen backstage (No. 4), and the tocsin is heard. An off-stage chorus of peasants cries out in terror at the approach of the enemy who is bringing fire and destruction. The chorus rushes in and prays for deliverance. To Thibaut's plea for information Bertrand, one of the peasants, reports that two big battles have been lost, and that the enemy has reached the Loire and laid siege to Orléans, with the treacherous Duke of Burgundy and Isabelle, the King's own mother, participating in the assault. All join in cursing her. Bertrand further reports that Orléans is nervously awaiting the assault, but he adds that the enemy, including the unvanquished Salisbury, will perish. The crowd is less sure, but Joan steps forward (No. 5) and tells them to dry their tears; a saviour is at hand and, she prophesies, an armed maid will lead the defeat of the enemy at Orléans. The crowd is bewildered. When Thibaut tells his daughter to be silent, the crowd adds its disbelief in miracles. 'There are miracles!' Joan retorts (bar 28), and she declares Salisbury to be already dead. As the crowd reaffirms its disbelief, a soldier rushes in to report that Joan's prophecy is indeed correct. Even Thibaut is awestruck by his daughter's prescience, and leaves the stage. Joan exhorts the people to pray and, abetted by Raimond and Bertrand, she leads a hymn (No. 6) of supplication for victory and peace, after which all leave except Joan. She now realizes her time for departure has come (No. 7), and with great sadness she begins (bar 39) her farewell to the hills, meadows, and companions of her childhood. 'You will never again see Joan; she is bidding farewell for ever (bar

47) . . . for it is my lot to tend another flock on the fields of murderous war' (bar 95).

During Joan's farewell the light has been fading. As the finale (No. 8) begins she laments further her destiny. 'O God, leave me in my humble station!' she begs (bar 8). The chapel bell begins to toll, and Joan is suddenly bathed in bright moonlight as an offstage women's chorus of heavenly voices addresses her. 'You must don the armour of battle and encase your young breast in iron. Beware of hopes, shun earthly love!' (bar 37) . . . God will place you above all earthly maidens,' the celestial chorus concludes. Joan, still in great distress of spirit, continues to beg fervently that 'the bitter cup may pass' from her, but the choir resumes its exhortation to hasten to the field of battle, where she will lead the French to victory. 'You will bring honour to the warrior, lustre and power to the throne, and you will bring Charles to Reims to take the crown' (bar 105). Joan perceives that her destiny is inescapable, and with the choir assuring her of God's support, she pledges herself to her mission. 'Everywhere I shall be victorious!' are her last confidently repeated words.

ACT 2. *A hall in the palace at Chinon.*
King Charles VII and his mistress, Agnès Sorel, are listening to a choir of minstrels (No. 10). The King finds their melancholy singing does nothing to raise his or Agnès's spirits, and he summons his gypsies, dwarfs and tumblers to restore their morale. After an extensive ballet (No. 11), he orders (No. 12) the dancers to be entertained and each to be rewarded with a golden chain. However, Dunois, a knight, contends that such gifts are impossible because the exchequer is empty and the King's own soldiers, having received no pay, are threatening to desert. The King would mortgage some of his land to raise money, but Dunois points out that the siege of Orléans threatens this land. Agnès pledges all her possessions to the King's cause, and leaves to collect them. As for the King, he declares that he would give up everything, including his kingdom, for the love of Agnès. Dunois reproves him sharply; this is no time for love, he insists, and launches (bar 62) into a vigorous exhortation to the King to remember his God-appointed role. At first (bar 88) Charles remains lost in his love for Agnès, but Dunois finally prevails, and the two men join (bar 148) in declaring their resolve to lift the siege of Orléans. A mortally wounded soldier, Lauret, enters to report a further defeat; the King should either flee or hurry to his troops, for hope yet remained. Having delivered his message, Lauret dies. Charles is in despair, and despite Dunois' exhortation to fight, he feels too much blood has already been shed, and he decides to withdraw across the Loire. In angry dismay Dunois upbraids him. 'We have no King!' he shouts (bar 221), declaring that he at least will go to perish in the ruins of Orléans. After Dunois' abrupt exit, Charles sinks exhausted on to his chair. His expressions of despair (No. 13) are interrupted by the entry of Agnès carrying her jewels. Charles turns to her for comfort, and she offers her wealth to him, including her lands and castles, to finance his campaign. But nothing can lift him from his despair, and he finally breaks down. Tenderly she tries to console him, and in an arioso (bar 70) she promises to go with him, come what may; as for Charles, he continues to find his only consolation in her. Finally they join (lento con anima) in a rapt expression of love.

As they embrace, off-stage trumpets and chorus greet the 'saviour-maid' (No. 14). Dunois and a crowd of knights and ladies rush in to tell a perplexed Charles and Agnès that fate has changed sides, and that the French have scored a great victory. Then the Archbishop [44] enters to confirm Dunois' tidings to an incredulous King: the army was on the verge of defeat when a miracle had happened. A maid had emerged from an oak grove and rallied the army, who had fallen anew upon the enemy and routed them. The Archbishop adds (bar 78) that Joan calls herself a prophetess and has promised to lift the siege of Orléans before the new moon.

Further off-stage praise of the 'saviour-maid' signals the arrival of Joan herself. To test her divine insights, the King instructs Dunois to take his place. When Joan enters (No. 15) with a body of knights and people, she quickly picks Charles out from the throng, though she has never before been in his presence. He asks her how she recognized him. 'I have seen you – but only where you were seen by no one but God,' she replies enigmatically (bar 27), and she offers to recount to him the three prayers he had secretly made one night (she tells him he may send away the crowd, but Charles says they may stay). 'First you prayed the Almighty to choose you as the sacrifice of reconciliation, and to pour for us upon your submissive head the whole cup of punishments' (bar 53). All are yet more astonished, and Joan goes on to disclose the King's second prayer – that if he should lose his throne, he should yet keep his spiritual peace, his friends, and his faithful Agnès. The crowd are again amazed. Asked by Joan (bar 85) whether she should recount the third prayer, Charles cuts her short. 'I believe!' he affirms (bar 91). 'No mortal by himself could do this. God is with you!' The crowd agree. The Archbishop asks her to tell them who she is, and Joan begins her narration (bar 130). She had been born in Domrémy, the daughter of a simple shepherd. Often she had heard how the English had tried to enslave her people, and she had prayed to the Virgin to protect them. Then once (bar 151), after she had prayed all night at the oak tree, a figure dressed like a shepherdess had appeared before her bearing a sword and banner, and had told her of her divine mission to free France and crown the King in Reims. [When Joan had questioned her own ability to do this, the figure had replied that everything was possible to a maid who rejected earthly love. The figure had touched her eyes, and the whole sky had been filled with winged cherubims bearing beautiful lilies, and a sweet voice was heard.] Three nights in a row the vision had appeared, but on the third night the figure had addressed her angrily (bar 196): 'Take up your cross, be obedient to heaven! In suffering lies purification on earth. Here you are lowly; there you will be raised up.' At this the figure had cast off her shepherdess's garb and had revealed herself to be the Virgin, had looked comfortingly upon Joan, and had then slowly disappeared upwards into heaven.

As the finale (No. 16) begins the Archbishop leads off an ensemble in which everyone accepts that Joan is divinely led, and they glorify God. After a further

---

[44] In fact the censor objected to this designation and changed 'Archbishop' to 'Pilgrim'. Tchaikovsky countered by suggesting that 'Cardinal' ought to be acceptable, since the Orthodox Church did not have cardinals.

assurance from Joan (bar 36) that she will return France to the King, Charles entrusts his army to her (bar 48) and offers her his sword. But she will not take it; the sword predestined for her is at the grave of St Catherine at Fierbois – and she wishes to bear a white banner with a purple stripe. The King orders Dunois to fetch the sword. Joan asks (bar 67) the Archbishop for his blessing and kneels before him as everyone reaffirms their faith in victory and urges Joan to lead the army to battle. Finally all go out in the wake of the King and Joan.

ACT 3, SCENE I. *A place near the battlefield. On the heights the English camp is burning.* Lionel, a Burgundian knight, rushes in. He is followed by Joan, who challenges him. In a heated exchange she discovers his identity as a follower of the treacherous Duke of Burgundy. Joan falls upon Lionel (bar 93), and in the struggle she tears his helmet from his head. Lionel is vanquished, but as Joan is about to despatch him, a shaft of moonlight falls upon his face. Struck by his appearance, Joan stays her hand. Lionel tells her (bar 113) not to delay; he asks no mercy. But she signals him (bar 119) to flee. He scorns thus to escape. Nevertheless, Joan cannot bring herself to kill him, despite his defiant rejection of her mercy. 'Kill me, and go!' she suddenly declares (bar 137). Lionel is utterly perplexed. For a second time Joan raises her sword, but again she is unable to strike. 'Holy Virgin!' she cries out in despair (bar 152). Startled by this invocation, and moved by Joan's evident distress, Lionel feels a welling sympathy for her. He asks her gently (bar 176) who she is. 'Come with me,' he finally pleads (bar 196). 'Leave your fatal sword!' 'Alas, I am unworthy to bear it!' she cries (bar 201). Her inner struggle gives rise to an impassioned outburst. 'O God, why, ah why did I give up my shepherd's crook for a warrior's sword?' she laments (allegro moderato). Lionel's feelings grow warmer still. 'Is it pity or love which suddenly creeps into my soul?' he asks in bewilderment (bar 265). This impassioned duet proceeds until, as Lionel takes Joan's hand (bar 300), Dunois is seen approaching. Again Joan tells Lionel to flee, but he refuses. Finally, to Joan's even greater distress, he declares (bar 418) he has fallen in love with her. Dunois enters hurriedly with a small detachment. Lionel picks up his sword, kneels before Dunois and offers it to him. Dunois returns it to him (andante), accepts Lionel's return to the French side, and then turns to Joan to report that victory is theirs, and that Reims has opened its gates to them. Suddenly Joan collapses exhausted into Lionel's arms, and it is seen that she is wounded in the shoulder. 'She is bleeding!' exclaims Lionel. 'Would that my life might flow away with my blood!' Joan replies in despair. Supported by Lionel and Dunois, she goes out slowly.

ACT 3, SCENE 2. *The square in front of Reims cathedral.*
A crowd is awaiting a procession. To a grand march (No. 18) a splendid coronation cavalcade appears, with Joan preceding the King, and enters the cathedral to the sound of the crowd's loud praise of the King and the 'saviour-maid'. When the procession has disappeared into the building, Thibaut and Raimond detach themselves from the crowd (No. 19). Raimond tries to persuade Thibaut to leave, but the latter refuses. He has seen Joan's pale, distressed face. 'The hour has come to save her!' he declares (bar 39) '. . . I want to make her return to the God from whom she has turned aside!' (bar

50). Raimond remonstrates desperately with him, but Thibaut is adamant; it is his duty to save his daughter, even if her body must be reduced to ashes.

As the finale (No. 20) begins, Thibaut and Raimond once again retreat into the crowd, which begs God's blessing, and praises Him. The King, Joan and the whole procession emerge from the cathedral. The King proceeds to a throne set on a dais, and Joan takes her place near him. The crowd praises Charles, who replies with thanks, extends pardon to his enemies, and ascribes victory to God's mercy. The crowd responds with praise. The King speaks of Joan as the agent of France's victory, and decrees that an altar shall be raised to her. Again the crowd gives praise, this time to Joan. The King addresses Joan as though she were divine, and begs her to reveal her 'immortal image' so that 'we may worship thee on earth' (bar 112). But as Joan stands silent, Thibaut steps forward. Joan cries out as she recognizes her father, and Thibaut straightway denounces her as an agent of the devil. The crowd declares him mad (bar 146), but he vigorously rejects their diagnosis. Then he challenges Joan to her face: 'In the name of the Trinity, do you hold yourself to be pure and holy?' (bar 168). But because of guilt at her love for Lionel, Joan remains silent, and the crowd is horror-struck. In their bewilderment the King and people join in a gigantic ensemble, ending with a plea to God to reveal the truth. Suddenly Dunois rises to Joan's defence. 'I challenge anyone here who dares accuse her!' he shouts (bar 256), but he is answered by a great clap of thunder. All recoil from Joan in horror. Thibaut again challenges Joan, but he too is answered by a great roll of thunder. Finally when the Archbishop confronts her, a third peal of thunder confirms the fears of everyone that Thibaut's accusation is indeed true. [Another vast ensemble unfolds in which all end by turning upon Joan for having deceived them as to the source of her powers; they tell her to flee from them. The King reinforces their demand, but assures her nevertheless of a safe conduct out of Reims. The people repeat their order.[45]] The King and his followers leave hurriedly; the crowd disperses in anger and dismay. Joan remains alone, her head still bowed. Then Lionel approaches her, offering his hand and protection. When Joan raises her head and recognizes him, she recoils in revulsion, crying out: 'Away! You are my hated enemy! You have destroyed my soul!' She rushes out, followed by Lionel.

ACT 4, SCENE 1. *A wood.*
Joan is seated deep in thought. She remains torn between her God-given mission and her love for Lionel. But it is the latter feeling which now triumphs. 'O Lionel!' she cries (bar 93). 'My dear beloved, I love you more than life. Where are you? Come to me!' Lionel enters precipitately and they embrace. An extensive love duet follows (No. 22). Their rapture is broken by an off-stage chorus of angels' voices. 'Heaven's decree is broken. You are a sinner!' they begin. Joan tears herself from Lionel's embrace, to his bewilderment. She listens transfixed to the choir. The sound of advancing English soldiers is heard. [Suddenly Joan awakes as from a reverie. 'Captivity and death! Yes,

---

[45] This cut involved the removal of some 140 bars and their replacement by thirty bars of new music.

yes, but for me, not for you!' she cries to Lionel (bar 244). She urges him to flee, declaring that she will remain. 'Fate has shown me my road, and I must submit to fate,' she affirms (bar 263), but Lionel still presses her not to forgo their love. Their desperate dialogue is interrupted when[46]] a group of English soldiers suddenly rushes in. Lionel draws his sword and attempts to defend Joan, but is mortally wounded. The soldiers try to bind Joan, but she tears herself away and rushes to Lionel as he dies. 'Receive my last kiss, and wait for me. Our meeting is at hand,' she announces quietly (andante). Then she turns and stretches out her hands to her captors to receive their chains. They rush out, dragging her with them.

ACT 4, SCENE 2. *A square in Rouen.*
A crowd is waiting for the procession to arrive with Joan. 'They're bringing her! There's the witch!' the people cry, looking off-stage towards the approaching cortège. Joan enters, a priest beside her, with soldiers and monks following. 'Holy father, support me! I'm afraid!' she gasps (bar 68). The crowd presses forward in pity, but is pushed back. 'Give me a cross,' begs Joan (bar 89), and one of the soldiers breaks a stick in two, ties the pieces together, and gives them to the priest.[47] Joan is bound to the stake. The executioner sets the pyre alight, and soldiers and monks throw on more wood. The priest blesses Joan and holds the cross high before her. As the flames mount Joan cries, 'O Lord, take me to your abode!' (bar 117). The off-stage chorus of angels joins its sounds to those of the crowd. Finally Joan, 'with an expression of joy on her face' [sic], declares 'The heavens have opened! My suffering is at an end!'[48]

Though, as we have already noted, Schiller afforded the main substance of Tchaikovsky's scenario, and Zhukovsky's translation a good many lines of the libretto, suggestions from other sources Tchaikovsky consulted also found their way into *The Maid of Orléans*; thus the idea for the opening chorus came from Mermet's libretto for his own opera, *Jeanne d'Arc*. The rest of Act 1 was drawn largely from Schiller, though Tchaikovsky transferred to this scene Joan's prescient announcement of Salisbury's death which, in *Die Jungfrau*, had been delivered to the King at Chinon. Significantly, most of the chorus's contributions, both here and elsewhere in the opera, were Tchaikovsky's inventions (as was the introduction of the mortally wounded Lauret in Act 2). The chorus of terrified peasants was his idea; so, too, were the angel voices which

---

[46] This section had accounted for some 100 bars.

[47] The censor objected to the representation of the cross on the stage, and this incident had to be excised in St Petersburg with the loss of some thirteen bars.

[48] In addition to the cuts indicated in this résumé of the plot of *The Maid*, Tchaikovsky made some other revisions. The final section (in F minor) of the Act 2 duet for the King and Dunois was rewritten and reduced from some fifty-odd bars to twenty, and a dozen bars in the first part of Joan's narration later in the same act were replaced by four bars of orchestral writing (bars 147–50). Finally the orchestral introduction (andante con moto) to the duet in the first scene of Act 4 was halved in length.

use part of God's command as Joan recalls it in her farewell soliloquy at the end of Schiller's prologue. In Act 2 the brief mention which Schiller made of the King's preoccupations with troubadours and entertainments for Agnès Sorel was the slender excuse for the minstrels' chorus and the ballet. Though most of what follows in this act observes the course of events as set out by Schiller, the libretto itself is almost entirely by Tchaikovsky up to the moment when the first tidings of victory are brought; after this it is drawn almost entirely from Zhukovsky's translation.

Whereas in these two acts Tchaikovsky had mostly been savagely truncating *Die Jungfrau von Orleans*, he had to supplement Schiller liberally in the first scene of Act 3, for Schiller had made the Joan/Lionel conflict very brief. Once the confessions of love begin no help was to be found in *Die Jungfrau*, though part of the final exchange between Joan and Lionel is from that play. It is in this scene that Tchaikovsky introduced the first substantial modification of plot, for Lionel, in Schiller an English officer, is now transformed into a Burgundian knight. This made it easier for him to change allegiance and thus figure in the coronation scene, and also more freely pursue his relationship with Joan in the last act. The end of this first scene of Act 3, where Lionel offers his sword to Dunois, was, of course, Tchaikovsky's invention, though Joan's wound and her last despairing utterance were not.

Schiller's real gift to Tchaikovsky was the coronation scene. The grand march, with its attendant tumult as the royal procession enters the cathedral of Reims, was all specified in *Die Jungfrau* and Tchaikovsky complied with Schiller's stage directions as closely as possible. Though he felt compelled to extend the Thibaut/Raimond dialogue and create a full triumphal chorus for the procession's re-entry from the cathedral, almost everything until Thibaut makes his first direct challenge to his daughter sets a virtually unabridged chunk from Schiller's fourth act. Tchaikovsky did, however, transfer some individual exclamations to the chorus, as well as inventing the texts in the huge ensemble which follows (and also in the second ensemble which he subsequently cut). By contrast, however, both the text and the basic idea of the scene's end, where Lionel approaches Joan to take her to safety, were Tchaikovsky's own. And with this scene Tchaikovsky's debt to Schiller virtually ceased. The first scene of the last act was entirely Tchaikovsky's conception, though Joan's opening words are drawn from her soliloquy at the beginning of Schiller's Act 4, and Schiller provided the suggestion for Joan's voluntary surrender at the end. As for the last scene, the idea for this came from Jules Barbier's tragedy, *Jeanne d'Arc*; in Schiller Joan had received a mortal wound on the field of battle.

Schiller described *Die Jungfrau von Orleans* as a 'romantic tragedy', a clear sign that he had not been concerned simply to filter through his personal vision of the human condition those historical events which had, in 1429, taken a young French peasant girl from her home to the royal court to become the instrument of victory against the invading English, and finally, in 1431, to a brutal end at the stake. For Schiller Joan was a figure of innocence, the reality of whose historical existence might be reshaped into a drama of sin and guilt ending in expiation and redemption. Thus he invented the romantic episode of Joan's love for the English knight, Lionel – an attachment which deflects her from the mission assigned to her by heaven. To be redeemed requires of Joan not merely a resumption of her mission but an act of atonement as emphatic as had been her sin. Had Schiller allowed her to perish through the sentence of an earthly court, as had the historical Joan, she might have appeared merely the helpless victim of events; hence in *Die Jungfrau* she received the mortal blow on the battlefield again actively struggling for her God-assigned cause.

This interpretation of Schiller's drama will scarcely cancel the offence many will feel at his violation of the real Joan, but for Tchaikovsky such distortions did not matter. What drew him to Joan was the image he could conjure of a young, sensitive girl, possessed by divine visions yet vulnerable to her own emotions, who is finally destroyed by circumstances from which she cannot escape. Tchaikovsky saw Joan, like Tatyana before her, as a victim of fate, and it was this, not historical scruples, which moved him to replace Schiller's allegorical end with something closer to chronicled fact. There is an element of fate in *Die Jungfrau*, yet when Schiller's Joan rushes to the field of battle she carries with her the possibility of survival; when Tchaikovsky's Joan enters the square at Rouen, the certainty of her end is absolute.

In the opera there is therefore nothing like Schiller's consistency of dramatic vision. But Tchaikovsky went further, not merely weakening the character of Joan, but debasing it. Schiller had presented her love for Lionel as a sudden involuntary response, scarcely to be condemned as a sin since no act of will was involved, yet sufficient to impair her singlemindedness. Nor was there any question of her yielding to temptation. On the contrary, she strove to master her feelings, begged for death rather than be confronted by Lionel again, and only saw him in captivity where she again unequivocally rejected his propositions. But Tchaikovsky's Joan fully indulges her emotions in a way which makes the attempt in the final scene to transform this languishing girl into an heroic martyr to whom is granted a place in the kingdom of heaven about as credible as turning Juliet into the Virgin herself.

As a piece of coherent, serious drama Tchaikovsky's scenario is therefore irredeemably flawed. Yet given the same basic stimulus as *Onegin* – that is, a central character who is a young girl caught up in a train of events which leads to misfortune – it might have been hoped that Tchaikovsky's inspiration would have been awakened. It was not. Tatyana and her fate had touched the sources of Tchaikovsky's creativity at their very deepest level, where had been born ideas of eloquent directness which embodied some of the central emotions and predicaments of the story; there, too, all-mastering fate had converted itself into pregnant thematic forms which could become generating forces within the musical tissue, or which could infiltrate a variety of musicodramatic situations, thus ubiquitously signalling the active workings of that ineluctable power. But Joan's plight never really gripped Tchaikovsky, and in *The Maid* there is nothing like the abundance of thematic significances to be found in *Onegin*. True, there is a kind of 'fate' theme associated with Joan's calling, this time embodied in a rising scale since her destiny is heaven-inspired. The words to which Tchaikovsky first devised this protoshape occur in the recognition scene in Act 2 (Ex. 153a), and it infiltrated some of the other music he subsequently wrote for contexts which allude to her calling in the earlier parts of the opera.[49] When Thibaut turns to Joan at the opera's opening, exhorting her to take an earthly protector in such perilous times, the oboe quietly enunciates a similar rising phrase (Ex. 153b) as an intimation of that factor which must override all considerations of earthly security. The idea haunts the following pages, even with a gentle irony affording Raimond his opening in the terzetto where he declares his readiness to forgo Joan's love if such be the will of God (later this same phrase explicitly dresses Joan's confession of her 'other calling' (Ex. 153c)). The protoshape is prominent in Joan's oblique disclosure to the people of Domrémy of her mission (Ex. 153d), and in her farewell aria later in the scene it may again be discerned (Ex. 153e) though, curiously, this seems to be an even more explicit, if inexplicable, quotation from Chopin's famous A major Polonaise (Gerald Abraham has drawn attention to Tchaikovsky's unconscious recollection of Mozart's Jupiter Symphony during the first duet of the second

---

[49] In Acts 3 and 4 this protoshape seems to have no part – except, that is, for one curious moment when Joan, during her first stormy encounter with Lionel, questions whether he had been sent by some infernal power.

act). For a moment, too, just before Joan's entry in Act 2, a hint of this same phrase is slipped in by the oboe as Charles changes place with Dunois, the King observing that Joan will be able to discover him if she truly possesses insight from heaven (Ex. 153f).

Ex. 153

a.

[That is the one to whom heaven has sent me!]

b.

[For a woman in such calamitous times]

c.

[voice part only]

[Ah, another calling has been decided for this humble maid!]

d. **Moderato** [voice part only]

Spa - si - tel zhiv, grya-det, grya-det on v si - le, mo - gu - chy vrag pa -

[The Saviour lives, he approaches in strength; the mighty foe will fall near Orleans]

- det pod Or - le - a - nom, no

e. [Andantino] **L'istesso tempo** [voice part only]

Tak vïsh - ne - ye na - zna-chi - lo iz - bra - nye; me -

[Thus the Almighty made his choice; it is not a desire for empty things which draws me!]

- nya vle - chet ne su - yet-nïkh zhe - la - nye!

f. **Ben sostenuto il tempo**

The King

- verg- nem, kog - da s ne - bes yei po - sla - no vse -

p

[when omniscience is sent her from heaven]

- zna - nye,

mf

g. [Allegro vivo] **Poco meno mosso** [voice part only]

Joan

Kto tï? te - bya po-slal ne - do - bry an - gel!

[Who are you? A wicked angel sent you!]

Tchaikovsky set about *The Maid of Orléans* with the avowed intention of purging his operatic style of what he felt were inappropriate 'symphonic' features. 'Opera should be the most popular of all musical forms,' he had declared to Nadezhda von Meck while deep in composing *The Maid*. 'Thus operatic style must relate to those of symphonic and chamber music as decorative painting relates to academic.'[50] Patently one consequence of this conviction was the suppression of any thematic working whose effect might be musical rather than overtly dramatic. Certainly there is a very reduced number of thematic cross-references in *The Maid* compared with *Onegin*, and when such repetitions do occur they are so explicit that their dramatic point is unmistakable; indeed, their bluntness often makes them seem trite. The most obvious of these labels is the 'heavenly voices' music which has its origins in Joan's Act 2 narration, and which Tchaikovsky simply slotted in at the two points where these angelic mentors address Joan. Exactly the same passage is quoted in the orchestra earlier in Act 2 to accompany the Archbishop's report of Joan's divinely ordained arrival on the field of battle. The stately music to which the saviour-maid had appeared before the King in Act 2, and which had loudly rounded off the scene, is likewise cited orchestrally in the coronation scene when the King reminds the people how Joan had saved his throne. Later, as Dunois comes forward to defend Joan, and the Archbishop to inquisition her, music associated with each in Act 2 is recalled. Perhaps the Archbishop's self-quotation was intended to be ironic; yet in neither case does the recollection sound like anything more than a formal stamp of identity of the most obvious kind. Nor is there any very compelling dramatic justification for repeating orchestrally the first half of the Hymn of Act I as the entr'acte to Act 2. Recall is used more subtly in the Act 4 entr'acte where faint thematic allusions to the end of the previous scene shadow Joan's thoughts as she broods upon her rejection by King and people, and on Lionel's final bid to persuade her to go with him. But this entr'acte is weakened by excessive use of diminished sevenths, as is the entr'acte to Act 3, where tritely explosive imagery does no more than forewarn of a tense situation when the curtain rises.

This dearth of thematic allusiveness is especially evident in the last stages of the opera where there is no accumulation of familiar material to draw together and finally focus major elements within the drama and music; similarly, at the opposite end of the opera, the overture provides less compendious forewarning of drama to come than some earlier

---

[50] *TLP8*, p. 67; *TPM2*, p. 37; *TZC2*, p. 259; *YDGC*, p. 205.

specimens. In the allegro vivo are represented only the French peasan-try (the alarm music preceding their first chorus in Act 1, followed by a derivative from this same chorus) and Joan (her theme of dedication from the end of Act 1, where she had signified her assent to her celestial instructors by briefly echoing their music). As for the attractive tune which provides the substance for the flanking sections, this has no direct connection with anything that follows. This overture's ternary structure, with its patent use of the solo flute as the symbol of innocence, must raise some suspicion that Tchaikovsky's contempt for Verdi's *Giovanna d'Arco* did not leave him unwilling to take suggestions from the earlier opera. Likewise that 'universal symbol, the descending semitone of grief', as Julian Budden calls it,[51] which occurs prominently in the opening of Verdi's opera, is a tiny melodic idea featuring occasionally but significantly in *The Maid*, presenting itself first in the overture's allegro vivo (in the middle of the peasants' alarm music), appearing in the orchestral preliminaries to Joan's farewell aria in Act 1, recurring in the orchestra during the first scene of Act 3 to embody something of Joan's anguish as love for Lionel begins to undermine her zeal for her divine mission (No. 17, bars 125ff.), and similarly disclosing the torment Thibaut experiences in the coronation scene as he braces himself to denounce his daughter for the sake of her immortal soul (No. 19, bars 38ff.).

But such connections with *Giovanna d'Arco* are superficial, and Tchaikovsky showed none of Verdi's crisply dramatic approach, and little of his psychological insight. All too often the music of *The Maid* seems little more than a step-by-step setting of a libretto. Tchaikovsky's avowed strivings for greater lucidity are evident above all in the ariosi of the dialogues, which are sometimes so functional melodically and so sparingly accompanied that they become virtually recitatives. Certain-ly the dialogue is efficiently despatched, but there is a cumulative impression of melodic parsimony. Only rarely in this flow of musical prose does some memorable phrase raise itself above the general level of the stream as a lyrical or dramatic landmark to give point to the listener's journey. This paucity of inner drama and lack of thematic distinctiveness are by no means compensated by positive qualities in the opera's numerous ensembles. And it is in Tchaikovsky's wide-spread use of the chorus, mostly in dramatic dialogue with the soloists but at other times united with them in more formal ensemble, that we find the strongest clue to his motivation in this opera. As Gerald Abraham has observed, there can be little doubt that with *The Maid of*

---

[51] Julian Budden, *The Operas of Verdi*, vol. 1 (London, 1973), p. 209.

Orléans Tchaikovsky was hoping to break into the international operatic scene. The subject of Joan was likely to have a far greater appeal to a non-Russian audience than any he had previously treated; likewise, Tchaikovsky had so shaped the scenario as to afford the sort of situations where he could achieve strong effects which might score ready success. For if Schiller was the source of Tchaikovsky's subject, the French grand opera tradition in general, and Meyerbeer in particular, were the begetters of the musical manners in this opera. Having, in *The Voyevoda* of 1868, succeeded in smothering much of the dramatic life under the sheer weight of the formal ensembles, Tchaikovsky had drastically reduced the use of such movements in the operas immediately following, using them only sparingly in *The Oprichnik* and abandoning them altogether in the original *Vakula*. There is a resurgence of such ensemble writing in *Onegin*, but in *The Maid* Tchaikovsky rehabilitated the solo/choral movement with a vengeance, at any excuse congealing the flow of events into a more formal ensemble, the greater part of the structure being spread across a frame built from a single melody, with the participants simply slotting themselves into the melodic/harmonic fabric. The expressive consistency which results from such a procedure inevitably renders such ensembles statuesque, consensus movements aiming to convey a single weighty emotion, not to demonstrate a diversity of dramatic stances. There is justification for such an approach in the Hymn (No. 6) of Act 1, though the theme with which Joan leads off this corporate prayer is too bland by far. The less extensive ensemble of acknowledgment which the King initiates in Act 2 after Joan has recounted to him his recent dreams is better, partly because it is kept within bounds, partly because the theme on which it is founded, though far from one of Tchaikovsky's best, is stronger. Much the same might be said of the balancing ensemble which follows Joan's narration, though the endeavour of the participants to assume more independent roles begins to expose the crippling constrictions within Tchaikovsky's ensemble technique. The largest of the formal ensemble movements occurs towards the end of the coronation scene as all stand stunned at Joan's refusal to deny her father's charge of impurity. Here Tchaikovsky's method could only spell disaster, for the essential diversity of viewpoint among the participants is engulfed in tumid textures. Drama has been replaced by emotional swell.

Even more disastrous, though for quite different reasons, is the final scene of the opera, which provides one of the two formal tableaux of the piece. The first of these had occupied the opening of the coronation scene which had unfolded against the background of a grand choral/ orchestral march, brilliant in manner (the scoring of this caused

Tchaikovsky many problems) but thematically unremarkable, even stodgy, with a particularly gross coda. The second tableau fills the whole last scene, the musical model for which was patently the slow movement of Mendelssohn's Italian Symphony, said to have been inspired by a religious procession seen in Naples. This symphony had long been one of Tchaikovsky's favourites, and he clearly decided that music using the same sort of measured pizzicato bass supporting a leisurely tune – and set, like Mendelssohn's slow movement, in D minor (one of Tchaikovsky's special keys of misfortune, even tragedy) – would make an apt background for the procession leading Joan to the stake. But background it remains. As for the deep emotion which had possessed Tchaikovsky on reading Wallon's account of Joan's end, this had by now been perverted, and the scene becomes a rosy sublimation of Joan's appalling sufferings. The hideous distastefulness of the end, where Joan, supported by angel chorus and thudding drum, ecstatically declares that the sufferings she has patently not endured are over and that heaven is opened to her, makes this one of Tchaikovsky's worst indiscretions. According to Modest, who had perceived the vulgarity of this ending, his brother came to share this view, and in the last weeks of his life was planning to substitute an ending based on Schiller.

Of course there are some positive things in *The Maid of Orléans* – even some fine ones. All Tchaikovsky's earlier operas had contained purely decorative choral movements, and one launches each of the first two acts of *The Maid*. That which opens the opera, it may be objected, places the locale not in France but Russia; nevertheless, one forgives this geographical ineptitude when offered such an enchanting example of that species of female chorus whose origins lay deep in Glinka's art. By contrast the chorus of minstrels at the beginning of Act 2 attempts self-consciously to confirm its location by employing the French song, *Mes belles amourettes*, which Tchaikovsky had used the previous year in his *Mélodie antique française*, No. 16 of his Children's Album, Op. 39. Yet even here Tchaikovsky could not completely silence his national voice, for this chorus's mild languor and melancholy oboe refrain draws it gently eastwards. The following ballet includes some worthwhile music, the dance for pages and dwarfs marking a sudden retreat towards the eighteenth century for another of Tchaikovsky's rococo stylizations, while the final tumblers' dance, vigorous and characterful, provides by far the best instrumental movement in the whole opera. Even the recitative sometimes flickers into life for an instant: for example, at the opening of the finale to Act 1 when Joan, having bade her decisive formal farewell to the familiar places and persons she must now leave, suddenly falters in her resolve as the pain of departure floods in upon her (Ex. 154), the orchestra sympathetically echoing her cry. The music to which Agnès offers the King her possessions in Act 2 has some genuine expressive substance; even more affecting is Joan's despairing entreaty at the end of her first fateful encounter with Lionel when, wounded, she pleads for death to escape the new torment brought into her life by the awakening of earthly love. Her phrase is taken up by the orchestra and brooded upon before sinking into silence in a final slow arpeggio. But the loveliest moment in all these wide acres of undernourished recitative is Joan's first direct address to Charles in the recognition scene. What man would not fall beneath the spell of a young girl who addressed him in such meltingly lyrical terms! (Ex. 155).

Ex. 154

[O God, leave me to my humble lot! You, my native home]

There are few formal solos in *The Maid*. The first is Joan's farewell aria at the end of Act 1, a piece of some musical substance employing that descending-chromaticism-over-a-pedal which was such a favoured and characteristic device with Russian composers ever since Glinka had discovered its potential. This time Tchaikovsky does not embed the chromaticism in the accompaniment but draws it out into full prominence by making it fundamental to the opening melody (Ex.

Ex. 155

[I have seen you, but only there where you were unseen by anyone but God.]

156). Its pathos is unfailing, while the firmness of melodic outline, already clearly displayed in Joan's first phrase and well maintained throughout the succeeding pages, ensures that pain is matched by resolve. Agnès, too, is favoured with an arioso in Act 2. Though the opening harmonic formula (see Ex. 158a) is perhaps the only readily recognizable Tchaikovskyan mark on this music, the King's devoted mistress roused Tchaikovsky's sympathy sufficiently for her to draw from him some touching music. The brief G flat duet in which she joins with Charles shows Tchaikovsky once again drawing his inspiration from the famous G flat 'Tu l'as dit' in *Les Huguenots*,* but this rapt expression of mutual love becomes very much Tchaikovsky's own with its characteristic chromaticism and ravishing emphasis upon the Neapolitan region. By comparison the earlier duet for Dunois and Charles is faceless, though conventionally effective, a compliment which cannot be paid to the duettino between Thibaut and Raimond in the coronation scene. This and the preceding scena, where the need to write music which might credibly be coming from the organ in the cathedral found Tchaikovsky at a loss how to maintain any musical focus, is one of the dreariest stretches in the whole opera.

*See Vol. 1, Ex. 54b.

Ex. 156

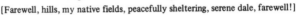

[Farewell, hills, my native fields, peacefully sheltering, serene dale, farewell!]

Fortunately the two duets for Joan and Lionel cannot be charged with dullness. As in *Onegin* Tchaikovsky employed two types of scene in *The Maid*: those using large forces, and those which centre exclusively (or almost so) on only two characters – and it is the more intimate scenes which draw the more consistent music from him. The second of these lovers' encounters contains the more formal duet, for here Joan ceases to struggle with her feelings, and both lovers surrender to their impulses with quiet rapture (Ex. 157). The C flat/C natural ambivalence of the motif which concludes Joan's answering phrase is subsequently exploited by Tchaikovsky to broaden the tonal field until the climax is reached in a shift to E major (Tchaikovsky's special key of ecstatic love)[52] for a new phrase (Ex. 158b) in which any lingering hesitancy is set aside for full commitment to mutual passion. That same progression with which Tchaikovsky had favoured Agnès in her Act 2 arioso (Ex. 158a) recurs as this key of joy is reached, and the

---

[52] That this key possessed special qualities for Tchaikovsky is clearly revealed in a letter he wrote to Nápravník before the first production of *The Maid*, in which, while agreeing to make a transposition of the duet, he added that he would prefer to rewrite the vocal part in the E major section rather than sacrifice the key. In the end, however, Tchaikovsky made a straightforward transposition of the whole duet.

Ex. 157

[*LIONEL:* O wonderful sweet dream! You are with me, my angel!

JOAN: O wonderful, sweet dream! You are with me, my dear!]

Ex. 158

a.

[If strength is not given you]

b.

Andantino

Chud - ny dar lyub - vi!   Chas ne - zab -

[*JOAN:* Wondrous gift of love! Unforgettable hour — joyous, blissful — O, if only you

- ven - ny,   svet - ly,   bla -

could last for ever. *LIONEL:* Wondrous gift of love!]

- zhen - ny,   O,   yes - li b

vech - no dlit - sya mog ti   vech - no, vech - no bez kont -

unobtrusive but all-pervading chromaticism, especially when set above a pedal, pronounces these lovers more Slav than Gallic. Yet, characteristic as it is, this duet lacks the melodic expansiveness of Tchaikovsky at his best. Taken as a whole, the earlier Joan/Lionel scene is the more notable achievement, for here Tchaikovsky had to confront the problem of how to effect the transition from extreme antagonism to mutual – if, on one side, undeclared – love. Though patchy, there is much worthy of admiration in his handling of this evolving dialogue, from the plangent C minor music to which Joan first admits the weakening of her lethal intent towards Lionel to that gentle, wondering phrase in which

Lionel confesses the spell Joan's femininity is weaving for him, opening out, as he begs her to come with him, into that same radiant E major in which they are to seal their passion in the next love scene (Ex. 159). There is also a quiet blend of warmth with pain in the phrase with which Joan begins the more formal duet which soon ensues.

Ex. 159

[I feel pity for your radiant beauty, pity for your youth; your sweet image impresses itself

on my soul, and I would wish to save you. But where is salvation? Follow me, abandon your terrible

alliance.]

But all these various moments and movements must yield place to Joan's narration in Act 2. The recognition scene, if inconsistent in quality, is by far the finest stretch in the whole opera: silver rather than gold, perhaps, but certainly more precious than the baser metals from which much of the rest of *The Maid* is cast. And in this silver setting Joan's narration is the jewel. It opens with simple dignity in A flat (Ex. 160a), shifting from its quietly firm diatonicism to a more mysterious chromaticism when Joan begins to describe her visions (Ex. 160b), and ending in the full brightness of E major, the key in which she is also to confess her greatest earthly happiness. It is the most spontaneous

Ex. 160

a.

[Holy father, I'm called Joan; I'm the daughter of a simple shepherd.]

b.

[And once, passing the whole night in diligent prayer with no thought of sleep,

I was sitting beneath a tree, when a beautiful figure appeared to me; in her hands were a sword and

banner, though she was dressed as a shepherdess like me.]

movement in the whole opera, the declaration of a simple soul who can speak of earthly things and heavenly visions with unaffected eloquence and visionary rapture in a manner so natural, so untainted by rhetoric, that for a moment the stage is occupied by a young girl as real as Tatyana.

In January 1878, less than a year before setting about *The Maid of Orléans*, Tchaikovsky had written to Taneyev from Sanremo defending his earlier choice of *Onegin* in the face of Taneyev's reservations.

> I worked [on *Onegin*] with indescribable enthusiasm and delight, caring little whether there were effects, movement, and so on. . . . If you find such things in something like *Aida*, for instance, then I'll assure you that not for all the riches in the world could I now write an opera with such a subject, for I need people, not dolls. I will willingly compose any opera where, even though there are no strong and startling effects, beings like myself experience feelings which I have experienced and understood. I don't know, I don't understand the feelings of an Egyptian princess, of a pharaoh, of some crazy Nubian woman. Some instinct suggests to me that these people must have moved, spoken, felt, but they must have expressed their feelings in some completely individual way, not as we do. . . . You ask me what I need. Let me tell you. I need [a subject] without kings, queens, tumultuous crowd effects, battles, marches – in a word, all those things which are the attributes of grand opera.[53]

And in describing what he did *not* need, Tchaikovsky could have been talking about *The Maid of Orléans*. Beguiled by the figure of Joan as a victim of fate, and prompted, perhaps, by less admirable commercial considerations, he had produced a work which ironically confirmed all too well the wisdom in his letter to Taneyev. Tchaikovsky simply had not been touched by his characters, had not felt with them, and in consequence he had been driven to dramatic formulae. *The Maid* is a work of effects without causes – or, at least, without causes offering adequate justification for the noisy sound edifices which Tchaikovsky so readily fabricated. Any listener who searches for deeper resonances, for those vastly varied, subtler sounds which reflect with truth the variety and richness within human emotion and behaviour – that is, any listener who comes to *The Maid* from *Onegin* – must quickly sense how hollow so much of it is.

[53] *TLP*7, pp. 21–2; *TZC*2, pp. 79–80; *TTP*, pp. 23–4.

A Note on the First Suite, and on
Certain Persons and Places

In Volume I of this study it was suggested that Tchaikovsky secretly embodied
a personal relationship from his own life in his symphonic poem, *Fatum*, and his
First Piano Concerto by the use of material cipher-generated from names. It is
possible that similar procedures may have produced some of the thematic
material of the First Suite. Again, however, the evidence cannot be considered
conclusive; thus I have excluded it from the main text of this last chapter.

The two main themes of the first movement, *Introduzione e Fuga*, of the
First Suite are scarcely characteristic of Tchaikovsky and, moreover, are dull.
This makes it difficult to believe they were really free conceptions. However, in
view of the deliberate mystery with which Tchaikovsky shrouded the identity
of the suite's dedicatee, it seems quite plausible that he should in some covert
way inscribe the dedication within the work itself. In fact, the fugue subject
could well be an abbreviated, but quite strict cipher derivative from one of
Tchaikovsky's forms of address to his patroness: 'Nadejda Filaretoffna, mily
drug' ('Nadezhda Filaretovna, dear friend') (Ex. 161a):

Ex. 161

That this fugue subject had fundamental significance in this suite is
confirmed by its influence upon thematic material elsewhere in the work. Its
conditioning of the main theme of the Gavotte is made explicit when, at the end
of the whole suite, this theme converts itself back into the fugue subject; less
obvious is the way the first theme of the Intermezzo (Ex. 161b) is built upon
the same contour which rises through a tenth from D to F and then sinks back
towards its initial note. The outline of the opening of the fugue subject is
reproduced at the beginning of the *Marche miniature*, and it recurs in the
gentle oboe theme in the middle of the Scherzo (since this movement was
sketched before the *Introduzione e Fuga*, this similarity could be coincidental;
otherwise it signifies that Tchaikovsky had already synthesized this thematic
tribute to his patroness before embarking on composition). The prominent
stepwise mediant-tonic descent at the apex of the fugue subject is reproduced
prominently in the second theme of the Intermezzo and towards the end of the
first section of the Divertimento.

The theme of the *Introduzione* is also a stiff invention. In view of Tchaikovsky's delight in the three main locations in which he spent the summer of 1878, and the joy and comfort he derived above all from the company of his sister, brother-in-law, and twin brothers, it seems equally plausible that he might wish these precious associations also to be secretly incorporated into this work which he began as the summer moved towards its close. It is a fact that if one takes the initial interval(s) which can be generated from the names of these places and persons (in two instances using inversions), every note of the initial theme of the work is neatly accounted for (though one minor modification is required for tonal reasons near the end) (Ex. 162).

Ex. 162

2

A NEW HOME:
SECOND PIANO CONCERTO

STRAVINSKY, ONCE ASKED what he loved most about his native Russia, replied: 'The violent Russian spring that seemed to begin in an hour and was like the whole earth cracking.'[1] As one reads the letters Tchaikovsky wrote from Kamenka in April 1879 it becomes obvious that he, too, responded sharply to this abrupt eruption of long-dormant nature – to (as he wrote) the sudden budding of the trees, the flowering of violet and lilac, the awakening of the nightingales, the splendour of the sunrises and the enchanting moonlit nights. Normally Tchaikovsky found little delight in the situation of his sister's home: the one thing which could reconcile him to the place, he told Anatoly, was a daily walk with Shibka, the Kamenka dog, through the neighbouring Trostyanka woods. But during that time when nature was being so magically transformed all Kamenka's shortcomings became tolerable. 'Spring's beauties are so bewitching that I forget the Yids, the smell of the factory, and so on,' he wrote cheerfully to Anatoly on 28 April, a week after his arrival for the summer of 1879.[2]

The arrangement on which Tchaikovsky returned to Kamenka this time was new. Reckoning that with his allowance from Mrs von Meck and receipts from his own compositions he had an annual income of some 7,000 to 8,000 roubles, he had insisted he should pay his own way – though whether this actually happened seems to have been a different matter. By so doing he could reasonably ask for accommodation more ideal for his requirements, he could install his personal belongings which had been sent from Moscow, and he could be free from some of the social constraints which had hedged round his visits as a family guest. If he had a home at all, then Kamenka was now that home. When he arrived there with Modest and Kolya he wasted no time in settling himself into a daily routine. A month earlier he had asked his benefac-

---

[1] I. Stravinsky: *Memories and Commentaries* (London, 1960), p. 30.
[2] *TLP*8, p. 176; *TPR*, p. 554.

tress whether he might spend some time in the peace of Brailov ahead of her own visit, but he had no intention of leaving Kamenka before Modest's departure in the middle of May; nor for the moment did he want anything to interrupt work on his First Suite. The fortunes of the Fourth Symphony had taught him how important it was to get a new work into print. If the preparation of the piano-duet version was entrusted to another, work might be delayed, and if a single manuscript score was all that was available, this severely restricted the number of performances which might be given. Tchaikovsky had already agreed with Jurgenson that the latter would begin engraving the score, parts and piano-duet transcription of his suite forthwith so that materials might be readily available to meet all demands, and he had determined to finish the orchestration and make the piano-duet version himself before leaving Kamenka. His faith in the successful future of his suite was fortified by the experience of playing it to a Kamenka audience. 'Everybody with me here is crazy about the Andante, and after my brother and I had played it as a piano duet, one girl had hysterics (that's a fact!!!)! To reduce the fair sex to hysterics is surely the height of artistic triumph!' he wrote jubilantly to Jurgenson.[3]

The first three weeks Tchaikovsky spent at Kamenka were marred only by universal concern for Sasha. There is no doubt that, though Lev ran the estate with admirable efficiency, the dominating personality in the Kamenka household was his wife. A few days after her brother's arrival Sasha heard that the French governess she had been trying to engage for her children was in Kiev. Not trusting anyone else to deal with this matter, she had rushed off to Kiev, where she had fallen ill. A telegram had arrived at Kamenka summoning Lev to bring her home, and leaving the rest of the family for two days in a state of alarm. The cares of being a mother and mistress of the estate, coupled with a congenital inability to relax, had reduced Sasha to a nervous state which was to afford much anxiety to the family during this summer, and which proved the harbinger of worse to come. Fortunately his sister's ailments did not impede Tchaikovsky's enjoyment of his own thirty-ninth birthday, celebrated by a day-long picnic in the Trostyanka woods. There was a similar event for Modest's birthday on 13 May; the next day Tchaikovsky left for Brailov.

Here, as intended, he rested entirely from work. Yet for all the peacefulness of his surroundings, Marcel's solicitude, the natural beauty of the place, he was restless. It was not simply that everything about the house was *too* new, that last year he had already exhausted his

[3] *TLP*8, p. 183; *TZC*2, pp. 285–6; *TPM*2, p. 610; *TPJ*1, p. 93.

subjects of conversation with Marcel – nor was it only that he soon became bored with inactivity and was killing time. Haunting him all the while was Antonina. Through Anatoly he had heard that she was again talking of divorce, but in the light of all her past behaviour Tchaikovsky responded very cautiously. He was ready to accept the blame, he wrote, and to pay up to 5,000 roubles of the costs, but he would only agree to begin proceedings if he was convinced that this time she was in earnest. As for the 10,000 roubles she would have received under an earlier settlement, she must understand that these were no longer available, though privately he instructed Anatoly to use his discretion about offering extra money payments if Anatoly thought these would advance his cause. A further reason for unease, even alarm, was to hear that Vladimir Shilovsky had been spreading rumours about Tchaikovsky's financial indebtedness to him. An angry Tchaikovsky wasted no time in denying the alleged debt of 28,000 roubles, claiming that it amounted to no more than 7,550 over the last ten years. Be that as it may, the details as set out by Tchaikovsky in his letter of repudiation indicate that between 1869 and 1876 he had received sums of an order which confirms a particularly close relationship between him and Shilovsky. Yet one suspects that Tchaikovsky was disquieted not by the facts of the relationship as known to himself, but only by the way they might appear to others. His condition for forgiving Shilovsky was unexpected. He began by arguing that if he did indeed owe 28,000 roubles, then 20,450 were still unpaid by Shilovsky. 'Now when I live solely by those casual sums which my morceaux malingres et rachitiques give me,' Tchaikovsky went on mendaciously, 'I cannot give Bochechkarov that firm and lasting support which I did before. And so the idea occurred to me to ask you to assign him a life pension of 300 roubles a year (that is, twenty-five a month). Nik[olay] Lvov[ich] is truly a pitiful, poor and sick old man. But to you this would be a negligible sum. As for my gratitude for this, it will be so great that I agree not to be in the least offended if I should hear that you are continuing to spread gossip about the 28,000 and about the blackness of my soul.'[4] The circumstances which could occasion Tchaikovsky's bursts of generosity could sometimes be strange indeed.

Tchaikovsky left Brailov on 25 May. During a prolonged delay at Kazatin he saw another train pull into the station drawing Nadezhda von Meck's personal coach. The curtains were drawn, so his patroness could know nothing of his presence, but for twenty minutes he pondered their proximity. It was a subject which would occupy him a good

[4] *TLP*8, p. 214.

deal over the next few months. If in Paris his patroness had seemed to be growing indifferent to their closeness, her old longing had now fully resurged. She had just heard of an estate near Kamenka which the owners might be persuaded to sell: if she moved there she would be nearer Tchaikovsky. She asked him to make enquiries and discover what would be the price, while in Brailov itself she was already revelling in the knowledge of his recent stay. 'Here, more than anywhere, I feel our spiritual closeness and I take unspeakable pleasure in it,' she wrote ecstatically. 'Already the rooms you occupied have been accorded the name of *Pyotr Ilich's bedroom* and *Pyotr Ilich's sitting room*. The trees in the Tartaksky and Vladimirsky woods beneath which both of us have drunk [tea], the benches on the crag where we have both sat, those same nightingales we have both heard, all, all *belong to both of us*, all bring us together, all make us still closer to each other. My God! what happiness there is in this!'[5] Even before this she had been planning an idyll of close residence such as they had experienced in Florence, but this time in Brailov itself. 'Near Brailov I have a cottage, Simaki,' she had explained on 17 May.

> . . . This cottage is very pretty, lying in a shady garden with a river at its end. Nightingales sing in the garden. . . . There are six rooms. This cottage stands about three miles from Brailov . . . I am sure you will like it. It is such a solitary, poetic spot that if you would agree to come to it for a whole month or even more during the time I am in Brailov, then I should be unspeakably happy. For me there would be a partial repetition of the most delightful time of my life at the Viale dei Colli [in Florence]. Although, of course, at Brailov I would not be able to walk near your apartment each day, yet each day I would feel you were near me, and from that thought I should likewise be calm and happy. I would also feel that with you close to me no evil could come near me.[6]

Tchaikovsky's response to this proposal was thoroughly ambivalent. In fact, he was clearly reluctant to visit Simaki, but equally he feared to upset his patroness, particularly when he might be needing more money from her to pay off Antonina. Ultimately he was to go there during the last half of August. Meanwhile in Kamenka, as we have seen, he settled down to scoring *The Maid of Orléans* and stepped up his daily work schedule on this, the largest score he had yet composed. His

---

[5] *TPM2*, p. 123.
[6] *TPM2*, p. 109.

brother Ippolit, who was now working for a steamship company on the Black Sea, had recently made a good speculation and had turned up to consult with Lev about the 50,000 roubles he had gained. The gap between Tchaikovsky and his brother had now much widened, and when Ippolit wanted to accompany him on his woodland walks Tchaikovsky was irritated. Then, after Ippolit's departure, Vera Butakova arrived. Despite the pretensions she had acquired to high society manners and acquaintances, Tchaikovsky still warmed to her personality, though he was a little troubled by a suspicion that her old attachment to him was not completely dead. As for his current and perpetual torment, Antonina, he had Anatoly acting as his agent in dealings with her, and at such a distance she seemed only half real.

Tchaikovsky always found solace at Kamenka, yet it is clear that these weeks with his sister's family were the most enjoyable he had spent for some years. He found himself becoming far more reconciled to Kamenka as a place, tried his hand at haymaking, grew poppies, read more of Dostoyevsky's *Brothers Karamazov* ('every single one of the characters is mad,' he observed to Modest. 'Usually only one instalment of a Dostoyevsky novel is tolerable; after this, confusion always comes'[7]); above all, he could enjoy the family life to as great (or as small) a degree as he chose. He watched with amused detachment the personality clashes between certain female members of the Kamenka company, especially the turmoil created among the incumbent governesses by the arrival of the new French teacher, Mlle Gautier. 'She's forty and a bit, her appearance is plain but not unpleasant: to wit, she has a good complexion, a slightly snub nose, and very kind eyes,' he wrote to Modest.

> She dresses well. *She eats with her knife!!!* . . . She behaves very decorously and very simply. From the beginning she has tried to display her talents, which are numerous. Amongst these she models in clay *and does it very well.* The day before yesterday we went to Verbovka. Lev brought her a piece of clay from which they make bricks there, and she modelled a very nice head with uncommon speed. *Tasya* [Tchaikovsky's niece Nataliya] has conceived a most ferocious hatred for her, and has suddenly been smitten with a very touching love for Miss Eastwood [the English governess at Kamenka]. The latter also received the Frenchwoman very grimly, and in her turn is suddenly manifesting a passionate partiality for Tasya. Yesterday there was quite a dramatic scene. Poor *Tasya*, who

[7] *TLP8*, p. 226; *TPM2*, p. 603; *TPR*, p. 571; *YDGC*, p. 215.

is now all miserable, tearful, won't eat, won't smile, wanted to go to Trostyanka with her brothers and Miss Eastwood. The English-woman expressed a willingness to take her. Sasha told Tasya she should ask for *Mlle Gautier's* permission. But Tasya ran to complain to Miss Eastwood, and a minute later the latter flew into the drawing-room looking white and grim, and let forth a stream of reproaches at Sasha. 'What! I've looked after Tasya for five years, I love her, she loves me, yet you won't let her go to the woods with me! You see how miserable she is, how awful she looks, yet you won't let her have a break!' and so on, and so on. Sasha calmed her down and explained that the Frenchwoman had been engaged *for Tasya*, and that Tasya had to be under her control . . . *Persephone* [Pelageya Kostetskaya, another governess] is triumphant. For some reason she looks upon Mlle Gautier as an ally, and received her with open arms. There now fly from her lips streams of such refined French words that it's getting awful. She's even stopped speaking Russian with us, and it's reached a point where yesterday, after supper, when Lev and I were finishing our tea and having a smoke, she started talking Lev's head off in French, and delivered at him the following memorable phrase: 'Je vois tout en beau je ne vois pas les! défections que de près!' Lev fled from her on to the balcony.[8]

But if this sharply observed, well relished account evidences the degree to which the Kamenka world could distract Tchaikovsky from his own inner cares, there was one deep-seated ache from which there was still no refuge. 'On this day exactly twenty-five years ago my mother died,' he wrote to Nadezhda von Meck on 25 June. '. . . I remember every moment of that terrible day as though it were yesterday.'[9]

On 2 July Tchaikovsky set out for Kondratyev's estate at Nizy. He had intended to delay this trip until late in the summer, but news of the precarious health of Bochechkarov, whom Kondratyev had taken from Moscow to his own home, persuaded Tchaikovsky to hasten his visit. He found Bochechkarov in a pitiful state, and during the next twelve days he took his share in keeping company with the old man, in enjoying as much as he could of this estate where, five years before, he had composed *Vakula* so quickly, and in waiting impatiently for Anatoly to join him in the middle of the month. Inactivity was again fretting him, and with the score of *The Maid of Orléans* awaiting his further attention, his impatience to resume work mounted irrepressibly. On 17

[8] *TLP8*, p. 250; *TPR*, pp. 581–2.
[9] *TLP8*, p. 255; *TPM2*, p. 140; *TZC2*, p. 294.

July, after Anatoly's arrival, he bade what he well knew would be his last farewell to Bochechkarov, and then set out for Kamenka.

Before leaving for Nizy Tchaikovsky had received cheering news from abroad of his ever-growing reputation as a composer. Bülow had played the First Piano Concerto in London and Wiesbaden, while also from Wiesbaden Fitzenhagen reported the great success of the Rococo Variations when he had played them at the festival. From Paris Colonne wrote declaring his intention of furthering the cause of Tchaikovsky's music. Nearer home Tchaikovsky was particularly pleased to hear that his Liturgy of St John Chrysostom had been sung several times in the University Church at Kiev (Jurgenson's lawsuit with Bakhmetyev, the director of the Imperial Chapel Choir, over the publication rights of this was, of course, in full swing). In addition, the Grand Duke Konstantin Nikolayevich had requested Rubinstein to mount for him a special performance of *Onegin* at the Moscow Conservatoire.

Fortified by these encouragements, Tchaikovsky pressed on with *The Maid of Orléans* as soon as he was back in Kamenka. As he observed to Jurgenson, if his divorce action was to begin in the autumn and he was condemned to spend a considerable time in Moscow engaged in most unpalatable proceedings, how would he then be able to work? 'Quite apart from this, I always hurry my labour,' he added. 'This always tells unfavourably upon my creations – but such is my nature. I'm always afraid I *shan't finish*. And how many further plans I have! I must make radical improvements to some of my earlier pieces; I must write a thousand more opuses! A hundred lives wouldn't suffice to accomplish all my plans.'[10] With such an inescapable sense of urgency, the scoring progressed steadily. He had lost his enthusiasm for hunting, and so was not tempted out on to those expeditions which claimed so much of Anatoly's time on this visit. He was thoroughly happy, however, to resume his role as prompter in the domestic theatricals which were planned for shortly before Anatoly's departure, mainly to divert Sasha, who was suffering violent fluctuations between a kind of euphoria and intense depression (it was, Tchaikovsky wrote to Nadezhda von Meck, a condition with which he was all too familiar himself). Tchaikovsky had asked to be allowed to invite Kotek for the last part of his stay, since it was intended that his violinist friend should prepare the vocal score of Act 3 of *The Maid*. Thus the pleasures of the dramatic entertainment were enhanced by Kotek playing his violin in the interval between the two plays, and the evening was rounded off with a dance. While all such

---

[10] *TLP*8, p. 287.

things and the music-making he could engage in with Kotek brought Tchaikovsky the greatest pleasure, he felt some alarm at the news that his father had been seriously ill. Sasha had decided it was time to enrol Nataliya in a boarding school in St Petersburg, and news of Ilya Petrovich's ailment made her the more anxious to speed thither. As soon as Anatoly's leave was up Tchaikovsky looked to his own departure for Simaki. Though he confided to his brother that he still had no wish to go there, it is quite certain that he was longing for a period of solitude. In any case his patroness had made clear her displeasure at the visit he had paid to Kondratyev at Nizy, and Tchaikovsky wanted to pacify her. On 20 August he was at Nadezhda von Meck's estate.

Immediately the problem of proximity again raised its disquieting head. Tchaikovsky was genuinely enraptured with Simaki itself.

A house as old as the hills, a well-stocked garden with ancient oaks and limes, very neglected and thus for some reason delightful, a river at the end of the garden, a wonderful view from the balcony on to the village and a distant wood, the remoteness from the factory, the village, and from all noise and bustle, the absolute quiet, the accommodation arranged with uncommon comfort, consisting of a hall, a large study, dining-room, bedroom and a room for Alyosha – all this couldn't correspond more with my tastes and inclinations. Around the cottage there are fields and copses where you can wander without meeting anyone, which I forthwith did with inexpressible pleasure. Finally, to cap it all, Léon, the old servant with whom I never feel constraint, has been assigned to me, as has a cook whom I don't see, and a coachman with a phaeton and four which I can use, though I would prefer not to have it, for this, as it were, compels me to ride, whereas I'd prefer to walk.

There were facilities for bathing in the river, and an abundance of mushrooms to pick in the woods. His hostess had furnished him with a pile of books but he quickly exhausted these, even though he only read in the evenings and at mealtimes (his special pleasure, he confessed). He asked her whether she had complete editions of Tolstoy and Dostoyevsky, and any volume of Dickens in Russian or French translation which she could lend him. The beauty – above all, the peacefulness – of Simaki, with rabbits in the fields and a family of cats in the roof to banish rats and mice, all conspired to relax him in a way not possible at Sasha's unpicturesque and hectic Kamenka.

But then the contented tone of this letter penned to Modest a day after his arrival changes abruptly. 'The nearness of N[adezhda]

F[ilaretovna] makes me feel uncomfortable – although, at bottom, this is silly, for I know that no one will disturb me. It's simply that I'm used to regarding N[adezhda] F[ilaretovna] as some distant and unseen good angel, and this consciousness that she's living a couple of miles off like an ordinary mortal disturbs me. Yesterday Pachulski met me and spent part of the evening with me, but I've forewarned him bluntly that I want to be completely alone for several days.'[11]

In fairness to his patroness, she had promised to furnish him with a daily schedule of her proposed movements to forestall any chance encounter between them, but Pachulski had proposed to bring Milochka to see Tchaikovsky, and even this, Tchaikovsky felt, was endangering that very special, idealized quality in his relationship with his 'good but unseen angel'. The letter in which he forestalled this suggestion is perhaps the most explicit confession of how he viewed Nadezhda von Meck's role in his existence.

My relations with you *as they are now* are for me the greatest joy and a necessary condition for my happiness. I would not wish them to be changed even one iota. As it is, I am accustomed to regard you as my good but unseen angel. All the inestimable charm and poetry of my friendship with you lies in the fact that you are so close, so infinitely dear to me – but, at the same time, we are *not acquainted* in the ordinary sense of the word – and this *non-acquaintance* must extend to those persons closest to you. I want to love Milochka as I have loved her up to this moment. If she were to appear before me – *la charme serait rompue.* All members of your family are close and dear to me, Milochka in particular – but for God's sake let everything stay as it has been. And how would I reply to Milochka who would start asking *why I did not visit her mama?* I would have to begin my acquaintance with a lie – very innocent, of course – but still a lie. That would be very distressing to me.[12]

Though Tchaikovsky's patroness acceded quickly to his appeal, the very worst disaster they had both feared was about to happen. One afternoon he miscalculated the time and set out for his walk too early, she inadvertently delayed her usual return to Brailov at four o'clock, and for the first time ever they suddenly confronted each other on a road through the woods. 'It was *frightfully* embarrassing,' Tchaikovsky wrote to Anatoly on the day following the mishap.

[11] *TLP8*, p. 309; *TZC2*, pp. 298–9; *YDGC*, p. 216 (partial).
[12] *TLP8*, p. 312; *TPM2*, p. 169; *TZC2*, p. 300.

Although we were face to face for only an instant, I was still terribly confused. Nevertheless I raised my hat politely. But she, so it seemed to me, was utterly disconcerted and didn't know what to do. It wasn't enough that she was riding in a barouche with Milochka, for behind were two more carriages with all her family. I wandered for a long time in the wood looking for mushrooms, and when I returned to the [picnic] table where tea had been prepared, letters and newspapers were lying on it. It seems she had sent a rider to look for me in the wood and to give me the post before tea. Altogether there are no bounds to her attentions. What a wonderful person she is for me![13]

The contretemps was quickly forgiven, and once again glimpses of each other became their closest intimacy. As she was boating on the river at Brailov a companion caught sight of Tchaikovsky crossing a bridge, and she strained shortsightedly to discern him. When she organized fancy-dress festivities on the lake at Brailov in celebration of her son Alexandr's nameday, she urged Tchaikovsky to watch them and the ensuing firework display from the opposite bank. He did as she asked, sitting in the darkness close enough to be able to report back to her snatches of conversation he had overheard as they passed close to him. She had earlier requested that Tchaikovsky should come to Brailov to see her recent acquisitions. Now, after both of them had taken stringent precautions to avoid a further collision, he visited Brailov itself, saw her pictures, played her pianos, and rewarded her with the rhapsody of delight for which she craved. All was as before.

Tchaikovsky's main mission at Simaki was to complete the score of *The Maid*. If he had earlier felt some reluctance to stay at his patroness's estate, this was fully dispelled by the conditions in which he lived. The one thing which really marred his stay was receiving the expected, yet still deeply distressing news of Bochechkarov's death. To Modest he summarized simply yet very humanly what this old man had meant to him.

I shall never be able to reconcile myself to the thought that N[ikolay] L[vovich] is no longer in this world. Moscow has become hateful to me. The memory of that huge share he had in the whole course of my Moscow life is like a knife in my heart. I can state unreservedly that he alone made my life in Moscow tolerable and possible. He possessed an astonishing capacity for reconciling himself with life; his presence and his company afforded diversion, calm and comfort which nothing can replace. What does one care that he was *insignificant* as regards moral and mental power? *He was agreeable always and to everybody*, and this took the place in him of a great mind and great gifts.[14]

Delight in his own comforts at Simaki had not made Tchaikovsky insensible to the needs of others. Suddenly filled with an awareness of his own mortality, he had turned his thoughts to Alexey's predicament if he should find himself masterless, and he had begged Nadezhda von Meck to take Alexey into her service if he, Tchaikovsky, should predecease her. Again while at Simaki he had acted as intermediary for the Polish Roman Catholic priest who lived on the estate. On his previous visit to Brailov Tchaikovsky had interceded with his patroness on behalf of the Catholic community, who wanted to enlarge their church, but who were prevented by one of Mrs von Meck's estate buildings which they wished to move to a new site. 'In my heart I have always been a most firm supporter of absolute freedom of conscience,' Tchaikovsky had explained. 'People must not be hindered from worshipping according to whatever rite they wish.'[15] Now Marcel had again approached Tchaikovsky on the priest's behalf, this time to gain Mrs von Meck's agreement to turning the slaughterhouse by the church into accommodation for the church's caretaker. Tchaikovsky's deep innate capacity for sympathy could also be recognized even by those with whom his contact was relatively slight. Marcel had obviously perceived it, despite all Tchaikovsky's insistence on a large measure of seclusion at Simaki, and his petition to Tchaikovsky proved fruitful in every way. An appeal to that same sympathy now came suddenly from Anatoly: a telegram arrived, begging Tchaikovsky to come straight from Simaki to St Petersburg where the twin, having had trouble at work, had resigned precipitately and wished to consult with his composer-brother. In the face of Anatoly's desperate entreaty it was to the Russian capital that he directed himself when he left Simaki on 13 September.

St Petersburg he found even more hateful than ever, and his depression was exacerbated by having to witness the tearful parting of Sasha and her daughter Nataliya when the former left for Kamenka. He went to the opera but met friends there, and had to endure their questions about his affairs, and parry their invitations to visit. Discovering that Anatoly's work crisis was a storm in a teacup only increased his

---

[14] *TLP8*, p. 322; *TZC2*, p. 302; *TPR*, p. 612; *YDGC*, p. 217 (partial).
[15] *TLP8*, p. 204; *TPM2*, p. 115; *TZC2*, p. 289.

irritation, and he would have left forthwith but for the deep obligation he felt to some of his family, above all to his distraught niece Nataliya and his enfeebled father. While in the Russian capital he took the opportunity of paving the way with Nápravník for a production of *The Maid*; then on 30 September he set off for Moscow. More and more of his time was being absorbed by matters relating to the publication of his works – by making or supervising various arrangements of his pieces, and by proof-reading – and direct discussions on these and financial matters with his publisher and staff were now imperative. He had hoped to stop in Moscow only one day, but he was quickly caught up in Rubinstein's and Jurgenson's drinking habits, and it took three days to complete the various business affairs requiring his attention. By now he seems to have drifted from these friends, and one suspects that this lubricated socializing was less a pleasure than a way of concealing the gap which divided them. 'My friends from the musical world of Moscow always receive me with expressions of great joy, and at first I myself am glad to see them. But as soon as the first moments have passed, and on both sides we have begun to enquire about one another's health and what we are doing, boredom and a certain awkwardness set in. Between us there has formed a gulf which is getting still deeper and deeper,' he confided to his benefactress.[16] Moscow without Bochechkarov was as unpalatable as St Petersburg, and it was with heartfelt relief that he left the city on 4 October. After a night in Kharkov he arrived in Grankino on 6 October.

In Moscow Jurgenson had omitted to tell Tchaikovsky that the piano-duet version of the Fourth Symphony was now issued, and the news reached the composer in a letter from Nadezhda von Meck. She had received a copy, and playing the work over and over again impelled her suddenly to pour out a naked confession of feelings which she had dammed up for over two years. 'I do not know whether you can understand the jealousy I feel regarding you in the absence of personal relations between us,' she began.

> Do you know that I am jealous of you in the same inexcusable way as a woman is jealous of the man she loves? Do you know that when you married I was *terribly* distressed; it was as though something had been torn from my heart. It hurt me, I became bitter; the thought of your nearness to that woman was unbearable to me – and, do you know, I am such a vile person that I rejoiced when things between you were bad. I reproached myself for this feeling, I believe I never in any way

[16] *TLP*8, p. 369; *TPM*2, p. 218.

let you notice it, but all the same I could not stifle it: a person cannot help her feelings. I hated that woman because you were *unhappy* with her, but I would have hated her a hundred times more if you had been *happy* with her. It seemed that she had taken from me what was *mine* alone, that to which I *alone* had a right because *I love you* as no one does, I value you more than anything in the world. If it is distasteful for you to know all this, forgive my involuntary confession. Your symphony is the reason for me pouring out all this. However, I think (and I know better than you) that I am not such an ideal person as you believe. Moreover, this cannot in any way change our relations. I do not want *any* change in them: I just want to be sure that *nothing* will change to the end of my life, that no one . . . but that is something I have no right to declare. Forgive me, and forget what I have said.[17]

Whether, despite her disclaimer, Tchaikovsky suspected she might be seeking a closer relationship cannot be said. He replied warmly, appreciatively, declared that he had always been convinced that she would understand the symphony better than anyone because it was *their* symphony, detailed for the hundredth time his debt to her, yet indicated frankly that she must place no hopes on receiving his love within some confining personal bond. 'I am indebted to you for everything: for life, for the possibility of going forward to a distant goal, for freedom, and for a degree of happiness such as previously I would have considered impossible,' he replied on 7 October. 'I read your letters with feelings of boundless gratitude and love such as I can express only in music, and for which there are no words.'[18] In any case, a direct link between them might in time prove superfluous, for during Tchaikovsky's stay at Simaki he had hatched with his benefactress the idea of engineering a marriage between one of her sons and one of his nieces; thus their relationship would be consummated in a vicarious union. Five years later, in 1884, their desires were to be fulfilled when Nikolay von Meck married Anna Davïdova.

Tchaikovsky's stay at Grankino was only brief, and on 11 October he, Modest and Kolya were in Kamenka. Feeling that the plans he had been conceiving with Nadezhda von Meck might give pleasure to Sasha, he broached the possibility of a von Meck–Davïdova union to Lev and Sasha, and (so he told Mrs von Meck) received their enthusiastic assent. At this stage it was Nataliya, whom Sasha had just installed in boarding school in St Petersburg, whom Tchaikovsky had nominated

---

[17] *TPM*2, pp. 212–13.
[18] *TLP*8, p. 371; *TPM*2, p. 220; *TZC*2, p. 322.

as the future bride, and the correspondence with his fellow conspirator was much filled over the next weeks with various schemes (in which Tchaikovsky showed the far greater understanding of human nature) for nurturing a developing relationship between the unsuspecting juveniles.

He was delighted to hear from his patroness that her immeasurable enthusiasm for the Fourth Symphony had consolidated into a scheme for subsidizing a Paris performance by Colonne, though the composer gloomily predicted that the work would fail with a French audience. Despite such a cheerless prospect, and notwithstanding the departure of Modest and Kolya for St Petersburg after only four days, Tchaikovsky's spirits rose at Kamenka. For three days he had toiled over the proofs of his First Suite, but then suddenly found himself for the first time in many months with no obligatory musical occupations. For some days he gave himself up to inactivity, idle occupations like hemming and marking towels, and to self-enjoyment. But quickly the charms of such an existence faded. 'These last days I've begun to observe in myself things which at first I didn't understand,' he admitted to Modest on 22 October. 'I experienced a certain vague dissatisfaction with myself, an over-frequent and almost irresistible desire to sleep, a certain emptiness, and finally *boredom*. There were times when I didn't know what to do with myself. Finally yesterday it became fully apparent to me what was the matter. I had to get on with something: I find myself absolutely incapable of living long without work. Today I began to create something, and the *boredom* vanished as if by magic.'[19] He had set about his Second Piano Concerto.

Tchaikovsky had a further fortnight in Kamenka and he determined that this time he would not rush to finish the piece. A week after starting upon the concerto he informed Anatoly of his progress. 'I work only in the morning before lunch – and, strange to say, I'm finding it some effort to compose. I don't feel a great inclination to composition – but, on the other hand, experience has taught me I can't live without work.'[20] Yet only three days later, on 1 November, he could report the sketches of the first movement complete. This done, he devoted the remaining time he felt he could spend at Kamenka to walking and reading. On his last day he discovered that Sasha had kept the letters which he had written to his parents from St Petersburg when he had been a schoolboy. 'It is difficult to convey to you what an agitating impression was made upon me by reading these letters carrying me

[19] *TLP*8, p. 388; *TPR*, p. 629; *TPB*, pp. 232–3.
[20] *TLP*8, p. 394; *TPR*, p. 631; *DTC*, pp. 452–3; *YDGC*, p. 219.

back nearly thirty years, reminding me vividly of my childhood sufferings which arose from a longing for my mother whom I loved with a
certain morbid, passionate love,' he revealed to Nadezhda von Meck,
knowing that this relationship would cause her no distress. '. . . Already
twenty-five years have passed since the day of her death.'[21] That night
he scarcely slept. It was a very tired Tchaikovsky who set out for
Moscow on 5 November.

Here he paused less than two days during which he toiled over
proof-reading, and was lost in admiration at Rubinstein's playing of his
Piano Sonata, which that pianist had first introduced to the public a
week earlier. He decided immediately that his new concerto should be
dedicated to Rubinstein. Arriving in St Petersburg on 10 November,
he felt again all his old antipathy for the place. He visited a circus
and found himself sitting close to two of Nadezhda von Meck's sons.
One of them was the sixteen-year-old Nikolay, now at the School of
Jurisprudence where Tchaikovsky himself had once been a pupil. He
recognized the lad from photographs his mother had sent him, but since
the two boys were ignorant of Tchaikovsky's identity he was able to
scrutinize them unobserved, taking special interest in the elected
bridegroom. 'I cannot express to you in words what a pleasant sensation I felt seeing two beings so close to you in front of me. Each of them
is, in his own way, very nice. Kolya took a very lively interest in the
show and talked a lot with his neighbours . . . I observed Kolya's habit
of twitching his facial muscles slightly, exactly as my brother Anatoly
does. It will seem odd to you, but even these nervous movements
appealed to me,' he wrote to their mother, as usual finding every feature
and idiosyncrasy of her family 'nice'.[22] She had now abandoned her
proposed visit to Naples; instead she had gone to Paris, where she had
reserved accommodation for Tchaikovsky. Thus France was his destination when he left St Petersburg on 21 November. In Berlin he saw
Kotek, was fascinated by a microscope museum, and was delighted by
a tolerable performance of Thomas's opera, Hamlet. On 25 November
he was in Paris.

Tchaikovsky discovered that his enthusiasm for the French capital
remained as strong as ever. Kondratyev was there recovering from a
bout of serious illness, and Tchaikovsky visited him, experiencing none
of the social strains he confessed to enduring from Kotek's eternal
chatter in Berlin. Nadezhda von Meck arranged that a fine Erard piano
should be delivered to Tchaikovsky's quarters, and on 29 November he

[21] *TLP*8, p. 402; *TPM*2, p. 239; *TZC*2, p. 328.
[22] *TLP*8, p. 407; *TPM*2, p. 244.

resumed work on the concerto, applying himself first to the finale. As with the first movement he found little enthusiasm within himself during the early stages of composition, but after some six days his creative faculties began to move more freely, and the sketches of the finale were swiftly completed, while the second movement, so he said, was already in his head. This went far better. 'My concerto is ready in rough, and I am very pleased with it, especially with the second movement, the *Andante*,' he could tell Mrs von Meck on 15 December.[23] When he resumed work on the concerto in Rome during February 1880 it was to make the transcription for two pianos so that Jurgenson might have this readily available for publication. The scoring was begun before the end of February, but was not completed until 10 May.

Although Tchaikovsky had determined to offer the dedication of the Second Piano Concerto to Rubinstein, memories of that artist's initial reception of its predecessor made him apprehensive. 'Yet though he [Rubinstein] may this time also be severely critical, this still won't matter if he plays it as splendidly as he does the first concerto,' he observed to Jurgenson on 3 March 1880. 'However, it's desirable that in this instance the gap between the denunciation and the performance should be shorter,' he added sardonically.[24] But it seems that Tchaikovsky's former assailant had decided to keep his peace. 'In the spring,' Tchaikovsky again wrote to Jurgenson on 24 August, 'I sent the concerto to Rub[instein] and asked him to comment upon it when he'd played it through, and to entrust Taneyev with changing as many details as he wished in the piano part, but not touching the essence [of the piece], of which *whatever advice I may receive, I will not change a single bar.* Taneyev has replied that *there's absolutely nothing to change.* This means that was Rubinstein's opinion.'[25] In fact Rubinstein did have reservations and communicated them to Tchaikovsky direct, who then transmitted them, and his own response, to Nadezhda von Meck on 10 October. 'N[ikolay] Gr[igoryevich] tells me in his opinion the piano part appears to be too episodic, and does not stand out sufficiently from the orchestra. . . . If he is right [which he was not] this will be very galling because I took pains precisely on this, to make the solo instrument stand out in as much relief as possible against the orchestral background.'[26]

It has usually been accepted that the première of the Second Piano Concerto took place in Moscow on 30 May 1882 with Taneyev playing

[23] *TLP*8, p. 457; *TPM*2, p. 276; *TZC*2, p. 345; *DTC*, p. 453; *YDGC*, p. 222 (partial).
[24] *TLP*9, p. 59; *TZC*2, p. 379; *TPJ*1, p. 140; *DTC*, p. 453.
[25] *TLP*9, p. 236; *TZC*2, p. 414; *TPJ*1, p. 165; *DTC*, p. 454.
[26] *TLP*9, p. 287; *TPM*2, p. 423; *TZC*2, p. 424; *DTC*, p. 454.

the solo part, but in fact the concerto was first heard in New York on 12 November 1881, when it was played by Madeleine Schiller with Theodore Thomas conducting.[27] In the Russian performance the conductor was Tchaikovsky's old teacher, Anton Rubinstein. By this time Taneyev had developed his own reservations about the piano writing, and exactly a month after giving the first Russian performance (at which the composer had not been present), he provided also a brief and frank digest of critical reaction to the work. 'Opinions about it are pretty varied, but they all agree on this – that the first and second movements are too long. . . . Few people approve the violin and cello solos in the second movement; they say the piano has nothing to do in it, with which I think one has to agree: there's an excessive preponderance of the other two instruments.'[28]

Tchaikovsky's reply, written from Grankino on 23 July, was tartly grateful. 'I'm extremely obliged to you for performing the concerto. I freely admit that it suffers from its length, and I regret that those persons to whom it was entrusted two years ago for critical scrutiny didn't indicate this failing at the proper time. In this they would have been doing me a great service – one perhaps even greater than the superb performance of the concerto in its present, so imperfect form. All the same – merci, merci, merci!'[29]

Among Tchaikovsky's major instrumental works the Second Piano Concerto was one about whose structure his own uncertainties seem to have persisted most obstinately. In November 1888 Tchaikovsky himself conducted the concerto in St Petersburg with the young Vasily Sapelnikov as the soloist, repeating the performance shortly afterwards in Prague and Moscow. At the very same time Alexandr Ziloti, Tchaikovsky's former pupil and now his friend, was preparing a revised edition of his own. It is apparent that Tchaikovsky himself had already made modifications for the performances with Sapelnikov,[30] but when Ziloti offered his more radical changes the composer rejected them flatly. 'I'm extremely grateful to you for your concern and interest, for your desire that my pieces should be made easier and more rewarding – but *emphatically* I can't agree with your cuts and especially with your re-ordering of the first movement,' he wrote on 8 January 1889. 'Perhaps I'm wrong and you're right – but my feelings as a composer rebel strongly against your transferences and changes. . . . The version

---

[27] I am grateful to John Warrack for drawing my attention to this.

[28] *TTP*, p. 80; *TZC2*, p. 536; *DTC*, p. 455.

[29] *TLP*11, p. 162; *TTP*, p. 81; *TZC2*, p. 538; *DTC*, p. 455.

[30] Probably the cut in the central ritornello of the first movement (bars 319–42), and the two in the Andante non troppo (bars 247–81 and 310–26; in orchestra bar 327).

of the Second Concerto I want is the one I made *Sapelnikov* play. . . .
With my changes the consistency and logical sequence of the parts is
not destroyed. My . . . hair stood on end at your idea of transferring the
cadenza to the end.'[31]

Ziloti did not let the matter rest there, and only three months before
his death Tchaikovsky was again having to resist his young friend's
persuasions to revise. When Jurgenson heard of this prolonged
tussle, he wrote to the composer urging him to hold his ground. 'I
agree to some of Ziloti's changes, but to others I emphatically can't,'
Tchaikovsky wrote in reply on 1 September. '. . . Those concessions
I've made and those cuts he and I have both thought up are quite
sufficient.'[32] Yet when Jurgenson printed a second edition four years
after Tchaikovsky's death the concerto appeared in a version heavily
revised by Ziloti, and it is in this mutilated form that it is still often
performed.

In writing to his patroness in July 1878 about his earlier compositions, Tchaikovsky had identified two clear categories: those which he
had set about from inner compulsion, and those which he had composed in a spirit of duty (i.e., commissions). That a work belonged to
one or other category was, he added, no sure pointer to its quality, for
inspiration might fade in works undertaken out of choice, while the
contracted task might suddenly fire his imagination. He might have
added that a commission was not without its incitements, for there was
the expression of faith in Tchaikovsky himself implicit in the very act of
commission, and there was the incentive of a fee in prospect. In fact,
except perhaps for the Piano Sonata, the Second Piano Concerto seems
to have been the first work Tchaikovsky undertook purely as an act of
will with no external stimulus except boredom at creative inactivity.
And in saying this, we have perhaps pointed straight at the source of the
work's weakness. The new piano concerto lacked any vital promptings,
and the melodic material reflects this. Nearly all of it is second-rate –
and with Tchaikovsky this meant that the work was irredeemably
handicapped. The material's identity, too, is sometimes questionable,
and the very opening theme suggests Schumann rather than
Tchaikovsky (Ex. 163a). The shade of the German master haunting a
work by Tchaikovsky rarely boded well, and this chunky beginning
collapses into impotence in its fourth two-bar phrase, its rigid sym-
metries prompting an equally mechanical phrase construction in
the ensuing pages. The second subject recalls the second fate motif of

---

[31] *TLP*14, p. 614; *DTC*, pp. 455–6 (partial).
[32] *TPJ*2, p. 271; *TZC*3, p. 63; *DTC*, p. 456.

Ex. 163

Onegin, and the imitative dialogue of clarinet and horn raises the melodic quality sharply (Ex. 164). Yet the portal which this opens upon richer thematic prospects is not passed, and the gentle, quasi-canonic invention to which this gives way has charm, but little else. Nor is this thematically unremarkable exposition strengthened by anything resembling the First Concerto's thoughtful deployment of materials. Here, from a reshuffling of themes in the recapitulation, had emerged a completely new balance of tonal tensions; in the Second Concerto the recapitulation is little more than an abbreviated review of the three thematic events of the exposition. Nor is there much significant development of exposition ideas beyond their prime form; the matrix of the concerto's opening is stamped upon the end of the second subject to round off the exposition, the work's opening phrase is seen in a new light by being made the rejoinder to a new melodic fragment at the E flat opening of the second of the central ritornelli (Ex. 163b), and there are some hints of developmental possibilities in the end of this, but that is about all. Indeed, since much of the material recurs in cadenza situations, its treatment tends to be loosely rhapsodic, combined with rhetorical flourishes and free interpolations.

Ex. 164

However, though these basic melodic deficiencies are sufficient to deny the Second Piano Concerto a place among Tchaikovsky's best works, it remains a piece of considerable significance, and of not negligible virtues. In the Violin Concerto Tchaikovsky's complete and well-founded confidence in the strength of his melodic invention to sustain the work had enabled him to remain within the well-tried sequence of events of the most traditional concerto structure. But in the Second Piano Concerto, with a solo instrument far less well adapted to melodic delivery, yet admirably suited to tumultuous rhetoric, and utterly self-sufficient, he was both driven and encouraged to essay a new synthesis of events. The result is a first movement with some very original structural features (Ex. 165). Its outlines are clear, even stark,

Ex. 165

SECOND PIANO CONCERTO: FIRST MOVEMENT

	Horizontal block indicates that a section centres upon one key (note), sloping block that tonal shifts occur.
■	Passage for orchestra
□	Passage for soloist
▨	Passage for soloist and orchestra

and there can be no doubt that the striving after clarity which Tchaikovsky had avowedly pursued in *The Maid*, and which was about to impel him to revise the Second Symphony, was also a powerful force in shaping this Allegro brillante. The harmonic structures, too, are remarkably forthright, with much use of sustained chords (there are some especially prolonged dominants), and the thematic workings are never involved. Thus, for instance, the ritornello which marks the beginning of the development has none of the briskly changing thematic engagements and equally swift tonal changes which mark the corresponding section of the First Concerto. Instead there is a dying rumination upon the melodic dialogue introduced in Ex. 164, all set within a magisterial, almost lapidary harmonic progress which is itself firmly embedded in C major/minor. Thus harmonic tension comes not from key shifts but from modal ambivalence and from the strong Neapolitan harmonies which engage implacably with the almost unbroken tonic pedal which underpins the whole section. Yet elsewhere in this movement it is tonal shifts that are of major importance, as the listener becomes acutely aware when, at the end of the G major-centred first subject, the second subject enters abruptly in E flat (see Ex. 164). As a piece of shock treatment this is, of course, thoroughly effective, but this move is also prophetic, for it is the harbinger of key behaviour in the whole movement. Rejecting any quasi-classical balance of keys, Tchaikovsky follows a procedure similar to that used by Schumann in his great C major Fantasia for piano, Op. 17, and operates almost exclusively on the flat side of the tonic, thus availing himself of that dark, potentially dramatic colouring which may be gained from a consistent probing towards flat regions. This early shift to E flat, by establishing the tonal antipodes to the tonic G major, defines the tonal territory of what follows: only in the second piano cadenza, the most overtly brilliant stretch of the whole movement, is there any significant probing of slightly sharper regions.

The striving for lucidity in this first movement also encourages the segregation of the solo instrument from the main body of sound, drama springing less from the direct and sometimes complex interaction of soloist and orchestra characteristic of the First Concerto than from a grandly spaced alternation of robust orchestral ritornello, grandiloquent cadenza, and even some contrasting passages of almost chamberlike intimacy. And if the exposition's structure is fairly orthodox, that of the development is not. Here Tchaikovsky completely abandons the traditional pattern of opening orchestral ritornello followed by close solo/orchestral collaboration used in the First Piano Concerto. Instead this central section is expanded to become the largest major division of the whole movement, and is boldly constructed from two ritornello/ cadenza sections, in the first of which the orchestra and then the soloist each hold rigidly to one tonality (C and B flat minor respectively), concentrating exclusively upon second subject ingredients, while in the far longer second section there is a contrasting tonal instability, with much greater emphasis upon first subject material with the addition of some new thematic matter. Such fitful, rhetorical discursiveness cannot match the closely argued course followed in this stretch of the First Concerto; what it does demonstrate most cheeringly is that the structural resourcefulness which Tchaikovsky had shown in so many of his finest instrumental works before his marriage, and which had appeared so paralyzed in the Piano Sonata, is again alive.

If this first movement is the most important Tchaikovsky had composed since that of the Fourth Symphony of 1877, the slow movement is the most ambitious since the Andante funèbre of the Third String Quartet of 1876. Yet its spiritual predecessor is far more the haunting Andante elegiaco of the Third Symphony. The opening theme (Ex. 166) is wholly admirable, starting almost naïvely like a recollection of Gounod's 'Ave Maria' on Bach's C major prelude, expanding its second phrase adroitly from four to six bars, adding sudden strength of profile in the abruptly shortened, twice-heard third

Ex. 166

phrase, relaxing briefly in a further two-bar phrase before resuming and reinforcing this new-found ardour in the following three-bar phrases, and finally retreating to end in the gentler realm in which the theme had begun. When it is repeated, starting from bar 11 of Ex. 166, with cello joining violin in amorous duet, the revised, much-expanded conclusion confirms the high fertility of Tchaikovsky's melodic inspiration in the first portion of this movement. His employment here of violin and cello soli on equal terms with the official soloist was patently determined by their ability to handle such a long-spun thread of lyrical melody superlatively well. But if this also occasions the first problem of the movement – that the piano simply cannot compete – there is a second flaw more fundamental to the music itself – that the melodic invention falters badly in the central section, which soon resorts to

mounting sequences upon a constricted melodic morsel, and culminates in pointless cadenzas after the interloping string soloists have
re-entered. Ziloti recognized this impoverishment, and his savagely
truncated version dispensed entirely with this central section. Nevertheless, Tchaikovsky's objections to the young pianist's mutilations
were fully justified, for Ziloti's reduction left nothing but a double
statement of the main theme, followed by a disproportionately long
coda. It is, in fact, still far better to perform the whole movement in its
original form without even Tchaikovsky's excisions of 1888.

The one movement to escape revision was the finale. This is not
surprising, for it is the most neatly packaged portion of the whole
concerto, affording impressive proof of how proficiently Tchaikovsky
could frame a movement which is largely compiled from virtually
discrete sections, ordered in a manner so mechanically balanced and
clear cut that criticism of their organization is silenced, yet which
manages to be less mechanical than it might appear to be at first
hearing. Though its melodic material is not as distinctive as that of the
parallel movement of the First Piano Concerto, this finale is in certain
respects more individual, for it is impossible to assign it confidently to a
particular structural category. The character of the first two themes
and their presentation in the tonic and relative minor respectively
promises the most routine of rondos, but the sudden intrusion, as the
tonic is regained, of a third theme proves this structural assumption
mistaken. A bird's eye view of the movement's thematic organization
might suggest another of Tchaikovsky's three-subject sonata patterns
with minimal development, but the tonal organization seems to exclude
this possibility. Yet, in fact, one way of viewing this movement is to see
it as an approach to sonata structure of the sort Tchaikovsky was to use
with far more pregnant results in the first movement of the Piano Trio –
that is, the reinterpretation of an apparently traditional thematic
scheme by irregular tonal organization. In this Allegro con fuoco
exposition and recapitulation are reversed; the exposition, instead of
concluding in a key other than the tonic, ends firmly back in G major.
After such a tonally enclosed section a full-scale development would
hardly be a natural consequence; yet to have merely prolonged the
tonic into a restatement of the first subject would have made this
recurrence a tonal non-event. Some tonal divergence is necessary, and
Tchaikovsky constructs a link made as a quasi-developmental extension of his third idea, thus enhancing a little the expressive world of the
movement, before passing to the recapitulation. This follows exactly
the thematic course of the exposition, but by setting the second theme in
the dominant minor (D minor), the third theme recurs in F. Thus the

greatest tonal tension is located towards the end of the movement, and the finality of the coda is reinforced by delaying the restatement of the tonic until this last stage. If such a view seems too sophisticated for a movement whose manner of address is so direct and uncomplicated, it at least warns us not to be too dismissive about this finale, even though it clearly makes no attempt to emulate the grander, more ambitious aspirations of the two large-scale organisms which have preceded it.

Tchaikovsky stayed nearly a month in Paris. His aversion to contacts with persons other than those very close to him remained as strong as ever. On the journey he had encountered Józef Wieniawski, pianist-brother of the famous Henryk, and to escape his companionship had pretended he was travelling with a lady – at which Wieniawski had winked and departed. In Paris he saw Kondratyev daily, but had insisted that his friend should introduce him as Mr Petrovsky to mask his identity. Tchaikovsky found most of his pleasures in walking, visits to the Louvre and the Palais de Justice, where the histrionics displayed by some of the participants caused him much amusement, and in the theatrical and musical life of the city. He saw Mozart's *Die Zauberflöte*, but the most momentous musical event of his stay was a con-cert performance by Colonne of Berlioz's entire *La Prise de Troie* in the presence of the French president. Berlioz fever was at its height in Paris, and only a week earlier, at a rival concert conducted by Pasdeloup, Tchaikovsky had heard extracts from this same opera. Thus he was afforded an opportunity for direct comparison between the merits of these two dominating conductors in the Parisian scene. 'The first's [Pasdeloup's] performance was less than middling, the second's [Colonne's] *very good*,' he declared to Mrs von Meck the next day, clearly relieved that the introduction of his Fourth Symphony to French ears had been placed in the latter's hands. 'The work itself, as always happens on closer acquaintance and in a better performance, pleased me considerably more, though I still consider the opera to be weak – even very weak if compared with Berlioz's masterpieces, i.e. *Faust* and *Romeo*.'[33]

A week before, he had passed judgement on a very different musical work to his patroness, who had just heard of the *Paraphrases* which Borodin, Cui, Lyadov and Rimsky-Korsakov had composed the pre-vious year on that best-known of all juvenile, two-fingered piano pieces, *Chopsticks*. Liszt had published a complimentary letter on this collection and he was to substantiate his praise by supplying a mazurka upon the

[33] *TLP*8, p. 440; *TPM*2, p. 265; *TZC*2, p. 338.

piece which was to be added to a later edition. In judging this set of pieces Tchaikovsky's critical aim found the bull's eye; his verdict on these trifles is a timely reminder of how sensible his musical judgements remained. As for his view on Liszt's role, it shows an equally shrewd, yet not ungenerous perception of part of that complex figure's character.

> This composition is, of course, an original piece of its kind, and it reveals in its composers remarkable talents for harmonization – but I find it unattractive. As a *joke* it is too ponderous, too bulky and indigestible because the endless repetitions of the theme are tiresome. As a work of art it is nothing. That several talented people should, for their own pleasure, set themselves the task of devising all kinds of variations upon a trivial, commonplace phrase is not surprising: what is surprising is that these dilettantish trifles should be printed and given currency. Only dilettantes can believe that every piquantly invented chord is worthy of being made public. As for Liszt, this old Jesuit responds with exaggeratedly enthusiastic compliments to every piece submitted to his most august scrutiny. He is a kind-hearted being, and one of the few outstanding artists in whose soul there has never been petty envy, a disposition to hinder the successes of his neighbour (Wagner and, in part, A[nton] Rubinstein are beholden to him for their successes; he also rendered many services to Berlioz) – but he is also too much a Jesuit to be truthful and honest. Returning to the variations, I will say that it is nevertheless a piquant musical curiosity, revealing in its composers great talents – but sadly onesided, i.e., directed solely towards *harmony*. If you should come by the piece, pay particular attention to *Requiem* by Borodin; this is a remarkably successful conceit.[34]

That same positive ability to see clearly the balance between virtues and inadequacies in music which had no great attraction to him led him to rise to Cui's defence when Mrs von Meck delivered herself unsympathetically upon a recently published set of that composer's songs which Tchaikovsky had sent her to look over. 'I am not in complete agreement, my dear friend, with your opinion of Cui,' he replied on 8 December.

> I do not perceive a great creative strength in him, but he has elegance, a pretty harmonic manner, and taste, in which respect he

---

[34] *TLP*8, pp. 421–2; *TPM*2, p. 253; *TZC*2, p. 331.

differs from the other representatives of that circle of musicians. . . .
Do you know *Cui's* opera *[William] Ratcliff*? There are delightful
things in it, though unfortunately they suffer from a certain sugari-
ness and *sleekness* in the harmony. It is obvious that the composer sat
a long while over each bar lovingly polishing it, as a result of which
the design is insufficiently free, the strokes too artificial, too contrived. . . . He took ten years writing *Ratcliff*! The opera was obviously written in bits very carefully finished off, but in consequence of
this one feels a lack of unity, and inconsistency of style.[35]

Though repeating in essentials the assessment he had made to Mrs von
Meck two years earlier of this journalistic tormentor and the other
members of Balakirev's group, the terms are now more balanced, and
the smouldering ferocity in the earlier judgement has died.

While in Paris Tchaikovsky was approached by the Berlin publisher,
Adolph Fürstner, with an offer to market his works in Germany. Much
flattered, Tchaikovsky had nevertheless replied that his relations with
Jurgenson made it impossible for him to accept (what he did not know
was that Fürstner had already issued pirated editions of his pieces).
Though he continued to feel that the good prospects which he believed
such an offer foretold for his music outside Russia did not apply to the
forthcoming performance of the Fourth Symphony in Paris, he was
afforded one other clear sign that his music was making considerable
headway in France; in January there would take place in Paris a concert
devoted entirely to his Third String Quartet and *Sérénade mélancolique*
(the latter with piano accompaniment). It was a somewhat more
self-assured Tchaikovsky who left for Rome on 17 December, the day
after his benefactress had also departed for Russia. Pausing for only a
day in Turin, he joined Modest and Kolya in the Italian capital on 20
December. On that same day in Moscow the First Suite was receiving
its première under Nikolay Rubinstein.

Much postal debate had preceded the decision that Rome should
become the base in which Tchaikovsky would spend the remainder of
the winter with Modest and Kolya. Modest had been the Italian
capital's most emphatic advocate, for he was attracted by the artistic
treasures of the place. Tchaikovsky had raised constant objections
to Modest's choice, but the latter had taken the matter into his own
hands and journeyed quietly to Rome, whence he wrote informing his
brother that he was awaiting his arrival. Tchaikovsky therefore had no

[35] *TLP8*, pp. 439–40; *TPM2*, p. 265; *TZC2*, pp. 337–8.

alternative but to proceed thither, but when he arrived he was surprised at the delight he discovered in it. The weather was wonderful, and there were none of those unpleasant reactions he had experienced two years before, when everything had been coloured by his post-marital gloom. With his Baedeker Modest had explored the city thoroughly, and he now acted as a well-informed guide to his brother. Tchaikovsky felt that the mists which had so obstinately clouded his appreciation of the visual arts had dispersed yet further. 'Michelangelo's frescos in the Sistine Chapel have ceased to be double Dutch to me, and I'm beginning to be filled with wonder at his powerful and original beauty,' he reported to Anatoly on 12 January 1880.[36] But reservations remained, and four days earlier he had given Nadezhda von Meck a clear glimpse of how he found himself affected by what he saw. Like Goethe before him, he found the superabundance of Rome's creative riches quite indigestible. In any case, his range of response was limited. Michelangelo's 'gloomy grandeur' and his muscular figures could impress him, but they could not delight or move him. An old parallel again rose in his mind. 'Is it not true that Beethoven and Michelangelo have very kindred natures?' he suggested to Nadezhda von Meck,[37] feeling that same discomfort at his own inability to respond to the Italian artist's majesty as he did at his antipathy to the rugged strength of the German composer. During this Roman interlude he was to return dutifully to long contemplations of Michelangelo's *Moses* and his Sistine Chapel frescos in the hope of some kind of inner illumination, and by the time of his departure he believed that the dawn of appreciation had truly broken (though one suspects this was more wish-fulfilment than true insight). But on another Italian master Tchaikovsky felt he could confer the highest compliment of which he was capable. 'My favourite is still Raphael, that Mozart of painting,' he had confessed to the same correspondent. Raphael's noble yet sweet lyricism, his poise, his elegant yet strong perfection, all addressed that side of Tchaikovsky which identified so readily with the musical world Mozart conjured for him. 'Paintings by Guercino still appeal to me in the highest degree,' he went on.

His *Florentine Endymion* [and] some of his Madonnas are of such angelic beauty that they fill my whole soul with a certain quiet rapture. However, I have to confess that in general I am by nature devoid of sensitivity to the plastic arts, and only a very few paintings and statues make a real impression on me. . . . Only today I experi-

---

[36] *TLP8*, p. 488; *TPR*, p. 655; *TPB*, p. 239; *YDGC*, p. 224.
[37] *TLP9*, p. 29; *TPM2*, p. 301; *TZC2*, p. 369.

enced just how important it is to gaze long and hard at a painting. I sat in front of Raphael's *Transfiguration*, and at first it seemed to me that there was nothing particular in this picture; but little by little I began to understand the facial expressions of each of the Apostles and other figures, and the more I peered, the more I was filled with fascination at the whole and the details.[38]

Here we may perceive the very essence of Tchaikovsky's response. Objective appraisal of the mastery in design or the magnificence of the craft had no real part in his reaction, nor were his sensibilities stirred by the pattern of contrasting tones and colours. Just as he felt drawn into the sound world of Mozart, so he needed to *absorb* himself in the world depicted by Raphael. But whereas the ultimate relish of Mozart's creations could be savoured by re-creating them, he had no power to do this with Raphael's. All he could do was sit before a picture until it ceased to be canvas covered with representations, and became a living world peopled by real beings with whom he could identify. When he had thus possessed it, then an emotional response could follow.

Tchaikovsky's new-found delight in Rome saturates the letters he wrote during his first days in the city. There was no music worth hearing, he said, but he used his spare time to begin systematically learning English, and he played Bach and duets with Modest on the piano he had imported into his hotel room. All will to compose had vanished. Then, predictably, his mood began to change, and the urge to work returned. Ten days after his arrival he set about the revision of the Second Symphony, completed the sketches in three days, and then wrote to Bessel (who had years before extracted from him the publication rights to this symphony), making it clear that he had no intention of letting him have the new version without an adequate fee. When abroad Tchaikovsky relied very much upon the good offices of his friends to keep him informed about the fortunes of his works. Ever since arriving in Rome he had been awaiting news of the First Suite, and he was much hurt that none of his friends in Moscow had thought to telegraph him of its success at its première. His dismay at Rubinstein's comments on the alleged difficulties in the piece have already been noted. He consoled himself by reflecting on the history of that same Rubinstein's reactions to the First Piano Concerto; 'what was impossible in 1875 became thoroughly possible in 1878,' he observed drily to Taneyev.[39] He gained no joy whatsoever from Mrs von Meck's adverse

[38] *TLP8*, p. 486; *TPM2*, p. 288; *TZC2*, p. 355.
[39] *TLP9*, p. 15; *TZC2*, p. 361; *TTP*, p. 47; *YDGC*, p. 224.

account of a performance of *Swan Lake* she had attended in Moscow, but at least she could report a full house.

However, the other news Tchaikovsky was really awaiting concerned the Paris performance of the Fourth Symphony. It was entirely his own fault that his secret hope of hearing the work was not fulfilled. 'He [Colonne] informs me that my symphony is to be given *tomorrow*, 25, at the Châtelet. This grieved me in the extreme. If he had written to me only one day earlier then I would still have been able to set out and arrive in Paris in time,' he lamented to the work's dedicatee. 'Of course I cannot blame *Colonne* for, wishing to ensure that I remained incognito, I wrote to him that my health prevented me from attending the performance of my symphony, and that he need not trouble to see that his letter arrived in time. But it is so disappointing that the one opportunity of hearing my symphony has eluded me. I was so rejoicing in this opportunity, I had promised myself such delight in being present at the performance of it unknown to and unnoticed by anyone!'[40] In his letter Colonne had confessed that the rehearsals had been long and hard, and he predicted that the Andantino and scherzo would score the greatest success. The event proved him right, and he declared that he would try to repeat these middle movements before the season was over, but there was no such proposal for the remaining two. The symphony's reception, as Tchaikovsky himself had prophesied, had not been brilliant. Despite this he was reluctant to allow his patroness to campaign for further performances of his works in Paris, and when he heard that she had returned to the attack on Colonne with a suggestion that he should conduct the First Suite and promote *The Maid of Orléans* he was firm in restraining her. 'It will be *embarrassing and distasteful* to me in the extreme if you again thank him [Colonne] in a material way for giving attention to my compositions,' he cautioned her on 28 February.[41]

Quite apart from fears that such a repeated arrangement might threaten the secrecy of his relationship with his patroness (Colonne had, in fact, had to be told something of it), Tchaikovsky must now have realized, though he might not have confessed it openly, that the international tide was beginning to run strongly in his favour, rendering such subsidized performances less necessary. From New York a little later he was to hear of the success of the First Suite under Leopold Damrosch and of a performance of the First Piano Concerto, while from Berlin came news of three performances of the concerto; the work was also heard in Budapest. All these performances were, according to

[40] *TLP*9, p. 26; *TPM*2, pp. 296–7; *TZC*2, p. 365.
[41] *TLP*9, p. 55; *TPM*2, p. 316; *TZC*2, p. 378.

Modest, highly successful. Indeed, Modest later declared that this period saw the beginning of his brother's international reputation.

Yet the most affecting news received by Tchaikovsky during his stay in Rome was of his father's end. On 20 January he heard from Anatoly of their parent's serious illness. Tchaikovsky would have sped dutifully to St Petersburg if this had been deemed necessary, the more so since the noise and bustle of Rome and the sheer volume of its cultural heritage were now weighing very heavily upon him. But such a journey quickly became pointless, for on 21 January Ilya Petrovich died. The loss did not strike Tchaikovsky very deeply. His father had never occupied that place at the very heart of his affections which his mother always had possessed, and always would. Anatoly wrote him a full account of their father's end, and Tchaikovsky recorded his own reaction to Nadezhda von Meck. 'I wept a lot as I read it, and I think these tears which I shed at the disappearance from this world of an upright man endowed with an angelic spirit had a beneficial effect on me. I feel enlightened and reconciled in spirit.'[42] Over the years Ilya Petrovich had become like a dear ornament to him, treasured because of its age and many associations, and wept over when broken with sentimental, not grief-stricken, tears. This melancholy event certainly had no effect upon the new work he was composing.

The first declaration of intent to compose the Italian Capriccio (or Italian Suite on folk melodies, as Tchaikovsky then envisaged it) was given in a letter to Taneyev of 16 January. In Rome Tchaikovsky had encountered the same propensity of Italians to sing everywhere which had been such a mixed joy during his stay in Florence in 1878, and the idea that such native melodies might be of use to him personally took a swift hold of him. 'Yesterday I heard a delightful folksong which I shall certainly use,' he had written to Nadezhda von Meck as early as 27 December 1879.[43] By 28 January 1880, when he had begun composition, his models had become specific; 'I want to compose something like the Spanish fantasias of *Glinka*,' he announced to his benefactress.[44] A week later he could report to her cheerfully that the basic work was done. 'I have already completed the sketches for an Italian fantasia on folk tunes for which I believe a good future may be predicted. It will be effective, thanks to the delightful tunes which I have succeeded in assembling partly from anthologies, partly through my own ears on the streets.'[45] The scoring was deferred until May, and it was only when

[42] *TLP*9, p. 33; *TPM*2, p. 303.
[43] *TLP*8, p. 466; *TPM*2, p. 281.
[44] *TLP*9, p. 29; *TPM*2, p. 301; *YDGC*, p. 225; *DTC*, p. 393.
[45] *TLP*9, p. 35; *TPM*2, p. 306; *DTC*, p. 393; *YDGC*, p. 226 (partial).

this was finally completed on 27 May that the title was changed to Italian Capriccio. By now Tchaikovsky had developed doubts about the musical substance of the piece, but for its orchestral effectiveness he had no fears. On 18 December 1880 Nikolay Rubinstein conducted the first performance at an RMS concert in Moscow so successfully that it was repeated at the next RMS concert a fortnight later. Such now was the Russian interest in a new work by Tchaikovsky that within a further fortnight it had been twice heard in St Petersburg.

Here apparently it scored less success, and some critics were already sharing the composer's own well-founded doubts about its musical substance. The opening fanfare, according to Modest, was a trumpet call his brother had heard daily from the barracks which lay alongside his hotel in Rome. Of the remaining four tunes, the only one to have been identified is that of the final tarantella, which was known in Italy as 'Ciccuzza'. The Italian Capriccio unfolds as a loose series of self-contained sections which grow by thematic repetition against changing backgrounds in the tradition of Glinka, or by simple developmental extension employing a good deal of sequence. It must remain uncertain whether the broader tonal planning was prompted by the highly appropriate Neapolitan chord which Tchaikovsky uses prominently in the coda to engineer a strong inflection of flat keys; certainly it relates perfectly to the placing, in the preceding music, of deep flat keys (E flat, D flat, and B flat major/minor itself) against the tonic A minor/major. This leaning towards the flat side of the tonic recalls the first movement of the Second Piano Concerto, the immediate predecessor of the Capriccio. But whereas the G major/E flat confrontation early in the concerto's first movement had defined the field of tonal operation for the following music, the even more extreme tritonal opposition (A major/E flat major) exhibited early in the Capriccio heralded a series of key contrasts used for purely colouristic purposes. In fact, the projection of bright, warm, contrasting colours through any means at Tchaikovsky's disposal is patently the main aim in the Capriccio.

Glinka's Spanish Overtures, which Tchaikovsky openly identified as the prototypes of the Italian Capriccio, were evocative pieces composed in response to the impressions made upon Glinka by Spain and its people during his visit there between 1845 and 1847. While the two pieces had been prompted by a common impulse and had been grown entirely from Spanish melodies, they had turned out very differently as designs, the first (*Capriccio brillante on the Jota aragonese*) being an essay in the free treatment of folk melody within a sonata pattern, while the second (*Recollection of a summer night in Madrid*) had abandoned any such formal mould in favour of a free scheme; in fact, Glinka described it as a pot-pourri, having based it on four themes instead of a single one, as in its predecessor. It was this Second Spanish Overture which was the true model for the Italian Capriccio. But whereas Glinka's vivid imagination and his flair for fantasy, with abrupt contrasts and unexpected juxtapositions, had enabled him to produce a colourful, highly inventive panorama of Mediterranean life, the Italian Capriccio, for all its arguable superiority as a well-made piece, shows Tchaikovsky thin in real inventiveness, and decidedly the inferior in power of suggestion. When the gregarious Glinka had lived in Spain he had soaked himself in the indigenous culture, and *Summer Night in Madrid* is Spain seen and felt from within; the Italian Capriccio is like Italy projected through the pages of a guide-book, evocative yet not real, and without the sheer allure of that technicolor gloss which Rimsky-Korsakov was to exhibit with such dazzling variety in his Spanish Capriccio.

In a letter inscribed to his patroness at the turn of the year, Tchaikovsky summarized what 1879 had meant to him.

As I look back on the passing year I must sing a hymn of thanksgiving to fate for the great number of good days I have spent both in Russia and abroad. I can say that for this whole year I have enjoyed undisturbed security, and have been happy as far as happiness is possible. Of course there have also been bitter moments – but only moments. What is more, these only arose from the misfortunes of people close to me while I, strictly speaking, have personally enjoyed unqualified happiness and contentment. This was the first year of my life during which I was the whole time a free man.[46]

The Italian Capriccio evidences forcefully the price of that freedom. In seeking the insulated conditions which he knew would be most favourable to his day-to-day contentment, Tchaikovsky had protected himself against those assaults on his nerve ends which alone could fully re-animate his creative powers, and had guarded himself from tensions which could broaden his experience and stretch his emotional awareness. The superficiality, even emptiness, of the Italian Capriccio suggests, perhaps more than any other work of this phase, the degree to which Tchaikovsky could not only retreat from the people around him (except for the chosen few), but also – paradoxically – detach himself from his environment. His capacity to withdraw into himself was now complete.

---

[46] *TLP*8, p. 491; *TPM*2, p. 291; *TZC*2, p. 363.

3

UKRAINIAN SUMMER:
TOTAL ISOLATION

WHEN A CREATIVE artist becomes as recluse as Tchaikovsky had grown over the last two years, his biographer becomes painfully aware of a deadening monotony invading his narrative. Just as his subject has shrunk from contacts with all but a very few dear and trusted persons, so the events of that subject's life have inevitably contracted towards the trivia of day-to-day existence. 1879 had established what was to be the pattern of Tchaikovsky's existence for several years to come, and it would be otiose to continue particularizing all the minutiae of his by now well-established routines. We may take it for granted that he instituted carefully regulated working practices wherever he was, that he went for daily walks, enjoyed the cultural or scenic fare offered by whatsoever location he found himself in, and read a great deal. Only when, in such matters, something of some significance occurred need it be sifted out for the record.

As for the further compositional activities of Tchaikovsky's present three months in Rome, no sooner were the sketches of the Italian Capriccio complete than he received from Karl Davïdov, the director of the St Petersburg Conservatoire, a commission to compose music for an event celebrating the silver jubilee of Alexandr II as Tsar. This was to take place in the Bolshoy Theatre in St Petersburg on 2 March, barely three weeks away in the future, and would consist of a series of tableaux vivants depicting major events in Alexandr's reign. 'These tableaux will be accompanied by appropriate music,' Davïdov informed Tchaikovsky.

The music is being composed by Rubinstein (Anton), Rimsky-Korsakov, Cui, Solovyev, Nápravník, Borodin, etc. We must have your name (an album with pictures and the music will subsequently be published). Each of the above-named composers has taken one tableau; because there's little time, and it's impossible to have long consultations between St Petersburg and Rome, I'm sending straight on to you the content of that tableau which is awaiting musical illustration from you. Bear in mind that there must not be more than seven minutes of music. In view of the facility with which you compose, I'm hoping that your score will be in St Petersburg ahead of many from the local composers.

TABLEAU 10[1]

Montenegro. The moment at which news is received in Montenegro of Russia's declaration of war on Turkey (the leader is reading the manifesto to the Montenegrins).

From 5–7 minutes of music.[2]

Tchaikovsky viewed this scheme balefully, and he suspected that the other composers had taken their pick of the various tableaux, leaving him with the least attractive. He countered by suggesting that his Slavonic March might prove a ready-made background for his tableau, and to encourage Davïdov's favour towards this idea, he promptly offered him the dedication of the new Italian Capriccio. Nevertheless, because there was no time to see whether Davïdov would bite at this suggestion, and feeling he simply could not be left out, Tchaikovsky set himself to discharge the formal request, and in four days had completed his offering. 'It goes without saying that I couldn't think up anything except the most filthy noise and crashes,' he confided gloomily to Anatoly on 12 February, the day after completing the work.[3] We have no way of judging the truth of Tchaikovsky's verdict, for the festal event never took place. In the growing political and social turmoil of the last years of Alexandr's reign the authorities had become increasingly nervous. Tchaikovsky had himself only recently felt the consequences of this when *The Oprichnik*, which was being rehearsed for a revival in Moscow, was suddenly withdrawn after the dress rehearsal, the authorities feeling that its subject matter was too subversive for the times. Then, only a fortnight before the tableaux vivants were to be exhibited, an attempt was made on the Tsar's life in his own Winter Palace in St Petersburg, and the presentation was cancelled. Tchaikovsky was as relieved at this as at the veto on *The Oprichnik*; the Montenegrin tableau music was never performed or published, and the score has disappeared.

Having completed this unwelcome chore, Tchaikovsky rested from active creation for some four months. After all, he had in little more than three months composed the Second Piano Concerto, the Italian

---

[1] In referring to this tableau in his letters, Tchaikovsky numbered it as 7.
[2] *TZC*2, pp. 372–3.
[3] *TLP*9, p. 41; *TPB*, p. 241; *YDGC*, p. 226.

Capriccio, the Montenegrin tableau, and had virtually written anew the first movement of the Second Symphony; now both the concerto and the capriccio were waiting to be brought to their finished forms. Scoring and making transcriptions of these pieces occupied him until the end of May, and in the meanwhile proofs of the vocal score of *The Maid* had begun to arrive and turned out to be so inaccurate that the labour of correction absorbed him until the end of July. As in Paris, he avoided meeting people as far as he could. Twice as a tourist he visited the Villa d'Este, but declined to call on Liszt, though he suspected he was in residence. Being in Rome encouraged him to turn his attention to an author from that city's greatest days, and he read Tacitus in a French translation which revealed to him what a 'great and powerful artist'[4] this ancient stylist was. He also recommended his patroness to read Metternich's memoirs. Certainly he found these books more congenial than the recent Violin Concerto by Brahms, a copy of which Nadezhda von Meck had sent him for his appraisal. This merely consolidated what was to be his lifelong reaction to Brahms's music. Tchaikovsky sensed clearly the inhibition in such music, the iron discipline which held the full emotional force in check. 'There are many preparations for something, many hints of something which must appear forthwith and must charm – yet nothing but tedium comes out of this. His music is not warmed by true feeling, there is no poetry in it, though it has great pretension to *depth*. Yet there is nothing in this depth. . . . For instance, let us take the opening of the concerto; as an introduction to something it is beautiful, it is an excellent pedestal for a column – but the column itself does not exist, and immediately after one pedestal there comes another. I do not know whether I am expressing well the thought – or, rather, the feeling which Brahms's music instils in me.' As so often happened when Tchaikovsky was faced with music he fundamentally disliked, he could display a degree of clear, even penetrating insight until the moment at which that music had to be submitted to the idiosyncrasies of his own most personal receptive faculties; then, if the subject was one he had to recognize as a major figure, the best he could do was to confess to incomprehension, as he freely did when ending this assessment of the Violin Concerto. 'As a musical personality Brahms is simply *antipathetic* to me, I cannot digest him. However hard I try [to respond to his music], I remain cold and hostile. It is a purely instinctive feeling.'[5]

While in Rome Tchaikovsky witnessed the noisy pre-Lenten revels,

[4] *TLP*9, p. 46; *TPM*2, p. 312; *TZC*2, p. 376.
[5] *TLP*9, p. 56; *TPM*2, p. 318; *TZC*2, pp. 378–9.

and concluded that Berlioz's overture, *Le Carnaval romain*, had caught their unrestrained ebullience perfectly. But while he was impressed by the unadulterated good nature of the carnival, and the complete absence of the drunkenness which so often marred similar Russian festivities, the sheer din and chaos weighed on his nerves. He was deeply worried, too, by the impending separation between Kolya's parents. The mother was the guilty party, and Kolya idolized her; now the idol would be seen to be flawed, and Tchaikovsky realized all too well the pain which would attend Kolya's disenchantment. As so often happened when Tchaikovsky was abroad, the identity of his next destination kept changing until the moment of final decision arrived. Modest and Kolya were to remain in Italy, and Tchaikovsky determined to leave Alexey with them to reduce Modest's burden as Kolya's custodian. Since Tchaikovsky would now have to return to Russia alone, he felt that only by a wide detour to his beloved Paris could he find some joy on this lonely journey. There, too, he could see Kondratyev, who had already visited him in Rome, had exasperated him with his drunkenness and general debauchery, but who still commanded a firm hold on his affections. Then he would spend a night in Berlin which was at that time enjoying a high place in his favours. On 9 March, his finances rejuvenated by the 300 roubles he had received from the Moscow branch of the RMS for the First Suite, Tchaikovsky left Rome. Using *Pendennis* on the train as a refuge into which he could retreat to escape the endless conversation of a certain Belgian count (Tchaikovsky decided that Thackeray's novel was as delightful as *David Copperfield*), he arrived in Paris two days later. Here he relished performances of Corneille's *Polyeucte* and Molière's *Les Femmes savantes* at the Comédie-Française, and derived equal delight from a brand new play, *La Petite Mère*, by Henri Meilhac and Ludovic Halévy. 'The play's enchanting,' he enthused to Modest. 'The hero's a young *composer-symphonist* with long hair and a nervous sensibility. I never saw anything funnier in my life – nor, despite some caricaturing, more true to life. In one scene, where he's sitting at the piano in his dressing-room composing the second movement of his symphony, I almost split my sides with laughter.'[6] Patently Tchaikovsky was not in the least solemn about his own profession. But in Berlin, where he arrived on 15 March, disappointment awaited him when, for the first time, he saw Wagner's *Die fliegende Holländer* ('terribly noisy and boring,' he judged it to Modest[7]); he found far more genuine pleasure in the chimpanzee and dog who

[6] *TLP*9, pp. 66–7; *TPB*, p. 242; *YDGC*, p. 228.
[7] *TLP*9, p. 72; *TZC*2, p. 382; *TPB*, p. 245.

shared a cage in the menagerie of the Aquarium. A visit to the Kaiser
Friedrich Museum confirmed his feeling that the spell in Rome had
advanced significantly his appreciation of the visual arts, especially
when he was able to recognize a Correggio without consulting the
catalogue.

On 19 March he arrived in St Petersburg. 'I have already begun my
periodic *martyrdom*,' he wrote to Nadezhda von Meck the following
day,[8] referring to the beginning of yet another spell of bolstering up a
depressed brother Anatoly. He had been well prepared for this by the
torrents of woe and self-doubtings which had poured from Anatoly's
letters to him in Paris and Rome; now, faced with Anatoly himself, with
the uncongenial ambience of the northern capital, and with the gap left
by the death of his father, whose grave he hastened to visit, his own
spirits plummeted. News of the mortal illness of the composer-violinist,
Henryk Wieniawski, whom Nadezhda von Meck had taken into her
Moscow home to nurse through his last days, depressed him yet
further. He spent a good deal of time with the Konradis, trying to
understand their domestic plight and to ensure that the blow to their
son would be lessened when, at last, he would have to be told of their
impending divorce. Tchaikovsky could not complain of boredom, for
there were far too many invitations from family and friends, far too
many business matters to attend to. But any sort of creative work was
impossible. Then, suddenly, the Grand Duke Konstantin Nikolayevich,
brother of the Tsar, president of the RMS, and for long an admirer of
Tchaikovsky's music, was insisting upon meeting him. Dreading the
prospect of this social contact with so elevated a personage, Tchaikovsky nevertheless accepted Nápravník's remorseless insistence that he
must endure such trials for the sake of his music, for Tchaikovsky's
main preoccupation in St Petersburg was to promote the production of
The Maid of Orléans, and the Grand Duke's support in this matter could
prove critical. Meanwhile, to aggravate his already frayed nerves, the
manuscript copy of the vocal score of *The Maid* submitted to the theatre
turned out to be grossly inaccurate, and much time had to be devoted to
correcting this. Not only did Tchaikovsky have to fulfil his obligation to
dine with the Grand Duke; the Grand Duke's son, the Grand Duke
Konstantin Konstantinovich, who was a friend of Vera Butakova, and
who was not only a great devotee of music but himself an amateur
composer and poet, also wanted to meet Tchaikovsky. Knowing,
however, of Tchaikovsky's aversion to formal social events, he asked
Vera Butakova to arrange an intimate evening at her own home.

[8] *TLP*9, p. 73; *TPM*2, p. 325.

Tchaikovsky could not escape. Yet when it came to the event, he found himself thoroughly disarmed by this twenty-two-year-old, and from nine until two in the morning they talked about music. For his part the Grand Duke was sufficiently taken by Tchaikovsky as a person to propose that the latter should accompany him on a three-year round-the-world trip upon which he was about to embark as a lieutenant in the Russian navy. Much flattered, Tchaikovsky nevertheless baulked at the thought of such protracted loss of freedom, and he declined the invitation. Nevertheless, this meeting marked the beginning of a friendship which was to last till the composer's death, and which was to result in the composition, upon the Grand Duke's own poems, of the Six Romances, Op. 63, and the male-voice chorus, 'Blessed is he who smiles', all of 1887.

Whatever the stresses of such meetings, they afforded Tchaikovsky yet more evidence from which he could take great heart. He could see he was passing from being simply a highly interesting, even respected composer to becoming an established figure whose music was one of the most admired ornaments of the cultural scene. From Moscow came news that, on 26 March, Nikolay Rubinstein was to perform not only Tchaikovsky's Piano Sonata but also the transcription which Liszt had already made of the Polonaise from *Eugene Onegin*, as well as a concert paraphrase on themes from the same opera by the German pianist and pupil of Liszt, Paul Pabst, now one of the professors at the Moscow Conservatoire. Meanwhile in St Petersburg itself there were, during Tchaikovsky's three-and-a-half-week stay, three concerts in which his own music was performed. On 30 March a quartet led by Auer played the Second String Quartet, Tchaikovsky receiving both an ovation and a wreath. Then five days later Nápravník conducted *Romeo and Juliet* at a musicians' benevolent fund concert, and two days later again directed the piece, this time in an all-Tchaikovsky programme in aid of a fund for establishing a scholarship to the St Petersburg Conservatoire. Besides *Romeo and Juliet*, there was the First Suite, the Andante cantabile from the First String Quartet arranged for solo violin, some romances, and Alexandra Panayeva, who had caused such romantic torment to Anatoly, singing the letter monologue from *Onegin*. The pleasure of witnessing a concert devoted entirely to his own music was offset only by comments from some of his acquaintances, and even from the press, who had decided that the concert was Tchaikovsky's own idea, and that he was responsible for the inflated ticket prices. The concert itself was well attended, especially by the aristocracy, and Turgenev was in the audience; it was a considerable personal success for Tchaikovsky himself. Even that unpalatable round of industrious visiting in which he engaged on behalf of *The Maid* furnished further firm evidence of his rising reputation. From Moscow, where he arrived on 14 April, he described to his patroness the social soliciting of his last two days in St Petersburg.

> On Sunday from two to five I was at Mrs Abaza's, where the Grand Duchess Ekater[ina] Mikhailovna's family were, to whom I had to play extracts from my new opera. Her daughter is a very talented singer, and sings my romances very nicely. Thence I directed myself to dinner with Isakov, the supreme head of the military schools. The beginning of the evening I spent with Count Litke, and from eleven at night until three I sat with the engaging and very musical Grand Duke Konst[antin] Konst[antinovich]. . . . On Monday I attended a grand dinner at Princess Vasilchikova's where I was, as they say, the hero of the festivities, and where there was a great gathering of titled people of every variety, among whom was the Prince Evg[eny] Maximil[ianovich] Leichtenbergsky, whose wife is an outstanding singer, and who does me the honour of declaring herself my admirer. I repeat: all this serves as very comforting proof to me of my growing success.[9]

By now Tchaikovsky was desperately tired, but also deeply re-assured; even he could see the affair of his marriage was beginning to pass into history, and his rehabilitation into Russian society had begun.

So much had this social hurly-burly dominated Tchaikovsky's St Petersburg existence that he decided he would in Moscow need first to keep his presence a secret so that he might finish the scoring of the Second Piano Concerto. Nikolay Rubinstein was mounting a Conservatoire performance of Beethoven's *Fidelio*, but Tchaikovsky chose to absent himself from the dress rehearsal which he would normally have felt obliged to attend. His attempt to remain incognito for two days proved vain, and his truancy was discovered. Filled with alarm at how Rubinstein would react, he hurried off to make his explanations, and was immediately engulfed in the social world of his Moscow friends. In consequence his stay had to be extended to more than a week so that he might do what was urgently required of him by Jurgenson and others. Little progress was made on scoring the concerto. On 23 April a very thankful composer was at last able to slip out of Moscow on the way to Kamenka.

*

[9] *TLP*9, p. 99; *TPM*2, p. 336; *TZC*2, pp. 389–90.

Tchaikovsky was beginning the longest single period he had so far spent in those special conditions of relaxation and freedom from worldly cares which the Ukraine afforded him. For seven months he was to find comfort in his sister's and patroness's homes, and the insulation this provided from the direct pressures of his wider existence was to be further reflected in some of the works he wrote during the next few months. Kamenka was in some turmoil when he arrived because of an influx of guests for Easter, including brother Ippolit with his wife and four-year-old daughter, as well as Anatoly. The need for the last to take up his new post in Moscow added urgency to Tchaikovsky's intention of finishing the Second Piano Concerto without delay, for he wished Anatoly to be his carrier, and when this brother left Kamenka on 14 May, he bore with him the completed score to pass over to Jurgenson. By now Modest had arrived with Kolya and Alexey. Tchaikovsky's distress at the situation within the Konradi household remained as acute as ever, and his heartfelt sympathy went out to all members of that unhappy clan. To Kolya's mother, now viewing the break from her husband with dread, he wrote one of his most touchingly sympathetic letters. 'Please, Alina Ivanovna,' it ended, 'arm yourself with courage, and bear the painful moment with philosophical calm. Remember that no decent person will ever blame you for anything, and will always understand that you are a victim of fateful circumstances beyond your control.'[10] There were times when a belief in fate had its comforts, it seems, for it could offer absolution from responsibility, and thus freedom from guilt.

Further testimony to Tchaikovsky's growing eminence was afforded soon after he arrived in Kamenka by a request from the Kiev branch of the RMS to become their musical director in charge of both concert and teaching activities. Much flattered, Tchaikovsky nevertheless declined the invitation without hesitation. Then, a fortnight later, came a letter from the St Petersburg Philharmonic Society, one of the oldest and most distinguished of Russia's musical associations, informing Tchaikovsky that the Society was planning to promote two concerts of his works, and asking him to propose what might be included. A delighted Tchaikovsky suggested the Second (revised) and Fourth Symphonies, *Francesca da Rimini* and the First Suite, as well as the still unperformed Violin Concerto and Italian Capriccio. Since the Society had a choir, he also put forward his Liturgy of St John Chrysostom, a clear indication that he viewed this work as far more than a purely functional piece of church music. Unfortunately these concerts did not materialize.

[10] *TLP*9, p. 115.

As for Tchaikovsky's more personal affairs, it is clear that Antonina had now realized nothing was to be gained from harassing her husband, and to confirm in her the wisdom of ignoring him totally, Tchaikovsky had twice sent her donations beyond his normal monthly payments made through Jurgenson. Now it became known that she was following her husband's suggestion that she should seek an appointment teaching music in a girls' school. Though Tchaikovsky would have much preferred her to find such a post in the provinces rather than in Moscow, he asked Jurgenson to give her what aid he could. 'The more she's occupied, the less she'll think of and bother me,' he observed pungently to his publisher on 12 May.[11] He brushed aside a proposal which emanated shortly afterwards from Antonina's mother that immediate divorce should again be discussed, for he did not intend to raise the matter with Antonina until September, when she had had a full year to think over his most recent proposals on this matter. A far more pressing cause for concern was Alexey's obligation to do military service. Though there was no escaping this, the period of conscription could be reduced from six to three years if Alexey passed an examination. For some time Tchaikovsky had been devoting time to coaching his valet, and at Kamenka he enrolled him in the local school, thus for a while losing some of his services.

Then Modest fell ill, and Tchaikovsky had to take over half the instruction of Kolya, who had just been told of his parents' divorce and who, for all Modest's careful preparation, had taken the news as badly as Tchaikovsky had feared he would. Finally, early in June, Sasha left for Western Europe with her elder daughters for a desperately needed rest, and Lev had to make a business trip; the result was that Uncle Pyotr was left in charge of the remaining children. Not only was his own work interrupted for a while; he had also to put off his departure for Simaki, where his patroness had hoped he would stay while she was at the great house of Brailov. Though Tchaikovsky expressed boundless regret at this enforced delay, his protestations were less than sincere. Patently the thought of close residence made him uneasy, especially after the unfortunate confrontation of the last visit. His discomforts at Kamenka were of a different order. However well he got on with children, he was simply not equipped by nature to be left in charge of them, and certainly not to handle the moods of girls approaching adolescence. Besides the twelve-year-old Nataliya, who took it upon herself to queen it over the others the moment their parents were gone, there was still in residence Evgeniya Olkhovskaya, daughter of

[11] *TLP*9, p. 117.

Tchaikovsky's half-sister, Zinaida, whom Sasha had taken into her own home after the death of her parents. Both girls attempted to dominate, and Uncly Pyotr was powerless to control the situation. 'Zhenya [Evgeniya], no longer being overshadowed by the other female figures, has emerged from the background very clearly and most offensively,' he unburdened himself to Anatoly on 11 June, three days after his regency had begun. 'God, what an unattractive little creature she is! Sometimes you want to take pity on her, to be nice to her through the friendly tone of your conversation, and in reply you'll unfailingly receive some disgusting nonsense from which it appears there's no way even of taking pity on her. Worst of all is that, in the absence of Tanya, Vera and Sasha, she constantly thrusts herself upon me with her endearments – and, my God, how repulsive this is! The children are charming, especially Bobik. Ah, what a delightful work of nature he is! I'm falling in love with him still more and more!'[12] Already from Sasha's children Tchaikovsky was singling out the nine-year-old Vladimir, the favourite nephew of his later years, the future dedicatee of the Sixth Symphony, and another of Modest's zealous allies in founding the Tchaikovsky Museum at Klin. When Lev returned a week later Tchaikovsky admitted that a 'small anarchy' had reigned during his absence. Relieved of these family responsibilities, yet still unable to go to Simaki even if he had wanted to because Alexey's examination had been put off until early July, he decided to utilize a break which had come in his work on the proofs of *The Maid*, and on 16 June set to work on the Six Duets, Op. 46.

'I've come to the conclusion that I'm writing too much, and I want for a whole year to compose nothing except trifles,' Tchaikovsky had written to Jurgenson at the end of April.[13] These duets and their companion romances, Op. 47, mostly answer this specification exactly. On 30 April, only days after his arrival at Kamenka, Tchaikovsky had told his patroness of his own musical contribution to the Good Friday service.

Today I made my début in the capacity of church precentor. My sister was desperately anxious that we should sing *Comely Joseph* when the shroud is carried out. We got hold of the music, made up a quartet from my sister, Tanya, Anatoly and me, and prepared Bortnyansky's setting of this anthem. At home our singing went well, but in the church Tanya got mixed up, and then we all did. My attempts to restore order were in vain, and we had to stop before the

12 *TLP*9, p. 142.
13 *TLP*9, p. 110.

end. My sister and Tanya are exceedingly distressed by this episode, but on Sunday an opportunity to redeem ourselves will present itself at mass. I have undertaken to practise with them Bortnyansky's seventh Cherubim's Song and the Lord's Prayer from my own Liturgy [of St John Chrysostom].[14]

It seems more than likely that these homely musical activities prompted Tchaikovsky to compose these six duets. Dedicated to his niece, Tatyana, they would have provided excellent domestic fare for mother and daughter, while in one – the setting of the Scottish ballad, 'Edward' – the second voice is a baritone which would have allowed Anatoly or Tchaikovsky himself to participate also. The first to be composed was 'Passion spent' (No. 5), based on a poem by Alexey Tolstoy ('an inexhaustible source of texts for music; to me he is one of the most attractive poets,' Tchaikovsky told his patroness a day after starting composition[15]). The epithet these duets continually prompt is 'charming'; certainly it aptly characterizes the modest music of the nature picture which opens and closes 'Evening' (No. 1) – music which captivates more strongly than that of the central section, where the singers perversely expend much vocal energy in begging to be allowed to rest. Charming, too, is the prettily sentimental vignette of the maiden weeping as the young man stands over her mockingly in 'In the garden, near the ford' (No. 4).

These last two duets set verse by Ivan Surikov, a dilettante-poet who had died only a few weeks earlier, and to whose work Tchaikovsky was strongly attracted; in both, as in 'Passion spent', Tchaikovsky repeated the opening portion of the poem at the end to permit a ternary structure. So strong was his commitment to this mechanical symmetry that in the languishing 'Tears' (No. 3), because he clearly felt that an already highly repetitive text could not be retraced yet again, he reviewed the material of the work's opening in an unexpectedly large piano postlude. Tchaikovsky declared that this was his own favourite, but by far the best are the remaining two. 'Scottish ballad' (No. 2), Alexey Tolstoy's translation of that remorselessly unfolding duologue of domestic tragedy, 'Edward', is aptly set to lean, even curt phrases, supported by the bleakest of piano accompaniments, the mounting tension heightened by the firm tonal shifts of verses three and four. Unable to break completely with the ternary structure, Tchaikovsky returned to the opening music for verse five, then plunged on to

---

[14] *TLP*9, p. 109; *TPM*2, p. 342; *TZC*2, p. 391.
[15] *TLP*9, p. 146; *TPM*2, p. 360; *TZC*2, p. 393; *YDGC*, p. 234; *DTC*, p. 288.

new invention for the final verse as the mother agonisedly asks her murderer-son what he will leave to her (Ex. 167a). Here for a moment Tchaikovsky echoes, though now with brutal force, that climactic moment of Tatyana's letter monologue in *Onegin* (also in D flat), where the musical embodiment of fate in action had impressed itself upon Tatyana's utterance with most poignant eloquence (see Vol. 2, Ex. 139a). The composer himself looked with much favour on this duet also, though he recognized its distinctive character, and feared it would never be performed as he wished ('it must not be sung but, rather, declaimed – and with the greatest fervour,' he told his patroness[16]). By contrast the final duet, 'Dawn' (No. 6) complements the first, setting Surikov's quietly blissful dawn greeting as a waltz in which Tchaikovsky's lyrical invention rises to a level above that of any of its companions. Whereas the previous songs – 'Scottish ballad', of course, excepted – had merely charmed, this one affords a measure of delight.

That same, seemingly indelible passage from Tatyana's letter monologue is recalled in 'Dusk fell on the earth', a Mickiewicz translation which is the third of the Seven Songs, Op. 47 (Ex. 167b). Here is yet another recrudescence of fate as the cause of sadness and dejection; indeed, the full scalic fate motif appears in the singer's final phrase (Ex. 167c). In some respects these songs are more interesting than the duets, for their treatment of the texts is more responsive, their unfolding of the musical ideas more flexible. Yet that fatal melodic flaw which dooms the Second Piano Concerto to second-rank status among Tchaikovsky's compositions is unremittingly evident in all these songs, whether it is pervasively present as in the limp sentimentality of 'Softly the spirit flew up to heaven' (No. 2, which, Tchaikovsky told Modest, was inspired by the duet between Christ and Mary Magdalene in Massenet's oratorio *Marie-Magdeleine*), or more intermittently as in the piano prelude to 'Dusk fell on the earth', which starts well with a shapely opening phrase strongly propelled by the harmonic anacrusis of three bars of supertonic driving into the dominant, but which by the end has sunk into both harmonic and melodic impotence; Tchaikovsky himself was, however, particularly proud of this song. He began sketching this collection before leaving for Mrs von Meck's estate on 13 July, but the main labour of composition was completed there and, like their companion duets, they were finished at the beginning of

---

[16] *TLP*10, p. 163; *TPM*2, p. 530; *TZC*2, p. 477. Besides resurging in the third of the Op. 47 songs, this crucial moment in Tatyana's letter monologue is also to round off the fifth of the Six Songs, Op. 65, which Tchaikovsky composed and dedicated to Désirée Artôt in 1888; this song also appears – significantly – to incorporate a strong hint of Mendelssohn's wedding march at its opening.

Ex. 167

a.

[But what will you leave to your mother, Edward?]

b.

["Why are you sad today, and all around you cheerless?"]

c.

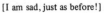

[I am sad, just as before!]

September. The set contains one of Tchaikovsky's better known songs, 'I bless you, forests' (No. 5), a setting of lines from Alexey Tolstoy's *John of Damascus*. Tolstoy's majestic benediction led Tchaikovsky into dignified melodic territory, with aspirations towards epic heights to match the poet's final shout of longing to gather all nature into his embrace. Though, sadly, the achievement scarcely equals the intention, 'I bless you, forests' impresses more deeply than the melancholy cradle song, 'Sleep, poor friend' (No. 4, another of the four Tolstoy settings in this set), where the hypnotic insistence upon a slender vocal phrase and a two-note piano sigh induces repose less through lulling charm than dulling monotony – though one may wonder whether any child could sleep when the ache within the lyric is projected with such noisy vehemence. Musorgsky managed cradle-side fantasizing with incomparably more moving pathos in 'Eremushka's cradle song'. The equally insistent accumulation of short-breathed phrases works better in 'If only I had known' (No. 1), for here it catches something of the breathless obsessiveness with which the image of the young horseman has infatuated the girl whose monologue this poem is, while the metrical straitjacket into which the various phrase contours are strapped conveys admirably her frustrated longing. Nevertheless, the quality of the melodic invention is again too insubstantial, and the sudden demisemiquaver howl of pain at the end of the second verse is an almost theatrical gesture which seeks to project the sheer force of feeling which the preceding music has lacked the substance to convey in full measure. The gay introduction had lightly sketched the carefree object of the girl's passion, and a touch of wistful irony is provided by ending the song with this same sprightly music which had found no part at all in the girl's utterance, just as the object of her adoration had remained unattainable.

The remaining two songs were later to be orchestrated by Tchaikovsky. According to the literary scholar, Fyodor Malinin, 'Does the day reign?' (No. 6) had been begun in St Petersburg in the spring. The words are by Apukhtin and were handed to Tchaikovsky, so Malinin stated, after the all-Tchaikovsky charity concert. Apukhtin had inscribed his verses to Alexandra Panayeva, who sang Tatyana's letter monologue in the same concert, and within days Tchaikovsky had sketched the music for these verses. Malinin's authority for this assertion is unknown; Tchaikovsky did, however, dedicate not only this song but also the others of Op. 47 to Panayeva. Though 'Does the day reign?' is one of the least distinguished in the set, the composer himself thought well enough of it to score it for performance in a concert he directed of his own works in Paris in 1888. Four years earlier he had similarly treated 'Was I not a little blade of grass' (No. 7). This was a far more worthwhile operation; the varying bar lengths ward off that metrical squareness to which Tchaikovsky was so prone to succumb when composing songs, while its modalism steers his invention into a freshly Russian world and away from the trite melodic particles from which some of its companion romances are built. As Gerald Abraham has pertinently observed, this Surikov translation of the Ukrainian Shevchenko's poem 'moved Tchaikovsky as far as he was capable of being moved in the direction of Musorgsky'.[17] The trouble is that Tchaikovsky now trod very unsurely in this special Russian world. As in 'Dusk fell on the earth', the melodic invention continually falters. Bars three to four of the piano introduction (Ex. 168a) provide the lamest of answers to the opening two; so, too, do the final two bars of Ex. 168b (especially the concluding melisma which is grossly inflated in the final verse) after the characterful first two phrases, the second of which had, with such heartfelt emotion, amplified the contour of the first. Yet for all its unevenness, the sadly resigned music of this young peasant girl, married against her will to an unkind, grey-haired old man, is more affecting than the shallow rhetoric of 'If only I had known' or 'Sleep, poor friend'.

When Tchaikovsky finally arrived at Brailov, Mrs von Meck had departed. Awaiting him was an expensive gold watch which she had ordered in Paris the preceding winter; it was intended, she explained, as a memento of her in case she should die soon. 'On one side is portrayed Joan of Arc, the subject of your great composition,' she added, 'and on the other Apollo and the Muses, the common companions of your inspirations – and in all this, impersonal and unseen, will lurk my spirit, for if a person possesses one, then *mine* will always be with you.'[18] Touched as he was by this gift, the impecunious Tchaikovsky would have infinitely preferred to receive the value of the watch in cash. 'Between ourselves,' he admitted to Anatoly the day after his arrival, 'I had hoped to find here not a *watch*, but some special sum of money. Nad[ezhda] Fil[aretovna] has so spoiled me by anticipating my wants and wishes that I had somehow calculated she would know by instinct what it is I now need. But I was mistaken, and now I see I shan't have a kopeck until the autumn.'[19]

His finances, in fact, were in utter disarray. He had already begged several months' advance on his allowance from his benefactress; now,

[17] Gerald Abraham: chapter on Russian song in Denis Stevens (ed.): *A History of Song* (London, 1960), p. 367.
[18] *TPM*2, p. 361.
[19] *TLP*9, p. 170; *TPM*2, p. 623.

Ex. 168

a.

b.

[Oh, you are my sorrow! Such it seems is my lot!]

with debts still amounting to 4,000 roubles, he turned in desperation to Jurgenson. Whether or not the latter would be able to make some arrangement, Tchaikovsky knew he would have to resign himself to remaining in Russia this summer. Spying on his benefactress's shelves a comprehensive collection of his own scores, he was taken aback by the quantity he had composed and by the shortcomings in its printed form. 'I have decided to write nothing for a while and busy myself solely with correcting and republishing all my former work,' he declared to Modest.[20] Meanwhile, during the month he was to enjoy his hostess's hospitality, he resolved to relax as much as possible. It proved a short-lived intention; as we have seen, both romances and duets were to exercise his creative faculties.

At Brailov, too, he found a collection of dances by Glinka, and this prompted him to survey to his patroness both the strengths and weaknesses of this much-flawed father-figure of Tchaikovsky's own native tradition. Though not quite right about Glinka's impatience of criticism or about which polka roused that composer's enthusiasm, it is an assessment far more balanced and perceptive than that which issues from most Russian musicians.

What an exceptional phenomenon Glinka is! When you read his *Memoirs*, which reveal a nice, amiable, but empty and even commonplace man: when you play his slighter compositions, it is just not possible to believe that all were written by the very same man who created, for instance . . . the Slavsya Chorus! And how many other amazing beauties are there in his operas, his overtures! What a stunningly original piece is *Kamarinskaya*, from which all later Russian composers up to the present time (and I, of course, among them) draw, in the most obvious fashion, contrapuntal and harmonic combinations as soon as they have to treat a Russian dance tune. . . . And suddenly this very same man, now in his full maturity, composes such a flat, shaming banality as the Coronation Polonaise (written a year before his death) or the Children's Polka about which he speaks with such self-satisfaction and such detail in his *Memoirs* as though it were some chef d'oeuvre. . . . Glinka was a talented Russian gentleman of his time, pettily proud, little developed, full of vanity and self-adoration, intolerant and pathologically touchy as soon as it came to the evaluation of his own compositions. All these qualities usually belong to mediocrity, but how they could find their place in a man who, it would seem, ought to have been assured and to have

[20] *TLP*9, p. 174; *TZC*2, p. 397; *TPB*, p. 250; *YDGC*, p. 235.

recognized his own strength with proud modesty – that I emphatically do not understand! . . . But all the same he wrote the Slavsya Chorus!'[21]

Feeling that the seclusion of his hostess's humbler accommodation would be far more to his liking, Tchaikovsky had within a week transferred to Simaki, and his rapturous joy is evident from many of his letters written during the first part of his three-week residence. Here he completed work on the proofs of *The Maid*, revelled yet again in Bizet's *Carmen*, investigated Massenet's *Marie-Magdeleine* ('a piece overflowing with virtues, elegance and charm,' he told Mrs von Meck[22]), but railed against contemporary French writers, castigating Zola and especially Victor Hugo, and confessing to Modest that when he had once read the latter's *Les Travailleurs de la Mer* at Usovo, his irritation had finally driven him to tear the book in pieces and fling it out of the window. It was still contemporary English novelists who particularly attracted him, and he continued his study of the English language in the hope that in six months he would be able to read Dickens and Thackeray as well as Shakespeare fluently. He listened to services not only in the Orthodox monastery but also in the new Catholic church in whose foundation he had himself played some part, deciding that the Orthodox service was vastly preferable to the Catholic mass. On a lower level he derived great amusement from a tiny libretto for an opera, *Sasha and Vanya*, which one of the villagers had concocted and which he now requested Tchaikovsky, as a 'musician of genius', to furnish with music so that they might perform it in their domestic theatre. It was to have piano accompaniment, must not be difficult, and must fall easily on the ear. Excusing himself from composing this ludicrous piece on the grounds of insufficient time, he nevertheless undertook to seek a volunteer from among other Russian composers, and circulated the literary bauble among his Moscow friends for their entertainment.

Even the sudden appearance of letters from Antonina and her mother only briefly ruffled his calm. His wife was incensed at gossip which had evidently been circulating in the Russian capital. 'I agree to your proposal [for settling our marriage affair]; I don't want to be even nominally the wife of a man who so basely slanders a woman who has done him no harm,' she wrote furiously on 7 July.

How could you and your brothers bring yourselves to tell all sorts of cock-and-bull stories to your relative, [Amaliya] Litke? What is

---

[21] *TLP*9, pp. 176–7; *TPM*2, pp. 369–70; *TZC*2, pp. 400–1.
[22] *TLP*9, p. 197; *TPM*2, p. 383.

more, she confirms her own good breeding by spreading these bits of tittle-tattle in St Petersburg! Why didn't you start with yourself, telling her about your own terrible vice, and then passing judgment on me? After all this you emphasize in your letters your own goodness and honourableness. But where are these qualities – and where is confirmation of them? Please don't trouble to reply. Maman has been so kind as to take upon herself negotiations with your lawyer to make an end of this matter.[23]

Antonina's terms still fell short of divorce, however, and she would sign nothing; in return for freedom of movement and guaranteed security, she would undertake to leave Moscow permanently and trouble him no more. A lightly veiled threat lurked unmistakably within the final assurance of 'maman's' letter. 'You are a man of genius, your good name is dear to you. Believe us, we will not sully it, and we will carry out the honourable undertaking we have given you as befits an honourable, noble family.'[24] But at remote Simaki even such embodiments of his most personal problems seemed almost unreal. For three days he was off his food and slept badly, but his initial agitation soon passed and, it seems, he dismissed Antonina as largely irrelevant.

Yet the truth is that, paradoxically, detachment itself was now becoming a strain. 'I confess I'm leaving here reluctantly; yet on the other hand, perhaps it's even harmful for me to stay too long,' he wrote to Modest on 7 August, four days before his return to Sasha's. 'I notice how the constant ecstasy in which I find myself here gets on my nerves. I have become pathologically susceptible to every kind of impression; often an utter trifle makes me weep, especially apropos some recollection or other from the irrevocable past, and especially its *irrevocability*.'[25] At Kamenka there was at least no danger of complete social isolation. Anatoly was daily expected, and Tchaikovsky's nieces had been waiting impatiently for his return so that they might set about mounting some more domestic theatricals – and for the success of such things Uncle Pyotr's participation was still considered essential. And without him there were no walks in the woods and no music making.

By now Jurgenson had arranged for some money to be made available through a bank in Kiev, and on 16 August, four days after his return to Kamenka, Tchaikovsky arrived in the city for a two-day stay so that he might also enjoy the kind of experience which a rural existence could not offer. For nearly four months he had heard little

[23] *TPM2*, p. 624.
[24] ibid.
[25] *TLP9*, p. 218; *TPM2*, p. 625; *TPB*, p. 256.

music except that which he made for himself, and the effect of encountering an orchestral performance again proved overwhelming. He went to one of his favourite places in Kiev, the Château des Fleurs, in which a small orchestra played. 'When, as I entered the garden, I heard the sounds of the celebrated overture to *Robert* [*le Diable* by Meyerbeer], the strength of the sensation I experienced almost made me faint,' he told Mrs von Meck.[26] Proofs of the Italian Capriccio and the Second Piano Concerto had now arrived, the new duets and romances had to be worked into their finished forms, and at the beginning of September he returned to his fantasy overture *Romeo and Juliet*, bringing it to that final perfection in which we know it today. Yet his determination to scrutinize all his earlier music remained. As his letter to Jurgenson of 13 September makes clear, a few pieces were satisfactory, while others required not to be reworked as compositions, merely to be corrected in their published form, and friends could be entrusted with this labour. 'Because I lack the strength to do all this properly by myself, I've asked Taneyev, Langer and Kashkin to apply their combined efforts to correcting the First and Third Symphonies, and also *The Tempest*. I hope they won't refuse. Please be so kind as to give them a copy each of these three pieces. Meanwhile be so kind as to send me my earlier piano pieces – i.e., everything except the [First] Concerto, the collection with the Bülow variations [Op. 19], and my last collection with the twelve pieces of moderate difficulty [Op. 40]. Please add to this my first six romances.'[27] The letter continued with a further request. 'I think that on the occasion of the Pushkin jubilee [the unveiling of a Pushkin memorial in Moscow], there was issued in Moscow a book in which were collected all the poems which hymned *Moscow*. I believe it's called *Moscow in the works of Russian poets*. I need this book very much, for I hope to find in it some theme for my exhibition music, to the composition of which I'm going to proceed shortly – and, to tell the truth, with indescribable aversion. . . . Have you told Nik[olay] Gr[igoryevich Rubinstein] that I want more precise and detailed directions about what's required of me?'[28] Ironically the work about which Tchaikovsky was setting with such aversion was to become one of his most famed compositions.

The first suggestion for the piece which was to emerge as the festival overture, *The year 1812*, had come from Rubinstein early in June. 'Rubinstein has been appointed by Grieg [the Minister of Finance] head of the musical section of the Exhibition [of Industry and the Arts]

[26] *TLP*9, p. 228; *TPM*2, p. 292; *TZC*2, pp. 412–13.
[27] *TLP*9, p. 253; *TZC*2, p. 419 (partial).
[28] *TLP*9, p. 253; *TPJ*1, p. 168; *TZC*2, pp. 419–20 (partial); *YDGC*, p. 240 (partial).

of 1881,' Jurgenson had written to Tchaikovsky on 10 June. '. . . He is proposing to ask you to choose and agree to compose one of the following pieces: (1) an overture to open the exhibition, or (2) [an overture] for the Tsar's silver jubilee, or (3) a cantata in whatever form or style you like, but with a hint of church music which must certainly be Orthodox, for the opening of the Cathedral of Christ the Saviour. Of course you'll be paid.'[29]

The freedom of choice left Tchaikovsky unimpressed, and he had no intention of agreeing to anything until he knew the precise conditions. 'It seems you think writing ceremonial pieces for an exhibition is some sort of ultimate bliss of which I shall hasten to avail myself, and that I shall straightway proceed to pour out my inspiration, not knowing properly where, how, what, why, when and so on. I won't lift a finger until something is *ordered* from me,' he replied testily on 5 July. '. . . [For commissioned pieces] I need stimulating, encouraging and galvanizing features in the form of precise indications, prescribed dates, and 100 rouble notes (a lot) coming in the more or less distant future. You give me the choice of this or that festal occasion as though one of these could attract me!'[30] Eleven days later he reinforced this distaste to the same correspondent. 'I wrote to you what I felt concerning the proposal, and I felt extreme repugnance. And it is impossible without repugnance to set about music which is destined for the glorification of what, at bottom, delights me not at all. Neither in the jubilee of the high-ranking person (who has always been fairly antipathetic to me) nor in the *cathedral*, which I don't like at all, is there anything of the sort which could kindle my inspiration.'[31] Having declared his position so un-equivocally, Tchaikovsky relegated the proposal to the back of his mind until the organizers responded as he required. Nearly three months passed before, on 30 September, a request arrived from Rubinstein. The latter had not lost his touch in handling Tchaikovsky. 'You will understand without any compliments that your composition would be dearer and more precious to me than all the others,' he wrote. 'It's not an order but a great favour to me – firstly, because of the occasion, secondly, yet again because of me. I shall not prescribe either a subject or a form. I ask that the composition should be from fifteen to twenty-five minutes long, with or without chorus – but, of course, without soloist.'[32]

[29] *TPJ*1, pp. 152–3; *DTC*, p. 396.
[30] *TLP*9, p. 157; *TZC*2, pp. 394–5; *TPJ*1, p. 154; *DTC*, p. 396 (first two sentences only).
[31] *TLP*9, p. 171; *TPJ*1, p. 156; *YDGC*, p. 235 (partial).
[32] *TPM*2, p. 626; also in 'P. I. Chaykovsky i N. G. Rubinstein' in *Istoriya russkoy muziki* (ed. by K. A. Kuznetsov) (Moscow, 1924), p. 182.

Tchaikovsky was persuaded but not reconciled. 'There is nothing less to my liking than composing for the sake of some *festivities*,' he promptly resumed his lament, this time to his patroness. 'Think, my dear friend! What, for instance, can you write *on the occasion of the opening of an exhibition* except banalities and generally noisy passages.'[33] Anxious to get this detestable chore out of the way, he decided upon an offering to mark the consecration of the cathedral, and on 12 October he set to work, composing the piece in a week. 'The overture will be very loud and noisy,' he further wrote to Nadezhda von Meck on 22 October, while buried in orchestrating the piece, 'but I wrote it with no warm feeling of love, and therefore there will probably be no artistic merits in it.'[34] The orchestration was completed on 19 November.

Despite his doubts about the overture's musical substance, Tchaikovsky did not believe it was necessarily unworthy the attention of the concert-going public, and when the exhibition was delayed for a year, he offered it to Nápravník for performance in St Petersburg. 'Nevertheless,' he wrote cautiously on 29 June 1881, 'I don't think it has any serious merits, and I shan't be at all surprised and offended if you find that it is in a style unsuitable for symphony concerts.'[35] In fact, Tchaikovsky had no business to be soliciting performance ahead of the event for which it had been commissioned, and Nápravník advised him to be patient until this had taken place. On 20 August 1882, in a hall specially constructed for the Exhibition, Ippolit Altani conducted the first performance of *1812*.

Since the Cathedral of Christ the Saviour was being built to commemorate the events of 1812, Tchaikovsky's choice of subject for his overture is easily understood. It was an equally obvious decision that he should take the national hymns of the warring powers as musical symbols, allowing the Marseillaise to range freely but fragmentarily in earlier portions of the work before retreating in the face of the Russian cannon which allies its explosions to the already full battery of percussion in the coda; this coda concludes with a full statement of 'God save the Tsar' as the emblem of Russian supremacy. Russia herself is represented by the Orthodox chant, *Save us, O Lord*, and by the folksong, 'U vorot', which Tchaikovsky had already arranged for piano duet in 1869.[36] From his own first opera, *The Voyevoda*, he appropriated part of the duet for Mariya and Olyona in Act 2, Scene 2, using this as the first eighteen bars of the G flat (written F sharp) second subject, an idea

[33] *TLP*9, p. 287; *TPM*2, p. 423; *TZC*2, p. 424; *YDGC*, p. 241 (partial).
[34] *TLP*9, p. 294; *TPM*2, p. 429; *TZC*2, pp. 425 and 484; *DTC*, p. 397; *YDGC*, p. 242.
[35] *TLP*10, p. 143; *DTC*, p. 397.
[36] *T50RF*, No. 48.

extended to lead into the folksong; this, now back in the tonic, acts as conclusion for the exposition. But whereas Tchaikovsky had modified his original harmony in the *Voyevoda* borrowing, he decided that his earlier folksong arrangement would do perfectly well in the new context, and the first eight bars of the resumed E flat minor are simply an orchestral transcription of the 1869 setting with a touch of metrical spicing from the tambourine. Add to all this that Tchaikovsky, consciously or unconsciously, also filched some thematic character from material invented for other recent works, and it becomes clear that a good deal of the basic conceptual labour of this unpalatable chore was eased.

1812 is therefore a thematic ragbag, yet its contemptuous dismissal by some critics is a little less than fair. The coda is insufferably tumid with its ridiculously heavy-handed preparation for the restatement of the Orthodox chant, followed by the national anthem stentoriously counterpointed to the jogging cavalry tune of the introduction. Yet the work's opening, with the chant intoned by solo sextet of two violas and four cellos, later joined by woodwind in simulation of choral antiphony, is solemnly impressive; effective, too, is the sudden eruption of the full orchestra and the beginning of the lament with the gruff interjections from lower strings (the oboe opening is surely a memory from *The Maid of Orléans*[37]). The first subject clearly gains its character from the new first subject of the recently revised first movement of the Second Symphony, while the descending string line, with its crotchet triplets, which counterpoints the restatement of the second subject material in that same movement (see Vol. 1, Ex. 62) is surely the suggestion for the string line which, at the corresponding point of *1812*, counterpoints the woodwind restatement of the *Voyevoda* material. This *Voyevoda* material was well worth rescuing, is nicely amplified in its new context, and pairs satisfactorily with the following folksong. Yet the development is inadequate, the recapitulation perfunctory, and the coda inexcusable. If the final impression left by *1812* is of a meretricious piece of bombast, Tchaikovsky had only himself to blame.

The Serenade for Strings, composed at the same time, is a very different matter, as Tchaikovsky himself recognized. 'I composed the serenade . . . from inner conviction. It is a heartfelt piece and so, I dare to think, is not lacking in real qualities,' he confessed to his benefactress in the same letter in which he had voiced such unloving doubts about *1812*.[38] Though by early September his various labours of proof-

[37] Act 3, Scene 1 (No. 17, bars 125ff.).
[38] *TLP*9, p. 294; *TPM*2, p. 429; *TZC*2, p. 425; *TPJ*1, p. 249; *DTC*, p. 477; *YDGC*, p. 242.

reading, copying duets and romances, and revising *Romeo and Juliet* had been brought to an end, he found himself again left in charge of the Kamenka children with all the strains which this entailed. On Sasha and Lev's return he had employed his new-found freedom in long walks, in enjoying the company of Modest and Kolya who had arrived immediately after Anatoly's departure, and in discovering anew some of the riches of Mozart's *Die Zauberflöte*. But as so often happened, within a day or two this freedom began to weigh on him, and on 21 September he began to sketch the Serenade, intending first that it should be either a symphony or a string quintet. By 7 October, with three movements complete, it had become a suite for string orchestra, but well before its completion on 26 October Tchaikovsky had decided it should be designated a serenade.

Full of enthusiasm for his new offspring, he was impatient to have it performed. His wish was to be granted sooner than ever he could have expected. On receiving the score Jurgenson turned to Nikolay Rubinstein, and on 3 December, only three weeks later, Tchaikovsky was greeted with a surprise performance given by Conservatoire forces when he visited his old teaching institution. The first public performance took place on 30 October 1881 in St Petersburg at an RMS concert under Nápravník; it was very successful and the Valse was encored. Moscow heard it the following January, and it was repeated in June with Anton Rubinstein conducting. 'At the first rehearsal Jupiter [Anton Rubinstein] declared to me: "I think this is Tchaikovsky's best piece",' Jurgenson reported to Tchaikovsky on 12 June. 'He praised the piece equally unconditionally to others, and at the final rehearsal said to me: "You can congratulate yourself on the publication of this opus".'[39] At last this St Petersburg pundit, who had growled with such consistent disapproval at Tchaikovsky's successive compositions, had found a work by his former pupil which he could endorse.

The Serenade for Strings provides yet further evidence of that complex interweaving of stylistic strands in Tchaikovsky's music. At the furthest extreme from his own most personal works had been the rococo stylizations of the *Vakula* minuet and the cello variations. Between these had lain the works with neo-classical leanings (notably the first movements of the Second String Quartet and Third Symphony). About the merits of his most recent exemplar of this strain, the Piano Sonata, Tchaikovsky was ambivalent, but he made no effort to provide a successor, and the First Suite was further proof that he felt he had more explorations to make if he were to discover an aspect of his

[39] *DTC*, p. 478; *YDGC*, p. 271; *TPJi*, p.249.

true self within some world other than that of his most personal music. In the Suite, as in the rococo stylizations, he had made no use of sonata principles (except, perhaps, in the Intermezzo), resorting to precedents from the Baroque (including fugue), ternary schemes, or loose rondo-type designs which permitted him to assemble a movement by shuffling a number of attractive, basically melodic units. In the Serenade, however, Tchaikovsky turned back to the four-movement sonata paradigm, though this time simply to fill its formal compartments as far as possible with sparkling or gracious melody. Proportions were schemed to have an elegant poise, while an enthusiastic appreciation was displayed for prolonged dominant pedals. Absolved from the weightier responsibilities which had oppressed him in his earlier neo-classical creations, Tchaikovsky abandoned the formal development altogether in the first movement, compiling this Pezzo in forma di Sonatina from a very neat, unfussy and (except for the key of the second subject) identical exposition and recapitulation, whose exactly balanced symmetry is further reinforced by a return to the stately andante non troppo introduction at the end of the movement. Within the main allegro moderato mechanical transition is avoided in both exposition and recapitulation; the first subject simply runs down on an extended dominant, and the second subject follows forthwith. This, like the first subject, is ternary in design, with a lightly developmental centre which draws in the main motif of the first subject, thus providing a gentle and satisfying engagement between the otherwise separated thematic elements of the movement.

To Mrs von Meck Tchaikovsky admitted that this first movement was a deliberate imitation of Mozart's manner. Yet the only melodic idea in this Serenade which explicitly suggests an eighteenth-century precedent is this second subject, with its bubbling moto perpetuo semiquavers which recall those sparkling inventions which so readily spilled over from Mozart's opera buffa world into that of his instrumental music. In fact, this music displays none of the style adopted by Tchaikovsky in his rococo stylizations. Rather it is a resurgent and far richer vein of neo-classicism, but one which looks to the eighteenth century for its models rather than to the nineteenth. Put simply: whereas the rococo stylizations represent the sort of music Mozart would have written if he had been of Tchaikovsky's generation, the Serenade is a quasi-symphonic piece such as Tchaikovsky imagined he would have composed, had he lived in Mozart's time. Thus Tchaikovsky's own creative personality is never masked in this delightful new creation, and the first subject of the first movement has clear aspirations to become a waltz, while the second movement commits itself expressly to this thematic world in which Tchaikovsky always ranged so happily. The third movement, *Elegia*, picks up the ascending scale which had opened the Valse (Ex. 169a), using it to launch a series of four ruminative phrases which, always starting identically, all end differently (Ex. 169b presents the first of these). When the main theme arrives (Ex. 169c) it, too, proves to be an elaboration of this same four-times-heard opening shape. Tchaikovsky's hand is discernible as surely in every bar of this beautiful movement as it had been in the Valse; meticulously scaled and as impeccably presented as is everything in the Serenade, this *Elegia* must count as one of the most comely pieces he had written.

Ex. 169

A few weeks before setting about this Serenade Tchaikovsky had received from Taneyev an energetic statement of his views on the only way forward for Russian music. 'We must not forget that only that is lasting which has embedded its roots in the people,' his former pupil had preached as the central part of his doctrine. 'Among the Western nations all art was *national* before it merged with the mainstream. This is a general rule from which you don't depart. The Netherlanders wrote their works upon folksongs; the Gregorian chants upon which the works of sixteenth-century Italians were founded were originally folk melodies. Bach created German music from the *chorale*, again a folk melody.'[40] However faulty Taneyev's view of music history, it might seem that Tchaikovsky had designed his Serenade's finale as a demonstration of belief in Taneyev's creed since, for the first time within a single movement, he employed not one but two folksongs, the first for the introduction, the second to act as the first subject. Both had already appeared in his folksong arrangements of 1869, and in both cases Tchaikovsky used these, the introduction up to bar 30 being simply a transcription of his earlier piano duet setting of 'A kak po lugu'.[41] By happy chance the outline of the treble line in the last four bars of this earlier arrangement anticipated the opening of the second folktune, 'Pod yablonyu zelyonoyu',[42] and Tchaikovsky was thus able to effect, *Kamarinskaya*-like, an easy transition to the allegro con spirito.[43] This, unlike the opening movement, has all the appurtenances of sonata structure, including an elaborate development. All is accomplished with deftness and energy, though without that verve and boldness which had made the finale of the Second Symphony so dazzling.

Yet the fact is that Tchaikovsky profoundly disagreed with Taneyev. 'If, thanks to Peter the Great, we have been *fatefully* caught on the tail of Europe, then thus we shall remain for ever,' he had countered on 13 August. 'I value very highly the wealth of material which the *slovenly and suffering people* [this had been Taneyev's expression] produce, but we, i.e., we who use this material, will always elaborate it in forms borrowed from Europe – for, born Russians, we are at the same time even far more Europeans, and we have so resolutely and deeply fostered and assimilated their forms that to tear ourselves from them we would have to strain and do violence to ourselves, and from such straining and violence nothing artistic could come. Where there is violence there is no inspiration, and where there is no inspiration there is no art.'[44] Tchaikovsky's own music is perpetual testimony to how deeply he held this belief, and this finale, far from being a recognition that Russian folksong is necessary, is more a pointed demonstration that such folksong might be absorbed into as complete a display of Western stylistic and structural methods as Tchaikovsky could invent. But the real coup de grâce remained. The whole Serenade had opened with a dignified theme wedded to a solemn, stiff harmonic support (Ex. 170a) – a formal gesture little related, it would seem, to Russian folksong; yet

[40] *TTP*, p. 55.
[41] *T50RF*, No. 28.
[42] *T50RF*, No. 42.
[43] The original piano harmonization appears in bars 60–75.
[44] *TLP9*, p. 223.

in the last movement, as the coda begins, Tchaikovsky suddenly reintroduces this solemn opening, only to go on to demonstrate with a touch of impishness that it is in fact fathered by that very same joyous Russian folksong which had acted as the main theme of the finale (Ex. 170b).

Ex. 170

Tchaikovsky remained at Kamenka until late November. Modest had begun to write a play, *The Benefactor*, and, prodded constantly by his brother, completed it to the admiration of the whole family. Tchaikovsky was convinced it would bring recognition to Modest in Russia's literary world, and was already scheming to have it produced in Moscow that season (it was to be given with little success in St Petersburg in February 1881). Nothing disturbed the even tenor of Tchaikovsky's own life. Antonina remained silent, and Zhenya's brother arrived early in October to remove his sister. Only Sasha's health occasioned anxiety. Finally the family discovered the real cause of the nervous tensions and pains which had afflicted and sometimes prostrated her during this summer; she had been concealing from them symptoms which made her fear she had a mortal illness. Now at last she confessed them, only to receive much reassurance from the doctor. Yet there remained the problem that she had for years been taking morphine for relief from various discomforts, and by now she had become addicted to it. In any case, family anxieties constantly beset her with her eldest children. In particular, Tanya, now nineteen, wanted to marry, but many doubts surrounded the prospects for her intended, and by mid-October the relationship was disintegrating. Uncle Pyotr shared in all these worries and sorrows, just as he did in the misfortunes of the Kamenka estate, which had had a bad year.

Yet his own affairs were prospering quietly. *The Maid* had been accepted by the Imperial Theatres in St Petersburg and would be produced during the winter, while in Moscow in January *Onegin* would be mounted at the Bolshoy. Thus Tchaikovsky would have operas being presented simultaneously in Russia's two greatest cities. He wanted publication of the revised versions of the Second Symphony and *Romeo and Juliet*, but the problem was that rights to these works had been assigned to publishers other than Jurgenson. His aim was to persuade Bote & Bock, the original publishers of *Romeo and Juliet*, to agree to engrave the new version and assign the rights to it within Russia to Jurgenson, even though in March he had already agreed that Bessel should have these rights. As for the Second Symphony, Tchaikovsky's relations with Bessel himself were now at so low an ebb that he had no wish to have any dealings with this publisher. In fact Tchaikovsky had got himself into a thorough mess, and he was only too ready to ask Jurgenson to act as his agent in all dealings with both publishing firms, just as he had been happy to transfer to others as far as possible the labour of correcting his own music, an ambitious scheme which proved abortive.

The one real cause for grief was the imminent departure of Alexey on military service. Tchaikovsky's valet had successfully passed the examination which would reduce his period of conscription, and his master still entertained, to the last, hopes that he might be exempted altogether. But Alexey's liability remained, and on 28 October he had to leave Kamenka. 'It's hard being deprived, perhaps for a long time, of a person with whom one has lived ten years,' Tchaikovsky wrote to Nadezhda von Meck on 26 October, even before Alexey's departure. 'I feel sorry for myself, but chiefly for him; he will have to endure a great deal before he becomes accustomed to his new situation. To alleviate my feeling of sadness I am working intensively.'[45] But promptly on Alexey's departure Tchaikovsky himself fell ill with nervous symptoms which may well have been caused by the loss of his servant. All work was forbidden him during his remaining days at Kamenka. On 23 November he arrived in Moscow.

While Tchaikovsky had been in the Ukraine his patroness had been travelling in Western Europe. Pachulski as usual journeyed with her, but on 22 July Nadezhda von Meck, now in Interlaken, informed Tchaikovsky of a new musical addition to her entourage. 'Two days ago a young pianist from Paris came to me. He has just finished his conservatoire course. . . . I have engaged him to work with the children

[45] *TLP*9, p. 298; *TPM*2, p. 431.

during the summer, to accompany Yuliya's singing, and to play piano duets with me. . . . He says he is twenty, but he looks no more than sixteen.'[46] Soon she had him playing Tchaikovsky's compositions, including the Fourth Symphony with her in its piano duet version. 'My partner did not play it well, though he performs magnificently,' she observed from Arcachon on 19 August. '. . . He is enraptured with your music. . . . Yesterday I also played your suite with him, and he was utterly delighted with the fugue, and expressed himself thus: "Dans les fugues modernes je n'ai jamais rien vu de si beau. Monsieur Massenet ne pourrait jamais faire rien de pareil." . . . He [the pianist] composes very nicely, and here he is also a true Frenchman.'[47]

Tchaikovsky was soon required to pronounce upon the creative activities of this young man. On 20 September from Florence his benefactress sent him the vocal score of Ponchielli's *La Giaconda* to look over, adding, 'I'm also sending a little composition for you to judge, one of *many* by my pianist . . . This young man is preparing to be a composer and he writes very nice pieces, but they are all echoes of his teacher, Massenet [in fact there is no evidence that this young man was ever Massenet's pupil]. He is now composing a trio.'[48] A month later Tchaikovsky replied dutifully and without enthusiasm; evidently he did not rate the young man's compositional abilities highly. Perhaps, too, he spied a potential rival for Mrs von Meck's affections, and decided to swat him without delay. 'The *Danse bohémienne is a very nice little piece*, but it is certainly too short. Not one idea is worked out to its conclusion, the form is too shrivelled, and it lacks wholeness.'[49]

Meanwhile the young Frenchman was sending his mistress into ecstasies by playing to her from the newly arrived vocal score of *The Maid*; in addition he was required to play Tchaikovsky's Piano Sonata, a number of the shorter piano pieces, as well as participate in the duet arrangement of the First Symphony. Mrs von Meck also set him to make piano arrangements of the Spanish, Neapolitan and Russian dances from *Swan Lake*, and was soon asking Tchaikovsky whether she might have them published. Tchaikovsky replied that Jurgenson held the Russian copyright of this ballet, and that he (Tchaikovsky) had no power to authorize publication; nevertheless, he was sure that Jurgenson would be only too happy to print these arrangements if they were sent to him (and, indeed, they did appear in 1881, though without the name of the arranger, who feared for some reason that

[46] *TPM2*, p. 374.
[47] *TPM2*, p. 394.
[48] *TPM2*, p. 408.
[49] *TLP9*, p. 295; *TPM2*, p. 429.

Massenet would be enraged if he got to hear about them). Early in
October a young cellist, Pyotr Danilchenko, arrived to take the pianist's place, but the latter was persuaded to stay on for an extra month so
that Nadezhda von Meck might be entertained with piano trios. 'Pyotr
Ilich, why have you not written a single trio?' she demanded to know on
30 October. 'I regret this every day because every day they play me a
trio, and I always sigh because you have not composed a single one.'[50]
Little did she realize that she was helping to sow a creative seed in
Tchaikovsky's mind, though it was to germinate only later. She had a
photograph taken of her trio and sent a copy to Tchaikovsky. '*Bussy's*
face and hands have a vague resemblance to Ant[on] Rubinstein's in
his youth,' Tchaikovsky noted. 'God grant that his fate may be as
fortunate as that of the "Tsar of pianists"!'[51] Indeed, the final reputation of the young man was to eclipse completely that of this keyboard
giant, though it was as composer, not as pianist. For 'Bussy' was, of
course, the eighteen-year-old Claude Debussy.

[50] *TPM*2, p. 434.
[51] *TLP*9, p. 298; *TPM*2, p. 431.

4

RESURGENT INDIVIDUALITY:
PIANO TRIO

THERE COULD NOT have been a greater contrast between the peaceful Ukrainian existence Tchaikovsky had enjoyed during the last seven months and the hectic round into which he was about to be caught in Moscow and St Petersburg. Proofs and inescapable social invitations filled his days, while his nights were troubled and sleepless. But to set against such trials was yet more hard evidence of the ever-increasing currency his music was gaining. His Liturgy was performed at the Conservatoire to his unqualified satisfaction. ('I experienced one of the sweetest moments of my composing career,' he confessed to Mrs von Meck[1]), and in the same private concert he heard his new Serenade for the first time. Then on 18 December Nikolay Rubinstein conducted the première of the Italian Capriccio. Tchaikovsky was not present as he had been required to visit St Petersburg for ten days to attend to various matters preparatory to the production of *The Maid*, but when he arrived back in Moscow on 20 December it was to hear of the success the work had enjoyed, a success confirmed when the piece was repeated on 1 January at another RMS concert.[2] Between these two performances the First Quartet had been given with its by now almost ritual encoring of the Andante cantabile, while on the very same evening *The Oprichnik*, from which the ban on presentation had been lifted, was being performed to an enthusiastic audience at the Bolshoy Theatre. Then on 30 December the Liturgy was sung publicly by the same choir which had delighted Tchaikovsky at the Conservatoire. 'The hall was full,' he wrote to Modest, 'and despite the forbidding of applause, there was a tremendous unexpected ovation with the presentation of a sort of lyre made from foliage from an unknown person.'[3] As one critic

[1] *TLP*9, p. 319; *TPM*2, p. 451; *TZC*2, p. 431; *YDGC*, p. 244.
[2] In the same concert was also performed the Second Symphony of Borodin, who visited Moscow for the occasion and who was present at the performance of Tchaikovsky's Liturgy.
[3] *TLP*9, p. 337; *TZC*2, p. 436; *TPB*, p. 261; *YDGC*, p. 246.

summarized it: 'The last week of the 1880 Moscow musical season might truly be called "Tchaikovsky week".'[4]

Yet more significant than all these events was the new production of *Onegin* at the Bolshoy Theatre. Tchaikovsky attended a number of the rehearsals and found himself delighted with the way the opera was being prepared. 'I can't deny Bevignani [who was to conduct the opera] his earnest request that I should attend the orchestral rehearsals and the performance,' he told Modest.[5] Despite this, Tchaikovsky slipped off to Kamenka for a fortnight's rest at the turn of the year. On 23 January 1881, four days after his return to Moscow, *Onegin* was given to the composer's complete satisfaction both with regard to the performance and to the opera's reception, though Modest remembered that scenically the staging was weak. A fortnight later Tchaikovsky left for St Petersburg to attend the final rehearsals and première of *The Maid* on 25 February. Though, as we have seen, the presentation of the opera had many shortcomings, and though he had to suffer the dictatorial interference of the management, he realized that his opera commanded great respect among the performers, and he himself enjoyed a personal audience success. Add to this that the Second Symphony was given in its revised form at an RMS concert on 12 February ('I was not there; they say it pleased,' he observed laconically to his patroness[6]) and it becomes obvious that these last three months had been a veritable Tchaikovsky festival. On his visit to St Petersburg barely a year before, he had been treated as a highly respected composer. Now, from being respected, he was beginning to become popular.

Needless to say, this had little effect upon his personal frame of mind. Some months earlier, when Taneyev had accused him of a modicum of hypocrisy about the success of his music, Tchaikovsky had been quick to distinguish between his pride in his compositions and his wishes for himself. 'I compose, i.e., I give vent to my moods and my feelings by way of musical language, and of course, as with anyone who talks and who has, or has pretensions to having, something to say, I need people to listen to me, and the more they listen to me, the more gratifying it is. In that sense I love *fame*, of course, and I strive after it with my whole heart. . . . But it doesn't follow from this that I love the manifestations of *fame* which are embodied in those dinners, suppers and musical

---

[4] *YDGC*, p. 247.
[5] *TLP*9, p. 331; *TPB*, pp. 260–1; *DTC*, p. 84; *YDGC*, p. 246.
[6] *TLP*10, p. 25; *TPM*2, p. 473; *DTC*, p. 352; *YDGC*, p. 249. Modest asserted that his brother had been present but had chosen to remain incognito, adding that none of the critics seem to have noticed that the symphony had been revised.

soirées at which I suffer as I always suffer in any company alien to me.'[7] As soon as he had arrived in Moscow to receive as warm a greeting to himself personally as to his music, his longing to escape surged up within him. Moscow became curiously unreal. 'My love for this old, dear (despite all its shortcomings) city has in no way diminished – on the contrary, has become keener and stronger – but it has taken on a certain morbid character,' he wrote to Nadezhda von Meck on 9 December from St Petersburg. 'It is as though I am already long dead, as though everything that once was has now sunk into the abyss of oblivion, as though I am some completely different person from another world and another time. It is difficult for me to express in words this extremely morbid and tormenting sensation. I have had to drown this mental pain either by increased work or by increased libations of Bacchus.'[8]

In St Petersburg he had hoped to recover from the strains of Moscow, but he was immediately confronted by a dispute over who should sing the part of Joan, then fell ill, and returned to Moscow no better than when he had left. By now he had to accept that his valet could not evade military service. He visited Alexey in barracks and was appalled at both his crushed appearance and his spartan and rigorous existence. 'And he has to live thus for four years!' he lamented to Modest on 31 December. 'The sergeant-major allowed Alyosha to accompany me to the gate. We were both silent because we both wanted terribly to weep, and Alyosha's voice trembled so much when he said goodbye that I could scarcely endure the agonizing moment. When I got home I wrote to *Fanya* [Tchaikovsky's cousin, Mitrofan] a despairing letter begging him to write to the regiment's commander, with whom he's friendly, so that somehow he might ease Alyosha's predicament. . . . I shall visit him again tomorrow.'[9] That evening, when visiting Hubert, Tchaikovsky had a sudden nervous attack 'such as I've never had before',[10] and which he thought was to be attributed primarily to his distressing encounter with Alexey. The extent to which Tchaikovsky had become dependent upon Alexey came home to him forcefully and repeatedly during these months. As for the protection he solicited for Alexey from his commanding officer, Tchaikovsky was to discover that a price had to be paid, for he found himself compelled to accompany the singing of the colonel's wife for whole evenings.

Nor was the position improved when he returned from Kamenka. It

[7] *TLP*9, p. 222; *TTP*, pp. 56–7.
[8] *TLP*9, p. 319; *TPM*2, pp. 450–1.
[9] *TLP*9, p. 337.
[10] *TLP*9, p. 339; *TZC*2, p. 437; *TPB*, p. 262; *YDGC*, p. 246.

was gratifying to have one's music praised in the press, and though he was sensitive to some reserved comments about *Onegin*, he was still not altogether discouraged either by these or by the still somewhat guarded applause on the first night. 'The success increased as the opera proceeded, and all ended more than happily,' he reported to Nadezhda von Meck. 'Of course an opera's success is not apparent on the first evening but afterwards, when it becomes clear how much drawing power it has.'[11] As he had observed to this same correspondent before the Bolshoy production, this would test whether the opera could become a repertoire piece. A vigorous attack upon his Liturgy by the Metropolitan of Moscow himself did upset him, but he knew perfectly well that this work would provoke a diversity of reactions which did not necessarily reflect upon its musical worth. Yet all this press comment could not but draw attention to Tchaikovsky himself, especially when it was supplemented by a good deal of tittle-tattle; it was like a constant exposure of his very being, and he would have fled from Moscow earlier, had it not been for yet another of Anatoly's turbulent affairs of the heart which called for all the moral support an elder brother could offer. On arriving in St Petersburg Tchaikovsky resolved to decline all invitations, for he had Modest and Kolya with him for company. The former had come for the first (and only) performance of his play, *The Benefactor*, which, through the assiduous efforts of his composer-brother, was produced at the Alexandrinsky Theatre on 21 February (later the play was revised, renamed, and enjoyed a moderate success on the Russian stage). Tchaikovsky himself was much absorbed by rehearsals, but even this could not protect him altogether from the endless unwanted attentions of his numerous relatives and acquaintances. His loathing for St Petersburg became more violent than ever, and on 26 February, the day after the première of *The Maid of Orléans*, he was on his way to Vienna. Though even before going to Kamenka he had spent all but ten of the thousand roubles which the RMS had paid him earlier in December, his finances were now again in good order, for he had just assigned thirty-seven of his shorter pieces to Jurgenson for a fee of 7,000 roubles. He thought that before him stretched a whole spring and summer of calm and freedom, as in 1880. During the next month, however, he was to receive three important pieces of news, one of which would contribute coincidentally to a brief rediscovery of his true individuality as a composer.

Tchaikovsky's response to the first of these, which concerned his patroness, cannot have been other than deeply apprehensive, though he did his utmost to mask this. For the last few weeks his letters had

---

[11] *TLP*10, p. 16; *TPM*2, p. 466; *TZC*2, p. 445; *DTC*, p. 84.

been marked with expressions of yearning for Italy and especially for Rome, in which he had lived the corresponding portion of the preceding year, and it was to Italy that he was now directing himself. As the train bore him towards Austria the press was already beginning its mainly unfavourable dissection of *The Maid*, and approaching Vienna, Tchaikovsky picked up a copy of *Neue freie Presse* from which he got his first taste of some of the things in store. Seeing the splendid production of *Oberon* in Vienna only pressed home how feebly *The Maid* had been mounted, though Weber's opera, which he had never seen before, impressed him less than its presentation: 'the music's rather tedious, though there are some delightful things,' he judged it to Anatoly the same day.[12] On 3 March he was in Florence, the next day in Rome. Then on 6 March he received the painful intelligence that Mrs von Meck had been compelled, because the affairs of the Brailov estate had been mismanaged, to lease Simaki. Tchaikovsky did his best to sound reassuring; she had been his salvation during the last three years, he affirmed, and a post at either of the Russian conservatoires was always available to him if he should be forced again to earn his own living. He was thoroughly aware that this was the last thing his benefactress wanted, and he knew the point would not be lost on her, but he was still to be beset during the summer by nagging fears that she might be unable to continue his allowance.

His current life in Rome gave little time to brood on this, however. Awaiting him at the station at six in the morning was Kondratyev and, with such a companion, Tchaikovsky was immediately drawn into the social whirl of his compatriots living in the city during his own eight-day visit. Prince Alexey Golitsïn, on whose estate at Trostinets Tchaikovsky had composed his first orchestral work, *The Storm*, nearly seventeen years before, was in residence and the Grand Duke Konstantin Konstantinovich's warship was anchored off Naples. The Grand Duke, with two of the Tsar's sons, the Grand Dukes Sergey and Pavel, had taken a villa in Rome and wanted to see Tchaikovsky, a request he could not refuse. Tchaikovsky felt the usual instinct to recoil violently from all the invitations he received, but for Kondratyev's company he was for the moment grateful. His spirits had risen when he had crossed the frontier and experienced the colour and warmth of the incipient Italian spring. But without Modest and Kolya, let alone Alexey, he became engulfed by his loneliness, and he gladly acceded to Kondratyev's proposal that they should together go to Naples, then to Nice, and finally to Paris.

It is yet another sign of Tchaikovsky's spreading fame that he was

[12] *TLP*10, p. 34; *YDGC*, p. 252.

now so sought after as a guest. Not only the Tsar's sons and the Grand Duke Konstantin, but the Russian ambassador wanted his company, and everywhere he was required to play and talk about his own music. In Naples he had hoped to relax, but on 13 March, the day after his arrival, came the second piece of crucial news. Jurgenson's researches had revealed that Antonina had taken a lover and given birth to a child. Now Tchaikovsky had incontrovertible grounds for divorce. 'I strongly approve of, and heartily thank you for your investigation into that creature of the female sex who has brought into the world an unfortunate being who is perhaps bearing my name,' he immediately wrote with fierce satisfaction to his publisher.

> How, I wonder, may I prevent her from registering it *as my* child? Has your spy thought of coping with this? In principle I *very much* want a divorce, but the question of money troubles me. *I know for certain* that at the present moment Mrs von Meck's affairs are in a far from brilliant condition, and I can't ask her for something over and above the sum I receive. In any case, after what is known to have happened, I consider it quite unnecessary to pay Ant[onina] Iv[anovna] any sort of compensation in the form of capital, such as was discussed earlier. If you wish to be my benefactor to the last in this matter, then try to see some specialist in divorce matters (for instance, the secretary of the consistory) and find out from him what I can do at this present moment. . . . *Of course there is no need to pay her a pension!*[13]

Yet relief was tempered with some apprehension, for dangers remained. Antonina could still make damaging accusations if she were pushed too far, and finally Tchaikovsky was to draw back from divorcing her. He felt the bitch was effectively kennelled and muzzled, and would trouble him no further unless roused.

Tchaikovsky's greatest adventure in Naples was to climb to the crater of Vesuvius; his most pleasant memory was of visiting Sorrento. There was a suggestion that he should abandon his prepared itinerary and instead travel with the Grand Dukes aboard their frigate to Athens and Jerusalem, but the assassination of Alexandr II on 13 March necessitated the immediate presence of all three in St Petersburg. Though Tchaikovsky had only a few months earlier expressed reserved feelings about the Tsar, the slaying of the Russian father brought forth a swell of emotion for the condition of his country. 'At such moments it's unpleasant to be abroad,' he wrote to Anatoly on 15 March, 'and with

---

[13] *TLP*10, pp. 53–4; *TPJ*1, pp. 185–6.

my whole soul I yearned for Russia so that I might be closer to the source of information, so that I might participate in the demonstrations for the new Tsar, know the details – in a word, share the common life of all my own people.'[14] With the departure of the three Grand Dukes the trip to the eastern Mediterranean was out of the question, and on 21 March Tchaikovsky and Kondratyev were in Nice.

Here the third and most crucial piece of news reached him. When Tchaikovsky had been in Moscow and St Petersburg, Nikolay Rubinstein's health had already been giving cause for concern. Rest had been urgently prescribed by the doctors, but Tchaikovsky knew that Rubinstein was congenitally incapable of staying inactive. Perceiving the seriousness of Rubinstein's condition, he was appalled at the prospect of his death. Then, while Tchaikovsky was in Naples, Anatoly had written that Rubinstein had been ordered abroad and was travelling to Nice. He did not arrive, and on 22 March Jurgenson telegraphed Tchaikovsky to say that Rubinstein was desperately ill in Paris. The next day he died.

No death had struck Tchaikovsky so hard since the passing of his own mother nearly twenty-seven years before. Rubinstein had given him his first professional appointment, had directed him, bullied him, but in his own rough, imperious way had nursed Tchaikovsky's gifts, sometimes criticizing his works unceremoniously, but always with unflagging energy presenting them to the world so that their worth might be assessed and their fame grow. No man had done more for the cause of Tchaikovsky's music than this difficult but true friend. Tchaikovsky was preoccupied with such thoughts as he sped towards Paris. So agitated was he that he dreaded having to view the body lest his self-control should give way. On 26 March a funeral service was held in the crowded Russian church in Paris, with Massenet, Colonne, Lalo, Pauline Viardot-Garcia and Turgenev among the congregation. 'Afterwards the coffin was carried into the lower chapel, and here I saw him for the last time,' Tchaikovsky concluded his account of Rubinstein's end given to Mrs von Meck the next day. 'He had altered beyond recognition. My God, my God, how terrible are such moments in life! Forgive me, my dear, that I write to you in such detail – I am terribly weighed down by grief.'[15]

Such was not the condition of Anton Rubinstein, who had hurried from Spain on hearing of his brother's illness. Jurgenson, who had come to Paris for the funeral, offered a convincing explanation of the

[14] *TLP*10, p. 55.
[15] *TLP*10, p. 68; *TPM*2, p. 491.

behaviour which now so affronted Tchaikovsky. 'It is difficult to convey
the sickening impression he [Anton Rubinstein] has produced on me
during these days,' Tchaikovsky wrote in indignant distress to Anatoly.
'He is not only not crushed by his brother's death but is, *apparently*, very
pleased about it. Jurgenson, with whom I spoke about this, explains
this incomprehensible fact by Anton's *jealousy* of Nikolay. For what?
Why? I don't understand. But if this is so, what could be more offensive
than such jealousy?'[16] To all these solemn, distressing events
Tchaikovsky responded with a sudden access of religious emotion.
'All's dark in my mind – but it could not be otherwise in view of such
questions, insoluble by the frail mind, as *death, the purpose and meaning of
life, its infinity or its finiteness* – but still the light of *faith* penetrates yet more
and more into my soul. Yes, dear friend,' he enthused to his sceptical
patroness.

> I feel that I am inclining more and more towards that only bulwark
> we have against all calamities. I feel I am beginning *to be able to love
> God*, which formerly I could not do. I am still visited by doubts: I still
> sometimes try to comprehend the incomprehensible with my weak
> and pitiful mind – but yet louder and louder the voice of divine truth
> begins to reach me. Already I often find an inexplicable delight in
> bowing before God's inscrutable yet, to me, unquestionable wisdom;
> often with tears I pray to *him* (where *he* is, who *he* is, I know not, but I
> know *he* exists), and I pray him to give me humility and love, I pray
> him to forgive me and enlighten me – but above all I say to him
> sweetly: *Lord, thy will be done*, for I know that his will is *holy*.[17]

All this was less a spiritual rebirth than a sentimental yearning for
something which might give purpose to, or at least numb the pain of
such distressing experiences. It had certainly helped at the Gare du
Nord when Tchaikovsky had watched Rubinstein's remains being
loaded into a luggage van on their way to Moscow. The indignity of this
exit struck him hard. 'But fortunately,' he consoled himself to his
patroness, 'I have seeds of *faith*, and I take comfort from the thought
that such is the *inexplicable* but *holy* will of God.'[18] For a moment it would
seem that fate and Christian destiny were conjoined. As a personal
service to this loyal yet abrasive supporter of his music he compiled a
detailed account of Rubinstein's last days which was printed in both the
Moscow Gazette and the *Russian Gazette*.

[16] *TLP*10, p. 73; *TPM*2, pp. 633–4; *TPB*, pp. 268–9.
[17] *TLP*10, p. 70; *TPM*2, pp. 491–2; *TZC*2, pp. 466–7.
[18] *TLP*10, p. 71; *TPM*2, p. 493.

By now Tchaikovsky's longing to be back in Russia was irresistible. The Tsar's violent end still weighed upon him, Rubinstein's death had caused him great grief and agitation, and Nadezhda von Meck had occasioned further anxiety by disclosing that her personal losses had been far greater than Tchaikovsky had been led to believe. She insisted that there was no risk to his allowance, but he remained unconvinced. 'In all probability there lies before me a sudden radical change in my life,' he predicted to his brother-in-law.[19] Yet such was Tchaikovsky's repugnance at Anton's indifference at his brother's death that he decided to delay in Paris for some days to avoid having to observe this at Nikolay's interment in Moscow. Thus it was 2 April before Tchaikovsky left. Pausing briefly in Berlin, he was four days later again in St Petersburg.

Tchaikovsky had not intended to spend a full month in the Russian capital, but Sasha had arrived with Tanya, had fallen ill, and within days of Tchaikovsky's own advent her condition had taken a turn for the worse. Lev was urgently summoned from the Ukraine, but could not stay indefinitely since the affairs of Kamenka required his presence. The doctors ordered Sasha to Carlsbad (now Karlovy Vary) as the only means of cure, but someone had to accompany her, and Tchaikovsky feared that this responsibility would of necessity fall upon him. His spirits remained black. Composition was out of the question, and he turned down flatly an unalluring request to write nine marches for a Moscow production of Alexey Tolstoy's tragedy, *Tsar Boris*. Finally, early in May, escape became possible. With all but one of her children in the Ukraine, Sasha was pining to a degree which persuaded the doctors that she should return there as soon as possible and travel abroad later; meanwhile, because both mother and father were still confined to St Petersburg, Uncle Pyotr was to hasten to Kamenka to fill the parental gap as best he could. Arriving in Moscow on 7 May, he saw Alexey and fought off an earnest appeal that he should become director of the Conservatoire in succession to Rubinstein.

Next day he was on his way south, still feeling no inclination to compose. The children made heavy demands on his time not only socially but musically, for the visiting music teacher, a certain Stanislav Blumenfeld, had remained absent some three months, and Tchaikovsky felt obliged to teach some of the children himself (had he known the role Blumenfeld was very soon to play in the life of one of Sasha's children, he could well have wished he would never visit Kamenka again). He did, however, give some thought to future

[19] *TLP* 10, p. 72.

creative projects. Hearing that other commitments were causing Karl Davïdov to despair of completing an opera he had already begun, Tchaikovsky asked the director of the St Petersburg Conservatoire whether the libretto might be assigned to him. 'I find the subject of [Pushkin's] *Poltava* very tempting,' he wrote to Davïdov on 17 May.[20] Meanwhile, still stirred by the religious thoughts and feelings which had been aroused by Rubinstein's death, he turned his attention again to Russian church music. 'I want to try to compose an *All-night Vigil*,' he wrote to Jurgenson on 20 May, 'and for this I need its complete *text*. . . . I've begun to learn *the rules of church singing*, but to have a full understanding of these I need Razumovsky's book (the history of church music), and so I'm asking you to send me a copy.'[21]

The task he was setting himself this time was very different from that he had faced in his Liturgy, for here he would be far less a creator than an arranger, though one whose aesthetic judgment would need to be fully alert. 'I wish not so much *theoretically* as *through the feeling* of an artist *to sober up* (to a certain degree) church music from excessive Europeanism,' he wrote to Modest on 5 June. 'I shall be an eclectic, i.e. something between Bortnyansky and Potulov. The All-night Vigil will be much less European than my mass; *however*, this will arise partly because here (in the All-night Vigil) there are fewer occasions when one can be carried away and compose. Here I shall be *someone setting the Ordinary* rather than a freely creating artist.'[22]

Unable still to discover all he needed from the work of Razumovsky, his old colleague who had officiated at his wedding, Tchaikovsky sent for a battery of service books from Jurgenson, but still found the path before him lay through a thicket of obstacles and uncertainties. At times he could trace neither text nor the correct chant, at others he found it impossible to understand the arrangements of the Propers. Such problems were also experienced by the Russian clergy, he discovered. 'I went to Father Alex[andr Tarnavich, the Kamenka parish priest] for explanations,' he told Modest on 3 July, by which time he had been struggling for at least a month, 'but he confessed to me that he himself knew nothing, and officiated according to some routine without consulting the Tipicon [the manual containing the order of services] or the [liturgical] rule . . . I asked Father Alex[andr] what his deacon did when performing the canon with canticles, and how he managed to find out what and how he should read and sing. . . . He replied: "I don't know. Before each service he tries to find something suitable for

---

[20] *TLP*10, p. 96.
[21] *TLP*10, p. 102; *TZC*2, pp. 469–70.
[22] *TLP*10, p. 120; *TPB*, p. 271; *DTC*, p. 283 (partial).

himself." '[23] Evidently stirred by Tchaikovsky's request to discover the correct order of events in the service he had so long celebrated defectively, Father Alexandr finally managed to compile for the composer a proper service order which set his feet on firmer liturgical ground, while correspondence with Razumovsky himself also brought some enlightenment. The sketches of the work were completed during July, though not brought to their final form until the following year.

After completing his All-night Vigil Tchaikovsky gave a brief summary of his work to Taneyev.

> In this instance, as always, I worked obeying my instinct rather than my cogitations or any preconceived theories. I treated the melodies of the Ordinary and the Hermologion quite freely, a little à la Bortnyansky, i.e. never hesitating to force them into metre, sometimes deviating from, changing and, in places, abandoning them altogether, and giving my own invention its head. There is no, or virtually no, contrapuntal element. *The melody is always in the top voice.* As for the harmony, it's always strict – that is, without chromaticism, without $\frac{6}{4}$ chords or sevenths. The dominant [seventh] chord appears only in a passing function.[24]

In fact, these restrictions on his harmonic resources are not always as strictly observed as Tchaikovsky asserted. The All-night Vigil consists of seventeen numbers, one containing various responses, the other sixteen setting longer, usually more continuous texts, including the Magnificat with a repeated trope, the Great Doxology, and various psalms. Some parts of the chant are presented unfettered by barlines, even occasionally there is free chanting, but elsewhere, as Tchaikovsky noted to Taneyev, he imposed clear metrical structures on the chant, though often preserving flexibility by the use of variable bar lengths, as at the work's opening (Ex. 171a). Most of the harmonizations are for four voices, but others divide a vocal line to permit simple antiphonal treatment or a fuller textural support, as in *O gladsome light* (No. 5: Ex. 171b), which also contains one of the only two brief passages in the whole Vigil which might claim to be contrapuntal. Another moment when an alien style invades the music is at the 'alleluias' in *Praise the name of the Lord* (No. 8: Ex. 171c) which might easily have escaped from a Western composition. Though no Western listener, ignorant of the traditions and ambience of the Orthodox Church liturgy, can be competent to pronounce on the validity of Tchaikovsky's arrangements, by far the greater part of the All-night Vigil gives the impression

---

[23] *TLP*10, p. 148; *TZC*2, p. 473.
[24] *TLP*10, p. 186; *TTP*, p. 72.

Ex. 171

[Bless the Lord, O my soul! Blessed be the Lord!]

[O gladsome light of the holy glory]

- vï,   sve - te   ti - khy   svya-tï - ya   sla - vï,   bez -
- vï,   sve - te   ti - khy   svya-tï - ya   sla - vï,   bez -
Sve - te   ti - khy svya - tï   -   ya   sla - vï,   bez -
Sve   -   te   ti - khy svya - tï   -   ya   sla - vï,   bez -

Not fast

Al - li-lu-i -ya,   al - li-lu-i - ya,   al - li - lu   -   i -
Al - li-lu-i - ya,   al - li-lu-i - ya,   al - li - lu   -   i -
c.
Al - li-lu-i -ya,   al - li-lu-i - ya,__al-li - lu   -   i -
Al - li-lu - i - ya,   al - li-lu-i - ya,   al-li-lu-i-

- ya,   al-li - lu - i-ya,   al - li - lu - i - ya,   al-li - lu - i - ya!
- ya,   al - li - lu - i - ya,   al   -   li-lu   -   i - ya!
- ya, _ al-li - lu - i-ya,   al   -   li - lu - i - ya,   al - li-lu-i   -   ya!
- ya, __ al-li - lu - i-ya,   al   -   li - lu - i - ya,   al-li-lu - i - ya!

of being as discreet and tasteful an adornment of the chant melodies as might be devised using a Western harmonic technique. Obviously harmonization, even when as simple as Tchaikovsky's, must alter the whole character of the chant, and thus produce something new; even so, the All-night Vigil, unlike the Liturgy, cannot claim a place in the canon of Tchaikovsky's original compositions.

It was Bortnyansky, identified by Tchaikovsky as one boundary mark to the stylistic world of the All-night Vigil, who provided the other major musical preoccupation of this summer of 1881. His funds being low, and having no impulse to compose, Tchaikovsky had requested from Jurgenson some routine commission which might stimulate him to work, and the publisher had replied with a suggestion that he should edit the complete works of this earlier Russian composer. Jurgenson had, of course, just won his right to publish Tchaikovsky's Liturgy,[25] and he was clearly anxious both to relish his victory and to capitalize on it. However, on receiving from Jurgenson a batch of the Imperial Chapel's editions of Bortnyansky's music, Tchaikovsky found himself very uncertain about the musical wisdom of Jurgenson's new venture, and uneasy about his own proposed part in it. 'I've . . . begun my editorial work which has proved to be pretty laborious and boring, mostly because the bulk of Bortnyansky's works are very commonplace trifles,' he wrote on 3 July. 'Why do you need to publish his complete edition? May I advise you to throw out this plan and instead undertake the following: *Publish an anthology of selected works by Bortn[yansky]*. This would be far better for your pocket and wiser in all respects. . . . I've even begun to waver about giving my name to such an edition with which I can have no sympathy. At this moment I'm composing some pieces of church music which are an attempt (very modest, let us grant) to counter the iniquitous style established by Bortnyansky and *tutti quanti*, and suddenly I'm simultaneously presenting the public with a project, of all of which my own work is a negation.'[26] But within a fortnight, through Jurgenson's persistence, he had capitulated. His task was to go over the musical text, correcting it and, where necessary, supplying a piano accompaniment for rehearsal purposes. Having now nearly completed the sketches for his All-night Vigil, Tchaikovsky was soon able to devote himself exclusively to this formidable labour, the results of which were to be issued in ten volumes. A little later, when deeply immersed in preparing his edition, he gave Jurgenson an assessment of Bortnyansky which shows that his critical values had in

[25] Despite the decree, the church authorities continued resolutely to forbid liturgical performance of Tchaikovsky's Liturgy.

[26] *TLP*10, p. 149; *TZC*2, p. 474; *TPJ*1, pp. 196–7; *DTC*, p. 535 (partial).

no way been unbalanced by the sheer tedium he found in the task. 'Bortnyansky was *a talent*, but a very second-class one, incapable of breaking even the smallest bit of new ground,' he wrote on 31 August.

He was an extremely good musician and an outstandingly accomplished technician, and therefore though you may not be doing art a great service by publishing his complete edition, you are not doing anything shameful. He has become hateful to me not because what he wrote was *bad*, but because he was prolific mediocrity incarnate, in the ocean of whose work there is not a single really live passage: everything's fluent, neat, pleasant, but monotonous and barren as a steppe.[27]

Distaste for this drudgery inflamed his zeal to be rid of it, and by 8 November virtually the entire edition was finished. It is obvious that such tasks as this and the All-night Vigil had crowded out any real opportunities for free composition. But not quite: Davïdov had willingly transferred his *Poltava* project, and on 6 September Tchaikovsky could report to Taneyev that it had sown seeds in his creative faculties, and some of these were beginning to germinate. 'I have a serviceable libretto to hand, and in my leisure hours I've already composed four numbers.'[28] Tchaikovsky had made a small beginning upon his seventh opera, *Mazepa*.

This summer at Kamenka was to be very different from the previous one. The wound inflicted by Alexey's departure remained as raw as ever, and constant memories of events and places associated with his valet kept the nerve ends sore. Though there is nothing to suggest an active homosexual relationship between the two men, Tchaikovsky's heightened tone in some of his letters to Alexey is that of a distraught lover, and the emotional depth to his loss is evidenced in many references to Alexey in his letters to others.[29] He had been assigned a new servant, Boris, while at Kamenka, but despite his recognition of Boris's virtues, no one could replace his old retainer. Though

[27] *TLP*10, p. 200; *TPJ*1, p. 205.
[28] *TLP*10, p. 204; *TZC*2, p. 481; *TTP*, p. 77; *YDGC*, p. 257.
[29] In this respect, Tchaikovsky's response in June 1879 to news of the illegitimate child Alexey was expecting by Marie Savion, a servant at the Pension Richelieu at Clarens, is interesting. 'My first feeling was of pity for poor *Marie*,' he wrote to Modest, 'and secondly, an upsurge of the strongest paternal tenderness towards the *embryo* in her womb. From this feeling I could gauge the strength of my deep-rooted love and affection for Alyosha. *His child!* It seems as though it's mine! I don't know whether this feeling will last, and how I should proceed. Sasha, whom I've consulted, says that I ought not to involve myself, and that I need help *Marie* only financially at this time. But, you know, she doesn't suspect how greatly I love Alyosha!' [*TPR*, p. 587].

Tchaikovsky was now uncomfortably aware of Jurgenson's growing irritation at his constant borrowings, he still periodically sent his Moscow publisher requests to make small allowances to Alexey so that his life might be easier. Tchaikovsky's own financial improvidence was worse than ever. Desperately needing 3,000 roubles, he turned to the Tsar himself, asking through an intermediary that this sum might be advanced to him against future performance royalties on *The Maid* and *Onegin*. He knew that the Tsar already looked favourably upon him as a composer, and within a fortnight an effusively grateful Tchaikovsky was acknowledging the Tsar's generosity.

But news from Moscow, whither Tanya had gone, was bad; she had broken her engagement to the officer, Vasily Trubetskoy, after the latter had appeared drunk in her apartment and had made improper advances to her. In the meantime Sasha had returned to Kamenka from St Petersburg much better if not cured, and all the family realized that her improvement was to be accounted for above all by her separation from her moody eldest daughter. Hearing that his niece had evidently not taken her broken engagement too much to heart, Tchaikovsky joined the rest of the Kamenka establishment in praying that the girl would remain in Moscow, and then accompany a friend to Lipetsk. But suddenly Tanya appeared in Kamenka. The reports of her condition in Moscow proved to be false, and on the way south she had been drinking heavily and dosing herself with morphine and chloroform. Sasha was reduced to hysterics, with consequences for her general condition such as the family had dreaded. 'My sister, who was beginning to get a little better, can already hardly move her legs today,' he reported gloomily to Mrs von Meck on 5 June. 'I assure you, my friend, that despite all my love for this family, I sometimes want to distance myself a little from them. Some evil fate denies them happiness.'[30] Lev being away, Tchaikovsky found himself the recipient of confidences from a completely distraught Tanya; Trubetskoy, it seems, had tried to rape her. Tchaikovsky did his best to divert her by playing duets with her, encouraging her to read, and turning her attention to subjects far removed from her own troubles.

It was to little avail. Then Lev returned, and sank into gloom. By 18 June the atmosphere had become so unbearable that Tchaikovsky was frantically seeking an avenue of escape. Then he remembered the stratagem which had rescued him from Antonina after his marriage. 'I beg you to send me a telegram containing roughly the following: *Your presence is needed in Moscow in connection with such-and-such a matter. Come*

---

[30] *TLP*10, p. 122; *TPM*2, p. 517.

quickly. I'll show them the telegram and then I shan't have such a conscience about leaving,' he confided to Jurgenson.[31] The latter did as he was bid, but when it came to the point Tchaikovsky stayed. 'There are a great number of places where I would now not only be able *to live* as I do here, but where I could enjoy life,' he unburdened himself to Anatoly on 30 June. 'However, I'm not leaving here because the most important thing for me now is that nothing and no one should disturb my habits. Every new place frightens me, for new conditions and a new situation will compel me to change my ways a little, and this is very painful to me. In another respect, to leave at this moment would be somehow awkward, as though I were casting them off when bad times have come to them. . . . How odd is a man's fate!' he continued, projecting light upon why his attitude to Kamenka was beginning to change, despite his continued attachment to it.

Thanks to N[adezhda] Fil[aretovna] I am a completely free man, always able to live where I wish. But here is proof for you that you don't buy *freedom* even by being provided for. Of all places on this earthly sphere I know none more unattractive (as regards natural beauties) than Kamenka. That which formerly was the single charm of life here, i.e. the contemplation of a family of people close to me living happily, has now turned into something quite the opposite. *However*, I'm doomed *to pass a large portion of my life precisely here*. And I have no right even to complain about this, . . . for no one and nothing hinders me from leaving – but I'm staying here for here I'm *at home*, in a thoroughly familiar spot, no one obstructing me in my habits. It's all very curious![32]

Curious or not, this frame of mind remained with him the whole summer. As for Mrs von Meck's personal affairs, these continued to be in disarray. Brailov was still losing money heavily, and Tchaikovsky tried to arrange that Lev should visit the estate to advise its owner on its efficient administration. Early in July Sasha departed for Carlsbad. Lev accompanied her part of the way, and a meeting was arranged en route between them and Mrs von Meck's sons, Alexandr and Nikolay, who was to become their son-in-law. With the absence of both Lev and Sasha, Tchaikovsky found himself again in loco parentis in a household which seemed to be increasingly overrun by hussars from a regiment stationed nearby. The attraction was, of course, the elder Davïdov girls. Early in the year the sixteen-year-old Varya, daughter of Lev's

---

[31] *TLP*10, p. 135; *TPJ*1, p. 195.
[32] *TLP*10, pp. 145–6.

brother Nikolay, had become engaged to Axel Sandberg, one of the hussar officers, and was married to him on 24 July. All Tchaikovsky's elaborate schemes to escape from Kamenka were finally reduced to a four-day visit to Kiev at the beginning of August, a stay long enough for him to buy a weighty supply of reading matter, exhaust his exchequer yet again, and become convinced that no sooner had he left Kamenka than he was yearning to be back.

Other blows fell upon him as the year dragged on. The new Tsar had decided that the period of conscription was too short and had extended it to six years, though as some compensation there was news that Alexey was to be granted two months' leave from August. In the middle of July his patroness had told Tchaikovsky that Brailov was again securely in her possession, and though he had earlier declined her invitation to stay at Simaki because it would be intolerable without Alexey, he had now decided to spend a month of this leave with his valet in this tranquil place. Mrs von Meck had attempted to persuade Lev to take over the entire management of the estate – though on condition that, as with Tchaikovsky, they should never meet face to face. But though she had disposed of some holdings in a railway line, this had proved insufficient to restore her financial position, and Brailov was again placed on the market. Then suddenly, at the beginning of September, came news that the estate had been sold, and that Simaki could never again be at Tchaikovsky's disposal.

Meanwhile in Moscow Hubert had been appointed director of the Conservatoire, but Klindworth had resigned, and the institution was frantically searching for eminent names to replace his and Rubinstein's. In response to an appeal from Jurgenson Tchaikovsky offered to allow himself to be nominated Professor of Theory, provided he was then given indefinite leave. Obviously, as Tchaikovsky must have realized, this would have been unprincipled, and Taneyev pressed home the attack begun by Jurgenson, working upon Tchaikovsky's conscience in a way which made him wretched. 'He demonstrated it was my duty [to teach at the Conservatoire],' Tchaikovsky moaned to Modest on 4 September. 'This got me very worked up, and I didn't sleep all night – rather, I slept badly, and that with the help of wine. No! Better to perish in poverty than make a stupid sacrifice,' he added vehemently,[33] then counter-attacking by suggesting, with complete sincerity, that it was Taneyev himself who could ultimately fill the gap left by Rubinstein. To set against such distressing matters were Anatoly's arrival in the middle of August and Modest's brief appearance at

[33] *TLP*10, pp. 201–2; *TPB*, p. 272; *YDGC*, p. 256.

the end. A promise of relief from personal strains was afforded when the planned winter migration of Lev and Sasha's entire family to Kiev began at the same time. Sasha returned in early September but stayed only a few days before going to Yalta to continue her cure for a further month. The next day Tchaikovsky learned that Alexey, whose leave had been reduced to a single month, had been forbidden to go beyond the outskirts of Moscow. His mind was quickly made up. Five days later, on 20 September, he left Kamenka, spent a day with those of the Davïdov family already in Kiev, took his two delighted young nephews, Dmitri and Bob, to see *Robert le Diable* at the opera, and on 22 September was reunited with Alexey.

His three weeks in Moscow did nothing to improve his morale, for he found Anatoly gloomily ruminating on his fate, the Conservatoire staff still demoralized by the death of Rubinstein, and Alexey further downcast by the prospect of a longer period of military service. With difficulty he endeavoured to amuse Alexey, spent a lot of money, gave some coaching to Pachulski, who was with Tchaikovsky's benefactress in Moscow, and on 13 October was on his way back to Kiev. In the train he brooded on *The Maid*'s evident lack of success, decided that *Mazepa* was not a subject which could fire him, and then settled down to plan an opera on that 'old, but eternally new subject, *Romeo and Juliet*. And now it's irrevocably decided: I shall write an opera on that theme,' he announced to Anatoly two days later.[34] It seems he may impetuously have begun work, for after his death there were found among his papers sketches for a love duet using some material from his earlier orchestral masterpiece. But on arriving at Kamenka on 17 October he had once again to engross himself with Bortnyansky, and *Romeo* faded as before. The peace and solitude of Sasha's now deserted house soothed his troubled nerves, and he had secretly to admit that he did not enjoy it as much when Lev returned from Kiev and talked incessantly about his own domestic worries. From Sasha, now in Odessa, came news that a second niece was engaged. The name of the future bridegroom must have made Uncle Pyotr start: on 16 November Vera was to marry Nikolay Rimsky-Korsakov, a naval officer and adjutant to the Grand Duke Konstantin Nikolayevich, but evidently no close relation of the composer. Tchaikovsky met Rimsky-Korsakov when Lev brought Vera to Kamenka to receive her grandmother's blessing, and took an instant liking to him. The unbounded joy of the young man in his bride-to-be touched Tchaikovsky deeply. 'Modya, what unfortunate fellows you and I are!' he exclaimed forlornly to his homosexual

[34] *TLP*10, p. 231; *TZC*2, p. 488; *TPB*, pp. 272–3; *YDGC*, p. 257.

brother. 'You know, we'll live a whole lifetime thus without experiencing for a single second the fullness of happiness in love!'[35]

There was reassurance in Mrs von Meck's response to his admission that he had been unwillingly devoting much time to editing Bortnyansky. Reproaching him roundly for not having applied to her for funds which would have made this labour unnecessary, she sent him an extra sum of money, thus tacitly confirming that her financial plight did not currently endanger her allowance. But there was a further, more uncomfortable confession he had to make; it was no longer Nataliya, but Vera whom they both were scheming should become the wife of one of her sons, but now this niece also was no longer available. Determined their matrimonial schemes should not be thwarted, Tchaikovsky offered an unsuspecting Anna as the new bridal candidate.

Modest identified three reasons for his brother's creative inertia during 1881: the death of Rubinstein, his increasing sensitivity to the family at Kamenka, and the loss of Alexey's company and services. There is no doubt that the stunning blow of Rubinstein's end did have an immediate effect upon Tchaikovsky's creative life, even if only to make him declare that he found no attraction in composing symphonic works now that the most perceptive advocate of his music was gone. Equally Alexey's absence, by denying him the close society of a loved companion and regulator of his day-to-day existence, deeply affected him, and made him more vulnerable to the discomforts of life. But when Modest defined the cause of his brother's changing relation to the Kamenka world as being his increasing love for that world, he was being disingenuous. 'From this time,' wrote Modest, 'Kamenka, which had so long served him as a refuge from all life's alarms and commotions, began to become the place where he found them most of all, because all his growing attachment to the members of Alexandra Ilinishna's family made him still more sensitive to their sorrows and joys.'[36] In his biography Modest quoted very little from the copious letters his composer-brother wrote to him and Anatoly during the summer of 1881, and the reason is plain to see, for the picture they draw of Kamenka is a very sorry one. It was not Tchaikovsky who was changing so much as the Kamenka family, as Tchaikovsky's own letter of 30 June to Anatoly confirms (see above, p. 145). Sasha was not only physically afflicted but in a dreadful mental condition. Tanya was even more emotionally disturbed, behaved with wild irresponsibility, smoked and drank heavily, and was already following her mother down

[35] *TLP*10, p. 244.
[36] *TZC*2, pp. 486–7.

the road to morphia addiction. Some of the other girls, though far less disordered than their eldest sister, were moody and contentious, while their father, weighed down by a situation which he plainly felt unable to handle, had lapsed into a helpless despondency which aroused more sympathy in Tchaikovsky than did the condition of anyone else. If Modest had been more frank he would, in fact, have been providing even stronger evidence to support his conclusion that Kamenka was a contributory factor in his brother's creative torpor.

Yet in the long term the absence of Alexey, the sad state of Kamenka affairs, and the loss of his havens at Brailov and Simaki were blessings in disguise. An existence such as Tchaikovsky had enjoyed in 1880 was dangerously protected, even cosy. Had this become the regular pattern of his living he would have been insulated too much from those sometimes painful experiences which were essential if his creative powers were again to be stimulated into full activity, once the stupefying emotional effect of his marital catastrophe had passed. Such experiences had been afforded in abundance by 1881; above all the death of Rubinstein was to liberate, if only briefly, something which had been imprisoned in him for four years. And the final factor in this year of 1881 was, of course, the birth of Antonina's child, for now she would be far less inclined to act in ways which would keep the paralyzing memory of the 1877 disaster alive. By now the shackles of that crippling event were beginning to slide from him, and when Tchaikovsky left Kamenka on 9 November with his ultimate destination Rome, his creative individuality was flexing itself to shape a work in which it would stand revealed more clearly and powerfully than in any piece since those two masterworks of 1877.

First, however, Tchaikovsky had to attend Vera's wedding in Kiev. At the theatre he saw *Vanka the steward*, a dramatization by Luka Antropov of a story by Dmitri Averkiev, and immediately decided that this, and not *Mazepa* or *Romeo and Juliet*, should be the subject of his next opera. After a whole year he felt his inclination to compose was again really stirring. All summer he had declared that his next work would be an opera, and in Rome he proposed to apply all his energies to this. He stayed nearly a fortnight in Kiev; on 25 November he was in Vienna, where he paused two nights, evidently in complete ignorance that a week later Brodsky was to give the première of the Violin Concerto with the Vienna Philharmonic Orchestra under Hans Richter. On 27 November he was in Venice, three days later in Florence. Here Nadezhda von Meck was in residence and, as in 1878, he made a special excursion to gaze at the villa in which she was living. On 2 December he settled in Rome where Modest, Kolya and Kondratyev had been awaiting him, together with a young lad, Grisha Sangursky, son of the chief bookkeeper at the Kamenka sugar refinery, who had been brought along as company for Kolya.

Arriving in time for the celebration of Liszt's recent seventieth birthday, he attended a special concert of Liszt's works. 'It was impossible not to feel some emotion at the sight of this old man of genius, overwhelmingly moved by the ovations of wildly enthusiastic Italians,' he wrote to Nadezhda von Meck on 8 December, two days later. 'But Liszt's compositions themselves leave me cold; they have in them more of poetic intentions than of real creative power, colours rather than draughtmanship.'[37] But other things in Rome's musical life did give him satisfaction. He found especial interest in the church music sung on important occasions, whether it was Palestrina performed in St Peter's at a papal mass for four newly canonized saints, or the singing in St John Lateran of a castrato, whose physical predicament drew both pity and a degree of revulsion from Tchaikovsky. At orchestral and chamber concerts he found the level of performance good.

The situation in Russia, however, gave him no encouragement to turn his own attention to orchestral composition. Nápravník, rated by Tchaikovsky the only remaining conductor to whom he could safely entrust his work, had been hounded by a press campaign from the conductorship of the St Petersburg RMS, while in Moscow Taneyev, whom Tchaikovsky was supporting as the man who could best occupy the rostrum left vacant by Rubinstein, would need to gain experience before his full capabilities could reveal themselves. Having already received a copy of *Vanka the steward*, Tchaikovsky decided he could not himself fashion a satisfactory libretto, and he requested Jurgenson to arrange that Averkiev or some other competent person should undertake this task. By now, however, Tchaikovsky was raring to compose, and *Mazepa* again claimed his attention as soon as he could find suitable accommodation in which he could both work and successfully defend himself from the barrage of social invitations with which he was continually pestered. What had attracted him to *Romeo and Juliet* a few weeks earlier had been the love scene, and a similar nocturnal episode in *Vanka the steward* had particularly drawn him to that subject. It was the same now with *Mazepa*. 'I have begun composing,' he informed his patroness on 13 December. 'I do not know what will come of it, but I have begun with music for the scene of *Mazepa and Mariya*. . . . If I am fired, then perhaps I shall write a whole opera on this subject.'[38] After this *Vanka the steward* sank from sight.

[37] *TLP*10, p. 277; *TPM*2, p. 578; *TZC*2, pp. 494–5.
[38] *TLP*10, p. 283; *TPM*2, p. 581; *TZC*2, p. 496; *DTC*, p. 119; *YDGC*, p. 260 (partial).

Yet, as Tchaikovsky's final sentence shows, his commitment to *Mazepa* was still not absolute, and within a fortnight his efforts were being directed into a very different project. 'Do you remember that you once counselled me to write a trio for piano, violin and cello, and do you remember my reply in which I openly declared to you my antipathy for this combination of instruments?' he asked Nadezhda von Meck on 27 December. 'And now suddenly, despite this antipathy, I have conceived the idea of testing myself in this sort of music which so far I have not touched. I have already written the beginning of *a trio*. Whether I shall finish it, whether it will come out successfully I do not know, but I would very much wish to bring what I have begun to a successful conclusion.'[39] He made no bones about the act of will which was still demanded of him in composing this piece, but he declared that joy in the pleasure the work would give her reconciled him to this.

Such was not the whole truth. Ever since Rubinstein's death Tchaikovsky had wished to enshrine his memory in a composition containing a substantial piano part in tribute to his friend's keyboard mastery, and this was the main prompting for the Trio. As for Tchaikovsky's doubts about his ability to complete the work, these were quickly resolved. Even picking up by chance a copy of the *Neue freie Presse* and reading in it Hanslick's blistering review of the Violin Concerto did not stun his now rampant creativity, and within three weeks, on 18 January 1882, the sketches for the Trio were complete. Though he felt increasing reassurance about the work's qualities as he brought it towards its final form, he feared that he might have handled the medium ineptly. 'Before you engrave it,' he wrote to Jurgenson on 11 February, two days after completing the piece, 'it's essential that Taneyev, Hřímalý, and Fitzenhagen should play it through. . . . I very much want *Karlusha* [Albrecht], *Kashkin, Hubert* and his wife, and our *whole circle* in general to be at this run-through. *It's absolutely essential* that Karlusha or another stringed instrument expert should give his attention to *my bow* markings and correct what is unsuitable.'[40] On 23 March, the first anniversary of Rubinstein's death, these three players performed the Trio privately at the Moscow Conservatoire. Tchaikovsky was still abroad, but on hearing the work played through a little later, he introduced substantial revisions. Especially anxious that this work, 'dedicated to the memory of a great artist', should be handsomely produced, he found himself well satisfied with Jurgenson's edition when it appeared in the early autumn. So, too, Taneyev's reactions gave him profound pleasure. 'I studied it for three and a half weeks,

[39] *TLP*10, p. 292; *TPM*2, p. 586; *DTC*, p. 499.
[40] *TLP*11, p. 47; *TZC*2, pp. 515–16; *DTC*, p. 500 (partial); *TPJ*1, p. 233.

playing it six hours each day,' Taneyev recorded on 5 November 1882, six days after the first public performance of the work at an RMS concert in Moscow. 'I've been going to write you a letter in which I wanted to express my delight in respect of your wonderful composition. I can't remember ever having experienced more pleasure when learning a new piece than in these three [and a half] weeks. . . . Most musicians are delighted with the Trio. It has also pleased the public. Nikolay Albertovich [Hubert] has received many letters asking for the Trio to be repeated.'[41] Tchaikovsky was the more appreciative of Taneyev's tribute because some of the reviews had been less favourable. 'My self-esteem as a composer is as gratified by your praise as it is indifferent to the press notices, to which experience has taught me to respond with philosophical indifference,' he replied five days later. 'I've read *Flerov's* article. I don't believe that anyone (among the musicians) informed him that the Trio's variations represent episodes from the life of Nik[olay] Grig[oryevich]. I think this brilliant idea must be his very own. But isn't it funny! You write music without any pretensions to represent anything, and suddenly you learn that it represents this or that!'[42] The Piano Trio achieved much popularity in Tchaikovsky's lifetime, and this tribute to a departed friend became an elegy to its own creator in November 1893 when, together with the Third Quartet, it was played in both Moscow and St Petersburg in memorial concerts for Tchaikovsky himself.

Such a purpose it fulfilled admirably, for if the Piano Trio cannot be placed in the very front rank of Tchaikovsky's compositions, it is an ambitious piece with many qualities. Its unusual planning recalls that of Beethoven's last piano sonata: two movements, the second of which is a set of variations. Kashkin related that the theme of these variations was inspired by memories of an enchanting day passed in a beauty spot near Moscow in 1873 when a company, including Tchaikovsky and Rubinstein, had dined al fresco with peasants singing and dancing for them. Kashkin also believed, despite Tchaikovsky's own written testimony, that the variations were some sort of composite character study of their dedicatee. Whatever the role of Rubinstein's personality in forming the piece, there is no doubt about that of Tchaikovsky's own; in no work of the last four years had his own self declared itself with such power and consistency. The first movement of the Second Piano Concerto had displayed admirable structural enterprise, but it had been handicapped by lack of characteristic melody of real quality, a deficiency which in any work of Tchaikovsky was fatal. Not so in the

41 *TZC*2, p. 557; *DTC*, p. 502; *TTP*, p. 88.
42 *TLP*11, p. 266; *TZC*2, p. 558; *TTP*, p. 89; *DTC*, pp. 502–3.

Piano Trio. True, little of it might claim a place among Tchaikovsky's finest thematic inventions, but from the very beginning there is a freely flowing stream of personal (if, at times, slightly Schumannesque) melody in which one fervent idea passes to the next in most natural succession. The theme of the 'introduction' (Ex. 172a) is made to grow into the 'first subject', while the 'transition to the second subject' (Ex. 172b) harks back to the characteristic rhythmic mould of the 'introduction', supported by a bass which spills over from the end of the preceding section. Such thematic overlaps occur elsewhere; thus the return of the opening key and theme (Ex. 172d) is accompanied by a four-note cello phrase which lingers from a shape prominent in the last stage of the development (see *x* in Ex. 172c and d; in the coda, yet

Ex. 172

d. **Adagio con duolo e ben sostenuto**

another derivative of this cello phrase generates an accompaniment motif to partner the concluding heavy-hearted, vastly stretched enunciation of the opening theme).

The structure of this first movement is equally striking. Heard against the background of a traditional first movement in which a slow introduction passes to an exposition set at a faster tempo, the function of the main thematic elements would seem to be those specified in raised commas in the preceding paragraph. And if one diagnoses the 'transition to the second subject' as the second subject itself, and construes the violin/cello dolce espressivo duet as a third subject, one perceives a pattern very close to the introduction and three-subject exposition of the Fourth Symphony's first movement. Yet the tonally more aware listener will have his suspicions aroused when, after the A minor opening, the first theme of the allegro giusto enters in the dominant. In fact Tchaikovsky had devised a radical tonal reinterpretation of the traditional functions of an apparently conventional thematic pattern. (Ex. 173) There is no introduction; the moderato assai opening theme *is* the true first subject, while the more chunky allegro giusto melody begins the second subject which goes on to spread itself generously and with wholehearted commitment to the dominant. The development, introduced by Ex. 172b, uses a principle of thematic evolution a little similar to that of the First Piano Concerto. But whereas, in the earlier work, themes had shown a protean ability to change into one another, in this development the single four-note cell which opens it (see Ex. 172b, bars five to six) displays a lively fertility in generating a swift succession of new thematic particles which finally arrive in E flat minor, a key which has exactly the same tritonal relationship to A minor as the E major central portion of the concerto's development had to the tonic of that work (B flat minor). What follows is the most memorable moment of the whole Trio: the harmonic movement settles into complete rest on a chord of E flat minor, the music's hectic progress is checked, and the two stringed instruments enter into an eloquent duet (Ex. 174) which inevitably brings to mind the slow movement of the Second Piano Concerto, but which has a more consistent strength of contour, a more muscular and closely argued contrapuntalism and greater harmonic richness than the violin/cello dialoguing of that earlier movement. This extensive, deeply expressive colloquy, at first tonally shifting, finally prepares the key of the recapitulation, which opens adagio con duolo e ben sostenuto (see Ex. 172d), thus wringing from the first subject every drop of its latent sorrow. Yet this recapitulation only emphasizes the structural ambiguities in what has gone before, for not only is the second subject

Ex. 173

PIANO TRIO: FIRST MOVEMENT

Sloping block indicates tonally unstable section
L = Link
Subjects are indicated by ① and ②

Ex. 174

recapitulated in toto; there follows the theme which had begun the development, as well as the dominant-supported conclusion to the violin/cello duet. Yet nowhere in all this is the tonic seriously challenged, and the movement ends with the first phrase of the first subject, vastly stretched by augmentation and internal repetitions, wearily drawing the movement to rest.

This Pezzo elegiaco, as Tchaikovsky expressly labelled it, is the most impressive piece he had composed since 1877. The following set of variations is matchingly large scale, though the theme upon which the variations are based makes it clear that the issues they are concerned with will be, at least initially, less weighty, for this neatly presented melody has much of the poise, even elegance, of that from which the Rococo Variations had sprung over five years earlier. Yet this ternary theme (Ex. 175a), built from modest two-bar phrases, already has a mild asymmetry which suggests its structure may not remain completely stable in what is to follow, and though the first variation is no more than this theme with its original harmony texturally elaborated, subsequent variations show an increasing readiness to modify the proportions of the theme's constituent parts (Ex. 175), stretching or compressing them until, by variation 5, the original ternary structure has been dissolved, the relationship with the theme asserting itself only in the characteristic contour which begins each half of this charming musical box confection (Ex. 175b). Variation 2 had already turned in the direction of the waltz, but in variation 6 this dance takes entire possession of the field. The Act 2 opening of Onegin, which this variation mysteriously – but, surely, significantly – quotes, had incorporated the 'fate embraced' motif; now converted into a waltz, it counterpoints with the first phrase of these variations' own theme in both the central section and the coda.

So far all has been admirable. The theme has been subjected to a number of inventive transformations, the definition of its new identities being further sharpened by a succession of matching key shifts (E major for the theme and first three variations, then a variation each in C sharp minor, C sharp major and A major). But successful as all this is, it has been a fatal miscalculation. Tchaikovsky has gone too far too fast; by removing the waltz from the orbit of the original theme, he has lost his thematic bearings. All he can do is turn back helplessly to the original theme, aping it in a graceless manner which betrays the influence of Schumann at its least beneficent, while the following fugue is an arid attempt to resume that masterly appropriation of new expressive territories so confidently pursued in the earlier part of this movement. These last two variations are the weakest portion of the whole Trio. Fortunately the following andante flebile recaptures something of the

Ex. 175

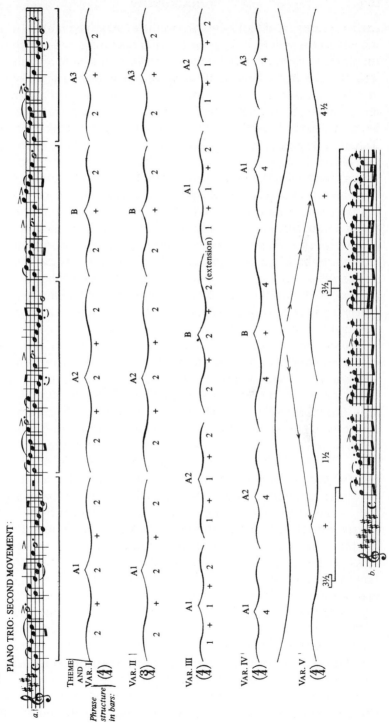

PIANO TRIO: SECOND MOVEMENT:

earlier quality, and looks forward to the expressive realm in which the whole piece is to end. Taking the familiar opening contour of the theme, though now rhythmically tautened with nervous pairs of semiquavers, Tchaikovsky here spins an affecting cantilena from a series of broadly arching phrases against an almost static harmonic background. A chirpy mazurka precedes the final variation, which leads back to the key and uncomplicated world of the original theme. There follows what Tchaikovsky described as a Variazione Finale e Coda, the finale being a full blown sonata structure with a derivative of the theme as first subject, and with the semiquaver motif from the transition of the first movement's exposition figuring prominently in the second subject and development. Finally in the coda the opening theme of the whole Trio is heard again. By means of the Variazione Finale Tchaikovsky aimed to give weight to the later stages of this essentially episodic movement, and also to build a substantial stretch of vigorous music as a strong foil to the return of that theme which had first established the elegiac purpose of the whole work. Now it bursts in, monumentally presented and extended before collapsing into a brief funeral march which quickly passes into silence.

Tchaikovsky's fatal misjudgment in the direction taken by the earlier variations produces the most serious flaw in the whole Trio. Later he was to sanction the omission of the fugue and the reduction of the breezy but rather tiresome Variazione Finale to the recapitulation only, but this merely diminishes the quantity of second-rate music. The certainty of course charted in the Rococo Variations in their authentic version appears the more impressive when set beside the disorientation of this Trio's variations. Nor can one but compare the textural refinement of the earlier work with the thickness of sound in so much of the Trio, an unattractive aspect of which Tchaikovsky was painfully aware. Yet in the nearly eight years separating the Fourth Symphony and Onegin from the Manfred Symphony the Piano Trio remained unique, for that very personal vein of invention which had suddenly been reopened in it by the emotional shock of Rubinstein's death became largely resealed until, three years later, the plight of Byron's hero fully exposed it yet again. In 1882 it was still beyond Tchaikovsky to express explicitly the full force of his own most intimate feelings, but a large measure of his very self could slip out when shielded within the formal grief-laden trappings of a public tribute, and it does so here. Almost inevitably there will be an element of posturing in such a self-consciously elegiac piece, nowhere more clearly heard in the Trio than in the final andante con moto with its monstrous piano textures, exaggeratedly delayed conclusion, and conventional marcia funebre postlude; another eleven years had to pass before Tchaikovsky could summon the confidence to offer a tragic conclusion so honest, so free of factitious attitudinizing as to be emotionally disconcerting. Yet elsewhere in the Trio there escaped inventions which are innocent of affectation – above all, that deeply touching dolce espressivo dialogue of the first movement. Uneven as it is, the Piano Trio is an imposing achievement. Rubinstein, who had served Tchaikovsky so well in life, had rendered a final service in his death.

5

FURTHER UNCERTAINTIES:
MAZEPA

JUST AS IT was the basic instinct of Tchaikovsky's nature for him to turn in upon himself, whether in the act of composition, or in the companionless walks, prolonged reading sessions, or more basic periods of solitary drinking which were regular elements in his daily existence, so in that portion of his life where he had to engage with his environment, he tended to confine as closely as possible his world, living entirely in the present, and responding solely to his immediate surroundings and to the happenings with which he was unavoidably faced. In consequence his reactions could be as limited in vision as they could be intense. In this, for instance, is the clue to his lifelong mishandling of his financial affairs. His current resources could always be drained by the impulses in day-to-day living, or by a sudden appeal from some outside source to his liberal, unthinking generosity. Tchaikovsky was simply incapable of a long-term financial strategy, and when such was required, as in his dealings with Antonina, it was better for someone else to administer the matter.

It was this propensity to live intensely but exclusively within the narrow orbit of the situation in which he found himself which also accounts for some of the apparent paradoxes, even contradictions, so prominent in Tchaikovsky's personality and pattern of existence. It explains, at least in part, the ambivalence in his relationship with his native land. Russia was as dear to him as to any of his musical contemporaries, yet it was also the scene of his greatest pains, both personal and musical. Despite the growing international currency of his music, his homeland was still the place where his works flourished most, where he most wished to be appreciated, and where failure was therefore the more keenly felt. This was just one reason why he would periodically experience the need to flee the land he loved (one notices how such rapid exits could follow hard upon the première of a new composition). But once he had removed himself from the scene of real or imagined failures, the fierce agony might abate to such a degree that he could, as now, lament such misfortunes, yet view them with some detachment. And here is yet another paradox: when he felt that the current fortunes of his music were at a low ebb and when discouragements abounded, his creativity did not necessarily falter. On 16 January, at the very moment when his most intensive work on the Piano Trio was drawing to a fruitful close, he noted bitterly to Jurgenson the setbacks which were besetting various of his pieces.

They're not giving *The Maid of Orléans*. . . they're not giving *Onegin*,[1] Auer is making mischief against the Violin Concerto, no one plays the Piano Concerto (the Second): in a word, it's bad. But what hurts, pains and vexes me terribly is that the theatres' directorate, not giving a kopeck to *The Maid of Orléans*, gives 30,000 to mount *The Snow Maiden* [by Rimsky-Korsakov]. Isn't it a fact – and isn't it disagreeable to you – that our *subject* has been taken from us, that *Lel* sings the very same words to different music; [it's] as though they've taken from me by force something that is mine, something native to me, close to me, and are presenting it to the public in new, brilliant attire. The pain of this reduces me to tears.[2]

Yet all these unpalatable, even distressing events (even Hanslick's diatribe against the Violin Concerto) had happened far from Rome. Distance lent detachment; such mortifications no more dammed his creative stream than they impeded his pleasure in his surroundings or in his day-to-day living with Modest and his charges.

It was the same with the situation in Sasha's family. Living in the middle of the Kamenka ferment the previous summer had deeply affected him in his work and his mode of living, but now, a thousand or so miles away, he could simply detail in letters the reports of turmoil in his sister's household, and then, it seems, brush them from his mind. In fact, news from Kiev was bad. Tanya was as intractable and disordered as ever, and this intensified the ambivalence in Tchaikovsky's attitude towards those people who afforded him some of the closest and most precious relationships of his whole life. For a moment he did ponder the prospect of returning there with alarm. 'I can't imagine anything more cheerless than life amidst this family,' he lamented to Anatoly on 14 January. '. . . Yet where, except at Kamenka, can I find a similar residence for myself?'[3] Indeed, Kamenka was irreplaceable, and he was to be drawn back there for the summer to risk the same miseries as

[1] In fact, this proved untrue, for only six days later *Onegin* was revived in Moscow.
[2] *TLP*11, p. 18; *TZC*2, p. 509; *TPJ*1, p. 226.
[3] *TLP*11, p. 17.

during 1881. Another piece of intelligence, however, brought both pleasure and relief: Anatoly had become engaged at last, and Tchaikovsky thankfully viewed the prospect this brought of an end to his own long-suffering role as comforter of a love-lorn brother. But here again, at this news of his brother's forthcoming nuptials, he looked in upon himself, reflecting upon his own attitude to the opposite sex – an attitude which had been gently challenged during the preceding weeks when he had become aware that Emma Genton, the governess to Kondratyev's sixteen-year-old daughter, Nadezhda, was exhibiting tender feelings ('more passionate than I would wish'[4]) towards him. Her departure from Rome with the Kondratyevs was a considerable relief. 'I'm terribly glad you feel you are happy,' he wrote to Anatoly on 20 February, 'and though I have never experienced anything of the sort, yet I think that I can understand perfectly everything you are going through. It's a certain kind of need for the care and caresses which only a woman can satisfy. Sometimes there comes over me an intense desire to be fondled by a woman's hand. Sometimes I see nice ladies (not, however, young ones) into whose lap I simply want to place my head and kiss their hands.'[5] The image of his mother (the lady with 'hands which, though not small, were unusually beautiful'[6]) remained as ineluctable as ever.

Though the Piano Trio and the need to copy out the All-night Vigil ensured that Tchaikovsky had work enough to occupy him fully, his dwindling funds heightened the attractiveness of a request for six piano pieces to be published in the *Nouvelliste*, the periodical which had already carried his *Seasons* in 1876. It was an easy way of making 600 roubles, but Tchaikovsky felt a moral obligation to consult Jurgenson before undertaking work for another publisher. Jurgenson had, it seems, already heard of this invitation, and his reaction was blunt. 'It would appear to me that you don't need this [commission]. I'm always your willing client,' he wrote brusquely on 26 January, thus smartly nipping Tchaikovsky's plan in the bud.[7] Attending a concert at which he heard for the second time a new quartet by Liszt's protégé, Giovanni Sgambati, he again judged the work worthless, and observed with distaste Liszt's ostentatious display of approbation. 'How I dislike this trait of Liszt!' he exploded to his patroness.

---

[4] *TLP*11, p. 37.
[5] *TLP*11, pp. 55–6; *TPM*3, p. 616; *YDGC*, p. 266 (partial); *TZC*2, p. 519 (with the words in parentheses omitted).
[6] See Vol. 1, p. 21.
[7] *TLP*11, p. 26; *TPJ*1, p. 230.

He never tells the truth, and always approves of everything un-reservedly. People keep telling me and writing to me that I'm wrong not to visit Liszt while living in the same city. But I will not call on him for nothing, for to his sugary compliments I shall also have to reply with flattery and falsehood, and that is very repugnant to me. In addition, he holds an eternal open house, and all the Russian ladies here are constantly in attendance – and I am avoiding these ladies, for last year I suffered not a little from their pressing invitations.[8]

By now it seems that Tchaikovsky's various compatriots in Rome had accepted that he was not to be drawn into either making or receiving visits. Bringing the Piano Trio to a successful conclusion was im-mensely beneficial to his morale, and his good spirits were heightened by news that Alexey had passed an examination which would reduce his army service to three years. There had been some discussion with Modest about visiting Algiers to which a maternal aunt of Kolya had invited them. But Kolya's father would not hear of such close contact with a sister of his by now divorced wife, and Naples was chosen instead as their next place of residence. Certainly it was imperative that they should leave Rome, partly because of the high cost of living, partly because Sergey Flerov, the Moscow music critic, had descended upon Tchaikovsky and was making heavy demands upon his time. On 21 February he left Rome alone, found a six-room flat with splendid views of Naples and Vesuvius, and on the 25th was joined by Modest and the two boys.

The new accommodation quickly revealed less attractive features. First there were mice – one of Tchaikovsky's life-long phobias: a whole army of them carried out manoeuvres in the attic above his room, he alleged. Secondly, when the bill was presented at the end of the first week's stay, it proved to be twice as much as expected. An enraged Tchaikovsky and brother promptly packed their bags and moved closer to the centre of Naples into lodgings more convenient for enjoying what the city could offer, but less attractive in themselves and, worst of all, intolerably noisy. Street singers and hurdy-gurdies – sometimes as many as three at a time – made impossible almost all work other than proof-reading or copying. Nevertheless, on 19 March he could announce that he had that day brought his All-night Vigil to its final form. Nor was casual strolling in the streets enjoyable because of the persistent badgering from hordes of beggars. Despite all this

[8] *TLP*11, p. 44; *TPM*3, p. 23; *TZC*2, p. 517.

Tchaikovsky was induced by the beauty of the scenery and the opportunities of visiting the places of interest around Naples itself to stay a full month in this southern city. The secularization of some of the Neapolitan monasteries saddened him. 'As a place where a man distances himself from the world's bustle for the sake of an ascetic life of contemplation, a monastery attracts me,' he wrote to Nadezhda von Meck,[9] further confirming that it was the poetic refuge religion could offer which was the basis of the church's appeal to him. Sarah Bernhardt was in Naples, and Tchaikovsky saw her both in *La Dame aux camélias* and in *Sphinx*, a play by that great favourite of his youth, Octave Feuillet. He also heard Verdi's *Il Trovatore* at the Teatro San Carlo, but this was the only music which gave him any pleasure in Naples.

For some time after receiving news of Anatoly's impending marriage he had been debating whether to return to Moscow for the event or wait in Italy for the arrival of Anatoly and his bride. His finances finally decided the matter. Realizing that his money would not hold out till then, and knowing, too, that business affairs also required his presence in Russia, he resolved to return. Leaving Naples on 23 March, he spent three days in Sorrento, a town whose peace so captivated him that he declared he would return thither for several weeks during next spring. Thence he returned to Naples for two nights, and on the 28th was in Florence, stayed four days, and then left for Vienna alone. Pausing here one night, he arrived in Moscow on 7 April.

It was here that Anatoly had done his courting, and Tchaikovsky was immediately drawn into the social life of the very numerous family into which his brother was to marry. Kondratyev, too, was in town, and his company proved inescapable. But these social distractions did not prevent Tchaikovsky from beginning negotiations with the impresario and producer, Mikhail Lentovsky, who had built a theatre in Moscow, and who wanted a new opera from Tchaikovsky for the next winter season. 'The subject will be either *Sadko*, or *The Tower of Koromïslov* (a legend), or Potekhin's [four-act folk drama] *A Measure of sorrow*,' he wrote to Modest on 13 April.[10] Lentovsky seems to have had something in common with Emanuel Schikaneder, Mozart's partner in *Die Zauberflöte*, in that his theatrical enterprises were aimed at a wide audience; certainly the choice of either a legend or a drama of a popular nature, rather than a literary classic or a subject attractive especially to an upper-class society, was determined by the breadth of appeal such themes might have. A week later the selection had fastened upon *Sadko*; after this the project was never mentioned again.

[9] *TLP*11, p. 79; *TPM*3, p. 38; *TZC*2, p. 524.
[10] *TLP*11, p. 98; *TZC*2, p. 528; *TPB*, p. 280; *YDGC*, p. 269.

The Tchaikovsky clan mustered in force in Moscow for the wedding. Nikolay and his wife appeared, as well as Lev and Sasha with the ungovernable Tanya. Vera and her new husband were also in attendance; they had left Paris hurriedly when rumours had begun to circulate that the Grand Duke Konstantin Nikolayevich, who was openly living with another woman, had married off his adjutant to a girl who had attracted him so that he might have her near him in Paris. After talking with Lev and Sasha, Tchaikovsky was able to report to his patroness upon the highly favourable impression made by her sons, Nikolay and Alexandr, when they had paid a four-day visit to the Davïdovs in Kiev during February. Uncle Pyotr had not been able to restrain himself from discovering Anna's reaction to Kolya. 'I asked Anna how she liked Kolya, and whether she would like him subsequently to become her husband,' he admitted to his fellow-conspirator. 'She replied without the slightest hesitation that she would like it very much, and was prepared to wait patiently until he had finished his studies, though she would have preferred this to have happened earlier. Now Anna is getting ready to go to St Petersburg and stay with my cousin, the Countess Litke. Would you allow Kolya to go to my cousin's house and see Anna? I know in advance, my dear, that you will agree to this,' he went on, but added a qualification: 'my only fear is that, if there should be kindled in Kolya a spark of serious feeling towards Anna, then how might these visits impair his studies?'[11]

The mother's order of priorities was clear. 'You were very right to remind me of his studies, my dear friend,' she replied forthwith. 'The main thing is that now he has examinations, and I fear anything which distracts him from diligent work. . . . And so I shall not hurry to tell him of Anna Lvovna's arrival in St Petersburg. I beg you, my dear, to write me . . . when Anna Lvovna will be in St Petersburg – secondly, the Countess Litke's address, and thirdly: will Anna Lvovna have returned to Kamenka by 13 June, because then both my boys, or perhaps Kolya alone . . . will come to Kamenka. What pleasure all these dreams afford me!' she added reassuringly, lest he should construe her restrictions upon her son's activities as future lover as a sign of indifference to the aim they both cherished.[12]

With Anatoly's wedding on 16 April some of the social pressures fell away a little. Tchaikovsky remained nearly three more weeks in Moscow, hearing for the first time his Piano Trio, an experience which led him to make some revisions of substance. Sasha and her family soon returned to the Ukraine, and life in Moscow was made more

[11] *TLP*11, p. 99; *TPM*3, p. 48.
[12] *TPM*3, pp. 50–1.

uncongenial by Alexey's confinement to barracks because of further examinations he had to pass. On 1 May Tchaikovsky received a simple telegram from a niece at Kamenka: 'The lilies of the valley are in flower. Vera.'[13] It was a summons he could not resist. Two days later he hastened from Moscow, spent his forty-second birthday in Kiev with Sasha and some of her family, and on 8 May was in Kamenka.

Once again Tchaikovsky's return to his homeland had been accompanied by very reserved feelings. 'The Russian porters seemed to me insolent Kalmucks, the gendarmes like bears, the snub-nosed officials who balefully examined my luggage and who subsequently appeared in the restaurant – and who with ostentatious slovenliness snatched what had fallen off the counter – all these aroused in me a wish to do them a mischief,' he had written to Modest from Warsaw on 5 April. 'Perhaps when I reach Russia proper this will pass.'[14] But these feelings had persisted. Moscow itself still had some charms, but the churlish behaviour of some of its inhabitants repelled him, making the attractions of Kamenka seem the greater, despite the prospect of what might confront him when he arrived. However, his first few days there proved pleasant, for Tanya had remained with Sasha in Kiev, while Modest and Kolya had joined Lev, Vera and her husband in Kamenka to make up a congenial ménage in which Tchaikovsky felt he could again turn his attention to *Mazepa*. His contentment was short-lived. Ten days after his arrival came news of the sudden death of Kolya's father, and Modest had to leave hastily for Grankino. Tchaikovsky realized, too, that Kamenka, whose noisy children were already making work difficult, would be overflowing when all Sasha's family with appendages collected there, and accommodation had to be found for the new tutor who was to teach the younger children. Tchaikovsky himself would be in the way, and he even made a half-hearted and unsuccessful expedition to find lodgings elsewhere in the Kamenka estate.

Nor was his restless mood eased by much progress on the opera. Constantly his thoughts turned longingly towards Italy. 'And yet I feel that in the summer it's only at Kamenka that I'm *at home*, and that if I had to go, I should *miss* even that *ennui* which torments me,' he concluded to Modest on 27 May. 'I'm working conscientiously – but I'm not inflamed; for the child I'm bringing forth I'm not experiencing a twentieth part of that inspiration and love which I have experienced before, especially in regard to some of my offspring.'[15] It would be best,

[13] *TLP*11, p. 107; *TPM*3, p. 53.
[14] *TLP*11, p. 94; *TZC*2, p. 528; *TPB*, p. 280; *YDGC*, p. 268 (partial).
[15] *TLP*11, p. 120; *DTC*, p. 119 (partial).

he decided, if he joined Modest after Anatoly and Parasha had left Kamenka; at Grankino he would also be able to work in far greater quiet and seclusion than was possible in his present situation. His presence would be especially welcomed by Modest, for Kolya was heir to the estate, and Modest had been entrusted by Kolya's father with his son's entire education. This responsibility, with its accompanying powers, had made Modest the target of pressures from other interested parties, including Kolya's mother, towards whom Tchaikovsky's feelings now became very different from what they had been at the time of her separation from her husband. Nor had the legacy of 10,000 roubles to Modest endeared him to the family. Meanwhile Tchaikovsky occupied some of his time by reading *Bleak House*. He had begun it on leaving Florence and, from the time he took to finish it, it would appear possible he read at least a part of it in English. 'I cried somewhat,' he confided to Modest, 'in the first place, because I pity Lady Dedlock, secondly, because it grieves me to part with all these people with whom I've lived exactly two months . . . thirdly, from tenderness and gratitude to such a great writer as Dickens.'[16] When Sasha finally arrived with Tanya she also brought with her Stanislav Blumenfeld, a circumstance which caused Tchaikovsky much disquiet, for he could see from the long tête-à-têtes his niece and the music teacher engaged in that there was some sort of liaison between them. Meanwhile from Grankino came news of ever-increasing pressures upon Modest; Konradi's will was being contested. On 12 June Anatoly and his wife arrived at last. Four days later Tchaikovsky left Kamenka to be at Modest's side.

Tchaikovsky had expected to spend at least two weeks at Grankino; he ended by staying nearly seven. He discovered with relief that Kolya's mother had departed, though in the matter of the will the advantage at present lay with her. If Modest were to press his case, it was clear that a visit to St Petersburg would be necessary, but his morale was much bedraggled from skirmishes with his rival, and his physical condition was low. For some time he had been suffering from a fistula, and it was apparent that an operation was essential. The local doctor performed this, but further abscesses erupted, leaving Modest almost prostrate. Realizing that his brother would need all his moral support when he was at last well enough to journey to the Russian capital, Tchaikovsky resolved to wait and travel with him. Meanwhile the enforced delay proved thoroughly acceptable, for in the calm of Grankino, with its pleasant bathing, he could work freely, and his rate of progress on *Mazepa* began to accelerate. But as the end of July

[16] *TLP*11, p. 126; *TZC*2, p. 532; *TPB*, p. 281; *YDGC*, p. 270.

approached he became restless, partly because of Grankino itself, partly because of anxiety over his brother's continuing ill-health. Kolya's mother had discovered a simple stratagem for obstructing Modest: she deprived him of money. Thus not only did Modest receive no part of the bequest he believed was due to him from his late employer; Kolya's mother made no move to pay Modest his arrears of salary and, in consequence, travelling to St Petersburg would have been impossible without funds from another source. Since there were no signs of the mother attempting to wrest control of Kolya from Modest, Tchaikovsky decided it would be better to delay the confrontation in St Petersburg until after his brother had recovered properly. And so, on leaving Grankino on 5 August, it was for Kamenka that they headed.

Here news awaited Tchaikovsky of the Czech production of *The Maid of Orléans*, first presented on 28 July. Sasha had taken another cure in Carlsbad, and on her return journey had delayed in Prague to attend a performance which, according to her, was well-meaning rather than meritorious – though Jurgenson reported that the opera had had a great success. For Tchaikovsky the most momentous event of his short stay in Kamenka was the visit of the von Meck boys. As soon as Kolya's examinations had finished, Tchaikovsky and Mrs von Meck had ensured that he should meet Anna in St Petersburg, and even while Tchaikovsky had been at Grankino the brothers had visited Kamenka. Nadezhda von Meck's enthusiasm for their marital scheme had now spilled over into a second project; perhaps her Alexandr could marry Nataliya Davïdova? Tchaikovsky had doubts, however, about Nataliya's compatibility with his patroness's other son, and did his best to extinguish the mother's hopes by painting an unflattering portrait of this niece. But on their original project he remained as committed as ever, and when the von Meck brothers returned, he wrote fulsomely to his confederate of the favourable impression they had created with the whole family. Their joint campaign to foster romance was thriving.

So, too, were the fortunes of Tchaikovsky's music at the Exhibition of Industry and the Arts. This had opened in Moscow two months earlier with attendant concerts in which Tchaikovsky's works were well represented. In the opening concert Taneyev had given the first Russian performance of the Second Piano Concerto with Anton Rubinstein conducting, nine days later the latter also directed the Serenade for Strings, and in other concerts the Hymn from Act 1 of *The Maid* and the Liturgy of St John Chrysostom were given. But most momentous of all from Tchaikovsky's point of view was the programme of 20 August devoted entirely to his own works, and on 17 August he left Kamenka to

attend this. Even before the Exhibition opened he had learned of the
Violin Concerto's great success in London when, on 8 May, Brodsky
had played it with Hans Richter conducting. Now, with Ippolit Altani,
the same soloist introduced it to Russia in a concert which included *The
Tempest*, the Italian Capriccio, some vocal items, and the first performance of *1812*. The concerto enjoyed a particular success. But despite
this, and the warm, welcome signs of esteem which were accorded him,
the inevitable Moscow gloom descended, further deepened by discovering Alexey in hospital and having to visit him daily. Rimsky-Korsakov
was in Moscow to conduct another of the Exhibition concerts, and
Tchaikovsky encountered him and his wife on two occasions. It was a
long time since the two men had met, and the Rimsky-Korsakovs
displayed much warmth towards Tchaikovsky to which he responded
with a good deal of reserve. 'I avoided their advances very decisively,
and neither visited them nor dined with them at the Huberts', and I'm
very glad I did so,' he wrote to Modest. 'This "mighty handful" is very
strange; they always thrust themselves upon me with sickly displays of
affection, and this is completely at odds with their actions towards
me.'[17] Obviously the matter of *The Snow Maiden* still rankled. Meanwhile, though Modest and Kolya had gone on to St Petersburg,
Tchaikovsky now decided he need not follow his brother thither, for
some of the rancour seemed to have gone out of the dispute over
Konradi's will, and Tchaikovsky clearly hoped that Modest would
reach some accommodation with Kolya's mother without his support.
He was also afraid the momentum achieved in composing *Mazepa* at
Grankino would be lost if he did not quickly resume work, and on 30
August he left Moscow for Kamenka, halting for two nights in Kiev,
and revelling in the solitude he could now enjoy after the distractions of
Moscow. He reached Kamenka on 2 September. The simultaneous
arrival of Blumenfeld, who was installed in the room next to his and
whose proximity inhibited Tchaikovsky in his habit of playing and
singing when composing, greatly irritated him. But otherwise
Kamenka was almost deserted. Sasha was in Sevastopol with Vera and
some of the younger children, Lev and Tanya were in St Petersburg,
and other members of the family were scattered in Moscow and Kiev.
Soon came news that Vera had been safely delivered of a daughter, and
that Modest and Kolya's mother had reached a compromise: he was to
be free to live where he chose with Kolya, and was to receive 6,000
roubles a year. In relative contentment Tchaikovsky set about bringing
his opera to a conclusion.

[17] *TLP*11, p. 193; *TPB*, pp. 283–4; *YDGC*, p. 274 (partial).

It is impossible to ascertain exactly what Tchaikovsky had by now composed of *Mazepa*. It was more than a year since Davïdov had sent him Viktor Burenin's libretto and, as we have seen, soon after this Tchaikovsky had begun tinkering with bits of it, composing 'four numbers' during the summer of 1881. In Rome in December he had begun the scene between Mazepa and Mariya in Act 2, reporting this to Mrs von Meck in terms suggesting that this was his first step in setting this libretto, i.e. that those pieces already composed were fairly insignificant in quantity, or only lightly sketched. The editors of the complete edition of Tchaikovsky's letters, having access to his sketchbooks, state that these indicate his efforts during May were directed primarily towards Act 3: to Andrey's aria and the finale, though he also gave some thought to the overture and the women's chorus which opens Act 1. His last work before leaving for Grankino was done on the following scene between Mariya and Andrey, and on the Act 1 finale. At Grankino, in conditions free from the bustle and distractions of Naples, Moscow and Kamenka, he disciplined himself to work more consistently, and after some three weeks of residence he could reveal that his enthusiasm for the subject had grown by degrees. 'I am working very diligently and methodically,' he wrote to Nadezhda von Meck on 12 July. 'Little by little there has come over me, if not a passionate enthusiasm for my subject, then at least a warm feeling for the dramatis personae. Like a mother who, the more her child occasions her worries, anxieties and alarms, the more she loves him, so I am already feeling a fatherly tenderness towards my new musical progeny who has so many times caused me painful moments of disillusionment with myself, almost of despair, but which now, despite all this, is already growing respectably and healthily.'[18] This new mood held, and on 25 July he could further disclose to his benefactress that he had that day finished 'a second third of the opera, i.e. one of the three acts'.[19]

Tchaikovsky clearly did little work after his return to Kamenka in early August, and certainly none during his Moscow visit in the latter half of the month, but in settling back into his sister's home at the beginning of September he picked up the threads of the piece again, and on 4 September, within two days of his arrival, he reported he had finished 'very successfully'[20] the entr'acte to Act 2. Work was interrupted for about a fortnight while he directed his attention to the set of Six Piano Pieces, Op. 51, for the Jurgenson brothers. These were

[18] *TLP*11, pp. 158–9; *TPM*3, pp. 70–1; *TZC*2, pp. 541–2; *DTC*, p. 120; *YDGC*, p. 272 (partial).
[19] *TLP*11, p. 165; *TPM*3, p. 74; *YDGC*, p. 272; *DTC*, p. 120.
[20] *TLP*11, p. 193; *TPB*, p. 283; *YDGC*, p. 276; *DTC*, p. 120.

delivered by Tchaikovsky for financial reasons, so he told Modest (paying 100 roubles for each piece, Pyotr Jurgenson had obviously proposed these pieces to compensate Tchaikovsky for having obstructed his *Nouvelliste* commission offered some months earlier). The return of Lev and Tanya from St Petersburg on 16 September brought a resumption of all those vexations now perpetually occasioned by his eldest niece's behaviour. Tchaikovsky's views on the proprieties in the relationship between members of the opposite sex were prim in the extreme, and the spectacle of his niece and Blumenfeld sitting opposite each other in a carriage and rubbing knees under a blanket so shocked him that, as he told Modest, he would have quit Kamenka there and then if he had had money for the journey. However, such constant affronts from Tanya made it easier for him resolutely to shut himself up in his own room, coming out only to eat and go for walks. The result was that by 22 September the piano pieces had been composed, and within a few days the sketches for *Mazepa* were finished. Tchaikovsky had worked on it for a year, and it had cost him much effort. 'I have never yet experienced such difficulty in composing any large piece as with this opera,' he reflected to Nadezhda von Meck on 26 September. 'I just do not know whether it is a decline in my talents or whether, perhaps, I have become more severe with myself – but remembering how formerly I worked without the slightest effort so that I did not know even the tiniest, transitory moments of self-doubt, or ever despaired of my own powers – I cannot fail to notice that I have become a different person. . . . Now I am like a man carrying a weighty, though dear burden which must at all costs be borne to the end.'[21] To Jurgenson the next day, however, he spoke more cheerfully of the result of his labours. '*I think* it'll be a good opera, *I think* that this time I'll not cause you to be out of pocket, *I think* that the public, and the singers, and I, and Jurgenson will be satisfied – but, yet, the devil only knows!'[22]

Without delay Tchaikovsky launched into orchestrating the opera. He viewed this operation with pleasure, and at first all went speedily. His hopes of finishing it by the spring so that it might be produced the next season were high. But just as scoring *The Maid* had proved more difficult than expected, so now he found his work on this new opera proceeding only slowly, for that increased self-criticism he had already perceived in the act of composition was equally evident when selecting the combination of timbres through which the sound would be projected. '*Mazepa* is coming along at a snail's pace, even though each

---

[21] *TLP*11, p. 216; *TPM*3, p. 102; *TZC*2, pp. 550–1; *TPB*, p. 595; *DTC*, p. 120; *YDGC*, p. 276 (partial).
[22] *TLP*11, p. 218; *TPJ*1, p. 259; *DTC*, pp. 120–1.

day I'm working several hours on it,' he lamented to Taneyev on 10 November.

> I can no longer explain to you why I've so changed in my attitudes. At first I thought it was that general decline of powers which goes with old age, but now I'm beginning to console myself with the thought that I've become more severe with myself, less self-confident, and perhaps it's from this that a bit I could once have orchestrated in a single day I now orchestrate in three or four. I'm very much against leaving Kamenka before I've finished the instrumentation of the first act. I'd thought I would manage to complete this by the middle of November, but it seems I have still at least fifteen days' work before me. But as soon as I finish I shall go to Moscow.[23]

In the event even more time was needed, and it was 24 December before he could report from Moscow that this labour was completed. Because it was only after this that he discovered the sketches for much of the rest of *Mazepa* had not been packed into his luggage when he had left Kamenka, he was unable to proceed further until the middle of January.

Meanwhile he had had some doubts about the dramatic structure of the piece, and on 9 January, now briefly in St Petersburg, he turned to Nápravník for advice. 'Please read the enclosed libretto and tell me whether you find any changes or cuts necessary. I particularly ask you, my dear chap, to direct your attention to Act 1. Would it not be better to divide this into two scenes – to finish the first scene with Mazepa's exit? I shall await your reply with the greatest impatience, and will not begin scoring Act 2 until I get your letter.'[24] In his reply Nápravník endorsed the division of Act 1 and also suggested, among other things, that the scene in Act 2 between Mazepa and Mariya might prove too long. Later Tchaikovsky was to concur with this view.

Despite what he had written to Nápravník, on 16 January Tchaikovsky, now in Paris, resumed work on *Mazepa*. He had passed to Act 3, perhaps because he had promised the conductor, Max Erdmannsdörfer, who had taken Nikolay Rubinstein's place in Moscow's orchestral world, that he would let him have for concert performance the entr'acte which depicts the Battle of Poltava – though when Tchaikovsky set to work he felt disenchantment with the piece

---

[23] *TLP*11, pp. 266–7; *TZC*2, p. 558 (partial); *TTP*, p. 89; *DTC*, p. 121 (partial); *YDGC*, p. 281 (partial).
[24] *TLP*11, p. 302.

and decided to set it aside for later revision; meanwhile he sent the gopak from Act 1 as a substitute, and Erdmannsdörfer conducted it at a special RMS concert in Moscow on 3 March. But otherwise initial progress on Act 3 was rapid and in a week, by 23 January, he had finished nearly half of it. Then, as before, his pace slackened. Fatigue and his increasing self-criticism intervened (and also problems with his niece, Tanya), though in the quality of the opera itself his confidence does not seem to have faltered. Commissions for a grand march and a cantata, *Moscow*, to grace the coronation of Alexandr III interrupted work during March, and it was 7 April before he could despatch the score of the third act. But Act 2 went more easily, and by 28 April the whole was completed. A fortnight later it was on its way to Jurgenson, together with the libretto in its final form, and the vocal score. 'I've spent two years on it,' Tchaikovsky wrote to his publisher on 10 May, 'and it's cost me a great many labours. I entrust its future fate to you!'[25]

What followed was something unprecedented in Tchaikovsky's relationship with his publisher. 'You know that I've never argued with you regarding the fees you have fixed, and indeed there has been no occasion to argue. . . . At times I have felt you have paid me too generously,' he wrote on 9 August.

> Now something completely the opposite has happened. The fee you propose for *Mazepa* [1,000 roubles] is *too* inequitable, and I can't let this remain without protest. Unless I'm mistaken, even for *The Maid of Orléans* I received from you more than 1,000 roubles. . . . But since then four years have passed. How can it be that my value in all this time has not increased one penny? In addition I didn't on that occasion make the transcription [for voices and piano]. . . . When you began engraving *The Maid* its production was undecided, its fate was unknown. Now, when the theatres of both our capitals are competing to get the [choral] parts, score and vocal score of *Mazepa* from you, you assign 1,000 roubles to me for an opera to which I've devoted two years and three months of assiduous labour.[26]

Jurgenson immediately and readily agreed, observing without irony that he was glad Tchaikovsky rated his own work highly, and accepting Tchaikovsky's named price of 2,400 roubles (in due course Tchaikovsky was able to argue the Imperial Theatres into paying him a royalty of ten per cent of the box office returns instead of the eight per cent which was the standard rate for three-act operas).

[25] *TLP*12, p. 146; *TZC*2, p. 585; *TPJ*1, p. 303; *DTC*, p. 122.
[26] *TLP*12, p. 200; *TPM*3, p. 624; *TZC*2, p. 593; *TPJ*1, p. 304; *DTC*, p. 122 (partial).

There were no grounds for complaint, however, about the swiftness with which Jurgenson issued the opera, and by August 1883 both the vocal score and the choral parts were already in print. His publisher's expeditiousness was to be expected: what did surprise Tchaikovsky was the response of the Imperial Theatres to his new opera. As his letter to Jurgenson shows, both the Bolshoy in Moscow and the Maryinsky in St Petersburg wanted to produce it. Not only that: both showed a willingness to accommodate Tchaikovsky's wishes and to allocate production resources such as they had never displayed before. It was all the most convincing proof Tchaikovsky had yet had of his now thoroughly established reputation as Russia's most admired composer, though he himself suspected there might be another explanation for this ardour. 'There must be some secret reason, and I cannot think of anything except that, perhaps, the Tsar himself has expressed a wish that my opera should be mounted as well as possible on the stages of both our capital cities,' he confided to Nadezhda von Meck.[27] It was even reported that the designer Bocharov had been sent from St Petersburg to the Ukraine to study the effect of moonlight there so that it might be properly reproduced on the stage. Be that as it may (and Modest attributed this zeal to the recent appointment of Ivan Vsevolozhsky as director of the Imperial Theatres), Tchaikovsky was asked to approve the costumes and observe the dance rehearsals for the Moscow production, as well as accompany the singers and supervise the musical preparations. Once rehearsals did start, the enthusiasm of everybody involved touched him deeply. 'I cannot complain of lack of zeal or sympathy,' he reported to Nadezhda von Meck on 8 February, a week before the première in Moscow. 'Everyone is treating the opera lovingly and with completely sincere delight.'[28] Even the first orchestral rehearsal did not cause him that disenchantment he had always, so he said, experienced with his previous operas.

The initial stages of the St Petersburg production went less smoothly. Though he had delegated to Nápravník the casting of the opera, disagreements arose, especially as to whether Wilhelmina Raab, who had caused Tchaikovsky much dissatisfaction when she had created the parts of Oxana in *Vakula the Smith* and Agnès Sorel in *The Maid*, should sing the role of Mariya, and these led to Tchaikovsky threatening to withdraw the opera until a more satisfactory singer could be found. Nápravník was angry, but Tchaikovsky's prestige, whether Tsar-inspired or personal, now lent his wishes great persuasive force.

[27] *TLP*12, p. 208; *TPM*3, p. 209; *TZC*2, pp. 595–6.
[28] *TLP*12, p. 304; *TPM*3, p. 253; *TZC*2, p. 617; *DTC*, pp. 124–5.

'Nápravník (between ourselves) is very offended by my letter and has written a reply which is not lacking in caustic observations,' he admitted to Modest on 24 September, 'but he strongly urges, even implores, that I should not approach the directorate with a request to postpone the production, promises *for the part of Mariya* some new singer who will shortly make her début, and assigns the part of Orlik to Stravinsky in accordance with my wish.'[29] Once this matter had been settled Tchaikovsky felt he could entrust everything to Nápravník. He could not be in two places at once, and despite pleas from St Petersburg, he decided to direct all his attention to what was happening in Moscow.

Mazepa was first heard in Moscow on 15 February 1884, conducted by Ippolit Altani. 'Immediately after the performance there was a dinner given to me by the performers at which, despite my terrible weariness, I had to be present till five o'clock in the morning,' he related to Nadezhda von Meck from Berlin on 19 February.[30] The last days before this had taken an appalling toll of his nerves, and the day after the performance he had hastened towards Western Europe, missing not only the première of his own Second Suite in Moscow that very evening, but also the opening night of the St Petersburg production on 18 February. '*Mazepa* was successful in the sense that both the performers and I received many ovations,' he continued to his patroness. '. . . My brothers, in view of my terrible nervous condition, persuaded me not to go to St Petersburg but to make haste abroad. . . . Here this morning I found a telegram from Modest informing me that yesterday's première of *Mazepa* in St Petersburg was also successful, and that the Tsar had stayed till the end and expressed complete satisfaction.'[31] He also, as Tchaikovsky was later to discover, expressed surprise at the composer's absence. Both Modest and Jurgenson observed that the opera's success would have been greater if Tchaikovsky had been present.

Of the Moscow production Modest remembered that the staging was excellent, the chorus first-rate, but that the solo singers without exception were all deficient in some way – though Tchaikovsky himself was full of praise for Emiliya Pavlovskaya as Mariya. The Moscow press was generally far more favourable than that of St Petersburg, where the staging, though perhaps even better than that of Moscow, was offset by some serious unevenness among the soloists. Cui led the attack with his by now well-known cry about Tchaikovsky's failing powers. Writing in *The Week*, he informed his readers that the libretto of *Mazepa* was

[29] *TLP*12, p. 230; *TZC*2, p. 603; *TPB*, p. 300.
[30] *TLP*12, p. 309; *TPM*3, p. 255.
[31] *TLP*12, p. 309; *TPM*3, p. 255; *TZC*2, p. 624 (partial).

superbly made. . . . Mr Tchaikovsky has, however, succeeded in spoiling it with his music to such a degree that almost all these wonderful scenes make no impression. . . . For ten years there has been noticeable a slow but continuous decline in Tchaikovsky's creative powers. . . . Once Mr Tchaikovsky's cantilenas were broad, melodious; they were not always equal to the situation, frequently fitted the words badly, but they caressed the ear and embodied sincere feeling and tender warmth. Now they have dwindled away, have faded, become impoverished. . . . The harmony in *Mazepa* is acceptable but rather ordinary – it lacks its former originality. . . . The whole opera has a drab colour, and is also persistently doleful because of the unbroken minor.'[32]

To these sentiments other critics added their voices.

Despite Modest's reassuring telegram Tchaikovsky was soon plunged into gloom when he received a reproachful letter and a dour report from Jurgenson, and news reached him of *Mazepa*'s unfavourable press reception in the Russian capital; his misery was exacerbated by an uneasy conscience about having stayed away from the St Petersburg première. But when Nápravník wrote assuring him that the opera had been successful and that it would become a repertoire piece, his spirits began to revive. Early in April he made some revisions, rewriting especially the end of the love scene for Mazepa and Mariya in Act 2 and shedding some sixty-five bars in the process, and also drastically truncating the end of the opera. These revisions were incorporated when *Mazepa* was revived in St Petersburg the next season. On 1 December 1885 the opera was produced in Tiflis. Despite Nápravník's prediction, however, it was not to hold its place in the Russian repertoire.

Whereas Pushkin had taken some seven years to complete *Eugene Onegin*, he wrote the greater part of *Poltava* in a single fortnight of ferocious activity, basing upon fact not only the broader plot of Mazepa's intrigue against Peter the Great to free the Ukraine, and the account of the tragic fates of Kochubey and Iskra, but also the tale of the disastrous relationship of the young Mariya with the elderly hetman (the apocryphal tale, used by Byron, of the young Mazepa's nightmare ride bound to a wild horse by the husband of a Polish noblewoman to whom he had been a lover, has no part in Pushkin's narrative). The last of Pushkin's three cantos is mainly a poetically vivid description of Peter the Great's victory at Poltava in 1709. The plot of the opera is as follows:

[32] *DTC*, p. 127; *TZC2*, pp. 622–3.

ACT I, SCENE I. *The garden of Kochubey's farmstead on the bank of a river.*
A chorus of girls is singing offstage. Throwing wreaths into the river to tell their fortunes, they enter in boats. Kochubey's daughter, Mariya, comes out of the house. They greet her, and she them, but she explains she cannot join them as the elderly hetman, Mazepa, has come to visit their house. Accepting that Mariya must stay to entertain the guests, the girls resume their song, and leave. Thoughtfully Mariya watches them as they disappear down the river. Left alone (No. 2), she reveals that her only pleasure is to see Mazepa and hear his voice, and she launches into an aria. 'Some incomprehensible power draws me to the hetman,' she confesses excitedly (bar 20). '. . . I love everything about him!' (bar 41). Her ecstatic outpouring is interrupted by the arrival of Andrey. When he tells her that he has long been aware that 'some fateful passion' has been tormenting her, she is upon the point of confiding her feelings to him, for she knows the friendship he feels for her. 'Friendship?' he exclaims (bar 109). 'No! It is not friendship which draws me to you: from my boyhood I have loved you passionately!' Moved by this revelation, and distressed by the anguish she has unwittingly caused Andrey, Mariya reveals her own torn feelings. 'And I, like you, am unhappy. Do not reproach me: I am borne along eternally by a secret fate' (poco più mosso); her passion for Mazepa is invincible. An impassioned duet of tormented love follows, at the end of which Andrey rushes out sobbing, while Mariya, also deeply distressed, re-enters the house.

For a while the stage remains empty. Then the doors on to the covered terrace in front of the house open (No. 3), and Kochubey, his wife Lyubov, and Mariya come out with Mazepa and other guests. Musicians and servants arrange themselves on the terrace. Mazepa thanks his host and family for their warm hospitality, and the chorus responds briefly with a burst of praise. When Mazepa asks to be entertained with singing and dancing, Kochubey gives the order, and there follows a chorus and gopak (No. 4). Mazepa is delighted with the diversions (No. 5). Before leaving, however, there is one other matter he wants to discuss with Kochubey. While the other guests disperse into the garden, the two men confer quietly. When they return to the forestage Kochubey is plainly agitated, for Mazepa has asked for Mariya's hand. Kochubey thinks he must be joking. 'You are a grey-haired old man, but my daughter is in the spring of youth,' he insists (bar 74). But Mazepa is adamant, and launches into a defence of his feelings (andante) in which he contrasts the fickle affections of youth with the constancy of which an older man is capable. Kochubey is unpersuaded, and a quarrel begins to develop (No. 6). He reminds Mazepa that Mariya is his god-daughter, to which Mazepa replies that he will seek from the church a dispensation to marry. What about Mariya's own feelings, asks Kochubey – but Mazepa answers that he knows Mariya loves him, for he has asked her and she has agreed to marry him. The exchanges become rapidly more heated, but Kochubey remains firm. 'I am severing our ties of friendship,' he finally shouts (bar 60). 'I ask you to leave my honourable house!' 'What! You throw me out of your house – me! Have you forgotten who I am?' roars Mazepa. The noise of the quarrel brings the others back on to the stage, and they now begin to join in, Lyubov supporting her husband, Andrey incredulous, yet equally determined Mazepa shall not marry Mariya, while Iskra and the chorus predict that the powerful Mazepa will get his own way. As for Mariya herself, she agonizes over how she may soothe her mother's aching heart and appease her father, but concludes there is no way: she will have to leave her parents' home, for death would be preferable to life without Mazepa. Finally Mazepa's patience gives way in the face of Kochubey's intransigence. Drawing his sabre, he calls to his men (vivacissimo). Kochubey immediately does the same, and the ensemble resumes. Suddenly Mariya tears herself from her mother's embrace and interposes herself between her father and Mazepa, begging them to stop quarrelling. Immediately Mazepa sheathes his sword and orders his men to stand back. Kochubey and his company do the same. In the brief calm which follows (andante non troppo) Mazepa turns contemptuously to his opponent. 'Kochubey, I should not have given rein to my anger; it did not befit a lion to fight against a sheep.' Drawing a pistol, he fires into the air. Immediately a second detachment of armed men enter and group themselves around him. Kochubey and the others draw back. In a last effort to justify himself, Mazepa observes with some restraint that he did not come as a plunderer but simply to claim what belonged to him. When Kochubey and his supporters still show themselves unyielding, Mazepa asks Mariya to make a free but final choice. Terribly divided, Mariya finally tears herself from her mother and rushes into Mazepa's embrace. 'I am yours!' she cries (bar 208). 'If you are mine, come with me!' he shouts in return (bar 210). After giving ironic thanks to Kochubey, he hurries out, taking Mariya with him. Kochubey and his followers would attempt to detain him, but Mazepa's men confront them. Lyubov faints.

ACT I, SCENE 2. *A room in Kochubey's house.*
A chorus of women, surrounding Lyubov on one side of the stage, sings a melancholy song of sympathy to their mistress, who voices her pain and grief at the eternal sorrow and disgrace her daughter has brought upon her parents. As this finishes, Lyubov signals the women to leave, and then approaches Kochubey, who is sitting on the opposite side of the stage with Andrey and Iskra. She exhorts her husband (No. 8) to direct action against Mazepa in his castle, but Kochubey refuses, for he has another plan. He prepares to reveal this, though not before all present, including the servants, have taken an oath of secrecy. All pledge to join in seeking revenge against Mazepa. Kochubey then tells them (bar 39) how, in past conversations with Mazepa, the hetman had darkly hinted at an intention which Kochubey had nevertheless been able to perceive. 'Fired by malice, Mazepa has conceived the idea of a perilous plot,' he reveals (bar 53). 'Traitor to the Russian Tsar, he wants to go over to the Swede, trusting in his victory. But it is time to frustrate the hetman's intrigues; I will reveal them to the Tsar!' Andrey, Iskra and the chorus warmly approve this scheme. Iskra affirms confidently that Mazepa's doom is now sealed, but Kochubey asks who will have the courage to transmit this information to the Tsar. Immediately Andrey offers himself as messenger. Kochubey willingly accepts the offer, but asks Andrey whether he is aware of the mortal danger in which he will place himself. Andrey replies that he is fully conscious of the risk, but that since Mazepa had dashed his hopes, his only

thought has been of revenging himself upon the hetman. 'Send me to the Tsar!' he cries (allegro moderato). 'I will fly like an arrow to the capital; swifter than a bird I will bring ruin to our enemy Mazepa!' Excitedly Iskra and the chorus echo his hopes. Kochubey thanks Andrey and the others, and then turns to brood upon the wrong done to him, and his longing for revenge. 'When you are in the hands of the Muscovite executioners . . . you will curse the day and hour when you became godfather to our daughter!' (bar 181). His wife takes up his cry, and the scene ends with a vigorous chorus of hate towards Mazepa.

ACT 2, SCENE 1. *A dungeon beneath a tower of Belotserkov Castle.*
Kochubey is sitting on a stone bench; he is chained to the wall. Not believing Kochubey's accusations, the Tsar has delivered him and Iskra into Mazepa's hands. The next day he is to die. What troubles him is not the fear of death, but the ignominy of his predicament – 'to fall silently before the feet of the villain like some dumb creature,' he groans (bar 132), 'to be given by the Tsar into the power of the Tsar's enemy to be abused, to lose one's life together with one's honour, to take one's friends with one to the scaffold, to hear their curses over one's grave, to go, though blameless, to execution, meeting the happy gaze of one's foe. . . .' He hears a key in the lock (bar 147), and believes it to be some holy hermit coming to give him absolution. But it is Mazepa's henchman, Orlik, who enters to interrogate him further. 'But why?' asks Kochubey (bar 180). 'I have confessed to everything you wanted.' But Orlik wants other information. Kochubey's estate will be forfeit to the Cossack treasury; where, however, is his hidden treasure? Indeed, Kochubey replies (bar 214), he did have three treasures. Two have gone: his honour, which he lost under torture, and his daughter, whom Mazepa stole. But the third – a holy vengeance upon Mazepa – still remains to him (bar 234). Orlik responds impatiently, demanding an answer. Still Kochubey refuses to give the information, telling Orlik to ransack his houses and gardens after he is dead, adding bitterly that he should take Mariya with him: she would readily show him all his treasures. 'But, for the Lord's sake, I beg you, beg you now to leave me in peace,' he pleads (bar 268), reminding Orlik that he, too, will on the Day of Judgement stand before God to answer for the blood he has shed and for all his deceit. Orlik, however, remains unimpressed, and when Kochubey still will not answer, he summons the torturers. 'O night of torments!' is Kochubey's final cry.

ACT 2, SCENE 2. *A room in Mazepa's castle, with an open door leading on to a terrace. Night.*
Mazepa is standing near the door, musing on the beauty of the night, and comparing the calm of the outer world with the gloom of his own thoughts. The stars seem to him like accusing eyes, the poplars like judges whispering among themselves. He broods upon the necessity of Kochubey's death. 'There is no way out! The informer and his minion must perish!' he ends in declaring (bar 120). 'God! How will she take the fateful sentence when she hears it?' Orlik enters to report that Kochubey still will not give way, and Mazepa confirms that he should arrange the execution for the next day. Orlik tries to say something to Mazepa, but the latter will hear nothing. Observing his master's mood, he leaves. Left alone, Mazepa turns his thoughts to Mariya, and

launches into an aria in praise of his young wife (No. 10a) 'O Mariya, in my declining years you, like a spring, have revived my spirit.' As he ends with an explicit confession of his love, Mariya herself enters unseen (No. 11), hesitating before approaching him. Though their greetings are affectionate, she immediately reproaches him for his recent coldness towards her, and reminds him (bar 42) of what she has sacrificed for him. She adds, however, that she does not regret this, for he had once sworn to love her: yet why does he not now love her? Quietly and tenderly Mazepa chides her for her accusations (moderato assai, quasi andantino). 'Mariya, believe me, I love you more than power and glory,' he concludes (bar 68). She continues to upbraid him, however, observing with bitterness that he is always engaged in consultations and affairs which leave no time for her. She has even, she believes, heard him toasting the health of another woman. Again Mazepa replies gently, denying that he is now capable of infatuation. 'You are jealous? Am I, at my age, going to seek the haughty compliments of proud beauty?' he replies soothingly (bar 94). 'Am I, a stern old man, to begin sighing like an idle youth?' She demands bluntly to know what is preoccupying him, and he resolves to tell her to allay her anxieties. After checking that no one is listening, he begins (allegro moderato) to reveal his plan: after years under the protection of Warsaw and the despotism of Moscow, the time is ripe to free the Ukraine. Everything is now prepared, and soon, perhaps, Mazepa himself could occupy a throne. Mariya's doubts are instantly dispelled, and she bursts out excitedly at her husband's prospects. But he checks her quickly, for nothing is yet certain. 'A storm is breaking; who can know what may be in store for me?' he cautions (bar 218). But nothing will now contain Mariya's feelings of excitement and devotion; if he fails, she will die with him. There begins a duet (andante non tanto) in which she continues to dwell on her absolute love and devotion, though his thoughts persist in running on the fate he has prepared for her father. 'Tell me, who is dearer to you, your father or your husband?' he asks (animato). 'Tell me, if he or I had to perish, to whom would you give preference?' Perceiving the urgency in his pleading, though ignorant of its cause, she assures him, 'O do not be angry. I am ready to sacrifice everything for you!' (bar 278) 'Then remember your words, Mariya,' he replies ominously. They bid each other farewell. Mazepa embraces Mariya, and she gazes after him as he leaves.

Mariya goes to the doorway into the garden (No. 12) and, as her husband had done at the beginning of the scene, observes how calm all is, contrasting this with the nagging, tormenting vision she has of her parents, and of their lonely future without her. Suddenly her mother is standing before her in the doorway. Mariya cries out in surprise, but Lyubov urges her to silence. She has come with one tearful request. 'Today is the execution!' she cries (bar 52). 'You alone can soften their rage; they want to execute your father!' Mariya is utterly uncomprehending, and her mother mistakes this for a changed allegiance. 'I see we have become strangers to each other,' she declares (bar 131), but nevertheless repeats her plea for Mariya to intercede for her father; the hetman will not refuse her. Gradually (moderato) the terrible truth begins to dawn upon Mariya, and Lyubov perceives that her daughter may indeed be ignorant of what has happened. With desperate urgency she tells Mariya of

Kochubey's approach to the Tsar and of the fearful consequences of this. When she comes to the matter of Kochubey's execution, Mariya cries out in terrible pain that she is responsible for all that has happened. Again Lyubov repeats (bar 220) that Mariya alone can save her father, but under the appalling strain of this revelation and of her own tormented conscience, Mariya faints. As Lyubov bends over her daughter, frantically trying to revive her, the sounds of a military march are heard, and she concludes that the execution is already in progress. On recovering, Mariya realizes quickly that she must act without delay, and the two women rush out.

ACT 2, SCENE 3. *A field with, at the back behind a rampart, a scaffold with two blocks on it.*

The crowd of people thronging the stage is restlessly awaiting the arrival of the execution party, and they reflect (bar 49) how great men may suddenly fall beneath the executioner's axe. As they ponder Mazepa's remorseless execution of his enemies, they pray to God (bar 81) that they may be spared such calamities. A drunken Cossack breaks into a song which causes the crowd to rebuke him for his untimely merriment. 'And should I not dance and sing?' he asks (bar 150). 'Look, they're going to cut off some landowners' heads. What's that to me?' The crowd is affronted, but he defiantly persists in his behaviour, claiming that it is his right as a free Cossack. Further protests from the crowd, and his resumed song, are interrupted by the sounds of an approaching procession (No. 14). Two executioners with axes enter and, as they go across the stage, they make passes at the women in the crowd, who recoil in horror. The procession then enters with Mazepa on a horse. The crowd makes an obeisance. Finally Kochubey and Iskra are led in, surrounded by guards and monks. Kochubey asks Iskra to join with him in a final prayer of confession, and the two men kneel. As the crowd echoes their prayers, the two men rise, embrace each other, and then mount the scaffold. The people crowd on to the rampart, hiding them from view. The drums roll and the axes appear above the heads of the people. Mariya and her mother rush in as the axes fall. Mariya cries out and falls into her mother's arms. A horrified gasp rises from the crowd, which begs for forgiveness for the dead men.

ACT 3. *The same setting as at the opening of the opera, but the garden is now neglected and the terrace half ruined. Night.*

After a symphonic tableau depicting the Battle of Poltava, the curtain rises. Swedish soldiers cross the stage, pursued by Russians. Then Andrey enters. He has been unsuccessfully searching for Mazepa, but concludes (bar 22) his enemy has fled the field of battle. He becomes aware (andante con moto) of his surroundings, and reflects painfully on the past happiness he had enjoyed here in Mariya's company. 'O, where are you, where, my darling?' he cries (bar 91), but there is no answer to his repeated call, and he returns to his former musings, finally (moderato) calling upon death to deliver him. Suddenly (No. 17) he hears two horsemen approaching. Thinking they may be Swedes, he hides. Mazepa and Orlik enter. They believe they have thrown off their pursuers, and Mazepa orders a halt to rest their horses. Orlik leads the animals away. Alone, Mazepa reflects upon the disastrous change in his fortunes; then suddenly realizing where he is, he finds his agony intensified. 'O fate, fate, how you have punished old Mazepa!' he cries (bar 73). Meanwhile Andrey has recognized a familiar voice, and re-enters to confront Mazepa. He launches into a denunciation of the hetman for what he has done, a denunciation which strikes Mazepa to the heart. He asks Andrey (bar 110) what he wants with him. 'What do I want? I want your death!' Andrey shouts (bar 114). Mazepa asks that his grey hairs and misery should win him some indulgence, but warns Andrey that if he attacks him, he will find he also is armed. At the end of a furious altercation Andrey draws his sabre and hurls himself upon Mazepa (bar 164). The latter fires his pistol and Andrey falls wounded. 'Unfortunate one!' Mazepa exclaims (No. 18). 'God is my witness – I did not want your ruin!' He summons Orlik, but at that moment the moon comes out to reveal Mariya emerging from the trees. Mazepa cries out at the sight of her. At first she does not notice him, but then hurries up to him. 'Ah, quiet, quiet, my friend,' she begins her wild ramblings (bar 30). 'My father and mother have just closed their eyes. Wait! Wait! They can hear us!' A mad scene develops, Mazepa watching his wife in helpless misery. He tries to bring her to her senses. 'I remember a field,' she recalls (andante) 'a noisy occasion, a mob, and dead bodies – my mother took me there . . . but where were you?' With mounting frenzy she asks him to go home with her, but then abruptly changes: this is not Mazepa she sees before her. 'He is handsome,' she bursts out (bar 109), 'love burns in his eyes, there is such comfort in his words, his moustache is whiter than snow – but yours is congealed with blood!' Orlik enters to warn Mazepa that their pursuers are approaching. Mazepa wants to take Mariya with them, but Orlik vigorously opposes this. In terrible indecision Mazepa gazes at Mariya, then quickly leaves with his henchman.

Mariya suddenly perceives the wounded Andrey (No. 19). At first she thinks it is her father's body; then, bending over Andrey (bar 15), she places his head in her lap. Though she sees it is not her father, she does not recognize Andrey. 'It is a child sleeping in the thick grass,' she concludes (bar 22); but when Andrey whispers her name, she knows that the voice is familiar. The dying man tries unsuccessfully to awaken her to reality (andante un poco rubato), but she begins to sing him a lullaby (andante non tanto), rocking him gently. Again he tries to make her understand, but again to no avail, though she recognizes that the voice had once sung songs to her in her parents' garden. As Andrey dies she resumes her lullaby, rocking him and staring blankly before her.

Though the musical conventions of Tchaikovsky's operas had always remained much the same, the characters of the works themselves had shown great variety. *The Maid of Orléans* had been a foray into a West European world, both in its subject and in its aggressive appropriation of the spectacular apparatus of grand opera. *Onegin* and *Vakula*, very different from each other as they were, had been quintessentially Russian, one digging deep into the strata of upper society to lay bare something of the predicaments and disasters which the mores of that society might bring about, the other revelling in a bright, fantastic country world in which pleasure and pain may take simpler forms, but are no less poignant. *The Oprichnik*, like *The Voyevoda* before it, had possessed none of the integrity of these last two; the plot was contrived, the characters too much like puppets manoeuvred into strong situations. *Mazepa*, frankly, turns back towards this operatic type. Like *The Oprichnik* it is set in the Russian past; a tsar hovers unseen in the background, the characters on stage include historical personages, but their role is not necessarily to reproduce veraciously what they may have done in life. For all the quality of the masterpiece from which the plot of *Mazepa* was drawn, the story as offered in Burenin's libretto can lay little claim to literary merit. It was here that Tchaikovsky's problems originated.

From the composer's request to Karl Davïdov, it is evident that it was reading Pushkin's original, and not the libretto, which aroused his interest. It is easy to see why. *Poltava* is a stirring subject, a substantial portion of the poem being written in dialogue which provided some precious, ready-made material to set within the newly constructed lines. The original libretto has disappeared, but Modest recorded that his brother left Burenin's framework essentially intact, though he made some excisions. 'Thus he cut out the scene of the executioners exchanging jokes with the womenfolk and the crowd before Kochubey's execution,' wrote Modest. 'Burenin had introduced this at the insistence of Davïdov, who wanted something "humorous and folky" as a contrast to the tragic element in the situation. Pyotr Ilich himself was keen on this stage situation, and cut it only on the advice of his friends, primarily Nápravník. In addition, instead of a scene for Mazepa and Orlik in the former's headquarters, Pyotr Ilich composed a symphonic tableau, *The Battle of Poltava*.'[33] Exactly how much Tchaikovsky revised the actual wording of the libretto we cannot know, but even without Modest's evidence it is apparent from the markings in Tchaikovsky's personal copies of *Poltava* that he himself went back to Pushkin's original and worked over it. In the final libretto everything which could be incorporated direct or adapted (usually simply by turning reported into direct speech) was used, and the middle two of the six scenes are virtual transcriptions from *Poltava*'s text; only the execution scene seems to owe nothing to Pushkin.[34] Significantly, it was Pushkin's own lines which inspired much of Tchaikovsky's best music in *Mazepa*.

---

[33] *TZC2*, p. 598.

[34] In the dungeon scene Kochubey's first thirteen and last ten bars (i.e. bars 272–81) have a newly written text. In the following scene words had to be provided for the short exchange between Mazepa and Orlik, for Mazepa's arioso (No. 10a: these were

The doubts Tchaikovsky felt on receiving Burenin's libretto are self-evident. He toyed only intermittently with setting it, more than once considered abandoning it altogether in favour of something else, and only settled to it wholeheartedly during his extensive stay with Modest at Grankino. What had attracted Pushkin to the theme in 1828 had been the figure of Peter the Great, here engaged in a struggle for national survival as momentous as that which Russia had faced only sixteen years earlier when Napoleon had invaded. Peter had faced separatism as well as incursion, for the encroaching Charles XII of Sweden was supported by Mazepa, the Cossack hetman of the Ukraine, who transferred his allegiance to Charles in the hope of securing Ukrainian independence from Russia. Peter's defeat of Charles and Mazepa at Poltava proved to be one of the most important victories in Russian history. As has been noted, the battle itself and Peter, the majestic Tsar, are the main themes of the last of Pushkin's three cantos, while the preceding two tell of Mazepa's treason and, above all, of his liaison with his own proud, calculating goddaughter, Mariya. *Poltava* is thus both a powerful national epic and a tragic romance, providing a splendidly broad setting in which the various traits of the old Cossack's character could emerge. 'Mazepa is one of the most remarkable figures of that epoch,' Pushkin wrote in his preface to the first edition. '. . . History shows him to be a man of ambition, steeped in perfidy and crime . . . the destroyer of his unfortunate mistress's father, traitor to Peter before victory, betrayer of Charles after his defeat.'[35] Pushkin amplified this in *Poltava*, explicitly characterizing Mazepa as a ruthless schemer and unfeeling cynic who holds nothing sacred, remembers no acts of kindness but who never forgets an insult, who loves nothing, is prepared to shed blood like water, who holds freedom in contempt, and whose plot to free the Ukraine is not a crusade to liberate a people but a bid to gain himself a throne.

We can discern little of this from the opera. Peter the Great has no part in it, and the crucial battle of Poltava is represented solely by the orchestral prelude to the last scene – an idea which must be credited to Tchaikovsky, not Burenin. From Pushkin's heroic panorama, with its confrontation of national leaders wheeling and clashing with the

---

specially written by Vasily Kandaurov), for the first part of the Mazepa/Mariya scene (to bar 40), for the first thirteen bars sung by Mariya when she is left alone (No. 12), and for the final stretch from just before Mariya's faint. In the first scene much of Andrey's, and all of Mazepa's declarations of love are from *Poltava* (No. 2, bars 112–32, and No. 5, bars 82–end respectively), as are a good deal of Kochubey's denunciation of Mazepa in Scene 2 and the ensuing finale, and nearly all the first part of the mad scene at the opera's end. Other lines from *Poltava* appear from time to time.

[35] Alexandr Pushkin, *Polnoye sobrany sochineny*, vol. 4 (Moscow, 1963), p. 519.

destinies of whole tribes and nations in the balance, Burenin merely sifted out the emotional entanglement of Mazepa and Mariya, which from the beginning some Pushkin commentators had criticized for marrying unhappily with the grander issues. Other events were brought in primarily because they were essential to the development of that relationship; everything was reduced to romantic melodrama where all was calculated to wring the heart or chill the nerves. The fact that the opera does intermittently make such an indelible impression must be credited solely to the quality of Tchaikovsky's music. Yet there was little he could do to bring to life the epic side of Mazepa, and the grim, wily figure of *Poltava* enters the opera as a bluff, elderly gentleman chatting with a friend, who declares his love in terms suggesting a provincial Gremin, then quarrels with his friend to music which begins well enough but grows into a finale which is one of the most faceless pieces of the entire opera, for all its carefully built vocal tumults and its pointed solo interventions designed to give some semblance of the cut and thrust of true drama.

The *Mazepa/Oprichnik* affinities have already been noted, and a comparison of the two operas is illuminating; nor is it always to the advantage of the later work. Their most clear point of similarity is in their use of folksongs, for in none of Tchaikovsky's intervening operas had he used as many. Five have been identified, the first providing the foundation for the engaging Act 1 chorus preceding the gopak (it recurs in the coda of the latter), a second turning up briefly in the finale of the same scene (vivacissimo),[36] though this time the national character is well smothered by its context. Indeed, there is a substantial resurgence of a national element in *Mazepa*. From Mazepa's entry until the gopak there is a good deal, and a certain amount is to be found in the overture (especially in the F sharp minor cor anglais theme). There is even more in the women's choruses, the first of which opens Act 1 enchantingly in $\frac{5}{4}$, while the second performs the same service more disconsolately for Act 2, with Lyubov supplying a plangently Slavonic centre. The woodwind arabesques of this chorus's final section make explicit its debt to the Persian chorus in *Ruslan and Lyudmila*. Another memory from *Ruslan*, this time of the spiky, lightly malicious music with which the evil enchantress Naina had been characterized, clearly fathered the musical embodiment of Mazepa's henchman, Orlik (Ex. 176). Yet *Mazepa's* most literal debt to Glinka comes during the love scene when, as the hero reflects upon his homeland's long bondage 'under the protection of Warsaw and the despotism of Moscow', Tchaikovsky slips in respectively the openings of the Act 2 mazurka and of the Slavsya Chorus from

---

[36] Rubets, *216 pesen*, No. 2.

Ex. 176

A Life for the Tsar (Ex. 177). The most extensive of the self-consciously national stretches of *Mazepa* occurs in the execution scene, the first part of which (No. 13) Tchaikovsky actually labelled 'folk scenes', employing one folksong to open, and a second for the intervention of the drunken Cossack.[37] The last of the opera's five known folksongs turns up in the entr'acte to Act 3, where not only did Tchaikovsky import the famous 'Slava', best known from its employment by Beethoven in the second Razumovsky quartet and by Musorgsky in the Coronation Scene in *Boris*, but also the liturgical chant which had already been incorporated in *1812*. Earlier in *Mazepa* the idiom of Orthodox church

---

[37] Rubets, *216 pesen*, No. 110, and Balakirev collection, No. 11, respectively.

Ex. 177

[Under the protection of Warsaw and the despotism of Moscow]

music had played a significant, if a less pervasive role than in *The Oprichnik*, materializing momentarily in the dungeon scene when Kochubey mistakes Orlik for a holy hermit come to absolve him, and far more extensively towards the end of the execution scene in the prayers of the condemned men and the people.

Yet except in their plentiful use of folksongs, their element of

Ex. 178

a.

b.

[In an instant the young heart bursts into flame, and is extinguished. In it love passes

and comes afresh.]

c.

[MARIYA: O how pale you are! Forgive me, my dear, and believe me: I love you!

MAZEPA: Forgive me, Mariya! My lovely darling, forgive me!]

Orthodox church music, and in their unbridled exploitation of strong situations, *Mazepa* and *The Oprichnik* are fundamentally different, and the sources of these differences lie in Tchaikovsky himself. In composing *The Oprichnik* he had still surveyed the drama from without, identifying the factors which were the moving forces of events, and then embodying them in musical materials which recurred and engaged as the tale ran its course. Though in *Mazepa* there is one theme which does range widely, Tchaikovsky now displayed a greatly reduced interest in such referential materials, and his use of thematic recall is more sparing. All but two of these instances are confined to the last scene; the exceptions are the introduction of Lyubov after the Mazepa/Mariya love duet by an orchestral quotation of the women's chorus which had supported her at the beginning of the second scene, and the recurrence of the brisk march, first heard during Mazepa's conspiracy revelation and again offstage at the end of the scene, to support the entry of Mazepa's forces before the execution.[38] Only one character, the second-rank Orlik, has a reminiscence theme (see Ex. 176b). Tchaikovsky, changed by the searing experiences of the intervening ten years (and with the creative achievement of *Onegin* behind him: we should remember he had described that opera as 'lyrical scenes'), now showed more interest in the emotional lives of his characters, probing deeply into their feelings to discover those creative springs which might then rise to the musical surface in a notable variety of embodiments, with a general consistency of melodic style rather than literal recall

[38] It must remain uncertain whether Tchaikovsky really intended to recall the gopak's introduction in the bass just before the andantino non troppo introducing the dungeon scene.

giving some expressive focus. This radical change straightway affects
the overture which is not, as had been that of *The Oprichnik*, a preview of
certain representative materials with incipient dramatic conflicts. Instead much of it seems more like a sketch of Mazepa himself, for though
the legendary ride of his youth is the substance of the initial allegro non
troppo (we have Tchaikovsky's authority for this), the following andantino con moto seems concerned solely with the hetman's emotional
involvement with Mariya, even opening with a tiny prefiguration of his
tender declaration of love in the first scene, and of the coda to the Act 2
love duet (Ex. 178).[39]

---

[39] In the original, longer conclusion to this scene, as Mazepa had pressed Mariya to
his breast, the orchestra had presented yet another version of this idea (Ex. 179)

Ex. 179

A price had to be paid for these dramaturgic shifts. A fundamental fault of *Mazepa* is a general lack of real precision, for in opting for a more abundant melodic fund, Tchaikovsky not only undermined the thematic definition of character and of the dramatic issues, but also put at risk that emotional concentration he had sometimes achieved with notable strength in *The Oprichnik*. Cui's observation that 'once Mr Tchaikovsky's cantilenas were broad, melodious . . . now they have dwindled away' contains more than a grain of truth, for though there are melodic passages of great emotional force in *Mazepa*, there is nothing as redblooded as Natalya's G flat arioso in *The Oprichnik*, for instance. Some of the dramatic associations of certain keys, as established in *Onegin* and used with less commitment in *The Maid*, do crop up again in *Mazepa*. E major can still be the key of happy or aspiring love, as when it is used soothingly by Mazepa in his love scene with Mariya, with pathetically faltering strength by the dying Andrey in the final scene. It had marked his entry at the beginning of the opera, though he had swiftly changed to E minor as he unhappily surveyed Mariya's obvious agitation. This key of doom closes both the first scene[40] and the execution scene. And even before composing the passage where, after her love scene with Mazepa, Mariya suddenly directs her thoughts to her distraught parents, Tchaikovsky had decided this should be in D minor; he had equally prescribed this key of despair and disaster for Mazepa's very last exit and what immediately followed.

Yet such tonal associations are looser in *Mazepa* than in *Onegin*. So, too, is much of the musico-dramatic organization when compared with *The Oprichnik*. Though nowhere in *Mazepa* is there anything as messily structured as the first scene of that earlier opera, neither is there anything as taut as the oath scene. The only comparable section is the Lyubov/Mariya duologue after the love scene, where the three statements of the mother's desperate plea for intercession provide structural cornerstones for this stretch of the opera, as well as hammering home the main dramatic point. Yet Tchaikovsky himself clearly felt that it hardly mattered if he paid less heed to such thematic and tonal operations and such structural procedures as the means of dramatic articulation, since there was an overriding force which made the use of these things almost incidental. For *Mazepa*, like *Onegin*, is an opera governed by fate. What finally fired Tchaikovsky to set purposefully

---

[40] In the original version, i.e. when this scene had been joined to that which followed, Tchaikovsky had ended this ensemble in C minor, thus leading up to the key of the following chorus. It is the more significant, therefore, that when he made such continuity inessential by separating the two scenes, he should have chosen to end in E minor instead.

about Burenin's libretto was the highly personal view he could take of the Mazepa/Mariya relationship. As with Tatyana and Joan, Mariya was the 'innocent' girl who became a victim of that all-governing force. But whereas Onegin had been fate's instrument through rejecting Tatyana, Mazepa had performed the same function through appropriation, becoming the central, ever-present factor in Mariya's existence, and therefore able to act as the direct surrogate of this irresistible power. This being so, the musical embodiments of fate and Mazepa could be joined in a single theme (Ex. 180) which leaps up powerfully and abruptly, only to be caught into that Tchaikovskyan symbol of fate, a descending scale, the end of which is twice repeated and unceremoniously amputated. As presented in Ex. 180 it launches the whole opera, demonstrating its absolute power at the end of the overture by remorselessly crushing out of existence Mazepa's more susceptible feelings which might have endangered its subsequent operations. It plays no part in the early stages of the opening scene, but resurges as Mazepa discloses to Kochubey that Mariya has declared to him her love – that emotion through which fate will finally claim its victim – and it plays an increasingly prominent role in the final stages of the action when Mariya's moment of decision approaches. Yet, aggressive as it is, this theme displays little of the potency of either fate theme in *Onegin*,[41] neither infiltrating itself as ubiquitously as had the 'fate in prospect' motif, nor stamping its shape indelibly upon new melodic conceptions as had the 'fate embraced' contour. Rarely does it exhibit even the implacable intrusiveness of the Fourth Symphony's motto theme. Instead its use is sparing, sometimes perfunctory. It has no part in the opera's second scene, and is heard only briefly and fragmentarily in the

Ex. 180

[41] Curiously, the second fate theme of *Onegin* does seem to play some part in the Mariya/Andrey encounter at the opening of the opera, haunting the aria in which Mariya feverishly reflects upon the 'unexpected power' which has drawn her to Mazepa (Ex. 181a), then repeatedly conditioning Andrey's vocal line as he begins to exercise himself over Mariya's evident inner agitation, finally appearing explicitly when Mariya replies (Ex. 181b). There are occasional suggestions of it subsequently, above all in Mariya's mad scene. Gerald Abraham has commented on other thematic legacies from *Onegin* (see his study of the operas in *Tchaikovsky: a symposium* (London, 1945), p. 163, and *Slavonic and romantic music* (London, 1968), p. 158).

Ex. 181

a.

[Some incomprehensible force draws me to the hetman]

b.

[If you would know my secret, I will not deny you,]

introduction to the dungeon scene. Even in the love scene it is relatively muted, its opening motif flickering nervously in the orchestral intro- duction, resonantly confirming Mazepa's sentence of death upon Kochubey, and then disappearing until Lyubov begins to open her daughter's eyes to Mazepa's ruthlessness. As the two women rush out on their fruitless mission to save Kochubey, it is this theme which abruptly brings down the curtain in E minor, just as it had done in the very first scene. And just as it had pronounced Kochubey's doom before the love scene, so it breaks out momentarily as the sentence is carried out. But in the final scene it loses its more portentous role, becoming little more than Mazepa's label, heralding his arrival and marking his ignominious exit in a muffled, expiring presentation.

It is this conjoining of the underlying force of the tale with the personality of Mazepa which is the pointer to Tchaikovsky's failure with his nominal hero, and to his relative success with Kochubey, Mariya and Lyubov – for the opera is by no means the lost cause it might appear to be from what has already been written. It was to these last three characters and, to a much lesser extent, to Andrey that Tchaikovsky really responded, just as he had done to Tatyana and Lensky rather than to Onegin. Mazepa himself, despite all his moments of conventional theatrical projection, is largely a cipher serving some- thing outside himself. His best bits are those where his emotions are most engaged by Mariya – for instance, in the first scene, where he declares his love in a touching arioso in E flat, Tchaikovsky's key of noble pathos (see Ex. 178b). Even more did he stir Tchaikovsky when Mariya's relationship with Mazepa places the Cossack himself under pressure, as when, in the preliminaries to the love scene with Mariya in the second act, he contemplates the beauty of the Ukrainian night in enchanted yet despondent music which grows out of the opening section of the preceding orchestral prelude (one of the loveliest passages in the whole opera, so superior to the Poltava entr'acte), agonizing on an implacable conscience and on the truth which she soon must know, then pouring out his love in an aria of rare tenderness.[42]

But when he engages with Mariya in duet, his soothing rejoinders to her scolding at his neglect are in danger of sounding bland when intersected by her more pointed utterances. This was evidently the first scene of the opera to be composed, and from the beginning it was Mariya who exercised the greater power over Tchaikovsky. Her re- proaches are spirited, not whining, and when, after Mazepa has

---

[42] This G flat aria was composed at the end of 1883 at the request of the baritone, Bogomir Korsov, who was to sing the title role.

uncovered his scheme for a free Ukraine, she hails him as a future tsar, a little of the seething ambition of Pushkin's heroine breaks through in the surging of the three-bar phrases from which her melodic line is mostly built (Ex. 182); Mazepa never achieves such vibrant self-projection. In the final scene, now defeated and finding himself in Kochubey's desolate garden, he is an ineffectual shadow who can do no more than lament fate's harshness, confront and reluctantly kill Andrey, then gaze helplessly at the sight of his deranged wife. Whatever dramatic life Mazepa now possesses stems from his tormented impotence at the heart-rending condition to which he has reduced Mariya.

Ex. 182

Kochubey makes an altogether more solid impression. If in the opening scene he had never emerged as much more than a costume figure, he does so assertively in what follows. Tchaikovsky's touch with Lyubov is admirably positive, too, for he had followed her lament over her daughter's abduction by furnishing her with a brief but vigorous exhortation to her husband, couched in musical terms which suggest she possesses something of the same spirit in adversity as the Boyarïna in *The Oprichnik*. Indeed, she is the only character in the opera who can match her own daughter in melodic breadth, as is impressively demonstrated by the vast melodic arc of her thrice-heard exhortation to Mariya to save Kochubey (Ex. 183). This whole duet is a brilliantly tense confrontation, Lyubov ever more remorselessly insistent in her determination to break through her daughter's incomprehension, Mariya almost disorientated as the truth dawns on her.

But Kochubey is yet more impressive, and the trenchant strength which begins to gather within his denunciation of Mazepa in the opera's second scene (Ex. 184) – so much richer in substance than the bustling end to the finale – re-emerges battered but indomitable in

Ex. 183

Moderato molto animato

Lyubov: Te - be od - noy, ___ te - be od - noy ___ svi - repstvo ikh
[You alone can soften their ferocity; they intend to execute your father, they are cruel and

piùanimando
cresc.
___ smyag-chit voz - mozh - no; o - ni ot-sa ___ kaz - nit khot - yat, ___
godless. Save your father, I beg you, my daughter, save your father!]

riten.   ff
___ o - ni zhe-sto - ki i bez - bozh - nï. Spa - si ot - sa, spa -

- si ot - sa, o doch mo - ya, mol - yu te-bya, spa - si ___ ot - sa!

Ex. 184

[Moderato] Più sostenuto
ad libitum

Kochubey: Tï ne ist-leyesh sred po-zha-ra, tï ne iz-dokh-nesh ot u-da-ra ka-
f colla parte
[You will not be reduced to ashes in the conflagration, you will not find rest

- zats-koy sab-li; net, ___ zlo - dey, net, ___ zlo - dey, net! Vru-

from the blows of a Cossack sabre; no, evil one, no!]

Ex. 185

[What is death? a longed-for sleep; I am ready to lie in a bloody grave.]

the dungeon scene which follows. Any charge that Tchaikovsky was incapable of treating the grimmer things of life except through conventionally melodramatic musical imagery or rhetoric is powerfully refuted by this imposing monologue. Now alone and imprisoned, Kochubey first ponders his predicament in austerely gloomy terms, then reflects upon death in music where intimations of a more wondrous, blissful prospect are conveyed in chords structured upon a bass which descends in alternating major and minor thirds (Ex. 185);[43] this same mechanical progression had been used to expose Joan's wonderment as she had begun to recall the vision of the Virgin which had inspired her crusade in *The Maid of Orléans* (see Ex. 160b). Racked less by fear of the ordeal before him than by bitterness at the injustice and ignominy of his situation, and sick at heart at the ruin he has innocently brought upon others, Kochubey is able at times to rise to a level of melodic inventiveness which admirably conveys the strength with which he confronts pain, as when he bursts out despairingly at the thought of his own daughter's betrayal of himself, then begs for some relief in the same music to which, a little earlier, he had reflected upon the one treasure which remained to him: vengeance upon Mazepa (Ex. 186). Nevertheless, his end in the execution scene strikes less for

[43] Striking harmonic structures synthesized by mechanically repeated bass shifts occur elsewhere in Kochubey's music (see No. 6, bars 54–59, No. 8, bars 53–58).

Ex. 186

[Take my daughter with you, she herself will tell you all, will show you all my

treasures.

But for God's sake, I beg you, leave me now in peace. I am prepared to submit to Him who [will be]

[your terrible [judge]]

anything it uncovers of Kochubey's inner world than for the extremity of his plight. The execution itself is grimly effective, the preceding prayers calculated to elicit a strong, but basically sentimental response, while the vigorous folkchorus and earthy contributions of the drunken Cossack, admirable as they are (though Nápravník disapproved of the latter), afford simply ironic background for the gruesome end.

Yet for all the sympathy with which Tchaikovsky conveys Kochubey's feelings, it was with Mariya that he identified most fully. From the moment when she is left alone on stage to declare her passion for Mazepa, and thus commit herself to the emotion through which fate will claim her for its own, Tchaikovsky invests her with an abundance of emotional life, her declaration of love being substantiated orchestrally by a sudden upward sweep of melody and a surge into appoggiatura-fortified, flat-key regions which suggests a delirious excitement (Ex. 187) found nowhere in *The Oprichnik*. Yet her following aria, with its nervous melody broken into short segments, is highly strung rather than passionate, as is the first part of her following duet with Andrey. Though an altogether weaker creation than Kochubey, Andrey, like Mazepa, takes on extra life when fired by Mariya. Yet even in this duet he cannot match the expressive eloquence of Mariya's finely projected misery at the opening of the G minor section,[44] while in the second scene his response to Kochubey likewise has a cramping stiffness; the short-breathed, repetitive melody of his C minor andante arioso sounds almost prim, certainly small-scale against Kochubey's declarations. His big solo scene opens Act 3, but apart from devising conventionally agitated or broken-hearted music, Tchaikovsky can do

---

[44] The opening sixteen bars of this were one of the first passages in the opera to be composed. Tchaikovsky noted it down in his copy of the Obikhod, using as text his favourite first phrase from the tale of Francesca da Rimini in Dante's *Inferno*; he dated it 25 May 1881.

Ex. 187

[But I have only one pleasure; to hear Mazepa's voice and see his proud face!]

little for him. All, however, is transformed by Mariya's entrance. From this point to the end it is she who dominates the stage. Mazepa soon slips away, and the dying Andrey is little more than a vocal prop necessary for a situation which is to give his demented beloved full scope for a deeply affecting scena. And deeply affecting it certainly is. Our capacity for sentimental compassion is especially vulnerable to the spectacle of a ruined, crazed heroine, and Tchaikovsky was heir to a cultural tradition which had recently bred a healthy crop of such ladies, whose common habitat was ruins or wilderness, and whose characteristic call was maniacal laughter. It is easy to deride such creatures, but

Tchaikovsky took Mariya very seriously, and from the moment when she emerges from the trees into the moonlight, and a solo violin recalls her avowal of love which had opened the final section of the Act 2 love duet, the whole musical level rises and maintains its most consistent height. A melancholy phrase introduced by the oboe obsessively haunts the orchestral background to her plaintive ramblings; faced with this, Mazepa suddenly acquires some true emotional response in his tonally tortuous interjections. In the section in G flat (a key which Tchaikovsky had always associated in his operas with particularly intense emotion) she snatches at memories of her father's execution, then turns on Mazepa with bitter reproach and a confused sense of recognition, and ends the first part of this scena with a frenzied recall of the image of Mazepa as she had once known him, ironically returning to that portion of their love music in which she had hailed him as a future tsar (see Ex. 182), and in which her husband had checked her ambitious dreams of their future together: 'A storm is breaking; who can know what may be in store for me?'

By now Tchaikovsky is again on the threshold of writing great opera, as he had been in Kochubey's prison monologue and the Lyubov/Mariya duet, and his drastic revision of the remaining portion of this fine scene is confirmation that Mariya finally took a grip upon his creative being almost as firm as that which Tatyana had exercised some five years before. For the original production he had written a much longer, elaborate finale. At the moment when Mariya had begun her lullaby for the second and last time (significantly, perhaps, set in D flat, also Tatyana's very special key), the chorus had started to drift back and, perceiving Mariya, had pitied her plight. When she had recognized among the crowd the same girls who had invited her at the beginning of the opera to join them in divining their fortunes by casting garlands on to the river, Mariya had issued the same invitation to them, actually quoting from their $\frac{5}{4}$ chorus; then suddenly leaping up, with demented laughter she had plunged into the river. With more noise than action the chorus had expressed horror at this sudden turn of events, though some of the men had taken to canoes to recover the body, which they had then placed alongside Andrey's on the forestage. After lamentations over this 'unfortunate victim of fate', the crowd had implored God's blessing, while the offstage band had played part of the Petrine march which had ended the Poltava entr'acte. Brutalized orchestral echoes of the first bar of Mariya's lullaby had loudly closed the scene.

This end was irremediably stagy, as Tchaikovsky quickly perceived, and his solution was as simple as it was masterly: cut all this gratuitous tableau, extend Mariya's lullaby, and let her alone sing the opera towards silence, rocking in her arms the body of the man who, if fate had allowed, might have brought her happiness. The momentary resurgence a little earlier of the Ukrainian march and of the G minor portion of her Act 1 love duet (the latter also touchingly recalled during Andrey's earlier scene) had marked the moments when her disordered mind had fleetingly fastened on her father's execution and her days with Andrey. But such memories would remain for ever her only contact with the outside world; the present itself was now shut out for ever. Tatyana had retained a loving husband, and some hope of a future; Mariya is not only crushed and out of her mind, but withdrawn and alone. It is an end of consummate, unashamed pathos – and absolutely right.

A fortnight after finishing the last sketch of *Mazepa*, a letter arrived for Tchaikovsky addressed in a hand he had not seen for eleven years. The writer had been looking over some of Tchaikovsky's scores of the intervening period. 'I have rejoiced to see your talent developing and getting stronger,' he observed. 'Your apogee is your two symphonic poems, *The Tempest* and *Francesca da Rimini*, especially the latter.'[45] These excellent impressions afforded by past achievements had persuaded the writer that he should intervene in Tchaikovsky's creative life. 'I should be happy to see you, and I have a programme for a symphony to impart to you which you should handle superbly.'[46] Such an intention might, in view of Tchaikovsky's reputation, seem impertinent, and the unqualified warmth of his reply to this long-lost correspondent is therefore the more striking.

> I can say quite simply that if I should live another ten or twenty years without seeing you, I would still never forget you, nor cease to think of you affectionately as of one of the brightest and undoubtedly most upright and talented artistic personalities whom I have ever met.
>
> I thank you most heartily for your intention of suggesting to me a subject for a symphonic poem, and I rejoice in your sympathy.
>
> If I should be in St Petersburg I will certainly come to see you. My inclination to seclusion and a life outside society cannot, of course, extend so far that I should deny myself the pleasure of seeing you and

[45] *BVP*, p. 164.
[46] ibid.

talking with you, and your summoning me is sufficient for me to consider it a pleasant duty to present myself before you.[47]

Balakirev was re-entering Tchaikovsky's life – with momentous consequences, as the last chapter of this volume will show.

[47] *TLP*11, pp. 241–2; *BVP*, p. 164.

6

A TIME OF CHILDREN:

SECOND SUITE

ON 8 OCTOBER 1882, the Sunday after he had completed the sketches for *Mazepa*, Tchaikovsky journeyed to Kiev to collect from a bank the latest instalment of his patroness's allowance. As had been his practice whenever the opportunity had presented itself, he attended mass at the Brothers' Monastery. And as had happened several times before, he fled from the service before the end. For a couple of days he pondered whether to write openly to a newspaper, but finally decided to address himself privately and bluntly to the bishop about what had given him such offence.

The cause is none other than the singing of the Brothers' Monastery choir. It will probably surprise you, your Grace, that their singing, famed throughout Kiev as uncommonly beautiful, should irritate, pain, even horrify me. But the point is that, in my capacity as a Russian musician who is endeavouring to foster the cause of Russian church singing, and who has expended much thought upon the subject, I stand unfortunately (I make bold to say) above the level of general discernment in what I require of singing within the liturgy – and, in any case, am at extreme variance with the tastes not only of the Orthodox public, but also the majority of the clergy. Without going into historical details I will only observe briefly that, because of a fateful conjunction of circumstances, the sickly sweet style of eighteenth-century Italian music has, from the end of the last century, become established with us. This, in my opinion, does not conform with the requirements of church style in general, and in particular has no relationship either in spirit or structure with our Orthodox liturgy . . .

So what is to be done? You cannot alter history, and against my will I have reconciled myself with the established style of church music, even as far as not disdaining to take upon myself the editing of a new printing of the works of Bortnyansky, who is the initiator, albeit gifted, of this trend which is so false and alien. . . . I repeat, I have reconciled myself with it, but only within certain bounds. . . . Last Sunday . . . I listened reluctantly to that strange, mazurka-like, nauseatingly affected three-fold *Lord have mercy* . . . with rather less patience to the *Unction of grace*. . . . But when they opened the central doors of the iconostasis, and the singers gabbled on one chord *Praise God from the heavens* as though casting aside the heavy burden of praising God in favour of their obligation to entertain the public with concert music, and, summoning up their strength, began performing a long, mindless, shapeless concerto, based on an alien mode, trivial, without talent, overflowing with vocal tricks ill-befitting a place of worship, I experienced a surge of indignation which increased the more they sang. Now a bass solo bawled out in a wild, howling roar, now a solo treble began to squeal, then a snatch of a phrase from some sort of Italian trepak was heard, now an operatic love motif rang out with unnatural sweetness in the most rough, bare, tame harmonization, now the whole choir faded to an exaggeratedly delicate pianissimo, now began to roar, to bellow at the tops of their voices.

O God! And just where, at what moment did this musical orgy occur? Precisely at that moment when the central act of the whole religious ceremony was being enacted, when your Grace and your officiants administered the body and blood of Christ![1]

And so on for many more unsparing lines. Manifestly Tchaikovsky was still capable, when roused, of that flow of blistering invective he had sometimes poured out during his toils as a music critic in the early 1870s. Yet this was but one of the torments which the later months of 1882 held for him. The troubles in his sister's unsettled, sometimes turbulent household seemed to come in waves, and now another broke over Kamenka, for news came that Sasha, who was still in the south after the birth of Vera's child, was suffering from kidney stones, while at Kamenka itself Tanya was becoming anorexic, though her behaviour had improved a good deal ('because there aren't any men about,' her uncle noted tartly[2]). Tchaikovsky, as so often before, observed pityingly the burden these anxieties placed upon his brother-in-law. He was longing to go abroad, but his finances would not yet permit it and, in any case, he would have had to go alone. It is no wonder that in such fraught circumstances he should have envisaged an ultimate

[1] *TLP*11, pp. 233–4.
[2] *TLP*11, p. 220.

withdrawal to another environment. When he wrote to his servant Alexey, conjuring a vision of their future life together, he was not merely attempting to cheer a very low spirited conscript; he was fortifying himself with a vision of escape. 'I dream that, when you've finished your period of military service, if I'm still alive, I shall cease living in other people's homes, and will settle for ever in some pleasant spot somewhere in Moscow. The two of us will make our home in a nice comfortable apartment, and we'll live in clover. . . . I pray God that the two years will pass the more quickly, and that these dreams may be fulfilled.'[3] And so they were to be – almost exactly.

But the wave, having broken, passed, and a calm followed. Sasha returned home, seemingly in good health, and Tanya continued to make an effort to control herself which won her uncle's deep gratitude. Even the new tutor for two of Sasha's sons, whose advent had deprived Tchaikovsky of part of his accommodation, brought a bonus, since the new arrival was also an enthusiast for vint, a card game to which Tchaikovsky himself was addicted. For a while he was again reconciled to Kamenka life, especially since Modest, who was now marooned in St Petersburg because Kolya's education required the services of other teachers also, was chafing at his confinement, while in Moscow Anatoly was endlessly worrying about his own health and the condition of his wife, who was pregnant. Tchaikovsky told both brothers roundly that St Petersburg and Moscow were bad enough in themselves, but with a miserable brother demanding moral support in each they would be intolerable.

But then the next wave rolled over Kamenka. Blumenfeld appeared, and the weather broke. During the music teacher's stay he and Tanya returned to those intimacies which had so shocked Tchaikovsky during an earlier residence. It was this wilful niece who finally roused him to make escape from Kamenka his central obsession. At dinner one day he innocently observed he would be going to Moscow and St Petersburg. 'Suddenly Tanya turns to me and says: "I can go with you, can't I?" I don't know what I muttered in reply,' continued a panic-stricken Tchaikovsky to Modest on 13 November, 'but I know that for a moment the blood rushed to my head, and I must have gone terribly red. . . . The painfulness of the feelings I experience in regard of her is such that no pen can describe it. Not only am I incapable of spending two days travelling with her tête-à-tête, but even here, with a lot of people, I become positively *ill* when she enters a room I'm in.'[4] To

[3] *TLP*II, p. 219.
[4] *TLP*II, p. 272; *YDGC*, p. 281 (partial).

outmanoeuvre Tanya, he decided he would have to leave unfinished his scoring of the first act of *Mazepa*, and instead bolt from Kamenka during the three days the family were to be away at a social occasion; he would leave a note that Nápravník had summoned him to St Petersburg in connection with the revival of *The Maid*. But Sasha suddenly suffered a new eruption of kidney stones and the trip was cancelled. So instead Tchaikovsky announced that he would be travelling with Jurgenson to see the Prague revival of the same opera, and that he would have to meet his publisher in Kiev; from there he would write that the performance had been postponed, and that he had instead gone to Moscow. Under this pretext he left Kamenka on 27 November. He was painfully aware of his ever more changing feelings towards his sister's home. 'I've left my *nook* without any regret,' he wrote to Modest three days later. 'Its cosiness vanished once I had become surrounded on all sides by neighbours, and I confess returning to Kamenka is something I shan't want at all – and, you know, that's sad. Having nowhere my own home, incapable of settling down anywhere else in Russia, fearing loneliness when abroad, I'm now at last a sort of nomad – and this thought distresses me.'[5] In Kiev he fell ill, and it was 2 December before he arrived in Moscow. Meanwhile Kamenskaya, who had created Joan in *The Maid* in 1881, had insisted she would only sing in the St Petersburg revival if the entire part were converted into a true mezzo-soprano role. Effecting this, as well as making some cuts suggested by Nápravník, had already cost him ten days of work on *Mazepa*, and the scoring was behind schedule. It is therefore no surprise that the idea he had hatched two months before of drawing a concert suite out of *Swan Lake* slipped into oblivion.

Life in Moscow proved as distracting as he expected. He was dined by his old Conservatoire colleagues, and scrutinized with especially close interest the musical gifts of Max Erdmannsdörfer, for this Leipzig-trained conductor and former musical director at Sondershausen would now be Tchaikovsky's principal advocate in Russia's second city. 'He is a very skilful, very experienced and expert conductor,' he concluded to Nadezhda von Meck after a fortnight.

But I have to admit that the Muscovites overrate his accomplishments. He is now the fashion, but I doubt this will last long. His shortcomings are as follows: 1. He cares too much about external effects, and is inclined to indulge the public's taste for exaggerated nuances. Thus, for instance, his *pp*s are so quiet that sometimes

[5] *TLP*11, p. 285.

neither the harmony nor the melody is at all audible, only a shadow of the sound being heard. This is terribly effective, but hardly artistic.
2. He is too much *a German*. His programmes are too German, and he doesn't play French music at all, for instance – and he is offhanded in his attitude to Russian music (except mine).[6]

Tchaikovsky had been quick to make Erdmannsdörfer's acquaintance, and readily recognized his flair for establishing a good relationship both with his fellow-professionals and the public. But for Tchaikovsky there was a painful side to the enthusiasm with which the RMS audience reciprocated, as he confided to his patroness: 'It is as though it [the audience] is trying to show it rates him much higher than Nik[olay] Grig[oryevich], whom it never received so enthusiastically. Not only has Moscow in general already acclimatized itself, as it were, to the loss of Nik[olay] Grig[oryevich], but it has begun to forget him. That is sad.'[7] The personal poignancy of this circumstance was heightened by attendance at a mass for Rubinstein, followed next day by a further requiem at the graveside.

In Moscow Tchaikovsky put the finishing touches to his All-night Vigil, and was also able to hear extracts from it at a public concert. He was greatly flattered that Pavel Tretyakov, a director of the Moscow RMS, and one of the founders of the picture gallery which still bears his name, should wish to augment the collection with a portrait of him by Vladimir Makovsky, though for this Tchaikovsky had to endure the penance of four long sittings.[8] He saw Alexey and was relieved to find that he was now reconciled to army life for the next two years. He was determined not to leave Moscow until the first act of *Mazepa* was scored, but it was 24 December before this was done. The next day he set out for St Petersburg to join a very impatient Modest. Here he met again Laroche, was deeply impressed by the performance of Lucien Guitry in the name part of Daudet's *Jack*, and revelled in a fine production of *Carmen* at the Maryinsky Theatre. He would have left the capital earlier, but illness enforced a delay. To his relief he saw little of Tanya, who was also in the city but installed with other relatives. On 9 January 1883 he slipped away en route for Berlin.

'I always adore Berlin when I'm travelling from Russia, though I can't bear it when I'm returning home,' he observed buoyantly to Modest. '. . . What a delight to be able to take a walk without being afraid of meeting people I know. . . . I'm enjoying *being abroad* exactly as

[6] *TLP*11, p. 293; *TPM*3, p. 128; *TZC*2, p. 564.
[7] *TLP*11, p. 287; *TPM*3, pp. 123–4; *TZC*2, pp. 562–3.
[8] The portrait subsequently disappeared, and no copy of it is known.

I did twenty-one years ago when I went for the first time.'[9] The one Berlin resident he did intend to see was Kotek, with whom his relations had become strained through the violinist's failure for so long to perform the concerto he had inspired five years before. But each day of his stay Tchaikovsky could not bring himself to call, and he ended by promising himself that he would make good this omission on the return journey, a resolution he did not keep. He stayed longer than expected in order to see *Tristan* for the first time in his life. He had heard that 'bad piece',[10] the *Siegfried Idyll*, on the eve of his departure from Moscow, but this performance of *Tristan* was a far more substantial opportunity to check the judgment on Wagner he had delivered so forcefully after the Bayreuth experience of six-and-a-half years earlier. It had not changed. 'I did not like the opera at all,' he began his broadside to Nadezhda von Meck.

... To make us listen four hours on end to an interminable symphony, rich in sumptuous orchestral colours but poor in ideas clearly and simply stated: to make singers for four hours on end perform not independent melodies but melodic fragments appended to that symphony (in addition to which, these fragments, though high in tessitura, are not infrequently swallowed up in the orchestra's thunder) – this, surely, is not the ideal towards which contemporary composers ought to be striving. Wagner has transferred the centre of gravity from the stage to the orchestra, and because this is a manifest absurdity, then his celebrated reform of the opera signifies nothing if you discount the above-mentioned negative consequences.[11]

He was convinced the audience was bored throughout, despite their favourable reception of each act, and he offered his patroness his own explanation for this troubling contradiction. 'It was probably a patriotic sympathy towards the composer, who has indeed dedicated his whole life to waxing poetic about Germanism.'[12] Yet, curiously, *Tristan*'s spell still seems to have lingered with Tchaikovsky, for just as *Der Ring* had conditioned *Francesca da Rimini* in 1876, so this other hateful creation of Wagner may well have contributed to the opening of the piece in which, in 1885, Tchaikovsky was to rediscover fully his own individual voice.

Tchaikovsky received more than adequate compensation for this

[9] *TLP*11, p. 303; *TZC*2, p. 565; *TPB*, pp. 290–1.
[10] *TLP*11, p. 293; *TPM*3, p. 128; *TZC*2, p. 564; *YDGC*, p. 283.
[11] *TLP*11, p. 304; *TPM*3, p. 131; *TZC*2, pp. 565–6.
[12] ibid.

unpalatable operatic experience when he settled in Paris on 14 January. 'I have just returned from the Opéra Comique, where I have heard *Le Nozze di Figaro* for the second time [since my arrival], and if there are to be more performances, then I shall go again, and again, and again,' he began one of his periodic bursts of Mozart enthusiasm to Nadezhda von Meck on 23 January.

> I know my worship of Mozart surprises you, dear friend. And even I myself am surprised that a man as flawed as I, not completely healthy either mentally or morally, has been able to preserve his ability to delight in Mozart, who possesses neither the depth nor the strength of Beethoven, neither the warmth nor the passion of Schumann, nor the brilliance of Meyerbeer, Berlioz, Wagner, etc. . . . Mozart neither overwhelms nor stuns me – but he captivates me, makes me happy, warms me. When I hear his music it is as though I am doing a good deed . . . and the longer I live, the more I get to know him, the more I love him.'[13]

During the previous performance of the opera Tchaikovsky had encountered the Grand Duke Konstantin Nikolayevich, and fearing this would be the preliminary to a dizzying social round, he was reduced to pretending that he would be leaving Paris in a couple of days. Modest was soon to join him – without Kolya this time – and in the meantime his single aim was to proceed with the scoring of *Mazepa* as expeditiously as possible. In any case, Paris was the one city in which Tchaikovsky knew he could be alone yet content. Quickly he established a routine which included frequent visits to the theatre. His old favourite, Musset's *On ne badine pas avec l'amour*, was but one of the pleasures offered by the Comédie-Française, though the most powerful impression of these first Paris days came from yet another of Sarah Bernhardt's performances, this time in Sardou's *Fédora* at the Vaudeville. Tchaikovsky had planned, after Modest's arrival, to spend some further days in Paris, and then to proceed with his brother to Rome. But Modest's arrival on 28 January brought an utterly unexpected and unpleasant shock. With him was Tanya. The declared purpose of her visit was that she should be placed under the supervision of the distinguished neurologist, Jean-Martin Charcot, in the hope of curing her morphine addiction. Since she would have to stay in Paris at least until the spring, Tchaikovsky accepted gloomily that he and Modest were also condemned to remain.

[13] *TLP*12, p. 27; *TPM*3, p. 139; *TZC*2, pp. 568–9; *YDGC*, p. 285 (partial).

Then work on scoring *Mazepa* was interrupted to complete the first of a batch of three commissions relating to the coronation of Tsar Alexandr III for whom, as Tsarevich, Tchaikovsky had composed his very first occasional piece, the Danish Festival Overture. Even before he had journeyed to Paris, Nikolay Alexeyev, a director of the Moscow branch of the RMS, had asked him to arrange the Slavsya Chorus from Glinka's *A Life for the Tsar* to be sung by a gargantuan choir of 7,500 students on the Red Square while the Tsar was crossing to enter the Kremlin. After four verses sung to the Slavsya tune Tchaikovsky was to devise a link leading to the Russian national anthem. The choir was to sing in unison, and the accompaniment would be for string orchestra. Tchaikovsky rebelled against the first condition, arguing that instinct and custom would cause some choralists to devise supporting lines of their own, and that if the spectators joined in this famous tune, as well they might, some of them would try to sing in parts also. Mindful of the vocal limitations of most of his singers and of the problems posed by the venue, Tchaikovsky completed the piece on 16 February, and promptly despatched it to Jurgenson. His own judgment on his labours is clear from the covering letter.

> In all this the only free *composition* is a few bars of transition, and also the third couplet of the text. The amount I should receive from the city of Moscow which, as you put it, is going to fork out a large sum for me, is as follows:

For simplifying the choral parts and orchestrating sixteen bars, repeated three times	–	3 roubles
For composing eight bars of transition to the hymn	–	4 roubles
For composing four lines for the third couplet, at 40 kopecks a line	–	1 rouble 60 kopecks
Total:		8 roubles, 60 kopecks

> These eight roubles, sixty kopecks I donate to the city of Moscow. No, but seriously – it's ridiculous even to raise the question of payment for such work, and I'd find it distasteful. Such things are to be done gratis, or not done at all.[14]

The requests for the remaining pieces arrived some three weeks later. 'The city of Moscow has commissioned from me a ceremonial march to

[14] *TLP*12, p. 57; *TZC*2, p. 572; *TPJ*1, p. 280. Only the chorus parts appear to have survived.

be played at the festivities which are to be organized for the Tsar at the Sokolniky Park, and the coronation commission has sent me the text written by Maikov for a big cantata which they have pressed me to compose. . . . My first thought was to refuse,' he confided to Nadezhda von Meck on 21 March, 'but then I decided I had at all costs to try to fulfil both commissions on time. I know from reliable sources that the Tsar is very disposed towards me (that is, to my music), and I would not want it to reach him that I *had refused*.'[15] The first approach for the cantata commission had been made to Anton Rubinstein, but he had declined because of the pressure of other commitments, and had suggested Tchaikovsky. Anxious to get these interruptions to *Mazepa* out of the way, Tchaikovsky applied himself to both without delay. The march was done first; it is, as might be expected, a thoroughly efficient response to the requirements of the situation, and it was conducted by Taneyev on 4 June, thirteen days after the Slavsya concoction had failed to impress because of the noise made by the spectators on the Red Square.

But the third piece was musically something much more than either of these works, as Tchaikovsky recognized. 'The march is noisy but bad . . . but the cantata is not nearly as poor as might be thought, considering how quickly it was composed,' he wrote to Taneyev.[16] Six days before, on 7 April, while still in the throes of composition, he had explained to his patroness what had fired him. 'The text Maikov has written for the cantata is very beautiful and poetic. There is a bit of patriotic vapouring, but apart from this the piece is deeply felt and written with originality. It has freshness and its tone is sincere, which is making it possible for me, too, somehow not only to stand aside from the difficulties of the task but, as long as I observe a proper decorum, to put into my music a measure of the feeling warmed in me by Maikov's beautiful lines.'[17] He had sufficient confidence in its musical virtues to hope it might be repeated at one of the RMS concerts in Moscow. Its première took place in the Kremlin on 27 May during the ceremonial act which immediately followed the coronation, when the Tsar dined alone in the presence of the others who had taken part in the main ceremony; the performers were the chorus and orchestra of the Bolshoy Theatre, conducted by Nápravník. Tchaikovsky had decided to accept payment for neither commission, for he remembered how indebted he had been to the Tsar when, two years before, he had solicited from

[15] *TLP*12, p. 80; *TPM*3, p. 159; *TZC*2, p. 576.
[16] *TLP*12, p. 102; *DTC*, p. 280; *TTP*, p. 97.
[17] *TLP*12, p. 97; *TPM*3, pp. 166–7; *DTC*, p. 280 (partial); *YDGC*, pp. 289–90 (partial).

Alexandr an advance of 3,000 roubles against future royalties for performances of his works in the Imperial Theatres, and had received instead the whole sum as a gift. In any case, if it was the city of Moscow which was commissioning the march, then the sum of 500 roubles being offered was an insult. Nevertheless, Alexandr himself now gave instructions that Tchaikovsky was to receive 1,500 roubles for his coronation offerings, but decided to disburse this in the form of a ring, just as he had for the Danish Festival Overture eighteen years earlier. Being currently insolvent, a dismayed Tchaikovsky promptly pawned the gift for 375 roubles, and on the same day lost both money and redemption ticket. The sole gain he made from his efforts was, as he shamefacedly told Nadezhda von Meck, 'a feeling of having committed some sort of improper act'.[18]

The cantata *Moscow* was the third and last of Tchaikovsky's major essays in the form, and it was by far the best. The first had been his 1865 graduation exercise on Schiller's 'An die Freude', while the second was composed for the opening of an exhibition celebrating the bicentenary of the birth of Peter the Great. Saddled with a poor text, Tchaikovsky had been able to find little to prompt musical inspiration in 1872, but Maikov's lines for *Moscow* were a very different matter. They sketched the history of the ancient capital from its peaceful origins through times of trouble to its peak of glory and its self-appointed role as protector of other Slav peoples. Their structure was simple and economical, their rhythms and images alive, and they unlocked in Tchaikovsky a vein of true, if less than first-rate lyricism, well able to support an extensive text without recourse to the shock treatment of abrupt tonal shifts or the grandiloquence of pedantic counterpoint, through which he had attempted to animate his earlier cantatas. And Tchaikovsky's music has not only much freshness; it is also impregnated with Russian intonations, at times intermittent and veiled, but at others sustained and explicit. Significantly, he had been concerned with Glinka's *A Life for the Tsar* in discharging the first of his coronation commissions, and during the cantata it becomes clear that within its fabric there lurk certain contexts from this opera so beloved by Tchaikovsky – above all, the opening phrase of the noble fourth act monologue in which Susanin greets his last dawn on this earth (Ex. 188b; the protoshape against which this and Tchaikovsky's derivatives are conceived is outlined in Ex. 188a). Yet it is Tchaikovsky's own *1812* overture which seems to have prompted the short andante religioso introduction for divided cellos. At the più mosso the mood becomes credibly arcadian; most

[18] *TLP*12, p. 199; *TPM*3, p. 203.

Ex. 188

[c, e, f, g, h and k are transposed]

striking here is the engaging flexibility of the choral phrases (Ex. 189a), and this flexibility is enhanced when the opening music later returns in three- instead of two-beat bars (Ex. 189b). The reduction to men's voices only, together with an increased agitation in the fertile orchestral ornamentation, is sufficient to signal the arrival of the alien hordes rolling wave after wave across Russia, and the voices finally die away as impenetrable night descends on Moscow, their concluding two-pitch phrase being taken up by the horns and hauntingly coupled with the

Ex. 189

a.

[From a tiny freezing spring there flowed a river.]

b.

[Is it really possible for Russia to perish in a cruel death?]

c.

[...impenetrable!]

[*In a and b the orchestral part is omitted*]

receding sounds of the chorus's opening theme (Ex. 189c). It is here that the first echo of Susanin is heard, for the horns finally give birth to a cadential phrase (Ex. 188c) whose outline summarizes Glinka's opening; it is surely not coincidence that it also comes close to the initial contour of the Russian national anthem, the other element which had featured in Tchaikovsky's first coronation offering (Ex. 188i). And out of this cadential fragment there flowers, in the most unaffected way, the following mezzo-soprano arioso (Ex. 188d). Quietly Moscow recovers, becoming a beacon to the surrounding peoples, and this rebirth is joyfully celebrated in the rousing chorus of the third movement. But the blessing of security and prosperity should be extended to brothers, and in the baritone monologue of the fourth movement the warrior of Moscow (a lightly masked symbol of Alexandr himself) goes forth to encounter the heavy plight of the Serbs, Montenegrins and Bulgarians. The echoes from *A Life for the Tsar* are now clearer, for not only is the baritone's succinct opening phrase (Ex. 188e) fathered by Susanin's monologue: it is also apparent that the brief imitative passage for strings which precedes this is conceived against the background of the fugal outburst in the opening chorus of Glinka's first opera (Ex. 188j and k record Glinka's and Tchaikovsky's phrases; Glinka's phrase is, in its turn, related to Susanin's opening). As for the baritone solo, Tchaikovsky here builds an arioso of imposing power, capped by the solid intervention of the chorus to echo the final words: 'Truly it is said of Moscow: "Two Romes have fallen – a third stands – there shall not be a fourth!"'. The orchestra celebrates the grandeur of this sentiment in a sonorous coda generated from yet another relative of the Susanin shape (Ex. 188f) and, even more, of the Russian anthem. The mezzo-soprano in the fifth movement also sings with a national accent as she voices the hero's sober reflections upon the responsibilities he must shoulder, shaping her opening (Ex. 188g) against a portion of the Susanin phrase, and then in the brief middle section pointedly borrowing the baritone's beginning when she ponders the possible fateful consequences paralleling those which had so implacably faced Susanin: 'If I am destined to die in battle, I am prepared to meet death face to face.' Then, to the music of her first section, she makes the act of dedication. In his preamble to the finale the baritone picks up thematic fragments from what has gone before, exhorting the people to brotherhood, truth and courage, and the chorus replies, finally rounding off the cantata with a shout of praise built from reiterations of yet another theme generated from the Susanin protoshape (Ex. 188h). Only in the noisy pealings of this finale does Tchaikovsky's response to a patriotic duty begin to sound dutiful; for the rest, *Moscow* is a piece with an attractiveness sufficient to merit it an occasional hearing, especially since, translated, it would be by no means difficult to perform.

The composition of these coronation commissions was not the only matter which slowed Tchaikovsky's progress on scoring *Mazepa*. Tanya's arrival had produced instant despondency, and a whole series of anxieties further distracted him at different times. Anatoly's wife was in the final stages of pregnancy, Sasha was still ailing in Kamenka, then Alexey fell seriously ill in Moscow. The expenses of Tanya's accommodation and treatment had been unforeseen, and the financial situation quickly deteriorated. Fearing, for a reason which will emerge later, to apply to Kamenka for the full cost of Tanya's budget, he looked in desperation to his patroness for a two-month advance on his allowance, to which she responded with customary alacrity. But these funds in due course became exhausted, and Tchaikovsky now turned to Jurgenson, extracting from him two sums of 1,000 roubles each to supplement the modest 600 roubles Tanya's father had despatched. 'I am a victim of fate, against which you can do nothing,' he was finally to reflect in self-justification.[19]

It was not long before Tchaikovsky was tiring of Paris itself, visiting the theatre less frequently and deriving even less pleasure from the local music. The death of Wagner on 13 February meant that the city's concert life was suddenly swamped by his works. 'The French are really funny! While Wagner was alive they didn't want to know him; now all the concerts are full of his works, and the furore is indescribable. You have to die to earn the attention of Paris,' he concluded sourly to Anatoly on 9 March.[20] This was not quite true, for an equal storm was being created by Saint-Saëns' new opera, *Henri VIII*, which had received its première at the Opéra four days before. Yet the French composer's success only deepened Tchaikovsky's pessimism over prospects for his own latest opera. 'I feel, I know that my *Mazepa* is much better than Saint-Saëns', and yet my opera will get no farther than the filthy stage of the Maryinsky, and I shall receive a miserable pittance for it,' he reflected.[21] He left Paris still ignorant of *Henri VIII*, but he did see *Figaro* at least four times, and was reduced to tears by Gounod's *Roméo et Juliette*. The death of Flotow had created a vacancy in the Académie des Beaux Arts for a foreign corresponding member, and Gounod had supported Tchaikovsky as one of five nominees for the place. But it was to be nearly ten more years before he gained election.

Predictably his longing to be back in Russia grew. Then he was troubled by a nagging conscience over Antonina. 'Perhaps I'm not acting completely impeccably in finally casting to the mercy of fate the unhappy being who is joined to me by the bonds of, as it were, matrimony. Now more and more often this thought disturbs me. If this being is in need, if she has been deserted by her lover (which is

[19] *TLP*12, p. 147; *TPJ*1, p. 303.
[20] *TLP*12, p. 70; *TPB*, p. 291; *TPM*3, p. 621; *TZC*2, p. 576.
[21] ibid.

exceedingly likely) and she's nowhere to lay her head, then I must come to her aid,' he wrote to Jurgenson on 12 March. 'And so I want to ask you to get hold of that gentleman who has already been employed to enquire about her, and again entrust him with seeking her out and discovering whether she needs material help. If so, then she must certainly be given money. Forgive me that I am imposing on your friendship.'[22] Nor was Antonina the only one to stir his compassion. Some weeks earlier he had received a letter from a Mrs Loginova who, as Mariya Palchikova, had once taught him the piano. She was in difficulties, and Tchaikovsky requested Jurgenson to send her fifty roubles against his account, for he remembered it was she who, over thirty-five years earlier, had begun his musical education.

But the chief preoccupation remained Tanya. She had been installed in a maison de santé, and Elizaveta Molas, a former governess in the Konradi household, had been hastily engaged from St Petersburg to act as nurse and companion. Since Tanya's personal maid, Sasha, was also in attendance and could give support to Elizaveta, the brothers felt able to take turns in visiting their niece on alternate days. Each stage of progressive withdrawal of the morphine caused violent physical and emotional reaction in the patient, and this was distressing to the spectators. Yet on other days Tanya would be in good spirits, able to enjoy the pleasures of Paris and accompany her uncle Modest to the theatre. Tchaikovsky himself was grateful for the appearance of Kondratyev for a fortnight at the end of March, though he was alarmed at the signs of premature age already appearing in this disorderly but engaging friend. But by now it was becoming imperative that Modest should return to Kolya in St Petersburg. Reluctant to leave his elder brother to cope with Tanya alone, he delayed his return until Tchaikovsky himself insisted he must go. On 18 April Modest finally left.

No one reading the copious letters which Tchaikovsky had written during the last eleven weeks could have guessed the event which he himself knew perfectly well was facing him. There had, in fact, been a far more compelling reason which had caused Modest to bring Tanya to Paris. She was pregnant by Blumenfeld. So far the secret had been guarded with extraordinary efficiency. Even Tanya's parents knew nothing about it. Modest was one of the first to be told, but he had withheld the information from his composer-brother while the latter was still in St Petersburg, and had told him nothing of the plan to bring their niece to Paris. Since it was imperative that Tanya should receive

[22] *TLP*12, pp. 72–3; *TPJ*1, p. 285.

Mily Balakirev
(1880)

Vladimir Stasov
(*c*.1870)

Alexandra [Sasha] Davïdova and
Nataliya [Nata] Pleskaya

Nikolay and Anna
[née Davïdova] von Meck

Tchaikovsky
in 1884

Tatyana [Tanya]
Davïdova

Above: Max
Erdmannsdörfer

Right: Eduard
Nápravník

Praskovya [Parasha]
Tchaikovskaya

treatment for her morphine addiction, the search for a cure through consultation with a distinguished – and distant – authority became the convincing excuse for removing her from Russia. Modest had to confide in his elder brother when he arrived in the French capital, but the secret was to remain until much later between them, Tanya's maid, Sasha, and Elizaveta Molas. Thus Tchaikovsky's letters to the family in Russia dealt solely with the cure for addiction, and when these are set beside the generally favourable reports on Tanya's health written to Modest after the latter had returned to Russia, there is some suspicion that the earlier accounts of Tanya's predicament and sufferings had been much heightened for the benefit of the family back home. In addition an operation to treat a condition resulting from the addiction was fabricated, presumably to account for the expense of the confinement, and to cover the possibility of death in childbirth.

Tchaikovsky's composure as the event neared is impressive, but he had every reason to believe that Elizaveta and Sasha could cope with everything more than competently. This they did. Being now without Modest, he found work on *Mazepa* an antidote for the loneliness of his situation, and his progress, both in scoring the opera and in devising the vocal score, accelerated accordingly. He did, however, find time to visit the recently opened exhibition of nineteenth-century portraits at the Académie des Beaux Arts ('very interesting and completely to my taste', he told Modest[23]), and he was also reading much, particularly enjoying Maupassant's recent collection of stories, *Mademoiselle Fifi*, and Zola's *Au bonheur des dames*.

The baby, a boy who was to be baptized Georges-Léon, was born at one o'clock on the morning of 8 May, the day after Tchaikovsky's own forty-third birthday. When he called at the maison de santé later that morning and saw Tanya with her son, he was struck by the strength of his own feelings towards this infant against whose arrival in this world he had seemed so steadfastly to set his thoughts. He had become aware of these emotions the day before: 'now I experienced them tenfold, and I told Tanya that while I had life in me she need have no worry on his [Georges-Léon's] account.'[24] He was the more upset, therefore, by the equanimity with which Tanya viewed the event and its implications, especially the prospect of having to live a lie when she returned to her parents' home. Tchaikovsky himself attended to the formalities of registering the birth and arranging the child's baptism. For the moment he was teased by the idea that he might himself in due course

[23] *TLP*12, p. 132; *TPB*, p. 296; *YDGC*, p. 292.
[24] *TLP*12, p. 140.

assume responsibility for the boy. But within a few days the wet nurse had borne Georges-Léon away to her home south of Paris at Villeneuve. He was to be kept in France for three years until, in 1886, Tchaikovsky's brother Nikolay and his wife adopted him.

The speed with which Georges-Léon had made his entrance and exit left Tchaikovsky suddenly free to plan his own departure from Paris. Tanya was to stay for a further six weeks, but with such sensible supervision as Elizaveta Molas could give, her uncle felt no unease about returning to Russia. Other causes, too, contributed to his much better mood. Anatoly's wife had been safely delivered of a daughter, Alexey had been granted a whole year's leave to recover from his illness, and *Mazepa* was finished. Together with Elizaveta he visited the wet nurse at her home in Villeneuve and returned fully confident that Georges-Léon would be well cared for. Preoccupations with the child's welfare could not prevent him inspecting the cathedral at Sens, where they had to spend a night on the return journey; Tchaikovsky rose at six the next morning to visit 'this vast, wonderful building', as he judged it to Modest.[25] And while in Paris he had heard that Jurgenson had been approached by the publishing house of Hamelle for French rights to the Piano Trio. Jurgenson, whose view of publishing was never timid, set the fee at 1,000 francs; expecting to be beaten down, he heard instead that Hamelle accepted the price, requesting in addition that Tchaikovsky's three works for violin and orchestra should be sold to him.

From the beginning of his time in Paris Nadezhda von Meck had been pressing Tchaikovsky to stay on her new estate at Pleshcheyevo near Moscow, and he had at first been much tempted by the idea, since it would be within easy distance of Anatoly and his wife. But his enthusiasm had progressively diminished, for it would also probably mean that he would be constantly visited by her sons and pestered for tuition by Pachulski. While in Paris he had received a batch of the latter's efforts, and though he had scrutinized them with that exemplary thoroughness and kindly rigour which seems to have marked all his teaching, he felt an increasing despair at Pachulski's lack of any gift for composition. Yet his own desperately straitened circumstances compelled him to think of spending the summer either as a guest or where the expenses would be minimal; the question of whether he should tear up his roots in Kamenka could not, therefore, yet be resolved. Anatoly had rented a villa at Podushkino outside Moscow, and Tchaikovsky excused himself from coming to Pleshcheyevo until the autumn, plead-

[25] *TLP*12, p. 157.

ing that his brother had prior claim to his company. Being again nearly penniless, he applied for a loan from brother Nikolay to pay his travel expenses, but this proved insufficient to cover also all Tanya's needs, and yet again his patroness's help had to be sought. On 22 May he left Paris. His parting act was to pen a letter to the newspaper *Gaulois*, clarifying Anton Rubinstein's position in the pre-history of the coronation cantata. Aware that rumours were impugning Rubinstein's patriotism in the matter, he rose strongly to the defence of his former teacher by publicly setting the record straight. His return through Berlin offered him a far more palatable Wagnerian experience than had his previous passage: a performance of that 'best of all *Wagner's* works', *Lohengrin*.[26] But Berlin itself seemed very provincial and barren when compared with Paris. On 27 May, the day his cantata was being offered to the Tsar in Moscow, he arrived in St Petersburg.

The relief felt by Tchaikovsky on leaving Paris was enormous, especially since he had the prospect of extended relaxation before him. The coronation taking place in Moscow had virtually emptied the Russian capital of those people he was always in fear of encountering; to have such freedom was compensation enough for missing the première of his cantata, especially since he was subsequently reassured that both performance and reception had been excellent. The fine weather and the chance of visiting favourite places with Modest and Kolya caused him to delay his departure for Podushkino, and it was 11 June before he was with Anatoly. He found that family life had wrought a vast improvement in this brother. The absence of Anatoly's former excitability and fussiness delighted him; so did his new niece (also called Tanya) and the presence of Alexey, as well as the news that Anna Davïdova and Nikolay von Meck were now officially betrothed. The location chosen by Anatoly for their summer residence proved idyllic. 'I am like a child revelling in all these delights,' he informed his patroness two days after his arrival, 'and literally the whole day yesterday I roamed through the surrounding woods.'[27] Every day, when circumstances permitted, he would collect mushrooms. He paid visits to Moscow to see Kondratyev and Vladimir Shilovsky, with whom his relations had recently been strained, as well as to deal with more weighty matters. Among these was a session with Pachulski, whose new symphony drove Tchaikovsky to the brink of telling him the blunt truth about his lack of talent. He took counsel about this with Nikolay von Meck, who was also in Moscow. 'For God's sake don't say anything;

---

[26] *TLP*12, p. 164; *TPM*3, p. 185; *TZC*2, p. 587; *YDGC*, p. 294.
[27] *TLP*12, p. 170; *TPM*3, p. 190.

mother will be terribly upset,' was the reply,[28] and Tchaikovsky remained silent not merely out of self-interest, but because his benefactress was already deeply distressed by the death of her youngest son, Mikhail, only days before.

Sympathy for the needs of others also impelled him to intercede with Karl Davïdov, director of the St Petersburg Conservatoire, on behalf of Laroche in the hope that appointment as professor of music history might help draw him out of the lethargy in which he still languished. He was very upset, too, that Nikolay Hubert, having been driven from the directorship of the Moscow Conservatoire by the recent troubles, had severed all connection with the institution. He knew Hubert was no administrator, but he acknowledged his gifts as a teacher, and he was alarmed at the idea that the twenty-two-year-old Anton Arensky should become head of the Conservatoire's theoretical studies, even though he already recognized Arensky's prodigious musical endowments. It was now five years since he himself had resigned from the Conservatoire, but it had been a major factor in his own past, and under Nikolay Rubinstein it had become an indispensable part of the musical life not only of Moscow but of Russia itself. A little earlier, while in Paris, he had been approached through Jurgenson to rejoin the staff, but even the bait of a two-room flat of his own could not entice him. Nevertheless, the surge of concern he felt for his old institution now drove him to devote several days to acting as an intermediary in trying to make possible Hubert's return to the professoriate. The hope proved impracticable, but since his plea to Davïdov on Laroche's behalf had been unfruitful, he was at length able (though with much misgiving) to persuade the Moscow Conservatoire to offer Hubert's vacant place to this long-standing but sadly unstable friend.

Tchaikovsky's period of relative relaxation was finally broken in early July when the proofs of *Mazepa* began to arrive. And once more his creative urges were proving irrepressible. 'I am also beginning to do a little work on a new suite, but I do not intend to hurry,' he confided to Nadezhda von Meck on 9 July[29]. But there would have been little time for this, even if his inspiration had been flowing freely. As has already been recorded, simultaneous productions of *Mazepa* were planned in Moscow and St Petersburg, and the roles were being allocated; thus the printed vocal score was urgently needed. To make matters worse, the engravings were deplorably inaccurate, and Tchaikovsky lamented bitterly that publishers in Russia did not have the excellent professional

[28] *TLP*12, p. 179; *TPM*3, p. 622.
[29] *TLP*12, p. 181; *TPM*3, p. 194; *TZC*2, p. 591; *DTC*, p. 400; *YDGC*, p. 296. In fact the sketches for the piece indicate he had actually started work on 13 June.

proof-readers who lightened the composer's task in Western Europe. Nor could he do anything about the constant procession of guests who visited Podushkino, and he found himself inescapably drawn into return invitations. In such conditions projected activities like resuming his study of the English language and exploring unknown Mozart had to be shelved.

So also, he decided, would he have to abandon his original plan to visit Pleshcheyevo that autumn. For the fact is that, ever since leaving Paris, he had been missing Kamenka badly, and the reproaches he constantly received from that quarter decided him that he should travel to the Ukraine for an extended stay. Pleshcheyevo would have to wait until the next spring, for in November rehearsals for *Mazepa* would demand his presence first in Moscow, then in St Petersburg, after which he planned to end the winter recovering in Italy. Tanya was remaining in Paris longer than expected, and by borrowing from his servant and his sister-in-law he scraped together some 200 roubles to send to her for maintenance of Georges-Léon. But the disaster with the Tsar's ring compelled him yet again to turn for an advance to his benefactress. By mid-August, having read three sets of proofs of *Mazepa*, he was suffering from nervous headaches and a persisting mild fever. Yet even now he could not rest; 'the demon of composition has taken possession of me with invincible power,' he wrote to Nadezhda von Meck,[30] and when he left Podushkino on 13 September, the sketches of the Second Suite were complete. After two days in Moscow, he headed for Kiev where, despite his outburst of the previous year to the bishop, he again attended mass at the Brothers' Monastery. Before leaving the city he bought a copy of Cui's opera, *A Prisoner in the Caucasus*, and of the First String Quartet by the eighteen-year-old Alexandr Glazunov. His judgments upon the two works were very divergent – and, one suspects, hardly impartial, for memories of the critical manglings he had received (and still was receiving) from one of the composers gnawed at him to the end of his life. Glazunov's work pleasantly surprised him. 'Despite its imitation of [Rimsky-]Korsakov, its unbearable way of restricting itself to countless repetitions of an idea in a thousand keys instead of *developing* it, despite its contempt for melody and its exclusive pursuit of harmonic curiosi-ties, a remarkable talent is discernible. The form is so fluent I'm astounded, and I suspect his teacher helped him,' he told Modest. '. . . I also bought *A Prisoner in the Caucasus*. This is trivial in the extreme, weak, childishly naïve – but, most of all, it's odd that a critic who has all his life persecuted *routine* should, in his declining years, produce an

[30] *TLP*12, p. 208; *TPM*3, p. 209; *TZC*2, p. 596.

opera so unashamedly *routine*.'[31] On 17 September he was in Kamenka; the next day he transferred to the much more congenial surroundings of Verbovka.

Tchaikovsky remained at Sasha's home for the next two and a half months. His first objective was to score his Second Suite; as he had explained to Nadezhda von Meck at the beginning of September, if it was not ready by the beginning of the winter season, he would not be able to discover how it sounded during his time in Moscow, which he was most anxious to do 'because I have used some new orchestral combinations which interest me greatly'.[32] The fact that he took more than five weeks to complete this operation, despite sometimes devoting six hours a day to it, is proof enough of the care he took. Even when the inevitable fatigue began to weigh on him, he remained convinced that the *Scherzo burlesque* and *Rêves d'enfant* at least would receive approbation. The work was finished on 25 October, and Erdmannsdörfer conducted the first performance on 16 February the next year in Moscow, where it had a success so brilliant that it had to be repeated a week later. But if the composer's eagerness to hear how it would sound was satisfied, then this must have been during rehearsal; at the performance itself he was absent. As already noted, the tensions of the première of *Mazepa* the previous evening had proved too much for him, and he had left for the West to recover.

The Second Suite is not a great piece, but it is a fascinating one, and very different from its predecessor. Why Tchaikovsky conceived it as he did is not as readily apparent as in the case of the First Suite, where the use of specific pre-classical types (Introduction and Fugue, and Gavotte) as the outer movements had defined the model as baroque, despite the expanses of Tchaikovskyan melody in the central movements – and despite his declared intention, when he started work on it, that it should be in the style of Lachner. The liberal doses of contrapuntalism in the Second Suite's opening *Jeu de sons* might suggest a parallel course in prospect, but this time the model is classical, with the allegro molto vivace designed as a sonata structure. For all its contrapuntal labours, the first subject still displays the Tchaikovskyan paradigm of tonic flanks with an extensive quasi-developmental centre. An explicit fugue provides a tonally undramatic substitute for the development, while the recapitulation is telescoped by the two subjects being played simultaneously, showing them to be in invertible counterpoint.

[31] *TLP*12, pp. 230–1; *TZC*2, p. 603; *TPB*, p. 300. In fact, *A Prisoner in the Caucasus* was an early work of Cui, composed in 1857–8, but revised in 1881–2 in anticipation of its première in 1883.

[32] *TLP*12, p. 216; *TPM*3, p. 212.

The anonymous counterpoint which occupies so much of this first movement renders it no more attractive than its counterpart in the First Suite. The remaining movements are not only more alive, but are something of a collective landmark in Tchaikovsky's evolution. His researches into new instrumental combinations, to which he had alluded at an early stage in the work's gestation, went well beyond the devising of brief orchestral piquancies and surprises, for in these four movements he undertook a reassessment of his orchestration sometimes as radical (but a good deal more profitable in creative dividends) as that he had conducted four years before when scoring *The Maid of Orléans*. It confirmed the bifurcation in his orchestral technique, for whereas the shift in the opera house had been towards generalization, in these new pieces, designed for the concert hall, it was towards greater particularization. In *The Maid* the sections of the orchestra had been treated more as choirs, the textures being more simply designed and sonorously presented. With this less detailed approach the brush strokes had become broader and simpler, with whole sections of dialogue now proceeding with spare chordal support scored only for strings, perhaps alternating with blocks of wind sound. Except in the more intimate scenes for Joan and Lionel there was much less use of solo wind instruments providing background counterpoints or decorative dialogues.

Similar preoccupations had seemed to condition the plainer approach to the organization and realization of orchestral colour in the First Suite, upon which Tchaikovsky had worked in parallel with *The Maid*, for even in the march each section had exploited a single, not a multiple sound world. Nor did the Italian Capriccio, his next orchestral work, mark any new departure, for its southern tunes were entities as self-contained as the melodic structures which were the main substance of the suite, and they had suggested matchingly broad areas of tone colour. The difference was that the pigments were now far more vivid, the contrasts fiercer, the backgrounds idiomatically designed to make possible strikingly projected accompaniments. But in the new suite Tchaikovsky sought to refine and detail his sound world to a degree which required some reappraisal of whole parameters of his technique. In the Valse there is a pronounced shift in the melodic manner. In earlier examples he had composed melodies mostly in sixteen-bar periods, each normally employing a limited range of rhythmic components; variety had come from an uncommon resourcefulness in diversifying the triple-time metre with duple-time inflections (see Vol. 2, p. 79, Ex. 115). Such tunes were customarily presented through one colour or divided between, at most, two; to broaden the rhythmic

field, contrasting melodic lines or fragments might be counterpointed
to the principal line. But Tchaikovsky's intention of introducing brisk
and varied colour changes into this new Valse prompted him not only
to widen the contrasts in melodic character between the different
sixteen-bar periods but, at a more local level, to absorb into the main
line the sort of variety formerly provided by subordinate fragments,
thus abetting melodically the new extra diversity of colour. And so the
agile quavers with which the violas complement the violins' benign
opening phrase (Ex. 190, bar 3) are soon transmitted to the principal
line (bar 8) which leaps up with new-found energy, while the repetition
of these sixteen bars brings modifications both in scoring and substance; the meticulous detail in the directions for performance is striking
throughout. The continuation, again of sixteen bars, broadens this
melodic world unprecedentedly; the two-beat ostinato-like figure in low
clarinet, punctuated by loudly chopped chords, can be accepted as a
waltz only by association with what has gone before. In the first section
of the First Suite's Divertimento (89 bars), which had many waltz
affinities, there had been some fifteen changes of orchestral colour; in
this Valse's first section (106 bars) there are nearly fifty, some lasting no
more than a single beat. By contrast, the centre of the movement, with
its sixteen-bar periods of unchanged scoring, emphasizes the newness
in what surrounds it.

Ex. 190

Yet the modification of melodic manner within this Valse is modest compared to the transformation of texture in the first section of the *Scherzo burlesque*; the optional introduction of four accordions later in the piece is only its most startling novelty. Gone are the stolidly functional basses and explicit harmonic supports of the First Suite; gone, too, is contrapuntal stodge in favour of a mercurial polyphony from which is spun a protean variety of textures, sometimes of such fineness that the harmony is only barely sketched. In this opening section everything from a single line, through two-part counterpoint, to tutti chords is used (though the last very sparingly, and never with the full orchestra). Merely to distribute among different permutations of instruments these fleeting lines, chords and other morsels which momentarily appear was to guarantee endless variety of sound; Tchaikovsky's achievement is to have used these resources so discriminatingly. It is no wonder that, with such fine judgements being demanded, the scoring should have taken so long. The first of the two episodes[33] affixes the quaver-two-semiquaver figure of the opening section to a series of pedal points which, being set a major third apart, reinforce the tonal uncertainty also created by the presentations of the new three-crotchet motif. Like the fourth movement of the Third Symphony, this *Scherzo burlesque* crosses into the musical territory of the Russian supernatural.

Nor is this the only context in these four movements which connects with the past, for the second episode suddenly flourishes a national manner redolent of the Second Symphony; it is difficult to believe (though it appears to be true) that the melody lustily sung by the horns is not a genuine folktune. Also of the Second Symphony's world is the last movement, the oddly named *Danse baroque* (i.e. 'quaint' or 'grotesque'). But it has equal affinity with the gopaks in Tchaikovsky's operas, though now possessing a more concentrated brilliance, with stretches in which the harmony is fragmented into a series of brilliant background splashes at different pitch levels. This dance is more helpfully defined by its sub-title: *Wild dance in imitation of Dargomïzhsky.* The specific model is that composer's *Kazachok*, though Tchaikovsky

---

[33] In Tchaikovsky's autograph score three pieces from this suite were considerably longer than when they were published in 1884. The *Scherzo burlesque* had started life as an extended rondo (ABACABA); after bar 333, at the end of the second episode (C) Tchaikovsky had continued for 44 further bars, then picked up the first section at bar 41, and continued to bar 205, concluding with 48 bars of coda which incorporated material from the second episode. The first section of *Rêves d'enfant* was longer by what was essentially a varied but reorganized version of the first 33 bars. In *Danse baroque*, starting from bar 219 (i.e. shortly before the coda), 90 bars were to be cut (these incorporated an exact repetition of bars 41–83). To smooth the gap Tchaikovsky added three new bars (bars 219–21 of the printed score).

takes no suggestion from the slow music in this roughly made but likeable piece. Predictably the model is far outstripped by the tribute; Dargomïzhsky's lively but crude inventiveness is transformed into a heady series of ear-enticing variations and digressions, never more engaging than when, just before the coda explodes, the dance pounds forward with earthy wit through some twenty bars of close two-part canon.

It is the remaining movement, *Rêves d'enfant* (No. 4), which contains both the most conventional and the most original music in the whole suite. The harmonic support to this gently folky berceuse is orthodox enough, and such it remains for over half the piece, though some of the textures have a rare fastidiousness. But the easy fantasies of the waking world give way to the evanescent images of unconsciousness as a series of E flat minor chords suddenly recalls those flutterings into which Miranda's first hesitant phrases of love had dissolved in *The Tempest* some ten years before. This time, however, the progress is not to a surge of physical passion but into a realm of yet more intangible images, conjured in textures so fragmented and chromatically ornamented that their harmonic foundation remains elusive (Ex. 191); only at the end of each does a shimmering harp-washed triad bring a brief stability. The convoluted oboe phrase introduces an image of some substance, but it dissipates within a progression of tonally unrelated triads before the whole impalpable creation sinks into limbo and vanishes. Like the opening of the Second String Quartet, this is a passage quite unprecedented in Tchaikovsky's work, and like that earlier music it seems to leap towards a distant future; the listener coming across it for the first time may momentarily wonder whether there will open before him the world of Bly, that other setting for disturbing childhood dreams and fantasies in Britten's *The Turn of the Screw*. Even within the enchanted music of *The Sleeping Beauty*, which it clearly presages, there is rarely quite the same disquieting sense of shapes indefinable and forces unknown. But in this present piece such things quickly pass; the conscious world returns and the child resumes its musings before falling into dreamless sleep.

Matters of childhood, though now seen very differently, are the whole subject of Tchaikovsky's remaining work of 1883, the Sixteen Songs for Children, Op. 54, upon which he started only a week after finishing the suite. The idea for such a collection was not new. In January 1881 he had set Axakov's 'Child's song' ('My Lizochek'), and five months later he told both Anatoly and Jurgenson that he intended to compose further songs of this kind. In the meantime 'Child's song' had been published as a supplement to the monthly *Recreation for*

Ex. 191

Children, and that autumn this periodical had approached Tchaikovsky for more of the same. He had firmly rejected the proposal, partly because of the unsuitability of the texts proposed, partly because of the inadequate fee. With this he seems to have set aside any idea of such creative work. It cannot have been entirely coincidence that, having just completed a piece in which a vision from the world of childhood had so deeply touched his creativity, he should now be impelled to return to this other project in which everything had been of that world. But it was a very long time since, in his daily existence, children had been such a close and absorbing factor as during the last few months. First Tanya's son, with whose welfare he had been so closely involved; then Anatoly's daughter, who had given him such delight during his weeks at Podushkino. And now, at Sasha's home, there was Irina, Vera's daughter born the previous year, whom he first thought un-attractive ('she reminds me very much of a widow, and such children aren't to my taste'[34]), but whom he admitted he very quickly came to adore. It was difficult any longer to look upon Sasha's offspring as a group of children. Two were already mothers, a third about to be married, and only Yury, now seven, remained at home. But suddenly a new generation had begun to spring up, and had become for a while a part of his life – and, it seems, of his creative world. 'I've set about composing children's songs, and I'm writing one regularly each day,' he told Modest on 5 November, three days after beginning work. 'But this is a light and very pleasant labour, for as my text I'm taking Pleshcheyev's *The Snowdrop,* where there are many delightful things.'[35] At this stage it seems he was confining himself to musical sketches, but the compulsion to bring these, and the others he drafted during the next week, to their final form soon turned leisurely recreation into assiduous toil, and by 15 November he could despatch fifteen completed songs to Jurgenson. 'So that this [collection] may serve as a rather special gift for children, it would be desirable to publish them as attractively as possible, and with pictures – but otherwise, as you think fit,' he wrote to his publisher. 'If you want you can add "Lizochek" to it.'[36] This last suggestion appealed to Jurgenson, and the earlier nonsense song was duly appended.

Tchaikovsky had known the minor poet, Alexey Plescheyev, from his first days in Moscow, and had already used two of his lyrics for much earlier romances. It must have been the appearance of 'Child's song' at the beginning of 1881 which had prompted Pleshcheyev to present

[34] *TLP*12, p. 232.
[35] *TLP*12, p. 264; *TPB*, p. 599; *YDGC*, p. 300.
[36] *TLP*12, p. 273; *TPJ*1, p. 310.

Tchaikovsky with a copy of his anthology for children, *The Snowdrop*, printed three years earlier. If the poet's hope was that this might lure the composer into setting more of his verses – and the inscription ('. . . as a mark of affection and gratitude for his beautiful music to my poor words') suggests that it was – then he was richly rewarded, for fourteen of the 1883 songs use Pleshcheyev's texts. Nearly all are sentimental; a number are translations, but in Pleshcheyev's jingle they mostly lose any real poetic quality they may once have possessed. There is the expected quota of seasonal ditties, though only the early arrival of autumn brings cheerlessness into any of them (No. 14). Spring gets three (Nos. 3 (a translation from Polish), 9 and 13) since it is the happiest time of all, and thoughts may run freely on budding nature, birds and insects. The two on winter skirt its less pleasant features, for one (No. 12) treats of children's excitement at the first snowfall, the other (No. 7) first paints a cosy domestic scene where mother tells her children a story in front of a blazing fire, then plays the piano for them to sing and dance, after which the poet reminds his young readers of less fortunate mortals ('paupers and orphans') who have to endure the howling blizzard and whom, he says, they ought to 'caress like brothers', should they ever come across any. A storm is also a distant background to a reassuring cradle song (No. 10). There is one other vignette of family life (No. 6, a translation from an English source): a fisherman's family is anxiously awaiting his return because he has been away three days, not two, and is the more excited when he does appear with a particularly good catch. Gardens, flowers and birds are not only liable to crop up anywhere, but have lyrics of their own; a modest patch is held to be much nicer than a grandly designed garden (No. 4), a solitary domestic plant resists the summons of its more fortunate confrères to join them in the garden because it must stay to gladden the sufferer and prisoner (No. 11, a translation from L. Ratisbonne), while God's bird intercedes with the Almighty for the poor ploughman (No. 2, another Polish translation). A swallow is the central figure in a more distinctive lyric (No. 15), bringing an orphan remembrances from her brother in prison: does she still weep for him? Significantly the text of this one is by Ivan Surikov from the Polish of Lenartowicz. But this worthier seriousness is also evident in Pleshcheyev's translation which produced the most famous song of the whole set, the 'Legend' (No. 5; the source is English), where the Christ-child in his garden is crowned with thorns by children who have ransacked all his flowers. Yet the set has humour, too, both in the opening song, which tells how a boy, bored with amusements, finally asks his grandmother to point the way to school, and in No. 8 (a translation from Gellert), in which a cuckoo, enraged that other singing birds are getting all the attention, determines to command notice by remorseless repetitions of its two notes.

With texts such as are used in the majority of these, the worst might be feared. In fact, this set is far from contemptible. Such songs are not upgraded nursery rhymes, but mostly simple romances, some for children, some about them. Most are slender in substance, a few are weak (Nos. 6, 12 and 14), but one or two are, of their kind, quite first-rate. It may be useful to approach them after reflecting upon the judgement made by Taneyev, that very perceptive critic of his former teacher's work. 'In the majority of these songs the required mood is fully achieved through simple means,' he wrote to Tchaikovsky on 4 July 1884. 'In addition, being harmonically uncomplicated (something it's impossible not to praise in a composition of the 80s), they are at the same time unusually interesting in the construction of their musical sentences and sections. . . . Among the individual numbers the first place without doubt belongs to "The Cuckoo" [No. 8] . . . "Christ" [No. 5] is a delight . . . "The Bird" [No. 2], "Spring" [No. 3], the second "Spring" [No. 9], the "Cradle song" [No. 10], "The Little Flower" [No. 11], "The Orphan" ["The Swallow": No. 15] are little masterpieces.'[37]

Taneyev's selection is thoroughly characteristic of a composer for whom resourceful musicianship rather than inventive brilliance was the central issue. His 'little masterpieces' are above all the well-made pieces, whose fluency could have become somniferous, had not Tchaikovsky incorporated phrases of doubled or halved length, for instance, or employed overlaps between voice and piano to diversify the jogtrot monotony which Pleshcheyev's prattle could so naturally have bred. The listener alert, like Taneyev, to such unobtrusive resourcefulness will find a good deal else to admire in this set. True, it is rare to find anything quite as sophisticated as the vocal opening of 'The Swallow' where the piano, having established the prevailing three-bar phrase structure (Ex. 192a; however, it pointedly dislocates this with a final phrase of four bars), then settles for a new kind of six-bar unit while the voice retraces the piano's first thoughts (Ex. 192b), at first out of phase, then delaying its final phrase to end simultaneously with its partner. This is certainly one of the best songs in the set, and the shift into the minor on the last page gently points up the pathos of the end. In the opening song, 'Granny and grandson', key is used to differentiate character, the grandmother's music being set in A minor, her grandson's in G or C major (it is surprising that Taneyev's list did not include

[37] *DTC*, pp. 307–8; *YDGC*, p. 321 (partial); *TTP*, p. 106.

Ex. 192

this thoughtful little sketch, which Tchaikovsky treats with charmingly ironic seriousness). Such shifts are between closely related keys, of course, and only very infrequently do any of these songs step outside the most narrow tonal boundaries; the expedition towards the flattened sub-mediant at the end of the first strophe of 'Spring' (No. 9) is quite an adventure. Even more surprising, perhaps, is the infrequency with which Tchaikovsky employs musical onomatopoeia in this set: the 'busy bees' in the prelude and postlude of 'My little garden' (No. 4), the children's laughter and the general din at the ends of the first two strophes of 'Winter evening', the stormy left-hand semiquavers in 'Spring' (No. 9) and the obvious bird noises in 'The Cuckoo' are about the only examples.

Whatever debate there may be over the list of 'little masterpieces' among these songs, there can surely be no disagreement with Taneyev about which are the finest two pieces. The 'Legend' quickly became, and has remained, one of Tchaikovsky's best-known short pieces. In April 1884 he transcribed the accompaniment for orchestra at the request of the tenor, Dmitri Usatov, and in 1889 he arranged the piece for unaccompanied chorus, which is the version most people know (usually under the title 'The Crown of Roses', with a first line: 'When Jesus Christ was yet a child'). The re-telling of one of the most pitiful incidents of the Passion story in terms of humanity's most innocent representatives has a poignancy which transcends its unblushing sentimentality, while the solemn procession of symmetrical phrases and the pervasive modalism of Tchaikovsky's setting bestow an almost hieratic quality which enables the piece to be both touching yet dignified. It affords the most substantial experience of the set – yet even among these unaffected pieces its simplicity is striking. There could scarcely be a stronger contrast of character than with 'The Cuckoo'. Humour rarely looms large in Tchaikovsky's music, but it does here, and with a lightness of touch which ensures that no point in this little scene is trampled upon. The cuckoo's disingenuous questions ('What are people saying about the singing of this or that bird?') have an arch simplicity which contrasts pointedly with the starling's chattery and mortifying replies; Taneyev thought Tchaikovsky had here worked bird-song into the accompaniment 'splendidly'. The end is hilarious, the piano petulantly thrashing (or flapping) in all directions until the starling explodes with laughter at the parasite's rage. Tchaikovsky wrote songs of greater substance, but none more delicious.

Tchaikovsky's return to Kamenka was greeted with much warmth from the whole clan. He found a special interest in encountering for the first time in nearly thirty years his cousin, Anastasiya Popova, a third of a century older than he, who had been a member of the Tchaikovsky household in his very earliest years, who had returned to take over the running of Ilya Petrovich's establishment on the death of Pyotr's mother in 1854, and who had now come to end her days in Sasha's care. Tchaikovsky had expected to find himself rather intimidated by Anastasiya, but instead found her to be amiable, grateful, yet hardly of this world, for her thoughts ran entirely on memories of thirty or forty years before. The kindness and attention which his sister was showing to this old lady, whose wits were gently slipping away, deeply touched

Tchaikovsky; whatever his views on Sasha's shortcomings, he freely admitted that responsibilities of this sort brought out the best in her. Tanya had already arrived from Paris with Elizaveta, but plans were being made for them to return, partly so that Tanya might continue her official treatment, partly to remove from her mother a presence which always adversely affected her health. Apart from concern for her child, Tanya had her own reasons for wishing to be back in France. One of the doctors who had attended her before her confinement was a certain Ferré. Tchaikovsky had noted he seemed attracted to Tanya, but the relationship had developed much farther after he had left, and the Frenchman had proposed marriage. In Paris Tanya would finally decide whether to accept his offer. Meanwhile, being in a highly nervous state, she soon removed herself to Kamenka to be nearer the local doctor, as a result of which the Verbovka establishment became far more relaxed.

Though Tchaikovsky believed that marriage to Ferré could be a good step for Tanya, he doubted the seriousness of her love. 'She talks to everyone too much about it for it to be a strong feeling,' he commented to Modest. But he was surprised at his own changed views about this troublesome niece. 'I'm exceedingly glad I've lost completely last year's feeling *of spite* towards Tanya. On the contrary, I feel a great deal of friendliness towards her, but not a trace of tenderness.'[38] For Blumenfeld her emotions were now violently hostile. But Tchaikovsky's judgements on the shallowness of her more recent attraction to Ferré was vindicated when an old aspirant, the merchant Otto Kern, appeared and immediately stimulated her interest. A proposal, swiftly made, that he should accompany her to Paris met with almost desperate opposition from her uncle. 'I have frankly advised her not to rush, but to attempt to visit Italy during the winter so as to try to entice some wealthy Englishman,' was his improbable counsel, as he told Modest. '. . . Lev isn't sending Tanya [to Paris] for the whole winter, but only for two months. Yet she will probably stay longer, and I foresee she's again going to cost me a lot of money. However, I shan't begrudge it, if only she gets married,' he added hopefully.[39] Within a fortnight of his arrival Tanya had left. His own emotions surprised him. 'My heart was wrung when she said goodbye,' he confessed to Anatoly. 'Somehow she's become pitiful and, above all, so distanced from her family that she's just like a stranger, and everyone breathed freely on being released from such a difficult guest. Even her parents, however much

[38] *TLP*12, p. 229.
[39] *TLP*12, pp. 235–6.

they love her, cannot hide that things are better and more carefree for them when she's far away.'[40] Once again with Tchaikovsky humanity had shown itself stronger than reflex. There could have been no greater contrast than the joy he felt at the celebrations of Anna and Nikolay's engagement. Yet even here, within the pleasure of seeing how the lovers 'sit all day in the corner and endlessly kiss each other', there was for him a pain which he knew Modest would understand. 'I look at them with envy, and think all the time that this indeed is real happiness, and that I shall never experience it.'[41]

When Tchaikovsky begins to gossip it is a sure sign that he is at his most relaxed, and the letters he wrote at Sasha's are well laced with small talk about the family. All such trivial matters of human behaviour, both generous and petty (and there was a vast number of the latter among the highly ramified tribe at Kamenka), provided an environment which he could both observe and share in a way not possible elsewhere. Kamenka, he discovered, remained necessary for him. And Kamenka still wanted him also, as he noted when Lev went to considerable trouble to install a fireplace in his room so that he might have more comfort and privacy as winter approached. Apart from spending a few days in Kiev in late October to avoid being left alone with Anastasiya while everyone else had gone to a family baptism, he spent all his time at Kamenka or Verbovka. His pattern of recreation was as before. Matters of geography and the history of Peter the Great featured in his reading, and operas seem to have been the most noteworthy element in his private music-making: Serov's *Judith*, but above all *Carmen*, which he played right through three times in as many days – though he also 'not without pleasure' investigated Rimsky-Korsakov's *May Night*.[42] He now found time to resume the study of English which had been impossible at Podushkino, and he made a start on *David Copperfield* in the original. Ippolit appeared for a few days, and both amused and aggravated everyone with his minor ailments. 'I very much love Ippolit's kindness, but God preserve me not only from living in the same house with him, but in the same town,' he confided to Modest.[43]

In fact, apart from intense irritations at the time-consuming inaccuracy of the Second Suite's proofs, and growing premonitions of the tensions he would have to face in Moscow and St Petersburg during the preparations for *Mazepa*, the only major disturbances during this two

[40] *TLP*12, p. 240.
[41] *TLP*12, p. 243.
[42] *TLP*12, p. 244; *TZC*2, p. 605; *YDGC*, p. 299; *TPB*, p. 599.
[43] *TLP*12, p. 270.

and a half months concerned Tanya. First she wrote from Paris telling him the cost of arrangements she was making for Georges-Léon, though she offered some hope that her uncle would soon be released from this financial burden, since she expected to marry that winter – but whether to Ferré or Kern she did not say. Then came the startling news that the former was no longer eligible, for on meeting Tanya he had told her calmly that he was now engaged to a French girl. Even worse was a sudden suspicion that Sasha had guessed the real truth behind her daughter's earlier stay in Paris. Yet most alarming of all was to be told all the essentials of Tanya's escapade by Alexey, who had picked them up from a former servant who had aided Blumenfeld in his nocturnal visits to Tanya's room. Then the story penetrated the fringes of the family itself, and for a few days Tchaikovsky lived in terror of the truth coming to the parents' ears. But before that could happen it was summarily dismissed as incredible; the very enormity of the scandal finally killed it, and he realized that for the moment at least the secret was safe.

Tchaikovsky left the Ukraine earlier than expected. The First Symphony had not been performed since its première in 1868; now, at Tchaikovsky's own instigation, it was to be played for a second time at an RMS concert on 1 December. On that very day he arrived in Moscow and received an ovation. The day following he attended a recital by the nineteen-year-old Glasgow-born German pianist, Eugen d'Albert, whose prodigious talents he was able to admire further at more private musical events. Within these encounters there began to germinate the seed of a future work for piano and orchestra.

A Note on the Second Suite, and on Certain Persons

It has already been suggested that two themes in the first movement of the First Suite may have been cipher-generated. The opening *Jeu de sons* of the Second Suite resembles that of its predecessor in that it is fugal and its thematic material is uncharacteristic of its composer – indeed, like that of the earlier movement, dull. Moreover, Tchaikovsky's sketches for this first movement indicate that it cost much effort to form it to his satisfaction, and since he had no lack of technical facility, it seems possible that certain constraints within the material were posing special problems. This offers some reinforcement to the suspicion that ciphers may be behind certain of the thematic ideas. The following suggestion concerning the first theme of the second subject cannot be considered any more conclusive than those made about the First Suite, and it is therefore excluded from the main text. It will be noted, however, that it is of a kind similar to that made with regard to the earlier piece.

The cipher system Tchaikovsky would appear to have used was that which both Ravel and Debussy, amongst others, are known to have employed later, and it provided a pitch equivalent for every letter of the alphabet (Ex. 193).

Ex. 193

Tchaikovsky composed the Second Suite while staying with his brother Anatoly and his family at Podushkino. The suite was dedicated to his sister-in-law, Praskovya, but her husband and their new daughter, Tanya, had an equal part in the composer's joy and affections during this summer episode. It would not be unreasonable, therefore, for him to incorporate these two as well as the work's dedicatee, though it would also be reasonable to assume that Praskovya would be the major element in any cipher generation. Applying a German transliteration of the three names to the system of Ex. 193 produces the following (Ex. 194):

Ex. 194

If we take the first five pitches of 'Praskowja', then the contours produced by the first three pitches each of 'Anatol' and 'Tanja', and finally the contour of the last five pitches of 'Praskowja', but overlapping these shapes, we create the note sequence of Ex. 195a. The overlapping might signify the family bond, the placings of the divided 'Praskowja' contour might symbolize the embracing love of the mother for the family. Be that as it may, if the thirteen-note shape of Ex. 195a is inverted by simply reversing the initial interval but then keeping to the white notes (the system is, of course, concerned only with white notes), we have the exact pitch sequence of the second subject in the exposition (Ex. 195b). If these suggestions are indeed valid, it seems highly probable that other elements in this movement's material are also cipher-generated.

Ex. 195

7

INTIMATE INSIGHTS AND MARKS OF
REHABILITATION: THIRD SUITE

The biographical portions of this study have been for the most
part a chronological charting of the events of Tchaikovsky's life,
blended with a selection from such passing evidence as illumines the
man himself, his attitudes to life and his art, and his relationships with
the people around him. Writing it has involved an increasingly drastic
sifting of the data, for what appears in the pages of this present volume
represents only a tiny portion of the information afforded by extant
materials. But among these abundant documents there are some
which, even though they contribute little of importance to the main
biographical narrative, do seem to merit extensive attention, simply
because of the unique illuminations they cast upon particular aspects of
Tchaikovsky and his behaviour patterns. This chapter draws heavily
upon two such bodies of material. The first consists of the letters to and
about one individual; the other is a personal diary.

The Odd Case of Leonty Tkachenko

During his last stay at Kamenka Tchaikovsky had ended a relationship
he had been conducting with a young man who, four years earlier, had
suddenly solicited his aid. The episode itself is bizarre but unimportant;
the interest lies in Tchaikovsky's part in it. It shows him plunging into a
deep involvement in the life and welfare of a person previously quite
unknown to him, but whose sudden cry for help had been sufficient to
engage his complete and sustained attention. It had begun, therefore,
in raw innocence, and because there was no conditioning from existing
ties of love or friendship, as in so many of his other numerous acts of
kindness and support, the whole affair reveals with an engaging
artlessness – indeed, perhaps more clearly than any other relationship
in his whole life – that mixture of wild impulse and measured sympathy,
of clear-headed insight and gullibility, which were such fundamental
traits of the real Tchaikovsky.

The beginning of it all had been documented to Nadezhda von Meck on 3 November 1879.

A fortnight ago from Poltava I received a letter written by a Mr Tkachenko, who is unknown to me, in which he informed me that, nourishing a passion for music and wishing to dedicate himself to the study of it, but having no means, he would like to become my man-servant, promising to carry out with all possible zeal the duties of a servant if only I would give him at least a chance of acquiring some knowledge, albeit small, of the theory of music. Because the letter was written very correctly and was shot through with sincerity, I replied that, although I could not accept his services in the capacity of a man-servant, I could help him to the means of acquiring a musical education if, from his next letter, I saw he was sufficiently gifted and young enough for study to lead to something. Yesterday I received his reply. He is twenty-two, and his musical knowledge is as weak as his wish to become a professional musician is strong. His letter was so written as to breed a great sympathy towards this youth. From all this it is evident that he is intelligent and talented. But what can you do with a person who for twenty-two years has only loved music, and can do nothing except what he has picked up by ear? I had to write in reply my frank opinion that he *had left it too late*, and that the years in which study might bear fruit had passed. I am very sorry for him.[1]

A full year went by. Then on 29 December 1880, Tchaikovsky picked up the tale.

The day before yesterday I received a letter from him; he is returning my letters to me, lest after his death they should fall into someone else's hands. He bids me farewell, and says he has decided on suicide because his struggle with life's misfortunes and his despair of ever being other than a man labouring solely for a morsel of bread have instilled in him an aversion to life. The letter exuded such sincerity, such a deep despair, that I was very shocked. From the postmark I learned that the letter had been written in Voronezh (formerly he had lived in Poltava), and I immediately decided to telegraph, asking one of the inhabitants of Voronezh to seek out Tkachenko through the police and to tell him, if it was not already too late, to await a letter from me. Fortunately Anatoly has a good friend, a certain

---

[1] *TLP*8, pp. 400–1; *TPM*2, pp. 237–8.

Stoikov, whom I quickly telegraphed. Yesterday evening I received a reply that *Tkachenko* has been found *in time*. He was in a frightful state. Now I have sent him money for the journey, and I am inviting him to come to Moscow by 22 January – i.e. the day on which I myself must return from Kamenka. What will come of all this I do not know, but I am happy that I have saved him from destruction. Judging from his letters he is a strange and wild young man – but intelligent, and very honourable and good.[2]

Tchaikovsky admitted that, on reading Tkachenko's letter, he had wept like a child. The day before writing to Nadezhda von Meck he had addressed himself directly to the unfortunate.

I certainly must become acquainted with you personally – and I want to . . . I have no idea at all in what way I shall be able to show you that moral support you need, but do not doubt that in me you have a firm friend, very disposed to be a support for you in enduring life's misfortunes. In any case, I think that I shall be able to draw you out of that painful moral condition in which you find yourself. But correspondence is not enough for this – I must see you, know you more closely, and then take action. . . . If I were at this moment a completely free person I would come *to Voronezh*, but for various reasons I cannot do this, and therefore it would be more convenient if you came to me here. I am sending you fifty roubles for the journey. . . . I have adequate means, and it costs me nothing to show *a friend*, such as I consider you to be, not only moral but also material support. . . . And so, farewell. Set aside gloomy thoughts, look more kindly on life and the future – and, most of all, do not doubt that, although I do not yet know you personally, I am already your sincere and firm friend.[3]

Within a fortnight this young man, in whose life Tchaikovsky had felt compelled to intervene 'in a fateful manner', had replied, but in terms Tchaikovsky had hardly expected.

His letter did not please me at all, and bred in me fear for the future. I confess I had expected him to say thank you to me for the helping hand I had extended to him. Not in the least. He hastens to assure me that it is useless for me *to take upon myself to assure him of the existence of*

---

[2] *TLP*9, pp. 333–4; *TPM*2, p. 457; *TCZ*2, pp. 434–5.
[3] *TLP*9, p. 335; *TCZ*2, pp. 435–6.

virtue (though I never thought to speak of anything of the sort), *that I shall not be able to prove to him that it is worth living in this world*, that he did not need the money I had sent him and would manage without it – but he promised, all the same, to come to Moscow on 22nd and to hear me out. All this is very strange and incomprehensible.[4]

A badly wounded Tchaikovsky now waited with much uncertainty the arrival of this odd character. But Tkachenko was punctual. 'I have met him,' he continued to Nadezhda von Meck two weeks later.

> . . . In general he is a sympathetic person. His sufferings have stemmed from the disparity between his aspirations and the gusts of stern reality. He is intelligent, developed – but nevertheless, for the sake of a morsel of bread he has been forced to serve as a guard on the railways. . . . He is very nervous, timid, abnormally shy. . . . Poverty, loneliness and circumstances of life have developed in him misanthropy and a hypochondriacal condition of the spirit. His views are rather queer – but, I repeat, he is far from stupid. I am extremely sorry for him, and I have resolved to take him into my care. I have now decided to send him for this half year to the Conservatoire. . . . I shall not find it difficult to cure him and turn him into a being both useful and reconciled with life because he inspires me with sincere sympathy.[5]

Fortified with this extraordinary prediction, Tchaikovsky had not long to await results. 'I will tell you, dear friend, a little about Tkachenko,' he began his letter of 8 February.

> He is a very strange person. I arranged everything for him thoroughly in every respect and, to be fair to him, he set about his studies with great zeal. On the eve of my departure he presented himself to me, and forewarned me that he had to have a serious talk with me. I settled myself to listen, and the more he developed his thoughts, the more and more I was convinced that here was a nature sick both morally and mentally. The following is the essence of his speech. The thought had entered his head that I had rendered him help and assistance *not for his good but for my own, in order to earn the reputation of a philanthropist*. He compared me with *those ladies* who occupy themselves with philanthropy because it is fashionable, and so that they

[4] *TLP*9, p. 347; *TPM*2, p. 463.
[5] *TLP*10, p. 17; *TPM*2, pp. 466–7; *TCZ*2, pp. 445–6.

will be much talked about. During this he stated that he did not want to be *a victim* of my weakness for making myself popular, that he emphatically refused to consider me his benefactor, and forewarned me I should not count upon gratitude on his part.[6]

Greatly affronted by this outburst, Tchaikovsky defended himself with dignity and reason, then dismissed Tkachenko. 'I told him I was leaving [Moscow], that I would not see him again, and asked him not to think about me at all, but only of his studies.'[7]

But Tkachenko was not to be shed that easily. Tchaikovsky spent the summer at Kamenka; then on 21 August he began a letter to Modest.

This morning I was going, as always, to write to you when suddenly Sila appeared from the station, informing me in confidence that some unknown young man wanted to see me. Because he didn't say who this was, I refused to go. Then Biryukov appeared; he had seen the strange young man, and been filled with pity for him. He had come from somewhere on foot, had spent a full day at the station, had had nothing to eat, had stubbornly refused all offers, and declared the police could take him if they wished. From the description I guessed it was Tkachenko, and ran in great agitation to the station. I thought he was waiting for me so that he could forthwith blow out his brains in front of me. I won't describe the desperate condition I found the unhappy man in. He was *inexpressibly* glad to see me and could not restrain his hysterical sobs. He's a strange person! I calmed him as best I could, told Sila to pour him some tea and let him sit alone in order to calm himself. Then I left, and at evening returned to him again, and sent him via Kharkov to Moscow [from where it seems he had walked all the way]. His object was to come to me to decline my allowance in view of his lack of ability, will, and his worthlessness in general. However, he has promised to send me from Kharkov [where he has a sister] his diary for the whole summer, which contains everything he wanted to say but couldn't *de vive voix*. I'm very exhausted from the upheavals I've suffered today – but Tkachenko has again become sympathetic; he has a good, but broken nature à la Dostoyevsky.[8]

The diary duly arrived – a fat volume with seven months'-worth of entries. It showed some flair with words, was disconcertingly frank ('he

[6] *TLP*10, p. 23; *TPM*2, pp. 471–2; *TZC*2, p. 448.

[7] *TLP*10, p. 24; *TPM*2, p. 472; *TCZ*2, p. 449.

[8] *TLP*10, p. 189; *TZC*2, p. 479.

discloses things such as even Rousseau wouldn't tell'[9]), and convinced Tchaikovsky he understood the roots of Tkachenko's problems. And in attempting to turn psychiatrist, his words suddenly take on a personal resonance which transcends the pathetic absurdity of the relationship which prompted them. Tkachenko's troubles all originated in the excessive tribute he had paid to sensuality in his youth, Tchaikovsky decided. 'As for the moral side of your *excesses*, in the first place I have no right to cast a stone at you, for I myself am not blameless,' he went on,

and secondly, in my opinion a man in this regard finds himself in a fateful dependence upon his temperament. Very often chastity is no more than the lack of an element of sensuality in the temperament. The whole point is this: to be able to stand above one's bodily desires and to be able to control them – and this comes with training. In your case this [training] was bad – or rather, there wasn't any, and so I do not label you *a profligate*. A profligate, in the true sense of the word, is one who makes physical pleasures *the aim of life*, whose spirit never protests against the pleasures of the flesh.[10]

Over the next week Tchaikovsky absorbed himself in Tkachenko's diary. Whether the lengthy analysis of the writer's problems with which he continued his letter really fitted the case is impossible to say, but there is much in it which is plausible. He identified Tkachenko as 'one of those *artistic natures* often met among Russians, who has a bent to artistic activity in general, but within his talents no specific inclination to this or that branch of art. Meanwhile,' he went on, '"step-mother fate", as though wilfully, cast you without rhyme or reason now into the Erivanskaya school, now into the army, now into the Consistory, now on to the railway – and everywhere. . . . Ah, Leonty Grigoryevich,' he cried, 'you are a good, nice person, but morally sick, for which of course you are not to blame, but circumstances.'[11] By now he was preparing Tkachenko to accept that, though he had managed to pass his Conservatoire examinations, as a musician he was unlikely to become more than a humble teacher; however, he thought that the diary offered powerful evidence of talent as a writer. What transpired during their meetings in Moscow we do not know, but from Rome in early December Tchaikovsky, who had meanwhile asked Modest's opinion of the diary, reinforced his advice to his protégé that he should turn his

[9]   *TLP*10, p. 210.
[10] *TLP*10, p. 215.
[11] *TLP*10, pp. 215–16.

mind to a literary career. Accordingly Tkachenko withdrew from the Conservatoire.

During the next year, 1882, Tchaikovsky continued to subsidize Tkachenko with twenty-five roubles a month to give him time to learn his new craft. The patient understanding which Tchaikovsky had sustained for so long now reaped its fullest reward. For the next year Tkachenko showed a remarkable persistence in trying to shape his talent as a writer, and from June a series of his literary efforts began to arrive for Tchaikovsky's perusal. The latter's judgements on them were frank, but kindly. He recognized that Tkachenko needed to write from within his own experience (he had already observed to Modest that the diary could make the basis of a novel), and he was unsparing in his verdict on the comedy Tkachenko included among these exercises because it attempted to deal with human matters the writer did not understand. But still Tkachenko persevered, though his constant changes of address presented persisting problems to Jurgenson, who had been charged with dispensing the monthly subsidy.

Yet it is apparent that, before the end of the year, a sense of realism had invaded Tchaikovsky's assessment of his protégé's literary abilities. Nor can he have failed to reflect that before him stretched the prospect of indefinite demands on both his moral and financial support. And so that powerful persuasiveness, which had earlier been directed towards encouraging Tkachenko's literary activities, was now applied to edge him towards a second objective. 'Since it is only very recently that you have begun to take your literary talent seriously, and since it will still be a long time before, through your own efforts, you will make up for the inadequacies in your schooling and become a mature writer, you will need to live for several years, despite having a firmly projected aim, without a definite position and, above all, without those *responsibilities* whose fulfilment completes [and] adorns our life,' Tchaikovsky wrote on 20 November. 'What you do need is occupations such as would interest you and make your life useful in the near future before you become a serious writer, while not distracting you from your main aim. And do you know what occupation I find completely suitable for your temperament? *The occupation of a village schoolteacher!* No, in my view there is no more honourable, more *holy* service to society than service as a village schoolteacher.'[12]

How Tkachenko really reacted to this sudden proposal we do not know for certain. He wrote one more hasty letter to Tchaikovsky, then a silence descended. 'How are you? Where are you? Let me know what

[12] *TLP*11, p. 276; *TZC*2, pp. 559–60.

you are up to. It's already more than two months since I had word from you,' Tchaikovsky wrote urgently from Paris on 26 January 1883.[13] But no reply came. It must be assumed that Tkachenko perceived in this new proposal a hidden verdict on his gifts as an author. Certainly that confidence which Tchaikovsky had enabled him to discover within himself had crumpled, and the relationship was to collapse as suddenly as it had arisen. The editors of the complete edition of Tchaikovsky's correspondence state that Tkachenko did indeed become a village schoolteacher with Tchaikovsky's help. But Modest, who must surely have known whether anything further passed between the two men, states that after this his brother's protégé soon vanished for ever. The final act of the relationship was told to Modest in the letter of 1 October 1883 from Verbovka. Everything ended almost as it had begun, except that, by now, Tchaikovsky's view of this strange bird of passage had once again suffered a harsh revision. His last words say it all.

When I arrived here I found awaiting me a parcel from *Tkachenko* who is in Poltava. On being opened it proved to be all my *letters* to him. Because the first time he wanted to kill himself he'd sent me my two letters, I understood this time he was, as it were, informing me of his impending suicide. Nevertheless, it was only for the first instant that I was a little worried; afterwards I somehow decided my Tkachenko was almost certainly alive. And, indeed, today I receive a request from him to send money, with no mention of my letters. His letter is, as always, ironical in tone. A pathetic, but rather unsympathetic person![14]

'The other day I was very touched by the ovation I was given at the Fisher High School for girls,' Tchaikovsky wrote to Nadezhda von Meck on 2 January 1884, a month after his arrival in Moscow to hear his First Symphony for the second time. 'The head of that institution had already several times written to me letters expressing ardent sympathy towards my music. Now she persuaded me to accept an invitation to a musical evening at the school, and the other day I went. I was met by *Miss Fisher*, surrounded by the mistresses and boarders. After this, choral performances of a whole series of my works began. These girls sang delightfully, and though I found it somewhat uncongenial to be the subject of general attention, I could not but be

[13] *TLP*12, p. 31.
[14] *TLP*12, p. 237; *TZC*2, p. 604.

touched by the unusually fervent sympathy which those present displayed towards me throughout the whole evening.'[15] Tchaikovsky was now becoming increasingly aware of the price of growing fame. The modesty of this occasion made such attentions easier to face than some he received at the more prestigious events, like the ovation on 1 December for his First Symphony ('both pleasant and flattering, but at the same time excruciatingly painful'[16]), or the prospect he faced on the first night of *Mazepa*. Being famous also made appalling demands on his time. Every would-be composer, however untalented (and most of them were), wanted to show him his work ('without exaggeration . . . not less than two or three each day,' he lamented to his patroness[17]). Not that this ever deterred him from exerting himself on behalf of the truly gifted, such as Arensky, whose abundantly inventive First Symphony had just received its première in Moscow under Erdmannsdörfer; Tchaikovsky interceded with Balakirev in the hope that it might be repeated in St Petersburg at a concert of the Free Music School, of which Balakirev had resumed direction in 1881.

But distractions of all kinds were the more difficult to avoid during these first weeks in Moscow because he could not plead that daily professional commitments were claiming his time. All the promises from Moscow and St Petersburg that *Mazepa* would be mounted before the end of 1883 had shown themselves to be worthless. Hardly had he arrived in Moscow than he was protesting to Vsevolozhsky about the delay, observing that if he had been forewarned he could have organized his winter differently. A flying visit to St Petersburg in mid-December to see Modest at least confirmed that, since he had to kill time, Moscow was the place to do it. He was staying at the same hotel as Laroche, whose indolence had become so extreme that Tchaikovsky decided he must act. 'I proposed that I should come to him each day for a couple of hours so that he could dictate to me an article for *The Russian Messenger*,' he told Nadezhda von Meck. 'This so flattered and touched him that half a big article, which you will probably read in the next number of *The Russian Messenger*, is already prepared and gone to the printers. . . . He needs *a nurse*; I've taken this role upon myself, because I have no business on my hands.'[18]

At the New Year this state of enforced inertia was at last broken. With the Russian Christmas Modest arrived for a fortnight, and both brothers were in St Petersburg for the wedding of Anna and Nikolay

[15] *TLP*12, p. 289; *TPM*3, p. 242; *TZC*2, p. 614.
[16] *TLP*12, p. 282; *TPM*3, p. 236; *TZC*2, p. 611; *YDGC*, p. 302.
[17] *TLP*12, p. 290; *TPM*3, p. 245.
[18] *TLP*12, pp. 288–9; *TPM*3, pp. 241–2; *TZC*2, pp. 613–14.

von Meck on 23 January. Needless to say, since Tchaikovsky was to be present, the bridegroom's mother did not return from Cannes for the event, but three of her daughters did appear and, as their mother had requested, Tchaikovsky recorded his frank and (predictably) favourable impressions of them. The première of *Mazepa* was now scheduled for 8 February. As noted earlier, Tchaikovsky committed the musical destiny of the St Petersburg production entirely into Nápravník's experienced hands, and devoted his personal energies to the Moscow preparations. He had predicted correctly that *Mazepa* would be yet again postponed, but on 15 February the opera was finally presented. His precipitate departure for the West the next day occasioned not only comment from the Tsar when the composer failed to appear at the first night of *Mazepa* in St Petersburg three days later; it also wounded Erdmannsdörfer that Tchaikovsky was not present to excite yet further the enthusiasm with which the Second Suite was greeted at its première, which was taking place at the moment the truant's train was pulling out of Moscow. To make his peace with this conductor he was to offer him the dedication of his next work, the Third Suite.

But for the moment Tchaikovsky's only concern was to put out of his mind everything connected with the strains and harassments of the last weeks. Pausing for two days in Berlin because his overwrought state had made it difficult to decide where to head next, he opted for Paris, and on 21 February settled himself into the same hotel room in which he had lived for five months in the previous year. His prime feeling was loneliness. Alexey had been unable to accompany him, for he had soon to return to the army, and Tchaikovsky confessed himself grateful even for Tanya's presence. He found her and Elizaveta comfortably installed, and noted with resignation that his niece had relapsed into her customary idleness. The Parisian theatre claimed him a few times, though apart from the Comédie-Française performing Molière's *Le Malade imaginaire* and *L'Ecole des femmes*, he seems to have found the plays on offer boring. The main experience of this three-week residence was offered by Massenet's *Manon Lescaut*, which had received its première a month earlier. He did not like it. 'I had expected something more. Very elegant, very individual, but not for one moment capable of touching, captivating, or arresting. . . . Because he [Massenet] cannot bear *dialogues*, everywhere conversation is going on he has fully developed music, and this never lets up for one moment, so that it actually becomes tiresome,' he told Modest.[19] Nor could he again avoid comparing the Parisian presentation ('*superb* performance . . . What a

[19] *TLP*12, pp. 317–18; *TPM*3, p. 626 (partial); *TZC*2, p. 625; *TPB*, p. 304.

production, what a superb musical performance!'[20]) with those his own operas customarily received in Russia. His main concern in France was to visit Georges-Léon. He went twice, giving no warning of his arrival the first time, and he left confident the child was being well cared for. Only two things really troubled him. First, the boy reminded him more of Blumenfeld than of his niece; second, what was to be Georges-Léon's future? 'How am I to place him in Russia? What name will he bear?' he wondered to Modest.[21] Whatever the answers, he knew *he* would have to find them.

Tchaikovsky had intended after Paris to proceed to Rome, where Anna and Nikolay were on honeymoon and had asked him to visit them. He had also been attracted by the idea of returning to Kamenka by boat from Naples to Odessa. But a decline in Tanya's health and an acute shortage of funds decided him he must stay in Paris. *Manon Lescaut* was already an enormous success and its press had been excellent; now Tchaikovsky received tidings about *Mazepa* which showed that Modest's favourable reports had been less than truthful. Yet he remained grateful that his brother had tried to spare him.

> You did well to lie, for indeed *the truth* might have killed me. . . . Only yesterday did I learn the facts from a letter of Jurgenson, who had the brutality not only to tell me the truth outright, but *to reproach* me for not going to St Petersburg. I don't know how I got through yesterday. It acted upon me like a crushing blow, and all day I suffered as terribly as though some colossal, irreparable misfortune had occurred. Of course this is my eternal [tendency to] exaggeration, but indeed at my age, in my position, when it is already difficult to have hope for the future, every even *relative* failure assumes the dimensions of a shameful fiasco.

'And,' he added bitterly – and uncomfortably, 'what is most galling of all is that, if I had been other than what I am and had upped and gone to St Petersburg, I would probably have left crowned with laurels.'[22]

Meanwhile the constant demands on his time which quickly built up from his acquaintances in Paris consolidated the yearning for a place of his own. Nadezhda von Meck had recently purchased a château at Belair in Touraine, and had invited him to spend some time there, but he had declined. His patroness was only one of the persons to whom, while he was in Paris, he confided this ever-strengthening wish.

[20] *TLP*12, p. 316; *TPM*3, p. 258.
[21] *TLP*12, p. 318.
[22] *TLP*12, p. 322; *TPM*3, p. 627; *TZC*2, p. 626; *TPB*, pp. 304–5.

'Nomadic life is beginning to weigh heavily on me. Whether this [home] will be somewhere on the outskirts of Moscow or somewhere a little farther away and a little more isolated I do not yet know. Thousands of plans crowd into my head – but, one way or another, I must finally have a place of my own.'[23] His immediate intention had been to return straight to Sasha's family circle, but a letter from Nápravník now told him of the Tsar's surprise at his truancy, and of his wish to see the composer. Tchaikovsky realized there was no escaping a visit to the Russian capital; to have stayed away would have been even more impolitic, since the Tsar had readily agreed to Nápravník's request to produce *Eugene Onegin* next season, declaring it to be his favourite opera. Because Anna and Nikolay were expected imminently from Italy, Tchaikovsky felt they could take over supervision of Tanya. On 12 March he left Paris, not knowing that the Tsar had decreed that the Order of St Vladimir (fourth class) should be conferred on him.

The investiture took place in the palace at Gatchina, just outside St Petersburg, on 19 March, four days after Tchaikovsky reached the Russian capital, where he learned that the Empress also wished to see him, and that there would be two audiences. She received him first, but though he had already sedated himself with a liberal quantity of bromide, his nerve nearly failed him, and at the very door he gulped down another dose lest he should fall senseless before his sovereign's consort. The kindly attentiveness with which he was treated soothed him, and by the second audience he was more self-possessed, though it was several days before his nerves returned to normal. This meeting certainly confirmed for Alexandr one subject's lifelong loyalty. 'I think that the man who has but once in his life had occasion to see the Tsar close to will be for ever his fervent admirer, for it is impossible to describe how charmingly attractive is his manner and whole way of behaving,' Tchaikovsky told Anatoly.[24] He summarized the especially pleasurable side of the occasion for Nadezhda von Meck. 'I was touched to the depths of my soul by the sympathy which the Tsar showed towards me. . . . [He] talked with me for a very long time, repeating several times that he loved my music very much, and altogether showed me an abundance of kindness.'[25]

This event was of profound importance to Tchaikovsky, not so much for the award itself as for what it signified. Though probably few others saw it as such, for the composer himself it was the visible symbol of full rehabilitation. The stigma which he felt had marked him in the eyes of

[23] *TLP*12, pp. 330–1; *TPM*3, p. 261; *YDGC*, p. 311 (partial).
[24] *TLP*12, p. 335; *TZC*2, pp. 629–30.
[25] *TLP*12, p. 334; *TPM*3, p. 263.

society ever since the scandal of his marriage nearly seven years before was now erased – or, at least, masked – by this public honour from the father of the Russian people. The people themselves might never forget, but at least they would now forgive. It was clearly much time before the full import of this awesome occasion sank in; what Tchaikovsky did immediately perceive, as he reflected on the Tsar's words and on what he could observe in St Petersburg itself, was that, despite Jurgenson's letter and the adverse press, *Mazepa* was no more an initial failure with the public than with their monarch. It was in a buoyant mood that he arrived in Moscow on 31 March.

Here he first devoted much time to making substantial revisions to *Mazepa*. This done, he once again took Laroche in hand, for a second time acting as amanuensis. By now he feared that his friend's oblomovshchina might force the Conservatoire to dismiss him, for though Laroche had begun the session conscientiously enough, he was now giving no classes. Tchaikovsky's main pleasures were found in Anatoly and his family, and in a Conservatoire performance of *Die Zauberflöte*, with which his acquaintance had been but sketchy, but which now took its place alongside *Figaro* – though a little lower than *Don Giovanni* – as one of his favourite operas. At a supper afterwards Arensky had proposed a toast to him, to which all had enthusiastically responded. He also had a chance at a grand musical soirée at Pavel Tretyakov's to assess the progress of his former student, the twenty-year-old pianist Alexandr Ziloti, who was to become a significant figure in Tchaikovsky's later years. He would have left Moscow sooner, but illness forced a delay, as did his personal endeavours to finalize the arrangements which others had successfully begun on his behalf to free Alexey from the remainder of his military service; he also wished to benefit from the abundance of Easter-tide services being celebrated, sometimes very splendidly, in the churches and cathedrals of Moscow. His three-week stay strengthened his longing for a home of his own to such a degree that for the first time he began inspecting possible properties. His searches were fruitless, but he left instructions with Anatoly to watch for anything which might be suitable near Moscow. Having mistakenly bought a ticket which took him via Kharkov instead of Kiev, he arrived in the city to discover that *Onegin* was being performed that evening. He would dearly have liked to see the performance, for he could have attended incognito, but he had already notified Lev that he would be in Kamenka on the 24th. On that day he began a new diary.

KAMENKA DIARY

Next to his letters, Tchaikovsky's personal diaries are the most important source of information on his outer biography and inner world.

According to Modest, his brother had kept a regular succession of daily diaries from the end of the 1870s to the end of the 1880s (and intermittently after this), but two years before his death had burned the greater number of these. This Kamenka diary was therefore only one from a whole mass of such notebooks of which ten have survived, though one of these perhaps hardly qualifies as a diary since it contains no information on day-to-day affairs, but was a receptacle for Tchaikovsky's views on creative individuals and matters of life, set down in a series of widely spaced entries between 1886 and 1888. Seven of the others relate to the period 1886–91; three are consecutive, covering a twenty-month period from February 1886 to October 1887. Of the remaining six, the longest runs for nearly six months, the shortest for five weeks. The scrappiest is the first, which contains some twenty-five irregular entries made between 23 June and 30 July 1873, from when Tchaikovsky left Russia for a trip through Germany and Switzerland to his arrival in Italy.

The one he was now beginning was to contain fifty-nine consecutive daily entries covering his entire stay at Kamenka. It differs from his first not only in its continuity, but in its content. The 1873 diary had been a record of external events – of places visited or traversed, persons whom Tchaikovsky encountered, trivia of his daily existence. It tells us a little about creative schemes which occurred to him during these weeks, and a good deal about his immediate reactions to the various situations he met, but apart from single entries on his love for his native Russia and on his yearning for solitude, it reveals nothing of his deeper desires and responses. The 1884 diary, on the other hand, exposes to us the pattern of his daily life, his work practices and his recreations amid a group of people with whom he shared the closest ties of family relationship or simple friendship. It records his emotional responses to the passing events and encounters of each day – responses all too often more violent than was warranted, as he himself frequently admitted. But it does much more. Letters, even when the recipient was as intimate and trusted as Modest or his patroness, were for the eyes of others; a diary, being a private repository, could harbour a degree of frankness which no letter could, and this Kamenka diary became a place of confession for the most private of feelings and most personal of secrets in a way that that of 1873 did not. This is what makes it so precious. The intimate letters written in the days after his marriage had mostly indicated what

Tchaikovsky's sexual nature was *not*; this Kamenka diary points to its positive characteristics, for there can be little doubt that the symbols X and Z which recur in it, and about which he writes so openly, denote homosexual drives. Most clearly of all, it vividly records an early stage of what was to be the central sexual attraction of his remaining years: his passion for his nephew, Bob.

Because of the unique insights afforded by this 1884 diary, there follows extensive quotation from it even though, apart from the composition of the Third Suite, the actual events of this two-month period at Kamenka were of no greater importance in themselves than were, for instance, the details of Tchaikovsky's relationship with Tkachenko. It is fortunate that, when these diaries were printed in 1923, they were overseen not by Modest, who had died seven years earlier, but by Ippolit, who was far less squeamish about those elements in his brother's personality which might be considered disfiguring or diminishing. In the following transcription[26] only four entries are given in full (the first, last, and those of 8 and 31 May); about one-third of the total text is reproduced. Because the entries use abbreviations liberally, the following pages would become irritatingly dense with square brackets if every editorial amplification was thus noted. Square brackets are therefore reserved for clarifications of the text, or for where significant matters have been incorporated to fill out the diary's record of these two months.

24 April.
Slept right up to Fundukleyevka. A sharp, cold wind. No one met me, but when I arrived [at Kamenka] I found Levushka was up. Chat, tea (I am in a mad-passion-for-tea phase). Letters. Visit to the old ladies [Lev's mother and her unmarried daughters, Alexandra and Elizaveta]. At the big house a most heartfelt meeting. How nice they are! Sat there a long time. Letters from Tasya [Tchaikovsky's niece, Nataliya]. Lev arrived. With him I visited Nikolay Vasilyevich [Lev's elder brother]. There I saw dear Varya [Nikolay's daughter], who's gone thin, and Axel [Sandberg]. Dinner for three: Lev, Sister [the family nickname for Anastasiya Popova] and I. Sister's incredible stories and complaints about Pelageya Osipovna [the Kamenka music teacher] during and after dinner. Walk to *Dubkovyar*. Violets. Cold. At home tea, letters to Modya, Tolya, Nadezhda Filaretovna, Jurgenson, Kondratyev. Supper for two with Lev. Flegont [the Kamenka tutor] arrived, and we played four rubbers of buy-vint. A cold north wind is howling outside.

---

[26] *TD*, pp. 11–29. There are twenty-one extracts from it, mostly very brief, in *TZC2*, pp. 634–45, and numerous even more fragmented ones, in *YDGC* and *TPM3*, pp. 628–9.

25 April.
Got up late. Still cold. After drinking tea, went to Lev who soon left, and I stayed to strum and think up something new. I hit on an idea for a *Concerto* for *piano*, but it turned out too wretched and wasn't new. Walked a little in the garden. Dinner for two: Sister's ill. Played Massenet's *Hérodiade*. Strolled for a bit . . . Drank tea at home . . . Read *Otto Jahn* [on Mozart] . . . After supper real vint. . . .

26 April.
Again got up late. Visit to Father Alexandr [Tarnavich, the Kamenka priest] . . . Sister was at dinner. . . . A terrible, incredible north-east wind continues to blow, but I heroically knocked off my obligatory walk . . . At home wrote letters . . . Read Lopukhin's memoirs. After supper vint for three . . . Terribly unlucky. Continue to do nothing and haven't the slightest inspiration.

27 April. Sunday.
The weather's improved a bit, but it was still with difficulty I completed my morning walk . . . Lunch at home . . . Read English, warmed myself by the fire . . . Dinner at the big house. For some reason it was tedious and heavy going . . . The Englishman frightened me with his proposal for [English] lessons. Vint at home . . . I won. Didn't get to mass today. . . .

28 April.
Rose at 9. The weather's clear . . . Spent all the time until dinner in the Trostyanka woods, gathering violets and deriving deep enjoyment . . . Tried to lay the foundations of a new symphony both in the Trostyanka woods and at home after dinner, but I'm dissatisfied with everything . . . Walked in the garden and conceived *the seed* not of a future symphony, but of a suite . . . Vint for three . . . My bad luck was colossal.

29 April.
In the morning, despite the cruelly cold wind, I went to the Trostyanka woods where I found comparative peace. Noted down some ideas. Dinner for two. Made music. English language. Vint for four . . . I had very bad luck.

30 April.
Trostyanka woods again, and noting down some wretched ideas . . . Visit to the big house . . . After tea English language. A walk to the mills . . . At dinner Nikolay Vasilyevich, Roman Efimovich [Derichenko, the Kamenka doctor] and Flegont. Vint. Lev's departure for Elizavetgrad [now Kirovograd].

1 May.
Woke up off colour . . . Completed a walk . . . Drank tea, played the piano a long time (unprofitably), dined at the big house . . . Read, drank tea, and played vint . . . Very dissatisfied with myself because of the banality of everything that comes into my head. Am I played out? . . .

2 May.
Wonderful weather. All morning in the Trostyanka woods . . . Read English after lunch . . . played the piano and jotted down something in my notebook . . . After dinner conversation about Schopenhauer, Tolstoy, and so on. I'm getting more and more stupid. As soon as there's serious conversation, my head's completely empty . . . Vint for two with Flegont. I lost . . .

3 May.
. . . Walked . . . Lev got back from Elizavetgrad at 7 a.m. and slept till 12 . . . Dined with Lev . . . Worked on English language, and in no time had to go and dine for a second time at the big house . . . Vint for four in the evening . . . Nikolay Vasilyevich came and frayed my nerves terribly with his gossip.

4 May.
. . . Went to the station to meet our people . . . A joyful meeting. Bob . . . Read for a long time . . . Collected *signatures* at home to send to Modya for his birthday . . . Vint for five. My luck was bad and I got terribly cross. Have just read the first Book of Kings.

5 May.
. . . Walked a distance in the field by the Trostyanka woods . . . Dinner with guests . . . Went to the big house . . . Sasha recounted the court news . . . Tea at home, a walk with no enjoyment . . . Two lots of vint. A lot of Z. Ah, what a depraved person I am!

6 May.
11 o'clock. Soon I'll be 44. How long have I lived and, in truth, without false modesty, how little have I done! Even in my regular occupation – for, putting my hand on my heart, there is nothing *perfect, exemplary*. Still I'm searching, wavering, unsteady. And for the rest? I read nothing [significant], I know nothing. Only on vint do I expend an abundance of precious time. But I believe *my health* will *come to no good* from it. Today I was so cross, so irritated, that I believe another moment, and I would have thrown an ugly scene of anger and hatred. My temper today is generally very bad, and my period of calm, quiet life, untroubled by anything, has passed. There's a lot of fuss, a lot of jars, a lot which a madman of my years cannot bear with indifference. No! it is time to live *in my own home* and *in my own way*.

[In his letters Tchaikovsky makes it clear that the return of Sasha and others two days earlier, and the ensuing extra bustle and fuss at Kamenka, accounted for this surge of feeling.]

The whole morning was spent on a pleasant walk . . . I'd hardly managed to get in my evening walk (to the mills) than I was summoned to supper – this is a new arrangement. I suffered from hunger and from *lack of attention* towards me. It's petty – but why hide that even such a trifle can anger me. Then vint and endless anger . . . The Elizavetgrad piano turned out to be a false trail: I'm without a piano [of my own]. I sent Alyosha with Vasily to look for one – as though there was any hope! All day Bob has rejoiced my eyes; how incomparably lovable he is in his white suit . . .

7 May.

Alyosha congratulated me with great affection . . . A very long walk . . . Judging from yesterday I thought everyone had forgotten my birthday, but I was wrong. I was congratulated, and we drank champagne . . . Tea at home . . . English language. Went to the big house . . . A piano from *Mr. Druzhin* . . . Vint. Irritability, but less than yesterday. . . .

8 May.

I'm a sort of walking malice! Because Sasha enjoyed getting me into difficulties at cards I was the more enraged because, out of magnanimity in view of her bad luck in the game today, I had only just previously let her have the bid in clubs (there were three of us playing). How do you like that? Are these the feelings of an artist who enjoys fame? Ugh! Pyotr Ilich, it's shameful, my good fellow! But then, since morning I've not been myself. The abominable state of my stomach is beginning seriously to poison my life. During the morning worked with the maximum effort (the scherzo). At dinner I was again in a rather bad mood. Walked to the Nikolayev field. It was damp, windy and overcast – but in the end it didn't rain. Drank tea in my room. Afterwards wrote a bit more. Bob walked about the garden with me, then came to my room. Ah, what a delight this Bob is! After supper (I was out of temper) vint for three. Ugh! What a life!

9 May.

. . . After a short walk worked all morning; it was now going better. Was angry at dinner because of the extreme chaos reigning in the household's arrangements . . . At home drank tea in company (Vera Vasilyevna [Butakova, Lev's sister]); sat at my window and chatted with Nata [Pleskaya, Lev's cousin] and Bob (. . . Ah, what a perfect being this Bob is!). . . .

10 May.

This vint for three so irritates me, I'm beginning to fear it will affect my health . . . But I haven't the strength to give up the game. Meanwhile today has been exceedingly successful – in the first place, because my work has gone excellently: secondly, because my stomach is in order . . . In the morning strolled in the garden with Bob (what a darling he is!) . . . *At teatime Sasha was eating her dinner* . . . It's very nice when they speak English at dinner. I'm beginning to understand – but Sister always butts in at the most interesting place. Worked after tea. Went to church for Vespers with Sasha . . . After supper there was . . . vint . . . Wrote to the directorate regarding *The Oprichnik.*

[A proposal put to the Imperial Theatres to revive Tchaikovsky's early opera was firmly resisted by the composer, who loathed the piece. He was able to thwart the current plans by pleading that he would need first to revise the work; he confided to Jurgenson, however, that he had no intention whatsoever of undertaking this operation.]

11 May.

. . . Finished the scherzo. After dinner (Pelageya Osipovna) walked . . . There was no game. . . .

12 May.
Why do I play vint? The only result is upset and bad temper . . . As regards the
weather, an abominable day. Spent all day writing the waltz for the suite, but
I'm far from certain it's completely satisfactory. After dinner . . . forced myself
to take a walk . . . to the Trostyanka woods.

13 May.
. . . Continued the waltz . . . Fearing the wind, walked about my room for an
hour . . . After supper (before which, to his great joy, I played duets with my
darling, the incomparable, wonderful, ideal Bob) played vint . . . In the breaks
between rubbers, I visited my angel Bob . . . Played vint till 1 a.m. . . .

14 May.
Walked the whole morning . . . The waltz came along with enormous difficulty. No, I'm growing old. After dinner sat in the drawing-room . . .
Laboured on the waltz until nearly 7 o'clock, but got nowhere. Walked in the
garden . . . After supper vint for four. A miracle – I won! . . .

15 May.
. . . After strolling in the garden a little . . . finished the sketch of the waltz . . .
The communal outing didn't take place. Lev went off with Bob. I wandered
about the vegetable garden and my room . . . Worked on English diligently.
Lev and Bob were away a long time – and, in fact, I got worried . . . We were
late sitting down to vint. . . .

16 May.
I decided in the morning . . . to walk to Zrubanets for lilies of the valley . . .
Having, with the greatest composure of spirit, sat down to play Mozart's
Zauberflöte I was, in the middle of the most exquisite pleasure, interrupted by
the entrance of *Bob*, with a horrified expression, to tell me of the death of Tusya
Bazilevskaya [the daughter of Lev's niece, Sasha (née Peresleny)]. Great
sorrow . . . Wrote letters till teatime, then worked . . . After supper . . . I first
wandered about aimlessly . . . At last, after all, our vint took place. I am very
weary. Darling Tusya! Ah, the poor things, the poor things! And why? But
God's will be done!

17 May.
. . . In the morning took a short walk . . . Worked . . . After dinner wandered
about with Bob . . . Until 7 o'clock struggled with one spot in the Andante. I
was tired. Went to Vespers. Sad thoughts and tears because of Tusya. Was late
for supper . . . Vint for two. . . .

18 May.
Wonderful weather . . . Went to mass. Was very susceptible to religious
impressions; stood nearly all the time with tears in my eyes. I'm always
touched to the depths of my soul by the manifestation of simple, wholesome
religious feeling in the common people . . . Was at the big house . . . Went to
the market with Bob. Worked very successfully . . . Strolled to the mills at

sunset. After supper played dances for the children . . . No vint at all. I confess
vint is almost a necessity for me – it's really disgraceful.

19 May.
A wonderful summer day. It tempted me to walk the whole morning . . . Only
managed to work a little . . . Picked lilies of the valley with Bob, drank tea,
revelled in the wonderful evening . . . Vint for four. When I was winning I was
embarrassed and tried to lose; when my luck changed I was angry. . . .

20 May.
. . . Worked all morning – not without effort, but my Andante is coming along
and I think it will come out very nicely. After dinner . . . walked . . . Drank tea
with Sasha and Nata. Tragic details of Tusya's death received – so painful,
they make you weep. Worked till 7 o'clock . . . English language . . . After
supper . . . a fairly quiet game of vint. I was less out-of-temper than usual.

21 May.
Put on my new clothes. Went to church . . . Called in at the big house . . .
Worked and finished the Andante, with which I'm very satisfied. Bob's ill.
Immediately after dinner . . . a pleasant stroll . . . Bob's well. Supper, Flegont
was late. Vint. . . .

22 May.
. . . Slept excellently . . . Strolled all morning . . . After dinner sat in the
drawing room, then worked a little . . . After supper vint, at which Flegont and
I won. . . .

23 May.
Again cold and windy . . . The first movement of the suite, called *Contrastes*,
with the themes –

[Ex. 196]

– is so loathsome to me that, having played about with it all day, I decided to
discard it and write something completely different . . . How hard has work
become for me! Is it old age at last? . . . English language . . . After supper (by
oil lamp) vint . . . In the morning received news from Pachulski about the
unsuccessful performance of the [Italian] Capriccio in Paris.

24 May.
At 9 o'clock went for a walk . . . Played Mozart. After tea was on the point of
struggling *again* with the loathsome *Contrastes*, but suddenly a new idea flashed
into my head, and the matter sorted itself out . . . Bob (in the end he will simply
drive me out of my mind with his unspeakable fascination) . . . Was terribly

angry during vint, but not on account of the cards but just generally because of something indefinable which might be called Z. Yes, this Z is less tormenting . . . than X – but all the same, it's unpleasant.

25 May. Sunday.
. . . Mass finished early, and for a long while I didn't know what to do with myself. Finally went to Alexandra Ivanovna [Lev's mother] and sat with her and Sister in the drawing-room. Worked. After dinner sat in my workroom with Bob . . . After tea composed a bit . . . Played [vint] with moderate luck . . . Today Z is especially tormenting me. May God forgive me such foul feelings! . . .

26 May.
. . . During the morning I walked a long time about the garden. Worked successfully until dinner. After dinner read Krïlov with Bob . . . Was at Sister's (at her invitation). She was upset that they're sending her to Verbovka [to make room for Nikolay and Anna and other expected guests], and wanted to go to a monastery. During the morning Sasha came to me to talk about this. At first (in the morning) I wasn't sympathetic towards Sister, but after visiting her I understood her feelings very well . . . Vint. I was incredibly irritable and angry, but not about the game, but because Z was tormenting me, which was the more annoying, seeing that during the morning it had subsided.

27 May.
. . . Strolled in the garden. Composed the final variation (the polonaise-finale). After dinner walked . . . Worked again after tea . . . After supper there was vint . . . As usual I was angry – at what I don't know – but most of all at Nikolay Vasilyevich who was talking loudly about this and that, and how he'd got his feet wet. . . .

28 May.
Walked in the garden in the morning . . . Wrote right up to dinner. Dined en petit-comité; Sister has gone off to a monastery . . . After tea again worked . . . Sat for a long time with Bob and Flegont on a bench in the conservatory . . . Worked at English. My successes in understanding what I read are significant, but I still don't understand anything when Miss Eastwood is talking . . . Vint . . . I won.

29 May. Ascension Day.
. . . Sat down to work without taking a walk and wrote until 12 o'clock. Walked with great pleasure . . . Dined at the big house . . . Tea for two with Nata. Worked with great effort . . . Played Mozart and was in ecstasy. Idea for a suite from Mozart . . . I declined to play vint. . . .

30 May.
I am working too hard, as though I'm being driven on. This straining is unhealthy, and it will probably show in the poor suite. In the morning (the weather was marvellous) I walked . . . Worked very successfully (the

variations before the finale). After this sat with Bob on the roof (I'd only climb up there for this angel!) . . . After this drank tea . . . and then worked furiously so as to be able to begin something new tomorrow. Sister's come back from the monastery. Dropped in on her before supper . . . Vint. I was very "tired and played withaut [Sic!] great pleasure" [Tchaikovsky wrote these words in English]. I lost.

31 May.

Tasya's sixteenth birthday was celebrated. Tolerable weather. In the morning I wrote a variation. Dinner was special, with champagne. Walked to the Trostyanka woods. Drank tea in my own room. Wrote letters. With Bob (the darling!) walked to the cliffs; there joined a boating party, and returned home with him. Dropped in at the conservatory with Bob and sat with Em. Fed. Played [my] children's songs to Bob. At Vespers. An evening with dancing: I was the pianist. Bob was amused beyond words that I played quadrilles on themes he gave me. At the end, when everyone had dispersed, Nata, who'd been very thoughtful, suddenly said to me: "Ah, Petichka, life isn't worth living!" Such words on the lips of so healthy and balanced a person as Nata made a very sad impression on me. In the course of the evening Vera Vasilyevna recalled the past – and apparently with regret. But all that she recalls is personally loathsome to me, and I wouldn't want any of it to return. [Seventeen years earlier, at Hapsal, Vera had been strongly attracted to Tchaikovsky, to his great embarrassment and distress.]

1 June. Sunday.

Was late for church . . . Afterwards walked to the big house . . . Was at Vera Vasilyevna's. Talked with her about Tanya. At home I managed to write a variation. After dinner a trip to Verbovka in the landau with Lev, Sasha and Bob . . . Vint after supper, at which I lost 7½ roubles. . . .

2 June.

. . . I worked well today, for I wrote a whole four variations. In the morning I only made a tour of the garden, and afterwards worked, finishing at 12.30 in expectation of Bob, who'd promised to come to learn singing, but who disappointed my expectations . . . Walked . . . Worked. Walked about vainly searching for Bob . . . Had supper (unusually tasty) at the Pleskys'. On returning home we played vint, and I won a little.

3 June.

Woke in the night because of a pain in my throat and nausea, and was off-colour all day, even though I worked well. Before dinner Bob came, and I played him my [children's] songs. After dinner got to the Trostyanka woods and back with the greatest effort. After tea was sitting down to work, but Bob lured me away . . . As soon as I'm not working or walking . . . I begin to long for Bob, and feel lonely without him. I love him terribly . . . A rehearsal. I accompanied Tasya's couplets. Unsympathetic performance, this. Vint with interruptions from Nikolay Vasilyevich. I won a lot.

4 June.
. . . Worked successfully . . . After dinner walked to the Trostyanka woods . . . *Finished the suite* . . . Wonderful evening . . . A rehearsal – *Les Femmes savantes*?!!? I was very nervy. Everything irritates me, and not without reason! The pain or, rather, the strange feeling in my throat . . . begins to worry me . . . Vint. I won. Despite this I was very out of spirits.

5 June.
A letter from Pachulski telling me of the sale of *Dvoryaninov* [an estate Tchaikovsky had considered buying]. Mixed feelings about this. Wrote a long letter to Nadezhda Filaretovna regarding my plans for purchasing an estate, which I have decided to set to one side. Walked to the big house, and talked a great deal with Vera Vasilyevna. Either I'm very mistaken, or she's not completely changed in her old feelings . . . After supper read Gogol with Bob – and dreams of producing *The Inspector-General* [by Gogol]. Tasya's performance is cancelled. Vint. Nikolay Vasilyevich.

6 June.
All day I was worried and extremely irritated by the persistent *strange* feeling in my throat. Worked during the morning on arranging the variations for piano duet. Walked after dinner . . . Wrote, worked at English, and still worried about my throat . . . Played vint with difficulty . . . Was very tortured not by the actual feeling Z, but by the fact that it's in me. . . .

7 June.
Woke . . . out of spirits and worried about *my throat* . . . What is it? Probably nothing, but it doesn't make my nerves more easy . . . Because of my slight indisposition and the marvellous weather, didn't work, but went to the Trostyanka woods . . . Lunch was late . . . Sat on the balcony steps with Bob and Tasya, who combed my hair . . . Afterwards did a little work at home . . . Wrote two variations . . . It was very nice at Vespers . . . Bob hurt his knee . . . My anxiety. The doctor. Vint. Appalling luck.

8 June. Whitsunday.
Mass . . . After dinner *the feeling* began again . . . I managed to do some work . . . After supper dancing. Vint for five.

9 June.
. . . Completed a splendid walk . . . Did a little work. After supper vint. . . .

10 June.
In the morning took a long walk . . . First I worked at the transcription of the variations, then at selecting my piano pieces for a volume of *Ausgewählte Werke* which Pyotr Ivanovich [Jurgenson] is projecting . . . A trip in the *landau* to Prussy: Sasha, Nata, Tasya, Sister and I. It would have been very pleasant if it hadn't been for *the feeling* which had seemed to be going, but which had returned with renewed strength. . . .

11 June.
Since the morning *the feeling*. Completed a long walk . . . Worked on (1) the variations, (2) proof-reading Mozart [Jurgenson was publishing a vocal score with the translation Tchaikovsky had made in 1875 of the libretto of *Figaro*] . . . After dinner *the feeling* vanished suddenly and completely unexpectedly – but in the evening it returned again. After dinner the proofs. Got Bob ready for his ride on horseback . . . Walked to the mills . . . After supper vint for two with Flegont . . . *The feeling*.

12 June.
. . . In the morning managed to get in my two hours walking . . . Worked and finished *Figaro*. For two hours after dinner was inseparable from my wonderful, incomparable Bob; at first he lounged about on a bench on the balcony, and was enchantingly *relaxed* and chatted about my compositions (*Stone Moscow* [the coronation cantata]). Then he sat in my room and made me play. After tea I worked . . . All day *the feeling*. . . .

13 June.
Marvellous weather. A long walk . . . Wrote the transcription of the finale. After dinner *the feeling* began to pass. Trip to Verbovka . . . At supper heard that Blumenfeld had summoned Vladimir Andreyevich [Plesky, Nata's brother] for some reason. Terrible, insane alarm, especially when Lev instructed that he should be summoned. Could hardly play two rubbers.

14 June.
A walk . . . Wrote the transcription of the finale. After dinner dropped in at the big house . . . Tea at home (for two with Sister . . .) . . . Wrote letters and worked on English. Unsuccessful attempt to get to Vespers at the Pokrov church . . . After supper sat in my study with Bob and talked about school matters. Vint. No luck . . . There was a bit of *the feeling*. . . .

15 June. Sunday.
. . . A trip to the great wood for the whole day . . . Supper and vint with Kern at home. Terribly strong feeling Z. My God! Forgive and calm me! *The feeling* has passed completely . . . A strange thing: I'm *terribly* unwilling to leave here. I think it's because of Bob.

16 June.
Dreamed about M and consequently was all day a little – and even more than a little – in love . . . It's nothing, nothing! Silence!!! In the morning was in the Trostyanka woods . . . At tea, and during the whole day in general, poor Sister irritated me; I am not nearly as affectionate towards her as I ought to be . . . After supper lots of people came to say goodbye to Sasha [who was going to Carlsbad]. Vint. I did very badly. Because of this, and most of all for a thousand other reasons constituting what I call Z, I was as angry as a vicious snake. Arrived home under the distressing, heavy pressure of this Z.

17 June.
Awoke with a severe pain in my throat . . . Made myself go for a walk. Worked at home. After dinner the pain began to get worse . . . so that each time I swallowed it was hellish torture. The night was terribly agonizing.

18 June.
A little better towards morning, thanks to a heavy sweat. How much friendship and sympathy Alyosha shows on such occasions! . . . Slept nearly all day. . . Ate very little . . . All the same, I played vint, and made myself survive two rubbers. Slept intermittently that night. Heard Sasha leave.

19 June.
Stayed indoors all day . . . Much better . . . Dined in my room . . . had supper at the house. Vint with Flegont, Lev and Dima [Lev's nephew]. . . .

20 June.
Walked to the Trostyanka woods. After dinner was at the big house . . . A ride through the fields in a wagonette . . . After supper, vint. At 11 o'clock left for the station with a drunken Alyosha and intolerable, good-for-nothing Mitya. At 1 in Znamenka. . . .

21 June.
Slept a lot. At four in Kharkov. Because of the exhibition I stayed not at the Grand Hotel, but at the Metropole. Idled about. The cathedral. The singers. Dinner at the Grand Hotel, tea at home. With Alyosha in the Tivoli Gardens.

The creative energies whose operations were to produce the Third Suite had begun quietly to collect themselves almost immediately following Tchaikovsky's post-*Mazepa* flight from Russia in February 1884. After only a fortnight in Paris he was thinking of starting upon a symphony when he returned to Kamenka, and in St Petersburg, after his audience with the Tsar, these intentions consolidated themselves. But, as his Kamenka diary reveals, within four days of his arrival in the Ukraine he had abandoned the idea of a symphony in favour of a suite because, as he explained to his patroness on that day (28 April: see above, p. 22), it was the freedom which the latter form offered which attracted him to it. Satisfactory ideas were slow to form themselves, however, and it was a further eleven days before he had decided on its overall shape; it would consist of five movements, and the last would be a set of variations. The ensuing birth process has been recorded in the Kamenka diary, and Tchaikovsky's letters of these same weeks confirm the dogged persistence which was demanded of him; indeed, the intended first movement (*Contrastes*) so dissatisfied him that he scrapped it. But the final stages of composition seem to have gone more easily. Certainly he now had much more confidence in its worth, and after completing the sketches on 4 June he felt it might prove to be the best of the three he had now composed. His faith in it increased during scoring at Grankino. It was finished on 31 July, and first performed at an RMS concert in St Petersburg on 24 January 1885, conducted by Hans von Bülow.

Tchaikovsky had thought the suite might score a success. 'But reality far exceeded my expectations,' he wrote to his patroness six days later. 'I have never before experienced such a triumph. I saw that the entire mass of the audience was moved, and grateful to me. These moments are the finest adornment of the artist's life. Thanks to these it is worth living and labouring.'[27] Modest remembered that his brother had never been more rapturously applauded, even declaring it was the greatest public triumph yet achieved by a Russian symphonic work. Moscow also greeted it with enthusiasm a week later, though Modest reported that its reception here was not so ecstatic as in St Petersburg, attributing this to the fact that Erdmannsdörfer's advocacy was less electrifying than that of Bülow. In both cities the press was unanimously favourable; even Laroche roused himself from his lethargy to claim that some of Tchaikovsky's works of the last three or four years had moved the centre of the musical world from Germany or France to Russia, and that the music of Tchaikovsky was now the true music of the future. Yet this din of public tribute and chorus of praise from the press for this one work had a still sweeter import for Tchaikovsky himself. It was another palpable endorsement by a wider public of what the Tsar's award had already symbolized.

Laroche's judgement was, of course, absurdly wrong, but it is a useful reminder that what may now strike us as merely conventional may have sounded very fresh at the time of its creation. There had certainly been little deep investigation of new expressive territories in Tchaikovsky's recent music, but there had been inventiveness – or, at least, real conviction – in the handling of old expressive issues and forms. Even the fugues of the earlier suites, dull as they had been, were not stale. The Third Suite is most notable for its further exploration of melodic and orchestral possibilities exposed in its immediate predecessor, and for Tchaikovsky's return to the challenge of the large-scale variation form. These matters are of concern in the last three movements; what most commands admiration in the opening Andantino molto cantabile is the skill with which well-tried practices are adapted

---

[27] *TLP*13, p. 25; *TPM*3, p. 337; *TZC*3, p. 20; *DTC*, p. 405; *YDGC*, p. 335 (partial).

to provide support for a very extensive flow of simple melody. Though it scarcely sounds like it, this *Elégie* is a sonata structure sharing many features with *Romeo and Juliet*. Thus both subjects are large ternary slabs, and while the middle section of the first opens up further the preceding melodic world, the central portion of the E flat paragraph is a new melody which gives this secondary tonal area the thematic dualism of *Romeo*'s second subject. Elements of the two subjects, or natural extensions from their melodic worlds, are set against one another in the development; as in *Romeo* there is a reordering of events in the recapitulation, though this time it is not a switch within the second subject, but a reversal of both subjects, for as G major is re-established the second subject is heard first. Yet when the first subject emerges out of its predecessor, it returns at a point within its middle section, as had the first subject of *Romeo*. As for the extensive rumination for cor anglais in the coda, this takes its departure from the drooping cadential phrase of the first subject, just as the new chorale-like melody in the coda of the Fourth Symphony's first movement had grown, also by augmentation, out of a portion of the fate theme.

Yet there have been none of the tensions or contrasts of true sonata thought in this lyrical movement. As was noted during discussion of the 1875 songs, $\frac{6}{8}$ rarely drew the melodic best from Tchaikovsky, and the narrow bars of the present movement, despite their $\frac{2}{4}$ shifts, foster a rhythmic sameness in both main themes, neither of which (especially the second) has much distinction. They possess charm, but their unvaried fluency becomes bland, whereas the first theme of the following *Valse mélancolique* has such ingenious variety that the stiff rhythmic personalities of its companions in the episodes of this simple rondo become positive assets. In the presentation of both these subsidiary themes running counterpoints have a prominent part; in view of what transpires in the finale, there must be some suspicion that these were incorporated as features which would especially please the German dedicatee. But the initial 22-bar waltz theme (Ex. 197) was even more novel than its counterpart in the Second Suite (see Ex. 190), with the rhythmic fluctuations taking on a yet more fundamental role, conditioning the momentum of the whole tune. Thus the energy released in the opening bar is promptly curbed in a single note B, is restored within three bars and enhanced in the two-bar sequence which builds from a natural extension of the opening configuration; then at bar nine it is fully released into a broad phrase which drives on, then winds down, first to rediscover something of its opening profile, finally to expire in a delayed, long-held E. Like its opposite number in the Second Suite, the repetition of this opening strain takes a new course, and this time

Ex. 197

reaches its harmonic destination in the penultimate phrase, its final four bars being merely a melodic postlude. A theme such as this, rather than a more conventional invention like the famous horn tune of the Fifth Symphony's Andante cantabile, emphasizes the rarity of Tchaikovsky's melodic gift; if the dancers of the first *Swan Lake* found the waltzes of that score bewildering, it is difficult to imagine what they would have made of this one.

This 'obligatory waltz' cost Tchaikovsky much effort, so his diary tells us, but it was labour well spent. By contrast the Scherzo seems to have come more easily. It continued the special researches of its predecessor, the *Scherzo burlesque*, in the spheres of texture and orchestration. The *Valse mélancolique* had especially explored the lower register of the orchestra, but this Scherzo lives in an altogether brighter world. The kaleidoscopic variety of colour of the *Scherzo burlesque* is here displayed with even sharper contrasts, and the central section, with its procession of piquant four-note phrases on trumpets and trombones, punctuated with delicate flecks from alternating strings and woodwind and the lightest of contributions from cymbals and snare drum, is one of the most ear-enchanting mixtures Tchaikovsky had yet confected. The incorporation of a pertly chattering phrase for oboes and bassoons provides the neatest of rhythmic connections with the flanking sections. Laroche saw in this music a lilliputian army, tiny elfin-soldiers on parade. One may question Laroche's particular image (and one certainly would the 'sense of sepulchral cold, of menacing, stony hopelessness'[28] he had detected in the *Valse mélancolique*), but not his instinct to discern in this brisk, spicy music suggestions of sprightly

[28] *TZC*3, p. 22.

miniature beings such as were, some seven years hence, to spring to life within the toy and tinsel world of *The Nutcracker*.

The theme and variations of this suite was only the fourth set in the official canon of Tchaikovsky's work; it also proved to be the last. His first, the twelve variations for piano, Op. 19, No. 6, of 1873, is an untidy set, handicapped by a theme of indifferent quality, a concern for enterprise in harmony and dissonance more ingenious than judicious, and textural turgidity. It foretold, however, Tchaikovsky's readiness to remodel, even rebuild his theme, a technique used more boldly in the vastly superior Rococo Variations, but with a control that ensured that the structural coherence and expressive focus of the whole was never impaired – that is, until Fitzenhagen laid his vandal's hands on it. In the finale of the Piano Trio the stylistic constraints of a rococo ideal had been absent, and Tchaikovsky had guaranteed the expressive gamut would be wide by laying a special emphasis on the character variation, as he was to do in this suite's finale, even though the theme of the latter could easily have fathered a second rococo set. As in the Trio there are twelve variations, some of which rigorously preserve, while others reject, the ternary structure of the theme. Similarly, there are numerous changes of metre and key, the one element always preserved being at least a portion of the theme's opening contour, even though the rhythm may be drastically restructured, additional notes may be inserted, or accidentals added to introduce a new key (Ex. 198).

Yet for all the variety of shape and character, and the thematic freedom of individual variations, this set's coherence is impressive for, unlike that of the Trio, it controls the range and pace of its expressive evolution, and it avoids the long-winded fugal labours and gargantuan sonata-patterned finale into which the heavy epicism of the earlier set had tempted Tchaikovsky. Nevertheless, it would appear from the evidence of the music itself that some of these variations, like those of the trio (if we are to believe Kashkin), were conditioned by the person of the dedicatee, and that the first four odd-numbered ones were kindly tributes to Erdmannsdörfer's nationality. Three are studiously contrapuntal; in variation 1, above the theme on pizzicato strings, flutes and clarinets paired in octaves weave unbroken florid counterpoints exactly as they had done in the first episode of the *Valse mélancolique*, while in variation 3, another cantus firmus study (scored only for three flutes, two clarinets and two bassoons), the tune is sustained against up to six supporting parts. Variation 5 is a fugato based on the theme's first four bars (Ex. 198c), the counterpoint having a studied gawkiness which ensures that the sort of thing which in the trio had sounded drily pedantic here sounds tongue-in-cheek, even mildly humorous. Variation

Ex. 198

7 converts the first three bars of the tune into the beginning of a four-line chorale. And if in the intervening variations Tchaikovsky has seemed intent on displaying a verve and capriciousness very much his own, there is in variation 4 a touch which cannot have been lost on Erdmannsdörfer when Tchaikovsky demonstrates impishly that he can surreptitiously turn his theme into the 'Dies irae'. But in the remaining five variations he is entirely himself. Indeed, after the Lutheran tones of variation 7, the theme fathers a plangent cor anglais cantilena, as Russian as could be (Ex. 198e), then for variation 9 generates a two-bar fragment which is repeated, *Kamarinskaya*-like, against a swift series of ever loudening backgrounds. After these variations-within-a-variation the sudden interruption of a violin cadenza signals a soloist's variation – a sort of hesitant waltz (Ex. 198f) which could easily have found a home in one of Tchaikovsky's ballets. The preceding two variations had raised the key a tone (to A minor and major respectively), and the move is repeated in variations 10 and 11, the latter moving back towards the original theme by restoring its rhythmic structure, though not its contours. The key is now B major, thus providing a neat balance to the opposite major third shift (G to E flat major) early in the first

movement. The unbroken tonic B pedal which has contributed so much to this variation's pervasive melancholy becomes finally a pivot upon which a series of G major chords can be swung into this B major context, thus forecasting the final return of the whole work's tonic. After portentous preliminaries G major is restored, and the polonaise-finale bursts in augustly, the opening pitches of the original theme now squeezed into a string of semiquavers which teasingly sounds like both an anacrusis and an opening bar (Ex. 198g). The disappointment in this sonorous finale is the theme of the second episode; otherwise this whole grand importation from the world of opera makes a colourful and bright end, neatly incorporating brief echoes from the scherzo's trio to remind us of but one of the delights that have gone before.

8

A HOME OF HIS OWN

'I WILL TELL you the details concerning my requirements. Land is quite unnecessary to me – i.e., I want only a modest house with a nice garden, *but established*. *A river* is certainly desirable. If there is a wood nearby, so much the better – but I mean, of course, a wood belonging to someone else – for, I repeat, I want to own only a modest house and garden. This dacha or cottage must be completely detached, and not in a row of other *dachas* and, most of all, it must be not far from a station so that *Moscow* is always at hand. . . . The most important and vital condition is that the location should be sympathetic, beautiful. If the house is situated somewhere low down so that there is no view from the windows, then it does not answer my requirements. A factory nearby is also very undesirable. That, I think, is everything.'[1] Thus, while at Kamenka, Tchaikovsky had set out the specifications for a home of his own so that his patroness could transmit them to Pachulski. This problem pupil had offered to help in the search, but he was only one of the agencies through which the composer had conducted enquiries during his early weeks at Sasha's. Though the disparity between his current resources and the price he would now have to pay brought a sudden sense of realism into his plans so that for the moment the project was shelved, within a year his hopes were to be realized.

After meeting Modest in Kharkov, Tchaikovsky headed for Grankino, where he planned to spend some time with his brother. The activity of the two months passed in the relatively uncongenial setting of Kamenka had wearied him, and in the peacefulness, fresh air and attractive living of the Konradi estate he found both rejuvenation and encouragement to work. Not only did he press ahead with scoring the Third Suite and further correcting the proofs of the vocal score of *Figaro* which contained his Russian version of da Ponte's libretto (an operation during which he decided that sometime he would perform the same translation service to *Don Giovanni*); he was soon making sketches

---

[1] *TLP*12, p. 372; *TPM*3, p. 279; *TZC*2, p. 643.

for a new piano concerto, a project which he quickly decided should be a two-movement concert piece instead. So contented was he that he delayed joining Anatoly and his family until after he had finished with the suite. The next day, 1 August, he left for Skabeyevo, where this brother had rented a villa and from which Moscow was easily accessible.

Skabeyevo he found yet more attractively situated than Podushkino, where he had passed the previous summer. It had been arranged that Laroche should share the villa, but this produced constant tensions. By now he was in an appalling condition, riddled with syphilis which Anatoly was in constant terror of contracting from him, and deteriorating intellectually, as even Tchaikovsky had to recognize. Once again he acted as scribe for this pathetic friend, but was dismayed at the 'empty-headed chatter'[2] about Mozart which he had to record, for he believed Laroche had once been without equal in Russia as a writer on music. Tchaikovsky's luggage containing the score of the suite and sketches for the new work for piano and orchestra had temporarily gone astray, but he would have been unable to work on it since the Skabeyevo villa owned no piano. Yet his equanimity held. Modest, who had been labouring on a new play at Grankino, was now in despair at his inability to find a satisfactory ending, and Tchaikovsky provided both moral support and a possible conclusion. And while bolstering Modest, he was also attempting to mollify Taneyev. The performance of *Die Zauberflöte* which Tchaikovsky had attended at the Conservatoire in April had been conducted by Karl Albrecht, even though it had been prepared by Taneyev – or so the latter claimed. Furious that Albrecht had plucked the glory from another's labours, Taneyev had turned to Tchaikovsky, who had gently reproached his former pupil for begrudging an older yet less publicly esteemed colleague a rare opportunity to gain some recognition. But Taneyev had remained unpersuaded by Tchaikovsky's balanced and sensitive words, and he now returned to the matter, provoking a substantial reply notable for its clear-headed perception of human character and relationships, and for its persuasive tact in both soothing yet chiding a badly ruffled friend. First he outlined the hard course of Albrecht's early professional career, then dwelt on his integrity, selflessness and conscientiousness, and ended by confronting squarely Taneyev's cause of offence, but with an evenhandedness which is both uncompromising yet disarming.

Even now the circumstance that you didn't conduct doesn't particularly trouble me. Let us suppose you had to do all the *menial work*. But

[2] *TLP*12, p. 411; *TZC*2, p. 652; *TPB*, pp. 313 and 601.

with your love of Mozart there cannot be any menial work when the matter concerns the performance of one of Mozart's best pieces. And most important: if Albrecht were a bad conductor, capable only of spoiling what you had prepared excellently, then I would very likely have been angry. But the point is that he directed the opera *superbly.* Whom, therefore, am I to pity? You, because you were deprived of the pleasure of conducting? But I cannot hide that I would have been even more sorry for Albrecht if, in his present position, being capable and worthy of occupying the conductor's rostrum, he had again for the thousandth time hidden in the shadow behind the scenes. Certainly I cannot deplore the fate of Mozart's opera, for though I don't doubt you would have conducted it superbly, Karlusha also conducted superbly.[3]

It was, of course, pure coincidence that Tchaikovsky should find himself in so short a time acting as nursemaid to Laroche and counsellor to both Modest and Taneyev. Yet the fact that he found such abundant reserves of wisdom and patient sympathy to deal so sensibly and amply with these three problem people is surely further confirmation of the increasing inner balance and confidence in himself which the Tsar's recognition and his ever-rising status in the public's eyes were fostering.

Tchaikovsky remained some six weeks at Skabeyevo. The new concert piece continued gently to form itself; his other musical activity was playing duets with Laroche, including items from Mozart's *Idomeneo*, Liszt's Faust Symphony and Borodin's *In Central Asia*. His reading again included Maupassant, in whose stories he found far more enjoyment than in Daudet's *Sapho*, where he suspected the author, under a pretence of offering a moral warning to his sons, of merely titillating French taste with a tale of debauchery. During one of two brief visits to Moscow he was introduced by Taneyev to his new Third Symphony, for which he admitted he could not feel much enthusiasm. The intention had been to return to Kamenka when Anatoly and his family left for the Crimea, but news came that Lev had journeyed to Paris to see Tanya and had brought her back to the family home. Since this would mean that no one would be on hand to guarantee Georges-Léon's continuing welfare, Tchaikovsky was quick to request Jurgenson to despatch a further 750 francs through a trusted agent in Paris to ensure that the child would remain secure until he himself could travel thither. Meanwhile, with Tanya present, Kamenka would be uncongenial, and since Anna and Nikolay were occupying

[3] *TLP*12, p. 407; *TZC*2, pp. 655–6; *TTP*, p. 111.

Tchaikovsky's own quarters there, he knew composition would be impracticable. So instead he turned to his patroness to ask whether he might at last take up her offer of a period at Pleshcheyevo when she left in mid-September. Her assent was immediate. Yet on leaving Skabeyevo on 13 September he headed first for Moscow, since he wanted to acquaint Taneyev with the finished sketch of the Concert Fantasia which he hoped his friend would introduce during the coming season. Tchaikovsky had asked that Laroche might periodically stay with him at Pleshcheyevo, partly so that their duet playing might continue, partly to gain Laroche's help in his study of English, and partly in the hope that he could fan further Laroche's fading literary spark. Otherwise, however, he had arranged that only Alexey and a cook should attend upon him, thus ensuring the maximum peace and privacy.

The house at Pleshcheyevo he found typical of his patroness's taste: overgrand and over-furnished, but well provided with musical instruments, books, music and wine. He would have preferred its situation to have been less enclosed, but the grounds, which ran extensively along the banks of a river, were delightful. Apart from a two-day visit to Moscow, Pleshcheyevo claimed him for a whole month, consolidating his longing for the quiet of a country environment, even though almost his sole visitor was Laroche, who returned with him from Moscow but only for one night, since he was again endeavouring to discipline himself into discharging properly his Conservatoire duties. In Moscow Tchaikovsky had heard Paul Pabst play his new *Grande fantaisie* on themes from *Mazepa*, which he judged 'very effective'.[4] He had much respect for Pabst; earlier at Kamenka, while planning that collection of his own piano works which Jurgenson wished to issue, he had entrusted Pabst with the final decision on what should be selected, giving him licence to edit them as seemed to him appropriate, though he was not to tamper with the substance.

At Pleshcheyevo Tchaikovsky re-read in Russian literature, discovering that as his regard for Tolstoy increased, so his enthusiasm for Turgenev cooled. He continued to work his way through *David Copperfield* in English, and made the acquaintance (in translation) of Goethe's *Wilhelm Meister* ('a complete *révélation* to me; I'd always thought it was terribly boring but, God! – what a delight it is!'[5]). He found among his benefactress's vocal scores Musorgsky's recently published *Khovanshchina* ('I discovered exactly what I had expected: pretension to realism in the peculiar way he understands and applies it, pitiful technique, poverty of invention – from time to time episodes with

[4] *TLP*12, p. 445.
[5] *TLP*12, p. 434; *TZC*2, p. 660; *TPB*, p. 317; *YDGC*, p. 324.

talent'[6]) and Wagner's *Parsifal* ('where, instead of people with characteristics and feelings with which we are familiar, there are fairy-tale
beings fit to adorn a ballet but in no way a drama . . . Their sufferings,
their feelings, their triumphs or misfortunes are completely alien to us –
and what is *alien* to the human heart cannot be the source of musical
inspiration'[7] – though he freely admitted that its 'harmonic richness is
amazing'[8]). From the Paris journal *Gaulois* he received a request to
contribute to an anthology of piano pieces in aid of impoverished
musicians, and responded with the *Impromptu caprice* which he inscribed to Sofya Jurgenson, and which her husband swiftly reprinted
for Russian musicians. Otherwise there was nothing to distract him
from completing the scoring of the Concert Fantasia, and this he did on
6 October. He now had no important outstanding commitments; all
that remained was to name to Jurgenson the prices for the suite (300
roubles) and the fantasia (200 roubles).

Just as Kotek had fired Tchaikovsky to compose his Violin Concerto,
so he had been spurred to write his Concert Fantasia by a particular
performer, 'a certain d'Albert', he told Nadezhda von Meck on 26 July,
some four weeks after starting upon the piece, 'a young man who
arrived in Moscow last winter, and whom I heard a great deal both at
concerts there and in a private house. In my opinion he is a pianist *of
genius*, and the true successor of the Rubinsteins.'[9] Yet though d'Albert
had been the original inspiration for the work, and though, when
writing to his patroness in July, Tchaikovsky had compared Taneyev
unfavourably with d'Albert, the former was Tchaikovsky's choice of
soloist when it received its première at an RMS concert conducted by
Erdmannsdörfer in Moscow on 6 March 1885, and he was delighted
both with Taneyev's account of the solo part and the audience's
response, which was equally enthusiastic when Taneyev introduced it
to St Petersburg on 16 April 1886, with Bülow conducting.

The Concert Fantasia enjoyed some popularity in Tchaikovsky's
lifetime, but has since sunk into complete neglect. Its crippling weakness is that it contains not one really strong idea, yet its very original
structure suffices to show that Tchaikovsky was concerned to fashion
something more than a mere showpiece to gratify a virtuoso pianist or
inflame a lionizing audience. His confessed dislike for the sound of
piano with orchestra had inclined him to segregate the soloist in the
Second Piano Concerto, nowhere more rigorously than in the develop-

---

[6] *TLP*12, p. 436; *TPM*3, p. 310; *TZC*2, p. 660; *YDGC*, p. 323 (partial).
[7] *TLP*12, p. 436; *TPM*3, p. 311; *TZC*2, p. 661.
[8] ibid.
[9] *TLP*12, p. 402; *TPM*3, p. 289; *TZC*2, p. 650; *DTC*, p. 457.

ment of the first movement, and the complete exclusion of the orchestra from the central section of this fantasia's first movement was the logical goal towards which this precedent had pointed. Elsewhere in the later work, however, Tchaikovsky seems to have been intent on exploiting that more selective approach to orchestral sound which had preoccupied him in his two recent suites (hence the time occupied in scoring the piece), and a glance through the opening pages of this fantasia's first movement quickly reveals the swiftly changing variety in the orchestral combinations, and the finely judged, yet sometimes highly detailed textures, so different from the Second Concerto's plain and solid slabs. The title of this first movement (*Quasi Rondo*) is unhelpful, since apart from the playfulness of the first two themes, which Tchaikovsky may have felt gave them some affinity with the sparkling ideas of classical rondo finales, there is no connection with rondo practice. Instead it resembles a sonata movement, with an exposition and recapitulation unfolded by soloist and orchestra, the development being replaced by a gigantic cadenza. This sonata view is well supported by the outer sections, for the first is a three-stage exposition much like that of the first movement of the Third Symphony, with the three themes (Ex. 199b, d and e) segregated tonally by being placed in the tonic, relative minor of the dominant, and dominant respectively (G, B minor and D), while the recapitulation simply shifts the last two themes into the relative minor and tonic (E minor and G). Despite the diversity of these themes, some simple protoshape (Ex. 199a) had haunted Tchaikovsky's creativity during their conception, and this same process also conditioned the two seemingly quite new ideas upon which the centre of the movement is based, the first (Ex. 199c) taking its contour from the movement's opening (Ex. 199b), the second (Ex. 199g) more distantly deriving from an inverted form of the 'third' subject (Ex. 199h); it is from this subject also that the extension of the first cadenza theme derives its shape (Ex. 199e and f).[10] The First Piano Concerto had employed thematic transformation, but whereas it had been in that work's development that the themes had progressively converted themselves into new forms, in this *Quasi Rondo*'s centre the two new themes retain their initial identities. And in one fundamental respect this enormous piano rhapsody rejects a developmental role, for instead of pursuing a consistently unstable tonal course, it is bounded by large slabs of G major and D major music. True, its central portion

[10] Nor, bearing in mind that, only the day before first hearing d'Albert, Tchaikovsky had once again listened to a performance of his own First Symphony, should we overlook the affinity between this first melody of the cadenza and the thematic world of the symphony's slow movement (see bars 46–9).

does explore flat key regions; but as it approaches its end, the calm cadencing and gentle thematic resolution denies to the orchestral re-entry any strongly marked function of being a tonic-resolving cul-mination; instead there is a modicum of surprise when the bright wind theme breaks in, its freshness redoubled after the textural ungainliness of much that has preceded it.

If the Andante mosso first movement had exhibited an unobtrusive thematic unity, the second, Andante cantabile, is built upon explicit melodic polarity; it was, in fact, the refugee conception from the Third Suite, and still carried the title *Contrastes*. When he had first had the idea

Ex. 199

for this movement at Kamenka in May, Tchaikovsky had quickly abandoned it, merely noting in his diary its two principal and highly contrasted themes (see Ex. 196). It is not known whether he intended the ramifications of this thematic dualism to be as far-reaching as they ultimately proved to be, but in this fantasia he not only effectively juxtaposes the two themes (first consecutively, then simultaneously), but makes them the initiators of very extensive sections which provide respectively the slow movement and finale elements of a conventional concerto's second and third movements. The mildly folky first theme begins as a pallid eight-bar invention, and comes to life only when a solo cello breaks in to reflect upon its cadence. The ensuing duologue is followed by a wistful string theme (più tranquillo), itself partnered by a rocking two-note horn line. Memories of *Romeo and Juliet* are inescapable, but this time the function of the quasi-ostinato is not to recall a theme just passed, but to provide a link to the future, for after the whole opening theme has been repeated, this oscillation suddenly re-emerges in the violas, foretelling the imminent intrusion of the contrasting theme which it also accompanies; the brief tussle for supremacy between these thematic opposites provides the most arresting passage in the whole fantasia. This second movement now reveals it has sonata-structure affiliations as had the first, for the course initially pursued by the molto vivace suggests that an exposition is being unfolded, though the brillante second subject is swiftly followed by a number of interrelated themes which only re-establish the dominant after an extended excursion through a variety of keys. After the abrupt return of the slow theme in the tonic, soon to be counterpointed by its capricious thematic antithesis (Ex. 200), the whole second subject section of the molto vivace is re-run, now also centring on the tonic. After such extrovert high spirits the repetition of the long-absent piu tranquillo string theme is in danger of sounding mawkish. The hectic coda begins by lightly echoing the opening of the whole fantasia.

For all its melodic shortcomings, the Concert Fantasia has some engaging qualities and a structural freshness which should win it the occasional hearing. Tchaikovsky himself clearly had reservations about the second movement, and appended to his autograph score an alternative ending to the first movement for use if it was wished to perform this separately. The conclusion of this corresponds to the final twenty-four bars of *Contrastes*.

With the Concert Fantasia completed, Tchaikovsky steeled himself for his visit to St Petersburg to attend the later rehearsals and first night of the new production of *Onegin* which the Tsar had authorized at the Bolshoy Theatre. Yet in the time which remained to him at Pleshcheyevo he could not remain entirely idle, and before leaving he had composed two of the six romances which were to make up his set, Op. 57. Besides reading copiously, he found much fascination in experimenting with the various stops on the harmonium his patroness had sent for his pleasure. On 15 October he set in order the books and music he had used, and confessed the single mischief he had committed during his stay. 'One night I wanted to wind up the big clock which

Ex. 200

hangs in my bedroom (it had stopped, and I'm terribly fond of the ticking of a clock at night), and I turned the key so vigorously that the weight fell with a crash, and the clock needs a substantial repair.'[11] Two days later he was in the Russian capital.

Even more than when *Mazepa* had been produced at the beginning of the year, Tchaikovsky was aware of the respect and cooperation with which the performers and staff of the Imperial Theatres were preparing *Onegin*. Nápravník had rehearsed the music thoroughly, and both the production and the principals were good, especially Pavlovskaya as Tatyana and Pryanishnikov as Onegin. In fact, the next few weeks were to be one of the most decisive phases in the relationship between Tchaikovsky's music and the public, though the first performance of *Onegin* at the Bolshoy Theatre on 31 October gave little sign of this; despite Modest's disclaimer, there even seems to have been some hissing after the first scene. Nevertheless, the applause strengthened as the evening proceeded; the ball was warmly received, the composer was given repeated ovations, and was presented with a laurel wreath, all of which signified at least a notable personal success, and which brought on an instant attack of nerves from which he took some days to recover. Yet the press produced its customary mixture of reactions. There was some enthusiasm ('all the sympathetic aspects of Mr Tchaikovsky's gift are boldly expressed . . . *Eugene Onegin* must be acknowledged . . . as Tchaikovsky's operatic masterpiece'[12]), but also incomprehension ('there is no doubt that *Eugene Onegin* was written under the influence of Dargomïzhsky's declamatory style [in *The Stone Guest*]'[13] . . . 'there is much, very much music, but in it the symphonist mercilessly crushes the operatic composer'[14] . . . 'many melodious bits . . . but little scenic movement'[15]). As for the opposition party within the press, it was led by the implacable Cui, whose malevolence reveals more about himself than his subject; the duel scene made 'a comic impression', Lensky's aria was 'a mournful diatonic whimper', the polonaise produced 'only boredom', Gremin's aria was 'banal' and Onegin's arioso 'commonplace'; even Tatyana's letter scene had only 'one or two successful phrases' to redeem the 'monotony, emptiness . . . and, in places, the vulgarity of the rest', and the whole opera was judged 'stillborn, absolutely worthless and weak', though Cui did concede it was excellently scored.[16]

[11] *TLP*12, p. 454; *TPM*3, p. 317; *TZC*2, p. 665.
[12] *DTC*, pp. 87–8; *YDGC*, p. 327 (partial); *TPM*3, p. 630 (partial).
[13] *DTC*, p. 87; *YDGC*, p. 326.
[14] *DTC*, p. 88; *TZC*2, p. 670; *YDGC*, p. 327.
[15] *DTC*, p. 88.
[16] *DTC*, pp. 88–9; *TZC*2, p. 669 (partial).

But when Tchaikovsky himself came to reflect upon all this a month later, he felt able to make a confident distinction. 'I hear that *Eugene Onegin* continues to please the public, but not the press. . . . Of the two evils, *dislike from the public* or *dislike from the press*, I, of course, prefer the latter.'[17] By this time events in St Petersburg had more than gratified this preference. Even before he had left the Russian capital on 13 November, the enthusiasm of the public for *Onegin* had powerfully demonstrated that his music was soaring to a quite new level of popularity which he admitted took him completely by surprise. Tickets for the second night had sold out by 1 o'clock on the day booking opened, and subsequent performances were playing to capacity houses. This, so Modest claimed, became the rule for years to come, and the popularity of the opera quickly spread to the rest of Russia, guaranteeing that Tchaikovsky would never lack for material means for the rest of his life. Reviewing this moment of his brother's life some fifteen years later, Modest had no doubts about its importance. Up till then Tchaikovsky's name had been famed only within the limited circles of fellow professionals and music lovers; after this it 'becomes known and appreciated by the masses, and Pyotr Ilich achieves the highest degree of popularity ever attained by a Russian composer within the borders of his native land'.[18] The events of Tchaikovsky's remaining years are incontrovertible proof that this time Modest was not exaggerating.

Tchaikovsky had planned to leave St Petersburg after the first night of *Onegin*, but because a period of court mourning had caused the Tsar to absent himself from the theatre, the composer decided it was prudent to delay his own departure, especially after the Tsar's observations on his non-appearance at the St Petersburg première of *Mazepa* earlier in the year. In the end his Imperial Majesty had his revenge, for it was only after three further performances with the Tsar still absent that Tchaikovsky felt he himself could decently depart. By now his plans were radically altered; news had come from Switzerland that Kotek was seriously ill with tuberculosis, and it was therefore for Berlin that he headed. The obvious success of *Onegin* had put him in an excellent frame of mind. Despite the urgency of his mission, he had no intention of rushing the journey. In any case the unremitting pressure of professional and family commitments during his three and a half weeks in St Petersburg had made it impossible to tackle other obligations, and he used his four days in Berlin to discharge two compositional tasks. Having misinterpreted something said at the audience in the spring,

[17] *TLP*12, p. 491; *TPM*3, p. 325; *TZC*2, p. 678; *DTC*, p. 89; *YDGC*, p. 331 (partial).
[18] *TZC*2, p. 671.

the Tsar had become puzzled that Tchaikovsky had written no further music for the church; now Tchaikovsky promptly set about sketching two Cherubim's Songs as a first step towards satisfying his sovereign's implied command.

The other order had arrived only a week before the first performance of *Onegin*. It was for a musical contribution to the celebrations surrounding the golden jubilee of the eminent actor, producer and playwright, Ivan Samarin who, as professor of drama at the Moscow Conservatoire, had been one of Tchaikovsky's former colleagues, and also the man responsible for mounting and producing *Onegin* when it had received its première at the Conservatoire in 1879. Now in Berlin Tchaikovsky could at last sit down to devise a *Grateful greeting* for strings, an elegantly shaped ternary piece of haunting melancholy, with a gently plangent introduction and a wistful coda. This musical tribute was duly performed at the celebrations in the Moscow Bolshoy Theatre on 28 December. Feeling the piece was too slight, Tchaikovsky at first denied it publication, but in 1890 he relented, dedicating it to the memory of Samarin who had died five years previously, but retaining the original designation (the title *Elegy* by which it is now usually known is therefore unauthorized). Tchaikovsky was right to feel that his initial verdict on the musical worth of this piece had been too harsh, and he thought well enough of it in 1891 to re-use it as the entr'acte to Act 4 in the music he provided for a production of *Hamlet* in St Petersburg.

What above all made his stay in Berlin so pleasant was his solitude. Even Alexey was not with him, and when he encountered the Polish violinist, Stanislaw Barcewicz, in one of the beer halls, he was quick to insist that news of his own presence should not reach either Anton Rubinstein or Karl Klindworth, both of whom he knew to be in the German capital. He attended two of Bilse's concerts, at one of which, just as in 1879, he heard his own Andante cantabile, noting that this piece seemed to have enslaved Berlin's ears to the exclusion of all his other music. Most pleasurable of all was hearing again Weber's *Oberon*. He was mistaken in believing it was the first time he had seen it, for he had attended a performance in Vienna in 1881, when he had been mostly unimpressed. This time he reacted rather differently. 'In places the music's delightful,' he told Modest, 'though the subject's nonsense like *Die Zauberflöte*. But it's fun to see, and . . . everywhere that he [Oberon] appears the music is inspired and poetic.'[19] Munich, where he arrived on 19 November, also pleased him; he spent two days in

[19] *TLP*12, p. 478; *TZC*2, p. 674; *TPB*, p. 320.

visiting the National Museum and the two main art galleries, then directed himself resolutely towards Davos, where Kotek awaited him.

Resolve was certainly required for the last stage of Tchaikovsky's journey. Further overnight stops at Lindau and Landquart preceded an eight-hour lone trek up into the mountains in a one-horse carriage. On arrival he was amazed at the contrast between the magnificent yet gloomy mountain setting and Davos itself, for he discovered the town to be well, even luxuriously appointed, and certainly self-sufficient, with its own theatre, newspaper, gas lighting, and a tolerable orchestra. But its dedication solely to the cause of curing consumptives depressed him. 'Davos inspires horror and despondency in me,' he confessed to Nadezhda von Meck the next day. '. . . My stay here will be very brief.'[20] He found Kotek outwardly better than he had dared to hope, but soon suspected that his true condition was far worse. Besides keeping his friend company, he added a further Cherubim's Song to the two composed in Berlin and posted all three to Balakirev, who was now reinstated in Russian musical life as director of the Imperial Chapel Choir, with instructions to select whichever he felt to be the best and to perform it with the Chapel Choir, if the Tsar so wished. Earlier in the year Tchaikovsky had asked Jurgenson to send him a score of Balakirev's recently published *Tamara*, and he was now finding much to admire in it. Before leaving Davos on 29 November he agreed in principle to Stasov's highly flattering request that certain manuscripts of his works should be deposited in the St Petersburg Public Library. As Stasov had explained: 'You are such a major Russian composer that your best pieces ought to be preserved in their originals in our national collection, along with the best pieces of Glinka, Dargomïzhsky, and such-like.'[21]

Tchaikovsky spent only six days in Davos. Before departure he secretly visited Kotek's doctor, and received an ambivalent prognosis. But to have remained longer would have been more than he could have borne. Leaving with Kotek some funds for use in an emergency, he passed through Zurich on his way to Paris, where he hoped to find some days of true relaxation, and to visit Georges-Léon. He found that a thriving lad was now resembling much more his mother than his father, and his morale was further improved by the care and attentions of his favourite hotel and the delights of the Parisian theatre, which he judged to be in peak form as regards its performers, if not its repertoire. However, the only opera he attended was Thomas's *Hamlet*, of

[20] *TLP*12, p. 482; *TPM*3, p. 324.
[21] *TLP*12, p. 490; *YDGC*, p. 330.

which, he said, he loved the first three acts. From St Petersburg, through Stasov, he heard that his *Romeo and Juliet* had earned him one of the newly instituted Glinka Awards, which had been anonymously endowed by the wealthy timber merchant and music publisher, Mitrofan Belyayev, for works by contemporary Russian composers. Tchaikovsky, however, seems to have been more pleased by the prospect of acquiring an instant 500 roubles than by the prestige of the award itself, for he had been unable to resist ordering a wardrobe of new clothes while in Paris.

But pleasure and idleness did not claim him completely during this fortnight. With both *Onegin* and *Mazepa* running in St Petersburg, and with the revival of *The Maid of Orléans* imminent, his thoughts returned to *Vakula the Smith*, 'one of my own favourites among my children. But,' he continued to Nadezhda von Meck, 'I am not so blind as not to see the fundamental faults from which it suffers, and which have prevented it from remaining in the repertoire.'[22] Nor was his creative work confined to projecting a whole series of revisions in this work; he also composed four new pieces, one a setting of *Thee we hymn*, a text he had treated once before in the Liturgy of St John Chrysostom, while the other three were romances. Although the Children's Songs had been composed only a year before, it was over four years since Tchaikovsky had produced a set of adult romances, the Seven Songs, Op. 47, and he was quick to group these new creations with the two Pleshcheyevo romances lying in his portfolio and a setting of Sollogub's 'Tell me, of what does the spring nightingale sing?' from earlier in the year, and to issue them as his Op. 57. All six were originally inscribed to singers, for though 'Sleep' (No. 4) was to be dedicated to Vera Butakova, it had first been given to Mariya Slavina, who had been Tchaikovsky's favoured choice for the role of Lyubov in the Moscow première of *Mazepa*. Since the dedicatees of three of the remaining five – Bogomir Korsov (No. 2), Emiliya Pavlovskaya (No. 3) and Dmitri Usatov (No. 5) – had created the roles of Mazepa, Mariya and Andrey respectively, it is no surprise that the musical world of *Mazepa* seems to linger in some of these six songs. Couple this occasional stylistic allegiance with the confined range of the subject-matter of the lyrics (all are monologues or meditations on love or loneliness), and it was to be expected that the music of the set would show less variety, both in style and quality, than had the Op. 47 songs.

Yet it was not Korsov but Fyodor Komissarzhevsky, creator of the role of Vakula eight years earlier, whose song, 'Tell me, of what does the

[22] *TLP*12, p. 498; *TPM*3, p. 326; *TZC*2, p. 679; *YDGC*, p. 332.

spring nightingale sing?', has the most explicit relationship with
Tchaikovsky's newest opera; singing the opening, Komissarzhevsky
must have wondered momentarily whether he was beginning Mazepa's
soothing assurance, also in E major, that Mariya need not doubt his
love and constancy. But in 'Tell me' passion is not a matter for
reaffirmation but for discovery; excitement quickly accumulates, the
vastly arching bass line of the opening supporting the singer's swelling
fervour as he prepares to disclose that magic word which answers all his
questions: 'Love!' Set as a ternary structure, 'Tell me' confirms
Tchaikovsky's skill for manufacturing a beautifully turned romance –
charmingly affecting, but not troubling our deeper responses. As for
Pavlovskaya, who had first sung Mariya, she may well have thought
that it was Slavina who had been given a fugitive invention from
Mariya's music early in Act 1, when the young girl still rejoiced in her
love for Mazepa with no inkling of the disasters it would breed. Though
'Sleep' makes no attempt to gather up the expressive weight its lightly
kindred music had borne in *Mazepa*, it serves its text nicely. This time
the single word towards which each of the three strophes moves
signifies not boundless joy but quiet repose, and in each strophe
Tchaikovsky pointedly avoids any cadential resolution until the last
imperative: 'Sleep!' Though designed as a plain strophic piece, it moves
at the very end on to new material to conclude, not in the relative minor
as in the first two strophes, but in the tonic, with a gentle coda to
confirm this true resolution.

Pavlovskaya herself was allotted Strugovshchikov's translation of
'Heiss mich nicht reden' from Goethe's *Wilhelm Meister*. It was
Tchaikovsky's third attempt at one of Mignon's songs, and his least
successful. The worlds of personalities become confused; Tatyana's
letter monologue of explicit confession soon threatens to burst in with
an uncontained passion which falsifies the suppressed love and longing
which are Mignon's predicament. But such a central outburst is seemly
in 'On the golden cornfields' (No. 2). The lyric has the widest range of
these six romances, for before the main substance of the song, which is a
lament of separation, there comes a brief picture of the country at
evening (Ex. 201). But this is seen, not with the charmed eyes which
had looked so easily upon that earlier pastoral scene in 'Evening' (Op.
27, No. 4; see Vol. 2, pp. 36–7, Ex. 103), but with the sombre gaze of the
lover who has failed to confess his love; it is not the bewitching sound of
birds and insects but the heavy tolling of a bell which finally marks this
dark image of the outer world.

By far the weakest of the set is the fifth. Treating a song entitled
'Death' in a manner not far removed from that of a waltz must seem

Ex. 201

[On the golden cornfields silence descends;

in the cooling air from the fading

settlements, trembling, there floats a sound . . .

My spirit is full. . .]

curious, even though the poet's mission is to persuade us cheerfully that the extinction we daily witness around us in nature should condition us to meet our own end 'submissively, with a gentle and triumphant smile'. 'Only thou alone' (No. 6), Pleshcheyev's translation of a lyric of love withheld, drew a far more pointed response; because sympathy and understanding cannot be transformed into love, the final naked cry of pain is here appropriate. Of the preceding five songs only one, 'Death', had employed Tchaikovsky's well-practised routine of repeating the piano prelude as postlude. In that song it had merely substantiated how perfunctory had been Tchaikovsky's response; in 'Only thou alone' it sets the seal on the piece. Frustration has found its voice, and there has been much restless freedom within the three strophes. But by the end nothing has changed.

The same was certainly not true of Tchaikovsky's mood during this Paris interlude. Suddenly, as had happened more than once before, the enthusiasm for Parisian existence which he had rediscovered on arrival evaporated. He ceased visiting the theatre, and that solitariness which had seemed such a blessing abruptly became an intolerable loneliness. 'I can't describe to you, dear Modest, how bored and depressed I've been during these last days,' he wrote on 15 December. '. . . It's longing for my native land, a wish to be *at home* which cannot find satisfaction in the fact that tomorrow I'm going to Russia, for there is still no *home* for me there. . . . One way or another, I must have a *home*.' But his current longing for the company of others raised a further tormenting dilemma. 'It means that to a certain extent I need *society*. All this confuses me. It means that to live alone in the country won't suit me. So where is my home to be? . . . How I long to talk with you! . . .'[23] The longing proved irresistible. He had intended going straight to Moscow, but on 19 December he was in St Petersburg with Modest.

Tchaikovsky's arrival proved timely, for Modest's play, *Lizaveta Nikolayevna*, which had caused such labour and anxiety at Grankino during the summer, was to receive its first performance at the Alexandrinsky Theatre, and a good deal of care had to be devoted to soothing a brother's nerves ahead of a modestly successful première, and subsequently bolstering that brother's spirits which fell in the face of what he believed was an unco-operative theatre management and a hostile press. But for Tchaikovsky himself this visit, and the next few weeks, were to afford further evidence of his own growing stature in his countrymen's eyes. The grip *Onegin* was taking on the public was confirmed for him when he attended the twelfth performance of the

[23] *TLP*12, pp. 508–9; *TPB*, pp. 324–5; *TZC*2, pp. 680–1 (partial).

season. On a more personal level came inscribed gifts: from Rimsky-Korsakov his new textbook on harmony, and from the young Glazunov a copy of his *Poème lyrique*, about which Tchaikovsky had waxed enthusiastic to Balakirev some weeks earlier, and which he had recommended to Jurgenson for publication. Even more flattering to him personally was to discover that, when Bülow came to Moscow a month later to give an enormously successful performance of the First Piano Concerto in the same concert which was to introduce the Third Suite to that city, he now had the personal authority to persuade the Bolshoy's management to put on *Mazepa* especially so that the German pianist could see the opera. He was also about to be unanimously elected a director of the Moscow branch of the RMS.

Tchaikovsky stayed ten days in St Petersburg, then left for Moscow to take up residence with Nikolay and Anna in Nadezhda von Meck's own house. But sadness abruptly descended upon him, for he found news awaiting him that Kotek had taken a turn for the worse, and within a week a telegram had announced his death. Tchaikovsky was entrusted with the painful task of breaking the news to Kotek's parents, and for three days he could not bring himself to do so. Deeply distressed personally, he found the need to immerse himself in proof-reading a welcome distraction.

The word 'fate' had cropped up in Tchaikovsky's letters more than once over the past weeks. Everything that now followed must have seemed yet further quiet confirmation of the operations of this overriding force; everything, unpleasant and pleasant, conspired to reinforce his need for a home of his own, and finally drove him to act. First there was his residence with Nikolay and Anna, for he discovered the negative side of their characters. He had always admitted that Anna could be acid in her comments on others, but Nikolay was now acquiring this trait, and the atmosphere which built up from their malicious strictures soon became intolerable. 'One story about *Nata* [Pleskaya] is enough to make you hate the lot of them,' he told Modest after enduring this a fortnight. 'Anna and I talked about *Nata*. She [Nata] is now not only a schemer, trying to alienate a mother from her daughters, but dishonourable, malicious, of use to nobody. In Anna's opinion I would do very well if I sent Nata off to Elizavetgrad, for (so she says) Sasha and Lev's only dream is to send her packing, but they can't bring themselves to say this to Nata. What sort of people are these? And your Molas is to go also! Every day Kolya Meck says again and again in every possible way that – 1. Nad[ezhda] Fil[aretovna] is, in essence, an unbalanced and unbearable old woman; that – 2. Vlad[imir von] Meck is a scoundrel and his wife a dissolute old hag;

that – 3. Yuliya [von Meck] is an evil virago; – 4. Sasha Beningsen [née von Meck] a *scandalmonger*; – 5. Sashok [von Meck] is wicked, vindictive, heartless; – 6. [Elizaveta] *Yolshina* [née von Meck] an arrant fool – and for some reason he praises only Sonya [née von Meck] to the skies. Do you remember that good-natured fellow – the Kolya who used to take photos of members of the family? What has Anna made of him! Today I learned from Sasha Bazilevskaya that Anna, Tanya and Liz[aveta] Mikh[ailovna Molas] consider that *Parasha* [Anatoly's wife] is a very unattractive, empty person, and *hangs* on the neck of every man.'[24] And now into this hideously spiteful world Tanya was about to return, bringing her own special brand of moody indolence. It is clear from the Kamenka diary alone that backbiting and malicious gossip were not confined to the newly weds, but were widespread in the family. How could he bear to commit himself to permanent residence with any of these?

Then there were the unremitting pressures of his professional life. What had brought him to Moscow was the urgent need to check the proofs of the Third Suite in readiness for the première which Bülow was imminently to conduct in St Petersburg. They were in a frightful mess, and for days on end Tchaikovsky was condemned to sit fuming over them, in the meantime warding off a deluge of invitations of varying kinds which would have absorbed any free time he might have had. And so the need to have a retreat where he could recover from labour also became more evident still during these three and a half weeks in Moscow. Nor could his home be within Moscow itself. There he would be too accessible; he had to distance himself sufficiently to ensure that his social participations would be at times and on terms of his own choosing.

Finally there were the swiftly mounting pressures of his own enormous success. These were brought home forcefully at the première of his Third Suite on 24 January, two days after his return to St Petersburg. As noted earlier, Tchaikovsky admitted he had never gained such a huge personal triumph, but six days later, having just arrived back in Moscow, he was detailing to Nadezhda von Meck something of the physical and social strains which were the price of such public acclamations. 'The weariness afterwards is enormous. The next day I was just like some sick person . . . I suffer rather than take pleasure in the awareness of my growing success. A wish to hide myself somewhere; a thirst for freedom, quiet, solitude prevailed over the feeling of a satisfied artistic self-esteem.' On the final day of his stay the Emperor had at last

[24] *TLP*13, p. 16; *TPM*3, p. 631 (partial).

attended a performance of *Onegin*, the fifteenth of the season. 'The Tsar wanted to see me, chatted with me for a very long while, was in the highest degree sweet and gracious towards me, with the utmost interest and in the greatest detail enquired about my life and my musical affairs, after which he took me to the Empress, who in her turn showed me the most touching attention.'[25] It all confirmed that his privacy would now be even further diminished, that he would be increasingly sought after, even lionized, and that self-protection was imperative. Before leaving Moscow he had inserted an advertisement in a Moscow paper: 'Single gentleman seeks a country dacha to rent.' The St Petersburg visit gave even stronger urgency to the search.

His first expedition to inspect a property proved disastrous. From the literature it looked ideal; the reality proved so disheartening that he almost determined to abandon everything and go abroad. But the decision, no sooner made, was reversed, and a new strategy evolved. 'A certain indescribable terror in the face of this impending journey enveloped me so strongly, a certain incomprehensible melancholy stifled me so terribly that yesterday I took an heroic decision and sent Alexey to rent a dacha which I had heard stood in a beautiful location and was provided with furniture, crockery and everything that was necessary,' he told Nadezhda von Meck on 15 February. 'Tomorrow I am going to St Petersburg, in a week everything will be ready, and I shall move into my own long-term quarters. . . . The dacha is situated in the village of *Maidanovo* about a mile and a half from *Klin*. The house has a lot of rooms, extremely well furnished; there is a magnificent park alongside the house, the view from the windows is very beautiful. . . . I shall have to live there a year, and if it proves that its upkeep is beyond my means, I shall manage to find something more suitable during the year.'[26] The location was certainly well-chosen, being some fifty miles to the north-west of Moscow on the railway joining the two capitals. The annual rent was to be 1,000 roubles.

Once again Tchaikovsky experienced a degree of disenchantment when he returned from St Petersburg a week later and saw what had been acquired for him. 'What Alyosha thought was luxurious and splendid seemed to me pretentious, tasteless, shabby and dingy. Immediately I decided most emphatically that Maidanovo won't be my continual and everlasting abode.' But then his tone softened as he reflected on its more positive virtues. 'Yet it's possible to live here a year, or at least until the beginning of next winter, and in summer it'll

[25] *TLP*13, p. 25; *TPM*3, p. 337; *TZC*3, pp. 20–1.
[26] *TLP*13, p. 31; *TPM*3, pp. 341–2; *TZC*3, pp. 23–4.

be really splendid . . . the situation's *delightful*. . . . The view from the windows, the quiet, the awareness that I'm in *my own home* – all this is so pleasant that I spent the whole day in the most agreeable state of mind. . . . Despite a certain disenchantment I'm happy, contented, glad, composed,' he told Modest.[27] His piano had been delivered, and he now engaged an excellent cook, arranged for a laundress, and within two days the drawbacks seemed still less serious. What mattered was not the shortcomings of the house itself, but what it signified. 'What a joy to be in my own home! What a bliss to know that no one will come and interfere with my work, my reading, my walks!' he exclaimed to his benefactress. 'Now I understand once and for all that my dream of settling for the rest of my days in the Russian countryside is not a passing whim, but a fundamental requirement of my nature.'[28] Three more days, and he was ordering his existence still better, he told Modest. 'I've begun receiving newspapers and journals, and this has greatly enriched my life here. I read a lot, I'm enjoying getting on with English, my work's going excellently, I eat, walk and sleep when I want and as much as I want: in a word, *I'm living!*'[29]

On Maidanovo, or nearby, he would base the rest of his life. His years of wandering were over.

Modest chose to call the period covered by this volume his brother's 'Kamenka years', partly because Sasha's Ukrainian home had been the chief haven for the composer during this restless phase of his life, but also because it was only in Kamenka, so Modest claimed, that his brother had found conditions which answered his spiritual needs. The sententiousness of Modest's title is understandable from a man anxious at all costs, as we have observed, to demonstrate his brother's dependence upon the support of a family whose loyalty and love were matched by a stability and orderliness which the world might envy and admire. But such was not, as we have also seen, the condition of Sasha's household – certainly not during the latter part of this period. Nor, perhaps, would it have been good for Tchaikovsky if it had been, for this might have encouraged him to linger further in the cosiness and comfort of her family circle. Instead he was inexorably driven from it. Yet the self-esteem fostered by the growing public enthusiasm for his music, the more than adequate means of livelihood which he now commanded, the reassurance he felt in his visible social rehabilitation – all created a confidence which enabled him once again to live indepen-

[27] *TLP*13, pp. 33–4; *TZC*3, p. 25; *TPB*, p. 327.
[28] *TLP*13, p. 35; *TPM*3, p. 344.
[29] *TLP*13, p. 36; *TZC*3, p. 26; *TPB*, p. 328.

dently. Meanwhile, this new self-sufficiency and self-assurance, which Modest rightly identified, seems to have fully and finally unstopped that blockage which, since the appalling events of 1877, had come between the composer's most personal inner world and his music. At last Tchaikovsky the creator could be completely himself again. And since this, rather than Tchaikovsky's enthusiastic words, is surely the most eloquent proof of what his newly begun existence really signified, the final chapter of this volume will leap beyond the natural biographical boundary afforded by this move to Maidanovo, and examine the first major work to be created within this new existence.

9

BALAKIREV RESURGENT:

MANFRED SYMPHONY

IN THE WINTER of 1867–8, on that visit to Russia which had first brought Balakirev into Tchaikovsky's personal life, Berlioz had conducted his own *Harold en Italie*. Both Balakirev and Vladimir Stasov had been hugely impressed, and it was this event, it seems, which prompted Stasov to outline a programme based on Byron's *Manfred* upon which Balakirev might also compose a four-movement symphony.

MANFRED

First movement
Manfred wandering in the Alps. His life is broken, his obsessive, fateful questions remain unanswered; in life nothing remains for him except memories. From time to time *memories of his ideal, Astarte*, creep in upon him. Memories, thoughts – burn, gnaw at him. He seeks and begs for oblivion, but no one can give him this.

Second movement
The way of life of the Alpine hunters, full of simplicity, good-nature, of a naïve patriarchal character, with which Manfred clashes, affording a sharp contrast. This is a quiet, idyllic adagio incorporating Manfred's theme which, like an idée fixe, must infiltrate the whole symphony.

Third movement
The Alpine fairy appearing to Manfred in a rainbow from the waterfall's spray.

Fourth movement
A wild, unbridled Allegro, full of savage audacity. Scene in the subterranean halls of the infernal Arimanes. Further on there follows the arrival of Manfred, arousing a general outburst from the subterranean spirits – and finally the *summons and appearance of Astarte* will

present a lovely contrast to this unbridled orgy: *this must be music light, limpid* as the air, and ideal. Further on the diablerie comes again, finishing Largo – Manfred's death.[1]

But when Stasov had offered this programme to Balakirev, the latter had felt it unsuited to him, and instead had tried to press Berlioz himself into composing it. Yet he, too, had refused. So the matter rested; in little more than a year Berlioz was dead, and by 1872 Balakirev himself was in the grip of that personal crisis which crushed his capacity to compose. The *Manfred* project, it seemed, was extinct.

Then in 1876 Balakirev began to creep back into the musical life of his native land. It was five years since he had made his exit from Tchaikovsky's professional world, and four since his last direct contact with his own former musical associates. The process of rehabilitation was slow, and even by 1881, when the ten-year silence between himself and Tchaikovsky was at last broken, this old campaigner for Russian music had still regained no position in the Russian musical scene of the sort he had once commanded with such energy and power. Yet when the initiative to renew contact was taken, it came not from this faded figure of the 1860s, but from his former willing protégé, now one of the chief ornaments of his country's music. In the summer of the previous year Tchaikovsky had made his second and final revision of that early masterpiece which Balakirev had, with such benevolent authority and stern coaxing, wrung from him a decade before, and the need to republish the score had enabled him to rectify an embarrassing omission.

'In the spring I had already corrected the proofs of my overture *Romeo and Juliet*, which Bock has printed in a new and somewhat improved form,' he wrote to Balakirev on 13 September 1881.

I asked him to send you a copy. Have you received it? I have always been a little tormented by the fact that, through an oversight, the first edition didn't carry the dedication to you on its title page. Now it's there – or, at least, it should be. I'm quite sure you are thoroughly indifferent to this dedication, but I do attach importance to it. I want you to know that I have not forgotten who was responsible for this score's appearance in this world, that I vividly recall the friendly sympathy you showed at the time, which I hope even now is not completely extinguished.[2]

[1] *BVP*, pp. 170–1.
[2] *TLP*10, pp. 217–18; *BVP*, p. 163.

Not knowing Balakirev's current address, Tchaikovsky had sent his letter to Bessel for forwarding. The publisher seems to have delayed shamelessly, however, and it was more than a year before a reply was received which proved as warm as Tchaikovsky's own letter had been. It also revealed that Balakirev's instincts to command remained undiminished. 'Your kind letter and dedication to me prove you have not completely struck me out of your heart's memory,' he wrote on 10 October 1882.

> And if this is so, then why should you not afford me the pleasure of coming to see me? . . . You will find no superfluous persons at my place – only the company you know, with the addition of its new member, the talented Glazunov. If you wish to meet no one, that's even possible – but give me warning at the above address of such a wish, and of your arrival. And so I shall hope to receive news of you, and that when you arrive in St Petersburg you'll remember also your old friend, who sincerely loves you,
>
>   M. Balakirev
> P.S. By the way, give your attention to a glaring error in the score of *Francesca*. On p. 92 the horns have been omitted, and the result's terrible.[3]

In this same letter, as we saw earlier (see above, p.204), Balakirev had offered to provide Tchaikovsky with a programme for a symphony which he thought would suit him admirably. Tchaikovsky had just finished sketching *Mazepa*, and though he knew it would be some months before he would complete scoring the opera, he also knew he would be restless for a new creative project, once this was done: Balakirev's proposal might therefore prove timely. Certainly his agreement to compose a piece on this undisclosed creative project was quite unequivocal, though for some reason he thought it was only to be a symphonic poem.

As might have been expected, Balakirev wasted little time, and on 9 November he despatched his plan. It proved to be Stasov's old scheme for a four-movement symphony on *Manfred*. 'I had originally offered the subject to Berlioz,' Balakirev confessed. 'He declined because of age and ill-health, not being disposed to compose anything more. Your *Francesca* suggested to me that you would be able to tackle this subject brilliantly – provided, of course, you *make an effort*, that you apply to your work just a little more criticism, allow your fantasy to mature in

[3] *BVP*, pp. 163–4.

your head, and don't hurry to finish at all costs.'[4] Balakirev went on to detail the programme, supplemented it with a number of requirements of his own, added some instructions on setting out the score such as one might offer to a student, and concluded with further commendation of his own proposal. 'Besides being profound, this subject is also contemporary, for the sickness of present-day mankind lies in this: it has not been able to preserve its ideals. They are shattered, nothing remaining to content the soul except bitterness. Every affliction of our time stems from this. How happy I shall be if this subject pleases you!'[5]

But it did not. It was now Tchaikovsky's turn to decline *Manfred*, as he did in his letter of 24 November.

I haven't a translation of *Manfred* to hand, and I don't want to give you a final reply regarding your programme until I've read through Byron's text. Perhaps closer acquaintance with it will change my attitude to the task you've proposed to me – although I very much doubt it. . . . In all probability your programme could indeed serve as a design for a symphonist inclined to imitate Berlioz . . . but for the present it leaves me completely cold, and if the heart and imagination are not warmed, it's scarcely worth setting about composing. To please you I might, perhaps – to use your expression – *make an effort*, and squeeze out of myself a whole series of more or less interesting episodes, in which you'd meet conventionally gloomy music to reproduce Manfred's hopeless disillusionment, and a lot of effective instrumental flashes in the Alpine fairy scherzo, and sunrise in the violins' high register, and Manfred's death with pianissimo trombones. I would be able to furnish these episodes with harmonic curiosities and piquancies, and I would then be able to send all this out into the world under the sonorous title: *Manfred – Symphonie d'après*, and so on. I might even receive praise for the fruits of my labours, but such composing in no way attracts me.[6]

He followed this by dismissing his own *Francesca da Rimini* and *The Tempest*, both so admired by Balakirev, and concluded by observing that his love for Schumann's *Manfred* made it impossible for him to conceive this subject in musical terms other than those already created by Schumann.

And there the matter remained for two years. But then something occurred to revive the *Manfred* project. Exactly what we will probably

[4] *BVP*, p. 165; *TZC*3, p. 51; *DTC*, p. 409.
[5] *BVP*, p. 167; *TZC*3, p. 53; *DTC*, p. 410.
[6] *TLP*11, pp. 280–1; *BVP*, pp. 167–8; *DTC*, p. 410 (partial).

never know, though we may guess. In the autumn of 1884, as we have
seen, Tchaikovsky had to be in St Petersburg for the new production of
Eugene Onegin. On 11 November, during this visit, Balakirev wrote to
him.

> Dear Pyotr Ilich,
>   I'm sending you the programme sheet copied out for me by
> Vladimir Stasov, and furnished with my notes. I sincerely wish and
> hope that *Manfred* will be one of your pearls.
>   It was so pleasant for me to talk with you today that, if only it is
> convenient for you tomorrow, don't refuse to come to the Chapel at
> the same time (11 o'clock). By then I shall have arrived and, taking
> you for a walk, will tell you much of great importance which I
> completely omitted today. I shall be disappointed if anything pre-
> vents you giving me a couple of hours during the morning . . . May
> Christ preserve you!
>
>   Ever yours,
>   M. Balakirev[7]

The two men had talked about religion. It was a subject which had
occupied Tchaikovsky's thoughts a good deal during the previous
months. In March he had read Tolstoy's *Confession*, still forbidden by
the spiritual censor, but which was circulating in manuscript. 'The
impression it made on me was all the stronger because the torments of
doubt and tragic perplexity through which Tolstoy has passed, and
which he expresses so amazingly well in his *Confession*, are known to me
also,' he had written to Nadezhda von Meck on 25 March. 'But
enlightenment came much earlier for me than for Tolstoy, probably
because my head is more simply constructed. . . . Every hour and every
minute I thank God He has given me faith in Him. In my fainthearted-
ness and my talent for losing heart to the point where I yearn *for oblivion*
because of some trivial blow, what would I be if I did not believe in God,
and did not submit to His will?'[8] Significantly this year he had attended
Easter services in Moscow with particular assiduity. But his response to
such rituals was primarily aesthetic and sentimental, and his religious
belief was largely self-persuasion which might bring certainty to counter troubling perplexities and assure final deliverance from irrepressible guilt. The confession made to his beloved cousin, Anna Merkling, a
few weeks later came much nearer the truth. 'What is needed is not to

---

[7] *BVP*, p. 170.
[8] *TLP*12, p. 336; *TPM*3, p. 266; *TZC*2, pp. 630–1.

be afraid of death. In this respect I have no grounds for complacency. I am not so imbued with religion as, with certainty, to see in death the beginning of a new life, nor enough a philosopher to reconcile myself to the abyss of non-existence into which I shall have to plunge.'[9]

Balakirev, however, no longer suffered from such uncertainties. Formerly he had been a free-thinker, but in the early 1870s he had come under the influence of a soothsayer, and had developed a very intense and eccentric brand of Christian faith. Might not that same Balakirev who, fifteen years before, had performed him such musical service, now also show him the way to spiritual salvation, delivering him from his sexual guilt, perhaps even thwarting his fate? Such must surely have been Tchaikovsky's thoughts. Certainly he had listened to Balakirev with longing and, perhaps, with renewed hope. The next day he replied.

I was deeply moved by our conversation of yesterday. How good you are! What a *true* friend you are to me! How I wish that that *enlightenment* which has come to your soul would also descend on me. I can say in all truth that more than ever I *thirst* for solace and support *in Christ*. I shall pray that faith in Him may be confirmed in me.[10]

It was within the closeness bred by this single religious exchange that Balakirev had reintroduced the *Manfred* project, and Tchaikovsky had agreed to compose it. Unfortunately the further meeting both men wanted could not materialize, for Tchaikovsky had now received his urgent summons to Switzerland to visit the dying Kotek. Nor does it seem that the further conversations which he and Balakirev planned ever took place. But this time he held to his resolve about Balakirev's other gift.

Tchaikovsky had now received two communications containing the *Manfred* programme.[11] In presenting his first version two years earlier, Balakirev had copied out Stasov's scheme, lightly paraphrasing it and fleshing out one or two details; upon remembering Astarte in the first movement Manfred 'calls upon her in vain', but 'only the echo from the cliffs repeats her name', while her appearance in the finale was to be 'the same as was in D major in the first movement, except that there this idea was fleeting, like a memory, and was immediately engulfed by Manfred's mood of suffering; here this same idea now appears in its full

[9] *TLP*12, p. 363; *TZC*2, p. 641.

[10] *TLP*12, p. 470; *BVP*, p. 172.

[11] The version of 1882 is printed in *BVP*, pp. 165–6, *DTC*, pp. 409–10 and *TZC*3, pp. 51–2.

and finished form'. Manfred's death would be preceded by a sunset. Far more important than such programmatic details had been the musical prescriptions. Balakirev had confirmed Stasov's requirement of an idée fixe recurring in all four movements, and had specified that the first movement was to begin in F sharp minor and end in F sharp major, while the Astarte music in between was to be in D. The second movement would be an Adagio pastorale in A major – and here Balakirev had added a caveat: 'Of course you should first have a hunters' tune, but in doing this, you must be *particularly careful not to fall into triviality*. God preserve you from vulgarities like German fanfares or Jägermusik!' The Alpine fairy movement would be a *Scherzo fantastique* in D, and the finale would begin in F sharp minor. Astarte's appearance would use her D major music from the first movement, though now in D flat.

When Balakirev sent Tchaikovsky the *Manfred* scheme for the second time, he enclosed Stasov's original hand-written programme (see above, pp. 296–7), and some of his own musical requirements had undergone changes. His obsession with keys not only of two sharps but of five flats had resurged; the symphony was to be in 'B flat minor without B flat major', while Astarte's first movement music was to begin in D major as before, but be repeated in D flat. The Adagio pastorale in A major was now envisaged as a Larghetto in G flat which, however, 'will not be difficult since the tempo is slow, and as supporting keys you can take B flat major and A major'. For some reason the scherzo was no longer *fantastique*, though the key remained, and Balakirev added that the idée fixe should provide material for the trio. The finale would begin in B flat minor, Astarte's music would still be in D flat, though now muted strings were stipulated, and the whole piece would end with a requiem (ideally with organ) and a final B flat major chord.

As significant as these revised musical supplementations was the list of 'helpful materials' which Balakirev supplied. In his 1882 directions he had reminded Tchaikovsky that the programme was like those of Berlioz's Symphonie Fantastique and *Harold en Italie*; now he specified particular pieces which he judged would help Tchaikovsky in each movement.

For the first and last movements:
  Francesca da Rimini by Tchaikovsky
  Hamlet by Liszt
  Finale from *Harold* by Berlioz
  Preludes in E minor, E flat minor and C sharp minor (No. 25, separate from the others) by Chopin

For the Larghetto:
  Adagio from the Symphonie Fantastique by Berlioz
For the Scherzo:
  La reine Mab [from *Romeo and Juliet*] by Berlioz
  Scherzo (B minor) from the Third Symphony by Tchaikovsky

Before leaving for Switzerland to attend Kotek, Tchaikovsky bought a copy of Byron's *Manfred*. He reflected that finding himself among the Alps might stimulate him to begin work, except that the distress at his friend's condition would probably make this impossible. But he did read the poem at Davos, and reaffirmed to Balakirev his intention of composing the symphony. He did not start composition until April 1885 at Maidanovo, however. The evidence of progress is very conflicting. Various notes on the sketches are themselves confused ('End of the symphony: 25 May – but before the end a very great deal still needs to be done. . . . Today's 18 July, but I still haven't gone very far. . . . And today's 12 August – and yet, oh, how far it is to the end!'[12]). In the full score the individual movements are clearly dated (first – 24 June; second – 3 August; third – 23 September; fourth – 24 September); yet the final date for the whole symphony is recorded as 4 October. Tchaikovsky's letters written during the period of composition sometimes seem to tell yet another story; what they do confirm is the labour which went into composition. He had intended to heed Balakirev's counsel not to rush, and first made only a few preliminary sketches. But by the end of June the urge to compose with his more characteristic intensity was beginning to grip him, though his feelings about the work he was forming were still equivocal. 'After some hesitation I've decided to compose Manfred, for I feel that, until I've fulfilled the promise I imprudently gave Balakirev during the winter, I shall not be at ease,' he confessed to Taneyev on 25 June. 'I don't know what will come out, but for the moment I'm dissatisfied with myself. No! It's a thousand times pleasanter to compose without a programme.'[13] But, as had happened many times before, as the labour progressed, so his feelings changed. 'Now I can't stop,' he told Emiliya Pavlovskaya on 1 August. 'The symphony's come out enormous, serious, difficult, absorbing all my time, sometimes wearying me in the extreme; but an inner voice tells me that I'm not labouring in vain, and that this will perhaps be the best of my symphonic compositions.'[14] Three weeks later, though he feared his

[12] *Avtografi P. I. Chaykovskovo v arkhive Doma-Muzeya v Klinu: Spravochnik* (Moscow/Leningrad, 1950), p. 28; *YDGC*, pp. 346, 348, 350.
[13] *TLP*13, p. 101; *TZC*3, p. 50; *YDGC*, p. 348; *DTC*, p. 411; *TTP*, p. 124; *TPM* 3, p. 634.
[14] *TLP*13, p. 118; *DTC*, p. 411 (partial); *YDGC*, p. 350 (partial).

involvement in the work was turning him into a Manfred himself, he
was acknowledging to Emiliya even greater confidence. 'I'm extracting
a promise from you that, when it's played in St Petersburg, you'll go to
hear it. I'm very proud of this work, and I want those persons whose
sympathy I value most in the world (and you are in the first rank of
these) to experience, when they hear it, a reverberation from the joy
with which I wrote this piece.'[15]

But it was still 25 September, a month later, before he could write to
Balakirev.

> I have carried out your wish. *Manfred* is finished . . . I think you will
> be somewhat displeased at the speed with which I've composed it . . .
> but the point is that I cannot do otherwise . . . I've sat over *Manfred* –
> not getting up from my seat, I may say – for nearly four months (from
> the beginning of June until today). It was very hard work – but also
> very pleasant, especially when, having begun with some effort, I got
> carried away. Of course, I cannot predict whether this symphony
> will please you or not, but *believe* me, never in my life have I tried so
> hard and become so weary from my work. The symphony is written
> in four movements in accordance with your programme. But I ask
> your forgiveness: I have not been able to keep to the keys and
> modulations you indicated, even though I wanted to . . . This piece
> is very difficult and demands a large orchestra – that is, a lot of
> strings. . . . Of course *Manfred* is dedicated to you.[16]

What followed was precisely what might have been expected after
the history of *Romeo and Juliet* nearly sixteen years earlier: Balakirev
pressed to be shown the piano-duet version so that he might suggest
improvements, and promptly told Tchaikovsky what sort of piece he
should compose next. Tchaikovsky tactfully but firmly parried this
attempt to take over his creative plans yet again, but he conceded that
Balakirev's opinion might be useful on details of pianistic layout in the
duet transcription, even though he had already sought the help of
Hubert's wife, whose advice on such matters he had always found
sufficient. Yet just as, when composing the piece, he had shown himself
perfectly prepared to ignore many of Balakirev's prescriptions, so now
he declined point-blank to listen to any requirements Balakirev might
have regarding the content of the piece.

Tchaikovsky felt that his confidence in his Manfred Symphony was
confirmed when the première under Erdmannsdörfer took place in

---

[15] *TLP*13, pp. 125–6.
[16] *TLP*13, pp. 145–6; *BVP*, p. 176; *DTC*, pp. 411–12; *TPJ* 2, p. 282 (partial).

Moscow at an RMS concert on 23 March 1886, the fifth anniversary of Nikolay Rubinstein's death. There had been five rehearsals and an 'excellent' performance. 'The first movement proved undoubtedly the best,' he wrote to Balakirev two days later. '*The scherzo* was taken very quickly, and when I heard it I didn't experience disenchantment as I frequently have. . . . The *Andante* doesn't sound bad. *The Finale* gains *very much* in performance, and proved to be the most effective movement *with the audience.*' Yet though at rehearsals the players had given increasingly open demonstrations of approval, he still felt the public had not much liked the symphony, while his friends were divided, some enthusiastic, others feeling that Tchaikovsky had concealed himself behind a mask. 'But I myself think it's my best symphonic work,' he continued defiantly, 'though because of its difficulty, impracticability and complexity it is doomed *to failure and to be ignored.*'[17] It was indeed the most extended orchestral piece he had yet written, using the largest complement of players, and bristling with formidable difficulties. Because of this complexity he had already offered it to Jurgenson free of charge.

Events quickly disproved his gloomy prediction. Before the end of the year it had been performed three times in St Petersburg or at nearby Pavlovsk; it had even reached New York. There was some very warm critical reaction, and Cui for once was full of praise, especially for the first movement.

But once the Manfred Symphony had begun to become history, and the composer himself could view it with some detachment, his satisfaction turned to hatred. In October 1888 he wrote blisteringly of it to the Grand Duke Konstantin Konstantinovich.

Without any wish to make a mere show of modesty, I will say that it is an abominable piece, and that I loathe it deeply, *with the one exception of the first movement.* Moreover, I must say to Your Highness that within a short time, with the agreement of my publisher, I shall destroy completely the remaining three movements, very poor as music (the finale in particular is something loathsome), and out of a large symphony which is quite impossibly long-winded I shall make a *Symphonische Dichtung.* Then I am sure my *Manfred* will be capable of pleasing. Indeed, it must be so: the first movement I wrote with enjoyment – the remaining ones are the result of straining from which, I remember, I felt myself for some time very unwell.[18]

[17] *TLP*13, pp. 298–9; *BVP*, p. 182; *DTC*, p. 414.
[18] *TLP*14, pp. 542–3; *TZC*3, pp. 274–5; *DTC*, p. 416 (partial); *YDGC*, pp. 453–4 (partial).

Thankfully, nothing more was heard of Tchaikovsky's destructive intentions towards the last three movements.

When Tchaikovsky came to know Byron's *Manfred* for himself in the days after giving his second promise to Balakirev, there might have seemed no reason why he should not have ended in rejecting the subject as before. Yet he did not, for Balakirev's new choice had been as inspired as that of *Romeo and Juliet*. True, its conventionally grand Alpine setting, its bevy of supernatural beings against whom the Abbot stands as representative of the other side of the spiritual equation – even its Chamois Hunter as a pattern of common humanity – probably left Tchaikovsky little stirred. But the figure of Manfred gripped him. Here was an outsider who from childhood had felt himself apart from other mortals. His solitariness had grown ever greater, his gloom ever deeper, his longing for forgetfulness was as strong as it was vain. Fate ruled his life; above all, Tchaikovsky must have perceived that Byron's hero was haunted by a very special sin – that he had been guilty of unnatural love. Byron had been impelled to write *Manfred* by his own attraction to his half-sister, Augusta, and though there is only bare mention of the wrong committed by Manfred with Astarte ('the only thing he seem'd to love – as he, indeed, by blood was bound to do'), it is clear that it was incest:

> Thou lovedst me
> Too much, as I loved thee: we were not made
> To torture thus each other, though it were
> The deadliest sin to love as we have loved.

There was, of course, no hint of this aberrant love in the programme Balakirev had transmitted. Stasov had obviously selected his elements to bring the scheme as close as possible to that which a moderately lively imagination might extract from Berlioz's *Harold en Italie*, as Tchaikovsky cannot have failed to notice, for as in *Harold* the first movement was to be concerned with the hero and his affairs, the second (in Tchaikovsky's sequence) shifted to a world outside that of the hero (religious in Berlioz, supernatural in Tchaikovsky), while the third returned to the plane of everyday life and simple mortals. The finale of both works was an orgiastic tableau of unbridled energy disrupted by the entry (or intimations) of the hero and, in the case of Manfred, ending in his death. Certainly Tchaikovsky seems to have heeded well Balakirev's admonition to take account of this other musical incarnation from Byron when setting about his own, and the acute-eared listener will find a variety of tiny musical moments in it which would probably not have come into being, but for the existence of Berlioz's *Harold*. Most striking of these is the clear echo of the harmonic structure supporting the second phrase of Berlioz's idée fixe (Ex. 202c), both at the opening of the trio in the Alpine fairy scherzo (Ex. 202a) and for the main theme of the slow movement (Ex. 202b; this harmonic parallel draws attention to the kinship of Tchaikovsky's themes, whose contours also seem not altogether unconditioned by those of Berlioz's first phrase (Ex. 202d)).[19]

Ex. 202

It was also to be expected that since Manfred, like Harold, stands apart from the other personalities and events of the drama, Tchaikovsky should have retained the musical personification of his hero unchanged throughout. The combination of an immutable theme with the material proper to the movement into which it has intruded could pose technical problems as great as were the expressive rewards to be reaped from such a confrontation of differing worlds and materials, for the idée fixe was likely to be at variance in pace, metre – and, consequently, in phrase structure – with its new, brief companions. The skill with which Berlioz had answered these challenges in the central

[19] Coincidentally the same progression was used by Bach in his C major keyboard prelude for which Gounod devised his Ave Maria obbligato, and which Tchaikovsky appears to quote at the beginning of Manfred's death scene (see below, p. 309).

movements of *Harold* is not the least impressive feature of that symphony, and was both a model and an inspiration to Tchaikovsky when he inserted Manfred's theme into the trio of his own scherzo. Yet elsewhere such combinations are mostly avoided – and here we begin to touch on the differences between the two pieces. Harold has the singularity of the individual, not the misanthropy of the recluse; his customary role may be that of detached observer, and he does not merge into a scene, but he can find a quiet corner to observe it from inside. Not so Manfred; he intrudes roughly (as did fate in the Fourth Symphony), for a moment sweeping aside other material – a scowling spectator, impotent to become part of the world he has briefly entered, and quickly forgotten by it.

For the fact is that *Harold en Italie* and the Manfred Symphony are really very different works, and nowhere is this more apparent than in the finale of each, in *Harold* the most implicitly, in the Manfred Symphony the most explicitly programmatic movement. While the Manfred Symphony is a fully romantic work of the 1880s, *Harold* remains a post-classical conception of the 1830s, and even the listener who is implacably convinced that the *Orgie de brigands* is a series of extra-musical representations will surely recognize that what prompted Berlioz to begin by recalling material from all three preceding movements was the example of Beethoven's Ninth Symphony as much as any pictorial purpose. So, too, when the brigands are at last allowed to sweep Harold aside and proceed to business, they organize their activities to shape out the events in a kind of abbreviated sonata structure. Only the startling recollection of the *Marche de pèlerins* after all these spirited proceedings brings a reminder that the movement is not controlled simply by musical considerations. If there is a model for Tchaikovsky's bacchanal, it is more the *Songe d'une nuit du Sabbat* in Berlioz's earlier Symphonie Fantastique; that much is suggested by the combination later devised between the two main thematic ingredients. Yet this is effected almost coincidentally, rather than because it might provide the movement's musical climax, as in Berlioz. In fact, almost the sole arbiter of events is Stasov's programme.

Yet the weakness of this finale derives less from the absence of any larger musical coherence than from the feebleness of the melodic material. Intended to be terse, this is merely short-winded. That abundant rhythmic variety, which had encouraged such a diversity of phrase structure in Berlioz's wild tableau, is here confined mostly to simplistic rhythmic restructuring of the initial phrase. Turning this orgy into a bacchanal was Tchaikovsky's idea, but the boozy improprieties of such occasions rarely have the spice of true villainy or the relish of an honest hellish debauch, and the invention soon becomes all too redolent of the colourful gopaks of Tchaikovsky's operas. The best of the music which here represents Manfred comes straight from the first movement, though when Astarte appears she adds a few poignant touches to her earlier material. Tchaikovsky's own brief summary of events in his autograph score claims erroneously that Manfred is finally forgiven, and this must explain the complacent rosiness in the death scene. If the opening of this sounds suspiciously like a quotation from Gounod's Ave Maria obbligato on Bach, with one note added to incorporate the contour of the first Manfred theme (compare x in Ex. 202e with the opening of Ex. 208a), there can be no doubt about the explicit appearance of the 'Dies irae' in the bass some bars later.

The central two movements have been far more successful. In substance both are mainly of the world of the suites, though much elaborated. As in the finale, Tchaikovsky rejected Balakirev's directions on key, selecting B minor for the scherzo and G for the slow movement. He also decided on andante con moto as the speed of the latter and called it *Pastorale*, though this label is rendered redundant by the opening oboe solo in compound duple time. The mood and material of this movement are certainly conditioned by those of the Adagio in the Symphonie Fantastique, but its structure owes nothing to Berlioz. As early as the slow movement of his First Symphony and as recently as the first movement of his Third Suite Tchaikovsky had shown an impressive capacity for organizing melodic materials into schemes whose totalities are rather more than the sum of their parts. As Ex. 203 shows, this *Pastorale* has a wide variety of materials in a large number of sections strung out with refreshing unpredictability. The brief intrusion of Manfred is external to the design, but it serves the useful function of breaking the movement into two clear but unequal parts. After this interruption, much of the earlier material is systematically recalled, the two A sentences and a fragment of F being blended to make a particularly extensive paragraph, while the fleeting demisemiquaver appendage to D is expanded to provide the first part of a tiny coda; this ends with echoes of the opening melody, now shaped to conform exactly with the last melodic contour of Berlioz's *Scène aux champs*. Most striking of all these modifications in this second half is the reharmonization of C, a horn theme based upon only three notes. On its first two appearances in this slow movement it had been harmonized by a sustained A minor triad, but now its repeated three-pitch cells are supported by a magical progression of chromatically related chords (Ex. 204b); enchantment, it seems, touches even the world of artless mortals – always assuming, that is, that this theme truly *is* the hunter's emblem, for with its

Ex. 203

MANFRED SYMPHONY: THIRD MOVEMENT

affiliations to a horn passage in the first movement (Ex. 204a), it might be yet another facet of Manfred himself. This is far from the only instance of thematic ambiguity in this symphony, as we shall see.

Ex. 204

This slow movement is decorated with all sorts of picturesque touches: a shepherd's musette, occasional bird-song, the 'sweet bells of the sauntering herd'. But enchantment had been the very essence of the preceding scherzo. Balakirev had said that Manfred should appear in the trio, and he intrudes twice, first merely as observer of the spirit he has conjured ('to look upon thy beauty – nothing further'), then as despairing interlocutor. Perhaps the main theme of the trio is indeed Tchaikovsky's personification of the 'Witch of the Alps', as Byron called her, but the similarity already noted between this cheerful theme and the oboe melody of the following *Pastorale* (see Ex. 202a and b) might suggest that it also contains intimations of the world of ordinary mortals. Yet within any study of Tchaikovsky's evolving style the materials of the scherzo itself and their presentation are of prime interest. The ten years which had passed since the scherzo of the Third Symphony provide a perspective which clarifies the novelty of that earlier movement. Like the Manfred scherzo its orchestration is critical

to its effect. But Tchaikovsky's craft has developed immensely in the
intervening years, and the two movements really share nothing except
their key. The 1875 scherzo had been a relatively simple affair – a single
line of undulating semiquavers presented in constantly changing colours as background to a variety of crisp phrases. Nothing as crystalized
as these stands out in the Manfred scherzo. Instead it spins a web of
intricate yet impeccably clear textures, unfolded on harmonic structures of great simplicity, as the opening demonstrates (Ex. 205); two
bars of tonic alternating with submediant follow upon two bars which
select components of a dominant ninth, delicately fragmented and
spiced with appoggiaturas.

Ex. 205

Nevertheless, though that fastidious variety of colour already exploited in parts of the Second and Third Suites is in this scherzo evolved into a chiaroscuro of a myriad fineness new in Tchaikovsky's music, it would be wrong to assume that this movement is merely a stream of bewitching orchestral sound. It displays a simple yet effective motivic growth; for instance, the slurred-note feature soon grows into a three-note cell which is first heard as accompaniment to the tiny melodic figure of which it is a simplification (bars 31ff.), then as a foreground motif of flexible contour (bars 39ff.) in a passage which reminds us that Naina's spiky dartings in *Ruslan and Lyudmila* are as much behind the hatching of this music as Berlioz's *Queen Mab* or Tchaikovsky's Third Symphony scherzo. As for matters of tonality, the listener is hard put to specify the key in force, once Glinka's witch has really taken possession, and it is only after much elusiveness that B minor is at last allowed to regain and confirm its hold. And just as, at the trio's opening, the Alpine fairy had seemingly materialized from the pulsing F sharp at the spellbound conclusion of the scherzo, so at the movement's end, as Manfred again stands as observer and his theme is heard for a third time, the spirit with 'hair of light and dazzling eyes of glory' vanishes upwards in the dying flickers of a B minor chord.

Tchaikovsky prefaced his autograph score of the first movement with a quite detailed account of its content, diverging a little from Stasov's prescription in both substance and emphasis.

Manfred wanders in the Alps. Tormented by fateful questions of existence, tortured by the burning anguish of hopelessness and memory of his guilty past, he experiences cruel spiritual torments. Manfred has penetrated deeply into the secrets of magic and communicates imperiously with the powerful forces of hell, but neither they nor anyone in the world can give him the *oblivion* which he yet vainly seeks and craves. Memories of his ruined Astarte, whom once he had passionately loved, gnaw and eat at his heart, and there is neither Grace nor an end to Manfred's boundless despair.[20]

It may seem curious that, though Tchaikovsky added Manfred's involvement in magic arts, there is no firm trace of those specific musical idioms of enchantment which he had used so pointedly in, for instance, *The Tempest*. In fact, it is a measure of his especially serious approach to this movement that he should have felt that such essentially ornamental elements, which had found a ready place elsewhere in the symphony, would be inept here, and the very existence of this more

[20] *DTC*, p. 408.

elaborate programme substantiates the importance he attached to this Lento lugubre. Balakirev, too, must have perceived it as the most significant part of the symphony, and he specified for it the longest list of pieces he felt might help Tchaikovsky's own thoughts to stir, for the only item which was obviously to relate to Tchaikovsky's finale was the brigands' movement from *Harold*. The other two orchestral works, Liszt's *Hamlet* and Tchaikovsky's own *Francesca da Rimini*, were musical portraits, as Tchaikovsky's first movement was to be. *Hamlet* seems to have left no direct marks on Tchaikovsky's invention, but *Francesca* may have bequeathed its ternary structure in which the heroine's music forms the centre. As for the preludes by Chopin, it could hardly be expected that pieces as idiomatically pianistic as those in E flat minor and C sharp minor could offer much, though the Largo in E minor was a different matter, and this gently melancholy piece may have played some part in forming the passage for solo horn (see Ex. 204a); both melodies are in E minor and are tightly confined, and both are supported by harmony proceeding solely by stepwise movement, often chromatic.

Yet it seems likely that Tchaikovsky selected his own models for the distinct musical worlds associated with Manfred and Astarte. He had already confessed to Balakirev his profound admiration for Schumann's incidental music for *Manfred*, and his determination to avoid its influence is suggested by the studied absence of any detectable connection between the earlier score and his own. Except, that is, for one small but crucial link: the hesitant and tender invention through which Tchaikovsky introduces Astarte in his first movement (Ex. 206a: andante) has a striking general affinity with the tiny, widely spaced phrases, also for muted strings, with which Schumann had punctuated Manfred's first words in the melodrama he devised to support Astarte's corresponding appearance (Ex. 206b). And if, by contrast, a musical antipathy should have driven Tchaikovsky to his choice of 'helpful material' for Manfred's own music, this need hardly cause surprise. Byron's hero had destroyed the woman who had become involved with him; Tristan, too, had been guilty of a kind of

Ex. 206

b.

[SCHUMANN]

c.

treachery in love, and Isolde had died. There any similarities
Tchaikovsky may have thought he could perceive with that tale ended;
nevertheless, as his creative urges prepared their incarnation of Manfred, their attention seems to have turned towards the music which
introduces the hero to Isolde in Wagner's opera (Ex. 207a). There is the

Ex. 207

same bluntness in the phrases on the well-reeded wind, the same
gruffness in the trenchant string chords which follow. Moreover, somewhere among Tchaikovsky's thoughts there seems to have lingered a
memory of the theme (Ex. 208e) which underpins Fricka's denunciation in *Walküre* of another act of incest: the union of Siegmund and
Sieglinde. Indeed, when Tchaikovsky widens the falling fourths to
fifths at Manfred's first climactic outburst (Ex. 208d), Wagner's contour is exactly matched. Yet Tchaikovsky's music (Ex. 207b) is all his
own. Though opening (it emerges) in E minor, resolution into a triad is
rigorously avoided until the ninth bar, the dissonances which promote
the absolute ascendency of the seventh chord arising almost entirely
from aggressive passing notes or appoggiaturas. Its terse masculinity is
consolidated when the strings present a rising line (bar 14) initiated by
a plunging seventh which steepens the contour of Manfred's very first

Ex. 208

notes, constituting a second Manfred theme (Ex. 208b), and confirming this as the toughest music Tchaikovsky had yet composed.

This process of thematic evolution is fundamental to the music of Manfred himself, and in the following quieter passage it is pursued at a motivic level when the twice-heard figure of three adjacent notes in the work's opening phrase (y in Ex. 208a) becomes an undulating quasi-ostinato thread (Ex. 208c) upon which is strung a series of new, brief ideas. Yet the progressive disclosure of a personality which such thematic unfolding admirably suggests is soon to be opposed by an obsessiveness which has already been foreshadowed in the nagging repetitions of this Manfred cell (y), though this is held in check until the entire first section has, Liszt-like, been repeated, now opening in the tonic key, and finally passing to yet another restatement of the symphony's first two bars, but with their contours widened, and with the second Manfred phrase annexed (Ex. 208d; further forms of these materials are set out in Ex. 208f and g).

But now, abruptly, thematic amplification suffers a reverse. Passages of great dynamic and expressive force had occurred before in Tchaikovsky's music. That last impetuous eruption of the lovers' music in *The Tempest* is but one example; yet the theme, once stated, had been allowed to range freely, then give place to other material. Not so this second Manfred phrase, for it is caught into a series of obsessive repetitions made more intense by diminution, and more frustrated by being trapped within a single chord which batters them with increasing violence. When at last Manfred's desperate writhings burst through these confining bonds, he can do no more than complete the earlier broken course of his original theme, then sink back exhausted towards E minor.

Some may feel that the dramatic analogies of the preceding prose are overheated. Yet one thing is surely clear from this music: even the most tempestuous passages in *Francesca* and the fiercest stretches of the Fourth Symphony had held back from the sheer violence which momentarily attends the climax of this first section. Without a readiness to hear such music as transmitting signals in addition to those received from the purely musical operations of the materials, it is doubtful whether the impact of this first movement could even be tolerated. This challenge to the listener's neural fortitude (the term is not used facetiously) is more powerful still after Manfred's music has detonated again to end the movement. Now enduringly marked by his encounter with his beloved, he returns morosely towards the original form of his opening phrase (Ex. 209a), restates it a fourth higher, then continues with a phrase impregnated by memories of Astarte's music –

by the descending fate-scale pattern which had proliferated so abundantly at the climax of her scene, above all by the two-quaver feminine
ending which had emerged unobtrusively when her opening music had
been heard for the second time (see z in Ex. 206c), and which had
become a stronger feature as her paragraph had unfolded (see Ex. 210).
It might be suspected that the brevity of this concluding section would
balance inadequately the earlier spacious deployment of Manfred's
material. But Tchaikovsky knew perfectly well what he was about.
After his vain pleas to Astarte, Manfred can but collapse into hopeless
and, finally, frantic misery, and this he does when the opening notes of
the Astarte-stamped phrase are broken off (Ex. 209b, bar 8) to be
repeated and decorated with ever-shortening note values while the
accompaniment pounds against it with increasingly brutal force. After
the trumpet scream which crowns this tumult, despair can go no
further; frenzy is bordering on hysteria, and Tchaikovsky's swift
conclusion is as right as it is necessary.

Ex. 209

There remains Astarte's music. Her first notes issue in the most natural way out of the brusque sounds which Manfred had uttered before falling into a characteristically abrupt silence (see Ex. 206a), for besides echoing his last two pitches, her first fragile phrase grows above yet another statement of his cell. The other moment when their worlds touch is in that last emotional vortex of the whole movement, both in the phrase which her music had so deeply conditioned (Ex. 209a, bars 8ff.), and even more when it is truncated (Ex. 209b) and so becomes yet another derivative of the three-note Manfred cell. Of all the thematic ambiguities of this symphony, this is the most subtle and perhaps the most significant. Yet otherwise Tchaikovsky could not conceive Astarte's music as anything but distinct from Manfred's, not simply because of the programme's requirements, but because to him it signified something far more poignant and pointed than anything in the literary subject. What had made Tchaikovsky's response to Manfred himself so strong was the irresistible invitation it provided for self-projection, and in the music he conceived for Byron's hero that autobiographical strain, so important in Tchaikovsky's work but for so long muted, reasserts itself with a vengeance. Nevertheless, an equally significant strand running through Tchaikovsky's work – and one which invariably lifts the level of his inspiration, sometimes to its greatest heights – is that of the suffering woman, almost always young and vulnerable, and almost always innocent – or, at least, enduring torments far greater than her failings. This strand goes back to his first important piece – that precocious student work, *The Storm*, where Katerina is destroyed through one lapse in love. In *Undine*, his second opera, the water nymph languishes and perishes through the faithlessness of her human lover, while in his next opera, *The Oprichnik*, it is the Boyarïna, tough and courageous in suffering, yet finally unable to survive the ordeal of her son's execution, who drew by far the strongest response from Tchaikovsky. In his orchestral music the suffering woman resurges powerfully in *Francesca da Rimini*. Nor should we forget Odette in *Swan Lake*: her final catastrophe inspired Tchaikovsky to a symphonic tableau of almost disconcerting power. In the years immediately following his marriage, with no more symphonic poems coming from his pen, the image lives on in his operas. After Tatyana comes Joan in *The Maid of Orléans*, for like her even more favoured predecessor in *Onegin*, it was she who prompted the opera's best music. Next Mariya in *Mazepa*, torn between her father and his murderer, the husband she loves: nothing in the nominal hero could rouse in Tchaikovsky a response as powerful as that stirred by Mariya's final crazed and hopeless predicament. And now Astarte. Insubstantial, yet still wonderfully beautiful, she haunts her lover's thoughts in the loveliest and most heartfelt music Tchaikovsky had discovered within himself since Tatyana had opened for him his richest and most personal vein some eight years before. Her floating ascent into Manfred's consciousness is exquisitely captured in the slender opening phrases (see Ex. 206a, bars 5ff.), each suggesting a brief delicate movement which is checked into a motionless silence. Then, as the phrases and the silences shorten, the tonal mists begin to lift and D major strengthens its pull in a string texture filled with the most telling chromatic detail and rich in seventh chords, though these now suggest a wistful yearning quite different from their abrasive contribution to Manfred's glowering appearance at the symphony's opening. But the ground is not even brushed; there is no hint of cadential resolution before the gentle ghost glides upwards to vanish as she receives renewed incarnation in the woodwind. The following duet for first violins and cellos (Ex. 210) has all the eloquence of that plangent dialogue which had formed the most memorable passage in the Piano Trio, though it possesses a more affecting simplicity of phrase, and combines in the most natural way with a fragment of Astarte's earlier music until both are swept aside by invading scales of fate. The re-entry of Astarte's first music as the climax of this outburst has a surprising vehemence: her sufferings still truly match those of Manfred. Finally, in a single line which faintly

Ex. 210

foreshadows a portion of that phrase which is about to bear the full burden of Manfred's response, she sinks down again to linger only in the recesses of her fateful lover's memory.

In November 1882, when Tchaikovsky had rejected the newly offered Manfred programme, his letter to Balakirev had also contained a dispirited assessment of his own achievement.

> Despite my venerable age and my considerable experience in composing, I must confess that *I am wandering* still in the boundless field of composition, trying vainly to discover my true pathway. I feel that such a pathway exists and I know that, once I find it, I shall write something really good – but some fateful blindness constantly leads me astray, and God knows whether sometime I shall hit upon where I ought to be going. . . . From time to time it's happened that I've come close to 'the pathway', and then pieces have emerged of which, to the end of my life, I shall not be ashamed, which please and maintain in me the energy for work. But this has happened rarely, and in no way can I number *Francesca* and *The Tempest* among these few exceptions. Both these pieces are written with affected ardour, with false pathos, with a pursuit of purely external effects – and at bottom they are cold, false and weak in the extreme. Their failings stem from the fact that these compositions of mine in no way *recreate* the given subject, but are only written *à propos* of it – that is, the kinship of the music and the programme is not an inner one, but external, incidental.[21]

It was, of course, a verdict too severe. Uneven as both pieces are, they contain, in the music of Miranda's love or Francesca's misery, passages which speak truly from the heart, though it is no surprise that Tchaikovsky would not wish (or, perhaps, have the capacity) to admit this, even to himself. Yet his assertion that other stretches of these works were no more than efficient responses to elements within his subjects was well founded, and his unsparing repudiation in 1888 of the last three movements of the Manfred Symphony was an equally valid recognition that, whatever the qualities of some of their musical invention or the craft with which this was deployed, they also were, as counterparts of Byron's poem, merely synthetic. In 1882 he had even censured *Romeo and Juliet* on the same grounds of non-commitment, even though only two years earlier he had felt sufficient regard for it to think it worth expending some of his creative energies upon a further

[21] *TLP*ii, p. 281; *BVP*, p. 168.

revision. Yet he continued to recognize that the first movement of the Manfred Symphony was something different, and three years after completing it his pride and trust in it remained as firm as ever, for he must have perceived that this time his identification with the subject had been total. The quality of the musical ideas and their application may be a matter for debate, but of one thing there can be no doubt: in this movement of such expressive extremes, Tchaikovsky was fully himself again.

And so, for a second time, Balakirev had rendered invaluable service. Yet for all the new hopes Tchaikovsky may in November 1884 have placed in his old mentor as a guide to personal salvation, his ambivalence remained. 'I have again taken a cordial farewell of Balakirev. He's a strange man (between ourselves, be it said, a *madman*), but all the same, essentially a wonderful person,' he had written to Jurgenson on 19 November, a week later.[22] It was predictable that Tchaikovsky should have wished to avoid direct contact with Balakirev while the Manfred Symphony remained unfinished; nor is it surprising that afterwards he should have done nothing to foster face-to-face encounters between himself and this autocrat who, with the symphony done, had promptly signalled that his next work should be a piano concerto in F sharp minor or C sharp minor, and who was threatening to pressurize him into making changes in *The Tempest* when they next met. In January 1886, when Tchaikovsky paid a visit to St Petersburg, they did consult over details of the piano-duet transcription of the symphony, but their religious exchanges do not seem to have been renewed.

The disintegration of their relationship is charted in their few remaining letters. Always it is Balakirev who attempts to engineer meetings. 'I'm inviting you . . . to my place on Thursday evening,' he wrote on 6 November 1886, when Tchaikovsky was in the city. 'But I won't tell anyone about this; I don't know whether you want to be completely alone, or whether you want me to invite anyone else. You'll tell me on Tuesday.'[23] It was the same four months later on Tchaikovsky's next visit. The party would include a few old friends they had in common – but 'if there's any of them you don't want to see, then let me know; it shall be as you wish, and the secret will remain *between us.*'[24] Whether they had met privately in November is unknown, but on this second visit Tchaikovsky simply could not face an intimate

[22] *TLP*12, p. 480; *TPJ*2, p. 20; *YDGC*, p. 329.
[23] *BVP*, p. 182.
[24] *BVP*, p. 183.

encounter. 'I haven't the strength to bear any longer my extreme weariness and nervous derangement, and today I've decided to go away into the country,' he pleaded. 'I'm very distressed I shan't be a witness to your triumph [the silver jubilee concert of the Free Music School which Balakirev was to conduct the next day]. Please, old chap, don't be angry. God knows, I have no more strength.'[25]

In November 1888, Balakirev tried for the last time. He had attended the première of Tchaikovsky's Fifth Symphony which the composer had conducted three days before, and he was determined to extract an answer to his invitation for the following Thursday. 'I shall send for a reply,' he promised on 20 November, 'so don't go out without leaving one for me.'[26] But again Tchaikovsky excused himself.

A three-year silence followed. Then in October 1891 Tchaikovsky wrote to Balakirev on behalf of a choirboy from St Sofiya's Cathedral in Kiev who had been inexplicably dismissed by the Metropolitan, despite possessing an unusually beautiful voice; perhaps Balakirev might have a place for him in the Imperial Chapel. But Balakirev wrote that he could offer no help. Their last two letters were exchanged some seven weeks later when Tchaikovsky was in St Petersburg to participate in a concert. Their tone and content tell all.

Wanting to hear your Slavonic March played by an orchestra, I earnestly beg you to inform me when your last rehearsal will be, and by *approximately* what time I need to come to the hall to hear the Slavonic March without having to waste more time than necessary. You will greatly oblige me by fulfilling my request.

Yours ever,
M. Balakirev[27]

Three days later, on 11 December, Tchaikovsky answered.

At today's rehearsal (it's the last one) the Slavonic March will be played second. I shall begin with the overture *exactly at 1 p.m.*; consequently the march will be played *at approximately* 1.20, since the

[25] *TLP*14, p. 61; *BVP*, p. 183.
[26] *BVP*, p. 184.
[27] *BVP*, p. 185.

overture's not especially long. The rehearsal's taking place in the hall
of the Assembly of the Nobility.

Sincerely devoted to you,
P. Tchaikovsky[28]

Not a hint of personal exchanges – not a hint of an invitation, nor even
of a wish to meet. Their relationship was finally over.

[28] *TLP*16A, p. 285; *BVP*, p. 186.

Volume IV

THE FINAL YEARS

(1885–1893)

CONTENTS

Preface to Volume IV 9

Main Literary Sources for Volume IV 12

1 *First Months at Maidanovo:* The Enchantress 13

2 *Growing Confidence: A Hard Winter and a Good Summer* 65

3 *A New Activity: Triumphs and Sorrows* 97

4 *International Conductor: Fifth Symphony* 127

5 *Second International Tour:* The Sleeping Beauty 166

6 *Eminent Relationships:* The Queen of Spades 216

7 *A Time of Change: End of a Relationship* 271

8 *American Tour* 313

9 *Double Bill:* The Nutcracker *and* Iolanta 332

10 *The Bonds of Fame: The Piano Music* 373

11 *The Russian Composer: Sixth Symphony* 421

12 *The Last Months* 460

Bibliography 489

Work List 492

Cumulative Index:
   Index of Works 505
   Index of Persons 511

ILLUSTRATIONS

Herman Laroche and Alexandr Glazunov

The Tchaikovsky brothers (1890): Anatoly, Nikolay, Ippolit, the composer, Modest

Nikolay Kashkin, the composer, Medea and Nikolay Figner

Anatoly Brandukov and the composer (1888)

Vasily Sapelnikov

Alexandr Ziloti and the composer (1888)

The composer and Bob Davïdov (1892)

Georges-Léon and Olga Tchaikovskaya

Eduard Epstein (a pianist), Varvara Zarudnaya, Mikhail Ippolitov-Ivanov, Karl Davïdov and Vasily Safonov

Tchaikovsky (1893)

PREFACE

THIS FINAL VOLUME covers the period of Tchaikovsky's greatest celebrity, when the supremacy he achieved as a composer within his native Russia was matched in some other countries by an almost equal fame consolidated by a series of expeditions as a conductor. It is also the period of some of his finest works (the Fifth Symphony and *The Queen of Spades*, for instance) – above all, of *The Sleeping Beauty* and Sixth Symphony (with the opera, *Eugene Onegin*, perhaps his greatest compositions).

This four-volume work has attempted to be no more than what is specified on the title page: a biographical and critical study. Such a fundamental work, spacious enough to be able to survey both life and compositions comprehensively and in some detail, has not existed up to now even in Tchaikovsky's native land (as the Russians themselves have admitted in a very generous appraisal of the first three volumes[1]). On the one hand it has sought to fix the successive events of the composer's life and define something of his personality, especially as it is projected through his surviving letters and diaries; on the other it has attempted to draw out those features which seem most noteworthy in individual pieces, make a qualitative assessment of these pieces, and identify some of the trends and evolutions perceptible in the different forms and genres in which Tchaikovsky composed. But it also seemed essential to attempt some sort of final drawing together of threads. I have not tried in the penultimate chapter to summarize his style, however, for this would have been impossible within the space available, if only because of the sheer variety within that style, and sometimes its inconsistencies. How, except in an additional volume, could one define the characteristics of a body of work which embraced both the Rococo Variations and the Sixth Symphony, or deal adequately with more specific but crucial matters such as orchestration or texture, in both of which there is a very significant evolution to be detected during the nearly three decades of Tchaikovsky's creative activity?

Instead I have attempted in this penultimate chapter something

[1] In *Sovyetskaya Muzïka*, issue of June, 1990.

more fundamental: to pinpoint a little of the Russianness of Tchaikovsky's music. His was a Russian mind forced to find its expression through techniques and forms that had been evolved by generations of alien Western creators, and, this being so, it would be unreasonable to expect stylistic consistency or uniform quality. But what is impressive about Tchaikovsky's work is the success with which he so often conducted this struggle (for struggle it was), and the sometimes extraordinary way in which he bent these Western resources to his creative will. For in his best and most characteristic works the ways of thinking most natural to the Russian mind are freely exercised to a remarkable degree. Had it been otherwise, his music could never have achieved that total individuality which grips so many listeners, nor could he have reached those pinnacles of achievement which it is now being increasingly recognized he attained. Inevitably I have been able only to scratch the surface of the subject, and I have had often to generalize more than I would have wished. But if in addition to any insights this chapter may offer to the non-specialist reader, it can suggest to other present or future Tchaikovsky scholars lines of investigation they might pursue much further than I, or if my approach offers ideas that scholars concerned with other Russian composers can find profitable, then I shall feel it to have been fully justified.

Had I been starting this work in 1990 I should, of course, have had a very different prospect before me. In 1975 I had to accept that Tchaikovsky's literary archives – his letters and diaries – would be firmly closed to me, and that any attempts to penetrate to his musical remains would be unsuccessful (my request for microfilm of his compositional sketches, for instance, was rejected on the grounds that they 'had not passed the censor'). Now, however, the advent of *glasnost* gives hope that such things will be readily available to my successors. But I have resisted any temptation to hold back the present volume in the hope of benefiting belatedly from this new openness myself, since the amount of time that would be required to sift through documents would certainly delay publication for at the very least two years – above all, because the terms of reference for this study are so immutably embodied in the three volumes already in print.

As in earlier volumes I owe many debts of gratitude. I must specially thank the Radcliffe Trust who awarded me their Musicology Fellowship for 1986–7. It was an especially valuable award as I began this final volume, for the quantity of biographical data that survives from Tchaikovsky's years of international fame is so great that it had to be sifted through a larger meshed net if the narrative pace of the preceding volumes was to be maintained, and this year-long deliverance from university teaching and administration provided a breathing space in which I could adjust to a new level of selection. This is the moment, too, when I review the various individuals whose help has been so invaluable. First Dr Anthea Baird of London University, who has been unfailing in making available books and scores, then two others who have had no part in this volume, but whose earlier assistance is remembered with undiminished gratitude: Mr A. Helliwell, now retired from London University, and Mrs Miriam Phillips, whose splendid services in preparing the typescripts for the first three volumes have now been performed by the most unglamorous of word processors. There is Alexandra Orlova whose researches have provided much material used in the final pages of this volume, and who made available to me her copy of that suppressed collection of the composer's letters, *Pisma k rodnïm*, which afforded especially invaluable insights into Tchaikovsky's tormented inner life at the time of his marriage. And there is my wife, who has borne the tedious burden of being my assistant in checking and proof reading, and to whom these volumes are dedicated. Finally, my thanks to the various efficient and helpful members of my publisher's staff, with whom I or my volumes have had dealings – to Elizabeth Dobson, Richard Wigmore – and especially to Livia Gollancz, whose expertise not only as book publisher but also as a former professional musician has been invaluable in shepherding these volumes into the wider world. In 1975 it had been intended that I should produce a single volume, but instead I have produced four. The patient tolerance with which the prospect of twins, then triplets, then quads was received is something for which I remain the more grateful, since Victor Gollancz Ltd would have been perfectly within its rights to stifle the others before birth. To these, and all others who have helped in various ways, my most heartfelt thanks.

BRAISHFIELD, HAMPSHIRE   DAVID BROWN
MAY 1990

MAIN LITERARY SOURCES FOR VOLUME IV
WITH ABBREVIATIONS

TLP 1–17   TCHAIKOVSKY (P.), *Polnoye sobraniye sochineny: literaturnïye proizvedeniya i perepiska* [Complete edition: literary works and correspondence], 17 vols. (Moscow, 1953–81)

TD   TCHAIKOVSKY (P.), *Dnevniki* [Diaries] (Moscow/Petrograd, 1923)

TPB   TCHAIKOVSKY (P.), *Pisma k blizkim* [Letters to his family] (Moscow, 1955)

TPJ 1–2   TCHAIKOVSKY (P.), *Perepiska s P. I. Jurgensonom* [Correspondence with Jurgenson], 2 vols. (Moscow, 1938–52)

TPM 1–3   TCHAIKOVSKY (P.), *Perepiska s N. F. von Meck* [Correspondence with Nadezhda von Meck], 3 vols. (Moscow/Leningrad, 1934–6)

TTP   *P. I. Chaykovsky: S. I. Taneyev. Pisma* [Tchaikovsky/Taneyev. Letters] (Moscow, 1951)

BVP   BALAKIREV (M.), *Perepiska s P. I. Chaykovskim* [Correspondence with Tchaikovsky], reprinted in FRID (E.) [ed.], *M. A. Balakirev: vospominaniya i pisma* [Balakirev: Recollections and letters] (Leningrad, 1962)

DTC   DOMBAYEV (G.), *Tvorchestvo P. I. Chaykovskovo* [Tchaikovsky's works] (Moscow, 1958)

PVC   PROTOPOPOV (V.) [ed.], *Vospominaniya o P. I. Chaykovskom* [Reminiscences of Tchaikovsky] (Moscow, 1962)

TZC 1–3   TCHAIKOVSKY (M.), *Zhizn P. I. Chaykovskovo* [Tchaikovsky's life], 3 vols. (Moscow, 1900–2)

TZM   ALEXEYEV (N.) [ed.], *Chaykovsky i zarubeznïye muzikanï: izbrannïye pisma inostrannïkh korrespondentov* [Tchaikovsky and foreign musicians: selected letters] (Leningrad, 1970)

YDGC   YAKOVLEV (V.) [ed.], *Dni i godï P. I. Chaykovskovo* [The days and years of Tchaikovsky] (Moscow/Leningrad, 1940)

One musical source is also abbreviated in references:

T50RF   TCHAIKOVSKY (P.), *50 Russian Folksongs*, arranged for piano duet by Tchaikovsky (Moscow, 1869)

I

FIRST MONTHS AT MAIDANOVO:

THE ENCHANTRESS

ON 31 JANUARY 1885 Russia's old capital heard Tchaikovsky's Third Suite for the first time. 'I was in Moscow for Erdmannsdörfer's concert,' Modest Tchaikovsky remembered in his biography of his brother, 'and on one occasion I happened to mention *The Enchantress*, and how effective the scene in which Kuma and the young prince meet would be in an opera – though I certainly was not recommending making a libretto from the drama itself. That very day Pyotr Ilich purchased a lithographed copy of I. V. Shpazhinsky's play and went into raptures about this scene. It settled the question: the next day a letter was written to the author of *The Enchantress*, proposing he should convert it into a libretto.'[1]

Deciding what his next opera should be was one of Tchaikovsky's lifelong occupations. Subjects came and went. Only weeks earlier, with *Eugene Onegin* consolidating its new-found, overwhelming popularity and edging its composer's thoughts once more towards operatic composition, Tchaikovsky's interest had been aroused in a scenario, *The Gipsies*, devised by Vasily Kandaurov. Yet, as had happened so often before, the project silently and swiftly sank without trace. But not *The Enchantress*. The play was new, and Tchaikovsky had already made two abortive attempts to see it; having now read it, he was gripped by the subject, even though there were currently politic reasons why Pushkin's *The Captain's Daughter* should have prior claim. The Tsar himself had suggested this subject during his meeting with Tchaikovsky at the *Onegin* performance only days before Modest had mentioned *The Enchantress*; he had even told the composer he need have no inhibitions about presenting the rebel leader, Pugachev, in his opera. A suggestion from His Imperial Majesty carried particular weight, and it had clearly circulated fairly widely, for others were soon adding their persuasions, including Emiliya Pavlovskaya, who had won such admiration and gratitude from Tchaikovsky for her creation of Mariya in his most

---

[1] *TZC*3, pp. 22–3; *DTC*, p. 146 (partial); *TLP*13, p. 29 (partial).

recent opera, *Mazepa*. Tchaikovsky's mind, however, was made up.
'Regarding *The Captain's Daughter*, I will tell you that if sometime I find
a librettist strong enough to cope with the formidable task of turning it
into an opera libretto, then I shall certainly work on it joyfully,' he
promised Pavlovskaya on 26 March. 'But meanwhile I'm counting on
The Enchantress by Shpazhinsky. The latter is now busy turning it into a
libretto. He is changing a lot and, unless I'm mistaken, a design very
good for music will result. Certainly it'll be the most ideal part for you!'
he added enticingly.[2]

Five weeks later he was equally adamant, if rather defensive. 'I did
indeed discuss the subject of *The Captain's Daughter* with some persons in
the theatre world . . . and on mature reflection I decided to drop the
idea . . .' he confessed to a certain Pavel Pereletsky, who was trying to
tempt him with Turgenev's *On the eve* (which Tchaikovsky rejected as
being too contemporary by far and, in any case, unsuitable for operatic
treatment). 'As for *The Enchantress*,' he continued, 'it will be unrecognizable as a libretto. Only its *essence* will remain; the treatment of the
subject will be completely different, and the main personages will be
given new shades of character which will make them more human,
sympathetic, more alive and warm. The dénouement will also be
subjected to fundamental change.'[3]

This transformation which Tchaikovsky believed Shpazhinsky was
effecting had enabled him to retain confidence in *The Enchantress*. But
three months had passed, not a note had been composed, and
Pavlovskaya had been joined by Modest in opposition to the subject.
Yet it was not faltering enthusiasm but a dilatory librettist that was
holding Tchaikovsky back. Since deciding upon the subject he had
avoided starting any major new work, but April was passing, and he felt
he could no longer delay. Accordingly he began to focus his thoughts
purposefully upon the Manfred Symphony. Composing *The Enchantress*
would have to be put off until the autumn.

In fact, Tchaikovsky had been far from barren during the earlier part
of 1885. The first month in his new home was happily devoted to the
revision of *Vakula the Smith* which three months earlier he had promised
himself he would make, and by 3 April *Cherevichki*, as the opera was now
to be called, was ready.[4] The other achievement of these first Maidanovo weeks was the addition of five pieces to the three Cherubim's
Songs and the setting of *Thee we hymn*, composed late the previous year.

---

[2] *TLP*13, p. 49; *TZC*3, pp. 31–2; *YDGC*, p. 341 (partial); *DTC*, p. 146 (partial).
[3] *TLP*13, p. 71.
[4] For details of the revisions, both to the plot and the music, see Vol. 1, pp. 315–20.

The prompting for these Nine Sacred Pieces had come from the Tsar, but it was Jurgenson who commissioned a tenth morsel, 'a hymn for four voices, but also suitable for one',[5] in honour of SS Cyril and Methodius, who had translated the Bible into Old Church Slavonic and invented the prototype of the Cyrillic alphabet. For all his native land's indebtedness to these two 'apostles of the Slavs', Tchaikovsky was unenthusiastic, and he suspected that the Slavonic Charitable Society, which had made the same request to him seven weeks earlier, was using his publisher's good offices. 'What hymn? Why? Who needs it? Why the hell, etc.,' he fumed in reply on 2 March. 'Some Slavonic society or other has already pestered me to compose something for a gala concert. I said no. And now you come crawling! And who asked you, you wretch, to trouble yourself with Slavonic founder-patriarchs???'[6] Nor did his mood improve when a fortnight later Jurgenson sent him the words and music of a Czech song in honour of the saints upon which he should base his own work. There was a covering note: 'The text is too long for Russians. Can you extract the quintessence in ten or fifteen lines?'[7] In consequence, Tchaikovsky claimed, he had to torment himself for six hours reducing the 'doggerel' to the required size. Yet by 19 March the hymn, a simple arrangement of an 'old Slavonic melody', had been composed. It was first performed at the Conservatoire on 18 April at what was thought to be the thousandth anniversary of the death of Methodius.

The Nine Sacred Pieces, which seem to have been completed in April, contain Tchaikovsky's last solution – and an impressive one – to the problem of marrying a Western harmonic technique to a melodic manner which, while not employing the perpetual metrical flexibility of Orthodox chants, would still be congruent with those chants. In the Liturgy of St John Chrysostom of 1878 Tchaikovsky had made free use of the resources of Western harmony. Whether traditional chants were being used or independent composition attempted, major and minor keys had prevailed, there had been a constant readiness to employ chromatic alterations to create or suggest tonal shifts, and cadential practices had almost always been rigidly conventional. Chromatic movement had occurred from time to time, diminished seventh chords had been included, and the intrusion of contrapuntal passages in a thoroughly Western idiom had caused some disconcerting wrenches of style. The All-night Vigil of 1881–2 had revealed a drastic shift,

[5] *TPJ*2, p. 25; *YDGC*, p. 338; *DTC*, pp. 283–4.
[6] *TLP*13, p. 37; *TPJ*2, p. 26; *TZC*3, p. 26; *DTC*, p. 286.
[7] *TPJ*2, p. 26.

Tchaikovsky now purging his style of those elements which had sounded outré in the Liturgy. Only the brief contrapuntal passages in *O gladsome light* (No. 5) and *Praise the name of the Lord* (No. 8) sound discrepant. The modes of the chants had been scrupulously respected, modulations within movements or integral sections had become rarities, vast areas of the work being completely void of accidentals. Chromatic movement and diminished sevenths had been banned completely; there had been no place for such a passage as had occurred in bars 15–17 of the Cherubim's Song in the Liturgy (see Vol. 2, Ex. 152).

This radically sifted style had offered an admirable support for the traditional chants which make up almost the entire All-night Vigil. What Tchaikovsky now set himself in most of these nine new pieces was to attempt once again free composition of the sort he had included in the earlier Liturgy, but profiting from the invaluable lessons learned in the Vigil. The stylistic abstentions of the latter are scarcely relaxed in the three Cherubim's Songs and *Thee we hymn* (No. 4), the first pieces to be composed (*Thee we hymn* is, in fact, chant-based). Each of the Cherubim's Songs is founded upon four statements of a single section, thus reflecting the repetitiveness of the chants of the Vigil; the final section is always varied and faster, and passes to an alleluia. As in *Thee we hymn* the modal integrity is maintained throughout; instead of a tonal cadence midway in each section, Tchaikovsky has used some modal conclusion of a sort he had rarely employed before. When accidentals do briefly appear ahead of the final alleluia in the second Cherubim's Song, the modulations to the dominant and its relative minor which these effect bring home how incongruous is functional tonality in this modal realm; where a contrapuntal passage does occur in any of these nine pieces it is normally built upon material which belongs to the melodic world of the set, and this softens the stylistic jar. The first two Cherubim's Songs are four-voice settings, but the third, based on an old Kiev chant, makes much use of vocal divisions, and to launch its concluding section presents a variant of the opening with distinctive parallel octave movement between the outer parts, a device already used in the Vigil (see Vol. 3, Ex. 171b). The popularity achieved by this fine piece seems to have given it a particular seminal importance in the evolution of later music for the Orthodox ritual.

While the three settings of the Cherubim's Song and *Thee we hymn* are mostly very different from those in the Liturgy, the remaining two pieces which use texts already treated in 1878 are closer to the world of the earlier settings. The stiffer melodic-harmonic manner of *Meet it is indeed* (No. 5) and its use of structural modulation set it apart from the first four pieces (the repeated phrase in bars 7–10 of Ex. 211 is particularly un-Russian). Similarly the very formal imitative passage at the centre of the Lord's Prayer (No. 6) fits uncomfortably. *Today the heavenly powers* (No. 9) vacillates stylistically between the gentle extremes represented within these two pieces. Of the five works composed at Maidanovo, the remaining two, *Bliss I chose* (No. 7) and *Let my prayer be set forth* (No. 8), are the most interesting. The latter, which uses four verses from Psalm 141, is a dialogue between three soloists and a four-voice choir, the repeated section for soloists suggesting momentarily that Tchaikovsky is to explore the limpid world of Renaissance polyphony, though by the end nineteenth-century Italian opera sounds a

Ex. 211

[Meet it is indeed to call thee blessed, O Mother of God, the ever-blessed and all-blameless]

more probable model. It is a curious conception, quite unlike anything elsewhere in Tchaikovsky's music. The opening of *Bliss I chose* strikes through its variety of scoring (Ex. 212).

Ex. 212

[Bliss I chose]

There follows the most fervent of these works, which reaches its climax when the music of the opening returns to set the final alleluias, extending itself urgently before subsiding into the calmest of conclusions. In the best of his other church music Tchaikovsky had mostly remained loyal to that spirit of universality which seems to the Western observer so fundamental to the Orthodox Church, revealing commitment while skirting the subjective; now he fractured the traditional constraints to make a more personal utterance which earns *Bliss I chose* a place among the most affecting of his shorter works.

Modest provided a full, sometimes very vivid picture of the personal domestic world his brother created for himself at Maidanovo,[8] and which remained in many respects unchanged to the end of his life. Alexey Sofronov, his valet, had been with him long enough to know 'what the master would like', and it was not only the organization and running of Tchaikovsky's day-to-day existence that was left entirely to him, but even such personal matters as the choice of furniture and furnishings. Tchaikovsky abhorred change, accustoming himself to anything new reluctantly, and parting even more unwillingly with anything old and familiar. 'From this time traditions were firmly established for a particular arrangement of his things, an arrangement which was preserved as far as possible through every change of residence so that, wherever Pyotr Ilich was living, the appearance of his rooms remained almost the same.' He was indifferent to fine things and luxuries; his home was furnished only with necessities, nor did he care about matters of good workmanship, good materials or good style. 'He did not complain that a table rocked or that the top had become warped, that a cupboard did not close properly, that a curtain was made of ticking and not of fine cretonne.' The only possessions which really mattered to him were his books and scores, about which he could be very proprietorial, chasing up friends who had not returned borrowed volumes, and lovingly rebinding those that had become worn. Yet he took inordinate pride in the knowledge of having his own home, 'his own cook, his own laundress, his own silver, his own tablecloth, his own dog'.

It was at Maidanovo, so Modest wrote, that he instituted a routine which he observed for the rest of his life when at home – though Tchaikovsky's own diaries make it clear that this was much modified from day to day according to prevailing circumstances. 'Pyotr Ilich got up between seven and eight o'clock. Between eight and nine he drank tea, usually (being an incorrigible smoker) without bread, and read the Bible. After the Bible he would occupy himself with English or with some reading which was not only pleasure but also work. Thus he read through Otto Jahn's book on Mozart in the German original, writing out the words he did not know and consulting the dictionary, then the

---

[8] *TZC*3, pp. 60–7. The following quotations are all from these pages. To avoid later confusion, 'Klin' in Modest's text has been changed throughout to 'Maidanovo'.

philosophical works of Spinoza, Schopenhauer and others. After tea
and reading came a walk lasting no more than three quarters of an
hour. Conversation during morning tea and a morning walk in the
company of a guest always meant that Pyotr Ilich would not be
composing that day, but scoring, writing letters, reading proofs. When
engaged in composing a new piece at Maidanovo he found any
company intolerable not only during the morning but all day. At one
time, when in Moscow, abroad, or at Kamenka, he had had to content
himself for his work hours with seclusion within the confines of the
room he was occupying, during which the one thing that did not inhibit
or distract him was the presence of his servant, Alexey Sofronov. The
latter, the sole witness of the compositional process of the majority of
his master's works, simply did not hear them, as it were, and only once
in his life burst out unexpectedly with enthusiastic approval (of the
girls' chorus in the third scene of *Eugene Onegin*), to the composer's great
surprise and distress – to his distress, because he was terrified at having
constantly by him a person who would "hear him", approve and
criticize. He was greatly gratified that this was the first and only
moment of illumination in the impenetrable night of Sofronov's
musicality.'

Yet if Alexey's presence continued to be of no account, the proximity
of others during the act of creation became an increasing irritant.
'Manfred was the last work Pyotr Ilich did not write in complete
isolation, and perhaps this was why it cost him so much effort, and why
his mood was irritable and gloomy. It seems that the most important
luxury of Pyotr Ilich's new situation was precisely this solitude during
the period of composition – and if not the sole, was certainly the chief
adornment of his stay at Maidanovo.'

But it was not merely that, while composing, he wanted no one near
him. 'In his first years as a musician, he could not have been more open.
Pyotr Ilich would show his works to all those living with him not only
when they were finished but of an evening, asking others for their
opinion of what he had done that morning, and willingly acceding to
requests that he should repeat something if it had pleased. . . . From
1885 he ceased almost completely showing his new works to anyone,
and usually the first person to get to know them was Jurgenson's
engraver.'

Modest described further how his brother divided each day between
creative work and other activities.

The period between half-past nine and midday Pyotr Ilich would
give up to no one, and . . . either composed, orchestrated, read

proofs, or wrote letters. Before setting about the pleasant task, Pyotr Ilich always hastened to get rid of the unpleasant. Consequently, every time he returned home after an absence, he began by devoting the first hours – and later, when his correspondence grew to great proportions, the first days – of his solitude at Maidanovo to this (after proof-reading) most hateful occupation. . . .

At twelve precisely Pyotr Ilich would have his lunch at which, thanks to his splendid appetite, he found whatever was given him to be excellently prepared, being profuse in his praises of the chef or cook and requiring Sofronov to convey to them his gratitude with a request to have it as well prepared more often. But because, in regard of his cuisine, the master of the house was very undemanding, it happened that guests would have preferred to convey not compliments to the kitchen, but the contrary. Pyotr Ilich always ate with pleasure, but very abstemiously, especially when he was alone.

After lunch he went for a walk, whatever the weather. Somewhere at sometime he had discovered that a man needs a two-hour walk for his health, and his observance of this rule was pedantic and superstitious, as though if he returned five minutes early he would fall ill, and unbelievable misfortunes of some sort would ensue. During his walks solitude was also as necessary as during his working hours. Not only people but his beloved dog was an impediment.

. . . For the most part his walk was a time of composition. During it the embryos of the principal ideas [were formed], consideration [was given to] the skeleton of a work, the noting down of the basic ideas took place. . . . The next morning he would place these sketches in front of him and would put the finishing touches of detail to them at the piano. As far as I know, except for two scenes in *Onegin* and some of his piano pieces and romances, he always developed his sketches at the piano, during which time, because he could not trust his appalling memory, he wrote down everything, even in places indicating the instrumentation. For the most part a composition was fully worked out in these sketches. When orchestrating he was only, as it were, making a fair copy, very rarely diverging and changing what he had written out in rough.

If music was not engaging his thoughts during a walk, he might improvise scenes from plays, declaiming them aloud, almost always in French. Insects fascinated him, and he would observe them carefully, especially ants. Like the more good-natured of the inhabitants of the surrounding dachas, he would give a tip to children he encountered. But what made Tchaikovsky's tips remarkable was their size, and news of this quickly spread among the local inhabitants. Not only did growing numbers of children seem to confront him in the village; when he attempted to evade them by walking in secluded woods, they would suddenly appear from among the trees. Worse was to follow, for soon the adults of the community were distributing themselves strategically to share in his largesse. Finally this cat-and-mouse situation became intolerable, and for a while Tchaikovsky had to confine his obligatory two-hour walk to the private park at Maidanovo. Modest continued:

> Towards four o'clock Pyotr Ilich returned home for tea. If he was alone he read the papers, historical journals, and if anyone was staying with him he very much liked to talk. From five until seven he again went off by himself to work.
>
> Before supper (which was served at eight) Pyotr Ilich would, if it was summer, take yet another walk in some open spot to admire the setting sun; this time he would be very willing to take it in company. In autumn and winter he would play the piano by himself for his own pleasure or, if Laroche or Kashkin [his favourite guests from outside the family] were staying with him, for four hands. After supper he would sit with his guests until eleven. When partners were available he loved three or four rubbers of vint, and when they were not he greatly liked to be read to aloud. His favourite reader was Laroche, not because he possessed some particular skill but because, when he read, the delight he was experiencing was expressed in every phrase, especially when the book was by Gogol or Flaubert. If there were no guests Pyotr Ilich for the most part read historical works about the late eighteenth and early nineteenth centuries, played patience, and always found himself a little bored. At eleven he went off to his room, wrote his diary, and again read for a long time before going to sleep. Since the summer of 1866 [when he had brought himself close to complete nervous collapse through over-work on his First Symphony] he had never composed a single note in the evening.

Even without Modest's memoir the externals of Tchaikovsky's biography would suffice to make clear the radical change which the move to Maidanovo wrought in his personal world. For more than a year scarcely anything except the demands of family relationships and of his personal affairs and professional commitments could drag him from his new home. But these still proved numerous. His recent appointment as a director of the Moscow branch of the Russian Musical Society (RMS) required periodic visits to the city, and his own creative projects sometimes necessitated trips to the outside world. Having pressed himself particularly hard to complete the revision of *Vakula*, on 10 April he was in St Petersburg to discuss with Polonsky the additional chunks of libretto he had himself devised. Back in Moscow he had to participate in the RMS's welcome to the Grand Duke Konstantin Nikolayevich, president of the Society, who had come for a Conservatoire performance of Cherubini's *Les deux journées*, an opera Tchaikovsky had once enjoyed, but now found 'very boring'.[9] A visit to Moscow in early May convinced him that Vsevolozhsky, who had been such a good friend in ensuring that *Mazepa* was well mounted, had overridden the reluctance some members of the Imperial Theatres' directorate had begun to show regarding the production of *Cherevichki*; no expense was to be spared to give it an excellent première. On the eve of his return home his birthday was celebrated by a lunch at Anatoly's and a dinner at the Conservatoire.

This visit had been cheering in all respects, and was in the sharpest contrast to the trip to St Petersburg a week later. He told his patroness he had gone there to show Polonsky the final libretto of *Cherevichki*, but the true purpose seems to have been to cope with the Kondratyevs' matrimonial affairs. This ill-suited couple had decided to separate, but Nikolay was proving unmanageable. His wife had already begged Modest's help, but he had proved powerless, and all hope now rested upon Tchaikovsky's influence with this difficult friend. Such turbulent passages had occurred in the Kondratyevs' relationship before, and yet again the storm was to pass, but it kept Tchaikovsky in the Russian capital for four precious days and caused him to arrive late in Moscow to begin his longest absence of the year. As a director of the RMS he had been required to share in the annual examining at the Conservatoire. He appeared on 22 May, and soon noted with surprised satisfaction that student numbers had grown and that the level of ability among them had become better in recent years. But what also became painfully evident was that the Conservatoire itself was in a terrible condition. Since Rubinstein's death four years earlier it had been disastrously run and the staff was demoralized. Hubert, who had held the directorship for the first two years, had possessed neither the required authority nor tact, and had been roughly ousted. His replacement, Albrecht, had incurred the hostility of both staff and students, and Tchaikovsky realized that this old friend, too, would simply have to be removed. In April he had sounded out Rimsky-Korsakov to discover whether he would be prepared to assume the directorship, should it be offered him, but he had flatly declined. Thus Taneyev seemed the best

[9] *TLP*13, p. 55; *TPM*3, p. 350; *TZC*3, p. 33; *YDGC*, p. 342.

choice, despite his youth, and on this visit Tchaikovsky was finally able to persuade the RMS to support the nomination of his former pupil.

All these manoeuvres involved a great measure of personal intervention. Taneyev's reluctance had to be overcome, each of Tchaikovsky's fellow-directors had to be canvassed individually, Albrecht had to be soothed and permitted to withdraw with honour, and a still very embittered Hubert had to be cajoled into forgetting, if possible, the shabby manner of his earlier dismissal, and persuaded to rejoin the professoriate. The conditions which the last imposed for his return were so extreme that Tchaikovsky decided he would himself have, in effect, to assume some of Hubert's responsibilities and become an unpaid teacher of composition. The success which crowned all these operations is yet another reflection of his understanding, patience and tact in assessing and resolving a problem outside himself. Exhausted as he was, he was content. 'I am convinced I have done the Conservatoire a service,' he told his benefactress on 12 June, the eve of his departure.[10] Events were to prove how right he was.

Tchaikovsky's three weeks of examining and negotiating were broken by a flying visit to Smolensk for the unveiling of a memorial to Glinka on 1 June. He had gone reluctantly to an occasion he knew would offer no respite from the stresses of Moscow, and it proved even worse than expected. Indeed, he found the unwanted and overwhelming attentions of multitudes of acquaintances so unpalatable, the manifest tensions between the musical factions present ('*of none of which am I a member*,' he observed acidly to Nadezhda von Meck[11]) so sickening, and the prospect of a crowded train journey home on which he would be forced to make conversation so dreadful that he invented an urgent telegram recalling him to Moscow, and left before the ceremony itself. Yet it is a further sign of the admirable conditions he found for his creative work at Maidanovo itself that he could, once he had returned thither, write so resignedly of all these wearisome and prolonged distractions from composition. But he was not a hermit in his country retreat, for those in Moscow whose company he really wanted could now come to him, and a regular trail of invited guests – family and friends – began to arrive. The house was uncongenial, but the surroundings – above all, the peace and quiet – more than compensated for this.

Now, however, a flaw had appeared in the Maidanovo situation itself. As the dachas around his own had begun to fill with their summer

[10] *TLP*13, pp. 90–1; *TPM*3, p. 362; *TZC*3, p. 46; *YDGC*, p. 347.
[11] *TLP*13, p. 89; *TPM*3, p. 360.

residents he became increasingly distressed at the loss of that privacy which it had offered back in the winter, and he made several enquiries about alternative accommodation in other localities. He also discovered that, being en route between Moscow and St Petersburg, he was at risk from the casual visitor who might decide to break his journey at Klin. Yet the continuing presence within the walls of his own house of Anatoly and his family, who had joined him in mid-May for the summer, did not hamper him in the least. Next Modest arrived, the Kondratyevs installed themselves in a neighbouring dacha, and Kolya Konradi appeared in August. But all these relatives and friends knew from experience that Tchaikovsky's work periods had to be strictly respected. In addition, between the middle of June and the beginning of September was a time of holidays, sometimes very prolonged, and there was a natural slackening in professional and business pressures.

But not a cessation. Taneyev was abroad, and certain matters relating to the Conservatoire, especially the need to fortify its future by strengthening its staff, required urgent attention. Tchaikovsky had no intention of allowing the good work he had begun earlier in the summer to be impaired. By now he had been told that he could not be both a director of the RMS and a professor at the Conservatoire, and he offered Taneyev the choice of deciding which position he should retain, though he made it clear he would prefer to maintain the *status quo*, to which Taneyev was to agree. But the RMS was responsible for the Conservatoire and for hiring and firing staff, and during the new director's absence Tchaikovsky conducted lengthy and sometimes delicate negotiations for Vasily Safonov to become one of the teachers of piano. According to Modest, it was Arensky who had put forward the name of this thirty-three-year-old who, like Tchaikovsky before him, had begun life in the civil service. Safonov had graduated from the St Petersburg Conservatoire with a gold medal only five years earlier, and had been teaching there ever since. Now Tchaikovsky personally negotiated the terms of employment. It was to prove a momentous appointment. Enthusiastic and successful as a piano teacher, Safonov was to succeed Taneyev as director of the Conservatoire in 1889, becoming also conductor of the concerts of the Moscow RMS.

Despite all such matters, and despite the arrival of all the proofs of *Cherevichki* and of the German-text edition of his recent set of Six Romances, Op. 57, the Manfred Symphony progressed. Brother Nikolay and his wife visited, Anna came for three days in mid-July, and Tchaikovsky reluctantly accepted the invitation to the whole Maidanovo entourage to make a short return visit to the Pleshcheyevo estate, where Anna was staying with her sister Vera and her children. On 22

August he was back in Maidanovo. He had felt unwell for much of the summer, and this he attributed to the strain of bringing the Manfred Symphony into the world. Yet he knew he could not afford to pause now, for the autumn was fast approaching. His obligatory visits to Moscow soon resumed – four over the next two months, mostly to attend to RMS business, each entailing several lost days. He parried a request from the Paris publisher, Félix Mackar, that he should read through and offer an opinion on some recent scores by young French composers, though he promised to do this later, for Mackar could be very useful to him, since he had negotiated with Jurgenson the right to publish Tchaikovsky's works in France. Modest said that his brother was surprised, though much heartened by Mackar's approach, for the 20,000 francs offered for publishing rights was enough to indicate that the publisher foresaw a significant market for Tchaikovsky's compositions in France. That Tchaikovsky's name was gaining prestige in that country had already been indicated by requests from the Paris Bach Society and the organization dedicated to publishing the works of Cherubini that he should become an honorary member of each. Both as publisher and concert promoter Mackar was to do Tchaikovsky good service, and a quiet friendship between the two men was to be cemented over the next few years through personal contact.

There were, in addition that autumn, new compositional requests Tchaikovsky found hard to refuse. Anxious to ensure *Onegin*'s continuing success, Vsevolozhsky asked him to compose a fresh dance for the ballroom scene, for which new scenery and costumes had been made, and on 3 September an écossaise was composed, scored, and on its way to St Petersburg. A month later he provided a choral piece for the School of Jurisprudence for the present pupils to sing at the fiftieth anniversary celebrations of this institution where he had once been a pupil. Though Tchaikovsky had been required to concoct both the words and music of this Jurists' Song himself, the committee still felt bold enough to approach him a second time; with barely a month to go, it wanted an orchestral piece. He capitulated wearily, as he told Nadezhda von Meck on 8 November from Kharkov while on his way to Kamenka: 'On the one hand writing these pieces is exceedingly unpalatable and boring: on the other, refusing is awkward.'[12] Normally he manufactured such works very quickly, but despite several hours' labour each day, it was more than a week before this one, a march, was done. The time it took is the more surprising, considering the indifferent quality of the result. But on his way through Moscow he had

[12] *TLP*13, p. 181; *TPM*3, p. 387.

paused for an RMS concert which had opened with his Coronation March of 1883. It was the first performance at which the composer had been present, and remembering his reception at the première of his Slavonic March nine years earlier, he had prepared himself for a similar ovation which did not occur. There is some justification for Tchaikovsky's disappointment, for the Coronation March is an admirable specimen of its kind. All too clearly the material had sprung from no true creative impulse, but he had put much care and resourcefulness into building upon it, and the scoring was colourful and contrasted. Its tepid reception can hardly have fired his enthusiasm as he prepared to begin the new march; nor was the occasion for the commission as grand, nor was there the challenge and stimulus of existing emblematic material to incorporate into the piece.[13] Be that as it may, Tchaikovsky's labours gained little musical return; compared with the Coronation March, the Jurists' March is a stodgy and less varied piece. By now Tchaikovsky's loyalty to his old school had been stretched beyond breaking point, and at the first performance on 17 December he was truant.

Most of the work on the Jurists' March was to be done in November at Kamenka where he had gone to join in Lev and Sasha's silver wedding celebrations. It was his first visit to his sister's home for seventeen months, and it proved an unhappy occasion, for domestic conditions had deteriorated further, and the behaviour he observed in his niece, Tasya, gave him deep offence. The party which had made much of the summer residence at Maidanovo so pleasant had begun to break up in early September. Modest left with Kolya Konradi on the eleventh, and three days earlier Anatoly had set off for Tiflis [now Tbilisi], where he had been appointed public prosecutor. The family considered the posting very fortunate, despite its distance. 'For me it will serve as a pretext for visiting at last the Caucasus, which has long attracted me,' was Tchaikovsky's own private confession to his cousin, Anna Merkling.[14] Parasha remained a further three weeks; then, on 26 September, Tchaikovsky accompanied his sister-in-law and young niece to Moscow, endured a further round of family farewells, and returned five days later to a new home. The proprietress of the dachas at Maidanovo, obviously somewhat in awe of Tchaikovsky's eminence, and knowing of his reservations about his present accommodation, had offered to let him transfer to that which she herself was currently

---

[13] The Coronation March had used the first phrase of the Danish national anthem (the Empress had formerly been a Danish princess), preceded by a paraphrase of the first phrase of the Russian national anthem (see bars 26–9).

[14] *TLP*13, p. 110; *TTP*, p. 223.

occupying, and during his absence Alexey had undertaken their removal to this smaller but much more pleasant and secluded dacha. On his return he felt justified in having taken a two-year lease on it. 'Everything's cosy, clean, nice, good,' he wrote to Anna Merkling the next day. 'Only the bedroom doesn't entirely satisfy me, but that's a trifle. In general it's excellent! God, what a delight to feel oneself in quiet, far from fuss, in one's own home and, moreover, alone!!! No one loves his nearest and dearest more than I – but all the same, my real *ideal* is solitude, the fellowship of books, scores, ink and paper.'[15] He admitted he had wept copiously on bidding Parasha goodbye, for she was a very special person for him. But now, with the Manfred Symphony all but finished, and with the added privacy his new home afforded, he could follow his 'real *ideal*'. The feeling of perpetual indisposition which had beset him the whole summer had gone. He continued to extol the merits of his new home and the virtues of Alexey who had arranged everything and was maintaining his domestic arrangements with faultless efficiency, while the extra resources which his music's growing public success was providing – or promising – enabled him to take over the two horses which Parasha had had to sell on leaving for the Caucasus (a very foolish purchase, so Modest stated, and one which Tchaikovsky was soon to regret; early the next year he sold them).

The succession of Saturday guests, often several at a time, provided a substantial but well controlled social life. Jurgenson, Kashkin, the Albrechts and Huberts, Laroche, Arensky – all from time to time were warmly welcomed, often staying overnight. Other guests were more shadowy figures. Some were family, others friends of a sort once epitomized by Bochechkarov, whose society Tchaikovsky had always found indispensable if his personal existence was to be complete and balanced. The happy chatter in his letters bears witness to his high morale. Three days after parting from Parasha and Tanya he signed the final date on the manuscript score of the Manfred Symphony; within five more days, having disposed of the first of the School of Jurisprudence commissions, he had begun *The Enchantress*.

Though *The Enchantress* was the eighth of Tchaikovsky's completed operas, it was the first for which an entire libretto was specially devised for him. Shpazhinsky had declared himself an enthusiastic collaborator, but he also proved a sluggish one, seeming to spend much of his time out of Moscow, with his wife, from whom he was in process of

---

[15] *TLP*13, p. 151; *TTP*, p. 224.

separating, acting as go-between. Earlier in the year he had failed to deliver the first act on time, and even now, some six months later, Tchaikovsky had no more than this portion of the libretto before him. His delight in it seems to have been unbounded. 'It is magnificently written,' he told Pavlovskaya on 21 October, by which time over half the music was drafted. 'There's an abundance of life and movement.'[16] So well was it going that he thought he had it in him to have the whole opera ready for the next season. But he was determined not to overstrain himself; if it was composed by the next spring, and polished and scored during the remainder of the year, it could go into the 1887/8 season. His visit to Kamenka and Moscow in November caused a month's break in composition which was probably timely, for he feared he was already pressing himself too hard. But it scarcely mattered that it was 21 December before he began the second act, for Shpazhinsky had still not provided all of it. So far the flow of ideas had come easily and the second act was finished on 13 February 1886. But he had now perceived a bad flaw in what remained; the five-act structure planned for *The Enchantress* would be too drawn out. Compressing three acts into two inevitably produced yet more delay, and though Tchaikovsky quickly received and composed the first scene of the third act, in mid-April he was still having to badger Shpazhinsky to let him have 'the *most important* scene of the opera',[17] the love scene between Kuma and the young prince. He was now in Tiflis and thoroughly behind schedule.

It is not clear whether the further two-and-a-half month delay in composition was caused by the librettist's slowness or solely by the distractions of his own extended stay with Anatoly and subsequent trip to Paris. Whatever the cause, it was 1 July before he resumed systematic work on *The Enchantress*, only to find that his mood had shifted. 'I'm composing, but without that rapture which the creator's heart sometimes feels,' he wrote to Modest on 7 July. '. . . I've been to the Shpazhinskys' and have received from him a *superb* fourth act.'[18] Eight days later he had arrived at this, but without much zest, which he attributed partly to his regular summer sense of indisposition, partly to his age. While he considered that the single act with which Shpazhinsky had replaced the projected fourth and fifth acts was 'unusually effective',[19] he also found it very problematic, and he told his librettist it would be mid-September before he would be through.

---

[16] *TLP*13, p. 167; *TZC*3, p. 70; *DTC*, p. 148.

[17] *TLP*13, p. 315.

[18] *TLP*13, p. 381; *TZC*3, p. 116 (which has 'without that relief'); *TPB*, p. 361; *DTC*, p. 150.

[19] *TLP*13, p. 414; *TZC*3, p. 122; *DTC*, p. 151; *YDGC*, p. 379.

Then, without warning, his mood changed yet again, work accelerated, and by 30 August everything had been sketched.

Having no manuscript paper suitable for an orchestral layout, Tchaikovsky now put *The Enchantress* aside for nearly a month and worked on the Twelve Romances, Op. 60, which had been prompted by the Empress's wish to have a work by Tchaikovsky dedicated to her. Returning afresh to the opera, he realized with alarm that it was far too long. Because Shpazhinsky was incommunicado Tchaikovsky was compelled to select the cuts himself, making them in each act ahead of the scoring, which he began on 1 October. The impatience of the Imperial Theatres to have the opera put enormous pressure upon him to complete an operation which for some years had been taking ever-increasing time. In any case he had to have Shpazhinsky's agreement to the cuts he had made, and there was also no escaping frequent and often extended trips to the two capitals for business and professional reasons. Above all, there was the production of *Cherevichki* which had been postponed from the previous season, and which Tchaikovsky had agreed to conduct himself. For some two months ahead of the première on 31 January 1887 he was much tied to Moscow because of rehearsals. By mid-December only the first act of *The Enchantress* had been scored, and it is no surprise that devising the vocal score, which was now urgently needed, took two months. On 6 March, less than a fortnight after he had passed the last page of this to his publisher, Taneyev introduced extracts from Act 1 at a special RMS concert in Moscow; eleven days later, at a Philharmonic Society concert in St Petersburg, Tchaikovsky himself was cajoled into conducting further excerpts. Less than a week, and rehearsals had begun in the theatre. By now the burden of work was almost intolerable. 'In St Petersburg for two-and-a-half weeks I wrote not a single real letter because of the complete impossibility of finding a free moment,' he lamented to Shpazhinskaya on 27 March from Maidanovo. 'And here I am forced against my will to sit at my writing table and work. By the end of the week I must at all costs correct all the proofs [of the vocal score] of *The Enchantress*, and as soon as I finish set about orchestrating, and again rush, for ever rush, and strain myself.'[20] Having managed to dispose of Act 2 by 19 April, he passed to Act 4 ('the most difficult'[21]). On 8 May it was done; on 18 May, except for a few markings, all was at last complete.

So he thought – for he soon discovered his labour was far from over. First Pavlovskaya, who was to create the title role, then Mariya

[20] *TLP*14, p. 65; *TTP*, pp. 314–15; *DTC*, p. 153 (partial).
[21] *TLP*14, p. 89; *DTC*, p. 154; *YDGC*, p. 410; *TTP*, p. 318.

Slavina, who sang the Princess, found problems in their parts, and Tchaikovsky made modifications to satisfy them. Then, on attending the first complete run-through of the opera in the Maryinsky Theatre on 19 September, he realized the surgery he had already performed before scoring had been insufficient. Above all, the love duet in the third act was too long, while further amputations were needed in the last act, and in the duet for Yury and the Princess in Act 2. But once these had been completed,[22] Tchaikovsky's confidence in his work grew. The orchestra, chorus, and in particular the production were beyond praise, he said, and the principal singers were thoroughly cooperative and satisfactory; only Pavlovskaya, who seemed to be losing her voice, gave any cause for concern. Tchaikovsky was to conduct the première himself, and from the first orchestral rehearsal on 12 October he felt assured of an audience success.

No doubt the public which had taken *Onegin* to its heart expected too much of this new offering, and the opening night on 1 November was not the occasion Tchaikovsky had anticipated. The first act was flawed by a bad mistake on stage, and though Tchaikovsky admitted the second went well, in the third Pavlovskaya overacted to compensate for her vocal problems. But the audience showed repeated approval during the fourth, and Melnikov, who sang Prince Nikita, excelled himself. Modest remembered that his brother had come from the opening night believing the opera had been a success, but subsequent performances progressively confirmed the public's disappointment, and by the seventh the house was only half full. 'Despite the ovations for me . . . the audience did not much like my opera and it was, in effect, unsuccessful,' he reflected to Nadezhda von Meck some three-and-a-half weeks later.[23]

As for the press reaction, 'I have encountered such malice, such hostility that I still cannot collect myself and explain to myself why and for what this should be,' he continued his lament. 'Over no other opera had I laboured so hard or with such industry, and yet never before have I been the object of such persecution on the part of *the press*.'[24] Modest

---

[22] The more significant changes made by Tchaikovsky during rehearsals were: 1. Act 2, No. 9. Coda to duet rewritten and shortened by 15 bars. 2. Act 3, No. 17. 13 bars cut from end of second E minor section: replaced by 1; 79 bars (mostly in C minor) cut before A flat minor section: replaced by 8; 67 bars cut from conclusion of vocal section: replaced by 30. Orchestral postlude remains identical except in details. 3. Act 4, No. 18. 80 bars cut from middle: replaced by 4. No. 21. 17 bars cut: replaced by 1. No. 22. 48 bars cut from first section. No. 23. 17 bars cut before entry of Prince; 29 bars cut before murder of Yury; 13 bars cut in funeral chorus.

[23] *TLP*14, p. 255; *TPM*3, p. 504; *TZC*3, p. 187.

[24] *ibid.*

was of a bluntly different opinion; in this instance the press had been over-kind. In fact, Tchaikovsky was much less than fair. True, from Cui there was the expected condemnation, though he did praise the orchestration, and especially Tchaikovsky's conducting. But other critics mingled much respect with their reservations, which largely concerned the dramatic side of the work. 'The Enchantress represents the work of a major talent including, besides vocal numbers, very many pages and separate episodes which are worthwhile and, in themselves, interesting to study,' noted Mikhail Ivanov, the critic of New Time and himself a composer, who had briefly been a pupil of Tchaikovsky. 'Perhaps it will add nothing to the already established reputation of its composer, nor will it become as popular as Onegin, but it will always encounter sympathy from persons of developed taste who are capable of turning their attention to individual details and of appreciating the talent with which the composer has invested them.'[25] Three days earlier in News Nikolay Solovyev had anticipated this last sentiment, but was more forthright about the shortcoming to which it pointed: 'As an opera composer Tchaikovsky has not moved forward. . . . His music represents a labour to be respected, a whole mass of very worthwhile details bears witness to the fact that the libretto of The Enchantress is being treated by a musician unquestionably gifted, but solely a musician, and not an opera composer from his head to his feet.'[26] An unsigned contribution to the St Petersburg Leaflet offered some specific, sometimes very warm compliments, though adding a major criticism: 'The folk element is most broadly worked out and developed in the first act of The Enchantress, which is the best and most polished of the whole opera. But it is virtually confined to this one alone. This act is full of life, fire, movement. . . . Tchaikovsky's noticeable efforts in The Enchantress to preserve as far as possible the correct accentuation and metre in the word setting, which formerly was a significant gap in his craft, is an important step forward in his creative evolution as regards opera. . . . In the symphonic working out of the music, in the wonders and ingenious complexity of its orchestration, Tchaikovsky has shown an inexhaustible inventiveness. The weak side [of the opera] is its inability to convey the dramatic situations through music.'[27] Pavel Makarov in the Stock Exchange Gazette voiced very similar views regarding the word setting, though he considered that The Enchantress showed an advance over Tchaikovsky's earlier operas as regards characterization and the handling of the stage action. But his final verdict was one

[25] DTC, p. 158; YDGC, p. 425; TPM3, p. 641 (partial).
[26] DTC, p. 158; YDGC, pp. 424–5.
[27] DTC, p. 157; YDGC, p. 424.

Tchaikovsky had often heard and lamented, and which, Modest claimed, was the common theme of all the notices of the opera: 'It is beyond Tchaikovsky the symphonist to turn himself into an operatic composer in the full meaning of that word.'[28]

Tchaikovsky continued defiantly to express faith in *The Enchantress*, and when, in May 1888, Shpazhinsky hinted at a possible revision, he refused point blank. 'It is not for the two of us to descend to the level of the public's incomprehension. . . . I consider *The Enchantress* the best of my operas, and I won't relinquish a single note of it,' he told his librettist bluntly.[29] He had consolation in the production mounted in Tiflis on 26 December 1887, especially since he heard it had been very well received. But in St Petersburg the twelfth performance of *The Enchantress*, given early the next season (29 October), proved to be the last until 1902. Moscow was to hear the opera only once during Tchaikovsky's lifetime: on 14 February 1890, when the sets of the St Petersburg production were specially brought over.

The plot of the opera runs as follows:

ACT 1. *The courtyard of an inn at the ferry crossing where the River Oka flows into the Volga. Nizhni-Novgorod in the background.*
Peasants and guests from the town are enjoying themselves. They are drawn to the inn by the hospitality and charms of its young hostess, Nastasya, nicknamed Kuma ('gossip' or 'god-mother'). Balakin, a visitor from Nizhni, reveals that Kuma is thought by some to be a witch, which will be bad for her if the ruthless Prince Nikita Kurlyatev, the governor-general, should hear of it. Foka, Kuma's uncle, mocks the attempts of Paisy, a drunken vagabond monk, to put superstitious fear into him, and persuades him, without difficulty, to drink. Potap, another local, quarrels with his opponent in a game they are playing; the other guests intervene. A women's chorus is heard approaching (No. 2). Kuma enters with Polya and other girls, to be greeted by all. She signals the drinkers to be served. A group of laughing girls surround Paisy, who drives them off. He upbraids Kuma for merriment unbecoming to a widow; she retorts that he should sober up before telling other people how to behave. The others are for throwing him out, and Foka leads him aside as a fresh group of revellers is seen approaching along the river. Balakin warns her that Mamïrov, a puritanical elderly deacon, has sworn to bring Prince Nikita to see for himself the iniquities that go on at her inn. Kuma reflects that she must think how best she can deal with him.

Two new boatloads of guests arrive (No. 3), including Kulash and Kichiga, a prize fighter. After greetings, Kichiga swaggers forward and demonstrates how to fight; all enjoy the spectacle. The city's church bells are heard (No. 4)

[28] *DTC*, p. 158; *YDGC*, p. 425.
[29] *TLP*14, p. 410.

as a song from Kuma is called for. Balakin asks how there can be singing while others are praying, but Lukash retorts that old men such as are at prayers are the ones who have ruined their pleasures, but at Kuma's they may still enjoy themselves. Kuma adds that the old men are hypocrites who deny themselves nothing. She sings a song (andante sostenuto) in praise of the Volga: 'From the steep hill of Nizhni let us look out upon our benefactress, Mother-Volga (bar 57) . . . What an expanse there is around! It has no boundary! . . . And thither, into that expanse, that space, the soul longs to fly, free as a bird' (bar 81).

Boats carrying Yury, the young prince (Nikita's son), the huntsman Zhuran, and a party returning from the chase appear on the river (No. 5). Kuma immediately shows agitation, and when Polya wonders what Yury is like, she bursts out with a rapt description of him; clearly she is already in love with him. The crowd greets Yury warmly as he passes by, and he returns their greetings, regretting he cannot delay with them. Before the boats disappear Zhuran springs ashore. While Lukash gaily invites some of the girls to pick flowers in the meadow and goes off with them, Zhuran asks Kuma why she is so silent and did not invite Yury to stay. Her quiet embarrassment is interrupted by the sudden return of Lukash (bar 109) with news that Prince Nikita himself is coming. There is immediate consternation. Balakin and some others leave. Foka and a servant begin clearing the tables, but Kuma stops them. Her firm resolve to confront the Prince restores their courage, and some of the others return to the stage. Having brought the crowd under control and ordered the table to be laid in a manner fit for a prince, she prepares to meet him.

Prince Nikita enters with Mamïrov (No. 6), who lists the evils of the place. Paisy joins in corroboratively, but the Prince silences him and calls for the hostess (bar 29). Her beauty and her modest mien strike him immediately. When Mamïrov reprimands her for being improperly dressed for a widow, the crowd turn on him, but Kuma silences them. 'Surely the Prince can judge without your help!' she insists (bar 47). Required to answer Mamïrov's charges, she replies with quiet dignity (andantino); when the Prince faces her with specific accusations of sorcery, she maintains her imposing self-control: 'My evil and sorcery are but this – that I greet my guests with kindness and a kind word, and that here there is no care' (bar 109). She invites him to be her guest. After brief hesitation he assents and she leads him to the table. Mamïrov tries again to incite the Prince against Kuma, but is cut short. Seeing her adversary in difficulties, Kuma presses her advantage, to the crowd's amazement and admiration. The Prince drinks, praises the wine, then takes a ring from his finger and throws it into the cup.

The finale (No. 7) opens with a 'decimet a capella' – Kuma overcome by the magnificence of the Prince's gift, the Prince clearly falling beneath her spell, a furious Mamïrov unable to believe his eyes, the others voicing amazement, happiness, and satisfaction at Mamïrov's discomfiture. At the end the Prince pats Kuma on the cheek, and she offers wine to Mamïrov. He refuses angrily, the others begin to tease him, and the merriment quickly and completely revives, the Prince joining in. Kuma offers him a tumblers' dance, and the Prince asks Mamïrov whether he would like it. The outraged reply prompts Kuma to suggest Mamïrov should dance with the tumblers. The dance begins.

After a while Kuma again draws the Prince's attention to Mamïrov. The Prince stops the dance and orders Mamïrov to dance. Mamïrov protests, but Kuma mischievously urges the Prince on. The dance resumes, Foka takes hold of Mamïrov and turns him round and round, to the amusement of all.

ACT 2. *The garden of Prince Nikita's house. Morning.*
The Princess Evpraksiya, Nikita's wife, is sitting within the porch. Troubled thoughts have driven away her sleep. A chorus of girls making lace inside the house only deepens her melancholy, and Nenila, her chamber maid and Mamïrov's sister, goes inside to silence them (bar 26). Mamïrov enters and she demands to know the truth (bar 43). He tells her what happened at Kuma's, revealing that the Prince has returned there often, and asserting he has made Kuma his mistress. 'Everything is possible for sorcery,' he explains (bar 79), begging the Princess not to betray him to her husband. Nenila tries to reassure her but is roughly silenced; Mamïrov says the best course with Kuma is 'to get rid of the witch' (bar 102). But instead the Princess orders Mamïrov to report to her all that happens; she then launches into a fierce reproach of her husband, finally becoming hysterical (bar 123). Mamïrov leaves and Nenila tries to calm and comfort her mistress, recommending ways in which magic may restore a wayward husband. The Princess impatiently interrupts and dismisses her. Left alone, she swears to be rid of Kuma.

As her son enters the Princess affects cheerfulness (No. 9). She tells him she and his father have chosen a fine bride for him, but he brushes that aside. He is more concerned at the moment with the signs of trouble within the family; his father has become irascible, and his mother preoccupied. She tries to dismiss this, but Yury is not deceived: 'Who has offended you? My father, perhaps?' (bar 57) Unable either to confess or draw confession, they join in a duet (moderato con moto): 'God grant we may live in happiness.' Despite a passage (poco più animato) where he again tries to uncover the cause of her sorrow, she continues to protest her contentment, finally kissing him and quickly leaving.

Left alone, Yury is confronted by Paisy (No. 10), who claims he has summoned him. Yury denies this. Paisy launches into an unctuous protestation which is cut off by the entry of Mamïrov, who appears angry on finding him there. Yury orders Paisy to be given something, and then leaves. Seeing he will in fact get nothing from Mamïrov, Paisy is about to slip away when Mamïrov detains him; he might be useful. Prince Nikita visits Kuma's inn. 'You must discover everything that goes on there by the Oka,' Mamïrov orders (bar 109). Paisy slips away, and Mamïrov vents his rage at the Prince for making him appear a fool during their first visit. He is bent on revenge.

Prince Nikita himself enters, deep in thought (No. 11). He commands Mamïrov to summon the Princess. Once the deacon has gone, he lays bare his feelings – his apathy towards his official duties and, above all, his misery at the distress he has caused his wife. But a storm rages within him: he cannot forget Kuma and he sings an arioso (andantino): 'But the image of that comely girl lives always with me, and tantalizes and lures me both day and night.' As he finishes the Princess comes from the house (No. 12). The Prince starts to talk about arrangements with the Boyar Sherstnev for their son's wedding with his daughter, but the Princess's thoughts are elsewhere – on Kuma. The Prince tries to dismiss the matter as rubbish. 'It is not nonsense, but a shame and your disgrace!' she retorts (allegro moderato). She begins a tirade of accusation and reproach. He attempts denial, but to no avail. 'Why pretend in vain?' she insists (poco meno mosso). He tries to browbeat her but she will have none of it. 'Who is she, your beloved beauty, Kuma? She is an evil witch!' (bar 112) – and the Princess sets out her plan for dealing with Kuma (l'istesso tempo): there is a holy father who will be their protector, she will go to him, and he will confine Kuma in his monastery's vault, and there she will have to repent her sins until she perishes. The Prince threatens to confine his wife instead: 'I'll find a cell for you where you may subdue your shrewish temper through prayer' (bar 172). But she remains defiant, and they finally rush out in opposite directions.

There is a noise offstage (No. 13). One of the Prince's dog handlers appears over the palisade carrying a bloodstained knife and runs off, followed by a shower of stones. More servants climb over, their clothes in tatters. The palisade begins to rock and is broken. Mamïrov enters; the servants tell him they were attacked by merchants after the market, and Mamïrov orders the guards to be summoned (bar 26). A crowd bursts through the palisade, led by Kichiga. Mamïrov confronts them, and others enter to support him. He orders Kichiga to be taken, but the two servants who attempt it are thrown aside and run off. A third approaches, but Kichiga threatens him with a stick. As a scuffle develops Yury enters and intervenes (bar 89). Everything subsides quickly. The crowd remove their hats and bow to him. Kichiga acts as spokesman: Prince Nikita's servants rob them, and they have no redress. Mamïrov is for taking them all to prison, but Yury will have none of it and tells them to go home. Thanking him (moderato assai), they disperse. Mamïrov predicts that Prince Nikita will be angry.

The Princess and Nenila come out of the house; at the same time Paisy appears. Yury defends himself against their reproaches for having intruded into his father's business (No. 14), and demands to know where his father is (bar 25). Paisy discloses he is at Kuma's. The Princess is furious and declares she will go there herself. Yury is bewildered and demands of his mother an explanation. She is silent and he falls on his knees (bar 63), then kisses her hands. But it is Nenila who has to tell him. 'Our Princess will be in her grave because of that peasant woman, the minx Kuma!' (bar 72). Yury instantly perceives the truth and his response is swift. 'I will kill her!' he cries (bar 86). His mother is overjoyed at his intention, and an ensemble develops, to be suddenly broken. 'I swear I will kill the evil one!' promises Yury (bar 179). 'My dear hope!' she replies.

Act 3. *Kuma's cottage.*

Prince Nikita is sitting at a table (No. 15). He seems downcast. His visits are now rousing public rumour, but he still cannot bear not to see Kuma. She is troubled, for she is sensitive to gossip – 'and what if it should reach the Princess? . . .' (bar 95). The Prince silences her and asks her to sit closer to him; she does so reluctantly. He draws her passionately towards him (allegro moderato) and begins a declaration of love (andante con moto). He kisses her but she turns away (più mosso). He tries again, but sees he cannot move her. 'She sits like a stone,' he laments (bar 148). His voice becomes tearful. She cannot understand his moods; she says she feels pity for him, 'but you yourself know that pity is not the same as love' (bar 166). As their duet draws to its climax she declares she has feelings for another. The Prince's mood changes to jealous fury (allegro non tanto), and he demands to know who his rival is. She tries to play it down, then defends herself against the Prince with simple dignity (moderato assai), setting out her dilemma; if another had attempted to take her, she might have shamed him into desisting, 'but I don't dare with you. I must do your will. You are the governor-general' (bar 241). However, when he threatens her (poco più animato) she becomes defiant, and as he forcibly embraces her she snatches a knife from the table and holds it to her throat. 'I would rather die than yield!' she shouts (bar 260). In a towering rage he leaves, swearing he will have his way. Exhausted, she sinks back on to a bench. She reflects (No. 16) on the reactions of the Prince and everyone else if it should become known that she is in love with Yury – yet she cannot get him out of her mind.

Suddenly Polya rushes in. She has news: the Princess has heard of her husband and Kuma, and Yury has sworn to kill Kuma. Foka enters to add that Kuma is also accused of using sorcery to tempt the Prince from his wife. 'And the young Prince believed this!' Kuma exclaims (bar 67). They advise her to secure her cottage at night, and Polya leaves. Kuma instructs Foka to tell no one of the threat. Foka cannot understand and also leaves. Alone, Kuma goes to the window, deep in thought (andante). Suddenly she jumps in terror (bar 130) as she thinks she sees two figures. She takes a candle, but then extinguishes it in case it should be observed. It is a moonlit night, and she sees two men come into the yard (allegro vivo), recognizing one as Yury. She climbs into bed and listens. Hearing them rattling the latch, she cries out: 'Save me, have mercy on me, O God!' (bar 170), and draws the curtain round the bed.

Yury and Zhuran enter carrying a lantern (No. 17). Seeing the bed Yury pulls back the curtain (andante (alla breve)). Kuma is reclining alluringly on her elbow, looking straight at Yury. He drops the dagger he is carrying, covers his eyes, and slowly backs towards the door. Kuma quickly leaves the bed to detain him. She addresses him very simply and openly, but he accuses her of causing division between his mother and father. 'That's not all,' she adds ironically (andantino). 'I have struck down the Prince with a potion in his cup, have driven him out of his mind with a devilish illusion. And have you brought a magic herb with you?' – one that will kill a witch. To his further angry but confused threats she begs to be allowed to speak openly without Zhuran. Yury sits and signals Zhuran to leave.

Kuma now tells Yury (allegro con spirito) of his father's visit, his threats, her manner of refusal, and his furious exit. Yury expresses disbelief. 'No, I speak the truth. God is my witness,' she replies (bar 201). She pleads further, finally covering his hand with kisses. Yury is partially persuaded (bar 225). Seeing the dagger on the floor, she picks it up and returns it to him; clumsily, he replaces it in its sheath. She sits beside him (bar 238), and begins to try to tell him of her love. Finally, taking his hand, she looks directly at him and confesses tenderly (andante): 'Long, my falcon, have I followed you stealthily . . . holding my breath, gazing upon you, I did not take my eyes off you!' Yury rises in confusion to leave, but is detained and quickly capitulates. 'I am your protector from all enemies!' he shouts (bar 311). She makes to kiss his hand, but he withdraws it. She smiles and looks a little guilty. Once again he goes towards the door (bar 331), but again she holds him back. 'It would have been better if you had fulfilled your curse, and had stabbed my breast with your dagger (bar 374) . . . Farewell then! God protect you! . . . It would not do for you to remain with Kuma, it would dishonour you . . . so go!' He feels pity for her – but under the force of her reproaches, her misery, and the spell of her beauty, pity turns to passion and mutual commitment. 'In your embraces is earthly paradise, and with you everything is forgotten!' are their final words.

ACT 4. *A dense, hill-enclosed forest on the banks of the Oka.*
Hunting horns are heard offstage. Kudma, a wizard, listens to them disgruntled, and withdraws into his cave. Zhuran and other hunters enter. He is to await his master; the others go off to hunt. Yury enters. He is planning to elope with Kuma, and Zhuran has made all the preparations, with relays of post horses arranged. Yury thanks Zhuran (bar 68), but Zhuran still attempts to dissuade him. For Yury there can be no question of this, and he begins an arioso (andante amoroso, con moto): 'She is now for me the dearest of all things in the world. How could I forget her?' Three hunters hurry in (No. 18) to report they have located a bear. All leave immediately.

Paisy enters with the Princess disguised as a pilgrim. She has come to get from the wizard the means to destroy Kuma. When the wizard appears, Paisy flees in terror (bar 40). Kudma complains (l'istesso tempo) it is 'sly old women' who are constantly coming to him for potions. The Princess angrily silences him: 'You would be ready to sink the world in poison to get its treasures,' she retorts (bar 75). She shows him a pouch with money in it. His interest is strongly aroused, and he decides not to turn her into a she-wolf. Has he the most deadly and agonizing of potions? He has, he replies, and they briefly revel (allegretto) in the thought of its devastating effects; then she hands him the money and he goes off to his cave to prepare it. The Princess follows.

A boat with Kuma, Kichiga, Lukash and Potap appears on the Oka (No. 20). They disembark, and the possessions Kuma has brought with her are unloaded. She thanks her companions, and they all sadly say farewell for what they believe will be the last time. Nevertheless, while she is still here they will remain close by in the boat to intercept any pursuers. Kuma sings an arioso of love (andante): 'Where are you, my beloved? I am here; come quickly!' As she finishes the Princess emerges from the cave (No. 21), sees Kuma, and approaches her with feigned meekness. She introduces herself as a pilgrim travelling to the Pechersky monastery; her companions have lagged behind and she will wait for them here. She sits beside Kuma. 'Something is wrong with you?' she asks (bar 30). 'Are you preparing to run away? With such rare beauty even a prince would be glad to fly away with you. Are we waiting for your dear beloved?' Kuma is thoroughly confused. The Princess offers to get her a cup of water from the spring, which she claims has magic restorative powers. Kuma gives the Princess a cup (bar 57). As the Princess fills the cup (bar 74) she covertly pours in the potion. Kuma drinks. 'What bitter water!' she observes (bar 81) – and the wizard's laughter is heard from the cave. Kuma is startled; it is only an owl in the wood, says the Princess. Hunting horns are heard offstage. The Princess withdraws hurriedly. 'Farewell! You will remember me!' are her parting words.

Kuma waits joyfully (No. 22). Yury rushes in and embraces her. They sing ecstatically of their untroubled future together, while the Princess from behind a tree and the wizard from his cave relish the terrible end in store for Kuma.

Suddenly Kuma feels strange (No. 23). Yury is alarmed; the Princess and the wizard add their satisfaction from the background. Kuma tells how she has been given water (bar 26). The Princess comes forward and reveals her true self, and the wizard hastily withdraws into the cave. 'I have brought death to the evildoer. I have purged the shame of my family,' she cries (andante con moto). Yury denounces his mother. Hunting horns are heard, and Kuma dies (bar 57) as the huntsmen return. Zhuran approaches Yury and gently raises him from Kuma's body. The Princess attempts self-justification, but Yury denounces her again, and throws himself on the neck of Zhuran, who leads him aside. The Princess orders the huntsmen to throw the body into the Oka, and they carry it off. Yury turns to his mother and asks (bar 91) where Kuma's body has gone. 'There in the Oka is her grave!' the Princess replies. She again withdraws to one side. Yury runs to the bank. The huntsmen come out of the river. He has lost everything. 'Nowhere is there happiness for me, nowhere is there a refuge!' (bar 115).

It begins to grow dark. Boats with Prince Nikita and servants appear. The Prince steps quickly ashore. He demands to know from his son where Kuma is. He now knows that she and Yury had planned to elope, and he does not believe Kuma is dead. He points to Kuma's belongings, and his temper rises yet further. When his son accuses him of causing Kuma's death, he stabs him (bar 168). The Princess cries out in horror. 'My thanks for that! You have united us for ever!' are Yury's dying words (bar 172). The Princess throws herself on her son's body. Servants gather round holding lanterns. Distant thunder, then a rising wind.

Yury's body is carried away to a men's chorus of mourning. The storm breaks, and the Prince's reason begins to give way. The wizard approaches the Prince (bar 289). The Prince sees him in a flash of lightning and recoils in horror; the wizard laughs demonically, supported by thunder. The Prince goes mad.

Any of Tchaikovsky's compatriots making acquaintance for the first time with one of his five operas from *The Oprichnik* to *Mazepa* must have felt that prior knowledge of any of the others had done little to prepare him for the experience he was now encountering. As noted in volume three, *Mazepa* had circled back towards that grim, overblown tragedy completed in 1872, but in the ten or so years since *The Oprichnik* Tchaikovsky's style had so evolved and, even more, Tchaikovsky himself had so changed that the two operas have little in common, except for being historical melodramas based on Russian history. With *The Enchantress* it was different. Admittedly its subject was purely fictional, but its general style was recognizably that of its predecessor. There were obvious parallels in dramatic content. Both operas charted the destruction of a family – father, mother and child – through passion for a fourth person, who likewise suffers disaster. Both open with a chorus promising a folk scene, both second acts begin with a lament for the older woman supported by female chorus; both operas close with a mad scene. Yet the dramatic natures of the two works were totally different. *Mazepa*, like *Onegin*, had been an episode opera, the plot accumulating through a series of scenes, often widely separated in time and place, with each embracing no more than one small span of action involving few of the principals (none sings in more than four of the six scenes, and Mazepa and Mariya in only three). By contrast *The Enchantress* offered a more organic plot, two of the four principals both appearing in all four acts and another in three, while in two acts, the second and fourth, the entrances and exits are numerous as incident follows incident, each systematically presenting the next in a chain of events.

The relatively smooth cohesion of the plot is matched by Tchaikovsky's music. Indeed, *The Enchantress* is, with the one-act *Iolanta*, perhaps the most fluently consistent of all his operas. Yet it is one of the least satisfactory. Why he should have chosen the plot in the first place may seem puzzling; why he should have held so firmly to his decision may appear yet more bewildering after the powerful dissuasion attempted by both Modest and Pavlovskaya. But when it came to choosing an operatic subject Tchaikovsky was very much his own man. In his excellent book, *Opera and Drama in Russia as Preached and Practiced in the 1860s*, Richard Taruskin has vividly described the polemics which racked the Russian operatic world during that turbulent decade of enlightenment and innovative achievement. The passions and inconsistencies of the debate, the clashes and animosities of the participants, the relationships it created or broke were central factors in Russia's musical life during those years when Tchaikovsky was first a student, then a young professional composer embarking on his own first opera. Yet there is little in *The Voyevoda* or its successors that hints at the existence of the diverse ideologies which did so much to shape the musico-dramatic works of Alexandr Serov, Dargomïzhsky and Musorgsky. In Smolensk only four months before setting about *The Enchantress* Tchaikovsky had distastefully observed the factionalism which still riddled the Russian musical world, and had tartly re-avowed his own refusal to have any part in it. He had no faith in theories. 'It is *the man* who renders service *to mankind*, and not the principles he embodies,' he had declared to Nadezhda von Meck in mid-March,[30] and it was a matchingly human pragmatism that he disclosed in his view of opera's function when, in October, his patroness had shifted the discussion from political to musical matters. 'You are right in taking this grudging view of what is, in essence, *a false kind of art*,' he had replied. 'But there is something irresistible which draws all composers to opera. It is this: that it alone gives you the means to communicate with *the masses* of the public. My Manfred will be played once, a second time, and will long disappear, and no one except the handful of connoisseurs who attend symphony concerts will know it. Whereas opera, and only opera, draws you close to people, relates your music to a real public, makes you accessible not only to tiny separate circles but, if conditions are favourable, to the whole nation. I do not think there is anything reprehensible in this aspiration – that is, it was not vanity that guided . . . Beethoven when he wrote his *Fidelio*.' For Brahms to have denied himself operatic composition was a kind of heroism, Tchaikovsky felt. But, he continued, 'in doing this [composing operas], you must not only pursue external effects, but choose subjects having artistic value, interesting, and which touch deeply'.[31]

The reference to Beethoven may seem inapposite, but what was now driving Tchaikovsky to *The Enchantress* was not unlike what had drawn the German composer to the subject of his only opera. Like Beethoven, Tchaikovsky could perceive in his central character the embodiment of an ideal – or, at least, that is what Kuma would be, once Shpazhinsky had reworked his play into a libretto. When Pavlovskaya had challenged the wisdom of Tchaikovsky's choice, he had conceded that Kuma's outer charms were precisely those mundane ones which would make her kind of hostelry a success. But these alone, Tchaikovsky maintained, could never have turned the young prince into a passionately devoted lover. 'The point is that in the depths of the soul of this loose country woman is *a moral force and beauty* which, until this happened, had merely had no place in which it could declare itself,' he had written on 24 April:

[30] *TLP*13, p. 45; *TPM*3, p. 347; *TZC*3, p. 30.
[31] *TLP*13, pp. 159–60; *TPM*3, p. 381; *TZC*3, pp. 74–5; *YDGC*, pp. 352–3 (partial).

This force is love. Her nature is strongly feminine, capable of falling in love only once and for ever, and of giving up *everything* for the sake of that love. While *love* was no more than an embryo Nastasya had disposed her *power* lightly – that is, she had amused herself with what made one and all who came across her fall in love with her. In this she is simply an engaging, attractive, though also depraved country woman. She knows she is *captivating*, she is content with this knowledge, and having been enlightened neither by [religious] belief nor by education while she was an orphan, she has made her sole mission in life to live gaily. But the man appears who is destined to touch the better strings of her *instincts* which till then have remained silent, and she is transformed. Life becomes *nothing* for her unless she attains her goal; *the power of her attractiveness*, which before had functioned instinctively, involuntarily, now becomes an invincible weapon which in an instant demolishes the alien power – that is, the *hatred* of the [young] prince. After this both surrender to the ungovernable torrent of their love which leads to inevitable catastrophe, to her *death*, and this death leaves in the spectator a sense of reconciliation and tenderness . . .

Shpazhinsky has grasped perfectly what I need . . . He is softening some of the *rough edges* in Nastasya's *manières d'être* and through her traits of character is bringing straight out the hidden strength *of her moral beauty*. He and I (and afterwards you, if you become reconciled to the role) will so do it that in the last act everyone will be in tears . . .

Since being tempted by *The Enchantress* I have remained completely faithful to my soul's fundamental need to illustrate in music what Goethe said: 'Das Ewig-Weibliche zieht uns hinan.' The fact that the *powerful beauty* of Nastasya's *femininity* has long been hidden within the shell of a *loose peasant woman* will tend to heighten all the more her attractiveness on the stage.[32]

It was, of course, a piece of engaging but monumental self-deception, especially if Tchaikovsky secretly imagined he was about to fashion a work whose central character somehow matched Beethoven's heroine in the pursuit of an ideal. Instinct is no substitute for choice; Kuma came to possess no moral purpose demanding passionate commitment to a course of action she knew required sustained courage and might demand complete self-sacrifice – simply a capacity for strong feelings which she now experienced more violently than ever before, and which led to her destruction. But not only is she no peasant Leonora; she is not

[32] *TLP*13, pp. 63–4; *TZC*3, pp. 39–40; *DTC*, pp. 147–8.

even a Tatyana or Mariya in pursuit of her love, for there is no evidence
that, in planning to elope with Yury, she has made a choice which she
could foresee, if only dimly, might set in motion a train of events leading
to disaster. When Kuma becomes the victim of passion, she has a
pathos which our sentimental pity may find hard to resist, but no more.
One factor which drew Tchaikovsky to her was, of course, that old,
familiar, irresistible concept: the woman who becomes the victim of
Fate. Yet he was probably little aware of this when he came to write the
opera. Certainly the Fate motif, born in that central crisis moment in
Tatyana's life, plays a smaller role even than in *Mazepa*, where its duties
had in any case been vigorously discharged by the hetman's own
theme. Though *The Enchantress* has a fair quota of prominent descending scales, the Fate motif appears explicitly only once[33] – at that
moment in the love duet (Ex. 213) when Kuma, having confided the

Ex. 213

[KUMA: Go!   YURY: I pity you   KUMA: No, you need not!]

        Go!   I am distressed!]

[33] A mediant-to-dominant stepwise descent occurs in a decorated form in the duet
for the Princess and Yury in Act 2 (No. 9: bars 200–3), but this is probably
coincidental. A prominent six-note descent has also been heard earlier (orchestra, bars
143–6; later, in a portion Tchaikovsky cut during rehearsals, it had recurred more
explicitly), and another also punctuates the memories of the Prince's soliloquy of love
in the orchestral passage following the quarrel with his wife. But nowhere is the descent
between the mediant and dominant.

fullness of her love, tells Yury to leave and, in an ambivalent A major/C sharp minor, he ponders the fateful decision that now confronts him.

Another pointer to Tchaikovsky's choice is contained in two further sentences in the letter to Pavlovskaya. 'Why do you *have* to love *Carmen*? Why . . . is *the beauty and strength* felt beneath the coarse exterior?'[34] That Bizet's last opera was one very real incitement to this subject, and that Tchaikovsky hoped to create in Kuma a species of Russian Carmen becomes clear at the very opening of *The Enchantress*. Just as the multi-layered society of soldiers, street urchins and cigarette girls with which Bizet fills his stage is indispensable if Carmen is to be perceived not only as an individual but as a social animal, so the peasantry revelling at Kuma's hostelry provides no mere decorative panorama, but projects an equally vibrant human world to which Kuma can be shown both to belong, yet from which she also stands apart. But within a few bars of the principals' entries the gulf which divides the two composers' dramatic perceptions is glaringly apparent. Bizet, while swiftly exposing externals, hints at a hidden side: is the quiet repetition in bars six to eight of Ex. 214a merely heightened coquetry, or does it

Ex. 214   [BIZET]

[34] *TLP*13, p. 64; *TZC*3, p. 40; *DTC*, p. 148.

[TCHAIKOVSKY]

[Where was I? In the green meadow looking for berries with the girls,

singing songs freely, and I summoned nice young men to walk with me]

contain a fleeting longing for something deeper than the easy amours with which his wanton gipsy has so freely stuffed her life? There is no such hint of ambivalence in Kuma's opening words, simply forthright self-exposure (Ex. 214b).

Yet Tchaikovsky is to establish one side of Kuma's individuality very appealingly in her arioso which is the centrepiece of this first act. If the opera's short orchestral introduction, with its two folksongs which are also to be the foundation of this arioso,[35] is intended as a portrayal of Kuma's 'femininity' as Tchaikovsky conceived it (with a more turbulent central section to foretell the dramatic storms into which she is to be caught), the buoyantly alive world revealed when the curtain rises is substantiated through Tchaikovsky's national style at its most extrovert and vigorous – a stream of racy ideas, many of which might well be folksongs, supported by seventh-spiced harmonies, bright orchestral colours, and much use of the changing-background principle – all confirming, even more than the folkscene in *Mazepa*, how consummately Tchaikovsky could re-work that Russian vein he had largely abandoned over the last eight years. Living, as he now did, closer to the Russian peasantry had doubtless sharpened his awareness of their nature and ambience (at Maidanovo he had himself collected the third of the identified folksongs in *The Enchantress* – that which is the foundation of the entr'acte before Act 4, and which recurs for the entry of Kuma and her friends). Likewise, the recent conversion of *Vakula* into *Cherevichki* had been a well-timed reminder for him of this rich musical source. The approach of the women's chorus has delicious freshness; Kuma makes her formal vocal entry (see Ex. 214b), brushes with Paisy, crushes him, ponders the implications of the Prince's impending visit, then prepares to receive new guests who are arriving to a sturdy chorus in $\frac{5}{4}$. All this, with the delightful cameo of the prize fighter, Kichiga, demonstrating his craft, is wholly admirable, as is the cloud of seriousness which passes over the scene as the distant bells of Nizhni-Novgorod are heard calling to prayer. The pacing, too, is excellent. Kuma's beautiful arioso is a moment of stillness at the heart of this folk scene. Its effect and purpose are not unlike those of Joan's narration in *The Maid*, though narrative self-disclosure is here replaced by lyrical self-projection. The musical terms being simpler and more confined than in the introduction, the exposure of Kuma herself is more explicit.

It is now that the action begins to move. Yury passes through the scene, his theme (see Ex. 217g) revealing no more of him than does his friendly greeting to those on the bank. But his father makes an instant and powerful impression; his stern octave introduction, with its grim-faced crotchets and whiplash demisemiquavers, is a succinct incarnation of this overbearing and harshly retributive governor (Ex. 215a). The confrontation which his entry occasions offers rich possibilities for disclosing more of Kuma, and Tchaikovsky's response is alert, whether

---

[35] The three folksongs identified in *The Enchantress* are: 'Sizoy golub po zoryam letal'; 'Ne shum shumit' (T5oRF, No. 21); 'Serezha-pastushok'. The first two are used in the introduction before Act 1 and in Kuma's arioso, the third in the entr'acte before Act 4 and in the Scena (No. 20).

Ex. 215

a.   Maestoso in tempo moderato assai

b.   Moderato assai

he is projecting the decisiveness and natural authority with which she
rallies and controls her forces ahead of his appearance, or the calculated campaign of bewitching charm and disarming vulnerability with
which she besieges, then subdues the Prince. The coy modesty of the
fluttering clarinet/flute phrase to which she first presents herself before
him, the unblushing simplicity of the music to which she begins to give
an account of herself (Ex. 216a), the firmness with which she paraphrases her own first folksong (see Ex. 217a) as her self-assurance

Ex. 216

a.

Kuma

Kto ya- bed -nïm na - ve - tom za - mïs- lil po - gu - bit,   iz   stra - [kha]

one who through sneaking slander plans to destroy, from fear . . .]

b.   Tempo 1 (Moderato)

Kuma

O nyom li   du-moy u -dru- chat mne

[Should my spirit be so depressed by the

du- shu?

thought of him?]

c.

Kuma

[That's not all: I have struck down the Prince with a potion in his cup; with a devilish illusion...]

be - sov - skim na - vazh - [deniyem]

grows (see Ex. 217h), the increasing strength of contour in her phrases as she persuades the Prince to accept her hospitality – all add firm and individual lines to the rapidly developing sketch of this peasant individual. The skilfully managed decimet, like the quartet in the first scene of *Onegin*, is a passage of reflection for all concerned. But a good deal of what follows is superfluous, and with the weakening of dramatic motivation, the musical level falls away. The tumblers' dance is efficient, but the final discomfiture of Mamïrov, though necessary for the plot, is treated as mere buffoonery.

Key usage has already shown evidence of thoughtful planning, though of a kind very different in many respects from that found in the earlier operas. Admittedly, some of the kinds of key association employed in *Onegin* do occur. E flat (with C minor) is very much the key of the Prince and his family, just as B flat (with G minor) had been of the Larins in *Onegin*. But whereas the earlier opera had been rich in such single keys associated with particular characters, dramatic forces or emotions, the most important tonal element in *The Enchantress* is a relationship: the tritone. Thus while B flat is Kuma's special key (that is, of Kuma the 'enchantress', the girl who possesses allure and knows how to use it to entice, command, enslave), E major, far from embodying happiness in love, as in *Onegin* and, to a lesser extent, in *Mazepa*, is

the key of the hatred and destructive forces which build against her.[36]
Perhaps surprisingly, while the introduction centres on B flat, the folk
chorus which opens the opera finally settles for E minor, which proves
to be very much a key of the habitués of Kuma's hostelry. However, the
route from B flat to E minor, via the tonic shared by their relatives (G
minor/G major), is far shorter than to E major; Kuma may be set apart
from her rustic companions, yet she is also easily connected with them,
and E minor may be as much the key of her more fundamental peasant
nature as of theirs. The folksongs and key of the introduction return for
Kuma's arioso at the centre of this first act, while following this are the
appearances of Yury and his father, both set in E flat; thus she is
already placed tonally close to the family whose destruction she is
unwittingly to cause. The abrupt wrench to A major, which Lukash
effects as soon as Yury has disappeared, brings home unceremoniously
the gulf between the worlds of country and city. As Kuma assumes firm
control of her forces B flat is re-established; later, when she begins to
master the Prince's affections and her confidence increases, it returns
yet again (andantino) and is the key of the decimet where her
ascendancy over the Prince is assured.

In general this first act, a tableau scene in the familiar Russian
pattern, makes an excellent beginning; conversely, the last ends in total
disaster. There is no need to look further than the plot for one reason for
this. Eight days after the première Tchaikovsky again wrote to
Shpazhinskaya: 'The fault is both mine and (chiefly) Ip[polit] Vas[il-
yevich Shpazhinsky]'s. He knows the [requirements of the theatre]
stage perfectly, but has not adjusted himself sufficiently to the demands
of opera. He has too many *words*; *dialogue* predominates excessively over
lyricism. However much I shortened the text . . . every scene came out
too long.'[37] And it is not simply too many words; in the last act, which
had originally been two but had been compressed into one at
Tchaikovsky's insistence, there is far too much action. Tchaikovsky
had already turned against it while scoring the opera. 'I don't love this
act – or, to put it better, I've fallen out-of-love with it,' he confessed
privately to his librettist's wife. 'It's a mess, stuck together artificially,
long, complicated, and terribly gloomy. But maybe I'm wrong.'[38] It
introduces yet another character – the wizard, whose sole function is

[36] The first version of the love duet for Kuma and Yury in Act 3 had ended in E
major; significantly, perhaps, in the revision it is transposed to E flat, the special key of
Yury and his family. It is also worth noting that the B flat/E tonal opposition is
fundamental to the first number in Act 1 of *Carmen*.
[37] *TLP*14, p. 250; *DTC*, p. 159; *TTP*, p. 327.
[38] *TLP*14, p. 89; *TTP*, p. 318; *YDGC*, p. 410 (partial).

the provision of a poison that would guarantee Kuma a particularly unpleasant end. To be fair, the poisoning is very well handled, and though Kuma dies too quickly to suffer much discomfort, Yury vents his grief affectingly (with strong hints of the Fate motif), and his death is touchingly mourned by his former comrades. But the deluge of incident, especially in the final fifteen or so minutes of the opera, swamps any sustained attempt Tchaikovsky might have made to crystallize a dramatic or emotional issue, and the effect of the concluding mad scene is in inverse proportion to the hysteria of the Prince's ravings and the violence of the encircling tempest, scored for the noisiest of orchestras, and cackling wizard.

The change in the principles governing this opera's tonal practices is matched by a less drastic, though significant, shift in thematic procedures. Throughout there is a powerful impression of melodic worlds created by constant variations against the background of unconscious protoshapes, or by constant evolution into new outlines which progressively achieve a more independent identity. To take just one example: the folktune which launches the introduction (Ex. 217a) generates a fresh entity (Ex. 217b) to open the stormy central section, later moving back towards its opening form (Ex. 217c), its redesigned second half then providing the contour for the phrase with which the peasants introduce themselves as Act 1 begins (Ex. 217d), which in turn yields Paisy's phrase (Ex. 217e) which is to underlie his conversation with Foka. Similarly the trend, already observed in *Mazepa*, away

Ex. 217

a. Introduction: bar 1

b. bar 24 [transposed]

c. bar 84

d. Act 1, No. 1, bar 9 — *bis* —

e. bar 42 [transposed]

f. Kuma's arioso (concluding orchestral phrase) [transposed]

g. Yury's theme: Act 1, No 5, bar 2

h. Act 1, No 6, bar 117

from referential themes is taken much farther in *The Enchantress*; especially noticeable is the lack of thematic recall towards the conclusion of the last act. Instead there is throughout an increased use of the situation motif – a thematic idea designed for a particular movement or stage of the plot, used perhaps intensively at the local level, but straying only a short way beyond the end of its area of origin, at most playing a small role in the following act. Thus any expectation that the opening folksong might become Kuma's musical badge disappears with Act 1, while the more personalized phrase with which she begins to impress herself upon the Prince (see Ex. 216a) recurs once early in Act 2, then vanishes. Neither Yury's phrase (which seems to spring from Kuma's folksong which immediately precedes it: see Ex. 217f and g) nor the far stronger invention in bare octaves which introduces his father (see Ex. 215a) develops any greater dramatic significance, the former being heard only as he quells the riot in Act 2, the latter briefly when the Princess abruptly silences Nenila's attempt to soothe her early in the same act. Echoes from the conclusion of the Prince's entrance theme in Act 2 (see Ex. 215b, bracketed portion ⌐*a*¬) twice infiltrate his attempt to win Kuma's love in Act 3, but memories of the Princess's phrase which begins the entr'acte before Act 2 (see Ex. 219, bracketed ⌐*x*¬) are even fainter in the third act.

A situation motif may be conditioned by the prevailing emotion or dramatic mood, but some appear to be deliberately personalized and, as in *Onegin* and *Mazepa*, it is the minor characters who tend to have the most self-conscious thematic identities. A malicious little phrase, whose ancestry goes back to Naina's music in Glinka's *Ruslan and Lyudmila*, forewarns us of the wizard during the Act 4 entr'acte (see bars 12–13). Ever adaptable to whatever situation or company he finds himself in, Paisy borrows the opening of this wizard's theme for his own Act 4 appearance, but in Act 1 takes his cue from the peasants (see Ex. 217e), while in Act 2 he filches a little from the chant world of the calling

he disgraces (Ex. 218), his wheedling unctuousness swelling its contours until Yury leaves impatiently. After this pious little rogue's
briefing by Mamïrov, his disappearance to the fidgety sounds of his
chant-motif, now transformed to expose him as the devious rascal he is,
is a delicious touch.

Ex. 218

   The two middle acts of *The Enchantress* are uneven, but they contain
much fine, sometimes very impressive music. If the first act had
belonged to the peasants, the second is dominated by the one principal
who has not yet appeared. Though the Prince is a firmly projected
figure, it is his wife who has the hotter blood, and the entr'acte, built
from the phrase in the first bar of Ex. 219, is as much concerned with the
Princess and her feelings as the introduction had been Kuma's domain,
her surrogate phrase assuming a variety of forms which uncover the
fertile workings of her obsession, then erupting into a full-scale melodic
expression of the torment this obsession has bred (Ex. 219). Like
Kuma, she is no introvert, and Mamïrov's words suffice to rouse her
quickly from her lament to a well projected decisiveness. Mamïrov is a
formidable, sinister figure. Less an individual than an activist, he lives

Ex. 219

in a devious, subversive world, rich in diminished sevenths and clipped orchestral motifs. While Mamïrov is in line from Orlik in *Mazepa*, Nenila's descent is from the Nurse in *Onegin*. She is of the same stock as Kuma, and her opening music is a curious anticipation of one of Kuma's most heartfelt moments in the love duet in Act 3 (see Ex. 226). Yet she is different. While retaining her warmth, she has lost her bloom. Age and earnest loyalty have made her garrulous, and the Princess finally cuts off impatiently her well-meant chatter. But, like Mamïrov, she draws a response which usefully uncovers more of her mistress; while the deacon prompts a quiet, iron firmness which points to a capacity for controlled reflection and resolute action, the irritation generated by her maid's ineffectual prattle finally releases a flood of rage and bitterness, leaving no doubt that she will prove a ruthless opponent.

The weakest of the four principals is Yury. Against the impressive composure his mother regains when he enters, his reply seems pallid. Distress at the division between his parents does rouse him, but to nothing like as distinctive or richly felt an utterance as his mother's reply (Ex. 220). Yet in gaining self-control, she masks her feelings and

Ex. 220

Pol - no!   A yes - li bï mne go-re pri - klyu- chi-los,

[Enough! And if I have suffered misfortune, I would not begin to depress you with it. No, I

ya im teb-ya ne sta - la b u - dru- chat.   Net, —

would not begin to depress you with it. No, no!]

the following duet with her son is too bland by far. Restraint has no part in her duet with the Prince. This encounter strips the covers from her feelings; unable to sustain the controlled formality of their first exchanges, she rounds upon her unfaithful husband with merciless denunciation (Ex. 221). But if her tirade of reproach seems to falter yet more each time she returns to this central musical thought, it is not weakening resolve but choking anger that breaks her vocal line, for

Ex. 221

[It is not nonsense,— but a shame and your disgrace! You are a wicked sinner,

you have forgotten your conscience, your family, and forgotten your honour!]

between these stanchions are phrases stretched tautly over vast, often precipitous contours (Ex. 222). While the prison scene in *Mazepa* had uncovered Tchaikovsky's capacity to probe the grimmer issues in human experience, his ability to explore the extremes of bitter anger is powerfully demonstrated here. Twice she struggles to check this torrent, but twice she is engulfed by her own feelings, and though her husband, hopelessly guilty, attempts to silence her with the full weight of his authority and personality, she remains implacably defiant.

Ex. 222

This is almost great opera, and the riotous peasant incursion which follows is also very efficiently handled. By contrast, the first stretch of the final scene may seem to be almost casual. But though its flow seems unruffled and its theme untroubled, passion has not been exhausted, nor anger purged; hatred has bored so deeply that the Princess cannot bear even to utter her rival's name, and when Nenila reveals it to her son, she passes the final threshold of bitterness. Now she has a champion. Vengeance upon Kuma is no longer a gnawing need; it can be a sublime crusade. Her unquestioning certainty in the justice of her cause and in its triumph heightens the illusory calm. The brief, rapt shift to G major, the radiance of her strong, broad lines, and the ecstasy of transcendental hatred in her last phrases are a stronger earnest of Kuma's doom than all the lashings and fury that have gone before.

The tonal principles underlying *The Enchantress* have unfolded further in this second act. It brings the first significant appearance of E major, established by the end of the Princess's aria of vengeance against Kuma, momentarily breaking through at the abrupt conclusion of her violent quarrel with her husband, and overspreading the act's end, where the thought of the peasant beauty's destruction possesses both mother and son. The duet of mutual care and affection, which they had earlier sung, had confirmed E flat as their family key, and it will bear the Prince's declaration of passion for Kuma early in the next act, and his son's confession of love at the end. G major seems to be the special key of love. In it the Prince admits Kuma's enslaving power, and in it the orchestral introduction to Act 3, a vignette of the Prince as despondent suitor, begins. The key predominates uncertainly in the early stages of the third act, where he presses himself upon her, but she resists. Perhaps there is intended irony that this girl, whose way of living has so often provoked outrage, should confess her behaviour yet defend her integrity not only in the same key but in musical terms (Ex. 223b) so close to those of the Prince's own confession of his improper passion for her in Act 2 (Ex. 223a). B flat – Kuma's own special key – returns as she exposes her impotence in the face of his orders, and appeals to his self-restraint with the full force of her defencelessness.

Ex. 223

a.

[But the image of that comely girl lives always with me,]

b.

[For my tender manner, my cheerful disposition,]

But when this proves vain, it is in E minor that her uncompromising
peasant nature bursts through and she defies him: she would rather cut
her own throat than submit.

This third act is very much Kuma's. The Prince as lover is a greatly
diminished figure. As the plea of an unrequited supplicant, his declaration in Act 2 (see Ex. 223a) had lacked the rapture of the hetman's
soliloquy before the love scene in *Mazepa*, and in this third act his
wooing of Kuma in the E flat arioso contains no trace of manly strength;
it lacks even the fervour of Agnès Sorel's avowal (in Act 2 of *The Maid*),
which it much resembles. His virility resurges when he is roused to
furious jealousy at the discovery of a rival, and he invades her tonal
territory (E minor), first to browbeat her, then to charge her with
harlotry, only to be opposed and driven off by her dignified defence of
her conduct (see Ex. 223b). Like Mariya's contributions during the
Mazepa love scene, Kuma's are the more pointed and characterful, as at
the centre of the Prince's E flat arioso where, despite her perplexity and
pity, she makes clear she has no love for him, significantly distancing
herself by manoeuvring back to her own remote ground, E minor.
Alone in the quiet and growing darkness after his stormy exit, her
thoughts fasten upon Yury, and the tenderness and intimacy of her
musings return her to her gentlest vein and key (see Ex. 216b). After the
short scene with Polya and Foka she ponders yet more intently his
arrival, the orchestra shadowing her thoughts in a committed E flat.
Fear at the prospect of confronting his murderous intentions only
sharpens awareness of her own secret love. Terror alternates with
longing; nowhere does the sense of tremulous feelings exposed find such
open or appealing expression as here.

With the rough entry of Yury and Zhuran there begins, as
Tchaikovsky himself put it, the '*most important* scene of the opera'[39]
(significantly, the very first sketches for *The Enchantress* relate to this).
And also quite certainly the finest – at times, indeed, offering stretches
of music that would have been worthy of a place in *Onegin*. The
crippling consequence of Shpazhinsky's prolixity was that it squeezed
out those moments when the momentum might be slowed or halted,
and a critical emotion or inner state might be investigated and musically exposed. But this love scene is a dynamic situation; the road from
hate to love for Yury is a long one, the stages of his journey numerous,
and Shpazhinsky was especially attentive to the construction of this
portion of the libretto. 'I am offering you the possibility, through your
lovely music, of conveying our heroes' sentiments through *nine* motifs,'

[39] *TLP*13, p. 315.

he explained when sending this portion of his finished work to Tchaikovsky.[40] It proved an excellent scheme, though Tchaikovsky broke it into ten rather than nine sections (Ex. 224). From the moment

Ex. 224

Stage/Character(s)/Situation	Keys
1. Allegro moderato Yury. Accusation (embarrassed)	F major – C major
2. Andantino Kuma. Gentle mockery Yury. Warning Kuma. Desire to explain	C major – E♭ major ∿∿∿ G major Kuma Yury Kuma
3. Allegro con spirito Kuma. Self-justification 1 (defiant: the peasant girl)	E minor – (B minor – F minor) – C minor
4. Moderato Kuma. Self-justification 2 (imploring: 'the enchantress') Yury. Weakening (embarrassed)	B♭ major ∿∿∿ (D minor) Kuma Yury Kuma
5. Bar 243 Kuma. Confession of love 1 (preparation) Yury. Confusion	G minor – B minor
6. Andante Kuma. Confession of love 2 (appealing)	B minor
7. Allegro Kuma. Confession of love 3 (assertive) Yury. Confused: finally promises Kuma protection	E minor – (B minor) – E minor Kuma Yury
8. Allegro moderato Kuma. Confession of love 4 (pleading) Yury. Confused; tries to leave but is powerless to do so	G major – (E minor) – G major/minor Kuma/Yury orch Kuma/Yury
9. Andante non tanto Kuma. Confession of love 5 (self-sacrificing) Yury. Final stage of capitulation	A♭ minor [fate theme] ∿∿∿ Kuma Kuma/Yury
10. Andante un poco rubato Kuma. ⎫ Yury. ⎭ Mutual love	E♭ major

∿∿∿ = tonally unstable passage
Bracketed keys are only transitory
⌐→ = sections employing identical material

[40] Quoted in Yarustovsky, *Opernaya dramaturgiya Chaykovskovo* (Moscow/Leningrad, 1947), pp. 208–9.

Yury draws back the bed curtain and reveals Kuma, she begins to take
command of the situation, slipping momentarily into her own B flat
and very firmly, but in the simplest and most transparent terms,
detaining him. Then in a clear C major, and exploiting that most
appealing melodic manner (see Ex. 216c) which she had used to such
effect upon his father in the first act, she settles into her campaign of
persuasion. In all that happens until they find a sure emotional haven
in their mutual love, she is the more secure, and her music the more
tonally stable. Disclosing first the charge against her of having bewitched his father, she slips disarmingly into E flat, his family's very
own territory, as she gently mocks the credence he has placed upon her
magic powers, then for the first time touches upon G major, the key of
love. Her shifts of mood are both a truthful reflection of her own inner
turmoil and a powerful weapon in her strategy of subjugation. Stunned
by her blunt account of his father's attempt upon her and her uncompromising refusal to yield, Yury's helplessness grows when she replaces
this fierce onslaught upon his feelings from the tougher side of her
peasant nature with the persuasions of the enchantress and, passing
from E minor to her other tonal extreme, implores his protection in the
most melting music of the whole opera (Ex. 225). Carmen never

Ex. 225

[As before God I have bared all my soul. My prince, hear my prayer also. In such cruel

misfortune only you can help me. Woe is the lonely one! All my life I endure sadness and torment!

riten.

Andante

- din, v ta - koy be - dè zhe - sto - koy, po-mo-zhesh mne.

Go - re o - di -

mp

Have pity upon me! Alone I am afraid; give me your hand!]

(♩ = ♩)

- no - koy! Ter - plyu vsyu zhizn tos - ku i mu - ku! Men-ya tĭ po-zha -

mf   mf

un poco string   Moderato (come sopra)

- lei!   Od - noy   mne strash - no; dai

fp espress.

3 3 3

3

ru - ku mne!

mf

sounded as vulnerable as this – nor as appealing. But, then, *The Enchantress* has long since parted company with Bizet's masterpiece.

Having disarmed him, she sets herself to win him. As Ex. 224 shows, the five stages (sections 5–9) through which she will gain his love are carefully and perceptively planned. Shyly in G minor she sets out towards her avowal, her self-control faltering when, with alarm, Yury begins to perceive where she is heading, then regaining command of herself and the situation as she directs the music to a firm B minor for a frank and tender confession of her love (Ex. 226a).

Ex. 226

[Long, my falcon, have I followed you stealthily, hiding from everyone! Holding my breath, gazing upon you, I did not take my eyes off you!]

[For whom is the Prince neglecting you? Your face radiates beauty, but he does not notice it.]

But having revealed her aim and frightened her quarry, she must retain the initiative and prevent his escape. And so she turns upon him with the more direct force of her peasant nature, going back to her earlier E minor music, and holding Yury within it until he vows his protection, then slipping easily to G major as she sees love begin to possess him. Finally confident he can no longer escape, she feigns a withdrawal which she knows will lure him into the trap: unworthy of him, she will bid him farewell. In Tchaikovsky's earlier operas G flat had normally appeared at least once at a moment of especially intense emotion. Kuma goes one flat deeper (to A flat minor); after this final assault upon his emotions, both calculated yet sincere, Yury can only capitulate, E flat exposing how completely his whole self is now contained within his words and how unconditionally he accepts her into his world and heart.

The richest contributions to the last act come, not surprisingly, from Kuma and the Princess, though Yury provides a very attractive love arioso, confirming his commitment to his beloved by choosing E minor, the key of her most artless nature. But his father has no such dramatic

opportunity as this, and his end, for all Tchaikovsky's furious orchestral imagery, lacks even a fraction of the pathos of his son's grief
for Kuma. Nor is the general tonal articulation as precise as in the
preceding acts, though with such a flood of incident there is less time for
single tonalities to underpin a particular character or force. There is a
predominance of flat keys while disasters gather and break. C minor,
the relative of E flat, is especially prominent as son, father and mother
hurtle towards their dooms, and it dominates the final stages of the
opera. Likewise the duet of malice which ends the scene for the Princess
and the wizard is in C sharp minor rather than E major. Kuma's
peasant companions had homed in upon their most characteristic E
minor during their farewells (a touchingly beautiful moment), and it is
the initial key of Kuma's soliloquy of love and longing. Perhaps the
most significant tonal feature of the act is what is not there: Kuma offers
not a hint of B flat, nor is there even a trace of that calculating charmer
from the days before Yury had given her his heart. Now secure in her
love, it is a simple, unaffected peasant girl who awaits him. The move to
E major during her aria may be intended as ironic, or simply signals a
confusing reversion to an old tonal metaphor, but who would wish to
fault Tchaikovsky when it supports so rightly the surge of truthful love
which will be this simple girl's last feeling on this earth?

But it is the Princess who makes the firmer impression. The outbursts with which she interrupts the wizard's misogynistic bumblings
have all the venomous ferocity which she had brought to the Act 2 duet
with her roaming husband, and momentarily but magnificently rekindle the dramatic blaze (though in the final section of their encounter
her ludicrous accomplice drags her down to his own level in what is
the feeblest passage in the whole opera). Equally impressive is the
ingratiating ruthlessness with which she insinuates herself into the
confidence of an unsuspecting Kuma, making her persuasions the more
familiar by adapting a little of her victim's own C major declaration to
Yury (see Ex. 216c) from early in the love scene. But with her rival's
extinction there is no further situation which could have drawn from
her those fierce responses which had already inspired some of the
opera's finest music; as distraught mother caught up in an implausible
welter of events she shrinks into impotence, and the opera's last flicker
of real dramatic life expires. It is a sad end to a piece which had begun
so excellently and continued for most of its course so well – even, at
times, so superbly.

2

GROWING CONFIDENCE:
A HARD WINTER AND A GOOD SUMMER

THE NEW LIFE at Maidanovo wrought in Tchaikovsky himself a change as great as in his existence, for while his acts of creation became more private, he displayed an increasing willingness to expose his personality to at least a limited circle of the outside world. It was not merely that his relationships with his long-standing Moscow friends became warmer than ever before; he showed greater readiness to make new acquaintances, to meet and talk with others where purposeful discussion might be pursued, or to collaborate where common interests might be served. And so to his energetic and continuing participation in the affairs of the Conservatoire and the RMS was to be added involvement with the choir of the Russian Choral Society and with the School of the Russian Synod, of whose management committee he became a member.

Modest's memories of his brother's intensified sense of social responsibility which grew in his new environment are liberally complemented in some of the letters Tchaikovsky himself wrote during his first year of residence. They reveal the enormous extent to which he gave of himself to help individuals, dispensing advice or offering moral support more unstintingly than ever, even though this absorbed much precious time. Taneyev profited yet again from his counsel. Tchaikovsky had been primarily responsible for his appointment as director of the Moscow Conservatoire, but his protégé was not yet thirty, and was finding the prospect of coping with some of the older, more established figures in the Moscow musical world intimidating. Above all he was apprehensive of Nikolay Alexeyev, one of the leading figures in Moscow's political life and about to become mayor of the city, who – so Taneyev suspected – was determined to consolidate his personal power within the Conservatoire and RMS by making them financially dependent upon himself. Tchaikovsky demolished this notion by subjecting his fellow-director's character to an analysis which seems both perceptive and balanced.

Alexeyev is very ambitious, and doesn't conceal this, but the targets of his ambition extend beyond dictatorship within the Mus[ical] Soc[iety] . . . He wishes to play the role of a strong and powerful man in wider circles . . . He's very *thrifty*, . . . takes no pleasure in his directorship, and would be very glad to get his money back. He is of a rather hard and dry character – but an exception in this regard was his devotion to Nikolay Grigoryevich [Rubinstein] which, after his death, was transferred to the affairs of the Mus[ical] Soc[iety] as a whole. [In this respect] he is making some sacrifice. I'm not saying this because I'm bemused by him, for I nourish no particular sympathy for him. But I have to value his *efficiency*, his mind [and] energy, and I should consider it a great loss for the cause if he were to leave. . . . I like his plain dealing; when you talk with him you know he says exactly what he's thinking. He's very open to persuasion, and you'll find he'll agree to all your proposals if they tend to the common good.[1]

More private predicaments opened his reserves of personal sympathy and wisdom. Emiliya Pavlovskaya, whom he was trying to reconcile to the part of Kuma in *The Enchantress*, lamented that during the three months when the opera season was closed, she could find no alternative activity to distract her. But she was now well into her career, Tchaikovsky reflected to himself; how then would she be able to face the ultimate void of retirement? Tactfully he broached the subject. 'Can you *walk* – that is, walk not in the sense of movement or simply mooching around, but in the sense of lively intercourse with the infinite and inexpressible beauty of nature? Can't you occupy yourself with translations from Russian *into Italian*, of which, it seems, you have an excellent command? Surely Russian literature is now a strong interest in the West? . . . Forgive me that I permit myself to give advice,' he added apologetically, 'but, you see, I'm not interested only in *Pavlovskaya* – that is, my best support on the stage – but also in Emiliya Karlovna, whom I shall love in twenty-five years' time as much as I do now.'[2] As Modest remembered, his brother's rapidly widening circle of friends and acquaintances initiated at this time a number of such correspondences – with Yuliya Shpazhinskaya, for instance, whom Tchaikovsky met through the collaboration with her husband over *The Enchantress*, and who, soon alone and with a family to rear, became the recipient during the next six years of over eighty kindly and caring

[1] *TLP*13, pp. 105–6; *TZC*3, p. 54; *TTP*, p. 128.
[2] *TLP*13, pp. 118–19.

letters. Even when the pressures of his other correspondence were at their greatest, his letters to her were always of generous length and filled with precise advice and encouragement on all sorts of matters; they revealed, too, his unstinting readiness to give of his own time to provide constructive criticism of her first fumbling efforts to turn herself into a writer, and to intercede vigorously though unsuccessfully with the Imperial Theatres to get her work performed.

Above all, perhaps, consciousness of the enormous success of his music and the personal prestige he enjoyed with his compatriots fortified the urge within this compassionate man to share with those less fortunate the material benefits fame was increasingly bringing him. One of his first acts after moving to Maidanovo was to instruct the St Petersburg branch of the RMS to donate to the Musicians' Benevolent Fund the total royalties from performances of his music in its past season's concerts. Conservatoire students, past, present and intending, increasingly received his support. He gave one hundred roubles each to Anna Alexandrova-Levenson, a former harmony pupil caught into the expenses of pregnancy, and to Zinaida Moiseyeva, who was seeking admission to study the piano, and whose surcharge for being entered as a supernumerary Tchaikovsky was prepared to pay secretly. Even the domestic plight of a certain Anna Pereselentseva, whom he encountered simply because she was one of Jurgenson's employees, drove him to intervene with financial help. His own family, of course, drew even quicker sympathy; his cousin Lidiya Olkhovskaya was given 150 roubles to help with home difficulties. But it was Georges-Léon who remained his most costly responsibility. In July 1885 Tchaikovsky had planned to bring the two-year-old to Russia, and Modest was poised to journey to Paris to collect him. But Tanya, who was not consulted until the last minute, had refused to consent; she hoped within the year to be in a position to have Georges-Léon nearer to her, she had said, and meanwhile it would be better for him to remain where he was. By now Tchaikovsky's brother Nikolay and his wife, who were childless and had been admitted to the secret of Georges-Léon's existence, were taking an active interest in the boy, but meanwhile the main financial responsibility remained with Tchaikovsky.

Yet the action which perhaps uncovers most clearly his unpretentious humanity was a service to his new, more lowly neighbours. In July, when two-thirds of Klin had been ravaged by fire, he had helped in combating the flames and had contributed to the relief fund, but he was also moved to more fundamental action by the enduring plight of the local peasantry. In the letter in which Nadezhda von Meck had wished him well as he settled into Maidanovo, she had also lamented the state of Russia, likening it to 'a theatre of marionettes. Learned societies gather,' she had continued, 'they discuss, mull over subjects *of the first importance*, but you know perfectly well that they will chat, wave their hands about, will go their separate ways – and nothing further will happen.'[3] Tchaikovsky's vision of his native land was less forlorn. There was much that was wrong, he admitted, but that was true of any country. At one time he had believed that political institutions, parliaments, and so on, were all that was required to set things right, but now he had doubts. Though recognizing he risked charges of being reactionary, he was currently more inclined to place his trust in a benign despot – more precisely, in the present Tsar.

Doubtless, whether Tchaikovsky realized it or not, his belief in the importance of benevolence from above was a powerful stimulus to his own actions within the restricted world of Maidanovo. Living as he now did so much closer to the Russian peasantry, he was the more alive to its problems and predicaments, and despite the importunate pressures upon his charity from individuals during his walks, he remained deeply disturbed by their deprivations. As the winter of 1885 closed in, he contrasted his own comfortable accommodation with that of the peasants. 'The cottages in the local village are of the most pitiful, tiny, dark sort,' he told his patroness. 'They must be terribly stuffy, and when you remember that they [the peasants] have to live in this dark and crowded state for eight months, your heart bleeds. I do not know why, but the people here are especially poor . . . Yet (and this is the most noticeable thing) all of them – the adults, old and young, and the children – have a thoroughly happy and contented appearance; in no way do they complain of their ill-starred fate – and the less they express their dissatisfaction with their life, the more I pity them and am touched by the Russian race's humility and long-suffering. The children have surprisingly sympathetic faces. There is no school: the nearest is four miles away . . . I should like to do something.'[4] Distress soon fathered action. He approached the local priest, who said something could be done if Tchaikovsky himself would finance it. The latter agreed, official permission was sought and granted, and on 1 February 1886 a Maidanovo school was inaugurated with proper ceremony. Three days later Tchaikovsky conducted a personal inspection, deciding that the teaching was marked more by good intentions than expertise. Nevertheless the annual commitment of 220 roubles for the sake of twenty-eight boys and girls was money well spent, he

[3] *TPM*3, p. 344.
[4] *TLP*13, pp. 170–1; *TPM*3, p. 384; *TZC*3, pp. 76–7.

concluded. Constant to his beliefs, he maintained his interest and support for the Maidanovo school for the rest of his life.

Another correspondence which began at this time was with the young conductor of the Tiflis opera company who had just had the courage, despite his very limited resources, to mount *Mazepa*, with his wife singing the part of Mariya. Tchaikovsky was both impressed and grateful, for his brother and sister-in-law had seen the production and given a favourable report. Mikhail Ippolitov-Ivanov was a twenty-six-year-old graduate from Rimsky-Korsakov's composition class at the St Petersburg Conservatoire. He had now been nearly three years in the Georgian capital as head of the new local branch of the RMS, and before he left in 1893 to join the staff of the Moscow Conservatoire (of which he was to be director from 1905 to 1922) he was to transform the musical life of this Caucasus city. Having scored a success with *Mazepa*, Ippolitov-Ivanov set his sights on *The Oprichnik*, the first opera he had heard and which had made an indelible impression upon him, he told Tchaikovsky. The latter, of course, discouraged this particular venture, recommending instead his new revision of *Vakula*, but adding that if *Cherevichki* was found to be unsuitable, *The Maid of Orléans* (Ippolitov-Ivanov's second choice) would be his preference, though he considered its music much inferior. Meanwhile Tchaikovsky's pleasure at what Ippolitov-Ivanov and his wife were doing for the fortunes of his music is reflected in the relaxed friendliness of his response. 'In Moscow the other day,' he ended his letter of 3 January 1886, 'while looking through *V. I. Safonov*'s photograph album, I stopped at a very sympathetic female face and asked who it was. It turned out to be your wife about whom earlier, especially in Kiev, I had always heard enthusiastic comments. Thus I took my first step to becoming acquainted with your wife thanks to a photograph, the second I take now in asking you to express to her my respect, and the third I shall take personally in Tiflis in the spring. Until a pleasant meeting!'[5]

This expedition to stay with Anatoly and his family had been projected months before. When it came, the sort of respite it provided was as desperately needed as Tchaikovsky could ever have envisaged. If during the earlier part of 1885 he had any doubts about the remorseless pressures his Moscow commitments and his sudden new fame would bring, this winter of 1885–6 disabused him. His letters detail the meetings, committees, official events, individual consultations, receptions, social occasions, concerts, opera and theatre trips,

[5] *TLP*13, p. 224; *TZC*3, p. 84 (last phrase omitted).

as well as visits to and from family, friends and acquaintances, which crammed the periods, often of a week or more, which he had to spend in Moscow. Yet these letters also tell of the halcyon contrast of his country home, where not only could work on *The Enchantress* progress happily, but where he could find instant relaxation, once he had completed the day's session of checking the Manfred Symphony proofs or of letter writing. His trip to Kamenka in November for Sasha and Lev's silver wedding had confirmed that he could never willingly return there to live. 'The former complete harmony has gone,' he reported sadly to his benefactress during what was clearly an uncomfortable, sometimes distressing visit. 'My relationship with the family has changed – although, I repeat, I love them as always.'[6] Transferring his remaining possessions to Maidanovo on his own return on 24 November now set the seal upon his new home.

Nor was there 'complete harmony' within the von Meck family. That backbiting which Tchaikovsky had observed in Anna and Nikolay towards other members of the family had now come to the attention of Nadezhda herself, who had reacted with distress to the couple's spiteful ingratitude towards Nikolay's eldest brother, Vladimir. Jealousy of Vladimir and exasperation at his inefficient control of the family's affairs were at the root of Nikolay's behaviour, while Anna had developed a massive inferiority complex which was driving her to trumpet her own family's supposed quality and importance. Above all, she had turned her husband against his own kind. But, protested her mother-in-law in a letter she begged Tchaikovsky to burn, 'if she wants Kolya to respect *her* parents, then she must respect *his* parents. She considers herself so brilliant that she does not understand such simple things.'[7] Tchaikovsky himself found no improvement in the couple when he encountered them during the winter until it was known that Anna was pregnant, and enforced rest brought a lull in her more active self-assertion. All this, coupled with further suspicions (fanned by Anna in depreciation of Vladimir) that his benefactress's financial affairs might again be in crisis, cast a heavy cloud over this very sensitive area of relationship.

Meanwhile in Moscow Tchaikovsky's well proven diplomatic skills were much in demand. He canvassed assiduously but unsuccessfully on behalf of Modest's play, *Lizaveta Nikolayevna*, which had been only tepidly received in St Petersburg, and he was also delegated to persuade Erdmannsdörfer to remain in Moscow for a further period after

[6] *TLP*13, pp. 188–9; *TPM*3, p. 388.
[7] *TPM*3, p. 390.

his contract expired. It had become imperative that this very popular German conductor should stay, for a rival society, the Philharmonic, was attracting members from the RMS. Quite apart from the latter's own fortunes, the Conservatoire depended heavily upon RMS profits for its income; thus a threat to the RMS was a threat to the Conservatoire. It was a point Tchaikovsky well understood, and he secured Erdmannsdörfer's agreement to a further three-year contract, but only after personal interventions he found highly distasteful.

The end of 1885 had also produced some happier occurrences. For a second time Tchaikovsky was the recipient of a 500-rouble Glinka Award given anonymously by Mitrofan Belyayev, this time for his symphonic fantasia, *The Tempest*. In November he was also elected the first honorary member of the Moscow Conservatoire in recognition of his distinction in composition and his services to Russian music. But his visit to St Petersburg for the New Year left him depressed. Performances of *Onegin* had been discontinued, *Mazepa* had not been seen all season, and now there seemed strong doubts that *Cherevichki* would be mounted in Moscow because Altani was ill. Meanwhile he had to witness another musician experiencing one of his greatest triumphs. On 16 January in St Petersburg Anton Rubinstein, Tchaikovsky's former teacher, had given the first in a series of seven 'historical concerts' which provided 'a survey of the continuous development of piano music', as Rubinstein himself wrote.[8] Three days later he began to repeat them in Moscow. The great pianist was approaching the end of his career as a virtuoso, and the series was also given, in whole or part, as a grand farewell gesture in eight other major European cities, including London. It was a remarkably novel and comprehensive project, opening with William Byrd's virginal piece, *The Carman's whistle*, and ending with works by Balakirev, Tchaikovsky[9] and Rubinstein himself.

This series was certainly the event of the musical season in Moscow. Tchaikovsky missed the first three recitals, attended the fourth from a sense of duty, encountered Rubinstein, and finding him especially touched by his presence, felt obliged to journey to Moscow for each of the three remaining, and for the gala evening in the visitor's honour at the Bolshoy on 22 February. The recitals themselves proved more than worth the time and effort; the problem was the cumulative effect of all the inescapable wining and dining of Rubinstein which followed these

---

[8] A. Rubinstein, 'Avtobiograficheskiye rasskazï'. Printed in A. G. Rubinstein, *Literaturnoye naslediye*, Vol. 1 (Moscow, 1983), p. 99.

[9] *Chant sans paroles*, Op. 2, No. 3, *Valse scherzo*, Op. 7, *Romance*, Op. 5, and *Scherzo à la russe*, Op. 1, No. 1.

weekly concerts, since each time a three-day absence from Maidanovo was entailed. For all Rubinstein's persisting coolness towards his compositions, Tchaikovsky recognised the quality of the man as well as the artist. 'Rubinstein is worthy the honours accorded him,' he reflected to Nadezhda von Meck four days after the gala. 'Besides being an exceptionally gifted artist, he is also without doubt an honourable, generous man.'[10] Yet a reservoir of bitterness at Rubinstein's indifference remained. Tchaikovsky had recently been browsing through one of Rubinstein's operas, and finally the dam burst. 'Played *Nero* after supper,' he confessed to his diary on 13 March. '. . . God! It makes you wild looking at this score. But, then, I play this abomination because the consciousness of my superiority, at least as regards integrity, sustains my power. You think you are writing badly, then you look at this trash . . . and you feel better!'[11]

All this while he had himself been busy on new compositions. Besides sketching at least half *The Enchantress* during the winter, he had completed two other shorter works. One was the *Dumka (Scène rustique russe)*, Op. 59, a substantial piece for piano which he finished on 5 March for Mackar to mark his new business relationship with the French publisher; the other was a curiosity – a melodrama for the Domovoy, or house-spirit, to be inserted into an imminent revival of Ostrovsky's play, *The Voyevoda*, upon which Tchaikovsky had based his own first opera nearly twenty years before. Shpazhinsky wrote to Tchaikovsky of Ostrovsky's request on 18 January, only six days before the planned first performance; the music was to express '*the noises of the night*'.[12] A further message warned Tchaikovsky that the orchestra at the Maly Theatre was 'so vile that you can't entrust any serious piece to it'.[13] In these dispiriting circumstances, what Tchaikovsky provided for a tiny orchestra of five woodwind, harp and strings was a little miracle of professional skill, making demands which even the wretched crew at the Maly could meet, yet conjuring an atmosphere of instant, translucent magic which Ostrovsky must surely have felt enhanced his own work. Yet the piece was heard once only, at the benefit performance for the actor Konstantin Rïbakov on 31 January.

But when to these creative labours was added the repeated shuttling between Moscow and Maidanovo for Rubinstein's recitals, the result was an intense depression, and a great reluctance to journey anywhere. Nevertheless, he had promised Anatoly and Parasha that he would

[10] *TLP*13, p. 278; *TPM*3, pp. 405–6; *TZC*3, p. 94; *YDGC*, pp. 361–2.
[11] *TD*, p. 41; *YDGC*, p. 364.
[12] *DTC*, p. 268. The performance was to be postponed until 31 January.
[13] *DTC*, p. 269.

come to Tiflis in the spring. After the première of the Manfred
Symphony on 23 March, he spent five days in St Petersburg dealing
with business affairs, and received an ovation at an RMS concert in
which Bülow played the solo part in the First Piano Concerto. Then on
4 April he left Moscow for Taganrog to spend two delightful days with
brother Ippolit and his wife. Forced to delay in Vladikavkaz (now
Ordzhonikidze) to await a carriage and horses, on 11 April he began
the last stage of his journey: the spectacular crossing of the Caucasus
Mountains along the Georgian Military Highway.

At first you approach the mountains rather slowly, despite the fact
that it seems they are right in front of your nose. . . . Then the valley
of the Terek becomes ever narrower, then you come out into the
Daryalskoye gorge – terrifying, gloomy, wild – then little by little you
enter the region of snow. . . . Finally we climbed up and up between
two high walls of snow. I had to put on my fur coat. At six in the
evening we descended into the valley of the Aragvi and spent
the night *at Mleti* . . . I dined, took a walk along the gallery in the
moonlight, and went to bed at nine. We left early next morning . . . all the time coming across picturesque villages and every
different kind of dwelling. The descent was made at a speed which
was sometimes truly frightening, particularly on the bends. Not far
from the station of Dushet there suddenly opens out a distant view so
amazingly wonderful that you want to weep for joy. The farther you
go, the more *the south* makes itself felt. Finally we passed through
Mtskheta . . . and at about 4.30 we were already in Tiflis.[14]

It was the most distant sortie Tchaikovsky had ever made within the
boundaries of the Russian Empire, and quite certainly the most
exciting. As for Tiflis, it blended the familiar with the exotic. 'The
town's delightfully picturesque,' he continued his rhapsody to Modest.

Not all the trees are yet in leaf – but then, all the fruit trees are in
blossom, in the gardens . . . the masses of flowers stand out vividly,
it's as warm as June and, in a word, it's the most true of springs,
exactly as it was in Naples when we left it four years ago. The main
streets are very lively, the shops are luxurious, and it smells totally of
Europe. But today, when I went into the native quarter (Maidan),
I found myself in a situation utterly new to me. The streets are
unusually narrow, as in Venice; downstairs on both sides is an

[14] *TLP*13, pp. 306–7; *TZC*3, pp. 98–9; *TPB*, p. 350.

endless row of small shops and craft establishments of all sorts where the locals sit cross-legged working in view of the passers-by. There are bakers and special kinds of food shops where they bake and fry various things. It's very interesting and novel.[15]

Just how thoroughly Europe had colonized this Asiatic outpost became apparent from a concert promoted by the new branch of the RMS, conducted by Ippolitov-Ivanov, in which the main work was Beethoven's Eroica Symphony; the programme also included Tchaikovsky's own *Sérénade mélancolique* for violin and orchestra. It was not an encouraging introduction to Tiflis's music, for the orchestra was poor, and the audience small. Nevertheless, he could see the future held promise, for the Society's classes already had 230 enrolled students, and there were now some outstanding musicians in the town, especially Ippolitov-Ivanov. Fearing that he would be fêted when he longed only for freedom and relaxation, he had firmly forewarned both Anatoly and Ippolitov-Ivanov that he wished to avoid social occasions, and no special events were to be mounted for him.

It was too much to hope. With a sister-in-law as socially conscious as Parasha there were endless invitations, including a charity ball and an evening of domestic theatricals in which Tchaikovsky was persuaded to accompany Anatoly in a reading from Turgenev's one-act play, *An Evening in Sorrento*. As for his music, knowledge of this had preceded him. 'My operas are given here more than anywhere, and *Mazepa* in particular enjoys a great success,' he reported to Nadezhda von Meck.[16] A fine performance of the opera was specially arranged by the company for his forty-sixth birthday on 7 May, and six days earlier a complete programme of his works conducted by Ippolitov-Ivanov, including *Romeo and Juliet*, the Serenade for Strings and Tatyana's Letter Monologue from *Onegin*, sung by Ippolitov-Ivanov's wife, Varvara Zarudnaya, had been given in his honour. It proved a far grander occasion than ever he had expected. First, as he entered the directors' box, there was a long standing ovation, then an address of welcome from a deputation of the local RMS and the presentation of various wreaths, including one made of beautifully wrought silver. The chorus and orchestra performed a chorus from *Mazepa* with a new text specially invented for the occasion; the audience demanded this should be repeated several times. Throughout the concert, which went on till nearly midnight, there were endless ovations. Finally there was a grand

[15] *TLP*13, p. 307; *TZC*3, p. 99; *TPB*, p. 350.
[16] *TLP*13, pp. 309–10; *TPM*3, p. 413; *TZC*3, p. 100.

supper, with more speeches. Tchaikovsky had viewed the prospect of this evening with no joy. But when, some days later, he came to review it for his patroness, the sincerity and genuine warmth with which the honest citizens of this remote but lively community had saluted him had taken on a very attractive aura. 'It all exhausted me terribly, but the memory of this triumph, with the like of which I have never before been favoured anywhere, will for my whole life remain pleasant for me.'[17] It was, as Modest put it, 'the first public acknowledgment of his service to the Russian peoples,'[18] – the strongest evidence yet of how universally popular his music had become.

Tchaikovsky stayed a month in Tiflis, delighting in the churches and the Easter-tide ceremonies and services, exploring the town so that he knew it better than Anatoly and Parasha, and soaking himself in the unfamiliar but enchanting atmosphere of the locality. He saw much of Ippolitov-Ivanov and his wife, quickly coming to like and respect them. But he spent more time in the company of a certain Ivan Verinovsky, a Russian artillery officer, whose attractiveness for him was of a special kind: that much is apparent from the diary Tchaikovsky was keeping, and especially from his deep and prolonged distress at news of Verinovsky's sudden suicide only three days after his own departure. The relationship was certainly observed disapprovingly by Parasha. But disapproval could cut both ways. Those scurrilous remarks made a year earlier by Nikolay and Anna contained a grain of truth; Parasha *did* flirt, enough to make Tchaikovsky remonstrate with her more than once during this visit. Yet in no way did she appear to bear resentment, and shortly before his departure she suddenly dissolved in tears at the thought of his going. 'I do not remember ever being so touched in my life,' he wrote in his diary that evening.[19] Once again it is clear some exceptionally strong bond united this very dissimilar pair at this time.

Parasha and Anatoly accompanied Tchaikovsky on the first part of his journey when he left Tiflis on 11 May. If he still harboured any doubts about his own celebrity status, the crowd who saw him off at the station and threw flowers into the train dispersed them. Though his destination was Paris, he had originally intended to take ship to Naples, then travel via Rome and Vichy, but this scheme had to be abandoned when an outbreak of cholera in Italy caused the French to impose a ten-day confinement in quarantine upon anyone entering from that country. In consequence he booked for Marseilles. The gloom from painful farewells to Anatoly and Parasha at Batum was dispelled by the

[17] *TLP*13, p. 326; *TPM*3, p. 414; *YDGC*, p. 369 (partial).
[18] *TZC*3, p. 104.
[19] *TD*, p. 53.

interest of the places he visited or saw during the leisurely cruise along the north coast of Turkey. His diary entries became fuller, and he provided a bulletin of each day's experiences both for Modest and for Anatoly and Parasha. The French steamer, *L'Arménie*, called at Trebizond ('very picturesque, very interesting – especially *the bazaar.* Drank coffee in a coffee shop and smoked a *hookah.* Went up a mountain on horseback to the monastery . . . only two Greek monks. Amazing view.'[20]), Keresun ('not especially interesting'[21]) and Samsun ('picturesque'[22]). On 16 May they docked at Constantinople for twenty-four hours. After enduring half a concert of Mozart, Beethoven and Dvořák, and a night ashore in a bug-infested room, Tchaikovsky took a guided tour of the city ('St Sofiya amazed and delighted me – but in general Constantinople is unsympathetic'[23]). The numerous and wretched dogs, for which the city was notorious, almost turned him against the whole canine race, he said. Off Greece the vessel passed close to Piraeus; a further day, and they were in sight of Sicily. Etna was in eruption and Alexey woke him at two in the morning to see the spectacle ('the sea . . . proved to be rough, and it is impossible to convey the beauty of this combination of moonlight with the fire of Etna and the stormy sea'[24]). Stromboli was smoking impressively, too, and they encountered a volcanic island which the captain said must be newly risen from the sea. After passing the Strait of Bonifacio ('Sardinia reminded me of a lunar landscape seen in some book of *Flammarion* . . . Corsica is grand and picturesque'[25]), on 23 May the steamer berthed in Marseilles.

For the pleasures of this sea voyage Tchaikovsky had paid a human price: confinement. There was simply no escaping his companions on deck, and his cabin had to become the refuge where he could weep over the end of Paul Bourget's newest novel, *Un crime d'amour*, and delight afresh in de Musset, lent to him by the captain. Most of all he could not abide anyone who wanted to talk to him about music, and he especially detested a certain Dr Gontard who had invented a monstrous new kind of piano and who dragooned him into reading the monograph he had written about it. Desperate to relieve the pressure, Tchaikovsky wrote a hypocritical letter of commendation to Saint-Saëns on his tormentor's

[20] Now Trabzon. *TLP*13, p. 330.
[21] Now Giresun. *TD*, p. 55.
[22] *ibid.*
[23] *TLP*13, p. 338; *TZC*3, p. 108; *YDGC*, p. 371.
[24] *TLP*13, p. 339; *TZC*3, p. 110; *YDGC*, p. 371 (partial).
[25] *TLP*13, p. 342; *TPB*, p. 356. Camille Flammarion (1842–1925) was a popularizer of astronomy.

behalf. Yet such was his frame of mind after Tiflis that he coped with the presence of most of the others during this twelve-day voyage remarkably well. He had, in fact, just passed six of the pleasantest weeks of his life, and on arriving in Paris on 28 May and settling into his familiar room in his familiar hotel, he extended this period of freedom for a few more days before confessing his presence to those people whom he had come to meet for professional reasons. Then, having sent Alexey ahead to Maidanovo to prepare for the time when he himself would at last be able to escape thither, he steeled himself for business. Sympathetically the weather broke at the same time, and it poured for days on end.

Professional matters could wait a little – but not Georges-Léon. It was now agreed that the three-year-old should be adopted by Nikolay and Olga, and the latter was coming to Paris for a period so that the child could become used to her; then she and Tchaikovsky would take him back to Russia. Tchaikovsky felt deep anxiety about the whole operation. Within hours of reaching Paris he had travelled to nearby Bicêtre where the Auclair family, which was fostering the lad, now lived. Georges-Léon was sitting in the window as he approached, and he was immediately dismayed at how like his mother he had grown 'so that Lev and Sasha will guess!!! He's an unusually sympathetic child,' he added more happily to Modest, 'affectionate, gentle – although he's very lively. When Mme Auclair asked him whether he wanted to go with me, he replied emphatically "Non!", and then, when I began showing that it would be nice, he said: "Et nous prendrons maman et papa aussi! Papa, va tout de suite t'habiller!" . . . This little scene touched me very much.'[26] He gave prompt attention to the legal formalities of Georges-Léon's adoption, and continued to see him frequently so that the lad would accept him too. His own feelings, he discovered, were ambivalent. The child was hyperactive, Mme Auclair had indulged him too much, Olga would have a battle instituting a more disciplined regime, and the journey back to Russia was likely to be difficult. But Georges-Léon was a charmer; they would survive one another.

By this time he had faced Mackar. So accustomed had he become to freedom that he dreaded the meeting. Ten times he approached the building before screwing up the resolve to enter; even a large absinth had not helped. But the Frenchman was quick to perceive his new composer's aversion to social contacts, and proceeded with a good deal of tact when taking Tchaikovsky under his wing in the matter of visits to

[26] *TLP*13, p. 346.

influential people. Tchaikovsky had come to Paris expecting to be a supplicant; he found he was as much sought after as seeking, and during the next three weeks Ambroise Thomas and Léo Delibes were only the most distinguished of the local musicians who called and had to leave their visiting cards because he was not at home. Later he met both, finding the former 'a very nice and gentle old man'[27] who invited him to observe the Conservatoire examinations, while the latter showed him a gratifying deference 'which I value especially because I consider him the most talented of French musicians after *Bizet*'.[28] He was unable to see Gounod, Saint-Saëns or Massenet, but he encountered Lalo and Fauré ('whom I liked extremely, both as man and musician'[29]), and made the acquaintance of a number of other highly regarded, though now almost forgotten, composers on the Parisian scene: men like Henri Maréchal, Charles Lefebvre – and another 'sympathetic' being, Louis Bourgault-Ducoudray, also a scholar, who was well versed in Russian culture and talked enthusiastically about Glinka and Tolstoy in particular. Of local performers Martin Marsick he knew already, and the Belgian violinist led a group which played one of Tchaikovsky's string quartets at a soirée on 19 June. Also performed were some of Tchaikovsky's songs and a quartet[30] by Fauré, likewise present, and which impressed Tchaikovsky deeply. Other acquaintances he now met included Lamoureux and Colonne, both full of promises to advance the cause of his music, and Antoine Marmontel, pianist and eminent piano teacher, to whom he dedicated the *Dumka* recently composed for Mackar.

But of all these new acquaintances by far the most memorable in every way was Pauline Viardot. Now long retired, she was an international legend; for a Russian she had especial significance as the first foreign performer to have sung Glinka and Dargomïzhsky in Russian, and an adoring Turgenev had been her companion for much of the last forty years of his life. Her aura made Tchaikovsky nervous, but he need have had no fears. 'I was completely enchanted by her,' he informed Parasha. 'Despite her seventy years [she was, in fact, sixty-four], she carries herself like a forty-year-old woman – lively, bright, kind, courteous – and she was able to make me feel at home with her from the very first moment.'[31] She talked to him freely about Turgenev, and how they had written *The Story of Love Triumphant* together. He sensed she

---

[27] *TLP*13, p. 366; *TZC*3, p. 114; *TPB*, p. 360.
[28] *TLP*13, p. 383; *TPM*3, p. 425; *YDGC*, p. 375.
[29] *TLP*13, p. 398; *TTP*, p. 139; *TZC*3, p. 119; *YDGC*, p. 375.
[30] The Second Piano Quartet.
[31] *TLP*13, p. 357; *TPM*3, p. 637; *TZC*3, p. 113; *TPB*, p. 359.

was as sincere as she was self-evidently knowledgeable and intelligent; of all his new Parisian acquaintances, she was the one he most liked. And she afforded him one other experience to treasure. Many years earlier her husband had purchased the autograph of that most revered of masterpieces, Mozart's *Don Giovanni*, and for two hours Tchaikovsky was able to examine it. 'I cannot express the feelings which engulfed me while looking through this musical *hallowed object*,' he recalled for Nadezhda von Meck. 'It was exactly as though I was grasping the hand of Mozart himself, and talking with him.'[32] For Tchaikovsky this was *the* event of his visit to Paris.

During his first days he engaged in his usual lively round of theatres, and was thoroughly bored by a meeting at Longchamps – the first time in his life he had been to horse races. He saw only one opera: Saint-Saëns's *Henri VIII*, whose wildly successful reception in 1883, while Tchaikovsky had been in Paris agonizing over the future fate of *Mazepa*, had roused his bitter envy. Now at last he heard the opera and found it, as he had expected, 'worse than mediocre'.[33] Lucien Guitry, whom he had met in Russia, and Alexey Golitsïn, on whose estate twenty-two years earlier he had composed that precocious student work, *The Storm*, were both in the French capital, but he spent more of his free time with his former pupil, the cellist Anatoly Brandukov, who had lived much of the last eight years abroad. Finding Brandukov's personal situation far from prosperous, he used his influence with Erdmannsdörfer to obtain the cellist an engagement in one of the following season's RMS concerts so that he might have the opportunity to visit his family in Russia; the next year he was to dedicate to Brandukov his own *Pezzo capriccioso* for cello and orchestra. But the pangs of longing for his homeland, which had beset him even before his arrival in France, became more importunate still. On 16 June Olga arrived, met Georges-Léon, and impressed her brother-in-law by the tact and patience with which she approached the formidable task confronting her. Yet there still remained a problem with the boy's documentation, for the Russian consul refused point-blank to incorporate him on Tchaikovsky's passport. Caught into the ponderous formalities of the local bureaucracy, Tchaikovsky applied for a French passport for Georges-Léon, initiating a procedure entailing various visits to various offices for the solemn recording of data, and delaying their departure from Paris. As Tchaikovsky informed Modest, it was Georges-Léon himself who at the last interview finally clinched matters with masterly innocence: 'Suddenly he broke the silence by

---

[32] *TLP*13, p. 383; *TPM*3, p. 426; *TZC*3, p. 113; *YDGC*, p. 374.
[33] *TD*, p. 63; *YDGC*, p. 374.

beginning to sing *The Marseillaise* at the top of his voice. Even the *chef de bureau*, a stern old man upon whom everything depended, started to roar with laughter.'[34] On 24 June they left for Russia. The three-day journey with their young charge was hectic, but still the burden of current preoccupations could not drive from Tchaikovsky's memory an event of thirty-two years before. Writing his diary in Berlin the next day, he ended: '*anniversary* of mother's death'.[35]

Tchaikovsky had been away from Russia for just on three months, and he had managed little or no composition. Now, however, the summer season was beginning; those affairs which would burden him would be in recession, those persons who would distract him would be away on their various tours, visits and vacations, and there was the prospect of some three months in which he could lead his own controlled and relatively undisturbed life at Maidanovo. Having delivered Olga and Georges-Léon into brother Nikolay's keeping in St Petersburg, delayed a day to see their new ward baptised into the Orthodox Church (Tchaikovsky himself standing as godfather), and laid the trail of deception which would hide the boy's origins from Anatoly and Parasha ('just imagine,' he wrote, 'they [Nikolay and Olga] want to adopt some orphan'[36]), on 30 June he was back in his own home, distributing presents to his delighted servants, fondling his dog, and playing vint in the evening with the Kondratyevs, who were in residence nearby. Determined to attack and despatch *The Enchantress*, he wanted no guests; even such as Kashkin and Albrecht were to be kept at bay for the moment, he told Jurgenson.

The first distraction came quickly and suddenly from an unexpected quarter: Antonina Ivanovna. It was seven years since Tchaikovsky had last seen his wife, five since she had given birth to an illegitimate child and effectively freed him from further obligation to her. But Antonina was irrational, and the distress she could still occasion was prodigious, as Tchaikovsky confided to Modest on 16 July:

The gist of her letters is that she now hopes I won't doubt her love, that she is now passionately in love, and proposes I should experience with her the supreme delights of love. *Her letters are completely mad.* I need hardly say that I was terribly upset. Of course, she can't force me to live with her, and there is no danger in her attempts at

[34] *TLP*13, p. 368.
[35] *TD*, p. 70; *YDGC*, p. 375.
[36] *TLP*13, p. 369.

reconciliation – but all the same, it was incredibly painful for me, and I even felt physically upset. But most of all, *despite everything*, I'm sorry for this unfortunate being . . . She is so deranged that in reply to my first letter, where I said she should abandon any hope of living with me, she sent me an invitation to visit her, to ask the hotel servant whether she had not [indeed] left her lover (but who is apparently still in love with her and might appear unexpectedly), and then to make love (according to her, she now knows how to arouse passion in me) . . . just as though I had once loved her . . . And now she's ready to be, as she says, 'all mine'. Finally I wrote her an appropriate letter, allotted her an allowance, and I think that now she'll finally leave me in peace. After this letter, which took me *a full two days* and which I tore up, I think, at least twenty-five times, I have calmed down and have set about the fourth act of the opera.[37]

The allowance was to be 600 roubles a year, which Tchaikovsky requested Jurgenson to pay on his behalf to avoid further contact with Antonina.

Jurgenson did as he was asked and saw Antonina, who had aged, was utterly confused and confusing, but who seemed satisfied with the allowance. Her sudden reappearance had produced a devastating effect upon her husband – haemorrhoid pains, and a feeling he would imminently die so extreme that he had drawn up a will. She continued to harass him periodically throughout the summer. A month later she claimed she had three children, all in a hospital for foundlings, that she had called one Pyotr after her husband, and that she was now proposing that he should adopt one or all of them. She enclosed an embroidered shirt, asked him to dedicate something to her, and begged for his photograph. His first reaction was to refuse, but on reflection he requested Jurgenson to find one and despatch it. Tchaikovsky's lingering concern for Antonina, and his readiness still to respond in such a trivial but personal matter, is curious yet touching. Jurgenson's intercessions and his willingness to act as a buffer between Tchaikovsky and Antonina earned Tchaikovsky's deep gratitude. Any relationship is bound to be under constant threat of strain when business matters loom so large in it and when one of the parties is as temperamental as Tchaikovsky, and Jurgenson's obvious affection for his most distinguished composer could only be sustained if in many things he exercised a great deal of forbearance and tact. Kindness itself could rebound unhappily; he had allocated a room in his own house for

[37] *TLP*13, p. 388.

Tchaikovsky's Moscow visits, but the previous winter disagreements had arisen and the close proximity had become uncomfortable for both. But if any serious constraint had remained, it was now dispelled.

In the sharpest contrast to assaults like Antonina's from the outside world was the growing richness of the inner life his new remote home made possible. One small sign of this is the quite separate diary he began earlier in the year in which, irregularly, he took the time to note his thoughtful response to any subject that was currently engrossing him. Often this was a composer, an author, or some musical or literary composition. His first contribution, made on 6 March after reading the Psalms, pondered the gulf separating the Old and New Testament views of divine mercy. Then, after a gap of four months, came a close packed set of entries upon Tolstoy, who seems to have afforded a large portion of Tchaikovsky's reading this summer. In two of these he set out his general views on the great novelist, whom he had met only once ten years earlier and some of whose more mundane thoughts and traits he had found painfully disenchanting.[38] Then, having finished that 'wonderful piece',[39] *Kholstomer*, and read another newly published short story, *The Death of Ivan Ilich* ('a work of tormenting genius'[40]), he was overtaken by a sense of awe. 'More than ever I'm convinced that Lev Tolstoy is the greatest of all writers who have ever existed at any time or anywhere,' he wrote that evening. 'He alone is enough for the Russian man not to have to bow his head in shame when everything that *Europe* has given humanity is reckoned up.'[41] He read another of the short stories, *The Woodfelling*, 'wept again',[42] and later re-visited *The Cossacks*. French literature, both fictional and critical, also occupied him much, but it was another Russian book that gave him the greater delight. Russia's past had always fascinated Tchaikovsky, and historical journals had always featured in his reading, but Sergey Axakov's *Family Chronicle*, the tale of the author's own patriarchal forebears on the newly opened Bashkirian steppes in the time of Catherine the Great, proved to be a real discovery – 'a wonderful, original work!'[43]

As for music, it was still primarily operas he played for his own recreation. He retained a strong allegiance to Serov, that now-forgotten figure who had taken the Russian operatic stage by storm in the sixties, and whose death in 1871 had created the situation which brought into

---

[38] These are quoted in Vol. 2, pp. 128–9.
[39] *TD*, p. 78; *YDGC*, p. 378.
[40] *ibid.*
[41] *TD*, pp. 211–12; *TZC3*, pp. 119–20; *TPB*, p. 606; *YDGC*, p. 378.
[42] *TD*, p. 79; *YDGC*, p. 378 (partial).
[43] *TD*, p. 98; *TZC3*, p. 134; *YDGC*, p. 388.

being one of Tchaikovsky's own best and most endearing works, *Vakula the Smith*. Both *Judith* and *Hostile Power* received his attentions. A year later he was to return to the latter with savagely divided feelings: 'a certain, almost disgusting musical ugliness – and along with this *talent, flair, imagination,*' as he noted in his diary on 28 April 1887. 'To tell the truth about all this, there's infinitely more in Serov than in the celebrated *mighty handful*. But then, they have *orderliness, a striving after elegance* – in a word, a comely exterior.'[44] But this, too, had its special attractions, and he also played through Rimsky-Korsakov's *May Night* and *Snowmaiden*, especially admiring the latter, and admitting that he even envied the mastery Rimsky displayed in it.

As for foreign, especially French composers, it was their newest pieces that interested him. He investigated further the piano quartet by Fauré which had so impressed him in Paris, but Massenet seems to have claimed a greater part of his time, and he spent some days studying both *Manon Lescaut* and *Le Cid*. He had seen the former in Paris within a month of its première in 1884, and had been greatly disappointed. Renewed acquaintance was initially more favourable, but finally damning – though his revulsion was linked with self-reproach. 'Ah, how nauseating Massenet is!!! But what's most unpleasant of all is that in this *nauseating quality* I feel something akin to myself.'[45] *Le Cid* showed that Massenet 'had written himself out'.[46] Neither Tchaikovsky's letters nor his diary give any hint of his reaction to Delibes' *Le roi l'a dit* or Wagner's *Parsifal*, though it is easy to guess which he preferred. His dislike of Brahms had become more uncompromising. He played one of the symphonies with Laroche during the piano-duet sessions which were a major pleasure of his friend's visits to Maidanovo. 'What an untalented s— ! It angers me that this presumptuous mediocrity is recognized *as a genius*. Why, Raff is a giant by comparison with him, to say nothing of Rubinstein who, despite everything, is a major and vital being.'[47] His furious contempt for the latter had much abated, it seems; both Rubinstein's Fourth Symphony (the 'Dramatic') and one by Glazunov provided further material for his duet playing with Laroche. Taneyev visited and brought his new Third Quartet; 'much that is good' was Tchaikovsky's judgement.[48]

Meanwhile a new young figure was rising in his esteem. At the end of

[44] *TD*, p. 139; *YDGC*, p. 411; *TZC3*, p. 165.
[45] *TD*, p. 85; *TZC3*, p. 125; *YDGC*, p. 380.
[46] *TD*, p. 102; *TZC3*, p. 137; *YDGC*, p. 389.
[47] *TD*, p. 101; *TZC3*, p. 136 (partial); *YDGC*, p. 389. Tchaikovsky confirmed his admiration for Raff by contributing to his memorial fund.
[48] *TD*, p. 90; *YDGC*, p. 382.

1885 Georgy Catoire, a maths graduate from Moscow University and a former piano pupil of Klindworth, had gone, on Tchaikovsky's advice, to Berlin to resume lessons with Klindworth and for belated study of composition. Catoire had become desperately homesick and Tchaikovsky had already provided generous moral comfort in letters to this youth for whom he saw a bright future. To encourage Catoire further he had asked him to send some of his work from Berlin. The evidence Catoire now brought when he visited Tchaikovsky so impressed him that he interceded with Rimsky-Korsakov to take him as a pupil. Sadly, Catoire's promise as a composer remained unfulfilled. Though he did become a professor of composition at the Moscow Conservatoire in 1916, his interest by then had shifted to the nature of music itself, and during his remaining ten years he developed into one of the leading Russian musical theorists of his time, investigating both harmony and structure, and exercising a powerful influence upon Soviet musical education.

This period at Maidanovo was, like its weather, mixed. Verinovsky's death continued to torment Tchaikovsky. He was haunted by a suspicion that if only he had remained in Tiflis a further week he could have intervened to save him, and he applied urgently for details surrounding the suicide from Ippolitov-Ivanov as well as Anatoly and Parasha, discovering that circumstances which he could not have influenced had driven his friend to take his own life. For all that, the memory of this relationship long remained painfully vivid, and any reminder of it could reduce him to uncontrollable tears. A further cause for emotional discomfort was Emma Genton's lingering attachment to him. It was five years since he had first noted signs of tender feelings in this governess to the Kondratyevs' daughter, and Emma was still with them in the neighbouring dacha. It was a relief when she left with the whole family early in August, but the absence of this strangely mixed group of friends left a void so great in Tchaikovsky's world that one evening he went down to the village, which he normally detested, simply to exchange a few words with anyone who might be about, then dropped in at a nearby dacha to chat with its inhabitants for a good hour about nothing in particular. Such seeking for society was a new and significant departure from his normal pattern of behaviour. By now he had resumed the particular types of social occasion which Maidanovo favoured so well and which he especially enjoyed. Among his prime guests were Jurgenson, Kashkin and Albrecht, that triumvirate whom he had first met in January 1866 as a novice teacher under Nikolay Rubinstein, and who ever since had been central associates within his professional life and beloved figures within his personal world. Their reunion was an informal celebration of twenty years of precious, if sometimes unsettled friendship. Brother Nikolay also passed through, reporting that Ippolit had seen Georges-Léon, noted how like Tanya he was, but had still suspected nothing.

Meanwhile, when not in company, Tchaikovsky was becoming more aware of those special, simple pleasures which the country offered. Having in April left Maidanovo covered in snow, he was the more struck by how green and colourful all had become. He found himself paying increasing attention to the flowers in his garden, and the nature around him on his walks became less merely an attractive, peaceful environment for escape, more a treasury of individual wonders. A simple occupation like feeding chickens gave him pleasure; so, less properly, did using his binoculars to spy on his neighbours, especially during their evening meals. And if he wished to blunt the sharper edges of reality, there was always another resource to hand. At the heart of the four entries on Tolstoy in his special diary is one provoked by reading a condemnation of alcohol; it is both a vigorous defence of its efficacy for such as he, and an exposé of a personal situation clearly hinted at almost daily in his ordinary diary. 'I, i.e. a sick man filled with *neuroses* – emphatically couldn't manage without the *poison* . . . Each evening I'm drunk. . . . In the first phase of inebriation I feel the most complete happiness and in that condition *I understand* infinitely more than I understand when making do without . . . the poison!!! Nor have I noticed that my health has particularly suffered in consequence of it. But then: *quod licet Jovi, non licet bovi*,' he added contentedly.[49]

There were visits to Moscow, including two for celebrations connected with the silver jubilee of Jurgenson's publishing house, and one to hear the Russian Choral Society, of which Tchaikovsky was a trustee, participate in two festal services. On 1 March some of his Nine Sacred Pieces had received their first performances in a concert at the Conservatoire; now on 9 August, in the second of these services, one of his Cherubim's Songs was sung – the first time he had ever heard any of his church music within the liturgy itself. Though the departure of the Kondratyevs had depressed him, the sudden full revival of his creative urges in mid-August and the equally sudden improvement in the weather brought a renewal of spirit, fortified by a fortnight's visit from Modest and Kolya Konradi. They arrived on 28 August; two days later the sketches of *The Enchantress* were complete, and before their departure no less than ten of the Twelve Romances, Op. 60, had been

[49] *TD*, p. 211.

composed. 'In the spring the Gr[and] Duke Konstantin Konstan-tinovich informed me that the Empress would like me to dedicate *one* romance to her, and the Gr[and] D[uke] counselled me very earnestly to do this; moreover, he took upon himself to be the intermediary,' Tchaikovsky explained to Nadezhda von Meck on 15 September.[50] Though he had already hugely exceeded Her Imperial Majesty's modest specification, he still decided to add two more ('Last night' (No. 1) and 'Exploit' (No. 11; a 'monologue for baritone')) to make up what would be, according to his own normal practice, a double set. The Empress was to convey her delight at Tchaikovsky's offering by sending him a signed portrait of herself.

Since Tchaikovsky had only completed sketching *The Enchantress* the day before beginning these romances, it could not be expected he would find much residual strength in his creativity as he faced it with this further challenge, and his diary confirms that it was loyal zeal rather than flooding inspiration which decided him on so large a set of songs. Only one of the two after-thoughts can be numbered among his better romances, despite his delight in Khomyakov's verses and his own opinion that the music of both 'had come out very successfully',[51] better than in any of the others. The latter claim may well be true but is more a pointer to the indifferent quality of the rest. Part of the trouble stemmed from the choice of verse, even more constricted in mood and content than in the Op. 57 songs of two years earlier. Though drawn from a variety of poets, a heavy pall hangs over the emotional world of nearly all of it. Love is mostly of the despairing, mute, past, lost, or long-suffering kind; in only one is it active and relished. Isolation and loneliness are recurring predicaments or situations, and in over half the songs night is the subject or the environment. Thus there is little in any of this verse that is bright or bracing, and the musical settings matchingly tread mostly rather drab and well worn expressive ground, facing the listener with easily assimilated ideas, garnished with har-monic dressing in which chromatic or brief dissonant touches provide an attractive light spice. There is scarcely a single moment which arrests, let alone disturbs. Whereas only two of the six songs in the preceding set, Op. 57, had formally prefigured the opening vocal phrase in the piano preamble (and on both occasions merely approx-imately), nine of the twelve new songs do so; moreover, the anticipation is almost always exact. In many such songs this initial idea, which may itself be highly repetitive or sequential, dominates what follows.

[50] *TLP*13, pp. 439–40; *TPM*3, p. 433.
[51] *TLP*13, p. 449; *TZC*3, p. 130; *TPB*, p. 364; *YDGC*, p. 384.

In the quality of its music, therefore, this set is at times dispiriting. There are even some dismally trite moments. A composer of Tchaikovsky's experience had no business to slide into so commonplace a sequence as in the last two bars of Ex. 227, even after music as

Ex. 227

[And why do I love you, gentle night? You do not send me — you send others peace!

What to me are the stars, the moon, the horizon, the clouds?]

watery as that which precedes it. 'Night' (No. 9), from which this example comes, is anonymous notespinning from beginning to end;

'Frenzied nights' (No. 6), to verses by his friend Apukhtin, is much the same in character and scarcely less tedious. Among their companions are better songs. Although 'I'll tell you nothing' (No. 2) is also in that compound metre into which dactyllic verse so easily tempted Tchaikovsky, and is as flaccid rhythmically as these last two, its melodic contours are stronger. So are those of 'O, if only you knew' (No. 3) which exploits expressive duality, chromaticism, and modifications within its last two strophes to project an ever-growing cry of loneliness. Both 'Forgive' (No. 8) and 'The mild stars shone for us' (No. 12) start well enough, but both falter, sometimes through loss of melodic distinctiveness, sometimes by running out of harmonic steam. Tchaikovsky's response to 'The nightingale' (No. 4), a translation by Pushkin (from Vuk Stefanović Karadzić) of a young man's grief at the loss of his beloved, shows that his interest, as with Mignon in his most famous romance, is less in inner suffering than the surface manifestations of misery – though in no way does this new setting match the melodic eloquence of 'None but the lonely heart' of seventeen years earlier. The mild gipsy tang of 'Gipsy's song' (No. 7) helps to make this one of the most attractive of the set, and 'Exploit' (No. 11) is suitably imposing in manner. The cheery enticements of 'Behind the window in the shadow' (No. 10) are matched with adequate impudence (and a mischievous out-of-key conclusion). Nor, having chosen a waltz to be the dressing for the 'Simple words' (No. 5) he himself devised as blatant tribute to his imperial dedicatee, could he fail completely.

But the best of these romances is the first, 'Last night', an ecstatic contemplation of nocturnal beauty. The source phrase (Ex. 228), though little more than charming, is still made to hold sway during more than half the song; nevertheless, the unusual metrical structure of Khomyakov's poem (doubtless this is what Tchaikovsky found so 'original'[52]) precluded a rigid symmetry in the musical sentences, and

Ex. 228

[52] *ibid.*

Tchaikovsky handled his source phrase with flexibility, sometimes using it complete, but more often without the last bar, and occasionally stretching the centre with an extra beat. Repetitiveness can convey admirably the intensity of rapture; equally, it makes more striking the breaking into new melodic and tonal territory when, as joy in this world turns into longing for heaven, the graceful source phrase can no longer contain all the poet's exaltation. The singer's subsequent return to the opening music is absolutely right; then a moment of quiet reflection, and the piano prelude is heard again, now infused with the ripplings of joy which have grown in the song.

'Last night' is not a great song – but it is endearing. That Tchaikovsky could have linked such a thoughtful creation to companions so often indifferent, even momentarily banal, is probably as much a reflection on his continuing view of the romance as upon his lack of critical discrimination. Though he was perfectly capable of producing distinguished songs within the conventions of the genre, worthy to be performed at concerts, romances were primarily fodder for domestic consumption, where the expressive demands and critical rigour of the concert hall or opera house scarcely applied. This being so, we should perhaps fret less over the slightness of songs like most of these, but rather fortify our respect for the modest distinctiveness of the better examples.

The onset of autumn brought some benefits. The summer malaise which perennially afflicted him began to disappear, that most substantial hindrance to his own occupation – the noise of pianos from the surrounding dachas – departed with the summer inhabitants, and the proprietress of the estate, who constantly irritated him, took herself off to Moscow. With the removal of all these aggravations the notion which had this year again constantly recurred to him of seeking new accommodation also receded. But the inevitable and unavoidable calls of Moscow resumed. There were formalities connected with the opening of the conservatoire session, and a special gala performance on 4 October of 'the best of Rubinstein's operas',[53] *The Demon*, conducted by the composer to celebrate twenty-five years of service to the Bolshoy Theatre by the designer, Karl Waltz. It was Waltz who, after an unhappy contribution to *Swan Lake*, had shared far more successfully in the premières of both *Onegin* and *Mazepa*, and he was the designated designer of *Cherevichki*. Tchaikovsky's visit uncovered anxieties about this impending production, for the new head of the Imperial Theatres in Moscow, Apollon Alexandrovich Maikov, was a novice in such

[53] *TLP*13, p. 460; *TPM*3, p. 439; *YDGC*, p. 386.

matters and, it seemed, ill-disposed to Russian music in general and to Tchaikovsky's in particular. At the supper after Rubinstein's performance rumours reached Tchaikovsky that Maikov was already intriguing against Altani, the conductor at the Bolshoy and a person Tchaikovsky liked and respected, both as man and musician. Incensed, he devoted his own speech to a eulogy of Altani, to the visible annoyance of Maikov who, he now feared, would probably revenge himself through non-cooperation during the preparations for mounting *Cherevichki*. A further cause for anxiety was Laroche. Taneyev had finally lost patience with his neglect of his conservatoire classes and was requiring his dismissal. But Tchaikovsky, perhaps recalling his own *modus exeundi* nine years earlier, proposed that the truant teacher should be granted a year's leave of absence, during which he could fade naturally from the scene.

The affairs of the RMS were an even greater cause of concern, for the membership had fallen by one third in a single season. Yet the greatest current tension came from his work on *The Enchantress*. In his anxiety to despatch the scoring, he was driving himself too hard; overwork finally took its toll, and headaches like a 'nail' driven into the brain beset him. From experience he knew the only cure was a complete break from work, and on 30 October he arrived in St Petersburg to stay with Modest. Apart from his swift passage through the city on his return from Paris, it was seven months since he had been there, and he reassured himself on how Georges-Léon had settled, and met a host of other family members. Above all, he spent much time with his nephew Bob, now fifteen, as tall as Tchaikovsky himself, and much more handsome than before. He also had a good deal of contact with Rimsky-Korsakov and those around him. The tone of Tchaikovsky's judgements upon these various fellow-professionals had changed greatly. Nearly nine years before, when his feelings of personal isolation and professional insecurity had been at their strongest, he had provided a ruthless dissection of the Kuchka for his patroness.[54] But Musorgsky, the most mutually antipathetic of the group, was dead (invited in December 1885 to attend the consecration of a memorial above his grave, Tchaikovsky had been grateful for an excuse to absent himself), and Cui, for all his damning reviews of Tchaikovsky's music, was by now no more than a predictable critical irritant, and certainly no threat as a rival composer. Meanwhile the technical expertise which Rimsky-Korsakov had laboriously acquired, and which was evident from the beginning in the work of a younger, professionally trained composer

[54] Printed in Vol. 2, pp. 228–30.

like Glazunov, was bound to win Tchaikovsky's respect. He remained prepared to be critical when necessary, and earlier in the year he had sent Rimsky-Korsakov an unsparingly frank judgement of his new textbook on harmony. Yet at the same time he had promised to ensure both Rimsky-Korsakov and Glazunov performances of their works in Moscow concerts, and when his plans had misfired, he had made urgent covert efforts to redeem his pledge, especially to the senior composer ('such an outstanding figure, and so worthy of every respect', as he had characterized Rimsky-Korsakov privately to Jurgenson[55]).

Tchaikovsky arrived in St Petersburg in time to hear several of the concerts of Russian music which Mitrofan Belyayev was promoting, one of which included what seems to have been the first complete performance in the capital of Tchaikovsky's First Symphony. For his own part, he certainly heard and admired Rimsky-Korsakov's newly revised Third Symphony, had good words for Glazunov's Second Overture on Greek themes, met Balakirev and Vladimir Stasov (through whom he learned that he had been awarded a third 500-rouble Glinka prize, this time for the Manfred Symphony), and made the personal acquaintance of Anatol Lyadov, another composer of Rimsky-Korsakov's circle towards whom his attitude had radically changed. Nearly seven years earlier, when Bessel had sent Tchaikovsky a new Arabesque for piano by this twenty-four-year-old former composition student of Rimsky-Korsakov, who had already won Musorgsky's warm approval, he had evaluated Lyadov very differently. 'It is impossible to envisage anything more vapid in content than this composer's music. He has many interesting chords and harmonic sequences, but not a single idea, even of the tiniest sort,' he had told Bessel.[56] But even before this present visit he had singled out Lyadov as a musician to whom a score of the Manfred Symphony should be presented, and the personal acquaintance he now made with this indolent, fastidious, very private, yet very engaging individual seems to have worked wonders; 'dear Lyadov' he was to become.[57] 'I have always tried to place myself *outside* all parties and to show in every way possible that I love and respect every honourable and gifted public figure in music, whatever his tendency,' Tchaikovsky was to write on 7 January 1889 to the recipient of his earlier adjudication of the Kuchka, having again that season been handsomely represented in Belyayev's concerts. '. . . And so I was very glad to use the opportunity to show publicly that, though Mr Cui, an individual deeply hateful to me,

[55] *TLP*13, p. 235; *TZC*3, p. 86; *TPJ*2, p. 35.
[56] *TLP*9, p. 36.
[57] *TLP*15A, p. 208.

belongs to the school which is called the "new Russian" or "the mighty handful", this in no way hinders me from respecting and loving such representatives of the school as Balakirev, Rimsky-Korsakov, Lyadov, Glazunov, or from considering myself flattered to appear on the concert platform alongside them.'[58] And in this declaration of wholehearted readiness to be heard with such skilled and accomplished creators is an implicit confidence that now he had absolutely nothing to fear from any comparisons which might be made.

Tchaikovsky took the opportunity to see the operas which interested him in the current repertoire (*Ruslan*, *Faust* and *Lohengrin*), but the main musical objective of this trip – to attend, diplomatically, the première of Nápravník's *Harold* – was thwarted when the opera had to be postponed. There was little rest to be found in all these activities, and he returned to Maidanovo on 21 November, grateful to be alone again. Yet it had been a very cheering three weeks. Quite apart from the obvious deep respect he enjoyed with his fellow musicians, he had again savoured that awareness which had grown on him in Tiflis: that his music was not merely liked but loved by a very wide public. 'From everywhere, at every step in St Petersburg I encountered so many expressions of sympathy and love that frequently I was moved to tears,' he recalled for his patroness the day after his return to Maidanovo.[59] Five days earlier the St Petersburg Chamber Music Society (CMS), which had just elected him an honorary member, had presented a concert devoted entirely to his works, including the Second String Quartet and the Piano Trio. 'The enthusiasm was genuine, and I left overwhelmed with a feeling of emotion and gratitude. Two days later I was still thoroughly out-of-sorts from the emotions I had experienced,' he continued.[60] Such high valuation by this particular society was especially significant, for, according to Modest, the membership was drawn mainly from the German community in the city, a group thoroughly familiar with the classics of Western chamber music. Meanwhile in the Imperial Theatres plans were already being made for a splendid production of the still unfinished *Enchantress*.

Greatly encouraged, Tchaikovsky returned to Maidanovo to resume scoring the opera. But soon the headaches and other symptoms returned, making work impossible. He was dismayed, therefore, when on 31 November a telegram from Moscow informed him that his presence was required urgently at the Bolshoy. His first thought was to telegraph that he could not come, and he was immediately overwhelmed by an

[58] *TLP*14, pp. 610–11; *TPM*3, pp. 560–1; *YDGC*, p. 460.
[59] *TLP*13, p. 493; *TPM*3, p. 448.
[60] *ibid.* and *YDGC*, p. 392 (partial).

attack of hysterics. But within half an hour, to his amazement, his symptoms had vanished. Like his haemorrhoidal pains, it had all been his nerves, he concluded. Leaving for Moscow, the following day he plunged into supervising the rehearsals of *Cherevichki*, the first three performances of which he was himself to conduct.

On balance it had been a good year. Tiflis and the cruise had provided one of the most truly enjoyable phases of his whole life: that much is apparent from the happy recollections of it which recur in his letters for weeks after his return from Paris. Paris itself had been worth enduring for the hopes it raised, and while the summer had been poor in weather, it had been productive. Yet as always, even in more cheerful periods, there had been those constant bouts of irritation and depression which make it difficult for the biographer to discern with any certainty whether the prevailing trend in his subject's morale is towards greater confidence and light, or deeper gloom and 'misanthropy'. In this regard there are two further pieces of evidence which, while setting themselves by their very nature to expose Tchaikovsky to a wider world, in fact disclose even more than was perhaps intended. The first is a letter. In July Jurgenson had received a request from Marie Lipsius, known as La Mara, who was compiling the second volume of her anthology of letters by eminent musicians of the last five hundred years: had he one of Tchaikovsky's which she might include? Finding none suitable, Jurgenson turned to Tchaikovsky himself. On 31 July the composer replied:

Dear friend,
  I understand very well the difficulty of your position. You are asked for some letter of mine to print; you have several hundred of them – yet there is not a single one which would be appropriate for the given situation. This is understandable: our correspondence has always been either too much of a business nature, or else too intimate. But how can I aid you in your misfortune? Might I not, for the pleasure of appearing in Miss *La Mara*'s book, commit forgery, i.e. write a letter especially for her collection, and use the occasion to display myself as musician, thinker and man in the most favourable light? Such a brand of sacrifice on the altar of European fame sickens me, though on the other hand I should tell a lie if I were to set about assuring you that I was not at all gratified by Miss *La Mara*'s desire to add me to the number of eminent musicians of our time. On the contrary, I am very touched and flattered by the attention of this well-known writer, and with complete sincerity I admit that I should

be happy to find myself in the company of Glinka, Dargomïzhsky and Serov. If there were plenty of time, it would have been possible to turn to one of my musical friends – for example, to *Laroche*, who has not a few letters of mine which contain detailed revelations of my musical likes and dislikes – in a word, letters where I speak my mind with complete openness as a musician. But time is lacking, and Laroche is far away.

Is it not curious that difficulty is encountered in finding a letter from a man who has conducted – and conducts – a most massive correspondence such as only a person engaged, not in material undertakings [sic], but in artistic labour would carry on? I engage in perpetual written correspondence with my four brothers, my sister, several cousins, a lot of friends and acquaintances – and in addition to this I have a huge casual correspondence with people whom often I do not know at all. Frequently I am so burdened by the need to give too large a portion of my time to correspondence that I inwardly curse all the postal organisations in the world. The post often causes me painful moments, but it also brings me the greatest joys. There is a being who has played a pre-eminent role in the story of my life for the last ten years. This being is my good fairy; I am obliged to her for all my happiness and for the possibility of devoting myself entirely to my beloved work – and yet I have never seen her, have never heard the sound of her voice, and all my relations with her are exclusively by post. Generally it might be said that I flood the whole world with my letters – and still I cannot extricate you from your difficulty.

There remains but one thing: to send to Miss *La Mara* my present letter. If it in no way characterizes me as a musician, then at least it enables you to satisfy this writer's flattering desire to number my person among the eminent.

Farewell!

P. Tchaikovsky[61]

Underlying this letter is a rare self-assurance. No one, surely, could believe that the thought of making this his contribution to La Mara's compendium had occurred to Tchaikovsky only as he began the last paragraph. Very self-consciously from the beginning it was to be his exhibition piece. It is casual but calculated – inconsequential yet designed teasingly to lift a little the corners of the mantle with which Tchaikovsky so habitually and closely cloaked his personal world.

---

[61] *TLP*13, pp. 407–8; *TPJ*2, pp. 46–7; *TZC*3, pp. 120–1. Before the end of the year Jurgenson's German translation had appeared in La Mara's anthology: *Musikerbriefe aus fünf Jahrhunderten*, Vol. 2 (Leipzig, 1886).

Most extraordinary of all is the explicit allusion to one of the most central, sensitive, and closely guarded secrets of his whole life: his relationship with his benefactress. Of course, a tantalizing morsel like this was bound to make him appear the more interesting – a man with an intriguing side, still more than half-hidden. But merely to mention his 'good fairy' was to hazard the unstoppable prying of the wider world. Tchaikovsky can hardly have been unaware of this; that he should have been prepared to face it is yet another telling sign of his new level of self-confidence and of his awareness – and relish – of his own celebrity.

The second is an entry in his special diary. On 2 October, some two months after his dicta on Tolstoy, he returned to this giant once again. Then, suddenly, the subject and purpose of his writing change. He begins to note down his own personal tastes in music, assesses a variety of composers, and confesses his own musical god. As a private record all this would, of course, be worth quoting for what it might teach us about Tchaikovsky himself, if not about the composers who are his subjects. But this time he is no longer writing simply a private record. He is writing for posterity, self-consciously revealing something of himself. He is now famous, he knows he fascinates others, is an object of their curiosity in a way few ever are; moreover, he is prepared to gratify that curiosity, albeit posthumously.

Probably after my death it will be not without interest to know what were my musical passions and prejudices, the more so since I rarely express them in conversation. . . .

I'll begin with *Beethoven*, whom it is unquestioningly assumed is to be praised to the skies, and to whom it is enjoined to bow as before God. And so what is Beethoven to me?

I bow before the greatness of some of his compositions – but I *do not love* Beethoven. My attitude to him reminds me of that which in childhood I experienced in regard of the God *of Sabaoth*. I nourished (and even now my feelings have not changed) for Him a feeling of wonder but, at the same time, of fear. He has created the heavens and the earth. He has also created me – and so I prostrate myself before Him – but *love* is not there. On the other hand, it is precisely and exclusively a feeling of *love* that *Christ* arouses. Though he was *God*, he was at the same time a man . . . And if *Beethoven* occupies in my heart a place like that of the God of Sabaoth, then I love *Mozart* like a musical Christ . . . Mozart was a being so angelic, of such child-like purity, his music is so full of unapproachable, divine beauty that if anyone may be named alongside Christ, then it is he . . . It is my profound conviction that *Mozart* is the highest, the supreme point attained by *beauty* in the sphere of music. No one other than he has made me weep, tremble with joy from recognition of the closeness to *something* which we call the *ideal* . . .

I do not know how *to discourse* on music and I shall not go into detail. However I will note two small points:

1. In *Beethoven* I like the middle period, sometimes the first, but in essence I *hate* the last, especially the last quartets. Here there are *flashes* – nothing more. The rest is *chaos* above which floats the spirit of that musical God of *Sabaoth* shrouded in impenetrable mist.

2. In *Mozart* I love *everything* . . . above all, *Don Giovanni*, for thanks to that I learned what *music* is . . . Of course, *loving* all Mozart, I shall not claim that every most insignificant piece of his is a *masterpiece*. No! For instance, I know that not one of his *sonatas* is a great work, but *yet* I love each *sonata* of his because it is *his* . . .

Of the predecessors of these two I will say that I willingly play *Bach* because *it is entertaining* to play a good fugue, but I do not recognize in him (as others do) great genius. For me *Handel* is completely fourth-rate, and he is not even entertaining. *Gluck*, despite the relative poverty of his creative work, I find sympathetic. I *love* a little of *Haydn*. But all these four *great men* come together in *Mozart*. He who knows Mozart knows what was good in these four, for being the greatest and most powerful of musical *creators*, he did not disdain both to take them under his wing and save them from oblivion. They are the rays lost in the sun of – Mozart.[62]

This summer Tchaikovsky had communed with the score of Mozart's supreme work; the next year, 1887, would be the centenary of its first revelation to the world. Already he was preparing his own tribute.

---

[62] *TD*, pp. 212–13; *TZC*3, pp. 132–3 (partial); *YDGC*, pp. 385–6 (partial).

3

A NEW ACTIVITY:
TRIUMPHS AND SORROWS

'WHAT HAVE YOU decided about conducting your opera yourself? I still do not know why your friends torment you with this advice. In my view it is not only unnecessary but much better *not* to profane your person by this mounting of the rostrum before the eyes and judgement of the whole public. I consider *a composer* too *sacred* a being to exhibit himself thus before the crowd.'[1]

Two days later, on 17 October, Tchaikovsky answered his patroness:

What you say about *my conducting* is absolute balm to my torn heart. Just imagine, my dear friend: all my life I have been tormented by awareness of my *inability* to conduct. It has seemed to me there is something shameful and disreputable in not being able to stop myself trembling with fear and horror at the very thought of going out in front of the public with a baton. I sense that this time also, when the moment comes, I shall not have the courage and shall back away, even though I have given a promise that I will myself conduct.[2]

Tchaikovsky's view of the act of directing his own music had been deeply ambivalent ever since that occasion in March 1868 when he had mounted the rostrum at the Bolshoy to conduct the dances from his first opera, *The Voyevoda*, and had felt that his head would fall sideways unless he fought to keep it upright. Nine years later he had made a second attempt and had coped better. But terror had merely been smothered, he had not risked the experience a third time, and his persisting dread that now, at the last moment, he would not be able to face the ordeal was very real. Yet he knew there were many powerful reasons for overcoming these nervous fears. For all Nadezhda von Meck's words, many of his fellow composers – Rubinstein, Balakirev, Rimsky-Korsakov, Taneyev, Nápravník, the young Ippolitov-Ivanov –

---

[1] *TPM*3, p. 442.
[2] *TLP*13, pp. 472–3; *TPM*3, p. 443; *TZC*3, p. 136.

were also conductors. Quite apart from the extra income which the activity might generate, it would enable Tchaikovsky to shape his music as he wished, it would mean that the occasions for performances of his works would increase greatly, and he would be able to take his music to places where the local musicians knew little or nothing of it. Nor can he have been unaware that a conductor could enjoy more celebrity in his own time than a composer. He had mooted the idea that he should take charge of the first performance of *Cherevichki* a year earlier when Altani's illness had caused postponement of the planned production, and during 1886 the urge to make the attempt had grown so strong that by the time he responded to the summons to Moscow, it had become as important a factor as the production itself.

When, after a fortnight of piano rehearsals, he had to face the orchestra, he fared better than he could have dared to hope. The preliminary rehearsals had gone well and his mood and physical condition were surprisingly good, despite still spending three or more hours each day scoring *The Enchantress*. He had sought private coaching from Altani, yet his suffering before the event itself was acute. 'Time after time I was on the point of deciding not to conduct. But in the end I somehow got control of myself, arrived, was enthusiastically received by the players, made quite a brave speech, and began waving my stick very confidently,' he told Modest. 'Now already I know *I can conduct*, and that at the performance I shall hardly be afraid.'[3]

Neither was he, once it had begun. Because preparations took longer than at first envisaged, the première was to be postponed until the last day of January, for to mount a new opera during the Christmas and New Year festivities could be disastrous. After a fortnight's break at Maidanovo with Modest and Laroche, during which he again made time to act as amanuensis for the latter, Tchaikovsky transferred to his benefactress's Moscow house, where he was better insulated from the outside world. There were seven orchestral rehearsals, in the course of which the singers and the orchestral players showed great consideration and support, and at the dress rehearsal all went well. On the morning of the première, 31 January 1887, he woke feeling ill. 'Nevertheless,' he wrote to Pavlovskaya,

neither dead nor alive, I appeared at the theatre at the appointed hour. Altani led me out to the orchestra – whereupon the curtain immediately rose and they started presenting wreaths from the

[3] *TLP*13, p. 518; *TPM*3, p. 639; *TPJ*2, p. 285; *TZC*3, p. 149; *DTC*, p. 135; *TPB*, p. 371.

orchestra, the choruses, etc., to thunderous applause. While this was going on I recovered somewhat, began the overture well, and by the overture's end was already conducting with complete confidence. The overture was vigorously applauded. The first act went through successfully, though much less well than at the dress rehearsal. After the first act more wreaths were presented . . . The performers and I were called out many times. I was now thoroughly composed and conducted the rest of the opera with total calm. The audience laughed a lot in the first scene of Act 2. Between the scenes in this act I got up and bowed several times. It seemed to me the third act pleased less than the second, but all the same there was applause, a little of it was encored, and both I and the performers took many calls. At the conclusion there were many very warm curtain calls. It's difficult to say whether the opera really pleased. Half the audience, if not more, were my friends, and it's not surprising I was given a lot of ovations. But time and the *real* audience at the following perform-ances will show whether the applause was for the opera or for me personally for previous services.[4]

However, the '*real* audience' was to have little chance to declare its verdict. Tchaikovsky himself was delighted with the performance in general, and with the production. Vsevolozhsky had been responsible for commissioning the scenery and costumes before the Moscow and St Petersburg administrations had been divided, and Waltz's sets were magnificent, though the costumes reflected the austerities of Maikov's new regime. Press reaction was highly respectful. The musical riches were gratefully acknowledged, but there was less appreciation of the dramatic qualities of the piece. Tchaikovsky piloted himself as well as his musicians through two more evenings, there were full houses despite the higher price tariff, each time the audience warmed as the opera proceeded, and the final applause was very enthusiastic. Yet after only five performances the management decided to withdraw the work. Tchaikovsky saw, perhaps with justification, the hand of Maikov behind this. Relations with the director had soured further when Maikov had refused a request to make the première of *Cherevichki* the orchestra's benefit performance. Tchaikovsky had enlisted the help of both Vsevolozhsky and the Grand Duke Konstantin Konstantinovich, but the former no longer had any power to intervene, and though the Grand Duke's approach to the Tsar drew a favourable response, it

---

[4] *TLP*14, pp. 20–1; *TZC*3, pp. 154–5; *DTC*, pp. 136–7; *TPM*3, p. 639 (partial); *TPJ*2, p. 285 (partial). For a summary of the plot, a critical examination of the opera, and some account of Tchaikovsky's revisions, see Vol. 1, pp. 313–35.

produced no action. Inevitably the incident did nothing to dispose Maikov more warmly towards *Cherevichki*. There were plans to present two further performances the following season, but these were to be cancelled. Thus the chance of hearing again this delightful opera, which always remained one of Tchaikovsky's own favourite creations, was never to be granted him.

Nevertheless, this production proved a watershed in Tchaikovsky's own professional life. Despite Modest's belief that the first-night audience was hardly aware of his brother's role as conductor, several critics commented favourably on Tchaikovsky's début. Most important of all for the future, perhaps, was Tchaikovsky's own view, and he was obviously as delighted as he was surprised at what he had discovered he could accomplish. Only a year later, with one international tour as conductor already behind him, he could himself weigh the significance of this venture, assess his own ability confidently, and point proudly to one 'first' he had scored. Like his pronouncements quoted earlier on Mozart and Beethoven, this record was intended for posterity.

> I was already almost forty-seven. At this age a real, true, born conductor already has, besides qualities which depend on his degree of natural talent, many years of experience. If you bear in mind that I did not possess this, then my début can be described as completely successful. I continue to think that I lack a conductor's real endowment, I know that I do not have in me that combination of mental and physical attributes which makes a musician *in general* into a conductor *in particular*. But this and all my subsequent attempts have proved that I *can* more or less successfully direct a performance of my own works – and for my greater well-being this is exactly what was necessary. . . . In the series of incalculably beneficial consequences of this there was, finally, that three-month concert tour of mine to Western Europe . . . If we exclude Glinka, who only once gave a concert in Paris, and A[nton] Rubinstein who, thanks to his genius as a virtuoso, has already long since penetrated abroad and acquired the right to citizenship of the stages and concert platforms of the whole world, then I was fated to be the first Russian composer personally to acquaint foreign listeners with his own works.[5]

And when he wrote this in April 1888, he had only just begun this process.

Nor was the dispute with Maikov the only diplomatic incident in

---

[5] *TMKS*, p. 335; *DTC*, p. 136 (partial).

which Tchaikovsky became embroiled during the preparations of
Cherevichki. The fiftieth anniversary of the first performance of Glinka's
A Life for the Tsar had fallen in the middle of rehearsals, and Cui had
published an article in Bessel's *Music Survey* à propos the event, during
which he had censured Nápravník for lack of sympathy towards
Russian music, citing in particular the case of Tchaikovsky's *Onegin.*
Tchaikovsky may privately have felt there was substance in Cui's
charge, but he knew that Nápravník had still been his best advocate in
the St Petersburg theatres, and he was depending on him to shape the
fortunes of *The Enchantress* during the following season. In his article Cui
had alleged an attempt by Nápravník to dissuade Tchaikovsky from
mounting *Onegin* in the Imperial Theatres, and Tchaikovsky realized
that to remain silent might seem confirmation of Cui's words. The
affair developed into an unseemly argument about who had said what,
Bessel claiming he had himself heard Nápravník offer this advice,
Tchaikovsky hotly protesting that, since he had never requested that
Onegin should be mounted by the Imperial Theatres in either St
Petersburg or Moscow, the conversation could never have taken place.
For many years his relations with Bessel had been deteriorating and the
latter's reply to his telegram of denial had already infuriated him. 'I
never engage in lying or fabrications, but I *serve truth*,' Bessel had begun
loftily, 'exactly as my esteemed contributor does. I am returning your
telegram because I do not wish it to serve as a demonstration of your
precipitate way of behaving. Memory may deceive a man, but facts
remain for ever.'[6] Nevertheless Bessel printed Tchaikovsky's letter
defending Nápravník, but added an unctuous editorial refutation of a
sort Tchaikovsky had expressly forbidden if Bessel chose to publish his
letter at all. This certainly provided good entertainment for *Music
Survey*'s readers, but it brought Tchaikovsky's anger to boiling point.
Scalded to the quick, on 10 January he wrote one of the most furious
and uncompromising letters of his life.

> I return to your demonstration of my, as you are pleased to call it,
> *'precipitate way of behaving'.*
>   1. I requested you to print a simple denial of a false fact. This you
> have not done.
>   2. I requested you not to add to my explanation your reservations
> which are, withal, based on a fact which in reality never existed and
> which, if it had, proves absolutely nothing, since no one can reprove
> Nápravník for an honestly expressed opinion about the opera lacking

[6] Quoted in *TLP*13, p. 527.

scenic effectiveness since I admit it is scenically ineffective. This also has not been done.

3. Not only have you not fulfilled my demand, but you have permitted yourself to add at the conclusion of your reservation hints that I had taken Nápravník's part only out of *self-interest*.

After all this I sever *once and for ever* all relations with your firm and with you personally.

I rejoice that you and your esteemed contributor serve *truth*. But I also serve *truth*, and because our *truths* diverge, it is not fitting that we should know each other.

P. Tchaikovsky[7]

Such matters, however distressing they may be, touch none of those more sensitive feelings which belong to the world of personal and especially family relationships; nor are the shocks they occasion likely to be as brutal as those which may come from human catastrophe. Tchaikovsky was cruelly reminded of this the day following the première of *Cherevichki*. Returning home with Modest at five in the morning in a radiantly happy mood such as his brother had rarely seen possess him, he retired to his room and fell sound asleep. Two hours later Modest was roused by the delivery of a telegram. He let his brother sleep till eleven; then, when he emerged still buoyant from the excitements of the previous day, Modest broke the news that their niece Tanya, whom they had both watched over during her pregnancy in Paris, of whose son Tchaikovsky had been the principal protector, and who, it seemed, had been gaining some control over her life in a way that gave hope of a future less disordered than her past, had collapsed and died during a masked ball in St Petersburg. For Tchaikovsky it was a grievous shock. He eased his sorrow by reflections on fate and upon memories of long-passed, happier times. His words to Parasha the next day would appear sentimental, were it not that they echoed so truly the joy in his eldest niece he had expressed during happier times at Kamenka. 'Poor Tanya! Now that all's finished, you involuntarily forget all her dark sides, and remember only what a marvellous girl she was twelve years ago.'[8] The blow, he said, made it more difficult for him when for a second time he had to guide the performers through his opera. 'It's time to go home! Oh, how it's time!' he wrote wearily to Modest after that performance.[9] He had to break the news to Anna, did

---

[7] *TLP*13, pp. 539–40.
[8] *TLP*14, p. 26.
[9] *TLP*14, p. 30; *TZC*3, p. 158; *TPB*, p. 374.

what he could to support her, and saw with much relief that preoccupation with her new-born daughter provided distraction. With the rest
of the Moscow relatives he attended a special celebration of the Office
for the Dead; then, his term as conductor of *Cherevichki* completed, on
10 February he was back in Maidanovo.

There was no chance to rest, however. Only Act 1 of *The Enchantress*
had been orchestrated, but even more pressing now was the need to
deliver the vocal score for engraving so that the chorus might begin to
learn their parts. It took eleven days to complete what had been started
many weeks earlier; the wonder is that it was completed so soon. Yet
Tchaikovsky seems to have had an extraordinary capacity to live each
day to the full. For a year now he had kept an unbroken diary whose
record shows that, even when the rehearsals of *Cherevichki* were at their
most demanding, he could cram in a multitude of other activities. On
that momentous day when, after a sleepless night and a dose of vodka,
he had for the first time stood smothering his agitation in front of the
orchestra, he could still return home, dine, visit the singer Alexandra
Panayeva whose faltering professional fortunes he was doing all in his
power to restore, then head for the Conservatoire to hear his Piano
Sonata, meet three people, and finally write two substantial letters, one
a further most sensitive expression of that understanding which
marked his continual moral support of Yuliya Shpazhinskaya. Then,
after only five days back in Maidanovo following upon his labours for
Cherevichki, he was caught in the fiasco of Alexey's wedding (the bride
had run away, and the groom who, Tchaikovsky thought, seemed
rather glad, insisted there should be a wild drinking party to justify the
200 roubles he had laid out on the occasion). That very evening
Tchaikovsky had to leave for Moscow to attend the wedding of Ziloti,
who was marrying one of Parasha's cousins, a daughter of the art
collector, Pavel Tretyakov. This was only one event in two turbulent
days. The pattern of the first, as recorded in his diary, is typical of such
visits. It began at Jurgenson's; then he visited his publisher's engraver,
listened to the choir of the Russian Synod's School, talked with one of
the officials, negotiated some arrangement with a bass soloist at the
Conservatoire, visited the class of Giacomo Galvani, one of the professors of singing, called on Albrecht's wife with his pianist-friend,
Nikolay Zverev, then lunched. After collecting his patroness's monthly
allowance from a bank, he dropped in upon the dress rehearsal of a new
opera, discussed Panayeva with Altani, had talks with the singer
Bogomir Korsov, returned to the Conservatoire to listen to a choir and
disapprove its choice of music, dined out with Albrecht, met Laroche,
and arrived home at midnight.

The consultation with Korsov doubtless concerned the affairs of the Imperial Opera. Maikov's inept handling of the benefit issue at *Cherevichki*'s première was only the first ominous sign of an autocratic ruthlessness which soon had all sections of the opera company against its director. Korsov, who had created the name part in *Mazepa* and had just delighted Tchaikovsky with his Devil in *Cherevichki*, had been one of the first to attempt a counter attack, and had already canvassed Tchaikovsky's support before the latter's return to Maidanovo. Though Tchaikovsky doubted his name carried the weight Korsov credited to it, by early May he had agreed to write to Count Vorontsov-Dashkov, Maikov's superior, protesting at the decimation of the opera company which Maikov was effecting by wholesale dismissals in the name of economy. A further fortnight, and Tchaikovsky was begging Vsevolozhsky to find a place in his St Petersburg company for Alexandra Krutikova, Tchaikovsky's choice for Solokha in *Cherevichki*, who was the latest victim of Maikov's austerity measures. Events now moved swiftly, and within a month the tyrant had been removed. What role Tchaikovsky's representations played in securing Maikov's departure is not clear; what is self-evident is, yet again, the readiness with which he would give of his time to help causes he valued and especially persons he respected.

The concern he felt for Arensky's creative welfare found a very different kind of expression – tough and uncompromising, though no less valuable to the young composer. During the three-and-a-half months Tchaikovsky was now to spend mostly at Maidanovo, he was to allow himself no true break, though during Easter week Bob visited and he was able to recapture with this fifteen-year-old something of that pleasure in childish things he had so enjoyed with Tanya and Bob's other sisters years before at Kamenka; in this instance he constructed with his nephew conduits and little canals for the water from melting snow, the two of them chattering all the while like a couple of magpies. Otherwise all Tchaikovsky's energies were devoted with ever increasing intensity to despatching *The Enchantress*, as well as checking the proofs of the choral parts and vocal score. He even excused himself from attending the two concerts Saint-Saëns gave in Moscow in early May, despite a personal invitation from the Frenchman. His reason, so he told his benefactress, was that he knew Saint-Saëns would be performing to a half-empty hall, and he did not wish to embarrass the visitor by witnessing his humiliation. But he was also aware that such a refusal would do nothing to help the cause of his own music in France.

Nevertheless, amid all this he still made time to scrutinize a new orchestral fantasia, *Marguerite Gautier*, which Arensky had composed, dedicated to Tchaikovsky, and sent him in December with a request for criticism. It was the more important Tchaikovsky should do this, for he had already told Taneyev something of his first impression, and this had come to Arensky's ears. The situation closely mirrored that of eighteen years earlier, when Balakirev, the dedicatee of Tchaikovsky's symphonic poem, *Fatum*, had written to Tchaikovsky his unsparing opinion of the piece.[10] The truths Tchaikovsky now had to set out were every bit as unpalatable, but there was a greater tact within his trenchant openness, and a more sensitive understanding of Arensky's inevitable reaction. The letter is worth quoting at length, for it also provides further evidence of certain of Tchaikovsky's tastes and attitudes, disclosing a notable primness in his view of what was an appropriate choice of subject, and a very acute perception of musical quality and character, even after no more than a cursory examination.

As Taneyev has correctly informed you, however much I might wish it, however much I may value your splendid talent, I indeed *do not like* your fantasia. It's easy to write a eulogy to a person you value highly, but very difficult to say to such a person: '*It's bad – I don't like it!*' unless you substantiate such a verdict with detailed explanation. If during all this past winter I had not had such an unusual accumulation of all sorts of affairs and troubles . . . then I should already have discharged the debt of gratitude and respect which is proper to such a talented artist as you. But . . . I kept postponing and postponing and have finally received your angry letter in which you make completely impossible and incredible suggestions that *I don't wish to reply to you*, that *I'm insulting you*, and so on. For what? Why? You know my opinion of you as an uncommonly gifted and well-schooled musician. As a person you have always inspired in me the most sincere sympathy, and to be able to suspect me of being capable of repaying with an insult the honour you have done me in the dedication of your fantasia you would have to suppose in me utter madness or unusual meanness of spirit. It would be much simpler to suppose (especially since Taneyev had told you my opinion) that I am procrastinating over my reply so as to postpone the unpleasantness of communicating to you *an uncomplimentary judgement*. Such an assumption would be much closer to the truth. . . . Again I thank you with my whole heart *for the dedication*. . . .

I'm not sending you a detailed critique of *Marguerite*, since for this it would be necessary to devote several days to careful study of it. . . . However, I'll give you my opinion in brief.

[10] For a major part of Balakirev's letter of 12 April 1869, see Vol. 1, pp. 170–1.

First, the choice of subject:

For me and for all your friends, it was simply *painful and distressing* to learn that you had chosen *La dame aux camélias* as the subject for your fantasia's programme. How can an educated musician choose a creation of M. *Dumas-fils*, portraying the adventures of a prostitute – and portraying these adventures, even though with an adroitness and *savoir faire* which is French, in a way that is in essence false, sentimental, and not devoid of vulgarity – when there is Homer, Shakespeare, Pushkin, Gogol, Tolstoy, Dante, Byron, Lermontov, and so on, and so on, and so on? Such a choice is comprehensible in *Verdi* [in *La traviata*] seeking a subject to strike at the nerves of people in a time of artistic decadence. But it is incomprehensible in a young, gifted Russian composer who has received a good education, is a pupil of R[imsky]-Korsakov . . . and a friend of *S. I. Taneyev*.

But the subject is a matter which lies outside my competence. I will pass over to the music:

1. *The orgy.* If we set aside the thought that by *orgy* here is understood a drinking party and ball at *some [slut's]* at which there is *a very large number of people*, that at this orgy they're drinking *champagne*, eating truffles with mayonnaise, and then dancing *the cancan* – then the music which depicts the orgy is not lacking in liveliness, fire, movement, sparkle. But it's steeped, as is the whole fantasia, in *Liszt*, and when it is examined closely, its beauty is *external, conventional*, and contains nothing within it to carry you away. Such *beauty* is not *absolute beauty*, but mere *prettiness* (conventional beauty) – and *continual prettiness* is a defect rather than a quality. *Rossini, Donizetti, Bellini, Mendelssohn, Massenet, Liszt*, and so on – their names are legion – are always pretty. Of course they are masters of their kind. But *their* predominant trait is not an ideal towards which we must strive, for neither *Beethoven* nor *Bach* (who is boring, but a genius all the same), nor *Glinka* nor *Mozart* pursued conventional *prettiness* but an ideal beauty which not infrequently manifests itself in a form which, at a first superficial glance, is not beautiful.

2. Pastoral in Bourgival . . . *is pretty* . . .

3. The love theme . . . is again very *pretty* and very much recalls Liszt – not some specific melody by Liszt, but his manner in general, the manner of his half-Italian melodies which yet lack the plasticity and simplicity of an Italian melody. However, the third and fourth bars of this theme and those following . . . contain something not merely *pretty* but also *beautiful*, able to enslave not only the ears but the heart.

It is obvious that in the development of these three themes, in the form, in the scoring, in the harmony, in the counterpoint you are in *Marguerite Gautier* the same master that you were before. . . .

To summarize all that has been said above . . . your fantasia is unsuccessful in its plan, unsympathetic in its subject, and its basic themes have little that captivates. It's infinitely less to my liking than your [First] Symphony and the three movements of your suite [Op. 7]. It emphatically is not *a step forward*, but a step, so to speak, sideways, and I would hope you would the more quickly return to your true path and rejoice us with new compositions even more sympathetic and perfect than the symphony and suite.[11]

Whether Arensky acquiesced in this unpalatable verdict as completely as Tchaikovsky had accepted Balakirev's strictures in 1869 seems unknown. But Tchaikovsky swiftly substantiated his continuing faith in Arensky by action. When in January he had told Nápravník he had written to Erdmannsdörfer, offering to sacrifice a performance of the Manfred Symphony in the RMS's concerts so that a work by Nápravník might be played, he was probably motivated less by idealism than a wish to sweeten the finest preparer and conductor of his operas ahead of the production of *The Enchantress*. But when in November he was to approach Rimsky-Korsakov suggesting that his (Tchaikovsky's) own *Romeo and Juliet* should be dropped from the Russian Symphony Concerts to make room for a piece by Arensky to help draw Rimsky-Korsakov's former pupil out of the depression into which he had sunk, he was acting from purely altruistic reasons. During the following years he was to give sterling support both to Arensky's work and to the composer himself. In 1890 he wrote to Arensky, à propos his opera, *A Dream on the Volga*, a letter of praise so warm and unqualified that the overwhelmed composer rushed from Moscow to Tchaikovsky's home at Frolovskoye to express his thanks. Two years later Tchaikovsky was using all his eloquence to persuade' Vsevolozhsky to set a time for the production of Arensky's still unfinished second opera, *Nal and Damayanti*, in the St Petersburg Imperial Theatres. He had already seen clearly signs of personal problems in prospect. 'Arensky's a man with an enormous talent,' he had written to Nadezhda von Meck in 1890, 'but there is something strange, unstable, unhealthily nervous and slightly, as it were, not quite normal mentally.'[12] Nevertheless, the years of Arensky's worst dissipations were still far ahead, and for the rest of Tchaikovsky's life Arensky remained a valued member of his social and musical circles.

[11] *TLP*14, pp. 79–80; *TZC*3, pp. 144–7; *YDGC*, p. 409 (partial).
[12] *TLP*15B, pp. 195–6; *TPM*3, p. 599; *TZC*3, p. 378 (partial).

As for the fortunes of Tchaikovsky's own music, the student concert which Taneyev conducted on 6 March, and which included four extracts from Act I of the as yet unfinished *Enchantress* (Kuma's arioso, the following chorus, the decimet, and the final chorus, 'Kak po lyudyam'), was as much a reminder to him of the urgency of his present labours as a proof of the keen interest being shown in the opera's forthcoming production. But the recital which Mackar had arranged eleven days earlier at the Salle Erard in Paris was a specially notable event, for it was the first time a concert consisting solely of Tchaikovsky's music had been mounted in a foreign country – moreover, without the composer present. True, for Mackar it was a promotional venture and admission was free; nevertheless, the hall overflowed, more than 200 of the 1000 patrons standing, and the programme – romances, piano pieces, the *Sérénade mélancolique* played by Marsick, and Brandukov performing a transcription of the Andante cantabile – was a great success. Yet for Tchaikovsky the real landmarks were the concerts he would himself conduct. The first was in St Petersburg on 17 March, with Panayeva as principal soloist. It was a touching idea to invite this singer to share in what Tchaikovsky hoped would be a highly successful occasion. Nine years earlier Anatoly had pursued her, but she had married their kinsman, Georgy Kartsov, and she was therefore within the family. Panayeva's problem was not her skill and artistry, which Tchaikovsky considered good if not outstanding, but her disorganized professional life. During his *Cherevichki* rehearsals he had spent much time with her and her husband trying to counsel and support, and his discussions with Altani when he revisited Moscow were, it seems, only one of a series of personal interventions he attempted on Panayeva's behalf. In St Petersburg he could now do something positive by asking the Philharmonic Society, whose concert it was, to invite her to participate.

When the Society had first approached Tchaikovsky in October he had refused to conduct, but after his success in the opera house he was longing to test himself on the concert platform. Though it was a charity concert the programme was substantial: the Second Suite, *Francesca da Rimini, 1812*, the middle movements from the Serenade for Strings, as well as the Tumblers' Dance and Kuma's Act I arioso from *The Enchantress*. Panayeva also sang three of Tchaikovsky's romances, and there were piano solos. Tchaikovsky had journeyed to St Petersburg immediately after Taneyev's student concert so that he might prepare himself thoroughly and also hear Eugen d'Albert, whose brilliance had prompted him to compose his Concert Fantasia for piano and orchestra and whom he had recently enthused about in Moscow, play concertos by Beethoven and d'Albert himself under Rubinstein's baton. There was poignancy in the occasion also, for the programme included the First Symphony and romances by Borodin, who had died suddenly only a week before. At the first rehearsal of his own concert on 12 March Tchaikovsky had again mastered his nerves and received an ovation from the performers, and at the third Balakirev had appeared with some of his associates. The concert itself was a huge success, several pieces being encored. The press was enthusiastic; even Cui was full of praise. But perhaps most significant for the future was the new self-awareness Tchaikovsky had experienced as a conductor. 'Of course I was very agitated before I went on,' he admitted to Nadezhda von Meck. 'But it was no longer fear but, rather, anticipation of that deep artistic joy which the composer experiences when he stands before a superb orchestra which is performing his work with love and enthusiasm. Delight of this kind was unknown to me until recently. It is so powerful and so extraordinary that it is impossible to express it in words. But if my attempts at conducting have cost me a colossal, painful struggle with myself, if they have cost me several years of life, I still do not regret it. I have experienced moments of unqualified happiness and bliss.'[13]

Ippolitov-Ivanov and his wife were visiting St Petersburg, had attended the concert, and on 26 March, two days after Tchaikovsky's own flight back to Maidanovo, they called upon him while en route for Moscow. Clearly they were a particularly engaging couple. At first he was angry at their intrusion – 'but afterwards these most dear people (she in particular has a rare sympathetic quality) made me forget everything except that the society of dear and good people is a priceless blessing,' as he wrote in his diary. '. . . Ivanov played and she sang delightful extracts from his opera (the duet in particular enchanted me).'[14] Tchaikovsky's enthusiasm was genuine, for at that time at least he felt he could detect some originality in Ippolitov-Ivanov's talent, and he was to try hard, but without success, to persuade the Bolshoy to produce *Ruth*.

The end of Tchaikovsky's time in St Petersburg had been both wearying and painful. On the last day he had visited Tanya's grave, but most distressing of all had been Kondratyev's health. In the summer he had realized his friend was sick, but now Kondratyev was obviously very seriously ill (in fact, he had syphilis), and the two men said goodbye almost as though they sensed they might never meet again. It

[13] *TLP*14, p. 58; *TPM*3, p. 468; *TZC*3, pp. 161–2; *TPB*, p. 608.
[14] *TD*, p. 132; *TZC*3, p. 163; *TLP*14, p. 63 (partial).

was Kondratyev's deteriorating condition which drew Tchaikovsky back to St Petersburg two months later for a week in which he spent time with his friend daily. After his especially concentrated labours on *The Enchantress* he knew he would be desperately in need of the summer break which had long been planned, but he feared Kondratyev was not much longer for this world, and even more than when they had parted earlier there was a sense of finality in their farewells. Now that Kondratyev was indeed dying, Tchaikovsky realized that fate had made him 'more than a friend – as it were, the closest of relatives'.[15] Nevertheless he felt he was in no condition to face any longer the pain and strain of observing Kondratyev's worsening condition; nor could he remain at Kondratyev's bedside, for he had to be present at the Conservatoire examinations in Moscow. After Tanya's sudden death he had decided his first summer call had to be on Lev and Sasha, but because he now learned that Sasha would be abroad, it was agreed he should visit Kamenka on his return journey. Thus his Conservatoire duties and *The Enchantress* completed, on 1 June he left Moscow for Nizhni-Novgorod.

This time his expedition to Tiflis began down the River Volga, a journey of which he had long dreamed. But his expectations had been set too high. At Nizhni he found even second-class accommodation on the best steamer difficult to obtain, the vessel was crowded, and solitude unobtainable. On 16 June, however, a fortnight later and five days after his arrival in Tiflis, he could review the trip for Shpazhinskaya and conclude that his nerves were in far better order, his mind was rested, and that it had been well worth the various discomforts.

It's not that during its course Mother-Volga offers an abundance of beautiful places . . . A hilly, sometimes wooded right bank and a completely deserted left bank – that's all. From time to time – but, nevertheless, very infrequently – there are villages and towns; very often steamers, barges, boats are met – all this just enough for it not to be too boring for a man who is looking for diversions. But Mother-Volga herself, majestically and calmly rolling for the several versts of her width her yellowish waters towards the sea, affords the Russian man accustomed to wide horizons, to breadth, and to level lines during his passage inexpressible delight. I'm completely in love with this divine, wonderful river, and would be capable of floating up and

[15] *TLP*14, p. 88.

down it all summer, but only on one condition: in my own steamer, by myself.[16]

Among the calls on the way were Kazan ('very beautiful from a distance'[17]), Simbirsk (now Ulyanovsk), Volsk, which had one of the best public gardens he had ever seen (on much later reflection, perhaps, the highlight of this trip), and Samara (now Kuybyshev), which he liked best of all so far, and where he saw posters for a performance of *Onegin* the previous evening. Saratov, where he attended mass at the cathedral, disappointed him, and Tsaritsyn (now Volgograd), visited the following day, he found unattractive for its incongruous mingling of East and West. He had now been able to transfer to the first-class, and he finished his descent of the Volga at Astrakhan ('much better than Saratov'[18]) in far more cheerful mood. What his diary reveals most distinctly is how much he was sometimes enjoying the society of some of his fellow-passengers, from all of whom he had successfully concealed his identity. Asked to accompany a young conservatoire student in one of his own songs during an impromptu musical evening, his understanding of his own music was found to be defective by his partner, who claimed the authority of her own teacher who had studied the song with Tchaikovsky himself. She also enquired whether he had seen Pavlovskaya in *Onegin*. Tchaikovsky positively delighted in all this – and in the rapidly developing relationship he was cultivating with an unusually sympathetic schoolboy. After a two-day crossing of the Caspian Sea, marred by a brief but frightening storm, they docked in Baku on 9 June. He spent a day there, finding the city interesting, clean and attractive, strongly conditioned by oriental influences, though lacking in vegetation and everywhere smelling of oil. He visited the oil installations, was fascinated by a gusher, and found the end of his journey spoiled only by having to travel in a train compartment where smoking was, incomprehensibly, prohibited.

In Tiflis a theatre company was visiting with the actress, Mariya Savina, at its head. Dumas' *Marguerite Gautier*, Arensky's unworthy choice of subject for his fantasia, was one of the plays on offer; another was *The Enchantress*. Tchaikovsky would happily have missed the latter, but Savina begged him to come to her benefit performance, and Shpazhinsky, it was said, had especially approved her conception of the title role. Tchaikovsky loathed it; it brought home to him how the character of Kuma had been transformed, so he thought, in his newly

[16] *TLP*14, pp. 118–19; *TTP*, p. 320. A verst is roughly two thirds of a mile.
[17] *TD*, p. 145; *YDGC*, p. 413.
[18] *TD*, p. 146; *YDGC*, p. 413.

finished opera. Since leaving Moscow he had felt no wish to compose, and the temperature rendered any work during the daytime almost impossible. The musical season was over; Zarudnaya was on tour in Kharkov, Ippolitov-Ivanov was with her, and apart from looking through Verdi's brand-new *Otello*, consolidating his knowledge of Ippolitov-Ivanov's *Ruth* and listening to a selection of pieces from his own *Onegin*, music seems to have had no part in Tchaikovsky's twelve days in Tiflis. Yet for the town itself his visit proved of critical importance. A new opera house was in process of construction, but there were insufficient funds to complete it. Such now was Tchaikovsky's prestige with the Tsar, however, that a personal letter requesting His Imperial Majesty to allocate the 235,000 roubles still needed was swiftly and wholly successful. A more exciting immediate prospect for the local operatic life was Tchaikovsky's agreement to conduct the first performance of the production of *The Enchantress* which was already being planned for November.

The remaining three-and-a-half weeks of Tchaikovsky's Caucasus interlude were to be spent with Anatoly and Parasha at Borzhom, midway between Tiflis and Batum. When he first saw this small and very new spa town on 23 June, his feelings were very reserved. Enclosed by mountains, it seemed gloomy and depressing. But a single stroll the next morning was sufficient to dispel this impression, for there was a vast variety of walks to choose from, the vegetation was surprisingly beautiful – above all, he found he could be alone, and after the close confinement of his journey and the social bustle which he had been unable to escape in Tiflis, solitude was what he craved most. The waters were like those of Vichy, in which he had great faith. He consulted a local doctor who concluded that pressure from his stomach had exiled his liver to some place it had no business to be. Placing total trust in this remarkable diagnosis, Tchaikovsky began the prescribed course of draughts and baths. In fact, he admitted he felt very well; the only depressions came now from St Petersburg, where the husband of his cousin, Amaliya Litke, a close companion of his childhood who had remained one of his favourites amongst his own kin, had died, and where Modest had been delayed by this family misfortune and by Kondratyev's condition. It was now over a month since Tchaikovsky had finished *The Enchantress*, but his creative forces still slumbered. To goad them into action, on 28 June he began tinkering with the beginning of a string sextet; the following day, in a rather more purposeful way, he set about his Fourth Suite.

Tchaikovsky's idea for a suite based on pieces by Mozart went back at least three years, to May 1884. It stirred again in December 1885 after hearing a performance of Beethoven's First Symphony. 'I myself had not suspected that I liked it so much,' he admitted to Taneyev. 'It must be that it resembles my god, Mozart. Don't forget that we shall have to celebrate the centenary of *Don Giovanni* on 8 November [in fact, 29 October] 1887.'[19] His mode of celebration – a set of arrangements of pieces by Mozart – had now been decided, and a couple of months later he bought some pieces by his idol. But despite investigating these over the next few days, he found himself unable to make a final selection. There the matter rested until the centenary's imminence forced him to act. His choice had now fallen on four pieces: the Gigue in G, K. 574, the Minuet in D, K. 355, the *Ave verum corpus* for voices, strings and organ, K. 618, and the Variations on 'Unser dummer Pöbel meint', K. 455. Since he selected as the basis for the third of these the piano transcription by Liszt, who had added an introduction and coda, all four movements were to be orchestrations from keyboard texts. Tchaikovsky began with the variations. 'I'm occupying myself about an hour each day with orchestrating the Mozart piano pieces,' he wrote to Jurgenson on 6 July after a week's work. '. . . I think there's a great future, especially abroad, for this suite, thanks to a successful choice of pieces and the *novelty* of its character (*the old given a contemporary treatment*) . . . The only thing I don't know is what to call it. It's necessary to devise a new word from the name "Mozart", for if the suite is successful, then I shall compile another and even a third. I don't want "Mozartiana", for that recalls "Kreisleriana" and so on.'[20] However, he was persuaded by Jurgenson that his suite was so different in intention from Schumann's set of piano pieces that the similarity of title would not cause confusion. On 9 August the work was complete. The first performance took place under the composer's direction on 26 November at an RMS concert in Moscow devoted entirely to Tchaikovsky's works.

Tchaikovsky prefaced the published score with a note: 'A great many of Mozart's outstanding short pieces are, for some incomprehensible reason, little known not only to the public but to many musicians also. The author who has arranged this suite entitled *Mozartiana* had in mind to provide a new occasion for the more frequent performance of these pearls of musical art, unpretentious in form, but filled with unrivalled beauties.'[21] Tchaikovsky's choice reveals the taste of a connoisseur. What must have attracted him to all four is a chromatic element which, in the Gigue and Minuet, is allied to pointed dissonance made the more

[19] *TLP*13, pp. 220–1; *TZC*3, p. 83; *TTP*, p. 137.
[20] *TLP*14, p. 133; *TZC*3, p. 170; *TPJ*2, p. 63; *DTC*, p. 418; *YDGC*, p. 415 (partial).
[21] *TZC*3, p. 196; *TPJ*2, p. 288; *DTC*, p. 417.

telling by their highly refined textures. Both are late pieces; *Ave verum corpus*, even later, is one of the most exquisite creations of eighteenth-century church music.

Throughout the suite Mozart's text is shown scrupulous respect, though it may be ingeniously transformed – for instance in bars 12–14 of the Gigue where, for two entries in this fugal-textured piece, the subject is deftly split between strings and woodwind to make possible a colour division more typical of post-classical scoring (Ex. 229). Apart from modifications and filling-out of texture required or suggested by

Ex. 229

the new medium, and the occasional provision of a harmonic detail, the only substantial revisions of notes are in the final movement, where certain of the arpeggio figures and scales of the ninth variation are re-thought in terms possible for, or more appropriate to a solo violin, while the cadenza in the middle of the tenth variation is rewritten to fit the range of the clarinet. Thus Tchaikovsky's approach is that not of a Tausig, but of a Liszt transcribing Bach; though a battery of four horns and a cymbal and bells may be intruders in a true Mozartian com-plement (at least, as used by Tchaikovsky), the orchestral sound is 'Mozartian' throughout the greater part of the suite. It is only when Tchaikovsky is faced with the highly idiomatic keyboard writing of the eighth variation that he prettily colours his rewritten texture with bells. His justification for their employment would doubtless have been Papageno's miniature Glockenspiel; when used here with pizzicato strings the more muted palette of a late-eighteenth-century orchestral canvas is flecked with tiny strokes from that range of bright, sparkling pigments from which *Nutcracker*'s kaleidoscopic enchantments will be manufactured.

The movement which may trouble, even offend, is the third, *Ave verum corpus* – or *Preghiera*, as both Liszt and Tchaikovsky labelled it. To be fair, Liszt had already laid his hands upon the piece, but Tchaikovsky has readily abetted him in what, from both, was an act of unconscious, even devout vandalism. But it is not merely the inclusion of Liszt's gratuitous introduction and postlude; Tchaikovsky's presen-tation of the rest, with celestial strings and twangling harp, transforms Mozart's ethereal delicacy into glutinous sentimentality. Yet, horrid as this may sound to our sanitized ears, Tchaikovsky can only be charged with misunderstanding, not bad taste. *Mozartiana* may now be a piece we do not want, and certainly no longer need, but in Tchaikovsky's own time it acquainted audiences with four excellent pieces many might otherwise not have known. Mozart's shade had greater cause for gratitude than censure at this highly practical homage to his memory – even, perhaps, for some regret that Tchaikovsky did not provide any successor.

Tchaikovsky had intended to stay at least six weeks in Borzhom to complete the prescribed course of waters and baths. Though he found irritating the increasingly persistent attempts of other visitors to make his acquaintance, he was completely in love with the town itself. On 4 July Modest and Kolya arrived. By now a remission in Kondratyev's illness had made possible his removal to Aachen, where it was hoped the waters might prolong his life a few months, and at first Tchaikovsky had thought this would make his own attendance upon his sick friend less necessary. Then on the 12 July a telegram arrived: 'Supplie venir; votre arrivée peut me ressusciter'. It was a hopeless appeal, but one he could not possibly ignore. The plans and promises to visit Ippolit, Nikolay and Sasha were laid aside. On 18 July he embarked from Batum for Odessa. It proved a slow journey, the vessel picking its way along the coast but including in its ports of call Sevastopol, where Tchaikovsky managed a brief meeting with Shpazhinskaya. Arriving in Odessa on 23 July, he spent a day enjoying this 'very beautiful . . . wonderful'[22] city and tormenting himself with reflections on the people and pleasures he had left behind him in Borzhom, and on the prospect of a lonely journey without Alexey, who was to return to Maidanovo. The train took him through Cracow, Vienna and Cologne. On 27 July he was with Kondratyev.

The year 1887 had already provided savage contrasts. The elation of conducting *Cherevichki* had been roughly countered by sudden grief from Tanya's death, and now the prolonged contentment of Tiflis and Borzhom was to be succeeded by weeks of pain and strain such as Tchaikovsky had long not known. 'I recall vividly all that happened exactly ten years ago!!!???' he ended his diary entry as he prepared to embark from Batum.[23] On 18 July 1877 he had married Antonina and had begun the most dreadful phase of his life; now again torment confronted him, for it was quickly apparent that Kondratyev was in a hopeless condition. Tchaikovsky did his best to prop the patient's spirits and to support the others who were caring for him when they had to endure his frequent outbursts of anger or ingratitude. Kondratyev's sufferings and moods fluctuated swiftly and violently; sometimes he seemed hopeful, even optimistic, at others despairing. By contrast, Tchaikovsky's moods, recorded in his diary in sudden, sometimes explosive outbursts, reveal a slow but inexorable trend. At first he felt mainly pity, an awareness of his own good fortune, some self-reproach, then growing despair.

> *29 July*: . . . Still more and more I see that I was very necessary to him, and that I did well in coming . . . *3 August*: . . . Now I'm . . . remorseful . . . Am I acting rightly? Take now, for instance. I sit here and all the while I rejoice in my *sacrifice*. But there is no sacrifice. I enjoy myself in peace, gorge myself at the *table d'hôte* . . . Am I not a quintessentially *self-centred individual*? Even in regard of those near to me I am not what I ought to be . . . *5 August*: . . . I found him

[22] *TD*, p. 159; *TZC3*, p. 174; *YDGC*, p. 417 (partial).
[23] *TD*, p. 157.

[Kondratyev] talking with Sasha [Legoshin, his servant] about the fact that in reality there's no improvement. He wept a lot. Ah! how painful this was! I can no longer remember what I said to him, only that little by little he became quieter . . . Lord, how sad I am! I want to rail at my fate – but I'm ashamed to. . . . *10 August*: . . . Talked with Sasha in his room. We are coming to the conclusion that things are bad . . . *12 August*: . . . N.D. [Kondratyev] was in a most agreeable state of mind. Unhappy man! If only he knew how vain are his hopes.[24]

After a fortnight within this situation Tchaikovsky realized there would be a limit to his capacity for enduring its increasing pressures. For a variety of reasons none of Kondratyev's kin had come with him; now Tchaikovsky wrote to Kondratyev's wife that someone from the family would soon have to take his place. Meanwhile a break, if only brief, was imperative. Paris was the obvious haven, for it was reasonably close and various friends, including Brandukov, were there. He arrived on 14 August and found a special sweetness in his familiar hotel, his accustomed cafés and restaurants, and his well-liked friends. Discovering everything was closed the following day for the Feast of the Assumption, he visited the delighted Auclairs at Bicêtre, then without reluctance delayed his return for twenty-four hours to meet Mackar, who greeted him effusively, and with whom he discussed business matters. This, he told Modest, had been the main object of his trip. Yet it was the contact with Brandukov which was to prove the more fruitful.

After Tchaikovsky's return to Aachen the effects of the pressures upon him began increasingly to show, and the diary entries become more impatient, even irritable.

19 August: . . . After my dinner and walk I found him still weaker and thoroughly poorly. I sat with him. Sudden anger at me. Although I could not get angry I was terribly *froid*. . . . Then it passed, but with difficulty. Pity took over. He was suffering terribly. . . . *23 August*: . . . N.D. roused painful thoughts in me. His self-centredness and lack of true goodness declare themselves so sharply and in so unattractive a manner that by now, except for pity, I nourish no feeling for him. Shall I soon tear myself from this hell? . . . It annoys and disturbs me that I cannot help being surprised and indignant at N.D. But this is beyond my strength.[25]

[24] *TD*, pp. 161–5; *YDGC*, pp. 417–18 (partial); *TZC3*, p. 176 (partial).
[25] *TD*, pp. 167–8.

At last Dmitri Zasyadko, Kondratyev's nephew, agreed to replace Tchaikovsky, and a term was fixed to Tchaikovsky's vigil. Now that an end came in sight, desperation to escape grew into an obsession, despite stabs of conscience. Not since the days of his marriage had any letters he wrote expressed such pain and frustration; nor was there a lessening of the private misery in his diary.

27 August: . . . Ten days to live in this hell!!! . . . *Sunday, 28 August*: N.D. much worse since this morning. . . . He's in utter despair. I cannot describe the scenes which took place: I shall never forget them. . . . Hours of torment. A strange thing – I was thoroughly weighed down by *horror* and *anguish*, but not by PITY!!! . . . And yet, God, how he suffers!!! And I do not understand why I have become so hardened. No! I know I'm not wicked and heartless. But it's my nerves and my *self-centredness* which whisper yet more loudly and more loudly in my ear: 'Go away, do not torment yourself, spare yourself!' But of departure I still dare not think. *30 August*: From this morning the *ray* of freedom has shone on me, for *in a week* I shall not be here . . . In the morning it seemed to me I was ill and wouldn't hold out. . . . *31 August*: . . . He was quiet and meek. In such a state he especially rouses my pity. I wanted to cry . . . Lying in bed I began to think of N.D., of his endless depression and suffering, and for a long time I sobbed like a child. . . . *2 September*: . . . N.D. is very weak. . . . From time to time he complains and weeps. Wearying, terrible hours![26]

On 4 September Zasyadko arrived. 'All today I was as in a nightmare. Furious self-centredness tears me to pieces. One thought: to leave!!! My patience can no longer be confined . . . Lord, is it possible a time will come when I shall no longer suffer thus! Poor N.D.! Poor Mitya [Zasyadko]! What lies before him!'[27] During these last days Tchaikovsky's secret dread had been that he would have to take Kondratyev with him to die in his native Russia. But on 6 September, with few tears, the two men said their last goodbyes, and Tchaikovsky headed for Maidanovo alone. So drained was he that he had to pause in Berlin. Delaying in St Petersburg to visit Kondratyev's wife, on 11 September he was home. Thoughts of mortality still possessed him so strongly that he drew up a new will, and three weeks later he again opened his more personal diary to take stock of how his view of things eternal had shifted during the past year.

[26] *TD*, pp. 168–70.
[27] *TD*, p. 173.

3 October: How short is life! How much you want to do, to think over, to say. You put off, imagining there is so much still ahead, but from a corner death is already beginning to lie in wait. . . . My *religion* has revealed itself infinitely more clearly. During all this time I have thought much of God, of life and death – and especially *in Aachen* the fateful questions: why? how? wherefore? often occupied me and hovered disturbingly before me. I should like sometime to set out my *religion* in detail for myself, if only so that once and for all I might clarify to myself my own beliefs and that boundary at which, after speculation, they begin. But life with its bustle rushes past, and I do not know whether I have succeeded in expressing that *Creed* which has evolved within me recently. It has evolved with great clarity, but all the same I don't yet apply it to my praying. I pray as of old, as I was taught to pray. But then God scarcely needs to know how and why we are praying. God does not need prayer. But *we need* it.[28]

His words tell us no more about his creed than perhaps they told Tchaikovsky himself, but they evidence the hold, albeit sentimental, that religious belief still retained upon him. Though when he wrote he did not know, it was the day of Kondratyev's death.

Modest chose to pass over Tchaikovsky's preoccupations at Aachen, though he fully recognized the personal distress his brother endured. Had Modest wished to record them, he had personally available as large a quantity of written evidence as from any comparable period of his brother's life, for it was in the detailed recounting of Kondratyev's sufferings in letters, as well as in the personal confessions of his diary, that Tchaikovsky found some relief from the feelings of each day. That he had little practical ability to cope with a predicament such as faced him is patently true, as Modest wrote. But this misses the main point – that, all the same, he stayed when he could so easily have pleaded his uselessness as an excuse to leave. For Tchaikovsky the dichotomy between his life as a private being and his role as a public, even international celebrity, was growing rapidly more extreme, and the danger that the latter would overwhelm the former was increasingly real. Yet it never happened. There was to be no loss of love for his family, no lessening in his relationships with those beings whose friendships he had cherished when he, too, had been unknown.

These weeks at Aachen reveal this in no uncertain way, exactly as the months immediately ahead were to show his public career moving on to yet broader and more exposed ground. There was barely adequate time

[28] *TD*, p. 213.

to rest at Maidanovo before he was required in St Petersburg for the rehearsals of *The Enchantress*. Unsettled in his present house, he spent much of his first few days scouting for a possible new residence, even resolving to buy a piece of woodland and build his own home, a project which soon fell through. Of Aachen he tried not to think; only in his sleep, as he told Modest, did the nightmare haunt him. But a quirk of memory recalled another painful incident from his distant past. Sixteen years before he had been passionately drawn to a seventeen-year-old, Eduard Zak, who two years later, in 1873, had taken his own life. Now, suddenly, vivid memories of this youth swelled up in him. The next day they returned. The entry in his ordinary diary is in part unclear, hinting, it would seem, at some dark secret, and certainly betraying a lingering agony within a precious remembrance. 'How amazingly well do I remember him: the sound of his voice, his movements, but in particular the uncommonly wonderful expression at times on his face. I cannot conceive to myself that he is *not* here *at all*. His death – that is, *his* complete non-existence – is beyond my comprehension. I think I never loved anyone as much as he. My God, but what did they not say to me *then* – and however much I soothe myself, my guilt before him is terrible! And yet I loved him – that is, I did not love [him enough?] – and now also I love him, and the memory of him is sacred to me.'[29] Tchaikovsky's services to Kondratyev reveal his capacity for devotion to a long-lived friendship with a still living friend; the strength of these involuntary memories discloses how enduring could be his feelings for a long-dead love.

The first general rehearsal of *The Enchantress* was on 19 September. Tchaikovsky visited St Petersburg for two days so that he might also attend the silver jubilee celebrations of the Conservatoire and receive honorary membership of the Imperial RMS. What became glaringly apparent from the rehearsal were the longueurs of the opera, and a good deal of the first ten days after his return to Maidanovo was devoted to cutting and resewing the seams. For musical recreation he had recently been playing Schumann: the opera *Genoveva* and that 'divine piece', *Das Paradies und die Peri*.[30] Laroche returned with him after a visit to Moscow at the end of the month, and yet again Tchaikovsky coaxed an article from his indolent friend by acting as scribe. The first orchestral rehearsal was on 12 October, Tchaikovsky conducting. Nápravník had done the groundwork excellently, the

[29] *TD*, pp. 176–7.
[30] *TD*, p. 178; *YDGC*, p. 420; *TZC3*, p. 182.

performers were enthusiastic, and the settings, costumes and production magnificent. After the première on 1 November Tchaikovsky was to have conducted only one further performance, but Nápravník was taken ill, and the composer directed the next two as well. He remained to see the fifth performance (and to note the house was not full); then the following day, 19 November, he left to begin preparations for his début as a concert conductor in Moscow.

The concert on 26 November was preceded by daily rehearsals. By now Tchaikovsky was desperately tired, and with much embarrassment he withdrew from his promise to conduct the opening night of the production of *The Enchantress* which Ippolitov-Ivanov was preparing in Tiflis. Apart from exhaustion from rehearsals, he faced other worries in Moscow. Parasha was ill with typhus, and the RMS was in grave difficulties. There were tensions between the Society and the Imperial Theatres whose orchestra provided the core of players for the former's concerts, and there were tensions with Erdsmanndörfer, whose contractual right to decide all programmes was being challenged by Taneyev, and who, moreover, had been reluctant that Tchaikovsky (so Taneyev claimed) should conduct the programme of his own works. Exhaustion was probably the reason he did not this time relish conducting as he had done in St Petersburg in March. But for Tchaikovsky personally the concert proved his greatest triumph to date. Besides *Francesca da Rimini* and *1812*, the programme comprised the Concert Fantasia, with Taneyev as soloist, Kuma's arioso from Act 1 of *The Enchantress*, two romances, and the first performance of *Mozartiana*. So successful was the whole event that it had to be repeated the following day. Tchaikovsky found the second occasion more pleasurable, perhaps because he had relieved some of his tensions in a burst of hysterics before going out to the rostrum; he certainly felt he conducted better. The Moscow press was as warm as the audience had been demonstrative. Among the notices was a brief assessment by Kashkin of Tchaikovsky as conductor. 'He has all the essential qualities for conducting an orchestra: complete self-control, extreme clarity and definition in his beat . . . His direction of the orchestra is distinguished by its utter simplicity, and if he has none of the virtuoso conductor's movements which come only with more or less prolonged practice, he has instead a quality which cannot be acquired . . . that inner fire, that animation which communicate themselves to the orchestra and which irresistibly act upon the audience through the integrity and inspired quality of the performance.'[31]

[31] *YDGC*, p. 429.

This over, Tchaikovsky could escape at last to Maidanovo for three weeks, broken only by two brief visits to Moscow, the first to attend a concert of his own chamber music, organized by the RMS and consisting of the first two string quartets and various of his piano pieces. Apart from finishing off the set of Six Romances, Op. 63, and composing a short choral piece, he did no work. A period of rest was the more necessary for he knew that shortly he would be embarking upon a fresh and perhaps even more demanding venture.

These triumphs in Tchaikovsky's public professional life during 1887 were not matched in creative achievements. It was one of his leanest years, producing only the Mozart scorings, a short concert piece for cello and orchestra, a set of six songs, and three tiny choral pieces. None of these is of great importance. He had managed to finish *Mozartiana* during his first fortnight with Kondratyev, and the urge quickly to set about some new piece was strong, partly because he had written no original work for months, partly because composition would afford the most effective of distractions from his friend's plight. The meeting with Brandukov in Paris proved critical, and on 24 August, a week after his return to Aachen, he began his *Pezzo capriccioso* for cello and orchestra, sketching it in two days, and completing the scoring by 11 September. The first performance took place on 28 February 1888 at a private occasion in Paris with Brandukov as soloist and Tchaikovsky conducting Colonne's orchestra. The Russian première, with the same soloist and conductor, was at an RMS concert in Moscow on 7 December 1889.

The *Pezzo capriccioso* is the last of Tchaikovsky's completed concert pieces for solo instrument and orchestra; it is also the weakest. The appalling emotional strains of the situation within which it was born plainly took a heavy toll of Tchaikovsky's creative energies, and the work is nondescript; though it opens well, its themes lack that freshness which makes the equally slender *Valse-scherzo* of 1877 so beguiling. Nor are they as distinctive as those of Tchaikovsky's other concert piece for violin and orchestra, the *Sérénade mélancolique* of 1875. Yet as further evidence of the working of Tchaikovsky's creative mind, the *Pezzo* is of some interest. Its main theme, like that of the *Valse-scherzo*, opens with a scalic ascent above a step-wise descending bass (Ex. 230b). But whereas the earlier work had subsequently offered a variety of completely new waltz tunes, the nine-note bass descent from B to A sharp (B flat) becomes the recurring feature of the piece. Even before supporting the main theme it had shaped the melody's course in the centre of the cellist's short introduction (Ex. 230a), and the middle portion of the scalic descent is also important in building the bass line of

Ex. 230

this whole first section. At the *Pezzo*'s centre, where the soloist moves into completely new thematic territory, the nine-note descent remains the most prominent single feature of the bass. Finally, towards the section's end, when the orchestra adds short, stepwise rising phrases against the cello's persisting chatter, the way is prepared for an almost seamless return of the opening theme. Here is another manifestation, though modified, of that kind of creative process which had formed the progressive thematic transformations of *Kamarinskaya*. It produces the most interesting moment in an otherwise unremarkable piece.

Of the remaining compositions of 1887, all vocal, the three choral pieces are very minor creations. 'An angel weeping' was written in early March, and 'The golden cloud has slept', a setting of Lermontov, in mid-July in Borzhom for a certain Mrs Kaitmazova. Unlike these, the third, 'Blessed is he who smiles', is for men's voices alone; it was composed on 19 December at the request of Albrecht, and was to be dedicated to the students' choir of Moscow University. This time Tchaikovsky had chosen verses by the Grand Duke Konstantin Konstantinovich. The interests of this young amateur pianist, composer and poet were wide, and subsequently he was to be president of both the Academy of Sciences and the Archaeological Society. Yet his main activity was as a poet, and in the 1880s he published three collections. He had presented Tchaikovsky with a copy of the first of these[32] in the

---

[32] *Poems* (St Petersburg, 1886).

autumn of the previous year, when he had been active as the intermediary to the Empress over the Twelve Romances, Op. 60, and it was from this volume that Tchaikovsky now took the texts for a new set of six songs to be issued as Op. 63. He had informed the Grand Duke of his intention at the beginning of 1887, but it was November before he began composition. The first news of the completed work was contained in a letter of 27 December.

Like the *Pezzo capriccioso*, the new songs were written under unfavourable conditions, and in a second letter a fortnight later, acknowledging the Grand Duke's gracious acceptance of the dedication, Tchaikovsky expressed a fear that they 'will appear to you (as, unfortunately, it seems is in fact the case) much weaker than my previous romances'.[33] Whether Tchaikovsky really believed this or not, his apprehension was well grounded, and Op. 63, like Op. 60, is among the least interesting of his collections; the songs' façades have a smooth and easy charm, but their content is mostly inconsequential. As such, they match well the lyrics they set, for the Grand Duke was no more than a facile, limited versifier, dealing with conventional imagery, moods and situations in sentimental and cosy terms, even when the rejected lover reflects that there will be no second chance (No. 3), or when the song of the nightingale awakens longing for his homeland in the expatriate (or exile?) (No. 2). Pain, sorrow, extroversion, humour have no real part in these texts. The lover beneath the window in 'Serenade' (No. 6) is no lusty wag enticing a coy girl, as in Polonsky's lively verse used for the tenth song of the Op. 60 set, but a sighing swain sweetening his sleeping beloved's dreams with his singing; Tchaikovsky's lilting music has more vitality and personality than the verse. 'I did not love you at first' (No. 1), 'I opened the window' (No. 2) and 'The first meeting' (No. 4), all in compound time, pass pleasantly but unmemorably, though the touches of harmonic pathos in the final section of the second, and the mild jolt of a distant modulation in the centre of the last, do briefly encourage more alert attention. The nostalgic world of 'The fires in the rooms were already out' (No. 5), with its silent lovers sitting in moonlit shadows as the nightingale voices their thoughts for them, is well matched by the general mood of Tchaikovsky's music, but that is about all. Only 'I do not please you' (No. 3) suggests some real attempt to provide more than just acceptable decoration for familiar sentiments and situations. Its melody is less fluently predictable both in phrase structure and in the course it follows, and the song moves on to new material on its last page as the disappointed lover utters his

---

[33] *TLP*14, p. 304.

melancholy warning. Yet to describe this as revelatory would be overstatement, and among less routine companions this romance's greater individuality would pass unnoticed.

The initiative which was to lead to Tchaikovsky's first European tour originated with the Hamburg and St Petersburg publisher, Daniel Rahter, who held the distribution rights to Tchaikovsky's music in Germany and the Austro-Hungarian Empire, and was proprietor of the firm of Bitner in St Petersburg. The speed with which Tchaikovsky's new accomplishment became known outside Russia was phenomenal. By July Rahter had organized an invitation from the Hamburg Philharmonic Society for him to conduct a concert of his own works the following January, and in September, Dmitri Friedrich, a concert agent in Berlin, secured him an engagement in Prague through the Umelecká Beseda; for this society, whose membership included personalities from all the arts, he was to conduct a similar concert in early December. Hard on the heels of that invitation came another from Otto Schneider, chairman of the Berlin Philharmonic Orchestra. Meanwhile in Paris Mackar wished the next concert he arranged to be presided over by the composer himself. By the time Tchaikovsky wrote to his French publisher on 9 November, only a fortnight after receiving Schneider's invitation, he could add Leipzig and Dresden to the venues where he would conduct before going to Paris. Though the Dresden and (later) Copenhagen concerts fell through, London was to be appended to Leipzig, Berlin, Hamburg, Prague and Paris. Tchaikovsky's repertoire was to contain *Francesca da Rimini*, *Romeo and Juliet* and *1812*, the Violin and First Piano Concertos, the Concert Fantasia, the First and Third Suites, Serenade for Strings, and the Andante cantabile.

There remained one major commitment before the tour: to conduct the St Petersburg première of *Mozartiana*. He fulfilled this at an RMS concert on 24 December. Again the work was an enormous success and, as in Moscow, the *Preghiera* had to be repeated. Two days later, on the eve of his departure for Berlin, he sat down with Rimsky-Korsakov, Glazunov and Lyadov to work out a detailed programme of Russian music which Tchaikovsky hoped he might, at his own risk, conduct in Paris at a second concert. This admirable intention could not be realized. That same evening in Tiflis *The Enchantress*, which he had promised to conduct, was being given for the first time.

1887 had proved quite extraordinary for Tchaikovsky. He had begun it quite unknown as a conductor; now, within less than a year of going out to control the first performance of *Cherevichki* in Moscow, he would be standing on the podium of the splendid new Gewandhaus in Leipzig, successor to the hall where Mozart had directed his own works, Mendelssohn had turned the orchestra into one of the finest in the world, and where Brahms and Wagner had both conducted.

4

INTERNATIONAL CONDUCTOR:
FIFTH SYMPHONY

TCHAIKOVSKY LEFT RUSSIA in a highly nervous condition. His agent, Friedrich, had schemed a public lunch in one of Berlin's best restaurants so that his '*numerous (!!!) friends and admirers (!!!!)*'[1] could meet him, but the guest of honour had already refused point blank to attend and was the more furious on arriving in the German capital to read in a newspaper that the event had been arranged for the next day. In consequence he remained incommunicado for twenty-four hours, visiting a museum instead, and laying in a good supply of books against the days ahead. As when he had been summoned from Maidanovo to rehearsals of *Cherevichki*, a fit of weeping did much to ease his tensions. Having confessed his whereabouts, he had to endure being shadowed everywhere by Friedrich, who took him to a performance of Berlioz's *Requiem*, where he could be introduced to certain notables. But because Friedrich's own interests lay with a rival orchestra, he did nothing to help the main matter which had brought Tchaikovsky to Berlin: the hope of finalizing with Schneider and others of the Philharmonic Orchestra the programme he would conduct in February. When, therefore, on 31 December he moved to Leipzig, where he was to conduct his First Suite, he knew he was doomed to return to the German capital to continue this negotiation. It all made a very bad beginning to his tour. If Brodsky and Ziloti had not met him at the station and taken charge of him, the strain, he thought, might have proved too much, and he would have returned to Russia.

In Leipzig the personal encounters proved as significant as the concert itself. While approaching Brodsky's house for lunch on the day following his arrival, he heard sounds of a piano and discovered Brodsky and Julius Klengel, principal cellist of the Gewandhaus Orchestra, engaged with Brahms himself in a rehearsal of that composer's recent C minor Piano Trio. It was the first encounter of what was to prove an uneasy, ambivalent relationship. In his *Autobiographical*

---

[1] *TLP*14, p. 292; *TPJ*2, p. 76.

Account of a Foreign Tour in 1888, written in Tiflis during April and envisaged for a wider readership, Tchaikovsky pictured Brahms as having 'an extremely sympathetic outward appearance. His handsome, almost patriarchal head recalls that of a benign, handsome, elderly Russian priest. . . . A certain softness of outline . . . rather long and thin grey hair, kind grey eyes, a thick beard with strong streaks of grey – all this recalls more the pure-blooded Great Russian type often met among our clergy.'[2] More privately to Modest the day following their first meeting he described Brahms as 'rubicund . . . pot-bellied . . . a dreadful toper'.[3] Yet Brahms improved on acquaintance, he discovered, and within three days he was writing warmly to Jurgenson that 'he's a very nice person, and not at all as proud as I'd imagined'.[4] At a Gewandhaus concert Tchaikovsky heard Brahms direct his new Double Concerto with Joachim and Robert Hausmann as soloists, but found the piece left him quite unmoved. What did impress him profoundly was the choir of the Thomaskirche singing choral works by Bach, and it made him revise his opinion of the excellence of Russian church choirs. In all their encounters of this six-day stay he admitted Brahms did everything he could to be agreeable, but he found him an easier drinking companion than conversationalist, more comfortable in retrospect than as a presence. As with the man, so with the musician: winning deep respect, but not affection. He still could find nothing to persuade him to like Brahms's music any better, or to believe that the German composer merited the reputation he enjoyed in his own land as well as with certain Russian expatriates such as Brodsky.

During the trio rehearsal another figure had entered the room, 'a very short man, middle-aged, of frail build, with shoulders of very unequal height, a head of prominent wavy fair hair and a very thin, almost youthful beard and moustaches . . . [and] unusually attractive, medium-sized blue eyes of an inexpressibly captivating nature recalling the look of a charming, innocent child'.[5] It was Edvard Grieg. Tchaikovsky already knew something of Grieg's music, and he recognized that his musical endowment was probably much less than Brahms's. But the attraction he had felt to Grieg's compositions was now reflected in his response to the man, Tchaikovsky immediately sensing that the mutual sympathy he detected could develop into friendship. He was also much taken by Grieg's wife Nina, and was

[2] *TMKS*, p. 342; *TZC*3, p. 202.
[3] *TLP*14, p. 296; *TPB*, p. 383; *TZC*3, p. 202 (modified).
[4] *TLP*14, p. 299; *TPJ*2, p. 77; *TZC*3, p. 203.
[5] *TMKS*, p. 345; *TZC*3, p. 202.

delighted to discover both of them were knowledgeable about Russian literature.

The third new acquaintance proved to be a bewildering curiosity whose herald preceded her. To Tchaikovsky's delight, the Brodskys preserved Russian Christmas traditions, but on Christmas Eve [5 January], 'when . . . we were sitting at the table for tea at Brodsky's, a beautiful, thoroughbred setter suddenly burst into the room and immediately began greeting the master, his ladies and little nephew in turn. "This means Miss Smyth will be here directly," they all declared with one voice, and in a few moments a tall Englishwoman, still young, unattractive, but with what is called "an expressive or intelligent face", entered the dining room, and I was forthwith introduced to her as a fellow-professional. Miss [Ethel] Smyth is one of the few women composers whom one may seriously consider a practitioner in the sphere of musical creativity,' he wrote in his *Autobiographical Account*. On the strength of a violin sonata which she and Brodsky performed for him, he heard promise of a future for this 'very serious and gifted composer'. But, Tchaikovsky continued, 'because no Englishwoman is capable of not possessing peculiarities and eccentricities, Miss Smyth has them – to wit: first, a superb dog, inseparable from this spinster and always announcing her appearance, as happened on this and other occasions of which I was witness; second, a passion for hunting, for the sake of which Miss Smyth sometimes goes for a time to England; and third, an incredible, incomprehensible adoration, amounting to a passion, for the enigmatic musical genius of Brahms.'[6]

Tchaikovsky's first rehearsal was on 2 January. That he should have been invited to conduct in so conservative an institution as the Gewandhaus was remarkable, and Tchaikovsky attributed much of the credit for this to Brodsky and Ziloti, who had prepared the ground well for him within the city. Yet the main engineer of this invitation was the seemingly ubiquitous Friedrich; the price was to have this Berlin agent haunt him again for most of his week in Leipzig. The night before the first rehearsal Tchaikovsky slept badly; on the day Carl Reinecke, the orchestra's conductor, introduced him to the players, he replied with a short speech in German, then set about his Suite. After the first movement the smiles he observed around the orchestra confirmed its approval, and terror vanished. Brahms was present, but refrained from direct comment; though it was reported that he, too, had expressed admiration for the Introduction and Fugue, he had praised nothing else, and had been scathing about the March. By contrast Grieg, who

6 *TMKS*, pp. 346–7.

attended the even more successful second rehearsal two days later to which a paying public, mostly young enthusiasts, was admitted, left Tchaikovsky a warmly complimentary visiting card. Tchaikovsky found the orchestra beyond praise, larger and better than any in Russia, and the Gewandhaus itself the most wonderful concert hall he had ever been in.

His part in the concert on 5 January was a success. Brodsky had warned him that he might enter and bow to a completely silent hall, but there was loud applause after the first two movements, less after the following, but two recalls at the end. By Leipzig standards this signified high approval, as the press made clear. Afterwards a reception was given for him by Reinecke, who enthralled him by recounting his memories of Schumann. The day following the Leipzig Liszt-Verein, a society dedicated to the promotion of new music, presented a concert in Tchaikovsky's honour, consisting of his Piano Trio, First String Quartet, and Ziloti playing the *Barcarolle* from *The Seasons* and Pabst's fantasia on themes from *Onegin*. The violinist in the Trio was the twenty-eight-year-old Karel Halíř, already a devoted advocate of Tchaikovsky's music, who had given the Violin Concerto its German première, and whose account delighted Tchaikovsky when he heard Halíř play it later that day, giving promise of an excellent performance under Tchaikovsky's own direction in Prague. The hall was packed for this Leipzig 'Tschaikowsky-Feier', and the composer was seated on the platform with Grieg and his wife beside him; afterwards he was told that one lady had been overheard telling her daughter that it was Tchaikovsky with his children. Of the other musical experiences Leipzig afforded him, the most significant was a performance of *Das Rheingold* under Nikisch whose conducting, though so very different from Bülow's, he quickly came to admire greatly.

On 7 January Tchaikovsky returned to Berlin. The concert planned in Copenhagen had not materialized, while his engagement in Hamburg was nearly a fortnight away. And so, having negotiated further his programme details with Schneider, the impresario Hermann Wolf, and others involved in the running of the Philharmonic Orchestra, on 9 January he left with Brodsky to travel overnight to Hamburg en route for Lübeck, where he intended to spend about a week, partly preparing for his Hamburg engagement, but mainly to rest. In Hamburg he attended both the rehearsal and the concert conducted that evening by Bülow, in which Brodsky was the soloist, and on 11 January he settled himself into Lübeck. But solitude was two-edged; it afforded relaxation, but also time to brood on loneliness, and that homesickness which had ebbed and flowed so freely during the past fortnight, but which receded during his first days in Lübeck, suddenly engulfed him. 'God! How much time still remains before May!' he wrote in his diary on 15 January. '. . . After dinner (in my room) I walked up and down my room for a long time, then dozed. But afterwards there ensued such *longing* and *ennui* that I was at my wits' end. Is it possible I shall hold out for another four months??? . . . My God, how I love our dear, precious Russia!'[7] Tchaikovsky's current reading was Maupassant's new novel, *Pierre et Jean*, to which he was now all too ready to respond with tears. Even the news that through Vsevolozhsky's efforts the Tsar had granted him an annual pension of three thousand roubles seems not to have especially cheered him. Nevertheless, with typical generosity, he decided that Antonina should share in this new income, and he asked Jurgenson whether he thought it right to double the allowance to her.

From the time of his arrival in Lübeck he had found the town and its surroundings attractive, while the cultural fare it offered included Shakespeare's *Othello* played by a touring troupe, and a tolerable performance of Meyerbeer's *L'Africaine* presented by the small but efficient local company. But at the latter Tchaikovsky discovered he had been recognized, and he now had to suffer the very sort of attentions he had come to Lübeck to escape. Returning to Hamburg on 16 January, he drank himself into a state of oblivion.

The concert with the Hamburg Philharmonic Society took place four days later. Tchaikovsky's portion of the programme consisted of the Serenade for Strings, the First Piano Concerto with the nineteen-year-old Vasily Sapelnikov as the brilliant soloist, and the variation-finale of the Third Suite. There had been four rehearsals, the last one for the public, with an orchestra which quickly became very co-operative, even enthusiastic. The concert was a success, the Serenade being especially well received. It was followed by a formal dinner for one hundred guests in Tchaikovsky's honour at which he made a well prepared speech in German. As in Leipzig, there were further performances of his music the following day. In one concert Julius Laube and his orchestra played *Romeo and Juliet* and the Italian Capriccio, while in another, organized by the Musical Society, Sapelnikov offered the *Scherzo à la russe*, the *Romance*, Op. 5, and the variations from Op. 19, while Johanna Nathan sang four romances. The social whirl was as great as in Leipzig, but there were some contacts which remained pleasurable memories: with the publisher, Daniel Rahter, who had set in motion this whole European tour and who, with his charming wife and children, now provided the kind of haven the Brodskys and Zilotis

[7] *TD*, p. 190; *TZC3*, pp. 206–7.

had afforded in Leipzig – and with Theodor Avé-Lallemant, a leading
teacher and still one of the most influential figures within the Hamburg
Philharmonic Society, who, despite his advanced years and entrenched
aversion to all new music, struggled to two of Tchaikovsky's rehearsals
and the concert, delighted Tchaikovsky by arranging for a special
photograph of him to be taken at the best Hamburg photographer so
that he might keep a personal memento of Tchaikovsky's visit, and
who, while telling him frankly he did not like his music with its noisy
scoring and especially its use of the percussion, nevertheless held out a
secure hope he could still become a good composer. 'Almost tearfully,'
Tchaikovsky recorded in his *Autobiographical Account*, 'he exhorted me to
leave Russia and settle permanently in Germany, where classical
traditions and conditions of the highest culture would quite certainly
free me from my shortcomings which, in his view, are easily explained
by my having been born and brought up in a land still little enlightened
and far behind Germany as regards progress.' Despite his brutal
frankness, Avé-Lallemant showed such warmth and kindness that, as
Tchaikovsky added, 'we parted great friends'.[8] His rejoinder to this
criticism was to be as charming as it was unexpected: the dedication
of his next symphony (significantly, perhaps, this was to use no
percussion except timpani).

Tchaikovsky's tolerant response to Avé-Lallemant's words is significant. He reacted in much the same way to the Hamburg musical press.
It offered some 'curiosities', but in general he expressed himself well
pleased with what had been at best very qualified praise – for, as he
explained to Shpazhinskaya, 'it's not that I roused never-ending
rapture, but [I did awaken] *great interest*'.[9] In fact, Tchaikovsky was
perfectly able to withstand adverse criticism, even public, provided he
detected no ill-will, and that it was well-informed and sincerely meant,
which he rarely believed it to be in Russia. Thus he accepted the
'honourable openness'[10] of Josef Sittard in the *Hamburgischer Correspondent* because Sittard had attended all the rehearsals and carefully
studied the works; then, before disclosing his criticisms to the larger
world, he had communicated them orally to Tchaikovsky 'in words
which conveyed such sincere goodwill, [and] had shown me so much
attention and friendly sympathy, that I retain an exceedingly pleasant
memory of my brief acquaintance with him'.[11] And within the reasons
which were at the roots of such Germans' reservations towards his own

[8] *TMKS*, p. 359.
[9] *TLP*14, p. 347; *TTP*, p. 333.
[10] *TMKS*, p. 359.
[11] *TMKS*, p. 360.

music, he sensed what made Brahms their god. The cult of Brahms reflected nothing but a desperate search by a large section of the German people for a musician who would have nothing to do with those who, like Liszt, had attempted to foist Wagner's ideals and objectives upon the concert hall. In the absence of a successor of true genius to Haydn, Mozart, Beethoven, Mendelssohn and Schumann, conservative Germans had fastened their support upon the honest Brahms; just as they criticized Tchaikovsky for his novelty, not because they felt he lacked talent, so they venerated Brahms for preserving a hallowed tradition, not because they believed he was a major genius. As Tchaikovsky observed, it was merely a case that 'in the land of the blind, the one-eyed is king'. This knowledge was comforting, and when he left Hamburg on 22 January, his worries about Brahms had much diminished.

There was now again nearly a fortnight before Tchaikovsky would be required for his next commitment: the first rehearsal of his Berlin concert. It had still proved impossible to agree the final programme, for the Philharmonic directors were nervous of including *Francesca da Rimini*, and the symphonic fantasia was sacrificed for *1812* which, to Tchaikovsky's surprise, was felt more likely to succeed not only by the Society's men, but also by Bülow. On this one-day visit to Berlin he was introduced to the precocious Richard Strauss, already greatly admired by Bülow. Hearing the twenty-three-year-old's Symphony in F minor, itself now four years old, Tchaikovsky found he could not share Bülow's enthusiasm, though on reflection he concluded his first judgement might have been over-severe. Most of the next ten days was spent in Leipzig, preceded by a forty-eight-hour visit to Magdeburg, where he delighted in the city but censured the singers in a performance of *Tannhäuser*, which he found a boring opera.

Meanwhile news of his successes was penetrating to other parts of Germany, and additional invitations to conduct came from Weimar and even Dresden, despite his having earlier cancelled an engagement there. From Paris came the suggestion he should conduct the second halves of two of Colonne's concerts. In one regard it was a particularly happy proposal for Tchaikovsky, who was not only freed from involvement in promotion and financial hazard, but was now guaranteed an excellent orchestra and an established audience. But since he bore no risk, he would receive no fee. Already Mackar was talking of concerts in Belgium to follow those in London.

Arriving in Leipzig on 26 January, Tchaikovsky again relaxed in the company of the Brodskys and Zilotis, refreshed his acquaintance with the Griegs and Miss Smyth, and was introduced to Ferruccio Busoni, still only twenty-one, whose personality he found charming and whose mastery as pianist and composer commanded his instant admiration, but whose repudiation of his native Italian tradition he deplored. At an evening of chamber music he heard a string quartet by Busoni, and at a musical evening at the Brodskys' was filled with delight by Grieg's new Third Violin Sonata, Op. 45. He saw Weber's unfinished opera, *Die drei Pintos* ('the music's very nice, but the subject's stupid'[12]) which had just been completed by one of the four resident opera conductors, the twenty-seven-year-old Gustav Mahler, who had directed its première only nine days earlier. He also made Mahler's acquaintance. Sapelnikov had been with Tchaikovsky most of the time since leaving Hamburg. Tchaikovsky was plainly drawn as much to the youth as to his playing ('since Kotek's time, I have still never loved anyone so passionately as he,' he confessed to Modest[13]), and he was determined to do what he could to advance the young virtuoso's career as much in Berlin as in Leipzig, just as he had already been vigorously endeavouring to forward Ziloti's fortunes in the German capital. When Sapelnikov returned with Tchaikovsky to Berlin on 2 February to participate in Tchaikovsky's concert, it was as accompanist to a mezzo-soprano in four of Tchaikovsky's romances; this time Ziloti was to be the soloist in the First Piano Concerto. But Sapelnikov was to have handsome compensation, for through Wolf Tchaikovsky organized a formal event at which Sapelnikov could play and commend himself. Two days before his own concert Tchaikovsky had a timely chance to sample contemporary British composition when Bülow conducted a hugely successful performance of the new Third Symphony (the 'Irish') by Charles Villiers Stanford.

The Berlin concert, unlike those in Leipzig and Hamburg, was to be entirely Tchaikovsky's own. Besides the concerto, romances and *1812*, it consisted of *Romeo and Juliet*, the Andante cantabile, and the Introduction and Fugue from the First Suite. The Berlin Philharmonic Orchestra was a new group, founded on the initiative of the players themselves, and self-governing. The musical tastes of the city were more eclectic than those of Leipzig or Hamburg, and the orchestra's repertoire was correspondingly broad, the players possessing a notable versatility, and great zeal when working. His three rehearsals aroused intense interest. Bülow appeared, as did the Polish-German pianist-composer, Moritz Moszkowski, whose tuneful music Tchaikovsky already knew and had found most attractive. Grieg travelled from Leipzig specially for the final rehearsal and concert, and the Brodskys

---

[12] *TLP*14, p. 345; *TZC*3, p. 213; *YDGC*, p. 436; *TPB*, p. 390.
[13] *TLP*14, p. 354; *TZC*3, p. 214; *YDGC*, p. 437; *TPB*, p. 391.

were there. Despite filthy weather the concert itself on 8 February was well attended, Ziloti played magnificently, and of the purely instrumental pieces, *1812* and the Introduction and Fugue were especially well received. The press was generally more openly favourable than in Leipzig or Hamburg. The social life which had inevitably monopolized a major part of Tchaikovsky's week in the city had further drained him, and an inner wound had been reopened by the constant recollections among the musicians he met there of his dead friend, Kotek, who had lived and worked in Berlin for his last eight years. But now that Tchaikovsky's concerts in Germany were over, and he could review not only the gratifying respect with which he had been received but also judge how he himself had survived the varied and severe demands made upon him, both as conductor and man, he admitted to a profound inner elation. 'Would you recognize in this Russian musician travelling across Europe that man who only a few years ago had absconded from life in society and lived in seclusion abroad or in the country!!!' he wrote in unconcealed triumph to his patroness.[14]

It was well he had learned to cope, for what was planned for him in Prague far exceeded in extent and tumult what he had already endured in the six weeks since leaving Russia. In Berlin he had finally – at a price – rid himself of Friedrich. His journey to the Bohemian capital took him to Leipzig yet again. Earlier the Liszt-Verein had planned a second concert of his music, to be conducted by Ziloti, but because this tribute had proved impossible to arrange, he was compensated by a performance under Nikisch of *Die Meistersinger*, mounted at his special request because he had never seen the opera before ('very interesting' was his only comment[15]). The next day, 11 February, he was awakened by the strains of the Russian national anthem; an ardent admirer, a bandmaster to one of the regiments stationed in the locality, had organized an early morning serenade beneath Tchaikovsky's hotel room by his large and excellent military band, a compliment which required the recipient to stand at an open window for about an hour on a bitterly cold morning. After a meal at the Brodskys' with the Griegs and Miss Smyth, and an evening at Ziloti's, the following morning he left with the latter for Prague.

Tchaikovsky knew he was to be fêted, but he can have little guessed what had been stored up for him. There was some embarrassment mingled with his pleasure, for he was well aware in advance that a political, anti-German leaven was fermenting within this rapturous welcome – and he had, after all, just been most courteously and

[14] *TLP*14, p. 357; *TPM*3, p. 516; *TZC*3, p. 215.
[15] *TLP*14, p. 359; *YDGC*, p. 438; *TPB*, p. 392.

respectfully received in three German cities. It began at the frontier. 'The senior guard enquired whether I was Tchaikovsky, and he looked after me all the way. *At Kralupy*, the station before Prague, a whole crowd and deputation [from the Umělecká Beseda] awaited us, accompanying us to Prague. At the terminus there were a mass of people, deputations, children with bouquets, [and finally] two speeches, one in Russian, the other, a long one, *in Czech*. I replied. I went to my carriage between two walls of people and cries of "Slava!"'[16]

The Umělecká Beseda, whose guest he was, had reserved a splendid hotel room for him, and placed a carriage at his disposal throughout his stay. That evening there was a performance of Verdi's *Otello*. The political import of his visit, as perceived by many Czechs, became yet clearer to Tchaikovsky himself when the first person to greet him at the theatre was František Rieger, one of the leading nationalist politicians, of whose daughter, Marie Červinková-Riegrová, already the librettist of two of Dvořák's operas, Tchaikovsky was to see a good deal during his time in Prague. On this same occasion he met Dvořák himself, who called the morning following and remained for two hours; then followed a tour of the city and sights with Adolf Patera, Librarian of the Czech Museum, who visited Tchaikovsky daily and seems to have functioned as his main guide and guardian during his stay. After dining with Eduard Valecka, writer, publisher, and Russophile, and one of the instigators of Tchaikovsky's visit, there was a ball where he sat in a place of honour. Next day, there was mass in the Russian church and a visit from a group of students, then lunch at Dvořák's, a further tour of the city with Patera and, to end, the Umělecká Beseda presented for him a grand musical evening, with his portrait displayed garlanded in laurels. The programme included Smetana's String Quartet, 'From my life', and the recently completed Piano Quintet by Dvořák, which Tchaikovsky found as appealing as its creator. 'All this is very pleasant,' he continued to Modest, 'very flattering, but you can imagine how tired I am and how, at bottom, I suffer.'[17] Suffering or not, he bore it. After all, as he had confessed in Germany, it was when he awoke in the morning that the prospect of such fuss produced a deep, indescribable despair; once it had all begun, he was swept up in it, and despair passed.

Tchaikovsky was to conduct in two concerts in Prague. He had declined a fee for the first, hearing that it would be one of a series of People's Concerts instituted the previous year by the Umělecká

[16] *TLP*14, pp. 359–60; *TPB*, p. 392.
[17] *TLP*14, p. 360; *TPB*, p. 393.

Beseda. He believed his gesture was an added factor in the warmth of his welcome, and it may account for the extension of his invitation to a second concert. At the first rehearsal he was greeted with a fanfare, Dvořák was but one of the numerous listeners at all three, and the concert on 19 February was a triumph. The programme was formidable: the First Piano Concerto played by Ziloti and the Violin Concerto by Halíř, *Romeo and Juliet*, the *Elégie* from the Third Suite, and *1812*. At the following banquet Tchaikovsky attempted a very substantial speech in Czech (carefully written out, Modest noted, phonetically in cyrillic letters with accents indicated). He had now been a week in Prague, and his feelings for his fellow-Slavs had grown ever warmer. 'For myself I assure you that the days I have passed here are quite the best and happiest of my whole life,' he ended his oration. 'My gratitude for this is boundless and cannot be expressed . . . Gentlemen, I propose the toast: To the Umělecká Beseda!'[18] Later that evening, concluding his diary entry, he confirmed the sincerity of his words: 'There's no doubt this is one of the most notable days of my life. I love these kind Czechs very much. With good reason, too!!! God! How much enthusiasm, and all this not for me at all, but for dear Russia.'[19] He had not realized before how much the Czechs hated the Germans.

The second concert was two days later. This time the venue was the National Theatre, and Tchaikovsky was in charge of the first half only. Rehearsals went less well, but the orchestra rose to the occasion, and again the performance itself was a huge success, Tchaikovsky conducting his Serenade for Strings, the variations from the Third Suite and *1812*, and Ziloti contributing the *Barcarolle* from *The Seasons*, the *Nocturne*, Op. 19, No. 4, and Pabst's *Onegin* fantasia. The second half was mounted by the theatre itself: a performance of Act 2 of *Swan Lake*. Perhaps Tchaikovsky contrasted what he now saw with the sad fortunes of this ballet during its first eleven years in his native land. '*A moment of complete happiness*,' he noted in his diary.[20]

It had been an extraordinary ten days – as Modest was to put it, 'the highest point of worldly fame Pyotr Ilich was destined to achieve during his lifetime'.[21] Tchaikovsky was the more upset therefore that the Russian press virtually ignored his triumph for Russia. The comprehensive detail in Tchaikovsky's diary entries reveals the concentration of appointments, visits, meetings, meals, receptions and so on, besides musical occasions, which packed even the days of his concerts.

[18] Quoted in *TLP*14, p. 622; *TZC*3, p. 222.
[19] *TD*, pp. 197–8; *TZC*3, p. 220; *YDGC*, p. 440.
[20] *TD*, p. 198; *TZC*3, p. 222; *YDGC*, p. 440.
[21] *TZC*3, p. 223.

There were photographs to be taken and inscribed, and things to be bought, the most important of the purchases he bore back to Russia being a marble clock in which he took great pride to the end of his days. It is well for posterity he was keeping a diary, for there was almost no time for letter writing. Among the more memorable of the other occasions was a performance of *The Bartered Bride*, an evening at the Russian circle with Dvořák who, when toasted by Tchaikovsky, managed a few words of Russian in reply and was embraced by Tchaikovsky in gratitude, a surprise torchlight serenade from the street to which he had to listen from a balcony and which covered him with confusion, a visit to the Rathaus where the assembled council rose to greet him, an ovation at the Civic Society, a grand welcome and send-off at the Students' Society – and a visit to '*Mozart's* room'.[22] Above all, perhaps, there was a concert at the Conservatoire where he heard an excellent performance of Dvořák's D minor Symphony, the autograph score of which (ironically, perhaps, the most Brahms-influenced of all his works) Dvořák presented to Tchaikovsky as a memento of his visit. The relationship between the two composers had developed rapidly and mutually.

Tchaikovsky's departure on 22 February was as much an occasion as his arrival, with friends, wellwishers and bouquets, and a certain Dr Buchal quoting Schiller:

> Die schönen Tage in Aranjuez
> Sind nun zu Ende.

Tchaikovsky was deeply touched, and sad to leave. But he was urgently required in Paris to prepare for his first concert. Outwardly his reception in the French capital much resembled that which he had just experienced in Prague, though it was spread over a period twice as long. But whereas, Modest believed, the Czech demonstrations had reflected a deep love for the Russian people founded upon racial affinity, a sense of brotherhood, and also upon a profound national musicality which was to continue feasting avidly upon his brother's music in the years following, the enthusiasm of the French was little more than a response to prevailing fashion. Tchaikovsky himself had fully realized before ever setting out for Paris that things Russian were *à la mode* – like Kronstadt hats, Franco-Russian cravats, Russian circus performers, the Russian national anthem alongside the Marseillaise, as Modest put it. But, the latter added, 'thirteen years have passed, and since then in Prague Pyotr Ilich's operas have held the stage and his

22 *TD*, p. 196.

symphonic music is known and loved as in Russia. In Paris he is . . . almost completely unperformed both in the theatre and on the concert platforms.'[23] Be that as it may – and Modest's account of this visit has a strong whiff of francophobia about it – Tchaikovsky's arrival in Paris on 24 February immersed him immediately in another maelstrom of activities in which, as in Prague, he was the centre of attention. His first commitment was to conduct Colonne's orchestra for a gala soirée at the grand home of Nikolay Benardaky, a wealthy expatriate Russian and musical Maecenas who, with Mackar, had been a leading figure in promoting Tchaikovsky's cause in France. Benardaky's wife, Marie, also Russian, was a former student at the St Petersburg Conservatoire, and Tchaikovsky orchestrated his song, 'Does the day reign?', for her to include in the same programme on 28 February. It was a sumptuous occasion, with a pleiad of most distinguished soloists including Jean Lassalle, principal baritone at the Opéra, the de Reszke brothers, Edouard and Jean, and Louis Diémer. Brandukov played the solo part in the première of the *Pezzo capriccioso* and in a transcription for cello and small orchestra that Tchaikovsky had recently made of his *Nocturne*, No. 4 of the Six pieces for piano, Op. 19, while Tchaikovsky himself conducted the *Elegia* and Valse from the Serenade for Strings, and the Andante cantabile, and also provided the piano accompaniment for the singers. There were three hundred invited guests, the cream of Parisian society, and it proved 'a famous evening',[24] Tchaikovsky leaving at half-past-four in the morning. In a city so ruled by fashion it was the aptest of beginnings for a visit such as his.

The two half-concerts were on 4 and 11 March. Tchaikovsky observed sardonically how Colonne was gathering in the receipts while he himself reaped nothing, and his feelings must have been very ambivalent when the conductor-promoter allocated him almost the entire second concert, contenting himself with an overture by Berlioz to begin. In the first concert Tchaikovsky conducted the Serenade for Strings, the variations from the Third Suite, as well as the Andante cantabile and *Nocturne*, again with Brandukov, Diémer was the soloist in the Concert Fantasia, and Juliette Conneau sang 'None but the lonely heart' and 'Does the day reign?'; in the second concert the variations, the *Nocturne* and the central two movements of the Serenade were repeated, *Francesca da Rimini* was added, Marsick was the soloist in the Violin Concerto, Diémer contributed three piano pieces (*Chant sans paroles*, Op. 40, No. 6, *Humoresque*, Op. 10, No. 2, and Liszt's transcription of the *Onegin* polonaise), and Alfred Giraudet, a baritone from the

[23] *TZC3*, p. 226.
[24] *TD*, p. 200; *YDGC*, p. 441.

Opéra, sang 'A Tear trembles' and 'Don Juan's serenade'. At rehearsal the players had greeted Tchaikovsky enthusiastically and at the concerts the Serenade and variations were especially well liked (at the first the Valse was encored). But Tchaikovsky sensed the problems posed to French listeners by the Concert Fantasia and *Francesca* in particular, and press reaction was cool. Modest believed that the influence of Cui's book, *La Musique en Russie*, accounted for the reserve among certain critics and their detection in Tchaikovsky's music of strong German elements.

Outside the concert hall he was lionized. There were press interviews and profiles, with *Le Figaro* mounting a special soirée in his honour at which the de Reszke brothers and Paul Taffanel, today regarded as the father of the French school of flute playing, performed; there was the predictable abundance of receptions (with or without his music), dinners, social events, and a plethora of appointments. At last he met Massenet as well as Gounod ('very amiable'[25]), who pointedly exhibited approval during Tchaikovsky's first concert. He was able to confirm his impression that, of all French composers, Delibes was the one he found personally 'most sympathetic'. He was dined by Widor, whose playing he admired at St Sulpice where the organist had already been installed eighteen years and would remain a further forty-six, and attended a recital by another rising star of the Ziloti-Sapelnikov-Busoni generation – also to be premier and foreign minister of Poland, and his country's signatory of the Versailles Treaty: Ignacy Jan Paderewski ('magnificent pianist'[26]). He consolidated his acquaintance with other leading musicians he had encountered on his last visit – notably Fauré, Marmontel and Lamoureux – met a number of leading writers, and was particularly delighted (so Modest stated) to hear that the fame of 'None but the lonely heart' was now sufficient for it to feature in the plot of a new novel, *Le Froc*, by Emile Goudeau; he was to bear back to Russia a number of books and scores presented to him by their creators and flatteringly inscribed. The chamber music society, *La trompette*, arranged an evening of his works including, besides the First String Quartet and numerous solo items, Tchaikovsky himself and Diémer playing the Concert Fantasia on two pianos. At a well filled Salle Erard Diémer presented an *audition* by himself and his pupils, all playing pieces by Tchaikovsky – some forty in all ('touched but weary,' the composer noted in his diary[27]). Again he was received by Viardot, who invited him to dine with her. Nor did he neglect to visit the Auclairs at

---

[25] *TD*, p. 201; *YDGC*, p. 441.
[26] *TD*, p. 201; *TZC*3, p. 228.
[27] *TD*, p. 204; *YDGC*, p. 444.

Bicêtre. His biggest regret was that there was so little time to go to theatres.

A few days before leaving for London Tchaikovsky reviewed the past weeks to Jurgenson. 'During all this time I have expended a very great deal of my money and even more of my health and strength – but I have gained a little fame. But constantly I ask myself: why? is it worth it? and so on – and I've come to the conclusion that to live without fame but quietly is far better than leading this mad existence. After London they're demanding that I should conduct various patriotic concerts here – but I've decided to spit on the lot of them and take myself off.'[28] He had not received a single franc as fee while in France, there had been no proposals that he should be paid anything for these future concerts which the new Société Franco-Russe was trying to promote, and all that was now taking him to London, he had admitted, was that he would be remunerated for his efforts. He had received further lucrative offers while in France – a thousand francs, for instance, to conduct in Angers – but he could face no more, and had firmly declined all such temptations as well as any proposal for a Belgian tour after England. It was in this dour frame of mind that on 19 March he endured a rough crossing from Calais to Dover. There was snow, too, and he arrived in London at midnight, five hours late. Two things restored his spirits somewhat; he had discovered he was not liable to seasickness, and his hotel, into which he had booked on the recommendation of Francesco Berger, secretary to the Philharmonic Society, who had conducted negotiations with him, was friendly and warm. French through and through, the Hotel Dieudonné in Ryder Street was particularly favoured by musicians and artists, and provided the comfortable retreat which made his five days in London bearable.[29]

While in Prague Tchaikovsky had conceived the idea of sharing his London concert with his new friend, Grieg, but it had proved impossible to match dates. There is no doubt that the two men had genuinely warmed to each other. After their Leipzig encounters Grieg had promptly written to Johan Svendsen, his fellow-composer, friend, and also the leading conductor in Scandinavia, gaining his agreement to invite Tchaikovsky to conduct in Oslo or Copenhagen in 1889. Back in Moscow later in the year Tchaikovsky reciprocated by engineering an invitation for Grieg to appear at an RMS concert performing his A minor Concerto and conducting others of his pieces. Meanwhile the two

[28] *TLP*14, p. 379; *TPJ*2, p. 86; *TZC*3, p. 233 (partial).
[29] For a very thorough account of the environment in which Tchaikovsky passed this visit to London, see Gerald Norris, *Stanford, the Cambridge Jubilee, and Tchaikovsky* (London, 1980), pp. 308–21.

men exchanged scores. 'If sometime you write an Adagio or, better still, a Largo and insert in it a truly Beethovenian pause – best of all, a whole bar of ⌒ – then use the pause for a free fantasy on the theme of "London",' Grieg wrote affably from Leipzig on 12 April, enquiring how Tchaikovsky's English visit had gone. 'And if you add another crotchet rest, then remember what you promised me: in the first place

[Ex. 231]

then the B flat minor piano concerto, and then . . . then a lot else. But no more – I'm already satisfied.'[30] Tchaikovsky responded, despatching not only the *1812* overture and the concerto, but *Romeo and Juliet* and the Third Suite. In return Grieg sent his overture, *Im Herbst*, G minor String Quartet, Third Violin Sonata, and First *Peer Gynt* suite. Friendly, flattering inscriptions graced all eight scores, and later in the year Tchaikovsky dedicated his fantasy overture, *Hamlet*, to Grieg. But then, as with some of Tchaikovsky's other relationships with fellow-musicians, the intimacy quickly faded. Grieg did not come to Moscow, nor Tchaikovsky to Scandinavia, and from a note in Tchaikovsky's personal diary the following year it seems he deliberately avoided the Norwegian composer while in Paris. They should have met in 1893 when both men were to receive honorary degrees from Cambridge University, but Grieg was ill and unable to attend. Thus after these close encounters in Leipzig and warm exchanges of scores and letters it seems the two men had no further contact.

Disappointed in his current hope of Grieg as fellow-conductor, Tchaikovsky had to divide the concert on 22 March with Frederic Cowen, after two rehearsals conducting his Serenade for Strings and variations from the Third Suite. He found the acoustics of the St James's Hall less satisfactory than those of the Châtelet where his Paris concerts had been held, and his ignorance of English meant that Cowen had to stand by the rostrum as interpreter. But on the credit side was the impressive sight-reading ability of an excellent English orchestra. He had heard that English audiences, like German, were undemonstrative, but the Serenade was self-evidently successful (three recalls), the variations rather less so. Press reaction was positively warm, and the management gave substantial proof of their view of his efforts, increasing his fee from the agreed £20 to £25. As Modest was to observe,

[30] Quoted in *TZM*, p. 207

of all his brother's visits during this European tour, the brief stay in London had the greatest significance for the future fame of his music. In England, despite the efforts of such as Dannreuther, it had remained relatively little known; now its creator had sowed the seeds of a popularity which, outside Russia, was to be matched only in America.

Tchaikovsky found London a cheerless city and, relieved as he was to be spared the social attentions of Paris, he was now frequently bored. Much of his freer time was occupied with deciding by which route he should return to Russia. He had relinquished the lease on his house in Maidanovo, and though Alexey had been searching for new accommodation, so far he had concluded no arrangement. This made it easier for Tchaikovsky to head for Tiflis, where he really longed to be since it was the only place where he could hope to relax. But still he could not settle by which route. He dearly wished to retrace in reverse a substantial part of the Black Sea-Mediterranean journey he had taken two years before, but fear of spring storms decided him finally to select a land passage. On 24 March he left London. Passing through Aachen, he thought much of Kondratyev, and his gloom was deepened by reading *La Terre*, the latest novel by Zola. The work of this naturalistic novelist possessed a special fascination for him, despite the violent physical reactions it could produce. Nearly three years earlier he had by accident come across Zola's *Germinal*. 'I began reading it, was carried away by it, and it happened I finished it very late at night. I was so agitated that I had palpitations which prevented me sleeping, and the next day I was *thoroughly* ill – and now I think of this novel as of some horrifying nightmare,' he had told Modest.[31] The same blend of attraction and revulsion marked his response to this newest novel of Zola; 'I positively hate the swine, for all his talent,' he noted in his diary on 25 March as he sped towards Vienna.[32] Here he delayed two days and caught up with his letter-writing, heartily thanking the Brodskys in Leipzig and Valecka and Patera in Prague for their hospitality and concern on his behalf, and greeting Dvořák with special warmth. 'I shall never forget how well and in how friendly a fashion you received me in Prague . . . Dear friend, convey my heartfelt greeting to your dear wife, and allow me to say again that I am very happy and fortunate to have gained your most precious friendship.'[33] London had afforded him a French play (Molière's *Tartuffe* excellently performed by Benoît-Constant Coquelin's company); now Vienna offered him an English opera – but even one act of *The Mikado* was too much. By now he was

[31] *TLP*13, p. 164; *TZC*3, p. 75; *TPB*, p. 334; *YDGC*, p. 352.
[32] *TD*, p. 206; *YDGC*, p. 445; *TZC*3, p. 238 (with 'swine' changed to 'writer').
[33] *TLP*14, pp. 391–2.

suffering a reaction from the turmoil of the past three months. 'Shall I write for the future?' he asked himself on 27 March in what for a while was to be his last diary entry. 'It's hardly worth it. Maybe with this I shall end my diary for ever. Old age advances, perhaps death is not far off. Is it worth it?'[34]

Yet there had been a very positive personal reward within all these activities. Even in London, once his concert was over, he had begun to admit this openly. 'Yesterday evening ended my torments, fears, upsets – but also, it must truthfully be said, my *joys*,' he wrote on 23 March. 'The point is that if my journey had comprised only rehearsals and concerts then, despite the strain on my nerves, I should have ex- perienced pleasure rather than feelings of weariness. Success, which I enjoyed everywhere, is very pleasant.'[35] And once he had recrossed the frontier of his native land, everything fell into a yet truer perspective. Not only were the benefits of the last three months more apparent; even more so were the attractions of repeating the experience. 'I shall try to get an invitation to conduct concerts in America next year or in two years' time,' he continued to his patroness on 3 April. 'Is it not strange that after more than three months of exhausting travelling abroad, I am already again dreaming of a journey?'[36] Next morning, after three days in Taganrog with Ippolit and his wife, he left for Tiflis. On 7 April he was with Anatoly and Parasha.

Nearly a year had passed since Tchaikovsky had finished an import- ant composition, and now, once he had recouped his strength in his three-week holiday and installed himself in the new accommodation Alexey had at last arranged for him, his overriding wish was to embark on major composition. For a while he was torn. On the one hand he longed to tackle a symphony, for it was eleven years since his last; on the other, he remained tormented by the recent history of his own operatic enterprises, and he was beset by an urge to prove he could still compose a successful opera. At the end of 1887 Modest had been working on a libretto for Tchaikovsky's former pupil, Nikolay Klenovsky, but the latter had backed away, and it had briefly seemed that brother Pyotr might take over the project. 'After the failure of *The Enchantress* I wanted *revenge* and was ready to rush at any subject, and at that time I felt envious that it wasn't I who was setting it. But now all that has passed,' he explained to his brother in finally declining this libretto, 'and first this summer *I shall without fail compose a symphony*, and I shall start upon an opera only if a subject turns up capable of stirring me deeply. A

[34] *TD*, p. 206; *YDGC*, p. 445 (partial).
[35] *TLP*14, p. 385; *TPM*3, p. 521; *TZC*3, p. 234 (partial).
[36] *TLP*14, p. 395; *TPM*3, p. 523; *TZC*3, p. 237.

subject such as *The Queen of Spades* does not touch me, and I should compose it indifferently.'[37] Within two years he was, of course, to take a very different view.

Nor for the moment was he prepared to commit himself to either of two other theatrical subjects which had earlier been offered him, though other persons had already concluded he was. 'Everything they are writing in the newspapers regarding my new works is *a lie*,' he wrote angrily to Nadezhda von Meck on 6 May, the day he arrived at last in his new home. 'I did indeed sometimes contemplate, and still do, an opera on *The Captain's Daughter*; I did indeed also contemplate accepting the proposal made to me *by the theatre's directorate* to write the music for a ballet, *Undine*, but all this is only one *possibility* and in no way a fact. After a trip to St Petersburg and some visits to Moscow in connection with the Conservatoire exams I intend above all to take in hand the composition of *a symphony*.'[38]

In fact, the summer was to be remarkably fruitful. His new home at Frolovskoye, a little farther from Klin than Maidanovo, delighted him. He had often seen the location from the train on his journeys to Moscow, and had long been attracted by its wooded environment and promise of a seclusion such as was impossible at Maidanovo. 'Alexey has arranged my new habitation wonderfully,' he enthused to Anatoly. 'It's not nearly as nice and elegant as at Maidanovo – but, then, the rooms are large, high, and there's wonderful very old furniture which gives the whole house a romantic touch. The house stands high; the view's superb . . . The garden is very sympathetic. But what's most precious of all is that you can go straight from the garden into the wood and stroll there the whole day. There's not a trace of the holiday inhabitants of the dachas.' He resolved to take gardening seriously and within days had everything ready for sowing and planting, once the weather had improved. He approved, too, of Alexey's new wife: 'extremely nice and sympathetic'[39] – though her best feature, he decided, was her excellent teeth. Before he could feel settled he had still to go to St Petersburg where he understood the Tsar wished to speak with him, and where many of his family were assembled for a wedding. The royal audience proved an official rather than informal occasion. No doubt a dutiful Tchaikovsky expressed his profound gratitude for the recent award of a pension, but His Majesty seemed in a hurry, and the newly returned ambassador for Russian music had no time to elaborate, as he had hoped, on the demonstrations of russophilia

---

[37] *TLP*14, p. 400; *TPB*, p. 400; *YDGC*; p. 446.
[38] *TLP*14, p. 416; *TPM*3, p. 529; *TZC*3, p. 240; *YDGC*, p. 446 (partial).
[39] *TLP*14, pp. 417–18; *TPB*, p. 401.

during his stay in Prague. His family brought even less joy during his ten-day visit. It was more than two years since he had seen his sister and her condition shocked him. Her addiction to morphine had become worse and she had aged, while Bob was growing unhealthily fat, and Tasya had lost her good looks.

Back in Frolovskoye on 21 May, he reviewed his creative schemes and came to one firm decision. *The Captain's Daughter* 'is too bitty; it calls for too many realizations of conversations, explanations and actions which are not amenable to music,' he told the Grand Duke Konstantin Konstantinovich.[40] The bitter lessons of *The Enchantress* had indeed been well absorbed. Nor, despite the Tsar's personal assurances, did he believe there would be no trouble with the censor if he were to present Pugachev truthfully. And there was another fundamental flaw. 'I found that there were no characters in it personally demanding to be realized musically, and the heroine in particular was quite painfully insipid. At one time when *The Captain's Daughter* was under discussion, I was probably tempted above all by the atmosphere of a past century and by the contrast between *gentlemen* in European costume and Pugachev with his wild horde. But a single contrast is not enough for an operatic subject; there must be living beings, affecting situations. I should like to write a concise opera in three acts with a subject of intimate character, where there is scope for lyrical outpourings. Can you think of something?' he continued to Yuliya Shpazhinskaya, whose literary impulses he had resumed prodding. 'And if you think of one, could you put together a scenario?'[41] Clearly, however, he placed little serious hope in Shpazhinskaya, and her search would take time anyway. Ten days later, on 31 May, having re-examined his Fourth Symphony, the orchestral material of which was being printed, and having been heartened to discover how good it seemed, he at last gave Modest the news he had begun work upon its successor.

It did not come easily, and the composer's letters over the next two months are laced with laments at the sluggishness of his inspiration, and with bursts of self-doubt. But there was an added complication, for he had been simultaneously but secretly gestating a second major work. Twelve years earlier, when he had been languishing in Vichy and lamenting his sterility, Modest had offered a programme for an orchestral piece on *Hamlet*. Tchaikovsky had warmly approved the subject but had also pronounced it very formidable, and soon was pouring his reawakened creative energies into *Francesca da Rimini*. His brother's suggestion had recurred to him in 1885, when he had

---

[40] *TLP*14, p. 442; *TZC*3, p. 245; *YDGC*, p. 448.
[41] *TLP*14, p. 427; *TTP*, p. 337; *TPB*, p. 611 (partial); *YDGC*, p. 447 (partial).

scribbled out a theme (never used) to match Hamlet's most famed words. Then on 21 September 1887 he had returned to the subject yet again, noting laconically in his diary that he had composed an 'unsuccessful second theme for *Hamlet*'.[42] Yet though his working sketchbook of the time includes a melody intended for *Hamlet* which he was to reject, the preliminary version of what was to become the opening theme is already there. Then on 6 February 1888, during his extended concert tour, he received a request from his actor-friend, Lucien Guitry, to provide incidental music for some scenes from Shakespeare's tragedy which were to be part of a charity performance only two months later in St Petersburg. Though a second letter soon notified Tchaikovsky that the event had been cancelled, the subject had finally seeded itself firmly, and during the remainder of his tour he had continued to jot down sketches, both verbal and musical.

However, once this summer's phase of purposeful composition began, the symphony took first place, and it was not until 29 June, after sketches for this were finished, that he set about the fantasy overture. But only five days later *Hamlet*, too, was drafted. This done, Tchaikovsky returned to the larger piece to score it, completing the work on 26 August. His own view of his new symphony had become more cheerful as this task neared its end, and when he introduced it to his Moscow friends in mid-September it was enthusiastically received, especially by Taneyev who had made the piano duet arrangement and thus already knew the piece well. Yet even when the symphony was completed, it was a month before Tchaikovsky could proceed to scoring *Hamlet*, and this operation was not concluded until 19 October, since he had also been engaged in orchestrating an overture, *Karmozina*, by Laroche for performance in November.

The Fifth Symphony and *Hamlet* received their premières within a week of each other, the symphony on 17 November and the fantasy overture on the 24th; on the latter occasion the symphony was heard for the second time. The performances, all in St Petersburg, were conducted by the composer. Both works were triumphs with the audiences. At the first concert, besides bouquets, there was a triple fanfare from the orchestra, and a deputation presented Tchaikovsky with an inscribed address admitting him to honorary membership of the St Petersburg Philharmonic Society. But neither piece was well received by the press. According to Modest, only two critics had a good word for the symphony; for the rest, including Cui in his well practised role as leader of the opposition, the work was routine and dependent upon

---

[42] *TD*, p. 178; *YDGC*, p. 420.

meretricious effect, and marked a further decline in Tchaikovsky's creative powers. The Second Piano Concerto, played by Sapelnikov, was also included in the first concert. Nearly nine years old but only now receiving its first performance in St Petersburg, it fared better, its age placing it in the unfriendly critics' ears among those former works in which the composer had been so much better than now.

What the critics could not know was that this new symphony shared an animating force with its predecessor, for though Tchaikovsky told the Grand Duke Konstantin Konstantinovich that the work had no programme, what was clearly a prescription for the first movement survives among the sketches:

> Intr[oduction]. Total submission before Fate – or, what is the same thing, the inscrutable design of Providence.
> Allegro. 1. Murmurs, doubts, laments, reproaches against . . . XXX.
>   2. Shall I cast myself into the embrace of *faith*?
> A wonderful programme, if only it can be fulfilled.[43]

Though we can only speculate whether the object for reproach which Tchaikovsky masked in the triple X was his homosexuality, one thing cannot be in doubt; his view of Fate has shifted radically, for the new identification of this all-governing force with divine will implies a confidence in ultimate clemency which is pointedly reflected at the symphony's opening (Ex. 232b), for while the familiar six-note scalic descent is there (though now set between the tonic and mediant), Gerald Abraham was surely right to spot a quotation from Glinka's *A Life for the Tsar* (Ex. 232a) whose text can be read as an exhortation to

Ex. 232

[Do not turn to sorrow]

[43] Quoted in Davïdova (K. Y.) and others [eds.], *Muzïkalnoye naslediye Chaykovskovo* etc. (Moscow, 1958), p. 239.

this new trust. Certainly the tone of the muted first bars confirms that the familiar force is no longer the strident assailant of the Fourth Symphony. And since the violence of any conflict is to be less extreme, there is less need for the respite afforded by shifting the central movements into personally uncommitted territory of no concern to this all-powerful force. Thus the slow movement continues the consideration of substantial personal issues. True, Fate remains intimidating, and twice it reminds of its power; yet now it may also be viewed as an integral, if painful, part of experience, not merely as a purely destructive challenge to it. At the untroubled opening of the third movement (see Ex. 236) acceptance turns almost to welcome; the familiar six-note symbol is unflinchingly allowed its special mediant-dominant niche, and its new Glinka-based companion rounds off the movement with an intrusion so mild as to seem positively benign. Any struggle being passed, the path away from sorrow may be securely trod; there is firm resolve when the finale's preliminaries review and revise the symphony's introduction, unfettered energy and fearless assimilation of the Fate themes in what follows, and a tone of triumph, even exultation, when they and the first movement's first subject are trumpeted at the end. The frantic defiance which had concluded the Fourth Symphony ('To live is still possible!') is replaced by firm, if hard-won, confidence.

Be all this as it may, there were also special musical considerations conditioning Tchaikovsky's view of what this symphony should be. The crucial clue to why he was aiming at a structural poise and consistency of expressive quality greater than in any of his more weighty instrumental pieces of the last dozen years is to be found in the dedication. Originally intending it for Grieg, Tchaikovsky was to transfer it to Theodor Avé-Lallemant, giving his Norwegian composer-friend the inscription of *Hamlet* instead.[44] Tchaikovsky left no expla-

---

[44] In view of Tchaikovsky's first intention of making Grieg the dedicatee, it is curious to note the similarities between the opening Allegro con anima and the finale of Grieg's Piano Sonata, also in E minor. Though composed in 1865, the sonata was revised and republished in Leipzig in 1887, and it is difficult to believe that this new version did not

nation for this change, but it may safely be assumed that he hoped his new symphony would win special approval from this highly conservative, though kindly pillar of the Hamburg Philharmonic Society, who had pleaded with him to seek deliverance from the rough mores of Russia's musical wilderness by cultivating the refined practices which prevailed in Germany's musical pastures. For just as in 1872, having been drawn increasingly into the circle of the Kuchka, he had composed his Second Symphony to show he also could command their musical world, and just as in the Serenade for Strings he had mixed Russian folksong with a Western style and technique to demonstrate to Taneyev that he could successfully compound them, so now, having recently had close contact with many of the leading European creative personalities (especially Brahms) and experienced more deeply than ever before their musical world, he sought to demonstrate to such as Avé-Lallemant that he could compose a symphony satisfying to Western ideals and criteria, yet uncompromisingly his own.

To begin with, the expressive balance between the four movements is far more even than in the Fourth Symphony; nor are there any of the disturbing tonal operations or asymmetries which had been such potent factors in the unique experience of that work's mighty first movement. Instead, the proportions of exposition, development and recapitulation are tidily balanced and the coda is content to round off neatly what has gone before. If there is a precedent it is the first movement of the Third Symphony, though confident maturity now enabled Tchaikovsky to avoid the inconsistencies and uncertainties of that badly flawed piece. As in the earlier movement there are still three subjects, the initial outline of the first clearly dependent upon the motto theme; each is allotted its own key (in the exposition E minor, B minor and its relative, D major, respectively; in the recapitulation adjusted, with little upheaval, to E minor, C sharp minor and E major) – though the adaptation of the second subject's opening (Ex. 233a) to become the answering phrase in the third (Ex. 233b) does recall the inter-subject connections of the Fourth Symphony. There are other similar touches that contribute to the exposition's fluency; above all, every fragment of the material is quintessentially Tchaikovsky's own. The development is of exemplary economy and shapeliness, favouring flat keys and redressing the sharp-key monopoly of the surrounding sections. Earlier

feature in the musical exchanges between its composer and Tchaikovsky in the same city early the following year. It is not merely that there are similarities within the first subjects of the two movements; there are also tiny touches which suggest this Molto allegro haunted Tchaikovsky's creativity as he composed his far more sophisticated sonata structure.

Ex. 233

materials are worked against one another, extended sequentially, though never tediously; there is an effective climax, and an untroubled entry into the recapitulation.

This is a very fine, if not a great movement. The slow movement is something more. Having spared his listener tumultuous expressive issues such as he had confronted him with in the Fourth Symphony's first movement, Tchaikovsky remained free to extend his investigation of weighty matters into the following Andante cantabile, con alcuna licenza. Indeed, not since the Andante funebre of the Third String Quartet had a slow movement been made to bear such heavy responsibility, and only once again would one ever be required to do so. Its playing time matches that of the entire first movement, and though its dynamic extremes had been paralleled in earlier scores, no movement had been so covered with expressive instructions and pointers. Creating it cost Tchaikovsky much uncertainty. Originally its main theme was to have been a version of the waltz tune which opens the third movement, and among the other sketches is one (Ex. 234a) which finally found no place in the symphony, though what was to become the opening of the slow movement's second theme, as first presented by the oboe (Ex. 234b), is contained within its contour. It also evidences how literally Tchaikovsky could tie programmatic concepts to particular musical materials, in this instance seeming to embody a fate-full antithesis in a fragment of tune and bass.[45] It is said that the melody

---

[45] Davïdova, *op. cit.*, p. 239. The editors suggest, however, that the lower words might refer to a musical idea not yet conceived, and never realized.

Ex. 234

Beneath the reply: 'No, there is no hope!'

finally chosen was paired with the words: 'O, que je t'aime! O mon amie!', which would confirm the impression that consolidates as the movement unfolds – that this is a profoundly personal outpouring of love and longing.

The sombre procession of slow chords at the opening impressed both Dvořák ('New World' Symphony) and Rakhmaninov (Second Piano Concerto), but whereas they were each to devise a chord structure to shift from the key of the first movement to the remote tonality of the slow movement, Tchaikovsky had no such distance to travel. Nevertheless, the first sounds are still within a minor key orbit, and the emergence of the main theme above these dark preliminaries as they gently settle into the new tonic of D major is perfectly judged. In fact, the theme (Ex. 235a) that follows is not one of Tchaikovsky's strongest, and certainly cannot compare with, for instance, that full-blooded melody which had embodied the youthful passions of Romeo and Juliet nearly twenty years earlier. But it scarcely mattered, for the issue now was certainly not the impetuous ardour of youth, but the disconsolate longing of age. Even when the contours steepen in the second half the falling sevenths are merely forlorn sighs. Its magic comes from its medium, for the yearning melancholy of the horn matches the theme perfectly, and none of its subsequent appearances is quite so affecting.

In any case, what follows is by no means dependent solely upon this first idea. Regardless of whatever programmatic significance the two appearances of the Fate materials may have, they conveniently mark the ends of the central and final sections in this ternary structure, on the second occasion enhancing the coda by ensuring it a more separate identity. Yet the frankness of this movement's melodic confession is made all the more effective by another of those simple yet perceptive ordering of events (Ex. 235) at which Tchaikovsky had shown himself

Ex. 235

FIFTH SYMPHONY: SLOW MOVEMENT

Tonal Outline:

so adept, most recently in the slow movement of the Manfred Symphony. The horn cantilena (Ai) is succeeded by a second theme (Bi), likewise cantabile, briefly introduced con moto by oboe in duet with horn before the strings resume the opening melody (Aii) with rich embellishment from wind counterpoints. But the modest oboe theme has merely foretold a little of what is to prove a melodic paragraph (Bii) as spacious as that of the horn theme, yet far more urgent and a great deal stronger in contour. After a full statement of this has ended the first major division of the movement, the centre brings with it a new theme and key (F sharp minor). As for the final section, just as in the slow movement of the Manfred Symphony Tchaikovsky had devised an expressive climax by welding into a single span three ideas earlier heard separately, so now, by excluding the oboe theme (Bi) and linking the statements of the two main themes into one huge, dynamically arching paragraph, the third section is given a grandeur to which the first had never aspired. The coda returns the music to the stillness from which this deeply eloquent movement had emerged.

The spirit of the waltz had haunted the first movement and lingered a little into the second; now it materializes in the third. Fate stoops to participate in the genial world of this interlude, leading the dance (Ex. 236) into a ternary structure less mechanically balanced than

Ex. 236

might at first appear. Simple, even naïve, this Valse may seem among its grander companions, but it executes its transitional function perfectly. While a deft overlapping of differing materials welds together the end of the central section and the return of the first (as in the Manfred Symphony's scherzo), an even more organic link is forged between the finale's Andante maestoso and the main Allegro vivace (Ex. 237a–d). Indeed, the emergence of the energetic first subject (Ex. 237d) from the dying conclusion of the introduction (Ex. 237c) is but one of a swift series of thematic evolutions (Ex. 237a–f). This Allegro vivace is Tchaikovsky at his most high spirited, with an elemental freshness almost unheard in his major symphonic works since the finale of the

Ex. 237

a. Motto theme, bars 5-6

b. bar 43

c. bar 50

d. bar 60

e. bar 82

f. bar 98

g. bar 128

h. Slow movement: horn theme

i. bar 195 (approached from C major)

Second Symphony. And if the real source of the fertile procession of materials which make up the first subject may be traced to the familiar Fate motif as it was reflected in the motto theme (Ex. 237a), the second subject (Ex. 237g) has an even more direct ancestry in the horn theme of the slow movement (Ex. 237h). One thematic metamorphosis is especially pointed: if Fate (in its true mediant-to-dominant form) had merely condescended to join the preceding waltz, it is now persuaded momentarily to plunge into the joyful celebration this finale must surely represent, and thus consummate the new relationship (Ex. 237i) – though its identity is immediately veiled as the key shifts to E minor. But whereas the Second Symphony's finale had succeeded splendidly, this one ends in failure, for the pompous parading of the Fate materials requires modest musical ideas to strain after an expressive significance beyond their strength. This conclusion fatally mars a splendid symphony which earlier had demonstrated how convincingly Tchaikovsky could now create a large-scale symphonic work of complete technical assurance and structural equilibrium, yet wholly his own in expression.

'*Hamlet* confronts the musician with a difficult task, for the philosophical basis of Shakespeare's tragedy is not amenable to musical treatment,' the critic of *New Time* reported after the fantasy overture's première. '. . . Judging from its [the overture's] sounds you could hardly believe the composer has made his principal aim the depiction of the Danish prince's spiritual torments. Clearly secondary episodes have been chosen.'[46] Privately Balakirev was less sparing. 'Shepherds from Vladimir. What are they doing here?' he wrote in his score à propos the oboe's B minor theme, adding 'Hamlet pays compliments to Ophelia, handing her an ice!' against the D major tune which follows.[47] Tchaikovsky's *Hamlet* is certainly not the finest of his shorter orchestral works any more than the fifth is the greatest of the symphonies, and the reservations of the first critic are understandable. But while it cannot compare with Liszt's remarkable portrayal of Shakespeare's hero (to which Tchaikovsky's owes not the slightest debt), neither did it deserve Balakirev's contempt. *Hamlet* was Tchaikovsky's fourth mature symphonic poem, his third upon a Shakespearean play, and the only one for which no kind of literary programme exists – though, as already noted, he had first entertained the possibility of an orchestral piece on this subject in 1876, and a little of the programme Modest had offered then (see Vol. 2, p. 91) may be discerned in what he now created. Yet his most important memory from that time seems to have been of the fragile woman who had won against the counter-claims of Shakespeare's hero, for to open the new piece he returned to the first notes with which he had represented Dante's pathetic Francesca da Rimini twelve years earlier (see Vol. 2, Ex. 124). But whatever relationship the theme this four-note fragment now introduces (Ex. 238) may have to

Ex. 238

---
[46] *DTC*, p. 425; *YDGC*, p. 458.
[47] Quoted in *BVP*, p. 203.

Hamlet himself, it also carries other significances. Most importantly it represents Fate; but just as in *Mazepa*, where the hetman's role as that force's executor had enabled Tchaikovsky to represent both the supernatural power and its human agent in a single theme, so now his perception of the ghost as Fate's surrogate made credible the projection of both through the grim-faced opening invention.

For all the lack of specific information, there can be little doubt about the links between much of Tchaikovsky's vivid imagery in this piece and its literary subject. *Romeo and Juliet* had been a musical drama, *The Tempest* a panorama, and *Francesca da Rimini* a portrait; *Hamlet* is something of all three. Like *Romeo and Juliet*, it is a sonata structure, but without central development in which dramatic conflicts could be played out. Instead it is content to embody a handful of the dramatis personae, a tiny selection of the drama's events, and its tragic dénouement. In the introduction Fate broods darkly, but once the twelve stopped horn notes have signalled midnight and the ghostly emissary appears, its chilling menace is exposed. Hamlet's response is instant, though his F minor music (Ex. 239a) finally suggests agitation of spirit

Ex. 239

a.   Allegro vivace

rather than decisive action. The hopeless divide between him and Ophelia (a Russian rather than Danish maiden, to judge from her melodic decorations (Ex. 239b)) is evident in their tritonal separation, and his rich-voiced answer to her disconsolate oboe melody in B minor is soon stamped by the Fate theme which draws nervously fluttering rejoinders from his beloved. Fortinbras passes across the scene (an annotation in the sketches specifies the march theme as his), Hamlet returns to his key and spiritual torments, and their undertow swirls beneath Ophelia's second appearance. The recurrence of his earlier answer emphasizes his fatal indecisiveness; he has advanced not at all, and only the re-entries of his father's ghost and Fortinbras stir him to action. He dies, and all-powerful Fate leads the dead march.

Such would seem to be one plausible interpretation of the musical images of this fantasy overture. But it is not enough. Though on the first page of his sketches Tchaikovsky had noted: 'Devise something at the start such that it will not be too like the beginning of Manfred',[48] the openings of the two works are almost interchangeable; both have tough initial phrases followed by descents of trenchant quavers into deeper regions – even the same rocking figure in triplets in what follows. Indeed, one of the clearest clues to a crucial element in this new work lies precisely in Tchaikovsky's failure to escape the marks of his earlier dramatic symphony. *Hamlet* is as much a portrait as a drama, though the nominal hero is merely part of this. For as in the first movement of the Manfred Symphony, it is as much Tchaikovsky himself who is projected. *Hamlet* is, in fact, a far more ramified piece than might at first be suspected, and within the opening theme lie the roots to four branches – Hamlet, Tchaikovsky himself, the ghost, Fate – and of these the last is predictably the strongest. But whereas, in the first page of that brief but telling orchestral prelude to *Onegin*, Fate had declared its power through the unchanging cadence on D into which each phrase end had been remorselessly gripped, it is now the phrase beginnings

[48] Davïdova, *op. cit.*, p. 303; *YDGC*, p. 515.

which are clamped. Five times[49] in this introduction the theme is heard, always seeking escape through fresh melodic and tonal sorties, but always resuming on the same pitch. Every search for freedom is doomed.

There being no clear pointers from Tchaikovsky's personal life at this time, we dare not even hazard a guess at any specific elements of self-projection in *Hamlet*. But his view of his Shakespearean alter ego is more discernible. Hamlet is seen as energetic, though the ultimate failure of his F minor music, for all its fury, to drive anywhere in particular is revealing. Ophelia is to be pitied; her theme has a plaintiveness in sharp contrast to the manly dignity of Hamlet's following address to her (Tchaikovsky here evidently permits him the licence of a declaration of love). Fortinbras's first appearance prompts momentary signs of purposefulness, as in Shakespeare. But still Hamlet fails to grapple with the issues confronting him (hence the absence of a development); despite enhanced activity in the recapitulation, nothing is added, and the frenzied sequences on the thematic morsel with which he responds to the ghost's stentorian address readily suggests impotent agitation. In Shakespeare's play Fortinbras enters after the tragedy is finished, but Tchaikovsky seems to have permitted himself a second licence by introducing the Norwegian prince earlier; the example of this admired soldier can thus be an added goad to Hamlet's indecision. But lest, because Fate has been subsumed within a musical idea with so many references that our perception of the identity of the final victor may have become misted, it is the long familiar, unequivocal symbol of this implacable power that suddenly emerges to stand present at the Prince's death (Ex. 240), extending its descent beyond the dominant to lead into the concluding death march.

Ex. 240

Hamlet is a fascinating piece: a compound of the various approaches displayed separately in Tchaikovsky's three preceding symphonic poems, and containing an autobiographical element as strong as in any

[49] In fact, four times in the first draft; bars 1–9 were added later.

of them. The consequences of this for the symphony that was being created at the same time could only be beneficial, for the fantasy overture could become the ready receptacle for many of those personal urges which might otherwise have invaded the larger work and endangered the poise and balance at which Tchaikovsky was so clearly aiming. And because *Hamlet* was a summation of a line of compositions there was really no place for a successor. Perhaps, therefore, what conditioned Tchaikovsky three years later to attempt to destroy the only other symphonic poem he was to create was not only his reservations about its musical worth and a recoiling from the intolerable resonances it may have sounded in his personal world, but also a sense that it was superfluous.

In Berlin on 30 December 1887, at the performance of Berlioz's *Requiem*, Tchaikovsky had once again come face to face with Désirée Artôt. Though during several seasons in the 1870s Artôt had sung with the Italian Opera companies in both Moscow and St Petersburg, she and Tchaikovsky seem to have had no contact, and it was nearly twenty years since he had met this Belgian singer who in 1868 had come to Moscow, enthralled him with her operatic personations, and for a brief while had seemed destined to become his wife. Then on 4 February, four days before his own concert with the Berlin Philharmonic Orchestra, Tchaikovsky had had dinner with the publisher Hugo Bock, and Artôt had been seated beside him. Three days later they met again at a reception Artôt herself had arranged. Tchaikovsky enjoyed the occasion greatly; she sang, and before he left had extracted a promise from him to compose a song for her. On 14 April she gently reminded him of his undertaking. 'I need not tell you that, in default of voice, I shall put all my soul into it,' this fifty-two-year-old promised.[50] Tchaikovsky reassured her, wrote warmly of their last meeting in Berlin, but pleaded that he had to dispose of other major commitments first. She hastened to reply; deadlines could do violence to inspiration – 'and I am too much your friend to impose such a piece of drudgery upon you. I am in no hurry; one day, when you're writing songs and you think I could perform one or another of them well, then just think of dedicating one to me. That's all I wish.'[51]

Nearly five months passed before Tchaikovsky wrote again. 'I have just delivered to my publisher, P. Jurgenson, 6 Mélodies which I have composed for you and of which I ask you to consent to accept the

[50] *TZM*, p. 193.
[51] *TZM*, pp. 193–4.

dedication,' he informed her on 29 October. '. . . . I think all six can be sung by you – that is, they will suit the present range of your voice. I would very much hope that these mélodies can please you – but unfortunately I am not at all sure, for I must confess to you that latterly I have been working too much and it is more than probable that my new compositions are rather the product *of good intentions* than true inspiration. And then, one is a little intimidated when one is composing for a singer one considers the greatest among the great.'[52]

There is some suspicion that Artôt, too, was a little intimidated by the magnitude of her former suitor's gift. 'I asked for but one song – and here so generously you have composed six for me. They say "generous like a king"; they have forgotten to add "or *like an artist*". Naturally I am very curious to make this new acquaintance but do not wish to cause you additional work. I will wait until Jurgenson has published them; but then ask him to send them to me immediately.'[53]

Artôt had to wait much longer than she can have expected, for it was May 1889 before they were printed; then Jurgenson failed to send her a copy, and it was only in August, after this reached the ears of a very embarrassed Tchaikovsky, that she received one. On 21 August she acknowledged the gift. 'At last, at last, dear friend, your songs are in my hands, waiting to be transferred to my voice. Yes, indeed, four, five and six are superb, but the first, "Sérénade", is adorable and has charming freshness. "La déception" also pleases me enormously. In a word, I am *in love* with your new offspring, and proud that you have created them while thinking of me.'[54]

Artôt had ranked them perceptively. Unable to reject the weakest, she had simply ignored it. Tchaikovsky had indeed compiled the set quickly, completing it on 22 October, only three days after finishing *Hamlet*. Yet it includes the most interesting songs he had composed for some years, and one of his finest. Even the second entitled 'Sérénade' (No. 3), passed over by Artôt, gains some distinctiveness from its gentle lilt – though, lightly French as it may intermittently be, its homage to the language of its poet and dedicatee is as nothing compared to the Gallic gaiety of the first song, also entitled 'Sérénade', one of the most captivating of all Tchaikovsky's lighter romances. But 'Déception' (No. 2), a lament on lost love, is more rooted in the composer's own land, and though 'Rondel' (No. 6) returns to the playful world in which the set had opened, it lacks the consistency of touch which had made

[52] *TLP*14, pp. 569–70; *TTP*, p. 373; *DTC*, p. 318; *TZM*, pp. 32–3 (last two sources in Russian only).

[53] *TZM*, p. 194; *DTC*, p. 318 (in Russian only).

[54] *TZM*, p. 195; *DTC*, p. 318 (partial; in Russian only).

the first song so enchanting. The two best songs remain, interesting not only for themselves but for the pointed signs they contain that their creator was composing for a woman who had once been fatefully poised to enter and share his own most personal life. The first lines in the three verses of Paul Collin's delicate poem of adoration, 'Qu'importe que l'hiver?' (No. 4), are set allegro, but for the last line of each the music suddenly slows to a rapt andante (Ex. 241a), and the voice softly hints

Ex. 241

at a familiar phrase. In the first two strophes it is the piano which finally amplifies and clarifies this a little; only in the last is the singer also allowed to reach the final note (Ex. 241b). Even now there would still remain a suspicion that this allusion to the most charged weapon in Tchaikovsky's melodic arsenal was simply coincidence, were it not that the entire phrase emerges at the centre of the following song (see *x* in Ex. 242c) and again in the postlude (Ex. 242d), this time almost exactly as at the climax of Tatyana's great Letter Monologue (see Vol. 2, Ex. 139a). 'Les larmes' (No. 5) is one of Tchaikovsky's most moving songs, with phrases which can develop unexpected breadth, a vocal line

Ex. 242

a.   **Andante doloroso**

b.   [MENDELSSOHN: transposed]

c.   [Andante doloroso]

più vivo *f*

O lar - mes,   lais - sez moi,_____ lais - sez moi!

d.   **Andante doloroso**

pas!

which passes from controlled bel canto to anguished declamation and back again, all within a single expressive arch.

A teasing point remains. Thematic similarities between works are not uncommon with Tchaikovsky. Hamlet's F minor music could be a metamorphosis of the Fifth Symphony's second subject (compare Exs. 233a and 239a), and the even more literal connection between the fantasy overture's opening theme and Francesca's melody has also been observed.[55] It has some obvious closeness, too, to the left-hand phrase at the opening of 'Les larmes' (Ex. 242a: notes 2–5). But if these first five notes are read as though in D minor, a far closer and more provocative parallel appears (Ex. 242b). 'Les larmes' dwells on lost dreams remembered; tears bring no relief, and the cry for deliverance is desperate (Ex. 242c). But it is not so much this central intervention of Fate as Tchaikovsky's thematic frame for the whole piece (Ex. 242a and d) which gives this setting a special point, a secret touch such as Artôt might well have understood – if she could have spotted it. A symbol of marriage has finally yielded to a symbol of Fate.

Quite apart from the generosity of his gift of songs, there is other clear evidence that Tchaikovsky had discovered a special pleasure in this renewed closeness with Artôt. In February 1889, when he visited Berlin again in the course of his second concert tour abroad and found his eight days there crammed with socializing, his gratitude to her was heartfelt. 'My sole comfort is *Artôt* who is invited everywhere with me and whom I like enormously,' he wrote to Modest.[56] His respect for her as an artist remained as secure as ever; 'I'm glad you are going to study with my old friend Artôt; she's a person of genius,' he wrote in June to a former pupil.[57] But Artôt could also present problems, for with his songs now safely received and performed, she suddenly confronted him with a second and far more demanding task. 'Yesterday evening the famous tenor, Capoul, read us the poem he has written for a grand opera, and since the subject is *Russian* we all exclaimed that only you ought to set it to music,' she wrote on 8 March 1890 to Tchaikovsky, who was in Florence engaged on the final sketches of *The Queen of Spades*. 'Capoul jumped for joy at this thought . . . [and] is ready to come to meet you and submit it to you personally. . . . Send me a word of reply, and if you wish to be even nicer – send a telegram saying "I await Capoul" – that will suffice. Two hours later he'll be *on his way!*'[58]

[55] This contour seems to have haunted Tchaikovsky's creativity at this time and is to be important in his next large-scale piece, *The Sleeping Beauty*.

[56] *TLP*15A, p. 51; *TZC*3, p. 296; *TPB*, p. 415; *YDGC*, p. 465.

[57] *TLP*15A, pp. 135–6; *YDGC*, p. 475.

[58] *TZM*, p. 196.

There was no matching enthusiasm from Tchaikovsky. Desperate to forestall the arrival of this would-be collaborator, he telegraphed Artôt that he could not undertake the opera, adding mendaciously that he was leaving Florence that very evening. A letter followed in which he uncompromisingly refused to entertain the idea of seeing M. Capoul and listed a largely fictitious series of composing commitments which would fill the next several years. But Artôt was a friend, and one deception had to be admitted – and, after all, she might discover the truth. 'I end by confessing to you *an untruth*. I am not leaving for Russia this evening. I told this untruth so that *M. Capoul* would be quite certain he would not find me; I feared that, encouraged by your friendship towards me (which I appreciate enormously), he would have come to find me here . . .

'Thank you, thank you a thousand times for singing my *songs* . . . I do not know when I shall come to Paris. I know only that if I should come I shall be enormously happy to see you again.'[59]

But Tchaikovsky had been badly frightened. There had been signs in their close relationship of 1868 that Artôt had been the more masterful, and this sudden evidence that she might, given the opportunity, seek an active role in his creative schemes must clearly have alerted him sharply to what close contact with her could risk. As for Artôt, she did not reply, and they never, it seems, met again.

[59] *TLP*15B, p. 75; *TTP*, p. 375.

5

SECOND INTERNATIONAL TOUR:

THE SLEEPING BEAUTY

THE TENOR OF Tchaikovsky's life, so turbulent in the first months of 1888, now entered an almost monotonous calm for the middle of the year. Delighted as ever by the situation at Frolovskoye, he continued to stock his garden with every kind of flower. But the late spring and early summer were bad, and in the unseasonal weather many of his plants faded and his own health wilted. Such woeful circumstances produced a special and, he admitted, surprisingly strong need of company to distract him when he was not in the act of composing. Modest visited twice, and Laroche, feckless as ever and now penniless, stayed a whole month with the woman he was preparing to make his third wife, the weeks the couple spent at Frolovskoye affording them less a pleasant change of surroundings than a refuge from total destitution. But Tchaikovsky still found a special pleasure in the company of Laroche, who well understood his host's habits, knew how to remain unseen during his working hours, and in the evenings read aloud to him, giving rich pleasure from his own self-evident relish of classics such as Gogol's *Dead Souls*. Earlier the wife of Kondratyev's former man-servant had come to stay with her young child. Whether it was the association with his old friend and the attentiveness which her husband had shown during his last dreadful weeks, there is no doubt that Tchaikovsky had developed a genuine affection for the Legoshin family, purchasing at his own expense a perambulator for their two-year-old daughter who suffered from rickets, and writing warmly of their visit in letters to various correspondents. During an interval between such guests loneliness had driven him to walk over and spend a day in his old haunts at Maidanovo, but this had only reminded him still more painfully of Kondratyev, who had once occupied a dacha there. Yet the Maidanovo circle itself remained necessary to him, if only because without it there was little chance of playing vint. He celebrated his name-day with a forty-eight-hour house party, including Jurgenson, Albrecht and Ziloti among the guests for the first day, and adding Maidanovo acquaintances for the second. Such two-way exchanges were to recur throughout the summer.

There were also, of course, periodic trips to Moscow and St Petersburg. The visit to the former for the Conservatoire examinations enabled him to observe how well the institution continued to be run under Taneyev, but left him concerned by its financial plight, for it relied heavily on revenues from the RMS concerts, and he feared that the number of subscribers to these would continue to dwindle. His own affairs were in no better order; the trip abroad had cost him much, moving to his new home had been expensive – and would his patroness advance him a third of next year's allowance? Less than three months later he was supplicating for the remaining two-thirds. Predictably she agreed to both petitions.

'You reprove me for sometimes doubting myself. But, my dear, I assure you that's better than being too self-assured. For it's inevitable that sometime I shall grow old and write myself out,' he wrote to the nineteen-year-old Vladimir Nápravník, son of his conductor-friend, who had recently settled for a period in Germany, and whose loneliness he had tried to alleviate. But, Tchaikovsky added, if this happened he would find something to occupy himself – and in any case 'I'm only *doubting*, and certainty that I'm good-for-nothing is still a long way off.'[1] For all the bursts of self-doubt that continued to pepper his letters when in the throes of composition, Tchaikovsky remained at bottom confident he still had more in him to give, and the progress he had been making on the new symphony and fantasy overture during these early weeks at Frolovskoye confirmed both this and the excellent working conditions his new home afforded. Any vestige of belief in *The Captain's Daughter* as a possible opera subject vanished when Shpazhinsky offered him a scenario drawn from it in five acts and twelve scenes. It would have resulted, Tchaikovsky reckoned, in an opera five to six hours long – though Shpazhinsky's scenario on Goethe's ballad, 'Der Gott und die Bajadere' did briefly engage his interest. A copy of the Grand Duke Konstantin Konstantinovich's new poem on St Sebastian, sent by the author for Tchaikovsky's comments, prompted a prolonged and detailed exchange on the nature and problems of poetic metre in which Tchaikovsky showed himself both thoughtful and very well informed about the craft of versifying. He also revealed himself impatient of those of his compatriots whose approach to their craft lacked professionalism. 'I believe Russian poetry would gain a great deal if the talented poets would interest themselves in the technique of

[1] *TLP*14, pp. 471–2.

their trade,' declared this most professional of Russian composers.[2] As he had earlier written to the Grand Duke: 'When you read *Goethe* you are astounded at his boldness in regard of foot, caesura, and so on, such that to the unaccustomed ear some verse scarcely seems even to be verse. Yet this merely surprises the ear, and doesn't offend it.'[3] Jurgenson proposed to employ Tchaikovsky's own literary abilities by commissioning a translation of Ulïbishev's three-volume biography of Mozart. But having spent two hours one evening on four pages, he concluded it would take him three years to complete, absorbing much time that would be better given to composition. In consequence, the task was given to a very willing Modest, Tchaikovsky offering to cast an eye over the musical portions of his brother's work, and provide a preface – though he was soon to assign Laroche responsibility for this editorial work. On the face of it this made a fair exchange, for Tchaikovsky had already undertaken to orchestrate Laroche's overture *Karmozina*. But really the debt was entirely Laroche's, for Tchaikovsky saw that this editorial task might provide a purposeful occupation to rouse his indolent friend. Tchaikovsky was the first to admit that Laroche could be intolerably self-centred and ill-natured, but his unstinting readiness to devote his own energies to supporting and encouraging this particular friend, often at personal and financial cost, seemed inexhaustible.

The summer's end brought a visit to Kamenka. It was nearly three years since he had been there, and he took stock of how he now viewed that place and those people among whom he had for several years gratefully centred his existence after the catastrophe of his marriage. 'Kamenka seemed to me uncommonly disagreeable, and I just couldn't understand how I could once have lived there. Of course, this relates to the place and not the people,' he wrote to Anatoly on 17 September, a day after his return to Frolovskoye. 'According to the degree of pleasure I felt on seeing the inhabitants of Kamenka it seems that (excluding Sasha, Lev and the three old ladies [Lev's mother and two elder sisters]) I like in particular Nikolay Vasilyevich [Davïdov, Lev's elder brother] . . . Vlad[imir] Andr[eyevich] Plesky also roused very pleasant feelings in me. On the other hand – goodness! how unsympathetic I find Lizaveta Serg[eyevna Davïdova, Lev's sister-in-law] and her son Vasya.' But this week with his sister was overshadowed by a gathering cloud of grief. 'The news from Paris is as bad as could be,' he continued. 'In the evenings I shed many tears thinking of poor Vera, for whom there's no hope. They're hiding the truth from Sasha as far as

[2] *TLP*14, p. 453; *TZC*3, p. 249.
[3] *TLP*14, p. 441; *TZC*3, p. 244; *YDGC*, p. 448 (partial).

possible, but she guesses . . . Poor Vera has tuberculosis of the lungs and bowels, and is melting away like a candle. Lev is going to Paris. Isn't it appallingly sad that it's just this nice, sympathetic Vera, who in no way seemed threatened with premature death, who is dying.'[4] He had already lost one niece, Tanya – and now to add to the impending loss of a second was yet another anguish. Even before leaving for the Ukraine he had realized that Nikolay Hubert, his fellow-student at the St Petersburg Conservatoire, his colleague at the Moscow, to whom he had drawn even closer in recent years, was very seriously ill. Within a month of Tchaikovsky's return from Kamenka Hubert was dead; another two, and Vera had gone. A year that had started with such gratifying triumphs for himself and his music ended in double sorrow.

Meanwhile preparations had continued for further forays to consolidate his reputation as an international conductor. Projects came and went. His first tour had relied on the initiatives and organization of foreign entrepreneurs; now he found himself an agent at home. But Julius Zet, a pianist and dealer in musical instruments, proved a thoroughly ineffective, if amiable representative, dreaming up schemes not only for a progress of some six weeks through Norway and Sweden during the next winter, but even of America, where in three months he would net 25,000 dollars. From the beginning Tchaikovsky had concluded this was too good to be true, but he had faith enough in Zet's less ambitious scheme to ask Alexandra Panayeva to travel with him as soprano soloist. Neither Zet's grandiose American project nor the Scandinavian tour materialized; nor did a separate proposal, put to Tchaikovsky in Paris during the spring and then taken up by Zet, that he should be the Russian musical delegate at the Paris Exhibition of 1889, as he could have been in 1878. Tchaikovsky would have been pleased to accept and conduct not only his own music but that of his compatriots, but the Exhibition would celebrate the centenary of the French Revolution, and any association would have to be both unofficial and discreet; under no circumstances could a loyal subject (and beneficiary) of the Tsar appear to be a celebrant of republicanism.

All the same, a more viable itinerary did begin to form itself during the middle months of the year. By the end of August he had committed himself in principle to conduct in Dresden and Berlin; by the end of October Frankfurt, Cologne and London had been added. But first he had to honour a promise to direct *Onegin* at the National Theatre in Prague, and even before this there were two conducting engagements in St Petersburg. In the first concert, on 17 November, the Fifth Sym-

4 *TLP*14, p. 521.

phony and his orchestrations of Laroche's *Karmozina* overture were to
be heard for the first time, along with the Second Piano Concerto and
some vocal and piano pieces, while in the second a week later the
symphony was to be repeated and *Hamlet* receive its première. On
11 November he journeyed to St Petersburg to begin rehearsals, endure
the strains these would entail, and engage in those business negotiations which now seemed an inevitable feature of any visit to the capital.
Yet he could still find time to exercise himself in the interests of others.
On the eve of his departure to St Petersburg he had specially reminded
Jurgenson to pay 'poor Ant[onina] Iv[anovna]'[5] her allowance, and he
had, since Hubert's death, concerned himself with the welfare of his
widow; now he secretly engineered a further loan for Kashkin who
remained in severe financial difficulties. Already, too, he had approached the Imperial Theatres on behalf of Shpazhinskaya, using all
his powers of innocent intrigue in the hope that the play he had at last
extracted from her might be produced. Discovering now that it was
unacceptable, he still found time to break the news to her in terms that
would, he hoped, not destroy her slender self-confidence. Yet his
greatest effort was again made for Laroche. At rehearsal distaste had
been expressed for the consistent brashness of his *Karmozina* overture –
yet so great was Tchaikovsky's determination it should succeed that,
with not a word to Laroche, he fabricated a programme which was
circulated at the concert, claiming that the overture had been envisaged to open an opera set in eighteenth-century Venetian carnival
orgies. When even this failed to justify it in the ears of the audience, he
took upon himself the responsibility for its failure, blaming his own
over-heavy scoring. Friendship could hardly go farther. It was well
that his own reception in both concerts had been so warm. On
25 November, inexpressibly weary, he left for Prague.

Tchaikovsky's arrival in the Czech capital was attended by none of
the festive ceremonial that had marked his approach earlier in the year.
Before the performance of *Onegin* there was a concert to conduct on
30 November at the National Theatre, the programme consisting of the
Fifth Symphony and Second Piano Concerto, again with Sapelnikov as
soloist. Though Tchaikovsky had forgone all concert fees on his last
visit, it had been agreed that this time he would receive half the takings.
But when a combination of bad timing and poor organization resulted
in a small audience and poor receipts, he donated his meagre share to a
musicians' pension fund. Whether this action was innocent or calculated, the press fell upon the theatre's directorate, news of his bounty

---

[5] *TLP*14, p. 586.

spread, and the opening of *Onegin* six days later was a personal triumph, with wreaths presented and endless ovations. Tchaikovsky had reservations about the staging of his opera, but the costumes were all at least reasonably designed, and the performance left him well satisfied, with a Tatyana in Berta Lautererová so ideal that he tried to arrange that she should sing the role in Moscow. He also invited Dvořák to conduct an RMS concert the following season. The Czech composer's first response was nervous (he would have to wait until he had learned Russian, he said), but in January Tchaikovsky's fellow-directors enthusiastically endorsed the invitation, for the current season would be Erdmannsdörfer's last, and as a way of revitalizing the Society's flagging fortunes Tchaikovsky suggested that for the following season a series of highly distinguished personalities should be invited to take charge of single concerts.

On 14 January 1889, even before the Society's meeting, Dvořák had written a charming letter of appreciation to Tchaikovsky personally:

My dear friend,

The last time you were with us in Prague I promised to write to you about your opera *Onegin*. Now I am impelled to do this not only by your request but also by my own wish to tell you everything I felt on hearing your work. I confess with joy that your opera made a very deep impression on me, just as I always expect from a true artistic creation. Without a moment's hesitation I'll say that none of your compositions so far has pleased me as much as *Onegin*. It is a wonderful piece, filled with warmth of feeling and poetry, likewise fine in detail; in a word, it is music that draws us to itself and penetrates the soul so deeply that it is unforgettable. As always when I go to the theatre I feel as in another world.

I congratulate both you and us on this work – and God grant you will leave the world many such compositions.

Yours sincerely,
Antonin Dvořák[6]

The simple sincerity of Dvořák's letter moved Tchaikovsky deeply:

Dear, kind, much respected friend,

You cannot imagine how happy your letter made me. I particularly value your opinion of my opera not only because you are a

---

[6] *TZM*, p. 219 (in Russian, pp. 179–80). Also in *TZC*3, p. 287 – and partially in *TLP*15A, p. 32; *TPJ*2, p. 294; *TPM*3, p. 645; *YDGC*, p. 461.

great artist, but because you are an upright and sincere person. I am
proud, I am happy to the last degree that it is from you that I have
succeeded in meriting a word of sincere sympathy, my dear, much
respected friend! Thank you again from my whole heart! . . .

For God's sake, dear friend, agree to come; all of us want this very
much. . . .

I embrace you, dear Dvořák!!!

Yours,

P. Cajkovskyj[7]

Tchaikovsky personally supervised the negotiations that were to bring
the Czech composer to Moscow, arranging that he should conduct in
Moscow the following season for a fee of 800 roubles – though not
earlier than March 1890 for fear of Russian frosts, Dvořák insisted.

On leaving Prague on 7 December Tchaikovsky had intended to
head for Moscow. But in a café in Vienna he chanced to pick up a
newspaper and learned of Vera's death in Nice. Thinking that his
niece's body would be brought back to St Petersburg for burial, and
anxious to have details of her end and discover how Sasha had taken
the news, he directed himself instead to the capital for a day. On
12 December, in a very sombre frame of mind, he was back home in
Frolovskoye.

He knew his rest would be only short. On 22 December at an RMS
concert in Moscow he had again to conduct the Fifth Symphony and
Second Piano Concerto, repeat the programme with Sapelnikov the
following evening for a wider public, then go straight to St Petersburg
to rehearse a performance of *The Tempest*. His last two concerts in the
capital had been for the Philharmonic Society and RMS respectively,
but this time the promoter was Belyayev, and pieces by the 'New
Russian School' would make up the rest of this, the fourth programme
of the Russian Symphony Concerts series. Tchaikovsky recognized that
he had long enjoyed good personal relations with members of the
Balakirev/Rimsky-Korsakov group – and much respect also; on his last
visit Glazunov had visited specially to present him with yet another
inscribed score, this time of his symphonic poem, *Stenka Razin*. But he
had never felt that he had been accepted as one of them. With this joint
participation that exclusion had become history, and the unqualified
ability he now knew his music possessed to sit comfortably and
confidently alongside any number of their compositions, yet in no way
to suffer in the ears of any audience, made it an occasion he could relish

[7] *TLP*15A, p. 32.

deeply, and he wrote of his satisfaction to Nadezhda von Meck (see above, pp. 91–2). Hearing from Prague that he had been elected an honorary member of the Umělecká Beseda was an added pleasure. Though there was still a week to the Russian Christmas Eve, he remained in St Petersburg to share that day with brother Nikolay and his family. In the meantime there was a chance to hear his Third String Quartet, and to check his opinion of *The Oprichnik* when his first published opera, which Ippolitov-Ivanov was so anxious to mount in Tiflis, was given a student performance at the Conservatoire. He went, so Modest said, hoping he might become at least a little reconciled to it; he left convinced he loathed it even more. On Christmas Day itself he was again in Frolovskoye, about to begin in earnest what he had for some months intended – and had, indeed, already begun: the composition of a ballet on *The Sleeping Beauty*.

Tchaikovsky now had before him some four weeks of almost unbroken freedom. The weather was excellent, his social life under control, and by the end of this period only the third act ('Aurora's wedding') remained to be sketched. He had even found time to satisfy a request for two pieces for a concert by the St Petersburg opera chorus in March, offering 'Blessed is he who smiles', a piece for men's voices written a year earlier for Albrecht, but still unperformed, and composing specially 'The Nightingale'. The text, concocted by Tchaikovsky himself as he contemplated his own imminent migration to southern European lands as his second concert tour approached, is charmingly pointed:

'A nightingale was flying away to a warm foreign clime. "You are bidding me farewell, dear people . . . And I thank you for your love and kindness . . . I would remain with you now . . . but I do not like your white winter . . . But as soon as lovely spring returns I shall come too with a new song."'

Tchaikovsky's setting, nevertheless, is innocent of humour or parody. 'The Nightingale' is the finest of his shorter choral pieces on secular texts – and the most Russian, with its solo-choral opening, irregular metres and phrasing, its modality and dynamic contrasts.

The only event to introduce any real sadness into this month of liberty was news of the death of Dmitri Razumovsky, his former Conservatoire colleague and the priest who had officiated at his wedding. A crucial meeting of the RMS did take him briefly to Moscow; even more was he drawn there by the prospect of meeting Ivan Klimenko, an old intimate from his student days and his early years in Moscow, whom he had not seen for seventeen years. Klimenko visited him at Frolovskoye, once with Jurgenson, a second time with

Ziloti and Taneyev, with whom Tchaikovsky was able to play Mozart from the beautifully bound set of Breitkopf and Härtel's complete edition, presented to him as a Christmas gift by Jurgenson and acknowledged by its almost dazed recipient as 'the best, most precious, most divine present I could ever hope to receive'.[8] It is no surprise that his current morning reading included Jahn's biography of Mozart, besides Dostoyevsky's *The Double*, the young Chekhov ('in my opinion he promises to become a very major literary force'[9]), and Tolstoy's *What I believe* ('I'm amazed at its combination of wisdom with childish naïveté'[10]). On the last day of January, well content with himself for his progress on the ballet, he left for St Petersburg. He was curious to hear Medea and Nikolay Figner in *Onegin*, but above all he already needed to discuss the still distant production of *The Sleeping Beauty* with Vsevolozhsky and Petipa. Having seen Victor Hugo's *Marion de Lorme* at the theatre, heard his own *Sérénade mélancolique* conducted by Rimsky-Korsakov and Second String Quartet led by Auer, on 5 February he set out upon his second concert tour of Europe.

His first destination was Berlin, where he spent three days mainly in the company of Wolf, whose services in organizing European tours remained indispensable, despite Zet's exertions. But he also passed time more relaxedly with Artôt and Klindworth, and since he had failed to secure Nikisch's services at an RMS concert next season, he arranged that Klindworth should conduct a Wagner programme. Tchaikovsky's first concert was in Cologne on 12 February, when he was to conduct his Third Suite. He found the orchestra surprisingly large and excellent. Though it seemed that the Germans in general knew little of Russian music, there were exceptions; Borodin, and in particular his First Symphony, had made an impression with some, and Tchaikovsky's own reception in Cologne was extremely enthusiastic, with a triple fanfare at the concert's end. Arriving in Frankfurt the following day, he found the orchestra less outstanding, though still very good. It had been planned to include *1812* as well as the Third Suite, but at rehearsals the promoters became nervous about the noisy ending of a piece which only a year earlier the Berliners had heard without flinching, and timidly asked that the overture be dropped from the programme. At the concert on 15 February Tchaikovsky received an ovation, despite Frankfurt's reputation for coolness and conservatism. So great was his success that he was to receive a pressing

[8] *TLP*15A, p. 14; *TPJ*2, p. 107; *TZC*3, p. 290.
[9] *TLP*15A, p. 27; *YDGC*, p. 461.
[10] *TD*, p. 221; *TZC*3, p. 290; *YDGC*, p. 462.

invitation to return before the year was out. By now he had been away from Russia ten days, and the almost unbroken social round which packed each day was already proving more and more wearying. When alone he often, he admitted, released his feelings in a flood of tears.

By 17 February he was in Dresden, where his musical commitment was larger: the Fourth Symphony and First Piano Concerto, with Emil Sauer as soloist. But the orchestra proved inferior, and he was furious with Wolf for not having warned him so that he could have chosen a less demanding programme. To make matters worse, though Tchaikovsky considered Sauer played the concerto excellently, his view of the work was idiosyncratic, making the conductor's task the more difficult. The first rehearsal went badly, and the concert on 20 was much less successful than those in Cologne and Frankfurt, though each movement of the symphony received more applause than the preceding, at the concert's end he was allotted a single fanfare, and the press pronounced the event a sensation. On 21 he was back in Berlin, where his four free days were filled with the obligatory meetings and meals, with Artôt his chief comforter. The Philharmonic Orchestra was magnificent, as he well knew, and the concert on 26 was played to an overflowing hall. His conducting was highly praised, though his music – the Serenade for Strings and *Francesca da Rimini* – had a mixed reception, the Serenade's Valse being encored, but *Francesca* (which the Philharmonic Society's directors had vetoed the previous year) having to face some noisy hissing from a minority of the audience. For all his attempts to put this hostility into perspective, it upset him badly, and the following day was marked by specially severe bouts of homesickness. He was shocked, too, by news of the death of Karl Davïdov, the cellist, composer, director of the St Petersburg Conservatoire, and dedicatee of the Italian Capriccio, whom he had respected as much as a musician as he had liked him as a man.

And all the while the fundamental ache remained. 'I cannot express to you how much *Heimweh*, as the Germans call it, fills me with misery, yearning, pining and pain,' he wrote to the Grand Duke Konstantin Konstantinovich. 'Last year also I felt this abnormally grievous longing for my homeland, but to an infinitely lesser degree. It is not the rehearsals for the concerts, nor the concerts themselves that are particularly burdensome, but the constant gyrating among strange people, even though they are sometimes extremely interesting. But worst of all is that I am scarcely ever alone.'[11] Ever since the tour had begun he had periodically declared that, but for Sapelnikov needing

[11] *TLP*15A, p. 58.

him to conduct the First Piano Concerto in London, he would have
instantly returned home. On the other hand he saw himself as an
ambassador for Russia, and he confessed that the sort of reception he
was receiving made him more than content. It was well that he had
planned, en route from Geneva, to stop in Leipzig to see the Brodskys,
write letters, and rest. At 11.30 at night on 28 February he arrived in
that city to be received like an old friend.

His two days there did something to restore his composure. At the
Brodskys' he heard a superb performance of his own Third String
Quartet, and met both Nováček and Sinding. At his first rehearsal in
Geneva on 5 March, the day after his arrival, he was confronted by an
orchestra that was pleasant and keen, but also bad and small; with only
three violas the prospect of conducting the Serenade for Strings, as well
as the First Suite and 'Don Juan's serenade', was dispiriting. Geneva
itself brought on a flood of nostalgia. 'I remember so vividly myself and
all of you thirteen years ago, and I feel so painfully how *irrevocable* is the
past,' he wrote to his nephew Bob, memories resurging of how he had
spent the first weeks of 1876 lodging in the city with Lev, Sasha and
their young family, two of whom had now so recently died. 'Yesterday I
went to the Boulevard Plainpalais where you lived. I remembered
Tanya and Vera so vividly, their arms red from running to school in the
cold, and all of you, and you with your tiny nose, and not that trunk
which you now have instead of a nose, and myself not as grey when I
was a whole thirteen years younger!!! I became terribly sad . . .

> *Nessun dolor maggiore*
> *Che ricordarsi del tempo felice*
> *Nella miseria!'*[12]

But the weather was excellent, and with daily rehearsals the orchestra
improved surprisingly so that the concert on 9 March was a notable
success, with a packed house and the presentation of a gilded wreath
from the local Russian colony; the Serenade's Valse, the Suite's
Miniature March and 'Don Juan's serenade' were all encored. Bitter
that the newspapers back home were reporting nothing of his exploits
for Russian music, he arrived two days later in Hamburg, went to his
hotel, and discovered that Brahms was installed in the next room. The
German composer had specially delayed his own departure from the
city for twenty-four hours so that he could hear the first rehearsal of
Tchaikovsky's Fifth Symphony the following day.

[12] *TLP*15A, p. 61.

Tchaikovsky was deeply flattered by Brahms's interest. Their first encounter in Leipzig a year before had done much to dispose him sympathetically towards Brahms as a person, and since then he had more than once reflected upon his music. The judgement he had passed to the Grand Duke Konstantin Konstantinovich in the intervening October was perhaps the most considered, and certainly the least unfavourable of his reflections upon his great contemporary.

In the music of this master (and mastery cannot, of course, be denied him) there is something dry, cold that alienates my heart. He has little melodic invention. His musical thought never gets to the point; hardly have you heard a hint of a viable melodic phrase than it has already fallen into a maelstrom of inconsequential harmonic progressions and modulations as though the composer had assigned himself the special task of being incomprehensible. It is as though he is tantalizing and exasperating your musical feeling, does not want to satisfy its demands, is ashamed to talk in a language that goes to the heart. His *depth* is not real; *elle est voulue*, he has decided once and for all that he should be deep, and the likeness is there – but only the likeness. *His is an empty chasm.* In no way can you say Brahms's music is weak and without significance. His style is always elevated; he never strives for external effect, he is never banal, everything of his is serious, noble – but the most important thing – *beauty* – is absent. It is impossible not to revere Brahms, it is impossible not to admire the virginal purity of his aspirations, not to admire his resolve. . . . But it is difficult to like him.[13]

Try as he might, Tchaikovsky could still find attractions only in a few of the earlier pieces – the B flat String Sextet, for instance. As for the symphonies, he judged them 'unimaginably boring and colourless'.[14]

His meeting with the man himself consolidated the more favourable of his earlier impressions. 'He is very amiable,' he wrote to Modest. 'After the rehearsal we had lunch and drank well together. He's a very sympathetic person, and I like his uprightness and simplicity.'[15] He tried unsuccessfully to add Brahms to the list of distinguished conductors who would transform the Moscow RMS's fortunes the next season. As for the Fifth Symphony, Brahms had told him frankly he did not like the finale, though he had strongly approved of the rest (so Tchaikovsky told Modest). In fact, as performance had succeeded performance at

[13] *TLP*14, pp. 553–4; *TZC*3, pp. 277–8.
[14] *ibid.*
[15] *TLP*15A, p. 68; *TPB*, p. 416; *YDGC*, p. 467 (partial).

the end of the previous year, Tchaikovsky himself had been turning against the whole work, and to his patroness he had compared it very unfavourably with 'our symphony' – the Fourth. But the growing enthusiasm he could sense among the players during the three Hamburg rehearsals revived his own liking for it; the final open rehearsal was a great success, and the concert on 15 March a triumph – though sadly Avé-Lallemant, the work's dedicatee, was prevented by illness from hearing and pronouncing on it. What marked out clearly these players for Tchaikovsky was that they were so warm towards him – and not surprisingly, for after his previous visit he had arranged that many of them, who were also members of Julius Laube's orchestra, should perform with that conductor at Pavlovsk, where they had scored much success. Back in their own city, they played a benefit concert for Laube two days before Tchaikovsky's, including two movements from the Serenade for Strings, and Tchaikovsky received an ovation from the audience and a fanfare from the players. But as soon as his own concert was over 'Heimweh' and depression descended again. What made it worse was that his next, final engagement was nearly a month away. Earlier he had thought of returning to the hotel at Clarens on Lake Geneva where he had found such comfort some eleven years earlier during the difficult months after his marriage, and where he had composed his Violin Concerto; there he would be able to continue with *The Sleeping Beauty*. But on enquiring he found the Mayor family was no longer in charge, and he decided it would be best to pass most of the intervening weeks in the European city always closest to his heart: Paris. There, however, he would be recognized and in demand; before this he needed a haven where he was quite unknown, where he could be alone for a while, and catch up on his correspondence. On 16 March he settled in Hanover for three days. The town he found attractive though unremarkable, despite some medieval buildings. But when he tried to compose a little more of *The Sleeping Beauty*, he found neither will nor much invention was in him. In the gloomiest frame of mind he toyed with the idea of passing through Aachen. 'I am drawn to look at the place where I was so unhappy, and where it will be pleasant to weep over N.D. [Kondratyev],' he reflected to Modest.[16] On 20 March he was installed in his familiar Paris hotel.

While this German-Swiss tour had certainly been a great personal success, the press reception had been mixed. According to Modest, the papers in Cologne had been unanimously approving, but in Frankfurt, where Brahms was much in favour, they had politely judged his Third

---

[16] *TLP*15A, p. 75; *TZC*3, p. 303; *TPB*, pp. 417–18.

Suite interesting rather than memorable, though all had commended his skill and originality. The Dresden critics had praised his conducting while censuring the orchestra for its performance, one paper roundly telling the wind section that they should have gone home and practised. But on the merits of the Fourth Symphony and First Piano Concerto they were divided though, again, all acknowledged Tchaikovsky's professionalism. All the same, there was some gratifyingly forthright praise for the symphony, especially its structure, and one critic observed approvingly the work's Russianness. The Berlin press was the most adverse; *Francesca da Rimini* was noted favourably by only one paper, and the reviews of the Serenade were condescending. The Hamburg critics divided on the Fifth Symphony. More than once since leaving Russia Tchaikovsky had repeated his view of hostile criticism; 'let them hiss, so long as they are interested,' he had declared to his patroness from Geneva,[17] and on his last tour he had readily accepted the honest reservations of such as Josef Sittard because he knew they were intelligent and founded on a good knowledge of his music. It must therefore have been a special pleasure to find this Hamburg correspondent considered the symphony one of 'the most significant compositions of recent times'.[18]

Paris offered an abundance of diversions and time to enjoy them. Tchaikovsky seems to have heard surprisingly little music other than his own during the last month – some Bach and an indifferent performance of Beethoven's Ninth Symphony in Berlin, and a few operas: Goldmark's *Die Königin von Saba* in Dresden ('I disliked the music very much'[19]), Cornelius's *Der Barbier von Bagdad* in Leipzig, *Rigoletto* in Geneva, and *Martha* in Hanover. Even his reading had been restricted, and he had visited only one art gallery (in Dresden to see Raphael's *Sistine Madonna*). But his three weeks in Paris were to be well provided with such pleasures: a comedy by Barrière and Thiboust, *Les excuses de l'amour*, on the second evening, and an enormously enjoyable account of Lalo's *Le roi d'Ys* on the next. Though an enveloping cloud of social engagements quickly precluded free choice in how he spent his following evenings, he was able to admire the 23-year-old American soprano, Emma Eames, invited by Gounod to make her Paris début a fortnight earlier opposite Jean de Reszke in *Roméo et Juliette* (a favourite opera of Tchaikovsky's), and to revel in Berlioz's 'best piece . . . *La damnation de Faust*. How I love this superb work!' he wrote to his nephew Bob,[20] who

[17] *TLP*15A, p. 63; *TPM*3, p. 567.
[18] *TZC*3, p. 301.
[19] *TD*, p. 224; *YDGC*, p. 464.
[20] *TLP*15A, p. 88; *TPB*, p. 421; *TZC*3, p. 306 (partial); *YDGC*, p. 469 (partial).

had just attended the first ever Russian *Ring* cycle, given by Angelo Neumann's travelling company in St Petersburg, and who now declared himself a Wagnerite (a similar disturbing confession was to come from Glazunov). During his stay in Paris Tchaikovsky was to discover how much Wagner's pernicious influence seemed also to have taken hold of the younger generation of French composers.

His personal condition, both without and within, was a different matter, for feverishness, toothache and drowziness marked his first days in Paris. A prime cause is plain; Antonina Ivanovna was once again besieging him for an increase in her allowance. A year before he had doubled it to 100 roubles a month; now she wanted it redoubled, and had written to her husband direct. As usual Jurgenson was the main party to negotiations, but the delays of correspondence prolonged the strain for Tchaikovsky. 'On mature reflection I have decided that Ant[onina] Iv[anovna] can be allotted 150 roubles [a month],' Tchaikovsky finally wrote on 2 April, in hope that a matter that had been preoccupying him for nearly a fortnight might be forgotten.

> . . . If you start reproving me, then I'll put it to you as follows. Three years ago, in consequence of Ant[onina] Iv[anovna] pestering me, you and I *decided* that you would forward to me none of her letters, that you would be the permanent intermediary between us, in regard of which I authorized you to arbitrate in all her requests. She was then given notice that she should not be so bold as to write to me. For two years she complied, but now she's again begun approaching me direct. According to our agreement, in no circumstances should you have sent me her letters, but should have opened them, read them, and made a decision. The point is (1): Ant[onina] Iv[anovna]'s letters literally make me ill, so unpleasant to me is every reminder of that person, and (2): through weakness of character I always end up doing what she wants. That's what's happened in the present instance. I'm not saying this by way of reproach – but with a view to the future,

he added, knowing how critically dependent he was on Jurgenson's continuing co-operation.[21]

The physical consequences of this wretched business at least justified a postponement of the social round. The Bélards, who ran the Hôtel Richepanse, were as solicitous as ever, and he had Brandukov again for company. When he emerged after two days it was to see the Mackars

---

[21] *TLP*15A, p. 84; *TPM*3, p. 647.

and meet Albert Noël, his publisher's new partner, to whom he took no liking, though he recognized Noël might profitably sharpen the firm's business edge. Paris had already begun to work its magic; 'my morbid melancholy and aversion *to a foreign country* have passed,' he ended his diary entry that evening.[22] This time he had come as a private citizen, not a celebrity, and he kept well clear of anything to do with the Exhibition; his closest involvement was to gaze at the new Eiffel Tower built specially for the occasion, then ascend it in a lift. But on 24 March there was a public event difficult to escape. Hearing Tchaikovsky was in Paris, Colonne planned to include the variations from the Third Suite in one of his concerts, and Tchaikovsky felt obliged to attend the first of Colonne's concerts after his arrival. That evening the conductor gave a reception at which some of Tchaikovsky's songs were sung, and he met Massenet, whom he had approached to conduct in Moscow next season. He was as delighted to have Massenet express his personal enthusiasm for the Suite's variations after Colonne's performance on 31 March as he had been to observe the public's enthusiasm at the concert itself, especially after their indifference at the final rehearsal. Having again met Paderewski and had his admiration for this 'pianist of genius, and very gifted composer' confirmed,[23] he invited him to play at an RMS concert he himself would conduct.

In Paris Tchaikovsky renewed acquaintance with the Benardakys, Fauré, Delibes, Lalo, Lefebvre, Diémer and Taffanel, and met for the first time d'Indy, Pierné, Chaminade – and another woman composer and remarkable personality, Augusta Holmès, born in France of Irish extraction (though it was said Alfred de Vigny was her real father), who had had Franck as a teacher and Saint-Saëns as a suitor, who was gifted enough to draw cool admiration from another woman composer, Ethel Smyth, and whose lively personality and famed good looks had secured her a prominent position in French artistic circles. Tchaikovsky had found Chaminade unsympathetic, but there is no record of what he made of Augusta, nor of her choral piece, *La vision de Ste-Thérèse*. He was equally silent on another composition by a woman, Pauline Viardot – a little opera given at a soirée at the great singer's home by some of her pupils and her two daughters. Of his pleasure in meeting Viardot again there can be no doubt. She had written her opera twenty years earlier on a text by Turgenev; now Tchaikovsky himself was faced with a proposition that he should set a libretto, *La courtisane*, by Louis Gallet. The subject roused his serious interest, and the text of Act 1 was

---

[22] *TD*, p. 229; *TZC3*, p. 304.
[23] *TLP15A*, p. 83; *TZC3*, p. 304; *TPJ2*, p. 119; *YDGC*, p. 469.

received during the summer. However, partly because of other commitments, but mainly because he could obtain no guarantee that it would be produced in Paris, he never began composition, though he was sufficiently attracted by the subject to reconsider it during the last year of his life.

His main purpose in visiting London, he had repeatedly said, was to provide Sapelnikov with the chance of being heard. The young pianist joined him on 30 March, halfway through his three weeks in Paris, and Tchaikovsky was determined to introduce him to French musical circles before they left, having him play to Mme Benardaky, then to Diémer, and persuading Colonne to let Sapelnikov exhibit himself at one of his soirées – all to such good purpose that the French conductor engaged him for the following season. On 9 April they were in London, waking next day to a London fog which, by the end of the morning's rehearsal, had turned into a 'peasouper' that even the local inhabitants said was exceptional for April. At the best of times Tchaikovsky had no love for London, and this indescribable murkiness, coupled with two rehearsals at which the orchestra had seemed to be cold towards him, did nothing to enhance his view of the English or their capital. But the players' excellence was indisputable, and the concert in St James's Hall, in which he conducted his First Suite as well as the First Piano Concerto, was a special success for Sapelnikov, who was to return to London repeatedly in subsequent years. Early the next morning, 12 April, Tchaikovsky slipped into Sapelnikov's room to kiss the sleeping youth farewell, then quietly left the Hotel Dieudonné. As his tour had progressed, a longing to head straight for Frolovskoye had grown ever stronger, but he had already promised to visit Anatoly and Parasha. Passing through Paris, he encountered Vera's widower at the railway terminus, and was deeply affected by the young man's continuing grief. The following day he was in Marseilles, ready to embark on a Mediterranean crossing to Batum, en route for Tiflis.

An eleven-day voyage lay before him. There was a good deal of unsettled, sometimes alarmingly rough weather, but the ship was comfortable, the captain and attendants pleasant, and the food excellent. His fellow-passengers proved uninteresting except for two, one a student from Moscow University, the other, Vladimir Sklifosovsky, the son of an eminent Moscow surgeon. Traversing the Strait of Bonifacio and passing within sight of the Lipari islands, where a volcano was in spectacular eruption, they weathered a gale off Messina before calling in at the island of Siros, which Tchaikovsky visited with the two youths. After a night broken by another terrifying storm the ship reached Smyrna (now Izmir), where the three again toured the sights and bought fezzes; the following day, 19 April, it berthed in Constantinople. Here Tchaikovsky had to say goodbye to his two companions. He had been strongly drawn to the fourteen-year-old Sklifosovsky, and it is no surprise that he should have wept on parting, or that he should have been upset at news of the boy's death the following year. But the impression had been deeper perhaps than even Tchaikovsky had realized at the time, and four years later he was to dedicate *Chant élégiaque*, No. 14 of the Eighteen Piano Pieces, Op. 72, to Sklifosovsky's memory.

Except for Tchaikovsky's obvious delight in this relationship, his diary gives little evidence that he found this voyage as interesting or stimulating as when he had made it in the opposite direction three years earlier. He read a little, including Gautier's *Le Capitaine Fracasse* ('both bad and superb at the same time'[24]) and managed to sketch a polonaise for *The Sleeping Beauty*. But the turmoil of his concert tour had drained him, and the three days steaming along the northern coast of Turkey became increasingly wearisome, for all the spring weather and calm sea. On 23 April the vessel docked in Batum. After a night in a bad hotel he boarded the train for Tiflis.

The visit was not an unqualified pleasure. Receiving copies of the journal *New Time* with two reports of Sapelnikov's success in London but no mention of his own part in the concert was simply too much to endure, and an angry letter was sent to the editor. His exploits were not of public interest because they were personal successes, he insisted, but because they were to the credit of Russian music. From London itself, however, there was an encouraging enquiry; through Jurgenson the impresario, Carl Rosa, had asked which of Tchaikovsky's operas the composer himself thought might be most suitable for production in England (*Mazepa* had already been ruled out on the mistaken ground that it was at odds with Byron). Tchaikovsky suggested *Onegin* and *The Maid of Orléans*; sadly, Rosa's sudden death ended the matter. In Tiflis the weather remained mostly excellent, the environment as enchanting as ever. But the reaction to his tour had now fully set in. 'A certain weariness, apathy, and indefinable melancholy often descend on me,' he wrote to his benefactress. 'I have not the slightest wish to work, somehow I have little wish even to read.'[25] Yet there was no escaping constant socializing when staying with Parasha – and all the time there was a gnawing urgency to proceed with the ballet. On 12 May the Artistic Society gave, in his honour, a concert of his works, including

[24] *TD*, p. 234; *YDGC*, p. 470.
[25] *TLP*15A, p. 100; *TPM*3, p. 572; *TZC*3, p. 310.

the Piano Trio; two days later he left to trace in reverse the route across the mountains which had provided him with such memorable vistas on his first visit to the Caucasus three years before. But this time he was in no mood to respond, and part of the way he had to share his carriage with a garrulous lady towards whom he maintained a stony silence until her 'twitterings'[26] faded. In Vladikavkaz he was sought out by Vasily Safonov's father, who took him, protesting, to his own home to share two bottles of wine.

On arriving in Moscow on 19 May, he found himself in the middle of a crisis. The Conservatoire had suffered, as he put it, a *coup d'état*. Drained by his teaching and administrative duties, deeply depressed by the recent death of his mother, and longing to return to composition and performance, Taneyev had resigned as director. All agreed that only Vasily Safonov could replace him, but he would not take the post unless Albrecht left the Conservatoire completely. Though Tchaikovsky was aware of the universal hostility his old friend now aroused, he could in no way understand its roots and, fiercely loyal, he insisted that if Albrecht were driven out, he would resign as an RMS director. A compromise followed much debate; Tchaikovsky would persuade Albrecht to retire on good financial terms, and there was to be no public hint that his departure had been other than at his own request. This entailed directors' meetings, consultations, sometimes difficult, with Taneyev (whom he persuaded to stay on as professor of counterpoint), Jurgenson, and Albrecht himself, whose resignation letter Tchaikovsky wrote out in his own hand. And while all this was boiling there were Conservatoire examinations and end-of-session performances to attend. But that humanity which he was exercising in public matters was as readily applied to private need; repeatedly he found time to give to Hubert's widow, and he was to be one of the main activists in arranging that she should take over the position at the Conservatoire vacated by Albrecht.

On 26 May he was with Modest and Kolya Konradi in St Petersburg, to be drawn into an even more pitiless round of visits and engagements. Between these he had consultations with Vsevolozhsky about the sets and costumes for *The Sleeping Beauty* and with Petipa about the choreography, attended a meeting of the committee constituted to oversee the celebrations of Anton Rubinstein's golden jubilee as a pianist, and tried to persuade Rubinstein himself to open the Moscow RMS's next season. When it became clear Rubinstein could come only in January 1890, he arranged for Rimsky-Korsakov to

[26] *TLP*15A, p. 106.

conduct the first concert instead, an occasion which was to witness Tchaikovsky's début as castanet player when he replaced an incompetent percussionist in Rimsky-Korsakov's *Capriccio espagnole*. A frenetic five days ended with a restaurant meal in the company of Rimsky-Korsakov and Lyadov beginning an hour before midnight and ending at two o'clock. On 31 May, after a four-month absence, he was home at last, determined to direct all his efforts into the ballet, the score of which was required by the Imperial Theatres in the middle of September.

The seed from which Tchaikovsky's second ballet grew had been sown by Vsevolozhsky just a year before. 'I have been thinking of writing a libretto on Perrault's fairy tale, *La belle au bois dormant*,' the director of the Imperial Theatres in St Petersburg had confided on 25 May 1888. 'I want to stage it in the style of Louis XIV, allowing the musical fantasy to run high and melodies to be written in the spirit of Lully, Bach, Rameau, and such-like. If this idea is to your liking, why shouldn't you undertake to compose the music? In the last act there needs to be a quadrille made from all Perrault's fairy stories – Puss in Boots, Tom Thumb, Cinderella, Bluebeard, and such-like.'[27] Vsevolozhsky had been showing sustained determination to have a ballet from Tchaikovsky, for some eighteen months before, in November 1886, he had proposed *Salammbô* or *Undine*. Tchaikovsky had instantly rejected the former, but Zhukovsky's touching tale, on which seventeen years earlier he had composed his second opera, once again detained him. The work would be for the following season; Modest was to be the librettist, Petipa the choreographer, and Tchaikovsky would receive the handsome fee of 5,000 roubles. Within two months, however, Tchaikovsky had realized the pressures of preparing to conduct *Cherevichki* and trying to complete *The Enchantress* would make the prospect of finishing the piece on time unrealistic. Yet already one suspects his initial enthusiasm for the subject was crumbling, and Modest's libretto failed to win either Vsevolozhsky's or his brother's approval. His immediate reaction to this other proposal is unknown. But Vsevolozhsky was persistent, and by 3 September Tchaikovsky was responding as he had hoped. 'I hasten to let you know that the manuscript of [the scenario of] *The Sleeping Beauty* has at last reached my address,' the composer wrote that day, '. . . and I very much want to tell you straight away that I'm charmed, delighted beyond all description. It suits me perfectly, and I ask for nothing more than to set it to music. It would be impossible to make a better stage arrangement of the elements in this delicious subject.'[28]

[27] *DTC*, p. 240.
[28] *TLP*14, p. 509; *DTC*, p. 240 (partial; in Russian only).

Tchaikovsky's enthusiasm was genuine, though to ensure his music would match the choreographer's requirements as closely as possible, he did not intend to start work until they had conferred. He had hoped to visit St Petersburg in September, but it was nearly mid-November before he was there to have a series of conferences with both Vsevolozhsky and Petipa, as a result of which agreement was reached on a detailed dramatic scheme which Petipa supplemented with requirements of character, metre, and exact length. But already so great had been Tchaikovsky's excitement with the subject that he had been unable to resist beginning, and during ten days in October, between completing work on the scores and proofs of the Fifth Symphony and *Hamlet* and conducting the St Petersburg premières of these two pieces, a large part of the Prologue (from the fairies' entrance (No. 2) to the moment in the Finale when the Lilac Fairy approaches Aurora's cradle) had been roughed out as best he could.

Nevertheless, the main labour of composition was deferred to the beginning of 1889 when he was back in Frolovskoye with Petipa's detailed scheme to hand. By 12 January the end of the Prologue was drafted, together with the opening Scène and Valse of Act 1. Then a newly begun diary recorded his successes and problems, excitements and depressions. The order in which he tackled the various movements sometimes seemed capricious. '*13 January*: . . . Worked all morning (Aurora's entrance). . . . *14 January*: . . . Wrote the big adagio in Act 1.[29] It was difficult. . . . *15 January*: . . . Work is going so-so . . . *16 January*: . . . As always now, I worked beyond my strength [on the Act 1 Finale]. It seems I'm played out! . . . *17 January*: . . . Generally worked well today. Finished Act 1. Played it through (it lasts half an hour).' Between 18 and 21 January there was a break to visit Moscow and deal with correspondence. '*22 January*: Work went well. Wrote the whole entr'acte to the *sleep* scene [No. 19] – not too badly, it seems . . . *23 January*: Worked especially well today, as of old. Did a lot. Finished Act 2, Scene 2 [remainder of No. 19, and No. 20].' Again there was an interruption, this time of two days. '*26 January*: Worked as diligently as ever [on the entr'acte with violin obbligato (No. 18)]. There's a hope I'll finish the first four scenes before leaving [on the concert tour].' Next day guests absorbed his time. '*28 January*: . . . Worked till I was weary [on Act 2, Scene 1]. . . . *29 January*: . . . Worked beyond my strength – I'm already very tired . . . *30 January*: Completed my work – that is, the

[29] 'Act 2' in *TD* (and also for entry of 17 January). These must be mistakes, though the latter might be 'Act 2, Scene 1'.

first four scenes.'[30] Three more days, and a preliminary rehearsal was taking place at the Bolshoy Theatre in St Petersburg.

The European tour now intervened, Tchaikovsky receiving from Petipa the detailed plan for the final act before leaving. What he composed in Hanover is unknown, though it must surely have been the march opening Act 3, and the following polonaise was certainly drafted during his Mediterranean journey. In fact, the Finale to Act 1 still had no ending, and this was provided at Tiflis, together with four numbers in Act 3: the Pas de quatre for the fairies, the mimes for Puss in Boots and the White Cat, and for Red Riding Hood and the Wolf, as well as the Pas berrichon. Nevertheless, Tchaikovsky's mood while in the Caucasus did not encourage work, and his ten days divided between Moscow and St Petersburg were too full of worrying distractions and social pressures to permit anything creative. Back in Frolovskoye on 31 May he was quick to resume, starting with the Pas de quatre (No. 25). For two days the unseasonal heat made work difficult; then again his diary becomes a record of swift progress. '*4 June*: Somehow I feel alright, probably because it's gone cold. Worked intensively and successfully (Pas de deux [No. 28]). . . . *5 June*: It's become very cold . . . Worked successfully [on the sarabande].' Later that day he read through the score of *Giselle*. '*6 June*: . . . My head aches a bit. All the same, I worked. Was composing the last number of the ballet, the mazurka. . . . *7 June*: Finished *composing* the ballet.'[31] He was proud of his rate of progress, though his arithmetic took no account of work not done at Frolovskoye. 'I finished the sketches on 7 June 1889 at 8 p.m.,' he wrote at their end. 'Praise be to God! In all I worked ten days in October, three weeks in January, and now a week; so, in all, about forty days.'[32]

The scoring was begun four days later. It was a slow process. 'I cannot now work as fast as I once did,' he wrote to Nadezhda von Meck after six weeks, the operation still far from completed, despite unbroken application. 'What is good is that I am satisfied with my new work, and I feel that for the time being I still have no need to worry about the decline in my inventive faculty with which I shall be threatened in the more or less near future.'[33] By now the Prologue and Act 1 were complete, a little work had been done on Act 2, but he had transferred his attention to Act 3. This intensive and sustained reviewing of what

---

[30] *TD*, pp. 219–21; *DTC*, p. 241 (except for final entry). A note in the sketches states that the first four scenes were completed a day earlier, on 29 January.

[31] *TD*, p. 241. Information in square brackets is provided from the sketches.

[32] *DTC*, p. 242; *YDGC*, p. 474; *TLP*15A, p. 156 (partial).

[33] *TLP*15A, p. 155; *TPM*3, p. 578; *TZC*3, p. 315; *DTC*, p. 243.

he had composed in no way diminished his pride in it. 'I think, my dear friend, that the music of this ballet will comprise one of my best works,' he continued on 6 August, the day Act 3 was completed. 'The subject is so poetic, musically so grateful, that I was completely carried away in composing it . . . As I think I have already written to you, the scoring is coming to me significantly less easily than in time past, and the work is going much more slowly – but perhaps this also is good.'[34] Three further weeks, and his enthusiasm still remained high. 'I have engaged in scoring it with special love and care, and I have devised several completely new orchestral combinations which I hope will be very beautiful and interesting.'[35] Three days later, on 28 August, Act 2 was done; four more days, and all was complete. The dedication was given to the man who had started it all, Vsevolozhsky, who took immense pride in the inscription.

'Very nice!!!!!' was the Tsar's comment at the dress rehearsal on 14 January 1890.[36] His Imperial Majesty had treated him very condescendingly, Tchaikovsky sensed, and neither his diary nor any of his letters contains a mention of the première the following day. Modest remembered how mortified his brother had been at the Tsar's words – but 'at the first performance the audience concurred completely with the Tsar's verdict, and their calls, their applause, lacking in any enthusiasm, also said "very nice" – no more . . . Pyotr Ilich felt very grieved at this – grieved because, having become familiar at rehearsals with the miracles of elegance, luxury, originality in the costumes and scenery, and with the inexhaustible grace and variety of Petipa's fantasy . . . [he] had expected that, in combination with his music, which he loved second only to that of *Eugene Onegin*, it would all elicit a storm of delight.'[37] But the audience did not appreciate any of this, Modest continued, and the popular press swooped. There was, he said (not quite accurately), only one review in the St Petersburg papers which greeted the ballet enthusiastically and predicted a successful future for it. This was from Mikhail Ivanov in *New Time*, which had already made amends for not reporting Tchaikovsky's foreign tour by printing a belated notice on it. 'The music for *The Sleeping Beauty* has been reproached by some reviewers for its excessive symphonism,' Ivanov declared. '. . . [But] this tendency is understandable, for Tchaikovsky cannot, because of the entrenched practices of earlier choreography,

[34] *TLP*15A, p. 160; *TPM*3, p. 580; *TZC*3, p. 315; *DTC*, p. 244; *YDGC*, p. 476 (partial).
[35] *TLP*15A, p. 169; *TPM*3, p. 583; *DTC*, p. 244; *YDGC*, p. 476.
[36] *TD*, p. 249; *TZC*3, p. 339; *DTC*, p. 244; *YDGC*, p. 482; *TLP*15A, p. 217.
[37] *TZC*3, p. 340.

renounce the means his art affords him. It declares itself even more in *The Sleeping Beauty*, where the very subject demands from him a larger infusion of the symphonic genre . . . I think it must be recognized the best music of *The Sleeping Beauty* is in the Prologue, Act 1, and almost all of Act 2 . . . In the ballet's final act there are some excellent character dances whose interest is reinforced by what happens on the stage itself.'[38]

Yet the most astute review was that written by Laroche for the *Moscow Gazette*. Reading this, with its perceptive assessment of the work's French and Russian elements and of its place within the tradition of Glinka, one can well understand Tchaikovsky's admiration for his friend's critical gifts. But first Laroche answered the charge that the story was trite.

> One of the artistic creations most truthful, most true to life, is the myth, provided it is an authentic *real* myth – not counterfeit, not a later invention, not specially fabricated. The fairy tale, for all its prosaic form, often embodies the most ancient, the most genuine of myths; *The Sleeping Beauty*, incidentally resembling in its basic motif Brünnhilde, guarded by fire, is one of the innumerable embodiments of earth, laid to rest by winter and awakened by the kiss of spring. In that sense Siegfried and Prince Désiré are one and the same person . . .
>
> Say as much as you wish against children's fairy tales: you will not destroy the fact that . . . within them are contained some of the profoundest ideas that stir mankind . . .
>
> In his youth Tchaikovsky composed one undemanding ballet . . . But in the music of *Swan Lake* could already be felt a symphonist with an unusual gift for the genre of ballet, an educated musician devoid of pedantry and snobbery, able at any time to divest himself of his professorial mantle and sit at the piano to improvise dances, even if only for a children's festivity. He is one of the foremost melodists of our time. But up to now he has exhibited that melodic gift for the most part in those kinds of music which are officially recognized as 'serious' – in the symphony, quartet, piano piece, symphonic poem, cantata, romance and opera of tragic content (only one opera, *Cherevichki*, is semi-comic). An elegist by nature, inclined to melancholy, and even to a certain despair, he has shown in these kinds of composition officially labelled 'serious' a seriousness of another kind, a seriousness of thought, a frequent sadness and melancholy, not

[38] *DTC*, pp. 246–7; *YDGC*, p. 485.

infrequently a nagging feeling of spiritual pain, and this, if one may so express it, *minor* part of his being (related to Chopin) has been more grasped and esteemed. But alongside this there is another Tchaikovsky: nice, happy, brimming with health, inclined to humour . . . and this Tchaikovsky, related not to Chopin but to Schumann, and above all to Glinka, has up to now been far less noticed and recognized, to judge from the obscurity in which the more optimistic part of his output resides. Meanwhile he has an inexhaustible fund of dance melodies, not of course like those which the operettas and ballets of the 'good old time' have schooled us in . . . but light, graceful, full of movement and sensual delight. In the accompaniment of these melodies (especially in *The Sleeping Beauty*) counterpoint plays an extensive role (usually a countermelody in a middle part). Those balletomanes who, having been brought up on Adam and Pugni, have still not managed to take in the waltzes of Strauss, may indict him for this device, which has long been employed in the waltzes of Strauss himself, though not as richly and skilfully as by Tchaikovsky.

The Russian musical manner, so strong in Tchaikovsky of recent years, makes itself felt time and again. The music fits the costume, the character entirely; there is a French tint in it, but at the same time it smells of Russia. . . . It is not a matter of local colour, which is excellently observed, but of an element more general and deep than colour – of the inner structuring of the music – above all, of the melodic basis. This fundamental element is unquestionably Russian. You could say . . . that the local colour is French, but *the style* is Russian . . .

If the production of *The Sleeping Beauty* is one of our theatre's pearls, then musically it is one of Tchaikovsky's. Together with *Eugene Onegin*, together with the composer's symphonies, his first and third suites, his [first] piano concerto and fantasy for piano and orchestra, together with some of his romances and with many episodes in his operas besides *Onegin*, it represents the highest point yet reached by the Glinka school – the point at which the school is already beginning to free itself from Glinka and open new horizons, still as yet unclear.[39]

Charles Perrault published his *Histoires et contes du temps passé*, which included *The Sleeping Beauty*, in 1697. The story as presented in

---

[39] Laroche (H. A.), *Izbrannïye stati*. Vol. 2 (Leningrad, 1975), pp. 140–3; *DTC*, pp. 245–6 (partial).

Tchaikovsky's ballet is summarized in the libretto printed in *Yezhegodnik imperatorskikh teatrov* (1890–1).[40] The libretto's content is not comprehensive; supplementations are provided in square brackets.

PROLOGUE. *The christening of Princess Aurora. A banquet in the King's palace.* [March (No. 1).] Courtiers are awaiting the entrance of the King and Queen. The masters of ceremonies show each to his place and explain the procedure for offering congratulations to the King, the Queen, and to the influential Fairies invited to the festivities as godmothers to Princess Aurora. Catalabutte, the senior master of ceremonies, checks the list of invitations sent to the Fairies. Everything is being done in accordance with the King's command, and all is ready for the opening of the festivities. The court is full. The sound of trumpets. Entrance of King Florestan and the Queen, preceded by pages; the nannies and wet nurses carry a cradle in which the newborn Princess Aurora sleeps. The King and Queen take their places on the platform on either side of the cradle, the masters of ceremonies announce the arrival of the Fairies. [Scène dansante (No. 2).] Entrance of the Fairies: Candide, Fleur de Farine, Violente, Canary, and Breadcrumb. The King and Queen meet them and show them to their places on the platform. Entrance of the Lilac Fairy, Princess Aurora's principal godmother. She is surrounded by her attendant spirits carrying large fans and censers, and bearing their mistress's mantle. At a signal from Catalabutte pages and young girls bring forward, on brocade pillows, gifts prepared by the King for his daughter's godmothers, and they explain to each Fairy that it is for her. [Pas de six (No. 3).] The Fairies come down from the platform so that they, for their part, may present gifts to their goddaughter. *Grand pas d'ensemble*: The Fairies' gifts. [Finale (No. 4).] In her turn the Lilac Fairy approaches the cradle to present her gift.

A noise is heard; a page runs in and tells of the arrival of the powerful and evil Fairy Carabosse, whom they have forgotten to invite to the feast. Catalabutte is in despair; how could he, always distinguished by his efficiency, have made such a frightful blunder – to forget to invite Fairy Carabosse! Trembling with fear, he approaches the King to admit his terrible mistake. The King and Queen are very alarmed; this mistake may bring after it much misfortune in the destiny of their dear child. The Fairies also express anxiety about this. Carabosse appears in a chariot drawn by six rats, accompanied by ugly pages. The King and Queen beg Fairy Carabosse not to blame them for this misdemeanour of Catalabutte, and they promise he will be punished according to her wish. Catalabutte, neither dead nor alive, throws himself at the evil Fairy's feet, begging forgiveness and promising to serve her faithfully

---

[40] As printed in Vol. 12g (1952), pp. 365–7, of the Tchaikovsky Complete Edition (*Polnoye sobraniye sochineny* (Moscow/Leningrad, 1940–71)). This summary version has been chosen here since it supplements the other more detailed accounts of the plot of *The Sleeping Beauty* printed in the appendices to Wiley (R. J.), *Tchaikovsky's ballets* (Oxford, 1985). In addition to a translation of the first edition of the libretto (St Petersburg, 1890), Wiley prints in full Petipa's specific instructions to Tchaikovsky regarding the kind of music required, as well as Petipa's ballet-master's notes. There are numerous differences of detail between the versions.

to the end of his days. Carabosse mocks Catalabutte, plucks out tufts of hair from his head and throws them to the rats to eat. The unfortunate man's head becomes completely bald. 'Although I am not Aurora's godmother,' says Carabosse, 'I still want to give her something.' The good Fairies entreat her to forgive the master of ceremonies' unintentional oversight, and not to poison the happiness of the best of kings. Carabosse laughs; her gaiety passes to her ugly pages and even her rats. The good Fairies turn away from their sister with revulsion. 'Aurora, thanks to the gifts of her six godmothers,' says Carabosse, 'will be the most beautiful, the most attractive, the most clever of all the princesses in the world. I do not have the power to deprive her of these qualities, but so that her happiness may never be destroyed – you see how good I am – she will fall asleep the first time she pricks her hand or finger, and her slumber will be eternal.' The King, Queen and all the court are dumbfounded. With her wand Carabosse makes signs over the cradle, pronouncing magic words and, happy at the trick she has played on her sisters, the good Fairies, laughs together with her ugly retinue. The Lilac Fairy, who has not yet managed to present a gift to her goddaughter, and who has been standing screened by Aurora's cradle, now comes forward. Carabosse looks at her with suspicion and malice. The good Fairy, leaning over the princess's cradle, says: 'Yes, you will fall asleep, my little Aurora, as our sister Carabosse wishes, but not for ever. The day will come when a handsome prince, captivated by your beauty, will give you a kiss that will awaken you from your long slumber, and you will be the bride of this prince, to live in happiness and contentment.' Carabosse, enraged, leaves in her chariot, and the good Fairies surround the cradle, expressing their wish to protect their goddaughter from the machinations of their evil sister.

ACT I. *The park in the palace of King Florestan XIV.* [Scène (No. 5).] Aurora is now twenty. Florestan is happy that Fairy Carabosse's predictions have not been fulfilled. Catalabutte, whose hair has not grown again, appears in a comical cap. Noticing several peasants arriving with needles to work in front of the palace, he reads them a declaration prohibiting the use of needles and pins within a hundred-mile radius of the royal residence. The frightened peasants beg forgiveness, but Catalabutte remains adamant and sends the offenders to prison. The King and Queen appear on the terrace of the castle accompanied by four princes, suitors for the hand of Princess Aurora. The King asks what the peasants who have been sent off to prison are guilty of. Catalabutte explains the reason for their arrest and shows the material evidence. The King and Queen are horrified. 'Let the guilty suffer for their crime and never more see God's light!' they say. The princes beg mercy for the guilty ones: 'Not one tear must be shed in Florestan's kingdom on that day when Aurora reaches twenty.' The King pardons the peasants. General rejoicing. [Valse (No. 6).] Dances of the peasants. [Scène (No. 7).] The princes have never seen Princess Aurora, though each of them has a medallion with her portrait. They are all burning with the desire to be Aurora's favourite, and tell this to the King and Queen, who say they have given their dear daughter full freedom of choice, and that the one she falls in love with will be their son-in-law and successor to the kingdom. Entrance of Aurora. She runs in, accompanied by her maids of honour carrying bouquets and wreaths. The four princes are astonished at the Princess's beauty. *Pas d'action* (No. 8). The King and Queen urge Aurora to make her choice of a husband. 'I am still so young,' Aurora says. 'Leave me to enjoy my freedom.' 'Do as you know best – but remember that the interests of the state require your marriage. Carabosse's prediction frightens us very much.' 'Don't worry; for her prediction to be fulfilled, I must pierce my hand or finger, and I never take into my hand either pins or needles. I sing, dance, make merry, but never sew,' says Aurora, dancing merrily – and suddenly she notices an old woman who, standing in the crowd, is beating time to her dance with a spindle. The Princess snatches the spindle from the old woman and begins to dance with it, now as with a sceptre, now imitating the work of spinners, trying to command the total admiration of her four suitors. [Finale (No. 9).] Suddenly her dances are interrupted, and in horror she looks at her hand, pricked by the spindle, and bloodstained. In horror Aurora throws herself from side to side and finally falls lifeless. The King and Queen rush to their daughter, and at the sight of her wounded hand, understand the full force of the misfortune that has befallen them. Then the old woman to whom the spindle had belonged throws off her cloak. They recognize her as the Fairy Carabosse, who laughs at the despair of Florestan and the Queen. The four princes unsheath their swords and rush towards her, but Carabosse, with a diabolical laugh, vanishes in a cloud of smoke and fire. The princes run out in fear. At this moment the fountain at the rear of the stage is illuminated with a magic light, and the Lilac Fairy appears. 'Be comforted,' she says to the despairing parents. 'Your daughter is sleeping and will sleep a hundred years. But in order that nothing of her happiness will change, you will fall asleep with her. Her awakening will be the signal for your awakening. Return to the castle. I will guarantee your safety.' They place the sleeping Princess on a litter and carry her out, accompanied by the King, the Queen and the highest officials. The cavaliers, pages and guards bow before this procession. The Fairy waves her wand in the direction of the castle, and all these groups on the threshold and on the staircase are at once overcome by sleep. Everything falls asleep, including the flowers and jets of the fountain. Ivy and creepers grow out from the earth and cover the castle and the sleeping people. Trees and large lilac bushes grow up magically under the influence of the Fairy, and transform the royal garden into an impenetrable wood. The Fairy's attendants gather around her, and she orders them to guard the castle so that none will dare disturb the quiet of those whom she is protecting.

ACT 2, SCENE 1. *Prince Désiré's hunt. A wooded place; a wide river flows at the rear of the stage. A dense forest stretches into the far distance. To the right of the audience, cliffs covered with vegetation. The landscape is filled with bright sunlight.* [Entr'acte et Scène (No. 10).] When the curtain opens the stage is empty, sounds of hunting horns are heard, then the hunt of Prince Désiré, who is pursuing wild animals in the nearby woods. Hunters (men and women) enter and spread themselves over the grass for lunch; Prince Désiré soon appears with his tutor, Galifron, and several courtiers of the King, his father. Lunch is prepared for the Prince and his retinue. [Colin-Maillard (No. 11).] Hunters and ladies, for diversion, organize dances, shoot with bows, and play at various games. [Scène (No. 12): Dance of the duchesses; Dance of the marchionesses; Dance of the countesses; Dance of the baronesses.] Young women try to please the Prince [each dance, it seems, involved only two aspirants. Farandole (No. 13): a general dance. Scène (No. 14).] People arrive to tell the Prince that a bear has been cornered in a thicket. The Prince is tired. 'Hunt without me,' he tells his retinue. 'I want to rest here; this place pleases me very much.'

The hunt has only just moved away when a boat of mother-of-pearl, decorated with gold and precious stones, appears on the river. From it on to the shore steps the Lilac Fairy, also the godmother of Prince Désiré. The Prince bows before the good Fairy, who behaves graciously towards him. 'I will show you your future bride,' she says. 'She is the most beautiful, the most enchanting and most intelligent princess in the world.' 'Where can I see her?' 'I will straightway call her spirit, and if she pleases you, you may fall in love with her.' The Fairy waves her wand towards the side of the cliffs, which open, and Aurora is seen sleeping with her retinue. At another sign from the Fairy, Aurora rises with her friends and appears on stage. Rays of the setting sun illumine her with a rose-coloured light. [Pas d'action (No. 15). Aurora's dancing increasingly delights the Prince. She finally disappears into a cleft of the rocks. Scène (No. 16).] The Prince, madly in love with Aurora, falls at his godmother's feet. 'Where is this heavenly creature you have shown me? Take me to her, I want to see her and press her to my heart.' 'Let us go,' says the Fairy, and leads him to her boat, which immediately moves on its way. The boat moves quickly and the landscape becomes more and more wild. *Panorama* (No. 17). Evening comes, night soon begins to fall, the moon illumines the boat with a silvery light; in the distance is seen the castle, which again disappears in a bend of the river. But then at last the castle again appears – the goal of their journey. The Prince and the Fairy get out of the boat. The Fairy, with a wave of her magic wand, makes the castle gates open; the walls, where the guards and the pages are sleeping, are seen. The Prince runs in, accompanied by the Fairy. The whole stage is enveloped in dense clouds, and quiet music is heard. *Musical entr'acte* (No. 19).

ACT 2, SCENE 2. *The Sleeping Beauty's castle*. The clouds disperse; a room is seen where Princess Aurora sleeps on a large bed beneath a canopy. The King and Queen are sleeping opposite in two armchairs; the court cavaliers, ladies and pages sleep standing up, leaning against one another and making up sleeping groups. A layer of dust and cobwebs covers the furniture and the people. The Fairy enters with Prince Désiré. The Prince rushes to the bed, calls upon the Princess in vain, stirs the King, Queen and Catalabutte, who is asleep on a stool at the King's feet. Nothing avails; only clouds of dust rise in the room. The Fairy remains a passive observer of the Prince's despair. Finally Désiré approaches the Sleeping Beauty and kisses her. [Finale (No. 20).] The magic spell of the wicked Carabosse vanishes. Princess Aurora awakens, and with her the entire court. The dust and cobwebs disappear, candles light up the room, the fire flares up. The Prince implores the King to agree to his marriage with his daughter. 'Such is her destiny,' replies the King, and joins the hands of the young people.

ACT 3. *The Wedding of Prince Désiré and Princess Aurora. The esplanade of King Florestan's palace.* [March (No. 21).] The courtiers gather for the festivity. Catalabutte, the chief master of ceremonies, allocates the guests their places. Entrance of the King, Queen, the newly-weds and their suite, and the Fairies: Diamond, Gold, Silver and Sapphire. At a signal from the King the festivity commences. Polonaise (No. 22). [Procession of Fairies, participants in the following Divertissement, and others].

Divertissement:

Pas de quatre (No. 23): Diamond Fairy, Gold Fairy, Silver Fairy, Sapphire Fairy.

Pas de caractère (No. 24): Puss in Boots and the White Cat.

Pas de deux (No. 25): The Bluebird and Princess Florine.

Pas de caractère (No. 26): Little Red Riding Hood and the Wolf.

Pas de caractère: Cinderella and Prince Fortuné.

Pas berrichon (No. 27): Tom Thumb, his brothers and the Ogre.

Pas de deux (No. 28): Aurora and Désiré.[41]

Entrance of the ballet:

Sarabande (No. 29): Roman, Persian, Indian, American and Turkish. General Coda [*Finale* (No. 30)].

Apotheosis (*Gloire des Fées*) [in the production changed to a tableau vivant representing Apollo].

Gluck's *Orfeo* had been a product of circumstance as much as genius, for without the reforming vision of the Viennese theatre Intendant, Giacomo Durazzo, and the shared dramatic perceptions of the librettist, Raniero Calzabigi, Gluck would never have conceived the powerful dramatic piece he did. *The Sleeping Beauty* was envisaged and grew in similar conditions, Durazzo's role taken by Vsevolozhsky, Calzabigi's by Petipa. In his fundamental study of Tchaikovsky's three ballets[42] Roland John Wiley has investigated the surviving sources and the evidence they and other contemporary documents yield on these works' creative backgrounds and first productions; he has also described the profound changes that took place in the cultural environment and administrative temper during the thirteen years separating the productions of *Swan Lake* and *The Sleeping Beauty*. Tchaikovsky's first ballet had been written in the mid-seventies for Moscow, where the musical expectations had been low and many of the resources inadequate, though some of the dancers had much technical skill. Then, in 1881,

---

[41] This appears in the libretto as a Pas de quatre, including also the Gold and Sapphire Fairies.

[42] Wiley, *op. cit.* In addition to the abundant information on Petipa and his role in preparing the ballet, there is a detailed description of the choreography in the first performances.

four years after *Swan Lake*'s première, Vsevolozhsky had been appointed to the Imperial Theatres. The new director had straightaway provided extra resources for the main St Petersburg companies, and Tchaikovsky had enjoyed his largesse in 1884 with the twin productions of his opera, *Mazepa*. But Vsevolozhsky was even more disposed towards ballet. True, he had done further damage to the Moscow company by severe financial constraints, but he saw Moscow as an outpost of his empire, and the economies there provided a further excuse for his lavish provision of the home company in the city of the Emperor and court. By the end of the decade the St Petersburg ballet was excellent in all respects.

Vsevolozhsky also aimed to raise the level of the music, and in 1886 he used the retirement of Minkus to abolish the post of resident ballet composer, thus making it easier to give commissions to an outsider like Tchaikovsky. But Vsevolozhsky was not simply a visionary administrator; like Durazzo, he was something of a creator, devising the scenarios of both *Sleeping Beauty* and perhaps of *Nutcracker*, and designing the costumes for the former. The third member of the team, Petipa, was a choreographer of genius, perhaps the greatest in the history of ballet in Russia. Twenty-two years older than Tchaikovsky, he had joined the St Petersburg company as a dancer when the future composer was only seven, had made his first deep mark as a choreographer in 1862 with *Pharoah's Daughter*, and for the next quarter of a century had devised a succession of pieces upon similar dramatic and choreographic schemes. Petipa crossed his watershed with *The Sleeping Beauty*, a fairy tale of a sort which preoccupied him for the remaining dozen or so years of his professional life. But it was also a watershed for the Russian ballet tradition itself. Until that moment the choreographer had been undisputed master before whom composer and librettist bowed; now that supremacy was broken, for Petipa was working with a composer of gifts and reputation such as he had never before encountered. It made for a hard time, he later admitted – and hard for the dancers too, for Tchaikovsky's rhythmic inventiveness remained as fertile as ever, posing formidable problems in learning and synchronization. But if Petipa had to accept that Tchaikovsky's music, once written, was almost a *fait accompli*, he was able in preliminary consultations to make clear to a highly attentive composer the requirements for his stage vision to be realized, and during rehearsals Tchaikovsky agreed a number of adjustments and cuts to accommodate his colleague's wishes. Many of these were relatively small; the really major piece of surgery was the excision of one of the pieces designed to display Auer's skill – the entr'acte with solo violin obbligato (No. 18) between the Panorama and the 'Sleep' entr'acte – on the very reasonable grounds that it held up the action.[43]

Setting the tale in the time of Louis XIV was an obvious invitation to incorporate an early-eighteenth-century musical style, though Tchaikovsky was careful to scale it judiciously so that its occurrences as an identifying mark of the highest society would be the more pointed. There is a whiff of it at the entry of the King and Queen with the four princes in Act 1, and more clearly still when Désiré arrives with his hunting party in Act 2. The preamble to the Scène (No. 12) lays the ground for the idiom's explicit use in the dignified Tempo di Menuetto of the duchesses' dance – though the baronesses who follow allow the stiff façade of their baroque Tempo di Gavotte to slip a little so that the lower ranking countesses and marchionesses subsequently feel no inhibition in dropping it completely. Though the stately Sarabande (No. 29)[44] following the Pas de deux for the lovers in Act 3 is surely intended as an evocation of a ceremonial dance from the court of the

---

[43] The situation, as revealed in the numerous source documents, seems chaotically inconclusive in many regards. Wiley's investigations indicate that very little was modified in the Prologue, and in Act 1 the only significant changes were the deletions of the princes' plea in the opening Scène (No. 5: bars 184–205), and of the parents' expressions of grief in the Finale (No. 9: bars 69–85). In the suite of four noblewomen's dances in Act 2 (No. 12), only that for the duchesses definitely survived to the première, and the order in Ziloti's transcription for solo piano (duchesses, baronesses, countesses, marchionesses) is different from that in the separately printed libretto of 1890 (see Wiley, *op. cit.*, p. 331). Aurora's variation in her Pas d'action with the Prince (No. 15) was replaced by the music of the Gold Fairy's variation in Act 3's first Pas de quatre (No. 23), which also lost the Sapphire Fairy's variation in $\frac{5}{4}$. The most numerous changes were made in Act 3. Tchaikovsky provided a ten-bar introduction to the cats' Pas de caractère (No. 24), and Petipa turned the second Pas de quatre (No. 25) into a Pas de deux for the Bluebird and Princess Florine 'without changing the music' (according to N. Cristoforov of the Imperial Theatres' Central Music Library; quoted in Wiley, *op. cit.*, p. 154); Cinderella and Prince Fortuné found a second home in a newly composed appendage to the following movement, the Pas de caractère for Red Riding Hood and the Wolf (No. 26). The *entrée* of the Pas de deux for Aurora and Désiré (No. 28: as noted earlier (footnote 41) this was at one stage re-planned as a third Pas de quatre, and was so described in both libretti) was evidently dropped. Having cut the entr'acte with solo violin obbligato (No. 18), Tchaikovsky had to devise a new ending for the Panorama (the original link is printed in Wiley, *op. cit.*, p. 406). Regardless of other changes made during late rehearsals, there are discrepancies between the specifications in the libretto and the published piano score (the full score was not printed until 1952). The differences in the piano score are: No. 23: the Diamond Fairy danced last. No. 25: a Pas de quatre for Cinderella, Prince Fortuné, the Bluebird and Princess Florine. No. 28: a Pas de deux for Aurora and Désiré.

[44] Though Petipa was more inclined to require cuts than extensions, this is one instance where Tchaikovsky's music proved too short, and to accommodate what was evidently a specially grand *entrée*, the second half of the dance was played three times (i.e. bar 33 to the end was repeated).

Sun King, it is the child of a German piece: the Sarabande, also in A minor, from Bach's Second English Suite. But the final Apotheosis returns this celebration of royal union, pomp and kingship to the land which had inspired it, being built upon a version of the tune 'Vive Henri IV' which Tchaikovsky was to re-use the following year during the bedroom scene in *The Queen of Spades*.

A gulf separates the musical worlds of *Swan Lake* and *The Sleeping Beauty*. The style of the former was a compromise, albeit a remarkable one. Tchaikovsky was already experienced in opera, and the bright, incisive, sometimes brash world of that theatrical genre was an influence upon the colourful scoring. Even more were there signs of the symphonic composer in the motivic generation of some melodies and textures, in the element of self-conscious contrapuntalism (certain countermelodies and imitations), in some of the spans of large-scale architecture with their powerfully built musical climaxes, and in the tendency, as much musical as dramatic, to use long-range repetitions as structural agents. The craft of *The Sleeping Beauty* is far more closely moulded to the form's requirements. It might be argued that the melodic world of the earlier ballet was stronger, that it had a more youthful energy, that there was something especially disarming in the rugged directness with which the unfolding events in some scènes had been confronted, that our emotional response to the tragic end of Odette and Siegfried is stronger than to the happy outcome of Aurora's and Désiré's adventures. But *The Sleeping Beauty* benefited not merely from the experience acquired in the dozen or more years between the ballets; there had been the specific researches of the suites, with their more refined and varied use of orchestral resource. The single most surprising instrumental novelty in *The Sleeping Beauty* is the substitution of piano for harp in the last act (in the concluding Apotheosis it fulfils, one suspects, what Tchaikovsky conceived as a continuo role). Earlier the harp, along with its familiar cadenza functions using arpeggios and flying glissandi, had added tiny brush strokes to enhance the delicate colours of the fairies' or Aurora's music – in the Adagio of the former's Pas de six (No. 3) in the Prologue, for instance. Some of the 'completely new orchestral combinations', of which Tchaikovsky wrote proudly to Nadezhda von Meck, are probably to be found in the variations that follow, especially in the collaboration of piccolo, flutes, bells and pizzicato strings to simulate the canary's song in No. 4, and in the contrasting timbres which are set against the line of pizzicato quavers through which the 'Fée aux miettes' scatters her breadcrumbs in No. 3.

And for Tchaikovsky there was also the experience of Delibes' two fine ballets. No doubt Petipa's 1884 production of *Coppélia* had been in Vsevolozhsky's mind when planning the new work. A fundamental weakness of *Swan Lake* had been the incessant intrusion of purely decorative dances, but in *Coppélia* such things had been concentrated into the festivities of the final scene, and the last act of *The Sleeping Beauty*, a celebration of the union of Aurora and Désiré, performed the same function, allowing Tchaikovsky to give almost undivided attention to dramatic issues in the Prologue and first two acts. But if Delibes' first ballet had the greater influence in giving *The Sleeping Beauty* its shape, for Tchaikovsky himself it was *Sylvia* that was the more suggestive. The first act of *Coppélia* had still accommodated a number of large formal dances, but in his second ballet Delibes had succeeded more consistently in blending divertissement with drama, and what is so striking about the music of *The Sleeping Beauty* is the almost total absence of gratuitous decoration. True, there are formal dances, notably the Valse (No. 6) in Act 1. But this is far better sited than that in *Swan Lake*, not clogging the action before it has barely begun; it is also far shorter (only three hundred against some five hundred bars), its lengthier introduction has a specified dramatic role, and the coda is less weighty, permitting a swift passage to the next portion of action. There may be no dramatic excuse for the Colin-maillard (No. 11) or the Farandole (No. 13) in Act 2, but the intervening suite of four dances (No. 12) for the noble ladies who would win the prince's favour is dramatically reasonable, concise, and nicely varied.

To describe *The Sleeping Beauty* as Wagnerian would be even more ludicrous than to liken *Swan Lake* to middle-period Verdi; but there is some parallel when one compares the later ballet's dramatic continuity with the more intermittent unfolding of plot in *Swan Lake*. Indeed, the truly important achievement of *The Sleeping Beauty* was not the reduction in the quantity of formal dances or their segregation; it was the far closer integration of music supportive of patterned physical movement with music that was primarily dramatic, and the organization of this amalgam into convincingly shaped musical movements. Dance and mime did not merely coexist but collaborated. Tchaikovsky had, in fact, been blessed in Vsevolozhsky's choice of subject. Regardless of its charm, enchantment, or any special resonances it may have sounded within Tchaikovsky himself, it was a plot full of physical movement which could be stylized to marry readily with music that was dance-like, if not actually *dansante*.

The problem was the first part of Act 2, introducing Désiré and his party; though a royal snack al fresco may merit a floor show, this remains dramatically peripheral, and it is not surprisingly the weakest stretch of the ballet. But the Prologue and Act 1 abounded in rich opportunities for stage action. A court must have its grand entrances both for its denizens and its honoured guests, important gifts must be presented with proper ceremony, rage may stimulate vigorous activity, courtship involves personal display (as, even more, does exhibition-ism), disaster can provoke violent nervous response. The Prologue immediately reveals the assurance with which Tchaikovsky faced the challenge within such stimuli. The brisk March (No. 1) is neatly designed as a simple rondo, the two episodes providing the locations for Catalabutte's 'récitations' before the entry of the King and Queen themselves is heralded by a particularly splendid preparation for the final reprise. The Scène dansante (No. 2) is in effect a three-section waltz, though at first heavily veiled. Five fairies float in to the delicate strains of harp with first violins divisi à 3 (see Ex. 244b),[45] with second violins doubling at the lower octave (a passage surely conditioned by Myrtha's entrance music in *Giselle*), the Lilac Fairy makes a separate, more energetic entry; then, as they receive their presents, the waltz becomes explicit, though with a delicacy and brevity that removes it far from the set-piece. In general outline the Pas de six (No. 3) matches that in Act 3 of *Swan Lake*, but each variation takes on average only half the time in performance, while the extensive opening section, formal and purely dance-like in the earlier ballet, is neither dance-like nor formal. Yet so far, for all its efficiency in supporting the plot, almost everything has been 'movement' rather than 'dramatic' music, and though the Finale (No. 4) is a scène entirely controlled by the events of a swiftly unfolding drama, the intervention of the Lilac Fairy justifies a return of the latter half of the introduction to provide an ending of true musical substance.

This recurrence creates a structural frame, especially since in the introduction, as here, the Lilac Fairy's music had been preceded by Carabosse's. The same will happen at the end of Act 1, and these three linkings of Carabosse/Lilac Fairy music become, in effect, structurally bracing ritornelli. But there are no repetitions within the Prologue itself, nor within Act 1 (though the 'Sleep' entr'acte in Act 2 is briefly foretold as the Lilac Fairy casts her spell). Such things are rarer in *The*

---

[45] Most of the musical examples here printed from *The Sleeping Beauty*, like those for *Swan Lake* in Vol. 2 and for *The Nutcracker* in the present volume, reproduce the piano transcriptions authorized by the composer. Tchaikovsky positively encouraged his transcribers (in the case of the ballets: Kashkin for *Swan Lake*, Ziloti for *The Sleeping Beauty*, and Taneyev for *The Nutcracker*) to reduce and modify the details of his orchestral texture to make the results more pianistic. Often the points I would most wish to make here are more clearly grasped from the transcription.

Sleeping Beauty than in *Swan Lake*; with Tchaikovsky's new-found confidence in responding to the requirements of ballet, he must have felt less inclination to draw in devices fundamental to symphonic music. In Act 2 the opening horn fanfares return as the second group of hunters approach, and the Prince's 'excitement' before the Panorama anticipates the music to which the sleepers will rise and he will greet his future bride when the spell is broken. But other instances are less exact, and make no special dramatic point; the Panorama is twice suggested in the final act, conditioning the opening sections of both the fairies' Pas de quatre (No. 23) and the lovers' Pas de deux (No. 28), and the second theme of the 'Rose' Adagio, its contour steepened, launches the long unwinding melody to which Aurora's shade rouses the Prince's desire in the big Pas d'action (No. 15; see Ex. 249).

The introduction sets out the musical embodiments of the forces of good and evil that are to contend for the destiny of Aurora. Glinka provided the musical principle for this contest, his *Ruslan* a specific model in its Act 4 confrontation. But whereas that outcome had been decided in the hurly-burly of a direct assault by Chernomor's anti-tonal forces upon Ruslan's staunch E major, the fairies decorously avoid such wand-to-wand tussling, and it is only after Carabosse has freely unleashed her malice in viciously energetic materials (Ex. 243a) which

Ex. 243

b. **L'istesso tempo [Allegro vivo]**

c. **Allegro vivo**

d. **Moderato**

e. **Allegro vivo**

f. **Moderato con moto**

g. **Allegro giusto**

h. **Allegro vivo**

scorn all attempts to impose tonal stability that the Lilac Fairy's theme (Ex. 244a) is heard in an E major as uncompromising as that of Ruslan himself. These are by far the most important recurring ideas, the Lilac Fairy's a smooth, elegantly curving line whose conjunct movement and

Ex. 244

b.   **Moderato con moto**

c.   **Adagio maestoso**

total tonal stability, so innocent of Carabosse's subversive chromaticism, seem to have marked materials associated with other benevolent forces in Aurora's life; its affinities with the music that introduces the good fairies (Ex. 244b) and the full-toned melody of the 'Rose' Adagio (the Princess's first brush with love; Ex. 244c) are generally self-evident. As for Carabosse's melodic badge, this is compounded of a variety of tiny elements which will operate singly or together, openly or covertly. It reveals its flexibility at the end of the Prologue when Carabosse and her cohort of pages and rats disrupt the christening party (Ex. 243b), heightening its grotesquerie with a vicious new repeated appendage, motif *c* of Ex. 243a then converting itself into a malicious cackle (Ex. 243c). In Act 1 as the King first questions Catalabutte (Ex. 243d), then hearing of the peasants' indiscretion, fastens his thoughts both angrily and fearfully upon Carabosse's curse (Ex. 243e), his three rising notes become infected with the violence of her motif *a*; when he goes on to pardon his subjects and unwittingly opens Carabosse's path to her goal, her music gains confidence, slyly taking possession of the whole orchestra (Ex. 243f), then extending itself and' with quiet irony leading the peasants into their waltz of gratitude. As the fateful needle pierces Aurora's finger (Ex. 243g), its refashioned semiquaver figure *b* reveals its potency, going on to weave the web that entangles her (Ex. 243h) while she dances wildly before dropping lifeless. Only when Carabosse throws off her cloak is her thematic persona heard undisguised. In the century-long stillness of Aurora's slumber her theme keeps quiet watch over monarch and court (see Ex. 251), and as Désiré approaches the sleeping Aurora it makes its last bid in frantic quavers (Ex. 243i), to be routed and disappear for ever as the Prince breaks the spell.

The Sleeping Beauty does not attempt the literal tonal opposition of *Swan Lake*, where the shifting intensity of sharp or flat keys had provided a barometer for calibrating changes in a climate of both benevolent and baleful forces. In fact the tonal planning is more ramified, for there are two systems of sharp/flat opposition, one highly personalized and concerned with the struggle between good and evil, the other with the weighty business of dynastic union, though at the heart of this lies the simple love of two young people. The introduction establishes what will become manifest as the tale unwinds: that Carabosse's nature is inclined to flat keys and is tonally disruptive, and that E major is the principal key of the Lilac Fairy and of benevolent forces. Though E minor can be a malevolent key, the real seat of Carabosse's power is F minor; in it she seals her curse in the Prologue, and caps her noisy gloating at its fulfilment in Act 1. Clearly Tchaikovsky made this choice of keys in part because of the neat opposition of four flats to four sharps, in part because the third of each tonic chord is the same pitch upon which he could pivot to move rapidly between them (as he does at the end of Act 1 when the Lilac Fairy hastens to mitigate her sister's curse). But the dominant seventh of F minor (Ex. 245a) is also the German sixth of E major (Ex. 245b), and can serve as a double edged weapon, capable of cutting either way – as Carabosse quickly discovers in this introduction; having flaunted herself, she makes as though she will retire unchallenged to her home key, only to be surprised by the enharmonic pull of the Lilac Fairy, and to hear her own dominant

Ex. 245

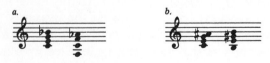

Дорогому Петру Ильичу на память от
горячего поклонника и искренно любящего ег

Ф 8 Марта
1892.

А Глазунов

Herman Laroche and Alexandr Glazunov

The Tchaikovsky brothers (1890):
Anatoly, Nikolay, Ippolit, the composer, Modest

Nikolay Kashkin, the composer, Medea and Nikolay Figner

Anatoly Brandukov and the composer (1888)

Vasily Sapelnikov

Alexandr Ziloti and the composer (1888)

The composer and Bob Davïdov (1892)

Georges-Léon and Olga Tchaikovskaya

Eduard Epstein (a pianist), Varvara Zarudnaya,
Mikhail Ippolitov-Ivanov, Karl Davïdov
and Vasily Safonov

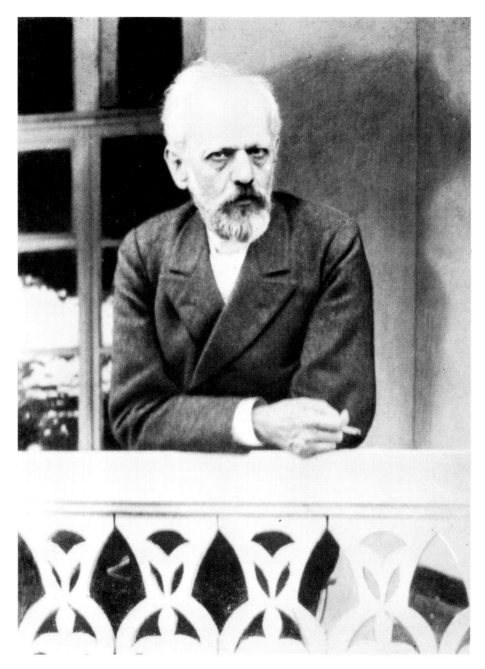

Tchaikovsky (1893)

seventh reverse its function to bring forward her good sister. This mode of conflict is resumed at the end of the Prologue (Ex. 246), the pull now the other way as Carabosse makes a frenzied effort to break the dominant pedal of her sister's E major – and for a moment succeeds (bar nine). But the good fairies cluster round the cradle, and her bid for her own F minor is thwarted.

The other sharp/flat division is between the diverse dynasties. Aurora and her parents, with the Lilac Fairy close by as guardian angel, share sharp-key regions, and the curtain rises upon A major as their court assembles. But the habitat of all Aurora's princely suitors is E flat, a tritone away. Though Act 1 opens in E major, the King and Queen enter in E flat, presumably in deference to the four contenders for their daughter's hand, and it is to be the key of the princes' collective courtship in the 'Rose' Adagio. But before this, when Aurora had first appeared, she had quickly retreated into her native A major, and after the new emotional adventure of the Adagio she again withdraws towards her family regions (to G major) before plunging recklessly back into the E flat heart of her admirers' own world as she seizes the spindle and her dance reaches its over-confident climax.

Act 2 is dominated by Désiré, and is mainly in flat keys.[46] Even the Lilac Fairy shifts her ground to D flat to be close to her other godchild whose destiny she is about to guide. Only as she summons Aurora's shade to rise and dance is there a switch to a sharp key (E major). Shifting abruptly towards Désiré's world by opening the Pas d'action (No. 15) in F major, the spirit teases him with a prospect of accessibility, shows its potential to enslave by drawing him deeper into its own sharp regions, then returns swiftly towards his tonal ground until, its work of enticement done, it is snatched away. The journey to Aurora's castle is undertaken in G major – but it is the Prince who ends sleep and makes a beginning to love, and the act concludes firmly in his E flat. It is teasing to speculate whether setting the last two sections of the ballet, the Tempo di Mazurka and Apotheosis, in two sharps and two flats respectively was a deliberate decision to symbolize the equal balance between the now united dynasties.[47]

Though the Scène (No. 5) which opens Act 1 can hardly match the tour de force Tchaikovsky had achieved when Carabosse and her cohort of rats and pages had rampaged through the happy celebration

[46] The Colin-maillard and courtly dances, like the national dances in *Swan Lake*, are decorative interpolations lying outside any dramatic scheme.

[47] Also, was scheming the Pas de six in the Prologue largely upon B flat and D major an equally deliberate decision to suggest the impartiality of these sisters – for Carabosse has not yet struck?

Ex. 246

of Aurora's christening, it is vibrant with life and bustling activity, supporting the action with unfailing fluency, and ending with a controlled slackening in the dramatic and musical thrust which makes the stasis of the Valse (No. 6) a natural outcome, not an unwelcome blockage. Aurora's entry is sprightly; the engaging pertness of a spirited maiden contrasts sharply with the corporate male ardour which instantly assails her in the 'Rose' Adagio. Though this is only the first section of an extensive Pas d'action (No. 8), it is in every way the centrepiece of the Act. In ballet there can be no time for the equivalents of the orchestral preambles or ritornelli of opera, and not the least impressive feature of this grand piece is the flexible continuity which is maintained as its simple rondo design unfolds. Phrase ends and cadences may be overlaid with decorative but significant movement (upward flashing scales, for instance); the return of the opening phrase gains rhythmic reinforcement from the twisting semiquaver figure decorating the bass (one of the great moments in the history of the tuba), and the final burst of 'broad grandiose music'[48] prescribed by Petipa manifests sudden eruptions of frenetic energy. In the repeated phrase of Ex. 247 the second, 'weak' bar, where a frenzied eruption of demisemiquavers is followed by a burst of swift harmonic movement, provides but one small instance from this score of Tchaikovsky's

Ex. 247

[48] Quoted in Wiley, *op. cit.*, p. 356.

unfailing ability to generate movement at the very point where, musically, it might otherwise falter.

After this Adagio the dance of the maids of honour and pages cannot
but sound lightweight. Neither, for all its charm, is Aurora's variation
of great substance – nor should it be. Her emotions are not yet engaged;
flirtation will rise to vicarious seduction only in the following act.
Though Carabosse's appearance, with its disastrous consequences, is
shorter than in the Prologue, the treatment is as masterly. And if the
emergence yet again of the Lilac Fairy's theme has something of the *déjà
entendu* about it, it pays its dividend when the familiar course is
dramatically broken as the spell of sleep is cast (Ex. 248). The magic
trick is again from *Ruslan*; upon a sustained high C a series of
chords, unrelated except for having this common note, produces tonal
disorientation, and all sink into deep slumber.[49]

Ex. 248

Apart from introducing the Prince, the first section of Act 2 has no
dramatic point, but this miniature *fête champêtre* provides a contrasting

[49] This spell is, of course, a kind of anathema for Carabosse; perhaps it is significant
that, of the six plain triads incorporating the note C, F minor is the one omitted. Nor,
when the chordal succession is rearranged in bars 23–29 of the 'Sleep' entr'acte, is it
sounded.

interlude of things bright and insouciant before Désiré himself is drawn into the main stream of the tale to become both the agent and beneficiary of its happy ending. The Pas d'action (No. 15) brings what is, in effect, the third of the Adagios which are among the special glories of this score. It is the most intimate, outwardly the least complex, but as impressive as any. The opening of Ex. 249 is yet another variant of that protoshape which had already launched the second theme of the 'Rose' Adagio, and had been observed within the past year in both *Hamlet* and the slow movement of the Fifth Symphony. In the last it had entered

Ex. 249

modestly on oboe, then shown its power to stir its creator's melodic fertility by generating the broad second theme. Now in this freely unwinding cello solo it ushers in one of the most impressive stretches of the ballet. Not since setting out the grief and anguish of guilty love at the centre of *Francesca da Rimini* had Tchaikovsky devised a melodic sweep as broad as this. Like Francesca's cantilena it grows by turning back upon itself. But whereas that theme had merged into its own repetition after some thirty bars, this passes after forty bars to a more urgent, animated phase (Ex. 250). Innocent grace becomes enchanting

Ex. 250

allure; fleeting scales provide decoration and momentum, and the cello line, now in the bass, becomes more restless, its contours steeper, the dissonance more exquisite and prolonged, the woodwind soon adding a touch of chromatic pathos as the spirit leads Désiré into the tonal heartland of the beauty she impersonates. Having roused her prey, she becomes yet bolder, and her main theme returns on the full battery of cellos, finally accelerating for the concluding Allegro which teases with coquetry. Whereas the 'Rose' Adagio had embodied a state of being, this one traces a process of becoming. Désiré is finally caught, and in an excited outburst begs to be taken where he may claim the embodiment of this illusion for his own.

As a composer Tchaikovsky was made for ballet. So was Delibes. But for all his gifts, the Frenchman was not in Tchaikovsky's league. His music has consummate shapeliness and grace ('le joli', as Tchaikovsky would have said), his melodies have attractiveness and life, sometimes distinctiveness, his structures have dramatic fluency. But he lacked passion; there is no suggestion of anything hidden behind his picturesque scenes in which fancifully attired shapes, attractive or grotesque, disport themselves in elegant movements which stir but never trouble the senses. It is decoration of the highest kind – and, let it be said, far from contemptible. Yet it is not simply that Tchaikovsky's gifts were of a higher order. *The Sleeping Beauty* succeeded precisely where

Tchaikovsky's own *Enchantress* had failed. The deeper significance with which Tchaikovsky had believed that operatic subject to be invested was a pitiful illusion; *The Sleeping Beauty*, on the other hand, was not only one of his greatest musical achievements, but one of his profoundest, for it treated a story which aspired to the condition of myth (as Laroche had perceived), and ballet was the ideal medium to set loose its rich and varied significances. Opera particularizes, its text adding enrichment, but fettering feelings and deeds to specific contexts; ballet is of sight and sound alone, grasped through the senses, leaving the mind free to respond as it will. We may take *The Sleeping Beauty* as entertainment at its simplest level, as children do, revelling in its fantasy and frissons, knowing all will come right in the end. But we may also understand it as multiple metaphor of life: childhood, youth, love, marriage – or of nature: autumn (sowing), winter (sleeping), spring (waking), summer (reaping) – or it may even waken a cosmic awareness: birth, death, regeneration, salvation. None of this emerges in *The Sleeping Beauty* as we see it on the stage; it is qualities within Tchaikovsky's music that may release such intuitions.

The events which more than anything lift this ballet from the plane of simple fairy tale into the regions of myth start with Désiré's journey, for it is here that Tchaikovsky's music begins to conjure a fantastic world where the laws which confine people and acts within time and place scarcely exist, and where the senses are liberated to experience feelings and sensations, to imagine images and thoughts that transcend those prompted by what is seen on the stage. The harmonic structure of the Panorama has a classic simplicity; its movement is of the slowest, the melodic unfolding stepwise and even (and clearly from within the Lilac Fairy's orbit), the washes of harp arpeggio light ripples on the water's surface. Never had Tchaikovsky achieved so much effect with such economy of means. The entr'acte with solo violin, fine in itself, was a hopeless miscalculation, and its exclusion essential; quite apart from retarding the drama, it returned towards the real world, whereas the 'Sleep' entr'acte takes us deep into the inner kingdom of magic itself, where no rational order survives, but only the single sustained high violin C of the spell of sleep binds all to itself. This 'Symphonic entr'acte' ranges more widely than had that earlier reconnaisance into dreams at the centre of the *Rêves d'enfant* of the Second Suite. It begins as when the spell was cast at the end of Act I (see Ex. 248), but is now haunted by the familiar themes of the opposing fairies, Carabosse's furtive (Ex. 251), but with a portion of the appendage in the final bar of Ex. 243b drawn out into a wail on high woodwind, the Lilac Fairy's stealthy on muted trumpet. Yet the real world remains close, and when

Ex. 251

the grand plagal cadence onto C swells as the clouds disperse, we seem
once again at its threshold. It is a false expectation; the spell instantly
reasserts its grip, and the interlude sinks into a stillness yet more
absolute.

What follows is expeditiously treated – and rightly so, for rejoicing
will come in the last act. After sounds so still and strange this music of
the mortals pulses with a special energy. At the Allegro vivace the
violins impose a tonal contour upon Carabosse's rhythm, and her F
minor is swiftly dislodged. Désiré approaches the sleeping girl, Carabosse makes her last frantic effort to retain her hold (see Ex. 243i), and
the violins again recall their binding note so that it may be ended once
and for all with the kiss. Aurora and the court rise and exult, and the
music of the spell which has been the means of defeating Carabosse
adds its benediction to the final cadencing.

Deliverance from evil and the joy of mutual love require proper
celebration. The criticism that has often been directed at the final act of
The Sleeping Beauty is based on a blinkered view of dramatic requirements and musical proprieties. If 'Aurora's Wedding' were omitted as
too cheerfully bathetic, a good many finales of classical symphonic
pieces might also be at high risk. Certainly the visible drama has been
completed in the previous act, but for the more primal joy that
culminates each of the ballet's other planes of significance this feast of
rejoicing is a necessary ritual. In any case, the visible and audible
experience broadens, for after the first release of joy and confidence in
the opening March (No. 21) and Polonaise (No. 22), the set pieces offer
a variety of musical and visual turns of kinds that have had no place in
what has gone before. All is in some way picturesque. There are witty,
sardonic character pieces. The two cats paw, claw, miaow and spit

vividly, the wolf roars fiercely at a very nervous Little Red Riding Hood, the ogre's seven-league boots stride monstrously, and Tom Thumb and his brothers scuttle about the stage. There are brief but brilliant dance numbers of dazzling variety to which the imaginativeness of Tchaikovsky's orchestration is often crucial. Finally the lovers take centre stage for their Pas de deux.[50] The entrée, the second reminder of the Panorama from Act 2, nicely balances that which had introduced the Divertissement. Their Adagio follows. Three of the four great Adagios of this ballet are love scenes, all different. The 'Rose' Adagio had been a first, grand declaration, corporate and self-consciously formal, that of the Pas d'action in Act 2 intimate and seductive. But this is an affirmation of mutual love. The opening oboe theme is tender but restrained, the syncopated string phrases nervous, the prolonged pauses with piano decoration betray lingering hesitancy. But suddenly, as with all true love, constraint breaks, the declaration is made frankly and fully, the midway break merely a breathless pause before the confession is renewed.

The coda of this final dance of love is the one moment in the ballet when a Russian voice is prominent, with what sounds like a fragment of a boisterous folk theme repeated against constantly changing backgrounds to produce a miniature gopak. But the decorous Sarabande, even if its model was German, supports an action that is French, for Petipa's stage picture was clearly designed to recreate a grand entrée of foreign nations from a court entertainment of Louis XIV – a point that was evidently lost on many in the first audience. It was sad if this tribute to one of royalty's most spectacular representatives from the past misfired; what was more vital, however, was that the score's topical message should not pass unnoticed. Though it was unspoken, this new ballet, mounted in the Imperial Theatres of the Tsar of all the Russias and under his imminent eye, was a pointed affirmation of monarchical grandeur; the general outburst of unbuttoned joy in the Mazurka could leave a dangerous impression of a court dedicated to unconfined merriment, and the concluding Apotheosis was a wholesome riposte – a mighty proclamation of the dignity and splendour of kingship in grand spectacle and stately dance.

---

[50] Though the libretto describes this as a Pas de quatre, the Gold and Silver Fairies also participating, the choreographic description by the dancer, Vladimir Stepanov, makes clear the Adagio was danced by the Prince and Aurora alone.

6

EMINENT RELATIONSHIPS:
THE QUEEN OF SPADES

As THE FIRST part of 1889 ran its course, it might have seemed that an annual cycle was emerging in Tchaikovsky's life; as in 1888, the early months were spent abroad in energetic concert-giving, the central months in assiduous creative work incorporating a visit to Kamenka, the later months in an increasing involvement in various administrative and concert activities in Moscow and St Petersburg. But there were to be differences. For all its blessings, Frolovskoye had revealed its limitations, and towards the end of July Tchaikovsky took also the tenancy of a flat in Moscow. He did this reluctantly, he admitted to his patroness, but 'of late I have had unbearable headaches in the evenings unless there has been the possibility of diverting myself from the weariness that follows work, and living in the country during the winter, I find no means of amusing myself except reading'.[1] He had been careful to ensure this alternative accommodation was quietly situated and that there was no risk of close neighbours who played the piano. A base in Moscow would make life easier once the season of winter concerts began, and the attractiveness of Frolovskoye had been badly impaired by the wholesale felling of trees that had begun while he had been away on tour, and against which he frequently raged in his letters. All the same, he would certainly remain in the country for the next two months until all work on *The Sleeping Beauty* had been completed.

None of this hindered his continuing initiatives on behalf of the ailing Moscow RMS. He negotiated with Brodsky to be soloist in the concert he himself would conduct on 9 November, and with Brodsky's quartet for a series of four recitals within the following fortnight;[2] he also finalized arrangements for the concert that would introduce Ippolitov-Ivanov and his wife to the RMS audience, and tactfully coaxed

[1] *TLP*15A, pp. 155–6; *TPM*3, p. 578; *TZC*3, p. 315.
[2] It appears that, because these concerts incurred a loss, Tchaikovsky made good the shortfall with a supplement of over 250 roubles out of his own pocket.

Nápravník into agreeing for his concert a fee much less than his fame merited. Knowing that this St Petersburg conductor had been forced to rest because of overwork, he tried to tempt him into taking over the less arduous role in Moscow which Erdmannsdörfer would soon resign. The single-handed labour of assembling a season's symphony concerts had cost Tchaikovsky dearly, and the thought that a single conductor might direct the 1890–91 season was very attractive.

The stresses of work were alleviated by the usual diversions. Mozart continued to figure prominently in his evening perusals of scores by other composers (*Don Giovanni, Idomeneo, Davidde penitente* and some symphonies (unspecified) are specially mentioned in his diary, as is Schumann's *Das Paradies und die Peri* and Rubinstein's Fifth Symphony). Mrs Legoshin was still living with Alexey and his wife in their quarters. The company of such simple, unaffected people meant much to Tchaikovsky, and the Legoshins' three-year-old daughter remained a special delight, Tchaikovsky even acting as nurse to her on occasions, so Modest remembered. But Alexey's wife seemed persistently ill, and Tchaikovsky's growing anxieties were to prove well founded, for early the following year she died of consumption (a fortnight earlier Fitzenhagen too had succumbed to a lingering illness). Bob stayed for a few days, Modest arrived at the beginning of July for the rest of the summer, and Laroche remained a long while, Tchaikovsky having assured his new wife that he would make him work and keep him from the temptations of alcohol. There were periodic visits from friends such as Jurgenson, Ziloti and Hubert's widow, and a house party for his name-day. But guests cost money, his finances sank desperately low, and when Kashkin joined Modest and Laroche for a residency, a crisis point was reached. As usual Alexey, who was as thrifty as his master was improvident, provided the solution; 'four gentlemen,' Tchaikovsky observed wryly to Anatoly, were all surviving 'on tick from a servant'.[3] His benefactress's unexpected suggestion that she should in future pay his annual allowance in one instalment during July because that was when she was usually in Russia was received with all the more delight. There may have been a further factor influencing this decision. Her youngest daughter, Milochka, who had figured so prominently in the earlier exchanges with her dear, unseen friend, had contracted a disastrous marriage which had produced a child and caused a complete rupture with her mother. Beset by such worry and torment, his benefactress would have been the more inclined to simplify and thus reduce the recurring burdens of ordinary life.

[3] *TLP*15A, p. 165; *TPB*, p. 424.

By 1 September, when *The Sleeping Beauty* was at last completed, Tchaikovsky was exhausted. Not only had the increasing fastidiousness with which he planned his orchestral textures made scoring the work a far more demanding operation; he had also satisfied a request for a piano piece to be included in the first issue of a new periodical, *Artist*, composing his *Valse scherzo* in A in time for September publication. But Kamenka, where he arrived on 4 September, was no place to relax, though it was excellent for his morale. 'The chief good is that all are completely well, which they were not at all before,' he wrote to Modest after a week. 'Sasha is surprisingly recovered; she's entirely the old, healthy Sasha. Living with Bob has given me indescribable delight. Alas! It has been too short. Seeing how the importance of Bob in my life is increasing all the time, I have finally decided that from next year I shall settle in St Petersburg. To see him, hear him and feel him close to me will soon become for me, it seems, the paramount condition for my happiness. Life goes on here very noisily: constant festivities, guests, trips, seeing off and meeting people without end. There's no thinking of work! And I don't regret this at all.'[4] To Shpazhinskaya he admitted he now coped with such social activities more easily. 'I don't recognize myself! Not more than some six or seven years ago I was a total recluse, an unsociable and totally confined toiler; now I'm one of the shavings whirled round in this social life. I admit the earlier way of living was much more congenial to me, but I do what I consider my duty.'[5] On the journey home he visited Nikolay and Anna on their new estate at Kopïlovo near Kiev, pausing in that city to see the production of *Onegin*, and receiving an unexpected but very flattering ovation. On 20 September he was again in Frolovskoye, refreshed yet hardly rested. Five days later he was himself presiding over the first rehearsal of a sumptuous new production of *Onegin* at the Bolshoy, conducting the opening night on 30 September.

Just how much the pressures on Tchaikovsky to exercise his late developed talent as conductor had grown in the last two years was to become clear during the next months as he shuttled to and fro between the two capitals. Moreover, he was now finding himself called upon to direct much music other than his own. He was clearly becoming a very effective conductor, and he himself had been well satisfied with the results in *Onegin*. Two days later he was in St Petersburg for ten days of rehearsals of *The Sleeping Beauty* and to attend meetings of the committee organizing the celebrations of Anton Rubinstein's golden jubilee.

---

[4] *TLP*15A, p. 174.
[5] *TLP*15A, p. 175; *TTP*, pp. 352–3.

Besides composing a chorus of greeting for the inauguration of these festivities on 30 November and also an *Impromptu* in A flat for piano to be included in a presentation album from Rubinstein's former pupils, he himself had charge of the two ensuing concerts of Rubinstein's own works. But before these he had to conduct the second concert of the RMS's new season, and on 13 October he was back in Moscow and installing himself in his new apartment. His achievement in controlling a mixed programme of Mozart, Glinka and Taneyev, with Brodsky playing Tchaikovsky's own Violin Concerto, pleased even Tchaikovsky. At a second concert a fortnight later he was directing the First Piano Concerto with Ziloti as soloist. After a month in Moscow he returned to St Petersburg for the two Rubinstein concerts which followed on consecutive days after the inaugural event; the first contained the Fifth Symphony, the musical picture *Russia* and the new Concertstück in A flat (with the composer himself as soloist), while the second offered pieces drawn from Rubinstein's vocal works and operas, including as second half the sacred opera, *Der Thurm zu Babel*, with Tchaikovsky having to control some 800 performers. Another five days, and he was again in Moscow conducting a charity concert which included Brandukov giving the *Pezzo capriccioso* its Russian première, and ended with Beethoven's Ninth Symphony. Then back to St Petersburg for rehearsals of *The Sleeping Beauty* and to conduct *Hamlet* and the Concert Fantasia as the first half of a Russian Symphony Concert.

It is no surprise that all this became at times unbearable. It was not only the concerts themselves; they entailed meetings with promoters and fellow musicians – and very taxing it was, however pleasant it might be to consolidate still further relationships with eminent colleagues like Rimsky-Korsakov, Lyadov and Glazunov. But he felt it his duty to serve the community while he could, he said, and he was to be rewarded, it seemed, by a sharp upward turn in the RMS's fortunes as a result of his persuading star conductors to undertake the journey to Moscow. For Rubinstein's concerts, however, Tchaikovsky himself was the chosen leader of homage. The critic in him was too perceptive and honest not to judge mercilessly the emptiness of much of Rubinstein's music, but he had great admiration for pieces like the Ocean Symphony, the musical pictures, *Ivan the Terrible* and *Don Quixote*, and the piano concertos, and his former teacher's personality retained its hold on him. 'In Anton Grigoryevich's presence he was always ill-at-ease, flustered as befits one who adores, regarding him as a being standing so far above himself as to exclude any possibility of equality in their relations,' Modest declared. This emerged in full at the meal after the second concert – and though his letters give no hint, Tchaikovsky cannot have come away from this without some feelings of deep chagrin, having endured his own martyrdom (as he described it) so unsparingly at the concert itself. 'When . . . someone tactlessly and ineptly expressed a wish that Anton Grigoryevich should drink a toast "as brothers" with Pyotr Ilich, the latter was not only confused but became indignant about it, and in reply protested sincerely and passionately that "his tongue could never bring itself to address Anton Grigoryevich as *tï*," that this "would impair the essence of their relationship, that he would be happy if Anton Grigoryevich called him *tï*, [but] refusing ever to change his own *vï* which expressed that sense of veneration which he nourished towards him, that distance which separated the pupil from the master, the man from the embodiment of his ideal."'[6]

For all Tchaikovsky's sincerity, he was by now alone in holding such a view of the proprieties which should govern their relationship. It was the moment, surely, when the master should have bowed with grace. But he did not. Modest was silent on what followed; Alexandra Panayeva was more open. She had sung in the first part of the concert and witnessed the violence of the nervous attack which Tchaikovsky had suffered in the interval, partly from the strain of the occasion, partly from sheer fatigue. She had also observed Tchaikovsky's personal triumph at the end. At the dinner afterwards she had been seated between Rubinstein and Tchaikovsky, and remembered the latter's speech. 'Suddenly Anton Grigoryevich, bending over me towards Pyotr Ilich, interrupted him with a laugh. "Now let us assume, Pyotr Ilich, you do not love me but love my brother – then I thank you for that!" Pyotr Ilich was about to protest in confusion, but Rubinstein repeated: "You love only my brother – and for that, thankyou!"'[7] Tchaikovsky's humiliation was complete; he crumpled in his chair, and there followed several moments of silence before Safonov jumped to his feet to make an indignant defence of his Moscow colleague.

The incident reveals more, perhaps, about Rubinstein than Tchaikovsky. In its peculiar way, for all its prolonged hiatuses, the relationship was one of the most fundamental of Tchaikovsky's whole life – even of Russian music itself, for in its later years the two men were the most famed and respected of all native musicians. Yet it was a relationship more of separation than closeness – puzzling yet very human. There was always a deep ambivalence in Rubinstein's attitude.

---

[6] *TZC3*, p. 331. *Tï* and *vï* in Russian are much like *tu* and *vous* in French.
[7] *PVC* (4th edit; Leningrad, 1980), pp. 134–5.

No doubt he felt little sympathy with the direction Tchaikovsky's creative searches took, once he had graduated from his Conservatoire class, and Tchaikovsky both perceived and, to a degree, understood this, though it did not lessen the wound. After all, Rubinstein had done more than anyone to form his craft as a composer, and Tchaikovsky had hoped he would help in his subsequent career. 'Yet I have the pain of confessing to you that A.R. did nothing, *but nothing at all* to further my plans and projects. . . . This has always deeply distressed me,' he wrote in 1892 to the German critic, Eugen Zabel.[8] But there was quite certainly another factor. Tchaikovsky had been shocked to perceive Anton's savage jealousy of his brother Nikolay at the time of the latter's death, and though in 1866 Tchaikovsky had gone to Moscow on the recommendation of Anton, the latter had not foreseen that the new graduate would fast become the greatest asset in his brother's musical empire, with Nikolay himself the performer most associated with Tchaikovsky's new works and drawing most glory from this association. In no way could Tchaikovsky have added more effectively to Anton's gall and fortified his disinclination either to conceal his very honest antipathy to much of Tchaikovsky's music or to advance its fortunes.

But Rubinstein's spell remained. 'Now I see him from time to time,' Tchaikovsky continued to Zabel, '[and] always with pleasure, for this extraordinary man has only to hold out his hand to you and direct a smile at you for you to be on your knees before him.' Always Rubinstein remained for Tchaikovsky the greatest personality among all living musicians. Modest remembered as a ten- or eleven-year-old being taken by his civil-servant brother to a charity performance in St Petersburg at which Anton was also in the audience. 'Forty years later, I recall vividly that emotion, that rapture, that veneration with which the future pupil gazed on his future teacher. Indeed, he did not look at the stage, but . . . never took his eyes off his "deity", shadowed him unnoticed in the intervals, tried to catch what he said, and envied those lucky ones who were able to squeeze his hand.'[9] And now at Rubinstein's jubilee nearly thirty years later nothing had changed.

But Tchaikovsky knew well the petty, even childish side of Rubinstein's nature. In his veneration there was little of love, and because the two men had never been close, there had never existed those more intimate, vulnerable bonds which might so easily have been ruptured by Anton's outburst. After the jubilee meal all remained as before.

---

8 *TLP*16B, p. 103; *TZC*3, p. 541.
9 *TZC*3, pp. 330–1.

Fearing that Anton might have observed his failure to call on him in St Petersburg the following May, he urgently requested Anton's daughter Anna to convey his apologies for not showing a proper respect – that is, if Anton had actually noticed his truancy. In 1891 he pressed Ippolitov-Ivanov to appoint a certain Armenian musical theorist to the staff of the Tiflis school of music for a variety of very good reasons – but above all because it would please Anton Grigoryevich.

Meanwhile on Anton's side there had developed far more respect for Tchaikovsky than ever the latter realized. The death of Nikolay in 1881 had probably made it easier to take Tchaikovsky for himself alone, and Modest was perhaps right in declaring that personal jealousy had no significant part in Rubinstein's view of Tchaikovsky, so that the latter's rapidly growing fame in the 1880s probably left Rubinstein untroubled. Ever anxious to continue broadening music's base in Russia, Rubinstein had in 1887 persuaded the St Petersburg RMS to establish an opera company performing operas only by Russian composers, all to be given in Russian. Besides affording openings for new talent, however, the venture would need the cachet that established figures could provide. Rubinstein knew Tchaikovsky had just completed an opera. 'If you haven't yet assigned *The Enchantress* to the Imperial Opera's directorate, then give it to us,' he wrote on 9 April. 'And if indeed it's already assigned, then compose us a new opera by 13 September. The make-up of the new company will be good . . . It'll be prepared carefully – you have nothing whatsoever to worry about. May I hope? Scribble a couple of words in reply.'[10] The tone is open, the appeal both respectful and friendly. Giving private counsel to the St Petersburg RMS on whom they should engage as conductors for the 1892–3 season, Rubinstein proposed that the main role should be assigned to Tchaikovsky 'for ten concerts on "indispensable" days [the most important concerts?], with an augmented fee and agreement there should be no constraints on [rehearsal?] time.'[11] Writing to his sister Sofya in Odessa in April 1893, he surveyed the musical pleasures the city was about to offer her – 'the Russian opera, and Tchaikovsky with Sapelnikov . . . You are a lucky person; I'm becoming envious!'[12]

But most revealing was his obviously heartfelt observation to this same sister some seven months later:

[10] Rubinstein (A.), *Literaturnoye naslediye*, vol. 3 (Moscow, 1986), pp. 95–6. Tchaikovsky replied that he could not oblige immediately, but that he would be delighted to do so in the future. In the end, however, Rubinstein's project foundered on the opposition of the Imperial Opera, who feared a rival.

[11] *Op. cit.*, p. 127.

[12] *Op. cit.*, p. 136.

What do you say about Tchaikovsky's death? Is it possible this is the will of God? What a loss for music in Russia! Yet you know, he was in the prime of life, he was only fifty – and all this for a glass of water! What a nonsense are all such tricks – and this life – and creation – and everything, and everything . . .[13]

Tchaikovsky's relationship with Anton Chekhov was far simpler, and far shorter. This time the roles were reversed, for during the brief period of their contact Chekhov was a young writer still in his twenties. He had begun publishing in 1880 while still a medical student in Moscow, but within a very few years the quality of his work was gaining it access to the more prestigious journals whose readers numbered Tchaikovsky. By 1887 Tchaikovsky was commenting enthusiastically on Chekhov's work to Modest who, as a writer himself, soon came to know the younger man personally. In December 1888, at Modest's home, Tchaikovsky and Chekhov met, to discover their admiration was mutual. Ten months later, on 24 October 1889, while Tchaikovsky was accustoming himself to his new flat in Moscow and looking ahead to the concert in which Brodsky was to play his Violin Concerto, Chekhov wrote to him:

This month I'm going to begin printing a little collection of my own stories. These stories are tedious and boring as is autumn, their tone is monotonous, and artistic elements in them are closely entwined with medical ones. Nevertheless this hasn't prevented me from daring to turn to you with a very humble request; permit me to dedicate this little collection to you. I very much wish to receive a favourable reply from you – in the first place because this dedication will afford me great pleasure, and secondly because it will gratify at least a little that deep feeling of respect which impels me to remember you daily. The idea of dedicating this anthology to you was sown in my head as far back as that very day when, dining with you at Modest Ilich's, I heard you had read my stories.

If, together with your assent, you would also send me your photograph, then I shall receive more than I'm worth, and I'll be happy to all eternity. Forgive me for troubling you.[14]

Despite the difference in their public fame, Tchaikovsky was delighted. He hastened round to Chekhov's to express his thanks, then wrote:

[13] *Op. cit.*, p. 140.
[14] Chekhov (A. P.), *Pisma v 12 tomakh* [*CP*] (Moscow, 1974–), Vol. 3, p. 259.

'I enclose my photograph, and earnestly beg you to entrust yours to the messenger. Did I adequately express my gratitude for the dedication? I think I did not, and so I'll tell you again that I am *deeply touched* by your kindness.'[15]

Chekhov was overwhelmed:

'I am very, very touched, dear Pyotr Ilich, and I give you boundless thanks. I am sending you both a photograph and a book, and I would send you the sun, too, if it belonged to me.'[16]

Faced with this extra gift, another of Chekhov's collections of short stories, Tchaikovsky responded with a season ticket to the new series of RMS concerts which was to begin the next day. 'I cannot deliver it myself, for all this week is being swallowed up in preparations for the first concert and in looking after our guest *Rimsky-Korsakov* [who was to conduct it],' he explained in his covering letter of 1 November. 'God grant that next week I shall be able to talk with you as I would like . . . I would point out that the ticket can be used by anyone.'[17]

But the most intriguing aspect of all this was the inscription in Chekhov's book:

'To Pyotr Ilich Tchaikovsky, from his future librettist: 26.X.89. A. Chekhov.'

The relationship had indeed developed with lightning speed. The libretto was to have been based on *Bela*, the first part of Lermontov's novel, *A Hero of Our Time*. According to Chekhov's brother, Mikhail, the proposal had originated from Tchaikovsky himself, who had even specified how the roles should be distributed among the voices, and had insisted that there should be no processions or marches. But how seriously he really took the project we do not know. If, as seems probable, he was scouting for an operatic subject, he was ripe to respond to anything which for an instant might seem feasible. But there is no mention of *Bela* in his letters, and behind him lay a trail of sudden enthusiasms which had sunk almost as rapidly as they had arisen. Lermontov's tale of the tragic relationship between a young Russian officer and a native girl from the Caucasus certainly offered scope for love music and for a powerful death scene. But in other regards it would have been less satisfactory, and if the story had indeed seeded itself in a corner of Tchaikovsky's brain, it was within a couple of months rooted out by the subject which was to inspire his second most popular opera.

Gloomy people, the volume dedicated to Tchaikovsky and containing

---

[15] *TLP*15A, p. 198.
[16] *CP*3, p. 262.
[17] *TLP*15A, p. 202.

ten stories, including some of Chekhov's best, appeared in the spring of 1890. There had been no flagging in the writer's assessment of his dedicatee.

'I am prepared day and night to mount a guard of honour at the porch of Pyotr Ilich's house – I revere him so much,' he enthused to Modest.

> If we're talking of ranks, then he now occupies in Russian art the second place after Lev Tolstoy, who has long occupied the first (I allot the third to Repin [the painter], and award myself the ninety-eighth). I have long harboured an impertinent wish to dedicate something to him. The dedication, I thought, would be a partial, minimal expression of that great critical opinion which I, as a writer, have formed concerning his magnificent talent, but which, because of my lack of musical gift, I cannot set down on paper. Unfortunately I have had to fulfil my dream through a book which I don't consider my best. It is made up of especially gloomy psychological studies and bears a gloomy title, such that my dedication must be little to the taste of Pyotr Ilich himself and his admirers.[18]

Yet Chekhov need not have worried. 'You can't imagine how pleasant I find *Chekhov*'s words about me,' Tchaikovsky wrote to Modest on 4 April 1890 from Florence. 'I'll write to him when I've come down to earth a little.'[19]

No doubt he did write, though no letter survives. But already the relationship's peak had been passed – and as for the season ticket, that had been used more by Chekhov's sister, Mariya, than the writer himself. By the time Tchaikovsky had returned from Italy Chekhov had left on his one-man sociological expedition to Sakhalin Island off the eastern shore of Siberia. He was away from Moscow the rest of the year, and on his return conceived a violent dislike for the city and kept away from it as much as possible. Their final letters were exchanged in November 1891. Chekhov had a cellist friend, Marian Semashko, who needed an appointment; could Tchaikovsky help? 'I am alive and well, and am writing a lot but printing little,' he went on. 'My extensive story *The Duel* will soon be published in *New Time*, but you don't need to read it in the paper: I'll send you the book [containing it] which will come out at the beginning of December.'[20]

[18] *CP*4, pp. 39–40; *TLP*15B, p. 108 (partial); *TPB*, p. 618 (final two sentences omitted).

[19] *TLP*15B, p. 108; *TPB*, p. 452.

[20] *CP*4, p. 286.

Tchaikovsky knew Semashko, was clearly unimpressed by the exclusive conditions the young cellist seemed to have set for any employment he might accept, and made it clear that such help as he might be able to give would be only towards enabling Semashko to gain a foothold in the profession. His letter is lengthy, thoughtful, helpful, but has a certain sternness about it. Then suddenly the tone changes.

> How glad I am, dear Anton Pavlovich, to see from your letter that you are in no way angry with me, for I did not really thank you for the dedication of *Gloomy people*, in which I take immense pride. I remember that during your expedition [to Sakhalin] I was always going to write a long letter to you, even attempting to explain which particular qualities in your talent so captivated and bewitched me. But there was not the time for it – and, above all, *I had not got it in me*. It is very difficult for a musician to express in words what and how he feels in regard of this or that artistic phenomenon.
>
> And so, thank you for not complaining about me. I am awaiting *The Duel* impatiently, and of course I shall in no way follow your advice to wait until December, although I warmly thank you in advance for the book. God grant that during this visit to Moscow we shall be able to see each other and have a chat. I press your hand warmly.[21]

But it seems circumstances never combined to bring them together again. As men and artists they were very different: Chekhov objective, capable of sharply imaging every conceivable type of humanity, Tchaikovsky subjective, able to project character with real conviction only when it displayed a trait or emotion shared or readily understood by Tchaikovsky himself. But their common humanity, as revealed both in themselves and their creations, drew each to the other. No two of Tchaikovsky's associations were more dissimilar than those with these two Antons, Rubinstein and Chekhov, for no two of his acquaintances were more unlike than they. Yet curiously, when death had made an end of both relationships, the final tributes from each were remarkably alike. The frank humanity within Rubinstein's letter to his sister surprises for the strength of feeling it exposes; the simple plainness of Chekhov's is nothing but what might be expected from a man whose work had revealed so much understanding for the predicaments and responses of a prodigious range of human types. Both are the worthiest of tributes to that humanity that all who knew Tchaikovsky seemed to

[21] *TLP*16A, p. 250; *TZC*3, pp. 327–8.

recognize within him. Chekhov's was contained in a telegram to Modest two days after Tchaikovsky's death: 'The news staggered me. It is a terrible anguish. I loved and revered Pyotr Ilich very deeply, and I am indebted to him for much. You have my heartfelt sympathy.'[22]

Antonina Ivanovna had long shown a devastating flair for the un-expected, and she scarred the end of 1889 for her husband by suddenly reappearing in Moscow and proposing that she and he might again live together. A second matter seemed to be equally important to her; despite two attempts, she had been unable to persuade the office to allocate her a complimentary ticket for the concert in which Tchaikovsky and Rubinstein would soon appear, and in a rage she had written to the former threatening to expose the facts of their marriage. For an instant Tchaikovsky decided to confront her, then could not face it, and once again asked Jurgenson to perform his well-practised role of seeing off this troublesome woman, and to ensure she got her ticket. However, for Tchaikovsky, already exhausted by the autumn's con-certs and commitments, it was the last straw. 'To go away, to go away somewhere or other quickly, to see no one, to know nothing, to work, work and work – that's what my soul thirsts for!' he moaned.[23] In fact he had already laid his plans, as the same letter to his patroness disclosed; he would settle somewhere in Italy for four months to rest and then work on an opera. 'I have chosen . . . Pushkin's *The Queen of Spades*. . . . Three years ago my brother Modest set about writing a libretto on *The Queen of Spades* at the request of a certain Klenovsky, and little by little during these three years he has devised a very successful libretto.'[24]

Modest remembered more precisely how his brother had finally taken his own decision to compose it. 'I had done the first three scenes of the libretto by order of Klenovsky, but that composer soon went back on his intention to compose the opera, and my work remained un-finished. Pyotr Ilich did not know it, and was little interested in becoming acquainted with it until the autumn of 1889, when I. A. Vsevolozhsky gave him the idea of using my work. Pyotr Ilich read through what I had done and, approving, decided forthwith to com-pose an opera on my libretto. At the end of December a meeting took place in the office of the Imperial Theatres' director attended by designers, office heads, V. Pogozhev, and Domershchikov of the ad-ministration department, at which I read through my scenario and

[22] *CP5*, p. 240.
[23] *TLP15A*, p. 220; *TPM3*, p. 590.
[24] *TLP15A*, p. 219; *TPM3*, p. 589; *TZC3*, p. 338; *YDGC*, p. 482.

where it was decided to transfer the action from the time of Alexandr I, where I had set it for Klenovsky, to the end of the reign of Catherine II. To fit in with this the scenario of the third scene – the ball – was altered completely, and the scene by the Winter Canal, which had been no part of my scheme, was added. Thus in the scenario of the complete libretto these two scenes belong as much to me as to all the other persons attending this meeting. In addition, I. A. Vsevolozhsky suggested to me many changes of detail in the remaining scenes.'[25]

Vsevolozhsky had proposed to mount the opera during the following season. It was a formidable hope, but it fitted in well with Tchaikovsky's independent decision to go abroad and settle himself into composing such a piece. 'I am longing to work,' he wrote to Nadezhda von Meck on 7 January 1890 from Moscow, 'and if I can contrive to find some comfortable corner abroad, I think I shall cope with my task and will deliver the vocal score to the directorate by May, and score it during the summer.'[26] He still could not decide where he should go; nevertheless, having attended the première of *The Sleeping Beauty* on 15 January, and three days later in Moscow conducted Anton Rubinstein's new Konzertstück with the composer as soloist, he left St Petersburg on 26 January, the question of his ultimate destination still unresolved. Two days later, in Berlin and in a thoroughly miserable frame of mind, he decided to buy a ticket for Florence simply 'so as not to prolong further my endless indecision'.[27] Hoping that work would alleviate his mood, on 31 January, the day after his arrival in the Italian city, he plunged into composing *The Queen of Spades*.

Tchaikovsky had been able to bring with him the libretto of only the first two scenes, and Modest was hard pressed to keep up with his brother's progress. Within ten days the first scene had been sketched; by 16 February, a week later, the second was also ready. In general Tchaikovsky seems to have warmly approved Modest's work, but he was quick to perceive in it the same wordiness which had crippled Shpazhinsky's libretto for *The Enchantress*, repeatedly exhorting his brother to brevity and, where necessary, ruthlessly pruning what he had received. Nor was Modest the only person whose expansionist tendencies had to be countered, for Vsevolozhsky wanted to enlarge the interlude inserted into the ballroom scene to entertain the guests. For this Modest had already offered the choice of two texts, one an allegory by Gavriil Derzhavin, the other a pastoral by Pyotr Karabanov. But

[25] *TZC*3, p. 388; *DTC*, p. 169.
[26] *TLP*15A, pp. 219–20; *TPM*3, p. 590; *TZC*3, p. 339.
[27] *TLP*15B, p. 19; *TZC*3, p. 341; *TPB*, p. 427.

before launching into this, Tchaikovsky was determined to compose the fourth scene, the encounter between Hermann and the Countess in her bedroom. For him this was the heart of the opera, and on 17 February he set about it, returning to the ballroom scene the very day he finished (23 February) and beginning with the interlude, for which he chose Karabanov's pastoral, also Modest's preference. He had found the bedroom scene harrowing to work upon – 'so terrible that a feeling of horror even now remains with me', he had admitted to Anna Merkling after working on it a couple of days.[28] However, retreating now into a rococo world to compose this pastoral interlude had a very different effect; 'at times I thought I was living in the eighteenth century, and that there was nothing beyond Mozart', he noted in his diary.[29] The whole third scene required nine days, but the fifth (the Countess's ghost appearing to Hermann in his barrack room) took only three; for the latter Modest searched out both a funeral chant and a trumpet call, and because neither of these had reached Tchaikovsky when he set about it, he had to begin composition at the point where there is a knock at the window. Tchaikovsky's work rate was now accelerating; the sixth scene (by the Winter Canal) was done in four days, a start was made on the introduction, and by 14 March, four days later, the last scene had been completed, except for Hermann's arioso. This, and the introduction, were finished the next day.

The urgency with which the vocal score was required in St Petersburg made the chore of preparing this the more gruelling, though it also provided an opportunity for reviewing the whole opera, and Tchaikovsky's confidence in it rose; he felt especially pleased with the bedroom scene. This operation was completed by 5 April; two days later he left Florence for Rome, and on 9 April began scoring the work. Within ten days the first act (Scenes 1 and 2) was finished, but the second (Scenes 3 and 4) took much longer, partly because work was interrupted by his return to Russia, partly because it proved more problematic. Having disposed of this act by 26 May, he required only ten days to score the remainder, though he continued tinkering with it a further fortnight.

Tchaikovsky admitted that composing Hermann's death scene caused an unexpected and violent reaction. 'I *pitied* Hermann so much that I suddenly began weeping copiously. This weeping went on an awfully long time, turning into a mild fit of hysteria of a very pleasant kind: that is, I found weeping awfully pleasant. Afterwards I began to

---

[28] *TLP*15B, p. 44; *TTP*, p. 237; *TZC*3, p. 349; *DTC*, p. 176; *YDGC*, p. 489.
[29] *TD*, p. 255; *TLP*15B, p. 111; *DTC*, p. 177; *YDGC*, p. 489.

ponder why,' he had reflected to Modest on 15 March, the day he finished composition, 'for there has never been a similar occasion when I have wept because of my hero's fate, and I tried to fathom why I wanted to weep so much. It seems to me that *Hermann* was not just a pretext for writing this or that music, but all the while a real, living human being, at the same time very sympathetic to me. Because *Figner* [the tenor who was to create the part] is very sympathetic to me, and because all the while I imagined Hermann in the shape of *Figner*, I also felt the most lively concern for his misfortunes. Now I think that this warm and lively relationship with the opera's hero has probably expressed itself beneficially in the music.'[30] Having completed everything, he discovered within himself a propensity to weep in all sorts of other places also. It had marred his complete run-through of the opera for Jurgenson and Kashkin at Frolovskoye early in July, and he wondered whether he was over-reacting – until he visited Figner later in the month to go through his role with him, and noted a similar response in this tenor who had done so much to warm his inspiration. 'He is in raptures about his part. He speaks of it with tears in his eyes,' he told Modest. 'A good sign!'[31] – though he was distressed that Figner had demanded a transposition downward of his 'brindisi' (as Tchaikovsky called it) in the last scene. Acknowledging the validity of his tenor's arguments, he dropped it from B to A major, later producing a compromise transposition in B flat. In any case he could not risk offending Figner, who was the darling of the St Petersburg operatic public and whose participation could be critical to the work's success. Nor could he ignore the tenor's preference regarding who should sing Liza, and though Tchaikovsky first envisaged Mravina in the part, he finally decided (though with little reluctance) that Medea, Figner's wife, should create the role. As for the production, Vsevolozhsky was fulfilling all expectations, and with the ever-reliable Nápravník to prepare and conduct the first performance, he felt absolute confidence.

Outwardly the première on 19 December seemed a complete vindication of his hopes. The designs were splendid, the furnishings for the Countess's bedroom being so artfully painted on to a backcloth that some in the audience would not believe the illusion until they had gone backstage to check for themselves. The costumes were specially made and were numerous. '*The Queen of Spades* was mounted with great splendour,' Pogozhev, the manager of the Imperial Theatres, remembered. '. . . The first performance went off brilliantly. The audience

[30] *TLP*15B, p. 87; *TZC*3, p. 357; *TPB*, pp. 447–8; *DTC*, pp. 190–1.
[31] *TLP*15B, p. 206; *TZC*3, p. 381; *TPB*, p. 466; *DTC*, p. 197; *YDGC*, p. 500.

endlessly called for Tchaikovsky and all the artists. The hero of the evening was Figner.'[32] Modest agreed. 'No opera by Pyotr Ilich was given such a splendid first performance,' he wrote in his biography.

Each of the principal performers displayed his or her talent at its best. At no time, in no respect was there occasion to regret that a part was not in better hands . . . The most difficult were discharged best of all: Nápravník in conducting the opera and Figner in the role of Hermann excelled themselves and without doubt contributed most of all to the opera's huge success. The settings and the costumes, faithful to the period down to tiny details – elegant, luxurious in the ballroom scene, striking through their imaginative richness – were on the same high level as the musical performance.

Success manifested itself from the first scene . . . The duet for Liza and Polina in the second scene, Eletsky's aria, the duet in the pastoral were encored.[33]

Yet as with the première of *The Enchantress*, there was something missing, Modest sensed. 'To judge from the first performance it would have been impossible to predict such a solid and lasting success as this opera now enjoys,' he continued.[34] The critical reaction swiftly confirmed this hollowness. If Tchaikovsky had felt dejected by the notices on *The Enchantress*, some of those for *The Queen of Spades* must have shattered him. They were merciless with the libretto – which was understandable; but as for the music, one critic even found 'that the new opera is by far the weakest of all Tchaikovsky's works in this genre . . . that even compared to . . . *The Enchantress*, *The Queen of Spades* represents a significant step backwards',[35] and predicted no future for it. Both because the subject was from Pushkin, and because its style and social world invited comparison with *Onegin* more than with any of the three intervening operas, this new work could not but suffer from the overwhelming love the Russian public had conceived for this now very familiar piece. It is no surprise, therefore, that another writer, Nikolay Solovyev in *News*, should have sensed in *The Queen of Spades* 'a certain striving after success, and hasty workmanship; there is not that solid and inspired writing which is to be felt so strongly in *Eugene Onegin*. . . . *The Queen of Spades* is interesting in parts; *Eugene Onegin* charms

[32] *DTC*, p. 200.
[33] *TZC*3, p. 412.
[34] *ibid.*
[35] *DTC*, p. 203; *YDGC*, p. 511; *TZC*3, pp. 412–13.

throughout.'[36] Writing the same day in the *St Petersburg Gazette* Vladimir Baskin found the subject and Modest's presentation of it unsympathetic. 'A lot of good music is wasted on thoroughly uninteresting figures . . . and so one has to direct one's attention to the unimportant bits instead, to episodic details, insertions made for purposes of variety. . . . Likewise, regarding the characters, there is nothing one can say definitely in favour of the new opera; indeed, it is simply impossible to consider Hermann as a musical character.'[37] Baskin conceded the Countess some individuality, felt Liza had been the most sympathetically treated by Tchaikovsky (and perhaps because of this, she reminded him of Tatyana in *Onegin*) and could not praise too highly the orchestration; as with *The Enchantress*, the critics were unanimous at least on this. Many of Solovyev's views were echoed the next day by Mikhail Ivanov in *New Time*. The dramatic scenes he found more impressive than the lyrical ones, and he singled out those in the bedroom and barracks; he enthused over the scoring, but felt the most interesting music was to be found in the secondary details. He considered Hermann, the Countess and (to a lesser extent) Liza had been well treated, but his final verdict was much like Solovyev's: 'Speaking of the general impression made by the music of *The Queen of Spades*, I have to admit that surface brilliance wins over inner content. In this regard *The Queen of Spades* stands unquestionably behind *Onegin*.'[38]

On 31 December, twelve days after the St Petersburg première, *The Queen of Spades* was mounted in Kiev. Tchaikovsky attended, was much impressed by the level of this provincial production, and was given a rapturous personal reception. However, it was 16 November 1891, nearly a year later, before it was heard in Moscow, when it was conducted at the Bolshoy by Altani. By now the critical reservations were falling away. It was introduced to Saratov on 5 December the next year, and to Odessa on 17 February 1893. It was first heard outside Russia in Prague, on 12 October 1892.

The action is set in St Petersburg towards the end of the eighteenth century. The plot of the opera is as follows[39]:

---

[36] *DTC*, p. 200; *YDGC*, p. 508; *TZC3*, p. 413 (partial).

[37] *DTC*, pp. 200–1; *YDGC*, p. 509.

[38] *DTC*, p. 201; *YDGC*, p. 510; *TZC3*, p. 413 (partial).

[39] Because the libretto of *The Queen of Spades*, like that of *Onegin*, is readily available in English translations, it seems unnecessary to identify the precise location of each portion of the action as has been done in other operas.

ACT I, SCENE I. *A recreation area in the Summer Garden. Spring.*
Nurses and governesses are sitting on benches or walking about, while their charges play; they all chatter happily (No. 1). A group of children with drums, toy trumpets and rifles marches in, and is drilled by its 'commander', to the admiration of the adults. The latter disperse as the 'soldiers' march off, followed by the other children. Chekalinsky, a noted gambler, and Surin, an officer in the horse guards, enter (No. 2). The former asks about the previous night's gambling session: was Hermann there? 'He was,' replies Surin, 'and . . . until eight in the morning he was riveted to the gambling table . . . watching the others play.' 'He's a strange man,' reflects Chekalinsky. '. . . I hear he's very poor.' 'He's not rich . . . Look, there he is – gloomy, like a demon from hell . . . pale,' observes Surin. Hermann, an officer in the engineers, and Tomsky, another guards officer, pass, engaged in conversation. Hermann confesses he is gloomy because he is in love, and launches into the first part of an arioso: 'I do not know her name, nor do I want to, for I do not wish to give her an earthly name!' Though Tomsky advises action, Hermann replies despairingly that he knows she is above him. 'We'll find another,' is Tomsky's solution, but Hermann resumes: he could not fall out-of-love with her, and he can live in peace only when his passions are slumbering. Thus calm is impossible. They leave, Tomsky voicing amazement that Hermann should be capable of such a consuming love.

A crowd of promenaders swarms in (No. 3), revelling in the spring day. Hermann and Tomsky re-enter, and Hermann declares that death alone will remain for him the moment he knows this unknown woman will never be his. Prince Eletsky appears, and Chekalinsky and Surin return. They congratulate the Prince on his engagement. Tomsky joins them, and the Prince openly, and Hermann to himself, voice their respective feelings of joy and misery in love. When they finish, the Prince is asked who his fiancée is. At that moment the Countess and her granddaughter, Liza, enter, and the Prince indicates Liza. Hermann is in despair. Both women observe that yet again they are confronted by Hermann.

There follows a Quintet (No. 4) for the two women, the two lovers, and Tomsky. All are disturbed: the women by this gloomy stranger who seems to haunt their steps, Hermann by the Countess who seems to him 'a fateful apparition', Tomsky by Hermann's reaction to Liza, the Prince by Liza's evident agitation on seeing Hermann.

Tomsky greets the Countess, and she wants to know who Hermann is. The Prince greets Liza, and Hermann reflects to himself that a tempest may follow upon a calm day. As he seats himself alone upon one of the benches, thunder is heard in the distance.

Chekalinsky and Surin resume their conversation with Tomsky (No. 5), asking who the old Countess is. 'It is not for nothing that she is called "the queen of spades",' he begins. In Paris in her youth she had been called 'la Vénus moscovite', and the Comte Saint Germain had pursued her, though unsuccessfully, since she preferred gambling to love. Once at Versailles, however, she had lost heavily. Saint Germain was present, and when the Countess had withdrawn in alarmed despondency at her own ruin, he had followed her and, for the price of one 'rendezvous', offered her a secret of three winning cards. Though outraged, she had the next evening appeared penniless at the table, knowing the secret; if she played them in order, she would win. This she had done. Once subsequently she had told her husband the secret, another time one of her lovers. But that very night a ghost had appeared to her. 'You will receive a mortal blow from a third man who, as a passionate and fervent lover, will come to learn by force the three cards.'

The listeners dismiss the story lightly (No. 6), but Chekalinsky points out to Hermann that here is an excellent way of winning while having no money. He and Surin cannot resist tormenting the engineers' officer with the ghost's prediction. 'You will receive a mortal blow . . .'

Suddenly the storm breaks, and all scatter to find shelter; only Hermann, repeating these words to himself, remains on the stage. But he rejects the temptation they offer, for he would still be without Liza. He resolves that the Prince shall not have her, and solemnly swears in the teeth of the storm: 'She shall be mine!'

ACT I, SCENE 2. *Liza's room. A door to the balcony leading on to the garden.*
Liza is sitting at the keyboard, entertaining a group of other girls by accompanying herself and her friend Polina in a sentimental duet-setting of Zhukovsky (No. 7). The listeners voice rapturous approval (No. 8), and request something else. Liza suggests Polina should perform a solo. She sings 'Liza's favourite romance'. Batyushkov's words tell how the singer had once shared with her beloved the joy of wandering in meadows, groves and fields. Love had promised her happiness – but what had she found in these happy places? A tomb. The other girls are very touched, though Polina wonders what could have made her sing such a tearful song. Liza is sad enough without it – but she is now betrothed: she should be happy – and so Polina launches into a Russian clapping song. Liza does not join in, but goes out on to the balcony.

This lively song, which turns into a dance, is interrupted by the entry of the governess (No. 9), who reproves them all sharply for unbecoming behaviour. The Countess is angry, she reports, and they should not be engaging in a Russian dance. After her short homily all leave except Polina and Liza (No. 10). Polina asks why Liza is so out of spirits, and playfully threatens to tell the Prince. Liza is alarmed. They kiss goodbye, and Liza accompanies her friend out. Masha, a maid, enters and extinguishes all the candles except one, going to lock the balcony door as Liza returns. But Liza stops her; the night is warm. Masha offers to help her undress, but Liza dismisses her. Alone, she stands thoughtfully, then quietly begins to weep. She questions why she is so unhappy, and reflects on the good fortune of having a husband such as the Prince, for he could have made a far better marriage. Again she weeps, then confesses to the night her secret obsession.

Suddenly her obsession is standing before her; Hermann has entered through the balcony door. Liza would flee, but he detains her. She orders him to leave, threatening to cry out if he refuses. 'Cry out! Summon them all! It's all the same to me whether I die alone or in the presence of others!' She stands looking silently downwards, and he begins his plea. It is his last hour on earth; would she grant him at least a moment alone with her in the wonderful silence of the night – 'then let death come, and with it peace'. She stands looking sadly at Hermann. He falls on his knees and begs forgiveness for having disturbed her tranquillity. She weeps yet again, and when he takes her hand she does not withdraw it. They are interrupted by a noise outside the door, and the Countess is heard demanding admittance. Liza signs Hermann to conceal himself behind a door curtain. The Countess enters with maids carrying candles. She insists upon knowing what Liza is doing, what the noise was, why Liza is still dressed, and why the balcony door remains open. Liza explains she could not sleep, and the Countess orders her to bed. Liza asks forgiveness and the old woman, grumpily repeating herself, leaves with her maids.

When Hermann emerges the ghost's words are on his lips, and he recoils in horror. Meanwhile Liza has closed the door, and she indicates to Hermann that he should leave via the balcony. But he resumes his plea. He no longer wishes to die forthwith, but to live and die with her. Seeing she is weakening, he makes as though to leave. Desperately she detains him. 'I am yours!' she cries.

ACT 2, SCENE 1. *A great hall.*
A masked ball is in progress (No. 11). After the contredanse the master of ceremonies invites the guests (No. 12) to go outside to witness a firework display. Chekalinsky, Surin and Tomsky linger to discuss Hermann; he is possessed by the hope of learning the secret of the three cards – and, Tomsky observes, 'he is one of those who, once he's conceived an idea, must carry it through to the end'.

The hall empties and servants prepare the centre of the room for the interlude. The Prince and Liza remain. He asks why she is so sad, but she evades his question and wants to leave. Nevertheless, he detains her to sing an aria of love, lamenting that she seems to distance herself from him, and declaring his own suffering at her evident unhappiness and remoteness. They leave, and Hermann enters (No. 13), in his hand a letter from Liza asking him to meet her in the hall after the interlude. Again the thought of the three cards possesses him. The guests begin to return, among them Chekalinsky and Surin, who steal up behind Hermann, whispering: 'And are you that third man who, as a passionate . . . ?' Hermann leaps to his feet in alarm, but his tormentors hide in the crowd from where, now joined by others, they teasingly repeat their question. Hermann's alarm increases. 'What if I should be mad!' he cries, and covers his face with his hands.

The master of ceremonies invites the guests to witness a pastoral: *The Faithful Shepherdess* (No. 14). The dancers are upper-class women, young men and girls, all in shepherd costume. They perform a quadrille, then a sarabande. Only a sadly pensive Prilepa does not join in, but instead weaves a garland. The dancers leave, and Prilepa reveals her sadness that her beloved has not come to join the dance. Milozvor (played by Polina) enters to declare his long-concealed love. They duet happily. Zlatogor (played by Tomsky[40]) and his suite enter, bearing costly presents. He asks Prilepa to choose between himself and Milozvor, and the latter agrees to accept her choice. Zlatogor

[40] Tchaikovsky did not consider the Milozvor/Polina and Zlatogor/Tomsky pairings immutable, and gave Nápravník complete freedom to assign the pastoral roles to others if he felt this would be better.

tempts with riches, Milozvor can offer only his love. Prilepa's choice is easy; she and Milozvor resume their love duet, and Amor and Hymen enter to bestow the nuptial crown. As the opening quadrille is repeated, the lovers join in.

The interlude over, the guests talk while Hermann again reflects on the fateful prediction (No. 15), and wonders whether he is truly in love. Suddenly he comes face to face with the Countess. Surin mocks him from behind as before: 'Look, there's your beloved!' – and again conceals himself. Hermann is yet more alarmed at this mysterious voice. Liza enters, slipping him the key of a door to the garden; beyond is a staircase leading, via the Countess's bedroom (she will not be there), to her own room. He should meet her there the next day; everything must be resolved. But Hermann insists upon coming that night. When she has left, Hermann declares: 'Now it is not I but fate that wills it thus, and I shall know the three cards!' He runs out.

The master of ceremonies announces that the Empress herself is coming. Great excitement. The guests line up on both sides of the entrance. The master of ceremonies signals the singers to begin their song of praise to Catherine; the men bow and the women curtsey as the curtain falls.

ACT 2, SCENE 2. *The Countess's bedroom.*
Hermann enters by a secret door (No. 16). He surveys the room, and remains for some time reflecting. He passes Liza's door and gazes at the Countess's portrait. Midnight strikes. 'So that's her, the "Moscow Venus" . . . I sense that one of us will perish through the other.' He would like to leave, but cannot.

He hears footsteps and hides behind a curtain. A maid appears and lights the candles. More enter, followed by the Countess and other maids, who chatter to her and lead her into her dressing room. Liza and Masha appear. Liza tells Masha to leave, and Masha guesses her secret. 'Yes, he will come. Be silent. Perhaps he's already there,' Liza says, extracting the silence of a very troubled servant. They leave.

The Countess's maids lead her back in and prepare to put her to bed. But she decides she does not wish to sleep there, and they place her in an armchair, packing cushions round her. Unaware of their continuing presence, she reflects to herself that society is not what it was, and her thoughts fly back to her youth in Paris. She recalls the exalted persons she knew, her conquests, and begins to sing an aria she remembers from an opera of that time. Suddenly aware her servants are still standing there, she impatiently dismisses them, then returns to her musings.

As she dozes off, Hermann emerges and stands before her (No. 17). She wakes and looks at him in dumb horror. He tells her not to be afraid; she holds the secret to his happiness, for she knows the three cards. He pleads with her to reveal them. Perhaps they are connected with some terrible sin. 'I am prepared to take your sin upon myself,' he declares. When she remains silent he loses patience and threatens her, pulling out a pistol. She raises her hand as though to protect herself, then falls back. Hermann approaches and takes her hand, thinking she is acting, but realizes she is dead – and that the secret has passed with her.

Liza enters from her room to see what has caused the noise below. In horror

Hermann points to the corpse, and Liza throws herself weeping on the Countess's body. 'I did not want her death; I only wanted to know the three cards!' he wails – and Liza realizes how Hermann has been using her. Desperately hurt and enraged, she turns on him. 'You monster! You murderer!' she cries. He would speak with her, but she points to the door, and he rushes out. Again she throws herself weeping on the Countess's body.

ACT 3, SCENE 1. *Hermann's room in the barracks.*
It is late evening (No. 18). In the background sounds of a drum and trumpet calls. Moonlight streams in through the window. Hermann is seated at the table reading a letter by the light of a candle. It is from Liza. She now believes he had no wish to cause the Countess's death, and begs him to meet her on the banks of the Winter Canal by midnight. If he does not come she will have to accept the worst. 'Forgive me, but I am suffering so much,' she ends. Hermann is distressed by it all. He sinks into an armchair, engrossed in his gloomy thoughts, and full of remorse for what he has done to Liza. He hears the sound of a distant choir and jumps up, for he recalls how he had gone to the church and, powerless to resist, had approached the open coffin, from which the Countess had winked at him.

Again he sits in his chair, and buries his face in his hands. There is a knock at the window (No. 19). Hermann looks up and listens. The wind howls. Someone appears at the window, then vanishes. Again there is a knocking, the wind blows open the window, and a shadow appears. The candle is blown out. In horror Hermann rises from his chair, goes to the door, and is confronted by the ghost of the Countess. It enters. 'I have come to you against my will, but I have been ordered to fulfil your request. Save Liza, marry her, and the three cards will win in turn. Remember: Three . . . Seven . . . Ace . . . Three . . . Seven . . . Ace . . .' Hermann is left repeating these words as she vanishes.

ACT 3, SCENE 2. *Beside the Winter Canal.*
Liza is standing beneath an archway in a dark corner (No. 20). She is dressed in black. It is close to midnight and Hermann has not appeared. Yet she has regained her faith in him and his innocence. She sings an arioso of love and longing.

The clock strikes twelve (No. 21). In utter despair, she has to accept that her terrible suspicions seem to have been well founded. 'So it is true! I have joined my fate with a scoundrel!' But as she is about to leave, Hermann enters. Overwhelmed with relief, she collapses into his embrace, and he kisses her. Together they sing of their mutual love. But when he says they must fly, and she asks whither, his reply stuns her: 'To the gambling house!' – for there riches await him. He tells Liza of the visit from the Countess's ghost. 'So it is true! I have joined my fate to a scoundrel!' she sings again, now knowing her worst fears are confirmed, while Hermann dwells obsessively upon the three cards. Nevertheless, she still tries to recall him to himself, assuring him that she is still his, and trying to persuade him to leave with her. But he only laughs and pushes her away; he no longer recognizes her. Driven beyond the limits of endurance, she throws herself into the canal.

ACT 3, SCENE 3. *A gambling house.*
Supper is being served to some guests, while others are playing cards (No. 22).
The atmosphere is relaxed and convivial. Besides Narumov, another officer in
the horse guards, those playing include Chekalinsky, Surin, Tomsky and the
Prince. The last has not been seen here before, and he explains his presence as
the consequence of the disastrous end to his love affair. 'They say: unlucky in
love – lucky in gambling,' he observes – adding 'but luck in love brings with
it ill-luck in gambling . . . You'll see!' The merriment of the other guests
resumes.

The gamblers join the supper guests, and demand a song from Tomsky,
whose reluctance they overcome. He sings a humorous love song (No. 23), to
the enthusiastic approval of the others. They all join in a lively gambling song
and dance.

The play resumes (No. 24) (the game apparently is faro). Hermann enters.
'My premonition did not deceive me,' observes the Prince to Tomsky.
'Perhaps I shall need a second. You will not refuse me?' Tomsky agrees.
Hermann is welcomed. 'I want to place a card,' he announces. All are
astounded. 'For how much?' asks Chekalinsky. 'Forty thousand,' replies
Hermann. General excited amazement. 'Surely you've learned the three cards
from the Countess?' Surin asks mockingly. Hermann is irritated. He chooses
the three; Chekalinsky deals, and Hermann wins. General stunned amazement. Chekalinsky asks Hermann whether he wants to pick up his winnings.
When he says no, the others think him mad. He plays again, staking on seven.
Chekalinsky deals again, and Hermann wins again. He laughs hysterically,
calls for wine, and with a glass in his hand, sings an arioso: 'What is our life? A
game! Good and evil are only dreams: work, honour are old wives' tales. Who
is right, who is fortunate here, friends? Today it's you, tomorrow 'tis I!'

Hermann insists upon playing a third time. Chekalinsky tries to get him to
take his winnings, but instead Hermann asks who will challenge him. The
Prince steps forward. The others try to dissuade him. 'I know what I am
doing,' he replies. 'We have an account to settle.' Chekalinsky deals. 'My ace!'
cries Hermann. 'No!' retorts the Prince. 'Your queen is beaten!' Hermann is
holding the queen of spades. At that moment the Countess's ghost appears to
Hermann and smiles at him. He curses her and stabs himself, falling senseless.
The ghost disappears. Briefly recovering his senses, Hermann tries to rise. He
begs the Prince's forgiveness, then thinks that he sees Liza before him. 'O how
I loved you, my angel! You beauty! You goddess!' He dies as the chorus prays
for the peace of his soul.

Thanks to the study of Tchaikovsky's operatic dramaturgy by Boris
Yarustovsky,[41] who had free access to the sketches, we know more
about the early conceptual stages of *The Queen of Spades* than of any other
opera by Tchaikovsky. His working method, so Yarustovsky confirms,
was always to create the basic material, in this instance storing it in the

---

[41] Yarustovsky (B.), *Opernaya dramaturgiya Chaykovskovo* (Moscow/Leningrad, 1947).

margins of his libretto or in a sketchbook if he had not yet received the text. Composition was not begun until he had decided how his materials should be used. Yarustovsky quotes a concrete instance – the clear prescription contained in the sketchbook for the introduction's structure: first a derivative from Tomsky's Act 1 ballad, then 'the cards[' theme] – it's played terribly ff, then woodwinds alone, and a pedal on A with the love theme in a broad form'.[42] Yarustovsky also revealed that Tchaikovsky began the more overtly dramatic scenes with their most critical moments, in the barracks scene starting near the end with the appearance of the Countess's ghost (though other factors influenced this decision; see above, p. 229), in the bedroom scene composing the opening, passing to the death scene, and only then completing the central portion.

In this last regard Tchaikovsky was simply reflecting a practice he had come to observe when faced with a whole opera. In each of his last four his creative attention had first been directed to a crucial scene of self-revelation or relationship (Tatyana's letter scene in *Onegin*, Joan's narration in *The Maid*, the love scenes in *Mazepa* and *The Enchantress*), and he was to do the same in *The Queen of Spades*. The fourth scene contains the crisis of the tale, the moment at which the forces which have defined themselves in the first three meet head-on, precipitating the disasters which follow, and Tchaikovsky's first sketches for the whole opera set out the three ideas upon which he was to build this scene's opening (Ex. 252). Among those which quickly followed were

Ex. 252

(somewhat mournful)

---

[42] *op. cit.*, p. 42.

two which defined the poles of Hermann's personality. One was for his arioso in the first scene ('Hermann the lover': see Ex. 257a), the other for his *brindisi* in the last ('Hermann the gambler'); this latter movement seems to have been envisaged with remarkable fullness.[43] Also included are the beginnings of Liza's arioso in Scene 2 and of her duet with Hermann in Scene 6, as well as Hermann's plea to the Countess in Scene 4.

But most important of all these preliminary sketches are those for the two themes which represent the main opposing forces of the story: the love theme which binds Hermann and Liza, and the theme of the three-card secret which enmeshes him with the Countess. The former had begun life as a three-bar phrase repeated almost sequentially a third higher (Ex. 253a); in the final version a simple change in bars two and three was to make the two phrases a more integral, broader unit (Ex. 253b) and bring the whole closer to what must surely have been lurking in Tchaikovsky's mind as he shaped his own idea: the climax of the Liebestod in *Tristan*.

Ex. 253

More interesting still seems to be the preparatory work on the card theme. As originally conceived (see Ex. 260a), it introduces the finale of Scene 4. But, Yarustovsky reveals, Tchaikovsky's sketches contain numerous harmonizations of this theme, many of which were never used, including one employing the whole-tone scale as bass and presumably intended for the Countess's disclosure of her secret in the

---

[43] Though it was subsequently to be transformed radically (see *op. cit.*, p. 91).

fifth scene (Ex. 254). Yarustovsky's study reinforces the impression that, while from the beginning the love theme was above all a melodic conception, the three-card theme provided a context in which the harmonic accessories were to be of equal importance.

Ex. 254

'As tense as a compressed spring' was how D. S. Mirsky described Pushkin's *The Queen of Spades*.[44] The finest of his prose works, it is terse narrative, the economy of its six short chapters ensuring that every detail tells, that in veering towards understatement its irony may be refined and sharpened, its passages of suspense or supernatural intrusion may strike with a more finely aimed and biting chill. It is a story which grows more impressive with every reading. But economy is not parsimony, for the main characters have a chiselled clarity. Hermann is the rigidly self-disciplined, thrifty German whose habitual self-control is threatened by fierce underlying passions and a vivid imagination. Though he refuses to risk 'the necessary in the hope of gaining the superfluous', he obsessively watches others play. Glimpsing an assured means of winning, he is ruthless in pursuit, and heartless in using Liza's emotional inexperience as his route to success. Seeing Liza crushed by the catastrophic consequence of his action and the uncovering of his duplicity, he feels little pity either for her or even for himself, only cold impassivity. At that moment he lacks even a qualm of conscience. Crashing to disaster at the very moment he believes final success to be his, he does not slide gently into the bleary lethe of drink, but plunges into the abyss of total madness.

Liza is pathetic, yet touching. As ward of the Countess (in Pushkin Tomsky, not she, is the grandchild) she has become the old woman's drudge, a young girl whose vision of the wider world has been formed by romantic novels, and who is all too disposed, both by naïve imagination and desperate hope, to see in this mysterious suitor the deliverer sent by Fate, and thus to respond to his cynical campaign to rouse her affections. But when she is so cruelly disabused, Pushkin

[44] Mirsky (D. S.), *A History of Russian Literature*, edit. and abridged by Francis J. Whitfield (London, 1968), p. 119.

denies her the romantic fulfilment of instant demise, insanity or slow decline; instead he marries her off to 'a pleasant young man . . . employed somewhere in the civil service . . . with a good income'. Yet it is the genre she represents, not Liza herself, that Pushkin is mocking, and because he refuses to identify her with her romantic stereotype, she has the chance to possess a modest but real life. So does the Countess, who might easily have been no more than a grotesque tool of the plot. A sad relic from a period long-past, she lives within her memories, scarcely aware of the present except in her own tightly enclosed environment, where she exercises what authority remains to her in a stream of whims and caprices of which the main victim is the hapless Liza.

While the richness of detail which contributes so much to Pushkin's narrative could be of little service to the opera composer, its structure was readily adaptable. Much of the tale is told in clearly articulated scenes, and Modest's appropriation of these was fairly comprehensive. His opening and conclusion are essentially Pushkin's first and last chapters, though the former is removed from Narumov's enclosed quarters to a public place where groups of promenaders may create a choral panorama, and some of the principals may converse and quickly set the plot in motion. Not surprisingly, the highly domestic scene between the Countess, Liza and Tomsky, which opens Pushkin's Chapter 2, is omitted. Chitchat and the prolonged harassment of a long-suffering Liza may uncover a good deal about the participants, but offered nothing to detain a librettist with Modest's intentions. However, projecting the heroine is now an urgent priority. And so Polina, who is barely mentioned in the story, is elevated to share with Liza a situation which makes plain the latter's personality and emotional condition, and which may end in the love scene (this, of course, is not in Pushkin). The ball, passed over quickly by Pushkin, begins the second act. It is here, instead of in an open street, that the exchanges between Hermann and Liza which gain him access to the Countess's bedroom take place; here, too, the obligatory ballet element may be accommodated. But most of what ensues follows Pushkin's structure closely. The scenes in the Countess's bedroom, in the barracks (where Modest incorporates a soliloquized account of Hermann's grisly imaginings at the Countess's funeral) and in the gambling room are all there. Only the canal scene is new, inserted at Tchaikovsky's insistence because otherwise 'the entire third act will have no women in it, and . . . also it's necessary for the spectator to know what has happened to *Liza*'.[45]

[45] *TLP*15B, p. 38; *TPB*, p. 431; *DTC*, pp. 175–6.

Yet the opera makes very little use of Pushkin's stretches of dialogue, partly because, unlike *Onegin* and *Mazepa*, *The Queen of Spades* is written in plain prose, but partly because the two main characters are so changed. Hermann's words to the Countess in her bedroom are the only significant adaptation. In Modest's scenario, Hermann is no longer Pushkin's 'rational man' but a fatalistic being – an ardent lover whose emotions are corrupted by the lure of gain. The change is apparent from his first entrance. Like *The Enchantress*, *The Queen of Spades* opens on to a choral tableau, the shadow of *Carmen* again apparent, this time in the children's imitation of parade ground exercises taken from the urchins in Bizet's opera. But while Carmen's natural habitat (and Kuma's) always remains that of her tribe, Hermann is already seen to stand apart from the bright secure society represented by this flock of pampered children with attendant guardians. The storm, which for the others merely necessitates a hasty retreat to avoid a drenching, becomes for Hermann a metaphor of his inner turmoil, the fitting confidant of his oath to possess Liza.

The latter is the matching romantic heroine; already betrothed to Prince Eletsky (an invention of the opera), she burns with secret yearning for the 'mysterious and gloomy stranger' who constantly appears before her and her grandmother during their excursions. Her resistance collapses dramatically when confronted by Hermann in the intimacy of her own room; later realizing obsession has overwhelmed his love, she leaps with equally sudden decisiveness to her end. As for the Countess, as hideous old crone recalling times long passed when she had possessed beauty, lovers and dark relationships, and who, in her welter of sleepy nostalgia, now unknowingly awaits her destroyer, she holds a macabre fascination which both repels yet grips, and which Modest exploited to the full.

Once Tchaikovsky had begun composition he was active not only in drastically pruning Modest's text,[46] but in modifying what remained. Details of rhyme and rhythm sometimes troubled him; short lines in arias could inhibit broad musical phrasing. Though he acknowledged that prose might have its own special rhythm, and in this regard was markedly warm about Modest's adaptation of Pushkin's text where Hermann addresses the Countess in the bedroom scene, he also felt the broader distinctions between prose and verse should be clearly maintained, both in the sung sound and the printed text, and he was particularly concerned to clarify such matters. Other changes he

---

[46] He was especially ruthless in shortening the first scene, making two savage cuts, the first in Hermann's arioso, the second disposing of much of his concluding monologue.

effected were more substantial, even fundamental. He transferred the romance in Scene 2 from Liza to Polina, partly to strengthen Polina's role, partly because he believed her contralto richness would enhance the effect of Liza's later soprano tones. The ballroom scene especially troubled him. Modest had proposed a formal polonaise to conclude, but this would not make a real ending; much better, Tchaikovsky felt, to build towards a grand appearance by the Empress herself, and to within only weeks of the première he was hoping the censor would allow a personation of the royal lady. But permission was not granted, and instead (and with equal dramatic effect) her entrance had to be forestalled at the last moment by the curtain. Tchaikovsky provided not only the words leading up to this, but also the texts for the Prince's earlier love aria, the chorus that rounds off the pastoral interlude, the Russian dance-song sung by Polina and the girls in the second scene, and for much of the canal scene (including Liza's arioso). Foreseeing that the censor would be unlikely to allow any part of the Orthodox liturgy to be used in a theatrical context, he devised a special text of his own for the funeral chant heard during the barracks scene. And if Tchaikovsky was unsparing in criticism of some of Modest's lines, so was the Grand Duke Konstantin Konstantinovich in regard of some of the composer's own word setting. As a keen amateur poet the Grand Duke was especially sensitive to false accentuation and redundant verbal repetition, and his representations persuaded Tchaikovsky to modify a little the text of Hermann's arioso in the first scene, and drastically revise that of the governess's arioso in the second.

Though *The Queen of Spades* contains no identified Russian folk-songs, it employs a greater quantity of borrowed material, literary and musical, than any other opera by Tchaikovsky. Besides the text for the pastoral interlude, drawn from Karabanov, verses by the early-nineteenth-century poets, Vasily Zhukovsky and Konstantin Batyushkov, were used for the opening numbers in Scene 2 (the duet for Liza and Polina, and Polina's romance respectively). Derzhavin, the poet dominating the late eighteenth century, was raided three times: for Tomsky's song in the final scene, and for the opening and closing choruses of the ballroom scene, the last of which also accounts for one of the musical borrowings – a polonaise with voices (original text: 'Let the thunder of victory ring out!') composed in 1791 by Jósef Kozlowski. Whether Tchaikovsky actually borrowed consciously for the pastoral interlude is uncertain. Nevertheless, while the opening theme of the duet for Prilepa and Milozvor (Ex. 255a) sounds much like the second main ritornello theme from the first movement of Mozart's C major Piano Concerto, K. 503 (Ex. 255b), extended by a portion of the second

Ex. 255

subject (Ex. 255c) from the C minor Wind Serenade, K. 388,[47] the first
theme of the following trio-finale (Ex. 255d) is virtually identical
(though with changed metre) with one in *Le fils-rival* by Bortnyansky
(Ex. 255e) – though Boris Asafyev pointed out that it is a mystery how
Tchaikovsky could have known Bortnyansky's opera, which was unpublished, and was not among the scores he took to Italy. The chant
used very effectively in the introduction to the barracks scene and as

---

[47] Probably known by Tchaikovsky in its transcription for string quintet in the same
key, K. 516b.

background to Hermann's memory of the dead Countess's wink is authentic, and an adaptation of the French song, 'Vive Henri IV', is heard on the cor anglais just before the most substantial of all these importations: the aria, 'Je crains de lui parler la nuit', from Grétry's *Richard Coeur-de-lion*, sung by the Countess as she muses on her past during the bedroom scene. Nevertheless, for all its fine effect here, it is, like the verses of Zhukovsky and Batyushkov, an anachronism, since *Richard Coeur-de-lion* was first produced in Paris in 1784, and therefore belongs to the old woman's dotage, not her youth.

Tchaikovsky engaged in more stylistic time-travelling in *The Queen of Spades* than in any other opera, for though the sentimental duet which opens Scene 2 and Tomsky's humorous song in the last reflect Tchaikovsky's personal view of rococo style,[48] the gigantic slabs of bright, fresh invention from which much of the ballroom scene is built show him intent on negating himself within what he understood as the persona of Mozart. And not only in the pastoral interlude: the opening entr'acte and chorus (forming respectively the exposition and re-capitulation of an abbreviated sonata movement) are the most deliber-ate imitation of his idol he had yet attempted, their character surely suggested by the opening of the Act 2 finale in *Don Giovanni*. We may only guess whether it was the private concert enjoyed by the Don as much as the real-world success enjoyed by Triquet's couplets in another dance scene which suggested the idea of a large-scale pastoral interlude with (it would seem) direct borrowings from Bortnyansky and Mozart himself. It contrasts effectively with the dignified melan-choly of the Prince's declaration of love, the baitings of Hermann, and the furtive furtherance of his relationship with Liza. But it is straining credibility to hear in the Milozvor-Prilepa-Zlatogor tale any ironic resonance from the Hermann-Liza-Eletsky drama of the opera itself, and this agreeable fifteen-minute idyll of arcadian rivalry in love is too otiose; worse still, the music is no more than pastiche,[49] devoid of that active fertilization by Tchaikovsky's own creativity which had given the hybrid style of the Rococo Variations such genuine life.

This excess of material not relevant to the central drama is one of Tchaikovsky's most serious miscalculations in an opera striking for its

---

[48] To help in devising such music Tchaikovsky had brought to Florence scores of seven eighteenth-century operas borrowed from the library of the Imperial Theatres, viz: Salieri, *La fiera di Venezia*; Astarita, *Rinaldo d'Asti*; Monsigny, *Le déserteur*; Galuppi, *Didone abbandonata*; Martin y Soler, *Il burbero di buon cuore*; Grétry, *Les deux avares* and *Richard Coeur-de-lion*.

[49] Tchaikovsky was the first to admit this, describing the choruses of this ballroom scene as 'a slavish imitation of the style of the past century, and not *composition* but, as it were, *borrowing*'. TLP15B, p. 293; TPJ2, p. 190; TZC3, p. 410; YDGC, p. 507.

very clear evidence of thoughtful planning in regard of key and especially of theme. The tritone relationship, though not as important as in *The Enchantress*, is evident three times in the second scene; when Polina shifts hastily to A to dispel the gloom cast by her doleful E flat minor romance, and when, after the girls' delicious dance-song in A, the governess returns to E flat to press home her extreme disapproval of her charges' frivolity; finally it effects the maximum contrast between the barely whispered pleading in F sharp minor with which Hermann begins his main campaign against Liza's resistance, and the flood of C major passion with which he reckons to surprise and swamp her defences. The interval is especially associated with Hermann. The central shift in his F major arioso of longing in Scene 1 is towards B minor, and elsewhere the E flat–A shift occurs three times: in the ballroom while he reads Liza's letter, in the bedroom during his questioning of the Countess (see Ex. 263), and in the barracks between the end of the chant and the preliminaries to the ghost's entrance.

To establish, by contrast, a relaxed mood, sharp major keys are employed. Scene 1 begins in D, Scene 2 in G, and the more formal passages which make up the greater part of Scene 3 (the beginning, interlude and end) are in D, A or E major, thus setting off the Prince's love aria in E flat, a key favoured by Tchaikovsky for noble pathos. After this grand ball there is little to encourage a return to such sharp keys until the last scene, where the gamblers choose A major to begin their revelry and, later, their play. Nevertheless, in the canal scene this key does become embroiled in more weighty matters; having battled for supremacy with B minor during Liza's desperate attempt to retain faith in Hermann, it survives to become the key of their duet of deceptive happiness, only to be finally dismissed when the tonal tussle is repeated after Hermann has revealed his emotional treachery.

The use of individual keys as the signifiers of particular dramatic forces or emotional predicaments can be as detailed as in *Onegin*. E minor seems again especially associated with the pain of doomed love. It is the key in which the preliminary version of the three-card theme, the symbol of that force which is to overwhelm Hermann's passion for Liza, appears in the introduction, in which mention is first made of Hermann, and in which he vents his despair to Tomsky. It is the key of the latter's impressive ballad through which the seed of obsession that will destroy love is planted in Hermann's mind. Polina's preliminaries to 'Liza's favourite romance' of tragic love, and the first exchanges of Hermann and Liza in Scene 2 are set in it, as is Hermann's cry of horror at the challenge to love that resurges as he watches the Countess from behind the door curtain; it is the key of Liza's last cry of delirious confusion before she yields. For an instant it reflects Hermann's divided feelings before his encounter with Liza in the ballroom and, entangled with B minor and F sharp minor, it contributes to the turmoil of conflicting feelings which follows the Countess's sudden, shocking death. It substantiates the pain of near-despair as Liza enters to await Hermann by the canal, returns when Hermann shows that his greed is greater than his passion, and for a moment in the final scene colours his dying words as he begs the Prince's forgiveness for stealing Liza and ruining his love.

As in *Onegin*, E major can support happiness in love. In it the Prince discloses his feelings for Liza in Scene 1, and in it Liza finally surrenders to Hermann at the end of Scene 2; in this second instance it confirms a joy whose openness is in the sharpest contrast to the ambivalence with which Hermann had employed the key a little earlier when he had resumed his protestations of passion, now confident that Liza would afford him his twin desires: her own self, and an avenue to the Countess. Greeting Hermann in the ballroom, Liza returns to E major; equally briefly (and again with fleeting reference to the love theme) it breaks into her urgent exchanges with Masha in the Countess's bedroom.

Surprisingly perhaps, D minor, the key of agitation or disaster in love, is little in evidence. While it colours the end of Hermann's love theme in Scene 1 (see Ex. 257a), its relative, F major, serves more appropriately for situations where passion, though tormented, is not without hope (Hermann's ariosi to Tomsky in Scene 1 and to Liza in Scene 2, and the final stage of Liza's response to Hermann before the moment of crisis arrives, is passed, and she gives way). As a tonal memory from the early scenes of the opera before Hermann's love had been corrupted, it becomes the key of his dying farewell to Liza's memory. B minor is the ally of F sharp minor, which Yarustovsky rightly identifies as the opera's 'key of Fate', and it occurs significantly five times (to open the introduction, at the conclusion of Scene 1, at the end of Hermann's opening monologue in Scene 4, for the aria by Grétry, and for Hermann's despair after the Countess's death). But three of these involve Hermann alone; by contrast, F sharp minor embraces all the protagonists, erupting for the first time as Hermann learns that Liza is already betrothed, then claiming the Quintet for its own. It is at the heart of Hermann's disastrously successful assault on Liza's affections, is the central key of the brief exchange between Liza and the Countess which fans Hermann's resolve, frames the bedroom scene in which the fateful act is performed, triumphs at Liza's annihilation, and materializes from the Countess's whole-tone subversions as Hermann stabs himself.

The thematic workings of *The Queen of Spades* mark a return to those extensive and inventive procedures which Tchaikovsky had employed to such striking effect in *Onegin*. Though situation themes are still used, the principle of the reminiscence theme is fully restored. The process of fertile thematic generation and variation, which encompasses the whole work, begins in the introduction, which is a laconic conspectus of what is to come: the prompting of events (Tomsky's ballad), followed by the two emblems of the drama's conflicting forces, exactly as Tchaikovsky had planned (see above, p. 239), though excluding 'the woodwinds'. Yet these are but the principal agents within a squad of thematic activists. The Countess as ghost employs that well-used Russian symbol of the supernatural – the whole-tone scale. It had momentarily penetrated the opera's introduction, but it parades itself more extensively in the barracks scene (Ex. 256), recurring in the canal scene when Hermann tells a horrified Liza of her grandmother's spectral visit, and in the gaming house while the old woman's ghost

Ex. 256

passes across the scene in mute triumph at her victim's disastrous gamble. A passage from the final verse of Tomsky's ballad predicting the fateful third visitor who will come to wring the secret from the Countess becomes Hermann's recurring scourge, whether whispered to him by teasing fellow-officers, irrepressibly surfacing in his own consciousness as the storm breaks, or goading him as he secretly observes the Countess in Liza's room (see Ex. 260b), or stands in crowded isolation in the ballroom.

More important still is the melody which had represented Hermann as lover (Ex. 257a) before suffering a Hyde-like transformation during

Ex. 257

[There he is, look. Gloomy, pale, like a demon from hell.]

b.

[three cards, three cards, three cards!]

Tomsky's ballad (Ex. 257b) to become the embodiment of the obsession which will overwhelm his longing for Liza. This greed theme grips him during the storm (see Ex. 262e), resurges in the ballroom, and breaks out violently when he approaches the dozing Countess, finally running through the orchestra with increasing force while he and Liza reel at the catastrophic consequence of his escapade. The scalic portion is heard alone in the barracks scene; recalling the cards he is to play, Hermann twice fastens upon it at the end of the canal scene.

The battle in which Hermann perishes is fought out by two highly differentiated thematic adversaries. Each grows from a motif that reveals remarkable flexibility. That of the card theme is angular, its separate notes clearly articulated and mostly presented on woodwind or brass, while that of the love theme (Ex. 258a) is conjunct, spreading itself sequentially into a broad melodic span above a dominant pedal, and is normally scored for strings.

This love theme is quite different from its counterpart in *Onegin* (see Vol. 2, Ex. 137). True, the earlier invention is the stronger, but

Ex. 258

a.

[Listen, Hermann]

[Here is the key to a secret door into the garden . . . there's a staircase . . . it'll take you to

my [grandmother's] bedroom.]

that in *The Queen of Spades* proves the more serviceable, for whereas the *Onegin* theme is only fully effective if used complete, the one-bar motif of the new theme suffices to send an instant dramatic signal, as during Liza's hasty exchanges with Hermann at the ball and with Masha in the bedroom. In addition, the motif is highly malleable.

Its rhythmic structure may be readily modified, as in the ballroom encounter, where prolongation of the drooping conclusion adds pathos to the dotted-rhythm agitation now stamped upon the opening (Ex. 258b). Apply this dotted rhythm more extensively, employ bassoons, and something of the baleful influence of the card secret is sensed (Ex. 258c). Though the theme has been content to retain its initial form on its first two appearances in the love scene, when Hermann launches his last assault the motif reveals its generative power, fathering a new melodic span far steeper in contour and possessing a new expressive force before which Liza's resistance quickly crumbles.

Besides the thematic connections established by explicit, if varied repetitions, other freer but no less interesting relationships are discernible. Whether or not the Liebestod was a factor in forming the love theme, it is noteworthy how the second form of the love motif (see ⌐—i—⌐ in Ex. 258a) draws close to the opening violin phrase in the bedroom scene (Ex. 259a), one of the first materials to be composed; the resemblance gains added point from the text which Hermann affixes to

Ex. 259

a.

b. Hermann
Ka-koy-to tay-noy si - loy   ya s ne-yu svya-zan   ro-kom
[Fate binds me to her through some secret force]

c. Liza
Ot - ku - da e - ti   slyo-zï?
[Whence come these tears?]

d.

e. [transposed]

f. [transposed]

g.

h. Hermann
Vsyo te zhe du - mï!
[always the same thoughts!]

i.

j.   ┌── retro.(?) ──┐

k. Liza ┌──── retro ────┐
Tak e - to   prav - da!   So slo - de - yem ...
[So it is true! With a scoundrel [I have joined my fate!]]

the latter (Ex. 259b). Whether or not this violin phrase is an additional
Fate motif peculiar to Hermann and the Countess, its characteristic
rising-four-note-opening-which-then-falls-back is reflected throughout
the very distinctive family of materials relating to loves which are
doomed because of this encounter. There is the motif in the form it
assumes in bars 3–4 of Ex. 258a (see ⌐–*i*–¬): Liza, searching within
herself the cause of her tearfulness before Hermann enters and the
reason becomes plain, merely interpolates one note into the motif to
form the opening phrase of her splendid scena (Ex. 259c). Hermann
decorates the motif's end as he begins his most intimate pleading
(Ex. 259d); by making his opening a paraphrase of 'Liza's favourite
romance' (Ex. 259e) which Polina had sung earlier in the scene,
Tchaikovsky manifestly strengthened Hermann's chances of success
with this susceptible girl. The concluding orchestral outburst moves
closer to the motif's shape (Ex. 259g); in both cases the love theme's
principle of ascending sequence is retained. By the fourth scene these
four rising notes possess an emotional resonance, and they break
through in the orchestra both there and in the barracks scene ('always
the same thoughts', Hermann also sings to them (Ex. 259h) in the
latter). They open the brief, forlorn duet in the canal scene (Ex. 259i).

Even the Prince employs them to hymn Liza, building from them a strong melodic arch befitting his maturer passion (Ex. 259j), but in which the reversed motif also lurks. Far more explicitly in the canal scene Liza's outburst of despair at the trick Fate has played upon her (Ex. 259k) will also reverse the motif (with the conclusion of Ex. 259a appended); love has turned sour for both. Nor in this chain of relationships should the resemblance between the opening theme of this canal scene (Ex. 259f) and Ex. 259d (bar two) and e be overlooked.

However much the love theme may reshape or redirect itself, its purpose is essentially expressive. But the card theme is a chameleon-like agent, active in determining the music's direction (or lack of it) as much as its character. It may operate as a single three-note motif, or it may be heard three times, either at the same level or, more often, as a rising sequence. Since each such transposition is commonly a whole tone, the nine-note version has no single key; when the whole sequence is continued upwards, the effect is total atonality, exacerbated by the harmonic ingredients being normally augmented triads as well as portions of seventh chords. This double application of the 3×3 version occurs three times (Hermann brooding on Tomsky's ballad during the storm, Chekalinsky and Surin whispering to him in the ballroom, and as Hermann prepares to confront the Countess in her bedroom (Ex. 260a)). Its broader foundation here is, of course, the ascending whole-tone scale; thus this symbol of the subversive powers of the Countess's secret while she yet lives complements neatly the descending whole-tone scale which is its counterpart after her death.

Tchaikovsky employed four different harmonizations of the sequential version of the card theme (Ex. 260a–d), accounting between them for more than a dozen of the thirty or so occasions when the motif or theme intrudes (some of these incursions are very prolonged; indeed, in all Tchaikovsky's operas, only the oprichniks' theme in *The Oprichnik* is comparably active). It is first heard as the Countess appears (Ex. 260c), where it unceremoniously twists the music to F sharp minor, the first appearance of this opera's key of fate. In massive bass

Ex. 260

b.

[Who, loving passionately, will come to know for certain from you . . .]

c.

[*HERMANN:* Who is your fiancée? *PRINCE:* That is she! *HERMANN:* She?]

d.

[[And when] a day later the beauty again appeared at the "jeu de la Reine" — alas, without a penny in her pocket —

she already knew the three cards . . .]

e.

Tomsky

"Pi - ko-voy Da - moy"! Ne mo-gu po-stig-nut ot-che - [vo]

["The Queen of Spades"! I still cannot grasp why [she does not gamble]]

augmentation it controls a whole six-bar stretch of Tomsky's ballad (Ex. 260d). After the Quintet it reveals other aspects of its versatility by both modifying its contour and proliferating into ornamentation. With sudden ferocity it appends itself to Tomsky's pointed transformation of Hermann's love theme (see ⌐——⌐ in Ex. 257b, bars 2–3) and in similar figuration flashes upwards on solo clarinet during Hermann's first exchanges with Liza in Scene 2 – a fleeting reminder of the second purpose behind his visit to Liza's room.

Sometimes the motif simply but tellingly decorates the harmony, content merely to signal its presence. In notes eight times shorter than in Ex. 260d it is heard in the preliminaries to Tomsky's ballad (Ex. 260e); again on bassoon(s), and even more naggingly, it attends the Countess's reproof of Liza in Scene 2 and Hermann's struggle with his twin desires in Scene 3. On low clarinet the repeated motif warns of the ghost's approach in Scene 5. The tritone leap in Ex. 260e quickly finds its proper resolution on the upper B, but it hints at the theme's moment of greatest potency: when Hermann challenges Fate – and loses. As the ghost had confided the fateful secret to Hermann, the naming of each card had been accompanied by the motif a tone higher, but at the third card the fourth had been quietly changed from perfect to diminished – a covert foretelling of where disaster will strike; now, in this critical final scene (Ex. 261), while the first two widely separated appearances of the constituent motif anticipate

Ex. 261

The game is played
① ② ③
Hermann prepares to play, ——— plays, —— and loses
[x3] [x3]

Hermann's first two successful wagers, the third supports magisterially his last gamble, going disastrously awry at the end by overshooting to a tritone, and thus wrenching the harmony off course – a brilliantly planned and executed *coup de grâce* in an opera whose thematic processes have shown impressive range, skill, insight, and organic power.

Yet there remains the most portentous theme of all – by no means the most obtrusive nor the most prolific, but certainly the most truly pervasive – the Fate theme, born thirteen years earlier at Tatyana's moment of supreme crisis (see Vol. 2, Ex. 139a). It quietly shapes the opera's first bass progression (see ⌐——⌐ in Ex. 262a, bars 2–3), recurs in this short introduction to take possession of the love theme (see Ex. 258a, bars 7–9), and affects jauntiness to introduce the untroubled preliminaries of the first scene (Ex. 262b) just as, even more actively, it will share in the initial convivialities of the last (Ex. 262c). That scalic

Ex. 262

[I do not know her name, nor do I want to!]

e. **Allegro moderato**

[[Three] cards, three cards, three cards!]

f. **Allegro moderato**

[O terrible apparition, death, I do not want you!]

g. **Moderato assai**

[A curse upon it! This thought will drive me out of my mind!]

h. **Allegro moderato**

[A curse upon it! How pitiful and absurd I am!]

[Ah, how I hate this world! Now, those were the days! Plainly they do not know how to enjoy themselves.

What manners!]

[Away with tears, torments and doubts! You are mine again, and I am yours!]

[Ah, how I love you, my angel, beauty, goddess! Ah!]

segment within the opening bar of Hermann's theme (and therefore of the greed theme also: see Ex. 257a and b) has been fathered by it, as the simple first-note transposition at the end of Hermann's arioso of confessed love reveals (Ex. 262d).[50] Its presence may be detected at other moments in this first scene; near the scene's end it finally drags the greed theme into its own mediant-to-dominant realm (Ex. 262e). Having in the second scene played its already established part in the love music (as in Ex. 258a), it matches Hermann's words in its barest form (Ex. 262f) when he secretly watches the departing Countess and, appalled at the avaricious thoughts she has inflamed, cries out at his sense of gathering disaster. Equally explicitly, both before and after the interlude in the ballroom, it again clothes his anguish (Ex. 262g and h). It is at its most assertive in the bedroom scene, thrusting itself into the nervous string phrases of the opening (Ex. 262i); it is worth observing how significantly Tchaikovsky expanded this idea beyond his initial conception (see Ex. 252c) so that the Fate theme's presence should be explicit. In its barest form on a solo bassoon it is the lone companion of the Countess's first musings (Ex. 262j). This is one of its most subtle intrusions. The Countess herself has introduced the pitches harmlessly between the tonic and mediant of D flat; its identity is thus still

[50] In this form, but in the minor, it had opened Lensky's aria in the duel scene of *Onegin* (see Vol. 2, Ex. 139k).

unconfirmed. But as the other instruments gather they steer the music towards B flat minor, establishing the theme's proper mediant-to-dominant identity, then allowing it to spread its workings throughout the orchestra to envelop this old woman who within a few minutes Fate will have claimed for its own. It recurs after both stanzas of the Grétry aria, and celebrates its triumph as Hermann stares despairingly at the old woman's body. Even as Liza greets him by the canal its presence belies her wishful words (Ex. 262k).[51] But its most momentous intervention comes at the very end. The dying Hermann's thoughts fasten upon Liza, and the love theme is heard (Ex. 262l); then suddenly the music slips from F into D flat, the key of its most memorable embodiment in *Onegin,* and the theme sinks through its authentic span, delaying its conclusion by chromatic insertions until the rest of the orchestra, and then Hermann, have fallen silent. By its last note all else has gone. The action is over; implacable Fate alone remains in possession.

The Queen of Spades is the most fully integrated of Tchaikovsky's operas. Yet the attention paid to other matters, both of detail and broader planning, is impressive, despite the speed of composition. To take just three differently scaled examples. Hermann's words to the Countess: 'Perhaps it [the secret] is linked *with a frightful sin, with the loss of [heavenly] bliss, with a pact with the devil?*' (Ex. 263) prompt not merely saturation of the vocal line by the 'diabolus in musica' (that is, the tritone) at the italicized words, but one of the tritonal key shifts. The

Ex. 263

[[Perhaps it is linked with] a frightful sin, with the loss of [heavenly] bliss, with a pact

---

[51] A six-note scalic figure runs through the bass as Hermann babbles his dreams of wealth to Liza. As in bars 38–40 of No. 2 of Scene 1, it is first heard between the submediant and tonic.

s pa - gu-boy bla - zhen - stva, s dya - vol-skim u - slo - vi -em?

with the devil?

Po - du - mai-te!

Think!]

interval also signifies the Countess's death (Ex. 264) when, after six
and a half bars on C sharp, the bass collapses on to G and descends
brokenly through whole tones (the mark of the dead Countess) to
C sharp, then confirms her death for Hermann by repeating the
tritone (the root progression of the central chords is to be echoed
when Hermann makes his final blunder; compare Ex. 261, ③). Finally,
there is evidence of proportions governed by the golden section

Ex. 264

c.f. ③ of ex. 261

whole tones
tritone

(0.618).[52] Yarustovsky observed that the entry of the love theme occurred at this point in Scene 2, but the figure is loose (0.605), and he appears to have investigated no further. Yet the appearance of the Countess's ghost in the barracks is uncannily exact within the second movement (No. 19) of the scene. Far more impressive still are the three figures yielded by the central bedroom scene. Not only is the division between the two main movements exact, but so are the proportions of four of the scenic sections within their movements of occurrence (Ex. 265); the one significant deviation is still no more than one per

Ex. 265

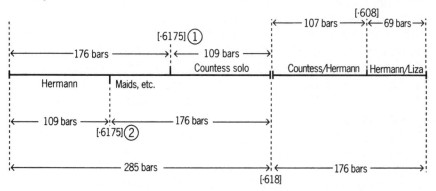

① The point of division has been taken as the change of time signature. If the Countess's vocal entry in the previous bar is taken, the reading is .614

② It is possible the golden section may control this division between sub-scenes 1 and 2. The point at which the music of the maids' chorus is first heard is well off target, but the scene on-stage overlaps with this. The bar in which the maids first sing is at the golden section, measuring from the opposite end.

[52] The golden section is produced by bisecting a line so that the ratio of the shorter to the longer portion is the same as that of the longer portion to the whole (i.e., so that AB is to BC as BC is to AC):

> A   B   C

To achieve this the line must be divided at a point between .618 and .619 of its length. The resulting proportion is considered to be visually particularly pleasing, and artists as diverse as Leonardo da Vinci and Pissarro have used it in planning the layout of paintings. Though it is obviously a proportion unrecognizable in time, composers have sometimes used it as a way of deciding ahead of composition the relative lengths (measured either in pulses or bars, not in 'real time') of sections within a piece. There is, for instance, clear internal evidence of its use by the late-fifteenth-century English composers represented in the Eton Choirbook; of recent composers who have employed it widely Bartók is perhaps the most notable.

cent. Difficult as it is to believe that Tchaikovsky pre-planned the scene with such exactitude, it is even harder to credit mere coincidence with these three figures.

It would be pointless to seek within *The Queen of Spades* those rich depths and subtleties of character possessed by the leading players in *Onegin*. Nevertheless, there is some penetrating observation of human behaviour and some well-drawn sketches. As the mysterious figure whose shadow falls across so many events in the opera, the Countess is seen remarkably little. Yet her appearances are well planned to be cumulatively revealing. As social participant she still shares in society's ferial recreations (Scene 1) and formal festivities (Scene 3); privately within her own unobserved world she no longer conceals the insecurity and impotence of age, as petty tyrant harassing Liza (Scene 2), and rummaging among memories of times long passed when she had commanded attention and influence (Scene 4). With Hermann's appearance terror renders her as mute as in the ballroom. Returning as ghost (see Ex. 256), she exploits her new power with quiet confidence to trick her destroyer into damnation.

Liza is observed more closely. Though she will have faced already (if at all) Tatyana's excruciating choice between caution and commitment, there remains a conflict for her, since it is against the background of an agreed match, seemingly contracted more for social suitability than emotional fulfilment, that her awakening to a greater passion is set. Her first notes in the Quintet (Ex. 266a) are already distantly conditioned by the love motif, testifying to the concealed longing beneath the alarm which Hermann stirs in her, and her vocal line swiftly builds in amplitude of phrase to leave no doubt that she, of all five participants, is animated by some uncommonly lively feeling. Joining with her friend Polina in a homely duet, she cannot suppress these melodic germs (Ex. 266b); while her words are of the peace of

Ex. 266

a.

Mne strash-no!   On o-pyat pe- re - do mnoy.
[I am terrified! Again he stands before me.]

b.

Uzh   ve - cher   ob - la - kov po - merk - nu - li kra - ya,
[Already it is evening . . . the edges of the clouds grow dark,]

c.

Ot- ku-da e - ti slyo- zï,   za- chem o - ne?   mo-i de-vi-chi gryo-zï, vï   iz-me -
[Whence, why these tears? My girlish daydreams, you have betrayed me,]

- ni - li mne,   mo-i de-vi-chi gryozï   vï   iz-me - ni - li mne,

d.

i   sno - va sta - la ya tvo - yei!
[and again I am yours!]

nature at evening, her thoughts run on a very different matter. Having,
like Tatyana, finally dismissed her attendant, she can explore her inner
being, reordering and reforming the two thematic elements and building a full melodic structure (Ex. 266c) in which she discovers, as much
for herself as for us, the strength of the emotion that has possessed her.
There is now no turning back on the heady voyage of self-knowledge.
C minor turns to C major, the orchestra accepts custody of the motifs
in which passion has grown, and the harmony beneath the quietly
rapturous figuration becomes almost static. No longer is Liza anxious,
bewildered, searching; instead she plunges into a new melodic world of
broad phrases, as firm as they are frank.

While Tchaikovsky has been developing with such insight this main
dramatic issue of the opera's earlier scenes, he has shown much
certainty of touch in sketching minor characters. Polina's surprisingly
serious romance, a fine reworking of the mezzo-soprano arioso (also
in E flat minor) from the cantata, *Moscow*, points to a capacity for
substantial feelings; this impression is reinforced by her solicitude for
Liza, and her attempt first to dispel her friend's heavy mood, then tease
away her gloom. Like Polina, the governess appears only once; her
breathless twitterings are reflected perfectly in an arioso whose nervous
elegance is rightly French. The Prince's set piece comes in the following
scene. Tchaikovsky's view of this 'distinguished . . . handsome . . .
stately' figure (to use Liza's words) is unclear. John Warrack's suggestion that the text owes something to Pushkin's poem *Priznaniye*
(*Confession*) seems well aimed, though what in Pushkin sounds like
tormented resignation becomes in Tchaikovsky's words self-abasement

('I am prepared to keep to myself to please you, to know the heat of jealous feelings'). The Prince's aria inevitably recalls Gremin's hymn to Tatyana and cannot but suffer from the memory of a greater emotional fullness and tonal richness. The cost in the *Onegin* aria had been increased scale, but it was a price that had been worth paying for such an expression of elderly, yet truly warm-blooded love.

Yet all these things, fine as many of them may be, are merely background to Tchaikovsky's central dramatic interest. In *The Queen of Spades* for the first time a male character exerted uncompromisingly the greatest pull on his sympathy. True, Hermann's role as lover in the early stages faced Tchaikovsky with a particularly difficult expressive challenge, and doubtless his hero's moroseness proved a convenient reason for not attempting the expression of full masculine passion. To end the first scene he avoided the issue by returning to the kind of situation which had concluded *The Enchantress*, substituting the din of the elements and the vehemence of an oath of possession for, in this instance, the delirium of true arousal. In the next Hermann pleads rather than lusts; the powerful sexual declaration Tchaikovsky might have found difficult to sustain is conveniently cut off by the Countess's entry, just as the rising temperature of the love theme's sequences has from its first version been quickly cooled by the opportune intervention of Fate. At the scene's end there is no celebration of mutual passion as Hermann breaches Liza's last defences, only a swift drop of the curtain.

With the ascendancy of Hermann's other objective, Tchaikovsky was dealing with a predicament he well understood: a man driven to destruction by a compulsion he is powerless to resist. Yet for such a being there is always a moment before which withdrawal was still possible, after which the course is fatefully set. For Tatyana it was as she composed and sealed her letter; for Hermann it is while he awaits the Countess. It is no surprise that the bedroom scene, like the letter scene, is by far the finest in the opera. Pacing is critical, nowhere more so than while Hermann divides the passing minutes between scrutiny of his surroundings and inner searchings. Even that deeply revealing introduction to *Onegin* had not suggested so strongly a sense of confinement as these spaced yet repetitive phrases, initially shooting upwards as though in search of a brighter world but finally caught by Fate (see Ex. 262i), continually circling back upon themselves, and partnered by a double ostinato, one measured, the other nervous and remorselessly nagging. Nor had Tchaikovsky ever used a more astringent harmonic language of seventh and ninth chords, so saturated with suspensions, appoggiaturas and simultaneous false relations. As a projection of tormented obsession these first six minutes of the bedroom scene are unsurpassed. Just as the enchanting maids' chorus affords the required contrast before the Countess settles to her memories, so the old woman's soliloquy provides the calm before catastrophe. Fear has no part in Hermann's feelings as he steps forward to confront the Countess and his fate; the card theme darkly on bass clarinet (see Ex. 260a), then bassoon, and the greed theme eruptively on cellos reflect only the excitement of a contestant anticipating the trial and his reward, the scurrying of chalumeau clarinets the terror of his opponent. Whether urging her to silence, appealing as persuasively as he knows how, or turning to more peremptory means of extraction, his self-control remains. When she dies there is no panic or regret, except that hope of wealth has gone. The resurgence of his obsession music with doubled force and pain is not only highly effective but profoundly truthful, his brief concluding encounter with Liza merely a confirmation that his monomania has throttled his ability to communicate.

It is the failure to pursue single-mindedly the consequences of this inward-turning neurosis which flaws so sadly what follows. Though the barracks scene works well, Hermann keeping within himself[53] as he relives the horror of the corpse's act of intimacy and passively receives the ghost's message, the canal scene, like the Polish act of *Boris* which Musorgsky added for much the same reasons, is something of a disaster. Inevitably Liza has become a casualty of Tchaikovsky's new preoccupation with Hermann. Admittedly, given the composer's determination to believe that she could experience a resurgence of feeling for Hermann (and he for her), he did his best in her heartbroken aria. The only other points in the score where a clearly Russian voice is heard are in Polina's romance, the two dance-songs (for the girls in Scene 2 and (less so) for the gamblers in Scene 7) and in the nursemaids' contribution to the opera's opening chorus. The particular idiom of this arioso had already been used for the Oxana/Solokha duet in *Vakula*, whose distant source is Gorislava's cavatina in *Ruslan*; it allows Liza to speak with an unaffected pathos which is never threatened by sentimentality. But it is only here, and momentarily when she greets Hermann and returns so clearly to her earlier thematic world (see Ex. 266d), that Tchaikovsky's music for her briefly regains something of the power and behavioural awareness that it had earlier shown, sometimes so impressively. Tchaikovsky simply did not know how to handle the emotional ambivalences of the love duet, and Liza's end is diminished

---

[53] Nikolay Figner, whose presence on stage in every scene had worried Tchaikovsky while composing the opera, especially requested that his part in this scene should be as far as possible parlando so that he could concentrate upon acting and rest his voice.

through being attended by one of the weakest musical inventions of the opera (see Ex. 259f).

At the end of the final scene there is more reason, perhaps, why Hermann's thoughts should return to his love for Liza, now that the self-inflicted blow has fixed his speedy exit from this world. Imminent death is a great persuader to scan the balance sheet for something worthy which may offer grounds for eleventh-hour redemption. But Hermann the penitent is difficult to credit; in fact, the end, with its choral prayer[54] and fragments of love theme, is shamelessly sentimental. Hermann was far more honest – and impressive – in the pessimistic defiance of his *brindisi*, a finely judged pause in the action, and a blunt declaration of the cynical fatalism which is the best hope he can muster before making his last, disastrous gamble.

The Queen of Spades is one of Tchaikovsky's most immediately gripping works, but it is not one of his most engaging. Far more uneven than *Onegin*, it suffers from what some (though not Tchaikovsky) find to be *Don Giovanni*'s greatest disability – that it contains not one truly sympathetic character. Even Liza lacks that disarming innocence with which Tatyana offered wholehearted commitment to Onegin. Prepared to violate an existing contract freely entered, she embarks on an amorous adventure, the failure of which leaves none of that regret for what might have been which stabs every spectator at Tatyana's abrupt dismissal of her would-be lover. Fewer still will be able to feel the sympathetic identification with which Hermann's plight filled Tchaikovsky, or feel a fraction of the pity that rises at Mariya's descent into lonely madness at *Mazepa*'s end. Whatever Hermann's more human feelings and motivations, it is neurosis that claims him, and his death is not so much a human tragedy as the closing of a case history. And for the student of Tchaikovsky's own case history *The Queen of Spades* evidences his increasing preoccupation with emotions bordering on hysteria, and a matching extension of his harmonic resources and a darkening of his orchestral palette. Above all in the bedroom scene, the clouded, tormented world of the last symphony can be distinctly foreheard.

[54] After the first performance it was decided to excise this male-voice chorus, and it was not performed for the rest of the run.

7

A TIME OF CHANGE:

END OF A RELATIONSHIP

'I AM LIVING through a very mysterious phase on my journey towards the grave. Something is happening within the depths of me which I myself do not comprehend: a certain weariness from life, a certain disenchantment, from time to time a dreadful melancholy – but not of the sort within whose depth one foresees a fresh surge of love for life, but something without hope, final.'[1]

It had been, of course, a recurring lament, but this time there may truly have been a new element of despair. Perhaps there is evidence of this in the work Tchaikovsky had begun a fortnight before this outpouring to Glazunov, for to set against the confident slabs of rococo brightness in *The Queen of Spades* is some of the darkest music he had yet composed. Certainly his arrival in Florence on 30 January had brought none of the pleasure he had anticipated from his previous visits to this city of boundless artistic riches, and the very day of his arrival he wrote imploringly to the Laroches to come and alleviate his depressed condition.

But as soon as he had started creative work his spirits eased, at least during the hours of labour. The hotel was inexpensive, his accommodation was well insulated from unwanted noise, he dined excellently at his own table, and there were at first few other guests to offer unwelcome attentions. On a typical day he rose before eight, read the papers, then worked until twelve-thirty, when he dined and went for a walk until three. Having a good view of the street outside, he would spend an hour with his valet watching the passing carriages, then work three more hours until dinner at seven. Finally there was letter writing, reading or a further walk, or else a visit to some place of entertainment. He sampled the local opera where *Aida* was the main, though very mixed attraction. But Florence had little else to offer as diversion at the end of the day, and so despite never managing to sit through an entire

---

[1] *TLP*15B, p. 30; *TZC*3, p. 345.

evening, he was repeatedly drawn back to this work, some of whose music (especially the opening of the scene between Aida and Amneris) he found compelling, but whose orchestration he condemned as crude. Nor could he survive a complete performance of Bellini's *I Puritani*, though he thought the opera itself delightful. As during his visit in 1878 the greatest musical pleasure came from a street singer, this time a certain Ferdinando. Sadly, he did not record his impressions at seeing Buffalo Bill, who was in the city with his Wild West Show as part of a European tour.

Because Alexey had remained in Russia to tend his dying wife, Tchaikovsky's companion was Modest's valet, Nazar. He was deeply grateful for Nazar's attentiveness, but not for his excessive curiosity. Like his temporary master Nazar kept a diary, and suspecting him of prying into the contents of his own journal, Tchaikovsky made one entry in French as a clear sign to Nazar that his improper activities were known. Nazar's own diary provides a fascinatingly vivid and unique record of Tchaikovsky's daily round as seen by a very close, engaging, but very artless observer, not subject to the vagaries of mood which so often colour the entries in Tchaikovsky's own journal, nor given to the dissimulations with which the composer not infrequently masked his true feelings in his letters. Nazar's entry for 10 February is typical.

> P.I. is in a good mood today. He had already begun the second scene yesterday and I can see it's going well. . . . Every time before he finishes work I go into his room and say that it's time for lunch or supper. I don't know – perhaps I disturb him by this, but he doesn't seem to show any displeasure. If I'd noticed this, of course I wouldn't have gone in . . . I went in at 7. P.I. hadn't yet finished. I said: 'It's time to stop.' He answered – and then goes on writing notes. 'Yes,' I say. 'It'll soon be seven o'clock.' 'Coming,' he says, and writes yet another note, striking a piano key. I stand. He pulls out his watch, opens it. 'There's twenty minutes to go. I can work another ten.' I said something – but he [replied]: 'Let me have just ten minutes.' I left. Ten minutes later he came in to me. 'Well, I've finished,' and he began asking what I was doing (I was writing; as he came in I closed my notebook), and went into his room. P.I. began walking up and down the room, but I stood by the table. He talked about Feklusha [Alexey's wife], Alexey and such-like.[2]

---

[2] Quoted in *TPB*, p. 614. Lazar's style was rough, with frequent shifts of tense.

Being so absorbed in his new opera, Tchaikovsky had only limited time and attention to give to what went on around him, whether pleasant or irritating. The Italian spring came early, brightening somewhat his view of Florence and enabling him as soon as mid-February to send a violet to Anna Merkling. Thoughts of the modest but stable domestic life of this favourite cousin seem to have recurred to him especially during this phase of Italian isolation. To her his situation had seemed desirable. 'Ah, Anna!' he retorted. 'Life's charm in no way lies in, as you say, rushing through other countries the whole year round, but in having in one's own home someone to love, someone to be interested in, someone to suffer for and to rejoice in. In a word, I'm sick to death of my solitude, my wandering life is repugnant to me, the absence of firm ground beneath my feet makes my life somehow artificial, unstable, empty!'[3] Inevitably thoughts of his homeland periodically welled up in him, and the ache was far stronger than he had expected; the Italian spring, he decided, was premature, untimely, quite unlike that of Russia, and the lifting of spirits it brought quickly passed. Nazar, to whom he had become increasingly attached and whose presence he found especially comforting while composing an opera which sometimes left him with feelings of terror, had a bad fall and was for a while incapacitated. The better weather meant the hotel would soon become more full and unwanted attentions from other guests would increase, while from Russia came news through Jurgenson of Bessel's latest manoeuvrings with the detested *Oprichnik*. The work had been produced in a private theatre in St Petersburg at the beginning of February, arousing the warm approval even of Laroche, who wrote to Tchaikovsky of the audience's enthusiasm for the 'freshness and beauty'[4] of its melodies. Two more performances had quickly followed. Tchaikovsky was incensed that a publisher should sanction a performance against the express wishes of the composer, but at such a distance the offence this opera offered his self-esteem seemed less, and he was content to leave the litigious Jurgenson to take such measures as would snuff out any further exploitation of it by the rival publisher.

The one serious interruption to progress on *The Queen of Spades* was occasioned by Antonina Ivanovna, who had followed up her recent demands for a) cohabitation and b) a concert ticket by writing an eight-page letter to Anton Rubinstein requesting a post at the St Petersburg Conservatoire similar to that held in Moscow by Hubert's widow. To Tchaikovsky himself there was no direct threat of the sort she had made

[3] *TLP*15B, p. 44; *TTP*, p. 237.
[4] Quoted in *TLP*15B, p. 50.

earlier, but this fresh evidence of her unbalanced state and potential for making trouble found him near the end of his tether. For a whole day he struggled to frame the sternest and most rational of letters, setting out his past generosity and declaring that, since she behaved like a child, she would have to be punished like a child. For a year he would reduce her allowance by one third; with good behaviour, it would be restored. Refusing to have any direct dealings with his wife, Tchaikovsky transmitted the letter through Jurgenson, instructing him not to send it if he thought it 'too gentle'.[5] Jurgenson did withhold it, though he implemented Tchaikovsky's financial sanction, which proved remarkably effective. At last a weapon had been discovered that could subdue this tiresome, pathetic woman, and Antonina Ivanovna was to vanish for ever from his life.

Another burden was also shed during his weeks in Florence. For the last season Tchaikovsky had been the main activist in forwarding the interests of the Moscow RMS, but his efforts had cost him dear. His labours as conductor in Moscow had brought him little or no personal gain, and the rapidly escalating demands for him to appear elsewhere in the country were something he contemplated with mounting concern. Already he had promised to conduct six programmes during the following Moscow season, and now another factor had intervened. Tchaikovsky had been the main instigator of Safonov's appointment as director of the Conservatoire, and he continued to recognize the invaluable personal qualities Safonov brought to this responsibility, as well as his power to draw much needed funds to the institution (his wife was a daughter of the minister of finance). But the pianist/conductor was becoming increasingly self-assertive within the RMS, and Tchaikovsky could see he and his fellow-director would imminently be at loggerheads. For some months Fitzenhagen had been mortally ill, and in the view of Tchaikovsky only Brandukov could replace him at the Conservatoire, but Safonov would have none of this. On 14 February, Fitzenhagen died; on 1 March Tchaikovsky acted. In a long letter to the Moscow RMS he set out with some passion his personal reasons for withdrawing from the six concerts he had undertaken, though he added that in each subsequent season he would be prepared to conduct a single programme. When he had been appointed a director of the RMS, he continued, he had thought that all decisions on musical matters would be unconditionally his, but now Safonov had twice refused to consider Brandukov's appointment, and Tchaikovsky's own position had become intolerable. But if one of them

[5] *TLP*15B, p. 35; *TPM*3, p. 648.

had to go, then for the sake of the Conservatoire it was far better that Safonov should remain. 'Vasily Ilich has displayed a great many excellent instincts as a director,' he added generously. '. . . He is intelligent, energetic, efficient, indefatigable, adroit, talented, and I will say with complete sincerity: I should be *terribly distressed* if the Conservatoire should lose him.'[6] This being so, it would be as well if Tchaikovsky resigned forthwith before he clashed openly with Safonov over the Fitzenhagen succession and precipitated a public scandal. Meanwhile he urged that Ziloti might be allocated at least three of the concerts he himself would leave without a conductor.

Tchaikovsky had intended to compose *The Queen of Spades* in Florence, then proceed to Rome to make the vocal score. But because it was impossible to find in the Italian capital accommodation as ideal for work as that he was still occupying, he decided to remain in Florence until this drudgery was over. By 6 April it was finished and despatched to Jurgenson for engraving. 'For the first time after nine weeks' work I've done nothing,' he informed Modest the next day. 'I spent the whole morning in *the Uffizi* and enjoyed myself tremendously, though not at all with what delights the rest of humanity.'[7] Once again he was confronted by the problem of what the visual arts had to offer him; once again he could discover within himself little response to the creative vision consummately crafted with colour and brush, but only to figures whose personalities and feelings he could sense or imagine, then enter for himself. He found this in a deserted corner he had visited once before in the Pitti Palace. 'I spent a whole two hours looking at old portraits of all kinds of princes, kings, popes and various historical figures. No one ever looks at them except me, it seems. Yet it's terribly interesting. Some stand or sit as though they were alive within their appropriate environment. I found an excellent portrait of Prince Ivan Chemodanov, the Muscovite ambassador. How alive!!! There's a wonderful, also surprisingly well preserved portrait of Catherine I and a lot of others.'[8] This, however, was merely the briefest of interludes. The opera had now to be scored, and for all his yearning to be back in Russia, he had no intention of returning until part of this operation was behind him. In any case, he had heard that *The Enchantress*, which had received its inadequately rehearsed and unsuccessful Moscow première at the Bolshoy on 14 February, was to be tried again in April; if he returned his attendance would certainly be required. Nevertheless

[6] *TLP*15B, p. 56.
[7] *TLP*15B, p. 112; *TZC*3, p. 361; *TPB*, p. 452.
[8] *TLP*15B, p. 112; *TZC*3, p. 362; *TPB*, p. 45B.

a change from his present situation was imperative. On 8 April he was in Rome.

The city had altered greatly since his last visit some eight years before, but its magic remained. Memories flooded in. 'I remember *Nik*[olay] *Dm*[itriyevich Kondratyev] every moment; it's both a sadness that brings tears, but at the same time it's somehow pleasant. . . . I can just see you and Kolya [Konradi] on every corner,' he continued to Modest after a quick stroll in the city. 'But thinking of you here is pleasant, both of you are certainly still alive, but poor N. D. Kondr[atyev] will not see Rome again . . . I shall stay here exactly three weeks . . . Dear, dear Rome!'[9] This excellent mood held for a week. Then news of his presence filtered down from Florence, he was besieged by invitations from other Russians in Rome, and Giovanni Sgambati slipped Tchaikovsky's D major quartet into one of his morning chamber concerts and requested the composer's presence. Worse was to follow; in the next concert Sgambati included his own quartet which Tchaikovsky had already heard during his visit to Rome in January 1882 and had disliked. Everything required that he should evade this second invitation, and his longing to be home became uncontainable. On 29 April he left Rome; on 4 May, with about half the opera scored, he was again in St Petersburg, where the proofs of the vocal score were already awaiting him. Remaining long enough for a family celebration of his fiftieth birthday and to attend the wedding of his niece Nataliya to her sister Vera's widower, Nikolay Rimsky-Korsakov, on 14 May he was in Moscow to see Jurgenson. That night he was back in Frolovskoye.

Glad as he was to be home, to be again with Alexey and have the unobtrusive but reassuring presence of Alexey's mother and of his own cook, Pavel, and his wife, Tchaikovsky's mood was made unsettled by outer circumstances. Fekla had died on 2 March and he visited her grave near the church, noting approvingly the memorial Alexey had placed over it. During his absence the Zilotis had moved to smaller accommodation and had loaned him some of their spare furniture which Alexey had installed. The result was a vast improvement to the house's interior, but the view outside was a very different matter; the surrounding woods, which had been Frolovskoye's principal attraction, had been completely felled. 'Only the grove behind the church remains,' he moaned to Modest. '*There's nowhere to walk!*'[10] So dismayed was he that he made a special journey to Maidanovo, only to discover

---

[9] *TLP*15B, p. 118; *TZC*3, p. 363; *TPB*, pp. 454–5.
[10] *TLP*15B, p. 144; *TZC*3, p. 366; *TPB*, p. 458.

that all the villas were taken. Nor was Moscow the same. In fact, the dispute within the RMS had wounded Tchaikovsky more sorely than he would admit. It had become for him more than just a clash of personalities, for mingled with this was a sense of betrayal by former associates, even friends, who had once been his staunchest allies, but whose support now seemed at best equivocal. Taneyev was the recipient of a particularly bitter letter. His only close ally seemed to be Jurgenson, who was likewise considering resignation. Nor in the end had his plans for a series of distinguished conductors to restore the fortunes of the RMS's concerts had the success he had anticipated. Dvořák's concert had been dogged by bad luck and had made little effect, Nápravník had misconceived his programme badly, and only Colonne had really impressed. Hearing rumours that Altani was likely to be removed as conductor of the Bolshoy, he made covert enquiries in the hope of securing the appointment for Ippolitov-Ivanov, though he admitted privately to Anatoly that he would pity him if he were to get the post. Resentment and disappointment had bitten deeper and deeper during his last lone weeks abroad, and with Frolovskoye mutilated and Moscow poisoned, the thought of settling in St Petersburg became for a moment yet stronger, especially since there seemed little prospect of organizing a reasonable flow of true friends to enliven his summer at Frolovskoye.

As always work provided the panacea, and for the next five weeks he immersed himself in scoring the second half of *The Queen of Spades* and correcting further proofs of the vocal score. Confidence in its worth did much to balance the increasing sourness he felt towards its predecessor, *The Enchantress*, which the Bolshoy had not remounted after Easter and which had clearly failed miserably. When he played the new opera to Jurgenson, Kashkin and Alexandra Hubert they enthusiastically endorsed his own judgement of it. Although this trio paid other visits to Frolovskoye during the summer, the companionship of such friends was rarer than he would have wished. Modest and Kolya Konradi stayed two days on their way to Grankino and Bob Davïdov stayed three. But Laroche could not be raised, Tchaikovsky later discovering that he had relapsed totally into his former inertia. Because he wished to avoid certain persons, especially Safonov, trips to Moscow were strictly for business and were as discreet as they were brief. There were now also disincentives to visit St Petersburg. A former pupil begged him to be godfather to her new-born child, but while being prepared to act by proxy, he refused to attend the ceremony, partly because he could not afford the time, partly because he feared he would drop the baby. More seriously: the artist Dmitry Benckendorf wrote on behalf of the Grand Duke Vladimir Alexandrovich, a brother of the Tsar, requesting forthwith an arrangement of 'the bluebird's dance'[sic] from *The Sleeping Beauty* for two cornets and military band. Declining the Grand Duke's request proved easier than evading Benckendorf, who was clearly waiting to lay siege to Tchaikovsky if he were to appear in St Petersburg.

There being no incentive to do other than remain at Frolovskoye and work, and his composer's morale being very high with the successful completion of the new opera, he turned to another long-planned project. Nearly four years before, in October 1886, the St Petersburg Chamber Music Society had elected him an honorary member, and for this he had promised he would compose and dedicate to the society a chamber work as soon as his current commitment, *The Enchantress*, was out of the way. Though he had failed to redeem this undertaking, in June the following year he had made a beginning on a string sextet while on holiday with Anatoly and Parasha at Borzhom, though within four days had given it up for want of any urge to work. According to Modest, it was while engaged on *The Queen of Spades* that his brother noted down the main theme of the slow movement (hence the name he was to give the sextet: *Souvenir de Florence*), and on 25 June, five days after putting the finishing touches to the opera, he set about the piece in earnest. This time the problem was of a different nature. 'I'm composing with unbelievable effort,' he wrote to Modest the same day. 'I'm hampered not by lack of ideas but by the novelty of the form. There must be six independent and at the same time homogeneous parts.'[11] As he had put it more precisely to Ziloti: he feared he was thinking in orchestral terms, then arranging what he had conceived for six solo strings. But the substance of the work delivered itself easily enough, and by 12 July all was sketched.

Over the next few days Tchaikovsky's good opinion of his latest work so grew that he began to cool towards *The Queen of Spades*; he was especially pleased with the fugue near the end. About the scoring, which he began on 26 July and completed by 6 August, he felt less secure. A private performance was arranged in St Petersburg on 7 December when Glazunov, Lyadov and Laroche were among the audience, and neither they nor the composer felt entirely happy; only the first two movements were really satisfactory. Nevertheless the work received its première three days later in an all-Tchaikovsky programme at the fourth concert of the Chamber Music Society's season.

[11] *TLP*15B, p. 184; *TZC*3, p. 375; *TPB*, p. 462; *TPM*3, p. 650; *DTC*, p. 483; *YDGC*, p. 499.

Tchaikovsky then laid the piece aside until December 1891, when he carried out the first stage of a thorough revision of the third and fourth movements, completing this operation during a further three days' work in Paris the next month.[12] Now confident that all was well, he allowed Jurgenson to publish, the score appearing in June 1892 and the parts in August. The first performance of the revised version took place on 6 December at the fourth chamber concert organized by the St Petersburg RMS, with Leopold Auer leading. The following day the CMS presented it with Evgeny Albrecht as first violin.

Except for the Sixth Symphony, the *Souvenir de Florence* was to be Tchaikovsky's last multi-movement work, and just as that stupendous final utterance proved to be the summation and consummation of all that was most personal and precious in his instrumental music, so the string sextet deftly drew together many of the diverse strands from which, over the past nearly twenty years, the textures and fabrics of his highly varied neo-classical works had been woven. Its most ready companion might seem to be the Serenade for Strings of ten years earlier, but that captivating creation had evaded almost all symphonic elaborations, and it is as much the more ambitious Second String Quartet that the *Souvenir de Florence* resembles, though it displays an expressive single-mindedness and a total technical facility which that earlier fascinating but flawed work had lacked. What the 1874 quartet had illumined so glaringly was the unbridgeable gulf that divided inherited classical forms, with their attendant expressive aims, from Tchaikovsky's own most personal creative materials and urges. The three orchestral suites had explored alternative solutions to the problem of remaining characteristic and alive within a multi-movement piece, and though in the splendid G major Suite the tangential line the first two had pursued now curved back sharply towards the main circle of Tchaikovsky's style, this final four-movement example had still made no attempt to face the grander symphonic responsibilities. Nor, of course, had the Serenade for Strings, which had simply redressed the balance of the Piano Sonata of two years earlier, for whereas that lifeless piece had sacrificed all that was most characteristic in its creator to the interests of what he fondly thought were continuing neo-classical practices, the serenade had given precedence to fresh and vital melody, quietly removing any structural or technical features that might have impeded the flow of lively invention. But the *Souvenir de Florence*

---

[12] The evidence of the sketches suggests that the most fundamental changes were made in the central section of the third movement, which had been a fugato, the second theme of the finale, the contour of which was made more interesting, and in the lead to the coda of the first movement; the last nine bars were new.

attempted a final and complete compromise, unreservedly adopting the entire sonata pattern in the first movement, and in the second working its melodic material diligently to squeeze every expressive drop it might yield.

In fact, however, Tchaikovsky's most impressive instrumental movements had come from the conflicts and tensions which were inherent between materials which had sprung from his most personal creative urges and the special demands of the established structures into which they were to fit. Such tensions forced new solutions. To take only examples drawn from opening movements based on sonata structure: the First Piano Concerto had radically reinterpreted the purpose of an introduction by basing it upon a melody complete in itself but pregnant with the embryos of themes to come; more importantly, it had confirmed the employment of three themes in the exposition, had demonstrated a new solution to the problem of transition, and gone on to show how thematic evolution could preserve the vital life so often threatened or even extinguished by the mechanical sequences and repetitions of other developments, and how a written-out cadenza and judicious reordering of earlier materials could first prolong, then resolve the tensions in the final third of the movement. The Piano Trio, too, had opened with an 'introduction' of profound import for what followed, and though a good deal of the movement's material did not represent Tchaikovsky at his best, the unprecedented relationship between the apparent thematic patterning and the associated keys had launched a truly organic succession of events in which the functions of many components had turned out to be not at all what they might have seemed. The Second Piano Concerto's material was positively second-rate, and not always very characteristic; what had made this first movement so arresting was the fearless abolition of much of the standard developmental procedures in favour of two ritornello/cadenza sections of majestic proportions followed by the most succinct of recapitulations. Most striking of all first movements, perhaps – and quite certainly the boldest – was that of the Fourth Symphony, which had allied the three-subject exposition with a seemingly reckless three-stage tonal scheme whose ramifications had profoundly reshaped the entire sonata design and produced a structure even bolder, perhaps, than that of its great counterpart in the last symphony.

In all these cases there had been, in truth, no compromise, only a hard-won accommodation. But always it was the structure that had had to bend, suffer expansion or compression, supplementations or amputations, even be fractured and then rewelded to allow for shifted proportions, modified functions, changed directions, different emphases – and this even when the material itself was less than first-class. When, conversely, the structure had been little more than a conventional mould adopted for the occasion the result had never been one of Tchaikovsky's supreme movements, even though the material might be among Tchaikovsky's most characteristic (the Fifth Symphony and Violin Concerto, for instance). And when both the pattern was conventional and the material not strong on individuality, the result could hardly be other than a second-rank creation, however fluently content and form may seem to fit. This is the condition of the *Souvenir de Florence*. That said, it is of its kind a fine piece, despite the relative brevity of the last two movements. It opens commandingly, the emphatic dominant of the first bar administering an unceremonious kick to the first subject whose momentum stems as much from the robust texture of six active strings as from the confident forthrightness of the theme itself (Ex. 267). This is one of the few passages in Tchaikovsky's music when the texture takes on a thoroughly Brahmsian sound; it is the first audible confirmation that he had not created in terms of this medium's possibilities, but made a *post factum* arrangement. If the abrupt move into the transition promises the most discrete of linking passages, its end confounds this expectation when the second subject glides in sweetly while transitional matters are still, it seems, not finalized (Ex. 268), for the three-crotchet figure, which had originated in bars 4–5 of the first subject (see Ex. 267) and then resurged in this transition, continues as main accompaniment to a passage whose breadth is the more surpris-

Ex. 267

Ex. 268

ing after so shy a beginning. Only a composer of uncommon skill and inventiveness could have devised a melodic paragraph as vast and compelling as the 200 or so bars which make up this indivisible expanse of transition and second subject. And while the development resorts initially to the means employed so synthetically in the Second String Quartet (that is, contrapuntally textured phrases, often grouped in pairs and then repeated at the same or a different level, these larger units themselves being subsequently repeated or sequenced[13]), there is

[13] See the scheme of the Second Quartet's development set out in Vol. 1, Ex. 81.

to be a drastic broadening of the expressive world as the fuguing gives way to reflections on the second subject. In the Third Quartet the recapitulation had widened further the expressive world by incorporating an entirely new theme, but there is to be no amplification here; instead, as in the first two quartets, a small adjustment ensures the arrival of the second subject in the tonic. All being as before, the coda does no more than rally the listener's responses a little with mounting sequences and hectic rhetoric.

The finale is also a sonata structure, though much slighter. The opening theme has an explicit Slavonic character which seems to have been carried over from the preceding Allegretto moderato, a ternary movement during the course of which the main theme had been subjected to a number of modestly varied backgrounds. But in the finale by far the strongest impression is made by the two chunks of vigorous counterpoint which provide the transitions in the exposition and recapitulation; the second becomes a full-scale fugato. Patently Tchaikovsky reckoned that the mainly German membership of the St Petersburg CMS would expect some evidence of academic expertise; equally he was relying upon the musical weight this section would afford, for the development had been barely more than a link between exposition and recapitulation. No doubt the first audience was much impressed by such a studied display of hectic fluency, but what lingers most in the memory from the *Souvenir de Florence* are those passages where Tchaikovsky's melodic inventiveness was allowed its freedom – above all in the slow movement. The Pas de deux in Act 2 of *Swan Lake* and the Andante non troppo of the Second Piano Concerto had amply demonstrated the power which duetting lines possessed to stir Tchaikovsky's melodic faculties, but this time the solo resources available were greater, and a viola was added to violin and cello for the climax to the first part of the Adagio cantabile e con moto. What impresses so strongly in this section is the measured melodic growth from an incipit that is little more than a decorated monotone through an ever more intense and eloquent duet to an impassioned colloquy whose power is heightened by studied tonal shifts. Just as the solemn introduction had merely set the scene,[14] so the furtive central section is little more than a breathing space before this deeply expressive paragraph is heard for a second time. If there had ever been a quality specifically Italian in the melodic opening then it has been engulfed as

---

[14] The main phrase of the introduction returns, though in the minor, during the finale (see bars 153ff.). It is difficult to judge whether this was coincidence. In the original version the phrase had been heard again between the central section of the slow movement and the return of the main theme.

Tchaikovsky has made it all his own. Certainly he wrote stronger and more individual melodies, but no paragraph that is, by its end, more affecting than this.

Socially 1890 had been the quietest of years. The three-and-a-half months of solitude in Italy had been succeeded by three of relative isolation in Frolovskoye, with trips to Moscow and St Petersburg as rare as might be, and few visitors; only Kashkin seems to have spent any significant time with Tchaikovsky at home. But now he was longing for the sight of other places and the renewal of contact with family and friends. Tiflis was certainly to be his ultimate destination, but he intended to do much before he reached there; he would repeat the trip of three years earlier, voyaging down the Volga and across the Caspian Sea to Baku. Next he dreamed of extending the first part yet further eastwards to Alapayevsk, where he had spent two happy years of childhood before boarding school in St Petersburg had brought that dreadful separation from his mother. But news of serious shoaling in the Volga and the wish to fit in more family visits prompted a new scheme: to visit Sasha at Kamenka, Ippolit at Taganrog, then travel up the Don to Kalach, make a land crossing to Tsaritsïn, and from there undertake the final stage of the Volga-Caspian journey. But Modest and Kolya would be at the Konradi estate, where he had so relished the quiet encircling steppes while composing much of *Mazepa*; he must, he decided, make Grankino his first destination. However, brother Nikolay should be incorporated; that would mean he would visit all four brothers and his sister during one trip. Anna and Nikolay von Meck at Kopïlovo near Kiev could also be slipped in. It would be a true odyssey, he observed.

It was all to be much simpler. The visit to Nikolay was abandoned and the Volga-Caspian excursion was forgotten; it would be Grankino, Kamenka, Kopïlovo, then Tiflis. Ippolit would have to wait till his return journey. First, however, he could not avoid spending a week in St Petersburg. On 7 August, the day after completing the sextet, he delivered the manuscript so that the parts might be copied, spent six days making adjustments to Hermann's final aria in *The Queen of Spades*, hearing a lot of music of which he had been sorely starved for months, and visiting family and friends. Then back home for three days and to Moscow to tie up various things with Jurgenson. On 20 August he settled at Grankino for a week with Bob Davïdov and Modest as well as Kolya, who it had been agreed should be his travelling companion. On 27 August the two men were at Kamenka.

This visit was to offer none of the pleasure experienced the previous year. Everyone seemed to have aged, the gaiety had gone, and Sasha was giving deep cause for concern. Quite apart from her gross over-weight, she had long sought escape from physical and domestic stress in morphine, and the doctor ascribed the fits she was suffering to her long dependence upon this and other drugs, to which was now added alcohol. After a fortnight of living in such a melancholy environment Tchaikovsky was relieved to move on to Kopïlovo for two contented days with Nikolay, Anna and their two children, though he found much cause for anxiety in the affairs of the estate. The one heartening encounter of all these travels was with the opera company in Kiev, where he found that the baritone Ippolit Pryanishnikov, who had sung Onegin in the triumphant production of Tchaikovsky's operatic masterpiece in St Petersburg in 1884, had reorganized the opera company into an association of the performers themselves. Tchaikovsky was clearly excited to find himself dealing not with an impresario but 'a whole company *of artists*', as he put it to Jurgenson. Discovering that Pryanishnikov wanted to mount *The Queen of Spades*, he was delighted. 'Please *don't set too high a price* for supplying performing materials; . . . their present resources are not great,' he added in his letter to his publisher,[15] for he judged the zeal and enthusiasm of the united company were matched by its artistic standards, in his assess-ment better than those of Moscow.

On arriving in Tiflis on 19 September the two men rented a flat, a manoeuvre which enabled Tchaikovsky to distance himself from the intensive social life into which his sister-in-law would inexorably have drawn him, had he stayed with her and her family. He paid frequent visits to the opera where he now had free admission, and used his first week of complete freedom to begin the orchestral piece he had already projected in St Petersburg: a symphonic ballad, *The Voyevoda*, founded not upon the Ostrovsky play which had been the basis of his first opera over twenty years before, but upon the very different subject of Pushkin's ballad after Mickiewicz. His enthusiasm for Tiflis was as strong as ever, and the steady progress he was soon making in sketching the new piece helped dispel the inner restlessness to which he had confessed on his arrival. Yet these seven weeks were also to prove a time of great anxiety. In St Petersburg Apukhtin was paying undue atten-tion to Bob. 'Apukhtin is a very pleasant being in society, and you may enjoy as much as you like of his wit when in the company of numerous other persons. But for God's sake don't extend it to friendship or private *tête-à-têtes*,' he wrote in alarm, knowing his former schoolfriend's sexual

---

[15] *TLP*15B, p. 252; *TPJ*2, p. 178; *TZC*3, p. 400; *YDGC*, p. 504 [partial].

disposition.[16] But the most perturbing – and fateful – event of this Tiflis visit was the arrival on 4 October of a letter from Nadezhda von Meck. Only days before she had written in her usual open terms.

'My dear, dear friend,' she had begun. 'I am very glad you are in Tiflis at last, in that beautiful Caucasus to which in my dreams I always aspire, though I myself can in no way get there.' She had gone on to chat about the weather, her own intentions for the immediate future, then given news of her family, so often by now unhappy or unfortunate. She was awaiting the return of her son Vladimir from the Crimea where the doctor had sent him to recover from total nervous collapse. Vladimir had been her most valued counsellor in business affairs, but she would not be able to discuss such matters since the doctor had ordered complete rest for him. Nikolay was already with her and had revealed the disastrous condition of his own affairs. She, of course, had always been against him purchasing the Kopïlovo estate, for he was too young and inexperienced – but Lev Vasilyevich had pushed him into it, though she could not understand why, since his own daughter's future was also tied up in it – and now everything was in an appalling, hopeless mess. 'My God! my God! How terrible all this is! You devote your whole life, all your abilities to affording your children a good secure life, you achieve this, but only to see very quickly the whole edifice you have erected with such labour and effort collapse like a house of cards. How cruel this is, how pitiless!' Alexandr had lost half his fortune in meat exporting because of the strong rouble, and the prospects of Milochka, still besotted by the worthless man she had married and completely subservient to him, looked bleak. But for all her manifest bitterness towards Lev for his bad advice to Nikolay, there was no cause for complaint against her own, special friend, and her last lines return abruptly to the warmth of the opening.

Forgive me, my dear, that I am plaguing you with my complainings; hearing them is no joy for anyone. Keep well, my dear, matchless friend, have a good rest, and do not forget one whose love for you is boundless.

Nadezhda von Meck

PS. Please address [your next letter] to Moscow.[17]

These were her last lines to Tchaikovsky to have survived. One more letter came, but it has disappeared. Yet we may easily guess its contents

[16] *TLP*15B, p. 272.
[17] *TPM*3, pp. 603–4.

from his reply. She too had now been engulfed in the disasters which had afflicted those close to her, her money was gone, and the subsidy which had been so reliable a part of his existence for thirteen years could no longer be paid. And with the ending of her allowance she wished their correspondence also to close.

It was the last blow Tchaikovsky could have expected, and his reply is a powerful crescendo of anguish and sorrow.

My dear, dear friend,

The news contained in your letter which I have only just received deeply saddened me, *though not for myself, but for you*. That is not at all an empty phrase. Of course I should be lying if I said that such a radical reduction of my budget will have no effect on my material welfare. But it will affect it to a much smaller degree than you probably think. The point is that in recent years my income has greatly increased, and there is no reason to doubt that it will continually and rapidly grow. Thus if, from the endless number of circumstances you have to worry about, you are sparing some small thought for me also – then, for God's sake I beg you, rest assured that I have not experienced even the slightest passing regret at the thought of the material deprivation that has befallen me. Believe me, all this is the simple truth: I have no talent for posing or for fabricating phrases. And so the point is not that for a while I shall reduce my expenditure: the point is that you, with your habits, with the grand scale of your life-style, will have to endure deprivations. That is frightfully painful and mortifying. I feel the need to place the blame for all that is happening on someone (for, of course, you are in no way to blame for it), and yet I do not know who is the true culprit. However, this anger is pointless and futile, for I do not consider I have the right to try and penetrate the sphere of what are purely your family affairs. It would be better if I asked Wladislaw Albertovich [Pachulski] to write to me when an opportunity offers about how you intend to manage, where you will live, to what extent you will be subject to deprivations. I cannot tell you how terribly sorry I feel for you. I cannot imagine you without wealth . . .

The last words of your letter hurt me a little, for I do not believe you can be serious about what you write. Do you really believe me capable of remembering you only while I was using your money? Could I really even for one moment forget what you have done for me, and how much I am indebted to you for? I can say without any exaggeration that you saved me, and that I should probably have gone out of my mind and perished if you had not come to my aid, and not sustained with your friendship, sympathy and material help (at that time it was the anchor that saved me) my utterly spent energy and my aspiration to go forward along my road! No, my dear friend, be assured that I shall remember this to my dying breath, and will bless you. I am glad that it is just now, when you can no longer share your resources with me, that I can with my whole heart express my boundless, fervent gratitude which is simply incapable of being expressed in words. Probably you yourself do not suspect the total, immeasurable scale of your act of goodness! If you had, it would not have entered your head that now, when you have become poor, I should think of you *sometimes*!!!! Without any exaggeration I can say that I have not forgotten you and shall not forget you for a single moment, for the thought I think about myself always and inevitably leads to you.

I fervently kiss your hand, and I beg you to know once and for all that no one sympathizes with you, and no one shares all your woes more than I.

> Yours,
> P. Tchaikovsky

About myself and what I am doing I will write another time. For God's sake forgive the hasty and bad writing, but I am too upset to write legibly.[18]

The pain is self-evident; the emotional intensity matches anything in their first exchanges of some thirteen years before. Many of the expressions of warmth and devotion in the intervening letters had sounded dutiful, and around the turn of the year there had been a four-and-a-half months' break in her writing, though since Pachulski was in correspondence with Tchaikovsky over his own compositions, there was a ready channel through which news of his patroness could be communicated. But for the last six months the exchange of letters had resumed much of its familiar tone and frequency.

But that there was another side to his feelings towards his patroness became apparent six days later when he broke the news to Jurgenson.

I have borne this blow philosophically, but all the same I was disagreeably struck and surprised. She had written so many times that I was guaranteed this subsidy to my dying breath . . . I have had

---

[18] *TLP*15B, pp. 263–5; *TPM*3, pp. 605–6; *TZC*3, pp. 394–6; *YDGC*, pp. 504–5 (partial).

to disabuse myself. Now I shall have to live quite differently, on a different scale, and shall probably even have to seek some employment with a good salary attached in St Petersburg. I'm very, very, very *hurt* – just *hurt*. My relations with N.F. von M[eck] were such that her lavish giving was never burdensome to me. Now retrospectively it is; my pride is wounded, my confidence in her unbounded readiness to support me materially and bear every kind of sacrifice for me has been deceived. Now I would wish that she was completely ruined so that she would need my help. But then, you see, I know perfectly well that, as *we* would see it, she's still terribly rich; in a word, a sort of sick, silly joke has occurred which I find shameful and sickening.[19]

This is one of Tchaikovsky's least admirable outpourings, but the selfishness and self-pity it exposes were far outweighed by his very genuine grief. Despite having to abandon his plans for an apartment of his own in St Petersburg, and despite the blow this dealt to his hopes of purchasing a dacha, the void her withdrawal left in his emotional life remained vast, and his bid to resume the relationship was not motivated solely by material considerations. Above all he remained bewildered. His friends offered a variety of explanations for her behaviour: Jurgenson that her affairs had crashed or that she had had a brain storm, Alexey that a jealous Pachulski had pressurized his mother-in-law into this action. Pachulski's part in the matter is certainly shadowy, and his subsequent brief role as intermediary between the two former correspondents placed him in the most favoured position to manipulate matters as he chose. What did soon emerge was that her financial affairs had recovered from any reversal they had suffered; what is also clear is that though his former benefactress never again wrote to him, he had reason to think she had not entirely excluded him from her inner world, since she continued to pass messages through Pachulski who remained for some months in regular correspondence with him. Her health, which was said to have accounted for the break in her writing earlier in the year, was bad. 'Yuliya Karlovna [Pachulski's wife] has just been entrusted by Nadezhda Filaretovna to tell you that she feels very ill and that the state of her morale is bad,' was reported in one letter; in another, 'Nadezhda Filaretovna has given instructions to convey to you a most heartfelt greeting and her deep gratitude for your attention'. Two months later,

[19] *TLP*15B, p. 268; *TPM*3, pp. 609–10; *TPJ*2, pp. 181–2; *TZC*3, pp. 396–7 (in fragments; partial).

in response to a letter from Tchaikovsky which has not been preserved, Pachulski reassured him: 'I beg you heartily to pardon me for leading you . . . to a conclusion which is the complete reverse of what everyone who has the joy of being close to you feels towards you. Nadezhda Filaretovna, to whom I gave your letter to read, has instructed me to inform you *"that it would be impossible for her ever to be angry with you and that her attitude towards you is immutable"*.'[20] Later letters wrote of her 'warm greeting', 'heartfelt greeting', and so on.

But after eight months Tchaikovsky could bear the remorseless coldness of such distant warmth no longer, and he poured out his feelings of misery and resentment.

I believe entirely that Nadezhda Filaretovna is ill, weak, that her nerves are disordered, and that she cannot write to me as before. And for nothing in the world would I want her to suffer on my account. What distresses, troubles and, speaking frankly, hurts me deeply is not that she does not write to me but that she has lost all interest in me. . . . Not once . . . has she entrusted you or her [Yuliya Karlovna] to ask me to tell her how I am living and what is happening to me. I have tried through you to establish a regular relationship with N.F. through correspondence, but every one of your letters has been merely a courteous reply to my attempt to preserve, even if only to a certain degree, a shadow of the past. . . . In the country in the autumn I read through N.F.'s earlier letters. Neither her illness nor her misfortunes nor her material difficulties, it would seem, could have altered those feelings which are expressed in these letters. Yet they have changed. Perhaps it is just because I never *personally* knew N.F. that I imagined her as an ideal being. I could not imagine fickleness in such a demigoddess; it seemed to me that the earth's globe would crumble to little pieces rather than that N.F. would become another person in relation to me. But the latter has happened, and this has turned topsy-turvy my attitudes towards people, my trust in the best of them; it has disrupted my calm, poisoned that portion of happiness given me by Fate.

Of course, [though] not wanting this, N.F. has behaved very cruelly towards me. Never have I felt myself so humbled, has my pride been so wounded as now. And what is most painful of all: in view of N.F.'s so badly disordered health I cannot, because I fear to distress and upset her, tell her all that torments me. I cannot express

[20] *TPM*3, p. 611.

myself – and that alone could relieve me. . . . Of course not a word of this to N.F.[21]

Pachulski's reply is of much interest.

> You misunderstand Nadezhda Filaretovna and are completely wrong about her. If, in addition to she herself being unable to write, much has changed, the main cause, I repeat, is and was the state of her health, alarm about which has pushed into the background everything except her treatment . . . Thanks to her condition, and indeed mine also, my relations with Nadezhda Filaretovna have also changed sharply, and in view of this it is not surprising she has no wish to make me the intermediary between her and you . . . You have something, whatever it may be, to say to Nadezhda Filaretovna, and if you were to write to her about yourself as of old and asked about her, then I guarantee she will respond whole-heartedly, and then you will discover how her attitude to you has changed not one bit; there is no need whatsoever to ask why she has changed *because there has been no change.* I do not consider I have the right to keep your letter of 18 June, and I beg you earnestly for permission to return it to you.[22]

Did Pachulski genuinely believe that the relationship needed no more than a personal approach from Tchaikovsky to restore it, or was he merely teasing the composer, reckoning that if Tchaikovsky did write he could safely intercept the letter so that a cynical suggestion would never be put to the test? Whatever the case, Tchaikovsky never wrote, and now that something between Nadezhda von Meck and Pachulski was denying him the latter as an intermediary, his correspondence with Pachulski ceased equally abruptly. What had precipitated her sudden withdrawal from their relationship is never likely to be known. At Kopïlovo Nikolay had raised with Tchaikovsky the increasing difficulty his mother was finding in letter writing, but the editors of the complete edition of their correspondence rejected the theory that it was a worsening disability of the arm which finally ended those written confidences and intimacies which she could never bring herself to transmit through an amanuensis. Instead they considered it more probable that the increasing jealousy of her children and brother had caused them to bring united pressure to bear on her (perhaps even

[21] *TLP*16A, pp. 131–2; *TPM*3, pp. 611–12; *TZC*3, pp. 398–9.
[22] *TPM*3, pp. 612–13.

involving exposure of his homosexuality), partly because her preoccupation with Tchaikovsky had reached the knowledge of a wider circle and had prompted some unflattering comment upon her part in it, and partly because resources they saw as theirs were being channelled to an outsider (and one they knew in recent years had no need of her money).

Modest attempted no explanation of her behaviour, merely attributing to his brother the view that what he had for thirteen years considered a unique and mutual relationship of two friends had been on her side no more than 'the passing caprice of a wealthy woman'.[23] Modest's judgement must be accepted with much reserve. For all his apparent adulation his feelings towards his brother were deeply ambivalent, for he was intensely jealous of his creative success and fame, and clearly equally jealous of this secret friend as being the closest rival for his brother's attention and affections. Just as the break with Antonina Ivanovna had brought joy to Nadezhda von Meck, so now the break with the latter brought joy to Modest, and this biographer-brother maintained that the composer's bitterness at this betrayal remained unassuaged so that on his deathbed 'he constantly repeated the name of Nadezhda Filaretovna von Meck angrily, reproaching her'.[24]

But a second tradition also grew within the family, for Galina von Meck, a child of Nikolay and Anna, believed the rift was secretly healed at the end.[25] Though she was too young to remember her great uncle, she recorded the family's conviction that it was fear on Nadezhda von Meck's side that the liaison which had produced Milochka would become known to Tchaikovsky that had decided her to make the break. On his side, Tchaikovsky was so deeply lacerated by what he saw as her emotional treachery that for three years he would countenance no

---

[23] *TZC3*, p. 397.

[24] *TZC3*, p. 652. Alexandr Litke, a nephew of the composer and Modest, who was also present at the composer's bedside, told Galina von Meck that Modest presented a false account of things the dying man uttered.

[25] See Meck (G. von), *As I remember them* (London, 1973), pp. 39–42. Shortly before her death in 1985 she confirmed to me orally that her grandmother had an 'atrophied' arm which made writing almost impossible in her last years; she also confirmed my own strong impression of Modest's fundamental feeling towards his brother. She had known this great-uncle well during the first twenty-five years of her life. When I asked her what was his strongest feeling towards his composer-brother, she answered in one word: 'Jealousy.' The gist of Galina von Meck's account is also contained in the recollections of her uncle, Yury Davïdov, who supported the view that Pachulski had a part in this break, using his position as Nadezhda von Meck's secretary to effect this. 'He [Pachulski] envied Pyotr Ilich his talent and his guaranteed material position which gave him complete independence in his later years.' (Davïdov (Y. L.), *Zapiski o P. I. Chaykovskom* (Moscow, 1962), p. 75).

mention of the subject from anyone. But in September 1893, only weeks before his death, he had approached Anna, who was about to leave for Nice to take a turn in nursing her dying mother-in-law, asking her to beg his former beloved friend to forgive him for his own silence, an apology that was wholeheartedly accepted and reciprocated. Galina von Meck's account of these years contains much hearsay and a good deal that is romantically heightened, but there is some plausibility in her record of this reconciliation, especially since she had the account direct from the intermediary, her own mother.

Almost certainly the truth will always remain clouded. What is clear is that the shadow of this rejection hung over the time that remained to Tchaikovsky; as Modest put it, his resentment 'unceasingly gnawed at him, darkening the last years of his life'.[26] It would be temptingly neat to hear the symphonic ballad, *The Voyevoda*, as a reflection of these sombre thoughts and feelings, but caution is needed, for the piece had been envisaged in St Petersburg where his nephew Bob, to whom he had told his intention, had expressed doubt about the subject. Nevertheless, only one of the three weeks spent composing it had passed when he received his benefactress's crucial letter. He had begun work by 27 September, and at first it had gone sluggishly, but by 16 October, when the sketches were completed, he felt well satisfied, and set about orchestrating these. By now, however, his life in Tiflis had too many distractions; the operation was discontinued, it was a year before he could return to it, and his promise to Rimsky-Korsakov to have it ready for a Russian Symphony Concert early in 1891 could not be honoured. Meanwhile in Paris he had heard a new instrument, the celeste, and he determined to include it in *The Voyevoda* as well as in his new ballet, *The Nutcracker*. The scoring was resumed on 18 September 1891 and completed sixteen days later.

Tchaikovsky himself conducted the first performance at a concert promoted by Ziloti in Moscow on 18 November. Even before the première he was having serious doubts about the piece and had been canvassing his friends' opinions. Among those who expressed strong reservations was Taneyev, and his view seems to have been decisive; Tchaikovsky's preparation became perfunctory, he conducted the performance offhandedly, and by its end had turned completely against the piece, despite its apparent success with the audience (in fact, the press also proved favourable). On returning to the artists' room he began ripping the score, then turned to the attendant and demanded he collect the orchestral parts immediately. Ziloti recalled what followed.

[26] *TZC*3, p. 399.

'Seeing his excitement and knowing that the score's fate threatened the parts, I decided on a desperate remedy and said: "Pardon me, Pyotr Ilich, here in this concert I am the master and not you, and only I can give the orders" – and I immediately instructed the attendant to collect all the orchestral parts and take them to my apartment. All this was spoken so sternly, so brazenly, that Pyotr Ilich was, as they say, flabbergasted. He only muttered quietly: "How dare you talk to me like that!" I replied: "We'll discuss this another time." At that moment visitors entered the room and with this our confrontation ended.'[27]

Though the following day Tchaikovsky carried out his threat to destroy the score, the parts were Ziloti's property and he retained them. Thus *The Voyevoda* became yet another of those pieces reconstructed after the composer's death from the orchestral material.[28] According to both Modest and Alexandr Goldenweiser, after its performance and publication in 1897 Taneyev radically revised his opinion of the piece, expressing bitter regret that he had so misjudged it and thus jeopardized its survival.

Nevertheless Taneyev's observation that one of the main themes (the viola/bassoon melody beginning in bar 276) seemed to fit remarkably closely with the lover's words in Pushkin's ballad, suggesting that it had grown more as the vocal part of a romance than as a free conception for orchestra, was very shrewd. Whether Taneyev was right, or whether his reservations about the love scene were justified, one thing is certain: unlike the *Souvenir de Florence*, *The Voyevoda*, though no master-piece, was written from creative necessity. In Pushkin's tartly ironic ballad a voyevoda (or provincial governor) returns home to find his wife in the garden with her lover. Ordering his servant to shoot the wife, he receives the bullet himself. The ternary design is that of *Francesca da Rimini*, though it runs for barely half the time. But whereas that substantial piece had been a musical picture, *The Voyevoda* is a compact drama – or more precisely, since there is no direct engagement between the conflicting forces of the tale, a triptych of which the main central panel is a love scene, the wings representations of the husband's discovery of his wife's love affair, and of his unexpected death. The extreme of separation between the opposing dramatis personae prompts an equally extreme tritonal separation, the outer sections centring upon A minor, the love scene beginning in, then returning to

---

[27] *TZC3*, p. 514; *DTC*, p. 429.
[28] David Lloyd-Jones suggested to me that one of the percussion parts may not have been collected. Certainly the complement of percussion instruments (timpani and a smaller drum) seems unusually small for a piece in which the orchestral palette is otherwise so richly varied.

E flat. This central section, like the splendid, far vaster love scene of *The Enchantress*, discloses a developing experience, though this involves none of the drastic emotional transformation which Prince Yury experiences in his entanglement with Kuma, but only an intensification of mutual adoration which readily allows Tchaikovsky to come full circle and end where he had begun – with the first love theme, its confidence enhanced by fuller scoring, its significance enriched by melodic amplification. Pushkin's unsentimental, even dry, sketch of his sad lovers offers no hint of passion gratified nor even of hope, but Tchaikovsky shows restraint neither in the warmth of his melody nor in the richness of his scoring, in which fervent strings eloquently reflect male passion while the gentle tinkling of the celeste enhances the wife's contrasting fragility.

The feverish stealth of the work's opening theme (Ex. 269a) clearly has a double significance, being not merely a forewarning of the voyevoda's approach but also a projection of his wife's agitation as she hurries to her tryst, for as the scene moves to the garden, its motion abruptly slows (Ex. 269b), and from this transformation issues most naturally the first love theme (Ex. 270). This gentle, sighing melody, built from sequences of Ex. 269c, both sets the scene and is her first tender admission of passion, and after her lover's more full-toned and forthright declaration, it returns on solo oboe, its breathless sequences now joined to firmer, more freely ranging and confident phrases

Ex. 269

Ex. 270

(Ex. 270) which fire him to still greater ardour. A new experience begins to open to her; yet the very repetitiveness of the new E minor melody also uncovers her lingering hesitation. But the briefest of persuasions from her lover suffices, and the firm return of her oboe theme, now on strings, surely marks their first close embrace, the subsequent entry into new melodic territory the new stage this brings in their lovers' relationship, the breathless Tristanesque sequences the preparation for their first kiss.

Against the opulence of such music, the voyevoda's musical world sounds harsh, cold and menacing. Whatever reservations Taneyev may have felt when he compared the central love scene with parallel passages in the earlier symphonic poems, he had no grounds for complaint about the originality and force of the opening and closing sections. If the references of the first stealthy sounds of the piece are ambivalent, there can be no doubt that the curt brass phrase which bursts from the crescendo represents only the voyevoda. All this is striking enough, especially when the whole passage is heard for a second time, building to a more extensive and savage climax; more intriguing still, however, are the cryptic contributions from the bass clarinet (Ex. 271) – a weird succession of fragments whose quasi parlando marking reinforces the impression of an enraged husband

Ex. 271

muttering as he digests the humiliation brought upon him by his wife's conduct.[29] This and the alternating woodwind and brass chords which, against the perpetual naggings of the work's opening phrase, progressively ease the pace in preparation for the love scene, is as original and arresting a passage as any Tchaikovsky had yet composed. So, too, is the work's end. First master and servant confer in furtive whispers (for surely the flute/clarinet phrases are the appalled servant's rejoinders?); then the fatal shot rings out and the voyevoda's fateful scale is heard for the last time, passing into solemn brass chords which are an uncanny anticipation of the conclusion of that last, most violent eruption in the Sixth Symphony's first movement.[30] With the singular darkness of this final outburst, as laconic as it is violent, this remarkable work ends as memorably as it had begun.

Nine days after the première Tchaikovsky wrote to Jurgenson. 'Do not regret *The Voyevoda* – it got its deserts. I'm not in the least sorry about this [its failure], for I'm profoundly convinced it is a work that compromises me. If I were an inexperienced youth it would be a different matter, but a hoary old man ought to go forward (even this is possible, for Verdi, for instance, continues to develop and he's nearly eighty), or he should remain on the height he's already reached. If such a thing recurs in the future I shall again tear it into pieces and then give up composing altogether.'[31]

It was an extraordinary judgement upon a work which contained some of the most novel passages Tchaikovsky had yet composed. But it is also profoundly indicative. In *The Voyevoda* he had overleaped himself; a new vein of experience within him had been unlocked and the novelty of what had come forth had been such as even he could not truly comprehend or assimilate – or, more likely, he could not bear to confront the reality signified in what he had done, and something within him had simply rejected it. So perhaps the clue *does* lie in what happened early in the period when the piece was in the forming. For all that Tchaikovsky had envisaged it before ever he could have known the blow awaiting him in his private world, it is still difficult to believe that the gloom and agitation which his best friend's betrayal had brought

[29] It has already been suggested that the opening of Scene 5 of Act 1 of Wagner's *Tristan* haunted Tchaikovsky's creative faculties as he conceived the opening of the Manfred Symphony (see Vol. 3, pp. 316–17). There is also a curious but very close parallel between the wind theme which runs through the first fifteen bars of that scene and the twelve-bar flute theme in *The Voyevoda* (bars 156–67) – the moment, presumably, when the voyevoda first sees his wife with her lover.

[30] Compare especially *The Voyevoda*, bars 484 ff. with the Sixth Symphony, first movement, bars 297 ff.

[31] *TLP*16A, pp. 276–7; *TPJ*2, p. 221; *DTC*, p. 430; *YDGC*, p. 540.

did not in some way contribute especially to the making of this concluding music, which mirrors so graphically the tragedy of this other man whom a woman had deceived.

Tchaikovsky left Tiflis on 3 November. He had passed nearly seven weeks there, and the social engagements he had so doggedly avoided on his arrival had finally engulfed him. For a visiting celebrity this was inevitable. Ziloti had arrived and given two concerts, in the second of which the Piano Trio had been included, and two days before Tchaikovsky's own departure came the climax of his visit: an all-Tchaikovsky concert in which he himself conducted the First Suite, Serenade for Strings, and *1812*. The reception at the end was as overwhelming as any he had experienced; wreaths, flowers, a diploma conferring honorary membership of the Tiflis Musical Circle, followed by a grand supper at the Artistic Society with innumerable speeches, toasts, and a special ode written in his honour. Two days later a whole crowd of relatives, friends and wellwishers accompanied him as far as Mtskheta on the first part of his journey home. It was the grandest of farewells – and the most fitting, for Tiflis would never see him again.

Once again Tchaikovsky had chosen the scenic route across the mountains to Vladikavkaz, completing the remainder of the journey to Taganrog by train. Partly at Ippolit's insistence and partly from the pleasure of seeing his niece Nataliya for the first time in twelve years, he stayed a day longer than planned. Arriving in Moscow on 12 November, he was met by a group of his closest friends who took him straight from the station to dine at the Hermitage Restaurant. The next day he was home in Frolovskoye.

Such now was the commercial value of some of Tchaikovsky's works that Jurgenson had earlier in the year begun issuing the piano music in a collected edition. Grouping separate sets of pieces within a single volume certainly reduced the cost, but Tchaikovsky had been appalled at the slovenliness with which the contents had been laid out and designated in the volumes he had seen. Jurgenson had now turned his attention to the songs, apparently proposing to issue volumes by voice, with transpositions as necessary. It was time to take a stand, Tchaikovsky realized. It would be far too great a labour for him to check the transposed editions, and anything that claimed to be a complete edition should present its contents in their original form anyway. Only if Jurgenson agreed to this would he permit it to go forward as having been newly corrected by the composer. As for transposed versions which might be published after this, they would have to conform with any changes he had made in the complete edition and would need to be checked by someone more reliable than the proofreaders currently used by Jurgenson. Jurgenson was stung by the uncompromising force with which this last condition was presented, claimed that a reissuing of the original edition had always been part of his scheme, defended his staff indignantly – but then capitulated; after all, Tchaikovsky was a friend – and far too prestigious and successful a composer to risk losing. On his side Tchaikovsky not only verified the text but took the opportunity to make revisions in some of the earlier songs. Having devoted his first five days in Frolovskoye to this, there were only another five in which he could relax before setting off for St Petersburg to share in preparations for the première of *The Queen of Spades*.

Though most of the following month was absorbed by these rehearsals, Tchaikovsky was also able to hear his Manfred Symphony conducted by Auer, and to discover in a private rehearsal both the strengths and weaknesses of his new *Souvenir de Florence*, then hear its over-hasty public presentation. The one event he would certainly have escaped if he could was the celebration at the Conservatoire of his silver jubilee as a composer. He had known for months that plans were being laid and had done all he could to thwart them, even publishing in mid-November a letter in Suvorin's *New Time* declaring his determination to avoid all such occasions. Though this certainly did not extinguish the ardour of those determined on marking the event, it may have dampened it, and he was spared the wider exposure of a public concert. The celebration took place on 15 December, four days before the première of *The Queen of Spades*. Three days after this he was on his way to Kiev for the production that Pryanishnikov was mounting.

Because his circle of family and friends in Kiev was far smaller, the social pressures he had endured in St Petersburg fell away. In his previous discussions with Pryanishnikov he had agreed to conduct the first performance of the opera, but subsequently he had pleaded to be released from his promise, readily offering to conduct a symphony concert instead. But as in Tiflis, the musicians of this provincial city were determined to make much of his presence among them. Only one small factor really marred his eleven-day stay; the concert on 27 December, the most significant of those he attended and which included his own Second Piano Concerto, opened with a Capriccioso by Stanislav Blumenfeld, who eight years before had entered so disastrously the life of his eldest niece, Tanya, and who was the father of Georges-Léon in whose earliest days Tchaikovsky himself had played such an important part. His one concern was to avoid a face-to-face encounter. More relaxing were the performances at the opera, where the repertoire was broad and he was able to see Meyerbeer's *Robert le diable*, Rubinstein's *Demon*, Thomas's *Mignon*, and *Lohengrin*. Compared with St Petersburg the resources of the Kiev company were very modest and their abilities more limited, but their zeal was irreproachable, the small orchestra played well, and the personalities of Pryanishnikov and the conductor, Josif Pribique, were not the only ones he found 'very sympathetic'. *The Queen of Spades* opened on 31 December, and the evidence of its instant success was chronicled in the local press. It was almost as though Kiev was trying to outdo Tiflis, with ovations starting after the first scene and increasing as the evening proceeded. 'The composer came on to the stage now with the performers, now by himself. In the interval after Act 2 the curtain behind Mr Tchaikovsky, who was standing by the footlights, was unexpectedly raised and he found himself surrounded by all the members of the company who presented him with a splendid silver wreath.'[32] Tchaikovsky summarized for Modest his own impressions of the occasion. 'Regarding the enthusiasm of the reception it would be ludicrous even to compare St Petersburg with Kiev. It was something incredible . . . In general the performance was very good, though "of course" after St Petersburg it all seemed pallid. I'm unimaginably tired and, at bottom, I'm constantly aching and suffering. Uncertainty about the immediate future also torments me. Should I turn down a concert tour abroad or not? Is it prudent to accept the directorate's proposal when the sextet has demonstrated that I'm beginning to go downhill? My head's empty and I haven't the slightest wish to work. "Hamlet" lies terribly heavily upon me. Today's the second performance; another prima donna is singing, thanks to which I've stayed.'[33] The next day he was in Kamenka.

His sister's home provided the best of antidotes. 'In appearance Sasha's very much better and not in the least like someone who's sick. . . . As usual Nata can still make me laugh a lot with the same old jokes . . . Miss Eastwood is in a state of bliss because all three boys [Sasha's youngest sons, Dmitri, Bob and Yury] are here, and every day she makes excellent "potted meat". Yesterday we welcomed in the New Year at the big house. It was very jolly.'[34] Ippolit was visiting also. But on the horizon there remained importunately new compositions proposed or promised. Already he had agreed to compose something for the Imperial Theatres in St Petersburg for the season 1891–2. 'Are you thinking about *King René's daughter*?' he continued his letter to Modest. 'In all probability it will end up with me going to Italy to compose, and

---

[32] *TZC3*, p. 415.

[33] *TLP15B*, pp. 304–5; *TZC3*, pp. 415–16; *TPB*, p. 472; *YDGC*, p. 511 (partial).

[34] *TLP16A*, p. 13; *TPB*, p. 472 (partial). The words 'potted meat' are written in English.

by early February I shall need to have the libretto in my hands. And the ballet?'[35] But before ever these were begun he had the *Hamlet* music to compose. On 17 January 1891 he was home in Frolovskoye, determined to discharge the promise he had given his friend, Lucien Guitry, to provide incidental music for Shakespeare's play.

'I never expected that I should hate Guitry. Now I have a deep hatred of him – though of course I have myself to blame,' Tchaikovsky wrote to Modest on 18 January.[36] Never, so Modest remembered, did his brother write anything with less relish than his *Hamlet* music. Guitry had first mooted the idea in 1888 when scenes from the play were to be included in a charity performance at the Maryinsky Theatre with, it was hoped, either an overture or an entr'acte provided by Tchaikovsky. That performance had been cancelled, but two years later Guitry had revived the idea, though this time the complete play would be mounted by the actor himself as his 'bénéfice d'adieu' to the Russian stage. The event having been scheduled for February 1891, it was imperative by Christmas 1890 that Tchaikovsky should begin to redeem his promise, but his attempt to begin work while at Kamenka bore no fruits, and even in the peace of Frolovskoye it took over a fortnight to assemble all that was required. His inspiration's apathy may be judged by the amount of music he adapted or even borrowed from earlier composi-tions. By 3 February all was done. Even though on 21 February Guitry was the hero of the evening, Tchaikovsky was surprised by his music's success, and his view of it softened. 'I have no objection to you publishing it since it pleased many people and everyone's in raptures about the [funeral] march,' he wrote to Jurgenson a week later[37] – but there could be no question of including anything taken bodily from earlier compositions. His music had aroused sufficient interest for it to be used in a performance in Moscow later in the year.

Though the 1888 proposal had proved abortive, Tchaikovsky's creativity had been roused and he had gone on to compose his fantasy overture on *Hamlet*. Clearly this was at the root of the current problem; creatively the subject was exhausted for him, and there was nothing to rekindle his interest when all that was required was a string of short, often fragmentary pieces for a third-rate, 29-strong theatre orchestra, despite Vsevolozhsky agreeing for this occasion to add another seven players to make a band as large as the pit could take.[38] In all

[35] *TLP*16A, p. 13; *TZC*3, p. 418; *TPB*, p. 472; *YDGC*, p. 512.
[36] *TLP*16A, p. 19; *TPB*, p. 473.
[37] *TLP*16A, p. 58; *TPJ*2, p. 205; *TZC*3, p. 426.
[38] These were Modest's figures. Guitry told Tchaikovsky there would be fifty players, but Modest, writing after the event, is probably the more reliable source.

Tchaikovsky supplied some seventeen pieces comprising an overture, four entr'actes and a concluding march, three vocal pieces, three melodramas and five fanfares.[39] The entr'actes before Acts 2, 3 and 4 were earlier pieces, the middle one (No. 7) having been a melodrama in Act 2 in *The Snow Maiden* music of 1873, while the last (No. 9), also for strings only and equally lovely, had been composed in 1884 in homage to another actor, Ivan Samarin. Now that Samarin was dead it had just been published as an *Elegy* to his memory. These two pieces had been taken over exactly as they were, and apart from minimal adjustments to the horn parts the entr'acte to Act 2 (No. 5) is as it was in the Third Symphony, where it had provided the first section and coda in the second movement (Alla tedesca). It is a sign of this symphony's lack of public success that Tchaikovsky could risk employing this music in this new context (ironically, that very evening at an RMS concert in St Petersburg Auer was conducting the whole piece).

Adapting the fantasy overture of 1888 was a formidable task, for the Mikhailovsky Theatre orchestra had no cor anglais or third flute, no cornetti à pistons or tuba, and only two horns and one trombone (bass). Apart from redistribution of the scoring and much simplification of the individual parts, especially those for strings, it needed drastic shortening also. To ease matters further for the players, Tchaikovsky rewrote the recapitulation to make it as exact a repeat of the exposition as possible.[40]

With two notable exceptions, by far the best of the *Hamlet* music is contained in these four second-hand items, even though the overture is an appalling mutilation of the original. The remaining entr'acte (No. 12: before Act 5) is the funeral march, the piece which made the most immediate impression and achieved for a while some popularity. The march's recurrence (No. 14) was required by Guitry ('avec cloches'[41]) to accompany Ophelia's funeral cortège. In Shakespeare a

---

[39] One fanfare has been discovered only recently and is not included in the Complete Edition. Three numbers are used twice (the last entr'acte which is also the funeral march, and the first and third melodramas; the last is shortened on its recurrence).

[40] The main excisions are:
Introduction: Bars 20–54 (from before the first demisemiquaver irruption until the horn's announcement of midnight). *Exposition*: Bars 117–44 (from Più allegro until the oboe's entry with the second subject (without anacrusis), which is transposed up a semitone into C minor). Bars 163–95 (from the end of the oboe theme until the march theme (the second theme of the second subject disappears altogether)). Bars 208–15 (eight-bar link to recapitulation replaced by two bars). *Recapitulation*: Bars 232–359 (in effect, the whole recapitulation after the first subject; replaced by repeat of the revised exposition, with oboe tune in B flat minor). *Coda*: Bars 394–end (replaced by 22-bar extension of preceding music).

[41] *TZM*, p. 212.

'dead march' is specified for the play's conclusion, but Guitry prescribed a 'Marche triomphale – très courte, pour Fortinbras',[42] to
which Tchaikovsky responded by beginning his last contribution with
the Norwegian prince's music from the overture.

Placing the four melodramas exactly in the play cannot be done with
complete certainty, for Tchaikovsky's original manuscript has disappeared, there appear to be no cues in any surviving sources, and in
1893, when Tchaikovsky was approached on the matter, he claimed he
could no longer remember where each belonged. Nevertheless there
can be no doubt that the first melodrama (No. 1), which is directed to
be used twice, accompanies the two appearances of the ghost in the first
scene, or that the second melodrama (No. 3) supports the spirit's
appearance before Hamlet himself in Scene 4. All are based on the
overture's opening theme. Since the extensive melodrama (No. 4)
recurs in shortened form in Act 3 (No. 8) where, from Guitry's
correspondence,[43] it is clear it provides a background for the mimed re-
enactment of the murder of Hamlet's father, it seems most probable
that its first appearance is as accompaniment to the ghost's narration of
his own death.

Apart from the brief and bright fanfares, the remaining pieces are
vocal. In *The Queen of Spades* Tomsky had been delegated to play
Zlatogor in the pastoral interlude; it is almost as though he has now
been drafted to be 'first clown' in the cemetery scene in *Hamlet*, for the
'Chant du fossoyeur' (No. 13) is the closest of relatives to Tomsky's
cheerful ditty in the final scene of that opera. Ophelia's songs are of
much more interest. Just as Balakirev over thirty years earlier had
incorporated a 'thème anglais' into his incidental music for *King Lear*,
so it is difficult not to believe that the basis of the concluding Allegro
vivace in Ophelia's first piece (No. 10: 'How should I your true love
know?') is founded on an English tune (Ex. 272). Nevertheless the tone
of this touching piece is mainly as French as the text to which it is

Ex. 272

Voi - ci le ma - tin   de Saint Va-len - tin,   et   je viens, mu - ti - ne, vous
di - re bon-jour, pour être à mon tour   vo - tre Va - len - ti - ne.

---

[42] *ibid.*

[43] In rehearsals it was found that the length of some pieces needed adjustment. The
funeral march required shortening, while the melodramas supporting 'the ghost's
conversation' and the mimed play had to be extended.

set; if any other composer comes to mind, it is Berlioz. The orchestral outburst that reflects her derangement is as emphatic as it is brief. Ophelia's other vocal piece (No. 11) relates to her second entry in the same scene; it splits into two, and is part melodrama. The text set by Tchaikovsky freely reorders Shakespeare's, providing a good many extra lines for the spoken part. Ex. 273 sets out the entire first part of this piece. Simple almost to the point of simplism, it achieves in all its thirty seconds a perfect projection of virginal sadness out-of-tune with itself. Just as Borodin, in his equally economical song-epigram, 'The false note', had used an unbroken mediant pedal to expose the dissonance of deceit within a confession of love, so as Ophelia falls silent

Ex. 273

the remorseless horn D throbs jarringly against the orchestra's continuation of her song. Her father's death has disordered her mind; it
remains her grating obsession. For a moment in these two weeks of
hateful activity assembling this collection of purely functional music
Tchaikovsky's most sensitive creative urges have been truly touched by
Shakespeare's pathetic maid, as they had been before by Pushkin's
Tatyana and Mariya, and Byron's Astarte.

Tchaikovsky's willingness to exert himself on behalf of young and
talented musicians was lifelong, but by now he was having to face the
limitations of Ippolitov-Ivanov as a composer. 'I have played it [*Azra*]
through. For the moment I will reserve judgement on the music. I like it
less than *Ruth* . . . and the libretto goes completely against the grain
with me,' he had written to Nápravník while in Tiflis.[44] Though he
claimed to have done what he could to promote the opera's fortunes in
St Petersburg, it is obvious he had neither much conviction of its worth
nor much hope for its future. With Arensky it was very different. The
one break he took while compiling the *Hamlet* music was to visit
Moscow for a performance of Arensky's *A Dream on the Volga* on 22
January. 'A beautiful opera! Some scenes are so good I was truly moved
to tears,' he enthused to Modest the next day,[45] endorsing his belief in a
long letter to Vsevolozhsky urging him to present it in St Petersburg.
Yet all Tchaikovsky's persuasions failed. The Intendant of the Imperial Theatres was, of course, subservient to the wishes and whims of his
Imperial master, but otherwise he remained very much his own man,

[44] *TLP*15B, p. 262.
[45] *TLP*16A, p. 27; *TZC*3, p. 424; *TPB*; p. 474; *YDGC*, p. 513.

making his judgements hardheadedly but shrewdly, when necessary softening the consequences by deploying his vast reserves of tact. Tchaikovsky was about to experience in full measure that side of the man for himself.

Having completed his chore for Guitry and spent some time revising the full score of *The Queen of Spades* prior to its publication, Tchaikovsky left Frolovskoye on 7 February for Moscow so that he could hear *The Tempest* rehearsed by Colonne. Unable to be at the concert itself, he sent a wreath to be presented in gratitude to the conductor. From Moscow he went straight to St Petersburg. Before attending Guitry's benefit he had, for the sake of the school run by the St Petersburg Women's Patriotic Society, to conduct his Third Suite in a charity concert in which Edouard de Reszke also sang 'Don Juan's serenade'. It was pre-eminently a society event, presided over by the Grand Duchess Ekaterina Mecklenburg-Strelitskaya, with a string of international soloists – Marcella Sembrich, Félia Litvinne, Nellie Melba and Antonio Cotogni, as well as Edouard de Reszke. A troublesome arm had already persuaded Tchaikovsky to decline a conducting tour abroad, but having first pleaded this handicap as grounds for not accepting the Grand Duchess's invitation, he reflected that it would be impolitic to refuse. Reversing his decision seems to have proved a grim mistake. The mindless adulation of singing superstars is by no means dead, but a century ago it was even more rampant. Only recently had Tchaikovsky observed how they were invading those very institutions which were the bastions of all that was most valuable in Russian musical life. At the beginning of the season he had spoken out forcefully against the Moscow RMS's decision to engage Adelina Patti to restore its fortunes; meanwhile in St Petersburg Melba and the de Reszke brothers were, at the Tsar's prompting, being engaged to sing in French and Italian on the stage of the Russian opera itself, and it seems there was worse to come next season. Now Tchaikovsky discovered for himself how powerless the native composer/conductor was against such competition, for though he told Anatoly he had a great success, Modest recorded that an audience who had come wishing only to hear foreign celebrity singers greeted his appearance on the platform in silence and dismissed him with feeble applause.

Whether or not Modest was the more accurate chronicler, a depressive cloud hung over Tchaikovsky all his time in the Russian capital, and the centre of offence was within the Imperial Russian Opera itself. Immediately on his return home on 24 February he released his feelings at great length to Vsevolozhsky. When he had arrived in St Petersburg some two-and-a-half weeks before he had heard rumours, which he had refused to credit, that *The Queen of Spades* was to be withdrawn for the rest of the season. Then he had met the chief producer, Kondratyev, who had confirmed this was so. But Vsevolozhsky had said nothing when they had met, and Tchaikovsky had been loath to introduce the subject himself in case it appeared his real concern was his royalties. Yet some explanation was due to him; otherwise how could he with any confidence proceed with the new opera and ballet the Imperial Theatres had commissioned? Was it Figner who did not want to sing opposite any woman other than his wife, or who was sulking because of having to shave off his beard? He had noticed that the Tsar, who had once showed such favour towards his music, especially *Onegin*, had clearly not liked *The Queen of Spades* and had not attended any performance after the première. Imperial displeasure must surely be the reason, since the opera itself had been performed to full houses. Of course he realized that the blame could not rest with Vsevolozhsky who, he knew, loved and valued the opera and had given him the new commission in the hope that its fruits would restore Tchaikovsky in the Tsar's favours. But in approaching this new work for the Imperial Theatres he felt like a guest entering a house where the host had made clear he was unwelcome. And after all, there was a musical world outside the theatre for which he could still compose. So would Vsevolozhsky discover whether the Tsar really considered there was too much of his music in the repertoire? If this was the case, then he would withdraw from the commission.

It was as wounded a letter as Tchaikovsky had ever sent – even more consistently so than that he had written to his patroness some five months earlier. In fact, he had guessed rightly in laying the blame at Figner's door: Medea had withdrawn through pregnancy and her husband would countenance no replacement. Vsevolozhsky was too much a politician to admit the truth, but his reply uncovers much about his side of this very crucial relationship in Tchaikovsky's creative life:

When I read your letter I simply gasped. What is this strange idea you have? I was straightway going to take my pen to reply – but preferred first to have a talk with Count Vorontsov[-Dashkov, the Minister of the Court] so as to be able to write to you reassuringly with all the more authority. *The Queen of Spades* greatly pleased the Tsar, and I even received an instruction to prepare a photographic album of all the performers and sets for His Majesty.

If you would begin your talk with me about the sudden withdrawal of your last opera, then I would be able to convey to you what the Tsar said to me: 'I am sorry I did not know Medea was singing for the

last time. I would have come.' Then there followed questions about
the replacement of Medea by Sionitskaya; he regretted that Mravina
could not sing the role.

It is partly my fault that I am not giving your opera with
Sionitskaya. I feared that the good impression created by Medea
would harm the opera if Sionitskaya replaced her. When the de
Reszke brothers suddenly left, I wanted to put the opera on at all
costs. Kondratyev scuppered that one; how and where could *The
Queen of Spades* be mounted so that it did not get into the subscrip-
tion series?[46] As for the dress rehearsal of *The Queen of Spades*, if you
recall, the Tsar summoned you at the very moment you were trying
to hide in the corridor, and at the end of the opera you likewise hid
yourself behind Count Vorontsov and the Grand Duke Vladimir
Alexandrovich. Morale de tout ceci – il ne faut pas trop être modeste
violette. I sent your letter to Count Vorontsov this morning. The
count said to me: 'Dites lui qu'on l'apprécie énormément. Tous les
dimanches on demande à l'orchestre des airs de son ballet et on a
souvent parlé de la *Dame de Pique* en se faisant un grand éloge.'
Yesterday at a court ball I was able to speak about your letter with
Volodya Obolensky. He was simply amazed that you doubted the
success of *The Queen of Spades*, and showered praise on your creative
genius and modesty; he recalled how confused you were when you
went to Gatchina to be presented to the Tsar. I do not know how to
soothe you and convince you that everything you write for us
interests the imperial box to the highest degree. I have placed all my
hopes for the coming season on *The Daughter of King René* and *Casse-
noisette*. Ce sera le clou de l'hiver prochain. In the whole of the
company's 1891–2 season this will be the only thing of interest
except, of course, for the revival of *The Queen of Spades* which has
remained [in performance] to just the point where the public has
taken a liking to it . . .

I think you know what a fervent admirer I am of your talent – but I
can say in all honesty that I think you have exposed something of
your real creativity in *The Queen of Spades*. Your dramatic strength has
declared itself to an extent that's staggering in two scenes: those of
the Countess's death and Hermann's ravings. From this I sense that
you must keep to intimate drama and not rush into grandiose
subjects. Jamais, au grand jamais, vous me n'avez impressioné
comme dans ces deux tableaux d'un réalisme saisissant. Le drame de

---

[46] This would have placed *The Queen of Spades* among the ordinary repertoire operas,
whereas it had been mounted as a special production with higher ticket prices.

votre *Enchantress* m'a laissé froid. Instinctivement je vous poussais à faire l'opéra de *Dame de Pique*, et je crois que votre oeuvre vivra et nous survivra.

You have a strange and unhappy character, dear Pyotr Ilich! You have a desire to torment and torture yourself with empty apparitions. Everyone knows your worth. To be precise, you are a Russian talent – real, not hollow – therefore you do not possess over-confidence but excessive modesty.

I beg you to forgive me for speaking so openly with you – but your letter elicited this openness.[47]

It was the reply of a consummate diplomat who, nevertheless, had a very deep regard for his correspondent. Its recipient was soothed, reassured; the opera and ballet were safe.

The first two months of 1891 were a time of creative urgency, for quite apart from Guitry's pressing deadline, there was the imminent prospect of a further foreign tour. The baritone, Ivan Melnikov, who since 1874 had been creating parts in Tchaikovsky's operas ranging from Vyazminsky in *The Oprichnik* to Tomsky in *The Queen of Spades*, had requested some unaccompanied choral pieces for the free choral class he ran in St Petersburg. Tchaikovsky responded with three four-voice pieces, 'Without time, without season', 'The voice of mirth grew silent' and ''Tis not the cuckoo in the damp pinewood' – for women's, men's, and mixed voices respectively. All three manuscripts are dated the same: 26 February, and there is no doubt Tchaikovsky could have despatched them all very quickly, though his unfaltering professionalism ensured that Melnikov received creations that genuinely delighted him and fully deserved their success when his choir sang them publicly two months later. These completed, and Vsevolozhsky's pacifying letter having done its work, Tchaikovsky directed his energies furiously into the new ballet, and though three further days were lost because of a visit to St Petersburg to see Modest's newest play and consult with Vsevolozhsky, by 11 March a significant start had been made on it.

All this had required a rigorous control of other distracting activities, and his letters from these weeks suggest he managed this with considerable success, though he maintained a reasonable social life at Frolovskoye with visits from his Moscow friends. The Grand Duke Konstantin Konstantinovich had now extended his activities within the Imperial Academy of Sciences into lexicography, planning an *Academic Dictionary* in which he asked Tchaikovsky to act as consultant

[47] *TZC3*, pp. 428–30.

on musical matters. Realizing the limitations in his knowledge when it came to music history, yet hardly able to refuse, he was quick to enlist the help of Taneyev, Laroche and Kashkin in discharging his part of the enterprise. But as always his customary kindly if, on occasions, uncompromisingly frank service to unknown, insignificant members of society was not neglected. A player in one of the Imperial Theatres' orchestras in St Petersburg had sent a score for Tchaikovsky to look over. This former pupil of Rimsky-Korsakov received the highest praise for his technical competence from the former professor of composition at the Moscow Conservatoire – 'but as yet you have no individuality and so your harmonic invention, like your melodic, is pallid and devoid of freshness. Of course I do not wish to say that you have no serious creative gift at all; perhaps later it will declare itself very palpably . . . In any case, you should continue to compose.'[48] Then there was a certain Vladimir Sherwood, a Moscow architect and enthusiast for things Russian, who wrote exhorting Tchaikovsky to busy himself with preserving the national tradition by engaging folk performers in concerts and promoting the study of folk music in conservatoires. In reply Tchaikovsky set out the fundamental differences within the traditions of folk and classical music, then told the reader with gentle bluntness that he did not know what he was talking about. But was there anything really to worry about? No, he ended cheerfully; we've got '*Glinka* – that alone is surely enough to guarantee it [Russian music] is taken seriously!'[49] Nor, as he was preparing to leave for the New World to which he had been invited as the distinguished international musician who would contribute to the celebrations inaugurating the new Carnegie Hall in New York, did he find it too much trouble to write to Jurgenson asking him to send the telegraph operator at Klin railway station, who also ran the station's choir, copies of his two textbooks on harmony.

But from this world of ordinary mortals he bore away one poignant memory as on 13 March he set out on the longest journey he would ever undertake. Alexey had just married the eighteen-year-old sister-in-law of Modest's valet, Nazar. Whether Tchaikovsky's absence from the wedding was premeditated or not, he was certainly distressed that Alexey had chosen the anniversary of his first wife's death. 'Alexey's [second] wife has turned out to be very pretty and delectable,' he admitted to Modest, '. . . but I get angry with her every time I go into Alexey's room while they are drinking tea and see how terribly in love

[48] *TLP*16A, p. 65.
[49] *TLP*16A, p. 32.

with his wife this man is. I remember poor, most gentle Feklusha, who is decomposing a few yards away from us. It must be because I often recall Feklusha that I find it melancholy here these days, and I contemplate my departure with pleasure.'[50]

It is abundantly clear that there was now no need for Tchaikovsky to solicit invitations to appear abroad as conductor of his own works. In October 1889 he had received a pressing invitation to conduct again in Frankfurt, but the production of *The Sleeping Beauty* and composition of *The Queen of Spades* had forced him to decline. Early in 1891 the invitation had been renewed and his Berlin agent, Wolf, had added concerts in Mainz and Budapest. This time it was the problem with his conducting arm that proved the obstacle. Already, however, Wolf had received a proposal from America for Carnegie Hall concerts in April. The fee would be $2,500. Such a sum could not be declined, Tchaikovsky reflected, for it might not be repeated. Meanwhile he had decided that a concert in Paris would be timely, and had given his publisher Mackar carte blanche for all the arrangements. After a brief visit to Moscow and a pause in St Petersburg to consult further, especially with Petipa, about *The Nutcracker*, on 18 March he set out for Paris. Passing through Berlin, he met Wolf and the publisher, Hugo Bock, whom he greatly liked, though he pretended to both that he was continuing his journey imminently, for he wished to spend the next twenty-four hours by himself; he had noticed a concert that evening in which both *1812* and the Andante cantabile were to be played, and he wanted the special pleasure of hearing them incognito. On 22 March he arrived in Paris.

Though he had managed a little work on the ballet during the first part of his journey, in the French capital all inclination vanished, and his first fortnight was mostly filled with inescapable visiting and dining, his only true pleasure deriving from the presence of Modest, Sapelnikov, Sophie Menter, and of his niece Tasya and family. Modest said he had never seen his brother so preoccupied when abroad, and he attributed this to the impending concert. Tchaikovsky was pleased with the first rehearsal and especially with the very sympathetic reception the players gave him. In the concert itself at the Châtelet on 5 April Sapelnikov was the soloist in the Second Piano Concerto, the rest of the programme consisting of the Third Suite, *Sérénade mélancolique* (with Johann Wolf as soloist), *The Tempest*, Slavonic March, Andante cantabile, and some vocal pieces. It was such a resounding success that, as Tchaikovsky himself put it, 'for a few days I drew the attention of the

[50] *TLP*16A, p. 64.

Paris public'.[51] Anxious to escape from the extra personal demands this brought, on 10 April he left for Rouen where he hoped to work on the ballet before embarking from Le Havre eight days later. On the day he arrived Modest had unexpectedly visited him, then equally abruptly returned to Paris and set out for Russia. Ever since leaving his homeland Tchaikovsky's underlying mood had been deeply gloomy and sometimes these feelings had broken to the surface in bursts of longing for his native land and those closest to him. In Rouen he rested somewhat, but the depression continued, and though he struggled to reach the end of Act 1, he finally wrote a long and desperate letter to Vsevolozhsky explaining that the opera and ballet would have to be postponed until the 1892–3 season. This done, he felt a wave of relief. Because there were three more days before embarkation and Rouen was unpleasant, he returned to Paris. From the station he set out for where Sophie Menter and Sapelnikov were staying. Finding himself in the Passage de l'Opéra, he turned into the Cabinet de lecture to glance at the papers from Russia. He picked up a copy of *New Time* and turned to the back page. What he read made him run out of the room as though he had been bitten.

Sasha was dead.

---

[51] *TLP*16A, p. 80; *TPB*, p. 479; *YDGC*, p. 521.

8

AMERICAN TOUR

IN FACT, MODEST already knew of Sasha's death, for on the day Tchaikovsky left for Rouen a telegram had arrived giving him the news. Though he had promptly set out to tell his brother personally, he had found his mood such that he had said nothing lest he should decide there and then to withdraw from the American tour. News like this, Modest reckoned, might be more easily handled amid the distractions of the concerts themselves, just as in 1887 preoccupation with conducting *Cherevichki* had made it easier to cope with the even more unexpected death of their eldest niece, Tanya. Thus he would inform his brother when he had arrived in America. To the question: what had brought him to Rouen, Modest had replied that homesickness was driving him back to Russia and he had come to say goodbye. Confident there were no Russian newspapers in Rouen, he instructed Tchaikovsky's hotel in Paris to forward all correspondence from Russia to the USA, and warned their Russian friends in Paris to write nothing of the matter in letters.

Modest could not, of course, know that his brother would impulsively return to Paris and then by chance stumble upon the information. Having done so, Tchaikovsky must for a long while have wandered the streets, for only much later did he head for where Menter and Sapelnikov were staying. His first reaction was as Modest had anticipated: to cancel everything. But though he had once been close to Sasha and had been especially dependent upon her during the years after his marriage when Kamenka had become his home, they had for a long time been drifting apart. Her ill health, and especially her addictions to drugs and alcohol, had warped her personality and distanced her from most of those once close to her, while his own restored social confidence and the enormous personal respect, even reverence, which he encountered as a musician wherever he went meant that his emotional dependence upon her had now shrunk to nothing. His main thought was for the effect upon her son, Bob; as for himself, it was a terrible shock, but one from which he must have known he would very soon recover. Menter and Sapelnikov gave him a bed for the night, and by next morning he had resolved to go on. Quite apart from his moral and contractual responsibilities, he had bought his ticket and incurred expenditure against a handsome advance. Supported by Menter, Sapelnikov and the young violinist Jules Konyus, who was working in Paris, he left for Rouen, stayed the night, and the next day boarded the steamship, *La Bretagne*, in Le Havre.

Because he thought he might later publish an account of his American venture, he kept a detailed diary of the whole trip from the moment he embarked. His sense of loneliness that evening became still more acute when he discovered that Laroche's wife, whom he had expected to accompany him to America, had not arrived. A young man throwing himself overboard on the first day further depressed him, especially since, as one of the few passengers who could read German, he was asked to decipher what he could of the suicide note. But the ship itself was very big, well appointed ('a real floating palace'[1]), and the food excellent. On the second day the vessel was rocked by 'une mer un peu grosse' (as one waiter had put it). 'But what would it be like if it were très grosse?!!!' Tchaikovsky wondered.[2] He was soon to know. But the calm of the other passengers, mostly seasoned travellers, dispelled his anxieties.

There was also a great variety of things to see and divert him: three huge seagulls following the ship would (he was told) continue all the way to Newfoundland, a large group of Alsatian emigrants organized their own dances to the accompaniment of an accordion, a whale spouted vigorously, and so on. But it was the varying moods and textures of the sea that fascinated him most, and he would go on deck to observe the effect of a sunset or of the moon on the ever-changing surface, or to gaze fascinated at its grandeur when in turmoil. By the third day he was trying to distance himself from all those things that troubled him by concentrating exclusively upon what was happening to him now or going on around him at that very moment. 'By this means I do not feel myself within myself but, as it were, someone else who is sailing across the ocean and living the interests of the moment.' It helped him to cope with one special torment. 'Sasha's death and everything that's painfully linked with thoughts of her seem like memories from a very distant past, which I am trying without particular difficulty to drive away by thinking afresh of the current interests of the one who is not me but who, *within me*, is travelling to America.'[3] That he

[1] *TLP*16A, p. 90; *TZC*3, p. 438; *TPB*, p. 481.
[2] *TLP*16A, p. 92; *TZC*3, p. 439; *TPB*, p. 483.
[3] *TLP*16A, p. 93; *TZC*3, p. 441; *TPB*, p. 484.

could fantasize thus so soon about the loss of an only sister is surely indicative of what that loss really meant to him.

There were some unpleasant things he could not ignore – such as a purse being stolen from his cabin. Even worse, in mid-Atlantic he experienced the sea's darker side – a full-scale storm which rudely shattered his belief that he was immune to seasickness. Another even greater terror awaited him off Newfoundland. A fog enveloped them, the ship slowed, and the roar every half-minute of its siren frayed his nerves further. When he learned that the 'unsympathetic' lady who had been placed beside him at table was the wife of a member of the Boston Symphony Orchestra, he was able to discover a good deal that was useful about American musical life, but he had found nearly all the other first-class passengers 'unusually empty American men and women, very dandified'.[4] The only one of interest was a Canadian bishop with his secretary returning from the Vatican; Tchaikovsky attended a private celebration of mass in his cabin. From the beginning he had discovered much more congenial company among the second-class passengers. It is no surprise that he should have sometimes sought escape in their quarters, for he had a lifelong need of ordinary human beings who were unsophisticated if occasionally individualistic, some-times rough yet still 'sympathetic'. The epitome of this need was, of course, his long-time servant, Alexey. But there were others also – and now it was a motley crew from the second class, necessary to him because he was firmly embedded, by the class division of a trans-Atlantic liner, in a group whose pretensions to style and taste blocked any open manifestation of their more basic humanity.

However, Tchaikovsky's choice of his covert social companions had been neither worthy nor wise. The character at the centre of the group, a travelling salesman he had fallen in with on the way from Rouen, turned out to be a womanizer who quickly engaged in a liaison with another passenger, the rest of the group acting as nursemaids to her baby son when he took her off to his cabin. Another had claimed to be the son of a wealthy cod-fisher in Newfoundland, but in New York he was to solicit money from Tchaikovsky, claiming to have been robbed in Central Park. Tchaikovsky refused his request, suspecting not only that his story of his father's wealth was untrue, but also that he now knew the identity of the thief who had taken his purse.

Yet even when the less salubrious sides of such companions had begun to show themselves, he still kept them company, for they were adept at entertaining themselves, and this diverted him too. Mean-

[4] *ibid.*

while in his own class, after a week at sea, the worst had happened. 'They have got to know who I am, and now various gentlemen constantly approach me and ask: am I so-and-so? After this there begin civilities, compliments, conversations. I have acquired a mass of acquaintances, and now I can't find any place where I can walk alone. Wherever I go there's someone I know who immediately begins to walk alongside me and gets into conversation. In addition they're insisting I play. I'm refusing – but I think I'll have to play something on the bad piano to get rid of them. My only thoughts: when will all this come to an end, and when shall I at last be home again?'[5] Then the ship was struck by a hurricane, and that night he slept wedged between his travelling trunk and the cabin wall. Finally on 25 April they took on the New York pilot. The following day he disembarked and was met by a delegation of five led by Morris Reno,[6] who had charge of the new Music Hall (as Carnegie Hall was called at that time); they piloted him through customs, then took him to his hotel. There to his horror he discovered that Wolf had accepted additional engagements for him of which he knew nothing, and that he would have to remain at least a further week. Begging to be excused any special appointment that evening, he gave way to a flood of tears, changed, and took a stroll up Broadway. He was struck both by the number of negroes on the streets and by the height of some of the buildings ('*nine* [sic] stories!'[7]). Back at the hotel he again relieved his feelings through tears; then, as always happened, he slept excellently. Such outpourings were merely an opening of the emotional safety valve; when the tour was over he would, he admitted to Anatoly and Parasha, recall it with pleasure.

Three things in particular struck him about America. First was the hotel accommodation, with its private bath and water closet, its hot and cold running water, speaking tube and lifts. Americans, he discovered, set great store by material comforts and pleasant living conditions, in which flowers might play a large part; one lady acquaintance was to send him so many to decorate his hotel room that he had to give most away (Americans, he also quickly discovered, never did anything by halves, and everything was on the grandest scale). Second was something he might have foreseen from the intense interest he had aroused among his American fellow-travellers: his fame was already immense. 'Tschaikowsky is here' was the headline to a biographical

---

  [5] *TLP*16A, pp. 95–6; *TZC*3, p. 444; *TPB*, p. 486.

  [6] One of the group was Reno's daughter, Alice, and the distant sight which two journalists caught of her entering the carriage with Tchaikovsky led to a newspaper report that he had arrived with his wife.

  [7] *TLP*16A, p. 97; *TZC*3, p. 446; *TPB*, p. 488.

piece in the *New York Herald* on the day he arrived. Everything that followed confirmed the scale of his reputation. 'It seems that in America I'm *ten times* better known than in Europe,' he wrote to Bob three days later. 'At first when I was told this I thought it was an exaggerated compliment. Now I see it's the truth. There are pieces of mine which they don't yet know in Moscow that here are played several times a season and about which whole articles and commentaries are written (for example, [the fantasy overture,] *Hamlet*).'[8]

Third was the openness of his reception. 'These Americans are amazing!' he noted in his diary after two days. 'Compared with the impression made by Paris, where in every advance, every kindness from a stranger one senses an attempt to exploit, the plain dealing, sincerity, generosity, cordiality without ulterior motive, the readiness to oblige and be nice which you find here is striking and at the same time touching. This and American ways in general, American manners and customs I find very sympathetic.'[9] On his first day he was taken by Reno to meet some of the people most closely involved in his visit: Walter Damrosch, the conductor, and Andrew Carnegie, the émigré Scotsman who was already diverting a portion of his vast wealth into public and philanthropic services, yet who had retained a fundamental simplicity, was still devoted to the folksongs of his homeland, and who immediately won Tchaikovsky's affection because of his enthusiasm for Moscow, which he had visited two years earlier. Then there were two he had already encountered, since they had been part of the dockside welcoming committee. One was Edwin Hyde, president of the New York Philharmonic Society, who conversed with him in a mixture of English, French and German with minute-long pauses between words during which he maintained the most serious yet affable expression; the other was Ferdinand Mayer, a very agreeable German who was the representative of Knabe's piano firm, who took him to be photographed and for a drive in Central Park, and whose assiduous and sustained attentions were such that Tchaikovsky had to remind himself that there was no self-interest involved. When Mayer was not free his associate, William Reinhard, would be sent instead, just to check Tchaikovsky did not need anything. Later Mayer took him to the top of one of the highest buildings ('I refuse to understand how you can live on the thirteenth floor'[10]), then into the treasury vaults where he was allowed to handle a bundle of new notes worth ten million dollars. In

---

[8] *TLP*16A, p. 99; *TZC*3, p. 451; *TPB*, pp. 488–9. In fact, it would be two more years before Moscow would hear *Hamlet*.

[9] *TD*, p. 265; *TZC*3, p. 448.

[10] *TD*, p. 268; *TZC*3, p. 453.

due course he met Gustav Schirmer, founder of the music publishing firm, who was over sixty but looked fifty, and at whose house he was introduced to the noted Wagnerian conductor of the New York Philharmonic Society, Anton Seidl, and to Willy von Sachs, 'a very courteous and elegant gentleman, a lover of music and a writer on it',[11] who lived in a large building reserved entirely for single men, and whose warm personality and knowledge of music made him, of all New Yorkers, the one with whom Tchaikovsky felt most at ease. Sachs was to provide one of the numerous splendid meals arranged specially for him, this one at the Manhattan Club, where each guest had a menu adorned with an excerpt from one of Tchaikovsky's compositions. It proved one of the most memorable social events of his days in New York, for another of those invited was Carl Schurz, who had fled his native Germany after the revolution of 1848 to become one of the most tireless and fearless of campaigners against political corruption in the USA. 'A man truly wise, educated and interesting,'[12] Schurz was much more than just a social activist, and with him Tchaikovsky talked into the early hours about Tolstoy, Turgenev and Dostoyevsky.

The warmth and lavishness of American hospitality in general surprised him. On some occasions he was dined in one of New York's best restaurants, on others entertainment was laid on for him privately. Sometimes its form took him aback, as when one evening at Damrosch's, 'the men alone went to the table, the poor women remaining somewhere nearby'. The cooking on this occasion was native American, 'that is, unusually revolting'.[13] Mostly such events were more comfortably organized. On the evening of his third day the Renos threw a dinner party in his honour. There were still some typically American touches.

The ladies were dressed in gowns as for a ball. The table was completely decked out with flowers. By each lady's place there lay a bouquet, and for the men buttonholes of lilies of the valley which each put into the button hole of his tailcoat when we sat down. Near each lady's setting was a picture of me in an elegant frame. Dinner started at 7.30 and finished exactly on 11. I write this without the slightest exaggeration; such is the custom here. To list all the dishes is impossible. In the middle of dinner ices were served, each in a sort of little box, and with them little slates, each with a slate pencil and

[11] *TD*, p. 266; *TZC3*, pp. 449–50.
[12] *TD*, p. 277; *TZC3*, p. 465.
[13] *TD*, p. 276; *TZC3*, p. 463.

wiper, on which were elegantly written excerpts from my compositions. There and then I had to autograph these slates. The conversation was very lively. I sat between Mme Reno and Mme Damrosch, a
very sympathetic and gracious lady. Opposite me *Carnegie* was sat, a
little old man, the admirer of Moscow and possessor of 40 million
dollars. His resemblance to Ostrovsky is amazing. All the time he
chatted about how we ought to bring one of our choirs *to New York*. At
11 o'clock, tormented by the need to have a smoke and by nausea
from endless eating, I decided to ask Mme Reno whether I might
rise.[14]

As he said some days later after he had lunched with Schirmer, who had
then taken charge of his entertainment for the rest of the day, finally
presenting him and his companion guests each with a bouquet of roses
and sending them home in his own carriage: 'One must be fair to
American hospitality; only amongst us could you meet something
similar.'[15]

Though Carnegie had contributed the hall and Reno was president
of the company which was to run it, the man responsible for
Tchaikovsky's visit was the very young Walter Damrosch, conductor of
the Symphony Orchestra. Tchaikovsky met Damrosch the day after his
arrival at the first rehearsal he was to conduct. As he advanced to greet
the conductor in the new hall the orchestra broke into loud applause,
Damrosch made a brief speech, and there was a second ovation.
Tchaikovsky found both the orchestra and the hall's acoustics excellent. Though there was a similar ovation at the choral rehearsal three
days later, his third rehearsal was a less happy occasion. The desperate
scramble to ensure the hall was ready for its opening meant that there
were workmen everywhere, and the way the orchestra had to be
deployed on stage produced problems of balance. Having played
perfunctorily through the Third Suite and Coronation March, he
passed to the First Piano Concerto but abandoned it halfway through
its first movement because the orchestra seemed tired and the parts
were in disarray. Nevertheless, his contribution to the opening concert
on 5 May went excellently. The event had all the enthusiastic ceremony
that might be expected of an American inauguration; first a speech by
Reno, then a choral rendition by the Oratorio Choir of the 'Old
Hundredth' followed by a eulogy and dedication of the hall by Bishop
Henry C. Potter. 'America' was sung by all present, Damrosch con-

[14] *TD*, pp. 266–7; *TZC*3, p. 450.
[15] *TD*, p. 271; *TZC*3, p. 457.

ducted Beethoven's *Leonora 3* Overture, Tchaikovsky following after the interval with his Coronation March. 'I was received with much noise,' he wrote in his diary. 'The march went excellently. A great success. I heard the rest of the concert from Hyde's box. Berlioz's *Te Deum* is rather tedious; only towards the end did I experience much pleasure. Reno invited me to his home. An impromptu supper. I slept like a dead man.'[16]

The choice of piece had not been Tchaikovsky's but Reno's, who had clearly wanted no more than a token contribution to what was something of a patriotic occasion. As music the march was at best politely received (although one critic, otherwise the greatest enthusiast for Tchaikovsky and his work, described it as 'musical claptrap'). But for the composer, and especially his conducting, there was nothing but praise. 'He seems a trifle embarrassed and responds to the applause by a succession of brusque and jerky bows,' the *New York Herald* reported the following day. 'But as soon as he grasps the baton his self-confidence returns. There is no sign of nervousness about him as he taps for silence. He conducts with the authoritative strength of a master and the band obeys his lead as one man.'[17] 'One of the few first-class composers who have also been great conductors,' was the *Evening Post*'s comment.[18] The rehearsal of the suite the following day ended with an enthusiastic demonstration of approval from the orchestra. But the spotlighting of himself as much as his music had taken its toll. The second concert was on the afternoon of 7 May, his fifty-first birthday. 'Never, I think, have I been so afraid. Is it that here they direct their attention to my exterior, and that in this my shyness reveals itself? However that may be, having endured several painful hours . . . I finally went out, again had an excellent reception, and produced, as they say in today's papers, a sensation. After the suite I sat in Reno's office and gave an interview to some reporters (O these reporters!) . . . I went to the box of Mme Reno who had sent me a mass of flowers, having guessed rightly that it was my birthday. I felt the need to be alone. And so, squeezing my way through the crowd of ladies who were surrounding me in the corridor and staring at me with eyes in which I could not but with pleasure read enthusiastic interest, [and] declining the Reno family's invitation, I rushed home.'[19]

With this performance of the Third Suite audience and critics could

[16] *TD*, p. 273; *TZC3*, pp. 459–60; *YDGC*, p. 525 (partial).
[17] Issue of 6 May. *TD*, p. 273 (in English) and *TZC3*, p. 460 (in Russian), both without final sentence. Quotations from the American press are as printed in Yoffe (E. O.), *Tchaikovsky in America* (New York, 1986).
[18] Issue of 6 May.
[19] *TD*, pp. 274–5; *TZC3*, pp. 461–2; *YDGC*, p. 525 (partial).

at last get the measure of how Tchaikovsky's music sounded when conducted by the composer himself. Never had he received such a batch of notices. 'A marvelous production. . . . Russian music certainly threatens that of Germany,' observed the *Morning Journal*. 'The sensation of the afternoon was Mr Tchaikovsky's Third Suite . . . original, unique, and full of local colour,' added the *Evening Post*. 'Heard yesterday as it was interpreted under the magnetic and magnificent conducting of the composer, it produced an overwhelmingly great effect,' was the *New York World*'s judgement. In fact, Tchaikovsky's conducting made as strong an immediate impression as his music. 'It would be impossible to play badly under such a conductor. Tchaikovsky's leading was a perfect revelation. He inspires his orchestra with his nervous force, and seems to hold every musician at the end of his baton. He roused the audience to a pitch of enthusiasm seldom witnessed,' reported the *Evening Telegram*, while the *Brooklyn Daily Eagle* revealed that his fellow-conductor was beginning to suffer from comparisons: 'a fresh, fascinating work . . . played with a fire which Mr Damrosch was not able to evoke from his orchestra'.[20]

The following day there was both a rehearsal and a concert. Having already had one unsatisfactory and abortive session on the piano concerto, he was the more angry with Damrosch for using up the greater portion of the rehearsal. His part went well, however. The ensuing concert included his setting of the Lord's Prayer from his Nine Sacred Pieces and his own choral arrangement of the 'Legend' from his Sixteen Children's Songs. These were placed between Schütz's 'boring'[21] *The Seven last words of our Saviour* and a 'fine oratorio',[22] *Sulamith*, by Damrosch's late father, Leopold. 'The choruses went well, but if I'd been less confused and agitated they would have gone better,' he decided.[23] Again press comment was unanimously favourable, though he can hardly have been pleased with the similarities some critics detected between his pieces and Schütz's.

His second great triumph came in the afternoon concert on 9 May. It included one of his songs, 'It's both bitter and sweet', and Tchaikovsky himself directing the First Piano Concerto with Adele aus der Ohe as soloist. Tchaikovsky had known nothing of this formidable player before his arrival in America. According to Reno she had been a pupil of Liszt, and four years earlier had arrived in New York penniless. Invited to play one of Liszt's concertos, she had impressed, and since

[20] All issues of 8 May.
[21] *TD*, pp. 270–1; *TZC*3, p. 456; *YDGC*, p. 524.
[22] *TD*, p. 275; *TZC*3, p. 463; *YDGC*, p. 526.
[23] *TD*, p. 275; *TZC*3, p. 462; *YDGC*, p. 526.

then had toured all America and built up considerable wealth. Personal acquaintance had given Tchaikovsky complete confidence in her, and he was surprised at his own calm before the concert. 'My concerto, outstandingly performed by Adele aus der Ohe, went off magnificently. The enthusiasm was such as I have never succeeded in arousing even in Russia. There were endless calls, they cried "Upwards"[sic!], waved their handkerchiefs – in a word, it was clear that I am indeed loved by the Americans. I particularly valued the orchestra's delight in me.'[24]

Though the *New York Times* had some reservations about the orchestra's and soloist's roles in the concerto, it had none about Tchaikovsky's. It was the *New York World* which most fully summarized the feelings which his four concerts had aroused among the musical public.

It is the first time in New York musical history that a European composer of the very highest rank has been specially invited to a musical festival here to produce some of his own works, and Mr Walter Damrosch deserves the sincerest thanks of the New York audiences for enabling them to hear Mr Tchaikovsky, a composer whom he ranks with Brahms and Saint-Saëns but whom we should be inclined to place higher. Some people have even styled the week's cycles a Tchaikovsky Festival.

The festival has in truth been made memorable by Mr Tchaikovsky's appearance at four concerts out of the six, and it is quite certain that if another series of concerts were arranged for the production especially of the works of the Russian guest, that festival would be a great success . . .

The first few bars of the opening 'Andante' [in fact, the opening of the concerto] proclaimed conductor and pianist in rapport . . . Mr Tchaikovsky is possessed of rare magnetism, and it is not surprising that the pianist should have felt this, as she came under the influence and direction of his conducting. He carried her along as he carries the orchestra and as he carries and sways his audiences with his orchestral music.[25]

Tchaikovsky's New York concerts were over – and he was dreadfully tired. There had been scarcely any free moments, and these only when he forcibly extricated himself from the well-intentioned commitments

[24] *TD*, p. 277; *TZC3*, p. 464; *YDGC*, p. 526. In his diary Tchaikovsky wrote 'upwards' in English; Modest translated it into German 'hoch!'.
[25] Issue of 10 May.

and events that others had planned for him. These had been legion. The very generosity of American hospitality had been strain enough, but there were concerts to attend also – a dreadful oratorio, *The Captivity*, by a certain Max Vogrich, presented by an orchestra and chorus of 500 ('I never heard worse or more commonplace music'[26]), and a recital by Charles Santley who, singing arias and romances in English ('very strictly in time, very colourlessly . . . with an English articulation and English squareness'[27]), made little impression. It provided, however, the opportunity to meet one of the most influential of American music critics, Henry Finck, who contributed to the *Evening Post*, and who had already written enthusiastically to Tchaikovsky in Russia about his fantasy overture, *Hamlet*. A performance of Mendelssohn's *Elijah* ('a beautiful, but rather long-winded piece'[28]) created a far better effect, and the inaugural festivities ended with an 'outstanding'[29] account of Handel's *Israel in Egypt*.

Finally there was the endless procession of callers. There were journalists, among them Ivy Ross of the *Morning Journal*, who asked for a statement of his views on Wagner, to which he responded with a brief article which appeared on 3 May. There were other musicians: the Scottish-born pianist and composer, Helen Hopekirk, a product of the Leipzig Conservatoire and Leschetizky, and an enthusiast for Russian music, whose first visit completely drained him ('after she'd left I sat like a statue on the divan for an hour-and-a-half, surrendering to the enjoyment of peace and solitude'[30]), and the London-born pianist, Franz Rummel, whom he had met in Berlin, and who now wanted him to conduct (without fee) at Rummel's own concert on 17 May, and who paid several visits in trying to further this end. There was the Hungarian singer, pianist and composer, Ferencz Korbay ('courteous, interesting'[31]), the composer and pianist, Bruno Klein ('young, very handsome'[32]), a woman pianist called Friend ('with gold fillings'[33]) and a flautist, Eugene Weiner, who seems to have wanted some concert commitment from Tchaikovsky.

And there was the trail of other visitors. Sometimes it demanded all his patience to endure their stay. One couple required to know whether he had composed a fantasy on 'The red sarafan', pointed out that

[26] *TD*, p. 265; *YDGC*, p. 523.
[27] *TD*, p. 272; *TZC3*, p. 458; *YDGC*, p. 524.
[28] *TD*, p. 274; *TZC3*, p. 461; *YDGC*, p. 525.
[29] *TD*, p. 277; *TZC3*, p. 465; *YDGC*, p. 526.
[30] *TD*, p. 267; *TZC3*, p. 452.
[31] *TD*, p. 278; *TZC3*, p. 465.
[32] *ibid.*
[33] *ibid.*

Thalberg had done so, declared that, being Russian, Tchaikovsky must certainly compose one, and promised to send a copy of Thalberg's so that he could remedy this omission. Others unwittingly brought strains of a different kind. One, an old man, who brought a libretto he had written, 'touched me deeply with his account of the death of his only son';[34] another, a lady correspondent of two Russian journals, unwittingly touched a most sensitive end among his already strained nerves. It was the first time during his travels he had talked heart-to-heart with a Russian woman. 'Suddenly tears welled up, my voice began to tremble and I couldn't hold back my sobs. I ran into the next room and didn't emerge for a long time. I burn with shame when recalling this unexpected turn of events.'[35] People from all over America wanted his autograph and he replied conscientiously to every request.

With the concerts on 9 May the inaugural festivities for the new Music Hall were over. The following day Carnegie gave a dinner for the principals in the preceding days' events, and once again Tchaikovsky found himself beside Mrs Damrosch. But it was Carnegie himself whom he most remembered from the event. He had warmed to him more and more during his fortnight in New York, and his admiration for the man who had gone from telegraph boy to become one of the richest men in America had deepened. But it had become a mutual admiration. 'During the whole evening he showed his affection for me in his own unusual way,' Tchaikovsky wrote in his diary. 'He seized my hands, crying that I was the uncrowned, though very real king of music, he embraced me (not kissing me: here men never kiss each other), in expressing my greatness stood on tiptoe and lifted his hands high in the air, and finally threw the whole company into raptures by showing how I conducted. He did this so seriously, so faithfully, so accurately, that I myself was delighted.'[36] At eleven o'clock Reno walked him to his hotel.

'What would I do without Mayer? How would I have obtained for myself the exact ticket I needed, how would I have got to the train, how would I have found out at what time, where, how, and what I had to do?'[37] It had been decided that Tchaikovsky should take a two-day break to visit Niagara Falls, and at eight-fifteen next morning Mayer was duly at his hotel to get him to the station. Mayer had indeed arranged everything, including two people to take charge of him when he changed trains at Buffalo. Most appreciated of all was the small hotel he had booked for him at Niagara, for whereas, once he had left

[34] *TD*, p. 275; *TZC3*, p. 462.
[35] *ibid.*
[36] *TD*, p. 279; *TZC3*, p. 467.
[37] *TD*, p. 280; *TZC3*, p. 467.

New York, all communication had to be in English, at the Hotel Kaltenbach everyone spoke German. Next morning, with no more guide than the driver of his landau with whom he communicated as much in sign language as in English, he crossed the bridge to Goat Island, then descended to where he could see the American side ('the beauty and grandeur of the spectacle is truly amazing'[38]). Resisting the temptation to pick the wild flowers, which was strictly forbidden, he visited Three Sisters Island, viewed the Horseshoe Fall, crossed to the Canadian side, and there summoned up courage to put on protective clothing and go down beneath the falls. He ended his excursion with a trip alongside the river to view the rapids, descending by the funicular railway to spend some time walking by the raging waters. After a meal in his hotel he returned for a last look at this spectacular work of nature, then caught the overnight train.

New York again meant visits and visiting. Damrosch was leaving for Europe; so impressed had he been by Tchaikovsky that, when saying goodbye, he enquired whether he might be prepared to accept him as his pupil. Tchaikovsky declined, of course, but feared afterwards that he had shown all too clearly his horror at the thought of Damrosch coming to his country home. Then Mayer took him across the East River and by train to his own house on the coast. Tchaikovsky endured this as best he could, for he found the Mayer family kind but dull. Next morning it was back again to New York and more visits. Seidl had replied to his attack on Wagner (or, rather, Wagnerism), suggesting that in condemning the Wagner cult Tchaikovsky was tilting at a windmill, then deftly adducing Tchaikovsky's own 'wonderful' Third Suite as evidence that elements of the symphonic and the operatic could be successfully compounded. Ivy Ross wanted a rejoinder from Tchaikovsky, but the time absorbed by other visitors prevented him writing anything, even had he wished to. He now discovered that Mayer's attentiveness had not been entirely unmotivated, for he hoped Tchaikovsky would be prepared to sign a testimonial that Knabe pianos were unquestionably the best in America. Having refused to do this on the grounds that he had insufficient knowledge of the American piano industry, and that he thought Steinway pianos were better anyway, he was collected in the Hydes' carriage to dine. This engaging couple represented what he found both the best and the worst in American life. The meal was interminable, even tastelessly pretentious, but the couple themselves were most open and natural. They could be unaffectedly serious, as when Hyde bowed his head and quietly recited

[38] *TD*, p. 281; *TZC3*, p. 469; *YDGC*, p. 527.

the Lord's Prayer before the meal, catching Tchaikovsky unawares –
but also merry and warm; Hyde, for instance, had obtained a Russian
primer and learned some phrases to throw at their guest, to everyone's
amusement. But it was Mrs Hyde who set the seal upon their welcome;
she insisted that Tchaikovsky 'should smoke a quick cigarette in *her*
drawing room – for an American lady the height of hospitality'.[39] At ten
he left. Again Mayer had taken care of everything. Reinhard was
waiting at his hotel and, shepherding him across the Hudson, saw him
safely settled into the night train to Baltimore.

For a second time Tchaikovsky found himself in a world where only
English was spoken. The concert would be in the Lyceum Theatre; the
players were the travelling Boston Festival Orchestra, good but small
(there were only four first violins, he discovered). Its conductor was the
cellist, Victor Herbert, who was to inspire Dvořák to compose his cello
concerto, and who was later still to make his own reputation as a
composer of operettas. It had already been agreed that the Third Suite
could not be played and would be replaced by the Serenade for Strings,
but no attempt had been made to rehearse it, as Tchaikovsky had been
promised. In consequence, much time had to be devoted to this, and
there was some friction with the players. In the afternoon concert
Adele aus der Ohe again played the First Piano Concerto. While
Tchaikovsky felt there was none of New York's rapture in his reception,
it was probably because the audience was small rather than because
those present were tepid; certainly the two press notices were as
enthusiastic as any in New York. Since Baltimore was the home of
Knabe pianos, the head of the firm, Ernest Knabe, took charge of the
distinguished visitor's entertainment. Knabe's table and cellar were
good, and it was nearly midnight before Tchaikovsky was returned to
his hotel. The following morning Knabe took him on an excursion
through the city ('nice, clean'[40]) and into his piano factory, then to the
Peabody Institute, part of which was a conservatoire impressively
planned and equipped, of which the Danish-born conductor and
composer, Asger Hamerik, was director. After a tour of the establishment, Knabe helped Tchaikovsky pack, then put him on the train to
Washington.

Tchaikovsky's musical appointment in the American capital was at a
soirée in the Russian Embassy that same evening – a diplomatic as
much as a musical event for about one hundred guests, all ambassadors
and their wives and daughters, or high officials. The programme

[39] *TD*, p. 284; *TZC*3, p. 473.
[40] *TD*, p. 286; *TZC*3, p. 475; *YDGC*, p. 528.

comprised Tchaikovsky's Piano Trio and a piano quartet by Brahms, in which the excellent pianist was the Embassy's first secretary. Tchaikovsky found himself far more relaxed at being in an environment where so many were Russian-speaking, with most others of the diplomatic community using French. The official soirée having been rounded off with an excellent supper, the ambassador, who had returned to Washington specially for the event, settled down to host a more intimate gathering which he plied with an equally excellent wine. Though it was three o'clock before Tchaikovsky regained his hotel, he woke next morning with a very pleasant memory of the occasion. Since the performers and programme for his concert in Philadelphia would be the same as in Baltimore, there would be no rehearsal, and he delayed a further day in Washington, lunching with the ambassador, and being taken on a tour of the sights. He visited the Washington Monument and the Capitol, then amused himself playing two-piano works with the first secretary-pianist before passing the evening listening to this amateur virtuoso perform two Beethoven concertos with a good student orchestra.

Tchaikovsky's final appearance as conductor was in Philadelphia on 18 May. The large auditorium of the Academy of Music was well filled, the enthusiasm great. As in so many press notices of his earlier concerts, there was a special interest in the appearance of the man himself. In America there was no escaping such scrutiny, and he probably found the observations in the *Daily Evening Telegraph* the next day the least offensive of all those offered, once he had passed the first two sentences. The notice is also, one suspects, the most objective assessment of his conducting:

He looks like a broker and clubman[41] rather than an artist. He seems to be rising sixty, but is well preserved and active. He is of middle height, slim, erect, with silvery gray hair and beard, florid complection, and small but piercing and expressive blue eyes: a self-contained and dignified personage, not without grace, but clearly giving no attention to stage niceties – altogether an attractive personality, if somewhat disconcerting to those who expected a more pronounced Slavic type, such as Rubinstein. It was agreeable to see the way in which he assumed that the great audience had not assembled to do him personal honour, but to hear certain pieces of music in which he was merely concerned with the interpretation. He

---

[41] The same day (19 May) a second Philadelphia paper, the *North American*, had written 'more like a prosperous merchant or a United States Senator'.

conveyed this idea without affectation, nor too much of brusqueness.
Taking up the baton without delay, he ceased at once to be the guest,
and was but one of a company of artists engaged in performing to a
Philadelphia audience. His work at the desk . . . showed good, if not
remarkable, powers as a conductor.

He had a firm grasp of the subject at all times, and one felt the
confidence of the players, that there was no instant of wavering or
uncertainty. In leading, Mr Tchaikovsky looks minutely, perhaps
too much so, after all the details of entrance and expression, but there
are no special points to be noted in his manner, unless it be the
peculiarity of beating from the wrist rather than with the full arm –
not an invariable custom, of course, but frequent with him. . . . Both
works were given with a delightful precision which yet did not
interfere with their strange and original rhythms.

The concert over, Tchaikovsky was very soon on the train to New
York. There remained one commitment: a concert of his works to be
mounted by the Composers' Club the next day in the assembly rooms of
the Metropolitan Opera House. Having slept till nine after his early
morning return, he received visitors, answered further innumerable
letters requesting his autograph, and agreed the wording of his letter of
recommendation for Knabe pianos. The remainder of the day was
spent with Adele aus der Ohe and the Renos above the Hudson River at
the summer residence of George Holls, a lawyer and patron of music.
The beautiful and tranquil environment and the easy company – above
all, the knowledge that tomorrow he would be embarked and on his
way home – sustained him cheerfully through the day. His first task
next morning was sad: to tell the elderly librettist that he would not be
setting his work. Then he had to attend a rehearsal of his Piano Trio
and Third Quartet in preparation for the evening concert. There were
formal farewells to Mrs Reno and her daughters, who heaped gifts upon
him, and to Mrs Hyde, then a splendid dinner of gratitude for Mayer
and Reinhard. The evening programme devoted entirely to his music
included a number of his songs, some of which were excellently done. In
the middle there was a speech addressed to him. He replied in French,
received an ovation, and a lady threw a bouquet of roses which hit him
full in the face. Afterwards there were many people to talk with, many
autographs to sign. At last with Reno, Mayer and Reinhard he escaped
to his hotel, packed, and shared in two bottles of champagne. Finally he
said goodbye to the hotel staff.

Throughout his three-and-a-half weeks in America there had been
the customary laments at the pressures upon him, the usual longing for

solitude, and the inevitable yearning for his native land and those close to him. But it had been in fact an exciting, immensely heartwarming experience. If Tchaikovsky needed reassurance about the worth of his music and its universal power to address and deeply excite those who would listen, then the reception he had enjoyed both as public celebrity and private guest had afforded this in abundance. And for a man who cherished the best that human affection and goodwill could provide, there would long be memories of the kindnesses shown to him. Some things puzzled him. Any society compounded from such a diversity of races as had formed the growing millions that were called Americans was bound to be filled with contradictions. Walking along Broadway on May Day, he encountered a gathering of five thousand socialists with banners proclaiming that they were slaves in free America, and objected to working more than eight hours a day. 'Yet all this demonstration seemed to me like some sort of buffoonery,' he reflected, 'and it seemed the native inhabitants viewed it in that way also, judging from how few showed curiosity and from how the public moved on as on a normal weekday.'[42] Against such a startling (to a Russian) evidence of a free society he found even more intolerable and hypocritical those 'remnants of English puritanism which manifest themselves in such stupid trifles as, for instance, only being able on Sundays to get a glass of *whisky* or *beer* by deceit. . . . It is said that the legislators responsible for this law in New York State are the most terrible drunkards.'[43] It was a small blemish on a great and very human society. Having bade farewell to his 'dear American friends',[44] he remained in his cabin to sleep, emerging as the *Fürst Bismarck* passed the Statue of Liberty. In his baggage was a model of this symbol of freedom presented to him by Mayer and Ernest Knabe. How, he continued to wonder, would he manage to get such a thing past the borders of his native land?

The return voyage was made in a frame of mind very different from that in which he had come nearly a month earlier. The thought that soon he would be home, the self-assurance he had built up in his relationships with the kinds of persons, especially Americans, who were to be encountered on such liners, his increased facility with the English language all produced a mood in which he needed fewer external distractions – though this time he could not have escaped into the company of ordinary beings even if he had wished, for there were no emigrants on board. Yet during the first few days he did not find even the sight of the sea enticed him. In fact, he was briefly in a mood to

[42] *TD*, p. 269; *TZC*3, p. 454.
[43] *TD*, p. 279; *TZC*3, p. 466.
[44] *TD*, p. 290; *TZC*3, p. 480.

begin thinking up ideas for a new symphony. His cabin, which he had rented from one of the ship's officers at an extortionate price, was excellent, as were both the cuisine and the service. In the morning when no one was about he could go into the saloon where there was an excellent Steinway piano and a presentable collection of music, including some of his own pieces. There was also a tolerable sixteen-man orchestra on board made up of stewards from the second class, though the selection of music they played was poor. There being so few third-class passengers, he could wander freely around the lower deck when he wanted to escape unwanted attentions. Since the ship, which was only on its second voyage, had made the outward crossing in six-and-a-half days, some two less than *La Bretagne*, his morale was raised yet further. But on the third day out the weather deteriorated, and for two days they were caught in a storm which Tchaikovsky endured miserably in his cabin with everything, including his trunk, rolling from one corner to the other. By the time it had abated his composure had disintegrated, and he felt again that all-too-familiar aversion to his fellow-passengers. Yet it quickly passed. That night, little more than a day off Southampton, he went on deck.

> It was a wonderful, calm, moonlit night. Having had my fill of reading in my cabin, I walked for a long while on deck. It was amazingly pleasant. Everyone without exception was asleep, and of the three hundred passengers in the first class I was the only one to go out and admire the night. The beauty was indescribable: you could not convey it in words. It's strange now to recall the terrible night of Sunday. . . . That night I promised myself I'd never travel the sea again. But my steward, *Schreber*, says that every time there's bad weather he promises himself he'll give up serving on a steamship, and every time he returns to harbour he longs for the sea and is bored without it. Perhaps it'll be like that with me also . . . There is some talk among the passengers of *a concert* today, and they're pestering me to play. It's this that poisons a sea voyage; it's the obligatory society of passengers.[45]

The following morning the appearance of fishing boats signalled the approach to land. After steaming along the English coast ('in some places rocky and picturesque, in others level, covered with fresh green grass'[46]), at two a.m. the ship called in at Southampton. Next day he

[45] *TD*, p. 293; *TZC3*, pp. 484–5.
[46] *TD*, p. 293; *TZC3*, p. 485.

watched a splendid sunrise, then spent much of the morning on deck admiring the English coast and the great number of ships, both steam and sailing. As they passed Folkestone and Dover and entered the North Sea, it became rougher. At eight the following morning they disembarked at Cuxhaven. By midday their train had arrived in Hamburg. Passing through Berlin, on 1 June he was in St Petersburg.

On 24 May, when Tchaikovsky was already in mid-Atlantic, the *New York Herald* took a final look at his visit. Its roll of honour is a curious one; nevertheless this afterthought evidences the depth of the impression he had made.

If we were to count up all the men and women of genius now adorning the world how long would that list be?

Should we be able to name twelve or ten or six such people? Men whose claim to the high honor would not be disputed by even the most skeptical and cold?

Let us try.

To head the list we should, of course, have Bismarck. Then might come Edison and Tolstoy, Sarah Bernhardt and perhaps Ibsen, with Herbert Spencer and two great composers – Dvořák and Tchaikovsky. The right of Tchaikovsky to a place on the roll will hardly, we think, be denied. He has that noblest of gifts – the gift creative. His works have unquestionable strength, originality and poetry.

The genius has been within our gates – has been here, indeed, for three weeks or more. And how have we shown our recognition of his presence? How have we honored this great Russian composer?

We have made much of such bright but far less wondrous lights, of actresses and artists of mere talent. But, apart from one reception and a few rounds of applause, we fail to see that public tribute or that private honor New York paid to Tchaikovsky.

Tchaikovsky is a modest, unassuming man. But no genius is unconscious of his genius.

What impression of New York will he take back to Europe, where his name is both a glory and a power?

9

DOUBLE BILL:

THE NUTCRACKER AND IOLANTA

In an interview given shortly before the première of *Iolanta* in December 1892, Tchaikovsky recalled when his interest had first been aroused in the subject of what was to prove his last opera:

'Eight [in fact, nine] years ago one of the *Russian Messenger*'s booklets containing the one-act play by the writer Henrik Hertz, entitled (in F. Müller's translation) *King René's daughter*, came into my hands. This subject enchanted me because of its poetical quality, originality, and abundance of lyrical moments. That was when I promised myself that some time I would set it to music. Because of a variety of obstacles it was only last year that I was able to carry out this resolve.'[1]

Five years later, in May 1888, Hertz's drama had been given a single performance in Moscow. Tchaikovsky saw it, promptly encountered Vsevolozhsky, and may there and then have agreed in principle to make an opera out of it.[2] The firm decision that he should compose not only a one-act opera but a two-act ballet for the Imperial Theatres in St Petersburg was made towards the end of 1890 as a result of further pressure from Vsevolozhsky. The librettist of the opera was to be Modest, who would base his work on Vladimir Zotov's translation of the Danish dramatist's play, while the ballet, *The Nutcracker*, founded upon E. T. A. Hoffmann's *Nussknacker und Mausekönig* in the version by Dumas *père*, would be devised by Petipa. Tchaikovsky's first efforts were directed into the ballet. He had become acquainted with Hoffmann's tale in 1882, but there is no evidence he had then considered it a possible subject for a stage piece, and it is clear that only Vsevolozhsky's persuasions now made him accept it. The first news that he had started composition was given to Modest on 9 March 1891, when he admitted that he was now becoming reconciled to the subject.

---

[1] *TMKS*, p. 368; *DTC*, pp. 219–20.

[2] Tchaikovsky's letter of 9 March 1890 to Désirée Artôt mentions 'a Russian opera, the libretto of which I've had for two years, and which I've given my word of honour to compose. And they want me to do another ballet'. (*TLP*15B, p. 74; *TTP*, p. 374).

But not entirely: though he composed a little on the journey to Berlin, his main thought was to get *The Nutcracker* out of the way so that he could set about *Iolanta*. By now much of Act 1 was sketched, and though no further work was possible in Paris, that act may have been finished during his five days in Rouen and a beginning was made upon Act 2. But the shock of his sister's death stunned totally his already unwilling capacity 'to reproduce Confiturenburg in music',[3] and nothing could be added during the American tour. The sketches were completed at Maidanovo on 6 July.

Though initially Tchaikovsky felt no greater satisfaction in the finished work than while it had been in progress, rating it far inferior to *The Sleeping Beauty*, he was within a month viewing it more favourably. By now he had turned his attention to the opera. Before beginning he had felt much ambivalence towards this story of the blind daughter of 'good King René' of Provence,[4] whose road to cure is opened by the force of love operating within her. Sometimes he felt drawn to it and believed it could be a masterpiece, at others he hated it, the prospect of setting it becoming a nightmare. When composition was started on 22 July, work went sluggishly for three weeks, even though Tchaikovsky had begun with the passage that most attracted him – the love scene, which he considered his brother had done 'excellently . . . But,' he continued, 'I don't think I've managed it particularly well; what's most sickening is that I'm beginning to fall into repeating myself, and a lot of this scene has come out like *The Enchantress*??!! Nevertheless, we'll see,' he added[5] – and, indeed, within days his mood had changed. 'I'm already writing the scene between *the king* and Ebn-Hakia,' he could tell Modest on 19 August. 'Then I shall only have to compose the scene where Robert and Vaudemont arrive and waken Iolanta. The duet itself and everything else is already composed. For several days now, once I'd settled down, I've been writing without effort and with enjoyment.'[6] He dared to believe that the flower duet and lullaby near the opera's opening had come out well.

Because of family visits to Ukolovo and Kamenka, *Iolanta* was not finished until 16 September. The scoring of the symphonic ballad, *The Voyevoda*, delayed that of the opera, but by 6 November this also had been completed, though the introduction was not done until December. In early February 1892 he returned to *The Nutcracker*, orchestrating first

---

[3] *TLP*16A, p. 88; *TZC*3, p. 437; *TPB*, p. 481.

[4] Another of René's daughters, Margaret of Anjou, became queen to Henry VI of England.

[5] *TLP*16A, p. 186; *TZC*3, p. 496; *TPB*, p. 497; *DTC*, p. 216; *YDGC*, p. 533.

[6] *TLP*16A, p. 190; *TZC*3, p. 501; *TPB*, p. 499; *DTC*, p. 216; *YDGC*, p. 534 (partial).

those numbers which would go into the suite he had devised to replace a second performance of *The Voyevoda*, which by now he had disowned. He conducted the suite at an RMS concert in St Petersburg on 19 March, though a further sixteen days' work remained before the entire ballet was scored.

During the remainder of 1892 he was heavily occupied in correcting the various versions of both works for the press, for the full scores would be issued ahead of their premières (the first time this had happened with any of his operas or ballets), and besides these there were the orchestral parts, the ballet's piano score (prepared by Taneyev – though because it was difficult Tchaikovsky himself also devised a second, simpler version), the opera's vocal score (also Taneyev's work, but unsatisfactorily printed so that it had to be revised and reissued), and the solo piano version (abominably done by Langer). There were also the needs of foreign musicians to consider, especially since the opera was already scheduled for productions in Hamburg and Schwerin, and one edition of the vocal score was to print a German translation.

In *Iolanta*, as in *The Queen of Spades*, the Figners were to sing leading roles, and during October at Nikolay's request Tchaikovsky composed an additional aria for him to sing ahead of the love duet. The premières of both works took place on 18 December, Nápravník conducting *Iolanta* and Riccardo Drigo *The Nutcracker*. The Hamburg production of the opera opened sixteen days later with Mahler conducting, followed after three further days by that in Schwerin. Both opera and ballet enjoyed huge success with the St Petersburg audience, and the staging was magnificent – in the case of the ballet almost too much so, Tchaikovsky concluded, for the splendour wearied the eyes. Gennady Kondratyev, chief producer at the Maryinsky, left a brief private account of the reception given the opera, which was performed first. 'At the beginning the aria for Medea [Figner, singing the name part, and] both women's choruses were warmly applauded . . . Serebryakov [the king] also sang his aria excellently . . . Medea and [Nikolay] Figner created a furore in the duet and, at the audience's insistence, repeated it. The whole opera produced the most favourable impression, and at the end Tchaikovsky, Nápravník and all the performers were called out many times.'[7] But though Modest also vouched for the opera's enthusiastic reception, he felt it was more a *succès d'estime*, while Rimsky-Korsakov, who had attended the dress rehearsal, had already damned it privately. He was in no mood to be favourable, for his own opera-

[7] *DTC*, p. 221.

ballet, *Mlada*, had had its indifferent première in the same theatre on
1 November, without the benediction of the Tsar's attendance at the
dress rehearsal, or performers as popular as the Figners to inflame
interest. Years later in his memoirs Rimsky was scathing, judging
Iolanta 'one of Tchaikovsky's weakest works. In my view everything in
the opera is unsuccessful – from the barefaced borrowings, like that of
the melody of Rubinstein's "Open my dungeon cell", to the orchestration, which Tchaikovsky did this time somehow the wrong way round;
the music suitable for the strings was entrusted to the wind and vice
versa, so that sometimes it actually sounded fantastic in thoroughly
inappropriate places (for instance, in the introduction, written for some
reason for wind instruments alone).'[8]

The press concurred. Modest summarized its reactions without
sparing himself.

> Everyone condemned the librettist, some for his bad verses, some
> for his prolixity. Everyone voted the opera's music weak ('in it
> Tchaikovsky repeats himself'), two thirds reiterated the phrase 'it
> has entwined no new laurel in the composer's wreath', and three
> quarters reproached it for filching a theme from Rubinstein for the
> duet of Vaudemont and Iolanta. To take them individually: M. M.
> Ivanov in *New Time* found that '[this time unfortunately the com-
> poser's melodic inspiration was far below its usual level.] Essentially
> *Iolanta*, with the exception of a couple of choral numbers, reveals
> itself as a collection of one- and two-voice romances, not to be
> considered particularly successful', Mr Baskin in the *St Petersburg
> Gazette* that, while *The Queen of Spades* is surely a weak repeating of
> *Onegin*, of *Iolanta* 'it would be saying a lot not to say that it was three steps
> backwards', Mr Domino in the *Stock Exchange Gazette* that it was 'a
> piece of craft work which could not pretend to artistic significance',
> Mr Weimarn in *Son of the Fatherland* that 'the opera is tiresomely long,
> the musical images of the characters are tediously sketched, and
> there are no new, fresh creative ideas in it'.[9]

Happily, the press was far less single-minded about Tchaikovsky's
share in *The Nutcracker*. There had been serious problems during

---

[8] Rimsky-Korsakov (N.A.), *Letopis moyei muzïkalnoy zhizni* (9th ed.) (Moscow, 1982),
p. 235. Quoted in *DTC*, p. 220. Ironically, Tchaikovsky was to express considerable
admiration for *Mlada*, the more surprising since he personally found no attraction in the
form of 'opera-ballet'.

[9] *TZC*3, pp. 579–80. The portion in square brackets is from the fuller quotation of
Ivanov's criticism in *DTC*, pp. 221–2.

preparations, for Petipa, who was to have been responsible for devising
and mounting the choreography, fell ill, and the task of completing this
devolved upon the second ballet-master, Lev Ivanov, who seems to
have been an excellent artisan thoroughly at home with formal dancing, but lacking in imagination and inventiveness where mime was
involved. The children's scenes, Modest remembered – and especially
the battle between the mice and the toys – were disastrous. In addition
Antonietta Dell'Era, who danced the Sugar Plum Fairy, was a good
technician but unattractive and overweight. Faced with the consequences of all this, and with the radically differing viewpoints of the
balletomane and the music critic, the press divided sharply, contradictions often appearing in the same paper. 'For instance,' Modest
continued, 'in one number of *New Time* it was said: "The music of
Nutcracker is much more interesting than that of *Iolanta*", while in
another a balletomane wrote that *Nutcracker* is much worse than *Iolanta*,
that the first act is "heavy and wooden", and the second "consists of
bits – true, delightful as sound, but making no overall impression".
[Yet] in a third issue of that same paper a balletomane wrote: "There
are so many brilliant pages in the score of the ballet that it would take'
too long to list them".'[10] One paper pronounced *The Nutcracker* second
only to *Onegin* among Tchaikovsky's works, another that it was a hack
piece unworthy of him; a third judged it an unqualified masterpiece of
scoring and fantasy, while a fourth found only boredom in it.

Though the first few nights of *Iolanta* and *Nutcracker* were given to full
houses, their success was not maintained, and in January 1893, after
eleven performances, they were withdrawn, never to be heard again in
Russia in the composer's lifetime.

The story of *The Nutcracker* as presented in Tchaikovsky's ballet
is summarized in the libretto printed in *Yezhegodnik imperatorskikh
teatrov* (1892–3).[11] The libretto's content is not comprehensive;
supplementations are provided in square brackets.

---

[10] *TZC3*, p. 580; *DTC*, p. 261 (partial).

[11] As printed in Vol. 13B of the Tchaikovsky Complete Edition (*Polnoye sobraniye
sochineny* (Moscow/Leningrad, 1940–71)). As with *The Sleeping Beauty*, this summary
version has been chosen since it supplements the more detailed accounts of the plot
printed in the appendices to Wiley (R. J.), *Tchaikovsky's ballets* (Oxford, 1985). In
addition to a translation of the first edition of the libretto (St Petersburg, 1892), Wiley
prints in full Petipa's instructions to Tchaikovsky regarding the kind of music required,
as well as Petipa's ballet-master's plan. There are numerous differences of detail
between these various versions, and also the rubrics in the score. In the last, for
instance, midnight strikes after Clara has re-entered the deserted room.

ACT I, SCENE I. *A hall in the house of the president, Silberhaus,* [Scène (No. 1)] where relatives and guests are preparing a luxuriously decorated Christmas tree for the children. The Silberhaus's children, Clara (Marie) and Fritz, and also their little guests, who are let into the room, feast their eyes on the brilliant spectacle, receive presents that have been prepared for them [Marche (No. 2)], prance and dance around [Petit galop (No. 3)] with the playthings they have been given. The general liveliness increases with the arrival of new guests who, dressed up as 'Incroyables' and 'Merveilleuses', perform a dance corresponding to the character of what they are representing: dandies of the time of the French Revolution.

[Scène dansante (No. 4)] As the last stroke of the clock indicates midnight Drosselmeyer, Clara's godfather, enters the hall and presents the children with four large mechanical dolls representing a sutler, a little soldier, Harlequin and Columbine. When they have been wound up with a key the dolls move mechanically, turn round and round, and dance. The children are in raptures [Scène et danse Grossvater (No. 5)], but Silberhaus, fearing for the safety of these expensive presents, orders them to be taken off into his study.

Wishing to console Clara and Fritz, who are upset, Drosselmeyer gives them from his pocket a very odd doll, a Nutcracker, and shows them how to make it work. Fritz takes the plaything from Clara and makes the Nutcracker crack the largest nuts, because of which he breaks his jaw. Clara picks up the abandoned Nutcracker, binds up his head, rocks him while dancing a 'polka-berceuse', and lays him in her favourite doll's bed. At Silberhaus's invitation all the guests, big and little, dance the old Grossvatertanz, at the end of which [Scène (No. 6)] Mrs Silberhaus reminds her husband that it is already late and time the children went to bed. Clara wants to take the Nutcracker with her but her father refuses. The children are taken out. The guests say goodbye to their hosts and gradually disperse.

For a while the hall remains empty. As soon as everything in the house is quiet, Clara, who is worried about the sick Nutcracker, decides to pay him a visit and enters the darkened hall. Rustling, scurrying, and the scratching of mice beneath the floor rivet Clara to the spot. [On the clock she sees Drosselmeyer like a great owl.] From chinks under the cornices a great many twinkling lights are seen, the room is filled with mice, and a petrified Clara runs to the sick Nutcracker's bed, seeking refuge there. The moon shines through the window, the Christmas tree grows by degrees and reaches gigantic proportions, the toys and playthings come to life. [Scène: la bataille (No. 7)] Hares sound the alarm, the sentry in his box presents arms and fires, the dolls flee in terror, waving their arms, seeking some place to hide. A detachment of gingerbread soldiers appears and falls into ranks. The hostile army of mice begins to advance, driving back the gingerbread soldiers and, gaining total victory, return with their spoils – lumps of gingerbread, which they devour on the spot.

The Nutcracker, seeing the failure of the gingerbread army, quickly jumps out of bed and orders the hares without delay again to sound the alarm. Lids fly off boxes in which tin soldiers lie, and riflemen, grenadiers, hussars and artillery men with brass cannon quickly slide out of them.

The Mouse King orders his army to renew their assault. Several times the mice attack the enemy but retreat with heavy casualties. Then the Mouse King steps forward for single combat with the Nutcracker. Clara, seeing the danger threatening her favourite, takes a shoe from her foot and hurls it with all her force at [the back of] the Mouse King. The Nutcracker wounds his enemy who saves himself by flight, together with his subjects. The Nutcracker, who has turned into a handsome prince, falls on his knees before Clara and begs her to follow him. They go towards the Christmas tree and disappear among its branches.

ACT 1, SCENE 2. [Scène (No. 8)] *The hall is transformed into a dense pine wood in winter.*
In great flakes snow begins to fall and a snowstorm rises. The entire corps de ballet, representing snowflakes, perform the big dance (Valse des flocons de neige (No. 9)), at the end forming picturesque groups like snowdrifts. Gradually the storm subsides and the winter landscape is illumined by the soft light of the moon, beneath which the snow sparkles like diamonds.

ACT 2. *Confiturenburg, the Palace of Sweets.* [Scène (No. 10)]
The Sugar Plum Fairy with Prince Coqueluche (Orgeat) are standing in a sugar kiosk (pavilion) decorated with dolphins, from whose mouths gush fountains of currant syrup, orangeade, lemonade, and other refreshing and sweet drinks. Awaiting the arrival of Clara and the Nutcracker Prince and preparing to greet them, the Sugar Plum Fairy and Prince Coqueluche leave their kiosk. The fairies of melodies, flowers, pictures, fruits, dolls, nights, dancers and dreams, and also sweets – caramel, barley sugar, chocolate, petits fours, nougat, mint cakes, dragée, pistachio and macaroons, picturesquely grouped – bow before her, and silver soldiers salute her.

[Scène (No. 11)] The major-domo, noting the approach of the expected guests, arranges the little Moors and pages, who have heads of pearls, trunks of rubies and emeralds, and legs of pure gold; they hold flaming torches. Clara and the Nutcracker float quietly along the river in a gilded nutshell. When they step onto the bank the silver soldiers salute, and the little Moors, in costumes made from iridescent humming-bird feathers, take Clara by the hand and carefully help her disembark.

The sugar kiosk on the rose-coloured river begins gradually to melt in the hot rays of the sun and finally disappears; the fountains stop gushing. The Sugar Plum Fairy with Prince Coqueluche and the princesses, the Nutcracker's sisters, meet the new arrivals; the suite respectfully bows, and the major-domo welcomes the Nutcracker Prince on his safe return to the Castle of Confiturenburg. The Nutcracker, touched by his reception, leads Clara by the hand and presents her to his sisters, explaining that it is to her alone that he is indebted for his miraculous rescue. The Sugar Plum Fairy orders the major-domo to begin the festivity, and herself withdraws with Prince Coqueluche and her suite so that the gaiety may not be inhibited.

A varied Divertissement (No. 12) begins. There are dances – chocolate (Spanish dance), coffee (Arabian dance), tea (Chinese dance), clowns (Danse des bouffons [Trépak]), sugar candies (Danse des mirlitons), polichinelles with Mère Gigogne, and others [Valse des fleurs (No. 13)]. At the end the

Sugar Plum Fairy appears with her suite and Prince Coqueluche, and herself takes part in the dances [Pas de deux (No. 14); this includes the so-called Dance of the Sugar Plum Fairy].

Clara is in raptures from all that is going on, and the Nutcracker Prince, radiant with joy that he is able to please his deliverer, tells her about the fairy-tale wonders of the Kingdom of Sweets.

The ballet's apotheosis [Valse finale (No. 15)] represents a huge beehive with bees flying round it, vigilantly guarding their riches.

Why Tchaikovsky should ever have let himself be persuaded to accept this tale as the subject for a ballet is bewildering. Both *Swan Lake* and *The Sleeping Beauty* had been dramatically meaty and deeply serious, the former, for all its decorative fat, moving through a series of super-naturally plausible incidents to a heartrendingly human conclusion, the latter lean and shapely, its end a justifiable, even essential consum-mation of a mythical tale that had suggested cycles of experience sensed less by the conscious mind than by some intuition deep within the human psyche. By contrast the story of *The Nutcracker* was not merely trite; it was pointless. Why on earth a young girl should, for a mild act of sentimental unselfishness and the heroic deed of hurling her shoe at the back of an unsuspecting mouse, be rewarded by the grossest offering of glitter and candy beggars comprehension. And since the piece leads to no true culmination, what was it all about anyway? *The Nutcracker* is meaningless in the profoundest sense.

Some, of course, will think this judgement too harsh. Yet the fact remains that *The Nutcracker* is the most inconsequential in all Tchaikovsky's mature theatrical pieces, and its dramatic structure the least satisfactory. The more to be admired, therefore, is Tchaikovsky's lively and fluent response to any dramatic potential within separate incidents and to any evocative suggestions within individual details. Indeed, given the appalling limitations of his subject, he did a remark-able job, and the fact that his part seems to have been accepted pretty well as it stood suggests that his collaborators thought so too. The one excision, made while his music was still only sketched, concerned dramatic structure. Vsevolozhsky, it seems, had invented the scenario, Petipa adapting it in great detail to the conventions of ballet, and Tchaikovsky working from the ballet-master's very precise prescrip-tions, which he followed respectfully though not slavishly. The dis-agreement had been between Vsevolozhsky and Petipa, for the latter had included a suite of five national dances and a coda to follow upon the March early in Act 1, and these were still in the initial plan from which Tchaikovsky worked at Frolovskoye before leaving for Paris and his American tour. No doubt the precedent Petipa had in mind was the Pas de six from the Prologue of *The Sleeping Beauty*. But while those variations could be dramatized as the good fairies' presentations of gifts to the infant princess, there was no such justification to be found here, and Vsevolozhsky vetoed this decorative insertion as representing an old-fashioned conception of what ballet should be; in his view such things should be confined (as in *The Sleeping Beauty*) to the final act (where the Spanish and Chinese Dances and a tarantella were indeed to find a haven). In any case they would have been danced by children from the theatre school, who were to be used to the full in this first act, and they would therefore have had to be limited in their technical demands and be correspondingly less effective. Certainly the excision of these miniature dances unclogged the momentum of Act 1, but it also exacerbated a fundamental flaw: that Act 1 was now almost exclusively dramatic, Act 2 very largely decorative, with only two characters, the Nutcracker-cum-Prince and Clara, appearing in both.

Yet, all this being said, the bulk of Tchaikovsky's music for the first act of *The Nutcracker* is a splendid achievement. The only large pure dance movement is the concluding waltz; for the rest, the most substantial is the brief dance engineered by Silberhaus to cut short his children's din, and employing the seventeenth-century Grossvatertanz (best known from Schumann's use of it in both *Papillons* and *Carnaval*). The overture establishes the ballet's musical world, its truncated sonata form exactly that of the 'Mozartean' entr'acte-plus-first-chorus of the ballroom scene in *The Queen of Spades*; its orchestra is classical in complement with only piccolo and triangle added, Tchaikovsky enhancing its textural fineness and rococo brightness by dispensing with cellos and basses and dividing violins and violas into six parts.

But this music is not eighteenth-century pastiche. Rather, it is Tchaikovsky's equivalent of the '*Magic Flute* idiom' – childlike, perfectly contained and controlled, elegant, enchanting the ear. Yet because the style is Tchaikovsky's own there is no wrench when the curtain rises and he raids his bottomless fund of *dansante* music to establish the mood, set the action moving, and provide a generalized background against which the excitement of the children's reactions can be projected. Though the March (No. 2) does produce a moment of musical stasis, there is an abundance of stage mime in the third number, with its children's galop, entry of more parents in fancy dress (to a lively minuet – the one brief moment in the score where a rococo idiom does assert itself), and resumption of the children's boisterous gaiety (for which Petipa specified the eighteenth-century tune, 'Bon voyage, cher Dumollet'). The swiftness of these events pushes the pace yet harder, before it is halted by the entry of Drosselmeyer.

The invention that characterizes Drosselmeyer (Ex. 274a) is inspired – bizarre yet not really frightening, its grotesquerie springing not only from its slightly eccentric melodic features but from its inventive harmonic manoeuvring within the clearest of G major pitch collections, and especially from its implacable evasion of the tonic chord till near the end. Drosselmeyer is a being who is never hedged in, is unfailingly resourceful, always free to act and to manipulate events; the momentary intrusion of the six-note Fate theme at the end (*x* in Ex. 274a) is

Ex. 274

a.   Andantino

b.   **Più andante**

c.   **Allegro molto vivace**

d.   **Allegro giusto**

perhaps pointed. His theme's chameleon capacity is reinforced by the variety of striking, though always simple orchestral combinations through which it is heard. Introduced on violas accompanied by trombones and tuba, it is then heard again on mildly raucous bassoon and bass clarinet with cello and double bass support. It can also redirect itself, softening its outlines as Drosselemeyer's presents are brought in (Ex. 274b), and adopting the reassuring manners of the waltz to make itself engagingly agreeable as, grinning, the ugly god-father makes his presentation (Ex. 274c). But though Drosselmeyer's is the most striking character theme in *The Nutcracker*, we should not disregard the brief representation of Harlequin and Columbine (Ex. 275) – Italian commedia dell'arte dolls perhaps, but thoroughly Russianized in their elementally energetic projection[12] – as Stravinsky was to remember when he devised the Infernal Dance for Kashchey and his subjects in *The Firebird*.

Ex. 275

Yet this theme, like almost all the others in *The Nutcracker*, is heard only once, for the plot provided few opportunities for recurrence. The beginning of Drosselmeyer's emblem appears in its final guise as Clara approaches the Nutcracker's bed (Drosselmeyer's face is about to be seen on the clock (see Ex. 274d)), and some of the following battle music is re-run in Act 2 as the Prince tells his sisters how Clara had

[12] In Petipa's ballet-master's plan these were also described as 'un diable et une diablesse'; see Wiley, *op. cit.*, p. 377.

saved him.[13] But that is about all. Nor is the tonal organization of more
than intermittent interest. That the whole ballet is consciously built
upon a tritonal arch, beginning and ending in B flat, with E major
concluding Act 1 and opening Act 2, might suggest otherwise, but the
planning of the intervening keys contains nothing that might brace this
span. There is perhaps more tonal purpose in Act 2. Initially that
purpose is colouristic, the key shifting from an E major opening to E flat
by the end of the Prince's narration, then becoming more structural as
it climbs back to A major through the six dances of the Divertissement
(though with an arresting jump between B flat and G in the centre), but
at the ballet's end suddenly plunging colouristically from D to B flat for
the Valse finale. Yet even in this act there seems to be no overall
strategy; there are certainly none of the rigorous tonal/dramatic
correspondences of *Swan Lake,* and few of the less schematized associations such as may be identified in *The Sleeping Beauty.* As for Act 1, that
begins in D major, and a mixture of keys of from one to three sharps is
central to much of what follows, giving a consistent colouring to the
general gaiety of the Silberhaus's Christmas party – though the swift
movement down the cycle of fifths in No. 3 (G-C-F) means that the
sudden twist on the very last quaver to a dominant seventh on A
produces the appropriate musical equivalent of the social dislocation
occasioned by Drosselmeyer's entrance, stopping the dancers in their
tracks, bringing the party sharply down to earth, and twisting towards
G major. There is no way of knowing whether some private instinct
within Tchaikovsky was stirred after the Nutcracker had been broken
and Clara took him in her arms – but at this point the music slides into
D flat and passes swiftly on to her lullaby (Ex. 276), within whose
melody the Fate motif ⌐——¬ finally but insistently takes shape. Though

Ex. 276

L'istesso tempo [Andante]

---

[13] His narrative had begun, for no reason that is clear, with a theme closely related to
the overture's opening.

it would be too much to draw parallels between the strength of Tatyana's feelings towards Onegin and the sentimental tenderness Clara suddenly conceives for her still hidden prince, there is in this music a brief influx of a feeling not found elsewhere in *The Nutcracker*.

The forthright melodies and firm colours of the Silberhaus's secure, normal world had given no hint of the plane of existence which Clara is about to discover. But as she re-enters on tiptoe the now darkened room, the idiom changes, lingering fragments of her lullaby pointing the nervousness with which she senses the imminence of things strange and unnerving in what had once been familiar and safe. It is the sound world which Tchaikovsky had first disclosed so briefly yet even more startlingly eight years before in the child's dream of the Second Suite, then explored further in the 'Sleep' entr'acte in *The Sleeping Beauty*, and in this new ballet had briefly foreshadowed before the March as the children had gazed at the Christmas tree, entranced and enchanted. Its main elements are tiny, often nervous melodic fragments, and the sharpest contrasts of colour and perhaps of register. It is often harmonically elusive and strange; when the normality of the triad emerges explicitly the chord is frequently static, for what it represents or suggests exists outside the changing, pressing momentum of human time. Wind timbre, whether solo or in finely judged ensemble, is exploited to the full, though the most fundamental single weapon is the harp scale or arpeggio, usually furtive and brief. Important, too, are the quietest of string backgrounds, often tremolando or trilled. The prevailing texture is of the most delicate, the prevailing dynamic pianissimo so that contrasts, whether the sudden forte stab or the broad measured crescendo, can be especially striking.

But as the creatures of this other world begin to reveal themselves we slip from this music of apprehensive imaginings into the music of representation, though all remains strange. Clara's inchoate dreams become reality, the mice intimate their presence, the tree grows awesomely, the dolls and hares (or rabbits, as they are designated in other sources) appear, and toy soldiers range themselves to engage with the mice. It is difficult to imagine how these preliminaries and the battle to come could have been better treated. In the turmoil keys often move swiftly and are often barely touched. The structuring of this lilliputian conflict (Ex. 277) depends upon three stretches of related music (the first covert appearance of the mice, then substantial parts of the two battles, where fanfares are added) and upon the variety of tiny fanfares which fulfil a role that is as potently motivic as pictorial. As for the musical organization of that broader portion of the action embracing this battle, it further confirms the care of Tchaikovsky's own planning. The flanks are two stretches of the most stable and expressively consistent C major music; the first is a return to Clara's lullaby to support the ebbing actions of the Silberhaus's party, the other is the second transformation scene where, after the turmoil of conflict, calm returns. Equally potent, though less literal, is the thematic relationship between the two transformation scenes. Determined not to waste a good idea, Tchaikovsky turned back to a theme (Ex. 278a) from the entr'acte with solo violin obbligato which he had rejected in *The Sleeping Beauty*, now vastly extending it sequentially and imitatively to suggest the growth of the Christmas tree (Ex. 278b), then simplifying it (Ex. 278c) to become the main building block for the second, even more majestic transformation scene which bears Clara and her Prince towards the land of Confiturenburg. Its shadow is to emerge again near the beginning of Act 2 to herald their arrival (Ex. 278d).

Regardless of any other considerations, the absence of a grand formal dance in anything that had gone before made it imperative that the closing number of Act 1 should fulfil this function. In any case, since there was to be a radical change of environment and dramatic character in the second act, forewarning of this wrench was urgently required. The idea of a Valse des flocons de neige (No. 9) was a pretty one, and to reflect the bright glitter of the scene Tchaikovsky drew in everything appropriate from his 'Nutcracker' orchestra. The fatal musical weakness of this waltz is melodic; no amount of orchestral magic, nor the allure of the women's wordless chorus can disguise the less-than-first-

Ex. 277

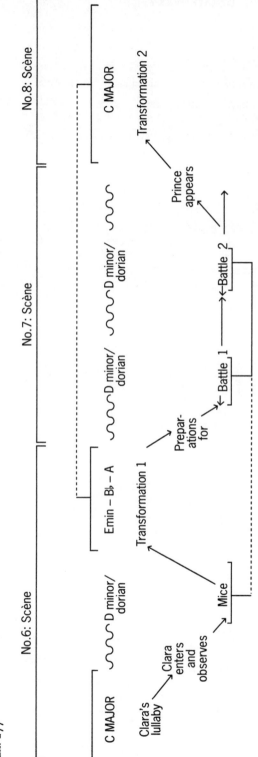

No.6: Scène   No.7: Scène   No.8: Scène

C MAJOR   D minor/dorian   E min – B♭ – A   D minor/dorian   D minor/dorian   C MAJOR

Clara's lullaby

Clara enters and observes

Mice

Transformation 1

Prepar-ations for

Battle 1

Battle 2

Prince appears

Transformation 2

～～～ passages of unstable tonality

identical passages

related passages

Ex. 278

a. Andante sostenuto

b. Moderato assai

c. Andante

d. Andante

rate quality of the material from which so much of it is built. The problem is basically one of rhythm. The strong character of the waltzes in *Swan Lake* of sixteen years before had come primarily from the rhythmic inventiveness of Tchaikovsky's tunes, but despite the first theme of this waltz holding persistently to a duple metre, there is little variety here. Nothing in *The Nutcracker* reveals more sadly than this the uncertainty which could now afflict Tchaikovsky's melodic inspiration when melodies were demanded from him strong enough to build substantial movements.

But *The Nutcracker* shows the very positive creative results that could come from broadening the orchestral palette. By the beginning of March 1891, as Tchaikovsky was marshalling his creative resources to begin work, he had decided to employ children's instruments such as Leopold Mozart had used in his Toy Symphony (formerly attributed to Haydn) and Bernhard Romberg in his Symphonie burlesque, and he incorporated these into the first act. During the first performances some were certainly played by the children on stage. According to one of the participants these were specially made trumpets, whistles, cuckoos, wooden and metal rattles; presumably they were to augment the notated noise of the toy trumpet and drum when Fritz and the others twice interrupt Clara's lullaby in No. 5. Another child's drum and a rattle were in the pit orchestra, the latter mimicking the sound of cracking nuts earlier in the same movement. Then during his subsequent time in Paris, Tchaikovsky had encountered a new orchestral instrument 'midway between a tiny piano and a Glockenspiel, with a divinely wonderful sound. I want to use this instrument in the symphonic poem, *The Voyevoda*, and the ballet,' he had told Jurgenson. '. . . It's called a "Celesta Mustel" . . . I want you to order this instrument. You won't lose anything on it, for you'll hire it out for all concerts where *The Voyevoda* is played. . . . Because this instrument will be required in St Petersburg earlier than in Moscow, it's advisable that it should be sent from Paris to Osip Ivanovich [Jurgenson's brother]. But regarding this I would wish him to show it to no one, for I fear that Rimsky-Korsakov and Glazunov will get wind of it and will use it for unusual effects ahead of me.'[14]

But it was not only that Tchaikovsky would find powerful creative stimulus in the novel possibilities offered by this; its presence encouraged him to explore also the possibilities for unusual combinations within the familiar complement – as all who know no more of *The*

---

[14] *TLP*16A, pp. 129–30; *TZC*3, p. 488; *TPJ*2, p. 212; *DTC*, p. 257 (partial); *YDGC*, p. 530 (partial).

Nutcracker than the suite Tchaikovsky himself drew from it will be fully aware. The suite was drawn mainly from the Divertissement (No. 12) in Act 2. The veiled scorn with which these movements are so often viewed is thoroughly unmerited. Whether the stimulus came from a new instrument (the celesta in the Sugar Plum Fairy's dance), familiar instruments in unusual combinations, or from the sound world of an imagined, exotic orient (the Arabian and Chinese dances), it sufficed to draw from Tchaikovsky a kind of material that was itself special in character, ideally suited to its purpose, and perfectly formed as music. There are no great melodies here, but there are some wonderfully individual ones. What other composer could have devised that so original, yet so right (and so piquantly harmonized) melody for the celesta (Ex. 279; any who still doubt Tchaikovsky's genius for

Ex. 279

stunningly original melody should take no more than the first bar and a half, then ask: how would I have continued?), or sketched a one-minute miniature of bobbing smiling Chinese with such flawless certainty and crystal clarity (the novel use of flute and bassoons with a great void between is only the first of the new textures in this piece), or devised a more distinctive and naïvely irresistible tune that exploited so consummately the 'close-harmony' potential of *three* flutes engaged melodically? True, the Russian Dance (Trépak), a chip off the Violin Concerto's finale, is more conventional, as is the Arabian Dance – though none of the precedents Tchaikovsky had before him had evoked oriental languor with such refinement and economy (the piece was founded upon a Georgian cradle song supplied by Ippolitov-Ivanov[15]). Significantly Tchaikovsky chose not to include the conventional Spanish Dance in the suite. Modelled as it was on the idiom established in Glinka's First Spanish Overture and most recently exemplified spectacularly in Rimsky's Spanish Capriccio, it sounds tame in such company. Nor does the hearty sketch of Mère Gigogne, whose children jump out from under her skirt, make a more individual mark, founded as it is on two engaging but unremarkable French popular songs ('Giroflé-girofla' and 'Cadet Rouselle'), though the scoring's echoes of (presumably) a fairground organ have charm.

There is much to admire in the music that precedes the Divertissement. Though the opening Scène (No. 10) prolongs further that melodic blandness which had marked the waltz ending Act 1, its leisurely harmonic tread and ever more scintillating decoration (capped by the first appearance of the Sugar Plum Fairy's special instrument, the celesta, here in concert with two harps to signal her entry) consolidates the task begun in the earlier movement: to leave no doubt that Clara is entering a totally new realm. Flutter-tongue flutes make their novel contribution[16] to this sound world that reflects the shimmering, rose-coloured waters of the river which bears Clara and her Prince into Confiturenburg; then, to descending scales, which clearly foretell the grand Pas de deux after the Divertissement, the Sugar Plum Fairy greets them, the music leaping into vigorous life as the little Moors and pages appear, and continuing with splendid pacing through the Prince's narrative. As has been noted, the ensuing dances are mostly excellent, though the Valse des fleurs (No. 13) that completes them is scarcely a rival to the great waltzes of the earlier ballets. It is with the Pas de deux (No. 14) that the lack of dramatic motivation makes itself felt with a vengeance. Too much is made of a scale repeated at different levels with different harmonizations, and it is soon painfully clear that Tchaikovsky was merely providing the accompaniment for a piece of formal decorative dancing ('Adage colossal d'effets,' as Petipa put it in his ballet-master's plan, showing that he too saw nothing of substance, either dramatic or expressive, that he could put into it[17]). By far the best section is the ballerina's variation (the Dance of the Sugar Plum Fairy, where the celeste enables us 'to hear drops of water

---

[15] Bars 1–8 of the muted violin theme.

[16] Tchaikovsky learned of this effect from his former harmony student, the flautist Alexandr Khimichenko, while in Kiev in the first days of 1892. Two months later, having forgotten both the terminology and the technique, he wrote to Khimichenko for information.

[17] Quoted in Wiley, *op. cit.*, p. 381.

spurting from the fountains', as Petipa had required). The preceding Tempo di Tarantella for the male dancer is the third piece salvaged from the suite of national dances intended for Act 1. The Valse finale (No. 15) opens well, but the Apotheosis, which returns to the music of the act's opening, finally sinks into total if loud harmonic inertia.

Having conducted his own examination of *The Nutcracker*, John Warrack summarized excellently what made Tchaikovsky so ideal a composer for the nineteenth-century ballet as he found it:

> Tchaikovsky had the genius for the melody that was essential to dance still entirely decorative, together with the fineness of ear to make his orchestration not merely an apt presentation of that melody but another expressive facet of it. Both were required to serve music as the highest form of décor. He did not seriously question these precepts, since for all his high respect for ballet music it was connected to a prettiment of life rather than an interpretation of life. And the decorative attracted him since it actually precluded, for its brief intoxication, any deeper emotional engagement, suggesting the illusion of prettiness as a quality sufficient in itself. It is an art whose limitations are part of its essence.[18]

For *The Nutcracker* as it is, this is impeccable, and if Tchaikovsky had written no other ballet, it could be left there. Yet in the light of what he had already added to the genre, there is an irrepressible question: what might also have resulted if the subject of his third ballet had been truly worthy of him, if Vsevolozhsky had not chosen so disastrously? In *Swan Lake* he had broken from the confining, crippling mould of the ballet tradition with a work so revolutionary that it was some twenty years before audiences could begin to come to terms with those very elements which were to give it its subsequent overwhelming appeal, even when the climax of the work had been as dreadfully traduced as it was in the revival of 1895. In *The Sleeping Beauty* he had gone on to create the greatest of nineteenth-century ballets, a masterpiece which had shown in an almost visionary way that the form could transcend its established bounds of virtuoso movement or graceful sentimentality and project significances hitherto the province only of play and opera. As it is, the very mastery with which Tchaikovsky extracted from *The Nutcracker* such potential as it did have only emphasizes the more mercilessly that it is the saddest case among all his mature works.

In the light of the enormous popularity *The Nutcracker* now enjoys, it seems extraordinary that the ballet was not seen in Moscow until

[18] Warrack (J.), *Tchaikovsky* (London, 1973), p. 260.

1919. There was, of course, no reason why the two works should be linked in a double bill, and *Iolanta* fared better, opening in Moscow on 23 November, seventeen days after the composer's death, and running for fourteen performances.

The plot of *Iolanta* is as follows:

A beautiful garden with luxuriant vegetation and a gothic-style pavilion. A small door at the back.

Four musicians are playing on stage. Iolanta's friends, Brigitta and Laura, together with some of the maidservants, are drawing branches towards Iolanta so that she may pick the fruits, gathering them by touch. Marta, her nurse, holds the basket. Iolanta's movements become slower, and finally she lowers her arms. She cannot understand what is missing in her life; everybody serves her but she has no way of repaying them for their love. When Marta tries to stop her, Iolanta calls them all around her (poco più mosso). Touching Marta's eyes she realizes she is weeping; but how, she asks, does Marta know when *she* weeps, for she never touches her eyes? The women remain in embarrassed silence. Brigitta suggests it is the music which is making Iolanta upset, and Marta dismisses the musicians. But Iolanta knows the music is not the cause. She thanks the players. 'Later when the sun is no longer warming us, you will come to cheer me,' she adds (largo). She declines the suggestions from Laura and Brigitta of things which might amuse her, admits she is tired, and asks them to gather flowers for her; enjoying their scent as she arranges them may perhaps restore her calm. When the others have left she turns to her nurse, asking whether it is really possible that eyes were given only for weeping (largo). Once tears and sadness had been unknown to her, but things have changed. 'Why is it that the coolness and silence of the night have become more dear to me? Why is it that I hear, as it were, sobbing where the nightingale sings? Why? Tell me, Marta.' (bar 140)

Marta attempts to comfort her (No. 2). Laura, Brigitta and the other women run in with a basket of flowers, which they offer to her in a chorus. Iolanta thanks them (No. 3), and asks how she may repay them (bar 7). Your love is our best reward, they reply. Iolanta requests Marta to sing her favourite song and let her rest her head on her shoulder as she used to as a child. One of the women gently fans Iolanta, who quickly falls asleep as the women sing a lullaby. Marta quietly lays Iolanta on the couch and indicates that the other servants should return and carefully carry Iolanta out. As all leave the song dies away.

For a while the stage is empty as hunting horns are heard (No. 4). Someone knocks at the door. Bertrand, the door-keeper and Marta's husband, enters and opens the door to Almerik, but will not let him proceed further, though Almerik says he is the king's messenger; this is forbidden territory on pain of death – and if King René has a message he would send his armour-bearer, Raoul. But Almerik tells him (andante non troppo) that Raoul had died the day before, that he is now the king's armour-bearer, producing a letter and the king's signet ring to confirm it. Bertrand admits Almerik, who is amazed at the paradise he has entered. He tells Bertrand the king is coming with a great Moorish physician. On learning that this place is the home of Iolanta, the king's blind daughter, Almerik replies that he did not know that she was blind – and, in any case, everyone knew she was in a convent in Spain. Bertrand disabuses him; Iolanta has lived here almost from birth so that her blindness could be kept from her betrothed, Robert, Duke of Burgundy, until after she had been cured. Marta enters to add that Iolanta knows nothing of her blindness; in her presence no one may speak of the light or of the beauty they see, and Iolanta is to believe her father is no more than a rich knight, not the king.

A trumpet call offstage signals the arrival of the king himself and Ebn-Hakia. René declares all his hopes now rest with the physician, who asks where Iolanta is. When Marta says she is sleeping, Ebn-Hakia is pleased, for he can examine her more easily, and the king orders him to be taken to Iolanta. Alone, he reveals his distress at his daughter's affliction, and his desperate hope that she should be cured. 'O Lord, if I am a sinner, why should my pure angel suffer?' he begins his aria (andante). Gladly he would give up crown and power, peace and happiness if only his child might see. He begs God to have pity upon him.

Ebn-Hakia returns (No. 5) to tell the king that cure is possible, but only if Iolanta is told of her blindness. He cannot promise to restore her sight – but with Allah all things are possible. René is appalled at the prospect that his daughter might come to suffer from the knowledge of her misfortune, yet remain uncured. He feels deceived in his hopes, and dismisses Ebn-Hakia. 'From henceforth I shall trust in no one!' he declares (bar 36). 'Farewell!' But the physician remains. 'In all aspects of existence there are two worlds – that of the flesh and that of the spirit,' he begins his monologue (adagio con moto). There is no feeling known only to the body, and the feeling of blindness must be known to the immortal soul before blind eyes can be opened. 'When the mind perceives this great truth, then it is possible, great master – yes, then it is possible that longing will awaken light in bodily darkness.' (bar 53) René is terribly torn by Ebn-Hakia's pronouncement, but the physician insists that he cannot proceed unless Iolanta is told and wishes to be cured. Saying he will wait until evening for the king's decision, he leaves. However, the king's mind is quickly made up; he will hold to his former resolve. 'Thus it is decided – and the doctor shall give way to the father!'

Again the stage is empty for a while. Then the voices of Duke Robert and Count Vaudemont, a Burgundian knight, are heard offstage (No. 6). They enter, and are as amazed as Almerik had been at what they see. The duke notices an inscription forbidding entry on pain of death. Vaudemont would leave, but the duke is tired after their journey; if anyone should find them, he reassures his companion, they have their swords. In any case, the longer he remains away from King René and his daughter, the better. Vaudemont tries to cheer him; surely the king, who is said to be good and wise, would annul his marriage contract – and what if Iolanta should prove to be beautiful? However, the duke is convinced she will be prim and proud. 'Don't you think I know nuns! With their benedicite and amen, they are cold and soulless as stone.' (moderato) He launches into an aria (vivace) in praise of his real beloved, Matilda.

The duke's precipitate and unrestrained passion contrasts sharply with that of Vaudemont (No. 6a); within him love still slumbers, he still dreams of some angel, some heavenly, wonderful form. 'O come, bright vision, source of love, warm the secret strings of my heart,' he cries (bar 39). Returning to himself (No. 7) after this romance, he observes footmarks and follows them until they take him to the door leading from the terrace. Finding it unlocked, he peers inside, sees the sleeping Iolanta, and cries out in rapture (bar 21). The duke, too, looks in, but reacts with indifference (bar 30), and tries repeatedly to drag away Vaudemont, who is now enthralled by Iolanta's appearance. Their exchanges finally wake her. She enters and asks who is there. Despite the duke's attempts to restrain him, Vaudemont introduces himself, explains they have lost their way, and Iolanta leaves to fetch wine to restore their strength.

The duke is so convinced his friend is bewitched that he declares he will fetch a detachment of troops to rescue him. As he leaves Iolanta returns. Vaudemont takes the goblet offered him (molto più mosso) and drinks while Iolanta holds the tray in expectation the duke will take his too. She is puzzled when he does not, and says she is sorry when Vaudemont tells her of the duke's departure. But Vaudemont launches into a confession of love: 'You have appeared before me like a vision of heavenly, pure beauty (moderato con moto) . . . but I see, yes, that you are no vision, and that fate has destined you to live, to inspire love, to suffer, to love!' (bar 122) Iolanta can understand nothing of this – 'yet your words are both strange and pleasant, and my head spins from them,' she admits (bar 140). Realizing this new experience has confused her, Vaudemont draws back. 'Your wish is to me a law,' he promises (quasi andante) – but he begs her to 'pluck a bloom for me from among your roses as a token of farewell, as a memory of our meeting and the fiery blush of your cheeks' (bar 181). Iolanta hands him a white rose instead (allegro moderato), and he points out her mistake, then says he will keep it, and asks for a red rose as well. Again Iolanta picks a white rose (bar 224). When she again realizes she has done something wrong she becomes more confused, and picks a third white rose. 'What does "red" mean?' she asks in bewilderment (bar 234) – and the truth begins to dawn on Vaudemont. He takes several roses and asks how many he is holding. 'She is blind!' he cries (bar 260) when it is plain she cannot answer.

Vaudemont lapses into a stunned silence, and Iolanta is bewildered and distressed by it (moderato). In great misery she begs him to teach her what she needs to know, but despairing of him remaining, she echoes his earlier words to her: 'Your wishes are to me a law (quasi andante) . . . Pluck and give me one of the roses as a token of farewell, as a memory of our meeting.' (bar 314) Instead Vaudemont takes her hand (moderato con moto), implores her not to weep – and in talking of her blindness begins to reveal to her the disability from which she suffers. 'Knight, what is light?' she asks at last (allegro moderato). 'It is nature's wonderful first creation, the Creator's first gift to his world,' he replies (moderato mosso); the man who knows not its blessing cannot love

God's world – and it is light that allows Vaudemont to see Iolanta's beauty. His words are so sweet that Iolanta declares she has never felt such happiness. But she has no need of light to praise God and experience his boundless bounty, for 'in the heat of the day, in fragrances, in sounds, and in myself, in all creations God, unseen and good, is reflected', she believes (bar 403). But while Vaudemont now understands something of how Iolanta feels, he has awakened in her a longing to see – so that she may be like him.

Voices are heard offstage calling for Iolanta (No. 8). The king, Ebn-Hakia, Almerik, Bertrand and the women enter. Iolanta embraces her father, who is furious when he notices Vaudemont. The latter briefly identifies himself and is immediately asked whether he has talked with Iolanta about anything. Iolanta herself replies (moderato): Vaudemont has told her much – what light is, and how he pitied her because she could not see. The others are horrified, and the king thinks this is a punishment from God. But Ebn-Hakia views it differently. 'It is not a punishment but your daughter's salvation,' he declares (bar 46). While the others voice their individual feelings in an ensemble, the king sinks on to a bench and buries his face in his hands. It begins to grow dark. The ensemble ended, the king tells Iolanta he has a doctor who can cure her; does she wish to see? 'Can I have a burning wish for something I understand only dimly?' she replies (andante). The physician quietly reminds the king that Iolanta can be cured only if she wishes it.

Suddenly the king sees a way of awakening his daughter's will. He orders the treatment to begin (bar 102), then turns to Vaudemont and asks whether he had read the notice forbidding entry, with its dire penalty. When Vaudemont admits he had, the king says he must die if the treatment does not work. There is general alarm, and Iolanta is especially distressed. She pleads with her father, but he insists that Vaudemont must die if the cure is unavailing. The others together plead with René to have pity on Iolanta – though Ebn-Hakia is now beginning to perceive the king's stratagem. Yet again the king loudly repeats his sentence, and Iolanta asks whether she will have to suffer to be cured. 'O no,' replies the physician (bar 154). 'All that is needed is for you to have a burning wish to see the light.' Iolanta states her readiness to suffer, if need be, to save Vaudemont – and now she knows that light is 'nature's wonderful first creation, the Creator's first gift to his world' (adagio con moto). Vaudemont falls on his knees in adoration of Iolanta (bar 192); he is still prepared to die for her. But she will have none of this, asks for his hand (bar 204) so that she may touch his face, begs her father's embrace, then goes off with Ebn-Hakia and the others, who pray that God may be with her. The king and Vaudemont remain. The former believes his daughter can be cured, though he dreads what she may have to suffer, and prays silently.

Fanfares are heard (No. 9); Duke Robert is approaching. The king goes to Vaudemont and discloses that his threat of execution was a ruse to make Iolanta wish to see. Vaudemont admits that René would have been technically within his rights to execute him – but not yet realizing the king's identity, he asks ingenuously 'yet who are you that you decide so imperiously people's fate?' (bar 14) 'I think that is a question I might rather ask of you,' replies the king. Vaudemont now reveals his full identity (and titles), adding that, however rich and exalted René may be, he would not be lowering himself if he gave Vaudemont his daughter's hand. But René says this is impossible because she has been promised to another from childhood.

Almerik rushes in to report that a group of armed men is approaching, and Vaudemont says it is Duke Robert. 'You will know forthwith who your rival is,' observes the king (bar 54). Almerik opens the gate and the duke enters with his followers. He sees Vaudemont, then the king, and does obeisance to the latter. Vaudemont is stunned now he knows the king's identity. The king points to the duke as Iolanta's betrothed, and Vaudemont immediately asks him (tempo 1) to admit his other affection. His friend feels that this is not the proper time or place, but when Vaudemont reveals that Iolanta is the object of his love, the duke turns to the king and states that he had been betrothed to his daughter as a child, that since then he had fallen in love with the Countess Matilda Lotaringy, that he would still keep his promise to marry Iolanta, but that Matilda would have his heart. Impressed by the duke's directness, the king releases him from his promise, and tells Vaudemont Iolanta is his if she can be cured. But the count says he will take her even if she remains blind, and the king gives his assent.

The sudden entry of Bertrand brings an anxious enquiry whether the treatment has succeeded. But the door-keeper cannot say; he had been unable to bear the strain when Iolanta had kept repeating 'O my knight, live!' The others' prayer for God's mercy is interrupted by offstage cries: 'Iolanta sees the light! O joy!' (moderato assai). Ebn-Hakia leads in Iolanta, and signals the others to withdraw to the back of the stage. It is now nearly dark; only the distant tops of the mountains are still illuminated by the evening sun, and the stars are visible. Iolanta's eyes are bandaged. All wait with bated breath. 'O let me see again the wonderful light which suddenly shone before me,' she pleads (bar 148). She cries out with joy when Ebn-Hakia removes the bandage (bar 152), but when she sees her garden it is so unfamiliar that she is overcome, even fearful (più mosso). The physician tells her to look upwards to the sky instead (bar 174), and she is overwhelmed by its loveliness. 'O how wonderful, how bright! What is it? God? the spirit of God?' she asks (bar 177). 'It is the light and the sky,' the physician replies. 'The sky? But is God not in the sky?' she rejoins. 'I am before you, O God!' She sinks to her knees. Ebn-Hakia tells her to look around her at the other people (bar 197). She sees her father for the first time, confirming his identity by touching his face, and he gives her into the protection of Vaudemont (bar 214). All join in praising the all-powerful Creator.

One critic was to rise uncompromisingly to *Iolanta*'s defence. 'Among all Tchaikovsky's works you will find scarcely another made with such care and refinement,' wrote Kashkin in *Artist* in December 1893, after St Petersburg had laid to rest both *Iolanta* and its creator. 'The music of *Iolanta* is so poetically delicate that it might be clearer and more understood on a small stage and in a small hall – in a word, it needs conditions, both for the performance and for the listener, approximating to those for chamber music . . . All the same, whatever *Iolanta*'s [lack of] success on the stage and with the public, it will always remain for the musician a dear, poetic work, and will occupy a place among the best works of its immortal composer.'[19]

Kashkin's verdict was perceptive; there is an intimacy about *Iolanta* that might have made it more effective as a chamber opera. As it is, we may easily – and perhaps fairly – dismiss the piece as a failure, though Kashkin was also right to observe the refinement and skill of its workmanship. Yet even here, ironically, he was pointing the finger at another deficiency – that, as the pseudonymous Domino had declared, the opera was the product of high craft, not true creativity. In fact, the evidence was heavily weighted towards the unfriendly critics; the melodic invention is mostly well below Tchaikovsky's best, for while the arioso/recitative through which most of the drama unfolds is convincingly handled, rarely do the more formal movements offer a truly memorable phrase, and there is some justification for Ivanov's impression of 'a collection of one- and two-voice romances'. Only the orchestral theme which accompanies Vaudemont's first surge of passion on beholding Iolanta has something of vintage Tchaikovsky about it (Ex. 280).

Ex. 280

[*VAUDEMONT:* [What do I] see? *ROBERT:* An enchantress? *VAUDEMONT:* No, an

19 *DTC*, p. 222.

Tvo - rets!___ kak kho-ro - sha   o - na!

angel! O Creator! How lovely she is!]

Rimsky's harsh verdict on the scoring was far less deserved. Tchaikovsky's decision to employ wind instruments alone for the short monothematic introduction can only seem surprising if no account is taken of what follows, for such instruments' bright, incisive sounds provide the most effective background for the sweet tones of strings and harp with which the stage musicians are serenading the blind princess when the curtain rises. But if the roots of this gentle music lie in Tchaikovsky's rococo world (though more precisely, perhaps, as Edward Garden has observed, in the celebrated minuet from Handel's *Berenice*), those of Iolanta's arioso are embedded in Kuma's arioso of longing in the final act of *The Enchantress*. Tchaikovsky himself had noted unenthusiastically that he had returned to the musical world of his earlier opera, but it is no surprise this should have happened. The two works were natural companions, the central character of each an unsophisticated young woman living in surroundings far removed from the grand centres of power and conflict (*The Oprichnik, The Maid, Mazepa*), the dehumanizing pressures of a metropolitan society (*Onegin, The Queen of Spades*), or a half-magic world of supernatural beings and fantastic happenings (*Vakula*). Like *The Enchantress*, *Iolanta* was non-episodic, its plot unfolding organically and smoothly, with each new incident a clear consequence of earlier happenings, and this had encouraged a radical shift towards a Wagnerian practice that formerly Tchaikovsky had condemned roundly – that of assigning to the orchestra the responsibility for musical evolution, thus permitting the singers maximum freedom in the enunciation and pacing of their parts.

The opening scene is a case in point; likewise the theme in Ex. 280, though heard some five times, is always in the orchestra.

The Enchantress had shown a much diminished interest in referential materials, but *Iolanta* abandons them altogether. For the first time in one of Tchaikovsky's operas the introduction has no thematic connection with what follows, and though within the opera there are a few long range recurrences of whole musical sections for dramatic reasons, there is no trace of thematic recall at the end.[20] Only the Fate theme continues to range at all widely, confirming that it is destiny, not disaster, that confronts Vaudemont and the duke in Iolanta's 'paradise' (Ex. 281a), and twisting itself in the orchestra as Vaudemont prepares to awaken his new beloved to the 'cruel fate' at whose hands she has unknowingly suffered (Ex. 281b). But a degree of mannerism has now infected the theme's usage, for though its crucial outline may be discerned in a half dozen other contexts, in none is there convincing reason for believing it signals the active presence of this force.[21]

Ex. 281

[*VAUDEMONT:* O, it is a paradise! *ROBERT:* No, it is a trap! Ruin threatens us, dear friend!]

---

[20] Except, that is, for the dramatically pointless and easily unnoticed return, during the finale, of the first four bars of Marta's contribution to the lullaby. Both texts speak of the 'Lord of the Universe', however, and it has also been pointed out (see below, p. 365, Ex. 284) that this phrase may deliberately echo one in the finale of Beethoven's Ninth Symphony.

[21] Except, perhaps ironically, when Vaudemont reveals his identity to the king, observing that he had come 'by chance' (No. 8, bar 22).

b.

[*VAUDEMONT:* Child, O no, there is no need for tears!

IOLANTA: You have not yet gone?

VAUDEMONT: Poor child!]

Equally the use of keys as dramatic signifiers is in no way as positive or unambiguous as in some of Tchaikovsky's earlier operas, and where such things may be traced, they seem even farther removed from many of Tchaikovsky's past usages than in *The Enchantress*. True, E major can once again become the key of happy love, as in Robert's aria in praise of his Matilda, though to reaffirm this to the king the duke adds an extra sharp, and it is likewise in B major that Vaudemont thrills at the first sight of the blind princess (see Ex. 280). But otherwise tonal-dramatic linkages seem to mark out strands particular to this tale and the characters involved in these, rather than emotional or dramatic states. Among the main strands are Iolanta's blindness, the possibility of cure offered by the skill of the Moorish physician in alliance with the irresistible incentive provided by the delectable young stranger, and the shifting predicaments this produces for the king and his daughter. There is, too, the bright, sighted world, and G major seems to be its key, as is suggested in the serenade which sets the scene. Also in G major Vaudemont begins his confession of love before discovering Iolanta's blindness, and in it, with some irony (for as yet she does not know she is not as he is), she begins her response after her confused giving of the roses; in it is set the end of the love scene, where Vaudemont begins to awaken her to the blessing she unknowingly lacks.

The keys most closely flanking G major (D and C) may also belong to this sighted world. While D seems to have some tenuous connection with Vaudemont and his responses to Iolanta's blindness, C appears to relate to sight itself (Ebn-Hakia's exhortation to place hope of cure in Allah, his perception that Iolanta's new-gained knowledge of her blindness will open the path to sight, the others' anxious enquiry whether the treatment has succeeded, the confirmation that it has, and Iolanta's greeting of the world around her when the bandages are removed). By contrast B minor can signify Iolanta's blindness. If the introduction has a separate key, it is this, and it constantly infiltrates the prevailing G major of the opera's opening, later covertly signalling why Iolanta (it is said) has been settled far away in Spain, and confirming the subject of discourse between king and physician at their first entrance. In B minor René bitterly rejects the physician's remedy and dismisses him, tacitly accepting his daughter's disability will remain total; even more absolutely, despite modal inflections, B minor takes total possession of Ebn-Hakia's ensuing monologue, where he confronts Iolanta's handicap squarely, setting out the facts that must be faced uncompromisingly if she is to be cured. And the key underpins Vaudemont's words when he begins to stir Iolanta's awareness of what her disability is costing her.

Just as three flats had been the tonal territory of the Prince and his family in *The Enchantress*, so for the king and his daughter in *Iolanta* it seems to be a special realm (literally, it would appear, in the scene between Bertrand and Almerik; after a conversation conducted exclusively in sharp keys, there is a sudden switch into flat-notated regions as Almerik is admitted to Iolanta's garden). C minor belongs especially to René. We first hear of him in it, in it he sets his aria of sorrow and pain at his daughter's affliction, through it his identity is confirmed for his daughter at the opera's end. But E flat is far more Iolanta's province, for ignorance of her disability has insulated her from the tensions and agonies which have remorselessly racked her father, and it is the key of her contentment, then of her road, albeit painful, to happiness. Her companions lull her asleep in it, in it she makes her first carefree gifts of roses to the bewitching young stranger, during the duet's conclusion voices the new happiness he has brought her (by far the best passage in this stiff and second-rate stretch), then ingenuously reveals to her father her excitement at the forbidden secret Vaudemont has begun to open for her; in it René perceives the stratagem through which he will rouse his daughter's desire for sight, then carries it through, first by his accusation of Vaudemont, then by his reaffirmation to Iolanta of the brutal sentence he has invented to drive her to her decision. It is in E flat, too, that Vaudemont introduces himself fully to the king, perhaps confirming that he is accepted by his beloved and is a worthy match for this royal princess.

Though C major may represent that human faculty over which Ebn-Hakia has such power, the Moorish doctor himself and his skill as physician appear to lean towards F minor, while Vaudemont, the other human agent in the healing, inclines to A flat; his romance is set in it, as is the transfigured recall of the love duet's conclusion which his beloved initiates, now that she has perceived the joyful hope of which he was the agent – and it is in A flat that the opera ends, for that hope which he has roused has now become reality, and she has committed herself to him.

Whether or not Tchaikovsky had been guilty of plagiarizing Rubinstein and others, *Iolanta* is a veritable anthology of resonances from Tchaikovsky's own operas. It is not merely that the music of the lovers' tenderly developing relationship at *Iolanta*'s heart (quite certainly the best invention in the score) was in direct line from that of *The Enchantress*; the brass fanfares heralding the various entrances (the nearest thing to a reminiscence theme in the opera, though the players are clearly all in René's employ, for they play the same for all comers) hark back yet more closely to those in the final act of that opera. But the more specific allusions within the love music of *Iolanta* are to a yet earlier piece for, as Gerald Abraham pointed out, it is the horn's answering phrase from the climactic moment of the letter monologue in *Onegin* that is the starting point for Vaudemont's thoughtful yet passionate revelation of his ideal in love; in addition Iolanta's distress that she has been unable to return properly the love shown her by her attendants (Ex. 282) borrows Onegin's cry of 'wearisome melancholy' as, isolated, he had observed the bright world of a St Petersburg ballroom (see Vol. 2, Ex. 143; this is one of the instances where, in the later opera, the resemblance to the Fate theme seems coincidental).

Ex. 282

[How can I repay you for this friendship?]

Such echoes from earlier operas are merely fleeting; so, too, is the memory of Joan's farewell (see Vol. 3, Ex. 153e), though in the scene of Robert and Vaudemont's first appearance the resemblance to Chopin's celebrated A major polonaise is even closer than it had been in *The Maid of Orléans. Mazepa* provided at least two contexts for recall; the passage, with its drooping oboe phrase, against which Iolanta dismisses her attendants before her aria of emotional bewilderment is adapted from Mariya's mad scene (Finale: Adagio), while the influence of that opera's dying end is more fundamental still, for not only is the charming song which speeds Iolanta's slumbers a child of Mariya's lullaby over the dead Andrey; for eight bars it lifts bodily an harmonic structure from the earlier piece.

Nor does *Iolanta* offer only memories from Tchaikovsky's operas. The end of the love duet (Ex. 283) is patently founded upon the motto of the

Ex. 283

Chud- ny per - ven-ets tvo-ren- ya,   per- vy mi - ru dar tvor- tsa,
[Wonderful first-born of creation, the Creator's first gift to the world, manifestation

sla - vï bo - zhey pro - yav-len - ye,
of God's glory,]

Fifth Symphony (compare Ex. 283 with Ex. 232b), though the theme and its repetitions prove no more adequate to convey the hopes and exultations of the new lovers than they had been to express triumph and exultation at the symphony's conclusion. There are suggestions of other composers, too – not only of the minuet from Handel's *Berenice* at the opening, but even of Beethoven's Ninth Symphony, for Yarustovsky has suggested that a phrase from the opera's finale (Ex. 284)

Ex. 284

expressing thanks to 'the Creator of the universe' (see also footnote 20) is a distant echo from that work's Andante maestoso. This relationship is perhaps debatable – but the opera begins with what is surely a close, yet highly transformed reworking of the opening of *Tristan* (Ex. 285a), though this time the four notes fall chromatically instead of rising towards the dominant seventh conclusion to each phrase, and the ensuing sequence matches this with a drop, not a rise of a minor third (Ex. 285b). Indeed, with the urgently piled sequences of the Poco più animato and then the dying conclusion, there must be some suspicion that this whole introduction is a parody of Wagner's prelude.

Ex. 285

Thus it is possible that *Iolanta* is framed by allusions to the two most seminal masterpieces of the nineteenth century, both being pieces in which the idea within the work may be considered as portentous as the music which carries it. Be that as it may, it is a pointer to what distinguishes *Iolanta* from all Tchaikovsky's other operas except, again, *The Enchantress*. None had concerned itself with anything beyond the challenges and stimuli of the human drama it projected; *Iolanta*, by contrast, has a message, albeit simple. If 'love, the redeeming power' might have superscribed *The Enchantress*, 'self-knowledge and will, the healing powers' might aptly have headed *Iolanta*. The condition essential for cure lies within the patient herself; whatever Ebn-Hakia's ministrations, the worlds of the spirit and body are so indivisible that it is only when Iolanta wills it that sight can come. We do not know whether Tchaikovsky himself was animated by this bit of metaphysics as he had been by the ideal of femininity he thought he could discern in Kuma. While composing the opera he had spotted a major problem inherent in Modest's libretto, one that could all too easily arise when an 'idea' is present requiring exposition (and probably debate), then translation into action. There was one stretch in particular: 'between the duet about *light* and the end there's too little *music*, and everything's narrative. I fear it'll be boring,' he had written on 6 August.[22] But while he had realized this stretch might well lack those more notable musical landmarks which earlier rise from time to time above the general level of the terrain, this was not the real problem. The very presentation of this idea was hopelessly flawed, for frightening Iolanta into acquiescence debased what should have been a voluntary decision to suffer the unknown in pursuit of a desirable end into an act enforced to avoid an intolerable disaster. In fact, to judge from the quality of his music, Tchaikovsky's creativity remained quite unstirred, and the transcendent tone of the opera's final stages sounds dutiful; one is almost grateful for the jolt of the whole-tone scale used to induce a mild attack of tonal vertigo as Iolanta finds the beauty of her garden too overwhelming for one so newly sighted. There must, of course, be a powerful pull at the emotions as she prepares to face the ordeal of treatment, then endures it; even stronger will be the tug at the moment she sees, just as when Leonora strips Florestan's chains. But in Beethoven's great glorification of fidelity and courageous love, a series of actions demanding herculean resolve and courage had been undertaken to gain this end; with *Iolanta* our response is dependent upon little except the sentimental appeal within any such moment, while the final joy, for which there was yet greater grounds than at the end of *Vakula* (Tchaikovsky's only other mature opera with a happy ending), is lifeless, for it is fettered within a four-phrase tune which begins regrettably and ends deplorably.

---

[22] *TLP*16A, p. 186; *TZC*3, p. 496; *TPB*, p. 497; *DTC*, p. 216; *YDGC*, p. 533.

But in any case, the real stimulus to Tchaikovsky's imagination was bound to come from the characters who are the agents of the idea, its beneficiaries, or engrossed observers of its consequences. Here is the key to Iolanta's failure. Few characters are of any substance, and some are mere ciphers. Bertrand and Almerik, for instance: their scene, stuffed with explanations, drove Tchaikovsky into plain recitative, his musical prose as efficient as it is mostly featureless. The duke is too peripheral to make any real mark, though his shout in praise of Matilda, intoxicated rather than passionate, usefully confirms him as a thoroughly unsuitable match for one as fragile as Iolanta. Vaudemont's fine aria, added at Figner's request, is well placed to emphasize the difference between the two men. But elsewhere the Burgundian knight comes to life only when fired by Iolanta, and the women are merely human decoration for her enclosed, unreal environment. The king is different; there is something from the painful, tough world of *Mazepa* in his music, and his aria is a noble piece, with a steeply profiled vocal line that confirms manliness beneath the grieving. There are moments elsewhere when René's music gains in harmonic richness and melodic eloquence to suggest flesh and blood within the royal costume (the preamble to his aria, for instance, his heavy-hearted rejoinder to Ebn-Hakia's uncompromising prescription, his own equally adamant determination to reject the physician's remedy, and his words of desperate hope as he watches his daughter leave to undergo Ebn-Hakia's treatment). And Ebn-Hakia makes a firm impression; his aria, which seems to promise no more than a mild dose of musical orientalism, accumulates quite surprising weight, for its insistent rotation around the same basic proposition relentlessly drives home the conditions essential for Iolanta's cure.

Yet, once again, as in *Onegin*, *The Maid*, *Mazepa* and *The Enchantress*, it was the young, vulnerable girl who captured Tchaikovsky's creative heart. Already in the opening scene the moments where Iolanta speaks alone are those which may suddenly open the springs of Tchaikovsky's tenderest invention, as when she thanks the musicians, asks her companions to pluck some blooms she may arrange to still her restlessness, and finally prepares to sleep. Perhaps we may feel that this first scene lies too close to Confiturenburg, that the opening serenade, the attractive flower chorus and the closing lullaby have little more than decorative prettiness, that Iolanta's aria is simply a misty-eyed expression of adolescent moodiness. But if all this does not yet move us, her pathetic condition surely touches our sentimental responses, and we are the more ready to react sympathetically when we see her confronted with a novel, bewildering experience which brings a new joy yet, in consequence of her blindness, agitation and pain. It was with this moment that Tchaikovsky began work on *Iolanta* and, as in all five of his most recent operas, the music he composed first remained the best in the score. He had likewise started upon *The Enchantress* with the love scene, and he schemed this new duet as carefully as that through which he had exposed the equally progressing relationship of Kuma and Yury. But the engagement between Vaudemont and Iolanta had less life and variety, for the blind princess was an innocent compared to the experienced and wily Kuma – and with Yury hate had first to be overcome; with Iolanta love had merely to be awakened. The duet in *Iolanta* is uneven, the fulfilment of human passion cheated by the final stiff glorification of light based upon the indifferent derivative from the Fifth Symphony's motto theme, and structured as a formal cabaletta conclusion. But earlier, while the exchanges between the young couple had remained intimate and personal, and while fresh, unknown feelings had been growing in both, the musical level had risen sharply. This portion of the duet unfolds easily and naturally, for all its careful organization; the central crisis (Vaudemont's perception of Iolanta's blindness) is neatly flanked by the identical beggings of tokens (in G sharp minor), with the final E flat section leading naturally forward towards the more recitative-like transition to the formal ending. Vaudemont's first avowal is tender, yet strongly arched and impassioned, his self-restraint the more impressive for the wealth of feeling within his music. Yet how much more affecting does this G sharp minor music sound the second time, when it is heard from Iolanta after her confused, misery-filled response to her suitor's stunned silence. This G major passage (Ex. 286), with its simple vocal phrases of pained bewilderment, and its at first halting, then eloquently free string line, is the emotional heart of the opera, nothing in it more beautiful than the

Ex. 286

[Your silence is bewildering, I do not know how my words could have been unpleasant ne zna-yu, chem moi slo - va te-be mog-li bĭt ne-pri - yat - nĭ.

to you. Tell me, wherein is my fault? I rarely meet strangers here, and there is much I do not yet

Ska - zhi mne, v chom mo-ya vi - na? Chu - zhikh ya

know: teach me, I am young,]

red - ko zdes vstre-cha - yu i mno - go-vo yesh-cho ne zna - yu;

tĭ na - u - chi, ya mo - lo - da,

sudden, pointed wrench into B minor as Iolanta's words uncover what her misfortune has cost her in relationship and experience. Tenderness, not passion is her lover's response (see Ex. 281b); trying to reassure and soothe her, his pity the stronger for her ignorance of her dreadful disability, he spares Tchaikovsky the need to explore a realm of rampant masculine sexuality that would have been alien to him. Had all of *Iolanta* been on this level, it would have been a masterpiece, not the slender, pretty, but also insipid piece it mostly is.

For all Tchaikovsky's readiness to set opera and ballet side by side, for him there could never have been any question of combining them, and when later in the year Karl Waltz offered him *Vanatabe*, a fairy tale subject in which Tchaikovsky found some attractive features, he was very clear what he would *not* attempt with it:

> I . . . do not understand that undefined and unsympathetic form of art which is called *opera-ballet*. It's one or the other; either my characters will *sing* or they'll *mime* . . . I allow a fantastic element into an opera only insofar as it does not impede real, simple people with their simple human passions and feelings from functioning . . . Only people – or, maybe, angels and devils who intervene in human affairs on a level with people – can sing.[23]

This, of course, had justified the angelic voices in *The Maid* or the Devil in *Vakula*. Among Tchaikovsky's operas, the latter stands apart. It was a piece with a special ambience, set in the real world though within the purview of the supernatural, peopled with warm-blooded mortals though incorporating a devil – but one that had enough of the human in him to experience feelings that might be projected through music. What Tchaikovsky had found so profitable in *Vakula*, and what helped make it one of his four finest operas, had been its range of stimulus: its fantasy, atmosphere, at times its vigour and movement – above all, of course, its vibrant humanity. But what had stirred him in the other three – his Pushkin-based operas – was the concentrated intensity of feeling experienced by certain characters at critical junctures in their lives. It is in these operas that the strip cartoon structure of the scenario is most evident, certain scenes focusing upon a character caught into some terrible predicament and exposing that character's emotional turmoil with a sustained intensity that is sometimes scarcely bearable. No one can remain unimpressed by the grand stage tableaux of these three operas (especially the dance scenes in *Onegin* and *The*

---

[23] *TLP*16A, p. 151; *YDGC*, p. 534.

Queen of Spades, the execution scene in *Mazepa*), but it is these intimate scenes at the other extreme that strike the more deeply – as we are confronted by the bitter outpouring of Kochubey enduring the torment of his betrayal to Mazepa and the apparent treachery of his daughter, by Hermann's destructive obsession which drives him to actions more than the Countess's nerves or his own sanity can survive, above all by the merciless baring of Tatyana's turmoil as she confronts the sudden, agonizing choice which is to ruin her life for ever. In January 1891, only months before beginning *Iolanta*, his last opera, Tchaikovsky had set out for Taneyev his operatic philosophy and method. This most lucid and truthful exposition is also a useful final reminder of the underlying consistency of intention and single-minded integrity behind a series of works which have shown much outward, sometimes confusing diversity and such wide, sometimes infuriating, variations in quality.

The question of *how an opera should be written* I have always decided, do decide, and shall decide extremely simply. You should write them (as, however, all other [forms] should be) as *God has decreed you should*. I have always striven as *truthfully*, as *sincerely* as possible to express in music that which is in the text. *Truthfulness* and *sincerity* are not just the result of intellect, but a direct product of inner feeling. So that the feeling should be alive, warm, I have always tried to choose subjects capable of warming me. Only those subjects can warm me in which real living people, feeling as I do, are participating. In consequence I find unbearable Wagnerian subjects which have nothing *human* in them . . . And so, having chosen my subject and set about composing the opera, I have given my feelings complete freedom, resorting neither to Wagner's recipe nor to the imitation of classical models, nor to a striving to be original. During this I in no way hinder the spirit of the time from influencing me. I recognize that if Wagner did not exist I should compose differently. I admit even *kuchkism* declares itself in my operatic works; probably also Italian music, which I loved passionately in my childhood, and *Glinka*, whom I worshipped in my youth, have also acted upon me strongly, to say nothing of Mozart. But I have never invoked one or another of these idols, but have let them take charge of my musical instincts as they wished. Perhaps in consequence of such a relationship to my work there is no direct indication in my operas of belonging to this or that school; perhaps not infrequently this or that force overcomes the others and I fall into imitation – but however this may be, all this happens of its own accord, and if I am sure of anything, it is that in my [operatic] compositions I am as God created me, and as I have been made by

my education, circumstances, the characteristics of that century
and that country in which I live and work. Not once have I been
unfaithful to myself. Whether I am good or bad let others decide.[24]

[24] *TLP*16A, p. 29; *TZC*3, pp. 421–2; *TTP*, p. 169.

IO

THE BONDS OF FAME:
THE PIANO MUSIC

'THEY HAD ALL . . . thought I was much older,' Tchaikovsky had noted in his American diary on 8 May 1891. The other guests at that curious supper at the Damroschs' had certainly been surprised to learn that the day before had been his fifty-first birthday. 'Have I aged of late?' he had continued dejectedly. 'It is very possible. I feel that something within me has gone to pieces . . . Under the influence of the talk about my aged appearance I had bad dreams all night.' The following ten lines are struck through; clearly the nature of his nightmare was such as should not be known to others – except its end. 'I was sliding helplessly down a gigantic stone incline into the sea, and was clutching at a small feature in some kind of rockface. All this, it seems, is an echo from the evening's conversations about my old age.'[1]

Laments about the gathering years, as about dwindling powers, provide a perpetual litany in Tchaikovsky's later life, but this time the evidence was there for all to see. True, some observers on his American expedition had noted the alertness in the 'expressive blue eyes', their 'wide awake, keen look', the quick, decisive manner. But the constant refrain had been that he looked older than he was. For us there is the harsh evidence facing p. 225, and though other photos present a less time-ravaged image, all, even the most carefully lit, suggest a subject around sixty rather than fifty. The Americans, so conscious of the outer man, had repeatedly confronted him with his aging image as they saw it, and their consensus had sunk deeply into his awareness. 'No! the old man is obviously in decline,' he wrote to Bob Davïdov from Maidanovo on 7 July, after a particularly exhausting bout of sketching the second act of *The Nutcracker*. 'Not only is his hair thinning and white as snow, not only are his teeth falling out and declining to chew his food, not only are his eyes weakening and wearying easily, not only are his legs shuffling rather than walking – but even the one and only ability he has

[1] *TD*, p. 276; *TZC3*, p. 463.

for any sort of occupation is failing and evaporating.'[2]

He had now been back from America a month, having passed the first eight days in St Petersburg relishing his return to familiar surroundings, relatives and friends. At Laroche's he had dined with Glazunov, who so enjoyed the evening that he had presented him with the autograph scores of his Quatuor slave, Op. 26, and two orchestral songs, Op. 27, as mementoes. Such gifts to Tchaikovsky had now become something of a habit with Glazunov. The deforestation at Frolovskoye had decided him that life there was no longer tolerable, and during his American tour Alexey had moved everything back to Maidanovo. But Maidanovo had its shortcomings: a serious fire had devastated a part of the village, and his former house was less solitary, though he admitted the other inhabitants kept to themselves. A further cause for depression was Alexey's condition; he was ailing so badly Tchaikovsky wondered whether his days were numbered. If he were to lose his faithful friend and servant country life of any sort would become intolerable, and he would settle in St Petersburg, he decided. Nor was this the only prospect of less attractive surroundings for living. Promotion for Anatoly had entailed a move to Revel [now Tallinn] in Estonia, and there would be no more visits to Tiflis unless Ippolitov-Ivanov could arrange for him to conduct concerts there. But this was not to be – nor did he find any comfort from his final urgent bid, if not to restore the intimacy, then at least to dispel the shadow of emotional treachery which hung over the memories of the long, precious relationship with his former patroness.

The fact is that the remaining two-and-a-half years of Tchaikovsky's life were to be a time of deepening inner gloom, despite all Modest's attempts to proclaim the opposite. Yet at the same time his outer, personal success constantly consolidated. The invitations to conduct not only his own, but others' compositions multiplied, the requests to attend performances of his own works and receive tumultuous ovations increased, and the conferring of honours from foreign institutions began. Gratifying as this might be, it cramped yet further his time for composition. Before the end of 1891 he would finish Iolanta, but in the nearly two years that would remain to him he would do no more than score The Nutcracker, then complete his last symphony, a one-movement piano concerto,[3] a set of eighteen piano pieces and a group of six songs. Yet in the preceding two years he had composed not only the double bill

---

[2] TLP16A, p. 156; TZC3, p. 490; TPB, p. 494.
[3] In fact drawn from the first movement of the rejected sketches for a four-movement symphony.

of opera and ballet, but also *The Queen of Spades*, the four-movement *Souvenir de Florence*, and the symphonic ballad, *The Voyevoda*. Doubtless the extra public commitments were partly to blame for this reduction – yet it is still impossible not to believe that some inner factor was diminishing his creative flow, and only one of these works to come can be placed among his very greatest.

Despite the constant public acknowledgments of his personal prestige, the grand foreign tours were over. Tchaikovsky had left America with pressing invitations to return, and he fully intended to if the terms were right. When Carnegie had visited Russia he had been enchanted by the sound of its church choirs, and Tchaikovsky opened negotiations with the choirmaster of St Sofiya's Cathedral in Kiev, Yakov Kalishevsky, whose boys had deeply impressed him in the performances of *The Queen of Spades* in that city, to discover whether Kalishevsky could muster a group and accompany him on a second American tour. Tchaikovsky's enthusiasm for the project was keen; if necessary he would make the trip the following January even though his wish had been to spend the whole of that winter in Russia. But when in September he received notification of the $4,000 for twenty concerts it was proposed to offer him personally, he was dismayed. Via Jurgenson he replied with a simple telegram: 'Non. Tschaikowsky'. A month later he made his own counter-proposal: $12,000 dollars for the twenty concerts. He had hardly expected it would be accepted, nor was it – but he seems to have harboured surprisingly little resentment, and in writing to Brodsky who through Tchaikovsky's representations had become leader of the New York Symphony Orchestra, he sent cordial greetings to the Renos, Damroschs, 'and the mass of my New York friends'.[4]

[4] *TLP*16A, p. 241. Modest claimed that his brother was especially bitter at this fee, having badly overestimated his success with the American public. However, Modest becomes an increasingly unreliable witness in matters concerning his brother's public prestige. In fact, the remuneration offered was not as paltry as Tchaikovsky imagined, for his previous fee had been unusually generous because the main occasion for his visit was of such special importance. Modest's attempts to diminish his brother's success were clearly motivated by intense jealousy at the far greater reputation the composer enjoyed. It is difficult to believe Tchaikovsky harboured any special resentment, for he added in this same letter: 'I retain the most gratifying memory of New York and of the cordiality of its inhabitants. The American people are unusually sympathetic, upright, simple and sincere.'

It could be predicted that nothing would come of a later, quite separate proposal that he should, in return for no more than accommodation costs, give a twenty- to thirty-minute conference paper on the state of music in Russia during the International Exhibition to be held in Chicago in 1893 to celebrate the 400th anniversary the previous year of Columbus's discovery of America. However, it was these national celebrations which prompted Mrs Jeannette M. Thurber to invite Dvořák to accept a two-year appointment as director of the National Conservatory of Music in New York.

A change was discernible is his social life also, for the house parties of Moscow friends and associates were over. Something of his antipathy to the Conservatoire had infected his view of the Moscow RMS, and those associated with either could not escape contamination. His guests were now mainly younger family or friends, and among his first were Modest, Bob Davïdov and his second cousin, Alexandr Litke, with whom in mid-July he transferred to Moscow to visit the Franco-Russian Exhibition. He had gone to it without enthusiasm but, once there, was captivated, staying in the city a week to revisit it. It was one welcome interlude in a very hectic summer. On returning to Maidanovo and further work on the second act of *The Nutcracker*, he was immediately distracted by proofs of *The Tempest* and *The Sleeping Beauty*. The former was being reissued in a revised edition, and Ziloti had proved a careless proofreader. As for the ballet, the four-hand transcription had been entrusted to Ziloti's cousin, the young Rakhmaninov, who was too inexperienced, Tchaikovsky concluded: 'It's lacking in boldness, craft, initiative – there's an over-slavish submission to the composer's authority, as a result of which there's no strength and brilliance.'[5] For Tchaikovsky transcriptions of his own pieces should not be pedantically literal. The effort demanded to correct no more than a portion of the defects had cost him several bad nights, and he begged Ziloti to complete the task for him – carefully. It all confirmed that he must supervise both proofs and transcriptions much more closely – even take such things upon himself.

Though Tchaikovsky found himself soon reconciled to Maidanovo, thoughts of settling in St Petersburg still lingered, and there remained the problem of how to spend his evenings in the solitude of the country, once he had finished the day's work. Reading was difficult, for it gave him a headache which prevented sleep, but he had found two ladies who were equal devotees of his favourite card game, vint. That, however, was the extent to which he was prepared to mix with his neighbours, and with the sketches of *The Nutcracker* finished on 6 July, he left for St Petersburg to avoid inviting them to the celebration of his nameday. But a week of freedom gave way to a further period of intensive activity, for besides setting about *Iolanta*, he had to correct the proofs of a new edition of *Onegin*, which incorporated all the revisions made during the past dozen years.

Also intensive seems to have been his study of Spinoza. Tchaikovsky's library contains a number of books by and on this seventeenth-century philosopher, and two years earlier he had already

5 *TLP*16A, p. 140.

confessed to the Grand Duke Konstantin Konstantinovich the attraction to be found in those who, 'like Spinoza and Count L. N. Tolstoy, do not distinguish between *good and bad people*'.[6] He had also confessed to knowing Spinoza only from the words of others, but now that he confronted the philosopher's metaphysical system for himself, he discovered an interest which was to remain. For one like Tchaikovsky, who longed to make the leap of faith but had never been able to perceive where lay the ground of certain belief, it was deeply reassuring to follow a great rationalist who identified God with nature itself, removing the need to search for a more transcendent deity. Even more, Spinoza offered hope when he emphasized that if we can understand our emotions and their causation, then we may free ourselves from their domination.

But especially, Tchaikovsky noted in his copy of Spinoza's *Correspondence*: 'Letter XXI must be read and re-read endlessly – to such an extent does everything in it correspond to my feelings and thoughts.'[7] No doubt it was comforting to hear a man of Spinoza's intellectual stature admit he sometimes could not understand the Holy Scriptures, assert the ascendancy of our natural understanding where it conflicted with the letter of these Scriptures, yet still declare that their authority, if not their literal record, provided him with a basis sufficient for belief. But equally must Tchaikovsky have grasped at the philosopher's refusal to accept that God recognized good and evil nature in man, such a moral distinction arising only through the exercise of human reason. '*When we consider the nature of the man who is led by his desire for pleasure,*' Spinoza had written, '*and when we compare his present desire with that which is felt by the upright, or with that which he himself had on another occasion, we assert that the man is deprived of a better desire because we judge that the desire of virtue then pertains to him. This we cannot do if we consider the nature of God's decree and His understanding. For in this respect the better desire belongs no more to that man's nature at that time than it does to the Nature of a Devil or of a stone . . .* Hence it is clear why the desire of Adam for earthly things was evil only in relation to our understanding and not in relation to that of God.'[8] However Spinoza's meaning may be perceived, Adam's fall gained a softer landing – a realization which held much comfort for one, like Tchaikovsky, aware of an irreparable flaw within himself.

Whether Spinozan speculations helped reconcile him to the theft of

---

[6] *TLP*15A, p. 204; *TZC*3, p. 328.

[7] Quoted in *TPB*, p. 622.

[8] Spinoza to Blyenbergh, 28 January 1665. Quoted from *The Correspondence of Spinoza*. Translated and edited by A. Wolf (London, 1928), p. 175.

the watch his former patroness had given him eleven years earlier, after he had composed *The Maid of Orléans*, is unknown. Certainly he found he was less upset by its disappearance than he might have expected, though his indifference was perhaps less a disinclination towards moral censure than an instinctive recoiling from this symbol of his one-time treasured relationship. The posture of the culprit, once caught, completely confounded him. Mrs Novïkova, the proprietress of Maidanovo, who was one of Tchaikovsky's partners in vint, had a son, and it was the latter's valet, Fedya, who had committed the offence. But having confessed, nothing could persuade or force him to reveal where the watch was. Next he implicated others, who were detained, then released. Finally he alleged he had given the watch to his master. Totally foxed, the police superintendent in charge of the investigation tried another approach; he suggested Tchaikovsky should confront the thief alone, who again confessed, then begged and received forgiveness – and thinking that this absolution closed the matter, retracted his confession, claiming he had never stolen the watch, and that his master, to whom he had given it, was therefore also cleared. On learning the matter was certainly not closed, he returned to his earlier tale.

For Tchaikovsky it was as distressing as it was bewildering. 'All *Klin*, all the peasants around are following the affair with feverish interest,' he wrote in discomfort to Modest.[9] With the whole neighbourhood feasting itself daily upon this delightfully unpredictable scandal, a break of four days with brother Nikolay at Ukolovo and a week in Kamenka were the more welcome. From Ukolovo he was able to visit the distinguished poet, Afanasy Fet, whose work had afforded him the lyric for his first surviving composition, and to whom he had repeatedly returned for song texts. Tchaikovsky had heard of Fet's extreme reserve, but discovered he was both pleasant and humorous. Their respect was mutual; Fet read for Tchaikovsky some of his newest work, then was to write and dedicate a poem to him as a memento of their meeting. At Kamenka Tchaikovsky found the family still grieving for Sasha, but their general condition appeared good. On 14 September, after four days in Moscow dealing with yet more proofs, he was back in Maidanovo. He had kept his presence in Moscow a secret, for the Conservatoire was marking its silver jubilee, and he was profoundly unwilling to be drawn into the celebrations. But with Laroche now also installed at Maidanovo piano duetting and reading aloud would resume in the evenings; such compensations made even correcting proofs of the full score of *The Queen of Spades* bearable. These done, and the sketches of *Iolanta* completed on 16 September, he began to orchestrate *The Voyevoda*.

Though Tchaikovsky had firmly declined the suggestion, made through Arensky, that he should conduct the production of *The Queen of Spades* planned in Odessa, the winter to come was to be marked out by a variety of conducting commitments which drew him increasingly away from Maidanovo, sometimes for extensive periods, and which was to culminate in the Black Sea city in his greatest personal triumph within his native land. But it was not only work that kept him at home for the remaining time. He was penniless. Currently there were no receipts to be had from the Imperial Theatres, nor were fees yet due from Jurgenson for the new opera and ballet, and it is no surprise that, apart from the briefest of visits to Moscow for a concert by the young Jules Konyus, he curtailed his expenses by remaining at Maidanovo for nearly two months until rehearsals for the Moscow première of *The Queen of Spades* drew him back there for three weeks.

Yet in no way did current financial constraints curb his largesse. In fact, his surviving letters show as much as at any other time of his life just how responsive he could be to anyone and everyone whose plight roused his sympathy. A credit note was sent to his cousin, Anna Merkling, to draw upon in case of need; Jules Konyus might get a poor audience for his concert – and if so, Jurgenson was to buy fifteen to twenty tickets on Tchaikovsky's account and distribute them to whom he chose. Nor was his generosity confined to money. During his weeks in Moscow in November his help was constantly solicited by young musicians, some entreating him to attend their performances, others wanting his support in obtaining financial assistance. More personal support was needed by Yuliya Shpazhinskaya, whose domestic situation had brought her to breaking point; she must separate, at least temporarily, from her family, Tchaikovsky urged her. But his greatest human concern at this moment was nearer home. Modest and Kolya Konradi still shared their existence, and the strain had increasingly told upon the younger man. Two years earlier Tchaikovsky had discovered the depth of Kolya's resentment at what he felt had been Modest's insulting treatment of his mother during the family disputes of Kolya's troubled childhood, and at Modest's lingering control of him. Kolya was also continuing to pay Modest a salary, and this rankled. So violent and bitter had been Kolya's outburst that Tchaikovsky had attempted to make his brother aware of how extreme the situation had become. But Modest had remained passive and Kolya's resentment had seemed to pass – that is, until the recent summer when he had again voiced his discontent, this time openly. For

Tchaikovsky personally the matter was deeply distressing. Though no doubt the strong physical attraction he had once felt towards Modest's former pupil had long since cooled, a bond remained, and while his loyalty to his brother was supreme, he hoped to preserve both relationships. In one of the longest of his surviving letters (and, to judge from the multitude of alterations, one of the most difficult he ever had to write), he counselled a complete break between the two men, analysing the whole situation and weighing its diverse factors, probabilities and possibilities with that clearheaded and wide ranging wisdom which he always seemed able to apply to a human problem outside himself. With a clean break the rift could perhaps be closed and a new relationship built, he suggested. But Modest had been dependent upon Kolya and would need support until he could find a position yielding an adequate income. Why not one in the theatre? Tchaikovsky would willingly write to Vsevolozhsky on his behalf; meanwhile he would be prepared to allocate him 300 roubles a month until Modest had found himself a paid position.

This written, and a second letter drafted to Bob, with whom he advised his brother to discuss the position, Tchaikovsky slept on the problem, and next day decided to send neither. Instead he framed his advice into a shorter, less frank, and far less effective document. Modest did not at this stage break with Kolya; that was to come nearly two years later. But it seems the financial arrangement was ended, for in writing of his brother's generosity to others at this time, Modest admitted that he was himself receiving from him 2,000 roubles a year – exactly the sum that Kolya had been paying.

The Moscow production of *The Queen of Spades* opened on 16 November. Tchaikovsky's pleasure in the production and the work's reception was offset by his total dissatisfaction with his new symphonic ballad, *The Voyevoda*, which he introduced two days later. But in other respects this second evening was a personal triumph, resonantly confirming the great success he could enjoy when conducting music other than his own, for the programme included Grieg's Concerto and Nápravník's Fantasia on Russian themes, with Ziloti as soloist in both, and Brandukov performing Glazunov's *Sérénade espagnole* as well as Tchaikovsky's arrangements of his own piano Nocturne, Op. 19, No. 4, and Andante cantabile. He would have left Moscow the day following this concert, but the performers in *The Queen of Spades* wanted to give a dinner in his honour, entailing a delay of a further three days. His last act was personal and completely characteristic. On behalf of the baritone, Pavel Khokhlov, who had created the Bolshoy's first Onegin and had just performed the same service with Eletsky in *The Queen of*

Spades, he addressed a letter to Pchelnikov, head of administration in the Moscow theatres:

Dear Pavel Mikhailovich,

The day before yesterday, when I was with you, I forgot to approach you with a further *very important* request. I had promised dear, sympathetic *Khokhlov* to petition you on his behalf: that when he performs the role of the Demon [in Rubinstein's opera] for the hundredth time, you would permit this to be advertised on the posters. I totally understand this fervent wish of his, and I consider he fully, fully merits those enthusiastic ovations which should be anticipated if the public are made aware of this jubilee, unprecedented on our stages. Please, I beg you most earnestly, respect *Khokhlov*'s petition. He is a favourite with his colleagues, the public, composers of operas, the Moscow ladies – in a word, he is a universal favourite, and you will afford pleasure to all if you accede to his request.

Yours very truly,
P. Tchaikovsky[10]

To Pchelnikov Tchaikovsky's wishes seem to have been law. Eleven days later Khokhlov received his deserved tribute.

Tchaikovsky's next public appearance was in St Petersburg. The pace of his engagements was accelerating, and there was only a fortnight at Maidanovo to continue the scoring of *Iolanta* before he had to be in the Russian capital for a charity event, in which he would conduct an excerpt from Verdi's *Ernani* besides his own Slavonic March and overture to *Cherevichki*. For Tchaikovsky personally it was less of a sensation than his Moscow concert. Figner had mounted it and was the star of the evening for most of the audience. It was an opportune moment for a four-day visit to Anatoly and his family in their new home in Revel. Back in Maidanovo on 21 December, he worked on revising the *Souvenir de Florence* as well as scoring the one piece of the opera that remained: the introduction. Ever since his return from America seven months earlier and his move back to Maidanovo he had debated with himself where he would settle permanently. He had thought much of St Petersburg, but now suddenly he had found what he needed in Klin itself. It was not an estate such as he had once dreamed of, but it was a house sufficient for his needs, the surroundings were pleasant, and he could bequeath it to Alexey, whom he now fully expected would outlive him. For three months of the winter he would

[10] *TLP*16A, p. 264.

rent a furnished apartment in St Petersburg. Though this purchase was to founder, he had taken the final decision that he would take up permanent residence in Klin. Within months he was to install himself in his last home.

All this was happening as he prepared for a series of engagements within both Russia and Western Europe. First there was Kiev. His visit had been planned in gratitude to Pryanishnikov and his opera company, whose production of *The Queen of Spades* the previous year had so delighted him that (so Modest wrote) he had been prepared to give them the première of *Iolanta* if the Imperial Theatres would agree. Permission was denied, of course, and as consolation Tchaikovsky promised to conduct a concert for the company, a decision which offended the local branch of the RMS, whose long-standing request that he should conduct for them remained unsatisfied. The solution was to give a concert for each, and on consecutive evenings he presided with great success over the same programme: the Third Suite, *1812*, and the overture and dances from *The Voyevoda*. With Kamenka close, he could pass the Russian Christmas there.

It is a paradox of the professional man's biography that its externals can become less interesting as its subject's distinction and fame grow. The range of activity in which youth may engage while pursuing its path to glory may be denied to many who have reached the pinnacles of their professions. Success makes life a prison of routines, and for Tchaikovsky these, as we have seen, were the increasing requests to conduct concerts, and those endless impositions which the public figure must accept as the price of fame – above all, the constant pressure for new works, and the need to supervise their presentation (and sometimes their re-presentation) to the world, and their publication (and often re-publication). Recently this last activity had increased to an almost intolerable degree. For all Tchaikovsky's persuadings, Jurgenson had still not felt able to engage a professional proofreader of his own such as the best German publishing houses employed. But this publisher-friend remained very conscious of the exceptional burden this placed on his most distinguished composer, and he now made an offer to take over Tchaikovsky's swelling business correspondence for him. Tchaikovsky was grateful for the thought, but he knew this was impracticable; he would simply have to use the time he could allocate to letter writing yet more productively. With ever more business and professional communications, personal letters had increasingly become documents penned in summary terms; rarely was there time for the leisurely, affectionate paragraphs encountered in earlier years recounting the trivial but sometimes so revealing details of his private life and activities. Nor are there any journals from his final two-and-a-half years; the record of his American tour is the last of his surviving diaries. And so the extended account he gave Bob Davïdov of his Christmas at Kamenka opened what was now a rare window on to his most personal world. His stay was clouded with sadness; Lev was away in St Petersburg, the children were dead or dispersed, and only the older members of the family seemed to remain. He arrived on Christmas Eve (5 January 1892) with Boris Plesky, son of the estate office's manager, who had been with him in Kiev and for whose company he felt much gratitude:

It was not without a painful feeling that I entered the courtyard, in the middle of which the empty, locked house produces a doleful impression. *Sister* [Nastasya Popova, Tchaikovsky's cousin, now eighty-four years old] met me and invited me to drink tea with her. During tea she said such strange and nonsensical things that Boris spluttered with laughter three times. It seems *she* . . . has declined greatly and become much more confused than before. After changing I directed myself to the big house. Al[exandra] Iv[anovna], Liz[aveta] Vas[ilyevna] and Alex[andra] V[asilye]vna [Lev's mother and elder sisters] are, by contrast, much better and more cheerful than they were in the summer. I visited Nik[olay] Vas[ilyevich, Lev's elder brother], (completely well), who again told me how he had stumbled over a bucket in the summer when Mariya Nikolayevna [his daughter] was sowing seed on the left and pushed him into the bucket, and several other already familiar tales which I listened to with great pleasure, for I love N[ikolay] V[asilyevich] terribly and am happy when I see he's still the same. Then I hurried off to *Sister* who simply can't understand that in no way have I come to drink tea with her all day, and is endlessly surprised that I don't confine myself to my own room and hers. Then there was dinner at the big house (lean and very tasty), then I looked in on *the Pleskys*, and again drank tea in the big house. The *Yashvils*, brother and sister, arrived – and unexpectedly, after them, *Mitya* [Dmitri Davïdov, one of Sasha's sons], very cheerful and much improved in appearance. Grandmother [Lev's mother], the aunts and Nik[olay] Vas[ilyevich] were *literally in tears* of pleasure at his unexpected arrival. At eleven-thirty I returned home with Mitya and went to bed. At six a creaking door awoke me, and from behind the wardrobe I heard *Sister*'s sepulchral voice: '*Darling, don't you want tea?*' I didn't reply. She went off, muttering some nonsense. After that I went to sleep again. Today, after tea at *Sister*'s, I walked, attended an endless mass, sat at home and chatted with Mitya, who told me how cheerless and boring it was living in his hole. I was terribly sorry for him. Then there was a sumptuous lunch at the big house, preceded by a little service. At the lunch Yashvil spoke very presumptuously and authoritatively about church music, of which he understands nothing. . . . Today it's the Christmas tree. *Kolya Sandberg* [Nikolay Vasilyevich's grandson] (for whom I nourish sympathy) is very busy with it. I leave tomorrow.[11]

Four days later, in a very different frame of mind, he again wrote to Bob:

You ask, my inestimable one, what my mood's like. Bad! Again, as during last year's tour, I am counting the days, hours and minutes to the end of my wandering. It's not that I'm physically tired from the journey – in no way. But what wearies me is that with strange people I can't be *myself* . . . As soon as I'm not alone, but with new and strange people, then without perceiving it myself I take on the part of a person who is amiable, mild, polite, and also apparently absolutely delighted in a new acquaintance, instinctively trying to charm them by all this, which for the most part I do successfully, but at the price of extreme strain, joined with an aversion to my own dissimulation and insincerity. I want to say to them: 'Go to the devil, the lot of you!', but I utter compliments, and sometimes am so carried away, even become so much the part, that it's difficult to tell where the real 'me' is speaking and where the false one, the one that seems. So in a word, all this is a mask which, with incredible relief, I shed when I remain alone . . .

Then the tone changes:

You are constantly in my thoughts, for at every feeling of sadness, melancholy, at every clouding of the mental horizon – like a ray of light the thought appears that you exist, and that I shall see you in the not so distant future. On my word of honour, I do not exaggerate. Incessantly, of its own accord, this ray of comfort breaks through . . . : 'Yes, it's bad, but it's nothing – Bob is still in this world.'[12]

Such words seem less those of an uncle to his nephew than of a husband to his wife or mistress.

[11] *TLP*16A, pp. 298–9.
[12] *TLP*16A, pp. 299–300; *TZC*3, p. 519 (partial).

Tchaikovsky was now in Warsaw. He had arrived on 9 January to conduct a concert of his own works: the Third Suite, Italian Capriccio, Violin Concerto and *Sérénade mélancolique*, together with the *Elegia* and Valse from the Serenade for Strings, and an aria from *The Maid of Orléans*. His former pupil, Stanislaw Barcewicz, would be the solo violinist, and Alisa Friede, who had recently created Milozvor in *The Queen of Spades*, would sing the aria, as well as five of his romances. The orchestra was good and the concert a predictable success. His two soloists took his entertainment upon themselves, though there was also a full-dress soirée in his honour at which he was especially struck by the charm and intelligence of the Polish ladies. More memorable still was acquaintance with Mascagni's very recent *Cavalleria rusticana*. For a moment *verismo* held a potent attraction for him; he was drawn back to a second performance, and wondered whether Modest would be able sometime to provide him with such a libretto. There was talk of mounting one of Tchaikovsky's own operas in the city. On 15 January, the day after his concert, he was escorted in style to the railway station, and on 17 he was in Hamburg where two days later he was due to conduct the first performance of *Onegin* in that city. But with only one rehearsal on the intervening day and with the opera being sung in German, the problems encountered in synchronizing the recitatives in this unfamiliar version decided him to withdraw. In any case, he had no fears in handing over to the local first conductor, who was not some middling Kapellmeister, but one 'of genius', with a burning desire to conduct the first performance. Yesterday I heard him conduct *the most amazing* performance of *Tannhäuser*.'[13] Indeed, under Gustav Mahler's direction *Onegin* was given a 'positively superb' presentation.[14] Yet Tchaikovsky sensed that the opera had not really pleased, though he had been called out respectfully after each scene. The press was reserved, but not unkind, and Tchaikovsky himself was more than delighted with the Tatyana of Kathi Bettaque, at least satisfied with the other principals, and had nothing but praise for the orchestra and chorus. The production was less consistent, and there were some incongruous touches, notably during the mazurka, when 'a sort of flower-filled wagon drawn by men with an unusual haircut came out and all the ladies grabbed the flowers and pinned them on their partners . . . My longing for my homeland ever increases,' he continued to Kolya Konradi. 'However, thank goodness, I have not long *to suffer*, and besides I hope to enjoy myself in Paris.'[15]

[13] *TLP16B*, p. 16; *TZC3*, pp. 521–2; *TPB*, p. 506; *YDGC*, p. 543 (partial).
[14] *TLP16B*, p. 17; *TZC3*, p. 524; *YDGC*, p. 544; *TTP*, p. 285.
[15] *TLP16B*, p. 17; *TZC3*, pp. 524–5; *TTP*, p. 285.

On 21 January he settled into his well-loved hotel, of which the warm
and trusted Bélards were still the proprietors, and where the Zilotis
were already staying. When this tour's schedule had been planned he
had expected he would now be at the first Prague performance of *The
Queen of Spades*, but this had been postponed for a season. His remaining
concerts were on 10 and 11 February in Amsterdam and The Hague,
and he planned to spend the intervening fortnight incognito, revising
the *Souvenir de Florence*. But within days he was thoroughly depressed,
despite the presence also of Sapelnikov and Sophie Menter. He went to
the theatre, even the Folies-Bergère, where the bill included a Russian
clown with 230 trained rats. It was all boring – and also rather
sickening, for while Massenet's *Esclarmonde* was drawing audiences to
the Maryinsky in St Petersburg, there was no Russian representation to
be found in any concerts or any theatrical and operatic performances in
Paris; this lowly act was the highest manifestation of that russophilia
in which the Parisians prided themselves. For want of anything better
to do he at last risked Zola's *La Bête humaine*. In his present frame of
mind it was the worst possible reading. After only three days' work the
sextet was completed, life became purposeless, then unbearable.
Postponing his Dutch concerts until the following season, on 31
January he left Paris. Two days later he was back in St Petersburg,
where he remained nearly a week to shake off the sense of isolation
which had gripped him so tightly while abroad.

Hard on the heels of his return to Maidanovo came news from
Amsterdam that the Maatschappij tot Bevordering der Toonkunst had
elected him a corresponding member of their Society. Even more
heartening was to find the house in which he would finally settle. It was
large, comfortable, on the edge of Klin, and had a more than adequate
garden. The move would occur in the middle of May, and meanwhile
his most pressing task was to score items from *The Nutcracker* to fill the
gap left by the now rejected *The Voyevoda* in the concert he was to
conduct for the St Petersburg RMS on 19 March. The engagement four
days before this can have afforded him little joy. As a distinguished
alumnus of the School of Jurisprudence he was to share in a concert
given by the school's amateur orchestra in the presence of the
Tsarevich, piloting them through his *Chant sans paroles*[16] and the waltz
from *The Sleeping Beauty*. For the RMS he conducted *Romeo and Juliet* as
well as the suite from *The Nutcracker*. The latter was an instant success,
almost every number was encored, and in June, to satisfy the requests
for copies which came from all directions, Jurgenson issued the score

---

[16] Presumably in the orchestration by Erdmannsdörfer.

and parts. *The Nutcracker Suite* was on the road to its still universal popularity.

In the middle of April Tchaikovsky was required in Moscow to honour a second promise given to Pryanishnikov and his company. While in Kiev before Christmas he had learned that the theatre would not be available to this excellent troupe for 1892–3, and they had taken the bold decision to promote themselves for a short season in Russia's second city ahead of this in the hope of installing themselves there for the following autumn. Tchaikovsky had openly doubted their wisdom, but had still offered to conduct three operas for them without fee and with his name appearing on posters alongside that of the resident conductor as though he were one of the company. This would guarantee success at least for their spring visit. First, however, on the anniversary of Sasha's death he had to attend a requiem mass in St Petersburg. He stayed there a week, then on 17 April headed straight for Moscow. As he arrived the idea for 'a symphony with a *secret* programme'[17] was already forming in his head.

Tchaikovsky had never conducted operas other than his own, and the three he was now to preside over were *Faust*, Rubinstein's *The Demon*, and *Onegin*. Pryanishnikov recalled the new insights he brought to *The Demon* and above all to the garden scene in Act 3 of *Faust*, as well as the warmth of the reception given him by both audiences and performers. Exciting this might be, but it was also very taxing, for besides having yet more proofs to correct, he had to cope with invitations, visitors of his own, and a constant trail of unknown individuals who wanted to play or sing for him, show him their compositions, or simply extract money. And when Tchaikovsky, having conducted four performances and received an especially enthusiastic ovation after *Onegin*, then been accompanied to the railway station by Pryanishnikov's entire company, left Moscow on 11 May, there was barely time to call in at Klin to act as godfather to Alexey's new son before he had to speed to St Petersburg to decide the casting of *Iolanta*. Only on 17 May could he savour properly what for him were the real qualities of his new and final home (and, after his death, his museum): its spacious rooms, splendid views, its privacy, and the numerous walks to which it gave easy access.

It was now eight months since Tchaikovsky had exercised his conceptual faculties, and he had an urge to compose. In November 1889, a year after completing his Fifth Symphony, he had confided to the Grand Duke Konstantin Konstantinovich that he had long aspired

[17] *TLP*16B, p. 70.

to crown his creative career with a grand symphony on some as yet undefined programme, but it was a further eighteen months before, evidently on his return voyage from America, he jotted down a few preliminary ideas for what might become such a piece. More important still was a programme he roughed out, possibly at the same time: 'The ultimate essence . . . of the symphony is *Life*. First part – all impulsive passion, confidence, thirst for activity. Must be short (the finale *death* – result of collapse). Second part love: third disappointments; fourth ends dying away (also short).'[18]

During the following months, while at work on *The Nutcracker* and *Iolanta*, he continued to note down further materials, but when at last he began systematic work on the piece, many of these and earlier ideas were discarded; nor was the programme to be used. Others were drawn in, however, progress was rapid, and by 8 June both the first movement and the finale were fully sketched. He had hoped to continue work in July and August, but further composition was delayed until October. Nevertheless, by 4 November the entire symphony was sketched, and within three days the first movement was scored up to the recapitulation. Already he had offered to conduct the première at a charity concert in Moscow in February. But there followed another enforced break, and when he returned to the piece he experienced total disenchantment. 'It's composed simply for the sake of composing something; there's nothing at all interesting or sympathetic in it,' he wrote to Bob Davïdov on 28 December. 'I've decided to discard and forget it . . . Perhaps,' he added, though he can hardly have realized how presciently, '*the subject* still has the potential to stir my inspiration.'[19] Two months later he told Bob the E flat symphony no longer existed.

In fact, it still did.[20] He first revealed his intention of using its sketches as the basis for a piano concerto early in April 1893, and he

---

[18] Davïdova (K.Y.) and others [eds.], *Muzïkalnoye naslediye Chaykovskovo* (Moscow, 1958), p. 245.

[19] *TLP*16B, p. 208; *TZC*3, p. 583; *TPB*, pp. 523–4; *YDGC*, p. 567.

[20] In the early 1950s the Soviet scholar, Semyon Bogatïrev, reconstructed the E flat Symphony ('No. 7', as it is now sometimes listed) from the sketches, scoring the first movement (beyond the point already reached by Tchaikovsky himself, but also using the version of this movement which the composer himself converted into his Piano Concerto No. 3, Op. 75), the scherzo and the finale (also referring in the case of the former to Tchaikovsky's own reworking of this movement into the *Scherzo-fantaisie* for piano, Op. 72, No. 10, and in the case of the latter to the Finale from the Andante and Finale for piano and orchestra, Op. 79, both as it survives in the composer's own piano score and in Taneyev's subsequent orchestrated version). Bogatïrev used the Andante from Op. 79 to provide the opening and closing sections of the slow movement. In the preface to his score of the E flat Symphony (Moscow, 1961) he provided full details of how his reconstruction was made.

began the conversion on 5 July, completing the first movement eight days later. But on reviewing what he had done, he judged it overlong, and decided to issue it as a single-movement Allegro de concert or Concertstück. 'As music it hasn't come out badly – but it's pretty ungrateful,' he observed to Ziloti. 'If that should be Taneyev's opinion, then perhaps I shall forthwith destroy it.'[21] Accordingly in October, after scoring the piece, he showed it to his most trusted critic who, with characteristic candour, told him its faults, above all that it lacked virtuosity. Modest stated that his brother in no way questioned Taneyev's verdict, but did not obliterate the piece since he had already promised it to Louis Diémer, with whom he had renewed acquaintance while in London in May, and he wished to show the score to the French pianist as evidence that he had not defaulted on his promise.

Tchaikovsky's attitude towards the piece remained ambivalent. In fact, the first movement was not abnormally long, and for all his declared intention to let it stand alone, he went on to convert the second and fourth movements of the E flat symphony into a slow movement and finale to make a three-movement piano concerto. After his death these transcriptions were put in order and scored by Taneyev, then published in 1897 as the Andante and Finale, Op. 79. The first performance of the authorized single movement was given in St Petersburg on 19 January 1895 with Taneyev as soloist, as he also was when, on 20 February 1897, the Andante and Finale were first heard, also in St Petersburg.

The defect specifically identified by Taneyev in the movement completed by Tchaikovsky himself and published in 1894 by Jurgenson as Piano Concerto No. 3, Op. 75, was an inevitable consequence of transcribing a largely completed orchestral movement into one for soloist and orchestra, for Tchaikovsky seems to have made no attempt to rewrite the substance of what he had composed, for the most part converting an orchestral texture into a piano solo, or drawing some idea out of the texture for the soloist to present, or else overlaying what was already there with piano figuration. In none of these ways was the result likely to be especially grateful. But the problem lay deeper than this. The Fifth Symphony had been a determined reconciliation of what Tchaikovsky saw as the Western symphonic pattern with his own most characteristic invention, and in many regards it was a remarkable success. Most important of all – where the requirements of these interests clashed irreconcilably, his musical creativity had taken precedence. If, when he set about the E flat symphony purposefully at the end of May 1892, he still intended to follow the programme already mapped out, he quickly abandoned it, for it is inconceivable that a design so conventional was articulating anything other than a purely musical experience – as Tchaikovsky himself certainly perceived when he came to scrutinize his finished sketches. If anything, the E flat symphony attempted to take the experiment of the Fifth Symphony further, hazarding a more total submission to the Western tradition, and despite Semyon Bogatïrev's conscientious attempt to realize Tchaikovsky's sketches, the piece remains faceless, giving not the slightest hint of the blazing originality and shattering expressive force of the symphony yet to come.

Thus it was not only that the Third Piano Concerto was handicapped by the nature of its earlier incarnation; that incarnation was less than first rate in materials. The exposition follows Tchaikovsky's familiar three-theme design, and there is some spiciness in the invention which follows the main theme. But the music quickly stagnates after the tutti reaffirmation of the opening theme and tonic, for it does not, as had the Second Piano Concerto, proceed to reinforce a tonal grip which is to be rudely broken by the shock of the second subject's distant key; instead Tchaikovsky seems to lose his nerve, and the most functional of transitions moves the music, with as much smoothness as is possible in conditions of such embarrassed haste, through a major third to the new tonal region (E flat to G – exactly that of the Second Concerto, though in reverse). Certainly the new gentle theme that follows is attractive, and its pathos is heightened when the oboe and bassoon counterpoint the piano with unapologetically unresolved dissonance (Ex. 287). Attractive, too, is its sprightly partner in this second subject. As for the sudden re-entry of an E flat chord, this and what follows brings to the codetta something of that contrast of harmonic colour which earlier had been so limply underplayed.

The development starts well by selecting the lively idea which had filled out the first subject's centre, heightening its piquancy by extending it over a whole-tone bass. Also admirable is the later augmentation of a portion of the first subject to produce a full, cantabile passage before the cadenza. Only now does Tchaikovsky break away from the symphony. The mammoth, written-out cadenza had been fundamental to the Second Piano Concerto and even more to the Concert Fantasia, in which it had substituted for the entire development. But whereas the two central cadenzas of the Second Concerto had fruitfully explored the further possibilities within the musical materials, adding a generous supply of effective, if not always elegant virtuosity, the cadenza which now intervenes before the recapitulation dwells almost myopically on

Ex. 287

the first theme of the second subject (especially the drooping figure in Ex. 287) in textures often remarkable for their turgidity.

There is one small saving touch in store; the recapitulation neatly modifies the first subject, taking a new direction from bar three, then extending this fresh idea. The point of this emerges later, after the dual second subject has been re-run, for in the coda the piano picks up the new extension which becomes a counterpoint for the widely striding portion of theme which it had earlier displaced.

While the conditions provided by his new home in Klin were as ideal as Tchaikovsky might reasonably hope to find within Russia, nothing could counter the fatigue which built up from the unbroken stream of proofs and the strain of drafting the E flat symphony's first two movements. A break was imperative. He had long felt out-of-sorts, and his ultimate destination was Vichy where he proposed to take a cure for 'catarrh of the stomach', and where he would stay incognito under the name of 'Pierre Davïdov'. Ahead of this he wanted to spend some days in Paris. On 9 June he left for St Petersburg, stayed six days, then headed for Berlin. In Paris he visited Colonne and conferred with his French publisher, Mackar, but his real aim was to introduce Bob to the attractions of his favourite West European city. Together they saw *Lohengrin* at the Opéra, *Manon* at the Opéra comique, and visited other places of entertainment.

Their pleasure was roughly shattered by the arrival of Parasha. By now Tchaikovsky was being forced to take a very different view of his sister-in-law. Anatoly had always been liable to bursts of depression and self-doubt, with a readiness to perceive ill-will, even malice in the attitudes and actions of those with whom he worked. As for Parasha, in Tiflis Tchaikovsky had observed her flightiness and her obvious social aspirations, as well as her plain insensitivity to her husband's problems. Nor had he failed to note that while she had been neglecting Anatoly she had become increasingly possessive of Tchaikovsky himself, and was quick to take offence if she felt he was neglecting her. Anatoly had just returned from a secondment to Samara from which he hoped preferment would follow, but everything had turned sour; yet now, while he was in a particularly depressed state, his wife ('hateful' Parasha, as Tchaikovsky described her) suddenly proposed to desert him and accompany Tchaikovsky and Bob to the West for a month.

What spurred Tchaikovsky to so vicious an epithet was his suspicion of her real motive. 'It is my deep conviction that *she is in love with Bob* and is going because of him,' he continued to Modest.[22] He could still find some pleasure in her company, but that joy which he had expressed in such sentimental terms in the first years after she had become his sister-in-law had completely gone, and with it much of his delight in sharing in her family life. On this occasion Anatoly had managed to persuade her to postpone her departure, but now she had broken away. Bob could not bear her, and Tchaikovsky hinted to Modest that she had indeed behaved in an unbecoming way towards their nephew. Another cherished, comforting element in his personal life had been irreparably flawed; what he had treasured as a secure and loving relationship was now a thing of the past.

There was nothing they could do but endure her company when they left for Vichy on 23 June. Tchaikovsky found the French spa as loathsome as when he had stayed there sixteen years before. The endless press of invalid humanity and the impossibility of ever being alone were almost intolerable, the boredom of a routine dedicated solely to obtaining a cure weighed heavily upon him, he had not the slightest urge to compose, and the longing to be back in Russia grew ever stronger during his three-week stay. But he believed the cure itself was benefiting him, and since the doctor diagnosed Bob as needing it urgently, he bore the tedium. In fact, the local theatre, orchestra, and opera were not at all bad, but the only other pleasures came from reading Russian papers at the Casino, from cycling (Bob on a bicycle, his uncle more decorously on a tricycle, both in 'lawn-tennis' outfits),

22 *TLP*16B, p. 108.

and discovering the pleasures (and chills) of the newly installed showers. Though everything he saw of Parasha confirmed his suspicions, he and Bob contrived to organize their days so as to be mostly separate from her. 'She's found acquaintances, dances at balls, and many admirers pay court to her, though from a distance,' he reported to Modest as they were preparing to leave.[23] She had one final shock in store for them. Though she was due to remain a further week, she abruptly announced she would depart with them. As Tchaikovsky noted to Modest, to do this would have revealed all too plainly the true motive behind her stay in Vichy, and after much argument she was made to think better of her decision. On 15 July Tchaikovsky and Bob left Vichy alone. Four days later they were in St Petersburg.

His return to Klin on 23 July found him somewhat restored in body but not in spirit. 'There now face me two months exclusively devoted to proofs, the simplified arrangement of the ballet, and so on,' he wrote to Taneyev, who had already lightened his burden by preparing not only the piano score of *The Nutcracker* but also the vocal score of *Iolanta*. 'I'm now looking through Langer's piano arrangement of *Iolanta* which, as usual, he's done *abominably*,' he added.[24] There were several versions of both works to oversee, including a German edition of the opera which Rahter was issuing in Hamburg, and during the next weeks his flow of letters to Jurgenson turned into a flood. Sometimes there was no escaping a journey to Moscow because problems had become too difficult to resolve by correspondence. He had no house guests, and the minor diversions around him assumed a special importance: the appearance of new flowers in his garden, even the distant wail of Alexey's baby son, who was teething. He read Flaubert's letters, writing excitedly to Modest about them, partly because of the image they projected of a most sympathetic man devoted to his art, partly because they supplemented Spinoza's insights, affording 'the most amazing answers to some of my own thoughts about the deity and religions'.[25] His impression of Zola's latest novel, *La Débâcle*, was very different from that which he had formed of *La Bête humaine* six months earlier. 'I'm surprised how Zola can be regarded as a serious writer,' he had declared distastefully to Bob Davïdov from Paris. 'What could be more impossible, devoid of truth, than the basis of this novel? There are, of course, scenes in it in which reality is depicted with truthfulness and life. But its very essence is so false that it's impossible for one second to take a lively interest in the affairs and circumstances of those

---

[23] *TLP*16B, p. 123.
[24] *TLP*16B, p. 128; *TTP*, p. 184; *TZC*3, p. 550 (partial).
[25] *TLP*16B, p. 137; *TZC*3, p. 552; *TPB*, p. 514; *YDGC*, p. 555.

participating. It's simply a crime novel *à la [Emile] Gaboriau*, larded with obscenity.'[26] By contrast *La Débâcle* he 'admired greatly', he told Modest.[27]

In his real world there were anxieties. He was deeply worried about Bob, to whom he had become still more attracted during their time abroad. The cure at Vichy seemed to have had little effect on the lad, and he feared he could discern in him traits that had marked his sister, Tanya, whose life had ended so tragically five years before. Would Bob, too, become a victim of Fate? Anatoly had left Revel for Nizhni-Novgorod, but there had been an outbreak of cholera which was also threatening the Konradi estate at Grankino, where Modest was staying. With proper precautions there was little need to fear – but neither was there absolute certainty they would not succumb to the disease which had killed their mother. Then, worst of all, Parasha's uncle, Sergey Tretyakov, who had seemed so hale and well when Tchaikovsky had met him in St Petersburg, died suddenly. The shock made him feel indisposed a whole day, and the funeral in Moscow left him still more depressed. Apologizing to Bob for not having sent a letter earlier, he pleaded that his silence had probably been a blessing. 'If I had written it would have been in a most melancholy and even gloomy tone. Such has been my perpetual mood. I won't go into details – but then, nothing special has occurred; it's simply that a phase of melancholia has set in.'[28]

Nothing happened to change his condition before his departure from Klin on 11 September. Proofs occupied him to the very last day. His destination was Vienna where he had been asked to conduct in one of the concerts organized in connection with a Musical-Theatrical Exhibition. Convinced that Vienna was infected with russophobia, but charmed by the terms in which the invitation had been issued, he accepted. The result was disastrous. The crowd of admirers in the hotel corridor besieging the neighbouring bedroom into which Mascagni had been booked forewarned him where Viennese musical admiration currently lay; the venue of his own concert – a stuffy and smelly restaurant, from which he had to insist all tables should be removed – confirmed how little importance was really attached to his own visit. The orchestra, though competent, was ludicrously small, and after two rehearsals he decided he had had enough. Sapelnikov and Sophie Menter had now arrived, and within two hours he was borne out of the city to Menter's castle at Itter.

26 *TLP16B*, p. 23; *TZC3*, p. 526; *TPB*, p. 509; *YDGC*, p. 545.
27 *TLP16B*, p. 144; *TZC3*, p. 553; *TPB*, p. 515; *YDGC*, p. 555.
28 *TLP16B*, p. 145.

It was the best thing that had happened to him for months. 'I'm completely well and am enjoying life in the full sense,' he wrote to Modest on 27 September, five days after his arrival. '*Itter* merits its reputation . . . For my sake a very regular and undisturbed daily order is observed. . . . This place is just enchantingly picturesque. Quiet, unruffled peace, and no guest of any sort. . . . In a word, it's a long time since I felt as well as here. I shall stay another five days. Then I shall go via Salzburg (I shall stop for the Mozarteum) and *Prague* (where I shall stop for *The Queen of Spades*) to St Petersburg.'[29] Delays in the Czech première of his opera caused him to linger more than a fortnight at Itter. By now, however, he was becoming impatient for news from Russia, and he had a longing to be back. The Prague performance on 12 October was excellent, he was rapturously received, and the press was approving. Yet in his letters there is scarcely a mention of any of this. It was not that he was unmoved or ungrateful; it was simply that such occasions were becoming almost routine, and he must have sensed that he was now falling into that category of internationally famous individuals to whom audiences come almost willing themselves to react as they do. The man who, nearly twenty-five years before, had been overcome with embarrassment at the applause for his First Symphony, who on his first visit to Prague in 1888 could still describe his reception as '*a moment of complete happiness*',[30] now found the extravagant receptions accorded him a matter almost of indifference. But there was nothing here of the repressed vanity or sated self-esteem of the complacent celebrity; rather, it was the inherent honesty of a truly modest man.

The day after the première he set off for St Petersburg, remaining four days to enjoy family visits. On 19 October he was home in Klin. More than a fortnight remained before he would be required in St Petersburg for rehearsals of *The Nutcracker* and *Iolanta*. He still had to compose an additional aria for Figner in the opera, but he also found time to complete the sketches and begin the orchestration of the E flat symphony. On 8 November the train brought him to St Petersburg in time for a very special reception at the hundredth performance of *Onegin* in the Russian capital.

Rehearsals of the double bill were spread over more than six weeks. As with proofs, so with these preparations Tchaikovsky seems to have involved himself to an unprecedented degree. Working constantly within the Imperial Theatres, it was opportune to press the case for scheduling Taneyev's still unfinished trilogy, *The Oresteia*, for the following season, thus forcing the composer to complete the piece.

[29] *TLP*16B, pp. 168–9; *TZC*3, p. 570; *TPB*, pp. 518–19.
[30] *TD*, p. 198; *TZC*3, pp. 222 and 563; *YDGC*, p. 440.

Vsevolozhsky's interest was certainly aroused – perhaps because he had never produced an opera on a classical subject in the Imperial Theatres, Tchaikovsky speculated. But the latter's attempt to extract an operatic commission for Arensky failed completely. The Theatres' director knew Arensky's fitful work habits too well; when he had completed his current enterprise, *Nal and Damayanti*, Vsevolozhsky would be prepared to consider it. Yet while Tchaikovsky was working so hard to further the cause of these two works, he showed little sympathy for Modest when his latest play, *A Day in St Petersburg*, flopped totally at the Alexandrinsky. It was a pretentious concoction – and Tchaikovsky had told his brother so; it would be a good lesson for Modest and would send him back to his real métier, which was writing straightforward theatre pieces. By contrast the performances on consecutive days of Tchaikovsky's own revised *Souvenir de Florence* reassured him that he now had the work as he wanted, and at the second he was presented with the medal of the CMS to thunderous applause. Simultaneously his international prestige was further recognized by election as a corresponding member of L'Institut de France. The *Moscow Gazette* recorded the details of the election with much pride. Tchaikovsky's sponsors had been Ambroise Thomas and Emile Paladilhe, his rivals Max Bruch and the Belgian composer, Peter Benoit. Tchaikovsky had received 32 out of the 35 votes cast, and was only the second Russian to be granted this distinction. Notification came also that Cambridge University wished to confer an honorary D.Mus. upon him. If he accepted, he would be required to attend the ceremony.

With his pleasure in the brilliantly successful presentation of his two new theatre pieces fractured by the hostile press reaction, he viewed the prospect immediately before him dourly. *Iolanta* was to be given in Hamburg on 3 January and in neighbouring Schwerin three days later. The thought of having to endure once again the strains of rehearsals preceding two more premières was too much. 'But suddenly I reflected that I was, in fact, in no way *obliged* to go to Hamburg *and Schwerin*, and that there they could get along without me,' he observed to Anatoly on 22 December. 'This calmed me completely, and now my plan is thus: the day after tomorrow, 24, I shall travel to Berlin. In Berlin I shall decide where I'll go to rest (most probably *Nice*). Then on 10 January I'll be in Brussels, then on 15 I shall proceed to Paris for three days, afterwards to *Montbéliard* to Mlle Fanny, and about 22 January I'll already be in Odessa where I'll conduct one or two concerts. At the end of January I'll be in St Petersburg.'[31] Much of this itinerary was to be

---

[31] *TLP*16B, p. 202; *TZC*3, p. 582; *TPB*, p. 522.

changed. Arriving in Berlin on 26 December for three days, he then directed himself to Basel, stayed a night, and the following day was in Montbéliard.

The mission that had brought Tchaikovsky to this small provincial French town was very special. In St Petersburg in March he had received a letter from Fanny Dürbach, the governess of his earliest years, to whom he had owed so much but whom he had not seen for forty-four years, and long thought dead. Her approach moved him very deeply; his feeling, he told Modest, was almost that which he would have experienced, knowing that his mother had returned from the grave. But it was a feeling mixed with dread that Fanny would have grown old, become enfeebled like 'Sister' at Kamenka, an unrecognizable shadow of the woman he had once so loved, and that if he should meet her he would wish her dead. All the same, he answered her letter and enclosed a photograph of himself. Her reply must have brought back a flood of memories and emotions:

Dear Pierre,
    Permit me to call you thus; otherwise, if I were not to address you as when you were my dear little pupil, it would seem to me as though I was not writing to you. This morning my sister came up to my room with your letter in her hand, saying: 'Here's something that will give you great pleasure!' I confess I had given up hope of the pleasure of seeing your handwriting again. When my present pupils had insisted that I should write to you, I had said to them: 'We shall see each other in heaven.'
    Because you are in France nearly every year, come the more quickly so that I may yet see you and talk with you about all those things which you and I so loved. How much there is about which only you can tell me! I know life well enough to foresee that there will be much that is sad. We will unite our memories and our regrets. You know how good your dear parents were to me, and how I loved you all, and I hope you will find it pleasant to chat about them with an old friend who has lived her life with such sweet memories.
    How much I would like to know how life has unfolded for all of you! I have thought a lot about Nikolay, that tall, handsome boy, about your dear sister Zina, about Ippolit and Lidiya. Do they, like you, still have dear memories of their old friend? . . .
    Come, we have so much to talk about. . . . You will not find yourself unknown in our town. But if it is quiet you want, then we

have here an hotel with a garden run by honest people. You will find it very good. In Russia it is possible to offer hospitality; everything is conducive to it. Here it is not so. We live very modestly in our own small house; we also have a garden and all that is necessary. All the same, I thank you heartily for the thought that it might be otherwise; again I thank you. Thank you for your good letter and the photograph. The more I look at it, the more I recognize you . . .

Your last letter, which I hold as something very precious and which I have re-read many times, was written in [18]56. You were then sixteen. You were telling me about your mother's death.

But your father: was he able to take pleasure in your successes? And your dear Sashenka: was she happy in her marriage? Tell me about your younger brothers – but most of all about yourself. Allow me to hope for a quick reply from you in expectation of our meeting.

I have written to you without constraint. When you come your presence will remind me that I must no longer talk with you as with my dear boy of time long past; I shall address you with all those titles that fame has conferred upon you. But meanwhile, as before, I kiss you and pray God to bless you and give you happiness.

Your old governess and friend,
Fanny Dürbach

My sister asks me to convey to you her feelings of deep respect. Do you remember how you used to try to work well during the week so as to receive a red bow on Sunday? Now you can wear it every day – but would it give you as much pleasure? From my heart I hope so.[32]

Over the next two months more letters were exchanged. When he came she could arrange for him to meet the parents of some of her former pupils who were musical (they came from the *best* society) – or if he wanted to play the organ for diversion, she could arrange it as she knew the organist and had a key to the church because of her Sunday School.

Then a little of the governess's habitual authority breaks through:

Dear Mr Tchaikovsky, why do you wish to make yourself out as old? When I lived with you your father was completely grey, but he was still not old. In 1856 you wrote to me: 'Papa has not aged at all.' Please, don't try to appear old. Leave that privilege to the one who

---

[32] *TZM*, pp. 127–8. The letters have been translated from French into Russian. Lidiya was a cousin of Tchaikovsky.

has acquired it through years and experience. In expectation of the meeting with the great Mr Tchaikovsky I kiss my dear little Pierre whom I love and shall always love with my whole heart.[33]

Tchaikovsky had thought to visit Fanny in July after his residence in Vichy, but he would have had to take Bob and he feared to risk boring his nephew. Now, however, the moment had arrived. To Nikolay, who had known Fanny as well as he, he wrote in full of their meeting. He had recognized her immediately and was astonished at how little she had changed in appearance.

I had been very afraid there would be tears, scenes – but there was none of this. She received me with joy, tenderness, and great simplicity, as though we hadn't seen each other for a whole year. Immediately I understood why both our parents and all of us had loved her very much. She is an unusually sympathetic, straightforward, intelligent being who exudes goodness and honesty. Soon there began endless recollections of the past and a whole stream of all sorts of the most interesting details about our childhood, about mother and all of us. Then she showed me *our exercise books* . . . your and my letters – but what was most interesting of all, several wonderfully sweet letters from Mama. I cannot describe the delectable, magical feeling I experienced as I listened to these tales and read all these letters and exercise books. The past in all its detail arose so clearly in my memory that it seemed I was breathing the air of our Votkinsk home, I was listening to the voice of Mama, Venichka, *Khamit*, Arisha, Akulina and so on. *Khamit*, for instance, I had completely forgotten, but here, as she recalled his figure and recounted how passionately he had loved Papa and us, the children, I suddenly saw him as though he were alive. . . . At times I was so carried back into that distant past that it became somehow awesome but at the same time sweet – and all the while both of us were holding back the tears. . . .

I sat with her from 3 to 8, and completely failed to notice how the time passed. I spent all the following day with her, except that she sent me off to the hotel to dine, saying frankly that her and her sister's table was too wretched, and that it would embarrass her to feed me. I had to pay two visits with her to very close friends and a relative who

[33] *TZM*, p. 130.

had long been interested to see me. . . . In the evening I exchanged
kisses *with Fanny* and left, having promised to return some time.[34]

It was one of the most deeply moving occasions of his later years. The
world famous composer and the unknown provincial governess, who
had shared what for both had been four wonderful years, relived not
merely the memory of events, but unselfconsciously recreated something of the precious intimacy of their old, very special relationship.
Whatever he might have become, and however aware she was of his
now immense fame, he remained for her the highly strung, vulnerable,
endearing, intelligent little boy whom she had nurtured, comforted,
loved. She wanted to recall how the other members of the family looked,
and he sent her some photographs. She thanked him with excited,
appreciative comments on each.

Yet in one special way he had disappointed her, though now she
forgave him. 'I am happy at your triumph in Brussels,' she ended her
reply. 'There can be no one more convinced of your talent than I. I saw
its emergence as the gift of a poet (which I would still have wished to see
you become). But nevertheless I still bless God for your successes, and
it seems to me he has sent down to you your reward. How many
renowned people are not recognized in their lifetime!'[35]

They continued to correspond, but sadly none of his letters have
survived. She worried endlessly about his health, tried to tempt him
back to Montbéliard as a place where he could find rest and quiet – and
where they could again talk. The strength of her enduring feelings for
him is evidenced in every line and epitomized in every letter ending:
'The friend of your first years and always' . . . 'Your oldest and most
devoted friend' . . . 'Your old friend who loves you more, perhaps, than
you would wish.' Her last letter was sent only weeks before his death,
and his reply was written as he prepared to leave Klin for the last time.
The meeting she had so hoped for never happened.

The Brussels concert on 14 January had, indeed, been a triumph.
Tchaikovsky had passed six of the intervening days in Paris, finding
some diversion in the Bélards, the Parisian restaurants and theatres,
but otherwise struggling to master his longing to return home. To Bob
he gave the clearest of all accounts of how his mood affected him during
this expedition abroad. '*All the time it's filthy, although* the character of

[34] *TLP*16B, pp. 213–14; *TZC*3, pp. 586–7; *TPB*, pp. 526–7. Khamit was a Cossack
servant of Tchaikovsky's father.
[35] *TZM*, p. 131.

this filthiness *changes* according to circumstances; now it's simply longing for my country, now agitation from the rehearsals and the [following] concert, now weariness from making acquaintances and conversations, now disenchantment with myself, now fear for the future, and so on, and so on. But all the while I am completely healthy, I sleep excellently, and only rarely am so upset that I lose my appetite.'[36] Part of the trouble, he insisted, was that he was travelling alone. He had sped to the Belgian capital on 9 January. The main works were the Third Suite, First Piano Concerto (with soloist Franz Rummel, who also contributed some of Tchaikovsky's piano pieces), the Suite from *The Nutcracker*, the two middle movements of the Serenade for Strings, and *1812*, while a singer from the local opera performed some of his romances. It was well that he had been allocated three rehearsals. There was no doubting the orchestra's ability or their goodwill towards him, but their discipline was slack, and quiet playing had to be imposed upon them. François Gevaert, whose textbook on instrumentation Tchaikovsky had translated in 1865 while still a student, was president of the benevolent fund for which the concert had been promoted, and during a break in rehearsals he welcomed Tchaikovsky on behalf of the orchestra, who were greatly touched by his decision to donate his fee to the fund.

The following day he was back in Paris, where he had contributed a letter to the newspaper *Paris* defending his country's musical honour against charges brought in an article by André Maurel, *Un voyage musical en Russie*, published in *Figaro* à propos the recent visit there of Lamoureux. Wagner had certainly not been ignored in Russia, Tchaikovsky insisted emphatically, nor was Lamoureux the first Frenchman to conduct for the RMS. As for the charge that Safonov and the singer Yakovlev had publicly 'decried' Bülow as a conductor at a dinner for Lamoureux, in Russia itself Bülow had been recognized as a great conductor and a champion of the cause of Russian music in his native Germany, with (Tchaikovsky added pointedly) a sincere enthusiasm for French music. Above all, it grieved Tchaikovsky that a dying man should be denigrated.

These six days in Paris offered no rest. His open letter had caused something of a stir (and drawn an embarrassed response from Lamoureux), and he knew he must thank personally those responsible for his election to L'Institut de France. Arriving in Odessa on 24 January, during nearly a fortnight in the city he attended a series of rehearsals leading up to the opening performance of *The Queen of Spades*,

[36] *TLP*17, p. 13.

endured a trail of receptions and social events in his honour, and participated as conductor in five concerts. Two were for charity and his role in these was nominal; his three main engagements were for the local branch of the RMS. In the first two Sophie Menter was the soloist, contributing some of Tchaikovsky's own piano pieces to the first, and in the second appearing as soloist in the première of her own Hungarian Rhapsody,[37] which Tchaikovsky had transcribed for piano and orchestra, and scored. The opening concert was an all-Tchaikovsky programme, the principal works being *The Tempest*, Rococo Variations (with Ladislaw Alois as soloist), the Andante cantabile, and the Suite from *The Nutcracker*; the second was a mixed programme with Borodin's First Symphony, Ernst's Violin Concerto in F sharp minor (played by Konstantin Gavrilov), a Scherzo by Porfiry Molchanov (a former pupil of Rimsky-Korsakov), Menter's new piece, and Tchaikovsky's own *1812*. In the third *The Tempest*, Andante cantabile, and the Suite from *The Nutcracker* were repeated, and two romances were added.

From the moment that a delegation of friends and RMS members met him at Odessa's railway station, Tchaikovsky encountered a reception even more frenetic than that he had faced in Prague in 1888. 'Never have I experienced anything like what I am experiencing now,' he wrote to Anna Merkling while in the middle of this maelstrom. 'They honour me here like some great man, almost like the saviour of my fatherland.'[38] At his entrance for the first opera rehearsal he was greeted with pomp, ceremony, and boundless applause. Several items in his first concert had to be played *four* times, so Modest recorded, while at the concert's end (reported one Odessa paper) 'the whole audience rose from its seats, cries of gratitude rang out from different directions . . . the ladies waved their handkerchiefs, the gentlemen their hats, while simultaneously on the platform the orchestra kept up a constant flourish . . . But this had seemed insufficient for the bemused members of the orchestra; recognizing what a great talent was among them, in the interval they had, one after the other, kissed his hands. This was not done on an enthusiastic impulse, but deliberately and reverentially. . . . Pyotr Ilich grasped the complete sincerity of their greeting, and thanked the players.'[39] As for the performance of *The Queen of Spades* on 31 January, it was not merely successful; it created a furore. In Tchaikovsky's second concert it was his own composition which pleased most; *1812* had to be repeated. His third concert was a

[37] It has been suggested that this work was in fact a now lost concerto by Liszt.
[38] *TLP*17, p. 24; *TZC*3, p. 595; *TTP*, p. 253.
[39] *TZC*3, pp. 596–7.

morning event, and that same evening he was present at his fourth performance of *The Queen of Spades*, to receive further ovations.

Tchaikovsky could not but be deeply moved by all this, yet his own accounts in his letters of these frantic ovations and ceaseless adulation were all laconic. 'Never have I been forced to weary myself by conducting as in Odessa, for I had to conduct five concerts – but then, never anytime or anywhere have I been so exalted or fêted as there . . . If only sometime I might receive in our capitals just a tenth part of what has happened in Odessa!' he wrote to Modest on 9 February, two days after his arrival in Kamenka for a five-day visit. 'But that's impossible – or rather, it's unnecessary. What I need is to believe in myself again – for my faith has been greatly undermined; it seems to me my role is over.'[40] Within twelve days of writing this he had finished the sketches of his greatest symphonic first movement.

Among the relentless procession of individuals soliciting Tchaikovsky's attention, and often his help, was one whose request yielded results which vastly pleased him. Nikolay Kuznetsov, a Ukrainian artist, wished to paint his portrait. Tchaikovsky agreed, and the painter worked first from sketches he made of the composer during rehearsals of *The Queen of Spades*, then requested him to pose formally in the theatre's foyer so that he might get not only the head but the hands right. Before Tchaikovsky left Odessa the canvas was completed. Kuznetsov's is the only surviving portrait of him from life, and is the more precious because the composer himself was so openly delighted with it. Modest also vouched for the remarkable way it had caught the 'tragic side' of his brother's mood at that time.[41]

Whether, before Tchaikovsky's return to Klin on 15 February, there had been any special factor which had stimulated his creativity to deliver a symphony of such rare originality and expressive richness as that which he was now beginning cannot be said for certain. Perhaps it was his solitary state during so much of his recent travelling that had left him free to ponder deeply the idea for *A Programme Symphony*, as he himself described it; perhaps it was a particular store of reawakened feelings and remembered experiences prompted by his recent visit to Fanny (and the rude awareness this had also brought of the remorseless passage of time) that had primed his emotional and spiritual responses to an unusual degree. Be that as it may, when he returned home he had already prepared a great deal of the work in his head, often to the

---

[40] *TLP*17, p. 27; *TZC*3, p. 599; *TPB*, p. 529; *YDGC*, p. 572.
[41] Tchaikovsky actively solicited for the painting to be shown in a travelling exhibition currently opening in St Petersburg. Thence it went to Moscow where Pavel Tretyakov was to purchase it for his collection.

accompaniment of tears, he admitted. On 16 February, the day following his arrival home, he set about it in earnest. 'The work went so fast and furious that I had the first movement completely ready in less than four days,' he wrote to Bob Davïdov on 23 February, 'and the remaining movements are already clearly outlined in my head. Half the third movement is already done. There will be much formal innovation in this symphony – and, incidentally, the finale will not be a noisy Allegro but, on the contrary, a most long drawn out Adagio. You can't imagine what bliss I feel, being convinced that my time is not yet passed and I can still work. Perhaps, of course, I'm mistaken – but I don't think so.'[42]

One thing was certain, even without Tchaikovsky's own declaration: this time he was writing to a programme, but one that was secret 'and would remain a mystery to all. . . . The programme is most thoroughly shot through with subjectivity,' he had also confided to Bob.[43] Secret or not, there can be no serious doubt that the programme he had mapped out, then abandoned before setting about the E flat symphony, had at the very least influenced that which was forming the new piece. Work was interrupted after a week when he journeyed to Moscow for an RMS concert on 26 February in which he introduced his fantasy overture, *Hamlet*, to the city, and also conducted his Concert Fantasia (with Taneyev as soloist) and the Suite from *The Nutcracker*. It was the first time he had appeared at an RMS concert in Moscow for three years, and was the result of a direct approach from Safonov the previous October, when the director of the Moscow Conservatoire had asked that they should bury their differences for the sake of Nikolay Rubinstein's creation, the Moscow branch of the RMS. Tchaikovsky's reception might have been foreseen: a flourish from the orchestra, wild applause from the hall, and enormous success after each piece (four numbers in the *Nutcracker* were encored). From Moscow he travelled on to Nizhni-Novgorod to visit Anatoly in his new home, returning to Klin on 3 March. Before leaving home he had made a note that his first task on being back would be to complete the new symphony's march 'in a solemnly triumphant manner',[44] and it is likely he had accomplished this before a second visit to Moscow for a concert on 9 March in which Safonov conducted Georgy Konyus's new suite for orchestra, *From a child's life*. The piece so impressed Tchaikovsky that he drafted an open letter to the *Russian Gazette* praising its qualities.[45]

[42] *TLP*17, p. 43; *TZC*3, pp. 602–3; *TPB*, p. 532; *DTC*, p. 432.
[43] *TLP*17, p. 41; *TZC*3, p. 602; *TPB*, p. 532; *DTC*, p. 432.
[44] *YDGC*, p. 574.
[45] For some reason the letter was never sent, but was discovered after Tchaikovsky's

Ahead of his visit to Moscow Tchaikovsky had passed a few days in St Petersburg, where something of a shock had awaited him; his widowed brother-in-law was to marry Ekaterina Olkhovskaya, a second cousin of his late wife. The family was divided sharply at the news. Lev had feared his children would be hostile, but Bob at least had taken it 'philosophically', and Tchaikovsky himself concluded it was not unreasonable for Lev, who was still young in body and spirit, to take another wife, even though his bride was nearly thirty years younger than he. But Anna Merkling, fanatically loyal to her cousin's memory, was outraged. 'Ah, Anna,' Tchaikovsky rejoined, having set out the case in the couple's favour as best he could, 'with our years we ought not to be so emphatic in saying yes and no. Remember how we were all angry with my father when he married Liz[aveta] Mikh[ailovna]. And so what? Nothing except unqualified happiness came from this late and, it seemed to us, unsuitable match. For a moment I myself found it distasteful to learn that Lev was marrying, but reflecting on his situation, not for one moment did I nourish any anger towards him, or wish to cast a stone.'[46] If at this stage Tchaikovsky was still struggling with divided inner feelings, he found reassuring what he was to see and hear of the couple during the months to come.

On 16 March he was in Moscow for a third time to share a concert three days later with Nápravník, again directing the Suite from *The Nutcracker*; two days later the programme was repeated. Then on 22 March he proceeded to Kharkov where, on 26, he conducted a concert of his own works for the RMS (*The Tempest*, Violin Concerto (with Konstantin Gorsky as soloist), the Second Symphony, *1812*, and some vocal pieces). There was the now regular delegation at the station to meet him, the orchestra greeted him at his initial rehearsal first with his own setting of the 'Slava' tune in the Battle of Poltava entr'acte in *Mazepa*, then with sustained applause. That evening as he entered the opera house for a performance of *Rigoletto*, he was received with furious clapping from the house and a three-fold fanfare from the orchestra. At the concert itself the orchestra, reinforced with a choir, repeated the 'Slava' greeting, Tchaikovsky was presented with an address of welcome from the RMS, was laden with wreaths and flowers, deafened with applause, called back repeatedly at the concert's end, and finally

death and shown to the Grand Duke Konstantin Konstantinovich who, in his turn, passed it on to the Tsar. Such had become the authority of Tchaikovsky's word in matters musical that, as a result of his expressed hope that Konyus would receive the support of those able to give it him, the Tsar conferred an annuity of 1200 roubles upon him.

[46] *TLP*17, p. 66; *TTP*, p. 254.

carried from the hall in a chair borne by a group of the local youth, to an incredible din. A banquet with a succession of toasts followed. A musical matinée in his honour the next day delayed his departure until 28. On 31 March, his first free day back in Klin, he resumed work on the symphony; five more days' application, first to the finale, then to the second movement, and on 5 April he could inscribe at its end: 'O Lord, I thank thee! Today . . . I have completed the sketches in their entirety.' The oscillation between moments of extravagant but gratifying public adulation and solitary sessions composing one of the most profoundly tragic, personal and pain-filled of all works may seem extraordinary. Yet a more bizarre contrast was to come; on the same day that he completed the symphony's sketches he composed, at the request of his cousin, Andrey Petrovich Tchaikovsky, who was commander of the 98th Yurevsky infantry regiment, a lively regimental march.[47]

This piece of trivia was not his only minor creation of these weeks. Between 13 and 15 March, having (presumably) just sketched the march from the Sixth Symphony, he devised a Quartet for four solo voices and piano based upon the B flat episode in Mozart's C minor Fantasia for piano, K. 475. In the spring of 1892 Nápravník's son, Vladimir, had spent some time lodging with Tchaikovsky in Maidanovo while preparing for an examination, and besides joining in piano duets with his host in the evenings, he had played a good deal of Mozart. The idea for this Quartet had been sown then. On 21 October 1893 it was performed at the Moscow Conservatoire by pupils of Lavrovskaya, and already Taneyev had orchestrated the piano part, to the composer's entire approval.

Suggestions for possible subjects for an opera were also offered during these weeks. Kolya Konradi proposed *The Merchant of Venice*, and Modest, it seems, had tried to tempt his brother with the libretto he had already written for Arensky on *Nal and Damayanti*, upon which that composer had made little progress. Tchaikovsky rejected both. What he needed, he said, was something like *Cavalleria rusticana* or *Carmen*. According to Modest, Tchaikovsky was giving a good deal of thought to the possibility of revising both *The Oprichnik* and *The Maid of Orléans*, and even made notes for a scenario on *Mr Gilfil's Love-Story* by George Eliot, whose works were especially attracting him at the time. As for Modest's next suggestion, *Undine*, Tchaikovsky had twenty-four years earlier composed (and later destroyed) an opera founded on de la

---

[47] Tchaikovsky composed it for piano, leaving it to the regiment's director of music to score for whatever forces were available to him.

Motte Fouqué's tale, and he found the subject no longer attractive. What was now occupying him (though only for the sake of making some money, he said) was a set of eighteen piano pieces. He began them on 19 April, composing at least one a day and completing the last on 3 May. During the early days he reported that he was working unwillingly, but as his toil approached its end he admitted he was finding it not only easier but more congenial. Ten were not entirely new, sketches for them existing among materials for the E flat symphony, and therefore dating from 1891 or 1892.[48] Tchaikovsky told Ziloti that at one stage he had envisaged arranging the pieces in three sets of six each, one of which would be dedicated to Ziloti himself, but that he had promised dedications to so many persons that he decided the pieces would have to remain together as Op. 72, each with a different inscription.

In fact, it seems particularly appropriate that what was to be almost his last, and one of his largest, grouping of pieces should become an anthology of various relationships, professional and personal. Some pieces were given to pianists, and are for the most part aptly brilliant: the *Polacca de concert* (No. 7) to Paul Pabst and the *Danse caractéristique* (No. 4) to Anatoly Galli, both members of staff at the Moscow Conservatoire. By contrast, a third teacher there, Nikolay Zverev, now past sixty, got a tenderly affectionate piece, *Passé lointain* (No. 17). Sergey Remezov (*Un poco di Chopin* (No. 15)) taught there, too; like Galli and Zverev, he was one of Tchaikovsky's personal circle. Even more intimate pianist-friends were allocated even more characterful pieces – Ziloti the *Scherzo-fantaisie* (No. 10), the largest item in the collection, and Sapelnikov the concluding *Scène dansante* (No. 18). The remaining professional musician was Vasily Safonov, director of the Conservatoire and until recently in conflict with Tchaikovsky: the reflective, touching *Méditation* (No. 5) was, presumably, something of a peace offering.

Two dedicatees were, like Tchaikovsky, former pupils of the School of Jurisprudence – Auguste Gerke (*Tendres reproches* (No. 3)) a contemporary and, from a later generation, Nikolay Lenz (*Valse à cinq temps* (No. 16)), who had been partially responsible for arrangements of both *Francesca da Rimini* and the Manfred Symphony for two pianos, eight hands. The remaining male dedicatees were more fleeting figures from Tchaikovsky's past. One was Vladimir Sklifosovsky, the lad who had enchanted him on his Mediterranean passage in 1889, and who had died the next year; appropriately he received the *Chant élégiaque* (No. 14). The other, a certain Pyotr Moskalev, was given *Berceuse* (No. 2).

[48] Nos. 2, 6, 9, 11–16 and 18.

All the rest were women. The Maslova sisters, Varvara and Anna, chaste intimates of Taneyev, received the contrasting *Impromptu* (No. 1) and *Un poco di Schumann* (No. 9), and Alina Bryullova, Kolya Konradi's mother, with whom Tchaikovsky seems to have preserved a cordial relationship despite the open hostility between her and Modest, was given *Echo rustique* (No. 13). Laroche's wife, Ekaterina, whom Tchaikovsky so respected (and by now so pitied) was allocated *Dialogue* (No. 8). The remaining three pieces were assigned to young women. Luiza Jurgenson, daughter of Osip, who a year earlier had solicited a dedication on her behalf, was allotted *Mazurque pour danser* (No. 6), Pyotr's daughter, now Alexandra Svetoslavskaya, received *L'Espiègle* (No. 12), and Nadezhda Kondratyeva, his old friend Nikolay's child, *Valse Bluette* (No. 11).

Tchaikovsky's piano music encompassed his whole creative life. His first opus comprised two piano pieces; his final set, Op. 72, was, as we have seen, compiled after he had completed the sketches of his last and greatest orchestral piece. Apart from the early Piano Sonata in C sharp minor, a student work which he never published (though its third movement was to afford the scherzo of his First Symphony), there is only one large-scale work, the G major Sonata of 1878. The rest consists of short- to medium-length pieces, some issued separately but others in groups, often of six or multiples thereof, as with the songs. The later pieces reveal no appreciable development in manner or style, for few sprang from any deep or personal creative impulse, and were in no way subject to the kind of evolution discernible in Tchaikovsky's more characteristic and important pieces. Since few even touch upon truly serious expressive issues, as do some of his songs, their quality is less uneven.

It would be easy, therefore, to dismiss the entire corpus as the epitome of competent mediocrity. To a point this would not be unfair. Nevertheless, there is more attractive music, more resourcefulness and sometimes more lively inventiveness in some of these hundred plus pieces than might be expected. The piano writing may lack flair, but is thoroughly workmanlike, for Tchaikovsky had learned to handle efficiently certain of the standard figurations of both routine and virtuoso style. His textures are mostly solid, sometimes thick. Leaning towards those of Schumann and Brahms rather than of Chopin and Liszt, they employ even more often the anonymous pianistic idiom of the drawing room, and frequently this conditions their melodic style also – which is not surprising, since they were mostly aimed at the domestic market. Quite often they have linear features, with a special inclination to duetting between treble and tenor lines of a sort often met elsewhere in his work. At times the polyphonic texture may suggest a transcription from a string quartet. From the beginning the most common structure is ternary, but occasionally with modifications to the reprise. Sometimes there are effective linking sections, at others a substantial coda which may do more than just close the piece tidily (very often recalling the central section).

Ops. 1 and 2 define the two main categories within all this, for Op. 1, No. 1 is a concert piece composed for and dedicated to a virtuoso, while Op. 2 is a group of three homely works intended even more for amateurs. The first category is by far the smaller, containing only the *Scherzo à la russe*, Op. 1, No. 1 (1867), dedicated to Nikolay Rubinstein, the *Valse caprice*, Op. 4 (1868), *Capriccio*, Op. 8 (1870), Six Pieces on a Single Theme, Op. 21 (1873), and *Dumka*, Op. 59 (1886). The last is inscribed to Antoine Marmontel, Ops. 4 and 8 to Anton Door and Karl Klindworth respectively (like Nikolay Rubinstein, colleagues at the Moscow Conservatoire; Klindworth was also the dedicatee of the G major Sonata). Of the Moscow pianists, Rubinstein was the best served in both the musical distinctiveness and brilliance of his piece, even though it was the earliest. Not surprisingly the *Valse caprice* leans towards Chopin, occasionally very explicitly. If the very extensive coda sounds like a deliberate move to appease Door, should he have found insufficient bravura in the main body of the piece, there was to be no such final compensation for Klindworth in the *Capriccio*, a slightly Schumannesque creation with that composer's mechanical rhythmic repetitiveness and passages of sustained metrical displacement.

These three pieces were written within a three-year period; *Dumka* dates from sixteen years later. Though composed at the prompting of his French publisher, Mackar, its dedication to the Parisian virtuoso confirms that Tchaikovsky recognized it as a concert piece. It is patently intended to provide the sort of local colour French listeners expected of a Russian, and in method, if not form, gravitates towards Balakirev's *Islamey*. A slow and broad folky theme frames the main body of the piece; it is in the lively central section, with its swift multiple repetitions of melodic fragments against changing backgrounds, that the debt to the Glinka tradition becomes especially apparent. But Tchaikovsky has none of Balakirev's flair for piano decoration and the impression is finally ponderous rather than powerful.

The remaining work in this category is of a very different order. The Six Pieces on a Single Theme, Op. 21, were composed for Tchaikovsky's former teacher, Anton Rubinstein, and were clearly designed not to provide a vehicle for pianistic brilliance, but to demonstrate to those, who (besides Rubinstein) he hoped would examine the score in some detail, inventive resourcefulness in transforming a theme to serve a variety of stylistic and expressive functions. *Prélude* (No. 1) introduces the theme (Ex. 288a), then reflects upon its two limbs (*a* and *b*) within a texture for the most part freely contrapuntal. Strict polyphony ensues as the theme is converted into a subject for the *Fugue à 4 voix* (No. 2; Ex. 288b), Tchaikovsky parading his total control of a Bachian technique. In what follows the theme is sometimes made to do more than provide the point of departure, and in *Impromptu* (No. 3) *b* is especially assertive, both during the hectic outer sections (bars 5, 6 and 10) and in the centre where, in bars 5 and 6, it slyly infiltrates this Schumannesque music.

The thematic metamorphoses in the remaining movements (Ex. 288d, e and h) confirm that in the most characteristic Tchaikovskyan variation it was the pitch outline that was the constant. A different kind of transformation occurs in the central section of the *Marche funèbre* (No.

Ex. 288

a. Prélude

b. Fugue à 4 voix

c. Impromptu [transposed]

d. Marche funèbre [key sig. reversed]

e. Mazurque [key sig. reversed]

f. Mazurque [transposed]

g. Mazurque

h. Scherzo [notation reversed]

4) when the 'Dies irae' emerges; it was a musical trick Tchaikovsky was to repeat in variation 4 of the Third Suite's finale. This sombre interloper recurs in the march's closing bars. The rising fifth in bar two of Ex. 288a had acquired some modest importance in both *Prélude* and *Fugue à 4 voix*, and now, with *b* appended (Ex. 288f), it slips into the first section of the *Mazurque* (No. 5) to generate a second melodic idea, while the opening of *b* provides the nucleus of the central section (Ex. 288g). The *Scherzo* (No. 6) is content to use the theme simply to provide its main idea.

The works designed for amateurs are almost all either dances, or else genre, descriptive or mood pieces. Impromptus and scherzi abound, as do dreamy evocations of various kinds – nocturnes, romances, and a variety of rêveries. Constantly in evidence is Tchaikovsky's sheer professionalism, the care with which he will engineer details, smooth joins, add telling touches, and shape neat, tasteful artefacts. They are his lowly offspring but not held in contempt, ranging from quite substantial and formidable challenges for (quasi-)professional pianists to morsels within the modest technique of a child. Tchaikovsky's first set, the three pieces of *Souvenir de Hapsal*, Op. 2 (1867), remained one of his most popular. *Ruines d'un château* (No. 1), with its measured ostinato bass, is picturesque in a mildly mysterious way, but it was above all *Chant sans paroles* (No. 3) which did most to introduce his name to a wider public before the Andante cantabile in the First String Quartet took over this function even more effectively. *Souvenir de Hapsal* was composed at the Estonian coastal town and dedicated to Vera Davïdova (later Butakova), Lev's sister, who during this summer holiday began showing warm feelings towards Tchaikovsky, to the latter's great embarrassment. The *Romance*, Op. 5 (1868), was composed during a second entanglement, this time his more serious encounter with the opera singer, Désirée Artôt, to whom he was briefly engaged. Tchaikovsky himself seems to have taken some pride in this piece, whose nocturne-like opening and closing sections are certainly attractive (see Ex. 41 in Vol. 1). The *Valse scherzo*, Op. 7 (1870), dedicated to his sister Sasha, suffers by comparison with the earlier *Valse caprice*, being melodically less consistent.

Each of the Three Pieces, Op. 9 (1870), is dedicated to a Moscow pianist. The first two were young women, Nadezhda Muromtseva and Alexandra Zograf, the third Alexandre Dubuque, one of the senior and most respected of Moscow piano teachers, who in 1867 had purchased from Tchaikovsky the cufflinks presented to him by the future Alexandr III in gratitude for the Festival Overture on the Danish national anthem, Op. 15. While the pieces are thoroughly pleasant trifles (the first, *Rêverie*, rather more interesting than the two dances that follow), the Two Pieces, Op. 10 (1872), have contrasting charms. The gently wayward melody and rippling accompaniment figuration offers no explanation for the choice of title for the first, *Nocturne*, though a texture not unlike that of the middle section may be found in the repeated quaver triplets of Chopin's example in A flat, Op. 32, No. 2. If the *Nocturne* is pretty salon music with some attractive harmonic touches, *Humoresque* is a more open-air piece, its material ranging from the piquant to the boisterous, and it was to become another of Tchaikovsky's better known piano works.

These two pieces were dedicated to his young pupil, Vladimir Shilovsky, and there is a similarly intimate and affectionate tone to *Rêverie du soir*, the first of the Six Pieces, Op. 19 (1873), inscribed to another of Tchaikovsky's closest friends, Nikolay Kondratyev. A trio of women pianists secure the next three. Vera Timanova, only eighteen, a pupil of Liszt and Tausig, receives the most brilliant, *Scherzo humoristique* (No. 2); the others were Anna Avramova and Monika Terminskaya, the former a product of the Moscow Conservatoire. Avramova was allotted *Feuillet d'album* (No. 3), which is one of the simplest and slightest of the set. Its opening sixteen bars (Ex. 289) are a microcosm of one of the most striking features of all these piano works: how a skilful composer can produce much from little, and animate music which might otherwise be of little consequence. The first half is no more than a pretty two-bar fragment heard four times – a static opening finally leading nowhere. A tiny shock is applied to restore momentum; *ai* becomes a fifth (*aii*) and generates a tight sequence with a small but telling elaboration at the cadence (*aiii*) in the next bar. This phrase is repeated before *aiii*, like *aii* before it, itself begins a new two-bar phrase which, also repeated, closes the sentence out-of-key. The imminent return of the opening becomes therefore a moment of newness in itself.

What was to prove the most popular of these pieces, *Nocturne* (No. 4), was given to Terminskaya. Terminology offers no puzzle here; texture and cantabile melody are what might be expected, and the delicate trickles of semiquavers which counterpoint the main theme's return are beautifully judged. Also admirable is the transformation of the central section's opening two bars (themselves drawn from the final two bars of the first section) when, as has happened so many times in earlier pieces, this central music returns to close the piece. *Capriccioso* (No. 5) was inscribed to a pianist colleague at the Moscow Conservatoire, Eduard Langer, whose ineptitude in making piano transcriptions was to cause Tchaikovsky so much exasperation. The main theme occurred to him in June 1873 while leaving Russia for Western Europe, and had

Ex. 289

originally been destined for a symphony 'which I intend shall eclipse all my previous ones'.[49] Heard in this leisurely Allegretto semplice, it is difficult to believe even Tchaikovsky could ever have made a piece built from material such as this fulfil so grand an ambition.

The last movement lies completely apart from its predecessors. Dedicated to his lifelong friend, Herman Laroche, it is a theme and variations in which, as in the Six Pieces on a Single Theme about to come, there would be points of interest to the connoisseur. Though only one of the twelve variations is labelled 'Alla Schumann', that composer's presence is to be felt from time to time elsewhere. The set is clearly an experimental work, Tchaikovsky mostly standing back from his material and subjecting it to a wide variety of treatments with results to be respected for the resourcefulness and good intentions they reveal, but giving little hint of that absolute assurance with which he

[49] *TD*, p. 3; *YDGC*, p. 94.

was to make the form his own only three years later in the Rococo Variations.

Tchaikovsky's best known piano collection, *The Seasons*, Op. 37b (1875–6), has already received attention in Vol. 2, as have the Piano Sonata, Op. 37, the *Album for Children*, Op. 39, and Twelve Pieces (moderate difficulty), Op. 40, all of 1878. Though both *The Seasons* and the Twelve Pieces were production line creations in that each item was composed within a single day as an act of will rather than creative impulse, the earlier set is by far the fresher. Op. 40 reflects all too clearly the inhibitions and blockages which had impeded the flow of Tchaikovsky's creativity after the trauma of his marriage in 1877, and apart from the unexpected experience which unfolds in *Rêverie interrompue* (No. 12), much of their music is all too obviously manufactured. Taken as a whole, this procession of prosaic pieces makes up the dullest of Tchaikovsky's piano sets.

Excepting the international virtuosi, the dedicatees of Tchaikovsky's piano works provide pointers to stages or events in his personal existence. Up to 1870 there are two close associations with women and his affection for his only sister, so far away in the Ukraine. Then in the 1870s it is first the world in which he moved as a professor at the Moscow Conservatoire, for his dedicatees become for the most part either colleagues or figures in the city's musical life. Having in 1877 passed through the central crisis of his life and withdrawn into the tighter circle of his family and closest friends, he now scattered his dedications within these groups, Modest being given the Twelve Pieces, and his six-year-old nephew, Bob Davïdov, the *Album for Children*. Each of the next set, the Six Pieces, Op. 51 (1882), have an individual inscription, all to persons close to Tchaikovsky. His nieces, Anna and Vera, receive *Polka peu dansante* (No. 2) and *Romance* (No. 5), and his cousin, Anna Merkling, *Menuetto scherzoso* (No. 3). Nata Pleskaya, Sasha's close friend at Kamenka, for whom Tchaikovsky felt a great warmth, receives *Natha-valse* (No. 4), a much extended version of a little piece he had composed for her four years earlier. The remaining two items are given to members of the family circle of his friend, Nikolay Kondratyev, Mariya, his wife, receiving the *Valse de salon* (No. 1), and their daughter's governess, Emma Genton, whose feelings towards Tchaikovsky had caused him some recent discomfort, *Valse sentimentale* (No. 6).

These dedications are clearly affectionate, and so are the pieces, all far more engaging than those of Op. 40, and far more inventive despite Tchaikovsky's assertion that he had composed them only to make some money. When she first played through her piece, Anna Merkling may

Ex. 290

well have been puzzled by the extended harmonic anacrusis leading to the perfect cadence in bars 4 to 5 (Ex. 290); music like this is not written without some thought and care, and his cousin would have gone on to discover this is but the beginning of a section rich in chromatic details. In its original form the *Natha-valse* has been the most modest of miniatures; now Tchaikovsky gave it greater sophistication, greatly expanding its range of textures and its length (the opening section of the later version is drawn from the original waltz, the central section is new). If *Polka peu dansante* suggests that niece Anna was a fairly lively girl with a more thoughtful side, her sister Vera's predominant trait, on the evidence of her *Romance*, was sentimentality both tender and passionate: the unexpected intrusion of her opening theme fortissimo towards the end of the increasingly urgent middle section is a nice touch.

Of Tchaikovsky's remaining four piano pieces from the 80s none except the *Dumka* for Marmontel adds anything significant to his legacy or to his stature. Two were contributions to journals. The *Impromptu caprice* (1884) was written for an album of pieces assembled by the Paris *Gaulois* for a musicians' benevolent fund, and was inscribed to his publisher Jurgenson's wife, Sofya. Like *Dumka*, it gave French music lovers what they expected of a Russian composer, the fast central section repeating a folky thematic fragment against different accompaniments. *Valse scherzo* (1889) was a commission from the Moscow-based *Artist*, made while Tchaikovsky was deep in scoring *The Sleeping Beauty*. It proved but a slight distraction, and the journal was delighted with what it received. The third piece, *Impromptu* (1889), was his contribution to the volume presented to Anton Rubinstein on his golden jubilee. Already saddled with conducting a large portion of the public celebrations as well as with a second commission for a song of greeting, and knowing all too well Rubinstein's apathy to his music generally, and in particular his indifference to the Six Pieces on a Single Theme which had been composed specially for him sixteen years earlier, Tchaikovsky patently felt no compulsion to strain himself over his contribution. If Rubinstein had judged his pupil's attitude from the effort patently *not* needed to produce this brief piece, he might have felt him lacking in gratitude and respect.

Apart from the *Impromptu* with the subtitle *Momento lirico*, published posthumously under the editorship of Taneyev, and Tchaikovsky's own piano transcription from the love scene in the rejected *Voyevoda* (labelled *Aveu passionné*), his only remaining piano work was the Op. 72 set. As noted earlier, the eighteen dedicatees provide a final conspectus of Tchaikovsky's relationships, and the pieces are correspondingly diverse, containing a far greater variety of expression and scale than any previous set, virtuoso concert pieces rubbing shoulders with modest pieces for domestic use. The set contains pieces as slight in content as any in earlier collections. *Passé lointain* opens with a simple, gently yearning theme, then comes close to note spinning; nor do any of the three pieces assigned to the daughters of friends (*Mazurque pour danser*, *L'Espiègle* and *Valse Bluette*) go beyond what might be expected; the first piece makes perfectly clear to Luiza Jurgenson how she may react physically, and while a more passive response was expected of Alexandra Svetoslavskaya and Nadezhda Kondratyeva, their youthful enjoyment was no doubt as complete. But the remainder, taken as a whole, make an unexpectedly impressive effect. Some pieces are strikingly individual, others work out expressive experiences more deeply than do the great majority of their earlier counterparts. The collection contains some of the largest and most imposing of Tchaikovsky's piano pieces. *Polacca de concert* is a ceremonial polonaise in Chopin's grandest manner, for it supplants the festive splendour of its orchestral counterparts in *Onegin*, *Vakula*, and the ballets by the aggressive power of the Polish master's examples, though without their textural variety. *Scherzo-fantaisie* was drawn from the sketches of the third movement from the rejected E flat Symphony, producing an effective vehicle for fleet fingerwork.

There are two other virtuoso pieces, both of which draw upon a Russian peasant world for much of their character. The thumping *Danse caractéristique* has a gentler central section, but in the set's concluding *Scène dansante*, subtitled *Invitation au trépak*, it is the centre which is furious. It is easy to believe that the first section is a mischievous parody of the instrumental recitative in the finale of Beethoven's Ninth Symphony, though the fragments which punctuate the recitative are not recollections of portentous things past, but very muted intimations of wild abandon to come. The allegro vivacissimo is surely also sportive, though now as much at the expense of the piece's dedicatee, the young Sapelnikov, for in overcoming the superhuman technical challenge some of it presents all visual dignity is bound to be lost. The short concluding section is so fragmented that the syntax almost dissolves, and the fff ending is a jest likely to swivel the pianist off his stool. This is one of Tchaikovsky's most unbuttoned bursts of humour.

The title of *Echo rustique* points also to pastoral content, and if there was some private association with Grankino, we may assume that Alina Bryullova at least would have spotted the point in the repeated interruption of what appears to be a straightforward chordal idea by a pretty, high-register tune marked 'quasi campanelli'. Like *Scène dansante* it is a wholly unique conception which lingers in the memory.

Two pieces are confessed stylizations of other composers. Tchaikovsky had grasped well the more facile idiom of Chopin's waltzes, but the very special traits of the mazurkas still eluded him, as *Un poco di Chopin* exposes all too well. Yet the D flat *Un poco di Schumann* is a pleasant and perceptive tribute. There is nothing 'fateful' in this music, and it must be only coincidence that it uses Tatyana's key and melodic outline from the heart of her Letter monologue. But the resemblance between the openings of *Chant élégiaque* and Liszt's third *Liebestraum* was surely deliberate,[50] for in this late tribute to a love now three years dead there was a special point in recalling a melody which had once set the words 'O love, thou canst love so long!' The recurring monotone within this melody is almost funereal, the texturally amplified repeat reinforces the strength of feeling more tactfully yet powerfully than the preceding forte crest, while the delicate più mosso theme which steals in upon both of these paragraphs provides a wistful contrast.

A number of pieces also end by creating a more substantial impression than might have been anticipated from their beginnings. The opening *Impromptu* plays as an engaging but straightforward ternary piece until the final section is built to a brief rhetorical climax, falling back abruptly to a coda which insistently reiterates the main motif

---

[50] Though it is also very like the central section (Più lento) of Liszt's symphonic poem, *Heroïde funèbre*.

above an unwinding harmonic descent. The nervous agitation that pulses from the opening of *Tendres reproches* suddenly finds its full voice in the impassioned imitative dialogue which closes the whole section. The beginning of *Méditation* is even more hushed, echoing something of the world of the Fifth Symphony's slow movement, though now scaled to the intimacy of the closet. After this so delicate opening the fff climax of the middle section provides as savage a contrast as any in these pieces. The melodic germ of this section is incorporated after the first music has returned, adding an expressive forcefulness which requires a very extensive coda to return the experience to the calm in which it had begun.

To judge from the weight and scale of this impressive piece Tchaikovsky viewed his reconciliation with Safonov very seriously. Equally serious, though in a more personal way, is *Dialogue*. Just as (no doubt) the exchanges Tchaikovsky had observed between Laroche and his wife had followed an unpredictable course, so does this colloquy, both in its details and in its broader outlines. It is a touching piece; Tchaikovsky still lived in hope for what he had increasingly had to recognize was a very troubled relationship. Structurally *Dialogue* is one of the freest creations in the set, and one of the most intriguing.

The remaining two pieces each have a root in the second movement of the recently sketched Sixth Symphony. *Valse à cinq temps* applies the same quintuple metre but is entirely lively and merry. *Berceuse* reflects the movement's pedal principle by maintaining the tonic of the first section as the bass of the central section in the relative minor, so that a mediant pedal results; only in the second half of this central section is this persistent ground broken. Melodically this lullaby is simple, yet it hints at depths sounded in no other piece in the collection, is expressively the most truly disquieting, and is the more telling for its total control. The deeper issues in store, which are only dimly foreheard in the recurring major/minor third oscillations of the opening two bars (Ex. 291a), become more apparent in the central section (Ex. 291b)

Ex. 291

sempre con Ped. *sempre pp in la mano sinistra*

b. **Andante mosso**

c. **Andante mosso**

with its tiny but constant dissonance and then its strong climax, and are finally confirmed in the coda (Ex. 291c), not through rhetorical contrasts, but simply by opening further the melodic vista and by twice climbing to a peak before descending to a calm conclusion. The harmonic language, now that the rocking minims have gained an offbeat counterpoint (bars 1–2), is uneasy, then tense, even strange. By its end there is nothing cosy or reassuring to be found in this lullaby; an impressionable child lulled by it might not slumber untroubled. Were we to know more of the dedicatee we might understand better what lay behind the haunting experience embodied in this undemonstrative piece. As it is, though evidently no child, 'M. Pierre Moskaleff à Odessa' seems likely to remain for ever a total mystery.

II

THE RUSSIAN COMPOSER:

SIXTH SYMPHONY

IN 1859, THE year in which Tchaikovsky left the School of Jurisprudence and began his short-lived career in the Ministry of Justice, Ivan Goncharov published his novel, *Oblomov*. The eponymous hero was quickly recognized by thinking Russians as epitomizing the negative side of their national personality, and 'oblomovshchina' (oblomovism) became an accepted word in the Russian vocabulary. The novel's first sentence reads: 'One morning Ilya Ilich Oblomov was lying in bed' – and it is eighteen closely packed pages in the Soviet edition before we read that Oblomov has got out of bed.

Thus Goncharov began to epitomize a cardinal flaw in the Russian character: inertia. It is a flaw that has conditioned every sector of the nation's life. It has dogged its history, which has tended to unfold as long periods of stasis, followed by short, sometimes very violent periods of activity when the state has been convulsed into progress. Peter the Great's radical measures in the early eighteenth century, the activities of those who set off the 1917 Revolution, the radical and breakneck reforms initiated by Gorbachev which have had such profound impact on both sides of Russia's political boundaries as our century approaches its end, are but the consequences of this inertia; they precipitate the periods of violent, often appallingly painful transition unavoidable if the political and social stagnation of decades, perhaps centuries, is to be corrected. Other active bids to effect change have been made and have failed, notably in 1825 and 1905, and there have been more passive attempts that have produced a short-lived amelioration. In the late 1850s and 60s, after the long and increasingly reactionary reign of Nikolay I, Alexandr II tried to create a freer society. His most spectacular act was the liberating of the Russian peasantry in 1861, but equally important was his liberalizing of the censorship laws, for in such a climate, with debate more open and productive, creative artists could discover their individual voices more freely. It is surely no accident that these were the years in which some of the major figures of Russian literature like Tolstoy and Dostoyevsky truly came into their own, and in which a major group of Russian composers emerged: Balakirev, Borodin, Musorgsky, Rimsky-Korsakov and Tchaikovsky himself.

Inertia of a kind is also intrinsic to Russian creativity. In literature it produces the novel that proceeds as a succession of self-contained sections, even set-piece scenes. *Oblomov* is a case in point – but take, for instance, the first part of Dostoyevsky's *The Idiot*. Though its sixteen chapters provide an unbroken record of Prince Mïshkin's arrival in St Petersburg after four years in Switzerland, and of his first day in the Russian capital, its organization is in discrete compartments, for no less than ten of these chapters are purely conversation pieces, as static and enclosed as may be. When the action shifts the narrative rushes on as though impatient to arrive at the next set piece, the last of which is that extraordinary scene in which Nastasya Filippovna is to decide whom she will marry, and which occupies the final four chapters, Dostoyevsky building it to an histrionic climax as contrived yet as convincing as any full scale operatic finale.

Indeed, such tableau organization is fundamental to the most Russian of operatic scenarios. Their method is the very opposite of that exemplified, for instance, in the libretti Lorenzo da Ponte had provided for Mozart. In these each character had spun one strand in the action; each act was an evolving, complex web of incident woven through the crossings and entwinings of these strands, and every new act picked up a tangle of strands left by what had gone before until at the opera's end all were sorted and neatly tied. By contrast, as we have noted in the discussion of *Onegin* – and could equally have observed of Tchaikovsky's other two Pushkin-based operas, *Mazepa* and *The Queen of Spades* (and of Musorgsky's *Boris Godunov*) – the most characteristic Russian scenario is like a strip cartoon, each scene presenting a crucial incident or stage in the plot, leaving the spectator to supply in his imagination what has happened in the gaps between these incidents. And such gaps can be chasms: Boris's first two appearances are separated by six years and the span of his entire reign – and a whole lifetime's-worth of experience separates our last glimpse of the dismayed, sobbing Tatyana at the calamitous end of her nameday party and our first sight of the mature society beauty commanding instant attention as her husband leads her into the grand St Petersburg ballroom.

Such a method is also at the root of the most characteristic structures of Russian composers. But before turning to these, we must consider for a moment the nature of the musical invention which these structures are required to deploy. Folksong affords the clearest clue to the characteristics of a nation's musicality, and Ex. 292b is a random Russian sample, the one with which Balakirev opened his collection of 1866 and Tchaikovsky closed his of 1868–9. The tune is typical of hundreds of Russian folksongs in that it evolves as a series of variations against a simple protoshape (Ex. 292a; the unbracketed notes are the fundamental ones). Its life stems above all from its rhythmic fertility,

Ex. 292

and despite the two-bar repetition at its close, it lacks that squarely balanced phrasing typical of so many of its Western counterparts. There are, of course, other Russian folksongs which do build upon this latter principle, though many of these are probably 'town' songs whose origins are later, and which were composed under the conditioning of Western practices. But a pure folksong such as Ex. 292b shapes out no structural span; rather it is a series of reflections upon a protoshape – a concentric, not an onward moving creation.

Such an example may help us understand why some Russian folksongs seem no more than melodic tags. There can, of course, be a special point in insistent and unchanging repetition, but fragments like these were surely intended less as final artefacts than as bases upon which variations might be improvised. Just such a tag is the dance tune[1] which gave its name to *Kamarinskaya*, that prodigy of Glinka's teeming inventiveness which had such influence upon later Russian composers, Tchaikovsky included (above all in the finale of his Second Symphony). *Kamarinskaya* is Russian folksong writ large, in that it uses the same principle of unfolding around a thematic constant (or, in this work, two constants, since there are two folktunes), though here Glinka varies the surroundings more than the tunes themselves. Like the Russian folksong already quoted, *Kamarinskaya* does not evolve to make an all-embracing point, complete only when the final note has been reached, as in the finest Western symphonic movements; rather, it says the same thing over and over again with ever new significances, consolidating rather than expanding the experience. Put simply, it is a

---

[1] The tune is quoted in Vol. 1, Ex. 66a.

decorative, not an organic creation – static rather than dynamic. And having said that, we have put our finger on the very essence of Russian creativity.

But we have also raised a paradox. The ability of Russians to express themselves through the elemental motion of the dance is as developed as any, and Russian folk music includes a wealth of vigorous dances and dance songs in which the impetus is colossal, seemingly unstoppable. The same is true of a good deal of Russian art music: Borodin's Polovtsian Dances from *Prince Igor* and Stravinsky's *The Rite of Spring*, to name but two instances. Perhaps the latter is a dangerous example to cite, for it has been said of *The Rite* that it is one work which does elevate rhythm to structural significance. Nonetheless, what we are hearing here is, like dance itself, externalized physical movement, not the dynamic of life itself. The powerful pulse patterns are a crucial part of the music's surface – but probe beneath the highly energized metrical patterns into the melodic and harmonic workings, and something very different emerges. The first two sections of *The Rite* are, in fact, demonstrations of all that has been already observed, for while 'L'adoration de la terre' is sustained entirely upon a melodic thread spun from three nuclei perpetually varied like the protoshape of a folksong, 'Les augures printaniers; danses des adolescentes' is harmonically static and melodically moves in circles, constantly returning to where it began. Only the metrical savagery devised by chopping the chords into violently dislocated pulses gives this music momentum.

It follows that a musical invention which is by its very nature static and reflective is totally unsuitable for building large-scale, evolving structures such as are the natural products of the best Western organic thought. During the discussion of Tchaikovsky's First Symphony in Vol. 1 attention was given to the dilemma this posed for the Russian composer. Endowed with a mind of this nature he was inclined, like his fellow-Russian novelists, to think most readily in terms of self-contained sections. The genius of most nineteenth-century Russian composers (and certainly of Tchaikovsky) was above all for melody, and especially for the sort that is designed as a broad, multi-phrased structure (that is, like 'town' songs rather than genuine folksongs). But such melodies, however extended they might be, had structures even more enclosed than those shaped out by folktunes of the sort we have considered; whereas these had led nowhere in particular, the former simply arrived at an end, thus requiring the composer to climb, as it were, a perimeter fence if he wished to move on, perhaps to explore a new melodic field.

This problem of transition was one of the most vexed the Russian composer faced, greater in many ways than that of development. In the latter at least he could fall back on his flair for ingenious manipulation within a system. In fact, the Russian mind seems to take an infinite delight in working such systems. For proof we need look no further than the work of Russian musical theorists, of whom there has been no shortage over the past hundred years. What has marked so many of them is a preoccupation with theory for its own sake rather than as a tool to open the secrets of the musical work. Their investigations have tended to be highly individual, often highly complex, logical in an often highly idiosyncratic way, exhibiting a delight in speculation for its own sake, a delight in systems unlikely to have much practical application, and sometimes plain potty. Some of these theorists have made little or no attempt to apply their systems to real music, often less (one suspects) because they feared they would collapse if confronted with reality as because they were not really interested in that reality. They have been engaged in a game of abstractions, of fathoming out ingenious relationships, of pitting their wits against one another. It is no surprise that such men and women come from a nation with a passion and genius for chess, or that Russian composers – Tchaikovsky included – were capable of producing fugatos expertly turned, though wholly sterile since they were no more than products of a consummately mastered system.

The world of Russian musical theory is a microcosm not only of the Russian's preoccupation with cause rather than effect, but also of his difficulty in connecting cause with effect, in imposing what his reason may tell him needs doing upon the world of hard reality (which has been a fundamental reason for those periods of stagnation in Russian history observed at the opening of this chapter). For just as it seems difficult for the Russian musical theorist to apply his active, controlled intelligence to the scrutiny of an imaginative conception, so it seems difficult for the Russian composer to harness his active, controlled intelligence to the unfolding of that imaginative conception – as Bach had done so pre-eminently in the fugue, or the classical masters in the symphony. To relate this to one hard musical situation: in the development sections of Russian symphonic works there is rarely lack of ingenuity in manipulating musical materials, but so often it seems a game played according to a well learned method, not the thoughtful, stage-by-stage uncovering of further positions in a unique and lively musical argument moving logically towards its conclusion. There is much truth in Musorgsky's dictum: 'The German, when he thinks, will first *examine and explore*, then *make his conclusion*: our [Russian] brother will first *make his conclusion*, then amuse himself with examination and exploration.'[2]

This can rarely produce totally satisfying results. Yet to discount the Russian symphony on this ground would be a gross error, for the best examples are totally different conceptions from their Western counterparts, despite their indebtedness to the same structural scheme and so many elements of the same method. For Tchaikovsky himself the symphony was 'the most lyrical of forms', but shot through with drama; its momentum stemmed not so much from continuity of thought as from striking juxtapositions, and its effect upon the listener came less from a rich and well ordered argument than from taking him through a succession of often highly charged sections which *added up* to a radically new kind of symphonic experience.

All the traits so far discussed are fundamental to Tchaikovsky's work. But they represent only one aspect. His training was thoroughly Western, and the problem of marrying the bundle of techniques which he had acquired in the St Petersburg Conservatoire with the kind of invention his native instincts drew from him was to be a formidable one. Tchaikovsky's style is so ramified that it would be quite impossible to describe and analyse it comprehensively within the scope of this chapter. It is not merely that there is a yawning dichotomy between his rococo stylizations and his most personal style; his creative instincts in general were as eclectic as those of any Russian, and produced many other and constant stylistic fissures. In working out his operatic style he could lean on a slender native tradition originating in Glinka's two examples, and subsequently continued more weakly by Dargomïzhsky and Serov. Tchaikovsky's operatic subjects, though inclining heavily to melodrama, even tragedy, were diverse enough to ensure musical variety, and different subjects prompted different emphases (above all, of course, in *Onegin*). But otherwise his operas simply extended this inherited line, nothing fundamental distinguishing *Iolanta* (1891) from *The Oprichnik* (1870–2). As for songs, there was a good supply of Russian models, and Tchaikovsky had none of Musorgsky's determination to break the mould of this mostly modest genre. Occasionally

[2] M. P. Musorgsky, *Pisma*, ed. E. Gordeyeva (Moscow, 1981), p. 75. This translation is somewhat free, since Musorgsky's original cannot be rendered literally into English. Other attempts have included: 'The German, when he thinks, first *theorizes* at length, and then *proves*, our Russian brother proves first, and then amuses himself with theory.' (J. Leyda and S. Bertensson [eds.], *The Musorgsky reader* (New York, 1947), p. 120). 'A German, when thinking, starts by analysing, and then proceeds to demonstrate. Our Russian brother begins by demonstrating, and afterwards may amuse himself with analysing.' (M. D. Calvocoressi, *Modest Musorgsky: his life and works* (London, 1956), p. 104).

a late song will expose a deeper, richer vein of experience than ever he could have opened in his earlier years (the most cursory comparison of 'None but the lonely heart', the last of his first set, Op. 9, with 'Again, as before, alone', the last of his final set, Op. 73, will make this point), but otherwise nothing differentiates his earlier from his later examples, except that the craft in the latter is sometimes more polished and sophisticated.

And so, despite all the achievements to be found within his operas and songs (above all within the former), neither genre is a satisfactory guide to the really essential Tchaikovsky. As for the ballets, *Swan Lake*, remarkable achievement that it is, is too imperfectly realized and *The Nutcracker* too dilute to offer consistent and clear evidence. In any case the constraints and pressures of this genre were too great for Tchaikovsky's full and unfettered individuality to be able to display itself, even in a masterpiece like *The Sleeping Beauty*. If we are seeking the heart of Tchaikovsky's work, where the grappling with basic principles is most evident and the greatest diversity and boldness are to be found, where his achievement is at its highest and his individuality at its strongest, we shall find it most consistently in his major instrumental pieces. What we may most usefully do here is pay special attention to, say, four of his most representative works or movements composed at seven- or eight-year intervals, excluding any piece which vacillates stylistically either through inexperience or choice, or which deliberately turns its back upon what was most personal within his music. And so we shall concentrate primarily upon *Romeo and Juliet* (begun 1869), and the first movements of the Fourth Symphony (1877–8), the Manfred Symphony (1885) and Sixth Symphony (1893).

The folk element, whether authentic or synthesized, had only sporadic importance in Tchaikovsky's work except during that brief period in the early 70s when he placed himself squarely in line with the ideals and practices of Balakirev and his group. The sources of his most characteristic melody are elusive, though Italian operatic cantilena is clearly one. In such themes Tchaikovsky's line unwinds broadly, is expressively full, and usually presents a clear periodic structure, though this may be disguised by the very expansiveness of the individual phrase and by its sequential extension, which may be prolonged. The first love theme of *Romeo and Juliet* exemplifies this kind of melody perfectly. In its basic form it is simply an eight-bar phrase, the second half a free sequence of the first, establishing the principle of growth to be used on the theme's recurrence to expand its dimensions beyond anything that could have been readily predicted. Thus when it resumes after the rocking love theme it is developed into a ternary structure nearly four times as large by evolving a new idea from its closing two bars (Ex. 293, bars three and four), extending it into a four-bar phrase *x*, then sequencing very inventively upon this for a further ten bars before returning to the opening by way of an equally smooth join. The

Ex. 293

result is as strong and integrated a melody as any; it is no surprise that this was a portion of the work that Tchaikovsky judged successful from the beginning, nor that some of the revisions made to the recapitulation were designed further to exploit melodic amplification.

This could have a claim as the greatest theme Tchaikovsky ever wrote: beside such a powerful declaration of passion the love theme of the symphonic ballad, *The Voyevoda*, merely pants (see Ex. 270). Only the melody which catches the full measure of Francesca's pain and sorrow[3] can in any way match it for breadth. And it is in the seven years that lie between his first Shakespeare-based masterpiece and *Francesca da Rimini* that nearly all Tchaikovsky's greatest melodies were created – that is, those with the strongest contours and most defined personalities, those which are the freest and most flexible, yet the most truly organic. Little that followed upon the terrible crisis of 1877 can match the melody of the love duet from *Undine* (which we know as the violin solo in the Act 2 Pas d'action of *Swan Lake*), or the swans' theme[4] which opens and closes the same act of this cornucopia of vital, vibrant melody – strong yet seemingly lakebound to begin with, taking wing so freely, settling, then rising in yet broader flight – or the expanse of cantilena that presents the love scene in *The Tempest*[5] – starting so modestly, then stage by stage swelling in strength of contour and then in breadth of phrase as nervous hesitation gives way to passion confessed. By contrast, the 'Rose' Adagio of *The Sleeping Beauty* (see Ex. 244c), great movement that it is, is more an assemblage of separate phrases, its power coming from their cumulative weight, not their protean ability to extend, expand and proliferate until, it seems, a single organism has revealed itself. Even the vastly spread solo cello tune of the Pas d'action in Act 2 of *The Sleeping Beauty* (see Ex. 249)

[3] See Vol. 2, Ex. 124.
[4] See Vol. 2, Exs. 117 and 118.
[5] See Vol. 1, Ex. 76.

sounds a little pallid in comparison to the best of the earlier tunes; like the 'Rose' Adagio also, it lacks their consistent quality.

Nor is it often that a later theme can match even such a smaller scale creation as Natalya's passionate arioso in Act 1 of *The Oprichnik*[6] or the hero's dignified lament in Act 2 of *Vakula*,[7] the Devil's taut incantation in the same opera[8] or the sinewy introductory theme of the First Piano Concerto, or Tatyana's theme of love[9] – a mere seven bars long, but presenting a single arch of such sudden and compact intensity of feeling as to strike more sharply and deeply than many a longer melody. All these are, in their various ways, monoliths: firm, even muscular, and unique. True, Joan's E major love theme in her Act 4 duet with Lionel in *The Maid of Orléans*[10] has an expressive fullness that contrasts refreshingly with the blowsiness of so many of that bombastic opera's other themes, but its phrases are more consistently conjunct, without that strength within the outlines of these earlier melodies. That which concludes the Manfred Symphony's first movement[11] is firmer, but reveals no power to grow further, instead becoming trapped into ever more frantic repetitions which yield surface excitement in plenty but no amplification,[12] as had the themes of *Romeo* and *Francesca*. Similarly the potential within the Princess's theme in the entr'acte to Act 2 of *The Enchantress* is never realized, for what follows upon the four bars of Ex. 219 is merely plain sequential extension over a dominant pedal. Not even the violin theme in the Second Piano Concerto's slow movement[13] nor the horn theme in the Fifth Symphony (see Ex. 237h) has the sturdiness of the finest earlier melodies, for all their spaciousness. Many of Tchaikovsky's best themes are now to be found in the more urbane world of the dance (whether in formal ballet or in an orchestral context), but such music inclines to the decorative; its function is not to scale expressive heights but to be attractively inventive.

Such, of course, is not the role of *The Sleeping Beauty*'s 'Rose' Adagio or Act 2 Pas d'action; nor should it be concluded that they are inferior to the best of Tchaikovsky's earlier creations, for while melodically they may be more the products of consummate craft than rampant inspiration, their creation was attended by insights and intuitions that had

[6] See Vol. 1, Ex. 54a. Laroche's comments on this opera were well judged, for its abundance of firm and distinctive melodies is its finest feature.
[7] See Vol. 1, Ex. 93.
[8] See Vol. 1, Ex. 87.
[9] See Vol. 2, Ex. 137.
[10] See Vol. 3, Ex. 158b.
[11] See Vol. 3, Ex. 209a.
[12] See Vol. 3, Ex. 209b.
[13] See Vol. 3, Ex. 166.

not been granted the younger, less experienced Tchaikovsky.[14] And there is no question, of course, that Tchaikovsky's melodic gift *per se* is to be written off during his last fifteen or so years, and he remained one of the nineteenth century's greatest melodists. There has, however, been a shift in its nature. Tchaikovsky's later themes tend to be more compact, sometimes almost epigrammatic, while the most arresting now rely more upon resourcefulness in their local structure or inventiveness of detail to make them memorable (this is true even of the exquisite Astarte music in the Manfred Symphony, one later theme that *does* rival in quality the finest of the earlier ones). We have noted, for instance, the sudden energy with which the Second Suite's valse theme climbs aloft,[15] the less impetuous but more powerful surge with which the Third Suite's valse theme discovers its own strength[16] – or the so simple, yet so unpredictable way in which, in *The Nutcracker*, the first two bars of the Chinese Dance are answered in bars three and four, or the opening of the Sugar Plum Fairy's Dance in bars two to four (see Ex. 279). Nor must we overlook Tchaikovsky's later ability to invent character themes that are totally unique. Certainly Caliban in *The Tempest*[17] was vividly personified, but Rotbart in *Swan Lake* had no invention to individualize him, nor were any of the supernaturals in *Vakula* projected through anything as uniquely personal as that with which Carabosse bounds into our mind's eye even before the curtain has risen on *The Sleeping Beauty* (see Ex. 243a). This unsurpassed flair for catching peculiarities of physical movement into music is magnificently confirmed in some of the miniature movements offered to Aurora and her Prince at their wedding entertainment: the cats' duet is but the most striking of these. Nor should the grotesque theme that characterizes Drosselmeyer in *The Nutcracker* go unnoted (see Ex. 274).

Yet while Tchaikovsky was fashioning melodies which have nothing of folksong about them, he sometimes revealed something of the

---

[14] Nor should we overlook Tchaikovsky's skill, especially in the later works, in creating melody that might serve a function other than being simply itself – for instance, the very contrasting expanses of melody which crown the development in the Piano Trio's first movement (see Vol. 3, Ex. 174) and Lyubov's desperate appeal to Mariya at the end of *Mazepa*'s second act (see Vol. 3, Ex. 183). Each is impressive in itself – more important, each is the culmination of a far broader musical design, and each concentrates mostly on a single phrase, building from this, through free sequences, a vast melodic vault. True, neither can rival the finest of the freely conceived melodies – or could, indeed, survive convincingly if the contexts were removed. But while there is a sense that these are constructs in a way that the *Romeo* and *Francesca* themes are not, they are perfectly calculated for their respective functions.

[15] See Vol. 3, Ex. 190.

[16] See Vol. 3, Ex. 197.

[17] See Vol. 1, Ex. 75.

Russian folk-composer's instinct to think in terms of foreground projections of a background outline. This was observed as early as in the oboe theme of the First Symphony's slow movement[18] where, in addition, a phrase from the centre of the melody was used as the point of departure for another theme. The linking process used in Ex. 293 relies to a degree upon this latter procedure, and elsewhere in *Romeo and Juliet* a swift succession of restructurings had demonstrated that two otherwise totally dissimilar tunes had a common element in their contours.[19] The great central theme of *Francesca da Rimini* unwinds further by turning back upon itself to unfold a new formation against an old shape.[20] To what extent Tchaikovsky was aware of creating these relationships while composing his themes is debatable, but there can surely be no doubt about the studied decision he took to synthesize the first subject of the Fourth Symphony's first movement from the contour of one, or perhaps two excerpts, both already in F minor, from Bizet's *Carmen* (Ex. 294). Thus something of this symphony's content is indicated yet more starkly than in the programme confided to Nadezhda von Meck; Fate is the all-powerful presence looming over both the Toreador's entrance and Carmen's ominous divination, for Escamillo is the force's agent in the opera, the reading of the cards the moment when Carmen is confronted with the inevitability of destruction at its hands. What is remarkable is the total assurance with which the radical transformation of musical character is effected and the complete conviction that this new melodic realization of the contour carries. To conjure such novelty from existing shapes was patently second nature to

Ex. 294   [BIZET]

[18] See Vol. 1, Ex. 8.

[19] See Vol. 1, Ex. 33. For other instances of contour relationships of various kinds and strengths between separate themes within the same work, see Vol. 1, Exs. 47 and 89, Vol. 2, Exs. 97, 110a and b, 123, 131, 138, 142 and 143, Vol. 3, Exs. 169, 178 and 179, 188, 199, 202 and 208, and Vol. 4, Exs. 217, 259 and 266. These exclude connections which are purely motivic or self-evidently deliberately devised.

[20] See Vol. 2, Ex. 124.

Tchaikovsky, as he was to confirm less spectacularly in the transformation of a folksong in the Serenade for Strings[21] and, more briefly but
literally, in the openings of several variations in the Third Suite's
finale.[22]

Yet what was probably the most important and fruitful product of
this ability was the line of melodic progeny fathered by the Fate contour
which had first appeared in *Onegin*[23] and which, as we have seen, was
constantly to resurface in his work.[24] Sometimes, as in the Second
Piano Concerto,[25] it is there for reasons that we cannot guess, but its
presence is pointed in some of the vocal works (the duet 'Scottish
ballad'[26] and the Artôt songs 'Qu'importe que l'hiver' and 'Les larmes'
(see Exs. 241, and 242c and d), for instance) and in the later operas
(above all, *The Queen of Spades*[27]). It seems particularly fitting that this
outline should overshadow the closing bars of 'Again, as before, alone'
(Ex. 296), the last of Tchaikovsky's Six Romances on texts by Rathaus,
Op. 73, and the last composition of importance that he ever completed.

Whether, when formulating the style of his own melodies,
Tchaikovsky was aware of any creative tension between a native
Russian's melodic impulses and those behind Western melody is
impossible to judge. All that can be said is that he settled any
difficulties with consummate skill. But there was a very real conflict to
resolve in the harmonic sector, for though Russian folk music was
unusual in having developed a practice of oral harmonization, this was
too rudimentary to offer an alternative method. Thus the problem was

---

[21] See Vol. 3, Ex. 170.

[22] See Vol. 3, Ex. 198.

[23] See Vol. 2, Ex. 139, (though the shape had also opened the central melody of the
elegiac slow movement of the Third String Quartet of the preceding year).

[24] Whether this theme, like the first subject of the Fourth Symphony, had its origin
in a French opera is less certain, but it is to be found in the final act of Gounod's *Roméo et
Juliette* (a favourite opera of Tchaikovsky) as a distraught Romeo bewails the fate that
has befallen his love (Ex. 295; this is virtually identical with the passage in *Onegin*
quoted in Vol. 2 as Ex. 139p).

Ex. 295   [GOUNOD]

[25] See Vol. 3, Ex. 164.

[26] See Vol. 3, Ex. 167a.

[27] See Exs. 258a and 262.

Ex. 296

a.

[Friend! Pray for me; I am praying for you!]

b.

not to establish a position in relation to two differing styles and techniques, but to effect some workable relationship between a Russian mind's creative instincts which, as we have repeatedly observed, were static rather than dynamic, and an organic, bass-rooted harmonic language which gave the music its propulsive power, and whose wider structures gave it shape.

Tchaikovsky had, of course, been thoroughly schooled in this Western harmonic method, at the foundation of which was the circle of fifths which was both a crucial element in harmonic movement and the very foundation of the modulatory apparatus. The most cursory glance at the tonal moves in *Romeo and Juliet* reveals much about his modulatory preferences:

Interval of shift	Number of occurrences
Semitone	7
Tone	3
Minor third	4 (three are from B minor to D major – i.e., between tonic and relative major)
Major third	1
Perfect fifth	4

By far the most common are semitonal shifts mostly involving a chromatic change to five of the seven degrees of the diatonic scale – a colouristic move par excellence, producing a striking local incident of no structural import except insofar as it may produce a particularly memorable moment. That there was little structural modulation scarcely mattered in a work which was so audibly based upon the familiar sonata blueprint, and whose dramatic representation of this tale of tragic love was so eloquent. Devising and operating a modulatory scheme was a skill learned easily enough; the far greater problem for Tchaikovsky was to apply the harmonic procedures learned in the Conservatoire without his individuality being unacceptably compromised or even annihilated. The first subject of *Romeo and Juliet* reveals how – and how well – he could manage this, even at so early a stage in his creative career. This extensive stretch of highly inventive and striking music presents a series of oscillations between passages of almost static harmony and others where the fundamental bass movement is solidly, sometimes swiftly, in fifths. Ex. 297 summarizes the harmonic support for the main theme[28] and what immediately follows. The first four bars are almost stationary, striking for their rich vocabul-

---

[28] This is quoted in full in Vol. 1, Ex. 31.

Ex. 297

ROMEO AND JULIET: FIRST SUBJECT (OPENING). HARMONIC ANALYSIS

Bracketed notes indicate an important harmonic detail. For purposes of clarity, the bass of the 'Detailed harmonic structure' has sometimes been simplified.

ary of seventh and even ninth chords, with the German sixth that is basic to bars two and three reinterpreting itself as a dominant seventh of C major to move to that chord in bar four. Harmonically this is music of sensation, not momentum. But during each of the next two bars there is a tiny flurry of harmonic fifths as this C major chord (the neapolitan) is decorated by its dominant-of-dominant, dominant, and then subdominant, briefly asserting C as the tonal centre before sideslipping semitonally to the tonic B in bar eight, as colouristic a manoeuvre as any earlier one. Yet in the ensuing modulation to D minor (bars 11–15) fundamental bass movement by fifths is far more crucial, and similarly directed movement, though fitful in rhythm, lies beneath a good deal of what follows in this substantial paragraph. Mostly, however, the colouristic and functional are kept apart; the most explicit blending of Russian instinct and Western method comes in the harmonic treatment of the great love theme itself where, after the magical semitonal shift (D to D flat), a chain of rich and characteristic chords are structured upon a bass that is the quintessence of Western harmonic practice.[29]

Tchaikovsky's harmony could merit a chapter of its own, but for present purposes we will do best to confine ourselves to the dichotomy so clearly evidenced in this first masterpiece. The first subject of the Fourth Symphony integrates the two sides more closely. The pace of harmonic change is mostly very slow, chords being often prolonged for four or more bars, with short intervening passages of swift harmonic movement. When a move to a new key is not instantaneous but is to be engineered, the circle of fifths is an important agent, as it had been in the first subject of *Romeo and Juliet*. The shift from the initial F minor to the tutti A minor restatement is effected through three steps down the circle (with a chromatic change at the centre: Ex. 298a), which also

Ex. 298

FOURTH SYMPHONY, FIRST MOVEMENT: FIRST SUBJECT. HARMONIC SUMMARY

[29] See Vol. 1, Ex. 29d.

plays some part in returning the music to the tonic for the second tutti restatement (Ex. 298b; in both parts of this example the harmony is reduced to the barest essentials). As in Ex. 297 Tchaikovsky's devotion to the German sixth is evident when this chord, rather than the usual dominant, is employed to approach the tonic (and to inflect the twelve bars of F minor triad which follow).

It may seem ironic that a composer who had already reduced to the minimum that very stage of the exposition (the transition) where the classical composer had been concerned to devise an extended and carefully timed process of modulation should reveal within the first subject itself, where his classical predecessor's prime aim had been the establishment of a single key, a mastery of well directed and well measured modulation. What is more, there is nothing pedantic or laboured about it; the process is as fundamental to the expressive aims of the work as the flow of melody which provides the thread of structure throughout this huge section. This control of musical space is evidenced even more impressively in the symphony's development. 'Artificial' this may be (if we are to believe what Tchaikovsky himself said), and insofar as it is 'worked out' the word is well chosen. But it is a splendidly paced section spread over a totally different kind of framework from that used in *Romeo and Juliet*. There considerations of drama had encouraged Tchaikovsky to engage his representative materials ever more feverishly in a series of phrases which were moved sequentially upward a step at a time; here nearly half the development (38 out of 83 bars) is spanned out upon a magisterial six-step descent through the circle of fifths before the pressure valve is tightened by a series of rising semitone shifts as the recapitulation is about to erupt. Yet the listener is barely conscious of this device itself, so richly is it embellished with all sorts of harmonic detail. It is exactly what it should be – the well built skeleton which the composer can clothe with living tissue.

But the first movement of the Manfred Symphony has no place for such mechanisms. Its method is much more that of the first four bars of Ex. 297, now vastly extended to embrace a whole movement. The abundance of seventh and ninth chords, their tensions often heightened by measured passing dissonances, appoggiaturas and suspensions, produces textural richness in plenty; whereas a plainer triadic language would have demanded chordal change if only for variety, sonorities such as these may be dwelt upon at length for their intrinsic allure. Ex. 299 attempts a summary of the harmonic content of the opening twenty-four bars[30] (there are some harmonic ambiguities,

---

[30] The first sixteen bars of this movement are quoted in Vol. 3, Ex. 207b.

Ex. 299

MANFRED SYMPHONY, FIRST MOVEMENT: OPENING. HARMONIC SUMMARY

and a number of tiny harmonic changes have been omitted). It is not merely that these two dozen bars of very measured music employ only ten fundamental chords; the movement between chords is achieved not by the operations of a harmonic bass generating progressions that urge the music on but largely by stepwise movement within the chords themselves, not infrequently chromatic. It is syntax of a kind associated with Liszt and Wagner rather than Schumann and Brahms, and there had already been a substantial dose of it in *Francesca da Rimini* (it was to recur in parts of *Hamlet*, and in *The Voyevoda*). And as this movement unfolds there are further extensive stretches where Tchaikovsky shows little urge to pursue a purposeful journey along a harmonically directed route, but instead, just as so many of his land's unnamed creators of folksongs delighted in dwelling upon some melodic *donnée*, seems to set quiet store by the tensions within a chord, or the colour or drama within a progression.

Yet his response has none of the obsession Skryabin was to develop for a particular sonority, nor any of Musorgsky's delight in searching out striking successions of drifting chords or in relentlessly repeating an arresting juxtaposition to extract the maximum possible sensation from it. Debussy would have found Tchaikovsky a poor substitute, had he not had Musorgsky to fertilize his creativity. The harmonic style of this first movement remains ambivalent, for there are passages where the harmonic thrust is clear. But what points up most clearly the prevailing shift is the procedures that are *not* there – for not only is there scarcely a shadow of a perfect cadence until the Astarte music, but not even a hint of a circle of fifths, and only one true structural application of the dominant chord (just before the tutti restatement of the opening theme). Rather, this music of Manfred himself seems hewn from immovable slabs of rock, no element contributing more to this epic grandeur than the harmonic idiom.

In music harmonically so inert the problem of transition can be resolved literally through silence, one section being simply brought to a halt on an inconclusive chord and a new section entering after a pregnant pause (as Liszt, for one, had profitably discovered).[31] But it

---

[31] In fact, in some cases the pause-as-transition may be an illusion, since the preceding music has already manoeuvred to the chord that is to be picked up after the pause. The silence is therefore no more than the simplest of punctuation marks.

could not always be so; mostly the harmonic momentum would not permit it. To return to what has been observed earlier: in the symphonic models which the Western tradition offered, the transition in exposition and recapitulation had been not a functional link but a frequently substantial stage in the experience. Tchaikovsky had lost no time in confronting the special challenge this posed for him, and since his nature urged him towards building huge, tonally enclosed first subjects and even more extensive melodic second subjects, his solution, as revealed in the First Symphony, had been to reduce the transition to the minimum, short of abolishing it altogether. Transitions in the next two symphonies are as economical, or almost so. The corresponding incident in the Second (original 1872 version) is five bars centring on a pivot chord, D flat (arrived at as the neapolitan of C minor, but quit as though it were the subdominant of A flat), in the Third a six-bar passage beginning with the neapolitan of the tonic D (E flat, but with an added C sharp), which, through minimum chromatic adjustment, shifts to the German sixth of B minor. This Third Symphony, like the Fourth and Fifth, has a three-subject exposition, and though the second transition is also effected by the simplest of chromatic moves, again to the German sixth of the key to come (A major), Tchaikovsky pauses on this chord, reinterpreting it as the dominant seventh of B flat and interpolating a new twelve-bar tune in this key before passing to his real tonal destination. This piece of opportunism both expands the section and produces one of the most attractive incidents in an otherwise mostly arid movement. Yet this manoeuvre, for all the expressive dividend it yields, is only a delaying tactic; the shift itself had taken no more than four bars, and when this is set within the context of the sections before and after it, each of which is centred upon a single key, it again reflects (like the other transitions just described) a method close to that already noted in the first subjects of both *Romeo and Juliet* and the Fourth Symphony – that is, short periods of dynamic activity between passages of relative stasis. The practice parallels exactly Dostoyevsky's as observed in the first part of *The Idiot*: set pieces linked by the swiftest of narrative transitions.

Three years after the First Symphony Tchaikovsky had repeated its transition process in *Romeo and Juliet*, though this time prolonging the dominant, partly to give the momentum time to slacken, partly to prepare more effectively for the highly dramatic tonal twist to come. However, in the three string quartets of the early and mid-70s he was composing with a profound awareness of venturing into the heartland of the Western tradition (and he knew that the connoisseur audience in Russia whose approval he would most want would be drawn from the communities of German extraction in the larger cities). In consequence his observance of traditional practice is at its most overtly respectful, and in the first-movement exposition of the first two quartets the transition is simply a section neatly stitched in, applying conventional harmonic mechanisms, with the use of local dominants. The Third Quartet is a very different affair. This still neglected piece merges first subject and transition – for in music which continues to occupy itself so singlemindedly with material which has already been constantly subverting the tonic, it will always be a matter for debate where precisely first subject ends and transition begins. To all intents and purposes they are indivisible; indeed, a major consequence is to give added significance to the second subject, for here at last we do feel on relatively stable tonal ground.

If nothing else, the first two quartets demonstrate the unremarkable fact that Tchaikovsky could devise a conventional transition as well as any competent student, and it was not only in subsequent chamber works that he continued to patch in such intersubject sections whenever he chose. In the Fourth Symphony's first movement he was truer to himself, following the precedents of the First Symphony and *Romeo and Juliet* by leaping directly to the dominant of the key to come, though this time moving aside to make a second approach, as though reaffirming that the new tonal centre truly has a drawing power of its own. Quite certainly this was the kind of transition that was troubling Tchaikovsky when he lamented the lack of organic continuity that resulted. In fact he did himself rather less than justice, for the very virtue of such a transition in music of this sort was that it marked the point of division between sections rather than obliterating it, acting less as a smooth join than as a punctuation mark. Yet it was an unsubtle procedure, and nothing could disguise the fact that something had been wilfully interpolated to effect a change of direction and prepare for something new. One solution was to avoid the problem altogether through a cryptic silence (as in the Manfred Symphony), another was to overlap first and second subjects (as in the First Piano Concerto). All these stratagems were viable, but all ducked the real challenge: to make the transition an integral but independent part of the unfolding experience. To address this squarely and devise a solution that was wholly satisfactory was to be one of the achievements of the last and greatest of the symphonies.

In Tchaikovsky's continuing campaign to conquer the problems of symphonic form two works are landmarks: the First and Fourth Symphonies. Viewed from the point in 1893 which the broader narrative of this volume has now reached and which affords a perspective on the First Symphony some twenty-seven years broad and deep, the achievement of this early piece seems remarkable indeed. To have created so fresh, so characteristic and well-formed a slow movement was feat enough; to have rethought and reshaped so successfully certain features of the sonata paradigm in the first movement compounded these achievements into a notable victory. The fruits of the latter battle are apparent in *Romeo and Juliet*, and the first movement of the Second Symphony of 1872 sought to broaden the conquest by enriching its substance with all the resources that contrapuntal and harmonic artifice could profitably provide. That there are moments when contrivance triumphs over inventiveness should not deafen the listener to the remarkable achievement this very substantial movement represents. Rarely did Tchaikovsky manage to maintain impetus so unflaggingly over so wide a span.

If Tchaikovsky's expansion of his Third Symphony to five movements was a sign that he felt the form as he had used it was no longer adequate, the solution he had chosen proved unsatisfactory. But within a very short span there would be no avoiding a more searching review of the whole symphonic experience; the turbulent inner changes precipitating the crisis that was so soon to break in his real world would see to that. Hence the radical innovations of the Fourth Symphony. The adjustments made in the first movement of the First Symphony had involved no shift in the overall proportions of the movement, nor in the nature or relative weightings of the three that followed. The greatly heightened expressive force of what was now to come made such adjustments unavoidable. The textural complexity of so much of the Second Symphony's original first movement may well have decided Tchaikovsky that the second movement must offer some breathing space and that the charming wedding march for a water nymph from the rejected opera, *Undine*, would serve well here. But what he put into the first movement of the Fourth made a greater respite imperative, and the relaxed mood of the two central movements was deliberate and well calculated.

But within the first movement itself structural matters could not stay as they had been. As in earlier works the main pressure was upon the exposition and was of two kinds. One was melodic – that it was here that Tchaikovsky's greatest single gift could be most freely deployed. This pressure was by no means new. As early as that precocious student work, *The Storm*, Tchaikovsky had favoured three distinct thematic areas, while in *Romeo and Juliet* the exposition had already grown to twice the length of the development. But the second pressure was new and changed the very nature of the symphony. As represented by the

Fourth, the symphony had become a human document – dramatic and in essence autobiographical, though concerned with matters psychological, not everyday. For Tchaikovsky's invention had now been invaded by an element that was unprecedentedly personal, urgent, capable of enormous expressive forcefulness, even violence, and which could be as disruptive structurally as it could be disconcerting expressively. Once unleashed, it could prove uncontainable, devouring musical space voraciously until it had, for the moment, expended itself. Only weeks before beginning the Fourth Symphony many of these traits had been exposed in the Allegro vivo of *Francesca da Rimini*, and though the Moderato con anima of the Fourth Symphony's first movement begins soberly enough, it is already possessed by a restlessness which forewarns of the remorseless persistence, even aggressiveness with which the idea will uncoil itself. The scale of this exposition, combined with its expressive weight, even forcefulness, make this unprecedented among Tchaikovsky's, and the symmetry which in earlier sonata structures he had retained fairly closely now disintegrates. As might be expected the development is relatively compact, but what persuaded Tchaikovsky to compress the recapitulation to half the length of the exposition was not merely that an equal balance would have expanded the movement to gargantuan proportions; so completely had he played his expressive cards earlier that to trump them was beyond him. Yet compression has its own power. Summarize the essentials of what has gone before, then once again free the most violent forces to lash themselves within the unyielding bounds of a concise coda, and the movement will end with a sense not of exhaustion but of energies yet unspent.

The structural asymmetry that resulted was to be taken still farther in later works. Neither the Manfred Symphony's first movement nor the symphonic ballad, *The Voyevoda*, are sonata structures, but each is an extensive movement ending with an unexpectedly terse account of earlier powerful and disturbing materials; while Manfred's climax is the most unremittingly violent Tchaikovsky ever devised, *The Voyevoda*'s end recalls the sinister, muttered ragings of the deceived husband, then shatters all with the fatal shot and its calamitous consequence. Both endings leave the listener discomforted. The Fifth Symphony which lay between these two works is at the antipodes of both, for though the melodic demands made upon the exposition resulted in a section of great size, Tchaikovsky's patent resolve this time not to upset the traditional equilibrium decided him not to risk expressive hyperbole. This permitted also a more traditional balance between it and the remaining movements, and in this regard the Fifth

Symphony comes closer to the First than any of the three intervening. It was in the first movement of the Sixth Symphony that the new kind of symphonism initiated in the Fourth and obliquely continued in the Manfred Symphony was to attain its ultimate fulfilment.

As recorded earlier Tchaikovsky sketched his last symphony between 16 February and 5 April, but delayed scoring it until the summer. He began this operation on 1 August, and at first found it difficult. 'Twenty years ago I'd have gone full steam ahead,' he wrote to Modest on 3 August. '. . . Now I've become timid, unsure of myself. All today I've sat over just two pages – and still it hasn't come out as I would wish.'[32] But then his confidence and his rate of progress increased, and on 13 August he could inform Taneyev optimistically: 'Already now I'm on the verge of finishing the scoring of the symphony's third movement, so that in three days I shall set about the finale, which won't take more than three days.'[33] In fact the scoring took longer than he had antici-pated, but by 31 August he could sign the completed manuscript. He was not dispirited at the time it had taken him. 'It's not the conse-quence of failing strength or old age,' he wrote to Anatoly that same day, 'but that I've become infinitely stricter with myself and I no longer have my former self-assurance. *I'm very proud* of the symphony, and I think it's the best of my works.'[34] Indeed, whatever other uncertainties may subsequently have returned or arisen, Tchaikovsky himself never had any doubts about the quality of what he had composed; it was a very special piece – as he declared to his nephew, Bob, to whom he proposed to dedicate the work. 'I shall consider it the usual [thing] and unsurprising if this symphony is torn to pieces or is little appreciated; it won't be the first time [this has happened]. But I definitely consider it the best and, in particular, *the most sincere* of all my works. I love it as I have never loved any other of my musical offspring.'[35]

To help with the details that remained Tchaikovsky invited to Klin two of the Konyus brothers; Jules, the violinist who through Tchaikovsky's recommendation had spent two years as joint leader with Brodsky of the New York Symphony Orchestra, was to take care of the bowings, while Lev, a pianist, would be a useful partner in working over the piano duet transcription which Tchaikovsky had decided to make himself. It seems that on 21 October Safonov conducted an

[32] *TLP*17, p. 142; *TZC*3, p. 628; *TPB*, p. 546; *YDGC*, pp. 587–8; *DTC*, p. 433.
[33] *TLP*17, p. 154; *TTP*, p. 196; *YDGC*, p. 588; *DTC*, p. 433.
[34] *TLP*17, p. 165; *TPB*, p. 547; *DTC*, p. 434; *YDGC*, p. 590.
[35] *TLP*17, p. 155; *TZC*3, p. 630; *TPB*, p. 547; *YDGC*, p. 588; *DTC*, p. 433.

orchestra of staff and students of the Moscow Conservatoire in a private reading of the symphony to enable corrections and revisions to be made to the orchestral material ahead of rehearsals for the première in St Petersburg a week later. Kashkin remembered that before leaving for the capital Tchaikovsky had expressed some doubts about the finale, saying that he might subsequently replace it with another. The rehearsals did little to reassure him about the overall effect, for the players were clearly puzzled by the new work, and Modest believed this made his brother fearful for the performance. The consequence was personal demoralization, Tchaikovsky conducting the rehearsals without his customary attention to detail (so Modest stated), and seeming unsure of himself at the première itself. The audience greeted the work politely, but there was no triumph. As for the press, they were respectful and mostly approving, but the piece was in general rated lower than its predecessors. However, Modest added, despite this collective lack of enthusiasm, his brother was now confident of its worth, for he seems to have understood perfectly well what a challenge it posed for all his listeners, sensing that their verdict was perhaps not final. 'It's not that it displeased, but it produced some bewilderment,' he wrote to Jurgenson on 30 October, two days after the première. 'As far as I myself am concerned, I take more pride in it than in any other of my works.'[36]

Despite the disquieting novelty of the experience presented both by the symphony as a whole and by its outer movements in particular, it might on first sight seem that in the opening Allegro non troppo Tchaikovsky had beaten a kind of retreat, since in its broadest outlines it conforms to the traditional sonata paradigm, even forming a two-subject (though three-theme) exposition, with the second in the conventional relative major. This retreat is merely apparent; Tchaikovsky has turned back not to capitulate, but to confront. In venturing into the freer forms of the Manfred Symphony's first movement and *The Voyevoda* he had been seeking a new way rather than blazing further an old trail. But the problem of a novel musical form is not unlike that of abstract art; it lacks both the ready references that define originality, and also the background of earlier experience that first excites a new response, then sharpens it by the continuing challenge which that familiar experience presents. In the first movement of the Fourth Symphony Tchaikovsky had fearlessly fractured the inherited mould, but what he did in the first movement of the Sixth was bolder still; he rebuilt that mould, but in the process refashioned it so that what it

[36] *TLP*17, p. 205; *TZC*3, pp. 645–6; *TPJ*2, p. 273; *YDGC*, p. 595; *DTC*, p. 437.

formed would have radically redesigned proportions, drastically shifted emphases, and sometimes mingled or even totally contorted functions. The result is the greatest and most articulate first movement he ever wrote.

Most immediately striking is the proportion of the main body of the movement occupied by the exposition (142 out of 335 bars; because of the slower speeds stipulated in the second subject it absorbs something like half the time in performance). As noted earlier, the urge to expand the exposition was bound to be strong in a composer with Tchaikovsky's melodic endowment; equally an inclination to compress what followed was natural to one who freely acknowledged that, for him, devising a development was an artificial process. The solution Tchaikovsky adopted (Ex. 300) was as effective in solving the latter problem as it was in widening the possibilities for melodic exploitation: compose a vast exposition, follow it by the most succinct of developments and proceed to the recapitulation; then, where the transition would come, open yet further the experience with new music that would precipitate the movement's climax; the second subject, represented by only one of its themes, would follow. Though what came between the two subjects was essentially new, the effect was to integrate development and recapitulation into a stretch of music of colossal power, after which the second subject took on a renewed significance. Finally the economy of the coda reinforced the sense of progressive compression that had informed the entire second half of the movement.

Such is the detached view that may be taken of this very large but totally assured movement. But, like it or not, no listener can come away from a performance without sensing that some inner experience of quite extraordinary turmoil and anguish has been externalized through it. Tchaikovsky stated openly that the symphony was written to a programme, albeit secret, and the title under which, after his death, it was published – 'Pateticheskaya Simfoniya' – was of his own choosing, though the adjective had been suggested to him by Modest the day following the première. The most striking formal innovation is the concluding Adagio lamentoso, which finally dies to nothing, and which is a patent legacy of the programme drafted before Tchaikovsky had set about the E flat Symphony – and not perhaps the only part of that programme to bear upon the present work.

The introduction, which provides a tonal upbeat by opening in E minor, was added to the first movement after the rest had been sketched. More clearly than the introduction to the Fifth Symphony, these dark subterranean sounds foretell the first subject to come

Ex. 300

SIXTH SYMPHONY: FIRST MOVEMENT

Ex. 301

(Ex. 301) – a nervous four-note motif, its first two quavers promptly fractured into semiquavers which make a second motif of considerable later importance, but which here take an immediate firm hold on proceedings and direct the music towards a world of gaiety and light. Already what we have heard within the first fifty bars is unique; never before had a symphonic movement staked out so wide an expressive area in so short a time. What follows is the kind of instant development familiar from earlier works by Tchaikovsky, though in contrast to the inward searching of *Romeo and Juliet* or, even more, the Fourth Symphony, the materials expand in scope. Nor is the tutti restatement as before; nor does the key return to the tonic for this restatement. Instead it enters in D sharp minor, sequences a third higher in F sharp minor; then, over a bass which sinks stepwise through a fifth to settle at last on D, the semiquaver activity subsides, a chord of D major is reached and finally falls silent. A single string line climbs arpeggio-wise aloft, slows, expires. A long silence – and then the string line begins to retrace its course downwards.[37] The weary, long-drawn second subject (Ex. 302) has arrived.

[37] In the first sketch the rising phrase had ended earlier (Ex. 303). Only later did Tchaikovsky extend it to create a closer mirror image of the second subject to come.

Ex. 303

Ex. 302

What we have just heard has turned the transition on its head. In classical movements its function had been to drive towards the second subject, and Tchaikovsky's own transitions had habitually made no attempt to mask their role of looking forward to a new stage, though they may have done no more than assert the dominant of the key to come. But this transition, inseparably welded to the departing first subject so that it is impossible to say exactly where it had begun,[38] settles unequivocally into the new key, then drains itself of any lingering vestige of dynamism.[39] It has therefore gone far beyond the kind of transition observed in the Manfred Symphony's first movement, where the chord preceding the silence had been unresolved, leaving no doubt that something would follow. Here nothing is promised; indeed, all seems to be over, and what is to follow could well be a hiatus or a non-sequitur. Instead what ensues proves to be precisely what this transition had indicated: a second subject in which harmonic movement remains minimal and harmonic thrust is nil, for it is supported by little more than a decorated D major triad, an almost entirely colouristic

[38] It might be argued that it had started some thirty bars earlier than suggested in Ex. 300 – that is, around bar 40, where new material had entered and B minor had been relinquished.

[39] It is therefore quite different from the Third Quartet's transition which, though also indivisible from the first subject, had manoeuvred to the dominant of the new key to drive straight into the second subject.

purpose being served by any deviation, whether it be a single diminished seventh (bar 2), a brief dominant (bar 4), a chromatically
decorated structure pulling against the D pedal (bars 5–6), or a seventh
chord which forcefully displaces the D major chord (bar 7), only to find
survival against its unremitting pull beyond its strength.

   This transition is the most perfectly calculated, truly organic that
Tchaikovsky ever devised. The second theme of this second subject is a
relaxed duet within the woodwind, the answering phrase a six-note
scalic idea split into two parts. This section brings some harmonic
movement, even modulation, but the return and subsequent extension
of the main theme first restores, then reinforces, and finally confirms
the total harmonic stasis towards which the exposition has been
moving, a calm reinforced by a ritardando molto and its final pppppp
marking, the quietest of the whole symphony. Conventional this
exposition may have been in many of its appropriations from traditional periodic and tonal practices, but in the way Tchaikovsky has
worked these out, and especially in the organization of its underlying
ebb and flow, it has become one of the most original ever composed.
And it has created the perfect background for what is to come.

   It would be inconceivable that Fate should not play a critical role in
an avowedly programmatic work of this temper. It appears in the
introduction (bar 15) growing out of the tail of the main motif, and then
early in the first subject, two manifestations overlapping as the music
shifts key (Ex. 304). The contour conditions the first theme of the
second subject (see *x* in Ex. 302), and though the answering phrase in
the second theme (bars 105–8) does not observe the median-to-
dominant placing, the six-note descent is there. But since the evidence
of the force's operations is to be so ubiquitous, restriction to the single
median-to-dominant form would become intolerable. Instead Fate
goes on to appropriate a full range of descending scales which some-

Ex. 304

times spread themselves over wide stretches of music, even influencing
the course of a whole section. If in the exposition Fate had seemed to
retain the relative benignity it had shown in the Fifth Symphony, its
marcatissimo eruption in the distant key of E flat early in the development proclaims uncompromisingly that both its power and its will
remain as implacable as ever. Tchaikovsky's response is the most
explicit of the entire symphony: to quote from the Russian requiem the
traditional chant: 'With thy saints, O Christ, give peace to the soul of
thy servant.' (Ex. 305)

Ex. 305

After the total stillness in which the exposition had ended, the
explosion of the development had produced the most violent of contrasts. It is the first subject that is first reconsidered, but with the
semiquavers no longer buoyant and untroubled, but generating one
of the most scorching bursts of energy to be found anywhere in
Tchaikovsky's work. The chant brings quiet but no calm, and with the
subsequent return to B minor and the reappearance of the first subject,
the fever resumes unabated. And just as the intrusion of Fate had
capped the first part of the development, so it is another peremptory
entry that redirects the music's course, not this time towards the soul's
Gethsemane, where hope of deliverance was yet alive, but its Calvary.
How Tchaikovsky, the doubter who longed for faith, would have
responded to that metaphor cannot be said. Whether he saw the
destiny-controlling agent in which he so fervently believed as the
executor of divine judgement, and whether, more specifically, the less
brutal image Fate had seemed to present in the Fifth Symphony
signified that he could now equate it with the stern redeeming power
within Christian belief is impossible to say. What follows in this
symphony suggests otherwise, for the crisis of suffering leads not to a
resurrection, but to final extinction. Whether such speculations can
have any validity – whether, indeed, they should be made – each must
decide for himself. What cannot be questioned is that this monolithic

section of new music, which with such labour heaves itself aloft, embodies the crisis of the experience made incarnate in this movement, and the gigantic slow scalic descent through more than two octaves leaves no question about what power is controlling destiny.

Tovey had no doubt about the merits of this passage: 'Undoubtedly the climax of Tchaikovsky's artistic career, as well as of this work.'[40] Yet it also fulfils something of the orthodox transition function, this time of restoring the tonic which had been regained at the recapitulation but then swiftly lost, for all the while, from the moment the Fate scale had heralded this cataclysmic section, a pedal F sharp had reaffirmed the dominant of B minor. The crisis endured, the resolution long promised can come and, with it, a kind of peace as the first theme of the second subject flows in, dispensing with its companion (a sacrifice the listener need regret little, for it was the weakest idea in the movement) and finally restoring the total stillness in which the exposition had ended. As in the Fourth Symphony, the coda is not a formal rounding off but the final stage in the experience. Its solemnity brings resignation as the symphony's opening idea is converted into a solemn, measured theme beneath which Fate stalks on pizzicato strings.

Like the first movement of the Manfred Symphony, this one has demanded that some attempt be made to guess the human experience that has provoked such a powerful series of musical events, organized so uniquely, yet so coherently. That said, the absolute musical control Tchaikovsky manifestly retains appears the more remarkable. The movement completely overshadows the two that follow. More relaxed they may be (of necessity, after what has gone before), but they are crucial to the total experience of the symphony and are, like all the central movements of Tchaikovsky's mature symphonies, perfectly formed. The Allegro con grazia is a sort of limping waltz, its $\frac{5}{4}$ metre casting a shadow of unease over its geniality. Set in D major, its tonic is prolonged to become a mediant pedal during the B minor trio (con dolcezza e flebile), and its unbroken pulsing on double bass and timpani fortifies the heavy melancholy produced by the plangent harmonies and persistent dissonance. The scale which descends through two octaves at the coda's opening shows Fate in a placid mood; the brief return to the trio has more tension to it, but this is dispelled when, as during the earlier link between the trio itself and the returning first section, it is mingled with the melodic figure which had opened the movement. The end of this ambivalently urbane movement is tranquil.

[40] D. F. Tovey, *Essays in musical analysis*, Vol. 2 (London, 1935), p. 86.

The ensuing Allegro molto vivace is second only to the first movement in structural interest. While the Allegro non troppo of the first
movement had ventured only briefly into the world of *Nutcracker*, this
seems, at least initially, totally committed to it. Its scale and complexity
is therefore the more surprising. Expressed in the plainest terms, it is
built from two large sections, the first, A, a miniature ternary structure
characterized by moto perpetuo triplet quavers, sometimes with a
thematic life of their own, but also acting as background to a succession
of ideas (including a foretaste of the main theme of B). It centres upon
G major, but also embraces E minor and B minor. It gives the
impression of being introductory, like a setting out of wares – that is,
until the sudden intrusion of the Fate scale in E flat (the same distant
key in which it had burst into the development of the first movement)
brings a heightened sense of purpose, and the music directs itself
towards the second section, B, set in E major. Here the march theme
comes into its own, forming the flanks of a ternary section. Though
during this section E major is inflected with telling touches from other
keys, its supremacy is never challenged. After this section A resumes, B
follows, now also in G major, and there is a substantial coda focusing
upon the main march theme.

Described thus, the movement is clearly unusual (though it has been
suggested that it shapes out a sonata structure without development),
but still apparently simple. Such, in fact, is not the case, for no account
has been taken of the significant amplifications as recurrence has
succeeded recurrence. Ex. 306 sets out the structure. The six shaded
areas make three pairs of correspondences, the second of each pair far
more extensive than the first. Between them they comprise over one
quarter of the movement, and it is above all through these that it makes
its critical effect. Each is a transitional section, driving the music
towards a destination; each recurrence is more insistent, more prolonged – the striving becomes more urgent, and a movement that had
begun as carefree betrays growing anxiety, then desperation, especially
when the main march theme returns for the last time, now fff, and
without the mitigation of the triplet quavers. In the earlier draft
programme the third movement was to be concerned with 'disappointments', and much of this intention has lingered. Though Tchaikovsky
had once envisaged its end as 'solemnly triumphant', this march is, in
fact, a deeply ironic, bitter conception – a desperate bid for happiness
so prolonged and vehement that it confirms not only the desperation of
the search, but also its futility. Twice Fate signals its presence, each
time wrenching this otherwise sharp-key music into deep flat regions;
then it retreats until, at the very end, in exuberant mockery, it assumes

Ex. 306

SIXTH SYMPHONY: THIRD MOVEMENT

= inexact relationship
= exact, or virtual identity

the tone and key of the movement itself. With this turn of events even hope against hope collapses, and the anguish is instant and total.

This is a fascinating movement. Its lively and perfectly judged textures have true musical substance, its detail is prodigious and its harmonic structures sometimes bold. The concluding bars of Ex. 307

Ex. 307

are but one instance; striking, too, is the shift towards the flat sub-mediant (C major) in bars seven and eight – a colouristic incident whose placing emphasizes the initial three-phrase grouping of the theme's two-bar phrases by throwing emphasis upon the fourth phrase as a change of direction. Those who would dismiss this movement as facile should listen and look again.

In the finale the descending scale becomes the melodic principle conditioning the entire piece; nowhere in Tchaikovsky's work is Fate so pervasive. Yet in presenting the conclusive battle between it and frail humanity Tchaikovsky also exploits the full range of his harmonic resources to project on the one hand the human urge to freedom and activity, on the other the tightening grip of a finally triumphant adversary. Thus the sturdy and unblushing parallel sevenths of the opening bar close into a dominant seventh (Ex. 308b), and the sequen-tial ascent of the string melody gains added lift from the dynamism within traditional harmonic method; but the section ends in harmonic inertia. The curious seesawing progress of the strings at the opening (Ex. 308a) has been the subject of much comment.[41] Daniel Koury[42] has stated that no seating plans of nineteenth-century Russian or-chestras have come to light, and we can only speculate whether it was the normal practice to place the violin sections on opposite sides of the stage so that the alternating notes of the opening theme would have seemed to come from different directions, or whether, as in the Renais-sance practice of 'eye music', the presence of Fate was to be initially obscured on the printed page; whatever the case, the string phrase that opens this Adagio lamentoso becomes in performance a five-note scalic segment.

As with the opening movement, a piece as patently 'about' some-thing as this demands an attempt at interpretation, for all the danger

[41] However, it was not entirely unprecedented in Tchaikovsky's work, having appeared as early as in his student overture, *The Storm* (bar 74), and again in the Third Suite (*Valse mélancolique*, bars 142 ff).

[42] Daniel J. Koury, *Orchestral performance practices in the nineteenth century: size, proportions and seating* (Ann Arbor, 1986), p. 209.

Ex. 308

a.

b.

with which this may be fraught, and the total polarity, both in timbre and material, of woodwind and strings in the movement's first paragraph provides surely some reasonable grounds for hearing them as presenting the two sides of the conflict. At first just a single note, then a three-note descent, the woodwind line permits itself to be drawn upward in parallel with the string phrases (though in constant, powerfully abrasive conflict with them), but then, with a spacious undulating descent through two octaves, it takes full possession of the conclusion to this first section. Yet after the opening returns (with an upward rushing anacrusis that is to have much importance later: see Ex. 308b, bar 19) Fate is to be less yielding, and the strings are permitted no ascent. Instead the woodwind line, strong enough to prevail even though represented by no more than the bassoons, presses the string phrases downwards, quickly ousting them and continuing its massive two-and-a-half-octave descent as the sole mournful occupant of the central stage. Even more in this second section have the dark, scarcely moving sonorities of Manfred's world been recalled, and even more than in that grim domain has all motion finally ceased, providing the perfect contrast to the D major section that follows, where the harmonic movement resumes and then presses forward, and where a new string theme is permitted to spread itself sequentially, vastly, and with increasing urgency, the woodwind now relinquishing their active role – for, as is revealed in the trail of ever more swiftly descending scales that bring an abrupt end to this section, Fate now has the power to invade and annex totally the string line itself.

Thus far a sonata structure might be in prospect. But to have played out the crisis in a development (thus suggesting that the final issue still remained to be decided), then attempted a recapitulation, would have been unthinkable. After the final critical encounter with Fate there could be little to add; only grief and anguish, then unceremonious oblivion. And so there is no development, and with the return of the home key, the final act of the drama is played out through a reworking of first subject material. If Fate had disguised its optical identity in the movement's opening string phrases it now drops its mask. The last encounter is fierce but brief; the last upward rushing anacruses are countered by implacable downward pulls, and finally expend themselves. All contest now over, a single gong stroke marks Fate's victory. Solemn chords follow, moving to the plainest, most familiar of cadences, but one which in this context has a chilling, even appalled finality. The drama is over; when the second subject enters, there is no striving upwards, for its four opening notes are now the first stage of a broken scale which can only sink still lower. The harmony darkens as the symphony re-enters the stygian gloom in which it had opened, and the scalic emblem of that force which Tchaikovsky so immutably believed had controlled his destiny sinks to a final subterranean silence.

Thus ends the greatest of Tchaikovsky's instrumental works, and surely the most truly original symphony to have been composed in the seventy years since Beethoven's Ninth. In the Fifth Symphony

Tchaikovsky had sought to prove he could submit to the externals of the Western view of the symphony, yet remain wholly himself. But in the Sixth there had been no compromise; the method, the form, the ethos were as personal as the musical invention and the expressive experience which shaped its structure. Had he lived, it is impossible to imagine any direction he could have taken beyond this. But the matter never arose. Within nine days of conducting its première he was dead.

12

THE LAST MONTHS

PYOTR ILICH'S LIFE proceeded like a spiral. On each twist in a given direction its course traversed zones identical in mood . . . Speaking earlier of the gloomy melancholy of his last years, I noticed the similarity of his mood[-pattern] at each abrupt turning point in his existence. And so, like the calming of his mental sufferings which, during the summer months of 1862, had preceded the abrupt change from a civil servant to a musician, [or] his serene spiritual state during February and March shortly before the crisis of 1877, so now we pass to the description of a period of tranquility and contentment, the prime cause of which is the creation of the Sixth Symphony . . . It was as though it absorbed the gloomy melancholy of the preceding years, and Pyotr Ilich for the moment experienced that lightening which is felt by the man who has confessed to a sympathetic soul everything that has long wearied and tormented him.[1]

Describing Tchaikovsky's state during the last months of his life cost Modest a good deal of discomfort. He could not deny there was much in it that was gloomy and depressed, but he took every opportunity to emphasize that there was another side. No doubt in the process of sketching the Sixth Symphony Tchaikovsky had exorcized (or at least placated) some of those tormenting phantoms that lurked within him, and his spirits were bound to be lifted by the equally unshakeable recognition that he had not only shaped a new creation, but shaped it well. Modest was honest enough to admit this. But as his brother's life approached its end he clutched at any straw that might provide evidence that his inner mood was constantly good. Tchaikovsky's view of death had changed radically, Modest said. Certainly there were events enough during these months to focus his thoughts upon this most final of matters. Vladimir Shilovsky, his pupil and close friend in the late 60s and 70s, whom he had allowed to compose the entr'acte before the second act of *The Oprichnik*, but from whom he had become

[1] *TZC3*, pp. 601–2.

distanced during the 80s, was now dying. Hearing this in February, Tchaikovsky had visited him, spent much time with him, and a measure of their former intimacy was restored. Shilovsky died on 6 July, just one month after his brother, Konstantin. Tchaikovsky had never been as intimate with the latter, but he had contributed modestly to the libretto of *Eugene Onegin*, and before this there had been some closeness between them. And while he was enduring the blows of these two passings, he knew that his classmate from the School of Jurisprudence, Apukhtin, was mortally sick. Most grievous of all was the death in June of his old friend and colleague, Karl Albrecht. He had learned that Albrecht was seriously ill just before leaving for Western Europe on his way to Cambridge to receive an honorary D.Mus. He had hastened to visit him, had perceived the extremity of his condition, and learned of his death from a newspaper while on his way home. He confessed to having shed many tears. But, Modest wrote, the effect upon him was not what it would once have been.

> Some years earlier a single piece of news like this would have acted upon Pyotr Ilich more strongly than all these taken together now did. He wept over 'his dear Karlusha', the closest of all these recently dead people, but when soon afterwards I saw him I was struck by the relative calm with which he took this loss, not to speak of the other two. He also talked about Apukhtin differently from how he had earlier about people who were dying. You felt now that he would not travel several hundred versts, as formerly he had done to Kotek, Kondratyev [and] Bochechkarov, just to see a friend before the eternal parting. It was as if death had become less terrible, mysterious and frightening. I cannot say whether this was a result of his sensitivity coarsening with age and experience, or whether the moral sufferings he endured in his last years had accustomed him to see death at such moments as a deliverer. But I am recording the undoubted fact that, for all this dire news from all directions, Pyotr Ilich was, from the time of his return from England until the very end, calm, serene, almost full of joie de vivre as in the best period of his life.[2]

By the end Modest is surely protesting too much. One cannot discount his testimony, of course. Though in his letters Tchaikovsky mentions these various deaths with much sadness, he dwells on none of them as though it was truly central to his thoughts. Yet Modest's

[2] *TZC3*, p. 626.

remarks about his brother's consistent cheerfulness during these last months consolidates the impression that he is desperate to stifle any thought that it could have been otherwise, and this merely deepens the suspicion that matters at the end may have been quite different from what the wider world was to believe. There is, in fact, every sign that Tchaikovsky coped adequately with the particular strains and problems with which he had to contend, that he was at times outwardly cheerful, just as at others he was not. But such cheerfulness in no way proves that there was not a depressive potential so extreme that, when activated, it could lead him to dire, even fatal action.

Nevertheless there were many things to cheer him. To the Tsar's decoration, the noisy salutations and ovations from audiences in three continents, and the more decorous but considered accolades of learned societies in Prague, France and Holland was to be added a musical honour as high as any Great Britain could bestow. The degree ceremony in Cambridge would be in mid-June, but he had to be in London a fortnight earlier to conduct in a concert of the Philharmonic Society. In the meantime he remained based on Klin, partly because he had certain commitments still to carry out in Moscow, partly because he intended to fulfil the promise given a year earlier to a young, obscure student from Kiev University to set some of his verses to music. On 4 May, the day after completing the Eighteen Piano Pieces, Op. 72, he was present at the dress rehearsal of an opera given by some of Lavrovskaya's students at the Moscow Conservatoire. He was as impressed by them as he was enchanted with the opera, Cimarosa's *Il matrimonio segreto*, and equal pleasure came from Rakhmaninov's 'delightful'[3] *Aleko*, whose première five days later he attended. This one-act opera had been composed the previous year as the nineteen-year-old's graduation exercise and had earned him the gold medal. Tchaikovsky's admiration was reinforced by hearing two of the piano pieces Rakhmaninov had also composed the previous year, and now issued as his Op. 3. One was *Mélodie*, the other the C sharp minor Prelude which was to perform for him much the same service in making his name known worldwide as the Andante cantabile had done for Tchaikovsky some twenty years earlier.

Between these two operatic events he was present at a concert by the Synod School's choir, went to the Maly Theatre to see Sardou's *Patrie* (which he found boring), and celebrated his fifty-third birthday. On 10 May he left for Nizhni-Novgorod to visit Anatoly, pausing on his return through Moscow to comfort the dying Albrecht. Seeing that the end

---

[3] *TLP*17, p. 91; *YDGC*, p. 581.

might come while he was away from Russia, he asked Jurgenson to provide out of his (Tchaikovsky's) own funds anything Albrecht's widow might need. That same day, 14 May, he was home in Klin. He had intended to remain only two days before leaving for St Petersburg on the first stage of his journey to England, but he delayed an extra day to complete the last of his Six Romances, Op. 73.

Daniil Rathaus had sent Tchaikovsky some of his own verses in August 1892, and the latter had immediately promised to set them. He had been especially struck by 'We sat together', and had forthwith sketched the vocal part for the first strophe, and also a portion of 'The sun has set'. He began composing the six songs purposefully on 5 May, but his intervening commitments delayed completion until 17 May. They proved to be his last completed work. It might seem curious that the fifty-three-year-old who had just created the Sixth Symphony should have remained so drawn to these verses of a twenty-four-year-old amateur he had never met. Tchaikovsky knew perfectly well what constituted good poetry, but the Olympian view of the littérateur was irrelevant to the song composer, as his choice of verse had repeatedly shown. What the former might here have judged as conventional and naïve was to him praiseworthy for its clarity and directness. Rathaus offered simply schemed verses, descriptions based on stock imagery but prettily picturesque, and feelings uncomplicated and familiar. Sentimentality reigned supreme and pointed a clear expressive path through verse which never encumbered the music. Actions that might demand a more varied, even complex response had no part in these mood pieces; even the lovers' communion in the fourth song was passive. Most of the rest were reflections on, or descriptions of, isolation: the failure to communicate (No. 1), then the distant beloved as the object of longing (No. 2), ecstatic memories (No. 5), and intercession (No. 6). Night shrouded most: it might be the time of loneliness (No. 2), confession (No. 3), rapture (No. 4), or benediction (No. 6).

Taken together, these settings are the closest Tchaikovsky came to composing a cycle. Unsurprisingly, it is not the situations of physical closeness or passionate but chaste communion to which he responded most strongly, but those of solitude. Throughout all six songs the vocal style is declamatory, and quaver movement predominates; individual phrases are mostly brief, and the structures are lucid even when, as in 'We sat together' (No. 1), the music in the second half moves into new territory to mark the passage of the years. Here the piano postlude is new, dwelling on the mediant-to-dominant move of that most basic form of that most basic of Fate themes, though this time placing more emphasis upon the rising scale (Ex. 309). It is, of course, derived from the unremarkable rising phrase before the singer's last words; what relates it to the Fate theme is the harmonic move in the third bar of Ex. 309 – above all, what ensues in the fourth.

Tchaikovsky dedicated the set to Nikolay Figner, who may well have felt the piano prelude to ''Mid sombre days' (No. 5) was a pale memory of the love theme in *The Queen of Spades*, the opera to whose success he had contributed so much. These songs, like 'In this moonlight' (No. 3)

Ex. 309

and 'The sun has set' (No. 4), reveal the hand of the totally assured craftsman, hitting their marks unerringly, matching Rathaus's intentions exactly. Yet none of them really matters. The remaining two are very different. The scalic phrases sinking disconsolately above a tonic pedal link 'Night' (No. 2) unmistakably with the end of the Sixth Symphony. It might be doubted whether Rathaus's conventional expression of romantic pining merits such desolate treatment, but there is no disparity between words and music in 'Again, as before, alone' (No. 6), not because Tchaikovsky's treatment is expressively less substantial, but because it is tauter. This is as close as he ever came in his adult songs to a song-epigram – and not merely because it is so compact; its material is matchingly economical, the drooping semitone of the opening expanding to encompass a minor third, and this three-note figure passing to the voice to become the dominating unit of the vocal line, just as the mournful semitone remains the burden of the piano part. As in 'Night' a tonic pedal runs unbroken through the song. 'Again, as before, alone' is a song of all-pervading melancholy, the climax no move towards fulfilment, merely a surge of yearning which quickly passes. As in ''Mid sombre days', the piano prelude is repeated to end (see Ex. 296). But whereas in that song it had simply provided a tidy conclusion, this postlude presents the final stage. Time has stood still, but something in the inner world has been quietly transformed. After longing has come a tempered resignation.

Tchaikovsky's last task before leaving for St Petersburg on 17 May was to despatch to his cousin, Andrey Petrovich, a trio for the regimental march he had composed a month earlier. He remained a week in the capital, during which he attended Rimsky-Korsakov's nameday party together with Lyadov, Belyayev and Glazunov (who presented him with yet another of his scores – the *Triumphal March*, Op. 40). Their host took the opportunity to approach Tchaikovsky with a request, resolved upon at a meeting of the St Petersburg RMS two days before, that he should conduct the Society's concerts during the coming season. Rimsky-Korsakov himself had made the proposal, and after some hesitation Tchaikovsky was to agree to direct four concerts. Arriving in Berlin on 27 May, he found his longing to return to Russia even greater than usual; this, together with the urge to proceed with the scoring of both the new symphony and the E flat Piano Concerto, made him for a moment consider abandoning the trip to London and Cambridge.

Two days later he was in London. Despite a quick journey through Cologne and a smooth crossing from Ostende, he reacted against London with his customary distaste. 'Several times during my journey yesterday, I decided to throw it up and turn tail, but somehow it's shameful to return empty-handed,' he wrote to Bob Davïdov, having with difficulty found a room in the Hotel Dieudonné.

> . . . I'm not only suffering from a melancholy for which there is no word (there's a place in my new symphony where I think it is well expressed), but from a hatred of strange people, and some undefined fear – and the devil knows from what else besides . . . But, of course, this is the last time I'll ever be doing all this; I shan't travel anywhere other than for a vast fee, and for not more than three days . . . London is a most disagreeable city. I can't find anything here. There are no *pissoirs*, no *shops that change money*, it was with difficulty I found a hat to fit me. On entering the hotel I encountered the Parisian pianist, *Diémer*, who's living here, and to my own surprise was terribly glad of this. He is, after all, an old acquaintance, very well disposed towards me. But a consequence was that almost immediately after my arrival I had to go to his *recital* – that is, a daytime concert.[4]

Whatever the tribulations in store, Tchaikovsky had now decided he would go through with this whole expedition. The course of the following fortnight's events has been charted in great detail, and with very liberal documentary support, by Gerald Norris.[5] 1893 was the fiftieth anniversary of the Cambridge University Musical Society (CUMS), and a proposal was made that the University should confer honorary degrees upon Brahms and Verdi to mark the occasion. Neither composer agreeing to come, the Society quickly assembled a remarkable clutch of alternative celebrities: Grieg, Max Bruch, Boito, Saint-Saëns and Tchaikovsky. It was Tchaikovsky's own idea that he might use his presence in England to conduct once again for the Philharmonic Society, and in the concert on 1 June he shared the rostrum with another of the graduands, Saint-Saëns. The latter was already hugely popular in England, both as composer and performer; it was the Philharmonic Society that seven years earlier had commissioned Saint-Saëns's Third Symphony, and for all Tchaikovsky's success on his previous two visits to London he started with a formidable disadvantage. The Frenchman was to play his own Second Piano Concerto, then conduct his *Le rouet d'Omphale*, while Tchaikovsky had charge of his Fourth Symphony which, though now some sixteen years old, London had never heard. He knew the work could prove problematic to the audience, and the two rehearsals seem to have been nervous

[4] *TLP*17, p. 97; *TPB*, pp. 539–40; *TZC*3, p. 618 (partial).
[5] G. Norris, *Stanford, the Cambridge jubilee, and Tchaikovsky* (London, 1980).

affairs, Tchaikovsky finally drawing the required spirit from the orchestra in the finale by exclaiming: 'Vodka – more vodka!' (according to the young Henry Wood, who was present at the final rehearsal). Alexander Mackenzie, who was to conduct the remaining items in the programme, was taken aback by Tchaikovsky's aging and exhausted appearance. 'The weak voice, intense nervousness, and exhaustion after rehearsal, plainly indicated failing health,' he remembered.[6]

Nevertheless, Tchaikovsky came away from the concert at the St James's Hall well satisfied with his reception. 'The concert went brilliantly,' he wrote to Modest two days later, 'that is, according to everyone's unanimous opinion, I enjoyed a real triumph, so that Saint-Saëns, who appeared after me, suffered somewhat as a result of my unusual success.'[7] Though it appears that Saint-Saëns was, in fact, enthusiastically received, Tchaikovsky still had no grounds for complaint; all four movements of the symphony were applauded by the capacity audience, they would have happily listened to the third a second time, and at the end gave him an ovation. Bernard Shaw, who was present as a music critic, noted especially the unusually high level of the playing both composers had drawn from the orchestra.

Eleven days remained before Tchaikovsky was due in Cambridge, and his public appearance and its success had drawn attention to him. The day following the concert the Philharmonic Society entertained the two foreign composers to dinner at the St Stephen's Club, Westminster. It was a sumptuous occasion, the meal beginning at seven and ending at eleven-thirty. Later Mackenzie recalled that he and Tchaikovsky had wandered the streets until after one o'clock discussing musical matters. The next day Sarasate, who had had to listen to Tchaikovsky from the back row under the gallery, invited him to return to the same hall to hear his own performances of Lalo's *Fantaisie norvégienne* and Beethoven's Violin Concerto, as well as the *Pibroch* Suite by Alexander Mackenzie. Following Sarasate's concert he sped to take tea with the wife of the Russian ambassador. The pressure of events was enormous, and the environment did nothing to help. His earlier visits to London had been during the winter, but the social season was now in full swing, and the press of traffic and pedestrians was at its most oppressive. 'Paris is a positive village compared to London,' he lamented to Modest. 'When people are driving in Regent Street or Hyde Park there are so many carriages, such colour and opulence, that one's dazzled.'[8]

[6] Sir A. Mackenzie, *A Musician's narrative* (London, 1927), p. 186.
[7] *TLP*17, p. 102; *TZC*3, p. 619; *TPB*, p. 540; *YDGC*, p. 583.
[8] *TLP*17, p. 102; *TZC*3, p. 619; *TPB*, p. 540.

There was no escaping the city's social whirl. The Stanfords, Henschels, the painter Alma-Tadema, the Cowens, the Bergers: all claimed him as a guest. When Boito arrived in London, Alberto Visetti, a professor of singing at the Royal College of Music (RCM), arranged a reception for his compatriot, and Tchaikovsky was one of a gathering of unusually distinguished guests. A number of resident musicians who met him at the time have left their memories of him, compounding between them a neat summary of many of his most fundamental traits. John Francis Barnett, composer and conductor, echoed the observations of some American writers during Tchaikovsky's tour of two years earlier: 'He was a finely built man, and held himself so well that he looked quite military in appearance.'⁹ But if such stiffness betrayed the effort required to retain an outer control in the face of powerful nervous pressures, others found that in intimate company he could be more at ease. Francesco Berger entertained him, Tchaikovsky having stipulated that 'there should be "no party" and "no evening dress". Accordingly we were only four. . . . His conversation, carried on in French and German (for I do not speak Russian), was easy without being brilliant, and in all he said there was apparent the modest, gentle spirit which was so characteristic of the man.'¹⁰ Mathilde Verne brought a woman's insight to bear; she found his appearance 'utterly opposed to the mental picture I had formed of the creator of such passionate and stirring music. I saw at once he was painfully shy and retiring.'¹¹ George Henschel, who had become acquainted with him in Moscow eighteen years earlier and now met him nearly every day during his stay in London, discovered even more of his moods, noting that, for all his immense fame, he was 'even more inclined to intervals of melancholy than when I had last met him; indeed, one afternoon, during a talk about the olden days in Petrograd and Moscow, and the many friends there who were no more, he suddenly got very depressed and, wondering what this world with all its life and strife was made for, expressed his own readiness at any moment to quit it'.¹² Another special insight came from the child's-eye view of Henschel's daughter, Helen. She sensed those qualities which had always endeared him to the young: 'The melancholy was naturally enough not evident to me as a small child, but the gentleness and kindness were. Nobody could have been more charming than he was. One of my life's minor tragedies is

⁹ J. F. Barnett, *Musical Reminiscences and Impressions* (London, 1906), p. 270.
¹⁰ F. Berger, *Reminiscences, Impressions and Anecdotes* (London, [n.d.]), p. 87.
¹¹ M. Verne, *Chords of remembrance* (London, 1936), pp. 86–7.
¹² Sir G. Henschel, *Musings & memories of a musician* (London, 1918), p. 365.

that he wrote me a long letter when he left London, that the wind blew it off the table into the waste-paper basket, and that the housemaid lit my fire with it.'[13] But it was Mackenzie who encapsulated many of the impressions made by their distinguished visitor: 'His unaffected modesty, kindly manner and real gratitude for any trifling service rendered, all contributed to the favourable impression made by a lovable man.'[14]

Alexandra Svyatlovskaya, who had created the part of Solokha when *Vakula the Smith* had been reincarnated as *Cherevichki*, was in London, and her recital on 7 June included pieces by Tchaikovsky. According to Henry Wood (though there is some conflicting evidence about this) the composer had agreed to accompany Svyatlovskaya but then withdrew, Wood himself (who the previous year had conducted the English première of *Onegin* with her as the nurse) substituting. There was to be a concert in Cambridge at which all the honorary graduands would be represented, and Tchaikovsky, who had chosen to conduct *Francesca da Rimini*, had his first rehearsal on 9 June at the RCM. That evening Stanford gave a soirée, including al fresco performances of English madrigals and partsongs by an amateur choir, the Magpie Minstrels, conducted by Lionel Benson. Now that all the graduands were in London (except Grieg, who was ill and unable to attend the ceremony), Tchaikovsky could summarize for Modest both his impressions of them and of his existence during the preceding fortnight.

It's the devil of a life! There's not one pleasant minute; only eternal anxiety, melancholy, fear, fatigue, aversion, and so on. But now the end's already close. On the other hand, in all fairness I must say there is a lot of nice people, and I've been shown much kindness of all sorts. All the future doctors have arrived except Grieg, who's ill. Among them besides Saint-Saëns I find *Boito* a sympathetic individual. But to make up for it *Bruch*'s a loathsome [Modest softened this to 'unsympathetic'], haughty figure. The morning of the day after tomorrow I travel to *Cambridge*, and I shan't be staying in an hotel but in a flat assigned to me at a Doctor *Maitland*'s [Downey Professor of English law, and a great enthusiast for music] from whom I have had a most kind letter of invitation. In all I shall spend one night there. On the day of my arrival there's a concert and a banquet, and the ceremony on the day following. In four hours it'll all be over.[15]

---

[13] H. Henschel, *When soft voices die* (London, 1944), p. 89.
[14] Sir A. Mackenzie, *op. cit.* p. 186.
[15] *TLP*17, p. 106; *TZC*3, p. 620; *TPB*, p. 541; *YDGC*, p. 583 (partial).

Tchaikovsky left for Cambridge early on 12 June, heading for the Guildhall to conduct his share of the morning's final rehearsal. Besides works by each of the five graduands (Grieg was still represented, since he would receive his degree at a later date), the afternoon concert included Stanford's setting of Swinburne's ode, *East to West*, for the concert also marked the professor of music's retirement after twenty-one years as conductor of CUMS. Tchaikovsky's contribution scored an enormous success with the audience – and also with Saint-Saëns who six years later eulogized it in his *Portraits et souvenirs*: 'Bristling with difficulties, Tchaikovsky's *Francesca da Rimini*, which lacks neither pungent flavours nor fireworks, shrinks from no violence; in it the gentlest and most kindly of men has unleashed a fearful tempest, and has had no more pity for his performers and listeners than Satan for the damned. But such are the composer's talent and supreme skill that one takes pleasure in this damnation and torture.'[16]

The concert over, there was a quick visit to Trinity College. The CUMS dinner was at King's College, and Tchaikovsky found himself seated next to Walter Damrosch, who was on holiday in England and whom Stanford had invited specially for the occasion. Then everyone moved off to a conversazione at the Fitzwilliam Museum, where Stanford was the central figure, and at which a presentation was made to him by CUMS. The degree congregation in the Senate House was at noon the following day. Tchaikovsky himself provided for Nápravník's son, Vladimir, an account of what happened.

At 11.30 we gathered at the appointed place and put on our doctoral robes, which consist of a white gown (silk) faced with crimson velvet, and a black velvet beret. Four doctors *of laws* were admitted to their degrees along with us, one of whom was an Indian ruler (rajah) who wore a turban adorned with precious stones with a value of several million [roubles], and one *a field marshal*. All the professors and doctors of the university in robes like ours but of a different colour collected in the same hall. At noon the procession set out on foot. I walked beside *Boito* and behind *Saint-Saëns*. Watched by a lot of people we crossed a big courtyard to the university's Senate [House], which was filled to overflowing. Each of us sat in an allotted place on a high platform, *the public orator* entered (that's what they call the gentleman whose special job it is to make the speeches at these ceremonies), and he delivered a speech in Latin to each of us in turn, which was a eulogy of our services to science and art. During the

---

[16] C. Saint-Saëns, *Portraits et souvenirs* (Paris, [n.d.]), p. 197.

speech the one in whose honour it was being delivered stood motion-less at the front. While this was going on, according to medieval tradition the students who filled the rows whistled, hooted, sang, cried – and to all this you must pay no attention. After the speech the orator leads the doctor by the hand and describes a semicircle with him towards the chancellor who is sitting in his special place. He takes the doctor by the hand and says in Latin: 'In the name of the Father, Son, and Holy Spirit I declare you to be a doctor.' There's a firm handshake, after which you are led off to your place. When this was over the procession returned to the first hall in the same order, and a half-hour later everyone in his own clothes set off for an official lunch, at the end of which an ancient loving-cup is passed round among the guests. Afterwards there's a reception at the chancellor's wife's, and with this it's all over.[17]

There is little doubt that the doctors of music were far outshone in the public's eyes by three of the other graduands. The 'Indian ruler' was a Maharajah (from whose conferment the Christian invocation was discreetly omitted), the 'field marshal' was Lord Roberts of Kandahar, while the third was Lord Herschell, the Lord Chancellor. Lord Roberts, very much a national hero, was rapturously received by the congregation, and saluted at the end with a rendering of 'For he's a jolly good fellow'. The *Pall Mall Gazette*, commenting on the music gradu-ands' reactions to a performance which was marked by 'more vigour than musical ability', observed that Saint-Saëns twisted his fingers and Tchaikovsky sank 'into ineffable meditations'. Tchaikovsky seems to have been spared the more boisterous sallies of undergraduate humour, though one bright spark raised roars of laughter by shouting 'Good old Shakemoffski!'.

The chancellor's luncheon and his wife's garden party over, Tchaikovsky hastened to return to London, for he was giving a farewell meal at the Dieudonné for various of his London friends. Afterwards he was taken to a new ballet, *Chicago*, at the Alhambra. The following day, 14 June, he was in Paris. Such letters as he had written while in England brim over with anguish at the inner sufferings the unbroken trail of concerts, public occasions and social events caused him, but in perspective there were good things that stood out. Cambridge itself had been very much to his taste, and so had his hosts, the Maitlands. '[Staying with them] would have made me feel terribly uncomfortable if he, and especially his wife, had not turned out to be the most

[17] *TLP*17, pp. 109–10.

charmingly sympathetic people I've ever met – and, moreover, also *russophiles*, which is a great rarity in England. Now it's all over I find it pleasant to recall my success in England and the unusual cordiality with which I was received everywhere. . . . Now I'm beginning to move in the direction of Grankino,' he continued his letter of 15 June to Kolya Konradi, 'but with delays. My route will be: Basel, Zurich, Innsbruck, Itter (at Menter's), Vienna.'[18]

Tchaikovsky spent four days in Paris recovering his equilibrium and his energies, and avoiding the local musical community; his only musical experience was a performance by the diseuse, Yvette Guilbert, at a café-chantant. Arriving at Itter on 19 June, he remained a week resting with Sophie Menter and Sapelnikov, and on 30 was in Grankino, rejoicing in his native land. 'I've already been here five days,' he wrote to Jurgenson on 5 July. 'From the Tyrol, with its mountains, crags, precipices, ravines, and so on, I've landed in a bare, endless steppe – and I find that a steppe is a hundred times more poetic, more spacious, more beautiful. What's more, life in a well organized Russian country estate is far more comfortable than staying in a decayed medieval castle.'[19] With Kolya Konradi and Bob in residence he found a human pleasure which balanced sadness at learning on his way home that Albrecht was no more, and shortly after his arrival that Vladimir Shilovsky had died. And he discovered more of the tensions that remained within the family at Kamenka, for awaiting him were half a dozen letters from Nata Pleskaya, who was still bitterly upset at Lev's 'betrayal' of his late wife. Tchaikovsky replied in terms both sympathetic yet stern. But it was not only Lev and his new wife with whom this old friend was at odds – so why, Tchaikovsky asked, did she not move into the big house, or even find a place of her own? He would do what he could to help financially. Then he heard distasteful rumours that his own arrival at Grankino had been interpreted by some in Kamenka as an opportunity to drive a wedge between Bob and his father. He had planned to stay a week, but remained more than two, combining relaxation with converting the first movement of the E flat Symphony into the Third Piano Concerto, and with once again giving attention to business matters. Proofs of the Op. 72 piano pieces and the Op. 73 romances had to be read, and concert arrangements for next season demanded attention. Auer had at last come round to playing the Violin Concerto which he had spurned for the past fifteen years. So indifferent had Tchaikovsky now become to Auer's attitude that he had

[18] *TLP*17, p. 108; *TTP*, p. 287; *TZC*3, p. 625 (partial).
[19] *TLP*17, pp. 122–3; *TPJ*2, p. 264.

forgotten to pass on to Safonov the virtuoso's hope that he could perform it during the coming season of the Moscow RMS. Now at last Tchaikovsky laid the matter before Safonov, begging him to tell a lie rather than reveal to Auer his forgetfulness. Relations with Safonov seem to have been very satisfactorily restored, and the cherished hopes that the director's connections with higher circles, as well as his administrative flair, might yield material benefits for the Conservatoire had been magnificently realized, for he had drawn from the Tsar a grant that would enable the institution's accommodation to be rebuilt. Tchaikovsky had arranged that both Menter and Sapelnikov should perform in St Petersburg during the following season in RMS and chamber concerts, and he interceded with Safonov to obtain engagements for them with the Moscow RMS. For his own part Tchaikovsky undertook to conduct the Moscow première of the Sixth Symphony in a charity concert for the musicians' benevolent fund.

After Grankino Tchaikovsky had promised to visit Nikolay at Ukolovo, and he arrived there on 17 July, remaining ten days until after Olga's nameday celebrations. Yet it was only at home that he could work properly, and both the Sixth Symphony and the new Piano Concerto needed to be scored by mid-September. Not only that: Tchaikovsky was already looking ahead to a new opera, and had asked Modest to give some thought to a possible subject. Arriving in Moscow on 28 July, he called on Albrecht's widow, and celebrated his return unstintingly with his Moscow friends. On 30 July he was home in Klin. It was two days before he could give attention to the symphony, for a pile of more than thirty letters awaited his attention. One was from Francesco Berger: a request, to which he agreed, that he would conduct the symphony in London the following May for the Philharmonic Society.

With his new home he was certainly well pleased. Alexey had attended to many things while he had been away, a new water closet had been installed, the fences and gates had been put in good order, and the garden was a mass of flowers. But he admitted he longed to be at Verbovka, where Modest and Bob were. 'I've noticed before after long trips and a life in society that during the first part of my return home I'm restless – at least, in recent years,' he continued to Modest. 'Probably it'll quickly pass.'[20] Already he had been asked to go abroad again, this time to Hamburg to attend the revival of *Iolanta*, and so that he could be consulted about the intended production of *The Queen of Spades*. The news from Kamenka was better; Lev seemed very contented in his

[20] *TLP*17, p. 142; *TZC*3, p. 628; *TPB*, p. 546.

new situation, and Katya, his wife, was conducting herself with a tact that was disarming many of her adversaries. Only Nata remained a cause for anxiety.

Tchaikovsky spent August bringing his last major composition to its final form. The tenor of life during these weeks was outwardly quiet. The St Petersburg RMS required details of what he proposed to conduct in his four concerts, and his choice is interesting. Two favourites of his youth – Schumann's *Das Paradies und die Peri* and Litolff's overture, *Die Girondisten*, are among the dozen items, which also included Smetana's *Vyšehrad* and some dances from Mozart's *Idomeneo*. What is notable is Tchaikovsky's concern to advance the cause of young composers; to the dances from Rakhmaninov's *Aleko* and the suite, *From a child's life*, by the eldest of the Konyus brothers, Georgy, he added a suite by Zygmunt Stojowski, a Paris-trained Polish composer whom he may have met recently in France. Once again he was prepared to risk Laroche's unloved *Karmozina* overture. As for established Russian composers, Taneyev (the overture to *Oresteia*) and Glazunov (fantasy: *The Forest*) were of a younger generation; the old guard was represented only by Rimsky-Korsakov (Third Symphony) and Tchaikovsky himself (the première of the Sixth Symphony).

At Klin itself Tchaikovsky found perpetual delight in his surroundings, in Alexey, his wife, and in their son, now some fifteen months old, whom he admitted he spoiled shamelessly. But in other relationships there was anxiety and even misery. Bob, now twenty-two, had grown into a restless and moody young man who did not reciprocate in any matching degree his uncle's devotion. The latter had done his best to smother the distress this caused him, but the intensity of his feelings mounted almost to panic when his nephew failed to reply promptly to letters. There was anxiety, too, at the abrupt and final break between Modest and Kolya Konradi, for the two had shared a flat with Bob, and Kolya, it seems, had been paying the rent. Now Modest and Bob would need financial support if they were to continue living in reasonable comfort. Tchaikovsky's disordered accounting had badly reduced his own funds; this, coupled with re-reading Nadezhda von Meck's letters, brought a surge of personal pain. 'O Nadezhda Filaretovna, why, perfidious woman, did you betray me?' he exclaimed suddenly during a mid-August letter to Jurgenson about his finances. '. . . Reading her letters, you could think fire would turn to water sooner than her allowance would cease, and you could be the more surprised also that I was content with such a paltry sum when she was prepared to give me almost everything. And suddenly – farewell! Most important: I almost believed she was ruined. But it turns out such wasn't the case at all. It was simply a woman's fickleness.'[21] Grief of another kind struck him on the eve of his departure from Klin for Hamburg on 1 September. 'At this moment, as I write this, *they're reading the burial service* over Lel Apukhtin!!!' he wrote to Bob. 'Though his death was not unexpected, it's still terrible and painful. He was once my closest friend.'[22]

It is the more surprising, therefore, to read Modest's insistence on his brother's 'cheerful frame of mind'[23] as he delayed in St Petersburg with Laroche for two days. Nor can anything have upset him in Hamburg, Modest continued, since he wrote no letters home; moreover, this mood persisted on his return ('It was long, long since I had seen him more radiant.'[24]). There is no way in which Modest's record can be tested, for Tchaikovsky's letters at this period are few and brief. In fact, September 1893 is the least documented month of his life as a mature composer. He left St Petersburg for Hamburg on 4 September, arrived on 6, attended the performance on 8 (at least, that was the day the posters announced the composer would be present), and was back in St Petersburg on 12. During the next few days, so Modest remembered, he interested himself in expediting the new living arrangements for Modest and Bob necessitated by the break with Kolya Konradi, and discussed with Modest possible subjects for an opera. As noted earlier, George Eliot had been particularly engaging Tchaikovsky's attention; he had now read *The Mill on the Floss*, *Silas Marner*, *Adam Bede*, *Middlemarch*, and all the *Scenes of clerical life*, and was minded to have a libretto made from the first of these scenes: *The Sad Fortunes of the Rev. Amos Barton*. Modest was against the idea, and for the moment no decision on any other subject was taken. What he did discuss further, so Modest recorded, was revisions of both *The Oprichnik* and *The Maid of Orléans*. This time, despite his oft expressed aversion to the former, Tchaikovsky seems to have been serious about reworking it, for he extracted the full score from the library of the Imperial Theatres. As for *The Maid*, he returned to Zhukovsky's translation of Schiller and seemed to be yielding to Modest's persuasions that he should recompose the last scene to end as had the German playwright.

On 19 September Tchaikovsky arrived in Moscow, stayed two days, and on 22 was in Mikhailovskoye, close to Nizhni-Novgorod, to visit Anatoly. His brother's new surroundings enchanted him, and he found the whole family in good spirits, Anatoly having just been awarded the Order of St Stanislav. He walked in the woods, picked mushrooms, and

[21] *TLP*17, p. 158.
[22] *TLP*17, p. 169; *TPB*, p. 549; *YDGC*, p. 590.
[23] *TZC*3, p. 632.
[24] *ibid.*

only returned to Moscow on 29 September because Modest's new comedy, *Prejudices*, was to have its première at the Maly Theatre. The play was excellently performed and well received – so the composer told Anatoly – though he added, with customary frankness, that it was overlong and spoiled by Modest's eternal failing: a poor last act. The following evening he visited Taneyev to hear some new pieces by Rakhmaninov: the *Fantaisie-tableaux* for two pianos, Op. 5, and the symphonic poem, *The Rock*, Op. 7.

One reason alone seems to have kept Tchaikovsky nearly ten days in Moscow; Alexey's wife was about to give birth for a second time, and he would not return to Klin until this was over. While awaiting news from Klin, he received from the Grand Duke Konstantin Konstantinovich a suggestion that he should set to music Apukhtin's 'Requiem' as a memorial to the poet. Tchaikovsky was doubtful. He could not recall the poem clearly, but he had just composed a symphony into which he had put 'without exaggeration' his own 'entire soul',[25] and he feared the mood demanded by the Apukhtin setting would require him to repeat himself. Back in Klin on 7 October he re-read the poem and excused himself from fulfilling the Grand Duke's request, pleading that Apukhtin's verses neither required nor were suitable for musical setting. But there was an additional reason.

> In 'Requiem' there is much talk of *God the judge, God the chastiser, God the avenger!!!* Forgive me, your Highness, but I take the liberty of confessing I do not believe in such a God – or, at least, such *a God* cannot draw from me those tears, that rapture, that veneration before the creator and source of every blessing which would inspire me. If it were possible, with the greatest joy I would try to set to music some texts of the Gospels. For instance, how often have I dreamed of illustrating through music Christ's words: '*Come unto me all ye that labour and are heavy laden*', and then '*for my yoke is easy and my burden is light*'. In these wonderful words how much is there of infinite love and compassion for man! What boundless poetry there is in this (one might say) *passionate* aspiration to dry the tears of sorrow and lighten the torment of suffering humanity![26]

He could not know how soon he himself would need the comfort words such as these might offer.

Tchaikovsky's spirits had become a little clouded by the hectic bustle of Moscow life, but, Modest insisted, they were completely restored as

[25] *TLP*17, p. 186; *TZC*3, p. 635.
[26] *TLP*17, p. 194; *TZC*3, pp. 637-8.

soon as he returned to Klin. This is difficult to credit. Alexey's wife had nearly died after giving birth, and for some days she lay in a critical condition. Tchaikovsky's first task in Klin was to score the Third Piano Concerto and he began this on 9 October, but progress was hampered by the need to remain quiet for the sake of the sick woman. Then before completing the concerto on 15 he heard of the death of Nikolay Zverev, an old colleague from Moscow Conservatoire days, and the dedicatee of *Passé lointain*, one of his most recent piano pieces. Modest would have us believe that his brother was no more affected by this death than by any of the recent others. In fact, it seems to have struck him very hard, and the failure of any of his Moscow acquaintances to inform him of the funeral arrangements caused him deep distress, to judge from his letters. Brandukov visited him to run through Saint-Saëns's A minor Cello Concerto, which he was to play in St Petersburg under Tchaikovsky's direction, and then journeyed with him to Moscow on 19, where Tchaikovsky attended a funeral banquet for his old friend, and visited his grave. This Moscow trip provided an opportunity to show the Third Piano Concerto to Taneyev, to hear his Mozart-based Quartet, *Night*, performed by some of Lavrovskaya's pupils at the Conservatoire, and, it seems, to benefit from the trial rehearsal of his new symphony. On the evening of 21 October he set out on his last journey to St Petersburg. Before leaving he dined with a group including Safonov and Pollini, the director of the Hamburg Opera, who had come to Russia with a proposal to muster a German orchestra which the following year would give two concerts in Moscow and then tour central and southern Russia, venturing as far as the shores of the Black Sea, the Caucasus and the towns on the Volga. The conductors would be Russian: Tchaikovsky to direct his own works, and Safonov for the rest of each programme. Such a tour of the Russian provinces would be unprecedented, and all present agreed it was an excellent project. The meal over, Tchaikovsky talked with Kashkin alone for a while. Whatever Tchaikovsky's mood may have been in the preceding days, he had never felt better or happier than at this moment, so Kashkin remembered him saying. Yet as the train passed Frolovskoye, Modest recorded, his brother pointed to the church and observed to his companions: 'That's where I shall be buried – and those who pass by will point to my grave.'[27]

Now once again there is a brief dearth of extant letters. Tchaikovsky conducted the first performance of the Sixth Symphony on 28 October, and much of his time, and certainly much of his energy, during the

[27] *TZC3*, p. 638.

preceding six days must have been absorbed in preparing for this. The programme also included the First Piano Concerto; the soloist was Adele aus der Ohe, who had performed the work with him in the United States two years before. As recorded earlier, Modest remembered his brother was ill-at-ease during rehearsals because the orchestra was evidently bewildered by the new piece, and the première was far from the triumph enjoyed by some of his earlier works at their first performances. On the programme the new work had been described simply as 'Sixth Symphony: B minor', and it was Modest who claimed responsibility for its special title. The score was due to be sent to Jurgenson the next day for engraving, and the composer was still wondering what to call it. He had no liking for either 'Programme' or 'Tragic'. 'I left the room with Pyotr Ilich still undecided,' Modest recalled. 'Then suddenly the title "Pathétique" came into my head. I returned, and I remember as though it were yesterday pronouncing this word while standing in the doorway. "Capital, Modest, bravo, *Pathétique!*" – and in my presence he inscribed on the score the name that has remained ever since.'[28] There was therefore no foundation, Modest insisted, for Hugo Riemann's suggestion that the title originated from the similarity between the work's initial phrase and that which opens Beethoven's piano sonata of the same name.

In all Tchaikovsky's biography the circumstances surrounding his death have proved the most contentious issue. The matter has been examined in great detail by the Soviet scholar, Alexandra Orlova, who came to the West in 1979, and the following discussion relies heavily upon material she has provided.[29] In his biography Modest recounted the events of the days following the Sixth Symphony's première, and until recent years his has been accepted as the authoritative record. Modest admitted that his brother's moods fluctuated a little, but insisted that these were cheerful rather than clouded, and denied they were such as to give any pointer towards what was so soon to happen.

On Tuesday, 31 [October], he [Tchaikovsky] attended A. Rubinstein's *Die Makkabäer* at the request of an operatic company who were giving a performance at the former Kononov theatre. On Wednesday, 1 [November], he was completely well. Walking with one of our nephews, Count A. N. Litke, he told him a great deal about

28 *TZC3*, pp. 644–5; *DTC*, p. 437.
29 See Alexandra Orlova, 'Tchaikovsky: the last chapter' in *Music & Letters*, Vol. 62 (1981), pp. 125–45, and *Tchaikovsky: a self-portrait* (Oxford, 1990), pp. 406–14.

Bochechkarov, about his oddities, expressions, jokes, and said that he missed him almost as much as just after his death in 1876 [in fact, 1879]. On that day he dined with our old friend, Vera Vasilyevna Butakova, *née* Davïdova. That evening he had a box at the Alexandrinsky Theatre, where Ostrovsky's *The Passionate Heart* was being given. During the interval he and I went to the dressing room of K[onstantin] A[lexandrovich] Varlamov [the leading actor]. He [Tchaikovsky] always greatly admired the latter's wonderful gift, and having become acquainted with him in the 90s, had come to like him personally. The talk was about spiritualism. Konstantin Alexandrovich, with his characteristic humour which cannot be caught on paper, expressed his total aversion for all 'this dirty rubbish', as for everything in general that reminded him of death. Nothing could have pleased Pyotr Ilich more; he agreed delightedly and laughed heartily at the original way in which this had been said. 'There'll be time enough for us to meet this repulsive snub-nosed monster,' he said – and then, turning to Varlamov as he went out: 'However, that's a long time off for both of us. I know I shall live a long time.'

From the theatre Pyotr Ilich went with our nephews, the Counts Litke, and Baron Buxhövden to Leiner's restaurant. I could not arrive until later and when, about an hour afterwards, I appeared I found all the aforementioned persons in the company of I. F. Gorbunov, A. K. Glazunov and F. F. Mühlbach. All of them had already finished eating, and I heard that Pyotr Ilich had eaten macaroni and washed it down, as was usual with him, with white wine and mineral water. The supper was quickly over and at two o'clock the two of us returned home on foot. Pyotr Ilich was completely calm and well.

On the morning of Thursday, 2 [November], when I came out of my bedroom Pyotr Ilich was not in the drawing-room drinking tea as usual, but in his own room, and he complained to me that he had had a bad night because of an upset stomach. This did not especially disturb me, because he often had such upsets which were always very violent and passed very quickly. Towards eleven o'clock he dressed and went off to Nápravník, but returned in half an hour without reaching him, and decided to resort to other remedies besides the flannel, which he had earlier put on [to keep himself warm]. I proposed we should send for Vasily Bernardovich Bertenson, his favourite doctor, but he firmly refused this. I did not insist, knowing that he was accustomed to similar indispositions, and always threw them off without help of any sort. Usually on these occasions he found castor oil was helpful. Convinced that on this occasion also he would resort to this, and knowing that in any case it could do no harm, I got on with my own business, quite unconcerned about his condition, and did not see him until one o'clock. After lunch he was to have a business meeting with F. F. Mühlbach. In any case from eleven to one Pyotr Ilich was well enough to be able to write two letters, but he did not have the patience to write a third in detail, and confined himself to a short note. At lunch he was not averse to food; he sat with us without eating only because, I think, he recognized it would be harmful. It was then he told us he had taken Guniadi water instead of castor oil.

I think this lunch proved fatal, for it was just while we were talking about the medicine he had taken that he poured out a glass of water and drank from it. The water was unboiled. We were all alarmed; he alone treated it with indifference and reassured us. Of all illnesses cholera was the one he feared least of all. Immediately after this he had to go out because he began to feel nausea. He did not return to the drawing-room but lay down in his own room to warm his stomach. All the same, neither he himself nor we, his companions, were at all alarmed. All this had happened often before. Although his disorder got worse we still put it down to the action of the bitter [Guniadi?] water. I again proposed sending for V. B. Bertenson, but again was told sharply not to; in addition, a little while afterwards he became better, asked that he might be allowed to sleep, remained alone in his room and, so I assumed, went to sleep. Convinced that all was quiet in his bedroom, I went about my own affairs, and was not home until five o'clock. When I returned his illness was so much worse that, despite his protest, I sent for V. B. Bertenson. All the same there were no alarming signs of a mortal illness.[30]

Over the next few hours Tchaikovsky's condition got rapidly worse. Whether Bertenson paid an immediate visit is not clear, but he was certainly there at a quarter past eight. Tchaikovsky was now vomiting frequently and had bad bouts of diarrhoea, but since no specimens had been preserved, 'the doctor could not at first confirm cholera'.[31] But Bertenson was convinced the illness was very serious and sent for his brother. In the meantime the symptoms became so violent that Tchaikovsky finally thought he was dying. At eleven the other Bertenson brother arrived 'and, after an examination of the sick man and his specimens, diagnosed cholera'.[32]

[30] *TZC3*, pp. 647–9.
[31] *TZC3*, p. 649.
[32] *ibid.*

This was implausible. The incubation period for cholera is normally twelve to twenty-eight hours, while Tchaikovsky's symptoms had begun within some four hours. Modest's statement that his brother feared cholera least of all illnesses is patent nonsense, and it is totally unbelievable that Modest would have had on his lunch table a supply of water that he must have known was potentially lethal. In any case it seems strange that, writing about his brother's death some years after the event, he should have felt the need to describe the course of his illness in such distasteful and minute detail (there are a further five harrowing pages to Modest's narrative). In fact he was largely quoting the highly specific account he had published in *Novoye vremya* on 13 November 1893, a week after his brother died, 'in order to dispel all the conflicting rumours'.[33] Modest's description had been intended to substantiate a similar though shorter description by Lev Bertenson printed in the same paper only two days after Tchaikovsky's end, in which the doctor had stated bluntly that when he had arrived he had found the composer 'in the so-called algide phase of the illness. The symptoms were thoroughly characteristic, and I could not but recognize immediately a very serious case of cholera.'[34] But these two accounts had only made matters worse, for they had disagreed in numerous details, Bertenson even losing a whole day of the composer's illness in the process. Nor does Modest's record accord with the bulletins fixed to the door of his apartment while the illness was running its course.[35] The fact is, as Modest confessed, that there had been rumours that needed silencing – and the two people who were in a position to do this most effectively had now made an extraordinary mess of it.

Yet even before these accounts had appeared, what had happened in Modest's flat after the composer's death on 6 November had been totally inconsistent with cholera. The authorities well knew how contagious the disease was and the regulations urged that the corpse of a victim should be removed immediately in a closed coffin. Yet Tchaikovsky's body was displayed in Modest's flat, which was freely opened to visitors wishing to pay their last respects. A series of requiems took place. Among the visitors was Rimsky-Korsakov who was bewildered by what he saw, and was to say so in his memoirs, *Manuscript of my musical life*: 'How odd that though his death was the result of cholera, there was free access to the requiems. I remember that

[33] Orlova, 'Tchaikovsky: the last chapter', p. 140.

[34] Orlova, *op. cit.*, p. 138.

[35] Lev Bertenson's and Modest Tchaikovsky's newspaper accounts, as well as the bulletins, are printed in full in Orlova, *op. cit.*, pp. 138–45.

Verzhbilovich, who was completely drunk after some drinking bout, kissed the body on the face and head.'[36]

From all this one thing is crystal clear; matters were not what they were meant to seem.[37] Yet it seems a conspiracy of silence was tacitly agreed by all, for they must have decided that, whatever the truth, it was better it were hid. There is one inescapable conclusion, which seems now to be universally accepted in the Soviet Union though it still is not spoken openly: that Tchaikovsky committed suicide. He had made one attempt in 1877, and his chief concern then had been to make his death appear to be from natural causes so that no disgrace would be brought to his family. By 1893 he was second only to Tolstoy in the fame and respect he enjoyed in his native Russia, and it seems that no one now wished to risk the public disclosure of something that might stain his memory and bring distress to his family. So all ignored the questions that shouted to be answered and have refused to be silenced. Even nearer our own time, some have evidently felt it necessary to emphasize the incident of the glass of water, transferring it from Modest's drawing-room to the public setting of Leiner's restaurant and so undermining yet further the credibility of this incident. This new version first appeared in the recollections, published in 1948, of the actor, Yury Yuryev, and was repeated in the memoirs of Tchaikovsky's youngest nephew, Yury Davïdov, written in 1943, but not printed until 1973, eight years after his death. According to the latter, who wrote as though he was present in the restaurant, his uncle asked for a glass of boiled water and, on being told they had only unboiled (there was presumably no reason why a high-class restaurant should expect such a request when mineral water was available, and the cholera season not completely over), demanded a glass of this and when it was brought promptly drank it off, actively frustrating with his elbow a desperate attempt to prevent him made by Modest, who had only just entered. If this incident really did take place, there seems only one possible explanation: that it was a publicly staged set-piece to give a visible explanation for some forthcoming eventuality.

But one story has come to light that may provide the answer to the

---

[36] N. Rimsky-Korsakov, Letopis moyei muzïkalnoy zhizni, 9th edit. (Moscow, 1982), p. 246.

[37] Further doubt is cast upon Modest's narration by Galina von Meck, daughter of Nikolay von Meck and Anna Davïdova, who knew well Alexandr Litke, one of those present at Tchaikovsky's end. She has stated that 'the interpretation of some of the things said by the dying man in his agony, according to what I know from the composer's nephew, young Count Alexander Litke . . . was completely different from the way his brother Modest related them'. (P. I. Tchaikovsky, Letters to his family: an autobiography. Trans. by Galina von Meck (London, 1981), p. 555.)

mystery. It was told to Alexandra Orlova in 1966 by Alexandr Voitov, former curator of coins at the Russian Museum in Leningrad, who had been a pupil at Tchaikovsky's old school, the School of Jurisprudence, during its last days before the First World War. Voitov had developed a passion for collecting data about the school while still a pupil there, and had amassed a huge fund of biographical details about its alumni. Mrs Orlova wrote down the story from Voitov's account:

Among the pupils who completed their studies at the School of Jurisprudence at the same time as Tchaikovsky there occurs the name of Jacobi. When I was at the school I spent all my holidays in Tsarskoye Selo with the family of Nikolay Borisovich Jacobi, who had been senior procurator to the Senate in the 1890s and who died in 1902. Jacobi's widow, Elizaveta Karlovna, was connected with my parents by ties of affinity and friendship. She was very fond of me and welcomed me warmly. In 1913, when I was in the last but one class in the school, the twentieth anniversary of Tchaikovsky's death was widely commemorated. It was then, apparently under the influence of surging recollections, that Mrs Jacobi, in great secret, told me the story which, she confessed, had long tormented her. She said that she had decided to reveal it to me because she was now old and felt she had not the right to take to her grave such an important and terrible secret. 'You,' she said, 'are interested in the history of the school and in the fate of its pupils, and therefore you ought to know the whole truth, the more so since it is such a sad page in the school's history.' And this is what she told me.

The incident took place in the autumn of 1893. Tchaikovsky was threatened with a terrible misfortune. Duke Stenbok-Fermor, disturbed by the attention which the composer was paying to his young nephew, wrote a letter of accusation to the Tsar and handed the letter to Jacobi to pass on to Alexandr III. Through exposure Tchaikovsky was threatened with the loss of all his rights, with exile to Siberia, with inevitable disgrace. Exposure would also bring disgrace upon the School of Jurisprudence and upon all old boys of the school, Tchaikovsky's fellow students. Yet the honour of the school uniform was sacred. To avoid publicity Jacobi decided upon the following: he invited all Tchaikovsky's former school-friends [he could trace in St Petersburg] and set up a court of honour which included himself. Altogether there were eight people present. Elizaveta Karlovna sat with her needlework in her usual place alongside her husband's study. From time to time from within she could hear voices, sometimes loud and agitated, sometimes dropping apparently to a whisper. This went on for a very long time, almost five hours. Then Tchaikovsky came headlong out of the study. He was almost running, he was unsteady, and he went out without saying a word. He was very white and agitated. All the others stayed a long time in the study talking quietly. When they had gone Jacobi told his wife, having made her swear absolute silence, what they had decided about the Stenbok-Fermor letter to the Tsar. Jacobi could not withhold it. And so the old boys [of the school] had come to a decision by which Tchaikovsky had promised to abide. They required him to kill himself . . . A day or two later news of the composer's mortal illness was circulating in St Petersburg.[38]

Alexandra Orlova has suggested that the court of honour could have been convened on 31 October, since it is the one day during which nothing is known about Tchaikovsky's movements until the evening. Perhaps it is significant that Modest only chronicles his brother's last days in detail from that evening, when he attended Rubinstein's opera. Tchaikovsky continued to write letters discussing future plans until the day he fell ill, but in retrospect this would merely reinforce the required impression that he anticipated any illness would be no more than a passing indisposition. If he did commit suicide, then the means, presumably, was a poison that would produce symptoms as close as possible to those of cholera. Tchaikovsky long refused to allow a doctor to be summoned, and this could have been to ensure that the poison had been absorbed beyond a point at which he could be saved.

This story has caused much interest in the West. Its mode of transmission is such that it must be treated with a good deal of reserve, and the accuracy of its detail must be judged with even more caution. But its validity is strengthened by the appearance some years later of the same story through a second source quite independent of the first.[39]

[38] Orlova, *op. cit.*, pp. 133–4.

[39] The new informant was Mrs Nataliya Kuznetsova-Vladimova, who now lives in Germany. She wrote to Alexandra Orlova in 1987 on reading an article the latter had written for the journal, *Kontinent*. The relevant parts of her very informal letter read: 'From my childhood I knew for certain of Pyotr Ilich Tchaikovsky's suicide through my paternal grandmother, Vera Sergeyevna Kuznetsova (*née* Denisyeva). Her elder sister, Olga Sergeyevna, was married to Tchaikovsky's brother, Nikolay Ilich. Vera Sergeyevna told the same version that you do. She lived in Leningrad . . . dying at the beginning of 1955 at a great age, but sound in mind and good in memory. [She had heard it] probably from Olga Sergeyevna, but in fact spoke of it most reluctantly, seeing in this court a kind of besmirching of a gentleman's honour for Tchaikovsky. But more than once she referred to Jacobi very aggressively . . . While writing to you I could hear how she pronounced that name . . . Vera Sergeyevna said that Alexandr III knew of the letter *after* Tchaikovsky's death. I well remember that at our home in 1952 my

It is doubtful we shall ever know the truth for certain. And in the light of patent inconsistencies between Bertenson's and Modest's published accounts, as well as the contradictions between what was seen to have happened and what was put forward as the truth, Modest's whole account of his brother's last days and hours must be held in serious question. But the presence towards the very end of so many others would have been a discouragement to misrepresentation of this stage, and by now the need to fabricate or distort had passed:

The doctors continued tirelessly to apply all possible means to maintain the action of the heart as though they still expected a miracle of recovery. During this time the following persons were at the dying man's bedside: the three doctors, the two Litke brothers, Buxhövden, N. N. Figner, Beyl [a young cellist], V.[Bob] Davïdov, my brother's valet Sofronov, Litrov, his wife, the medical attendant, brother Nikolay and I. Lev Bernardovich decided there were too many people for the small room. They opened the window. Figner and Beyl left. Bertenson, deciding all hope was lost, left in extreme exhaustion, entrusting supervision of the final moments to [Dr] N. N. Mamonov. His breathing became less frequent, though questions about something to drink could bring a degree of consciousness. Now he was no longer replying in words, but in positive or negative sounds. Suddenly his eyes, which up to now had been half-closed and glazed, opened. A certain indescribable expression of clear consciousness appeared. In turn he fixed his gaze upon the three persons standing close, then looked up to the sky. For a few moments something lit up his eyes and faded with his final breath. It was a little after three o'clock.[40]

grandmother talked with Yury Iosifovich Slonimsky, the author of books on ballet, and when he said that the cause of Tchaikovsky's suicide was that he had paid improper attention to the heir [to the throne], she had corrected him. "No, it was to the nephew of Count Stenbok and not to the heir . . ."' In a contribution to 'Comment & Chronicle' in *19th Century Music* (Vol. XIII, No. 3 (spring 1990), pp. 273–4) Mary Woodside reports on information included in the unpublished memoirs of Aloys Mooser, the Swiss musicologist and critic, who worked in St Petersburg from 1896 to 1909. According to Dr Woodside, Mooser heard from Riccardo Drigo that Tchaikovsky had committed suicide to avoid a homosexual relationship becoming public knowledge (the affair having been brought to the attention of the Tsar who had declared that the man concerned 'must disappear immediately'). Finding the story difficult to believe, Mooser had turned to Glazunov, who had confirmed Drigo's account.

At the time of writing this, the present author has heard from a seemingly reliable source that it will soon be officially admitted in print in the Soviet Union that the circumstances surrounding Tchaikovsky's death are unclear.

[40] *TZC3*, p. 654.

The news, it seems, began to spread through St Petersburg ahead of the formal announcement in the press. Lidiya Konisskaya has reconstructed a full account of what ensued.[41] The staircase to Modest's apartment on the fifth floor was soon filled by two lines, one ascending, the other descending, as an unbroken stream of people filed in to pay their respects. Requiems were conducted around the body, those unable to get into the room listening from the landing or staircase. At eleven o'clock the School of Jurisprudence paid its tribute, at noon the chorus of the Imperial Opera sang. Nápravník was in charge, and Rimsky-Korsakov and Glazunov were present. An hour later there was another requiem, at six o'clock a fourth. A death mask was taken. That evening the composer's portrait was placed in the foyer of the Maryinsky Theatre wreathed in black and garlanded in flowers.

The procession of personal tribute continued the next day. By now more than three hundred wreaths had arrived. They came not only from within Russia itself, but from abroad: from France and Italy, from the Hamburg and Czech Operas, and from private individuals like Guitry and Colonne. The directorate of the Imperial Theatres was entrusted with the funeral arrangements, for which the state paid. Vladimir Pogozhev, director of the Theatres' administration, was given the main responsibility. As far as he could remember, the Tsar allocated 5,000 roubles. Pogozhev's task was daunting not only for the demands that the externals of the event should be lavish, but because of the pressing requests of both private individuals and public institutions for places at the funeral service. From both St Petersburg and Moscow the opera companies, the branches of the RMS and the Conservatoires wished to be represented, as did the School of Jurisprudence, other educational institutions and various cities of Russia. The cortège was finally divided into sections, and staff from the Theatres acted as marshals. The funeral service would be in the Kazan Cathedral, the first time such an honour had been granted a commoner. The building could hold 6,000, and admission would be by ticket. More than 60,000 applied, and finally 8,000 were crammed in.

The coffin was borne from Modest's apartment by members of the family and two singers representing the generations who had worked with Tchaikovsky: Ivan Melnikov, who had created Vyazminsky in *The Oprichnik* nearly thirty years earlier, and Nikolay Figner, so important in his two most recent operas. As the procession passed the Maryinsky, which had been draped in mourning, it stopped in the crowded square. More wreaths were added and speeches made.

---

[41] L. M. Konisskaya, *Chaykovsky v Peterburge* (Leningrad, 1969).

The service in the Cathedral was attended by members of the royal family, and music by Tchaikovsky himself was sung by the chorus of the Imperial Opera. A detail remained in Yury Davïdov's memory fifty years after the event. Beside the coffin one wreath, woven from forget-me-nots and blue ribbons, stood out for its size. It proved to be Antonina Ivanovna's final caprice.

The route to the Alexandr Nevsky Cemetery was lined on either side by a wall of totally silent spectators. It is said that Alexandr III watched the procession. 'We have many dukes and barons, but only one Tchaikovsky,' he is reported to have said. As the cortège passed many joined it from behind. All traffic had been diverted from the funeral route, but it was still four o'clock, four hours after the service had begun in the Cathedral, before the procession reached its destination. There, with a crowd filling the cemetery and overflowing into its surroundings, Tchaikovsky was buried near Glinka, Borodin and Musorgsky.

It had been an extraordinary occasion,[42] for what had brought so many into the church and on to the streets was not that dutiful, remote reverence that may be felt for a tsar or a great national or military leader, but grief at the passing of a commoner – an ordinary Russian who had lived as they did, knew their existence, but had possessed a gift that had afforded an enrichment of life for all those who could and would listen. The formal tributes followed. Obituaries continued to appear, and memorial concerts proliferated. The second performance of the Sixth Symphony in St Petersburg under Nápravník provided a particularly moving occasion. In due course more solid memorials were set up. In 1897 a monument was erected over his grave incorporating a

---

[42] One of those present in the Kazan Cathedral was Nikolay Sklifosovsky, father of the youth to whom Tchaikovsky had been strongly attracted during a Mediterranean crossing in 1889, and who had been posthumously remembered in the dedication of the piano piece, *Chant élégiaque*, Op. 72, No. 14. Sklifosovsky had recently received a surgical appointment in St Petersburg University. His observations in a letter written to his daughter immediately after the event offer a private and trustworthy confirmation of the reaction to Tchaikovsky's death. I have to thank Sklifosovsky's great-granddaughter, Kupava Birkett, for making this letter available to me. 'Indeed everyone was staggered by the news of Tchaikovsky's death. Many were unwilling to believe it, and demanded it be confirmed by newspaper reports . . . The day of the funeral was an extraordinary ceremonial occasion, and I do not remember ever having witnessed anything like it. You know, nearly all the population of St Petersburg gathered into the Kazan Cathedral and along the Nevsky Prospect. The church was full, even though admission was by ticket. I was in the Kazan Cathedral with Mama. The splendid singing was so moving that it was difficult to hold back the tears . . . They [the people] loved the dead man dearly, though this had not been outwardly apparent.'

bust, and a seated statue was placed in the St Petersburg Conservatoire the following year.

But for those who had known Tchaikovsky such things were really of small importance. Often he had been difficult, of course, and seemingly distant, but this had stemmed not from arrogance or aloofness, and those who had come at all close to him seem to have sensed this, while those who were intimate with him, if only for a short time, grasped this in full measure. Above all they knew, or had sensed, that humanity which had been exercised for so many through individual and usually private acts of kindness. The man and his music were inseparable, and Laroche, who had known Tchaikovsky as long and as well as any, recognized this in his obituary notice. But in the end it was not grasping what gave the man or his creations their greatness that really mattered about this dear, dead friend. The concluding words of Laroche's final sentence are those which surely would have given Tchaikovsky the deepest satisfaction and comfort:

> You can analyse the technical merits of a score, you can indicate and enumerate the moral qualities and talents of the person in question, but it is not technical qualities – at least, not they alone – that embody what is fascinating in his music, nor do his talents or virtues impart to his personality its magnetic power. As in artistic creation, so in human personality: when all analytical and critical efforts have been made, there remains something undiscovered, something secret, and it is this very secret that is the most important element, the true essence of the subject. While making no claim to have explained the phenomenon, we still have to recall that phenomenon; we cannot forget that, without any effort or intention on his own part, Pyotr Ilich through his presence alone brought into everything light and warmth. And if Europe mourns in him a major artistic force, one of the greatest in the second half of the nineteenth century, then it is only those persons who had the happiness of knowing him closely who know what *a man* has been lost through his death.[43]

---

[43] Reprinted in H. A. Laroche, *Izbrannïye stati*, Vol. 2: *P. I. Chaykovsky* (Leningrad, 1975), p. 189.

BIBLIOGRAPHY

This is a working bibliography and is not comprehensive. The only Russian-language sources listed are the principal ones used in writing this study. The selection of English-language titles is broader, though articles have been included only when they contain material or comment of some substance. For a comprehensive bibliography the reader should consult that which I compiled for my entry on Tchaikovsky in *The New Grove Dictionary of Music and Musicians*, vol. 18 (London, 1980); a supplemented reprint is included in Brown (D.) and others, *Russian Masters 1* (London, 1986).

RUSSIAN-LANGUAGE TITLES

1. *Catalogues, studies of the sources and chronology of composition:*

Davïdova (K. Y.) and others [eds.], *Muzïkalnoye naslediye Chaykovskovo: iz istory yevo proizvedeny* [Tchaikovsky's musical legacy: history of his works] (Moscow, 1958)

Dombayev (G.), *Tvorchestvo P. I. Chaykovskovo v materialakh i dokumentakh* [Tchaikovsky's works in materials and documents] (Moscow, 1958)

Jurgenson (B.) [ed.], *Catalogue thématique des oeuvres de P. Tschaikowsky* (Moscow, 1897; repr. London, 1965)

Korotkova-Leviton (Z. V.) and others [eds.], *Avtografï P. I. Chaykovskovo v arkhive Doma-Muzeya v Klinu* [Tchaikovsky's autographs in the Klin Museum archive (Moscow/Leningrad, 1950)

2. *Documentary sources (letters, diaries, documentary biography, etc.):*

Alexeyev (N. A.) and others [eds.], *Chaykovsky i zarubezhnïye muzïkantï: izbrannïye pisma inostrannïkh korrespondentov* [Tchaikovsky and foreign musicians: selected letters from foreign correspondents] (Leningrad, 1970)

Tchaikovsky (P.), *Polnoye sobraniye sochineny: literaturnïye proizvedeniya i perepiska* [Complete edition: literary works and correspondence], 17 vols. (Moscow, 1953–81)

Tchaikovsky (P.), *Dnevniki* [Diaries], ed. I. I. Tchaikovsky (Moscow/Petrograd, 1923) [see also ENGLISH-LANGUAGE TITLES]

Tchaikovsky (P.), *Pisma k blizkim: izbrannoye* [Letters to his family; selected], ed. V. A. Zhdanov (Moscow, 1955)

Tchaikovsky (P.), *Pisma k rodnïm* [Letters to his relatives], ed. V. A. Zhdanov (Moscow, 1940)

Orlova (A. A.) [ed.], *M. A. Balakirev: perepiska s P. I. Chaykovskim* [Balakirev: correspondence with Tchaikovsky]. Printed in Frid (E.) and others [eds.], *M. I. Balakirev: vospominaniya i pisma* [Balakirev: recollections and letters] (Leningrad, 1962)

Yakovlev (V.) and others [eds.], *Dni i godï P. I. Chaykovskovo* [Days and years of Tchaikovsky] (Moscow/Leningrad, 1940)

Yakovlev (V.) [ed.], *P. I. Chaykovsky: muzïkalno-kriticheskiye stati* [Tchaikovsky: musical-critical articles] (Moscow, 1953)
Zhdanov (V. A.) [ed.], *P. I. Chaykovsky: S. I. Taneyev. Pisma* [Tchaikovsky: Taneyev. Letters] (Moscow, 1951)
Zhdanov (V. A.) and Zhegin (N. T.) [eds.], *P. I. Chaykovsky: perepiska s N. F. von Meck* [Tchaikovsky: correspondence with Nadezhda von Meck], 3 vols. (Moscow/Leningrad, 1934–36)
Zhdanov (V. A.) and Zhegin (N. T.) [eds.], *P. I. Chaykovsky: perepiska s P. I. Jurgensonom* [Tchaikovsky: correspondence with Jurgenson], 2 vols. (Moscow/Leningrad, 1938–52)

3. *Biographies and studies:*

Glebov (I.) [ed.], *Proshloye russkoy muzïki: materiali i issledovaniya. 1. P. I. Chaikovsky* [The past of Russian music: materials and researches. 1. Tchaikovsky] (Petrograd, 1920)
Kashkin (N.), *Vospominaniya o P. I. Chaykovskom* [Recollections of Tchaikovsky] (Moscow, 1896)
Konisskaya (L. M.), *Chaykovsky v Peterburge* [Tchaikovsky in St Petersburg] (Leningrad, 1969)
Orlova (A. A.), *P. I. Chaykovsky: o muzïke, o zhizni, o sebe* [Tchaikovsky: on music, on life, on himself] (Leningrad, 1976) [see also ENGLISH-LANGUAGE TITLES]
Protopopov (V. V.) and others [eds.], *Vospominaniya o P. I. Chaykovskom* [Reminiscences of Tchaikovsky] (Moscow, 1962) [subsequent editions amplify the contents]
Rabinovich (B. I.), *P. I. Chaykovsky i narodnaya pesnya* [Tchaikovsky and folksong] (Moscow, 1963)
Tchaikovsky (M.), *Zhizn P. I. Chaykovskovo* [Tchaikovsky's life], 3 vols. (Moscow, 1900–02) [see also ENGLISH-LANGUAGE TITLES under Newmarch (R.)]
Yarustovsky (B.), *Opernaya dramaturgiya Chaykovskovo* [Tchaikovsky's operatic dramaturgy] (Moscow/Leningrad, 1947)

ENGLISH-LANGUAGE TITLES

Abraham (G.) [ed.], *Tchaikovsky: a symposium* (London, 1945)
Abraham (G.), 'Tchaikovsky' in *Masters of Russian music* [with M. D. Calvocoressi] (London, 1936) [rev. and reprinted in 1944 as *Tchaikovsky: a short biography*]
Abraham (G.), '*Eugene Onegin* and Tchaikovsky's marriage' in *On Russian music* (London, 1939)
Abraham (G.), 'The programme of the *Pathétique* Symphony' in *On Russian music* (London, 1939)
Abraham (G.), 'Russia' in Stevens (D.) [ed.], *A History of song* (London, 1960) [reprinted in *Essays on Russian and East European music* (Oxford, 1985)]
Abraham (G.), 'Tchaikovsky revalued' in *Studies in Russian music* (London, 1935)
Abraham (G.), 'Tchaikovsky's first opera' in Hüschen (H.) [ed.], *Festschrift Karl Gustav Fellerer* (Regensburg, 1962)
Abraham (G.), 'Tchaikovsky: operas and incidental music' in *Tchaikovsky: a symposium* [see above; rev. reprint in *Slavonic and romantic music* (London, 1968)]
Abraham, (G.), 'Tchaikovsky: some centennial reflections' in *Music & Letters*, vol. 21 (1940), p. 110 [reprinted in *Slavonic and romantic music* (London, 1968)]
Brown (D.), *Tchaikovsky: a biographical and critical study*, vol. 1 (1840–74), vol. 2 (1874–78), vol. 3 (1878–85) (London, 1978–86) [the predecessors to the present volume]

Brown (D.), 'Tchaikovsky' in *Russian Masters 1* (London, 1986) [Revised reprint of the entry in *The New Grove dictionary of music and musicians* (London, 1980)]

Brown (D.), 'Balakirev, Tchaikovsky and nationalism' in *Music & Letters*, vol. 42 (1961), p. 227

Brown (D.), 'Tchaikovsky and Chekhov' in Brown (M. H.) and Wiley (R. J.) [eds.], *Slavonic and Western music; essays for Gerald Abraham* (Ann Arbor, 1985)

Brown (D.), 'Tchaikovsky's marriage' in *The Musical Times*, vol. cxxiii (1982), p. 754

Brown (D.), 'Tchaikovsky's *Mazepa*' in *The Musical Times*, vol. cxxv (1984), p. 696

Friskin (J.), 'The Text of Tchaikovsky's B flat minor concerto' in *Music & Letters*, vol. 50 (1969), p. 246

Garden (E.), *Tchaikovsky* [Master Musicians Series] (London, 1973)

Garden (E.), 'The influence of Balakirev on Tchaikovsky' in *Proceedings of the Royal Musical Association*, vol. 107 (1980–1), p. 86

Garden (E.), 'Three Russian piano concertos' in *Music & Letters*, vol. 60 (1979), p. 166

Garden (E.), 'Tchaikovsky and Tolstoy' in *Music & Letters*, vol. 55 (1974), p. 307

John (N.) [ed.], *Eugene Onegin* [Opera Guide 38] (London, 1988)

Lloyd-Jones (D.), 'A Background to *Iolanta*' in *The Musical Times*, vol. cix (1968), p. 225

Newmarch (R.) [ed.], *The Life and letters of Peter Ilich Tchaikovsky by Modeste Tchaikovsky. Edited from the Russian . . . by Rosa Newmarch* (London, 1906)

Orlova (A.), *Tchaikovsky: a self-portrait* (Oxford, 1990)

Orlova (A.), 'Tchaikovsky: the last chapter' in *Music & Letters*, vol. 62 (1981), p. 125

Poznansky (A.), 'Tchaikovsky's suicide: myth and reality' in *19th-century Music*, vol. 11 (1988), p. 199

Tchaikovsky (P.), *The Diaries of Tchaikovsky*. Translated by W. Lakond (New York, 1945)

Tchaikovsky (P.), *Letters to his family: an autobiography*. Trans. by G. von Meck, with add. material by P. Young (London, 1981)

Tovey (D. F.), 'Tchaikovsky: Symphony . . . No. 5' in *Essays in musical analysis*, vol. vi (London, 1939)

Tovey (D. F.), 'Tchaikovsky: Pathetic symphony . . . No. 6' in *Essays in musical analysis*, vol. ii (London, 1935)

Volkoff (V.), *Tchaikovsky: a self-portrait* (London, 1975)

Warrack (J.), *Tchaikovsky* (London, 1973)

Warrack (J.), *Tchaikovsky's ballet music* [BBC Music Guides] (London, 1979)

Warrack (J.), *Tchaikovsky's symphonies and concertos* [BBC Music Guides] (London, 1969)

Weinstock (H.), *Tchaikovsky* (London, 1946)

Westrup (J.), 'Tchaikovsky and the symphony' in *The Musical Times*, vol. lxxxi (1940), p. 249

Wiley (R. J.), *Tchaikovsky's ballets* (Oxford, 1985)

Wiley (R. J.), 'Dramatic time and music in Tchaikovsky's ballets' in Brown (M. H.) and Wiley (R. J.) [eds.], *Slavonic and Western music; essays for Gerald Abraham* (Ann Arbor, 1985)

Wiley (R. J.), 'The Symphonic element in *Nutcracker*' in *The Musical Times*, vol. cxxv (1984), p. 693

Yoffe (E. O.), *Tchaikovsky in America: the composer's visit in 1891* (New York, 1986)

Zajaczkowski (H.), *Tchaikovsky's musical style* (Ann Arbor, 1987)

Zajaczkowski (H.), 'The Function of obsessive elements in Tchaikovsky's style' in *The Music Review*, vol. 43 (1982), p. 24

Zajaczkowski (H.), 'Tchaikovsky: the missing piece of the jigsaw puzzle' in *The Musical Times*, vol. cxxxi (1990), p. 238

WORK LIST

All Tchaikovsky's surviving works except the church music have been printed in the Russian Complete Edition (*Polnoye sobraniye sochineny* (Moscow/Leningrad, 1940–71)), and for a number of pieces this was their first publication. The list below records only editions which preceded this. As a result of further more precise data becoming available, the information in this Work List differs in some details from that given in the four volumes of the hardback edition.

Each entry sets out the following information (if known): Title (date of composition). Place and date of first public performance (place and date of publication).

In the case of works using the orchestra, publication data refer to the full score.

ORCHESTRAL WORKS
(all for full orchestra unless otherwise stated)

Allegro non tanto in G, for strings (1863–4)
Largo and Allegro in D, for 2 flutes and strings (1863–4)
Andante ma non troppo [and ?Allegro moderato] in A (1863–4)
Agitato and Allegro in E minor, for small orchestra (1863–4)
Allegro vivo in C minor (1863–4)
The Romans at the Coliseum (1863–4) [lost]
The Storm: overture to Ostrovsky's play, Op. 76 (sum. 1864). St Petersburg, 7 Mar 1896 (St Petersburg, 1896)
Characteristic Dances [later used as *Dances of the Hay Maidens* in the opera, *The Voyevoda*] (1865). Pavlovsk, 11 Sept 1865
Overture in F:
    1st version: small orchestra (27 Aug–27 Nov 1865). St Petersburg, 9 Dec 1865
    2nd version: full orchestra (Feb 1866). Moscow, 16 Mar 1866
Overture in C minor (sum. 1865–by 31 Jan 1866). Voronezh, 1931
Symphony No. 1 in G minor, Op. 13, *Winter daydreams*:
    1st version: (Mar–Sept 1866)
    2nd version: (Nov–Dec 1866). Moscow, 15 Feb 1868
    3rd version: (1874). Moscow, 1 Dec 1883 (Moscow, 1875)
Festival Overture on the Danish national anthem, Op. 15 (22 Sept–24 Nov 1866). Moscow, 10 Feb 1867 (Moscow, 1892)
Fatum: symphonic poem, Op. 77 (by 7 Oct–Dec 1868). Moscow, 27 Feb 1869 (St Petersburg, 1896)
Romeo and Juliet: fantasy overture after Shakespeare:
    1st version: (7 Oct–27 Nov 1869). Moscow, 16 Mar 1870
    2nd version: (sum. 1870). St Petersburg, 17 Feb 1872 (Berlin, 1871)
    3rd version: (completed 10 Sept 1880). Tiflis, 1 May 1886 (Berlin, 1881)
Serenade for Nikolay Rubinstein's nameday [see CHAMBER MUSIC]
Symphony No. 2 in C minor, Op. 17, *Little Russian*:

1st version: (June–Nov 1872). Moscow, 7 Feb 1873 (piano duet arrangement: St Petersburg, 1873)

2nd version: (30 Dec 1879–2 Jan 1880). St Petersburg, 12 Feb 1881 (St Petersburg, 1881)

The Tempest: symphonic fantasia after Shakespeare, Op. 18 (19 Aug–22 Oct 1873). Moscow, 19 Dec 1873 (Moscow, 1877)

Symphony No. 3 in D, Op. 29, *Polish* (17 June–13 Aug 1875). Moscow, 19 Nov 1875 (Moscow, 1877)

Slavonic March, Op. 31 (completed by 7 Oct 1876). Moscow, 17 Nov 1876 (Moscow, 1880)

Francesca da Rimini: symphonic fantasia after Dante, Op. 32 (7 Oct–17 Nov 1876). Moscow, 9 Mar 1877 (Moscow, 1878)

Symphony No. 4 in F minor, Op. 36 (by May 1877–7 Jan 1878). Moscow, 22 Feb 1878 (Moscow, 1880)

Suite No. 1 in D, Op. 43 (27 Aug 1878–2 Sept 1879). Moscow, 20 Dec 1879 (Moscow, 1879)

Italian Capriccio, Op. 45 (by 28 Jan–27 May 1880). Moscow, 18 Dec 1880 (Moscow, 1880)

Serenade in C, for string orchestra, Op. 48 (21 Sept–26 Oct 1880). St Petersburg, 30 Oct 1881 (Moscow, 1881)

The Year 1812: festival overture, Op. 49 (12 Oct–19 Nov 1880). Moscow, 20 Aug 1882 (Moscow, 1882)

Coronation March (17 Mar–by 4 Apr 1883). Moscow, 4 June 1883 (Moscow, 1883)

Suite No. 2 in C, Op. 53 (13 June–25 Oct 1883). Moscow, 16 Feb 1884 (Moscow, 1884)

Suite No. 3 in G, Op. 55 (Apr–31 July 1884). St Petersburg, 24 Jan 1885 (Moscow, 1885)

A Grateful Greeting: later, *Elegy*, in honour of Ivan Samarin, for string orchestra (by 18 Nov 1884). Moscow, 28 Dec 1884 (Moscow, 1890)

Manfred Symphony (after Byron), Op. 58 (Apr–4 Oct 1885). Moscow, 23 Mar 1886 (Moscow, 1886)

Jurists' March (8–17 Nov 1885). St Petersburg, 17 Dec 1885 (Moscow, 1894)

Suite No. 4 in G, Op. 61, *Mozartiana* [based on works by Mozart] (29 June–9 Aug 1887). Moscow, 26 Nov 1887 (Moscow, 1887)

Symphony No. 5 in E minor, Op. 64 (May–26 Aug 1888). St Petersburg, 17 Nov 1888 (Moscow, 1888)

Hamlet: fantasy overture after Shakespeare, Op. 67 (29 June–19 Oct 1888). St Petersburg, 24 Nov 1888 (Moscow, 1890)

The Voyevoda: symphonic ballad after Pushkin (after Mickiewicz), Op. 78 (by 27 Sep 1890 – 4 Oct 1891). Moscow, 18 Nov 1891 (St Petersburg, 1897)

The Nutcracker: suite from the ballet, Op. 71a (scored: 9–20 Feb 1892). St Petersburg, 19 Mar 1892 (Moscow, 1892)

Symphony [No. 7] in E flat [unfinished: sketches used for Piano Concerto No. 3 in E flat, Op. 75, Andante and Finale, Op. 79, and *Scherzo-fantasie*, Op. 72, No. 10, for piano] (May–7 Nov 1892). [From the original sketches Semyon Bogatïrev reconstructed a version which was performed in Moscow on 7 Feb 1957 (Moscow, 1951)]

Symphony No. 6 in B minor, Op. 74, *Pathétique* (16 Feb–31 Aug 1893). St Petersburg, 28 Oct 1893 (Moscow, 1894)

SOLO INSTRUMENT AND ORCHESTRA

Piano Concerto No. 1 in B flat minor, Op. 23 (Nov 1874–21 Feb 1875). Boston, USA, 25 Oct 1875 (Moscow, 1879)

Sérénade mélancolique, for violin and orchestra, Op. 26 (?Feb 1875). Moscow, 28 Jan 1876 (Moscow, 1879)

Variations on a Rococo Theme, for cello and small orchestra, Op. 33 (Dec 1876). Moscow, 30 Nov 1877 (Moscow, 1889)

Valse-scherzo, for violin and orchestra, Op. 34 (early 1877). Paris, 20 Sept 1878 (Moscow, 1895)

Violin Concerto in D, Op. 35 (17 Mar–11 Apr 1878). Vienna, 4 Dec 1881 (Moscow, 1888)

Piano Concerto No. 2 in G, Op. 44 (22 Oct 1879–10 May 1880). New York, 12 Nov 1881 (Moscow, 1881)

Concert Fantasia for piano and orchestra, Op. 56 (June–6 Oct 1884). Moscow, 6 Mar 1885 (Moscow, 1893)

Pezzo capriccioso, for cello and orchestra, Op. 62 (24 Aug–by 11 Sept 1887). Paris, 28 Feb 1888 (Moscow, 1888)

Piano Concerto No. 3 in E flat, Op. 75 [also referred to as Allegro de concert and *Konzertstück*. A reworking of the first movement of the uncompleted Symphony in E flat] (5 July–15 Oct 1893). St Petersburg, 19 Jan 1895 (Moscow, 1894)

Andante and Finale, for piano and orchestra, Op. 79 [a reworking of the slow movement and finale of the uncompleted Symphony in E flat] (begun after 15 Oct 1893 [Unfinished: completed and orchestrated by Taneyev]). St Petersburg, 20 Feb 1897 (St Petersburg, 1897)

CHAMBER MUSIC

Adagio in C, for 4 horns (1863–4)

Adagio in F, for 2 flutes, 2 oboes, 2 clarinets, cor anglais and bass clarinet (1863–4)

Adagio molto in E flat, for string quartet and harp (1863–4)

Allegretto in E, for string quartet (1863–4)

Allegretto moderato in D, for string trio (1863–4)

Allegro in C minor, for piano sextet (including double bass) (1863–4)

Allegro vivace in B flat, for string quartet (1863–4)

Andante ma non troppo in E minor, for string quintet (1863–4)

Andante molto in G, for string quartet (1863–4)

String Quartet in B flat [one movement only] (27 Aug–by 11 Nov 1865). Moscow, 11 Nov 1865 (Moscow, 1940)

String Quartet No. 1 in D, Op. 11 (Feb–?Mar 1871). Moscow, 28 Mar 1871 (Moscow, 1872) [second movement, Andante cantabile, arranged for cello and string orchestra by Tchaikovsky (?1886–7)]

Serenade for Nikolay Rubinstein's name day, for 2 flutes, 2 clarinets, horn, bassoon and string quartet (13 Dec 1872). Moscow, 18 Dec 1872

String Quartet No. 2 in F, Op. 22 (completed 30 Jan 1874). Moscow, 22 Mar 1874 (Moscow, 1876)

String Quartet No. 3 in E flat minor, Op. 30 (Jan–1 Mar 1876). Moscow, 30 Mar 1876 (Moscow, 1876) [Andante funebre arranged for violin and piano by Tchaikovsky (Moscow, 1877)]

Souvenir d'un lieu cher, for violin and piano, Op. 42 (Mar–May 1878). (Moscow, 1879):
Méditation [original slow movement of the Violin Concerto] (23–25 Mar, 1878)
Scherzo
Mélodie

Piano Trio in A minor ('To the memory of a great artist'), Op. 50 (Dec 1881–9 Feb 1882). Moscow, 30 Oct 1882 (Moscow, 1882)

String Sextet in D, Op. 70, *Souvenir de Florence* (25 June–6 Aug 1890 [opening sketched

28 June 1887]). St Petersburg, 10 Dec 1890. Revised version (Dec 1891–28 Jan 1892). St Petersburg, 6 Dec 1892 (Moscow, 1892)

PIANO WORKS
(for solo piano unless otherwise stated)

Anastasie Valse, in F (Aug 1854). (Moscow, 1913)

Piece based on the tune 'Vozle rechki, vozle mostu' [By the river, by the bridge]: musical joke after Konstantin Lyadov (aut. 1862) [lost]

Allegro in F minor (1863–4) [incomplete; central portion used as the *Scherzo* in *Souvenir de Hapsal*, Op. 2]

Theme and variations in A minor (1863–4). (Moscow, 1909)

Sonata in C sharp minor, Op. 80 (1865). (Moscow, 1900) [third movement used as the Scherzo of the First Symphony]

Two Pieces, Op. 1. (Moscow, 1867):
1. *Scherzo à la russe*, in B flat (1867). Moscow, 12 Apr 1867
2. *Impromptu*, in E flat minor (1863–4)

Souvenir de Hapsal, Op. 2 (June–July 1867). (Moscow, 1868):
1. *Ruines d'un château*, in E minor
2. *Scherzo*, in F [founded on the central portion of the Allegro in F minor (1863–4)]. Moscow, 10 Mar 1868
3. *Chant sans paroles*, in F

Potpourri on themes from the opera, *The Voyevoda* [published under pseudonym of Cramer] (1868). (Moscow, 1868)

Valse caprice, in D, Op. 4 (Oct 1868). Moscow, 20 Apr 1869 (Moscow, 1868)

Romance, in F minor, Op. 5 (Nov 1868). Moscow, 20 Dec 1868 (Moscow, 1868)

Valse scherzo, [No. 1] in A, Op. 7 (by 15 Feb 1870). (Moscow, 1870)

Capriccio, in G flat, Op. 8 (by 15 Feb 1870). (Moscow, 1870)

Three Pieces, Op. 9 (by 7 Nov 1870). (Moscow, 1871):
1. *Rêverie*, in D. Moscow, 28 Mar 1871
2. *Polka de salon*, in B flat
3. *Mazurka de salon*, in D minor [a reworking of the Mazurka composed for Ostrovsky's play, *Dmitri the Pretender and Vasily Shuisky* (by 11 Feb 1867). See STAGE WORKS]. Moscow, 28 Mar 1871

Two Pieces, Op. 10 (Jan 1872) (Moscow, 1874 [*Nocturne*], 1875 [*Humoresque*]):
1. *Nocturne*, in F (Moscow, 1874)
2. *Humoresque*, in E minor (Moscow, 1875) [arranged for violin and piano by Tchaikovsky (by 1877)]

Six Pieces, Op. 19 (Oct–by 8 Nov 1873). (Moscow, 1874):
1. *Rêverie du soir*, in G minor. Moscow, 6 Mar 1874
2. *Scherzo humoristique*, in D
3. *Feuillet d'album*, in D
4. *Nocturne*, in C sharp minor [transcribed for cello and small orchestra by Tchaikovsky (1888)]
5. *Capriccioso*, in B flat
6. *Thème original et variations*, in F. Moscow, Apr 1874

Six Pieces on a Single Theme, Op. 21 (Oct–by 20 Dec 1873). (St Petersburg, 1873):
1. *Prélude*, in B
2. *Fugue à 4 voix*, in G sharp minor
3. *Impromptu*, in C sharp minor
4. *Marche funèbre*, in A flat minor
5. *Mazurque*, in A flat minor

6. *Scherzo*, in A flat

The Seasons, Op. 37b (Dec 1875–?May 1876). (Moscow, 1876):
1. *Janvier: Au coin du feu*, in A
2. *Février: Carnaval*, in D
3. *Mars: Chant de l'alouette*, in G minor
4. *Avril: Perce-neige*, in B flat
5. *Mai: Les nuits de mai*, in G
6. *Juin: Barcarolle*, in G minor
7. *Juillet: Chant du faucheur*, in E flat
8. *Août: La moisson*, in B minor
9. *Septembre: La chasse*, in G
10. *Octobre: Chant d'automne*, in D minor
11. *Novembre: Troika*, in E
12. *Décembre: Noël*, in A flat

Funeral march on themes from *The Oprichnik* (by 28 Mar 1877). [lost]

Twelve Pieces (moderate difficulty), Op. 40 (24 Feb–12 May 1878). (Moscow, 1879):
1. *Etude*, in G
2. *Chanson triste*, in G minor
3. *Marche funèbre*, in C minor
4. *Mazurka*, in C
5. *Mazurka*, in D
6. *Chant sans paroles*, in A minor
7. *Au village*, in A minor
8. *Valse*, in A flat
9. *Valse*, in F sharp minor (first version: June or July 1876)
10. *Danse russe*, in A minor [originally composed as a supplementary dance for the ballet, *Swan Lake* (1877)]
11. *Scherzo*, in D minor
12. *Rêverie interrompue*, in F minor

Album for children: 24 easy pieces, Op. 39 (13–16 May 1878). (Moscow, 1878) [Tchaikovsky's original sequence; nos. in brackets indicate Jurgenson's published order]:
1. (1) *Prière de matin*, in G
2. (2) *Le matin en hiver*, in D
3. (4) *Maman*, in G
4. (3) *Le petit cavalier*, in D
5. (5) *Marche des soldats de bois*, in D
6. (9) *La nouvelle poupée*, in B flat
7. (6) *La poupée malade*, in G minor
8. (7) *Enterrement de la poupée*, in C minor
9. (8) *Valse*, in E flat
10. (14) *Polka*, in B flat
11. (10) *Mazurka*, in D minor
12. (11) *Chanson russe*, in F
13. (12) *Le paysan prélude*, in B flat
14. (13) *Chanson populaire (Kamarinskaya)*, in D
15. (15) *Chanson italienne*, in D
16. (16) *Mélodie antique française*, in G minor
17. (17) *Chanson allemande*, in E flat
18. (18) *Chanson napolitaine*, in E flat
19. (19) *Conte de la vieille bonne*, in C
20. (20) *La sorcière (Baba Yaga)*, in E minor

21. (21) *Douce rêverie*, in C
22. (22) *Chant de l'alouette*, in G
23. (24) *A l'église*, in E minor
24. (23) *L'orgue de barberie*, in G

Sonata in G, Op. 37 (13 Mar–7 Aug 1878). Moscow, 2 Nov 1879 (Moscow, 1879)

March for the Volunteer Fleet, in C [published under the pseudonym of P. Sinopov] (6 May 1878). (Moscow, 1878)

Six Pieces, Op. 51 (?5–22 Sept 1882). (Moscow, 1882):
1. *Valse de salon*, in A flat
2. *Polka peu dansante*, in B minor
3. *Menuetto scherzoso*, in E flat
4. *Natha-valse*, in A (first version: 17 Aug 1878)
5. *Romance*, in F
6. *Valse sentimentale*, in F minor

Impromptu caprice, in G (30 Sept 1884). (Paris, 1885)

Dumka: Russian rustic scene, in C minor, Op. 59 (27 Feb–5 Mar 1886). (Moscow, 1886)

Valse scherzo, [No. 2] in A (by 27 Aug 1889). (Moscow, 1889)

Impromptu, in A flat (2–12 Oct 1889). (St Petersburg, 1889)

Aveu passioné, in E minor (?1892) [largely a transcription of an episode in the symphonic ballad, *The Voyevoda*]. (Moscow/Leningrad, 1949)

Military March [for the Yurevsky Regiment], in B flat (5 Apr and 17 May 1893). (Moscow, 1894)

Eighteen Pieces, Op. 72 (19 Apr–3 May 1893). (Moscow, 1893):
1. *Impromptu*, in F minor
2. *Berceuse*, in A flat
3. *Tendres reproches*, in C sharp minor
4. *Danse caractéristique*, in D
5. *Méditation*, in D
6. *Mazurque pour danser*, in B flat
7. *Polacca de concert*, in E flat
8. *Dialogue*, in B
9. *Un poco di Schumann*, in D flat
10. *Scherzo-fantaisie*, in E flat minor [reworked from the Scherzo of the abandoned Symphony [No. 7] in E flat. See ORCHESTRAL WORKS]
11. *Valse Bluette*, in E flat
12. *L'Espiègle*, in E
13. *Echo rustique*, in E flat
14. *Chant élégiaque*, in D flat
15. *Un poco di Chopin*, in C sharp minor
16. *Valse à cinq temps*, in D
17. *Passé lointain*, in E flat
18. *Scène dansante (invitation au trépak)*, in C

Impromptu (Momento lirico), in A flat (?1892–3) [completed by Taneyev]. (Moscow, 1894)

STAGE WORKS
(* = vocal score, or piano score in the case of ballets; + = full score)

Hyperbole: opera in one act (V. Olkhovsky); (1854) [incomplete; lost]

Music for the fountain scene in *Boris Godunov* (Pushkin); (?1863–4) [lost]

Introduction and Mazurka for *Dmitry the Pretender and Vasily Shuisky* (Ostrovsky); (by 11

Feb 1867) [Mazurka later reworked as *Mazurka de salon* in Three Pieces, Op. 9. See PIANO WORKS]

Couplets for a vaudeville, *The Tangle* (Fyodorov); (Dec 1867). Moscow, Dec 1867 [lost]

The Voyevoda: opera in 3 acts, Op. 3 (Ostrovsky and Tchaikovsky, after Ostrovsky's *A Dream on the Volga*); (20 Mar 1867–10 Aug 1868). Moscow, 11 Feb 1869 [score destroyed by Tchaikovsky, reconstructed from performing materials by Pavel Lamm]

Recitatives and chorus for Auber's *Le domino noir* (Nov 1868). Moscow, 22 Jan 1870 [lost]

Undine: opera in 3 acts (Sollogub, after Zhukovsky's translation of F. de la Motte Fouqué); (Jan–July 1869). Moscow, 28 Mar 1870 [concert performance: excerpts only]

'Chorus of flowers and insects' for an opera, *Mandragora* (Rachinsky); (by 8–25 Jan 1870). Concert performance: Moscow, 30 Dec 1870

Couplets for tenor and two violins for Beaumarchais's *Le Barbier de Séville* (translated by Sadovsky); (by 24 Feb 1872). Moscow, 24 Feb 1872 (Moscow, 1906)

The Oprichnik: opera in 4 acts (Tchaikovsky, after Lazhechnikov); (Feb 1870–1 Apr 1872). St Petersburg, 24 Apr 1874 (*St Petersburg, 1874; + St Petersburg, 1896)

The Snow Maiden (Ostrovsky): incidental music, Op. 12 (Mar–Apr 1873). Moscow, 23 May 1873 (*Moscow, 1873; + Moscow, 1895)

Vakula the Smith: opera in 3 acts, Op. 14 (Polonsky, after Gogol's *Christmas Eve*); (June–2 Sept 1874: overture by 17 Oct 1874). St Petersburg, 6 Dec 1876 (*Moscow, 1876)

Swan Lake: ballet in 4 acts, Op. 20 (V. Begichev and V. Heltser); (Aug 1875–22 Apr 1876). Moscow, 4 Mar 1877 (*Moscow, 1877; + Moscow, 1895)

Eugene Onegin: lyrical scenes in 3 acts, Op. 24 (Tchaikovsky and K. Shilovsky, after Pushkin); (May 1877–1 Feb 1878). Moscow, 29 Mar 1879 (*Moscow, 1880; + Moscow, 1880)

The Maid of Orléans: opera in 4 acts (Tchaikovsky, after Zhukovsky's translation of Schiller's *Die Jungfrau von Orleans*, and other sources); (17 Dec 1878–4 Sept 1879: revised 1882). St Petersburg, 25 Feb 1881 (*Moscow, 1880; + Moscow, 1899)

Cradle song for a play, *La Fée* (O. Feuillet); (13 July 1879). Kamenka, ?14 Aug 1879 [lost]

Music for a tableau, *Montenegrins receiving the news of Russia's declaration of war on Turkey* (8–11 Feb 1880) [lost]

Mazepa: opera in 3 acts (Burenin (revised by Tchaikovsky), after Pushkin's *Poltava*); (June 1881–28 Apr 1883). Moscow, 15 Feb 1884 (* Moscow, 1883; + Moscow, 1899)

Cherevichki: opera in 4 acts [a revision of *Vakula the Smith*] (Polonsky, after Gogol's *Christmas Eve*, with additions by Tchaikovsky and N. Chayev); (28 Feb–3 Apr 1885). Moscow, 31 Jan 1887 (*Moscow, 1885; + Moscow, 1898)

The Enchantress: opera in 4 acts (Shpazhinsky); (Oct 1885–18 May 1887). St Petersburg, 1 Nov 1887 (*Moscow, 1887; + Moscow, 1901)

Domovoy's monologue: melodrama for the play, *The Voyevoda* (Ostrovsky); (25–29 Jan 1886). Moscow, 31 Jan 1886 (facsimile of score: Moscow/Leningrad, 1940)

The Sleeping Beauty: ballet in a prologue and 3 acts, Op. 66 (Petipa and Vsevolozhsky, after Perrault's *La belle au bois dormant*); (Oct 1888–1 Sept 1889). St Petersburg, 15 Jan 1890 (*Moscow, 1889; no copy of the full score listed in the Jurgenson 1897 Catalogue has come to light)

The Queen of Spades: opera in 3 acts, Op. 68 (M. and P. Tchaikovsky, after Pushkin); (31 Jan–20 June 1890). St Petersburg, 19 Dec 1890 (* Moscow, 1890; + Moscow, 1891)

Incidental music to *Hamlet*, Op. 67a (Shakespeare); (19 Jan–3 Feb 1891). St Petersburg, 21 Feb 1891 (+ Moscow, 1892; * Moscow, 1896)

Iolanta: lyric opera in one act, Op. 69 (M. Tchaikovsky, after V. Zotov's translation of

Hertz's *King René's daughter*); (22 July–27 Dec 1891). St Petersburg, 18 Dec 1892 (*and + Moscow, 1892)

The Nutcracker: ballet in 2 acts, Op. 71 (?Vsevolozhsky and Petipa, after Dumas *père*'s version of E. T. A. Hoffmann's *Nussknacker und Mausekönig*); (Feb 1891–4 Apr 1892). St Petersburg, 18 Dec 1892 (*and + Moscow, 1892).

Duet for an opera on *Romeo and Juliet* (Shakespeare, translated by Sokolovsky) [partly based on the fantasy overture; completed by Taneyev]; (Oct 1881 or 1893). (Moscow, 1895)

CHORAL WORKS

An oratorio (?1863–4) [lost]

'At bedtime' (Ogaryov), for unaccompanied chorus [also provided with an orchestral accompaniment by Tchaikovsky] (1863–4)

Cantata: 'An die Freude' (Schiller, translated Axakov and others), for SATB soli, chorus and orchestra (Nov–Dec 1865). St Petersburg, 10 Jan 1866

'Nature and love' (Tchaikovsky), for SSA and piano (Dec 1870). Moscow, 28 Mar 1871 (Moscow, 1894)

Cantata in commemoration of the bicentenary of the birth of Peter the Great (Polonsky), for T solo, chorus and orchestra (Feb–Mar 1872). Moscow, 12 June 1872

Cantata (Hymn, or Chorus) in celebration of the golden jubilee of Osip Petrov (Nekrasov), for T solo, chorus and orchestra (by 29 Dec 1875). St Petersburg, 6 May 1876

Liturgy of St John Chrysostom, Op. 41, for unaccompanied chorus (16 May–6 Aug 1878). Kiev, June 1879 (Moscow, 1879)

Cantata, for unaccompanied women's chorus à4 (?Sept 1881) [composed for his niece, Anna, at school; lost]

'Evening' (?Tchaikovsky), for unaccompanied men's chorus à3 (by 25 Dec 1881). (Moscow, 1881)

All-night Vigil, Op. 52, for unaccompanied chorus (May 1881–19 Mar 1882). Moscow, 9 July 1882 (Moscow, 1883)

Moscow: coronation cantata (Maikov), for Mez and Bar soli, chorus and orchestra (17 Mar–5 Apr 1883). Moscow, 27 May 1883 (Moscow, 1885 [vocal score], 1888 [full score])

Nine Sacred Pieces, for unaccompanied chorus (Nov 1884–Apr (possibly Aug) 1885). Moscow, 1 Mar 1886 [nos. 1 and 4 only] (Moscow, 1885):

1. Cherubim's song in F [No. 1] (Nov 1884)
2. Cherubim's song in D [No. 2] (Nov 1884)
3. Cherubim's song in C [No. 3] (Dec 1884)
4. *Thee we hymn* (Dec 1884)
5. *Meet it is indeed*
6. Lord's Prayer
7. *Bliss I chose*
8. *Let my prayer be set forth*, for SSA soli and chorus (Apr 1885)
9. *Today the heavenly powers*

Hymn in honour of SS Cyril and Methodius (Tchaikovsky), for unaccompanied chorus (19 Mar 1885). Moscow, 18 Apr 1885 (Moscow, 1885)

Jurists' Song for the golden jubilee of the School of Jurisprudence (Tchaikovsky), for unaccompanied chorus (by 9 Oct 1885). St Petersburg, 17 Dec 1885 (St Petersburg, 1885)

'An angel weeping', for unaccompanied chorus (2 Mar 1887). Moscow, 20 Mar 1887 (Moscow, 1906)

'The golden cloud has slept' (Lermontov), for unaccompanied chorus (17 July 1887). (Moscow, 1922)

'Blessed is he who smiles' (Grand Duke Konstantin Konstantinovich Romanov), for unaccompanied men's chorus à4 (19 Dec 1887). Moscow, 20 Mar 1892 (Moscow, 1889)

'The Nightingale' (Tchaikovsky), for unaccompanied chorus (21–24 Jan 1889). St Petersburg, 31 Mar 1889 (Moscow, 1890)

A Greeting to Anton Rubinstein for his golden jubilee as an artist (Polonsky), for unaccompanied chorus (2–12 Oct 1889). St Petersburg, 30 Nov 1889 (Moscow, 1889)

'Legend', Op. 54, No. 5 (Pleshcheyev), for unaccompanied chorus [arrangement of the solo song] (Jan 1889). St Petersburg, 31 Mar 1889 (Moscow, 1890)

''Tis not the cuckoo in the damp pinewood' (Tsïganov), for unaccompanied chorus (by 26 Feb 1891). St Petersburg, 5 May 1891 (Moscow, 1894)

'Without time, without season' (Tsïganov), for unaccompanied women's chorus à4 (by 26 Feb 1891). St Petersburg, 5 May 1891 (Moscow, 1894)

'The voice of mirth grew silent' (Pushkin), for unaccompanied men's chorus à4 (by 26 Feb 1891). St Petersburg, 5 May 1891 (Moscow, 1894)

'Night' (Tchaikovsky), for SATB and piano [reworking of an episode from Mozart's Fantasia for piano, in C minor, K. 475] (13–15 Mar 1893). Moscow, 21 Oct 1893 (Moscow, 1893)

'Spring', for unaccompanied women's chorus [lost]

SONGS AND DUETS

(Of the versions of certain of these pieces made by Tchaikovsky only orchestrations of the piano parts are here noted)

'My genius, my angel, my friend' (Fet) (c. 1857–8; just possibly 1854)

'Zemfira's song' (Pushkin) (c. 1857–60)

'Mezza notte' (?1860–1). (St Petersburg, ?1862)

Six Romances, Op. 6 (5–12 Dec 1869). (Moscow, 1870):
  1. 'Do not believe, my friend' (A. Tolstoy)
  2. 'Not a word, O my friend' (Pleshcheyev, after M. Hartmann)
  3. 'It's both bitter and sweet' (Rostopchina)
  4. 'A tear trembles' (A. Tolstoy)
  5. 'Why?' (Mey, after Heine)
  6. 'No, only he who knows' (Mey, after Goethe) [usually known in English as 'None but the lonely heart']

'To forget so soon' (Apukhtin) (1870). (Moscow, 1873)

Six Romances, Op. 16 (?Dec 1872–Jan 1873). (St Petersburg, 1873):
  1. 'Cradle song' (Maikov)
  2. 'Wait a while' (Grekov)
  3. 'Accept but once' (Fet)
  4. 'O sing that song' (Pleshcheyev, after F. Hemans)
  5. 'Thy radiant, angelic image' (Tchaikovsky)
  6. 'Modern Greek song' (Maikov)

'Take my heart away' (Fet) (by 11 Oct 1873). (*Nouvelliste*, Nov 1873)

'Blue eyes of spring' (Mikhaylov, after Heine) (by 11 Oct 1873). (*Nouvelliste*, Jan 1874)

Six Romances, Op. 25 (?Feb–Mar 1875). (St Petersburg, 1875):
  1. 'Reconciliation' (Shcherbina)

2. 'As o'er the burning ashes' (Tyutchev)
3. 'Mignon's song' (Tyutchev, after Goethe)
4. 'The canary' (Mey)
5. 'I never spoke to her' (Mey)
6. 'As they reiterated: "Fool!"' (Mey)

Six Romances, Op. 27 (by 19 Apr 1875). (Moscow, 1875):
  1. 'At bedtime' (Ogaryov)
  2. 'Look, yonder cloud' (Grekov)
  3. 'Do not leave me' (Fet)
  4. 'Evening' (Mey, after Shevchenko)
  5. 'Was it the mother who bore me?' (Mey, after Mickiewicz)
  6. 'My spoiled darling' (Mey, after Mickiewicz)

Six Romances, Op. 28 (by 23 Apr 1875). (Moscow, 1875):
  1. 'No, I shall never tell' (Grekov, after de Musset)
  2. 'The corals' (Mey, after Kondratowicz)
  3. 'Why did I dream of you?' (Mey)
  4. 'He loved me so much' (?Apukhtin)
  5. 'No response, or word, or greeting' (Apukhtin)
  6. 'The fearful minute' (Tchaikovsky)

'I should like in a single word' (Mey, after Heine) (by 15 May 1875). (*Nouvelliste*, Sept 1875)

'We have not far to walk' (Grekov) (by 15 May 1875). (*Nouvelliste*, Nov 1875)

Six Romances, Op. 38 (23 Feb–25 July 1878). (Moscow, 1878):
  1. 'Don Juan's serenade' (A. Tolstoy)
  2. 'It was in the early spring' (A. Tolstoy)
  3. 'Amid the din of the ball' (A. Tolstoy)
  4. 'O, if only you could for one moment' (A. Tolstoy)
  5. 'The love of a dead man' (Lermontov)
  6. 'Pimpinella' (Tchaikovsky, after a Florentine popular song)

Six duets, Op. 46 (16 Jun–5 Sept 1880). (Moscow, 1881):
  1. 'Evening' [S Mez] (Surikov)
  2. 'Scottish ballad' [S Bar] (Scottish ballad, 'Edward': translated A. Tolstoy)
  3. 'Tears' [S Mez] (Tyutchev)
  4. 'In the garden, near the ford' [S Mez] (Surikov, after Shevchenko)
  5. 'Passion spent' [ST] (A. Tolstoy)
  6. 'Dawn' [S Mez] (Surikov) [orchestrated: Nov–Dec 1889]

Seven Romances, Op. 47 (July–Aug 1880). (Moscow, 1881):
  1. 'If only I had known' (A. Tolstoy)
  2. 'Softly the spirit flew up to heaven' (A. Tolstoy)
  3. 'Dusk fell on the earth' (Berg, after Mickiewicz)
  4. 'Sleep, poor friend' (A. Tolstoy)
  5. 'I bless you, forests' (A. Tolstoy)
  6. 'Does the day reign?' (Apukhtin) [orchestrated: 24 Feb 1888 [lost]]
  7. 'Was I not a little blade of grass' (Surikov, after Shevchenko) [orchestrated by 27 Sept 1884]

Sixteen Children's Songs, Op. 54 (nos. 1–14, Pleshcheyev; no. 15, Surikov, after Lenartowicz; no. 16, Axakov); (nos. 1–15: 2–15 Nov 1883; no. 16: by 19 Jan 1881). (Moscow, 1884):
  1. 'Granny and grandson'
  2. 'The little bird' (after Kondratowicz)
  3. 'Spring'
  4. 'My little garden'

5. 'Legend' (from an English source) [orchestrated: 14 Apr 1884 (Moscow, 1892); arr. for mixed chorus: Jan 1889 (Moscow, 1889)]
6. 'On the bank'
7. 'Winter evening'
8. 'The cuckoo' (after Gellert)
9. 'Spring'
10. 'Lullaby in a storm'
11. 'The flower' (after L. Ratisbonne)
12. 'Winter'
13. 'Spring song'
14. 'Autumn'
15. 'The swallow'
16. 'Child's song: (My Lizochek)' (Moscow, 1881)

Six Romances, Op. 57 (no. 1: ?early 1884; nos. 2–6: Oct–13 Dec 1884). (Moscow, 1885):
1. 'Tell me, of what does the spring nightingale sing?' (Sollogub)
2. 'On the golden cornfields' (A. Tolstoy)
3. 'Do not ask' (Strugovshchikov, after Goethe)
4. 'Sleep' (Merezhkovsky)
5. 'Death' (Merezhkovsky)
6. 'Only thou alone' (Pleshcheyev, after A. Kristen)

Twelve Romances, Op. 60 (31 Aug–20 Sept 1886). (Moscow, 1886 [nos. 1–6], 1887 [nos. 7–12]):
1. 'Last night' (Khomyakov)
2. 'I'll tell you nothing' (Fet)
3. 'O, if only you knew' (Pleshcheyev)
4. 'The nightingale' (Pushkin, after V. S. Karadzić)
5. 'Simple words' (Tchaikovsky)
6. 'Frenzied nights' (Apukhtin)
7. 'Gipsy's song' (Polonsky)
8. 'Forgive' (Nekrasov)
9. 'Night' (Polonsky)
10. 'Behind the window in the shadow' (Polonsky)
11. 'Exploit' (Khomyakov)
12. 'The mild stars shone for us' (Pleshcheyev)

Six Romances, Op. 63 (Grand Duke Konstantin Konstantinovich Romanov); (Nov–Dec 1887). (Moscow, 1888):
1. 'I did not love you at first'
2. 'I opened the window'
3. 'I do not please you'
4. 'The first meeting'
5. 'The fires in the rooms were already out'
6. 'Serenade (O child, beneath thy window)'

Six Romances (on French texts), Op. 65 (completed 22 Oct 1888). (Moscow, 1889):
1. 'Sérénade (Où vas-tu, souffle d'aurore?)' (E. Turquéty)
2. 'Déception' (Collin)
3. 'Sérénade (J'aime dans le rayon de la limpide aurore)' (Collin)
4. 'Qu'importe que l'hiver?' (Collin)
5. 'Les larmes' (A.-M. Blanchecotte)
6. 'Rondel' (Collin)

Six Romances, Op. 73 (Rathaus); (5–17 May 1893). (Moscow, 1893):
1. 'We sat together'
2. 'Night'
3. 'In this moonlight'

4. 'The sun has set'
5. "Mid sombre days'
6. 'Again, as before, alone'
'Who goes?' (Apukhtin) [lost]

ARRANGEMENTS AND EDITIONS

Weber, Scherzo of Piano Sonata, Op. 39 (J199). Orchestrated (1863)
Beethoven, First movement of Piano Sonata, Op. 31, No. 2. Orchestrated (4 versions) (?1863)
Beethoven, First movement of Violin Sonata, Op. 47 ('Kreutzer'). Orchestrated (1863–4)
Gung'l, *Le retour* (valse) for piano. Orchestrated (1863–4)
Schumann, Adagio and Allegro brillante from *Etudes symphoniques*, Op. 13. Orchestrated (1864)
K. Kral, Festival March for piano. Orchestrated (1867). Moscow, May 1867
Dargomïzhsky, *Little Russian kazachok*: fantasia. Arranged for piano (?1868). (Moscow, 1868)
E. Tarnovskaya, 'I remember all': song, transcribed for piano by Dubuque. Arranged for piano duet (?1868). (Moscow, 1868)
Fifty Russian Folksongs. Arranged for piano duet (nos. 1–25: aut. 1868; nos. 26–50: by 7 Oct 1869). (Moscow, 1869)
A. Rubinstein, *Ivan the Terrible*: musical picture for orchestra. Arranged for piano duet (?8 Oct–?11 Nov 1869). (St Petersburg, 1869)
A. Dubuque, *Maria-Dagmar*: polka for piano. Orchestrated (?1869)
Dargomïzhsky, 'The golden cloud has slept' (for 3 voices and piano). Piano part orchestrated (?1870 or ?1876). St Petersburg, 7 Jan 1877
Stradella, 'O del mio dolce': aria. Piano part orchestrated (10 Nov 1870). Moscow, 18 Nov 1870
A. Rubinstein, *Don Quixote*: musical picture for orchestra. Arranged for piano duet (Jan–Feb 1871). (St Petersburg, ?1871)
Cimarosa, 'Le faccio un inchino': trio from *Il matrimonio segreto*. Piano part in vocal score orchestrated (?1871)
Weber, Finale (perpetuum mobile) from Piano Sonata, Op. 24 (J138). Transcribed for piano, left hand (?1871). (Moscow, ?1871)
V. Prokunin, 65 Russian Folksongs. Edition (1872). (Moscow, 1872 and 1873)
M. A. Mamontova, A collection of children's songs on Russian and Ukrainian melodies. Harmonized (nos. 1–24: by 8 May 1872; nos. 25–39: by May 1877). (Moscow, 1872; nos. 25–39 unpublished)
Anon, 'Gaudeamus igitur'. Arranged for men's chorus à4 and piano (1874). (Moscow, 1874)
Haydn, 'Gott erhalte' (Austrian national anthem). Orchestrated (1874). ?Moscow, 24 Feb 1874
Schumann, *Ballade vom Haideknaben*, Op. 122, No. 1 (declamation for voice and piano). Piano part orchestrated (11 Mar 1874). Moscow, 19 Apr 1874
Liszt, 'Der König in Thule': song. Piano part orchestrated (3 Nov 1874)
Bortnyansky, Complete church music. Edited (2 July–8 Nov 1881). (Moscow, 1881–2)
Couplets on a theme from Glinka's *A Life for the Tsar*, linked with the Russian national anthem of A. Lvov. Arrangement for chorus and string orchestra (14–16 Feb 1883). Moscow, 22 May 1883 (Moscow, after 1897)
Mozart, 4 pieces. Orchestrated (1887) [see ORCHESTRAL WORKS: Suite No. 4 in G, Op. 61, *Mozartiana*].

Laroche, *Karmozina*: overture. Orchestrated (27 Aug–21 Sept 1888). St Petersburg, 17 Nov 1888

S. Menter, *Ungarische Zigeunerweisen*, for piano. Arranged for piano and orchestra (?1893). Odessa, 4 Feb 1893. [It has been suggested the work is a lost concerto by Liszt]

WRITINGS

Diaries. Many destroyed by Tchaikovsky; surviving ones published in 1923 [see Bibliography]

'Autobiographical description of a journey abroad in 1888', in *Russky vestnik* (1894, no. 2)

Reviews and critical articles; first published as *P. I. Chaykovsky: muzïkalnïye feletonï i zametki*, ed. H. Laroche (Moscow, 1898)

Guide to the practical study of harmony (completed 14 Aug 1871). (Moscow, 1872)

A short manual of harmony adapted to the study of religious music in Russia (1874–5). (Moscow, 1875)

'Wagner and his music', in *Morning Journal* (New York, 3 May 1891)

'A conversation with Tchaikovsky in November 1892 in St Petersburg', in *Peterburgskaya zhizn* (24 Nov 1892)

Editing and correcting of musical terms in *Slovar russkovo yazïka* [Dictionary of the Russian language] (Oct 1892–1893). (St Petersburg, 1892 and 1895)

TRANSLATIONS, ETC.

F.-A. Gevaert, *Traité général d'instrumentation* (sum. 1865). (Moscow, 1866)

Urbain's cavatina, 'Une dame noble et sage', from Meyerbeer's *Les Huguenots* (by 17 June 1868). (Moscow, 1868)

Schumann, *Musikalische Haus- und Lebensregeln* (by 1 Aug 1868). (Moscow, 1869)

J. C. Lobe, *Katechismus der Musik* (completed 20 Nov 1869). (Moscow, 1870)

Translations of German texts used by A. Rubinstein:
12 persische Lieder, Op. 34 (by 24 Dec 1869). (St Petersburg, 1870)
4 songs (Op. 32, Nos. 1 and 6, and Op. 33, Nos. 2 and 4) (?1870–1). (St Petersburg, ?1871)
6 romances, Op. 72 (?1870–1). (St Petersburg, ?1871)
6 romances, Op. 76 (?1871). (St Petersburg, ?1872)
3 songs, Op. 83, Nos. 1, 5 and 9 (?1871). (St Petersburg, ?1872)

Mozart, *Le nozze di Figaro*. Translation of recitatives (1875). Moscow, 17 May 1876 (* Moscow, 1884)

Glinka, six Italian texts used in vocal pieces (by 27 Dec 1877). (Moscow, 1878):
Mio ben, ricordati
Ho perduto il mio tesoro
Mi sento il cor traffigere
Pur non sonno
Tu sei figlio

Glinka, Quartet for SATB (without words).
Text ('Prayer') (and, perhaps, piano accompaniment) provided by Tchaikovsky (?1877). (Moscow, 1878)

Handel, *Israel in Egypt* (in collaboration with Taneyev) (1886)

CUMULATIVE INDEX OF WORKS

ORCHESTRAL WORKS

The Romans at the Coliseum (1863–4) [lost], I: 73
The Storm: overture to Ostrovsky's play, Op. 76 (1864), I: 74–80, 87–8, 103, 105, 123, 132, 145, 148, 167, 189, 222. II: 44. III: 133, 320. IV: 79, 441, 455
Characteristic Dances (1864–5) [later used as the *Dances of the Hay Maidens* in the opera, *The Voyevoda*], I: 83, 119–20, 127, 129–30, 136, 149. IV: 97, 382
Overture in F (1865: rev. 1866), I: 80, 83, 86–8, 95, 99
Overture in C minor (1865–6), I: 80–1, 86–8, 90, 95, 146, 148, 268
Symphony No. 1 in G minor, Op. 13 (*Winter Daydreams*) (1866: rev. 1874), I: 74, 78, 81, 96, 99–115, 117, 120, 129, 186–7, 217, 250, 257, 259. II: 16, 21, 49, 125, 264. III: 117, 127, 241, 150–1, 279, 309. IV: 22, 91, 395, 408, 424, 431, 439–41, 443
Festival Overture on the Danish national anthem, Op. 15 (1866), I: 101, 116–17. III: 213, 215. IV: 27, 411
Fatum: symphonic poem, Op. 77 (1868), I: 163, 165–8, 172, 174, 186, 197–8, 206, 209, 233. III: 62. IV: 105
Romeo and Juliet: fantasy overture (1869: rev. 1870 and 1880), I: 13, 77–8, 81, 131, 135, 173, 180, 182–95, 197, 201, 209, 211–12, 217–18, 221, 226, 236, 240, 247, 251, 253, 260, 264–5, 282–3, 294–5, 302. II: 16, 22, 24, 26, 44, 55, 102, 108, 112, 114, 167, 232, 299. III: 103, 117, 121, 126, 147, 269, 281, 287, 297, 304, 306, 322. IV: 74, 107, 125, 131, 134, 137, 142, 152, 157, 427–31, 434–7, 439–41, 447
Symphony No. 2 in C minor, Op. 17 (*Little Russian*) (1872: rev. 1879–80), I: 87, 155, 176, 189, 253–69, 281, 283, 290. II: 22, 24, 49, 162, 167, 174, 176, 269. III: 85, 93, 100, 105, 120, 124, 126, 130, 229. IV: 150, 154–6, 405, 423, 439, 441
The Tempest: symphonic fantasia, Op. 18 (1873), I: 131, 283–4, 291–8, 306. II: 16, 47, 112–13, 134, 144, 237, 271. III: 30–1, 117, 171, 204, 230, 299, 313, 318, 322–3. IV: 71, 157, 172, 306, 311, 376, 402, 405, 428, 430
Symphony No. 3 in D, Op. 29 (*Polish*) (1875), I: 200, 250–1. II: 41–50, 52, 60–1, 63, 66, 68, 87, 169, 171, 174, 219, 241. III: 22, 86, 117, 121, 229, 279, 311–13. IV: 150, 302, 439, 441
Slavonic March, Op. 31 (1876), II: 99–102, 133, 246. III: 99, 324. IV: 27, 311, 381
Francesca da Rimini: symphonic fantasia, Op. 32 (1876), II: 54, 68, 92–3, 98, 106–16, 133, 161, 168, 174, 237, 264, 270. III: 105, 204, 211, 298–9, 302, 314, 318, 320, 322. IV: 108, 121, 125, 133, 139–40, 146, 157, 164, 175, 179, 211, 294, 407, 428–31, 438, 442, 469–70
Symphony No. 4 in F minor, Op. 36 (1877–8), I: 105, 189. II: 23, 44, 112, 133, 136–7, 142–3, 153, 159–76, 180, 199, 216, 223, 232, 237, 239, 241, 245, 248–51, 253, 256, 263, 270. III: 17, 22, 65, 75–7, 86, 89, 91, 94, 105, 127, 155, 160, 194, 269, 308, 318. IV: 146, 149–51, 175, 178–9, 280, 427, 431–2, 436–7, 439–44, 451, 466–7
Suite No. 1 in D, Op. 43 (1878–9), II: 293. III: 15–16, 19–23, 25, 30, 34, 62–3, 65, 77, 91, 93–4, 101, 103, 105, 121–2, 127, 226–9, 241, 268. IV: 125, 127, 129–30, 134–5, 176, 182, 190, 279, 298
Italian Capriccio, Op. 45 (1880), III: 95–100, 105, 117, 129, 171, 227, 262. IV: 131, 175, 385
Serenade in C, for string orchestra, Op. 48 (1880), III: 120–5, 129, 170. IV: 74, 108, 125, 131, 137, 139–40, 142, 150, 175–6, 178–9, 279, 295, 326, 385, 401, 432
1812: festival overture, Op. 49 (1880), I: 116, 152–3. III: 117–20, 171, 215. IV: 108, 121, 125, 133–5, 137, 142, 174, 298, 311, 382, 401–2, 405
Coronation March (1883), III: 175, 213–15. IV: 27, 319–20
Suite No. 2 in C, Op. 53 (1883), III: 177, 224–33, 240–2, 252, 268–70, 279, 313. IV: 108, 213, 279, 430
Suite No. 3 in G, Op. 55 (1884), III: 22, 252, 257–8, 260–75, 278–80, 291–2, 309, 313. IV: 13, 125, 131, 137, 139–40, 142, 174, 178–9, 181, 190, 279, 306, 311, 319–21, 325–6, 382, 385, 401, 411, 430–1, 455

A Grateful Greeting: Elegy, in honour of Ivan Samarin, for string orchestra (1884), III: 285. IV: 302

Manfred Symphony, Op. 58 (1885), I: 81, 197. II: 47, 239. III: 160, 204, 211, 296–323. IV: 14, 20, 25–6, 28, 41, 70, 73, 91, 107, 154, 158, 297, 299, 407, 427, 429–30, 437–8, 440, 442–4, 448, 451, 458

Jurists' March (1885), IV: 26–7

Suite No. 4 in G, Op. 61, *Mozartiana* (1887), IV: 112–15, 121–2, 125

Symphony No. 5 in E minor, Op. 64 (1888), III: 270, 324. IV: 133, 146–56, 160, 164, 167, 169–70, 172, 176–9, 186, 211, 281, 365, 368, 387, 389–90, 418, 429, 439, 442, 445, 447, 450, 458

Hamlet: fantasy overture, Op. 67 (1888), IV: 142, 146–7, 149, 156–61, 164, 167, 170, 186, 211, 219, 317, 323, 404, 438

The Voyevoda: symphonic ballad, Op. 78 (1890–1), IV: 285, 293–7, 333–4, 349, 375, 379–80, 386, 416, 428, 438, 442, 444

The Nutcracker: suite from the ballet, Op. 71a (1892), IV: 386–7, 401–2, 404–5

Symphony [No. 7] in E flat (1892) [incomplete], IV: 330, 388–91, 395, 404, 407, 416, 472

Symphony No. 6 in B minor, Op. 74 (*Pathétique*) (1893), I: 194. II: 168, 173, 176. III: 107, 161. IV: 270, 279, 297, 374, 403–4, 406, 418, 427, 443–60, 463, 465, 473–4, 477–8, 487

CONCERTOS, ETC.

Piano Concerto No. 1 in B flat minor, Op. 23 (1874–5), I: 197–9, 335. II: 15–29, 40, 42–4, 52, 65, 67, 87, 168–9, 262–4, 271. III: 16, 62, 70, 83, 85–6, 88, 93–4, 117, 155, 279, 291. IV: 73, 125, 131, 134, 137, 142, 175–6, 179, 182, 190, 217, 280, 319, 321–2, 326, 401, 429, 440, 478

Sérénade mélancolique for violin and orchestra, Op. 26 (1875), II: 28–9, 261, 271. III: 91, 222. IV: 74, 108, 122, 174, 311, 385

Rococo Variations for cello and orchestra, Op. 33 (1876), I: 215, 261. II: 116–23, 253, 264. III: 22, 70, 121–2, 158, 160, 271. IV: 246, 402, 414

Valse-scherzo for violin and orchestra, Op. 34 (1877), II: 253, 261, 271. III: 222. IV: 122

Violin Concerto in D, Op. 35 (1878), I: 262. II: 26, 260–70, 281, 289. III: 83, 105, 149, 151, 163, 171, 211, 222, 278. IV: 125, 130, 137, 141, 178, 219, 223, 281, 350, 385, 405, 472

Piano Concerto No. 2 in G, Op. 44 ((1879–80), III: 77, 79–89, 96, 99, 104–5, 109, 117, 152, 155, 163, 170, 279. IV: 148, 170, 172, 280, 283, 299, 311, 390, 429, 432

Concert Fantasia in G for piano and orchestra, Op. 56 (1884), III: 241, 262, 275–82. IV: 108, 121, 125, 139–40, 190, 219, 390, 404

Pezzo capriccioso for cello and orchestra, Op. 62 (1887), IV: 79, 122–4, 139, 219

Piano Concerto No. 3 in E flat, Op. 75 (1893), IV: 374, 388–91, 465, 472–3, 477

Andante and Finale for piano and orchestra, Op. 79 (1893) [incomplete], IV: 388–9

CHAMBER MUSIC

String Quartet Movement in B flat (1865), I: 80, 83, 118

String Quartet No. 1 in D, Op. 11 (1871), I: 161, 175, 215–20, 251, 257, 281, 298, 300, 302, 305, 310. II: 16, 28, 40, 62, 67, 102, 125, 256, 265, 273. III: 31, 103, 129, 285. IV: 108, 125, 130, 134, 139–40, 276, 311, 380, 402, 411, 439–40, 462

Andante cantabile [*see* String Quartet No. 1]

Serenade for Nikolay Rubinstein's name-day (1872), I: 269

String Quartet No. 2 in F, Op. 22 (1874), I: 298–306. II: 16, 28, 40, 42, 50, 52, 61–2, 116, 133, 273. III: 22, 103, 121, 230. IV: 92, 174, 279, 282, 439–40

String Quartet No. 3 in E flat minor, Op. 30 (1876), II: 40, 61–8, 87, 116, 269. III: 86, 91, 152. IV: 151, 173, 176, 283, 328, 432, 439–40, 448

Souvenir d'un lieu cher for violin and piano, Op. 42 (1878), II: 281, 285, 289
    1. *Méditation*, II: 261

Piano Trio in A minor, Op. 50 (1881–2), I: 105. III: 88, 128, 151–61, 163–5, 167, 222, 271, 321. IV: 92, 130, 185, 280, 298, 327–8, 375, 430

String Sextet in D: *Souvenir de Florence*, Op. 70 (1890: rev. 1891), IV: 113, 278–84, 294, 299, 381, 386, 396

PIANO WORKS

Anastasie Valse (1854), I: 44
Piece on the Russian folksong, 'Vozle rechki, vozle mostu' (1862) [lost], I: 72–3
Allegro in F minor (1863–4) [incomplete], I: 73
Theme and Variations in A minor (1863–4), I: 73–4, 117
Piano Sonata in C sharp minor, Op. 80 (1865), I: 80–1, 87, 102. IV: 408
Two Pieces, Op. 1:
    1. *Scherzo à la russe* (1867), I: 80, 117–18. IV: 71, 131, 409
    2. *Impromptu* (1863–4?), I: 118
Souvenir de Hapsal, Op. 2 (1867), I: 123. IV: 409, 411
    2. *Scherzo*, I: 73
    3. *Chant sans paroles*, II: 271. IV: 71, 386
Pot-pourri on themes from the opera, *The Voyevoda* [published under the pseudonym of 'Cramer'] (1868), I: 136
Valse caprice, Op. 4 (1868), I: 160. II: 66. IV: 409, 411
Romance, Op. 5 (1868), I: 157–8, 160, 197, 200. IV: 71, 131, 411
Valse scherzo [No. 1], Op. 7 (1870), I: 208. IV: 71, 411
Capriccio, Op. 8 (1870), I: 208. IV: 409
Three Pieces, Op. 9 (1870), I: 214, 221. IV: 411–12
    1. *Rêverie*, I: 215
    3. *Mazurka de salon*, I: 117, 215
Two Pieces, Op. 10 (1872), I: 249. IV: 412
    2. *Humoresque*, IV: 139
Six Pieces, Op. 19 (1873), I: 298. II: 125. III: 117, 271. IV: 412–14
    4. *Nocturne*, IV: 137, 139, 380
    5. *Capriccioso*, I: 290
    6. *Thème original et variations*, IV: 131
Six Pieces on a Single Theme, Op. 21 (1873), I: 298. III: 22. IV: 409–11, 416
The Seasons, Op. 37b (1875–6), II: 56, 122–5. III: 164. IV: 414
    Juin: Barcarolle, IV: 130, 137
Funeral March on themes from the opera, *The Oprichnik* (1877) [lost], II: 221
Piano Sonata in G, Op. 37 (1878), II: 66, 260, 263, 265, 273–6, 285, 287, 289. III: 78, 81, 86, 103, 121, 127. IV: 103, 279, 408–9, 414
Album for children: 24 Easy Pieces (à la Schumann), Op. 39 (1878), II: 273, 277–8, 289. III: 51. IV: 414
    18. *Chanson napolitaine*, II: 80
    23. *L'orgue de barbarie*, II: 276, 279
Twelve Pieces (moderate difficulty), Op. 40 (1878), II: 260, 273, 276–7, 289. III: 117. IV: 414
    6. *Chant sans paroles*, IV: 139
    10. *Danse russe*, II: 75
    12. *Rêverie interrompue*, II: 257
March for the Volunteer Fleet [published under the pseudonym of P. Sinopov] (1878), II: 273
Six Pieces, Op. 51 (1882), III: 172–3. IV: 414–15
Impromptu caprice (1884), III: 278. IV: 415
Dumka, Op. 59 (1886), IV: 72, 78, 409, 415
Valse scherzo [No. 2] (1889), IV: 218, 415
Impromptu (1889), IV: 219, 416
Aveu passioné (?1892), IV: 416
Military March (1893), IV: 406, 465
Eighteen Pieces, Op. 72 (1893), II: 77. IV: 374, 407–8, 416–20, 462, 472
    10. *Scherzo-fantaisie*, IV: 388
    14. *Chant élégiaque*, IV: 183, 487
    17. *Passé lointain*, IV: 477
Impromptu (Momento lirico) (?1892–3) [completed by Taneyev], IV: 416

STAGE WORKS

Hyperbole: opera in one act (Viktor Olkhovsky) (1854) [incomplete: lost], I: 45

Music for the fountain scene in *Boris Godunov* (Pushkin) (1863–4) [lost], I: 73
Couplets for the vaudeville, *The Tangle* (Fyodorov) (1867) [lost], I: 124, 175
Introduction and Mazurka for *Dmitry the Pretender and Vasily Shuisky* (Ostrovsky) (1867), I: 117, 214
The Voyevoda: opera in three acts, Op. 3 (Ostrovsky: Tchaikovsky) (1867–8), I: 13, 83, 87, 117–18, 121, 123, 128, 134–56, 158, 160, 168, 174, 176, 204, 215, 227, 232–7, 239, 241, 321. II: 74, 85, 102, 182. III: 50, 119–20, 185. IV: 40, 72, 382
Recitatives and chorus for Auber's *Le Domino noir* (1868) [lost], I: 156–7, 160
Undine: opera in three acts (de la Motte Fouqué (translated Zhukovsky): Sollogub) (1869) [destroyed; fragments only survive], I: 174–7, 206, 209–10, 214, 225, 227, 257, 288, 290. II: 74, 273. III: 36, 320. IV: 428, 441
'Chorus of flowers and insects', for an opera, *Mandragora* (Rachinsky) (1869–70), I: 196, 206–8, 211, 214, 248
The Oprichnik: opera in four acts (Lazhechnikov: Tchaikovsky) (1870–2), I: 97, 154, 196, 208–9, 213–15, 221–2, 224–45, 248, 251, 253, 255, 282–4, 298, 306–9, 311–12, 318, 320–1, 328. II: 16, 40, 74, 102, 182, 221, 295–6. III: 35, 50, 99, 129, 185, 187, 189, 191–3, 197, 201, 260, 320. IV: 39–40, 69, 173, 256, 273, 309, 359, 406, 426, 429, 460, 475, 486
Couplets for Beaumarchais's *Le Barbier de Séville* (translated Sadovsky) (1872), I: 250
Incidental music to *The Snowmaiden*, Op. 12 (Ostrovsky) (1873), I: 176, 284–90, 298. III: 163, 171. IV: 302
Vakula the Smith: opera in four acts, Op. 14 (Gogol: Polonsky) (1874: rev. and renamed *Cherevichki*, 1885), I: 155, 308–35. II: 16, 20, 24, 28–9, 41, 51–2, 61, 87–8, 102, 107, 116, 120, 157, 195, 198–9, 217. III: 15, 27, 34–5, 50, 69, 121, 176, 184, 287. IV: 14, 23, 25, 30, 46, 69, 71, 83, 89–90, 93, 98–104, 116, 125, 127, 185, 189, 269, 313, 359, 366, 370, 381, 416, 429, 469
Les caprices d'Oxane [see *Vakula the Smith*]
Swan Lake: ballet in four acts, Op. 20 (Begichev and Heltser) (1875–6), I: 152–3, 176, 221–2. II: 41–2, 50, 53–4, 67–87, 93, 114, 125, 133, 194, 247, 276, 278. III: 94, 127, 209, 270, 320. IV: 89, 137, 189, 195–6, 198–201, 206–7, 283, 339, 344, 349, 352, 427–8
Eugene Onegin: lyric scenes in three acts, Op. 24 (Pushkin: K. Shilovsky and Tchaikovsky) (1877–8), I: 97, 144, 150, 204, 241, 313, 335. II: 30, 38, 60, 67, 86, 124, 137, 143–4, 146, 153, 159–60, 168, 176–219, 239, 241, 246–7, 249, 253, 256, 259, 280–1, 293. III: 31–2, 44–5, 48, 50, 54, 61, 70, 83, 103, 109, 111, 126, 130, 132, 144, 158, 160, 163, 184, 191, 193–6, 203–4, 254–5, 281, 283–5, 287–8, 290, 293, 300, 320–1. IV: 13, 20–1, 26, 31–2, 40, 43, 49, 52, 54, 58, 71, 74, 89, 101, 111–12, 158, 162, 169–71, 174, 183, 188, 190, 218, 231–2, 239, 243, 246–9, 251, 253, 259, 262–3, 266–8, 270, 285, 307, 336, 359, 367, 370, 376, 385, 387, 395, 416–17, 422, 426, 429, 432, 461, 469
The Maid of Orléans: opera in four acts (Schiller (translated Zhukovsky): Tchaikovsky) (1878–9), II: 278. III: 16, 19, 23–31, 34–61, 67, 69–70, 73, 75, 85, 94, 100, 102, 104, 107, 115, 120, 126–7, 129–33, 144, 147, 163, 170, 173, 175–6, 184, 193, 199, 209, 227, 287, 320. IV: 46, 58, 69, 183, 239, 359, 364, 367, 370, 378, 385, 406, 429, 475
Montenegrin tableau (1880) [lost], III: 98–100
Duet from *Romeo and Juliet* (Shakespeare (translated Sokolovsky)) (1881 or 1893) [unfinished: completed by Taneyev], II: 280. III: 147, 149–50
Mazepa: opera in three acts (Pushkin: Burenin, rev. Tchaikovsky) (1881–3), I: 335. III: 138, 143, 147, 149–51, 168–9, 171–205, 209–10, 212–14, 218–19, 221–2, 224–6, 240, 251–3, 255, 277, 283–4, 287–8, 291, 298, 320. IV: 13–14, 23, 39–40, 43, 48, 49, 52, 54, 56, 58, 69, 71, 74, 79, 89, 104, 157, 183, 196, 239, 243, 270, 284, 359, 364, 367, 371, 405, 422
Cherevichki (1885) [see *Vakula the Smith*]
The Enchantress: opera in four acts (Shpazhinsky) (1885–7), I: 335. IV: 13–14, 28–64, 66, 70, 72, 80, 85–6, 90, 92, 101, 103–4, 107–8, 110–12, 120–1, 125, 144, 146, 185, 213, 222, 228, 231–2, 239, 243, 247, 268, 275, 277–8, 295, 309, 333, 359–62, 366–8, 429–30
The Sorceress [see *The Enchantress*]
Domovoy's Monologue: melodrama for the play, *The Voyevoda* (Ostrovsky) (1886), IV: 72
The Sleeping Beauty: ballet in a prologue and three acts, Op. 66 (Perrault: Vsevolozhsky and Petipa) (1888–9), II: 75, 85, 217. III: 230. IV: 164, 173–4, 178, 183–216, 218–19, 228, 278, 311, 333, 339–40, 344–6, 352, 376, 386, 415, 427–30
The Queen of Spades: opera in three acts, Op. 68 (Pushkin: M. and P. Tchaikovsky) (1890), I: 334. II: 120. IV: 145, 164, 198, 227–73, 275–8, 284–5, 299–300, 303, 306–9, 311, 334, 340, 359, 371, 375, 378–80, 382, 385–6, 395, 401–3, 422, 432, 464, 473, 486
Incidental music for *Hamlet* (Shakespeare) (1891), III: 285. IV: 300–5

Iolanta: opera in one act (H. Hertz (translated Zotov): M. Tchaikovsky) (1891), IV: 40, 300, 308, 332–6, 353–71, 373, 376, 379, 381–2, 387–8, 393, 395–6, 426, 473

The Nutcracker: ballet in two acts, Op. 71 (Dumas *père*, after E. T. A. Hoffmann: Petipa) (1891–2), I: 114. II: 76. III: 23, 271. IV: 115, 196, 200, 293, 301, 308–9, 311–12, 332–53, 367, 373–4, 376, 386–8, 393, 395, 427, 430, 452

CHORAL WORKS

An oratorio (1863–4) [lost], I: 73. II: 35
'At bedtime' (Ogaryov), for unaccompanied chorus (1863–4), I: 73–4. II: 35
Cantata: 'An die Freude' (Schiller (translated Axakov and others)) (1865), I: 83–6, 89, 95, 127, 130, 146, 169, 250–1. II: 52. III: 215
'Nature and love' (Tchaikovsky): trio for SSA and piano (1870), I: 214–15
Cantata in commemoration of the bicentenary of Peter the Great (Polonsky) (1872), I: 248, 250–1, 253. II: 46, 52. III: 215
Cantata in celebration of the golden jubilee of Osip Petrov (Nekrasov) (1875), II: 52
Liturgy of St John Chrysostom, for unaccompanied chorus, Op. 41 (1878), II: 231, 281, 283–6, 289. III: 71, 105, 108, 129, 132, 138, 142, 170, 287. IV: 15–16
All-night Vigil, for unaccompanied chorus, Op. 52 (1881–2), III: 138–43, 164–5, 210. IV: 15–16
Couplets on Glinka's *A Life for the Tsar*, linked with the Russian National Anthem (1883), III: 213–14, 218
Moscow: coronation cantata (Maikov) (1883), III: 175, 214–18, 223, 266. IV: 267
Nine Sacred Pieces for unaccompanied chorus (1884–5), III: 285–7. IV 14–19, 85
    6. Lord's Prayer, IV: 321
Hymn in honour of SS Cyril and Methodius (Tchaikovsky), for unaccompanied chorus (1885), IV: 15
Jurists' Song (Tchaikovsky), for unaccompanied chorus (1885), IV: 26–8
'An angel weeping', for unaccompanied chorus (1887), IV: 122–3
'The golden cloud has slept' (Lermontov), for unaccompanied chorus (1887), IV: 122–3
'Blessed is he who smiles' (Grand Duke Konstantin Konstantinovich), for unaccompanied men's chorus (1887), III: 103. IV: 122–3, 173
'The Nightingale' (Tchaikovsky), for unaccompanied chorus (1889), IV: 173
A Greeting to Anton Rubinstein (Polonsky), for unaccompanied chorus (1889), IV: 219, 416
'Legend' (Pleshcheyev), for unaccompanied chorus [arrangement of the solo song, Op. 54, No. 5] (1889), IV: 321
''Tis not the cuckoo' (Tsïganov), for unaccompanied chorus (1891), IV: 309
'Without time, without season' (Tsïganov), for unaccompanied women's chorus (1891), IV: 309
'The voice of mirth grew silent' (Pushkin), for unaccompanied men's chorus (1891), IV: 309
'Night' (Tchaikovsky), for SATB and piano [reworked from Mozart's Fantasia, K.475], IV: 406, 477

SONGS

'Our mama in St Petersburg' (with sister Sasha) (1844) [lost], I: 22, 28
'My genius, my angel, my friend' (Fet) (*c.* 1857–8), I: 45, 73
'Zemfira's Song' (Pushkin) (*c.* 1857–60), I: 73
'Mezza notte' (anon) (?1860–1), I: 73, 118
Six Romances, Op. 6 (1869), I: 201–6, 208. III: 117
    1. 'Do not believe, my friend' (A. Tolstoy), I: 273
    2. 'Not a word, O my friend' (Pleshcheyev, after Hartmann), I: 273
    3. 'It's both bitter and sweet' (Rostopchina), I: 208, 215. IV: 321
    4. 'A tear trembles' (A. Tolstoy), IV: 140
    6. 'None but the lonely heart' (Mey, after Goethe), I: 214, 273. II: 31. IV: 139, 427
'To forget so soon' (Apukhtin) (1870), I: 214–15, 270
Six Romances, Op. 16 (1872–3), I: 269–73, 290. II: 29
'Blue eyes of spring' (Mikhaylov, after Heine) (1873), I: 298. II: 29

'Take my heart away' (Fet) (1873), I: 298. II: 29–31
Six Romances, Op. 25 (1874–5), II: 29–35
Six Romances, Op. 27 (1875), II: 29–30, 35–8. III: 288
Six Romances, Op. 28 (1875), II: 29–30, 35, 38–40
'We have not far to walk' (Grekov) (1875), II: 30
'I should like in a single word' (Mey, after Heine) (1875), II: 30–1
Six Romances, Op. 38 (1878), II: 281–2, 289
    1. 'Don Juan's serenade' (A. Tolstoy), IV: 140, 176, 306
    5. 'The love of a dead man' (Lermontov), II: 257
    6. 'Pimpinella' (Tchaikovsky, after a Florentine popular song), II: 258–9
Six Duets, Op. 46 (1880), III: 107–9, 117, 121
    2. 'Scottish ballad' (Scottish ballad 'Edward': translated A. Tolstoy), IV: 432
Seven Romances, Op. 47 (1880), II: 258. III: 107, 109–12, 117, 121, 287
    6. 'Does the day reign?' (Apukhtin), IV: 139
Sixteen Children's Songs, Op. 54 (1881–3), III: 230, 234–8, 264, 287
Six Romances, Op. 57 (1884), III: 281, 287–90. IV: 25, 86
Twelve Romances, Op. 60 (1886), IV: 30, 85–9, 124
Six Romances, Op. 63 (Grand Duke Konstantin Konstantinovich) (1887), III: 103. IV: 122, 124–5
Six Romances (on French texts), Op. 65 (1888), I: 197. III: 109. IV: 160–6
    4. 'Qu'importe que l'hiver?' (Collin), IV: 432
Six Romances, Op. 73 (Rathaus), IV: 374, 463–5, 472
    6. 'Again, as before, alone', IV: 427, 432–3

ARRANGEMENTS

Schumann, Adagio and Allegro brillante from *Etudes symphoniques*, Op. 13. Orchestrated (1864), I: 75
K. Kral, Festival March. Orchestrated (1867) [lost], I: 120
Dargomïzhsky, *Little Russian Kazachok*. Arranged for piano (1868), I: 120
50 Russian Folksongs. Arranged for piano duet (1868–9), I: 77, 143, 160–4, 179, 220, 234, 257, 287, 324. II: 102, 278. III: 119–20, 124
A. Rubinstein, *Ivan the Terrible*: musical picture for orchestra. Arranged for piano duet (1869), I: 180
A. Rubinstein, *Don Quixote*: musical picture for orchestra. Arranged for piano duet (1870), I: 214
V. Prokunin, 65 Russian Folksongs. Edited, with piano arrangements by Tchaikovsky (1872), I: 107, 287, 324
M. A. Mamontova, A collection of children's songs on Russian and Ukrainian melodies. Harmonised (1872 and 1877), I: 251, 265. II: 136, 289–90
Laroche, *Karmozina*: overture. Orchestrated (1888), IV: 168, 170, 474
?S. Menter [perhaps Liszt], *Ungarische Zigeunerweisen*, for piano. Arranged for piano and orchestra (?1893), IV: 402

MAJOR LITERARY WORKS

Translation into Russian of F.-A. Gevaert, *Traité général d'instrumentation* (1865), I: 80, 83, 93, 128. IV: 401
Guide to the practical study of harmony (1871), I: 223
A short manual of harmony adapted to the study of religious music in Russia (1874–5), II: 28
Translation of da Ponte's libretto for Mozart's *Le nozze di Figaro* (1875), II: 56. III: 266, 274

CUMULATIVE INDEX OF PERSONS

Abaza, Yuliya Fyodorovna (d. 1915), II: 180. III: 104

Abraham, Gerald, I: 13, 137, 153, 243. II: 30, 193. III: 45, 49, 112, 195. IV: 148, 363

Adam, Adolphe (1803–56), I: 39, 52. IV: 187, 190, 200

Adamov, Vladimir Stepanovich (1838–77), I: 42, 59, 179, 212, 215. II: 152

Adamova, Sofya Stepanovna (fl. 1860), I: 52

Akulina [inhabitant of Votkinsk], IV: 399

Albert, Eugen d' (1864–1932), III: 241, 278–9. IV: 108–9

Albrecht, Anna Leontyevna, IV: 28, 103, 463, 473

Albrecht, Evgeny Karlovich (1842–94), IV: 279

Albrecht, Konstantin [Karl] Karlovich (1836–93), I: 93, 101, 172–3, 223. II: 17, 69, 94, 146, 155, 157, 179, 241, 243, 249–50, 295, 297. III: 151, 275–6. IV: 23–4, 28, 80, 84, 103, 123, 166, 173, 184, 461–3, 472

Alexandr I, Tsar (1777–1825), IV: 228

Alexandr II, Tsar (1818–81), I: 60, 97. II: 99, 226. III: 98–9, 118, 134, 137. IV: 421

Alexandr III, Tsar (1845–94), I: 101, 116–17, 126. III: 135, 144, 146, 175–7, 213–15, 218, 223, 225, 252, 254–5, 267–8, 276, 281, 284–6. IV: 13, 15, 99, 112, 131, 145–6, 188, 307–8, 335, 405, 411, 462, 473, 483–5, 487

Alexandrova, Elizaveta Mikhailovna [see Tchaikovskaya]

Alexandrova-Kochetova, Alexandra Dormidontovna (1833–1902), II: 180

Alexandrova-Levenson, Anna Yakovlevna (1856–1930), IV: 67

Alexey [footman], II: 88, 288

Alexeyev, Nikolay Alexandrovich (1852–93), III: 213. IV: 65–6

Alexeyev, Venedikt, IV: 399

Alexeyeva, Ekaterina Andreyevna (1805–82), I: 20, 43–4

Alma-Tadema, Lawrence (1836–1912), IV: 468

Alois, Ladislaw, IV: 402

Alopeus, Ivan Samoylovich (1824–1904), I: 40

Altani, Ippolit Karlovich (1846–1919), III: 119, 171, 177. IV: 71, 90, 98, 103, 108, 232, 277

Alyabyev, Alexandr Alexandrovich (1787–1851), I: 39. II: 223

Alyosha [see Davïdov, Alexey Vasilyevich]

Alyosha [see Sofronov, Alexey Ivanovich]

Amici [Roman boy street singer], II: 257

Antonini, Giacomo, II: 218–19

Antropov, Luka Nikolayevich (1843–84), III: 149

Apukhtin, Alexey Nikolayevich (1840–93), I: 41, 52, 59, 66, 82, 94, 99–100, 134–5, 179, 214–15, 270, 290. II: 38, 293–4. III: 15, 111. IV: 88, 285, 461, 474, 476

Arensky, Anton Stepanovich (1861–1906), III: 224, 251, 255. IV: 25, 28, 104–7, 111, 305, 379, 396, 406

Arisha [inhabitant of Votkinsk], IV: 399

Artôt, Désirée (1835–1907), I: 156–60, 174, 184, 197–200, 208, 275. II: 20, 24, 43, 56. III: 109. IV: 160–5, 174–5, 332, 411

Asafyev, Boris Vladimirovich (1884–1949), IV: 245

Assier, Alexandra Andreyevna [see Tchaikovskaya]

Assier, Andrey (fl. 1805–13), I: 20

Assier, Ekaterina Andreyevna [see Alexeyeva]

Assier, Mikhail [Misha] Andreyevich, II: 132

Assier, Olga Grigoryevna, II: 132

Astarita, Gennaro (c. 1745/6–after 1803), IV: 246

Auber, Daniel (1782–1871), I: 156–7, 160, 276

Auclair [family], IV: 77, 117, 140

Auer, Leopold (1845–1930), I: 216. II: 28, 261–2. III: 103, 163. IV: 174, 196, 279, 299, 302, 472–3

Avé-Lallemant, Theodor (1806–90), IV: 132, 149–50, 178

Avenarius, Vasily Petrovich (1839–1919), II: 116

Averkiev, Dmitri Vasilyevich (1836–1905), III: 149–50

Avramova, Anna Konstantinovna (1848–1918), IV: 412

Axakov, Konstantin Sergeyevich (1817–60), III: 230

Axakov, Sergey Timofeyevich (1791–1859), IV: 82

Axel [see Samberg, Axel Ivanovich]

Azanchevsky, Mikhail Pavlovich (1839–81), II: 60, 254

Baccarat, Eduard-Prosper, Baron de (fl. 1852), I: 40

Bach, Johann Sebastian (1685–1750), I: 45, 63, 69, 277. II: 53. III: 86, 93, 124, 307, 309. IV: 26, 96, 106, 115, 128, 179, 185, 198, 410

Bakhireva, Avdotya Yakovlevna (d. 1880), I: 210

Bakhmetyev, Nikolay Ivanovich (1807–91), II: 283. III: 70

Balakirev, Mily Alexeyevich (1837–1910), I: 18–19, 43, 60, 68, 71, 84, 124–8, 130–3, 154, 161–3, 167–75, 178–87, 189, 195–7, 201, 207–8, 210–11, 214, 221, 224, 227, 233, 247–8, 265, 277, 279, 281–3, 293, 295, 308. II: 35, 91, 112, 114, 126, 174–5, 228–30, 299. III: 91, 204–5, 251, 286, 291, 296–306, 309, 311, 314, 322–5. IV: 71, 91–2, 97, 105, 107, 109, 156, 172, 303, 409, 422–3, 427

Barbier, Jules (1822–1901), III: 25–6, 43

Barcewicz, Stanislaw (1858–1929), II: 261, 271. III: 285. IV: 385

Barnett, John Francis (1837–1916), IV: 468

Barrière, Théodore (1823–77), IV: 179

Bartók, Béla (1881–1945), I: 301. IV: 265

Baskin, Vladimir Sergeyevich (1855–1913), IV: 232, 335

Batyushkov, Konstantin Nikolayevich (1787–1855), I: 165. IV: 244, 246

Bazilevskaya, Alexandra [Sasha] Vladimirovna (1862–1937), III: 261, 292

Bazilevskaya, Ekaterina [Tusya] Petrovna (d. 1884), III: 261–2

Beaumarchais, Pierre (1732–99), I: 250

Beauplan, II: 192

Becker [piano maker], II: 133

Becker, Franz Davidovich (fl. 1850–2), I: 43

Beethoven, Ludwig van (1770–1827), I: 45, 58–60, 63, 67, 70–1, 83, 109, 173, 204, 211, 265, 277–80, 284, 309. II: 49, 55, 96, 127, 129, 162–3, 168, 172, 174, 256. III: 27, 92, 104, 152, 188, 212, 308. IV: 41, 74, 76, 95–6, 100, 106, 109, 113, 133, 179, 219, 320, 360, 365–6, 417, 458, 467, 478

Begichev, Vladimir Petrovich (1828–91), I: 97, 134, 175, 284. II: 70

Begicheva, Mariya Vasilyevna (1830–79), I: 97

Bekleshev, Pyotr Platonovich (fl. 1856), I: 49

Bélard [family], IV: 180, 386, 400

Bellermann, Gottfried Heinrich (1832–1903), I: 60

Bellini, Vincenzo (1801–35), I: 27, 45, 52, 275. II: 243. IV: 106, 272

Belyayev, Mitrofan Petrovich (1836–1904), III: 287. IV: 71, 91, 172, 465

Benardaky, Mariya Pavlovna (d. 1913), IV: 139, 181–2

Benardaky, Nikolay Dmitriyevich (d. 1910), IV: 139, 181

Benckendorf, Dmitri Alexandrovich, IV: 277–8

Beningsen, Alexandra Karlovna (1849–1929), III: 292

Benoit, Peter (1834–1901), IV: 396

Benson, Lionel, IV: 469

Berezovsky, Maxim Sozontovich (1745–77), II: 283

Berg, Fyodor Nikolayevich (1840–1909), II: 16

Berger, Francesco (1834–1933), IV: 141, 468, 473

Berlioz, Hector (1803–69), I: 60, 70, 72, 77–8, 125–6, 170–1, 174, 196, 207, 258, 279. II: 47–9. III: 29, 89–90, 101, 212, 296–9, 302–3, 306–8, 313–14. IV: 127, 139, 160, 179, 304, 320

Bernard, Nikolay Matveyevich (1844–1905), II: 56, 122

Bernhardt, Sarah (1844–1923), III: 24, 166, 212. IV: 331

Berrard, Joseph (1800–83), I: 36, 39

Bertenson, Lev Bernadovich, IV: 480–1, 485

Bertenson, Vasily Bernardovich (1853–1933), IV: 479–80, 485

Bessel, Vasily Vasilyevich (1843–1907), I: 63, 68, 83, 180, 214, 224–6, 256, 281–2, 290, 298, 308, 311. II: 28–31, 35, 67, 149, 295. III: 93, 126, 298. IV: 91, 101, 273

Bettaque, Kathi, IV: 385

Bevignani, Enrico (1841–1903), III: 130

Beyl [cellist], IV: 485

Bial, Karl (1833–92), I: 221

Bilse, Benjamin (1816–1902), II: 108. III: 31, 285

Birkett, Kupava, IV: 487

Biryukov, Alexandr Ivanovich, II: 291. III: 247

Bismarck, Otto von (1815–98), IV: 331

Bizet, Georges (1838–75), I: 262, 277. II: 58–60, 199, 260. III: 17, 22, 115, 210, 240. IV: 44, 50, 62, 78, 243, 406, 431

Blumenfeld, Stanislav Mikhailovich (1850–97), III: 137, 169, 171, 173, 208, 220, 239, 241, 253, 266, 286. IV: 299

Bob [see Davidov, Vladimir Lvovich]

Bocharov, Mikhail Ilich (1831–95), III: 176

Bochechkarov, Nikolay Lvovich (d. 1879), I: 246. II: 287, 295–6. III: 66, 69–70, 73–5. IV: 28, 461, 478

Bock,Hugo[Gustav](1848–1932),IV:160,311
Bogatïrev, Semyon, IV: 388, 390
Bogoslovsky, Mikhail Izmaylovich (*fl.* 1850–2), I: 40–1
Boito, Arrigo (1842–1918), IV: 466, 468–70
Bonnet, Mariya (*fl.* 1861), I: 58
Boris [servant at Kamenka], III: 143
Borodin, Alexandr Porfirevich (1833–87), I: 18, 126, 132, 136, 173, 178, 201–3, 236, 247, 258–9, 282–3, 325. II: 22–3, 228–9. III: 89–90, 98, 129, 276. IV: 109, 174, 304, 402, 422, 424, 487
Bortnyansky, Dmitri Stepanovich (1751–1825), II: 283. III: 107–8, 138–9, 142–3, 147–8, 206. IV: 245–6
Bosset, Vera de, II: 218
Bourgault-Ducoudray, Louis (1840–1910), IV: 78
Bourget, Paul (1852–1935), IV: 76
Bowen, Catherine Drinker, I: 14
Brahms, Johannes (1833–97), I: 160, 280. II: 15, 96, 108, 247. III: 100. IV: 41, 83, 126–9, 133, 138, 150, 176–8, 281, 322, 327, 408, 435, 466
Brandukov, Anatoly Andreyevich (1859–1930), II: 121. IV: 79, 108, 117, 122, 139, 180, 219, 274, 380
Britten, Benjamin (1913–76), III: 230
Brodsky, Adolf (1851–1929), II: 28, 262–3. III: 149, 171. IV: 127–31, 133–5, 143, 176, 216–17, 223, 375, 443
Bruch, Max (1838–1920), IV: 396, 466, 469
Bryullova, Alina Ivanovna (1849–1932), II: 77, 270–1. III: 101–2, 105, 165, 169–70. IV: 379, 408, 417
Buchal, Dr, IV: 138
Budden, Julian, III: 49
Buffalo Bill [*see* Cody, William]
Bugayev, Nikolay Vasilyevich (1837–1903), I: 120
Bülow, Hans von (1830–94), I: 274. II: 15–16, 18–19, 66–7, 96, 102, 108. III: 70, 268, 278, 291–2. IV: 73, 130, 133–4, 401
Burenin, Viktor Petrovich (1841–1926), III: 172, 185–7, 194
Busoni, Ferruccio (1866–1924), IV: 133–4
Butakova, Vera Vasilyevna (1848–1923), I: 66–7, 122–3, 133–4, 174, 208, 213. II: 132. III: 31, 68, 102, 260, 264–5, 287. IV: 411, 479
Buxhövden, Rudolf (*b.* 1870), IV: 479
Byrd, William (1543–1623), IV: 71
Byron, George (1788–1824), I: 126, 170. II: 182. III: 160, 178, 296–303, 306, 311, 314, 320, 322. IV: 106, 183, 305

Calvocoressi, M. D. (1877–1944), IV: 426
Calzabigi, Raniero de (1714–95), IV: 195

Canova, Antonio (1757–1822), I: 307
Capoul, Joseph (1839–1924), IV: 164–5
Carnegie, Andrew (1835–1919), IV: 317, 319, 324, 375
Catherine I (1684–1727), IV: 275
Catherine II (the Great), Tsaritsa (1729–96), I: 334. IV: 82, 228
Catoire, Georgy Lvovich (1861–1926), IV: 84
Červinková-Riegrová, Marie (1854–95), IV: 136
Chaminade, Cécile (1857–1944), IV: 181
Charcot, Jean-Martin (1825–93), III: 212, 221
Charles XII, King (1682–1718), III: 186
Chateaubriand, François Auguste, Vicomte de (1768–1848), I: 32
Chayev, Nikolay Alexandrovich (1824–1906), I: 313
Chekhov, Anton Pavlovich (1860–1904), IV: 174, 222–7
Chekhov, Mikhail Pavlovich (1865–1936), IV: 224
Chekhova, Mariya Pavlovna (1863–1957), IV: 225
Chemodanov, Ivan Ivanovich, Prince (*fl.* 1656), IV: 275
Cherubini, Luigi (1760–1842), II: 247. IV: 23, 26
Chopin, Frédéric (1810–49), I: 163, 279. II: 274–5. III: 45, 302, 314. IV: 190, 364, 408–9, 412, 416–17
Ciardi, Cesare (1817–77), I: 62, 67
Cimarosa, Domenico (1749–1801), IV: 462
Cody, William (1846–1917), IV: 272
Collin, Paul (1843–1915), IV: 162
Colonne, Edouard (1838–1910), III: 29–31, 70, 77, 89, 94, 135. IV: 78, 122, 133, 139, 181–2, 277, 306, 391, 486
Columbus, Christopher (1451–1506), IV: 375
Conneau, Juliette, IV: 139
Coquelin, Constant (1841–1909), IV: 143
Corneille, Pierre (1606–84), III: 101
Cornelius, Peter (1824–74), IV: 179
Correggio (1494–1534), III: 102
Cotogni, Antonio (1831–1918), IV: 306
Cowen, Frederic (1852–1935), IV: 142, 468
Cristoforov, Nikolay Iosifovich (1836–92), IV: 197
Cui, César Antonovich (1835–1918), I: 18, 84, 95–6, 125, 127–8, 169, 179, 227–8, 247–8, 256, 282, 285, 293, 298, 312. II: 16, 19, 46, 60–1, 67, 94, 107–8, 229, 262, 270. III: 36, 89–91, 98, 177, 193, 225–6, 283, 305. IV: 32, 90–1, 101, 109, 140, 147
Czajkowski, Michael (1804–86), I: 282

Dagmar, Princess [*see* Mariya Fyodorovna, Tsaritsa]

Damrosch, Leopold (1832–85), II: 262. III: 94. IV: 321

Damrosch, Walter (1862–1950), IV: 317–19, 321–2, 325, 373, 375, 470

Damrosch, Mrs Walter, IV: 318–19, 324, 373, 375

Danilchenko, Pyotr Antonovich (1857–1908), III: 128

Dannreuther, Edward (1844–1905), II: 19. IV: 143

Dante Alighieri (1265–1321), II: 90, 92–3, 108, 110, 114. III: 201. IV: 106, 156, 176

Dargomïzhsky, Alexandr Sergeyevich (1813–69), I: 120, 126, 131, 133, 279–81. II: 51. III: 229–30, 283, 286. IV: 41, 78, 94, 426

Daudet, Alphonse (1840–97), III: 210, 276

David, Félicien (1810–76), I: 196

Davïdov, Alexey [Alyosha] Vasilyevich (1846–1909), I: 62

Davïdov, Dmitri [Dima] Lvovich (1870–1930), III: 147. IV: 300, 383–4

Davïdov, Karl Yulevich (1838–89), II: 107–8, 149, 240, 294. III: 98–9, 138, 143, 172, 185, 224. IV: 175

Davïdov, Lev Vasilyevich (1837–96), I: 53–4, 62, 66, 80, 95, 175, 209. II: 28, 41–2, 57, 88–9, 99–100, 106, 145, 150, 154, 241, 243, 248–9, 279, 288, 291. III: 16, 63, 65, 68–9, 76, 106–7, 121, 137, 144–7, 149, 167–8, 171, 173, 207, 219, 239–40, 255, 257–9, 261, 264, 266–7, 276, 291. IV: 27, 70, 110, 168–9, 176, 286, 383, 405, 472–3

Davïdov, Nikolay Vasilyevich (1826–1916), I: 80. III: 257–9, 263–5. IV: 168, 383

Davïdov, Vasily Petrovich (1870–97), IV: 168

Davïdov, Vasily Vasilyevich (1829–73), I: 221

Davïdov, Vladimir [Bob] Lvovich (1871–1906), I: 53. II: 57. III: 107, 147, 257, 259–66. IV: 90, 104, 146, 176, 179, 217–18, 277, 284–5, 293, 300, 313, 317, 373, 376, 380, 383–4, 388, 391–4, 399–400, 404–5, 414, 443, 466, 472–5, 482, 485

Davïdov, Yury Lvovich (1876–1965), I: 221–2. II: 88, 241. III: 234. IV: 292, 300, 487

Davïdova, Adèle Alexandrovna (b. 1808?), I: 66

Davïdova, Alexandra [Sasha] Ilinishna (1842–91), I: 22, 34, 36–7, 47–8, 53–4, 56–8, 61–2, 64, 66, 75, 80, 82, 89, 95, 98, 121–2, 133–4, 175, 179, 208, 211, 213, 221, 225, 248–9, 253–4, 308, 335. II: 28, 41–2, 57, 88–9, 98–100, 104–6, 133, 144–5, 149–50, 152–4, 160, 177, 225, 240–1, 243–4, 248–9, 253, 272–3, 279, 288, 291, 293–4, 298. III: 15–16, 63, 65, 68–71, 74, 76–7, 105–8, 121, 125, 137, 143–5, 147–8, 163, 167–71, 207–9, 219, 226, 234, 238–41, 254, 259–60, 262–7, 291, 294. IV: 27, 70, 110, 116, 146, 168, 172, 176,

218, 284–5, 300, 312–14, 333, 378, 387, 398, 405, 411, 414, 472

Davïdova, Alexandra Ivanovna (1802–95), I: 66, 212. III: 257, 263. IV: 168, 383

Davïdova, Alexandra Vasilyevna (1827–1917), III: 257. IV: 168, 383

Davïdova, Anna Lvovna (1864–1942), I: 221–2. II: 224, 293. III: 33, 76, 148, 167, 170, 223, 240, 251, 253–4, 263, 277, 291–2. IV: 25, 70, 76, 102, 218, 284–6, 292–3, 414–15, 482

Davïdova, Elizaveta Sergeyevna (1831–1918), IV: 168

Davïdova, Elizaveta Vasilyevna (1823–1904), I: 66, 212. III: 257. IV: 168, 383

Davïdova, Kseniya Yurevna, IV: 148, 151, 388

Davïdova, Mariya Nikolayevna, IV: 383

Davïdova, Nataliya [Tasya] Lvovna (1868–1956), III: 68–9, 71, 74–5, 106, 148, 170, 257, 264–5. IV: 27, 146, 276, 311

Davïdova, Tatyana [Tanya] Lvovna (1861–87), I: 53, 62, 221. II: 57, 154, 291. III: 107–8, 125, 137, 144, 148, 163, 167–9, 171, 173, 175, 207–10, 212, 218–23, 225, 234, 239–41, 252–4, 264, 276, 286, 292. IV: 67, 85, 102, 104, 109–10, 116, 169, 176, 299, 313, 394

Davïdova, Varvara [Varya] Nikolayevna (1864–1942), III: 145, 257

Davïdova, Vera Lvovna (1863–89), I: 221. III: 107, 147–9, 167–8, 171, 207, 234. IV: 25, 168–9, 172, 176, 182, 276, 414–15

Davïdova, Vera Vasilyevna [see Butakova]

Debussy, Claude (1862–1918), III: 126–8, 241. IV: 438

Dehn, Siegfried (1799–1858), I: 17, 68

Delavigne, Casimir (1793–1843), I: 26

Delibes, Léo (1836–91), I: 262. II: 59, 77, 93, 247, 260. III: 25. IV: 78, 83, 140, 181, 198–9, 212

Dell'Era, Antonietta (b. 1863), IV: 336

Denisyeva, Olga Sergeyevna [see Tchaikovskaya]

Derichenko, Roman Efimovich, II: 291. III: 258

Derzhavin, Gavriil Romanovich (1743–1816), IV: 228, 244

Dickens, Charles (1812–70), I: 91, 120. III: 27, 71, 101, 115, 169, 240, 277

Diémer, Louis (1843–1919), IV: 139–40, 181–2, 389, 466

Dima [see Davïdov, Dmitri Lvovich]

Dima [see Peresleny, Vadim Vladimirovich]

Domenichino [Zampieri, Domenico] (1581–1641), II: 246

Domershchikov, Platon Pavlovich (1850–1900), IV: 227

Domino [pseudonym: critic], IV: 335, 358

Donaurov, Sergey Ivanovich (1838–97), I: 253

Donizetti, Gaetano (1797–1848), I: 27, 45, 52, 67, 275. IV: 106
Door, Anton (1833–1919), I: 160. II: 66, 241, 247. III: 19. IV: 409
Doré, Gustave (1832–83), II: 107
Dostoyevsky, Fyodor Mikhailovich (1821–81), I: 72, 120. III: 29, 68, 71, 247. IV: 174, 318, 421–2, 430
Drigo, Riccardo (1846–1930), II: 76, 78. IV: 334, 485
Druzhin [piano supplier], III: 260
Dubuque, Alexandre (1812–98), I: 63, 91, 117, 123. IV: 411
Dumas (père), Alexandre (1802–70), IV: 332
Dumas (fils), Alexandre (1824–95), IV: 104–7, 111
Durazzo, Giacomo (1717–94), IV: 195–6
Dürbach, Fanny (1822–95), I: 22–8, 30–4, 47, 50. IV: 396–400, 403
Dvořák, Antonín (1841–1904), IV: 76, 136–8, 143, 152, 171–2, 277, 326, 331, 375
Dyagilev, Sergey Pavlovich (1872–1929), II: 217

Eames, Emma (1865–1952), IV: 179
Eastwood, Martha (d. 1909–10?), II: 291. III: 68–9, 263. IV: 300
Edison, Thomas (1847–1931), IV: 331
Ekaterina Mikhailovna, Grand Duchess (1827–94), III: 104
Elena Pavlovna, Grand Duchess (1806–73), I: 59–60, 67–8, 125–6, 171–2, 255
Eliot, George (1819–80), IV: 406, 475
Emilya Konstantinovna [cook] (fl. 1862), I: 61
Erdmannsdörfer, Max (1848–1905), III: 174–5, 209–10, 226, 251–2, 268, 271–2, 278, 304. IV: 13, 70–1, 79, 107, 121, 171, 217, 386
Ernst, Heinrich Wilhelm (1814–65), IV: 402
Ershova, Sofya Alexandrovna (fl. 1876), II: 92
Euripides (d. 406 BC), II: 248

Famintsïn, Alexandr Sergeyevich (1841–96), I: 173, 225. II: 19, 94
Fauré, Gabriel (1845–1924), IV: 78, 83, 140, 181
Fedya [valet], IV: 378
Fénelon, François de Salignac de la Mothe (1651–1715), I: 32
Ferdinando [Florentine boy street singer], IV: 272
Ferré, Dr, III: 239, 241
Fet, Afanasy Afanasyevich (1820–92), II: 29, 257. IV: 378
Feuillet, Octave (1812–90), I: 53. III: 166
Figner, Medea Ivanovna (1859–1952), IV: 174, 230, 269, 307–8, 334–5

Figner, Nikolay Nikolayevich (1857–1918), IV: 174, 230–1, 307, 334–5, 367, 381, 395, 464, 485–6
Fillipov [piano teacher] (fl. 1848), I: 31
Finck, Henry (1854–1926), IV: 323
Fisher, Sofya Nikolayevna (d. 1913), III: 250
Fitzenhagen, Wilhelm Fyodorovich (1848–90), I: 215. II: 117, 120–3, 127. III: 70, 151, 271. IV: 217, 274–5
Flammarion, Camille (1842–1925), IV: 76
Flaubert, Gustave (1821–80), IV: 22, 185, 393
Flegont [Kamenka tutor], III: 208, 257–9, 262–3, 266–7
Flerov, Sergey Vasilyevich (1841–1901), III: 152, 165
Flotow, Friedrich von (1812–83), III: 219. IV: 179
Fouqué, Friedrich, Baron de la Motte (1698–1774), I: 174. II: 273. III: 37. IV: 145, 185, 407
Franck, César (1822–90), IV: 181
Friede, Alisa, IV: 385
Friedrich, Dmitri Avgustovich, IV: 125, 127, 129, 135
Friend [woman pianist], IV: 323
Friskin, James (1886–1967), II: 19
Fürstner, Adolph (1833–1908), III: 91
Fyodorov, Pavel Stepanovich (1803–79), I: 124, 175

Gaboriau, Emile (1835–73), IV: 394
Gabrieli, Andrea(?) (1520–96), I: 180
Galler, Konstantin Petrovich (1845–88), II: 88
Gallet, Louis (1835–98), IV: 181
Galli, Anatoly Ivanovich (1845–1918), IV: 407
Galli-Marié, Célestine (1840–1905), II: 58–9
Galuppi, Baldassare (1706–85), IV: 246
Galvani, Giacomo (1827–89), IV: 103
Garden, Edward, I: 13. IV: 359
Gautier, G. [governess at Kamenka], III: 65, 68–9
Gautier, Théophile (1811–72), IV: 183
Gavrilov, Konstantin, IV: 402
Gedeonov, Stepan Alexandrovich (1816–78), I: 135–6, 156, 175
Gellert, Christian (1715–69), III: 235
Genton, Emma, III: 164. IV: 84, 414
Georges-Léon [see Tchaikovsky, Georgy Nikolayevich]
Gerard, Vladimir Nikolayevich (1839–1903), I: 41. II: 232
Gerke, Auguste Antonovich (1841–1902), IV: 407
Gevaert, François (1828–1908), I: 80, 83, 93. IV: 401
Giraudet, Alfred, IV: 139

Glazunov, Alexandr Konstantinovich (1865–1936), III: 225, 291, 298. IV: 83, 91–2, 125, 172, 180, 219, 271, 278, 349, 374, 380, 465, 474, 479, 485–6

Glinka, Mikhail Ivanovich (1804–57), I: 17–19, 34, 45, 60, 64, 66, 68–9, 71–3, 77, 83, 85, 94, 97–8, 103, 115, 125–6, 131, 143–4, 146, 148–9, 162–3, 168, 170, 176–7, 185, 189–91, 201, 207, 211, 234–5, 238–9, 241, 244, 257, 264–5, 267, 276, 287, 293–4, 300, 306, 308, 321–2, 325, 328. II: 16, 21, 26, 31–3, 36, 39, 43, 47, 51, 78, 80, 99, 114, 174, 217, 236, 243, 249, 278, 281, 285. III: 23, 51–2, 95–7, 114–15, 187–8, 213, 215–16, 218, 272, 286, 313. IV: 24, 52, 78, 92, 94, 100–1, 106, 123, 148–9, 189–90, 201, 219, 269, 310, 351, 371, 409, 423, 426, 487

Gluck, Christoph Willibald (1714–87), IV: 96, 195

Goethe, Johann Wolfgang von (1749–1832), I: 202, 204–5. II: 31. III: 92, 277, 288. IV: 42, 167–8

Gogol, Nikolay Vasilyevich (1809–52), I: 32, 66, 91, 120, 222, 283, 306, 308, 313–14, 321, 325, 335. II: 291. III: 265. IV: 22, 106, 166

Goldenweiser, Alexandr Borisovich (1875–1961), IV: 294

Goldmark, Carl (1838–1915), IV: 179

Golitsïn, Alexey Vasilyevich, Prince (1832–1901), I: 76, 212, 222. III: 133. IV: 79

Golitsïn, Vasily, Prince, II: 41

Golovina, Mariya Alexeyevna (d. 1878), II: 287

Goncharov, Ivan Alexandrovich (1812–91), I: 58. IV: 421–2

Gontard, Dr, IV: 76

Gorbachev, Mikhail, IV: 421

Gorbunov, I. F., IV: 479

Gorsky, Konstantin, IV: 405

Goudeau, Emile, IV: 140

Gounod, Charles (1818–93), I: 72, 157, 160, 179, 276. II: 55, 96, 137, 252. III: 24–5, 86, 219, 307, 309. IV: 78, 92, 140, 179, 387, 432

Grekov, Nikolay Perfilyevich (1810–66), II: 38

Grétry, André-Ernest-Modeste (1741–1813), IV: 246, 248, 263

Grieg, Edvard (1843–1907), IV: 128–30, 133–5, 141–2, 149, 380, 466, 469–70

Grieg, Nina (1845–1935), IV: 128, 130, 133, 135

Grieg, Samuil Alexeyevich (1827–87), III: 117

Griepenkerl, Wolfgang (1810–68), I: 72

Gropius, Paul (1821–88), II: 69

Guercino (1591–1666), III: 92

Guilbert, Yvette (1867–1944), IV: 472

Guitry, Lucien (1860–1925), III: 210. IV: 79, 147, 301–3, 306, 309, 486

Halévy, Ludovic (1834–1908), III: 101

Halíř, Karel (1859–1909), IV: 130, 137

Hamelle, Jacques (d. 1917), III: 222

Hamerik, Asger (1843–1923), IV: 326

Handel, George Frederick (1685–1759), I: 55, 277. IV: 96, 359, 365

Hansen, Joseph, II: 70, 75

Hanslick, Eduard (1825–1904), II: 102, 262–3. III: 151, 163

Hartmann, Moritz (1821–72), I: 202

Hausmann, Robert (1852–1909), IV: 128

Haydn, Joseph (1732–1809), I: 63, 184, 277, 280. II: 285. IV: 96, 133

Heine, Heinrich (1797–1856), I: 202. II: 29–30

Heltser, Vasily Fyodorovich (1840–1908), II: 70–1

Hemans, Felicia (1793–1835), I: 271

Henry VI (1421–71), IV: 333

Henschel, George (1850–1934), IV: 468

Henschel, Helen, I: 67. IV: 468

Herbert, Victor (1859–1924), IV: 326

Herke, Anton (fl. 1862), I: 62

Herschell, Farrer, Lord (1837–99), IV: 471

Hertz, Henrik (1797–1870), IV: 332

Hoffmann, E. T. A. (1776–1822), IV: 332

Holls, George, IV: 328

Holmès, Augusta (1847–1903), IV: 181

Homer, IV: 106

Hopekirk, Helen (1856–1945), IV: 323

Hřímalý, Jan (1844–1915), III: 151

Hubert, Alexandra Ivanovna (1850–1937), III: 151, 171, 304. IV: 28, 170, 184, 217, 273, 277

Hubert, Nikolay Albertovich (1840–88), I: 223, 247. II: 17–19, 94. III: 131, 146, 151–2, 171, 224. IV: 23–4, 28, 169–70

Hugo, Victor (1802–85), III: 115. IV: 174

Hyde, Edward, IV: 317, 320, 325–6

Hyde, Mrs Edward, IV: 325–6, 328

Ibsen, Henrik (1828–1906), IV: 331

Indy, Vincent d' (1851–1931), IV: 181

Ippolitov-Ivanov, Mikhail Mikhailovich (1859–1935), IV: 69, 74–5, 84, 97, 109, 112, 121, 173, 216, 222, 277, 305, 374

Isakov, Vasily Nikolayevich (1821–91), III: 104

Ivan IV (the Terrible), Tsar (1534–84), I: 227–8, 238

Ivanov, Lev Ivanovich (1833–1901), II: 75–6. IV: 336

Ivanov, Mikhail Mikhailovich (1849–1927), II: 149. IV: 32, 188, 232, 335, 358

Jacobi, Elizaveta Karlovna, IV: 483–4

Jacobi, Nikolay Borisovich (d. 1902), IV: 483–4

Jahn, Otto (1813–69), III: 258. IV: 19, 174

Janáček, Leoš (1854–1928), I: 75
Joachim, Joseph (1831–1907), II: 96, 108, 260. IV: 128
Joan of Arc (c. 1412–31), I: 26. III: 16, 25, 44, 112
Jurgenson, Luiza Osipovna, IV: 408, 416
Jurgenson, Osip Ivanovich (1829–1910), I: 61, 93. IV: 349
Jurgenson Pyotr Ivanovich (1836–1903), I: 28, 64, 80, 93–4, 118, 120, 131, 136, 160, 180, 185, 220, 223, 246, 288, 290, 298, 311, 313. II: 28–30, 35, 38, 52, 69, 71, 121, 150, 155–6, 180, 240–1, 243, 246, 249, 253–4, 262–3, 273, 277, 283–4, 287–90, 295, 297. III: 16, 20–1, 24, 31, 65, 70, 75, 79, 81, 91, 104–7, 114, 116–18, 121, 126–7, 132, 134–6, 138, 142, 144–6, 150–1, 163–4, 170, 172–3, 175–8, 209, 213, 219–20, 222, 224, 230, 234, 249, 253, 255, 257, 260, 265–6, 276–8, 286, 291, 305, 323. IV: 15, 20, 26, 28, 30, 67, 80–1, 84–5, 91, 93–4, 103, 113, 128, 131, 141, 160–1, 166, 168, 170, 173–4, 180, 183–4, 217, 227, 230, 273–5, 277, 279, 284–5, 288–9, 297–9, 301, 310, 349, 375, 379, 382, 386, 389, 393, 444, 463, 472, 474, 478
Jurgenson, Sofya Ivanovna (1840–1911), IV: 415

Kaitmazova, Mrs, IV: 123
Kalishevsky, Yakov Stepanovich (1856–1923), IV: 375
Kamenskaya, Mariya Danilovna (1854–1925), III: 35–6, 209
Kandaurov, Vasily Alexeyevich (1830–88), III: 186. IV: 13
Kapnist, Emiliya Alexeyevna (fl. 1868), I: 129
Karabanov, Pyotr Matveyevich (1764–1829), IV: 228–9, 244
Karadzić, Vuk Stefanović (1787–1864), IV: 88
Karakozov, Dmitri Vasilyevich (1840–66), I: 97
Karpakova, Pelageya [Polina] Mikhailovna (1845–1920), II: 69, 74–5
Kartsov, Georgy Pavlovich (1862–1930), IV: 108
Kartsova, Alexandra Petrovna (1836–99), I: 54
Kashkin, Nikolay Dmitriyevich (1839–1920), I: 61, 89–92, 96–8, 107, 120, 124–5, 129, 137, 146, 153, 160, 165, 180, 198, 206, 215, 220, 225, 246–7, 250, 256, 259, 278, 284, 295. II: 17–18, 41, 59, 69–71, 74, 77, 100–1, 107, 122, 137–8, 142–3, 146, 148, 155–7, 182, 217, 250, 257, 274, 295, 297. III: 117, 151–2, 271. IV: 22, 28, 80, 84, 121, 170, 200, 217, 230, 277, 284, 310, 357–8, 444, 477
Kashkina, Elizaveta Konstantinovna (1846–1910), I: 92

Kashperov, Vladimir Nikitich (1827–94), I: 75, 123, 179
Katya [see Olkhovskaya, Ekaterina Nikolayevna]
Katya [see Schobert, Ekaterina Vasilyevna]
Keiser, Ilya Karlovich (fl. 1850), I: 35
Keiser, Mariya Karlovna [see Tchaikovskaya]
Kern, Otto Romanovich, III: 239, 241, 266
Khamit [Cossack servant], IV: 399–400
Khimichenko, Alexandr Vasilyevich (1856–1947), IV: 351
Khokhlov, Pavel Akinfiyevich (1854–1919), IV: 380–1
Khomyakov, Alexey Stepanovich (1804–60), IV: 86, 88
Klein, Bruno, IV: 323
Klengel, Julius (1859–1933), IV: 127
Klenovsky, Nikolay Semyonovich (1857–1915), IV: 144, 227–8
Klimenko, Ivan Alexandrovich (fl. 1860–1908), I: 124, 185, 209, 215, 225, 255. II: 138. IV: 173
Klindworth, Karl (1830–1916), I: 221. II: 54, 92, 94. III: 146, 285. IV: 84, 174, 409
Knabe, Ernest, IV: 326, 329
Kohne [composer], II: 221, 223, 225
Kolya [see Konradi, Nikolay Hermanovich]
Kolya [see Peresleny, Nikolay Vladimirovich]
Komissarzhevsky, Fyodor Petrovich (1838–1905), II: 180. III: 287–8
Kondratowicz, Ludwig-Wladislaw (1823–62), II: 38
Kondratyev, Gennady Petrovich (1834–1905), I: 226, 310. IV: 307–8, 334
Kondratyev, Mikhail Sergeyevich (d. 1872), I: 227
Kondratyev, Nikolay Dmitriyevich (1832–87), I: 222–3, 253–5, 290, 308. II: 41, 88, 99, 102, 288, 292. III: 69, 71, 78, 89, 101, 133, 135, 149, 164, 166, 220, 223, 257. IV: 23, 25, 80, 84–5, 109–10, 112, 115–20, 122, 143, 166, 178, 276, 408, 412, 414, 461
Kondratyeva, Mariya Sergeyevna, IV: 23, 25, 80, 84–5, 117–18, 414
Kondratyeva, Nadezhda Nikolayevna (b. 1865), III: 164. IV: 85, 408, 416
Konisskaya, Lidiya Mikhailovna, IV: 486
Konradi, Alina Ivanovna [see Bryullova]
Konradi, Herman Karlovich (1833–82), II: 57, 88, 144, 245, 247, 249, 270–1. III: 101–2, 105, 165, 168–70
Konradi, Nikolay [Kolya] Hermanovich (1868–1923), II: 57, 77, 89, 92–3, 104, 245, 247, 249, 251–2, 254, 270–2, 292. III: 33–4, 64, 76–7, 91, 101–2, 105–6, 121, 132–3, 149–50, 163, 165, 168–71, 208, 212, 220, 223. IV: 25, 27, 85, 115, 184, 276–7, 284–5, 379–80, 385, 406, 408, 472, 474–5

Konstantin Konstantinovich, Grand Duke (1858–1915), II: 127. III: 102–4, 133–5, 305. IV: 86, 99, 123–4, 146, 148, 167–8, 175, 177, 244, 309, 377, 387, 405, 476

Konstantin Nikolayevich, Grand Duke (1827–92), I: 253, 310. II: 61. III: 70, 102, 147, 167, 212. IV: 23

Konyus, Georgy Eduardovich (1862–1933), IV: 404–5, 474

Konyus, Jules Eduardovich (1869–1942), IV: 314, 379, 443

Konyus, Lev Eduardovich (1871–1944), IV: 443

Korbay, Ferencz (1846–1913), IV: 323

Korsov, Bogomir Bogomirovich (1845–1920), II: 295–6. III: 196, 287. IV: 103–4

Koryakin, Mikhail Mikhailovich (1850–97), II: 217

Kostetskaya, Pelageya Osipovna, III: 69, 257, 260

Kotek, Iosif Iosifovich (1855–85), II: 129–30, 144–7, 150, 152, 243, 247–8, 260–3, 265, 270–1. III: 17, 24–5, 31, 70–1, 78, 211, 278, 284, 286, 291, 301, 303. IV: 134–5, 461

Koury, Daniel, IV: 455

Kozidub, Pyotr Gerasimovich (fl. 1872), I: 265

Kozlowski Jósef (1757–1831), IV: 244

Kral, K. I. (fl. 1867), I: 120

Krïlov, Ivan Andreyevich (1769–1844), III: 263

Kross, Gustav Gustavovich (1831–85), I: 69. II: 19, 52

Krovishein, Apollon Konstantinovich (fl. 1870), I: 213

Krutikova, Alexandra Pavlovna (1851–1919), IV: 104

Kudravtsev [acquaintance of Tchaikovsky's wife], II: 151

Kündinger, Auguste (b. 1827), I: 46

Kündinger, Rudolf (b. 1832), I: 45–6, 49, 73

Kuznetsov, Nikolay Dmitriyevich (1850–1930), IV: 403

Kuznetsova, Vera Sergeyevna (d. 1955), IV: 484

Kuznetsova-Vladimova, Nataliya, IV: 484

Lachner, Franz Paul (1803–90), III: 19, 226

Lakond, Wladimir, I: 14

Lalo, Eduard (1823–92), II: 260. III: 17, 135. IV: 78, 179, 181, 467

La Mara [see Lipsius, Marie]

Lamoureux, Charles (1834–99), IV: 78, 140, 401

Langer, Eduard Leontyevich (1835–1908), II: 140. III: 117. IV: 334, 393, 412

Laroche, Anastasiya Petrovna (1847–75), II: 40

Laroche, Ekaterina Ivanovna, IV: 166, 217, 271, 314, 408, 418

Laroche, Herman Avgustovich (1845–1904), I: 63, 67, 70–3, 76–7, 83–4, 87, 89–90, 92–3, 120, 124, 128, 138, 143, 153, 156, 165, 170, 180, 207–8, 223, 227, 246–7, 250, 293, 295, 302, 311–12. II: 19, 40, 66–7, 76, 94–5, 107, 110, 148–9, 182, 227, 295. III: 17, 210, 224, 251, 255, 268, 270, 275–7. IV: 22, 28, 83, 90, 94, 98, 103, 120, 147, 166, 168, 170, 189–90, 217, 271, 273, 277–8, 310, 374, 378, 413, 418, 429, 474–5, 488

Lassalle, Jean (1847–1909), IV: 139

Lassus, Orlande de (1532–94), I: 180

Laub, Ferdinand (1832–75), I: 215, 224, 274. II: 40, 61–2, 65–6

Laube, Julius, IV: 131, 178

Lautererová, Berta (1869–1936), IV: 171

Lavrovskaya [Lawrowska], Elizaveta Andreyevna (1845–1919), I: 214. II: 142, 176, 183. IV: 406, 462, 477

Lazari, Konstantin Nikolayevich de (1838–1903), I: 96, 134, 159

Lazhechnikov, Ivan Ivanovich (1792–1869), I: 208, 228, 232

Lefebvre, Charles (1843–1917), IV: 78, 181

Legnani, Pierina, II: 75

Legoshin, Alexandr A., IV: 117, 166

Legoshin, Mrs, IV: 166, 217

Leichtenbergsky, Evgeny Maximilianovich, Duke (1847–1901), III: 104

Leigh, Augusta, III: 306

Lenartowicz, Teofil, III: 235

Lentovsky, Mikhail Valentinovich (1843–1906), III: 166

Lenz, Nikolay Konstantinovich (b. 1858), IV: 407

Léon [Leonty], III: 71

Leonardo da Vinci (1452–1519), II: 252. IV: 265

Lermontov, Mikhail Yurevich (1814–41), I: 122, 170. II: 91, 257. IV: 106, 224

Leschetizky, Theodor (1830–1915), I: 62. IV: 323

Levenson, Osip Yakovlevich (d. 1892), II: 182

Lichine, Grigory Andreyevich (1854–88), II: 296

Lipsius, Marie [La Mara] (1837–1927), IV: 93–4

Liszt, Franz (1811–86), I: 67–8, 70, 72, 77–8, 126, 167, 170, 183, 189, 272, 279, 290, 293. II: 94–5, 107, 110–11, 121, 274–5. III: 89–90, 100, 103, 150, 164–5, 276, 302, 314, 318. IV: 106, 113, 115, 133, 139, 156, 321, 402, 408, 412, 417, 438

Litke, Alexandr Nikolayevich (1879–1918), IV: 292, 376, 478–9, 482, 485

Litke, Amaliya Vasilyevna (1841–1912), III: 115–16, 167. IV: 112
Litke, Nikolay Fyodorovich (1839–87), III: 104
Litolff, Henry (1818–91), I: 72. IV: 474
Litrov, Nazar Firsovich (d. 1900), IV: 272–3, 310, 485
Litvinne, Félia (1860–1936), IV: 306
Litvinov, Alexandr Alexandrovich (1861–1933), II: 253
Lloyd-Jones, David, IV: 294
Lobe, Johann Christian (1797–1881), I: 180
Loginova [see Palchikova, Mariya Markovna]
Lomakin, Gavriil Joachimovich (1812–85), I: 43, 126–7
Lopukhin [family of], I: 124, 175
Lopukhin, Ivan Vladimirovich (1756–1815), III: 258
Louis XIV, King (1638–1715), I: 26. IV: 185, 197, 215
Louis XVII, King (1785–95), I: 26, 223
Louis XVIII, King (1755–1824), I: 26
Lukashevich, Nikolay Alexandrovich (1821–after 1894), III: 35
Lully, Jean Baptiste (1632–87), IV: 185
Lvov, Alexey Fyodorovich (1798–1870), I: 174. II: 283. III: 216–17
Lyadov, Anatol Konstantinovich (1855–1914), III: 89. IV: 91–2, 125, 185, 219, 278, 465
Lyadov, Konstantin Nikolayevich (1820–68), I: 73, 87, 128

Mackenzie, Alexander (1847–1935), IV: 467, 469
Mackar, Félix (1837–1903), IV: 26, 72, 77–8, 108, 117, 125, 133, 139, 180, 311, 391, 409
Mahler, Gustav (1860–1911), IV: 134, 334, 385
Maikov, Apollon Alexandrovich (1826–1902), IV: 89–90, 99–100, 104
Maikov, Apollon Nikolayevich (1821–97), III: 214–15
Maitland, Florence, IV: 471
Maitland, Frederic (1850–1906), IV: 469, 471
Makarov, Pavel Semyonovich (1841–91), III: 36. IV: 32
Makovsky, Vladimir Egorovich (1846–1920), III: 210
Malinin, Fyodor Nikolayevich (d. 1947), III: 111
Malozemova, Sofya Alexandrovna (1846–1908), II: 149
Malya [see Schobert, Amaliya Vasilyevna]
Mamonov, N. N., IV: 485
Mamontova, Mariya Alexandrovna (d. 1904), I: 251, 265. II: 136, 289–90
Manns, Sir August (1825–1907), II: 43

Marcel Karlovich [servant at Brailov], II: 280, 285. III: 65–6, 74
Maréchal, Henri (1842–1924), IV: 78
Margaret of Anjou (1430–82), IV: 333
Mariya Fyodorovna, Tsaritsa (1847–1928), I: 101, 116, 126. III: 254, 293. IV: 30, 86
Marmontel, Antoine (1816–98), IV: 78, 140, 409, 415
Marsick, Martin (1848–1924), IV: 78, 108, 139
Martin y Soler, Vicente (1754–1806), IV: 246
Marx, Adolphe (1795–1866), I: 60, 63
Mascagni, Pietro (1863–1945), IV: 385, 394, 406
Maslov, Fyodor Ivanovich (1840–1915), I: 41–2, 44
Maslova, Anna Ivanovna, IV: 408
Maslova, Varvara Ivanovna (d. 1905), IV: 408
Massenet, Jules (1842–1912), III: 17, 25, 109, 115, 127–8, 135, 252–3, 258. IV: 78, 83, 106, 140, 181, 386, 391
Masson, Michel, I: 26
Maszewski [Polish amateur pianist] (fl. 1845), I: 28
Maupassant, Guy de (1850–93), III: 221, 276. IV: 131
Maurel, André, IV: 401
Mayer, Ferdinand, IV: 317, 324–6, 328–9
Mayor [family], III: 28. IV: 178
Mazepa, Ivan Stepanovich (c. 1644–1709), III: 178, 186–7
Meck, Alexandr [Sashok] Karlovich von (1864–1911), III: 73, 145, 167, 170, 292. IV: 286
Meck, Alexandra Karlovna von (1849–1920), II: 221, 224
Meck, Anna von [see Davïdova, Anna Lvovna]
Meck, Barbara von, I: 14
Meck, Elizaveta Mikhailovna von, III: 291
Meck, Galina von, IV: 292–3, 482
Meck, Karl Fyodorovich von (1819–76), II: 220–1, 224–5
Meck, Lyudmila [Milochka] Karlovna von (1872–1946), II: 224. III: 72–3. IV: 217, 286, 292
Meck, Mikhail Karlovich von (1871–83), III: 224
Meck, Nadezhda Filaretovna von (1831–94), I: 14, 102, 259, 267, 282–3, 286, 293, 313, 319. II: 17, 20, 59, 80, 103, 130–1, 133–6, 140–1, 143, 145–6, 149–53, 159–60, 162–3, 166–7, 174, 177, 179, 220–39, 241–51, 253, 255–7, 259–60, 262, 271, 276, 279–81, 283, 287, 290, 292–4, 296–8. III: 15–19, 22, 24–6, 28–9, 31–6, 48, 62, 64, 66–7, 69–79, 81, 89–95, 97, 100, 102, 104–5, 108–9, 112, 114–15, 117, 119–20, 122, 126–36, 144–51, 164, 166–7, 170, 172–3, 176–7, 206, 209–12,

Meck, Nadezhda Filaretovna von – *cont.*
214–15, 222–6, 244–6, 250–4, 256–7, 265,
267–8, 274, 277–8, 281, 286, 291–4, 300. IV:
24, 26, 31, 41, 67–8, 70, 72, 74–5, 79, 86, 91–
2, 94–5, 97, 103–4, 107, 109, 135, 144–5,
167, 173, 179, 183, 187–8, 198, 216–17, 227–
8, 286–93, 378, 431, 474
Meck, Nikolay Karlovich von (1863–1929), II:
224. III: 76, 78, 145, 167, 170, 223, 240, 251,
253–4, 263, 277, 291–2. IV: 70, 75, 218,
284–5, 291–2, 482
Meck, Vladimir Karlovich von (1852–92), III:
291. IV: 70, 286
Meck, Yuliya Karlovna von (1853–1913), III:
127, 292. IV: 289–90
Mecklenburg-Strelitskaya, Ekaterina Mikhailovna, Grand Duchess (1824–94), IV:
306
Meilhac, Henri (1832–97), III: 101
Melba, Nellie (1859–1931), IV: 306
Melnikov, Ivan Alexandrovich (1832–1906),
IV: 31, 309, 486
Mendelssohn, Felix (1809–47), I: 60, 67–8,
70–1, 100, 102, 257, 279, 295. II: 31, 47, 65,
264. III: 51, 109. IV: 106, 126, 133, 165, 323
Menshikova, Alexandra Grigoryevna (1840–
1902), I: 136
Menter, Sophie (1846–1918), IV: 311–14, 386,
394, 402, 472–3
Mercadante, Saverio (1795–1870), I: 179
Merelli, Eugenio (*fl.* 1868–73), I: 156, 275
Merkling, Anna Petrovna (1830–1911), I:
307–8. III: 300. IV: 27–8, 229, 273, 379,
402, 405, 414
Mermet, Auguste (1815–89), III: 16, 23, 25, 42
Merten, Eduard Nikolayevich (1840–1905), I:
137
Meshchersky, Vladimir Petrovich (1839–
1914), II: 146–7
Metternich, Klemens (1773–1859), III: 100
Mey, Lev Alexandrovich (1822–62), I: 204,
206. II: 30, 36, 38, 257
Meyerbeer, Giacomo (1791–1864), I: 52, 56,
70–2, 241, 243–4, 276. II: 56–7, 249. III: 16,
50, 53, 117, 147, 212. IV: 131, 299
Michelangelo (1475–1564), II: 256. III: 92
Michelet, Jules (1798–1874), III: 25
Mickiewicz, Adam (1798–1855), I: 282. II:
36–7. III: 109. IV: 285
Mikhaylov, Mikhail Larionovich (1829–65),
II: 29
Milochka [*see* Meck, Lyudmila Karlovna von]
Milyukov, Alexandr Ivanovich (*d.* 1887), II:
149
Milyukov, Ivan Andreyevich, II: 149
Milyukova, Adel Ivanovna, II: 149
Milyukova, Antonina Ivanovna [*see* Tchai-
kovskaya]

Milyukova, Olga Nikanorovna (*d.* 1881), II:
149, 151, 296. III: 106, 115–16
Mina [*see* Schobert, Wilhelmina Vasilyevna]
Minkus, Léon (1826–1907), II: 75, 78. IV: 196
Mirsky, D. S., IV: 241
Misha [*see* Assier, Mikhail Andreyevich]
Mitya [Kamenka servant], III: 267
Mitya [*see* Davïdov, Dmitri Lvovich]
Moiseyeva, Zinaida, IV: 67
Molas, Elizaveta Mikhailovna (*b.* 1839), III:
220–2, 239, 252, 291–2
Molchanov, Porfiry Iustinovich (1863–1945),
IV: 402
Molière, Jean Baptiste Poquelin (1622–73), I:
40, 123, 222. II: 291. III: 101, 252, 265. IV:
143
Monsigny, Pierre-Alexandre (1729–1817), IV:
246
Mooser, Aloys (1876–1969), IV: 485
Moskalev, Pyotr, IV: 407, 420
Moszkowski, Moritz (1854–1925), IV: 134
Mozart, Leopold (1719–1787), IV: 349
Mozart, Wolfgang Amadeus (1756–91), I: 27,
44, 52, 63, 67, 71, 146, 216–18, 277–9, 302,
335. II: 56, 225, 285. III: 27, 45, 89, 92–3,
121–2, 166, 212, 219, 225, 255, 258, 261–3,
266, 275–6, 285. IV: 19, 76, 79, 95–6, 100,
106, 112–15, 126, 133, 138, 168, 174, 217,
219, 229, 244–6, 270, 340, 371, 422, 474
Mravina, Evgeniya Konstantinovna (1864–
1914), IV: 230, 308
Mühlbach, Fyodor Fyodorovich, IV: 479–80
Müller, F., IV: 332
Muromtseva, Nadezhda Alexandrovna (*d.*
1909), IV: 411
Musorgsky, Modest Petrovich (1839–81), I:
18, 60, 77, 126, 131–2, 139, 149, 173, 177,
201–2, 225–6, 234, 244, 265, 269, 272, 281–
2, 333. II: 35, 51, 78, 117, 184, 193, 198, 217–
19, 228–9, 278. III: 111–12, 188, 277. IV:
41, 90–1, 269, 422, 425–6, 438, 487
Musset, Alfred de (1810–57), I: 121. II: 38,
292. III: 212. IV: 76

Napoléon Bonaparte (1769–1821), I: 26. II:
248. III: 186
Nápravník, Eduard (1839–1916), I: 186, 226–
7, 247, 256, 293, 310–12. II: 19, 52, 61, 107,
109, 157. III: 35, 54, 75, 98, 102–3, 119, 121,
150, 174, 176–8, 185, 201, 209, 214, 252, 254,
283. IV: 92, 97, 101–2, 107, 120–1, 217,
230–1, 235, 277, 305, 334, 380, 405, 479,
486–7
Nápravník, Vladimir Eduardovich (1869–
1948), IV: 167, 406, 470
Nata [*see* Pleskaya, Nataliya Andreyevna]
Nathan, Johanna, IV: 131
Nazar [*see* Litrov, Nazar Firsovich]

Nekrasov, Nikolay Alexeyevich (1821–78), II: 52

Neumann, Angelo (1838–1910), IV: 180

Nikisch, Artur (1855–1922), IV: 130, 135, 174

Nikolay I, Tsar (1796–1855), I: 36. IV: 421

Nikolay, Tsarevich (d. 1865), I: 126

Nilsson, Christine (1843–1921), I: 274

Nilus [family of], I: 96

Nodier, Charles (1780–1844), II: 142

Noël, Albert, IV: 181

Norris, Gerald, IV: 141, 466

Novácek, Ottokar (1866–1900), IV: 176

Novello, Alfred (1810–96), I: 93

Novïkov, Nikolay N., IV: 378

Novíkova, Nadezhda Vasilyevna, IV: 378

Obolensky, Vladimir, IV: 308

Odoyevsky, Vladimir Petrovich, Prince (1804–69), I: 94, 96, 139

Offenbach, Jacques (1819–80), I: 55

Ogaryov, Nikolay Platonovich (1813–77), I: 74

Ohe, Adele aus der (1864–1937), IV: 321–2, 326, 328, 478

Oldenburg, Pyotr Georgiyevich, Prince (1812–81), I: 40

Olkhovskaya, Ekaterina Nikolayevna (b. 1866), IV: 405, 472, 474

Olkhovskaya, Evgeniya [Zhenya] Evgeniyevna, III: 106–7, 125

Olkhovskaya, Lidiya Vladimirovna (1830–92), I: 22, 25, 27, 32, 40, 48, 56. IV: 67, 397–8

Olkhovskaya, Zinaida Ilinishna (1829–78), I: 21–2, 26, 29–32, 34–5, 40, 45, 47, 66, 82, 99, 120, 123. II: 240, 255. III: 107. IV: 397

Olkhovsky, Evgeny Ivanovich (d. 1877), I: 45, 48

Olkhovsky, Nikolay Ivanovich (1819–92), I: 48

Olkhovsky, Viktor Ivanovich (fl. 1854–5), I: 44–5

Orlova, Alexandra, II: 232. IV: 478, 483–4

Ostrovsky, Alexandr Nikolayevich (1823–86), I: 75–7, 87, 94, 107, 117–20, 123, 136, 139, 144, 174, 214, 232, 284–6, 288–9. IV: 72, 285, 319, 479

Pabst, Paul (1854–97), III: 103, 277. IV: 130, 137, 407

Pachulski, Wladislaw (d. 1919), III: 17, 19, 30, 72, 126, 147, 222–3, 262, 265, 274. IV: 287–92

Pacini, Giovanni (1796–1867), I: 179

Paderewski, Ignacy Jan (1860–1941), IV: 140, 181

Padilla y Ramos, Mariano (1842–1906), I: 159–60

Paladilhe, Emile (1844–1926), IV: 396

Palchikova, Mariya Markovna (d. 1888), I: 27–8, 34. III: 220

Palestrina, Giovanni Pierluigi da (1525–94), III: 150

Panayeva, Alexandra Valeryanovna (1853–1942), II: 259, 270. III: 103, 111. IV: 103, 108, 169, 220

Parasha [see Tchaikovskaya, Praskovya Vladimirovna]

Pasdeloup, Jules (1819–87), II: 102. III: 89

Patera, Adolf (1836–1912), IV: 136, 143

Patti, Adelina (1843–1919), I: 56, 274. IV: 306

Pavel [cook], IV: 276

Pavel Alexandrovich, Grand Duke (1860–1919), III: 133–5

Pavlovskaya, Emiliya Karlovna (1856–1935), III: 177, 283, 287–8, 303–4. IV: 13–14, 29–31, 40–2, 44, 66, 98, 111

Pchelnikov, Pavel Mikhailovich (1851–1913), IV: 381

Pelageya Osipovna [see Kostetskaya]

Pereletsky, Pavel Alexeyevich, IV: 14

Pereselentseva, Anna Vasilyevna, IV: 67

Peresleny, Alexandra [Sasha] Vladimirovna (1862–1937), II: 291

Peresleny, Ekaterina Vasilyevna (1822–98), II: 291

Peresleny, Nikolay [Kolya] Vladimirovich, II: 291

Peresleny, Sofiya Vladimirovna, II: 106

Peresleny, Vadim [Dima] Vladimirovich, II: 291. III: 267

Perrault, Charles (1628–1703), IV: 185, 190

Persephone [see Kostetskaya, Pelageya Osipovna]

Peter (the Great), Tsar (1672–1725), I: 19, 26, 248, 250. III: 124, 178, 186, 215, 240. IV: 421

Petipa, Marius Ivanovich (1822–1910), II: 75–7. IV: 174, 184–8, 191, 195–7, 199, 209, 215, 311, 332, 336, 339–40, 343, 351–2

Petrov, Osip Afanasyevich (1807–78), II: 51, 56

Petrova, Anastasiya Petrovna (1824–93), I: 32–3, 44

Phillips, Miriam, II: 166

Piccioli, Luigi (1812–68), I: 45, 52, 58, 82

Pierné, Gabriel (1863–1937), IV: 181

Pisarev, Vasily Vasilyevich (fl. 1861), I: 54–7

Pissarro, Camille (1830–1903), IV: 265

Platonova, Yuliya Fyodorovna (1841–92), I: 226

Pleshcheyev, Alexey Nikolayevich (1825–93), I: 95, 178, 271. III: 234–6, 290

Pleskaya, Nataliya [Nata] Andreyevna (*b.* 1837), II: 291. III: 260, 262–5, 291. IV: 300, 414, 472, 474

Plesky, Boris Vladimirovich, IV: 383

Plesky, Vladimir Andreyevich, II: 291. III: 268

Pogozhev, Vladimir Petrovich (1851–1935), IV: 227, 230, 486

Pollini, Bernhard (1835–97), IV: 477

Polonsky, Yakov Petrovich (1819–98), I: 250, 253, 306, 308. IV: 23, 124

Polya [*see* Tchaikovsky, Ippolit Ilich]

Ponchielli, Amilcare (1834–86), III: 127

Ponte, Lorenzo da (1749–1838), II: 56. III: 274. IV: 422

Popova, Anastasiya Vasilyevna (1807–94), I: 27. III: 238, 240, 257–8, 260, 263–6. IV: 383, 397

Potekhin, Nikolay Antipovich (1834–96), III: 166

Potter, Henry C., Bishop, IV: 319

Potulov, Nikolay Mikhailovich (1810–73), III: 138

Prach, Johann [Ivan] Gottfried (*d.* 1818), I: 287

Pribique, Iosif Vyacheslavovich (1855–1937), IV: 300

Prokofiev, Sergey Sergeyevich (1891–1953), II: 217–19. III: 23

Prokunin, Vasily Pavlovich (1848–1910), I: 107, 287, 324. II: 126

Pryanishnikov, Ippolit Petrovich (1847–1921), III: 36, 283. IV: 285, 299–300, 382, 387

Pugachev, Emelyan Ivanovich (1726–1775), IV: 13, 146

Pugni, Cesari (1802–70), I: 39, 72. IV: 190

Purgold, Nadezhda Nikolayevna [*see* Rimskaya-Korsakova]

Pushkin, Alexandr Sergeyevich (1799–1837), I: 18, 26, 66, 73, 120, 212, 313. II: 60, 68, 142–3, 153, 176, 179, 181–90, 193, 199, 210, 215–19. III: 117, 138, 143, 178, 185–7, 197. IV: 13–14, 88, 106, 145–6, 167, 227, 231, 241–3, 267, 285, 294–5, 305, 370

Pyotr Gerasimovich [butler at Kamenka: *see* Kozidub]

Raab, Wilhelmina Ivanovna (1848–1917), I: 226, 312. III: 176

Rachinsky, Sergey Alexandrovich (1836–1902), I: 165, 206–8, 215

Racine, Jean Baptiste (1639–99), I: 40. III: 24

Raff, Joachim (1822–82), I: 280. II: 96. IV: 83

Rahter, Daniel (1828–1891), IV: 125, 131, 393

Rakhmaninov, Sergey Vasilyevich (1873–1943), IV: 152, 376, 462, 474, 476

Rameau, Jean Philippe (1683–1764), IV: 185

Raphael (1483–1520), III: 92–3. IV: 179

Rathaus, Daniil Maximovich (1868–1937), IV: 462–5

Ratisbonne, Louis (1827–1900), III: 235

Ravel, Maurice (1875–1937), III: 241

Rayevsky [relatives of the Davïdovs], II: 291

Razumovsky, Dmitri Vasilyevich (1818–89), II: 146, 290. III: 138–9. IV: 173

Reinecke, Carl (1824–1910), IV: 129–30

Reinhard, William, IV: 317, 326, 328

Reinthaler, Karl (1822–96), I: 84

Reisinger, Julius (*b.* 1827), II: 69–70, 75, 77

Remezov, Sergey Mikhailovich (*b.* 1854), IV: 407

René I, King (1409–80), IV: 333

Reno, Alice, IV: 316, 328

Reno, Mary, IV: 318–20, 328, 375

Reno, Morris, IV: 316–21, 324, 328, 375

Repin, Ilya Efimovich (1844–1930), IV: 225

Reszke, Edouard de (1855–1917), IV: 139–40, 306, 308

Reszke, Jean de (1850–1925), IV: 139–40, 179, 306, 308

Rïbakov, Konstantin Nikolayevich (1856–1916), IV: 72

Richter, Hans (1843–1916), II: 95, 102, 241, 262. III: 149, 171

Rieger, Frantisek (1818–1903), IV: 136

Riemann, Hugo (1849–1919), IV: 478

Rimskaya-Korsakova, Irina Nikolayevna (*b.* 1882), III: 234

Rimskaya-Korsakova, Nadezhda Nikolayevna (1848–1919), I: 221, 255–6, 269. III: 171

Rimskaya-Korsakova, Sofya Karlovna (1867–1936), III: 292

Rimskaya-Korsakova, Vera Lvovna [*see* Davïdova]

Rimsky-Korsakov, Nikolay Alexandrovich (1852–1908/9), III: 147, 167–8. IV: 182, 276

Rimsky-Korsakov, Nikolay Andreyevich (1844–1908), I: 18, 84, 126–7, 130–2, 144, 173, 184, 208, 214, 220–1, 255, 269, 281–3, 285, 287–8, 293, 295, 308, 311. II: 19, 42, 51–3, 68, 83, 102, 108, 217, 228–9. III: 89, 97–8, 163, 171, 225, 240, 291. IV: 23, 69, 83–4, 90–2, 97, 106–7, 125, 172, 174, 184–5, 219, 224, 293, 310, 334–5, 349, 351, 359, 402, 422, 465, 474, 481, 486

Roberts, Frederick, Lord (1832–1914), IV: 470–1

Roman [*see* Derichenko, Roman Efimovich]

Romberg, Bernhard (1767–1841), IV: 349

Rosa, Carl (1842–1889), IV: 183

Ross, Ivy, IV: 323, 325

Rossini Gioacchino (1792–1868), I: 27, 41, 43–5, 52, 156, 179, 275–6. II: 89. IV: 106

Rostopchina, Evdokiya Petrovna (1811–58), I: 202

Rousseau, Jean-Jacques (1712–78), III: 29, 32, 248

Rubets, Alexandr Ivanovich (1837–1913), I: 69, 324

Rubinstein, Anna Antonovna (1869–1915), IV: 222

Rubinstein, Anton Grigoryevich (1829–94), I: 59–64, 67–72, 76, 80, 82–4, 86–90, 92, 98–100, 107, 125–7, 132, 158–9, 180, 209, 213–14, 222–3, 274, 280, 298, 308. II: 28, 67, 96, 100, 102, 181–2. III: 80, 90, 98, 121, 128, 135–7, 170, 214, 223, 278, 285. IV: 71–2, 83, 89–90, 97, 100, 109, 184, 217–23, 226–8, 273, 300, 327, 335, 363, 381, 387, 409–10, 416, 478, 484

Rubinstein, Nikolay Grigoryevich (1835–81), I: 69, 82, 87–97, 99, 101–2, 117–18, 120, 124–5, 132, 134, 136, 158–9, 165, 171, 178, 184–5, 207, 210–11, 214–15, 223–4, 227, 246–8, 250, 255–6, 269–70, 274, 285, 293, 298, 310–12. II: 15–19, 28, 40, 42, 55–6, 61, 87, 94, 107, 117, 125, 127, 130, 149, 155, 157, 161–2, 178–82, 227–8, 240, 243, 250, 253–4, 271–2, 274, 287, 294, 296–8. III: 16, 21, 27–8, 30, 70, 75, 78–9, 91, 93, 96, 103–4, 117–18, 121, 129, 135–8, 146–52, 160–1, 174, 210, 224, 278, 305. IV: 23, 66, 84, 221–2, 404, 409

Rubinstein, Sofya Grigoryevna (1841–1919), II: 149. IV: 222, 226

Rummel, Franz (1853–1901), IV: 323, 401

Ryabov, Stepan Yakovlevich (1831–1919), II: 69

Ryumin, Konstantin Ivanovich (d. 1880–90), I: 209–10

Sachs, Willy von, IV: 318

Sadovsky, Prov Mikhailovich (1818–72), I: 96, 107, 250

Safonov, Ilya Ivanovich (1824–96), IV: 184, 407

Safonov, Vasily Ilich (1852–1918), IV: 25, 69, 184, 220, 222, 274–5, 277, 401, 404, 443, 473, 477

Saint-Saëns, Camille (1835–1921), II: 54–6, 58, 102. III: 25, 219. IV: 76, 78–9, 104, 181, 332, 466–7, 469–71, 477

Sakharov, Pyotr Ionovich (1848–95), II: 284

Salieri, Antonio (1750–1825), IV: 246

Saligoux, Dr, II: 243–4

Samarin, Ivan Vasilyevich (1817–85), III: 285. IV: 302

Sandberg, Axel Ivanovich, III: 146, 257

Sandberg, Nikolay Axelevich, IV: 384

Sangursky, Grigory [Grisha] Matveyevich, III: 150, 163, 165

Santley, Charles (1834–1922), IV: 323

Sapelnikov, Vasily Lvovich (1868–1941), III: 80–1. IV: 131, 134, 148, 170, 172, 175, 182–3, 311–14, 386, 394, 407, 417, 472–3

Sarasate, Pablo (1844–1908), IV: 467

Sardou, Victorien (1831–1908), III: 212. IV: 462

Sasha [maid], III: 220–1

Sasha [see Davïdova, Alexandra Ilinishna]

Sasha [see Peresleny, Alexandra Vladimirovna]

Sashok [see Meck, Alexandr Karlovich von]

Sauer, Emil (1862–1942), IV: 175

Sauret, Emile (1852–1920), II: 262

Savina, Mariya Gavrilovna (1854–1916), IV: 111

Savion, Marie, III: 28, 143

Schikaneder, Emanuel (1751–1812), III: 166

Schiller, Friedrich (1759–1805), I: 83. II: 280. III: 16, 24–5, 36, 42–4, 50–1, 215. IV: 138, 475

Schiller, Madeleine, III: 80

Schirmer, Gustav, IV: 318–19

Schneider, Otto (1851–90), IV: 125, 127, 130

Schobert, Amaliya Vasilyevna (1841–1912), I: 32, 36, 53

Schobert, Ekaterina Vasilyevna (d. 1866), I: 36

Schobert, Elizaveta Andreyevna (b. 1823), I: 36, 47, 53, 82

Schobert, Wilhelmina Vasilyevna (fl. 1850), I: 36

Schopenhauer, Arthur (1788–1860), III: 259. IV: 20

Schramek, Ivan Osipovich (1815–74), I: 137

Schreber [steward], IV: 330

Schubert, Franz (1797–1828), I: 71, 204, 206, 217–18, 279. II: 30–1

Schumann, Clara (1819–96), I: 63

Schumann, Robert (1810–56), I: 59–60, 64, 67–8, 70–1, 75, 81, 100, 126, 138, 143, 153, 173, 179, 199, 204, 213, 280, 293, 309. II: 31, 44, 124, 274–5, 277. III: 81, 85, 153, 158, 212, 299, 314. IV: 113, 120, 133, 190, 217, 340, 408–10, 413, 417, 438, 478

Schurz, Carl (1829–1906), IV: 318

Schütz, Heinrich (1585–1672), IV: 321

Scott, Walter (1771–1832), I: 283

Seidl, Anton (1850–98), IV: 318, 325

Semashko, Marian Romualdovich, IV: 225–6

Sembrich, Marcella (1858–1935), IV: 306

Serebryakov, Konstantin Terentyevich (1852–1919), IV: 334

Sergey Alexandrovich, Grand Duke (1857–1905), III: 133–5

Serov, Alexandr Nikolayevich (1820–71), I: 64, 71–2, 84, 89, 124, 274, 306. II: 51. III: 240. IV: 41, 82–3, 94, 426

Sgambati, Giovanni (1841–1914), III: 164. IV: 276

Shakespeare, William (1564–1616), I: 126, 180–1, 185, 283, 292. II: 47, 91–2, 116–17, 256, 279–80, 292. III: 27, 115. IV: 106, 131, 147, 156, 302–5, 406

Shalyapin, Fyodor Ivanovich (1873–1938), II: 218

Shangin, Ivan Ilich, II: 69

Shaw, George Bernard (1856–1950), IV: 467

Sherwood, Vladimir Osipovich (1833–97), IV: 310

Shestakova, Lyudmila Ivanovna (1816–1906), I: 125, 185. II: 51

Shevchenko, Taras Grigoryevich (1814–61), II: 36. III: 112

Shilovsky, Konstantin Stepanovich (1849–93), I: 97. II: 54, 67–8, 87, 142–4, 176, 188–9. IV: 461

Shilovsky, Vladimir Stepanovich (1852–93), I: 97, 134, 178–9, 209–12, 223–4, 234, 248–9, 253, 291–3, 305, 309. II: 41, 47, 58, 68, 99, 138, 144, 146. III: 66, 223. IV: 412, 460–1, 472

Shpazhinskaya, Yuliya Petrovna (d. 1919), IV: 28, 30, 50, 66–7, 103, 110, 116, 132, 146, 170, 218, 379

Shpazhinsky, Ippolit Vasilyevich (1848–1917), IV: 13–14, 28–30, 33, 41–2, 50, 58, 66, 72, 111, 167, 228

Sila [see Uzlenko, Sila]

Sinding, Christian (1856–1941), IV: 176

Sionitskaya, Mariya Adrianovna Deisha- (1859–1932), IV: 308

Sister [see Popova, Anastasiya Vasilyevna]

Sittard, Josef (1846–1903), IV: 132, 179

Sklifosovsky, Nikolay, IV: 182, 487

Sklifosovsky, Vladimir Nikolayevich (d. 1890), IV: 182–3, 407, 487

Skobolev, Mikhail Dmitriyevich (1843–82), II: 246

Skryabin, Alexandr Nikolayevich (1872–1915), IV: 438

Slavina, Mariya Alexandrovna (1858–1951), III: 287–8. IV: 31

Slonimsky, Yury Iosifovich, IV: 485

Smetana, Bedřich (1824–84), IV: 136, 138, 474

Smyth, Ethel (1858–1944), IV: 129, 133, 135, 181

Sobeshchanskaya, Anna Osipovna (1842–1918), II: 75

Sofronov, Alexey [Alyosha] Ivanovich (1859–1925), I: 224. II: 41, 93, 122, 144, 160, 241–2, 245, 247–9, 253, 270, 279–80. III: 15–16, 24–5, 28, 71, 74, 101, 105–7, 126, 131, 133, 137, 143–4, 146–9, 165, 168, 171, 208, 210, 219, 222–3, 225, 241, 252, 255, 259–60, 267,

277, 285, 293. IV: 19–21, 28, 76–7, 103, 116, 143–5, 217, 272, 276, 289, 310, 315, 374, 381, 387, 393, 473–4, 476, 585

Sofronov, Mikhail Ivanovich (1848–1932), I: 224. II: 41, 93, 150, 243

Sofronova, Ekaterina Yakovlevna (b. 1873), IV: 310, 474, 476–7

Sofronova, Fekla Grigoryevna (d. 1890), IV: 145, 217, 272, 276, 310–11

Sollogub, Vladimir Alexandrovich (1814–82), I: 174. III: 287

Solovyev, Nikolay Feopemptovich (1847–1916), III: 98. IV: 32, 231–2

Sonya [see Rimskaya-Korsakova, Sofya Karlovna]

Spasskaya, Adelaida Lvovna (fl. 1862–5), I: 68

Spencer, Herbert (1820–1903), IV: 331

Spinoza, Benedict de (1632–77), IV: 20, 376–7, 393

Stagno, Roberto (1836–97), I: 156

Stanford, Charles Villiers (1852–1924), IV: 134, 468–70

Stasov, Dmitri Vasilyevich (1828–1918), I: 126

Stasov, Vladimir Vasilyevich (1824–1906), I: 7, 125–6, 131, 185, 256, 282–4, 286, 291–5. II: 116–17, 136–7. III: 27–8, 286–7, 296–8, 300–2, 306, 308, 313. IV: 91

Stenbok-Fermor, Duke, IV: 483–5

Stepanov, Vladimir Ivanovich (1866–96), IV: 215

Stiehl, Heinrich (1829–86), I: 63

Stoikov [friend of Anatoly Tchaikovsky], III: 244

Stojowski, Zygmunt (1869–1946), IV: 474

Strauss, Johann (1825–99), I: 83, 119. IV: 190

Strauss, Richard (1864–1949), IV: 133

Stravinsky, Fyodor Ignatyevich (1843–1902), I: 228. III: 36, 177

Stravinsky, Igor Fyodorovich (1882–1971), I: 228, 334–5. II: 86, 217–19. III: 64. IV: 343, 424

Strugovshchikov, Alexandr Nikolayevich (1808–78), III: 288

Sullivan, Arthur (1842–1900), IV: 143

Surikov, Ivan Zakharovich (1842–80), III: 108–9, 112, 235

Susanin, Ivan (fl. 1612–13), I: 7

Suvorin, Alexey Sergeyevich (1834–1912), III: 27. IV: 299

Svendsen, Johan (1840–1911), IV: 141

Svetoslavskaya, Alexandra Petrovna (1869–1945), IV: 408, 416

Svyatlovskaya, Alexandra Vladimirovna (1856–1923), IV: 469

Swinburne, Algernon (1837–1909), IV: 470

Tacitus, Cornelius (*c.* 56–*c.* 120), III: 100
Taffanel, Paul (1844–1908), IV: 140, 181
Tamberlik, Enrico (1820–89), I: 213
Taneyev, Sergey Ivanovich (1856–1915), I: 259–60, 311–12. II: 15, 18–19, 42, 52, 60, 100, 102, 107–9, 161–3, 166, 174, 176, 181, 276, 287, 297. III: 21, 61, 79–80, 93, 95, 117, 123–4, 130, 139, 143, 146, 150–2, 170, 174, 214, 236, 238, 275–8, 303. IV: 23–5, 30, 65, 83, 90, 97, 105–6, 108, 113, 121, 147, 150, 167, 174, 184, 200, 219, 277, 293–4, 296, 310, 334, 371, 385–9, 393, 395, 404, 406, 416, 443, 474, 476–7
Tanya [*see* Davïdova, Tatyana Lvovna]
Tanya [*see* Tchaikovskaya, Tatyana Anatolyevna]
Tarnavich, Alexandr Danilevich (1843–1923), III: 138–9, 258
Tarnovskaya, Elizaveta Petrovna (*fl.* 1866), I: 90
Tarnovsky, Konstantin Avgustovich (1826–92), I: 90, 95–6, 99
Taruskin, Richard, IV: 40
Tasya [*see* Davïdova, Nataliya Lvovna]
Tausig, Carl (1841–71), IV: 115, 412
Tchaikovskaya, Alexandra Andreyevna (1813–54), I: 20–3, 29–31, 33–8. II: 231, 293. III: 69, 77–8, 95, 164, 238. IV: 80, 397–9
Tchaikovskaya, Alexandra [Sasha] Ilinishna [*see* Davïdova]
Tchaikovskaya, Antonina Ivanovna (1849–1917), II: 137–60, 178, 224, 239–40, 242–4, 248–9, 251, 253–4, 272, 280, 288, 290, 296. III: 24–5, 32–4, 66–8, 75–6, 106, 115–16, 125, 134, 144, 149, 162, 219–20. IV: 80–2, 116, 131, 170, 180, 227, 273–4, 292, 487
Tchaikovskaya, Ekaterina Ilinishna (*b.* and *d. c.* 1835), I: 22
Tchaikovskaya, Elizaveta Mikhailovna (*fl.* 1862–93), I: 82, 90, 100, 179. II: 98, 133, 145, 148, 240. IV: 405
Tchaikovskaya, Elizaveta Petrovna (*fl.* 1854–7), I: 48
Tchaikovskaya, Lidiya Vladimirovna [*see* Olkhovskaya]
Tchaikovskaya, Mariya Karlovna (*d. c.* 1830), I: 21
Tchaikovskaya, Nataliya Ippolitovna (*b.* 1876), III: 105. IV: 298
Tchaikovskaya, Olga Sergeyevna (*fl.* 1872–93), I: 255. II: 40. III: 167, 222. IV: 25, 67, 77, 79–80, 473, 484
Tchaikovskaya, Praskovya [Parasha] Vladimirovna (1864–1956), III: 166, 169, 208, 219, 222, 225, 242, 292. IV: 27–8, 69, 72, 74–6, 78, 80, 84, 102–3, 112, 121, 144, 182–3, 278, 285, 316, 391–4

Tchaikovskaya, Sofya Petrovna (1843–1920), II: 292. III: 105. IV: 73, 144, 173
Tchaikovskaya, Tatyana [Tanya] Anatolyevna (*b.* 1883), III: 222–3, 234, 242. IV: 27–8
Tchaikovskaya, Zinaida Ilinishna [*see* Olkhovskaya]
Tchaikovsky [postmaster] (*fl.* 1872), I: 254
Tchaikovsky, Anatoly Ilich (1850–1915), I: 34, 45, 48, 55, 61–2, 66–7, 80, 88–91, 94, 96, 98–102, 117, 119–21, 124, 129, 135, 156–7, 159–60, 165, 174–5, 178, 210–13, 215, 221–4, 227, 247–9, 255. II: 17, 27–8, 40–1, 57, 68, 90, 98–9, 105, 107, 117, 132, 145–50, 153–4, 157, 161, 177, 180, 225–6, 240–8, 251–2, 254–5, 257–8, 260–1, 263, 270, 272, 287–8, 291–3, 295, 297. III: 15–17, 24–7, 31–3, 63–4, 66, 68–72, 74, 77–8, 92, 95, 99, 102–3, 105, 107–8, 112, 116, 121, 132–6, 144, 146–8, 163–4, 166–7, 169, 177, 208, 219–23, 230, 234, 239, 242, 244, 254–5, 257, 268, 275–6. IV: 23, 25, 27, 29, 69, 72, 74–5, 80, 84, 108, 112, 144–5, 168, 182, 217, 277–8, 306, 316, 374, 381, 392, 394, 396, 398, 404, 443, 475–6
Tchaikovsky, Andrey Petrovich (1841–1920), IV: 406, 465
Tchaikovsky, Fyodor (*fl.* 1709), I: 19
Tchaikovsky, Georgy [Georges-Léon] Nikolayevich (1883–1940), III: 221–2, 225, 234, 239, 241, 253, 276, 286. IV: 67, 77, 79–80, 85, 91, 102, 299
Tchaikovsky, Ilya Petrovich (1795–1880), I: 19–24, 26–7, 30–1, 34, 37–8, 45, 47–9, 51–6, 62, 64–7, 82, 99–100, 120, 123, 157, 159, 179, 212, 215, 225, 253. II: 41, 98, 133, 145, 240, 255, 293. III: 15, 32, 71, 75, 77, 95, 102, 238. IV: 397–9, 405
Tchaikovsky, Ippolit Ilich (1843–1927), I: 22, 34, 36–7, 47–8, 61, 175. II: 98, 292. III: 68, 105, 240, 257. IV: 73, 85, 116, 144, 284, 298, 300, 397
Tchaikovsky, Ivan Petrovich (*d.* 1814), I: 20
Tchaikovsky, Mikhail [*see* Czajkowski, Michael]
Tchaikovsky, Mitrofan [Fanya] Petrovich (1840–1903), III: 131
Tchaikovsky, Modest Ilich (1850–1916), I: 19–21, 23–4, 26–8, 30–1, 34–5, 40–2, 45, 47–8, 50–1, 55, 58–9, 61–2, 66–7, 71, 75, 77, 80, 82, 89–90, 94–5, 98–101, 118–19, 121–2, 125, 131, 135–6, 139, 157, 160, 174–5, 179, 206–7, 210–13, 216, 220–4, 227, 232, 238, 249, 253–4, 269, 294, 298, 305–9, 313, 335. II: 16–18, 27, 40, 52–61, 66–9, 76, 87–94, 96–9, 103–6, 116, 125, 127, 132, 136, 138, 142, 144–5, 153, 160, 177–8, 181, 183, 220–1, 224–5, 232, 244–5, 247, 249, 251–6, 260–

3, 270–2, 279–80, 292–3, 295–7. III: 15–20, 22, 27, 30, 32 -3, 36, 51, 63–5, 68, 71, 73, 91–3, 95–6, 101, 105–7, 109, 112, 115–16, 121, 125, 129–33, 138, 143, 146–9, 163, 165–6, 168–71, 173, 176–8, 185–6, 208–10, 212, 220–3, 225, 234, 239–40, 247–53, 256–7, 259, 274–6, 283–5, 290–1, 294–5. IV: 13–14, 19–23, 25–9, 31, 33, 40, 65–7, 70, 73, 75–7, 79–80, 85, 90, 92, 98, 100, 102, 112, 115, 117, 119–20, 128, 134, 137–40, 142–4, 146–7, 156, 164, 166, 168, 173, 177–8, 184–5, 188, 217–23, 225, 227–32, 242–4, 272, 275–8, 284, 292–4, 300–1, 305–6, 309–13, 332–6, 366, 374–6, 378–80, 382, 385, 389, 392–8, 402–3, 406, 408, 414, 443–5, 460–1, 467, 469, 473–8, 481–2, 484–6

Tchaikovsky, Nikolay Ilich (1838–1910), I: 22–5, 27, 30–4, 36–7, 40, 61, 64, 212, 221, 224, 248, 255. II: 40, 89. III: 76–7, 167, 222–3. IV: 25, 67, 77, 80, 85, 116, 173, 284, 378, 397, 399, 473, 484–5

Tchaikovsky, Pyotr Petrovich (1788–1871), I: 20, 48, 215, 246

Terminskaya, Monika Vikentyevna (b. 1850), IV: 412

Thackeray, William Makepeace (1811–63), I: 120. II: 248. III: 27, 101, 115

Thalberg, Sigismondo (1812–71), IV: 324

Thiboust, Lambert (1826–67), IV: 179

Thomas, Ambroise (1811–96), I: 276. II: 96. III: 77, 286. IV: 79, 300, 396

Thomas, Theodore (1835–1905), III: 80

Thurber, Jeannette, IV: 375

Tikhon [servant at Kamenka], II: 291

Timanova, Vera Viktorovna (1855–1942), IV: 412

Tintoretto, Jacopo (Robusti), (1518–94), I: 307

Titian (c. 1477–1576), I: 307

Tkachenko, Leonty Grigoryevich (1857–1921), III: 243–50, 257

Tolstoy, Alexey Konstantinovich (1817–75), I: 202. II: 257, 281. III: 108, 111, 137

Tolstoy, Lev Nikolayevich (1828–1910), I: 120, 202, 216. II: 125–9, 166–7, 298. III: 29, 71, 259, 277, 300. IV: 78, 82, 85, 95, 106, 174, 225, 318, 331, 377, 421, 482

Tovey, Donald (1875–1940), IV: 451

Trepov, Fyodor Fyodorovich (1812–89), II: 226

Tretyakov, Pavel Mikhailovich (1832–98), III: 210, 255. IV: 103, 403

Tretyakov, Sergey Mikhailovich (1834–92), IV: 394

Trubetskoy, Vasily Andreyevich, Prince (1856–1920), III: 144

Turgenev, Ivan Sergeyevich (1818–83), I: 120, 215–16. II: 127, 298. III: 29, 103, 135, 277. IV: 14, 74, 78, 181, 318

Tusya [see Bazilevskaya, Ekaterina Petrovna]

Tyutchev, Fyodor Ivanovich (1803–73), II: 31, 257

Ulïbïshev, Alexandr Dmitriyevich (1794–1858), I: 125. IV: 168

Usatov, Dmitri Andreyevich (1847–1913), I: 313. III: 238, 287

Uzlenko, Sila, III: 247

Vakar, Mariya Petrovna (fl. 1850–2), I: 38

Vakar, Modest Alexeyevich (fl. 1850), I: 34–6

Vakar, Nikolay Modestovich (d. 1850), I: 35

Vakar, Platon Alexeyevich (1826–99), I: 36, 38

Valecka, Eduard, IV: 136, 143

Valzek, Bertha Osipovna (d. after 1903), I 96, 215. II: 94

Varenka [family], I: 52

Varlamov, Konstantin Alexandrovich (1851–1915), IV: 479

Varya [see Davïdova, Varvara Nikolayevna]

Vasilchikova, Mariya Nikolayevna, Princess, III: 104

Vasily [Kamenka servant?], III: 259

Venichka [see Alexeyev, Venedikt]

Vera Vasilyevna [see Davïdova]

Verdi, Giuseppe (1813–1901), I: 45, 52, 56, 213, 276. II: 56, 96, 154. III: 16, 49, 61, 166. IV: 106, 112, 136, 179, 199, 271–2, 297, 381, 405, 466

Verinovsky, Ivan Alexandrovich (d. 1886), IV: 75, 84

Verne, Mathilde (1868–1936), IV: 468

Verstovsky, Alexey Nikolayevich (1799–1862), I: 72

Verzhbilovich, Alexandr Valerianovich (1850–1911), IV: 482

Viardot-Garcia, Pauline (1821–1910), I: 156. II: 58. III: 135. IV: 78–9, 140, 181

Victor Emmanuel II, King (1820–78), II: 252

Vigny, Alfred de (1797–1863), II: 136–7. IV: 181

Villebois, Konstantin Petrovich (1817–82), I: 160–1, 163, 287

Visetti, Alberto (1846–1928), IV: 468

Vishnitsky, Timofey Vikentyevich, II: 291

Vittorio [Florentine boy street singer], II: 257–9, 278

Vladimir Alexandrovich, Grand Duke (1847–1909), IV: 278, 308

Vogrich, Max (1852–1916), IV: 323

Voitov, Alexandr (d. 1966), IV: 483

Volkmann, Robert (1815–83), I: 84

Volkoff, Vladimir, I: 13–14. II: 103

Volokhov [employee at Kamenka], II: 291

Vorontsov-Dashkov, Illarion Ivanovich (1837–1917), IV: 104, 307–8

Vsevolozhsky, Ivan Alexandrovich (1835–1909), II: 75–6, 184. III: 176, 251. IV: 23, 26, 99, 104, 107, 131, 174, 184–6, 188, 195–6, 199, 227–8, 230, 301, 305–9, 312, 332, 339–40, 352, 380, 396

Wagner, Richard (1813–83), I: 64, 70–2, 93, 221, 257, 274, 276, 280–1, 295, 300–1. II: 54, 60, 68, 88, 92–8, 108–10, 114, 168–9, 247. III: 34, 90, 101, 211–12, 219, 223, 278, 316–17. IV: 83, 92, 126,.130, 133, 135, 174, 180, 189, 199, 240, 254, 296–7, 300, 323, 325, 359, 365, 370, 385, 391, 401, 438
Wallon, Henri (1812–1904), III: 24, 51
Waltz, Karl Fyodorovich (1846–1929), II: 69, 181–2. IV: 89, 99, 370
Warrack, John, I: 13. II: 83, 85. III: 80. IV: 267, 352
Weber, Carl Maria von (1786–1826), I: 39, 52, 71, 275. II: 56. III: 29, 133, 285. IV: 134
Weimarn, Pavel Platonovich (1857–1905), IV: 335
Weiner, Eugene, IV: 323
Weitz, Ivan Ivanovich (d. 1858), I: 36
Widor, Charles Marie (1845–1937), IV: 140
Wieniawski, Henryk (1835–80), I: 62, 94. II: 28. III: 89, 102
Wieniawski, Jósef (1837–1912), III: 89
Wiley, Roland John, IV: 191, 195, 197, 336
Wilhelm I, Kaiser (1797–1888), II: 95
Wolf, Hermann (1845–1902), IV: 130, 134, 174–5, 311, 316
Wolf, Johann, IV: 311
Wood, Henry (1869–1944), IV: 467, 469
Woodside, Mary, IV: 485

Yachmeneva, Nataliya Grigoryevna (fl. 1856), I: 49
Yakovlev, Leonid Georgiyevich (1858–1919), IV: 401
Yarustovsky, Boris, I: 13. II: 198–9. IV: 238–41, 248, 265, 365
Yashvil, Vladimir Vladimirovich, IV: 383–4

Yazïkov, Alexandr Petrovich (1802–78), I: 40
Yazïkova, Nadezhda, II: 144
Yazïkova, Yuliya Sergeyevna (1824–86), II: 144
Yoffe, Elkhonen, IV: 320
Yolshin, Alexandr, II: 224–5
Yolshina, Elizaveta Karlovna (1848–1903), III: 292
Yuryev, Yury, IV: 482

Zabel, Eugen, IV: 221
Zak, Eduard (1854–73), I: 248–9. IV: 121
Zaremba, Nikolay Ivanovich (1821–79), I: 60–2, 67, 69–70, 99–100, 107, 120, 127, 132, 170, 180
Zarudnaya, Varvara Mikhailovna (1857–1939), IV: 69, 74–5, 109, 112, 216
Zasulich, Vera Ivanovna (1851–1919), II: 226
Zasyadko, Dmitri Ivanovich, IV: 118
Zet, Julius, IV: 169, 174
Zhdanov, V., II: 103
Zhegin, N., II: 103
Zhenya [see Olkhovskaya, Evgeniya Evgenyevna]
Zhukovsky, Vasily Andreyevich (1783–1852), I: 69, 174. II: 183, 189, 273, 280. III: 16, 24, 26, 37, 42–3. IV: 185, 244, 246, 475
Ziloti, Alexandr Ilich (1863–1945), III: 80–1, 88, 255. IV: 103, 127, 129–31, 133–5, 137, 166, 173, 197, 200, 217, 219, 275–6, 278, 293–4, 298, 376, 380, 386, 389, 407
Ziloti, Vera Pavlovna (1866–1940), IV: 103, 132–3, 276, 386
Zograf, Alexandra Yuryevna (1850–1919), IV: 411
Zola, Emile (1840–1902), III: 115, 221. IV: 143, 386, 393–4
Zotov, Vladimir Rafailovich (1821–96), IV: 332
Zvantsev, Konstantin Ivanovich (1823–90), II: 54, 68
Zverev, Nikolay Sergeyevich (1832–93), IV: 103, 407, 477